THE CHILD CARE GUIDE
AND FAMILY ADVISER

Compiled from Parents' Magazine

by PHYLLIS B. KATZ

Associate Editor, Parents' Magazine

Illustrated by Meg Wholberg
Photographs by Suzanne Szasz

Published by
THE PARENTS' INSTITUTE, INC.
52 Vanderbilt Avenue, New York 17, N.Y.

FOREWORD

BY KATHERINE B. OETTINGER

Chief, Children's Bureau
U. S. Department of Health, Education and Welfare

I wonder if the young parent of today realizes how lucky he is! He has at his fingertips a vast body of knowledge about the physical and social growth processes his child will experience as he grows and develops.

This knowledge has been distilled by experts into popular form so that parents need not grapple with the nomenclature of medicine, psychology or the social sciences, to help gain understanding of their child's needs and growth patterns.

A number of magazines contribute to this service to parents through the articles they carry in their columns.

PARENTS' MAGAZINE is one of these. I am pleased to see PARENTS' carry the service a step further in THE CHILD CARE GUIDE AND FAMILY ADVISER. This compendium of articles, which have appeared in the magazine over recent years, is intended to provide parents with a ready reference and current guide in identifying and meeting the needs of their children in this decade, which has brought more profound changes in external factors affecting children than any comparable period in history.

This type of material which translates modern, scientific findings into usable, practical terms may be valuable not only to parents. Professional workers who find themselves constantly required to absorb scientific information from fields related to their own and to explain it to parents will find here concise, organized material on a wide variety of pertinent subjects.

Today's parents need above all trust in themselves and their ability to judge what is best for their child. Nothing that is written or printed can substitute for this. Yet parents with firm faith in their own competence, and those striving to build it, can always employ new and sound knowledge to smooth the road ahead for the advancing child. The expanding world of children holds more wonders and fewer fears when confident, loving and knowing parents share it.

CONTRIBUTORS

Harold A. Abramson, M.D.
Author of "The Patient Speaks"; Research Psychiatrist, the Biological Laboratory, Cold Spring Harbor, New York; Consultant in Research Psychiatry, State Hospital, Central Islip, New York

Milton R. Aisenson, M.D.
Member of American Academy of Pediatrics

Carmen Stone Allen

Jennie H. Allen

Stella Applebaum
Author of "Working Wives and Mothers"

Rhoda W. Bacmeister
Lecturer on Early Childhood Education at City College of New York; author of "Caring for the Runabout Child" and "All in the Family"

Margaret H. Bacon

Anne Barnes

Joel Berg

Harold W. Bernard
Director, Psycho-Education Clinic, University of Oregon

Maja Bernath
Executive Editor, Your New Baby; Associate Editor, Parents' Magazine

Bruno Bettelheim, Ph.D.
Principal of the Sonia Shankman Orthogenic School at the University of Chicago; author of "Love Is Not Enough" and "Truants From Life"; Fellow and Diplomate of the American Psychological Association; Fellow of the American Orthopsychiatric Association

Evelyn Beyer
Director, Nursery School, Sarah Lawrence College, New York

Irma Simonton Black
Formerly Instructor at Bank Street College of Education, New York City; author of "Off to a Good Start" and "Busy Water," the latest in a series of books for children

Earl W. Blank
Professor of English in charge of dramatics, Berea College, Kentucky

Mary A. Boncquet

Ethel Greenfield Booth

Ruth and Edward Brecher

Doris P. Buck

Adeline Bullock, R.N.
Author of "Parents' Magazine Book for Expectant Mothers"

Bradley Burch

Helen Steers Burgess
Member of Board of Directors, Child Study Association of America

Gladys Toler Burris

Vivian Cadden
Co-author of "An Intelligent Man's Guide to Women"

Jane Lynott Carroll

Ruth Carson

Earl Clark

Katherine Clifford

Louise Fox Connell

Dolly Connelly

Betty Cunkle

Norma E. Cutts, Ph.D.
Co-author of "Better Home Discipline" and "Teaching the Bright and Gifted"

George Davenel
Placement Director, Assistant Professor of Student Personnel, Queens College, New York

Ida Davidoff, Ed.D.
Marriage Counselor

Hedley S. Dimock, Ph.D.
Director of Group Guidance, Montreal Children's Hospital; author of "Camping and Character"

Louis I. Dublin, Ph.D.
President, Committee to Protect Our Children's Teeth, Inc.

Evelyn Millis Duvall, Ph.D.
Consultant, National Council on Family Relations; author of "Facts of Life and Love"

Virginia and Morton Edwards

Jon Eisenson, Ph.D.
Director of Queens College Speech Clinic, New York

Louise Ellison
Nursery School Teacher

Tinka D. Engel
Former psychiatric social worker

Ralph G. Engelsman
Author, lecturer, life underwriter

Naomi L. Engelsman

O. Spurgeon English, M.D.
Professor of Psychiatry, Temple University Medical School; co-author of "Fathers Are Parents, Too"

Margaret Ione Etzell

Arnold A. Fenton, D.D.

N. C. Ferguson
Manager, Editorial Service Bureau, Eastman Kodak Company

Florence Mary Fitch
Author of One God: "The Way We Worship Him"

Constance J. Foster
Co-author of "Fathers Are Parents, Too"

Ruth C. Fredericks

John E. French
Supervisor of Art Education Elementary School, University of California

Betty Friedan

Katherine Earls Gerwin

Arnold Gesell, Ph.D., M.D.
Founder of the Clinic of Child Develop-

ment, Yale University; Director of Gesell Institute of Child Development; noted author and educator

Donna Geyer

Margaret Albrecht Gillmor
Formerly Articles Editor, Parents' Magazine

Katherine Glover

Robert M. Goldenson, Ph.D.
Professor of Psychology, Hunter College, New York City; co-author of "The Complete Book of Play and Playthings"

Ruth Schley Goldman
Deputy Commissioner, Social Services, Department of Welfare, Chicago, Illinois

Edith Harwin Goodman

Jack Goodman
Radio Station News Director

Sidney L. Green, M.D.
Psychiatrist, Brooklyn, New York

Andrew W. Grieve
High School Football Coach

Benjamin C. Gruenberg, Ph.D.
Biologist, lecturer; author of "Biology and Human Life" and "Biology and Man"

Margaret M. Hall
Kindergarten specialist

Fred M. Hechinger
Author of "The Big Red Schoolhouse"; Education Editor, New York Times

Susan Stampfer Heller

Barbara V. Hertz
Managing Editor, Parents' Magazine

Leone Ann Heuer

Marjorie S. Hildebrand

Reuben Hill, Ph.D.
Professor of Sociology, University of North Carolina; co-author of "When You Marry"

Mary B. Hoover

Theodore Irwin

Janet Jackson
Teacher

Irving Jaffee
Former Olympic Skating Champion

Gladys Gardner Jenkins
Member of Advisory Board, Association for Family Living, Chicago, Illinois

Lydia Joel
Editor of Dance Magazine

Martha Collins Johnson

Goldie Ruth Kaback, Ph.D.
Consulting Psychologist, New York City

Bernard Katz

Helen L. Kaufman
Author of "The Little Music Library"

Paul W. Kearney

Flora H. Kimball, R.N.

Mary Margaret Kern

Jean R. Komaiko

C. H. Kramer, M.D.
Member of the American Psychiatric Association

Paul A. Krooks, D.D.S.

Irving Ladimer, S.J.D.
Consultant, Institute for the Advancement of Medical Communication

Margaret L. Lane

Grace Langdon, Ph.D.
Lecturer, New York University and Child Education Foundation; toy consultant; author of "Home Guidance for Young Children"

Herbert Lawrence, M.D.
Dermatologist, author of "The Care of Your Skin"

George Lawton, Ph.D.
Psychologist, author of "How To Be Happy Though Young"

Eda J. LeShan
Director of Education, Guidance Center of New Rochelle, Inc., and Parent Group Leader

Lena Levine, M.D.
Psychiatrist and gynecologist; consultant in marriage counseling program of Planned Parenthood Federation of Amer-

ica; Director of Marriage Consultation Service of Margaret Sanger Research Bureau; lecturer, author of "The Doctor Talks to the Bride"

Maxine Livingston
Family Home Editor, Parents' Magazine

Jean A. Lyons

Charles E. Marrow
Engineer

Merabe Marshall

Grace B. Martin

Corinne Weil Mattuck
Faculty member, Goddard College; Parent Education Chairman, Vermont Congress of Parents and Teachers

Margaret McEathron
Specialist in remedial reading

John W. McLeod, AIA
Vice Chairman, AIA National Committee on School Building; member U.S. delegation to the 1957 International Conference on Public Education, Geneva, Switzerland

Francis Drewry McMullen
Specialist in psychological testing

Elizabeth G. Meier
Associate Professor, New York School of Social Work, Columbia University

Evelyn Emig Mellon

Dorothy Melrose

Betty Thayer Miller
Teacher

Margaret Mochrie

James V. Moffatt
Director of Admissions, The Hill School, Pottstown, Pennsylvania

Dudley J. Morton, M.D.
Formerly Assistant Professor of Anatomy, Columbia University; Research Assistant, Museum of Natural History, New York City

Nicholas Moseley, Ph.D.
Co-author of "Better Home Discipline" and "Teaching the Bright and Gifted"

Eleanor Neal, R.N.

Edith G. Neisser
Author of "Brothers and Sisters" and "The Eldest Child"

Ruth Newman
Remedial Education Center, Washington, D.C.

Andre Norton
Children's Librarian, Cleveland, Ohio

Elizabeth C. O'Daly
Author of "Dear Parents: Candid Advice From a School Principal"

Patricia Rayburn Olson

Eveline Omwake
Director, Child Study Center Nursery School, Yale University

Garrett Oppenheim
Former Copy Editor, N.Y. Herald Tribune

Warren Page
Shooting Editor, Field and Stream

Emily S. Parcher

Joan W. Parks
Health and Welfare Division, Metropolitan Life Insurance Company

Katherine Peavy

Maria Massey Pelikan

Doris Pennant

Harriet D. Pennington

Lola Pergament

Maria W. Piers, Ph.D.
Faculty member of the University of Illinois School of Social Work; faculty member of the Child Care Program of the Chicago Institute for Psychoanalysis

Jack Harrison Pollack

Shirley Pollock

Elenore Thomas Pounds

Helen Puner
Author of "Freud: His Life and His Mind"; Associate Editor, Parents' Magazine

Fritz Redl, Ph.D.
Professor of Behavioral Sciences, School of Education, Wayne State University; formerly chief, Child Research Bureau,

National Institute for Mental Health; co-author of "The Aggressive Child"

Helen Reid
Formerly with the Ryther Child Care Center and the Family Life Education Program, Seattle, Washington

Bea Renaud

Barbara Leonard Reynolds

Margaret A. Ribble, M.D.
Psychiatrist, New York City; author of "The Personality of the Young Child" and "The Rights of Infants"

Audrey Palm Riker, R.N., Ed.D.

Estelle R. Roddy
Publications Department, Oak Lane Country Day School of Temple University, Philadelphia, Pennsylvania

Allan B. Rothenberg
Author of "A Manual of First Aid for Mental Health in Childhood and Adolescence"

Priscilla Rosten
Late member of the Child Study Association Book Review Committee

Ruth Kenyon Russell, M.D.

Herman Schneider
Author of "Everyday Weather and How It Works"

Elizabeth Lee Schweiger

Ruth Newburn Sedam
Formerly Editor of Baby Talk Magazine

Amy Selwyn

Everette E. Sentman
Editor-in-Chief, The United Educators, Inc., Lake Bluff, Illinois

Joseph Shallit

Helen S. Sharpe

May Reynolds Sherwin, Ph.D.
Child Psychologist; author of "Children From Seed to Saplings"; Advisory Editor, Parents' Magazine

Dorothy Edwards Shuttlesworth
Author of "Exploring Nature With Your Child"

Dorothy Siegel

Josephine Courtney Sisk
Teacher

Fletcher D. Slater

Gardner Soule

Shirley Southcott
Social Worker

Benjamin Spock, M.D.
Professor of Child Development, Medical School of Western Reserve University; well known pediatrician and author of "Baby and Child Care"

Thomas F. Staton
Chief of Educational Advisors, Air Command and Staff School, Air University, Maxwell Air Force Base, Alabama

Edith M. Stern
Author of "Mental Illness: A Guide for the Family"

Mrs. A. W. Stirling

Nora Stirling
Consultant and playwright for the "Plays for Living" series, Family Service Association of America

Quentin C. Stodola
Director of Counseling and Testing, North Dakota Agricultural College

Herbert R. Stolz, M.D.
Assistant Superintendent of Schools, Oakland, California

Jack Stone

Elizabeth F. Stonorov
Director, Charlestown Play House, Charlestown, Pennsylvania

C. K. Thomas
Director, Cornell Speech Clinic, Cornell University

Helen Thomson
Former psychiatric social worker

Elsieliese Thrope

Charles A. Tompkins, M.D.
Pediatrician

Walter A. Tompkins

John Thomas Urwin

Amy Vanderbilt
Author of "Amy Vanderbilt's Complete Book of Etiquette"

Hermann Vollmer, M.D.
Late pediatrician

Donald N. Von Pein
Psychologist

Helen Macomber Walker
Director of School Lunch Program, Polk County Board of Public Instruction, Florida

Sonya Weber, D.Sc.
Instructor in Physical Medicine, Columbia University

Mort Weisinger

Jack Allan Weiss, M.D.
Surgeon and Associate Professor, Chicago Medical College; author of "A Handbook for Parents on Preparing a Child for the Hospital"

Ronnie Welch

Sara Welles
Senior Editor, Printer's Ink

Dorothy V. Whipple, M.D.
Pediatrician; author of "Our American Babies"

Jane Whitbread
Co-author of "An Intelligent Man's Guide to Women"

Edward T. Wilkes, M.D.
Associate Clinical Professor of Pediatrics, New York University Bellevue Post Graduate Medical School; author of "Family Guide to Teen-age Health"

Lou Williams
Geology instructor, Stephens College, Missouri

Sloan Wilson
Formerly Assistant Director, White House Conference on Education; author of "The Man in the Gray Flannel Suit" and "A Summer Place"

David Wineman
*Co-author of "Controls From Within"
and "The Aggressive Child"*

Rudolph M. Wittenberg, Ph.D.
*Author of "On Call For Youth" and
"Adolescence and Discipline"*

Henry H. Work, M.D.
*Associate Professor of Psychiatry, School
of Medicine, University of California*

Bee Wyndham

Margaret S. Young
Children's Librarian, Cleveland, Ohio

CONTENTS

SPECIAL PROBLEMS

PERSONALITY AND CHARACTER DEVELOPMENT

DISCIPLINE

FEARS

SPEECH—THE ART OF COMMUNICATION

CREATIVE AND RECREATIONAL ACTIVITIES

PREPARATION FOR SCHOOL

CHARACTER AND SOCIAL DEVELOPMENT

DISCIPLINE AND MANNERS

HELPING CHILDREN LEARN

CREATIVE ACTIVITIES

SPECIAL PROBLEMS

Section Seven · HEALTH AND SAFETY

ACCIDENT PREVENTION

HOME CARE AND CONVALESCENCE

NUTRITION

GROWTH

FOOT HEALTH AND POSTURE

EARS, EYES AND TEETH

MENTAL HYGIENE

Section Eight • EDUCATION

CHOOSING A SCHOOL

HOME HELP WITH SCHOOL WORK

SPECIAL ASPECTS

Section Nine · HOME MANAGEMENT 809

EFFICIENCY IN THE HOUSEHOLD

SECURITY FOR THE FAMILY

WORK AND HELP ARRANGEMENTS

SPECIAL PROBLEMS

BABIES

THE NEWBORN BABY • PHYSICAL CARE
SLEEP NEEDS • WHY BABIES CRY • SOLID FOODS
FORMULA MAKING • WEANING • UNDERFEEDING
FIRST TEETH • MAKING FRIENDS WITH THE DOCTOR
SPOILING • LEARNING INDEPENDENCE
PREMATURITY • CIRCUMCISION • TOILET TRAINING
THUMB-SUCKING • THE OVERACTIVE BABY • COLIC

WHAT YOU SHOULD KNOW
ABOUT A NEWBORN BABY

WITHOUT question, the newborn baby has a charm and appeal all his own. Also without question—except to eyes that look on him with love —the appeal definitely doesn't lie in his looks. His head, which seems enormous compared to his body, may be covered with long or short hair. The skin, often wrinkled, is usually red and sometimes mottled but it isn't long before it fades to peaches and cream. The chin may look inadequate—and a good thing, too, for it's easier this way for the baby to nurse.

The sometimes "lopsided" appearance of a newborn's head is the result of an amazing ability to adapt to the process of birth. The skull is composed of separate plates which do not quite meet and do not fuse until after birth. They can be pressed together, even overlap, if compression is needed during passage through the birth canal, but a few days or weeks after birth the head resumes its normal shape.

The newborn's proportions may surprise you. The head is one-fourth of the body length. The shoulders are scarcely wider than the head, which makes for easier traveling through the birth canal. His abdomen is large and domed—it almost seems bloated—and his arms and legs are skinny and short by comparison. He still holds for a while to the prenatal position, arms flexed and knees bent, with feet usually crossed. The little legs are bowed from knee to ankle. These too will straighten out within a few weeks. His buttocks are small, his genitals large in comparison to his body's size.

Occasionally an infant's breasts look somewhat swollen during the first week of life, and they may ooze milk. This may happen to either a boy or a girl baby. It is the result of hormones absorbed from the mother and disappears within a few days. No attempt should be made to massage or squeeze the breasts. This can be harmful.

What It Means To Be Born

Being born is one of life's major experiences—and something of a shock. The baby, before birth, lies closely, darkly and softly protected in his liquid-filled sac. Perhaps what he feels is somewhat akin to the comfort we feel drowsing in a tub of warm water. He doesn't even have to breathe or eat. Oxygen and nourishment come to him through the pulsing umbilical tube.

Suddenly this idyllic retreat is disturbed by a series of vigorous muscular contractions which drain its waters and force the baby downward. His body stiffens, his back arches as he is pushed through the birth canal. As he comes out into the world the air strikes sensitive skin which has never felt cold before. The baby begins his new life as a separate person, and the lungs must draw their first breath. Like a bellows they fill and empty, bringing forth his first cry—the cry that is music to his waiting mother's ears. Then the cord is cut.

What he can do. If his mother did not have a heavy dose of anesthesia during childbirth, which would make the baby sleepy also, the newborn may open his blue eyes when his mother speaks to him. All new babies' eyes are blue or blue-gray. The color will begin to change, if your child is going to be brown-eyed, when he is several months old. His vision is not yet coordinated, though, and you are little more than a blur of light and shadow to him.

His sense of smell is more acute. Almost from birth it inspires him to nuzzle for food if he is held near your breast. His face turns toward a touch on his cheek. His hands clutch fast to your finger if you press it gently to his palm.

He can cry, which from the beginning of time has summoned mothers to their babies' aid. He doesn't "decide" to cry when he feels discomfort of some sort. The cry is automatic, the way your eye blinks when something comes near it. The baby will be at least three months old before he will be aware enough to realize that a cry can be an appeal.

Interpreting Behavior

Some of the things the newborn is or can do, bring anxious wrinkles to the brow of inexperienced parents. His eyes often look "crossed." The nerve connections between eyes and brain are not yet mature enough to enable him to focus both eyes together. Nevertheless, his eyes will turn automatically toward a light, and within a few weeks will follow a lighted or a moving object.

His stools during the first few days look greenish-black, because the intestines at birth contain a dark green substance called meconium. The normal yellowish stool appears in a few days.

He sometimes jerks suddenly. The newborn's brain and nervous system are quite unfinished. The tiny nerve fibers which will eventually connect his brain with his muscles do not form until after birth so he cannot yet move his body purposefully. For now, his muscles move his arms and legs by reflex action. The jerking movements that may worry his mother actually keep his circulation going and his heart pumping evenly.

He sneezes and coughs without apparent reason. But there is reason—it serves to keep his nose and throat clear of secretions. He's not "catching cold," not even if his feet feel chilly, too. It is natural for a baby's feet to be cool.

The queer little snorts and grunts a baby sometimes makes while sleeping are quite normal, too. They occur because his tongue slips back occasionally against the roof of his mouth, pressing slightly against the air passage, and because once in a while he "forgets" to breathe for a moment. The breathing itself is, for him, such a new accomplishment.

Learning to Breathe

Breathing is shallow and uneven during the first weeks of life. The baby's chest is small, its muscles tiny. He looks as though he's "breathing with his stomach." In the hospital a special watch is generally placed on newborn babies the first day of life to insure that breathing develops normally.

You actually help your baby learn to breathe when you cuddle him. Holding him close, stroking him gently, accelerates the flow of blood to his brain and prods the breathing mechanisms. So does suckling which he attempts from time to time.

Crying also is a stimulus to breathing during the early weeks. The baby who cries suddenly may be trying in his own way to stimulate his breathing mechanism. But crying for more than a couple of minutes, you have to remember, is exhausting and defeats this objective instead of helping.

The newborn's mouth is equipped with special muscles having a strong sucking reflex, but the hazards of birth and of strange surroundings may add difficulties to his first attempts. He must "learn" through practice how to hold the nipple far back in his mouth, and his mother must learn how to hold him and support his head close to the breast so that his lips come well over the areola. Untried mouth muscles tire easily, and his natural rhythm during the early weeks of life is to nurse sparingly and often.

Learning to sleep. The newborn infant does not actually sleep; he dozes in an uneasy continuation of the prenatal state. He dozes most securely when his surroundings are most like that state—when he is cuddled close in loving arms or nestled in a snug bassinet. He needs to be largely undisturbed, so that the rapid growth which is taking place in his nervous system and in his brain can continue. Gradually he will stay awake for tiny intervals. Psychologists tell us that a baby must learn to stay awake before he will be able to relax and really sleep.

He needs time to get used to life outside his mother's body. For a while, he needs an environment as similar as possible to his snug prenatal existence. Primitive mothers cuddle their babies beside them, or wrap them in a sling and carry them against their own bodies. The baby is somehow reassured by the feel of another skin against his own.

He is accustomed to a stable temperature and may cry if too much of his skin is exposed to the chilling air in diapering or bathing. He may also cry in fright if he is laid on a hard flat surface which does not yield to his body as the uterus did before birth. He is used to motion, very gentle motion, and is generally soothed by being rocked or carried. He is used to muted sounds. Even before birth a baby receives some sound vibrations and may respond by body movement to regular rhythms, such as music or applause in a theater. Now lullabies, soft crooning, are pleasing to him.

He is born in a state of semiconsciousness, and this state may continue for some time, with only brief periods of wakefulness when he is suckled or bathed. Slow and gentle his mother must be, slow and easy, in waking him from the drowsy fog of prenatal existence to the satisfactions of being alive.

—By Evelyn Emig Mellon

BATHING THE NEW BABY

WHY do you bathe your baby? To help keep his skin healthy and comfortable, and to protect his health. To make him sweet and clean. To give him a joyous chance to kick and stretch without a stitch of clothes to hamper him.

To soothe and relax him for sounder sleep. Bathtime offers a wonderful opportunity to laugh and play and talk with your baby.

At first, when you're perhaps a bit wobbly or uncertain about handling your baby, it's comforting to know that his daily bath can be considered a "maybe" not a "must." In fact, some doctors suggest once-a-week baths during the early weeks, with sponge-offs between baths. So any day you don't feel up to bathing your baby—don't.

When to bathe. The best time is when you're unhurried and relaxed. Many mothers like mid-morning, before the 10 A.M. feeding.

Late afternoon, when some babies get fussy, is another good bathtime if that fits in with your household schedule. As your baby grows older and stays awake longer, you may settle for an early supper with his bath a little later, so your husband can get in on the fun. But wait at least an hour after any mealtime.

As a general rule, sticking to the same bath schedule every day works to the advantage of both of you. Exception to the rule: hot weather. In summertime, your baby appreciates extra baths and sponge-offs during the day—and occasionally on sticky midsummer nights.

Where should you bathe your baby? Any comfortably warm room—kitchen, bedroom or bath—where he won't be in a draft. A temperature of 75° is about right.

A folding bath-table-and-tub is a convenience. Some mothers like a plastic or enamel tub, a dishpan (reserved for baby, please!) or the well scrubbed kitchen sink. The family tub requires too much stooping and bending for you to be able to hold your baby comfortably when he's tiny. Later a baby bath seat will help you keep him safe in the big tub.

If you want to sit during the bath, put the tub on a sturdy table or on a broad-based straight chair. If you prefer to stand, the folding table-tub is designed to save your back. A kitchen table is usually a fairly comfortable height for a separate tub.

Pre-Bath Preparations

What should you assemble before the bath begins? Get together everything you'll need during and after the bath because *a baby must never be left alone on the table or in the tub!*

One good plan, which the Maternity Center Association teaches Expectant Parents' Classes, is to arrange the things in layers on a chair back or table in the order you need them.

At the bottom of the pile goes a rubberized pad and a cotton pad. Next, two diapers—ready for use. Then a fresh shirt and a gown or dress. Next, a clean washcloth. On the top of the pile, a fresh cotton receiving blanket and big bath towel.

On a tray or shelf within easy reach you'll need mild soap in a soap dish, large rustproof safety pins in a covered container (well away from the baby's reach), cotton twists and baby oil, lotion or powder. You'll find a newspaper on the floor handy to catch soiled clothes and a paper bag or basket for used cotton.

Some mothers who use a metal tub put a diaper or bath towel in the bottom to keep their babies from slipping. Folding tubs may have a little hammock for the baby.

Pour warm water into the tub—just a few inches. Fill a pitcher with very hot water and keep it nearby, in case the bath water cools off too much before you're ready. Water temperatures should be about 90° to 100° on a bath thermometer—or feel just comfortably warm to your wrist.

One more thing before you start: get the baby's bottle out to be warmed if he eats after the bath.

After washing *your* hands, take off your wristwatch and rings or pins that might scratch and have your fingernails short and smooth. Are you wearing a big splash-proof apron?

How do you bathe a baby? Your own way, really. But a few basic steps make you more easy and certain. Whatever way you choose, you're likely to breathe easier if you have someone with you during the first bath. Not only for moral support, but just in case you forget something!

Let's begin with a *sponge bath*. When you're first home from the hospital you may want to sit and sponge-bathe your baby. Many doctors think it advisable to give sponge baths until the navel has healed.

In one arm, hold your baby, wrapped in the receiving blanket he's been in. With your free hand, pick up the towel and clean receiving blanket from the top of the pile you've prepared. Now have a seat.

Lay the baby's fresh blanket and towel on your lap and put him on top. He can still have his clothes on or he can be undressed down to his diaper. Keep his shoulders and tummy covered.

The Face and Hair

Nature normally cleans your baby's eyes and mouth without help, so don't do anything except admire them. If his eyelid corners need cleaning, wipe them gently with moistened cotton, working out from the inside corner. Use a moistened twist of cotton to clean the baby's nostrils. His outer ears can be cleaned the same way or with a soft washcloth. Wipe gently, never dig. Do *not* try to clean the inner ear.

To wash your little one's face, no soap is needed. Wrap a soft washcloth around your hand like a mitten so water can't drip from the corners. (Some mothers like a bath sponge better, as long as it stays clean and fresh.) Gently wash the baby's forehead, then cheeks and chin—or chins! Pat him dry with the towel.

If he's having a shampoo (two or three a week are usually plenty) lather his head, tilted back a little to keep the soap out of his eyes. It's a good idea to wrap the baby's blanket around his arms for a minute, so he can't wave them about.

Scalp care. Don't be afraid to wash the "soft spot" on the top of his head —its covering is really quite tough. Thorough scalp care helps ward off "cradle cap," the yellowish crust that may form from the secretions of glands in his scalp.

Rinse the soap out quickly but carefully—from his forehead back—holding his head (well supported) over the tub. He may not like his shampoo very much, so do it quickly and talk soothingly. Slant his head downward slightly, so the rinse water won't run on his face, then pat dry.

Now for the body bath—and off go all the baby's clothes, diaper last, onto the paper on the floor. Time to test the bath water. If it has cooled off, add hot water from your pitcher.

Rub a little soap on your hands or on the washcloth and lather the baby's neck, shoulders, arms and fingers, chest, tummy and legs. Always wash and wipe a girl baby's genitals from front to back, gently separating the folds of the vulva. If a boy baby has been circumcised, gently cleanse the tip of his penis. If he is uncircumcised, retract—do not force—the foreskin, cleanse the penis and ease the foreskin back into place.

Now roll your baby over (toward you) and soap his back. Soaping done, be especially careful to rinse the soap from every part of his body so that his skin doesn't become irritated.

Slide the soiled receiving blanket off your lap. This leaves a rosy clean baby lying on a clean bath towel and blanket. Pat him dry—don't rub. Pay special attention to creases and folds around the neck, under the arms, at elbows and knees, between the legs, fingers and toes.

Finishing Touches

As a finishing touch, you may like to use baby oil or lotion. A sprinkling of baby powder, spread on with your hand, is soothing in hot weather. Be careful to keep the powder away from the baby's face—breathing powder into the lungs can be harmful.

Slip the towel out from under him. On go the diaper and shirt, and maybe nightie or kimono. Put the fresh pads under him. He's sweet and clean and, if it's mealtime, ready to eat!

An *oil bath*, which some doctors recommend be given to newborns for a few weeks and to premature or sick babies, follows a routine similar to the sponge bath. The difference is that you use warm baby oil instead of soap and water, cotton instead of a washcloth. Warm the oil by letting the bottle stand in warm water. Pour a little into a saucer.

Dip a bit of cotton into the oil and wipe the baby's body gently, a small area at a time, keeping the rest of his body well covered. Wipe off excess oil with clean cotton.

Giving a tub bath. Sitting down or standing at a bath table, you follow the same step-by-step procedure as in a sponge bath until rinsing time, when you ease the baby into the tub. Or, if you like, you can wash and dry his face, ears and head while he's lying on your lap or the bath table. Then soap and rinse the rest of his body after he's in the tub. Use as little soap as possible—it's slippery!

When a baby goes into the bathtub, water can be fun or frightening to him— and a lot depends on first impressions. Let your baby down easily into his bath, and have just an inch or two of water in the tub at first. Talk to him gently and move in slow motion—with no quick flips from front to back. Hold him securely, so he won't get the feeling he's falling—another common cause of bathtub fright. Here's a good safe grip: let his neck and shoulders rest on your wrist and forearm, with your thumb around his shoulder and your fingers under his armpit. To turn him tummy down, hold his shoulder and armpit the same way and rest his chest on your wrist and forearm.

As a baby gets to be a veteran of the tub, he usually views it as a great time for play. Trickle a little water on his tummy or back—and you get a lopsided smile or a gleeful gurgle. An older baby likes to have time to frolic in the tub. Before long, you find bathtime is not a chore but one of the day's brightest spots.

—By Ruth Newburn Sedam

YOUR BABY'S SLEEP NEEDS

FEW things are more beautiful to see than a sleeping child—and few are more mysterious.

If you ask the scientists, they'll agree that sleep is one of the great mysteries. They know that it is an essential, primitive function, as important to the maintenance of life as nutrition is. They know that during sleep a kind of re-fueling process takes place: something like an overhaul of the entire organism, especially the nervous system—but they don't know just *how* this overhaul works. We are told by authorities on the subject that sleep is *behavior*, just like talking, walking, laughing, and so on.

By watching your child, or children, sleep, you can see for yourself how sleep behavior differs from baby to baby—and from month to month: this six-month-old looks as if he's working hard at staying asleep; that one-year-old is so utterly relaxed, so poured into sleep you envy his perfect repose; this three-year-old's sensitive face reflects the dreams that amuse or plague him. One child needs a lot of sleep, another relatively little.

Children's ways of falling asleep and waking up are just as varied as their ways of *staying* asleep. It's the business of *going* to sleep that most often presents a problem.

The new baby. The brand-new baby needs all the sleep he can get and—unless he's colicky or hungry—gets all the sleep he needs without your having to do much about it. Actually at this early stage he can't be said to be properly asleep, just as he isn't properly awake yet. He spends his days and nights in a kind of doze from which he emerges only in order to drink. Drinking is the one thing he seems to do in a really intense way. There's something wonderfully dedicated, something downright passionate in the way a new baby sucks in nourishment. When he's had his fill, he sinks back into that semiconscious, restless, shallow kind of slumber that is typical of the new baby's sleep.

If possible, the new baby should have a room of his own. (A screen or partition helps, if a separate room is not available.) He does not need complete darkness or silence for sleeping. In fact, it's better to let him get used to sleeping with a certain amount of gentle, diffused noise than to accustom him to absolute silence. As he gets older, he'll find noises less disturbing if he's been sleeping amidst them from the beginning. Of course, sudden violent noises such as slamming doors or shouts, should be avoided.

You should also make sure he is neither too hot nor too cool for comfort. You can tell whether he's chilly or over-warm by touching his back or abdomen. A baby's hands and feet are cooler than the rest of him so you can't tell from them if he's comfortable.

Sleep at Three to Six Months

As your baby gets older, his sleep behavior changes. He may take longer to fall asleep now, but once asleep he'll sleep more quietly and deeply and—best of all—for more hours at a stretch. One blissful morning you'll wake up and find that he has slept right through the night. He's practically civilized!

His waking periods, too, are more active now. He looks around, is pleased when he sees something moving, something colorful such as a bright toy. He reaches for things and kicks his legs high in the air. Sometimes he succeeds in turning over from his back to his stomach or vice versa.

Naturally, when the world is so full of things to see and do, it's hard to let it all go by falling asleep. That's why your 3 to 6-month-old often takes longer to fall asleep. You can help him relax into sleep by leading him toward it gently: a little quiet play, a little singing and rocking, everything done in a calm unhurried way, will soon help your youngster let go of the day and give himself up to sleep—the contented kind that refreshes.

At this age and older he may be bothered by new teeth. The discomfort of teething is worse, of course, at bedtime, because then there's nothing else to catch his attention. Rocking and a soothing lullaby or two may help him forget his woes.

New routines—6 months to a year. Between the ages of 6 months and one year, your baby may give up his mid-morning nap in favor of one long afternoon nap. Or he may shift about in his nap pattern for a few months. He now should sleep straight through 11 to 12 hours at night. His sleep at this age will be so deep that waking up may be quite a chore for him.

A lot of babies are cranky and weepy when they wake from their long nap. It's a good idea to give them lots of time to wake up, not to rush them into any activity, such as getting dressed or washing. Once they are fully awake it helps to have a cheerful suggestion ready, like: "Let's go bye-bye," or "Let's have juice," or "Let's put a hat on Teddy bear"—anything to get the baby started on his afternoon in a good mood.

A one-year-old knows quite well what sleep is all about and seems to have a certain amount of control over it. That is, he can relax into sleep if he is willing. Relaxing (or "releasing" as it's often called) into sleep is a skill that a baby must acquire, like the trick of opening his hand and letting things drop.

Often, though, the older baby refuses to let go. He may keep himself awake consciously, because he's afraid of missing any fun. Or, he may be kept from sleep unconsciously, by inner tensions.

If your child shows signs of becoming a "poor sleeper," ask yourself if you aren't riding him a little too hard. Do you scold him for things like spilling his milk? Is his waking day a round of "no's"? It is easier than you think to slide into such a pattern, no matter how good your intentions! Try relaxing your demands and giving your baby more affection, freedom and fun, and very likely you'll find him relaxing into sleep more easily.

It is important to remember that some babies are naturally "poor sleepers." It is harder for them to fall asleep, to stay asleep or to adjust to changes in routine. Remember too that thumb-sucking should not be interfered with—it is a natural help for relaxing that many babies need.

The Toddler and Sleep

When your baby reaches the toddler stage, a whole raft of new problems enters his life. Around this time, many ambitious mothers begin toilet training and weaning from bottle to cup. These are big upheavals in a toddler's life— and so are learning to walk and talk, for that matter!

If he himself is anxious to excel at these new skills (because he wants to please you, or for his own satisfaction) he may experience the frustration of not being able to live up to his own expectations. Now, that is something we grownups know only too well and we have more or less become used to accepting minor frustrations. But for a toddler these first encounters with his own inadequacy can be unsettling. They may make him tense and fretful at bedtime and keep him from releasing into sleep. Here, again, you can help him along by not insisting too strictly on toilet training or weaning and by praising him when he succeeds but not making an issue of it when he fails, or even comforting him in case of accident. Above all, show him your love. It's his most important possession and he is still too young to take it for granted!

Incidentally, if you wish to wean your child from the bottle, it's better never to let him go to sleep with a bottle in his bed. On the other hand, if you've decided to let the youngster do his own weaning (they all, eventually, give up the bottle of their own accord) you'll find that letting him fall asleep with a bedtime bottle in his mouth is a good way of making sure he'll fall asleep happily.

Your toddler may, like so many at this age, develop little rituals for himself. They help to get him into the proper frame of mind for sleep. One little girl tucks in her Teddy bear while mother pulls down the shades; another must have three hugs and a kiss; one little boy likes a kiss on each eye for pleasant dreams, and so on. You can even help your toddler work up a going-to-sleep routine, such as carrying him around the room while he says "good night" to the pictures on the wall, letting him switch off the lights—or whatever may please him.

Once a ritual like this has been established, let him stick to it until he gives it up himself. If you try to leave out any part of his going-to-bed routine or change the sequence of it, you might find yourself with a wakeful and rebellious toddler on your hands.

Parents need patience and tact. One of the distressing things about a child who won't or can't sleep is the effect his restlessness has on his parents. At the end of a day with your baby or toddler, you need and deserve some rest. If you don't get it, because the baby refuses to sleep, your temper is apt to become very short indeed. And even if you are the world's most patient woman—being waked too many times during the night is bound to have a demoralizing effect on you. That's when you'll be tempted to drive your toddler back to bed with scoldings and threats. Don't do it! Forcing a baby to go back to sleep may work at first, but in the long run it may turn him into an even worse sleeper than he was before.

Because sleep is so important for your child's growth and development, it is worth devoting all your patience, love and ingenuity to the job of getting him started on good, healthful, common-sense sleeping habits.

—By Maria Massey Pelikan

WHY DO BABIES CRY?

HOW can a mother tell what her baby is crying for? Why is it that some babies cry so much more than others? Do babies always cry for a reason? People who have studied a great many infants have found some answers to questions like these.

"There probably is always a reason behind a baby's cry and we should try to find it, but even skilled observers don't always succeed," says Dr. Sally Ann Provence of the Department of Pediatrics, Yale University School of Medicine.

"The early weeks are bound to be a period of instability. The baby's nervous system, his breathing apparatus, his eating and sleeping rhythms, are all immature. Some babies take longer than others to settle down.

"Besides," Dr. Provence points out, "as any mother of two or more has noticed, what makes one baby cry may not bother another at all. Infants differ a great deal in sensitivity—in their reaction to the same situation.

"Wet diapers, for instance, disturb some babies—especially during the first six weeks—but others pay little attention. One infant will raise the roof when he's hungry; he's the kind that can't wait a minute for food without crying. Another, more easygoing, manages to be more patient before he protests.

"When you have a baby with an entirely different temperament or built-in set of traits than you have," says Dr. Provence, "it's often harder to figure out what's making him cry. But after a few months, almost every mother manages to work out a system she can rely on pretty well."

The First Three Months

It's comforting news, if you're having trouble interpreting your baby's cry-language, that the first two or three months are the hardest! It's also nice to know that even if you can only *guess* at the reason behind this fuss, you usually help your baby by going to him and trying to soothe him. That famous "tender loving care" by and large will cut down—not increase—the total amount of crying. Studies show that babies are more apt to get "spoiled" not when their cries are answered but when they're ignored.

This doesn't mean you seize your little friend in your arms every time he utters a chirp. A few minutes' crying, now and then, is nothing to worry about. The discomfort—or whatever his reason for crying—may be temporary and correct itself. Some babies, for instance, often fuss for a few minutes before they fall asleep, for no apparent reason. Sometimes all a whimpering baby seems to want is a pat or two, a shift in position, a little more covering—or less. However, if these measures don't work, you'll find many a sob can be soothed quickly by a little cuddling.

Causes of Crying

Have you heard that an infant *ought* to cry some because it's good exercise for his lungs? A popular old theory—one not supported by modern findings. A baby's lungs fill gradually with air for the first ten days or so of his life. Crying does abet that process but he's not crying just to inflate his lungs.

In understanding what does cause a baby's cries, it helps to know about how his needs keep changing as he grows. In the first few weeks of life, *hunger* is high on the list of what can make him unhappy enough to cry.

Many mothers say they learn to recognize a hunger cry by its sound sooner than other cries. Still, hunger rhythms don't go by the clock in a little baby, so he's apt to cry from hunger at quite irregular intervals—which can be confusing to new parents. There's one clue that helps make a hunger cry easier to spot. If your baby is restless instead of quiet after you pick him up—and if he searches around with his mouth and sucks frantically on his fists—chances are he's trying to tell you he'd like some nourishment. Timing, too, offers valuable hints. If your baby cries two hours or more after a meal, he may be feeling hunger pangs. If he consistently wakes up and yells within an hour or two after eating he may be ready for more food at a time: a longer session at the breast or a strengthened or increased formula.

Hunger Cries

When your baby sounds off soon after a feeding, his problem may be an unburped bubble—even though he performed nicely both during and after his meal. Turn him on his tummy and listen for the sound effects that will probably make him more comfortable.

Servicing a cry for food should be prompt. Reasonable speed when he's small helps him learn to wait a little as he grows bigger. He begins to understand that you're *for* him, that he can count on you to take care of his needs. This growth of trust is a wonderful bonus for answering his cries promptly.

Did you know that your child may cry because *you're* tired and tense? Studies of "colicky" babies have indicated that fatigue, tension and discord in the family may be a large contributing factor. (See separate article on "Colic.")

Another cause of young babies' cries can be just plain noise. Any loud noise —the doorbell, a blast from TV, even your voice when you call out suddenly— may make your baby let out a shriek. He may also evidence the startle reaction of drawing up his legs and seeming to clutch at the air. Loud noises bother some babies more than others, but there's usually less crying when the newcomer's family remembers to keep the household noise reasonably low.

A sudden jarring or a feeling of losing his balance can also startle a baby. Move slowly and gently—no jerky motions—when you bathe and dress your child. As you pick him up or turn him over, make sure to give him good support.

Even when he's lying in his crib a young baby gets a feeling of falling, because he can't help rolling sideways. Dr. Samuel Wishik, Professor of Maternal and Child Health at the University of Pittsburg, offers a solution to this problem which may sound surprisingly "old-fashioned."

"Little babies ought to be *swaddled*," declares Dr. Wishik. "A young baby likes and needs close wrapping. I hope we resume the custom."

How do you swaddle a baby? "Lay him on a small blanket and fold one corner up over his feet," says Dr. Wishik, "but *don't* hold his legs down straight —that's a restraint many babies object to! Let him lie in the position he's been accustomed to in his prenatal months—legs drawn up and arms bent. Fold both sides of the blanket over him almost up to the shoulders and pin the blanket snugly. His arms should be covered.

"When a baby gets to be about three months old and begins to outgrow the startle reflex, he won't need this 'cocoon' for a feeling of security. But there'd be a lot less crying by young babies," says Dr. Wishik, "if we went back to swaddling during the first two or three months."

When a Pacifier May Help

What about pacifiers? Some physicians feel a pacifier is fine—*provided* the baby has had plenty of sucking time at the bottle or breast, as well as all the attention he needs. Some infants require more sucking than others, and with them a pacifier is often a success. But don't pop a pacifier in your baby's mouth every time he fusses—it may be hard for him to part with if it becomes a handy substitute for your own arms around him.

In the early weeks, babies' cries come mostly from what might be called "internal" causes, such as hunger and other inner discomforts or tensions. But as your child's body and mind develop, new needs develop too. If these needs are satisfied, you'll find your baby crying less as he grows older. For example, as his eyes become more efficient and gradually learn to focus, he wants to use them. First he likes to look at a soft light. Later, he's fascinated by bright-colored toys hung over his crib, or curtains flapping in the breeze. At about four weeks, if he frets in the late afternoon and before he falls asleep, he may simply be telling you he's begun to grow up and is able to stay awake for longer intervals. Sometimes he'd like a little company. Gentle rocking or a few minutes' conversation may calm his cries. Music will often soothe him. Sometimes all it takes to sweeten up a late-afternoon crosspatch is to switch his bath to that time of day. The warm bath water is soothing in itself. And most babies enjoy a social hour along toward evening, just as grownups do.

The older your baby gets, the more he wants to see and hear what's going on. By around four months, his whimper sometimes has a forlorn sound, as if he were asking, "Where *is* everybody?" Moving his carriage or playpen near where you're working often changes his tune from fussing to contentedly "talking" to himself.

While it's important to respect his growing abilities and give him what he needs—remember that he doesn't *always* need to be picked up! Just as every baby requires care and attention, his development also benefits from a little time-to-himself, a few "islands of quiet," as Dr. Provence puts it, that let him look and listen. Overdoses of being lifted up and carried around and played with over-stimulate him and can make him more unhappy and fretful in the long run.

It's well known that babies often cry from sheer boredom. What a pity—since there's no one so eager to learn as a baby, if he's given half a chance. One easy way to avoid boredom is often overlooked: just make sure your baby's toys are right for his particular stage in growing. Many toy departments are well equipped to guide you in selecting toys to suit a growing baby's play abilities. Who wouldn't be bored if he's asked to amuse himself with gadgets much too young or too old for him?

Frustration is a frequent cause of crying. There's the leg-stuck-through-the-crib-bars kind, which is easy enough to take care of. But another frustration cry, not so simple to cope with, may appear when your child has almost—but not quite—mastered a new skill. You can't imagine what he's fussing about, but a few days later you'll see frowns and tears give way to smiles. He has finally managed to roll over or sit up! (For crying due to teething see article "First Teeth.")

When your baby gets to be seven or eight months old, he may startle you by crying whenever he sees an unfamiliar face or even a familiar face, in strange surroundings. He's always been such a friendly fellow—what suddenly makes him scream and turn away? This cry has a "developmental" source, too. The eight-month-old is beginning to know the difference between people. He clings tightly to mommy to make sure she won't go away. If your baby howls at the sight of his doting grandma or aunts, explain the situation. When he's not *forced* to be sociable, he'll soon outgrow this cry too.

—By Ruth Newburn Sedam

HOW TO KEEP YOUR BABY WELL IN WINTER

MOTHERS today appreciate the medical advances made in the past fifty years which have helped safeguard their babies' health during the winter months. Miracle drugs to combat colds, ear infections and pneumonia; vitamins to build healthy bodies and resistance to disease; serums to prevent or modify whooping cough and measles—all have helped make the winter season a more healthful time of year. However, winter still holds some hazards and discomforts for young babies. Here are some general rules to guide you in keeping your baby well in cold weather.

Room temperature. In the daytime—68 to 72 degrees (F.) is a good room temperature for the healthy baby. Dressed in his shirt (cotton or part wool mixture), diaper and kimono, he should be comfortable while he's awake. A lightweight blanket may be added while he sleeps.

At night do not let the baby's room get colder than about 60 degrees (F.). In addition to his shirt, diaper and nightdress he will need two lightweight blankets or tuck him in a warm, safe, roomy sleeping garment.

Your baby's airings. In winter weather, healthy newborn babies are generally aired indoors and on clear days only, until they are four to six weeks old. Do not allow the temperature of the room to go below 60 degrees (F.) during these airings. A ten-minute airing once a day is sufficient for the new baby.

Do not let the air blow directly on your baby. Place a screen in front of the open window or hang a blanket or folded sheet over the side of the crib. Protect the baby's head with a knitted cap or with the folds of the shawl or blanket in which you have wrapped him. Cover him with his usual night covering. Remove the extra covering after the airing when the room temperature reaches 68 to 72 degrees.

After a healthy baby of normal weight is six weeks old, outdoor airing in good weather is usually recommended. But notice those words "in good weather." They don't mean just any sunny day. They mean a sunny day in which no strong, dust-laden wind is blowing, in which the temperature is above freezing and snow is not melting. Melting snow makes the air damp, even though the sun is shining. Damp air has no benefits for your baby.

What outdoor temperature is best for a baby? Dr. Benjamin Spock's advice is to be guided by your baby's weight. If your baby weighs from eight to ten pounds, an outdoor temperature of 60 degrees or more is perfectly safe for his daily airing. When he weighs ten pounds he can enjoy clear days in which the temperature is above freezing (above 32 degrees). When he weighs twelve pounds or more you can put him in a sunny sheltered spot even though the temperature in the shade is slightly below freezing. But watch the thermometer and see that the sun shines on his carriage all the while.

How long should his airing last? Start this outdoor airing with 20 to 30-minute periods between the hours of 11 and 1 when the sun is high. Increase the time gradually to two to three hours daily starting around midday when the sun is apt to be at its warmest.

Dressing your baby for outdoors. Be guided by two things: the temperature outside rather than the calendar, and where and how you plan to air your baby. For example, a baby who is sleeping in his carriage, protected by its hood and sides, will need less bundling than the older baby who takes his airing in an open playpen.

Be guided by the way your baby feels to your touch. Slip your fingers inside his neck band and inside his bonnet. If his skin is moist with perspiration you'll know you've dressed him too warmly. If his body (not his hands or feet) feels cool to your fingers you can be sure that he needs a bit more covering.

Food Needs

A baby's food requirements are somewhat higher in winter than in summer. His appetite is often keener, especially if he has outdoor airings regularly. He usually accepts new foods, new textures with hungry willingness. Moreover, the danger of food spoilage or contamination of food by flies or other insects is lessened.

In addition to his food your baby will need some form of vitamin D. Today doctors advise giving vitamin D all year round.

Mothers often ask, does my baby need other vitamins or minerals in cold weather? Your doctor must decide this. Your baby probably gets sufficient vitamin A from the milk he drinks and from the fish oils. Vitamin C is essential in every season. If your baby doesn't take at least two ounces of orange juice or four ounces of tomato juice each day (unless he's breast-fed) your doctor will probably suggest giving him vitamin C in some other form.

If your baby needs it, your doctor may advise some of the B-complex vitamins. If he's anemic he may need additional iron. Or examination may indicate that he needs more calcium but never give any of these things except on your doctor's order.

Guard against illness. There are diseases babies used to have which your baby need never have today if he gets every protective shot to which he is entitled.

Colds. Someone once said, "Contentment preserves one even from catching cold." Perhaps that is one reason why babies up to a year old have so few colds, and those they do have are very mild. For when you stop to think of it, all the loving care young babies get must add up to contentment. And all the things that make up that care—food, rest, cleanliness and comfort—are also cold-preventive measures.

An infant doesn't usually have a fever with his cold. But take his temperature to be sure. If it is 101 or over consult your doctor. Never treat a baby's cold without your doctor's advice. Never give your baby medicine—not even little doses, not even nose drops—without a doctor's order.

Despite caution and conscientious care, older babies of a year or more do catch cold. And these colds can be severe. Doctors tell us that babies catch cold from other people far more frequently than from being chilled. That's why it's best to keep your baby away from anyone who has a cold.

If you have a cold or a sinus infection, turn the baby's care and formula-making over to someone else if this is possible. If not, take every precaution to prevent spreading germs. Keep your distance except when actually tending to your baby's needs. Then wear a mask but be sure to touch only the tapes. Never touch the portion which covers your mouth and nose. Use a fresh mask daily. Boil it or discard it for another after each day's use—oftener, if your cold is fresh and in its most infectious stage. Wash your hands with soap and water before you touch your baby or his food.

Avoid crowds. The fewer people who come in contact with your baby, the less chance he has of catching cold. If you have to take your baby with you when you market, go when the stores are less crowded, or telephone for supplies. Often a few pennies more spent for groceries to be delivered mean dollars and worry saved by preventing sickness.

Don't dress your baby too warmly. Don't take him out in winter directly after his bath. Wait at least one hour.

Avoid overheated, over-dry rooms. Avoid chilling. Diaper him with several thicknesses to prevent nighttime sopping. If you change him during the night do it in a warm room.

Give him regular outdoor airings in good weather.

Signs of a Cold

The older baby's cold often seems to come on quite suddenly. He may seem perfectly well, but in the late afternoon get cross and fretful. Perhaps he looks flushed and his eyes appear dull and heavy. You take his temperature and he has a fever—101 or 102, maybe even higher. Of course you call your doctor. Not because this is an unusual pattern for a baby's cold, but because you know that you need a doctor's advice any time a child has a fever of 101 or more. A cold treated promptly and properly will soon be better and there are not apt to be complications. When any baby has a persistent cough, with or without fever, he should be taken to the doctor.

When you call your doctor tell him the child's symptoms—temperature, cough, wheezing, running nose, appearance. He'll no doubt tell you to put the baby to bed, keep him warm, give him all he wants to drink and may suggest further treatment before he gets there. Or he will tell you what to do and ask you to report to him in 24 hours.

When your baby has a cold, keep his room a bit warmer (72–74 degrees F.)

day and night. Don't open the window. Keep the air moist. Keep him in bed at least 24 hours after his temperature is normal; longer if he has been quite sick.

Don't take him out too soon after a winter cold, even though the day is mild. Wait until a day or so after the cold is completely gone, then keep him out only for twenty to thirty minutes the first day, in a sunny sheltered spot. If no symptoms reappear that night, increase the time the second day to an hour or so, then to his usual out-of-doors time.

When a baby one year old or more starts a cold with a fever, even a high one, it's more or less the usual course of events. You don't minimize its importance but you don't become unduly alarmed either. But if a baby who has had a cold for several days with little or no fever suddenly runs a temperature it's a different matter. Get in touch with your doctor. He'll want to determine the cause.

Ear infections can be a complication of any illness that started with a stuffy nose, a cold or a sore throat. It can be a mild infection; in fact mild ear infections are quite common in young children. The more serious infections can be checked with modern drugs if your doctor is called promptly.

The child of two or older can usually tell you if his ear aches. He may point to it or pull on it or say it hurts. As the younger baby can't do this, you must be aware of certain signs. If a baby who usually sleeps well, especially one who has had a cold, suddenly sleeps fitfully and cries out sharply during his sleep for no apparent cause, you can suspect an earache. He may shake his head from side to side, cry when you lay him on one side or when you touch his ear. Possibly the area behind the ear will be red and swollen, but not always. He may have a fever. He may just seem listless and refuse his food. Any one or more of these signs can indicate ear infection. Call your doctor promptly. Serious trouble can be prevented if treatment is started immediately.

Your doctor will suggest relief measures you can use until he gets there. A well covered, warm (not hot) water bottle often gives partial relief and can do no harm.

Frostbite. If a white spot that feels hard when you touch it appears on your baby's cheeks, fingers, ears or nose, you can suspect frostbite. The spot remains white or sometimes turns blue after the baby is brought indoors. It's best, of course, to keep your baby in when the weather is below freezing. And when the temperature is on the borderline, check the thermometer occasionally after you put the baby out, to see that the temperature hasn't dropped to freezing.

If frostbite does occur, consult your doctor for proper treatment. Do not rub or massage it unless he tells you to. Sometimes it is several weeks before the spot disappears.

Mottled or marbled skin tends to make many mothers think their babies are cold when they really aren't. Many babies' skin takes on a bluish-red mottled look when exposed to cold. It's the reaction of the network of surface veins to the cold. If his body feels comfortably warm don't worry about the mottling.

Sneezing in the young baby doesn't necessarily mean he's catching cold. So hold off with those extra blankets. As a matter of fact, the blankets may be the cause. Blanket lint is often irritating to the delicate membranes in the baby's nose because he has no protective hair on the lining of his nostrils. If your baby sneezes often, suspect the blankets and try covering them with a non-linty material. —*By Adeline Bullock, R.N.*

SUMMER CARE FOR BABIES

B ABIES grow irritable and uncomfortable in hot weather in much the same way as adults. Fortunately, there's a good deal you can do to help your baby weather summer's sultriness in comfort.

A daily bath is a must—and more than one a day in the hottest weather. When you bathe your baby more than once daily, go easy on the soap. A few tablespoonsful of cornstarch, added to the water, make a soothing bath. Older infants who can sit alone will enjoy spending longer periods, playing and splashing. Baby bath seats are available to keep them safe. However, never leave your baby alone in the tub and protect him from drafts.

After the bath, careful drying of his folds and creases reduces the possibility of chafing. A light sprinkling of baby powder or lotion, especially around the buttocks, helps prevent irritation. If you prefer a solution to powder, you can make a soothing effective one from a cup of boiled water and one tablespoonful of baking soda. Store in a clean covered jar and apply it cooled with clean absorbent cotton.

Despite precautions, prickly heat and other minor rashes sometimes occur. Prickly heat is a baby's most common minor summer malady. A non-contagious eruption of tiny red pimples caused by the inflammation of the skin around the sweat ducts, it usually appears around the neck and shoulders, causing itchiness and discomfort. But there are safe and practical ways to prevent and treat it. Cleanliness and exposure to air promote healing. Before or after his bath, let your naked baby kick in a protected, well ventilated place. Put him on an absorbent pad or some folded diapers for short periods during the day— about ten or fifteen minutes or longer if his room is draft-free and he's enjoying the airing. There are also good powders on the market, specifically for prickly heat.

Clothing can often be an inadvertent source of discomfort to newborn babies. Dress your infant according to the temperature. Overdressing may lead to persistent skin discomfort. Avoid tight or constricting garments. Our present knowledge of infant care points to the virtue of free, unhampered body movements for even the youngest baby.

Choosing Summer Clothes

Several basic principles can be kept in mind in choosing summer clothes for the baby. The less fussing the better is a good rule of thumb. Babies are comfortable in simple, loose cotton shirts and diapers, so avoid bulky folds and bunchy gathers. Avoid shoes, too, during the baby's first summer. He will be cooler without them. Check to be sure that lined protective pants and diaper covers have loose, non-constricting leg openings. If you must dress him for a special occasion, remember that some fabrics are more absorbent and less irritating than others—for example, cotton or soft challis.

There was a time when babies were protected from all rays of the sun, kept tightly bundled and covered during infrequent outings. Today, most parents are familiar with sunlight's benefits—in pleasure, in health, in preventing and helping to clear up minor skin irritations and rashes—so familiar that often we go to the opposite extreme of overexposure. Your baby shouldn't be exposed to the sun's direct rays indiscriminately. He should be exposed only moderately and gradually—and a planned program will be the most helpful to him. One minute a day at about one month of age is a safe rate at first. Start by exposing his legs to the sun, then his trunk and back. At all times, protect his eyes by placing him with the top of his head toward the sun. Since bright sunlight is likely to annoy him, put a visored cap or bonnet on him.

With these precautions taken, get your baby exposed to the sun in moderate amounts as often as possible. (Don't of course expose him during heat waves.) Find a warm spot out of drafts and expose him for brief periods in the early morning and late afternoon. Later, as he grows more used to the sun, longer outings with less clothing will be safe and healthful. (If possible, put him on a quilted pad or in a playpen—for these combine safety with freely circulating air. A playpen cover of absorbent cloth will feel cool and fresh to the baby. A partially shaded outdoor spot in which you can anticipate the approach of the sun may be used for longer outings or naps. If your baby does sleep outside it's wise to select a spot you can watch from a window—preferably a level one protected from leaves and insects. If there is danger of insect bites, a thin netting over the carriage will help prevent them.

Airings for City Babies

A city mother can use her ingenuity to provide fresh air and sunshine for her baby. Many frustrated apartment dwellers find it difficult to give their babies the two to three hours' outing most doctors consider advisable. But the sunlit apartment window is an ideal substitute for an outing, since it isn't necessary to be in the direct rays of the sun to profit from its health-giving rays. Open the window wide and put your baby in front of it in his carriage or on a pad— making sure that he's protected from drafts. This is a good time to initiate sunbath and exercise time—again carefully limiting and increasing the amount of exposure.

As your baby grows, you'll want to include him in family outings. There are lightweight aluminum and canvas travel cribs available which fit neatly into the back seat of a car and double as daytime playpens. Parents themselves can fix a light plywood board secured in the back seat and extending to the back of the front seat which, spread with a pad, will make a roomy and comfortable play place for a traveling baby. Adjustable platforms can also be purchased ready made.

If a beach, lake or any place near water is your destination, you'll need to take special protective measures for him. The sun's reflected rays will be much stronger than any he has known in the back yard or at a window. Since babies burn much more quickly than adults, and the effect of sun and wind may lead to serious complications—it's wise to protect a young baby from all direct rays of the sun on summer trips.

In the first year of life, summer will coincide with a period of rapid change and growth. Infants seem to be more susceptible to infectious diarrhea and other disturbances in hot weather. The ever present danger of diarrhea should be kept in mind and precautions taken to avert it. Changes in water and milk are a frequent cause of diarrhea. For short one day excursions, jars or cans of baby food and juice, bottles packed in an insulated picnic bag and home boiled water will offer a baby a safe and familiar diet. For longer trips, consult your doctor about what to do.

Always be careful to prevent contamination of milk. Once milk has been heated and used for feeding a baby, the remaining portions should be discarded, for bacteria multiply rapidly in warm milk. When milk has been unrefrigerated for any length of time, don't use it for a young child. In using commercially prepared sterilized baby foods, heat only as much as you need for one feeding and keep the rest under refrigeration in the original container. Studies show that fewer bacteria are present when the food isn't transferred to another container. Careful attention to clean hands, bottles and nipples prevents unnecessary mishap in the hot months.

Avoid Changes in Feeding

Weaning from breast or bottle to cup is a major adjustment, one that can well wait until cooler weather. A fussy irritable baby is in no mood to take such momentous change in his accustomed feeding routine. Changes in diet and new foods can also be postponed. Just as adults often eat less in summer, a baby's appetite may suffer too. Introducing new foods at a time when his appetite is poor may condition him against a valuable food which he might otherwise accept.

There's usually no need for concern when a baby occasionally refuses a meal or fails to eat his regular portion. If he has no temperature, no sign of a cold or diarrhea, and he continues to take fluids well, he's undoubtedly all right. Make sure, though, that you offer him extra fluids in the hot months—juice or cooled boiled water, or boiled water mixed with his favorite fruit juice.

Established sleeping habits can be upset by weather changes. For infants, a diaper can take the place of a cover on a warm night. Older babies often need nothing more than light cotton pajamas, a zippered cotton sack, or a nightgown over their nighttime diapers. A small fan placed to promote air circulation, but not directly aimed at the baby, is an excellent way to keep his room comfortable for sleep. —*By Audrey Palm Riker, R.N., Ed.D.*

BREAST OR BOTTLE FEEDING— PROS AND CONS

WILL you and your baby be happiest and will your baby be healthiest with breast feeding or with bottle feeding? It will pay to take an unbiased look at both sides of this important question in the light of recent findings and also to find out how your doctor feels about it in your particular case.

Which does your doctor recommend? Well in advance of the baby's birth, you and your doctor will be talking over the feeding question. Some physicians feel strongly that babies are better off breast-fed. Others think bottle feeding has a lot of advantages. Your doctor's recommendation may be influenced by your physical condition or by your emotional makeup (which he probably knows more about than you think). Your baby's size and condition at birth may also affect your doctor's decision. But by and large, your physician will be guided by how you feel about feeding the baby. If you earnestly want to breast feed—or just as definitely don't want to—be sure to say so. Tell your obstetrician—and also, if possible, the doctor who will take care of your baby after he's born—which feeding system you think would work out best.

Will you be able to nurse your baby? Many women with small breasts wonder whether they'll be able to produce enough milk to satisfy a hungry baby. Size of breasts, experience shows, gives no indication of a mother's ability to produce milk—small-breasted women are often very successful at it. If you really want to nurse, the chances are good that you can. Many women, who were unable to breast feed their first baby, manage beautifully with the second. Often the difference lies in whether or not you get plenty of encouragement from your doctor, your husband and the hospital where the baby is born.

Does the idea of breast feeding appeal to you? Some mothers haven't the slightest doubt. They put it this way: "Breast feeding sounds natural and happy. It must make you feel close to your baby—knowing you're helping him grow and develop as no other person can—and it must give the baby a nice feeling of security, too." Breast milk is pure, nourishing and easy to digest. And recent tests show that colostrum, which comes in before the milk, definitely does give the baby some early protection against disease. Besides being good for the baby, breast milk is cheap—and as some mothers put it "so much less bother than messing around making formula and boiling bottles!"

That's how an "I-like-breast-feeding" mother feels. But what about the mother—just as "good" and loving a mother—to whom the idea of breast feeding seems both unattractive and inconvenient: "All those pads and that leaking milk! The very thought of being a nursing mother makes me squirm. My baby is going to get a good nutritious formula!"

If you feel uncomfortable about it should you force yourself to breast feed? Many doctors say not. Millions of babies have thrived on carefully prepared formulas—and there are plenty of nourishing, easy-to-digest formulas to choose from. True, breast-fed babies sometimes seem to have fewer digestive upsets than those fed by bottle. And tests do indicate that colostrum—the yellowish fluid the baby gets from the mother's breasts for the first few days or so—provides early immunity to certain diseases. But every baby is born with immunity—he gets it chiefly from his nine months' nourishment through the placenta.

As for his emotional start in life: a bottle-fed baby can get a fine sense of security and contentment if meals are served in mother's arms in the same cozy atmosphere a nursing baby enjoys. He'll look forward to feeding as eagerly as his breast-fed friends if he's given the breast feeder's privilege of stopping when he's full—or, on lazy days, if he's allowed plenty of sucking.

It's actually better, child care experts conclude, for a baby to be served cow's milk by a happy and relaxed mother than to get breast milk from a discontented mother who hates the whole business and is gingerly "doing her duty."

The bottle-fed baby who does get cheated, doctors say, is the fellow who is not held but propped up with a pillow for all his feedings. That makes bottle feeding a lonely rather than a friendly experience. These substitutes for mother's arms should be used only in cases of emergency when there's no other way to feed him.

What is husband's attitude? It's important to know his opinion. If he is strongly for (or against) breast feeding, that's something to consider when you're making up your mind. It's hard for either breast feeding or bottle feeding to be completely successful or happy if you're worrying because the baby's daddy disapproves. Here again, find out what's bothering him and try to come to a sensible conclusion. However, you'll probably find he's in favor of whichever system you want, particularly after you talk it over and explain your reasons.

Are you afraid breast feeding will spoil your figure? Your doctor will explain that nursing needn't cause your breasts to droop. According to Dr. Edwin Gold, Obstetric Consultant of the New York City Department of Health, breast changes take place during pregnancy, not during nursing. Says Dr. Gold, "Breasts properly supported by a good brassiere before the baby is born as well as during nursing, won't sag because of stretched skin and tissues."

However, it is important to watch your weight. Breasts can sag if you're over-fat, even if you've never been pregnant. Doctors point out that just because a nursing mother must eat extra food, she needn't put on extra weight. Skim milk can be used for that required quart a day. It contains the necessary calcium and protein, but not the fat.

Today's mothers (nursing or not) are taught to steer clear of excess starch and sugar after the baby arrives as well as during pregnancy—when physicians normally like to limit a mother's weight gain to about 20 pounds. Sensible diet, plus exercises, will get rid of most new-mother fat.

Breast feeding, in one way, actually improves a mother's figure because as the baby nurses the muscle wall of the uterus contracts—which helps it back to normal size and position.

Do you think "self-demand" won't work with bottle feeding? Millions of mothers who are enthusiastic about a flexible schedule—and also about bottle feeding—have found that the two work together perfectly well. True, babies who are breast fed get food more promptly when they ask for it than bottle-fed babies who have to wait around while dinner is being warmed. Also, if a self-demand baby is bottle fed, it's a little harder on mother to meet the irregular hunger calls of those first few weeks. It means making up extra formula, which may or may not get used.

Will breast feeding tie you down? Doctors say it needn't, if you make use of a "freedom bottle." When the milk supply is well established and the baby's feeding schedule has settled down to a pretty regular routine, many physicians recommend a "freedom bottle" to let the nursing mother get a little change of scenery. They suggest that every other day is often enough at first. Many working mothers who nurse find they can go back to the office in a month or two, with the aid of one bottle feeding daily. The milk can be expressed from the breast (this method keeps the breast from becoming uncomfortably full—and it also lessens the likelihood of reducing the milk supply). Or the "freedom bottle" may be formula, made one bottle at a time.

Getting the breast-fed baby accustomed to a bottle early in life has other advantages: When you begin to wean him, he won't be so set in his ways. Father often benefits from the "freedom bottle," too, because it lets him have the fun of feeding the baby once in a while.

Is formula trouble to make? Most formulas are quite simple to make. They're a mixture of milk, water and sweetening. The doctor may recommend evaporated milk, pasteurized fresh milk, dried whole milk or some special kind—depending on your baby's needs and what kind of milk is available.

Is breast feeding painful? With proper preparation during pregnancy and caution during the early days of nursing, breast feeding is normally not painful. If a mother plans to breast feed, many physicians suggest anointing and massaging nipples regularly, beginning about three months before the baby is born. If nipples are sensitive when the baby first starts to nurse, the doctor usually cuts down nursing time to five minutes at each breast to help the tenderness clear up. As the nipples get accustomed to nursing, the time can be increased.

Doctors say breast feeding need not be exhausting, either, if a mother adopts a design for living which includes proper nutrition and plenty of rest—and eliminates a few housekeeping and social frills for a while. Several short rests during a day—even five or ten minutes at a time—can do much to keep up a nursing mother's strength and milk supply.

What is hospital's attitude? This is an important question—particularly if you're a mother who earnestly wants to breast feed her baby. In hospitals with "rooming-in" facilities—where mother and baby bunk within peeking distance—breast feeding is taken for granted and made easy in every way. Many hospitals, however, are not staffed to bring the baby in for the frequent nursing that is so helpful in stimulating and increasing the supply of breast milk.

But if you insist firmly that you're anxious to breast feed the baby, and the doctor makes it clear that you should be helped to succeed, the hospital staff will usually do the best they can to cooperate.

These days, people concerned with the welfare of mothers and babies are realizing that whether a baby is breast-fed or bottle-fed isn't as important as the confidence building, two-way feeling of warmth and tenderness that develops when a baby and his mother thoroughly enjoy each other's company. Being held is part of your baby's enjoyment of eating.

When is this really important goal—mother-and-baby happiness—most likely to be reached? When you, having carefully considered all aspects of the question, are feeding your baby in the way that *you* feel is best.

—By Ruth Newburn Sedam

HOW TO PREPARE FORMULA

A QUICK, safe way to prepare formula is by the terminal heating method. Good equipment is important. You will need:

A container for sterilizing. It can be a large kettle or pail that has a tight cover, a sterilizer designed especially for terminal heating or a pressure cooker. Whatever you use must be tall enough to hold the bottles in an upright position so that the nipple shields or screw caps do not touch the lid, allowing the steam to circulate completely around the bottles.

Formula-making equipment: Measuring cup, pitcher, funnel, measuring spoons, bottle brush.

Bottles, nipples and shields or screw caps. Enough for a twenty-four hour supply of formula and drinking water.

Scrub all equipment with hot soapy water, using your bottle brush on the insides of bottles and nipples. Check the nipple holes. They should permit the formula to drop as fast as it can without running in a stream. When everything is thoroughly scrubbed, rinse well with hot water.

Make up the formula according to your doctor's instructions. If he has included lactic acid or any other acid, find out if it is suitable for terminal heating. Pour formula through funnel into clean bottles. Put the nipples on the bottles and set the shields over them lightly. If you use the bottles with disk-and-screw cap, place the nipples in the bottles upside down, cover with the sealing disks, and screw caps down to snug fit. Then loosen caps with a one-quarter to one-half turn back.

Sterilization technique. Now you are ready to sterilize. Place bottles on a rack in the sterilizer. If your utensil has no rack, a piece of heavy wire mesh cut to fit the bottom will do. Or arrange a folded towel around the bottles to prevent them from tipping. Pour water in the sterilizer to the level of formula in the bottles and cover tightly. Heat and boil for 20 minutes.

In a pressure cooker, only an inch or so of water is necessary. Follow your usual procedure for pressure-cooking, using a pressure of five pounds for ten minutes. Remove from heat and let stand at room temperature for about five minutes. If the pressure is not entirely reduced after five minutes, run cold water over the cooker. Too rapid reduction of pressure causes boiling over of formula and clogged nipples. (If nipples tend to clog during feeding, insert a square of sterilized gauze between bottle rim and nipple before capping.) Remove bottles after the pressure is exhausted.

Tighten nipple shields or screw caps. Cool bottles in lukewarm water, then cold water. When cool to the touch, dry each bottle and refrigerate.

—By Adeline Bullock, R.N.

FIVE IMPORTANT RULES
FOR BABY FEEDING

IF your baby is allowed to fill himself to the brim at every feeding most feeding problems vanish. So if you want to prevent colic, if you want to find out your baby's normal, natural schedule of sleeping and eating, and if you want to minimize vomiting, then it's important to know *how* to let him get full.

"But why," you may ask, "will filling my baby full do all this?"

Simply because, if he's fed full, there is no air in his stomach to displace the milk. Furthermore, the baby's schedule can then be set up properly, based on the emptying time of his stomach. If he's always filled full to the top, he will always take the same time to empty his stomach (provided you give him the same kind of food, which, naturally, is what occurs with the newborn). This, in infants, as in all the animal kingdom, automatically determines the schedule.

A painstaking series of X-ray studies were made at the University of Nebraska Hospital to show exactly what happens in the stomachs of babies who are fed in right or in wrong ways. As a result of those studies it is possible to state the following five rules for baby feeding.

Feed your baby in an upright position. Hold him as nearly upright as can be done with comfort. As the X-rays showed, if he is fed lying down a large air bubble forms on top of the milk in his stomach. It can't escape, so he never gets completely full when he's fed in a lying-down position.

Feed him only when he cries for it. Before he cries for a meal is too soon. If things are going along in nature's way, an infant eats till he's full and then goes to sleep. He sleeps till his stomach gets empty and hunger pains wake him. Then he wants to eat again.

So, in feeding a little baby, wait till he cries. In the newborn, this crying will be synonymous with waking, if he was full when he went to sleep and if he wasn't wakened before he awoke with hunger pangs. Such a flexible feeding program is popularly called "self-demand."

By waiting till he cries, you know he's hungry, and he'll eat till he's full. Then he'll go back to sleep. If fed *before* he's hungry, he doesn't go to sleep properly, simply because he won't eat a full meal. Here, again, we see an intimate connection between eating and sleeping. A full stomach diverts blood from the brain and helps induce sleep.

Feed him promptly when he does cry for it. Some mothers let the baby cry for maybe half an hour before feeding, in the mistaken notion that crying is good for the lungs, or because it may not be convenient to fix the bottle right away. Or they may be waiting for a predetermined time—an artificial schedule that doesn't jibe with the baby's stomach.

But what happens when he gets fed too late? Apart from building up early resentment in the baby toward his mother because he has to wait for food, these things happen: his stomach gets all filled up with air from his crying and he gets too tired to eat properly. Between the air and the fatigue, he'll eat only a partial meal and then drop off to sleep before he's full.

A baby who is fed too late usually wakes up before he's supposed to, for the simple reason that he wasn't filled full and hunger wakes him up before his sleep is out.

Feed him with a nipple that doesn't starve him. If the holes are too small he can't get enough milk from the nipple, so he'll get tired before he's full and go to sleep. And then he'll wake up too soon, hungry, and presto! you've got a "feeding problem."

The remedy is simple. Test the nipple before warming the milk, by turning the bottle upside down. If the milk does not come out in a steady drip (about

20 drops per minute) the holes are too small. If such is the case, heat a fine needle red hot and plunge it into the nipple. If you place the eye end of the needle into a cork or raw potato, it will be easier to hold. If you get the holes too large, heat the needle again and partially seal up the enlarged holes. If this doesn't work, put that nipple aside for use when your baby is older, when he can take milk faster, and fix another. Some doctors recommend making two cross cuts with a razor blade.

Feed him all he wants. Give him all he can hold every meal. If he's bottle fed keep on bringing out the bottles as long as he'll take them. Of course this assumes you are using the formula recommended by your pediatrician.

You don't need to worry about measuring his intake. We don't know how much milk a breast-fed baby gets. We don't need to know, either with breast-fed or bottle-fed babies. Just give 'em all they want. Have plenty of the formula on hand and keep offering seconds. When he finally stops sucking and all the other factors are under control, you'll know he's full.

The same basic advice applies to older babies. Whenever they're hungry, feed them. And when you feed them, feed them full. As the intervals between feedings gradually lengthen, and as the need for sleep lessens, the baby will be eating less often. In fact, when a child gets into his second or third year, his growth slows down, and if he seems to have no desire to eat three meals a day, it's often better to give him two big meals a day that he'll enjoy.

SYMPTOMS OF UNDERFEEDING

IN the newborn clinic of a hospital, five babies had been brought in by five worried mothers. One baby had diarrhea. Another was vomiting. Still another had colic. The fourth was losing weight in spite of an increased number of feedings, and the last wasn't sleeping right.

The treatment eventually prescribed, although the symptoms differed widely, was essentially the same for each baby: feed him full.

This is not to say that any mother whose baby is showing such symptoms should take it upon herself to diagnose his trouble as undernourishment, and neglect to call the doctor. There is always the possibility that a more serious cause is behind the symptom.

Take the first baby, for example. On questioning, his mother said the baby's stools were loose and frequent. Obviously, she reasoned, the thing to do was to feed him less—"give his insides a rest" so they could get back to more normal movements.

Reduced food intake and other dietary restrictions are proper treatment for many diarrheas, but examination ruled out infection or other disorders as the cause in this case. Here's what was happening to the baby:

Normally, after a meal, there is increased activity of the whole gastrointestinal tract. If feedings are small but frequent, as is usually the case when the baby's stomach isn't filled full at each feeding, bowel movements are also frequent. A hungry baby also has increased hunger contractions, which step up intestinal activity still more.

This abnormal activity causes rapid emptying of the intestinal tract. Green stools often result, because the food doesn't stay in the intestines long enough for the green bile pigments to be absorbed normally. The looseness or liquidity of the stools is due to lack of time in the lower bowel where the absorption of fluids normally takes place. Explosive movements are also apt to result because the baby's stomach, not completely filled with milk, contains a lot of air which is passed along in the intestinal tract.

The second baby examined had alarmed his parents because of much vomiting. A careful evaluation ruled out any abnormality in the gastrointestinal tract. The mother disclosed that her baby took his formula lying down from a propped bottle. Because of his spitting up, she figured he must be getting too much, and she cut down on his milk.

Causes of Vomiting

Sometimes vomiting in infants is caused by a fat intolerance and may be helped by a reduction in fat and increase in protein. And some vomiting occurs in babies at about six months because they become more active. Occasionally, too, a baby may be overfed with too concentrated a diet. More often, however, it is the other way around.

But at least 90 per cent of the time, vomiting is due to the baby's not getting his fill. When a baby is not filled up to the brim, the air in his stomach is not displaced with food, and a sudden burp may cause a too strong contraction of the stomach and a loss of the feeding.

A baby can retain air in his stomach even when he's held at his feedings, of course, if he's not fed properly. But a propped bottle makes matters worse. Because a propped bottle almost inevitably means a baby will *swallow* a lot of air with his food, it is one of the most common causes of vomiting. He'll quit taking his bottle and often will vomit part or all of his meal. So it may seem as though he is getting too full. But it's air he's full of, not milk.

The usual approach to the colic that bothered the third baby is to change the feedings around, change the formula and cut the feedings. There are some 400-odd formulas for baby feeding, and the normal baby will thrive on almost any of them. But not if he doesn't get enough.

Except for the exceptional baby whose colic may be due to a genuine allergy, which will be shown by a rash or other symptom, colic is caused by air in the intestines. Improper feeding, inadequate filling, causes the air to collect in the stomach and pass down into the intestines.

Why do some improperly fed babies have colic and others not? It may be due to the fact that some babies can propel air through the intestinal tract because of a better developed nerve-muscle mechanism; others can't readily expel air and pain results.

Burping the baby during and after feeding is common practice. But a baby often needs to be burped *before* feeding to get rid of air swallowed in crying.

With a colicky baby already on your hands, of course, it's a little tougher. He'll wiggle and fret while he is feeding, often swallowing more air and continuing the colic cycle. Your doctor may interrupt the cycle with sedation at night. Then the baby wakes up relaxed from a good rest, hungry and ready—with proper feeding technique—to fill himself full.

Don't Feed Too Often

Very frequently babies don't eat well or gain properly because they are *fed too often*. That was the case with the fourth infant in the hospital. "He's not growing and gaining," his mother said, "so I've been trying to feed him more often." This baby was never allowed to get hungry so he never really ate a full meal.

Waiting till a baby is hungry before feeding him is quite different from making a hungry baby wait for food. A feeding schedule should never be imposed on a baby. He should be fed whenever he is hungry and eventually, as his system develops regularity, his hunger-rhythm will determine his feeding schedule.

How can you tell when your baby is hungry? A young baby's lusty crying almost always means hunger. When he's full up with food he goes to sleep. Normally, he sleeps till hunger pangs wake him. If he wakes up and doesn't cry, you'll know he's not hungry enough for a full meal.

Queer as it may seem, too frequent feeding can make a baby lose weight. The solution is to feed him when he's hungry, and feed him full then.

The fifth baby in the clinic wasn't sleeping right. "He doesn't go to sleep well after his last feeding," complained his mother. "So lately we've been cutting down, but he's getting worse, not better."

Sleeping problem. The only reason this mother had a sleeping problem was that she had a feeding problem. Her baby wasn't sleepy because his stomach was only partially filled. Not enough blood was transferred from brain to stomach.

The trouble started when she saw that her baby was still hungry after one bottle. Sensibly, she tried a second bottle once or twice, but since he didn't take it all she stopped.

No wonder he wasn't sleeping. His hunger wasn't satisfied, his stomach emptied too soon, and hunger pangs woke him up before he was through sleeping.

This sleeping problem was immediately resolved, as it is in the vast majority of cases, by increasing the amount of the feedings and teaching the mother how to fill her baby full.

We won't quite say a baby *can't* be overfed, but our experience teaches us the reverse—underfeeding—is very common. Let your baby tell you when he is hungry, then feed him full, and you'll avoid almost all feeding problems.

WHEN AND HOW TO WEAN YOUR BABY

FROM a medical point of view, there is no need to wean your baby from the breast until he is a year old or older. Some primitive tribes, with different customs, keep their children at breast for several years, with no apparent bad results.

From the standpoint of Western practice and custom, however, six to nine months is the usual time, assuming that the mother has a choice and has plenty of milk.

Weaning from the bottle is usually accomplished by the time the baby reaches a year and a half—though the child may still want to take a bottle to bed with him at night. Any time up to this is all right, depending on the individual baby. For it cannot be stressed too often that all babies are different. The need to suck varies greatly from one baby to another.

The advice of your own doctor on weaning plus your own good sense are the best guides to rely on. Your doctor knows your baby, his needs, patterns and home background. He knows, too, the needs of the baby's parents. What we shall try to do here is to set forth principles and facts which apply in different measure to all babies, and which will act as a guide at this important time of your baby's life.

First of all, whether weaning from the breast or the bottle, *follow your baby's lead*. Don't pull the breast or the bottle away when he still wants it, and don't force the cup before he's ready for it. To withhold the bottle increases his psychological need for it and to force the cup results in rebellion. Either act makes the baby angry, for it forces him into independence before he is ready for it, and then we find the weaning process going in reverse.

Weaning from the Breast

Though here we are helping a child to change his way of taking nourishment, just as in weaning from the bottle, there are important differences. Chief of these is the emotional satisfaction enjoyed by both the baby and the mother in the act of nursing, which can be approached, but not quite duplicated, by the mother holding the baby in her arms while he takes his bottle.

Another difference is that sometimes the baby at the breast is ready to give it up earlier than the baby on the bottle. We are not sure whether this is due to the fact that he has a more satisfactory emotional and sucking experience on breast than on the bottle, or whether his newly stirring independence, his impatience at being held so close, impels him to leave off such dependent contact with his mother.

Maybe it's some of both. For it is certain that most babies, from six to nine months of age, begin to want to hold their own bottles, to ease away from having everything done for them.

We advise weaning from the breast to the bottle to the cup, rather than directly from breast to cup. The reason is simple: it's more gradual.

So from the beginning, breast-fed babies should get a bottle occasionally, along with the breast. We often recommend that the bottle supersede the breast entirely for the middle feeding. This gives the mother's milk supply a boost for the afternoon feeding and also further acquaints the baby with the bottle, which by now should be an old friend.

If at any time, due to sickness, teething or other cause, the baby seems to reject this bottle feeding and want the breast again without interruption, don't hesitate to let him nurse again for awhile. Here again, don't push.

After several days of substituting the bottle for the breast for one feeding per day, substitute the bottle for the breast at the first feeding and then, a few days later, for the final feeding. Ordinarily, if managed this way, somewhere between six and nine months the transition is made easily and naturally from breast to bottle. But do it gradually and without coercion. Babies' patterns don't change abruptly. They take time.

From bottle to cup. Here again we need to follow nature. It is much more complex to drink liquid than it is to suck it in.

Some parents, over-eager to have a grownup child, start pouring milk into the baby almost at birth. They forget that if a newborn gets milk from a cup, he gets it by sucking it off the edge, not by true drinking.

One mother, feeling that her baby was unusually precocious, tried to wean him abruptly from the bottle to the cup at six months. This is ill-advised.

Because this mother assumed that her baby could change from bottle to cup overnight, she soon had a rebellious baby on her hands. He would have nothing to do with a cup, and without the bottle, his old, tried and familiar source of food supply, he was unhappy. His mother made it worse because she figured he ought to be taking as much milk from the cup as he used to from his bottle and it just doesn't work that way at first. It is a punitive and purposeless act for a parent to jump a baby suddenly, without preparation, from the bottle to the cup. It may be the beginning of all sorts of emotional conflicts and often results in the child's building up an aversion to milk itself, which may last for years.

The transition from bottle to cup should be made in these gradual steps:

How to Make Transition

First, at about six months of age (again being guided by the baby for he will develop to the point where he is sitting up and showing interest in anything he can pick up, including a cup) put an empty cup, preferably an unbreakable one, on the baby's tray during mealtime.

Give him an occasional sip of milk from a glass which you hold. Any sip he takes is one less from the bottle.

He'll next accept the pouring of milk from your glass to his cup, just a little in the bottom at first, which he will gradually be able to get into his mouth without spilling all of it on the way. Be patient and don't care how long it takes him to master this skill; it's a complex one and it's amazing how quickly he does learn.

We are here assuming that he goes through all the steps; if he skips one or more that's all to the good, if he does it easily and naturally.

He'll gradually get adept with the cup and will be drinking all his milk from it, except just before naps and bedtime. Most babies still want a bottle then.

Gradually, too, he'll lose interest in a bottle at naptime. Now it's just the bedtime bottle.

He'll be taking other things to bed, for sucking and chewing. Since they help him avoid thumb-sucking, parents should be perfectly willing.

So, his sucking needs well satisfied, your child will soon drink out of his cup at meals and take his bottle only at night. No attempt should be made to deprive him of this last-ditch sucking satisfaction. Taking the bottle to bed doesn't mean it will be hard for him to give it up if you are permissive about his taking other things to bed, too.

Usually between 15 to 18 months, if his sucking needs are met in the ways described, a baby's instinctive drive to suck seems to fade out naturally and he gives up the bottle of his own accord. If his need for it persists after 18 months, it may be an indication that other deep needs for love or acceptance have been denied, or the parents have missed the cue when he would have willingly gone to bed without a bottle.

We do not mean to imply that his need for the bottle at bedtime should not be occasionally tested. If not tested, some babies just keep on with it because it's the easiest thing to do, so testing is good. Give him a chance to do without it, but give him the chance not caring which way it comes out.

One mother brought her three-year-old boy to us because he still demanded his bottle when he went to bed. As we talked with her, we soon learned that she had set a deadline for weaning her baby from the bottle at nine months and had tried doing it all at once, except that she had given in and let her child have a bottle at bedtime because he had fussed so much then.

As a result, because of his mother's insistence that he drink from a cup and give up all bottles except one, this baby hung on to his bedtime bottle for dear life.

Here the bottle was being used, not to satisfy a need for sucking, but as an indirect way of getting attention and effectively getting back at his mother for taking his other bottles away too soon.

In such cases where the transition from bottle to cup has been made too abruptly, the following method of treatment often corrects a difficult situation.

Corrective treatment
1. Be completely accepting of or, at least, completely neutral about his bedtime bottle.
2. Give him a bottle of water, not milk, to take to bed.
3. A few nights later, give him an empty bottle.
4. Then give him a nipple, along with other things to suck and chew.
The child himself will eventually eliminate the nipple.

If you haven't followed this kind of easy-going plan in weaning your baby and are having trouble now, start over again. Begin by changing your own attitude and accepting the fact that there's no hurry, that it is best to let your baby proceed at his own pace. Then help your child learn that he really has no need for the milk bottle at bedtime.

With this lack of a compulsive deadline, and with a warmly understanding attitude, watch your baby gradually leave off the breast or the bottle and reach out to take care of his own needs with a cup in his hands.

—*By Charles A. Tompkins, M.D., and Fletcher D. Slater*

SOLID FOOD FOR THE BABY

PETER is three months old. He is lying on the examining table in the doctor's office, waving his arms, kicking his legs, making cooing and gurgling noises. He has been examined and his mother is now sitting by the doctor's desk.

Peter has come along splendidly since he left the hospital. He has taken his evaporated milk formula with great gusto and gained an average of six pounds a week. He has spit up a little milk once a day and had the usual amount of hiccoughing. But, aside from these common signs that his stomach is young and inexperienced, he has had no indigestion. He has been contented and pleased with life.

The doctor is talking about cereal and is listing the brands which are pre-cooked for a mother's convenience. All she has to do is to add water or formula and serve. The doctor says to start with a teaspoonful at the morning and evening feedings and increase by about a teaspoonful each day up to a total of two or three tablespoons. However, he emphasizes the point that Peter's appetite is to be the guide and that if he doesn't want more than one teaspoonful for two or three weeks, then one teaspoonful is the right amount.

A day passes. Peter's mother is happily mixing a small portion of cereal. This is a milestone in Peter's development and she is appropriately excited. She cradles him in her left arm, dips into the miniature serving and inserts the spoon into Peter's mouth. Peter looks puzzled; his brow wrinkles and the rest of his face looks more surprised than pleased. He clacks his tongue and opens and shuts his mouth with no sign of efficiency. The cereal, instead of disappearing inwards, oozes out over his lower lip. His mother scrapes the cereal up from his chin like a barber shaving a customer and tries to get it back into his mouth. She withdraws the spoon, holding it against his upper lip, thus using his lip as a scraper to empty the bowl of the spoon. Again more of the cereal comes out than goes down, but each time she repeats the operation she gains a little ground and after a while the job is done.

When Resistance Develops

The next day and the day after Peter seems to get less rather than more skillful and his mother is glad to stop after getting one teaspoonful into him. After a few more days it begins to look as though it weren't so much lack of eating skill on Peter's part as plain cussedness. He ejects the whole teaspoonful promptly and efficiently and then clamps his jaw shut and turns his head away to dodge the second teaspoonful. Peter's mother is beginning to get a little panicky and a little riled. The doctor said it was time to begin solids, and besides everybody has to learn sooner or later to eat them. Is she going to be defied by this twelve-pound bundle that seems so helpless in every other respect? She has an impulse to call the doctor for help, but when she gets to the telephone she decides that that would be silly. She determines to fight it out alone. And fight she does. But Peter, in spite of his tender age, gets his back up in proportion.

It is now ten days since the struggle began. It is 10:15 A.M. The battle of the cereal has been won as usual by Peter. His mother gets the bottle from the warmer, resentful, but anticipating the relief of seeing Peter go at that with his usual gusto. Instead the battle look comes into his eye. He clamps his jaws shut against the nipple and turns his head to the side. His mother is really frightened now. She rushes to the telephone and confesses the whole tragic story. The doctor, of course, advises her to lay off and relax, to stop the cereal for a few days and to offer the bottle casually and gingerly. He says, "Don't worry if he goes hungry for one or even two extra feedings; his appetite will build up and compel him to drink sooner or later." Peter did get his appetite back and his old enthusiasm for eating but it was a gradual process. For several days the old suspicion would crop up now and then making him suddenly turn away from his half-finished bottle with jerky determination.

This story is not at all uncommon. Sometimes the rebellion is milder and sometimes it becomes so intense that a permanent problem results. A long feeding problem is sad indeed. It wastes hours and it wastes patience and it usually makes a thin child in the long run. But worse than these are the effects on the attitudes of the child and the mother, and on their relationship with each other. The baby's attitude toward life is based on his eating, since eating is what he spends his first year doing. If he comes to think of food as something which the world, in the person of his mother, is always forcing upon him, he is compelled to develop psychologically in a balky direction, instead of preserving his natural outgoingness. He learns to wait suspiciously to see what is going to be done to him.

What Mother Should Do

How could Peter's problem have been avoided? His mother needed to know that food never should become a matter of solemn duty. An infant is born, not only with a terrific appetite for calories, but with an instinct to choose a well balanced diet. Nature will make him experiment with new foods even if his mother is so unnatural as never to offer him any. By the time he is crawling he will taste everything that he can pick up, food or nonfood. But it is our present-day style to start solids before the infant can reach or hold them. Since we adults are going to be depositing food in his mouth before he is old enough to have any choice in the business, we have a responsibility to be tactful about it. The first mouthful of solid food feels different, tastes different, and gets into his mouth in a different way from any he has had before. He is bound, unless he is a glutton, to be puzzled and to need time to get used to it.

If cereal is the first solid food, it usually works best to make it much thinner than the usual proportions at first, and to make it with formula. In this way its taste and consistency will be close to what the baby likes already. It is also best to let the baby attempt to suck it from the tip of the spoon rather than to dump it on the tip of his tongue. If after a few days he gets less rather than more pleasure from it, the doctor may suggest a change to some other cereal or to some other food altogether. Cereal is a food which evokes little enthusiasm at first from some infants. Whereas nearly 50 per cent of babies remain doubtful about cereal for many days after starting it, 90 per cent of them become delighted with fruit within a couple of days. Some pediatricians, for this reason, think it is a much better bet to start all infants on applesauce or mashed bananas. Then after two weeks they come to enjoy solid foods and will welcome the addition of cereal.

Mothers usually ask, "Should solid foods be given before or after the bottle?" The pediatrician might well answer, "Ask the baby!" There are some infants who, when they are hungry, want milk and only milk at first. They become furious if offered solids at such a moment. These are the infants who when assuaged by milk are always ready to try something else afterwards. Other infants are quite willing to start with solid food and some of these with smaller appetites will not touch solids after the bottle anyway. Here, as in so many other situations, the baby knows exactly what he is ready for, better than all the rest of us put together. —*By Benjamin Spock, M.D.*

HOW TO HELP YOUR BABY GROW STRAIGHT AND STRONG

THE newborn baby has much the same curled-up position that he had before birth. But many changes must take place beneath his soft flesh if his body is to become strong and straight. And he hasn't much time to accomplish them. In just a few years his body segments—head, trunk and legs—must be aligned vertically. Just as your baby will someday build a column of blocks, so these segments of his body must someday balance as squarely as possible on top of each other. Muscles hold those body segments in place. Muscles that *bend* the joints are opposed by muscles that *straighten* the joints. If one muscle group is strong, well developed and its opposing group is weak, some part of the body will be pulled out of alignment. At the same time, all the muscles must increase in strength and some must increase in elasticity and length as well.

All these fundamental changes take place gradually in the first two years of growth—crucial postural years. There are many things that mothers and fathers can do, or refrain from doing, to promote the development of good posture.

What you give your baby to lie on is important. When you provide him with a firm, flat mattress, his flexible spine can lie straight. This applies to carriage and bassinet as well as to crib. If your infant is resting on a folded blanket or a pillow when he's out for his airings, put a piece of plywood or several layers of heavy cardboard underneath, so that the foundation at least is firm. The proper mattress has another advantage. Soon, when you place him on his stomach, he will want to raise his head and he can lift and turn it easily if he doesn't have to cope with the humps of a soft mattress or a pillow. His urge to get that wobbly head up uses upper back and neck muscles.

Exercise is necessary for good posture development. Some of the things you may do just for fun are fine exercise for your baby. Once he is getting along well with that head-lifting, you can start pulling him up slowly by the hands into a sitting position, letting him exert as much effort himself as he wants. This is not a suggestion, of course, that you teach him to sit up. Babies do that when they're ready for it. But the raising and lowering call many parts of his body into use. Almost every baby, at first, will flex his arms and not allow the pull to reach to his abdomen. Pretty soon, however, in pulling himself up he will be using abdominal muscles. Another exercise is playing peek-a-boo while he is on his stomach, encouraging the lifting and turning of his head, which uses back muscles.

Give Baby Room to Flex His Muscles

Give your baby room to move about. Think of some of the effects of confinement on those bones and muscles that are eager to get into action. When a baby begins to roll around, the sides of an outgrown bassinet may hamper his activity. Whenever you can, give him freedom to squirm about on a blanket on the floor. Sleeping garments that aren't spacious enough or blankets that weigh him down discourage his incipient urge to move about. Perhaps you've set up a sparkling crib toy or "gym" to furnish incentive for stretching and reaching. This is fine, for it gives his abdominal muscles a workout. But if his sweaters and shirts are too tight, will he feel it's worth the struggle? Even clothes that chafe may inhibit the most determined muscles. If the legs of his pants are tight and irritate his skin, a baby may keep his knees bent in some special way to minimize the chafing—and then what chance do those muscles that work to straighten the joints have to come into play?

When he starts to creep, balls and bright toys that he can push across the room give him something to go after. Pushing the legs to make the creeping movements lengthens and brings into better alignment the muscles he will have to use for erect posture. Certainly, a playpen is a blessing when you're busy and don't want the creeper under your feet—but don't overdo confinement. Folding gates can shut off dangers such as stairs if you want to give your young explorer the wide open spaces of a whole room. Of course, the time will come when nothing in the world will keep him from the challenge of those stairs. He should have the chance to climb them under your watchful eye or be given some substitute like a short flight of steps.

Climbing stairs uses practically all of his muscles. At first he moves carefully on hands and knees, and the benefits are the same as those of creeping. When he begins to walk up and down the stairs, it is principally the leg and thigh muscles that are strengthened. At the same time, a great deal is required in the way of coordination of all body muscles in order to raise and lower himself from step to step and still keep balance in shifting his weight. If you watch, you will see your child return momentarily to the creeping position, baffled by this great problem of balance. But then he tries, tries again and someday discards the supporting hand or rail with a triumphant smile which broadens at your applause.

Restrain That Helping Hand

When your baby begins to pull himself up in those first efforts to stand, let him be, even though the impulse to help is hard to control at times. Of course a helping hand is needed once in a while to get him out of a bad spot. But the more he can work at pulling himself up and letting himself down, the better it is for him. As the muscles he needs to lift himself up contract and shorten, the opposing muscle groups must relax and lengthen. In letting himself down, the reverse occurs—so that strength and elasticity in all muscles are improved. In connection with standing, a point not often considered is that long periods of standing on soft surfaces can have bad effects on posture. No matter how firm his crib mattress, if a baby spends too much time standing up on it, flat feet and knock-knees may develop. The feet spread and turn in on their sides, for the arch is not yet well developed.

Never urge a child to stand and walk before he is ready. The necessary muscle changes take place before he shows that he is completely ready to do it himself. If the adjustment at knee and hip joints is not completed, the baby will compensate, if forced into a standing position, by curving the lower back in order to bring his head up. This is potential sway-back—an abnormal increase in the forward curve of the lower spine. It pushes the abdomen forward, too. Thus shifted forward, the weight of the abdomen must later be compensated for by an increase of the backward curve in the upper back—result: a rounded back or humped shoulders. Carrying the process further still, the round back and forward humped shoulders interfere with breathing and normal chest expansion. The ribs are pushed down and in turn push down on the abdomen, increasing the sway-back. So your baby is showing common sense in waiting until his body feels capable of standing and walking.

Socks are important. How often do you get new ones for your infant? Most parents are well aware of the need for room in shoes, but it is amazing how many cases of curled toes occur because socks are too short. They can be just as restricting as shoes that are tight or too short, so it is a good idea to check up on fit of socks at regular intervals of a few weeks.

Emotional Aspects of Growth

Growth isn't entirely physical. It has its emotional aspects, too, and your love for your baby and your respect for his individuality help him grow straight and stride high. The creeper who is reined in by "no" every time he makes a move in the direction of some forbidden object (which could just as well be kept out of reach) can feel the disapproval bringing his muscles up short. The youngster who comes to feel inadequate because from a parent's point of view he isn't walking soon enough or talking soon enough or is "behind" in toilet training, isn't likely to be the one who swings along with his chin up, free, self-assured and untrammeled.

We have all experienced muscular tension due to some emotional upset— anger, perhaps, or anxiety. And we have all occasionally had that tired, no-muscle-at-all feeling from sorrow or frustration. If a child is never really happy, his shoulders can't very well be straight or his stomach muscles firm. A classic example of emotional-muscular interaction is that of the teen-age girl who humps her shoulders to hide developing breasts, embarrassed by her approaching womanliness.

Just what then does good posture mean? For most of us, it still calls up some vision of a figure standing still with an imaginary book on his head—"chin up . . . shoulders back . . . stomach in!" This stationary ramrod is not necessarily enjoying good posture at all. Good posture means using all the parts of the body with maximum ease and grace, with a minimum expenditure of energy. Those parts are constantly shifting in their relationship to each other. The muscles and bones are constantly at work. If he gets off to a bad start as a baby, poor posture can eventually keep your child from functioning at his best. With good posture, he is poised, alive, energetic—not merely standing erect, but moving through the world with a strong, straight backbone, a sense of well-being and enthusiasm for living.   —*By Sonya Weber, D.Sc.*

FIRST TEETH

IT should comfort a mother whose baby is about four months old and probably beginning to cut his first teeth to know that many babies go through
teething without any trouble at all. The first sign of a tooth may be the click of
a tiny point against the edge of a cup. For other babies there will be two days of
discomfort before the first tooth erupts, then no difficulty at all until the first
molars come through. Only a few babies are fretful for several days with each
tooth. They may also have a cold or stomach upset while teething. Since the
eruption of the twenty baby teeth is spread over a little more than two years, it
means that this last group of infants will spend a lot of time being miserable.
Doctors just don't know why some children have more trouble with teething
than others.

Nowadays doctors do not believe that a cough, fever or diarrhea which
comes on at the time a tooth is pushing through the gum is due to the tooth. In
the past even convulsions were blamed on teething. Today your doctor will
want to know about any sign of illness but he will treat it quite apart from
teething. There is probably no doubt that in many cases teething does lower
resistance to infections, especially colds. Some babies have digestive upsets
marked by vomiting and diarrhea. For them the doctor will advise a simple
diet that is sure to agree with them.

When you look at the swollen red area that marks the place where a tooth
is coming through you can understand why lancing the gum seemed like a good
idea many years ago. Very few doctors feel it is necessary to lance the gum today. If the baby is comforted by the good old remedy of rubbing the gum
with the back of a spoon, this is a good idea. The teething baby will try to chew
on things and will like firm rubber toys, a cup or pliable plastic object for this
purpose. Firm plastic objects are apt to crack and have sharp edges, long
objects may be jammed too far into his mouth—so don't give them to him.

Night Crying

Often babies who get along all right during the day awake screaming at night.
A little comforting and a few ounces of warm milk usually put them back to
sleep. For a few days you may notice that the baby stops sucking after taking
about an ounce of milk, then starts again and stops. It may be that sucking
makes the gums swell. For this short period you can give quite a bit of milk
in a cup and put extra amounts on the baby's cereal and in his puddings. If
night crying continues, tell your doctor.

The age for cutting teeth may vary by several months but it is interesting
that the sequence is practically always the same. There are four lower and four

AVERAGE TIMES OF ERUPTION OF BABY TEETH

UPPER

1. Central Incisor—8 to 12 months
2. Lateral Incisor—8 to 12 months
3. Canine (Eyetooth)—18 to 24 months
4. First Molar—12 to 18 months
5. Second Molar—24 to 30 months

LOWER

1. Central Incisor—5 to 9 months
2. Lateral Incisor—8 to 14 months
3. Canine (Eyetooth)—18 to 24 months
4. First Molar—12 to 18 months
5. Second Molar—24 to 30 months

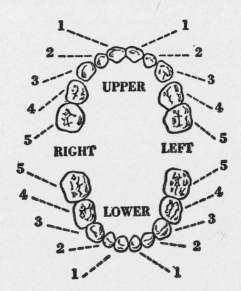

upper biting or incisor teeth, and your baby's first tooth will be a lower central incisor. In about two weeks the other central incisor appears, then the four upper incisors, covering a period of three months. Most babies have six teeth at a year of age, and there is usually a pause of several months before the lower lateral incisors and the four molars come in. A baby is apt to be fretful with his first tooth, then again with some of the molars. The canines are in by his second birthday. These are the pointed teeth (eyeteeth) known as dog teeth and stomach teeth. After the second birthday the last four molars erupt. This gives the baby twenty teeth.

Prenatal growth. The temporary teeth start to form at the fifth month of pregnancy. At birth these teeth are present and almost complete in the jaw bones. During the first fourteen months of life the permanent teeth are forming lower down in the bone. This is another reason why it is important that the mother have plenty of calcium and vitamins A and D in her diet during pregnancy. Unless there is a long illness or a milk allergy to alter the usual diet for an infant, you can feel sure that your baby is getting plenty of material for tooth formation. It's true, though, that some people are born with teeth which are resistant to decay while others have teeth which are less so.

What about using a swab to clean a baby's mouth, and how soon should a toothbrush be used? Never use a swab and never try to wipe out the mouth of an infant, because there is danger of starting an infection. The tissues are so delicate that they are injured by even a light touch. As to a toothbrush—there is very little point in a child's using one before the age of two. Most children of this age love brushing their teeth and mothers have to be careful that they do not damage the gums. A gentle brushing is enough. It is a good idea for the child to eat fruit between meals rather than candy. The constant presence of sugar on teeth encourages the growth of acid-producing bacteria.

Combating Tooth Decay

Research is still active on the ammoniated and anti-enzyme toothpastes and the fluoride compounds. Your own dentist is the one to give advice. In some localities fluorides occur naturally in the water or have been added in just the right concentration. In other regions dentists apply a fluoride solution to the teeth. When the enamel is still forming, as it is right after eruption, fluorine will combine with it to make it harder and more resistant to decay. Both of these methods are said to reduce decay. Dentists have different routines when it comes to applying the fluoride, but they usually do so when the child is about three years old and all his baby teeth are in, then again when he is nine and has some of his permanent teeth. When the child is thirteen it is applied again.

A child usually makes his first visit to the dentist around three years of age, though of course you should take him right away if he has toothaches before this or if he breaks a tooth. Some young children have a greenish deposit on their teeth. Though harmless, the dentist should remove it.

Choosing a dentist. Mothers try to hide their feelings but are naturally anxious when the child first visits the dentist. If you can find a dentist who is especially interested in children or who specializes in work for children, you will be delighted by the pleasant way in which your children are handled. There are small dental chairs which are comfortable, and most visits will be only for cleaning and inspection. When there is a cavity, modern dental tools make filling almost painless. Visits should be frequent enough so that tiny cracks or cavities can be filled before they become larger. Baby teeth can even develop abscesses which are painful and may harm the permanent teeth. First teeth should be well cared for so that they will last long enough to preserve the shape of the jaw. Sometimes people don't remember that these baby molars have to last for twelve years!

Don't worry because your baby has begun to drool. At birth there is very little saliva, but it increases at about four months as the glands develop. The little baby just doesn't know how to swallow well enough to handle all this fluid, and if gums are swollen there is bound to be a good deal of drooling. This stage won't last long. You can use bibs to protect your baby's clothes, but take them off when he sleeps.

When to expect first tooth. Six months is the average time for the first tooth to erupt, but there isn't anything to worry about if it doesn't show up until the baby is nine or ten months old. If a tooth hasn't appeared when your baby is a year old, your doctor may recommend an X-ray of his jaw, to see if any teeth are present, and he might prescribe thyroid. Sometimes an illness will delay teething. It may be helpful to ask one of your relatives about teething in your family, because it usually does run in families to have teeth early or late. Such things as extra teeth or missing teeth are in the nature of family characteristics, too. Once in awhile we read of a baby being born with teeth, but this is not an advantage. These teeth are usually very loose and must be pulled before they fall out as there is danger of the baby's choking on them.

As soon as the baby has a few teeth you will be happy to notice that he relishes his strained or mashed foods more than ever. He has an instinct to chew and can manage crackers and toast nicely. Soon he will be ready for chopped foods.

Your child is now well started on the miraculous and orderly process of acquiring teeth—one which begins early and continues for some years. Your task is to see that he gets the food that will help to make strong teeth, and that they are well cared for from babyhood on through his growing years.
—*By Ruth Kenyon Russell, M.D.*

HOW YOUR BABY LEARNS TO TALK

MOST babies are born with the ability to make noises, out of which they must learn to fashion a language that will let their wants be known to those around them. Among other things, he notices the sounds that he inadvertently makes. He tries, and out comes another sound. Soon he's amusing himself with gurgles, snorts, lip smackings and all sorts of odd noises, some of which may resemble English sounds, French or Zulu.

At this early stage it doesn't matter whether he's babbling in Kansas City, in Quebec or deep in the heart of Zululand. He's making random noises, and they're likely to be as random in one part of the globe as another. The normal baby's vocal equipment is the same everywhere, regardless of the color of his skin or the shape of his skull. Some of the sounds will be useful to him, no matter what his native language turns out to be. Some will be useful only in this preliminary exercising of the muscles that he will need to use when he really gets around to speaking.

The next stage comes when he begins to mimic the sounds that other people make. His mother appears at the side of his crib while he's opening and closing his lips and experimenting with sounds, and she optimistically interprets his noises as "Mama," even though to a less prejudiced observer they might sound more like "muh muh muh." At any rate she says, "Mama" and her baby, who has been getting bored with his solo, joins in enthusiastically if not very accurately. From now on, however, he has a new game, and if the family continues to play it with him he'll stop experimenting with the sounds that might have turned into Zulu clicks and French nasal vowels. His models will be Kansas City, New Orleans or New London, and they will help to teach him the particular American sound system that his family happens to use. Eventually he'll be limited chiefly to the forty-odd sounds on which English is built.

When Sounds Take on Meaning

So far, all is echo. There comes a time, however, when a familiar sequence of sounds is associated with a particular thing, at which point the sound takes on meaning and becomes a word. If his mother always says "bottle" when she gives it to him, sooner or later the association will be formed and the baby will know what "Mama" and "bottle" mean. He mimics what he hears and pangs of hunger may remind him to try to say "bottle" before he sees the bottle. Of course he won't score a perfect bull's eye the first time. He hasn't learned to hear "bottle" with complete accuracy yet, nor have his tongue and lip muscles learned to reproduce accurately what he does hear. By the end of the first year, however, your baby is apt to have two or three words that he can use meaningfully.

Actually, he knows more than he seems to. Every baby has a stock of words waiting to be practiced. Some youngsters whose speaking has been delayed have large passive vocabularies, as can be demonstrated by naming objects in the room and watching the youngster's eyes turn from one object to another.

You can stimulate your baby's speech development by calling objects by their names in your baby's hearing long before he is ready to talk and by keeping on naming objects for a long time after he has begun to try to talk. Start when he's about six months old. When you appear by the side of his crib say "Mama" or "Daddy" or "Susie." Say "bottle" when you give it to him. Say "bath" when you lower him into it. Say "knee" when you soap it and "nose" when you touch it.

Then when he's learned to say "bottle" or "ball" or "Daddy" make a point of getting him to use the right word at the right time. Encourage him to say "bottle" before you give it to him. Don't, of course, expect an adult pronunciation at first. If he comes no closer to "bottle" than "woffoo" he should get a passing grade for effort—and the bottle.

What meaning the baby attaches to these first words usually has a somewhat wider range than adults intend. He may surprise you by saying "Mama" to a neighbor who has dropped in. He may greet a puddle in the road with "bath." And the family cocker and his Teddy bear may have to share the name "cat" till he learns that there are different kinds of furry animals. The words may have additional meanings at different times: at one time "Mama" may mean, "There you are"; at another, "Pick me up"; at still another, "Where are you?" The single word "up" may mean, "Pick me up," or "The cat just jumped up on the table," or "The ball over there on the high shelf." Gradually he learns to narrow the meaning until "cat up" becomes a statement, and "baby up" is a request, if not a demand.

Range of Meaning

The shades of meaning that result from putting words together present baffling new obstacles. An "if" can change the whole meaning of a sentence. "You" means Mama and "me" means the baby when he talks to Mama, but have exactly reversed meanings when Mama talks to him. Some of his linguistic productions at this stage represent mimicry, but a day comes when he says, "Kitty runned away," and you know he hasn't heard "runned," not in your house. He made it up on the pattern of "walked" and "climbed" and "hurried." Now you know that he has attached a past tense ending to a simple verb, and that's a big step forward. He'll learn "ran" later.

On the average the one-year-old will be able to use one or two words, and the two-year-old will begin to put several words together in what passes for a sentence. But an average is only an average, and there's no cause for alarm if your youngster falls slightly behind. If he hasn't done any real talking by the age of three, then it's time to investigate. He may have difficulty in hearing some tones.

Effect of physical defects. Physical defects can also hamper the development of speech, though their importance is often exaggerated. To be sure, the cleft-palate youngster requires either surgery or learning to use an artificial palate of the type with which some speech clinics have had a good deal of success. He'll need help with his speech in either case. The youngster with cerebral palsy, whose muscular control has been damaged, may need special help.

Minor physical deviations, however, are usually an excuse rather than a reason for poor speech.

Speaking doesn't depend on the pattern of the teeth or the form of the jaw, but on the cooperation of the moving parts—tongue, lips and soft palate—with the relatively fixed jaw and teeth. Since no two of us have identical teeth patterns, probably no two of us adjust the tongue in exactly the same relationship to the teeth for a sound like "s." If the tongue habitually remains too far forward in the mouth, a whistling "s" or even a lisp may develop. With slight irregularities, then, the best treatment is patience and good speech at home.

Whether your child has buck teeth or not, the kind of speech he first learns to use will largely reflect your own. If you have a tendency to mumble or whine, so will he. If your voice is tense and harsh, the chances are that his will be too. If yours, however, is pleasant, distinct and relaxed, his voice will pattern itself on yours. You can help your youngster most by encouraging him to speak clearly from the age of six months on, and by setting him an example of clear, pleasant, relaxed speech.

—By C. K. Thomas

HOW CHARACTER DEVELOPS

FROM the side of the crib, a mother and father contemplate their sleeping baby. They wonder, "What will he be like?" "What can we do to help him be a good person?" Honest, generous, independent, responsible, respectful of others—these are some of the things they mean by "good person," traits of character that develop from experiences of living and learning as distinguished from the varieties of temperament children seem to be born with. One baby may from birth have a take-it-easy sort of personality. His brother is born with an up-and-at-'em approach. These are basic constitutional differences. But placid or energetic, either can turn out truthful or dishonest, industrious or negligent, "good" or "bad" as a result of what they experience from life.

Not so long ago, the answer to "What can we do to help?" would have been a sort of no-nonsense "Teach him good character!" That was sound enough, and still is. The trouble was that the method of teaching was often approached somewhat as seasoning a roast. You can rub the seasoning all over the surface, but the rubbing affects only the outside.

Ideas change as knowledge deepens, and with our increased knowledge of the human being, we've come to realize that using seasoning methods with a child gets comparable results. The most conscientious rubbing-in of good character ideals goes only skin-deep: "Honesty is the best policy" hung over a child's headboard soon becomes part of the wallpaper to him. Daily bombardment with "Well begun is half done" and "Respect your elders" and "Don't blow your own horn" can't make a youngster industrious, respectful or modest.

For character grows from within. It has roots in good bodily function as well as emotional and mental roots. Today's parents standing there at the side of the crib know that. They know, too, that they play an important role in how their child's character will grow. Do they realize, though, how early their influence is felt?

Character formation begins right there—while the baby is still in his crib, in his infancy. For it is rooted, we've come to see, in a sound sense of one's own goodness, and of one's personal value to others. We tend to associate our own part in developing this self-confidence with the older child who is able to understand verbal approval. But long before they can bolster their baby's self-esteem with words of approval for something he has done, a mother and father can give him support in other ways just by accepting him as he is and guiding him with gentleness. The self-belief that underlies good character can be nourished from the time a baby is born.

Satisfying Basic Needs

An important requisite for a child's early character growth is confidence in the goodness of his own body and its functions. An infant comes into the world with one important want: the need for pleasant body sensation. The only thing he is aware of for a while is simply the difference between bodily pleasure and pain. All that he's capable of wanting is to exercise those bodily functions which have proven to give him pleasure—to eat, eliminate, suck, feel full, warm and safe. He develops awareness in this way through his body and its functions.

Here is a mother who is helping to form her child's character while he's only an infant, with never an understandable word spoken between them: she feeds him when he's hungry; as she does so, her arms are sure but relaxed—a warm and comforting haven; she lets him indulge happily in the sucking he enjoys so much; she holds him close, caresses him, rocks him, hums or sings. She makes those little sounds usually described as "meaningless" that are actually so pleasantly meaningful to her baby's developing hearing sense. Confidence and trust in another human being grow in response to this early parental care.

About the time a baby can sit up, pleasure feeling has grown stronger in the lower part of his body. He finds it feels good to play with his feet, put them in his mouth, to pass his hands over his thighs and abdomen. By the time his first birthday comes around, his delight in his own body is pretty evident. Around this time, the questing hands begin to grope in the genital region.

Interest in genital region. It's at this point—the point where he discovers there is a pleasant sensation in the genital parts of his body—that a baby often meets sudden disapproval where before there was only approval and love. Often there's a sharp "No!" His hand is pulled away. Sometimes it's slapped.

What's happened? Something important has been lost in the relationship between parent and child. The broad term "sensual" suddenly focuses down to "sexual" for the once-approving parents. And the change in term represents an emotional change in attitude, charged with all our old taboos, loaded with fear of "sex habits," with distorted and exaggerated notions of what this exploration means to the baby. All it really does mean to him is another area of strong body pleasure. Instead of imposing their own fears on the child, this is a time when parents who are really bothered can substitute diversion for the slap or the "No." He'll turn gladly to a hand game like pat-a-cake or clap hands. And he'll welcome toys that satisfy his desire to explore by touching.

Something of the same censoring attitude in adults comes into play when, toward the end of his second year, the baby shows interest in urination and his bowel movements. His fascination with the products of his body makes most grownups feel uneasy and critical of him. With too many such experiences of disapproval, the child's good feelings about himself begin to get shaky, and his growing confidence in his parents is disturbed. On the other hand, when he can feel free of such incomprehensible disapproval, his sense of well-being, his self-confidence and his increasing functional control can grow on unimpaired by these unnecessary hindrances.

Developing Muscular Control

In the second year of life, a child's next big "want" or drive becomes evident, the urge to unrestricted movement. We can call it aggression, though the word has come to stand for destructive aggressiveness only. But aggression in a human being is a good thing when it is properly channeled. In the toddler, it is a drive to explore and master the world around him—and it is shown mostly in his muscular activities. It is what first impels him toward mastery of his own body, for instance, in acquiring balance and skill in moving around. It also takes, in his experimenting and learning of control, other forms not quite so acceptable to grownups—including breaking, tearing and getting into danger. And once again, how parents handle this basic drive is important to the child's character development. Sudden interference with instinctual urges, rather than redirecting, is unwise, and clever parents know how to prevent breakage and danger.

Look at that youngster now! His muscles are growing rapidly and he runs—walking is a rare thing. He pulls and pushes and seizes. And with this new ability comes the new keen satisfaction of doing things and getting things by himself, of deciding where he is going and going there on his own. The muscles of the two and three-year-old, like the initial sensations and awareness of the one-year-old, have a flare-up of energy that may be startling to adults. Inevitably, since his knowledge of what is acceptable to others and what isn't doesn't come along as fast as his muscular, aggressive development, some of his experiments are going to be unintentionally destructive. When they are, his self-confidence can run into a variety of parental reactions.

There is, first, the "Stop—you're a bad boy!" or this-child-needs-discipline reaction. A second kind is one of complete permissiveness—"When Johnny hits his cousin, we know he's just expressing his aggressive urge."

Provide outlets for energy. Neither of these extremes contributes anything positive to a child's character growth. The first leaves him no outlet for an inborn, crude but natural, basically important drive. The second gives him outlets without helping him to develop a sense of mastery over that drive, some idea of what is the acceptable thing to do with this excess of energy. A child left floundering without such guidance can become terribly unhappy in a year or so, when he begins to play and work with other children.

But when parents know what aggression really is and are neither frightened nor confused by outbursts of vigorous energy, there is an alternative method of handling it. Aggressive urges can be redirected into vigorous play by such sensible means, for instance, as providing a place where the urge to run and climb and generally bang around can do no harm to the rest of the household —a play space of some sort. They furnish this place, furthermore, with things that allow for the desire for free movement and activities: blocks, boxes, steps to climb, drawers to open and shut, toys that are unbreakable and toys whose breakage doesn't matter anyway. At the same time, they are not hesitant about redirecting the child when he is doing something harmful to himself or others. Where there is genuine understanding, this can be accomplished with firmness but without blame.

When this kind of approach is consistent, the aggressive drive is mostly funneled into character traits that every parent wants his child to have later in life—a readiness to work and to face difficult situations, for instance, with a desire to overcome them rather than run away or fight blindly; a willingness to compete when necessary; a desire to broaden, to acquire more knowledge.

—By Margaret A. Ribble, M.D., and Margaret Albrecht Gillmor

DOES A BABY THINK?

PARENTS are justified if they look for signs of intelligence and awareness in even the tiniest infant. Of course, we can't apply our adult standards to a baby's intelligence. When a baby "thinks" he doesn't think the way we do. He doesn't mull over things. He doesn't look back and he doesn't look ahead. When a baby thinks he deals, literally, with the matter at hand. To touch, to feel, to grasp, these are among his first impressions and what to do with the things he comes in contact with are his first problems. Although his first movements are uncoordinated, after a few days they begin to become better coordinated, more purposeful. Your baby is starting to "think."

Studies have shown that the mind begins to develop at an incredibly early age. According to Dr. Arnold Gesell this growth is profoundly bound up with the growth of the nervous system. As early as five months before the baby is born, all of the nerve cells he will ever possess have already been formed and many of them are prepared to function in an orderly way. At this time the fetus makes movements of arms and legs so vigorous that they can be seen and felt through the mother's abdominal wall (quickening). The eyelids can wink, the eyeballs can roll, the hands can clasp, the mouth can open and close, the throat can swallow. The chest makes rhythmic movements in preparation for the event of birth when the breath of postnatal life will rush into the lungs.

What about the mind? How does it grow? Basically it grows as does the nervous system. It grows with the nervous system. Growth is a patterning process. It reproduces patterned changes in the nerve cells and corresponding changes in behavior.

To give an example: early in life when the baby is only a few weeks old, he learns that crying brings results. First, he only cries because he is hungry—he feels uncomfortable, the body tissues need nourishment, his nervous tension is high. While this is only an automatic reflex at first, he soon learns that crying brings results—the warm bottle, the mother's soft breast. He begins to divine some kind of connection between crying and satisfaction. When he cries now, there is a demanding quality to his call. He has mastered lesson number one in learning to think.

Shortly after that, and remember that your baby is only about three or four weeks old, he makes another interesting discovery: he recognizes the source of his satisfaction. When mother approaches, he turns toward her, mouth open, ready for nursing. This is another step toward thinking.

Formation of Visual Images

At about four weeks of age the baby begins to take an interest in the world in which he lives. Along with his sense of hearing, the sense of sight has been developing. Through his eyes he has been forming visual images. That is why blind babies learn much more slowly than do babies with normal sight. The normal four-week-old baby is beginning to widen his horizon quite literally. It's still a small horizon for his range of vision is limited, but he is progressing. When he was born, his eyeballs would rove aimlessly. After several days, his eyeballs would stand still for brief periods at a time. He seemed to be "looking" at things. Actually, though, he doesn't really perceive them at this age. But he continues his exercises, strengthening his eye muscles by this means. Nature is helping him, too, and along with the development of his eyes goes the development of other body muscles, such as those of his hands, arms, neck. Then comes the wonderful moment, at four weeks, when a baby definitely *sees* an object. More than that, he will follow it with his eyes, as if he couldn't tear himself away from it. His mind is beginning to wake up, it wants to explore its surroundings, it wants to learn. Even Einstein started with such modest beginnings!

At about four weeks of age the baby develops, too, a distinct awareness of faces. He smiles, usually when somebody bends over him for he knows by now that people are good to babies! He doesn't recognize different faces yet, of course; that will take another three or four months.

Interest in people. At three months he will be very much interested in the movements of people around him—at four months he will show obvious pleasure at someone's approach. The four-month-old is beginning to "think" of people as more than feeders and cleaners and pacifiers. People are good company, especially mother—and when she leaves he is apt to cry and protest; his alert mind rebels at such treatment.

At that age, too, the baby can hold a rattle and look at it while he is holding it in his hands. Hands and eyes are doing teamwork, coming into more effective coordination. It's still a crude kind of grasping, and the baby couldn't pick up the rattle all by himself. It has to be handed to him. That finer coordination of fingers and hands involved in picking up something won't exist for another four or five months. But as the baby's behavior patterns advance in degree and in kind, we realize that an advance in his mental maturity must also take place.

When a baby is about six months old, his mother can finally claim that Junior knows her. His thinking has progressed to the stage where he can tell faces apart. Some babies cry when a stranger approaches them—that's only a sign of an infant's awareness of differences and not unfriendliness as some mothers fear. Usually, after he has had a chance to study the stranger soberly, he will go to him and start "exploring" him, with hands, eyes and sometimes his mouth.

Sense of ownership. At about the same time, too, the baby is beginning to display a sense of ownership. When toys are taken out of his hand, he will protest by crying or screaming. Later on, when he is nine months old, he will show some selectiveness in the choice of his toys. He will pick up a favorite toy and hold on to it until another toy claims his attention.

By the time he is one year old a baby has definite patterns of thinking. His world has expanded tremendously. He has preferences, he has learned to enjoy the company of others, he picks out his favorite toys. And all the time he is learning and learning . . .

The most interesting thing about this whole learning process, this advance in the baby's thinking, is that nobody taught him to do the things he can now do. His increasing powers are due to changes within his nervous system. True, a favorable environment will encourage and hasten his development, but it does not create it. Changes come from within and physical and mental development work together.

Individual children will differ, of course, from the norms set down here but they all develop along these general lines. *—By Elsieliese Thrope*

HELP YOUR BABY MAKE FRIENDS WITH THE DOCTOR

TOO many youngsters look upon a visit to their doctor as an unpleasant or even fearful "must," instead of what it should be—a visit with a friend who wants to keep them in the best of health. Actually, any child can be prepared to take a visit to his doctor casually—even to enjoy it—but not without preparation and cooperation on the part of his parents.

Let's begin with your baby's initial visits to the doctor. First of all, make the appointment for a time which doesn't conflict with his feeding schedule, if possible. Right after feeding is a good time, for then a baby is relaxed and content. Second, begin planning for "doctor's visit day" the day before. Make formula in the evening if possible and do any other routine work which can be done ahead of time. Try to make the day one of less rush than usual so you will not tend to be tense and impatient. Third, and this is very important, have your baby comfortably dressed. He gets off to a bad start if he has to have a lot of fussy clothing removed and replaced in the doctor's office. Dressing the baby simply saves time for the doctor and energy for you, too.

As you go to keep your appointment, it's important that the baby feels you are relaxed, that the doctor's office is a pleasant place, that you and the doctor are friends. If your baby has reached the toast or cracker stage, take a piece of his favorite cruncher with you and give it to him when the doctor finishes his examination. You may even give him a new rattle or toy. That way he will soon learn that something pleasant follows the examination.

Next come the visits when your baby has more than a weighing, measuring and general checkup. When he is about six weeks to three months old, it is time for immunization. The first inoculation is usually a combined one for diphtheria, tetanus and pertussis (whooping cough), commonly known as a "DPT." It consists of three injections, one month apart.

Smallpox immunization is usually given one month after the last DPT and produces an active immunity for a period of five years, when it should be repeated. The first polio shot should be given around the fifth month, with a second three or four weeks later and boosters after seven months and a year.

It's important to keep your own record of the dates and nature of your child's immunizations. Should you ever find it necessary to take him to another doctor, this information is of inestimable value.

Baby's First Injection

Let your baby have a new rattle or toy just before an injection is given. He'll be so busy looking at it, feeling it, tasting it, that usually he won't even feel the prick of the needle and he certainly won't think of the little hurt for very long. See if your doctor will let you hold the baby as the injection is given, if you can do it without reacting too emotionally yourself. Some physicians prefer this—provided they see that the mother can really be a help and not a hindrance. Babies and small children are extremely susceptible to the power of suggestion in the tone of a mother's voice. If you show that you are worried or that you expect your child to fuss and scream, he will sense it and probably live up to your expectations. Naturally, if he does cry, you will soothe and cuddle him, and not say there's nothing to cry about. If there weren't anything to cry about he wouldn't be crying.

Simply show that you understand his feelings and want to comfort him. If you can take a few minutes out to play with your baby after you return home from the doctor's office, by all means do so.

All of this is a good investment in the future, for not only will it make further visits to the doctor's office happier but it will ease the situation when you have an ill child who requires medical attention at home. Furthermore, a child who is friendly with his doctor is likely to recover much more quickly from an illness than one who has built up feelings of unpleasantness and fear that make him unwilling to follow the doctor's instructions.

As the baby becomes older, the same parental attitude still applies. It's up to mother to plan ahead for the visit to the doctor and make that day somewhat special. Talk about it a little ahead of time. Just how far ahead and how much talking depend, of course, on the child's age—his capacity to understand. Too much talk too far in advance can make a child unnecessarily anxious.

Sometimes it helps to play-act with the child what the doctor will probably do. If he doesn't have a toy "doctor kit," tongue depressors and cotton swabs can be purchased at the drug store for a very small sum. Some string and a small funnel make quite a satisfactory stethoscope. "I think this is what the doctor is going to do when we go to see him," you say, and show him. Then let him show you, examining your throat, holding a flashlight to your ears, listening to your heart, thumping your chest. Tell him why it is important to have a checkup with the doctor and why we have immunizations. Don't dwell on these things, but casually mention them so they become something to be accepted just as eating and sleeping are accepted. Remark that it is pretty wonderful to have such a good friend as his doctor to keep him well and to care for him when he is ill.

Build mutual trust. Nurture the mutual trust between you so he knows that if a mother says it is going to hurt a little, but only a little, he knows it's true. Above all, don't say injections don't hurt, because they do—but not very much or very long. If the child expects a little hurt, he is prepared for it and he will most likely accept it. When he is able to do it without too much fussing, praise him. If he does cry or fuss, don't scold him or pay undue attention. He's working off his fear, most likely, and it will pass.

Just as you did when he was an infant, you can give him a treat of some kind after his visit to the doctor. You might even mention it beforehand. Plan the day so you can take an extra half hour after the appointment with the doctor is over. He will count on that special event and it will bolster his courage should it need an extra boost. He can even come to see, after a while, that going to the doctor's can be fun!

—*By Flora H. Kimball, R.N.*

WHEN AND HOW
IS A CHILD SPOILED?

THERE are many old wives' tales about spoiling children that need to be dispelled. The popular concept is that spoiling is caused by letting a child have his own way too much, and that whether you are dealing with an infant or an older child, it amounts to the same thing. It doesn't. The very things which can spoil an older child have exactly the opposite effect on an infant.

No one wants a spoiled child. With trepidation parents set out to strike a balance between giving a child the love, attention and encouragement that authorities agree he needs, yet exercising enough control so that he does not become spoiled. What does spoiling mean and what causes it?

Spoiling and Babies

The child called "spoiled" is the poor sport, the one who must always have his own way, the demanding child who expects to be given to but never to give. In short, he is self-centered. Such a child is all too apt to be incapable of giving or loving in a mature sense, and expects to continue dependent upon others.

It's safe to say that you can't spoil an infant, at least not by doing the things for him that most people think of as spoiling. You can't spoil him by rocking him, holding him too much, by being with him a lot, feeding him when he wants it, or comforting him when he cries. You can give in to his demands as freely as you like, and it won't spoil him. In certain cases it might create some inconvenient habits (from your point of view), but it won't make him into the kind of self-centered person described above.

It is often the infant who has been "spoiled" in the popular sense of the word who becomes the unspoiled adult. Infancy is full of paradoxes. The more the baby is allowed extreme dependence for as long as he needs it, the sooner he is able to grow into independence. The more you give freely, the less he demands. The more he is cuddled and attended to, the better able he is to love and give to others when he is older. When people have been generous with him, he can be generous with others.

What people really mean when they denounce certain practices as tending to spoil a baby is that these practices will create bad habits—"bad" in the sense that they are inconvenient for the adult. The baby who is rocked to sleep every night will come to expect it every night, and if the parent isn't inclined or able to do it, it is an undesirable habit. It usually isn't necessary and perhaps shouldn't be started as a regular thing. But the point is, whether it is done or not, it won't harm the child's character. Anyone who has seen the serenity on the face of a child who has fallen asleep in the warmth of his mother's arms senses this.

Babies Need Attention

The main thing to remember is that a person becomes self-centered (spoiled) because somewhere along the line he hasn't gotten the love and security he needs, and turning inward and looking out for himself are his ways of assuring himself that someone cares for his welfare. The demanding person is the one who, deep down, fears that his demands won't be met, and so tests out those about him. The person who remains immature and dependent into adulthood is the one whose legitimate dependency needs were not gratified in infancy. When too much stress is placed on not spoiling the baby, so that love and attention are meted out to him in quantities thought to be enough but not too much, frustrations and anxieties result that make him the kind of person described as spoiled. The more the parent arbitrarily tries to instill traits of independence and unselfishness into the unready baby, the more dependent and selfish he becomes.

We have been talking about the infant. What of the older child? Can he be spoiled by having his own way too much? Yes. Whereas the infant is spoiled when his parents expect too much of him, the older child is spoiled when they don't expect enough. The older child also needs flexible parents who are not afraid to give to him and love him. But when the unlimited coddling so essential to the infant is continued beyond where it is appropriate, it reaches a point of diminishing returns. As a child grows physically and emotionally, we expect things of him that we could never ask of an infant. There are, for instance, legitimate limits to his behavior: he must learn not to run in the street. We expect him to assume some responsibilities: there comes a time when he shares in the family chores. We expect that at times he will have to be on the giving rather than the receiving end: Johnny must give up his Saturday plans because it's his sister's birthday and the family is going on a picnic. As he grows, the child needs a certain amount of discipline.

The difference is that the infant is allowed his own way because he alone knows his needs; the child is not always given his way because sometimes he chooses wrongly. The child is ready to accept curbs and responsibilities, whereas the infant is not. When the child does not have guidance, when he is never expected to give and is never disciplined, his conception of the world becomes warped, and he gets the idea that he is the center of it. He is spoiled.

Don't push baby's development. Where does one draw the line between the taking, dependent period of babyhood and the time when the child is ready to give in a more mature sense? When do we stop coddling the infant and start expecting something of him? There is no set age. Some babies need to be babies longer than others. The child himself will give the clues to his readiness, in little everyday things. When he is old enough to master holding a cup, he must begin to take some responsibility for not spilling the contents. When he is able to move about and is faced with a choice of which things to play with, he must begin to learn which things he mustn't touch. These are only beginnings, but they preface the larger responsibilities and limits he will come to know. The mother's demands on him must keep pace with his ability to comply. The child who has had a free and wholesome period of infant dependency is capable of assuming later responsibilities. The infant who has been given to almost limitlessly becomes the child who can give to others and abide by limits.

So when we talk about spoiling, let's know that there is a difference between the effect of giving an infant his own way and the effect of always giving an older child his way. The infant thrives on it; the older child can be harmed. The older child can be spoiled by it; the infant cannot. —*By Shirley Southcott*

HELP YOURS TO BE A DO-IT-YOURSELF BABY

WHEN and how can we best help a baby with his urge toward independence? Probably the soundest starting point is for us to learn the fascinating facts of growth and development. If we know what's happening now and going to happen next, it's easier to allow a child to progress—and do what he can when he can. It's also easier to quit pushing; to stop asking him to do bigger and better things than his bones, muscles and nerves are ready for.

Even though we can do everything better than he can—and five times as fast!—we must persuade ourselves to let the baby try, let him learn through practice. As each new accomplishment becomes due we can watch for signs, provide encouragement and remove unnecessary obstacles.

We can, for example, arrange a reasonably clear track for the neophyte creeper. He has trouble enough getting from here to there without detouring around antiques and decorative objects he's forbidden to touch. When he's ready to walk, we can't hurry him by a day. But we can refrain from keeping him cooped up when he obviously wants out. We can provide him with clothes not bothered by dirt and, perhaps more important, a mother not bothered by dirt!

The "Me-do-it" dresser can do it better with zippers, big armholes, big buttons. When he finally becomes interested in do-it-yourself toileting, overalls and underpants that pull down easily will encourage his sense of accomplishment—and also help him win your approval.

Approval and accomplishment are goals and rewards of every do-it-yourselfer. Watch your baby's elation—and his pleasure in your praise—when he finally takes his first step alone! According to people who have studied children, accomplishment and approval are basic ingredients of security. In "America's Baby Book," Dr. John C. Montgomery says: "The more sure a child is of his own worth and his own ability to do things for himself, the more secure he is."

Children need to feel a constant glow of affection and support. Without this they have noticeably less spunk and initiative, fewer moments of triumph that come with accomplishment.

"But when our child is trying to accomplish something and can't, he gets so mad!" parents complain. "Should we step in and do it for him—which usually makes him madder—or let him struggle alone?"

A certain amount of frustration—which Dr. Arnold Gesell has described as a kind of "thrustration"—is a fundamental part of learning. A child thrusts forward from one accomplishment to the next, pauses to rest on a plateau in between, sometimes slips backward a little. Parents familiar with the child-development pattern can frequently figure out what the child is doing—or trying to do—that makes him seem so cross and contrary. When he has almost—but not quite—conquered a new skill, he sometimes gets frantically determined to succeed.

Practice Periods

Practice periods are important and necessary. With parents alert to the problem, practicing sessions that are overlong and frustrating can usually be avoided.

For instance, suppose your child is learning to feed himself. You give him good tools to help him along: a short easy-to-hold spoon, a dish with straight sides to shove food against, a comfortable chair and table. When his spoon and his mouth begin to make connections, you leave him to feed himself. But before he gets tired and discouraged with this exciting but difficult feed-yourself system, you'll come back and quietly help him.

Children who have learned to walk still like to be carried occasionally. The independent "I-can-do-it" dresser sometimes likes a little help, too—especially when he's tired or hungry or just getting over an illness.

Insisting that a youngster finish every single thing he starts is more apt to kill interest than build character. When someone helps button the last few buttons or pick up the remaining toys, the job seems not too hard and worth tackling again.

We can help, too, by not expecting a more finished performance than a child is able to give. Sweaters pulled on wrong side out, pants and polo shirts on backward got that way through serious if inaccurate effort. Must the work really be done over?

And consider that small face with its clean shiny circle framed by a ring of dirt and the hands that suddenly change color at the wrists. Washing talents will improve eventually—but a good job usually comes sooner if we don't expect perfection at the start.

The new self-feeder, too, is certain to make a mess. He misses the target—spills food on his face, hair and the floor around him. Manners are beyond his comprehension—and he couldn't care less!

The mother who knows the child-development facts-of-life prepares for the inevitable—mentally and physically. She frequently serves "finger foods" like diced cooked carrot, small pieces of meat. She provides a cover-up bib, protects the floor and surrounding territory—then concentrates on looking out the window. She may go back and help but she knows better than to show her impatience by saying "Hurry up!"

Requests for speed would discourage—and probably slow down—a small person working hard to clean his plate. "Come on!" is no help to a fellow trying to bend a shoe lace into a bow knot. Walks that can't include an occasional side trip to explore a neighbor's doorstep are dull indeed.

Learning to Recognize Limits

It is not fun—but it's vitally necessary—for children to learn what they can't do, too. The knife that cuts apples is sharp and not for children to use. Step ladders should be climbed only by people who are good at climbing stairs. The electric train belongs to Big Brother. Mommy is resting now—she'll get out the finger paints later. Rights, limits, dangers must be gradually recognized and accepted.

We can guide ourselves in our guidance of children by double-checking: Are these "no's" necessary, or mostly due to unreasonable fears or a lack of understanding on our part?

Too much being-done-for dampens enthusiasm for doing. Too many don'ts discourage the drive for self-help. Doing and learning the things a child wants to learn and do—which may or may not be what we want!—are as basic as growing. "How-to" experiments begin in early babyhood and, with nourishment, never stop. How to make hands take hold of a rattle, pick up a string, put a peg in a hole. Soon—how to flush the toilet, answer the telephone, tie a bib, feed the new baby, ride the new bike, see what's inside the clock.

As a youngster grows, his ideas inevitably get bigger than his abilities. Words won't come that say what he means, blocks won't build the beautiful garage he can see in his imagination, roller skates won't go right. Rage and tears ensue.

How can parents help? We sympathize with his problem, praise his desire to try again—but divert him or lend a hand when he's attempting too much, too soon. And we never cease to be amazed at his fierce determination to conquer his current objective.

The long-range objective—the goals every parent wants for his child—are happiness and independence. The ability to make decisions (and mistakes!) and take both in stride. Zest and curiosity that keep him interested in learning new skills and listening to new ideas.

If there is family love and approval he can feel and count on—and help when he needs it, but hands off when he doesn't—the chances are your young do-it-yourself enthusiast will continue to enjoy doing things himself all through his life.   —*By Ruth Newburn Sedam*

HOW TO LIVE WITH A TWO-YEAR-OLD

EVERY mother can see the physical changes in her child during his second year—can see him literally transformed from dependent baby to sturdy, exploring, independent youngster.

She can see his greater skill in handling things. Now he runs where before he toddled, climbs where he once crawled. He develops control over his bladder and bowels, and drops his morning nap.

These physical changes, while wonderful, are easy to trace and accept. But his emotional and psychological changes, though equally enormous, are not so apparent nor so well understood.

As parents, we are apt to forget that our child is a personality. He is becoming—and rapidly, during this second year!—an individual. The first year he was a mother-centered infant. Now he is becoming a self-centered person, increasingly aware of father, brothers and sisters, playmates.

He is developing a mind of his own. During the first year he pretty much took what mother gave him. He depended on her to feed him, change him and put him to bed, to cuddle and protect him.

Now he is learning to talk and speak his own mind, and the word he seems to prefer with distressing partiality is "No!" It seems much easier for him to say "No!" than to express positive wants. It's as if he were glorying in his new-found power of choice.

This is one of the emotional changes that needs to be understood by every mother. Her child is not being "ornery." He is simply growing, exercising a new-found ability, just as he runs for the pure fun of running. He's trying out this "No" business, and it's fascinating. Bear with him. He'll get over it, probably during this tumultuous second year, if his mother is wise enough not to engage in too many battles.

Is this to suggest that the "No" phase be ignored? Exactly. Nothing is to be gained by conflict, and everything is to be lost. The understanding mother will learn somehow to divert her child's attention into another channel. During this second year, it is easy to refocus the child's interest. Ignore the No and suggest another activity.

How two mothers reacted. Two devoted young mothers illustrate this point very well. Mrs. C., well meaning and conscientious, was afraid that "giving in" to her year-and-a-half-old son would teach him to be selfish. Mrs. N. had found out that she got along better with her seventeen-month-old boy if she did what ought to be done for him as casually as possible, and the fewer the issues raised, the better.

Both women happened to bring their children into the doctor's office for periodic physical checkups one afternoon. Each child was asked to let mother undress him for the examination. "No!" was the almost automatic response from each small patient.

Mrs. C. coaxed. Then she threatened. "Jimmy, you come here this minute or Mother will spank. The doctor won't let you keep the pretty balloon if you don't behave."

The battlelines were drawn. It ended up with a slap on the child's rear, a sobbing, sullen child, and the impression on Jimmy's part that his mother didn't love him when he stood up for his rights, and that doctors are his personal enemies.

Mrs. N., faced with a similar defiant, testing "No!" calmly went over to her child, gathered him up and started to undress him, at the same time pointing to the doctor's stethoscope.

"See the doctor's little telephone, Robbie?" she said, untying his shoes. "He's going to listen to your chest. Won't that be fun? Now, let's take off your playsuit while we blow up your balloon."

And Robbie, his attention passing from the stethoscope to the swelling red balloon, helped get his clothes off and they all had a fine time during the examination.

One mother was telling her child that if he was independent, she didn't love him. The other mother accepted her child's independence and, even though she guided him into the activity needed at the moment, he felt loved all the time.

Avoid Harsh Discipline

The stumbling block with many of us is the old, disproved notion that a child cannot be taught without harsh discipline. Actually, he learns far faster and better to leave the gas stove controls alone if he is persistently and firmly removed every time he goes to touch them, with a passing "No, no," and his attention diverted to another absorbing activity. Scolding and punishment fix

his attention on the forbidden act, while removal and diversion show by actions that the thing which is tabooed just isn't done.

The second year is the child's long, long year of discovery. The understanding mother will recognize her child's inordinate curiosity and allow for it. This little chap has the whole world ahead of him.

Has it ever rocked you back on your heels to think what an enormous number of things a little child has to learn? Well, he's digging into his job heroically. His drive to explore is insatiable. He has to examine everything he can lay his hands on. He wants to test its weight and smell, its taste, texture and moving parts, if any. He shakes it to see if it rattles.

One mother telephoned her doctor. She sounded exhausted.

"Doctor," she sighed, "Billy just wears me out! I can't keep up with him. And he cries, now, if I leave him in his playpen more than ten minutes. What can I do?"

The trouble was, she was trying to lead a normal, ordered adult life, entirely surrounded by a young explorer beside whom Columbus, by comparison, was a piker.

It helps immeasurably, first, if we recognize the exploring urge as normal. It's a sure sign the child is bright and as he should be. It's the way he learns.

Second, we must either change his environment reasonably to suit his bursting energy or change him (God forbid!) to suit our staid, adult ways.

There is only one choice open to thinking parents. Get the things that he mustn't get at out of his reach. Jam shut the drawers that he mustn't open; move the precious glass menagerie off the lower shelves; keep the bathroom door shut; shockproof all wall plugs; wedge the good books tight in the bookcase. See that he has plenty of things of his own to play with. Then, you'll have to say "No, no" only a bearable number of times, and both you and he will get through the year with fewer scars.

The child's reaching out to try new things brings on many an emotional crisis. Take, for example, the desire to feed himself, which becomes marked, if not beaten down by parental disapproval, during this second year. His hands, which could only hold things, can now pick them up. This ability naturally and easily translates into ability to feed himself.

Desire for Self-Feeding

Feeding himself can become a very satisfying experience for the child. The use of new muscular abilities serves the double purpose of trying out those abilities (in itself a most exciting thing) and satisfying hunger.

True, it can only be done when the child is ready. All children are not ready at the same time, but usually the urge definitely shows itself early in the second year. When he is ready, he will grasp any food available and put it in his mouth.

No mother should be surprised if at times her child regresses and wants her to feed him again. She should follow his lead, for if she accepts and understands that this abrupt change from independence to dependence is natural enough at times, he will soon again be reaching out to feed himself.

For this child of yours, this second-year storm center, is a curious mixture of dependence and independence. And paradoxically, the more he is reassured when he returns to you for mothering, the more venturesome he will become. It's as if he needed a firm base from which to venture out into the unknown. Every so often he has to come back and make sure that base is still there.

The wise mother will show him by her actions and the tone of her voice that she loves him both ways—dependent and independent.

Another area of emotional crisis is in the growing control of bladder and bowel. Most children develop this control during the second year. The mother who tries too hard to see that her child becomes "trained" often defeats her own purpose. The child, who is usually trying to please, to imitate and still to show that he is someone, often appears to the mother to be spiting her by having accidents and getting soiled. Often her efforts to help him seem only to intensify his stubbornness.

The solution is to avoid giving him anything to be stubborn about. Let him decide when he needs to go to the bathroom and take the responsibility for his bowel and bladder control when he shows himself ready to do so. But don't hurry him. Let him come to it in his own good time. Until then, be casual; clean up the accidents; don't insist on impossible control. He'll learn it, himself, when he is really ready.

Interest in Other People

As the child swings wider from his mother-orbit and becomes increasingly aware of others outside the family, he is again a curious mixture of trust and apprehension, dependence and independence. He wants to be friends but he wants to do it his way.

It is certainly in order, here, for the mother to protect her child. Well-meaning friends often want to hurry the friend-making process. They rush, they gush, they overwhelm. Usually, a whisper aside to them will do the trick, such as, "Johnny will want to make friends but he likes to take it slow. Just say 'Hello' to him and then wait till he warms up."

Up to now, we have been talking about the child. Let's think briefly about the mother.

She's been having a rough time of it, this second year. In the first year, her baby was quite content to let her care for his every need. Now, he is showing independence and rebellion, because he is becoming able to do things for himself. No wonder she is often at sea. On the one hand, she is proud of his growing ability to take care of himself in feeding, in elimination, in play and in many other ways; on the other, she has the feeling that he is deserting her, that she is no longer needed as much as she was.

But if she understands that there are two sides to her child and always will be, she will feel comforted. One, the baby part, needs to be comforted and cuddled and loved and protected. It's this part that shows up every night. No matter how aggressive, stubborn, resentful and unwilling her child has been during the day, he now becomes again her trusting little baby, demanding her love, her care and feeding, her tenderness in putting him to bed in the evening.

He is learning by trial and error, you see, how to reconcile his new surge for independence and his old habit of being taken care of. It is a great comfort to him every night to be able to come back like a little baby to his mother and be cuddled and cared for.

Reversion to baby patterns. So too, at other times, when fatigue, fright or any emotional upset makes him feel unsure of this new, larger world he is stepping into, he reverts to baby patterns which make him feel secure again, such as wanting a bottle, crawling instead of walking, sucking his thumb, wanting desperately to be held, even wetting.

Understanding this dual nature of her child helps a mother over one of the hardest spots in this crowded second year: her uneasiness because he wants to be babied some of the time but not all of the time. The wise mother just follows his lead and gives him babying when he needs it, and comradeship and acceptance of his new independence when he needs that. She loves him both ways because both ways are his. In all of our thinking about the child and his needs, we must not forget that a mother is an individual, too. She still has responsibilities to herself and to the rest of the family, as well as to her child. Her ability to be herself, a person as well as a mother, is of vital importance to her emotional balance and perspective.

What Parents Can Do

A child changes rapidly during his second year. The more we understand about those changes, the better parents we will be. On the other hand, the child needs to feel that his parents remain loving, understanding and strong. In his changing world, here is something he can bank on.

Here are six pieces of specific advice for the parents of a child approaching or in his second year:

1. Recognize the child's growing physical and mental ability, his urge to explore and his drive to do things for himself. When he tries to do things, he's ready for them.

2. Meet also his need to be babied when he shows it.

3. Avoid conflict. Put forbidden objects out of reach. In teaching him the safe limits of activity, distract rather than scold or punish.

4. Protect your child from friends who tend to overwhelm him with affection. Suggest that they go slow.

5. Remain, yourself, a person as well as a mother. Don't become utterly submerged in your child. Try to keep your perspective.

6. Love and accept your child in all his moods and all his blunderings. He's doing his best to learn.

Finally, the second year is all-important; it also can be fun. Tremendous changes will occur. Parents need only to accept those changes and give a child their steadfast love, support and confidence. *—By Henry H. Work, M.D.*

PREMATURE BABIES

THE story of the premature baby has changed dramatically in the past fifty years. Once, 75 per cent of them perished shortly after birth. Today, three out of four prematures not only survive but most of them go on to be husky, happy youngsters.

By international agreement, a premature is any baby weighing less than five and one-half pounds. Also, babies weighing as much as nine pounds may be considered premature if mentally or organically they are still not mature. The human baby is completely formed in his mother's womb three to four months after conception. After that he simply grows in size and strength. Can you imagine, then, a child weighing less than two pounds as some babies do? Think of anything that size. A box of granulated sugar, a grapefruit, and then remember that this small package is a human being complete with vital organs, blood, bones, even hair.

Doctors today believe that there are a number of reasons for premature births. A mother may have had a poor diet or inadequate medical care during her pregnancy. She may have overworked or contracted an illness during the early months of her pregnancy. Certain families seem to have a tendency to prematurity and mothers who have given birth to one tiny baby often give birth to others. Twins and triplets are frequently premature, and interestingly enough, statistics indicate that certain races have a tendency toward smaller babies. If because of the mother's health a Caesarean section must be performed early the baby will be small. And finally, there are still the unfathomable cases of healthy mothers who carry their babies the full nine months and yet deliver tiny infants.

Is there anything an expectant mother can do to prevent the birth of a premature? The answer is yes, although there are no absolute guarantees. First, early in pregnancy arrange for prenatal care under a competent physician. Second, eat a properly balanced diet rich in protein foods. Third, avoid overfatigue, particularly in the final three months of pregnancy.

Today, much is known about premature care, for medical men have learned how to carry on where nature left off. Conditions inside the mother's womb have been simulated artificially for prematures, allowing the infant to make up for the extra months and pounds denied him by premature birth.

Pioneer Premature Baby Care

How has this been done? An excellent place to find the answer is at Michael Reese Hospital in Chicago, Illinois. Michael Reese is only one of many premature stations in the United States, but it was the pioneer in this field. There, Dr. Julius H. Hess and Evelyn Lundeen, the nurse who assisted him, first set up their pilot nursery and designed the special Hess incubators. Today the nursery has a special isolation room, a main incubator section, graduation room, quarters for formula-making, linen and sterilization.

A staff on three shifts a day tends to babies resting and growing in the three types of incubator with which the station is equipped. Every facility of a great general hospital is available for the tiny patients.

The birth of any premature is an emergency. Aware that the first days, even the first hours of life, are critical for these babies, the City Board of Health has a ruling that all premature births must be reported within the first hour of life.

To save these children, the city of Chicago and most other large towns in America provide special ambulances equipped with portable incubators and staffed by health nurses.

At Reese the staff is alerted as the health nurse steps into the nursery, portable incubator firm in her hands. What is the baby inside like? Like most prematures, he has arms and legs skeleton-like in appearance. His skin seems wrinkled and so transparent that you can see the vessels beneath the surface. His head is large, and his breathing is difficult. But this baby can cry with the best of them.

Quickly the infant is placed in a glass-enclosed incubator (called "the womb with a window") in which an even and warm temperature is maintained. The humidity inside is high to assist in thinning out the mucus in the back of the baby's throat and his bronchial tubes. The moist air and the warmth of the incubator help cut down deaths from hyaline disease, the respiratory ailment which is the commonest killer of prematures.

A resident physician is on hand to take careful note of the baby's condition and to give instructions. He will order oxygen for as brief a period as possible if the baby has difficulty in breathing. Today the giving of oxygen is carefully watched! Modern research indicates that an overdose may cause retrolental fibroplasia, a scar formation in the eye, which once left many prematures blind. Fewer cases are seen now. But there are still some which are not due to an excess of oxygen in the baby's incubator.

Constant Nursing Care

For the nurse handling the new arrival, there are endless details which demand constant care. She must be patient, for progress in a premature station is slow. Often an infant may take 14 days simply to regain weight lost after birth. She must be scrupulously clean, for infection is a constant danger with all babies, but particularly with prematures, who have less immunity to disease. Her uniform must not touch the baby; nor is she allowed to move from child to child without washing hands and arms up to the elbow. In her busy eight-hour shift she may have as many as 100 functions to perform for her five or six patients.

From the layman's point of view, perhaps the most fascinating thing about premature care is the feeding. In the early hours of life, no attempt is made to give any nourishment. Babies under two pounds sometimes go two or three days without food. Big four-pounders wait twelve hours or more, at which time their diet consists of a teaspoon of sterile water given by medicine dropper, and followed later by a teaspoonful of milk given the same way. The bigger babies quickly progress to a doll-size bottle. The smaller must hit two and three-fourth pounds before they can suck from the one-ounce bottle.

During feeding the infant's head rests in the nurse's left hand. The dropper, equipped with a piece of soft rubber tubing, is pressed gently on the back of the tongue to stimulate sucking.

Through years of experience the staff has learned that the best policy is to give the least amount of food possible which still permits a weight gain. By not overfeeding, intestinal disturbance can largely be prevented.

All milk given to these tiny babies at Michael Reese is human milk. Each new mother is taught how to extract milk from her breasts (either manually or with a pump) four times a day at home. Each is cautioned that lactation may take as long as three weeks to start for the mother of a premature. For those mothers who have no milk, there is the city's Free Fund, and the hospital keeps a supply of this. Once the baby reaches four pounds a formula may, if necessary, be substituted for breast milk.

Often the patient is hospitalized for a number of months, though the average stay is about 30 days. How long the baby must remain will depend on the time it takes for him to gain sufficient weight and maturity.

Visiting Nurse Assists Parents

To help the anxious parents about to take over where the hospital leaves off, there is the visiting nurse. She calls on the family early. She discusses sleeping arrangements, inspects the bassinet, teaches the non-nursing mother to make formula and, above all, tries to answer the many questions that are asked. Later, when the baby is a part of the family, she will visit again to check on his progress. This transition period is often a difficult one. The mother may be anxious about her ability to care for the small infant. To remedy this, she is invited to the nursery before the baby is discharged. Under supervision, she feeds, bathes and dresses her child. This direct contact does much to dispel anxiety and fear. When going-home day arrives, the mother has been well prepared. With baby in arms (now weighing about five pounds) she leaves with written instructions and definite know-how.

Once at home the premature must be protected against infection, for he is still not as strong as a full-term baby. At three months the acute problems of most prematures stop but, because he started life so small, he should be checked by a physician once a month for six or eight months. The slightest illness should be reported to the doctor. Emotionally, he will fare best if his mother can treat him like any healthy human being. This isn't easy, for there is more anxiety, more curiosity about a premature.

With the premature, patience is the thing which pays the largest dividends. Because he started extra small it may take him extra time to match his peers.

In about two years, the majority of prematures equal their peers mentally. By the time they are three they have caught up with their friends in dexterity and ambulatory ability. Sometimes it may take five to eight years before they match playmates in height and weight.

What happens to the premature who does not get such an excellent start as he might at Michael Reese? What if he happens to be born in another city? Or on a farm miles away from a hospital?

Today general hospitals throughout the country are well equipped with nurseries and incubators. Moreover many communities now have ambulance service and mother's milk.

For the mother who lives far from any general hospital, there is much, too, that can be done at home. The less a premature is moved the first 24 hours of life, the better. A cardboard box bedded down with blankets and kept warm either by a hot pad underneath or light bulb suspended overhead, has more than once served as an incubator. The important thing is to keep the temperature constant so that the baby has no extra strain or unnecessary adjustment to make.

Daily care. The premature infant's skin should be washed as little as possible. Nature protects all babies against infection by a skin coating called vernix caseosa. All that need be done is to clean the buttocks with water or oil.

Since food is not required the first days of life, and since here again nature provides all babies with excess fluids at birth, nourishment can wait for one or several days. It is important to secure the services of a competent physician.

The science of caring for the premature which has been pioneered at Michael Reese, is now being taught to students who come from all parts of this country and from abroad.

Having learned to care for the premature, these men and women will be better able to care for all children. Knowledge, patience, devotion and skill are the watchwords of all good medicine and nursing.   —*By Jean R. Komaiko*

CIRCUMCISION—
THE PROS AND CONS

SHOULD our baby boy be circumcised?" is a question asked by many new parents—unless, of course, the operation is automatically performed in accordance with religious doctrine. All doctors are not in agreement about the merits of circumcision—some even refuse to perform it unless the parents insist. But almost all doctors find many parents know little or nothing about the operation. A brief description and history may help you decide whether it is indicated for your baby.

Circumcision, meaning to cut around, is the surgical removal of the prepuce or foreskin, the fold of skin surrounding the head of the penis. The prepuce may vary in length from less than three-eighths of an inch to more than one and a half inches and is removed in its entirety as a complete ring of skin. The professional Jewish circumciser, called a Mohel, uses a sharp knife for the operation (he may also use a clamp as does the surgeon) and relies on tight bandaging to stop the slight flow of blood. Surgeons frequently use sutures (stitches) to arrest bleeding. Nowadays they often perform the operation using a clamp that fits over the head of the penis. The foreskin is drawn up and around a metal ring to measure the amount of skin to be removed. The doctor then cuts off the exposed skin with a stroke of the knife. The tight clamp which shuts off the blood supply is left in place for a minute to prevent later bleeding. Some doctors use a special type of clamp that eliminates stitches.

The operation is not very painful, especially if it is performed no later than eight days after birth. Jewish ritual requires circumcision on the eighth day. Vitamin K given to the mother just before delivery or to the baby at the time of birth insures that the coagulating properties in his blood are at a safe level. If the baby is much older—six months or more—when the operation is performed, a general anesthetic is usually recommended.

Hospitals Set Health Standards

Many hospitals now perform routine blood and coagulation tests for each infant before permitting circumcision and insist that the operation be performed by a skilled person known to them. The Jewish professional circumciser, although not a doctor, is required to meet definite standards.

If your baby is to be circumcised, you will naturally follow your own doctor's advice on aftercare. He may suggest applying medicated ointment or sterile petroleum jelly on a single layer of gauze, just large enough to be wrapped around the penis, to permit urine to pass freely through the bandage to the diaper. Of course, the bandage will require changing when the baby is diapered. Some doctors recommend a light application of an antiseptic once a day, probably at bathtime.

The earliest written record of circumcision is the Old Testament account of Abraham's circumcision of himself, his son and his male servants—in all, nearly four hundred persons—by which he solemnized the covenant made with Jehovah. Since then, Jewish law has required that all Jewish male infants be circumcised to signify membership in their religious group. There is evidence that after Abraham's time the practice spread to Phoenicia and later to Egypt. At first the operation was performed on members of the priesthood and nobility, who adopted it for reasons of cleanliness and hygiene. In time it was performed on all boys of ten or twelve. Among the Arabs, circumcision is performed at age thirteen, and among several African and South Pacific tribes, it is also performed at puberty as a ceremonial initiation into manhood. In many parts of India and the Near East circumcision is frequently practiced, but it is unknown in parts of the Orient and Scandinavia.

Few other practices have been subject to such long-standing and bitter controversy, with the reasons for and against such a mixture of fact and fancy, superstition and scientific knowledge. What are the pros and cons of the argument today?

Those in favor of circumcision claim that it promotes cleanliness, since uncircumcised boys may develop a sticky secretion between the foreskin and the penis which can cause an odor and be a source of itching. Opponents reply to this argument that children taught to bathe the genitals daily with soap and water do not suffer from excessive secretions. Only boys having an extremely long foreskin, difficult to keep clean, accumulate such secretions.

Circumcision is frequently advised for boys having a very tight foreskin that may misdirect the flow of urine. In some cases adhesions form between the foreskin and the penis, but these may frequently be broken naturally by applying slight manual pressure to retract the foreskin. Even if the adhesions remain for some time, they may be broken by the first erections of the penis.

Medical Considerations

A basic objection to circumcision is that, since the foreskin protects the head of the penis, its removal is contrary to what is natural and best. In support of this claim, it has been observed that ulcers often develop in the tip of a circumcised penis, but practically never occur in an uncircumcised one. On the other hand, circumcision is thought to prevent cancer of the penis. Fortunately, this type of cancer is extremely rare, even among uncircumcised men. Some claim that since circumcision removes skin tissue having specialized sensory nerves with a sexual function, it is a deprivation to remove this tissue.

There is statistical evidence to support the claim that circumcision affords a slight measure of protection against venereal disease and other local infections. In particular, the bacteria that cause gonorrhea may remain in the prepuce after exposure to the disease. It has been conjectured, although it hasn't been proved, that the low incidence of uterine cancer among Jewish women is attributable to their husbands' circumcision.

How can parents weigh the arguments for and against circumcision? If their decision is not determined by religious requirements, parents should ask the advice of their family doctor or pediatrician. The decision to circumcise should always be made with the individual child in mind, not as a merely routine matter, as there are cases where circumcision is medically unwise. For instance, a malnourished infant or one who weighs less than five or six pounds should not be circumcised. Most physicians also advise against circumcising an infant who has jaundice or any illness or congenital defect that may cause complications.

If you decide on circumcision for your child, be sure that a skilled person performs the operation. Your baby's first operation—even a minor one—is an important experience, not to be undertaken casually without serious attention to his unique needs. —*By Edward T. Wilkes, M.D.*

TOILET TRAINING

THE term "toilet training" seems to place upon the parent the responsibility for a child's mastery of the eliminating processes. At best, all a parent can do is help guide the child *as he learns control*.

The testimony of hundreds of mothers gives convincing evidence that the great majority of toilet-training problems are psychological and start with the mother's disgust and abhorrence with the whole "filthy" business of elimination. If mothers didn't think of it as nasty, the whole matter could be approached in a matter-of-fact way and many problems would never develop.

Yet mothers cannot be blamed for their feelings. They got them from their own mothers. But it's time for the unreasoning circle to be broken.

After all, stools or feces are merely the waste product coming from the gastrointestinal processing plant.

So, in handling toilet training, first of all be neutral about stools and urine. Think of them simply as waste products. Don't be in an unreasonable hurry to flush the toilet or empty the pot. If you feel disgust your child may sense your feeling and make it his own.

Control develops gradually. Realize, too, that the sphincter muscles which control the movement of the lower bowel and bladder develop gradually in the child, and that the times at which children develop control varies considerably. Control over all body functions develops slowly, from the head downward. Usually it does not extend to the muscles controlling elimination until some time during the second year. Control of the bladder develops somewhat later than does command over the anal sphincter. That is why many children keep on wetting, even after they can control their bowel movements.

Mothers often say proudly, "Why, my Jimmy's only ten months old, and he's perfectly trained already. He always goes, right after a meal."

Actually, that mother is trained, not her baby. Seldom does a baby have any control that early in his development. What the mother really does is to recognize and time her baby's involuntary "mass action."

When the lower bowel fills up, it distends, stimulating the nerves that govern the sphincter muscles which keep the lower bowel closed, so the baby has a movement. The reason this happens so often following a big meal is that digestive activity starts in the stomach, which in turn affects the nerves that govern the gastrointestinal tract. Contractions are set up in the lower bowel, the sphincter relaxes and often a movement results. That's why letting the child get hungry and eat a big meal helps elimination.

How Conflict Arises

There probably is little danger in trying to start toilet training *before* the child's physical equipment is capable of exercising control, *if the child doesn't object*. But if he does object, conflicts are set up. A child is always angered when he is made to do anything he doesn't want to do. If set on his toilet seat before he has any conscious control, he may feel rejected and unloved if he doesn't perform as expected. And, of course, he can't perform. He's got the equipment, the sphincter muscles, but they aren't ready yet to function on request.

If the child rebels, he will probably resist later on when he does have control, perhaps not by open rebellion, but by sitting quietly on the seat and having no movement. He may have it later in his pants or in a corner.

Only when the mother tries to take over does this conflict arise. A child simply cannot react in this way to a relaxed, nonurgent attitude, which is what the wise mother should strive for.

With the repugnance to elimination which so many persons have inherited, mothers naturally want to get the whole "filthy" business of soiling and wetting over with in a hurry. This urgency is bound to be reflected in their impatience and anger whenever Junior has an accident or when he doesn't "go" as expected. This is sure to result in difficulty. That is why a more matter-of-fact "this is just waste" attitude is advisable.

The wise mother doesn't go overboard in the other direction either, praising her child to the skies whenever he eliminates successfully. That takes the whole thing out of its proper realm of a normal body function. She may casually approve but that is enough.

Aside from the emotional reaction which too-early toilet training is apt to induce in the child, it just doesn't pay from the parents' viewpoint. In the majority of cases, arrested training, resistance, deliberate accidents and constipation, have come from the mother's attempt to hurry the child into control before he is ready. And in these cases, the ultimate goal of complete control is immeasurably delayed, rather than hastened. Some of these children still aren't toilet trained at four or five years of age!

Eagerness to get toilet training over with is understandable, but unwise.

Suppose your baby is a year old. After a big meal, he shows signs of being ready to eliminate—he is very still or he starts to strain or "gets that look in his eye" as mothers say. Then you put him on his toilet seat if he doesn't object. If he functions, you show approval casually. If he doesn't and has an accident later, you stay calm, because if you react strongly, the baby reacts, too. Don't even smile as if to say, "I love you anyway," because then he may get the mistaken idea that you approve of accidents. Children have a great way of connecting things as cause and effect. Just be neutral.

Parental Attitudes

In just the same cause-and-effect way he may think, if you turn up your nose and show disgust at stools, "Mother hates BMs, so I won't have any." And then you have a child who may hold back movements through either submissiveness or rebellion. He will either have his movements in undesirable places or become constipated for psychological reasons.

None of these things happens if a mother keeps calm and relaxed.

Remember, the real goal of toilet training is to help the child take the responsibility for elimination. If the mother assumes the responsibility—always asks him, "Isn't it time to go, dear?"—he is not being trained.

It helps his feeling of responsibility to have his toilet seat where he can get on and off by himself. He should be allowed to as soon as he wants to.

Constipation in children doesn't mean infrequent movements, but hard stools. All during the toilet-training period in the second year of life, it is important that the stools be soft so fear of pain in passing hard stools never develops. Your doctor can give you dietary help to this end.

Actually, constipation due to physical causes is not nearly as common as supposed. But a state of anxiety over bowel movements has become all too frequent in our society, focusing undue attention on the anal area.

There isn't nearly the emotional reaction to urination that there is to defecation. Yet wetting continues longer than soiling. The important thing to remember is that the child should never be shamed for wetting. Usually, he just can't help himself, for control of urination seems to be acquired later and much more gradually than bowel control. Greet an accident casually and help your child into dry clothes.

Quite early, say in his second year, get the child used to urinating in different places, so he won't be unable to go except on his toilet at home.

—*By Charles A. Tompkins, M.D., and Fletcher D. Slater*

GO EASY WITH A BALKY BABY

EVEN the sweetest-tempered babies can develop, without warning, fits of resistance toward some ordinary aspect of daily life. Suddenly, they stage passionate rebellions against having their faces washed, being dressed or being toileted. And pressing them usually only increases their irritation, leaving mother feeling baffled and frustrated.

Even worse, pressure often serves to fix the incident or object in his memory so that next day he reacts the same way. This can establish a pattern of repeat performances whenever the situation comes up. In addition, resistance on one point is all too likely to carry over to others, until you may find yourself at odds with your baby most of the time.

When a baby develops a balky streak the first thing to consider is whether his reaction is due to an unpleasant experience of some sort. It may be

purely physical: he is tired or chafed or getting a new tooth or coming down with a cold.

If he seems all right physically, maybe an experience of another nature is behind his fretfulness. If you've a bit of Sherlock Holmes about you, you may be able to figure out what happened. Perhaps yesterday morning the cereal was too warm and hurt going down. Maybe in bathing him you almost let him slip or got a smidgin of soap in his eye—something you forgot the next moment but which the wary baby remembers. An older baby sometimes is frightened by the water gurgling down the drain in the tub or the flushing sound of the toilet and may screw up his face and back off at the mere sight of these utilities.

Possibly someone was upset or rushed and handled the baby in a hurried or preoccupied manner. Any mother sometimes becomes so involved in her own responsibilities that her mind isn't "there" when she is caring for her baby, and any self-respecting infant resents and is disturbed by feeling ignored. Another thing—if the adults around him are emotionally upset, the baby can pick up some of their feeling and be disturbed by it. This also may be expressed as balkiness.

Sometimes too many shifts in schedule make a baby leery of changes. On the other hand, he may be ready for a change in schedule, such as a later naptime, but mother clings to the established routine, so that he puts up a vigorous protest against a bed he no longer wants to go to quite so early. Moreover, as he grows older the excitement of a new accomplishment sometimes makes it difficult for him to sleep.

That touches on the most general reason for a baby's balkiness: he is growing older and the adults about him do not recognize or appreciate new developments that are taking place.

Desire for Physical Exercise

Learning to use his body and to explore his world is a baby's business. From the time he can first turn over, he is gripped by a continual urge to exercise his maturing nerves and muscles so that practice can give him mastery over them. Where he once lay supine while mother diapered or dressed him, it is now an insult to his prowess to expect him to lie still.

The baby feels physically restrained when his arms are being thrust into sleeves and when dresses or sweaters are being wriggled over his head. To be pulled into clothing or out of it is an interference with his liberty. He will writhe and squirm—unless you are smart enough to capture his interest with a tinkling toy or a cracker or a song, while you finish the job.

There's no doubt about it—a baby's life is full of frustrations that adults don't appreciate. For example, his developing powers of manipulation give him a compelling urge to feel and finger all the minutiae of his environment. He must scrape away at the expanse of fuzzy carpet or tug at the window drapes. He wants to taste, too—so anything at all finds its way to his mouth.

The older baby must explore everything in his path as he creeps about the house. Cigarette ashes are delightful to sample. The wastebasket is a bonanza! The stairs would be exciting to climb if somebody would take away that folding gate and let him try. (It is not too difficult to initiate him into the art of safely backing down, one knee after the other, if mother will take the time to show him how.) Even before a year, he is trying to imitate the activities his canny eye sees performed by those about him. If you watch closely you will notice how often the baby tries to do something and then finds he cannot. It is amazing that nature has given him the persistence to continue trying in the face of so much discouragement.

He learns to pull himself to a standing position—a milestone in his parade of accomplishments—but he cannot get down again. He frets. Yet the minute he is set down he must struggle to pull himself up again.

He learns how to open his fingers and let his rattle drop from his chair to the floor, looking after it with interest. His mother says "No" when, on recovering it, he tries this new and fascinating feat once more.

Frustration Leads to Rebellion

"No"—a word he may interpret variously as a warning of danger or as a sign that his mother is inexplicably angry with him—is sometimes a sad and serious threat to his security. Learning to respond to a mother's note of warning is an ability human babies share with most warm-blooded animals. The baby is equipped to "freeze" when his mother warns of danger. But if she tries too early or too often to discipline him by calling "No," she confuses him and weakens the effect of her teaching. From such mounting frustrations the baby often develops an increasing rebellion.

How can we help the balky baby? First, we can understand what he needs and what the world is like to him. Then we can try to minimize the conflict between his needs and ours. One of the enchanting things about a baby is that everything interests him—he is eminently distractible. Is he tadpoling toward the bookcase? Head him off by offering him a tin cup to bang, a piece of silky cloth to fondle; or give him an old magazine to look at, crumple and tear. Does he balk at playing with his toys, clamor for things he can't have? Give him the joy of delving into a low cupboard shelf filled with pans and lids and other safe kitchen paraphernalia.

Babies who are learning to toddle need to spend endless time inching up on tables or chairs, increasing their ability to balance on small, unsteady feet. And they love to clamber in and out of a simple carton.

If a baby rejects his playpen it is time to leave him out for longer periods of time, so he can practice his new motor skills and explore his world as nature is prodding him to do. Supply him with new interests to entertain him when you feel it is necessary to put him back again.

Does he object to having his face washed? Maybe it's washed too often. Having his face rubbed with a wet rough cloth must seem pretty meaningless to a baby. He can be given a sketchy mop-up while you talk to him.

When the baby balks at mealtime it may be because you've been urging him to eat too much. A drop in appetite is natural as his rate of growing slows down. If he objects to a particular food, omit it for several days. When you reintroduce it, serve it in a new bright-colored bowl; perhaps in a different room too—to help him forget his distaste.

It may be the baby is eager to "help" with the feeding, even if he seems much too young. Cover the floor beneath his chair with newspapers and let him go! Touching the spoon with which you're feeding him, or holding another spoon of his own, or having the freedom to dabble in the exquisitely mushy food—these will give him a sweet sense of satisfaction. The look of triumph on a baby's face when his first awkward motions toward self-help are praised is wonderful to see.

Magic formula. For the baby who has developed an over-all crankiness, unhappiness or balkiness for whatever reason, there is a Magic Three Days formula which can help to begin the return to a happier attitude. Of course, you have to pick a time when you feel secure. For three days, see if you can avoid any difficulty with the baby before it starts. Let him go where he wants as much as you can. Other times, see that he is quietly amused. Omit those aspects of feeding, dressing and toileting situations which you suspect have aroused resistance. Divert him skillfully from any circumstance you think might occasion a protest. These few days aren't enough to "spoil" a baby, even if such a program would spoil him, but they are usually enough to restore a good deal of his old serenity.

Inexperienced parents sometimes fear they are "giving in" to a baby when they defer to his preferences, and that this will encourage him to become even more resistant and demanding. Almost the opposite is true.

There is no substitute for good humor, fun and loving sympathy in handling a baby. The amount of frustration which he can accept is limited. A wise mother will try to figure out the emotions behind her baby's balkiness and be mature and gentle in reacting to them. It is not only good strategy but a golden opportunity to lay a foundation for later cooperation.

—*By Evelyn Emig Mellon*

BABY FEARS

A BABY'S fears are often taken for granted as a part of the process of growing up. It is true that many baby fears have no lasting effect upon later behavior, that they are "outgrown." But it is also true that some of these fears carry over into childhood and adulthood with far-reaching results. Fears of the dark, of thunderstorms, of countless animals and crawling creatures are common.

Most studies of childhood fears deal with children of nursery-school age, but many fears have their origin at a much earlier age, which we adults are either unaware of or have forgotten.

The prevention of such fears is important, for not only do they make the child an object of ridicule among his playmates and the butt of practical jokes but later on they may become social and occupational handicaps and in some cases an actual danger to health.

Many fears are taught—the idea of danger is planted in the child's mind by someone who is himself a victim of that particular fear or who merely shows concern in the presence of a young child over the approach of an animal or over a thunderstorm, a heavy wind or a torrential rain.

It is important that those who are afraid of one thing or another keep their apprehensions and anxieties well under control in the presence of small children. Even a facial expression or a mere gesture will give the child the feeling of imminent danger. A young child can very well be cautioned against real danger, such as the snapping of a dog, by telling him that many dogs do not like to be petted by strangers and that it is best to leave them alone.

With regard to other fears, observing parents and psychologists agree that most fears are caused by an unpleasant experience and that fear is merely exaggerated caution against a possible repetition of unpleasantness. The experience may have inflicted pain, as in the case of a burn or a dogbite, or it may have startled the child, or it may have merely upset the even tenor of his life.

It does not matter at all whether the fear-provoking situation contains an element of danger or not when viewed through adult eyes. A baby cannot make this distinction. He is unaware of the danger from sharp knives, scissors and fire. The mistake most often made is to force upon the child the adult view that there is nothing to be afraid of and to try to compel him to master his fear in one fell swoop. Emotions cannot be quieted by a mere command. They must subside of their own accord. But the right handling of frightening experiences may prevent the child from acquiring an unconquerable dread of objects, animals and situations which in themselves are neither repulsive nor dangerous.

Familiarity Dispels Fear

In one family a baby was crawling about the room while his mother was cleaning the rug with a vacuum cleaner. Suddenly, he came in direct line with the exhaust end of the cylinder and a blast of air struck him. A piercing cry was the result. Nothing anyone did to soothe and reassure him was of any help; the baby continued to cry and sob, and kept this up after he was carried out of the room.

When he was brought back into the room, he burst into a new fit of crying at the sight of the cleaner. Again he was taken to another room until the cleaner had been put away. Even then he looked with visible apprehension at the place where he had seen the fearful object a few minutes before.

On the day after he was frightened by the cleaner the youngster would not go near it, but he was quite willing to watch the cleaning process from the safe retreat of his crib in the next room. While he at first eyed the procedure with some mistrust, he didn't cry or show the terror of the preceding day.

For two or three days he watched the cleaning process from his crib. Then he was left to sit or creep on the floor while the cleaning was going on. When the work was completed, the cleaner was left on the floor for awhile, apparently forgotten. Time after time he came near the dreaded object, until after three or four days he sat beside it, inspected it and finally ventured to touch it. Eventually, he showed no more fear of the cleaner.

Some adults may think this baby should have been taken right back to face the vacuum cleaner. But a small child cannot be expected to reason like an adult. His fears must be dealt with in a different manner.

Each fear needs its own kind of treatment. Another little boy had become extremely afraid of rain. His family believes that this was caused by a gloomy-minded houseworker who often expressed great concern over rain and frequently told the child stories of terrible happenings due to heavy rain: homes washed away by floods, tracks washed out, trains derailed and similar accidents from which the little boy concluded that rain was something to be dreaded. This is a typical example of fear that was taught to the child.

In order to help him outgrow this fear, his family tried to see that he did not have to go out in the rain. But they told him how well the grass would grow because of rain and how much good food the cows and horses would have as a result. They showed him how the ponds and brooks filled up with good fresh water so that the animals could drink all they wanted. The little boy had become very much interested in cows and horses and gradually he came to think of rain in a normal and understanding way.

Strong emotion inhibits reasoning. The important thing in dealing with a child's fear is not to force sudden contact with the dreaded object or situation. Instead, grownups should at first shield the baby from whatever frightens him and be casual about the matter.

This course of action has a sound scientific basis: strong emotion interferes with the functioning of reasoning power; it is impossible—especially for a young child—to recognize the absence of danger when his intelligence is inactive because of fear. Familiarity with the cause of the fear must be established gradually after the child's interest in the dreaded object has been aroused, either through his natural curiosity, as in the case of the vacuum cleaner, or through his liking for things which have no visible connection with the cause of his fear, as in the case of the horses and cows.

In the last analysis a child masters his fears himself. All we can do is to set the stage and provide the props. *—By Mary A. Boncquet*

IF YOU HAVE A VERY ACTIVE BABY

IF you have what is described as a very active baby, you'll know almost better than we do what is meant—a tense, wiry, jack-rabbity child who is wound up tighter than all get-out. He'll have some or all of these earmarks (and there are just as many "she's" as "he's"). He doesn't gain much weight; he's very alert—his senses seem to be more acute than other children's; he requires little sleep; he's inclined to have feeding problems; he touches depths and heights of emotion. Fight him, and he's a little demon; go along with him, and he's the most responsive, loving little person imaginable.

There doesn't seem to be an apparent cause for him to be this way, but he is from birth. So far as we are able to find out, it's not due to any glandular imbalance. The best guess would be that it's simply heredity. One thing is certain—common problems of eating and sleeping seem to be aggravated in the very active baby. So proper feeding is doubly important. Briefly—let him eat and sleep *as he needs it*. Feed him upright, feed him full and feed him *after* he cries for it to minimize crying and tenseness.

Not too much is known as yet about prenatal influences, or how they affect the child before birth. Perhaps chemical changes in the mother's bloodstream bring about changes in the developing fetus. Maybe—this is still speculative—emotional disturbances in the mother cause little-known changes in blood chemistry and endocrine activity which in turn work changes in the intra-uterine, developing personality.

It must be admitted that even the newborn baby has a personality, or at least an individual potential for personality. Here is the package, unique and totally different, the product of two people. There's nothing quite like it on earth, and sometimes it's a very lively package, indeed—a wailing, red-faced little mite, legs and arms kicking and waving frantically. Put to the breast or bottle he sucks greedily, avidly. He seems to sleep with the trigger set.

All pediatricians have a number of these hair-trigger children as patients. Mothers, particularly, often feel a sense of guilt and worry for fear that they're not handling these children as they should; they try too hard, and this very trying often upsets them and the child.

Growth of Tension

It is certainly true, too, that the naturally hyperactive child often kicks off tensions in the parents. These tensions, in turn, add steam to the parents' dealing with their already hair-triggered child, and a vicious cycle may easily be set up.

The fact should be stressed that the hyperactive child is entirely normal, varying only in the degree of his aliveness; there's nothing at all wrong with him, and he'll turn out all right—probably a bit better than all right.

Let's go a little further in describing the very active child. All normal babies at birth give a start and cry when equilibrium is lost, or when there's a sudden, loud noise, like a sneeze or a door banging shut.

This startle reflex gets stronger during the first two weeks, then gradually fades, though babies never entirely lose it.

The very active child will react with a violent start to a noise which would scarcely disturb a more placid infant. He'll lie poised like a coiled spring even when resting, and will show the startle reflex even when he's rolled over, ever so gently, in bed.

He demonstrates the other defenses more quickly and strongly, too, than does the ordinary baby. He withdraws more quickly from painful stimuli; he blinks more at sudden light; he shivers and mottles more easily when cold; he struggles more violently if restrained; he seems to hate clothes, unless they're kept to a minimum and very comfortable.

Of course, some movements at birth are not defensive—raising the head when placed on the stomach; stretching; grasping objects when his hand touches them; hand-to-mouth movements; aimless kicking and waving. But your very active child does all these things harder and better than the average.

When hungry, the placid, well mannered, "good" baby often signals that fact with a mild, reasonable protest. The very active baby, on the contrary, bludgeons your ears with angry screams, and flails his arms and legs.

Well, take him as he is, and be thankful. For the overactive baby has got something extra the average baby hasn't. To quote Dr. C. Anderson Aldrich, the late author of "Babies Are Human Beings," "The most definite personalities put on the biggest show."

"But Doctor," protested a worried mother, "my baby's just *impossible*. Why, it's all I can do to change his diapers. He doubles his legs up so tight I can't straighten them out."

"Okay," is the reply, "so you just change him with his legs doubled up!"

And really, that's the whole secret. You've got an "extra" baby, a pepped-up model. Don't fight him; accept him. It's not an evidence of cantankerousness. He's built that way; he'll probably always be like that. Dr. Margaret Fries, while admitting that very little is known about the inborn personality, concludes that "markedly active infants are likely to be markedly active at later ages, too."

Compensations for Overactive Child

You can learn to live with his added zing. And there are compensations. If these "extra" babies seem to be "affected more acutely by the disturbing things in their routine, as though they were more aware of themselves as individuals," as Dr. and Mrs. Aldrich put it, they are equally keen in appreciation when their needs are satisfied. Such a child, if handled with respect, and not frustrated by blocking and disapproving, "becomes highly responsive and fairly sparkles with the zest of living," to quote again from the Aldriches. The first year of life for and with the very active child is the hardest. In the first year a placid baby's mother feels that her baby is wholly dependent on her. She can lavish on him all her protecting love and care. But the mother with the very active baby doesn't ever quite feel she has even that first year of a wholly dependent, mother-focused baby. He's not like the others; he doesn't seem to need his mother as much because his drive for self-expression constantly finds an outlet.

But this is only appearance, and a misleading one. Actually, the very active baby is just as dependent on his mother for survival as any other baby. In spite of his independence, he wants and needs her love and care quite as much as the most helpless-seeming infant, and he's louder and more demanding than he ever was.

With the overactive child it is even more important than with the average baby to look to his needs. He is only trying the best way he knows to satisfy his instinctive, natural cravings. If satisfied, he will not revolt. "Satisfied people never start a revolution"—and by "revolution" we mean using the weapons of the angry, unsatisfied child—disobedience, teasing, whining, demanding, fussing.

Instead of cracking down—which is what mother feels like doing—she needs to find out what the unmet needs are, and to help him gratify them if at all possible. For remember, it is satisfaction of natural needs, not denial of them, that gives a child ability to grow and develop.

People in general—even parents—are apt to label the strident, vigorous babies as "bad" children, and the placid, easy-going ones as "good" children. Yet as a matter of fact, said Dr. Aldrich, "from the standpoint of ability to defend themselves and to live independently, the 'sparklers' are decidedly more efficient."

The mother of a very active nine-week-old baby, at her wits' end, brought him in to her doctor.

"He's already quit taking his afternoon nap," she said. "He cries when I put him to bed after dinner. John and I are just worn out, getting up with him all night. I don't know what to do!"

A Classic Example

Here was an "extra" baby—a classic example. Examination showed a perfect baby, normal in every respect—except that he was an overactive child.

Directions were given for filling him full, in an erect position, after he gave his hunger cry, and getting him to bed right afterward in a dark, quiet room, without any play period following the 6 o'clock feeding.

Although she tried it, and found it helped some, the child's mother reported over the telephone, "He still wakes up at all hours of the night and cries. He refuses the bottle—he just acts mad!"

Little babies don't act mad for no reason. If they're angry, it's always because some need is not being satisfied. It was doubtful that at that age the baby's social instincts were so strong he needed company on demand all night.

"How do you cover him?" the doctor asked.

The mother described the nightclothes—sleepers with feet. "And we pin down the blankets so he won't get uncovered in the cold room. He kicks and squirms so."

The doctor suggested that she keep the window shut at night and forget about the blanket, for the hyperactive child desperately hates any hampering of his freedom. Typically he's a "rolling stone" while he sleeps. He changes position dozens of times a night.

"And you can assure his grandmother," the doctor added, "that he'll get plenty of fresh air through the wall seams, around the windows and doors."

His mother reported a few days later that her child was sleeping much better. Closing the window, too, meant shutting out night sounds, which often awaken sensitive sleepers. It was also explained to this mother that the very active child seems to need less sleep than the average.

The very active child is often quick of perception, emotion and intellect. His motor is racing from birth, and he does more moving, feeling, tasting, yelling, investigating with all his senses, than does the average infant.

Does all this mean that if you are blessed with one of these fireballs you can only accept him and help him to meet his needs as he expresses them?

Not quite. It is also true that you can, with your doctor's help, guide his growth in a way that will be more satisfying to him.

Mrs. Jones found her extremely active baby was tired when night came and found it hard to go to sleep. On questioning, the doctor found that her baby had developed a habit of demanding that the door be left open, and all the sounds and some of the light of the workaday world were seeping in.

No baby can protect himself against undue stimulation and this very active baby was being worn out by sounds and sights which the ordinary baby would sleep right through.

Once she understood this, Mrs. Jones put his bed in the back bedroom, installed tight window shades, and shutting the door, stayed with him till he went to sleep.

The baby, protected from overstimulation, got his sleep regularly (though it was much less than she thought he needed), and became a rested, if still high-strung baby.

Avoid Undue Stimulation

Be sure there is no undue stimulation, for sensitive babies no doubt find the world far more colorful and full of sounds than less sensitive ones. If it is not toned down at sleep or naptime, they may get little rest.

It is also true that infants who eat and digest rapidly also seem to move quickly. It is probable that they utilize their food better, and so tend to need less and to be more slender than the average.

Often tailormade for the overactive child is the two-meal, split-dinner scheme that has been found to work wonders with feeding problems in some children. This means feeding him when he's hungry—his first meal a brunch, perhaps about 10 in the morning and his dinner with the family, but splitting that dinner into an orange-juice, 4 o'clock snack, and the main course at 6 or 6:30 or later. Play with dad then comes before dinner, not after, and the full baby feels like going to sleep.

Your doctor should always be consulted, of course, when anything disrupts the normal life of your baby. Nothing can take the place of a regular, routine checkup, or a phone call to report unusual symptoms. This is even more true of a very active baby than of the average infant—for one thing, his mother needs more reassurance that he is normal. As an example, overactivity often includes the digestive tract, so frequent stools may be perfectly normal.

What about the older child? As one mother put it, "Jimmy just runs himself to death. He's always on the go. He has absolutely no sense when it comes to activity. He'll play like a fire engine all day, come in exhausted and ravenous, eat a big dinner and want to keep going at top speed till bedtime. He gets furious when we try to put limits on his activity."

What's to be done? Perhaps the first step is for the parents to realize that their child is an "extra," and seems to require more activity than the average. Consult your doctor.

If the doctor decides, after careful study, that the child is harming himself or wrecking the family by his endless activity, let the doctor discuss all this with him in a reasonable way, pointing out that his enthusiasm is leading him past safe limits of his endurance (or of family endurance).

—*By Charles A. Tompkins, M.D., and Fletcher D. Slater*

THE FACTS ABOUT THUMB-SUCKING

FOR a great many babies, thumb-sucking is a comforting pastime. And authoritative advice tells us there's no need to worry about it, since this is one of the natural things a little baby does. But for parents who don't feel quite easy about the thumb-sucking habit, it helps to examine some of the reasons behind this typical baby behavior. Why do babies suck their thumbs? What satisfaction does it give them? Is it sometimes a sign that the baby needs other kinds of satisfaction which we could supply?

Every baby is born with the instinctive urge to suck—a remarkable ability which not only enables him to be fed but at the same time exercises and so helps to develop the jaw. Some babies have actually been known to suck their thumbs before leaving the hospital delivery room! Moreover, there is evidence, as Dr. C. Anderson Aldrich has stated, "which points to the possibility that thumb-sucking is a favorite intra-uterine occupation. If this is true such exercise affords the baby his only opportunity to get his sucking muscles into trim before this vital function is required."

Aside from the biological necessity for sucking, there is also a lot of pleasure associated with this activity. A new baby finds his first real happiness in life while being fed, cradled cozily in his mother's arms. So it stands to reason that the process which helps to give him this warm satisfaction—the sucking instinct—is in itself a source of pleasure to the baby.

While the sucking instinct is strongest during the first six months of life, it is more pronounced in some babies than in others. One baby will be completely satisfied with the sucking he gets at feeding time. If ever he pops finger or thumb into his mouth his mother knows that it's simply a sign that he's hungry. In fact, some youngsters continue to suck their thumbs when they're hungry until around the age of three. But many a baby will want more sucking time than breast or bottle provides and so may turn to his thumb following a feeding while drifting off to sleep. This extra sucking at sleep time gives him a necessary feeling of cozy contentment. Many babies—and some older children who are well past the age of three—seem to need the thumb as a kind of bedtime "tranquilizer."

According to Dr. John C. Montgomery: "Around three months all babies put thumbs, fingers or fists into their mouths. It is normal behavior. First they develop control of muscles of the face, then muscles of the hands. Soon they combine the two. Hand-to-mouth control is a new physical accomplishment. Baby must spend time practicing it, if he is ever to be able to feed himself."

Can We Cut Down on Thumb-Sucking?

While perfectly natural, early thumb-sucking does deserve some attention. Since it may indicate that a baby isn't satisfied with the amount of sucking he gets at mealtimes, mother can try to give him a chance to suck longer at feedings.

It is thought that a breast-fed baby is less likely to become a thumb-sucker than a bottle-fed baby. This is because, although he may quickly get most of the milk he wants within the first ten minutes of his feeding, he may go right on nursing for 20 minutes or longer, lured on by a trickle of milk left in the breast. On the other hand, a bottle-fed baby who promptly empties the bottle and satisfies his hunger in a hurry must rely on his thumb for more sucking satisfaction. He can't be allowed to suck on an empty bottle because swallowing air would give him a stomachache.

If a bottle-fed baby finishes his formula in less than 20 minutes it is probably time to make him work just a little harder for his dinner—not so hard that he gets discouraged before he's had enough to eat, but hard enough to satisfy his need to suck. Dr. Benjamin Spock refers to a study made by Dr. David Levy who found that babies who are fed every 3 hours don't suck their thumbs as much as babies fed every 4 hours, and that babies who empty their bottles in 10 minutes (because the nipple holes are large) are much more likely to suck their thumbs than babies who take longer to feed.

There are certain types of nipple-bottle-collar combination on the market which regulate the flow of milk to meet the individual baby's nursing requirements. It is important to replace used nipples regularly, since both sterilizing and the baby's sucking soon make them weak and flabby. If, even with a brand-new nipple, the baby finishes his feeding within 10 minutes or so, it is a good idea to buy blind nipples and puncture them yourself with a hot needle. To do this: push a cork into the eye end of a fine needle and hold the point over a flame until the needle is red hot. Then puncture the nipple in only one or two places instead of the usual three. You may have to experiment and waste a couple of nipples before getting the desired results.

Use of a Pacifier

Some doctors advise the use of a pacifier for babies who suck their thumbs. But it is important to remember that a pacifier cannot substitute either for food or for the cuddling and attention which every baby needs in order to be really happy. Popping a pacifier into his mouth every time he whimpers may well add up to being slipshod about some of the baby's other basic requirements quite aside from his sucking need. There are times, for instance, when a baby just wants to be affectionately cuddled and rocked gently to sleep instead of having to use either his thumb or a pacifier for comfort. Since every baby is different, don't be surprised if yours is one who says "thumbs down" to a pacifier and prefers his thumb!

Self-demand or flexible feeding schedules come closer to meeting a little baby's sucking requirements than the stopwatch schedules which once were so popular. It is the frequency of feedings as well as the time spent at any one particular feeding which add up to an adequate amount of sucking exercise. The baby may nurse only a few minutes at one feeding and spend half an hour or more at another meal. By catering to his individual wants during the first few months, instead of imposing an arbitrary schedule, you not only help to gratify his sucking need, but are more apt to help your baby develop a happy feeling about his life in general. All this may mean that he won't need thumb-sucking for any kind of comfort at any time.

With a baby who sucks his thumb, it is wise to go slow on omitting feedings. Even though, for the sake of convenience, mother may be eager to skip the late evening or wee-hours-of-the-morning feeding, it is better to continue these mealtimes for a while if the baby's sucking tendency shows up in thumb-sucking. For the same reason, it is better not to try to rush a thumb-sucker onto a three-meal-a-day schedule, nor to wean him to cup drinking if he still seems to want his bottle.

Now, supposing you follow all these suggestions "to the letter" and still your baby sucks his thumb. What to do? Nothing at all! Knowing that your baby knows best what he's doing, you can relax and use that "don't worry" advice of the baby care experts. Your baby happens to be one of the many who requires an extra measure of sucking—and he is satisfying this need in a perfectly acceptable way. The more he is allowed to suck now—without any restrictive measures taken on your part—the less likely he is to continue the practice after his sucking urge begins to diminish.

How diversion works. Is it ever advisable to cut down on thumb-sucking by trying to divert the baby's attention from his thumb? For example, many mothers will put a toy into the baby's hand the moment they notice thumb moving toward mouth. This trick may work temporarily—but let's never underestimate the power of a baby's will! He's pretty quick to catch on to the fact that something or someone is deliberately detouring that thumb. Such repeated attempts at diverting baby's attention may actually have the opposite effect, intensifying his interest in thumb-sucking. The same holds true for constantly removing baby's thumb from his mouth—or using "police" methods in an effort to control thumb-sucking. Under no circumstances should you use mechanical devices—splints, thumb guards, mittens—or bad-tasting medicine applied to the thumb, to stop thumb-sucking. Such harsh measures actually punish a baby for trying to do something which is perfectly natural for him to do. And, in the long run, this type of prevention merely adds fuel to the flame by frustrating a baby into wanting and needing his thumb all the more to comfort his upset feelings.

When the Older Baby Sucks His Thumb

Thumb-sucking helps to satisfy a young baby's naturally strong urge to suck. In addition, it comforts him when he's fussy, helps him to relax and go to sleep more easily. The older baby or toddler sucks his thumb for the same reasons but with one exception: his early need for sucking is no longer as pronounced as it was during the first six months or so of his babyhood. He is simply using this younger-baby practice for comfort when he feels irritable, bored, apprehensive, or tired. If thumb-sucking helps him through these occasional periods of stress, well and good!

We don't need to feel concerned about a toddler's thumb-sucking unless he seems to be relying on this form of comfort a very great deal of the time. Then we ought to ask: What is it that's missing from his life which causes him to depend so heavily on thumb-sucking? Does he need a little more attention or show of affection? This may be particularly so if there's a new baby in the family who seems to be demanding most of mother's time. Or is his life a bit too strenuous? Sometimes trying to keep pace with an older brother or sister makes a child turn to his thumb for release from tension. On the other hand, many a child sucks his thumb when life gets dull and there's nothing much to do. Does he have enough interesting toys—adequate space and opportunity for play? Is he lonely? Maybe he needs a playmate or two—perhaps a few hours a day at a playschool or nursery school to make life more interesting. Or, if he's already attending a nursery school, is this routine a little too demanding or tiring for him at his age? Any number of things may be causing him to use his thumb for comfort or relaxation.

If we can discover and correct the reasons for it, we may find that thumb-sucking will gradually disappear. If not, the main thing to remember is that without this form of comfort a child who thumb-sucks might be cranky and unhappy much of the time. He wouldn't suck his thumb if he didn't feel the need for it, so it's useless to punish, bribe, scold or threaten him into giving up this behavior. When he's ready, he'll give it up of his own accord.

Don't overemphasize problem. Of course, if prolonged thumb-sucking is a source of worry to a child's parents, it helps to talk over the situation with someone outside the family—a pediatrician or child-guidance expert who may be able to shed new light on the question. But it's important to know that a child is not necessarily a "problem child" just because he sucks his thumb! Many children who apparently have perfectly happy and well adjusted lives do suck their thumbs often or occasionally. In many cases, it may simply be a matter of "temperament." Some children are more sensitive, more tense, sometimes more fearful than other children. Such a sensitive boy or girl may have more need for comfort and therefore turns to thumb-sucking for part-time consolation.

Some parents worry that thumb-sucking may make their child's teeth protrude. If discontinued before the second teeth come through, thumb-sucking has no lasting effect. In an older child, whose second teeth are coming in, thumb-sucking may *sometimes* cause protruding teeth. But in a large majority of cases, displaced teeth are caused by other factors, such as heredity. Dr. Benjamin Spock says only about one-quarter of the children with displaced teeth have ever been thumb-suckers.

Whatever the reasons for thumb-sucking, it does supply a basic need and comfort for many babies and toddlers. We can help to fulfill this need in other ways while still remembering that the behavior itself is nothing to worry about.

—By Joan W. Parks

WHAT TO DO ABOUT A COLICKY BABY

WHEN an infant who appears healthy and well fed has spells of irritability, fussing or crying for a total of more than three hours a day, on more than three days a week, the answer more often than not is colic. The spells come at irregular intervals and last anywhere from a few minutes to several hours. In severe cases the baby's crying may develop into agonized screaming, with his knees drawn up against his abdomen as if in pain. The baby may seem hungry, but feeding doesn't relieve him. In fact, his crying may start shortly after feeding. The paroxysms usually begin when the infant is a week old and usually disappear spontaneously in the eighth week.

Colic can arise from many different causes and your doctor must do considerable sleuthing to find out which one applies to your baby. There may be a hereditary factor. There may be an allergy or a mechanical fault in the digestive system. Maybe improper diet is at the root of it—or poor handling.

The most common cause for the kind of colic that is just excessive crying is inadequate feeding. That may mean "more" in the sense of quantity, but it doesn't necessarily. A diet higher in calories may be what's needed, or more frequent feedings in smaller amounts. Occasionally we see infants whose stomach capacity is unusually small and they must be fed small concentrated quantities of formula more frequently than usual.

When the colic isn't simply irritability and crying, but obviously involves abdominal pain, the cause for the stomach or intestinal spasms has to be uncovered. Excessive gas formation that makes intestinal muscles contract painfully may be one. Often this can be corrected by decreasing the amount of carbohydrate or fat in the formula.

Sensitivity to Food

Another cause may be excess sensitivity to food—commonly an allergy to cow's milk—which brings on a spasm of the small intestine. This is suspected when there is a family history of allergy. Often one of the parents dislikes milk or rarely takes it. Substituting a non-allergic milk product helps determine whether or not milk allergy is causing the colic.

Some babies just seem to be born more tense than others. A baby who awakens at the slightest sound and is sensitive to light, for instance, may be more susceptible to colic. In such cases, the best remedy may lie in giving him a sedative if the doctor prescribes it. Other babies may require drugs to relieve the spasms of the stomach muscles, especially if they tend to vomit.

Overfeeding may also result in a spasm of the intestines, but usually this is accompanied by some distension of the abdomen and vomiting. It seems that the gas gets caught in a part of the intestine and the muscles contract to get rid of it, sometimes causing a slight kinking and pain.

There has been evidence that tension in people around them causes colic in some babies. For instance, a study of married students and their families, made at Yale University by a group of pediatricians and psychiatrists, showed that of the 98 babies studied, 48 were colicky babies who cried and fussed several hours every day, usually in the late afternoon. The cause varied with different individuals, but the most prominent factor was family tension. In 22 of these 48 babies, family tension was judged to be the predominant cause of their colic. (In the group of contented babies, family tension was rare.)

In the Yale experiment, 25 of the colicky babies responded to motion such as rocking, walking, gentle bouncing. They were soothed, too, when a mechanical rocking cradle was used. Even when the rocking mechanism of the cradle failed, the babies continued to be soothed by the continuing monotonous sound of the motor. The mothers also told the researchers that with different babies the sound of a vacuum cleaner, washing machine, running water or even the buzzing of an electric clock appeared to help.

Another successful remedy was the use of a pacifier. A few years ago Dr. Milton Levine studied 28 babies who had colic and found that they were relieved by pacifiers. These infants gave them up spontaneously by 13 months of age. Dr. Benjamin Spock has also reported that many mothers have written him about their success in relieving a colicky baby by the use of a pacifier.

The majority of these babies dropped its use between their third and sixth month. These studies have also shown that few of the pacifier babies became thumb-suckers.

The Yale study also confirmed the theory that colic is more common in a first-born. Of 72 first-born babies, 42 were colicky. Of 22 with older siblings, only 6 had colic.

Colic, as you can see, is not a simple problem, and not easily solved. But a skilled physician, by giving each individual infant careful attention, can nearly always analyze the cause. He is helped a lot by a mother who observes carefully the nature of her own baby's symptoms.

—*By Edward T. Wilkes, M.D.*

PRESCHOOLERS

CHARACTER DEVELOPMENT • LEARNING TO SHARE • JEALOUSY
HANDLING ANGER • BACK TALK AND BAD LANGUAGE
MENTAL GROWTH • DISCIPLINE • GUIDANCE OR GIVING IN
BRIBERY • EMBARRASSING BEHAVIOR • COMMON FEARS
IMPORTANCE OF LISTENING • CREATIVE PLAY
LEARNING TO GET DRESSED • PREPARING FOR SCHOOL
ENCOURAGING READING AND WRITING ABILITY

THE BASIS OF CHARACTER

APPARENTLY it is when a youngster is somewhere around two or three that a lot of mothers and fathers first become concerned about "good" and "bad" character. Actually, he won't really begin to display fixed traits of character for another two or three years, but nevertheless certain things he does worry his parents. It is at this age that many a mother thinks of her child, "He's so selfish—he takes things that don't belong to him."

It's true that such a young child looks upon anything interesting as "his," whether it really belongs to him or not. He wants to take toys from playmates, candy from grocery shelves; he wants to rifle through visitors' pocketbooks. But to judge such acts in a moral light is at best meaningless to the child and at worst damaging. He can't make fine distinctions between right and wrong.

Another concern is that a youngster is going to grow up to be a bully, because he attacks other children. There's no question that a three-year-old's first meetings with other children have to be guided, especially when the others are younger. He has no concept of what can result from hitting a playmate with a shovel. Though he must be stopped, simply repeating, "Don't hit," is no help to him. One thing that will help, with time, is his own growing power of observation. He sees that a playmate who is kicked or bitten or hit cries and runs away.

Parental Discussion

Another real help is calm, easy-going discussion by parents of the possible consequences of his acts. Young as he is, if this early teaching is not too reproachful or threatening or too insistent he can begin to understand. One way of teaching that is comprehensible to him is telling a brief, simple but dramatic story in words he knows that illustrates what happens when some-one is hurt. "So the children who were hurt decided that the boy with the shovel was no good to play with," can help the shovel swinger understand in advance what the consequences may be.

"Is he going to be a liar?" is still another common worry. And usually it's because grownups have forgotten how much of a child's mental life is taken up with fantasy. Or if they do remember, or recognize it in the three-year-old, they expect it to come to an end too soon. Even at the age of five, a youngster can still be involved with imaginary playmates, animals or things that could happen—so real to him that they *did* happen. While a part of the parent's job is to clarify the difference between make-believe and reality, it shouldn't be done in such a fashion as to make the child feel his make-believing is deceitful. Even when an element of deceit is present, it is often because a child is beginning to want to do or say things to please his parents, as well as himself.

Avoid Stern Disapproval

Calling a youngster a liar is one of the worst things a parent can do. The child who meets stern disapproval or punishment is apt to use make-believe as a solace. And if deceit is persistent it is usually an indication of unhappiness, of a need for more companionship with parents.

Sometimes, too, when a child gets to be three, four or five, he finds himself confronted with the word "ungrateful." While he knows only too well what the accompanying disapproval means, the word in itself means nothing to him. To parents who use it, however, it means an expectation of gratitude, a loving response for something they have done, where it can't yet be understood. A mother and father know how much they sacrifice on behalf of their child, but their sacrifice is something he can't possibly understand. They can only continue to give generously while the child's love feeling grows and becomes steady. Perhaps they have to budget strictly to take care of his physical and material needs. That this is love or something to be grateful for is completely beyond the child's ken at this time. But he can respond better to a few minutes of roughhousing with his father or having a story told to him.

At about four or five, character begins to "set." This doesn't mean that whatever a child is by this time is unchangeable. On the contrary, teachers, friends, church—all of the people and experiences life brings to him—are going to have a great influence on what he is. "Set" means simply that his character is pointed generally in the direction it will go on growing.

By four or five, he has begun to recognize his own urges and to have some notion of the proper way to use them, some idea of what he can and can't do. The consistent love and unblameful guidance from his parents that have strengthened his self-confidence have simultaneously worked in another important way to influence his character development. They have led him to trust his parents and believe in them, because they have believed in his essential goodness and have led him gently through the early stages of immaturity; so now he is ready to accept more direct teaching in matters of what is honest, truthful and just. In other words, out of his trust he is more inclined to accept their judgments and values than to disbelieve them. In so simple a thing as "It sounds nicer to say 'please,'" he's more likely to feel you really have *his* well-being in mind and not just your own satisfaction.

At this point, a good thing for parents to keep in mind is the tremendous importance of a positive attitude in presenting their social and moral ideas. Teaching that always takes the form of warnings, for instance, is not positive. It assumes that the child will be "bad" and has to be kept from it by the presentation of dire consequences. What should be assumed is that the child is good and will want to continue to be so, to continue growing into an interesting, intelligent and well loved person.

And it is an accurate assumption. The child who has been guided with love through his initial strong sensuous and aggressive phases, who has experienced genuine companionship with his parents and has good examples in them, both anticipates the best from the world and the people in it and is able to give his best in return—to be the "good person" they want him to be.

—By Margaret A. Ribble, M.D., and Margaret Albrecht Gillmor

SEX AND THE YOUNG CHILD

IT is early Sunday morning and the playground is deserted. Near the swings Bobby and Ann play noisily, running and shouting. Suddenly the little boy jumps on a swing as his companion leaps for the one beside him. They begin a contest to see who can swing higher, but Bobby wins easily and they shuffle to a stop.

"Let's play bunking," says six-year-old Ann.

"Okay," her playmate agrees, and they each throw one of their legs across the swing seats, so they face each other. Gradually, like two opposing pendulums, they begin to rock back and forth. The game goes on until the seats collide with such force that Ann shouts protestingly.

Bobby and Ann take delight in this and other simple forms of play. They are at the blissful age of discovery. Is there a greater significance than mere play in what they are doing?

Peggy, a sandy-haired girl of eighteen, is sitting on a dock at the edge of a lake when a young man rushes by, gives her a playful shove and leaves her in a cloud of spray as he dives into the water. "Hey!" shouts Peggy as she jumps to her feet and follows her attacker headlong into the lake. Swimming up behind him she gets a good hold on one of his toes and pulls him under. Not to be outdone, he dunks her, and then the couple swim quietly out to a raft to get better acquainted in the sun.

Interest in Sex

To the adult mind the second episode is clearly an example of love play. If Peggy's parents had been watching they might have reacted in one of two ways. They might have smiled knowingly, pleased by the evidence of their daughter's coming of age—or they might have been filled with dire misgivings and apprehension born out of failure to understand where their daughter's sex drives came from and where they were going.

It is no less than astonishing to discover how few parents realize that sex is something which grows, just as teeth and hair and other parts of the body grow. Were Bobby and Ann playing at sex? They certainly were. Not like Peggy and her friend, naturally. Not with the same consciousness and understanding. But in their way they were making discoveries, too, learning the ways of the body and the moods and temperament of each other. At the age of six, Bobby and Ann know more about sex than grownups would dare give them credit for.

We are living in an era of enlightenment. Already shrouds of mystery have been peeled away by increased frankness and instruction in our schools, churches and homes. But as yet we are just emerging. The scars of prudishness have only been given a chance to heal in the last few decades.

Today's mother knows that what is unsaid between herself and her children will be said in the dangerous classroom of the street. Becoming aware of sex as it grows in her child is the privilege of the modern woman. But parents are still baffled by their own frustrations when it comes time to explain the facts of life. The reason for this is, in a way, simple. They do not always know them.

Gradual Sexual Growth

Fact one is that sex grows. It does not suddenly and mysteriously appear in a person's twelfth or thirteenth year, to be reckoned with in the few years prior to marriage. It takes shape during a gradual development, beginning with, believe it or not, the very first moments of life in the newborn!

Until recently it seemed that the most convenient course was to ignore sex entirely in our children until the growth of their bodies and the extent of their activities made it impossible to ignore it any longer. Living in a world of "sex for adults, games for children," we were astonished, even hurt when our youngsters suddenly showed themselves as full-sized human beings. And then, faced with the full realization of what could no longer be ignored, we were filled with misgivings. Had we told them enough? The answer was: no, because we did not know enough ourselves.

One of the first desires of the tiny infant is for something to soothe his aching stomach. He is irritated and, never having tasted food, he does not know what he wants. But a warm object between his lips does the trick. And with it comes a sip of milk and the first moment of pleasure.

Oral Stage

It is a fact that the baby derives bodily satisfaction by holding something between his lips. This is the beginning of what scientists call the oral stage of sexual development, in which all things find their way into the baby's mouth. Gradually the infant comes to savor the sucking experience. We find it hard to believe that this is a sex manifestation because it seems only to concern the baby's getting fed, and the fact that he is kept warm if he is at his mother's breast. But babies want to suck aside from being fed.

A baby associates the pleasure of sucking and eating with the good warmth of the person who supplies the food, and so comes to need the comfort of being held, hugged or caressed. So important is this second means of bodily satisfaction that in the baby wards of certain hospitals and foundling homes attempts are being made to organize groups of women volunteers to come in regularly and pick up and play with the babies. Doctors realize how important cuddling is for normal development.

In the first and second years of a child's life, every parent has the constant problem of pulling out of the baby's mouth things that do not belong there. Anything that interests the child will find its way between his lips if possible. The reason for this is partly curiosity, partly the fact that in an infant pleasure is associated with his mouth.

Anal Stage

Just as many objects get into a baby's mouth sooner or later, it isn't long before he finds another part of his body that affords him tactual pleasure. Roughly, between the ages of one and a half to six years old, boys and girls discover the rectum. This is as natural as finding out that the nipple on a feeding bottle is a means to a pleasant end. As the parent puts more and more emphasis on toilet training, the child comes to know that rectal stimulation is pleasurable.

It is usually at moments like this that the unwise parent turns the first key on a long series of locked doors between the child and himself. Sudden scolding or a terrifying scene will do more harm than good—for to put fear into the child's heart at an early age is to cut him off from the power to reason and to figure things out correctly later on.

You can keep from being shocked by being prepared for such interests and knowing that they are normal—a part of your child's sexual development. If you keep your head in such a situation, you will let your child know that he need not fear your presence when he "discovers" parts of his body. Handled understandingly the first time, a child will come back to his parents again and again for help when things seem puzzling. But if frightened, he will keep such things to himself. That is why it is vital to recognize sex as it develops.

The names that the psychologist gives the various stages of your child's sexual growth are not, in themselves, important. They do serve, however, to point out the framework, and so we use them here. Following the oral stage, when sex, if we choose to call it that, is a matter of stimulating the lips and mouth, the young human being passes into the anal stage, which we have just described—(anal comes from anus, or rectum). These two periods are forerunners of the third, the genital stage.

Genital Stage

Here again can we actually mean that little children, say between the ages of six and ten, are prone to sexual stimulation of some sort? Yes, strange as it may seem to you if you've become used to shutting your eyes to it, they do have sex lives.

Although the stages that a child passes through do eventually lead up to a relation between the sexes, there is a great deal of overlapping and a great deal of backtracking before they get anywhere near that point.

To the child of seven, sex play is already a familiar occurrence. In the course of exploratory touching, the parts of the body which provide a "good feeling" are discovered. Even at seven the nerve endings in the genitals are already considerably developed, and command much of the normal child's attention. But here again, if this childhood masturbation is viewed with horror by the parent, the results can be harmful. No amount of scolding is going to force a little girl to keep her hands behind her back. In fact, scolding only serves to focus attention on the kind of thing the parent wishes her to forget. The parent need wish nothing of the kind. It is the child's right to explore. The parent needs to understand and to adopt an intelligent attitude. Explain if you feel it necessary, divert attention if you think it wise, prevent tight clothing or lack of cleanliness from overstimulating, but never help to create fear or an overburdening sense of shame.

Normal children differ greatly in the amount of attention they give to sexual interests. Some youngsters are perfectly frank about stimulating and showing off their bodies, while others seem to give their parents no cause for worry in this respect. These differences are due partly to the fact that physical development and psychological tendencies differ from child to child. But just as important is the basic attitude of the parent and that of the society in which the parent and child live.

A child's discovery of himself and the world is a beautiful thing to watch. In growing up, he needs your strength to build his own. You, more than anyone, can shake the props out from under him by making his natural needs seem fearful or evil. You can swathe him in guilt for what he cannot help, or bolster him by teaching acceptance of his changing body and happy anticipation of his future.

—By Bradley Burch in consultation with Milton R. Aisenson, M.D.

JEALOUSY IN CHILDREN

PARENTS should not be too upset by behavior and personality difficulties with their children. Many so-called problem children—we used to call them bad children—turn out in later life to be sensitive, intelligent and highly creative individuals.

Good children, to be wholly good (and were there ever any outside fiction?) would have to be children who had everything they wanted, no conflicts, no jealousies; or else children who avoided such conflicts by being utterly submissive. They would have no difficulties to overcome, no rights to fight for.

A bad child is often only one in revolt. For instance, Balzac, who as a child was thought to be dull-witted and lazy, obstinate and disagreeable, who was punished more than any of his classmates, was actually revolting against a loveless home environment. He was bored and fatigued by unimaginative school work and found release in fantasy. Secretly he lived a double life. Into this second existence, which was at first nothing but a wish-dream and an escape, he poured all the energies of his life, reacting at first with "badness" to the unbearable circumstances of his youth. He developed into one of the most creative geniuses of 19th-century France.

All children are born with a strong will to get what they want and need. But they cannot have everything they want and cannot change their environment according to their wishes. They react to this early disappointment and frustration with so-called badness. This at least indicates a healthy ability to fight back and is, in many respects, better than submissive conforming.

New Baby in the Family

Consider jealousy, one of the most frequent sources of conflict in early childhood. You know how a child commonly reacts to the arrival of a new baby. He revolts against the intruder. He doesn't want to share parental love with him. He suddenly refuses to eat. He wets his bed again. He regresses in every respect to an earlier infantile state. He becomes hard to handle, breaks out into temper tantrums, spits and bites, tips over the newcomer's bassinet—"accidentally" of course. He hates the new baby, but hides his hostility behind exaggerated affection, hugging the child with such ardor that he hurts him. Thoughtful parents can do much to ease this trying situation but I do not think it can be prevented altogether, for the following reasons.

A child regards his mother as an indispensable possession, as a source of life, love and security. Who can expect him, in the beginning, to share this unique possession with anyone else? If he has to, he will be jealous. He will be jealous not only of the new baby who has just arrived, but of everybody with whom he has to share his mother's affection and love. This means he will be jealous of his sisters and brothers, of his father, of everything and everybody in whom his mother is interested. To prevent this is just as impossible as to prevent the child's love for and dependency on his mother. For this love and this jealousy both have the same source in the child's feeling of helplessness, of belonging to his mother and of his mother's belonging to him.

Jealousy Will Out

You may be able to avoid emotional excesses by tactful handling of the situation, by reassuring the child of your love, but as soon as you try to suppress jealousy altogether, to eradicate it as a bad thing, you certainly will get into trouble. The child's suppressed emotion will reappear in other ways and with bad effect. If you repress it altogether, you may harm the child. He may become generally hostile, not only to the one of whom he is jealous. His emotional development may come to a standstill. He may withdraw from everybody and appear to be obstinate and stubborn. He may become generally irritable and depressed because he cannot digest what is going on inside of him. Or he may turn his aggressiveness against himself, blame everything on himself and indulge in self-punishment.

The violence with which jealousy—if it is suppressed—may disturb and destroy a personality only proves the overwhelming power of this emotion. It should be possible to turn this powerful element into positive channels where it no longer destroys and distorts but contributes something constructive to human development.

What Parents Can Do

Occasionally when a child suffers from jealousy this emotion can be a spur to effort. If this constructive use of an undesirable but inescapable reaction to a situation is to be made, one must look behind the "badness" of the jealous child and see what really is going on. Show him sympathetic understanding. Help him to admit that he is jealous and tell you why he is, convince him that his jealousy is nothing bad, but that it is quite natural.

If the child is not compelled to hide and repress this emotion, he feels relieved from emotional distress, tension and feelings of guilt. This prevents excessive and unreasonable reactions to his jealousy. And while he is allowed to express—within limits—his jealousy as well as his other emotions, he simultaneously learns to express himself freely in words and play and simple creative acts.

By experiencing delight and satisfaction in self-expression, he is compensated for what he construes as lack of sufficient love.

When parents see that a child suffers from jealousy, let them try to help him realize that they value him for himself and are not comparing him with others to his disadvantage. If the jealous child finds himself cherished and sees his achievements acclaimed, he becomes conscious of his value and gains self-confidence. He no longer depends helplessly on his mother and bursts into a rage when he fancies he is neglected, but depends in part on himself and enjoys his growing independence. His rivals—whether brothers, sisters or schoolmates—no longer arouse destructive fury accompanied by a sense of inferiority on his part, but rather provide a stimulus to creative competition. When he reaches this stage, his world looks brighter to him. He will soon be ready to accept his rival as playmate and companion, someone he no longer fears but from whom he can receive and to whom he can give.

—By Hermann Vollmer, M.D.

TEACH YOUR CHILD
TO GIVE AS WELL AS TAKE

SELFISHNESS is an ugly thing. We hate to have our children exhibit it.

But young children *are* greedy, because they were born so and haven't yet had time to get over it. Growing into genuine unselfishness is a slow process. Most of us have not achieved it fully ourselves. Fortunately, all of us, children as well as adults, have generous impulses to help us along the way. They are quite as basic and nearly as powerful as our selfish ones. Most of us enjoy owning things but we are willing, even happy, to give some of them to others as loans or as gifts. Being able to do so gives us as much satisfaction as having them. In time we can reasonably hope to develop similar attitudes in our children.

Our chances seem better when we remember how early babies take pleasure in social exchanges. At first the baby hardly recognizes his mother as a person separate from himself, but in a few months he does. Before he is a year old he recognizes members of the family and has developed a repertoire of cute tricks that delight them. These he repeats endlessly and enjoys the family's response—he begins to feel his power to affect others.

Then along comes the open-the-hand-at-will stage. At four or five months he learns to reach out and grasp objects, and he hangs on until he is tired. But at around a year he learns to release his grip purposely. That is the time when he drops toys as fast as you pick them up for him. He's not perverse; he's practicing.

Teaching Sharing

Then you have a chance to start training in sharing. You give him something, then put out your hand to receive it as he releases it. He gives it to you! Soon he gets the idea, receiving and giving, getting a social response, sharing.

This is a good time to send your baby toddling across the room on a "giving" errand—"Take it to Daddy. Give the paper to Daddy." A most satisfactory achievement, sure to be rewarded by praise! Every experience in which sharing, giving or pleasing others is fun helps to lay important foundations for generosity.

Soon the baby is learning conscious control of the tensing and relaxing of other muscles than those of his hands. His functions of elimination interest him. He can withhold or "give" at will, and what he does in this way obviously interests others. Let us hope that when he does so he is not shamed, not made to feel that his offering is despised as filthy. If he is, then it may seem better not to give out what one has. In such infantile experiences, say the psychiatrists, may lie roots of later giving or refusing to give.

Respecting Property of Others

Before long the child comes to know the limits of his own self very well and begins to explore the mysteries of *mine, yours* and even *ours.* This is a complicated subject, but in the beginning it will be satisfactory if he thinks in terms of "to each his own."

How can a child respect other people's property rights unless he knows what ownership means? He must have his own things and realize that he may do pretty much what he likes with them. No one else will take them without his permission. Once he understands that, he can comprehend the idea of respecting the property rights of others—though he may not do as well as he knows.

Muriel seemed determined to snatch every toy away from Nancy.

Actually Muriel was at a highly imitative age. What she saw someone else do fascinated her and made her feel *that* was the one thing in the world she wanted to do herself. There being only one toy of each sort, the rest was inevitable.

Provide Similar Toys

This gives us a clue to one simple device for teaching young children to enjoy sharing. When possible, provide two toys practically alike. Before children are ready for genuine joint play they will often sit happily together doing the same thing, each independently. There is no actual sharing of the toys but there is companionship.

Books are often enjoyed in this way. So is clay or crayon work. With older children we often see the sense of companionship especially strong in a group occupied with individual creative or artistic activities.

Playthings such as dolls that encourage "pretend" play promote social sharing, and a tea set will inevitably start it. A wagon usually helps, for it is more fun to pull it with a passenger than empty. A tricycle with a back step also invites joint play, as does a swing. They all teach sharing because of the simple fact that they provide more fun when shared than when used alone. With older children organized games supply incentive: you have to get up a crowd to play them.

But with the little ones there are times when there is only one available toy and perhaps two children want it. Then we can suggest ways of cooperative play. Perhaps one child can load the toy truck and deliver it to the other who unloads and returns the empty. Or we can explain taking turns. Deprivation is endurable if not too long continued.

Use Impersonal Methods

Of course each child wants first turn and as they get to the argumentative age we must teach devices for settling such squabbles too. One can flip a coin, draw straws, guess nearest a chosen number or perform any of a dozen such rituals. Their virtue lies in being impersonal.

Children can learn all three ways of sharing: share the object (cut the apple in two), share the time (take turns), share the use (you ride while I pull). One or another will usually work and after a while the children come to understand equal sharing as fair and just.

Oddly enough, outright giving is sometimes easier than sharing and so can be a step toward learning to share. For one thing the child does not particularly want the pictureless book that he gives father as a birthday gift, or the soap he wraps up for mother. But there is more to it than that. We all feel bigger and more important when people are affected by what we do.

One aspect of this satisfaction comes out in malicious teasing or "you can't play with us." If the victim doesn't care, it's no fun. But a pleasanter aspect is just as gratifying. How youngsters love to make a baby laugh!

Emphasize Joy of Giving

We encourage children to give gifts and the recipient usually thanks the giver with enthusiasm; but do we, as bystanders, point up the experience? Are we as sure to say "Look how happy you have made him!" If we want to cultivate generosity we should emphasize the joys of giving.

While the child is learning to enjoy being generous other members of the family must set a good example.

And it is best to keep the positive attitude in the foreground even when the small fry can't be as open-handed as their elders. If definite propaganda is necessary, it comes best at a moment when the child is benefiting from the sharing. "Yes, I'll give you a piece of my candy. It's nice to share, and I know some day when you have some you will give me a piece."

Quite painlessly you have planted the idea that sharing is pleasant and that he plans to do it himself next time. Maybe he will, too, if it is made easy for him.

The same principle applies in helping a child overcome selfishness when he has company. Don't demand too much. There is today less emphasis on formal good manners for children than there used to be. We tend to be content if they are reasonably friendly with each other, and an occasional squabble doesn't disturb us much more than it does them.

If one knows of the visit in advance, plans can be made with the young host or hostess. Mother may suggest the use of materials and toys that work well for more than one child. It may even be wise to suggest putting away a favorite toy temporarily if the child cannot bear to share it. Some families have a "company box" of special toys to be brought out to share with guests. The contents should be ample but may be very simple—bright papers to cut and paste, crayons or a collection of tiny cars and trucks. Their value lies in their not being used too often and so remaining "special."

In the last analysis selfishness and hoarding arise from a fear of not having enough left for oneself. But not enough of what? Possessions, perhaps, as extensions of ourselves or as necessary for play possibilities present and future; food, for its delicious taste and because it also represents love, and power and importance—all the things that go to build that elusive and vital feeling we call "security."

The child who does not feel sure of himself, of his world, and of his own satisfying place in it, is going to need to bolster his confidence. He may use hoarding and stinginess for the purpose.

We all know the things a child needs to build his inner security: plenty of dependable love coupled with firm, reasonable controls, some possessions of his own that others respect, a position of dignity and importance in the family and a realization of his growing competence and independence.

Building Security

The child who feels there is enough of what he treasures to share without danger of depriving himself will seldom be very greedy. But he will still have moments of anxiety and insecurity. In them he will reach out for support. Each of us has his favorite ways of doing this, ways built into us by our temperament and experiences. We may lean on ownership for prestige, on the attention and admiration of others, on proving our own strength or skill or, oddly enough, on *sharing*. That proves our strength, too, doesn't it?

Some children buy the goodwill of their peers and the approval of adults by giving or sharing; but the motive may be a deeper one. Sharing an activity, a pleasure, or even a trouble builds that we-feeling which is balm to the soul.

Children first learn the satisfaction of belonging through daily family living. When the feeling of the family as a united group is strong, sharing is the foundation of home life. When fun and work are shared according to the needs and abilities of each member, the child breathes in an atmosphere of happy group membership. Soon it is not too hard to transfer this attitude to his playmates.

The more happy experiences of working and playing with others a child has, the more willing he becomes to risk his personal desires and importance in such adventures. There are temperamental differences, of course. Some children are cautious and hesitant, some impulsive and rash.

How Parents Can Help

If he seems too slow in outgrowing babyish greed we may help a child by seeing that he develops other kinds of buttress for the ego, such as new skills of which he can be proud. A fundamentally cheerful, courageous and generous spirit is a tremendous achievement, rarely to be attained quickly. We must be content to see our children working toward it and to give them what help we can.

While they are little we can keep the demands for sharing their own things infrequent enough to be endurable, and can teach them the satisfactions of family sharing. As they grow stronger and more sure of themselves, more can be expected. At each step we must try to ask only what can be given and still leave the experience a happy one for the child.

If we are friendly and outgoing, placing human values above material ones, our children will come to feel this is the natural approach to life.

—By Rhoda W. Bacmeister

RESPONSIBILITY AND THE CHILD

PARENTS usually think of responsibility in preschoolers as: can they take care of themselves, can they take care of possessions? Actually—and without being at all aware of it most of the time—we're constantly instilling in even very young children a far deeper concept of responsibility. But let's take these other things up first—the beginnings of neatness, cleanliness, promptness, physical safety, care of property.

Usually when somebody says, "Can he be responsible for . . . ?" he's asking, "Is he old enough to . . . ?" But "old enough," when it means simply if the birthday cake has had two or three, four or five candles, is a warped yardstick. It's accurate enough as an over-all gauge of some things, of course—you can see with your own eyes that a two-year-old doesn't have the small muscle development necessary to conquer buttons and buttonholes that a five-year-old has. But thinking of *all* a child's equipment is a better way to look at "old enough"—and that equipment is different for each child.

A pretty self-evident part of being old enough is *experience*. "You know better than that!" isn't an irrational thing (though maybe a little useless) to say to a five-year-old if he takes his stuffed kangaroo for a swim in the bathtub; the likelihood is that he really does know better. But the two-year-old might not yet have learned what happens to stuffed toys, or to any large object made of absorbent material, in water. Like his buttoning muscles, his experience muscles haven't grown that far.

Phase of Development

Part of experience, of course, is a child's *phase of development*. At three, for instance, did your youngster delight in tidying, neatly hoarding, stacking? Now at five does he take an opposite but equal joy in disorder, leaving a wake of scatter and shatter in his room, the yard, throughout the house? Three, perhaps, loved to scrub the basin after a wash-up. Five, while he can be held responsible (with an encouraging eye occasionally looking in) for washing his face and hands, likely as not leaves the sopping cloth crumpled in a grime-gray sink. Does this mean that Three is "responsible" and Five mysteriously, disappointingly "irresponsible"?

No. For most Threes are natural stackers-up of things, because for them there's pleasure and achievement—and approval—in being a stacker-up. And Three—or Two, for that matter—can become very proficient at washing his hands. Because he's responsible? Because water is fun and feels good and may bring memories of happy bathtimes. If you show almost any of the little ones how to wring out a cloth before scrubbing up, they're quite delighted to wring it out—and then douse it again just to wring it out again.

But Five can be as natural a scatterer as Three is a stacker—for equally good reason: he has a much bigger world on his mind. Putting away and stacking up take time from more important things like finishing a cow of clay. Even water, while it's still alluring, runs second to the call of the children in the street. In washing up, he's likely to get more dirt on the towel than in the basin unless he's watched. Because washing has become a job —not play—and he wants to get it done as quickly as possible.

What Matters Most

What matters most to a child is another aspect of being "old enough" at any age. Sometimes we insist he put his toys away at a time that's right for us, but wrong for him—he's in the middle of a game or some creative project important to him.

In nursery school, some mothers and fathers ask, even of the Two's, "Don't you try to get them to put their blocks away?" What's more important is getting them to build with the blocks, to learn how to do their work with them. Gradually, they work into the putting-away. But even when they've learned this, they're not always held responsible for it.

Akin to this is *how much energy* a child has at a particular time for his responsibilities. Those blocks, for instance. Even the Five's who have become accustomed to stashing them away are not expected to do it "as usual" if they've been out on a trip and have spent their energy on that. A longer-term influence might be something that's upset a youngster, so that his energy is taken up with what is disturbing him and he needs extra help with something he's been doing himself. One wouldn't expect a five-year-old to feed his dog if he had some variation of "flu." An emotional flu can be just as wearing.

Patient Teaching

Something we don't ordinarily think of as part of "old enough" is what and how a child has been taught. *Patient teaching* is pretty necessary for all the tasks a child must learn to assume for himself. And part of patient teaching is *patient waiting.* At nursery school, two-year-olds can usually shove their arms into their jackets by themselves, though they can't manage the intricacies of the zippers. But once a zipper is started they often want to finish it—and usually can if you'll wait long enough to let them. At two or three a youngster tries to pull his pants and leggings up and down. He can shove his arms into his undershirt, his sweater. At about three, some children try to put on their undershirts by themselves. We should let them try—and help only when frustration begins to verge on desperation. It's best if we can help without seeming to help.

Along with patient waiting, *respect for effort* is a factor in the teaching, too. When a child doesn't feel a failure too deeply, he'll tackle a job again and sooner than if he'd been allowed to get really discouraged. When he does manage to do something difficult like putting on his undershirt or sweater, a smile or word of appreciation is worth everything—even if the clothing is on him inside out and backwards. That doesn't mean trumpets must sound—just a warm "That was a pretty hard thing to do" is enough.

One way of keeping a child and his responsibilities on an even keel is to avoid imposing too quickly those obligations which are primarily for our own comfort and convenience. It's perfectly human for a busy mother to look forward to the time when Julie can part her own hair and Pat is able to tie his own shoelaces. But it's easy to fall into the too-soon and too-much trap. Without taking pause, that mother's mind can run on, "If Julie's old enough to part her own hair, she's old enough to help with the dishes; if Pat ties those shoelaces, he can scrub carrots, too."

Too Much Too Soon

It doesn't work that way, though. Too much too soon can make a youngster back off even from those responsibilities he's already used to—and from new ones he might like.

For children do *want* to grow, do want to be "responsible," do want to be independent and do for themselves—and perhaps that's the heart of the matter for all of us. It's a child's own interest we have to recognize and nurture when we help him assume jobs like feeding, dressing or cleaning himself, and later on, taking care of his clothes, his toys, his share of the household chores. We can nurture this interest in simple day-by-day ways, like making sure hooks and clothes hangers are placed low enough in the closet for a child to reach comfortably or providing a toy chest for putting away toys.

Is it part of teaching responsibility to "let them take the consequences"? So many parents ask that—usually in connection with lost or broken possessions. Whether a three-year-old truck driver bangs the fender off a $2.50 truck or a $17.50 truck makes a difference to us—but does it to him? Does even a five-year-old really know the difference, and could he possibly out of his limited experience really learn it from the "consequences"? Well, he could perhaps learn something this way: if he had been warned frequently that banging the truck into the wall would take off the wheels, then the consequences might be having to wait until it could be repaired, seeing the time and effort that had to go into the repairing. This would be teaching something. But to make the consequence the loss of the toy would be interfering with something more important—the fact that he needs that truck in his business, in his work, in broadening his experience.

Pattern Set Early

A while back, we mentioned that the children learn more important aspects of responsibility than the ones we've been talking about. And these more profound aspects they learn not so much by what we tell them to do, but by what we ourselves are. The fact is, by the time a child is five, he has been started on the road to becoming either a responsible or an irresponsible person. At five, most children know pretty well what their parents mean by responsible behavior, whether they use the word or just act out their knowledge. What they know depends almost completely on their reaction to the things they've seen and heard in their family life.

You can hear it when they play: "She said that I was the one to take care of this" . . . or even, "I'm responsible for . . ."

The children exchange guns or dolls with a warning to the friend to "Be careful," "Don't lose it," "Put it back when you're finished."

We'd certainly describe as responsible the way in which they enact the roles of fireman, cop, ditchdigger, bandit, doctor, nurse, father, mother. They collect their properties, set the stage, learn their lines and develop the plot as they go along like any good company of players. Sometimes the ideas are more noteworthy for their originality than for their practicality, but this is a matter of limited experience and the closeness of fantasy to real life. At five, children usually stay with an idea until something has been accomplished —the fire put out, the patient cured, the bandit captured or the building erected.

Awareness of Responsibility

In her make-believe play, which closely mirrors her real home life, Cathy has shown that she's aware of her responsibilities, her place in her family's life and, furthermore, that she accepts and appreciates her parents' outside responsibilities to the community. To a great extent she's shown that she knows what's expected of her now, and quite a bit about what will be expected of her in the adult world. At play, Cathy has acted out a child's-eye view of her own future. She's behaved like a responsible five-year-old. For she carried through on a project, shared in the fun, relinquished first place, waited her turn and created new activity to interest herself and her playmate.

Of course, Cathy doesn't always do what's expected of her. Who does? Sometimes she waits until the last minute before bedtime to put away her toys. Often she manages to "lose" her mittens, particularly when she doesn't want to wear them. But her parents don't expect Cathy to be a paragon. They're aware that inconsistencies coexist in the wholesome growth of a child.

Some parents aren't aware of this. To some, responsibility has as limited a meaning as it does to five-year-old Bobby, who said that responsibility means "to do what people tell you to." Bobby's definition, with its implication of complete dependency, might well mean irresponsibility to Cathy's parents.

Various Meanings of Responsibility

Other five-year-olds have different ideas. Donny, for example, says that responsibility means "you take care of your little brother." When he adds, "If you don't take care of your little brother you might get hit by a car yourself," it's evident that for Donny responsibility has been largely determined by fear. When Cathy was asked what responsibility meant, she simply said, "It means taking care of your clothes and your toys."

Every child's understanding of the meaning of responsibility is influenced by what the concept means to his parents. Bobby's statement suggests that he's learning blind obedience and conformity. Anxiety enters into Donny's understanding of responsibility. On the other hand, Cathy shows that she has something definite and practical to work with—and plenty of time ahead to broaden her understanding.

The family group is the most effective setting for learning responsibility as it is for learning many other things. Living in the family teaches the way in which one person talks to, listens to, helps, protects, supports, understands, shows affection toward or takes responsibility for another. In this way one finds out about consideration, patience, control and the whole long list of human attributes. The child learns from his parents' response to him and his siblings what it means to be a grownup man or woman—a mother or a daddy.   —By Eveline Omwake

HOW TO HANDLE ANGER

A NGER is a frightening emotion—both to the person who expresses anger and to the person against whom it is directed. It may help you to realize, right at the start, that every child, no matter how well behaved, gets angry. The normal child is a small person with strong emotions which he expresses with violence.

None of this means that he should be free to rage about with no control, doing damage to himself or others. Your part as a parent is to help your child channel these perfectly normal strong emotions in socially acceptable ways.

To an adult a child's anger often seems to spring from surprisingly trivial causes. Tommy at three goes into a spasm because he can't quite manage his new tricycle. He kicks it over and pummels it with his fists. Or he is found pinching or biting his new baby sister. Again he may take his anger out on himself and vomit or have nightmares.

It's pretty futile trying to convince him that he's getting himself all worked up over nothing. Don't waste time arguing with him.

Avoid Anger-Rousing Situations

It's more sensible, whenever possible, to try to avoid the situations that are bound to arouse his anger. Frequently a child loses his temper because his parents persist in a routine that no longer fits or satisfies his need. At two, for instance, Johnny suddenly refused to go contentedly to bed as he had in the past. When he saw his mother coming with his pajamas in hand, he would fly into a rage that upset him and the whole family.

Johnny's mother thought it over and decided to change her handling of the situation. First she adopted a warning system, a wise procedure for parents of all small children. Fifteen minutes before bedtime she let Johnny know that it was almost time to stop playing. She also bought Johnny a boy rag doll and dressed it in pajamas like his. In time he came to accept the doll as a pleasant signal that bedtime was near. Making an issue over the matter of going to bed was discontinued.

The whole bedtime routine was made into a little ritual with the same songs every night and always a piggy-back ride up the stairs on daddy's back. Johnny came to accept going to bed and to sleep as the natural end of the performance.

Another situation that parents need to handle with foresight is the child's request for special attention. Ignored, it almost invariably brings on an explosion of frustrated rage. When Jane insists that you come out to the back yard and see her sand castle, you should go. Even if you feel that she is being unreasonably demanding lately, you should not refuse her request. Don't thwart her desire for your attention but try to discover why she wants so much of it.

When Children Need Attention

Is there a new baby in the family? Then Jane will, of course, need special expressions of love and interest until she realizes that the newcomer is not going to take her place in her parents' affections. Have social engagements taken you away from home more often recently, or is some personal worry occupying the forefront of your mind? Whatever the reason, if Jane demands special attention it is because she needs it. To refuse her demands will merely intensify the problem. She will only feel more strongly that she is not loved as much as she wants to be.

Here the best procedure is to grant Jane's immediate request and then work out a way to meet her need for more attention by letting her go along on shopping trips, perhaps, or giving her an extra half-hour of your time for bedtime reading. It is never perverseness or a desire to be "pesty" that makes children so demanding of your time and energy. It is a deep-down need to feel surer of you and more confident of your love for them. There's no clearer proof of this than the blind rage that seizes them if they meet with refusal of the thing they are searching for—more of you than you have been giving.

All parents know how it maddens children to be kept from doing something they very much want to do. Sometimes, of course, this is unavoidable. Billy must not play with matches nor can Mary be allowed to eat all the chocolates she wants.

On the whole, however, the less interference parents practice the better. This doesn't mean that you must endure all sorts of inconveniences and destruction in order to let your child do whatever he likes. It does mean that within the limits of common sense you should try to say no as little as possible.

Let Youngsters Explore

If your three-year-old is determined to empty your lower bureau drawer why not keep things in the upper drawers which he cannot reach, putting a few old articles of clothing in the lower one, where he can pull it out as much as he pleases? It is possible, of course, just to close the bedroom door and keep your little explorer out. But that isn't the best solution. It deprives him of a lot of harmless fun, once you have bothered to go to the slight trouble of arranging things so he can do no harm. Moreover, a child resents being shut out of places to which the rest of the family has free access.

Contrary to much popular hope and belief, no toddler learns any moral lesson about property rights by being spanked when he meddles with things that don't belong to him. All he learns is that mother and father get angry with him if he's interested and curious enough to touch and explore. Why they should be angry he doesn't understand. It's quite beyond his powers of comprehension at this age. Punishment only builds up considerable hostility toward those who force him to deny his joyous inner urges to touch and explore all manner of things.

The more a youngster's interest and energy are directed toward what he may do, rather than what is forbidden, the better for his healthy development and the whole family's happiness. Often all this involves is merely distracting his attention from the dangerous or undesirable activity and substituting something more attractive. This isn't bribery but an intelligent way of avoiding unnecessary trouble.

Parents who are sensitive to rising tensions in their children can often prevent crises by engineering activities that drain off feelings of anger. "Rainy day trouble," for instance, is frequently averted by helping young ones dress up and organize a parade in which everyone marches "upstairs and downstairs and in my lady's chamber," singing all the while. This helps to discharge the excess energy that can otherwise degenerate into wrangling and quarreling. A good lively pillow fight with some old cushions can achieve the same result. For younger children try a vigorous game of "Ring Around A-Rosey" or "Three Times Around Went Our Gallant Ship."

Encourage Creative Activity

Creative activities are a constructive channel for emotional relief. Such activities as finger painting and clay modeling enable the tense or "wound-up" youngster to express his feelings in wholesome, satisfying ways just as an adult may work himself out of a grouch by buying a new hat or playing golf. In such ways adult or child achieves an infinitely better adjustment than the person who vents his wrath on his employees and family or takes it out on himself.

No matter how clever you are at keeping a jump ahead of them and forestalling wrath, there inevitably come times when Billy kicks and screams because he is not allowed to cross the street on his tricycle and Janet breaks all her crayons in cold fury because she cannot have her sister's coloring book.

When confronted with an enraged child, parents have two obligations. First, they must deal with the symptom of anger, whether it takes the form of a temper tantrum, a recurring nightmare, smashing things or hitting the baby. Second, they must do something constructive about whatever is precipitating the rages.

Sometimes the symptom itself has to be controlled. Linda can't be allowed free expression of her feelings at the cost of tearing her best dress or smashing her sister's favorite doll. Parents should remember, however, that it is risky business to punish a child for displaying his emotions. This only teaches him to repress them and hidden feelings can be a lifelong threat to healthy emotional growth. Moreover, when feelings go unexpressed the parents get a false sense that all is well. If your child gives no apparent sign of trouble, you are not forewarned when he needs special help.

Don't Forbid Expressions of Anger

When a youngster is allowed to express his anger within reasonable limits, he can get it out of his system much as he throws up a meal that doesn't agree with him. Then he feels better. In the long run his parents are amply repaid for the wear and tear of the scenes that may occur occasionally.

Verbal expressions of anger are nothing more than an indication that children still have to do some growing toward emotional maturity, just as they have to do more physical growing. In the long view one need be no more alarming than the other.

Many parents fear that back talk, unless it is promptly checked, will become a habit with their children. Like all other expressions of anger, it is just another way in which a youngster gets his bad feelings out of his system where they will do him less harm. The child who is forced to hide his natural inclination to tell his parents what he thinks of them often becomes the adult whose repressed anger eventually reappears in such guises as obstinacy or sullenness, unhappy traits which are hard to cure.

Far better if you can take it in good grace and let him blow off steam while he is little. There is no danger that back talk will persist in the child who grows up in a family where he is loved and understood. Give him time and he will realize that it is childish behavior not practiced by his mother and father. Since he wants to be like them, he will eventually drop it, not because he is forced but because he himself wishes to. This is the best form of control because it is self-control.

Recognizing Feelings

Since young children react without much awareness of what is making them feel as they do, it is sometimes good practice to clarify an anger situation for a youngster by giving him what psychiatrists call recognition of his feelings. You can do this by putting into words the fact that he is angry, why he is angry and your willingness to accept his feelings. Thus when Bruce was furiously hitting at his mother, she said firmly but sympathetically, "I know you are angry at me because I wouldn't let you go barefoot, Bruce. I can understand why you feel cross. But I can't let you go without your shoes because there is sharp gravel on which you could cut your feet."

With the exception of such a simple statement, it is wise to avoid discussing a child's anger with him. Such discussions are for the most part useless since they seldom reach the feelings that have caused the rage. Furthermore, to talk a child into behaving better through threat of punishment or, even worse, the withholding of parental love is a very dangerous procedure. It is far wiser to take action that helps a child to feel differently, rather than requiring him to act differently.

Parental understanding does not mean that the parent tries to bring up his child in an unreal atmosphere of sweetness and light. The ability to accept the unpleasant and frustrating aspects of life philosophically is one of the hallmarks of maturity. Everyone must learn to endure disappointment and the capacity to do so is best developed at home where, with the support of understanding parents, a child learns that there are some things he cannot do no matter how much he rages or coaxes.

Father and mother may realize Ann's irritability is a consequence of the rainstorm that upset her plans for a back-yard tea party. But if her quarrelsomeness upsets the whole family's dinner, she had best finish the meal in her room.

Parents Need Compassion

Ours is not an easy culture for children to grow up in. Parents should look with compassion on the struggling, resisting and backsliding a youngster goes through in trying to adjust to our complex civilization. Too often adults tend to underestimate the depth of a child's feelings. At the same time they may overestimate his capacity to control those feelings.

It is a hard job for a child to learn to relinquish the very human desire to have what he wants when he wants it. No wonder then that growing up emotionally sometimes engenders anger. Yet all child psychiatrists agree that the way a child learns to deal with that anger is a dynamic force in the development of his personality.

Will he become greedy and embittered, an adult whose neurotic hostility shows itself in race prejudice, malicious gossip, constant criticism and fault-finding? Or will his anger be for the most part a constructive aspect of his adult personality so that he can speak out against injustice, cruelty or an invasion of his own rights? If the latter is the case he will have learned to use his anger in constructive, creative ways. —*By Helen Thomson*

IF YOUR CHILD SAYS "I DON'T LIKE YOU"

LITTLE children's greatest need is for their parents' love. Punishment or even criticism can be potent evidence to a child that he can't really be certain of it. Put that knowledge together with something else we know: a child's learning is based on exploring his world. Some things like a hot stove are "hurts." Others are "not-hurts." But his exploration isn't limited to the physical world; it applies to relationships, too. People are "hurts" and "not-hurts." Some can be counted on. Some can't. One way of finding out which is which can follow along these lines: "My parents are cross. Maybe they don't like me any more. I'll see. I'll say *I* don't like *them!*"

No one can say for sure that a child of three or four goes through this reasoning process. But if you listen carefully to his voice, not his words, you'll often hear this undertone of "Do you like me?" Just as he holds a hand near the stove to find out if it's hot, he tries out, "I don't like you," to see what effect it has on you and if he's still safe with you.

Parental Reactions

As to parents' reactions, they are as varied, naturally, as are parents and their relationships with their children. Whether you're tired and harassed or calm and happy at the moment obviously has an effect. And the surrounding circumstances matter, too. The clarion quality of your youngster's remark in the supermarket, for example, can rouse embarrassment you wouldn't feel in the privacy of your home. Public or private, though, one sub-surface re-action seems common to many parents. We feel we've failed somehow. We take the words seriously—in the wrong way. They are certainly to be taken seriously as meaning something to the child at the time. But as a statement of lasting and profound feeling? No. Children's emotions are intense and shortlived. Look at their friendships. Best friends one minute and foes the next. Look at the impulsive hugs they give us, just as swift and unexpected as "I don't like you."

Whether a youngster is simply getting momentary resentment off his chest or is testing us out, one thing he is definitely not doing is taking an un-alterable stand. He's very likely to be loving and happy again within five minutes, if his "I don't like you" is handled properly.

Now there's the heart of the matter—what is "properly"? Mothers and fathers seem to have three fundamental responses. One is to ignore the child. The second is a snap back, "I don't like you, either." The third is, in essence, "Well, I like you."

Don't Ignore the Child

Ignoring the child leaves him with vague feelings of uncertainty and dis-trust, while the need to find out if you still love him persists. Therefore, he finds other ways of testing. "Buy me some gum," he demands. Or suddenly he is very tired and wants to be carried. At home he wants you to read to him, play with him. The "ignoring treatment" actually forces him to try something different.

One can't say of "I don't like you, either"—that it evades the issue. His fears are substantiated. But does any mother or father knowingly want to confirm a child's suspicion that he isn't loved? Of course, some parents say they want to "toughen" their boy or girl. But it doesn't work that way. No one is strengthened by being made to feel unaccepted. And even though a few minutes later you may be buying him ice cream or inviting him to play—evidence that you do love him—that original suspicion isn't completely erased. After all, you *said* you didn't like him.

There is the third way, the one of saying to the child, "Well, I like you." It's positive. It settles on the spot his anxiety about your acceptance. He need not take to other types of behavior to try you out.

I'm not suggesting that we automatically recite, "Well, I like you." There are times when only those words will do. But it mustn't be a mechanical response. Far more important than the particular words you use is whether your child senses that your not liking the way he behaves doesn't threaten your basic liking for him. How this feeling is conveyed depends on how close you are to each other, on the circumstances and on your own mood.

Matter-of-Fact Attitude

For instance, a harried mother who was shopping in a supermarket ignored the remark—the remark, not the child. "Come on, Bobby," she responded, "let's find the applesauce shelf."

In print, it may look like evasion. But the mother's voice and eyes, the hand she put out to her son, said plainer than words: "I'm sorry you feel that way. I don't like what you did and I don't want you to do it again. But it's over with now, isn't it? You and I are always friends."

On another occasion, a father took an equally matter-of-fact attitude with his young daughter who had to be stopped from squeezing loaves of bread in the store. She had shouted "I don't like you."

"I guess you don't right now," this father said. "But the bread doesn't belong to us and people don't want to buy it when it's been squeezed."

He didn't say, "I like you," but neither did he imply in any way, "I don't like you." His whole manner indicated it was the treatment of the bread, the lack of consideration for others, that he disliked. She pouted a minute; then they were pushing the grocery cart together companionably.

Express Your Affection

You can prove all this to yourself. Next time you're blasted with "I don't like you," try letting your youngster know you do like him. Do it your own way. But if you've kept any hint of "I don't like you" out of your voice, just watch him. The child who isn't used to "But I do like you" as an answer usually pauses. This is what he wanted—but not necessarily what he expected. He may repeat his challenge. He wants to be sure. There's a change, though. His voice may calm down a bit. His belligerency isn't as potent as before. This time, his words may smack simply of face-saving.

Once we understand what's behind them, those sharp words, "I don't like you," become less of a shock and just something not so hard to live with after all.

—By Donald N. Von Pein

WATCH YOUR CHILD'S MENTAL GROWTH

PARENTS take great pride in the intelligent things children do. It is natural to boast about the first cute sayings and feel on top of the world when a neighbor says, "He certainly is a smart little boy." We do compete keenly, and are equally sensitive about our children's unintelligence. Sometimes we even prod our youngster, or overstimulate him in an effort to prove that he is "smart."

Good mental ability does contribute to the richness of living. But too often we confuse mental ability with scholastic ability and value book learning above other ways of showing intelligence. Mrs. Brown had two boys, Phil and Tom. Phil did well in school. He always brought home a fine report card and rated well with his teachers. Tom did not take to books. He spent hours on the floor with his drawing materials. He was busy making plans for houses—plans which took much thought and careful drawing, a knowledge of how to measure and apply arithmetic. But Mrs. Brown was so anxious for Tom to bring home the same grades as his brother that she hid his drawing materials in an attempt to make him "learn something." Tom was learning all the time, just as Phil was learning, but his mother did not realize this.

All children do not learn in the same way. We can help each of our children to develop the abilities which he has if we are willing to recognize differences in children, and help each one learn in his own way. Wise guidance, good opportunities for learning experiences, and encouragement may help an average child go even further than one of higher native ability whose interest has not been aroused or whose intelligence has not been fully encouraged to develop.

Encourage Curiosity

A baby has no ideas in his head, but as he develops the use of his senses, he gradually builds up the ability to understand and interpret the world about him. The tiny child wants to touch, feel and taste everything which he can reach. This is his way of learning. Yet so often mother follows him around turning aside his interest and his curiosity with "Don't touch that," "Don't put that in your mouth." Yet, later, when the baby is grown and in school this same mother complains, "I can't make Susan take an interest in anything. She just wastes time." True, the toddler must be protected from dangers, but there are many things he may be allowed to explore. His curiosity is important in the total pattern of growing mentally.

The "into everything" days are soon left behind, but as the child grows older he continues to reach out for new experiences. He no longer goes from one thing to another, but is able to concentrate for a short time on something which really interests him. Two-and-a-half-year-old Steven was fascinated with trying to take one of his pull-toys apart. He tried hard to put it together again, and with a look of intent interest experimented with the pegs and holes until finally he put it together after a fashion. We should try not to call a child or interrupt him when he really seems absorbed in what he is doing, for concentration will be a valuable trait when he is older.

The little child's mind develops by making things, finding out about things, doing things, acting out experiences. Give the youngster blocks and toys, suitable for his age, of the kind which can be taken apart and put together again, or combined in many ways. Let the child experiment with many types of material. Give him crayons, paper, paint and clay, finger paints, simple musical instruments, the drum, cymbals, a bell or a triangle. Encourage him to sing, to use his body in rhythms, to enjoy dramatic play. All these things should be done for fun. Fortunate is the child in whose home these things are done freely, simply and spontaneously. We need to avoid the attitude of a task. We need to avoid also, too much adult guidance. Let the child draw or paint in his own way. If mother says, "A man doesn't look like that—do it this way," a child is often discouraged and his initial delight in creating is destroyed. Help only when the child asks for it, and then carefully, trying not to destroy the idea or plan which he has in mind or to offer suggestions which he is not able to carry out. As he gets older he will become interested in techniques and will ask for definite help in acquiring them.

Finishing Tasks Come Later

Often a child will not finish what he has begun. This distresses many adults who fear he is forming bad habits of not carrying through. Finishing will come later—these early years are years of experiment, not of complete or perfect work. Let the child experiment with dashes of color, with half-finished carpentry, with the clay dishes which are never finished. Put the things aside when he tires; perhaps he will come back to them, perhaps he will forget them, but he is learning nevertheless through his efforts to make something, crude and unfinished though they may be.

We need, too, to avoid showing off the creative activities of a little child. Too often we destroy the spontaneity of learning and make a child self-conscious by saying, "Sing a little song for Grandma and Aunt Lucy."

The mental growth of a little child should be encouraged through experiences related to his understanding, and his feeling of spontaneous pleasure in what he is doing. Showing off or forced performances may delight the ego of mother or father but all too often slow up and discourage the real learning of the little child. Sometimes the child will want to "dance for Grandma and Aunt Lucy"; if the desire comes from the child, then the adults can enter into her eagerness and make the experience valuable by their encouragement and pleasure in it.

"Do It Myself"

"Do it myself" is the key to much of the learning of the preschool child. Mary's mother knew that it was best to let a three-year-old try things out for herself, whenever possible. So when the new red tricycle was unwrapped, she held back her urge to say, "Put your feet here, Mary, this is how you do it," and stood back watching while Mary tried to ride it herself. Mary made it go backwards, but couldn't get the knack of going forward. She would get off and look at the tricycle, turn the pedals, push it this way and that, then get on again and go backwards again. But just before lunch when mother went out to call her, there she was riding forward with a look of triumph on her small face. If a situation is too difficult, if the "do it myself" fails, then a helping hand or a suggestion should always be ready. As far as possible the preschool child should be protected from situations which are beyond his ability to handle, by seeing that his toys and play equipment are suitable for his age, and that he is not exposed to experiences which will be too much for him. This is not always possible, but it is possible within measure.

The attitude of "wanting to know" is one of the most permanent gifts we can give a child. It is this attitude, not the specific knowledge which he acquires, which is important during the preschool years. He wants to find out about the world around him and his relationship to it. We need to answer his questions simply, clearly, and in such a way that he can understand. If he wants more of an answer than we have given he will ask again, if we have given him the feeling that questions are welcome and not a nuisance. If we don't know we can always say, "Let's find out." A child's mental growth thrives in an atmosphere of "finding out."

Seek Out Simple Experiences

All of us are not lucky enough to be able to provide all experiences first-hand, but there are many questions which we can answer by seeing. Sometimes, however, in our enthusiasm to show our children things, we overdo it. Simple, near-at-home and understandable experiences are usually more effective than those that might be overwhelming. It is better to watch the building of a house which will be finished within a reasonable period of time than the building of a city skyscraper which, to the child, never seems finished.

A child needs time to look at the things in which he is interested, whether they are in real situations or in stories or pictures. Too often we hurry him along, continually talking and explaining or pointing things out to him. If we give him a chance to see for himself, he will look and ask questions when he is ready.

Let the little child get used to his own immediate world before we extend the horizon too far. There is lots of time ahead to explore the larger world. When we read to the little child stories of here and now, they are more understandable to him than stories about other lands and faraway people. Imaginative stories, fairy tales, yes, but all in their own time. As the child learns to understand his own small world he will be able to extend himself into fantasy and the unreal, to learn to love and enjoy it, yet to distinguish between fantasy and reality. —*By Gladys Gardner Jenkins*

WHAT IS DISCIPLINE?

SOME parents are wondering whether modern methods of child training are too soft. Their fear is that consistently gentle treatment will not prepare a child for the rugged realities of adult life but will render him incapable of making his way in a tough world. They put it this way: Shouldn't children be prepared to face reality and learn that undesirable conduct usually will bring painful results?

This is certainly true in adult life—the person who does a slipshod job gets fired, the one who breaks a traffic law is fined or jailed. Since this is so, don't parents owe it to their children to mete out fair but definite punishment for all misdemeanors?

Shouldn't a child learn early that life holds both pain and frustration, quite apart from whether one deserves it or not?

Shouldn't every child realize that disagreeable or boring tasks occupy a sizable percentage of most people's time, and the sooner he learns to accept such uninteresting tasks without question, the better off he is likely to be?

Constructive Discipline

Let's take a closer look at what underlies these questions. First, undesirable behavior should automatically result in some kind of painful experience, in other words, punishment. Is this necessary or advisable? Actually there is confusion here, and where there is a chance for constructive discipline, punishment is being substituted.

Here, for example, is a rule that is perfectly fair and practically universal in American homes: everyone washes before dinner. If the children in a family always observe the rule, there is no occasion for punishment. But if a three-year-old turns up at the table with suspiciously grimy hands, a casual reminder may be all that is needed to send him scurrying for soap and water before he begins his meal. Certainly there is no need for punishment.

But let's say that Eddie, three and a half, flatly refuses to wash his hands one day. He's tired and cross to start with, and it is obvious that he is trying to work up some kind of excitement. Or he may be testing the adults to see whether they will stand firm or not.

There are several ways in which this situation might be handled. An affectionate parent might pick up Eddie and cuddle him a bit, perhaps give him a drink of fruit juice since he may be hungry and say, "Here, let me help you, darling." An imaginative parent might work in a bit of dramatic play by telling Eddie that Dr. Anderson, who takes care of Eddie, scrubs up with a little brush when he is getting especially clean. "Here, you are, Dr. Eddie," along with a proffered nail brush, might transform the stubborn one into an energetic actor. You get the results you want and no punishment is involved.

Another mother might say, "Very well, Eddie, unwashed hands just do not come to our table." Said calmly and matter-of-factly, with a firm though friendly air, the chances are that this too would convince Eddie.

The Wrong Approach

But suppose mother turns on Eddie and says, "You go upstairs to your room. You've got to learn to obey and no questions asked!" Whereupon she gives Eddie a firm smack in the nether region and propels him in the direction of the stairs. It's quite natural that Eddie should give loud voice to his anger. Do you think that spanking Eddie has really taught him any more than the other children learned without being spanked? To my mind, the mothers who weren't too tired to use understanding and imagination were far more effective disciplinarians and teachers. They got their children washed and to the table, thereby giving them a demonstration that there are rules which must be obeyed. If children can learn pleasantly, why not? Is there any real reason for making them miserable?

As to pain and frustration being inevitable in life, every mature grownup knows that everyone has his share of physical and mental suffering, that disappointment, sickness and death happen to us all. But to burden a child unnecessarily with pain and disappointment serves no constructive purpose. A child needs to experience the world's harshness in little ways before he can take it in big ways. He needs to experience, too, the world's goodness before he can get a perspective on misfortune.

A child learns best in ways that he understands. Perhaps some unfriendly child will snatch a prized toy from him one day and break it. Nature will deal him an unkind blow by giving him a fever on the day of his best friend's party.

What about the belief that children are better off if they learn to do disagreeable or boring tasks early in life? Here again we must consider the age and maturity of the child.

Age and Maturity

A woman cleans house because she and her family want to live in an attractive, pleasant place. A man adds up long columns of figures—even though he doesn't enjoy doing so—because he knows he must send in his income tax return in good order and on time. He and his wife put aside money for their children's education—even though they might like to spend it for other things—because they know education is important.

The young child, on the other hand, has few over-all aims. He'll pick up his toys if mother picks up, too, because he enjoys her company and approval. He won't care about learning to read, however, at the age of three or four, because he can't see any need for it. (But he may work himself to a frazzle learning to stand up on skates.) The six-year-old, on the other hand, is often eager to know which letters mean what. The seven-year-old wants to read and is willing to struggle to learn. His interests have expanded and he realizes reading will be useful to him. The high school student will work for creditable grades because he knows his entrance into college depends on them.

To be willing to do work that is not immediately rewarding requires a mature point of view that the little child simply does not have. To try to make a preschool child perform unpleasant tasks for the sake of character development is about as realistic and sound as to expect him to earn his school tuition. In fifteen short years, he may do both. But then he will understand the reason for it.

Even if we accept the fact, however, that a child cannot face all the realities of adult life in his early years, we certainly do not want to fall into the fault of overindulgence. This is every bit as crippling to a child's growth as is arbitrary strictness.

Beware of Overindulgence

For instance, Teddy, age three, refused to sit down in the car when his mother drove. He preferred to stand up and look out of the front window. His mother, though a bit apprehensive about this, gave up and let him do as he wanted to. Another mother gave in when her four-year-old daughter Jill refused to wear rubbers and let her go out into a muddy yard without them.

Neither mother could bear to say no and stick to it—even though she knew she was right and the child wrong. They had heard about children being harmed by frustration. They were also afraid that if they said no their children wouldn't love them.

Here are cases where reality should have been faced, not for any fancy educational reason, but because the children would have been better off for it. Teddy's mother should have realized that small children want to look outside when they ride in a car and she should have provided Teddy with a small seat that lifted him up high enough so that he could see out of the windows. Then she could have insisted that when he rode in the car he must stay in his seat.

Jill could have been told that either she wore rubbers or played indoors. As it was, you could hardly blame either of these children for feeling that there weren't any rules in their families that could not be set aside if they refused to obey them.

Disobedience Results

The child who finds that he can override any and all family rules gets to the point where he doesn't take any rules seriously. As a result, it becomes quite impossible to make a calm and quiet request and have the child obey it. Instead, the overindulgent parent has to work himself into a lather before the child realizes that he means what he says. Naturally, this does not make for pleasant family relations. There are upsetting scenes and more lost tempers in homes where this attitude prevails than in those where parents are not afraid to be firm.

Discipline is important in any family. It is important not so much for the sake of helping the child face some future theoretical world but to help him to live with the least pain and friction in his own child's world. It is a big part of a parent's job to let a youngster know what is expected of him, and this knowledge is an important part of the child's security.

Expectations may vary pretty widely from family to family. That's all right too. Some parents, for instance, are quite willing to let their young children dig holes all over the yard. Others who love adult order and beauty won't stand for this. These parents are wise to limit digging to a specified place.

One set of parents with several lively children may thoroughly enjoy an informal and often noisy evening meal together, even when guests are present. That's just fine if they are happy that way. But if parents or their guests are irritated by children's arguments and their tendency to take over the conversation, everyone may be happier if the children eat at a separate table.

Act Consistently

There isn't necessarily anything good or bad about these differences. They are simply due to the fact that people are different. The parent who is a reasonably well adjusted human being is going to help—not harm—his children by acting consistently like himself.

Family discipline, no matter how firm, can be kept friendly. As a matter of fact, it is an extremely valuable experience in human relations for a child to know that his parents can say no and yet be loving and kind. Ideally, discipline should be a teaching process rather than a punishing one. The fact that this never works out 100 per cent is merely another proof that all of us, adult and child alike, may make mistakes.

The most important emotional experience of infancy and early childhood is that of being loved and loving in return. The sternness and justice that may be admirable in a court of law are not the qualities to stress in a relationship with one's own small children. But fair and simple rules, on the other hand, are necessary since they help a child to know what is expected and to feel he has parents who are capable of and willing to give him the guidance he needs so much.

—By Irma Simonton Black

GUIDANCE OR GIVING IN?

WHILE generations of parents have had little trouble making a child understand that there are many things he should not do, they've had considerably more trouble making the child obey their warnings. Maybe they have gone about it in the wrong way—maybe saying "No" doesn't always do the job. Maybe saying "Yes" a little more often might be just what is needed to turn the trick! It boils down to this: let a child have his way when there is no physical danger threatening, when nobody else's rights are being flouted. Let him have his way when no generally accepted social convention is being violated. Will such a course of action spoil your child? Those who have studied children think not.

Just how does this theory work? Here are a few concrete examples.

Douglas is a bright, lively little boy just approaching his second birthday. Up to a month ago he'd been very good about going to bed. At any time from six-thirty to seven o'clock, he was prepared to have his mother tuck him into bed and close the door. Then one evening, without any warning, this delightful situation changed. Douglas let it be known with great vehemence that he didn't want to go to bed. For a seemingly endless week his parents struggled through a scene every night. When their son found them adamant so far as going to bed was concerned, he demanded a bottle he never drank, a blanket he didn't need, toys he didn't want to play with.

Finding a Solution

Today, as if by magic, peace has once more been restored. How was the situation handled? In a very special way—his parents gave up thinking of it as a struggle and decided to let him have his way. But not the way of a screaming, fretful, overtired child. It was, instead, the parents' way, but they had taken their cue from the child. A new bedtime ritual was substituted for the old one, a somewhat more elaborate one, but it took far less time than quieting a rebellious boy. Now when Douglas starts his requests, instead of trying to reason with him, mother produces the items he asks for. If he wants a pillow, she gives him one; if he asks for his Teddy bear, he gets it. Sometimes she suggests something first and so diverts him before he makes some other wilder demand. Dr. Gesell, in "Infant and Child in the Culture of Today," tells us that going to sleep is full of tensions and new difficulties for the toddler and that he needs all the help we can give him. So don't let him cry it out at this age; let him have his way! Try to grant his requests even when they seem a bit unreasonable, and let him feel he has won a point when you hand over the doll or give him a cracker. In due time this too will pass, although the phase seems endless while it's on.

The Independent Child

Then there's the case of Chrissie who is suddenly becoming very independent. When mother has served her lunch, Chrissie waves her spoon impatiently and says imperiously, "Go 'way!" There is little harm in giving in to this request, provided mother stays close enough to take a quick look from time to time to see that all is well. But what about bathtime, when once again our prima donna, now in the tub, tells her mother to go away? Here is a situation where mother must become a bit of an actress, as Chrissie's mother learned one day after carrying a screaming and kicking child from the bathroom.

The next day Chrissie allowed herself to be put into the tub again. Again she began with "Go 'way!" but mother was prepared, and this time they both wound up laughing. What did mother do? Nothing very elaborate or remarkable—she just made a game of "going away" and hid behind the bath towel. Now Chrissie and mother play peekaboo in the bathroom every day and Chrissie seems to have forgotten what started it.

Suppose your child should suddenly refuse to take a bath. Here it would be wiser to accept his refusal than to force him into what might be a dangerous situation. A bathtub is no place in which to discipline a stubborn child. But why not, while letting him have his way, be ready with a counter-proposal? You might enjoy his having a sponge bath, or perhaps he'd be amused sitting on his toilet-chair with his feet in a basin. He'll come around in time, and meanwhile you will have spared yourself and your child the excitement and fatigue of a wearing and avoidable scene.

Learning by Experience

Stephen is physically small for his age, but emotionally and in every other way he's developing as any normal child should. He seems to have a tremendous urge to climb on everything from ordinary chairs to tree stumps in the back yard, fences and many other objects, even as other children of his age.

His mother is quite understandably alarmed and snatches him down with great cries of "No, no!" every time she sees him climbing. It has now become a kind of diabolical game they play, the child scheming to outwit his mother, while she spies on him through the window. Not too long ago Stephen fell from a swinging gate when he saw his mother coming after him, and sprained his ankle.

But Stephen's accident need never have happened. A child should be taught how to climb carefully where there is a reasonable degree of safety. His urge to climb is a natural, healthy one but he must be given intelligent supervision and protection against harm. A child must learn caution but he can't learn it by being overprotected. He must learn through experience. Whether or not you snatch him away from what you consider the danger of being hurt should depend on the degree of hurt he might receive. Stephen's mother would have been wiser to help her son learn how and where to climb rather than to forbid all climbing.

When to Give In

Actually, very few parents are prepared to handle all of the things their children think up to do. Reading, helpful though it is, can't be expected to provide all the answers. It can help a great deal if we consciously try to formulate a philosophy of child guidance, based on all we can learn about a child's nature and needs at different ages.

The solution to many of the problems which parents encounter in bringing up children lies in giving the child every reasonable opportunity to have his way. Don't misunderstand. It is not suggested that you drop the word "no" from your vocabulary, that you throw all ideas of good discipline to the winds. Nor can you be expected to reason with a very young child. He must be trained not to go into the streets. He must be taught to respect other people's property. He must not be allowed to play with matches. But just because there are so many things he will wish to do, it becomes doubly important to give him the chance to do what he wishes whenever it is safe for him, and whenever it will not harm others.

The vigorous child, curious, fun-loving, quick to cry and show temper, not always obedient, too often possessive of his own toys, is definitely *not* the spoiled child. It is the whining, fussy child who is spoiled, rather than the happy, positive one. You will not be spoiling or bringing up an un-disciplined child by letting your small son or daughter have his way whenever and wherever it is safe, sensible and possible: you *may* spoil a child by insisting on absolute obedience from a youngster of this age who is neither emotionally nor mentally ready to give it. —*By Ethel Greenfield Booth*

BRIBERY DOESN'T PAY

IT was 8:30 P.M. but five-year-old Johnny Baxter didn't want to go to bed. "If you go right up now I'll read you *two* stories," mother promised.

Johnny cocked his head at the ceiling, master of the situation. "I tell you what, men," he said, in drawling imitation of his favorite television hero, "I'll go to bed if I can have a lollipop to take along."

The elder Baxters heaved a sigh of relief. The nightly deal had at last been made. They were not particularly happy about it, but it seemed the best they could do. For somehow, after years of bargaining with their son, they had lost sight of the fact that a little boy could be put to bed simply and naturally, without any bribes or threats.

The Baxters are by no means an extreme example of what can happen to parents of young children who come to rely on threats and bribes for discipline. Most of us know better, but many of us slide from time to time into the lazy habit of trying to get the behavior we want, fast, by these methods. So it's a good idea to stop every once in a while and figure out afresh: just what is wrong with bribes and threats?

Discipline Weakened

Bribes and threats are wrong because they weaken discipline, turn home into a battleground of argumentative bargaining and, used as a long-term method of control, produce belligerent, hostile children. While it is true that the first, second or third time you use a particular bribe or threat you are apt to get results, in the long run its efficiency is bound to decrease.

Every time Johnny's mother bribed him to eat his spinach with the promise of an ice cream cone as his reward, spinach became less desirable to him, since he learned to think of it as a barrier he must hurdle in order to get the ice cream.

Once parents start bargaining with their child over some aspect of his life —say, going to bed or eating—this way of handling conflicts is apt to spread throughout their whole relationship. Even in this day and age, it is pretty upsetting to hear a six-year-old ask her mother, "What'll you give me if I clean up my room?" But this is just what can happen when children are regularly bribed or threatened into going through with the simple routines which should be a matter of course in a happy family relationship.

Difficulties May Increase

It is going to be hard, over the years, for a mother to deal with a child who has learned, through constant bargaining, to be belligerent and argumentative. But it is going to be even harder for that child to grow up and accept the responsibilities of maturity. First, it is a tragic blow to his security to have learned to think of his parents as adversaries to be bargained with, instead of as friends who see his side of things. Second, he will perhaps never learn the profound lesson that in all the important relationships of life we must work together and do things for each other for no other reward than each other's happiness. The parents who grumble that with children it is "all give and no get," the housewife who regrets her marriage because she has had to make "such a sacrifice," may have been children who learned never to do anything for nothing, early in life.

Because threatening seems, offhand, a more severe form of discipline than bribing, you might think it would be more effective, even if less desirable. Actually, the constantly threatened child is probably even more undisciplined than the constantly bribed one. Few mothers have either the heart or the sheer physical stamina to carry out all the threats, veiled or otherwise, which are used to get a small child, handled in this manner, through a single day. And once he has learned that at least some of the threats will never be carried out, he soon begins to turn a deaf ear to all of them. "Selective in-attention" is a fancy name for an ability, possessed by children whose parents threaten them, to "tune out" 99 and 44/100 per cent of the time.

Threats May Induce Misbehavior

The threat of punishment, moreover, sometimes acts as a positive spur to misbehavior. Suppose your husband always wanted dinner ready on the dot but that after months of being on time, you were late with dinner preparations one afternoon and were frantically opening cans when your husband got home. Suppose you came to meet him, but before you could get out your words of explanation and apology, he blew up and shouted that if this happened again he was going to cut your monthly allowance. Wouldn't you be tempted to "show him" by staying out the very next afternoon? And this is just the way it works with a child.

Perhaps the worst charge that can be made against the bribing and threatening method of controlling young children is that it blinds the parents who use it to the real basis for happy and effective discipline. It is natural and right that children start out in life with a strong "me first" urge. But modifying it from babyhood onward are two other strong drives—the desire to grow up and the desire to be acceptable to his parents. The parents who have learned to recognize and work with their child's unique growth pattern so that they do not ask too much or too little of him, the parents who manage to maintain a friendly relationship with their child, invariably have better behaved offspring than those who go in for bribes and threats. Several modern methods of child care, while inherently good, can easily lead to bargaining if abused. Since a bribe-threat relationship, like a feeding problem, is much more easily avoided than cured, it is helpful to know the pitfalls.

Pitfall number one can occur when a parent uses the perfectly good technique of distraction. It is certainly an excellent idea to distract a very small child before trouble arises and to get him pleasantly, rather than grimly, through the routines of the day. But once trouble has arisen, once the child has encountered frustration and is perhaps screaming with rage, it is neither necessary nor right that the parents buy back his good spirits with offers of a lollipop, a ride in the car, anything if he will only stop crying. Yet many new mothers have made this mistake of appeasing their children in the name of distraction, and so have laid the groundwork for later bargains and deals.

Another very common pitfall among modern parents is the tendency to try to reason with a child who is too young to be reasoned with. It seems, for instance, only sensible to explain to a small child who is sick in bed that the reason you want him to stay under the covers is to get over his cold, and the reason you want him to get over his cold is so that he can go to the birthday party on Saturday. This, however, is grownup logic. To the child, Saturday is eons away and meanwhile it is far more fun to bounce on the bed than to sit still. If you continue to try to reason with him you are bound to lose patience and end up by saying, "Stay under those covers or no party!"

There is still another and more all-pervading reason why we modern parents are apt to bargain with our children. Having become convinced that it is wrong to assert our authority all over the place and compel obedience from our children, we have swung to the other extreme and are afraid to show any leadership at all. Those of us who have attempted to leave our children completely uncurbed often resort to bribes or threats whenever it becomes absolutely essential that we exert some control.

Children Need Control

Actually, of course, as child specialists are busy pointing out these days, children most certainly do need some control and are miserable if they don't know to what limits they may go. Parents who are generally on good terms with their children can and should be able to say firmly what can and cannot be done in a given situation. Children feel much more secure with parents who are sufficiently sure of themselves not to have to bargain over important matters.

On the other hand, it is also possible to start bargaining with your child because you are asking too much of him. A mother who feels that her four-year-old *must* tie his shoelaces, clean his room and play nicely at all times with his little brother, is in for trouble—because her child just isn't mature enough to meet her demands and if she cannot understand and make allowances for the child's normal inability to obey her requests, she is almost certain to resort to bribes or threats.

But whatever the royal road that may have led you to the place where you find yourself more or less regularly bargaining with your child, the big thing

is to get out of the situation as quickly as possible. The important thing is to make it clear to your child, and to yourself, that from now on you do things for each other, not for the promise of a bribe or the fear of a threat, but just because you care about each other and want to live together happily. Though he may have seemed like a born little bargain driver, you may be surprised to find how quickly your child will adjust to a wiser, happier way of family life.
—By Margaret H. Bacon

DOES YOUR CHILD EMBARRASS YOU IN PUBLIC?

EVERY thoughtful parent knows that even the mildest mannered, easiest-to-handle children occasionally throw a scene in public, especially during the preschool years. It may be in the grocery store or during a shopping expedition for the youngster's clothes, on a bus or other public conveyance, in a restaurant or watching a parade. The child's rebellion may be born of boredom, tiredness, hunger, a perfectly normal desire for attention, or any of a thousand other needs.

Still, mothers wish that they were better at handling misbehavior in public. "If only I didn't get so embarrassed," said one, "that I take things out on Billy which really aren't his fault." And another: "At home I can usually reason with Sue, but in public she gets me on the spot and before I know it I'm furious and she's screaming."

Maybe the initial step toward improved handling is to recognize the fact that it's the audience—however unwittingly—that is the real troublemaker. Young and old, we react to being exposed to the public eye. An audience, especially an audience of strangers, puts us under pressure. At home if David bursts into tears because you have to take something away from him, you offer a permissible substitute in a friendly manner and go on about your business. But let this happen in the grocery store or on a train and immediately David's tears put you on the defensive. You feel everybody is watching—and unfortunately it's usually true. Then you may feel a totally unwarranted fear that both you as a parent and your child are on trial. This is the feeling that can turn what should be a temporary clash into a prolonged battle of wills.

Influence of Public Opinion

Of course, strangers often do pass judgment on us and on our children on the basis of how our youngsters behave in public and any number of other inadequate criteria. And, perhaps partly due to the temper of our times, it's hard to be poised and inwardly confident when we feel that we are being rated unfavorably, no matter how unfairly. Yet being able to maintain one's self-assurance in an unfriendly atmosphere is not only the secret of avoiding soul-shattering tussles with Mary Jane in the grocery store but essential to satisfactory living in all adult activity.

For many mothers, awareness of this basic truth is sufficient to relieve their embarrassment when their children act up in public. Once freed from the notion that their youngsters' behavior connotes some kind of failure on their own part, they are able to deal with the behavior in the same friendly but firm manner they would use in the privacy of their homes. And nearly always the youngster, given the security of feeling himself on familiar ground, quickly becomes, if not a cherub, at least manageable.

Another help toward relieving oneself of embarrassment in such circumstances is to try to understand how your child is feeling. Why does he grab the cookies, refuse to try on the new shoes, struggle to stand up by the window on the bus, hit a playmate or perhaps hit you? Does he feel unjustly treated, unduly shoved about, fearful, or is he just trying to prove his independence? You may not be able to fathom the reason why he does, but in the process of trying you will almost certainly think a little more clearly about the welfare of your small beleaguered youngster. You'll be free to do whatever is most likely to help him become secure and satisfied again in the shortest possible time, and that's what constitutes successful handling of any scene with a child, at home or in public.

Skillful Planning Helps

Searching for the reasons will also give you some important clues as to how such scenes may be avoided in the future. It goes almost without saying that children are most likely to be difficult when they are tired, hot, hungry, overstimulated, taxed beyond their years or bored. Toss into the picture a mother who is operating on a tight schedule and you have a pretty sure-fire recipe for trouble. What all this adds up to is that one way to avoid public scenes is through skillful planning.

In these servantless days it's tempting to take the youngest with us wherever we go, instead of hiring an expensive baby sitter. This practice has much to recommend it for young and old alike, as long as parents use discretion and never expect or demand of their children behavior beyond their years. If your toddler seems to enjoy going places with you, fine. But if he tends, whenever you're out in public, to be fussier, more excited or much harder to control, you'd be wiser to protect him from such unsettling experiences as much as possible until he's old enough—three and a half, perhaps, or four—

to handle them better. Many women arrange "baby-sitting swaps" with a neighbor in order to do errands unencumbered.

If you take a child to a movie, circus or any other public entertainment, you have to be prepared to leave sooner than you might like. When you want to take more than one, better arrange for both parents to be along, so one of you can leave with the youngest child, if necessary.

Shopping with Children

Shopping expeditions are usually more satisfactory if they're planned for days when you don't have any other special engagements and no deadline for being back home. It's surprising how much smoother they go when your child doesn't feel rushed. Generally, the best time to shop with a child is on weekdays as soon as possible after the stores open. This way you not only avoid the big shopping crowds and the transportation rush hours but also your youngster is probably at his freshest. If you must go at other times, chances are you'll do a successful job if you're relaxed and unhurried.

For a small child, having to sit in one place any length of time is an excruciatingly trying experience. Keep this in mind not only when you have to travel long distances, but also when you take your youngster on a public conveyance. Looking out the window soon palls—but you can make a game of it: "Soon we're going to pass the fire station, Johnny. Can you spot it before I do?" Or, "Let's see who spies the first man with a beard (or the first blue car, big dog, baby carriage, and so forth)."

One mother keeps her three-year-old boy fascinated by singing very softly into his ear, just loud enough for him to hear. Another mother, with equal success, tells stories about what it was like to ride on streetcars and subways when she was a little girl. Actually, just about anything you do with a small child that involves paying him attention will generally keep him happy for as long as it takes to get to town—if you start the activity while he is still content. If you wait until he has already become restless, a change of position may be the only salvation for you, the child and the other passengers. If there's no room for Johnny to stand on the seat, try letting him kneel in your lap facing you, or stand facing you with his hands holding on to your knees.

Bringing Snacks and Toys

Any expedition with a child—shopping, traveling or just visiting friends—is likely to go more smoothly if you take along a few small toys and between-meal snacks against the time he shows signs of becoming bored, hungry or obstreperous. Inexpensive items from the ten-cent store are ideal—anything small, regardless of how perishable it may be. This is one time when you needn't be concerned about the lasting qualities of a toy. Many mothers keep a small emergency supply of small items on hand for just such occasions, together with some purse-size plastic bags in which to carry crackers, gum, dried fruit or any other treats that your child is allowed to have between meals. Certainly when you take your one-to-four-year-old youngster with you to the grocery store, where he will be surrounded by tempting edibles, you should be prepared to offer him fruit or something else to eat.

Parents are often concerned about their children's table manners in public. Until a child is four or five years old, parents really should be pleased—and tell their youngster so—if, having a meal in a public place, he simply enjoys the occasion. With a preschooler, it's important, whenever possible, to pick a rather informal, rapid-service place where children are welcome. Either bring along crackers for your offspring to nibble on while you are waiting for your order or ask the waitress to serve the child his milk right away. Many a restaurant experience gets off on the wrong foot because Mary Jane grows restless with waiting too long for food. Little children usually much prefer drive-ins and cafeterias to more formal eating places, but even the latter can afford a pleasant change if parents are thoughtful and relaxed about manners. Embarrassing scenes in public sometimes are precipitated by the fact that a child feels left out, temporarily rejected. You may not realize it, but while you are talking earnestly with a saleslady about sizes and materials, your Susie, completely unmindful of the fact that it's a snowsuit for her which is under discussion, may begin to feel that a strange grownup has usurped her mother's attention. She makes a sudden dash behind the counter and begins to pull out boxes. "Showing off" is her way of letting you know that she feels neglected. Couldn't the incident have been prevented if you had included Susie in the talk?

Children Need Attention

Children don't just *want* attention, they *need* it—some perhaps more than others and all of them more at some times than at other times. It's a pretty safe idea to operate on the premise that when your child shows off, it indicates that he is genuinely in need of attention, which to him signifies love and security. Naturally you don't want to encourage such behavior, but giving more attention at other times and handling the show-off episodes sympathetically—"Now, Susie, enough of that. Come sit in Mother's lap"—is usually your best bet for lowering the incidence of these lapses.

No matter how skillfully you plan, how many clever techniques you employ in an effort to ward off trouble in public, at some time or other an explosion is sure to occur. Does it really matter? Almost before you know it, your toddler will be an adolescent and concerned about the impression *you* make in public!
—*By Mary B. Hoover*

WHAT IS
YOUR CHILD AFRAID OF?

FEAR and pain are normal and useful parts of our lives, serving to warn us away from dangers and notify us when we have overstepped nature's limitations. We could hardly expect to bring a child up safely if he were totally indifferent to danger. Fires, knives, mechanical devices and traffic, for example, all are interesting to him and he will naturally be drawn to investigate and experiment with them unless attraction is balanced by the emotion of fear. Just telling him to let them alone will not work. It takes emotion to counteract emotion.

Our particular culture tends to exalt courage above caution. We admire the person who will take a risk, counting upon his own skill and resourcefulness to pull him through safely.

We all take chances daily, of course, and often no harm comes of what may be considered a calculated risk. However, we may refuse without shame what we consider a bad risk. Certainly no one ridicules the pedestrian who waits for the green traffic light. We cannot avoid some risk, but each of us must draw his own line between reasonable courage and foolhardy rashness. We judge by the nature of the danger, our knowledge of how to deal with it and our estimate of our own skill.

Developing Good Judgment

None of these things is easy for a child to judge. He knows little of the real extent of the danger, has only our word for how to cope with it and often misjudges his own skill. The whole problem of developing courage without rashness, caution without panic, lies in gradually increasing his power to judge wisely. Much of it must come from experience.

For example, it is delightfully challenging to a child to walk along the top of a wall, delightful because it is dangerous! Success means triumph and self-confidence; failure a skinned knee—or a broken bone. Is the wall too high or too narrow? How can he tell except by trying?

One parent cries, "Edward, come down at once! Don't you know you're apt to fall and break your leg?"

Another looks at the wall, feels that it is not too high or too narrow and says, "Well, maybe you can if you go carefully. I'll walk along beside you and you can grab me if you slip."

If the first child learns anything it is fear. High places are dangerous; keep off them. Well they may be, and a warning is in order, but we should be careful how it is given. Our voices should induce caution, not terror.

The second child is being trained in judgment. He can be told how to balance with his arms and place his feet well. He will know how this risk is to be met. If he falls, his injury will not be serious enough to create an all-time fear, yet he will have learned that he may fall.

Above all, he is getting an experience that helps him to understand degrees of danger and degrees of skill. He sees that the world includes not only safe things that one may do and others too dangerous to attempt but also doubtful things one must approach carefully and learn how to do. Judgment and caution are developing instead of fear.

While we want children to develop caution, we wish that they might be spared all unfounded and excessive fears. But the world is not so kind. They are bound to encounter experiences that throw them into panic, from the time when a cut and bleeding finger seems an incomprehensible tragedy to the moment when the high school orator's mouth goes dry and his knees turn to water as he faces a full auditorium. These are shock experiences, the psychologists tell us, but they need have no serious after-effects if the whirlwind of emotion they generate is allowed to blow itself out.

Be Sympathetic

We do not say to the baby, "Stop that screaming. Be a big boy." We let him know we understand and accept the way he feels. Instead of adding our disapproval to his pain and fear we stand by his side against disaster, sympathetic but undaunted. "Oh, too bad," we say to the young child. "It does hurt, doesn't it? But I know how to fix it. It will be better soon." Then when the treatment is over we admire the bandaged finger. Later we may encourage the wounded hero to exhibit it proudly and tell daddy all about it, including how much it hurt and how hard he cried at first. Treated in that way the fright works itself off, is happily over and done with, and there is nothing left to cause undue future fears.

Many of the fears that young children get from experience can be handled in this way—if you are on hand at the right moment. But a big dog passing by may bark at your toddler, terrify him and be gone by the time you arrive on the scene. Only later do you see that the sight of a dog throws him into a frenzy.

It is too late then to treat this experience like the cut finger, but you can give your child reassuring experiences to counteract it. He may like to watch a dog at some distance, provided you hold him in your arms. It may seem fun to watch from a window while someone else plays with a dog. Stories and pictures and toys may help. Your purpose is to help create many pleasant associations with the idea of dog. Finally these will overbalance the one fright experience.

Avoid Ridicule

Never deny or ridicule the child's fear and do not emphasize it by unnecessary comment. When the small child pulls back and clings to your skirt, it is more helpful to pick him up and say casually, "Yes, I know how you feel. That dog is big and noisy, isn't he? But he's only playing. Let's stand here and watch. Someday when you're more used to them you will probably like dogs."

It is worse than useless to try to cure a young child's fright by forcing him to repeat a frightening experience. Perhaps you will drive the car again as soon as possible after an accident in order to overcome your dread of it. But you are mature enough to realize your dread is irrational. Building up happy associations with whatever frightens a child is the surest way to cure his fears.

Fear of the dark seems to appear suddenly in children and without apparent cause. The shadows in the corner become wolves, tigers or "bad men," and they seem very real to him. Bad dreams often increase at this time and a child who may have been cheerfully venturesome shrinks back from anything unfamiliar.

Various explanations of this "scaredy-cat" stage between three and six are offered. For practical purposes, however, it is not too hard to understand on the basis of the child's rapidly expanding world and his limited understanding of it.

Parental Support Needed

Children suffering from fears need plenty of support. They need to realize that you understand their fears though you do not share them, and that, for instance, you will leave a little light on in their room at night so that they can make sure there is no tiger under the chair. But they need to know also that if there *is* and they see him there, you are still not afraid and will stay with them awhile and leave the door open.

As the child's grasp on reality becomes stronger, these fears are gradually outgrown unless there is someone around who reinforces them by his own superstitions, by teasing or by pegging down specific fears by comment so that they become a part of the child's own picture of himself.

Fears by contagion, fears based on shock experiences, fears of the unknown and unfamiliar—these are all fairly easy to understand and deal with. They yield to patient, understanding guidance, including moral support, reassuring experiences and training in how to handle the dangerous, or supposedly dangerous, situations. Gradually the child acquires judgment and confidence.

Most parents, however, encounter signs of a much more elusive type of fear at some time before their children are grown. These fears may appear at any age and reflect in each case the deeper worries appropriate to that age. Tracing down the basic and underlying fear may be quite a problem. Some of the most common are variations on these themes:

Common Fears

My parents don't love me, or they won't if they know what I did (or thought, or even dreamed).

I am going to lose Mommy or Daddy: they will leave or send me away.

I hate the people I also love.

I'm bad and can't help it.

There are bad or secret things I am afraid or ashamed to know about.

Fortunately we can often help a child overcome these deep fears. Look at the list—lack of love, fear of loss, guilt and shame, taboos and mysteries, fear for one's own integrity and worth, personal or physical.

The best cure is prevention, obviously. The child who feels securely loved, wanted, valued for himself, has a good start toward moral courage. We can also help by letting in the sunshine of frank discussion to dissolve the miasma of fear which surrounds the old mysteries of sex and death.

All this we can do for prevention, and it will help, but still we must not be surprised if our children develop some unconscious worries. They come to all of us. The better we know our children, the more likely we are to be able to guess the real trouble and give our child specific support. Sometimes we even have to examine our own hearts to see whether the child's fear may be a reflection of our anxieties or fears.

Seeking Outside Help

In the few cases where symptoms persist over a long time and tend to get worse, parents can turn to a guidance clinic, a capable counselor, or if necessary, to a psychiatrist.

But what we want for our children is more than a freedom from fear. We want them to have courage.

And courage is based on a sense of personal security and personal worth. These qualities produce the strength that enables us to admit our failures and weaknesses as well as our strengths. The person who has courage will proceed with caution and sometimes he will let well enough alone, even if somebody dares him to go ahead. One of the fears we all have to some extent is the fear of social criticism if we do what we believe to be right and wise. The courage for that, too, depends upon the development of self-respect.

—By Rhoda W. Bacmeister

IF NIGHT FEARS DISTURB SLEEP

AT one time or another nearly every parent has run into difficulties in trying to get his child to go to bed in the evening or to fall asleep. The particular nature of a child's resistance to going to sleep differs from child to child. Each parent will have to try to find out why his child has a hard time getting settled for his much-needed rest and then act accordingly. On the other hand, there are difficulties about falling asleep which nearly every child encounters at one time or another and these seem so universal that their discussion may be useful to all parents, although the most important advice will still be to look for the specific causes of your own child's difficulties around bedtime.

First of all, some of a child's difficulties about falling asleep are perfectly normal and not due to any mistakes on the part of the parent. (The only danger is that once these normal sleep difficulties appear a parent may find himself upset, may try to force the issue and then may handle it poorly. He may unwillingly make mistakes which aggravate what was originally just a minor disturbance.)

By and large, there are two major causes of a child's resistance to falling asleep. Both are necessary consequences of growing up. For instance, although the child is tired after an active day, he still wants to stay awake, either to keep on doing exciting things or to be sure not to miss out on anything that may take place while he sleeps. These are perfectly normal desires but may still lead to quite a battle when the child ought to be going to bed. This kind of sleep difficulty starts at a time in the child's life when he begins to be fascinated with the world, when each new experience is so exciting that he can never get enough of it.

The Anxious Child

Basically, in most instances, this is the result of a healthy desire to learn more about the world, not to give up the contact with reality, to continue as long as possible to enjoy a parent's company.

Of course, in the anxious child, the same device may serve mainly to postpone bedtime because of the anxiety connected with going to sleep. Although outwardly the child's behavior will seem the same, our reaction to it will have to be different depending on whether the child wishes mainly to continue an enjoyable contact with the world or is mainly afraid of what the night may have in store. In either case, the child's excited demands, the arguments that follow, the battle of wills—all these will interfere with the child's ability to fall asleep. Therefore, to help him, it is a good idea to make things less and less exciting, less and less attractive, as bedtime approaches.

For example, while it is a good idea to introduce new stories from time to time during the day, a new story asks for the child's full concentration. This is fine in the daytime, but at night it cannot help but make him more wide awake, and even more so if the content of the story is exciting or provides much food for thought and for questions. In this case, reading the new story will effectively prevent him from settling down to sleep. The very familiar, on the other hand, while less stimulating is also less exciting, and is always the most reassuring. So he is much more willing to fall asleep.

Fear of Parents' Absence

Some children are afraid their parents may leave them after they have fallen asleep or that they may begin an exciting game with an older brother or sister or that a visitor may come. Any experience the child has had of suddenly awakening from sleep to find the parent unexpectedly not at home or with a visitor, will feed into such fears of missing out.

For this reason it is always a good idea to tell children what is going to be happening around the house while they sleep and to be sure to paint things in not too attractive colors so that they do not get the feeling that they miss out on too much. The more the child gets the feeling that he knows pretty much what will happen during the night, the less reluctant he will be to go to sleep.

A general fear of what may happen to him when he cannot pay close attention because he is sleeping lies behind many a child's sleep disturbances.

Sometimes relatively innocuous events have far-reaching consequences here. The child who is carried to another room in his sleep is startled, on awakening, because he does not know how he came to be there. He cannot fully understand such a thing and if this can happen in his sleep, how can he be sure that the next time he may not be carried out of the house? If a child needs to be moved at night it is better to wake him up first and then carry him into another room. This is advisable even if the child resents being awakened—his resentment will be short-lived and relatively unimportant when compared with the fears that are created by moving him around in his sleep.

"Separation Fears"

Closely connected is the child's fear of what may happen to those who are important to him, most of all to his parents.

In this connection it should be stressed that the younger the child is, the more convinced he is that what he does not see, hear or feel does not exist. This is what psychologists mean when they speak of the "separation fears" so common in small children. Such children are terrified by the idea that a parent, particularly their mother, may leave them. How can they be sure that once the parent is out of sight, he has not left them for good?

Incidentally, that is why small children love peek-a-boo games. Their pleasure derives from the repeated experience that, contrary to the anxiety they feel, they have only to open their eyes and the loved person is still right where he was.

This fear of losing the beloved person or loved things, this separation anxiety is so central—particularly at night—that when free to do so, children themselves will find the best remedy against it: they will hold on, even in sleep, to some preferred toy. It is as if they wanted to feel that the pleasant reality on which their security depends during the day has not deserted them at night, in their sleep, even if they no longer see it. Therefore a cuddly animal taken to bed with him not only serves as a protector against night fears originating in a child's internal world but on a much more primitive level serves as tangible evidence that things do not disappear during the night.

All of us, at one time or another, fear that we may lose our ability to take care of ourselves, and so does the child. Therefore, in terms of what constitutes his being taken care of, one of the most basic fears of the child is that food, the main sustenance of his life, may disappear or may not be readily available should he feel hungry at night. This is why night fears of considerable severity will sometimes disappear if the child is allowed to take a bottle to hold on to—and this long after the child has been weaned from the bottle during the day.

Sleep, as such, is a regressive phenomenon. More mature abilities, those acquired later in childhood, must be given up in order to enjoy the very primitive rest that only sleep can provide. Therefore it becomes understandable that perhaps for a long time a child who no longer plays mainly with stuffed animals during the day and certainly no longer drinks from a bottle when he is wide awake, feels the impulse to return, in the regressive state of sleep or of falling asleep, to what has given him security at an earlier stage of development. Consequently he insists on taking a stuffed animal and perhaps a bottle to bed with him.

Anxiety or fears which prevent a child from falling asleep can at least be alleviated by letting the child suck on some hard food or munch a cookie after the lights are turned out. Such pleasurable chewing relieves tension, which can keep a child from falling asleep. But much more important is the fact that it convinces the child that pleasure does not disappear even though he is now falling asleep. At the same time the sucking encourages the child to give up, for the time being, his growing interest in what is going on about him and encourages him to give up his defenses against being infantile again —both of which would interfere with his falling asleep.

Toys as Protectors

Quite different in its psychological meaning from the holding on to an animal as a token of pleasurable reality is the child's use of his toy animals as protectors. To him the same toy animals may also offer a very different protection: as watchdogs, so to speak, against inner tendencies of which the child disapproves.

The more awake the child is, the more he is in control of his instincts. But the more tired he gets, the less energy he has available for the fight to live up to parental demands and the more overwhelming grows his wish to give in and enjoy more primitive satisfaction.

A typical example is the child who has given up thumb-sucking during the day. He has learned to enjoy play with other children and doesn't need to find enjoyment in infantile sucking. But when he is tired of playing or when he is expected to stay by himself and go to sleep, he will return to earlier sources of satisfaction, and once more suck his thumb.

In his sucking before falling asleep, we can observe how the child reverts to baby ways. Actually he is afraid that in his sleep he may lose control altogether. The child who has recently acquired the ability to keep dry during the day and to use the toilet, may be very much afraid that in his sleep he may lose his newly acquired control and wet the bed. If this is what he fears, he clings to his Teddy bear more because he expects the bear to watch out that he doesn't do anything bad (such as wetting his bed) than because he wants him to be a watchdog against dangers from the outside.

Fear of Masturbation

A child who suffers from sleeplessness may also be afraid that in his sleep he may indulge in masturbation of which the parents have shown disapproval. There, too, the assurance from a parent that he does not mind will often give immediate relief from night fears and do away with the resistance to sleep.

Any type of "nice behavior" a parent tries to teach his child, but which a child is not yet able to live up to, may become a source of fear lest in his sleep or dreams he may transgress against it. Dreams to a child seem much more real than they do to adults and are another frequent source of night fears. In his dream the child does what he is not supposed to do, which creates anxiety; so, rather than risk the anxiety the dream may create, the child prefers not to fall asleep.

This is not usually too serious a situation as long as the child is concerned only with such relatively harmless matters as eating forbidden candy. It becomes much more serious when the desires of the child are in conflict with what our society believes to be right and acceptable. For example, the child may act out in his dream the jealousy he feels for a newly arrived baby. He may dream he is throwing the baby out of the window.

Repression of Desires

Usually, as the child grows older, dreams no longer express the child's wishes and antisocial desires so directly. The child learns finally to repress such unacceptable desires even to the point where he can't believe he really feels them. This is the age when the child claims somebody has done the thing, but not he. One five-year-old boy who was fully toilet trained wet his bed one night and woke up screaming with anxiety. When the parent came into the child's bedroom he was standing in a corner of his bed pointing to the wet spot and screaming, "Somebody wet my bed!"

When the child can no longer recognize the wish as his own, it will appear to him as something strange and dangerous, which persecutes him. Instead of dreaming about his wish to hurt baby brother, he now dreams mainly about the punishment he will have to endure as a result of such wishes. He will then dream of being chased by a policeman, a big wolf or perhaps the dog across the street.

One reason why animals are so often the form in which the persecutor appears in dreams is that the child can easily observe on the street or on the farm how animals are permitted to freely fulfill their instinctual desires. Therefore, the animal, to whom the child often feels closer than to adults, becomes the bad tempter to undesirable behavior as well as the persecutor.

How Parents Can Help

The child's fight against his own asocial and instinctual desires is a normal step in the process of growing up and we can do little to protect the child against such inner conflicts. All we can do is to avoid aggravating them. This means we should avoid putting too many restrictions on the young child and assure him of our enduring affection even if occasional transgressions occur. We can explain to the child that none of us is perfect, that all learning takes time and that there is nothing wrong with bad wishes or dreams as long as they do not lead to bad actions when awake. Moreover, we should explain to him that dreams are not real and that everyone, including mothers and daddies, has bad dreams sometimes; that he is safe and need not be afraid even if he sometimes does something his parents would not like. We should assure him that he will not be punished for it. In general, the secure child who feels well protected by the love of his parents will overcome even these night fears in a relatively short time. —*By Bruno Bettelheim, Ph.D.*

FEAR OF THE DENTIST

HAVE you ever sat in a dentist's waiting room and listened to a child screaming, "No, no, I won't let you! I want to go home! Mommy, take me home!"

If you've witnessed such a scene, which is duplicated in thousands of dentists' offices daily, you probably squirmed and wondered for whom you felt most sorry: the hysterical, frightened child? the upset and embarrassed mother? the exhausted and frustrated dentist? Or it could be you suddenly felt sorry for yourself. You may have remembered it would soon be time for your own child to make his first trip to the dentist.

Are ordeals like this a necessary part of visits to the dentist, either for a young child on his first trip or for subsequent follow-up visits? Experience proves that they're not. When parents and dentists tackle the problem intelligently, most childhood fears of dentistry can be prevented or conquered. With understanding preparation and handling, a youngster can come to think of the man in the white coat as friend instead of foe—someone who helps, even though he may have to hurt occasionally.

But there are no simple rules for success in achieving this happy state of affairs. Only by understanding the sources of a child's fears can we help prevent those fears, or help the child overcome them. Parents who fail to understand the *why* of fears tend to be impatient and critical, instead of sympathetic and helpful.

How Fear Develops

How does fear of the dentist get started in the first place? One simple but important source is other people's conversation. "Last Tuesday I went to the dentist and he nearly killed me." Frightening words take on literal meaning in young people's minds.

Talk of playmates and friends, parents can't control. Talk at home, they can. This sometimes takes the form of fear-talk about dentists a child overhears or making a bogey-man out of the dentist to enforce discipline. "You be good or I'll take you to the dentist and he'll fix you!" Such comments will not mark the beginning of a pleasant relationship.

Parents' attitudes, too, and tone of voice children sense, absorb and file away for future reference. If mother is afraid of the dentist, her fear may show in spite of the fact that she is careful not to put it in words. When it's time for young Johnny to go to the dentist, she may be amazed that he puts up a fight. She looks at the dentist and says honestly, "Why I never talked about dentistry in front of Johnny!" Her statement may be entirely true, but it's also true that she underestimates Johnny's ability to notice when she's upset, his ability to observe attitudes as well as words.

If a mother is afraid of the dentist she'll help her child most by looking her fear in the eye and doing her best to get rid of it. When parents are calm and matter-of-fact in their own feelings toward dentistry the child usually reflects that attitude.

Knowledge Conquers Fear

A frightened child, on the other hand, can often be relieved by a man-to-man explanation that even dads and mothers are sometimes frightened too—but that after it was all over, it almost always turned out they were scared of something not worth being scared of (like a loud noise or mice—or maybe even dentists!). Just the realization that he's not the only person who was ever afraid of anything can help clear up a youngster's fears. And the knowledge that others have conquered fear can help him do the same.

A child can get over fear more quickly if he's given plenty of comfort and support. Not smothered in pity—just reassured in a friendly matter-of-fact way to the effect that fear is nothing unusual, and that it can be conquered.

One psychologist reports how a little girl, who used to kick and scream every time she had to go to the dentist, was helped to get rid of her terror. At first, her parents urged her to "be a big girl" and "stop acting like a baby." They promised her gifts, ice cream, all sorts of rewards to be "good." And with no success.

They were advised to change their tack. So on the next visit the parents told the child, "It's perfectly all right to cry. Some little girls are worried when they go to the dentist. But going to the dentist is important, so we're going. If you want to cry, you can cry. We'll stay with you and love you just the same." The results were astounding. The reason was simple. As soon as the child realized it wasn't wrong or unusual to be afraid, the hysterics gave way to a mild whimper. She could then concentrate on the fear itself and try to master it, knowing her parents were helping her.

Feelings of Inadequacy

Fear is often tied up closely in a child's mind with a feeling of inadequacy. The child may secretly wonder why he's so frightened. If mother and dentist ignore his fear or make fun of him and assure him he's acting like a baby he becomes convinced they're right. Shaming serves to decrease his self-confidence, makes him feel less secure. And his hysterics at the dentist's increase.

What he really needs, instead of "Be a man!" is to be allowed to go ahead and "Be a little boy." We must accept his fears as real, important and natural, then get to work helping him to overcome them.

Above all, we mustn't expect too much heroism from a child at the dentist's. If he has to be hurt, he has a right to cry. This has been his way of handling pain since babyhood. But there is a difference between crying and hysteria. With our help, he can gradually learn the grownup art of control.

Fear thrives on ignorance—and a parent can often dispel fear by telling the child what to expect at the dentist's. Not a fairy tale that pretends the whole thing is a picnic, nor a gruesome and detailed description of drills, forceps and hypodermic syringes. Just a realistic story told in words the child can understand, an explanation which helps make dental care acceptable as one of the experiences we must all learn to face.

Explain Dentist's Function

Our explanation to a child will stress the fact that we should be grateful to the dentist for keeping our teeth strong and useful.

In simple, unemotional terms we can tell the child about the dentist's chair that goes up as tall as a highchair, about the little tools and lights that help the dentist examine our teeth carefully, the drill that makes a buzzing noise as it gets rid of decay and makes a clean place for the filling to go—and that sometimes hurts for a minute or so.

We must be careful not to promise—or even imply—that going to the dentist won't ever hurt a bit. Fears multiply by leaps and bounds if a child discovers that people whom he trusted have been deceiving him. A matter-of-fact statement that dental treatment may be uncomfortable—but not for long at a time—gives the child a realistic concept of this new experience he's facing.

To help build up a friendly relationship, many dentists encourage parents to bring a child along on an adult dental visit that involves merely cleaning or filling—an occasion when the youngster can see for himself that mother or dad is relaxed and comfortable in the dentist's chair. This is a much better way to introduce a child to the dentist than to have him arrive at the office for the first time complete with a tremendous cavity, a swollen jaw and a sleepless night from an aching tooth.

Establish Early Acquaintance

When a youngster comes to the family dentist before he has trouble—say about the age of two—he can get acquainted in easy and friendly stages: by riding in the "elevator" chair, making funny noises with the air syringe, maybe having his teeth cleaned with the whirring little brush.

When it's time later on to fill a tooth, the whole business won't seem so strange and frightening. If the child is old enough to understand, the dentist can catch his interest and take the edge off his uneasiness by explaining the fascinating modern instruments and techniques he may use to cut down discomfort in dentistry. Possibly the air-water vapor spray, which reduces heat —and therefore much of the pain—connected with drilling; perhaps the drilling instruments that contain tiny diamonds (the only known surface harder than enamel) which cut with great speed and less friction; or any of the improved new anesthetics.

The dentist can also help by keeping appointments short. And by setting definite limits to any discomfort that the child must bear. When a child understands that this may hurt—but only for a short time—perhaps he can endure the pain more easily.

When a so-called "baby" tooth must be pulled, the youngster can more readily accept the situation if he's convinced a bigger and better tooth is coming through—which the dentist can prove by showing him an X-ray picture of the new tooth sitting there ready to come up through the gum. Emphasis on replacement and restoration helps children accept dental care with greater ease.

Accentuate the Positive

Parents can also "accentuate the positive" by stressing some interesting side trip or pleasant occurrence that's going to follow a visit to the dentist. Not a bribe for being good, but something that's fun to look forward to—like a call at the monkey house at the zoo, or buying a new book, or maybe seeing a movie.

But in spite of intelligent preparation by parents and understanding handling by the dentist—fears of dentistry frequently develop in a child's mind and are nourished by his playmates' remarks. And in this case the strong instinct for self-defense—which every baby has in abundance at birth—sometimes plays a part in the fear-picture. A frightened child at the dentist is often reacting with a deep-seated urge to protect his body from harm. Faced with an alarming array of instruments, strange antiseptic odors and unknown persons in white gowns, he knows something is going to be done to him. Just what, he isn't sure—but from things he's heard and things he can see for himself, he's convinced it won't be good!

The youngster who screams at the dentist, "No, I won't let you!" may really mean, "No, you might do something to my body!" In the mind of a young child, harm to his tooth can easily multiply into harm to his whole body. When the instinct to protect himself from physical harm joins forces with fear caused by unflattering reports he's heard about what goes on at the dentist's—it's not surprising that he won't submit quietly.

Patience needed. Most of children's fears and difficulties—simple or subtle —can be resolved through patience and understanding. If not, parents should seek professional guidance.

Clearly, there is no one way to help every child adopt a more relaxed attitude toward dentistry. But given parents who understand the problems involved, and a dentist who is sympathetic to the needs of the child, the youngster will usually learn to cope with his fears and become a good patient.

—*By Paul A. Krooks, D.D.S., and Eda J. LeShan*

THERE'S A RIGHT WAY
TO TALK TO CHILDREN

THE way you talk to your child, your choice of language can make all the difference in the world when it comes to getting along happily and securing cooperation from two, three and four-year-olds. One mother frankly admits having learned how to talk to her three-year-old child while observing a nursery school class. It seemed as if there was some magic or wonderful force at work in this room containing thirty-six children and four teachers. A feeling of fun and play pervaded, plus a good noise of children living together and liking it. The mother began listening to see if she could find out why this school was such a happy place.

One small boy approached another and kicked him experimentally. The normal reaction (one which would have been common in many mothers) would have been to swoop down on the offender with a "Stop your kicking, you bad boy!" and forcibly separate him from the first child. Instead, the nursery school teacher said in a firm but kind voice, "Feet belong on the floor, Johnny."

Johnny looked at his feet, seemed to be thinking about what the teacher had said, and then wandered off to another activity. No one had gotten angry with him. He had been told simply that feet belonged on the floor and he was willing to accept that fact when he would probably have rebelled at being called a "bad boy."

Old Concepts Discarded

The old concepts of "good" and "bad" had been discarded for something better. A child who behaved in a manner which we consider "good" was called, instead, "big." Anne was a "big rester." She was not a "good girl because she took her nap." Probing the philosophy behind these and other carefully chosen phrases which the teachers used, this mother realized that the word "big" was helping the child to grow as an individual and develop a sense of responsibility. Anne was beginning to realize that she takes a nap because she needs to rest, not just because mother or teacher wants her to.

The old idea was not to coddle children. If they had to do something, one told them so briefly, even curtly, and no nonsense about it. It was coddling to persuade them to do things which were necessary for their own good. But what had been heard at nursery school was not wheedling. It was affirmative and gently firm. To be sure, the children were handled with tact and diplomacy. But is there anything wrong with that? Civilized man has invented many beautiful expressions with which to oil the machinery of living together. Why should we use them only with adults? Have you ever stopped to think how many times you say a curt "no" or "don't" to your preschool child? Count them some day, and consider how much more pleasant the home atmosphere would be if these words were seldom used.

There are times, of course, when a direct command is necessary—as in cases of danger. But actually most of our "no's" pop out by habit, or are the natural result of being bigger and having more knowledge than our children. Some of them express the tendency toward dictatorship which lurks in the best of us.

There was no such approach at the nursery school. Instead the following remarks were heard which seemed admirably adaptable to home use.

"Brooms are for sweeping." This was said to a child about to use a broom as a weapon.

Instill Order and Security

"Paint brushes are for painting," and "Clay stays at the table." These words instill in the child, without pitting mother's will against his own, an idea of an orderly procedure in living. He accepts it as he has learned to accept the fact that night follows day, and it gives him a sense of security.

One child who had an urge to pinch and hurt other children was led gently to the clay table and told "Clay is for squeezing and pinching." He tore into the clay, pummeling and pinching it to his heart's content. Another child who made an effort to throw the clay was told that "Balls are for throwing." In adult language these remarks are like saying, "That's life" and accepting it!

The word "let's," which is used in all sorts of situations at nursery school, engenders in the child a nice sense of togetherness in a world of adults in which he may sometimes feel small and lonely.

When Mary, about to hit Susan, is asked "What are you trying to tell Susan?" she is stopped short. Perhaps it makes her ask herself, "What *am* I trying to tell Susan? And is this the best way to tell her?"

The friend of all nursery school teachers is the word "Time." Wonderful impersonal Time! It is time for rest, for picking up toys, for going to the bathroom, and so forth. Even adults know that one cannot fight with Time.

Use of "We"

Then there is the "we" which nursery school teachers use when speaking to small children. It implies that all of us, big and little, must live by certain rules and regulations. It helps a child to be willing to do the necessary things, for he realizes that not only he and the other children but grownups, too, must do them.

Children were constantly bringing their drawings, their paintings or their clay-workings to the teachers for praise.

"Wasn't it *fun?*" the teachers invariably remarked, or "I'll bet you had *fun* doing that." Not once the usual "Good! Johnny," or "Fine!" It is always difficult to praise a child's art work sincerely. We can't possibly know how much these apparent scrawls mean to the child who has created them. They are the expression of his feelings, perhaps of inner tensions. As a consequence the child is first to feel the almost inevitable insincerity when an adult tries to praise something which he does not really understand.

Encouraging Self-Expression

But when the adult says, "Wasn't it fun?" he is, first of all, expressing a sincere reaction. And he is also encouraging the child to express himself for the sake of the inner, glowing satisfaction he gets out of it, rather than for adult approbation which may not always be forthcoming. It is important to teach our children not to depend upon praise for their sense of worth and self-respect. What happy adults we would be if more of us could go about doing the world's work "for fun," for our own self-satisfaction instead of because we hope the boss will pat us on the back or because we must have approval to bolster our self-confidence.

Learning how to talk to your toddler can be one of the most rewarding and important experiences. And it can make a world of difference at your house!

—By Grace B. Martin

DO YOU TALK TOO MUCH?

SPEECH is a complicated tool. Because we grownups use it so easily we forget how difficult it is for small children and how much they still have to learn about it. How many words have meaning for a child? Only a few hundred before school age and most of these are acquired during the later preschool years. All the rest of the many thousands that we adults pour out in daily conversation may be meaningless to him or at best half-understood, guessed at by such clues as tone of voice, accompanying gesture or situation. By repetition associated with the same situation they acquire meaning. They get worked into the child's own vocabulary. But it is a long, complicated process.

Meantime, talk, talk, talk, go the grownups, pouring over the youngsters' defenseless heads a stream of words of which they recognize only a few—if they bother to listen. It's very fatiguing!

Why should mother say to two-year-old Johnny, "We have to go into the house now, Johnny, so Mother can cook your dinner. You're going to be hungry pretty soon, you know, and Johnny wants a good dinner, doesn't he?" Why make him undertake the translation of all that when she could just smile and hold out her hand to him? Or she could reinforce it with, "Come on, Johnny. Dinnertime soon," picking out the words she knows he understands.

Substitutes for Words

A smile, a nod, a headshake, a wave and dozens of other little gestures make themselves clear to the child at once and so do facial expressions of amusement, approval, disapproval and so on. Almost any woman finds it fun to practice making comments and giving directions in pantomime. And the youngsters' quick perception is gratifying.

Words are useful and important, of course. We want the children to be learning new ones all the time. But most of us are too lavish with them. They have more interest and meaning if we use only a few at a time.

When you are beginning to learn a foreign language, you get along pretty well as long as people go slowly and don't give you too much at once. So it is with little children. They respond best to brief, unhurried remarks with periods of quiet between.

Very young children cannot think of two things at once. They can work *or* listen, not both. If a youngster is in the habit of being talked to as he plays, he may become so dependent upon this that he is restless without it and does not develop strong play drives.

Learning Not to Listen

Or he may learn not to listen. A great deal of what he hears is beyond his understanding anyhow, so he ignores it. But if he doesn't do as mother says, she may consider him naughty or stubborn.

Maybe a shell of protective deafness prevented his hearing. Maybe he didn't understand because the key words were buried in a lot of others. Maybe he heard vaguely but knew there was time enough—"She didn't yell yet," as one child put it. Maybe he's tired of being told what to do.

If you find that sort of thing happens very often it would be a good idea to ask yourself how often you give directions or speak to your child. Keep track for half an hour.

If you let the blessed silences develop and if, when you speak, you do it simply and clearly, your child will learn to listen. Words will be interesting and have meaning for him.

If he has already lost the habit of listening, you will need to be sure that you catch his attention before you talk to him. Then you can avoid repeating what you have said.

Getting a Child's Attention

If his name, followed by a pause, doesn't get his attention, you may need to go to him, perhaps touch him, before he notices you, but this phase should not last long. After he realizes that you are not going to keep interrupting his activities, he will probably respond to his name alone.

Then say what you have to say, simply. Speak distinctly and not too fast, but, above all, naturally. Nothing is more deadening than that ter-ri-bly distinct speech that one sometimes hears overconscientious persons use. Don't hesitate to use gestures or facial expression to supplement words.

When you have finished, stop. Don't explain or repeat. It takes time for your message to get through and for the child to reorganize his responses accordingly. Allow plenty of time, more than seems necessary, before you say anything more. Nine times out of ten you won't need to.

Just how simply you must speak and how slow the response will be depends upon the temperament as well as the age of your child. The youngest ones all need much consideration in these respects but, by the time they are four or five, some are expanding their vocabularies by leaps and bounds. Their ability to hold in mind a complex thought is increasing greatly, as is their speed of response.

Age Determines Abilities

But remember that the ability to hold in mind and carry out three very simple commands, repeated once, is a five-year test on the Stanford-Binet intelligence scale. ("Put this key on that chair, then shut the door, then bring me that box," with gestures used to clarify.) That means that most fives can do it, but it is too hard for some.

A young mother sent her five-year-old on an errand. "Run upstairs for me, will you, dear, and bring me my white doeskin gloves. They're right in a box in the top drawer of my bureau. It's over at one side, sort of, under the picture of Grandma on the top of the bureau."

He was looking puzzled, so she added, "You know the picture of Grandma, don't you, dear?" He nodded.

"Well, that's where they are. And while you're there, just get my blue silk scarf out of the pocket of my fur coat in the closet, won't you please?"

He trotted off and she said, "I might as well go in the first place, but I want him to learn. He's just as sweet as he can be but so scatterbrained! I do everything I possibly can to make things clear but he never gets it straight."

You will not be surprised to learn that he brought back the picture of Grandma!

Watch Language Development

As a guide to how much to talk to your child, watch his language development. You know pretty well what words he understands, responds to correctly and uses. These should be the nucleus of your own vocabulary in talking with him—the words you can depend on. You will use others, of course. How would his vocabulary increase unless you did?

Vocabulary building will go faster and easier if you help him with clues to the new words. If you use the name of a new object, show him the object, if you can. If it is a new action word, illustrate it.

A good, rich vocabulary develops through varied experiences. When he sees a bulldozer or a cricket he will want to know what it is. Tell him, but don't smother him with explanations. He will learn more by looking and listening.

Try to keep your sentences almost as short as those the child himself is currently using. Keep remarks down to two or three sentences. If the child wants to know more he will ask.

If You Are Talkative

If you are naturally talkative and find that this does not satisfy you and if there are no older people around that you can talk to, try talking to yourself. Or recite poetry—a fine excuse for learning some that you enjoy—or sing. In those ways you can have a good time without demanding any of your child's attention, unless he cares to listen.

He will very likely be carrying on his own monologues. Some young children chatter pretty steadily as they play, some talk very little. In either case the young child will be talking chiefly to himself. It is a game of matching the word to the thing, language play, not an attempt at communication.

"Get a block. Get a block," says Joey, doing so. "Up on top, up on top." Such speech is self-centered and to answer it is to interrupt. The situation is quite different when the child talks to you or asks questions. Then he shows a need for either information or social exchange. He wants to be talked to.

He may want only a few words to show your interest in him and his activity. He may want real conversation practice. We all know the endless "why" sequence:

"Come and get your coat now, Estelle."

"Why?"

"Because we're going for a walk."

"Why?"

"Well, for fun, and to get the groceries for dinner."

"Why?"

Conversational Exchange

Perhaps Estelle is stalling to prolong her present play. Very likely she just enjoys the conversational exchange and has hit on an easy way to keep it going. It's not likely that she is curious about all those whys. Search for information more often appears in a single question, a pause to think over the answer, then maybe another question, maybe not.

Such a child can absorb more conversation than his less social-minded contemporaries. He can learn the words that go with all sorts of things around the house. He is an excellent candidate for little trips to widen his horizons, accompanied by casual conversation about things he knows and understands. He might even enjoy a tale about a giant in seven-league boots but only because he likes to hear you talking to him! If you want to keep his belief that words mean something, stick to the familiar.

Or of course you may go off into nonsense noises just for fun. "Hey-diddle-diddle" is a comical sound and just about as sensible as the rest of Mother Goose to a modern child. But nonsense has its own hilarious "sense" now and then.

If children are not swamped with words but get them in reasonably small batches so that they can savor and enjoy them, they develop a lovely word sensitivity of their own. One child called ocean breakers "the smash-water" and another, waking before dawn, observed that "the stars clinged on all night long." Words are too lovely, as well as too useful, for us to allow their significance and charm to be lost to our children in the confusion of continual chatter. —*By Rhoda W. Bacmeister*

IF YOUR CHILD
USES BAD LANGUAGE

MOST children discover the delights of using what we call "bad language" somewhere in the process of growing up.

Where do they pick up this inelegant, offensive kind of language? It doesn't take much detective listening to discover that some of it comes from us! Some of it is picked up from other children in the neighborhood. The child who hears daddy using an explosive word or phrase, when he has cut himself while shaving, is likely to try it out himself. Or if the big boy down the street says certain words that sound big and tough, four-year-old Jim is likely to try them out at home, to show how big and tough he is.

Some of it, then, is chiefly imitative, delivered experimentally, without much feeling. Much of this particular kind of "bad language" would fall by the wayside if it were not fixed by the response it receives from shocked and annoyed grownups. The parent who responds with a bang, verbal or otherwise, when his preschool youngster tries out one of the words that he has heard, is likely to succeed in enhancing the value of the word, rather than diminishing its value or importance. What started out as just another word suddenly acquires importance; it becomes something to remember, a weapon to use, an effective teasing tool.

Joking Can Help

Adults subjected to a barrage of such verbiage usually feel helpless as well as annoyed. And yet it can often be somewhat deflected if it is accepted as a joke, laughing *with* it, rather than *at* it, or converting it into legitimate nonsense talk by changing it slightly.

This kind of treatment tends to take the glamour out of teasingly offensive talk. It becomes officially accepted silly talk and is more likely to fade away as new words are discovered. However, don't try this method of diversion by conversion unless it's fun for you. Children are likely to sense it if you find it painful and be confused by your seeming good cheer when you are really disgusted and annoyed.

Some of these words like "stinker," "dummy dope" and "stupid" may be relatively harmless outlets for angry feelings. Whatever their purpose, they are painful to live with, and sometimes it seems as if they will never be outgrown.

What are children trying to tell us when they use these words that irk our ears and patience? One thing they are telling us is that they are feeling big and important and powerful. It is a kind of intoxication with one's self.

Recognize Child's Needs

It is usually at this point that well-meaning parents decide this is about all they can stand, and they bear down with assorted devices of disapproval, ranging from discouraging comments, "That's not nice to say," to mild threats and mouth washing with soap or even spanking. The trouble is that none of these methods works. The words continue to come forth with a blithe lack of concern for the sensitive and condemning ears of parents.

If the need to be and sound important is the chief motivating reason for some tough talk, then what really needs to be done is to give full recognition to the toughness itself. "You really are strong, aren't you? Boy, you can do hard things. You are as tough as a cowboy. It feels good, doesn't it, to be strong like that? It even makes you want to talk tough."

This is not guaranteed to dispel all tough language, but it may diminish the need to try to impress you with the wonderful feeling of bigness and toughness by using certain words.

What about the bathroom variety of language? Probably it has somewhat the same value to four and five-year-olds that slightly risqué stories have to their parents. There is the feeling that there is something slightly wicked and exciting about these words. Certainly the shocked reaction of grownups to them tends to encourage this feeling of wickedness. However, if such language is treated in a somewhat matter-of-fact way, these words lose their charm. Half of the fun is the response they bring—the giggling rejoinder from their age-mates or the shocked disapproval of adults.

Expression of Anger

Some "bad language" expresses attack. It is an expression of anger. "You dummy dope!" or "I'll cut you up and throw you in the garbage," is delivered in anger. Telling him that he shouldn't call his mother such names, that it isn't nice, that it makes her feel bad and so forth—none of these attempts at stopping such talk is likely to meet with much success. Some children may stop for the moment and store away a little slice of guilt because of their wickedness. But most children will continue to express their anger with words even though we find them hard to endure.

Actually this is evidence of a step toward a more mature handling of their angry feelings. They no longer beat at you with fists and feet. They are now able to translate the anger from their muscles to their tongue. Maybe you could talk about it with your young child. "Remember when you were little, how you used to kick and hit when you were angry? Now, you don't need to do that. You still say angry words when you get mad. But when you get bigger maybe you won't need to say them." Or, "I know you get awfully cross at grownups, sometimes. They make you do things you don't like to do. And so you feel like calling them names. The trouble with that is that then they get mad, and that doesn't help. Maybe you could just talk about it, just tell your mother or your teacher what makes you cross and she'll try to help you."

Then there are all the expletives that accompany explosive behavior, the words that daddy says when he's mad or maybe mommy when she drops something. What about them? Some families have made a game of substituting nonsense words that seem just as satisfying.

Use Direct Approach

Most parents have discovered the relative ineffectiveness of soap and warnings about wickedness, although some children may seem to respond to such treatment. Actually many of these children may be carrying on an underground out-of-parents'-earshot practice of forbidden language. It is true also that some grownups swear, and whip their children for imitating them.

We seem to have moved several notches away from this point of view. Now we tend to tell parents to ignore bad language, and it will disappear. But that doesn't always work either. In the first place, we grownups aren't very good at ignoring. We say nothing, do not express our disapproval, and yet they feel it hovering about. This is confusing to children and certainly not helpful.

Let's be honest with them. If we don't like it, let's let them know it. "I get awfully tired of hearing you say those words. I'll be glad when you don't need to say them any more. If you have to say them—then go somewhere else and say them, but not here. I'm tired of them." Such an approach is not condemning—not even wholly prohibitive. It is honest, it is direct. In fact it seems to make the words seem tiresome and not too important.

Don't Be Too Alarmed

Obviously the important thing about the treatment of "bad language" is our attitude toward it. If we label it wicked, and condemn it as something to be punished for and to feel guilty about, we may succeed in sending it underground or in keeping it out of range of our ears so that we may have the illusion that we have stopped it. But it is doubtful that this is the case.

If we accept the fact that children are likely to experiment in this field, as they do in others, and if we do not attach too much importance to it, we are more likely to be successful in helping children to grow out of it. If our feelings are hurt and we look upon bad language as a personal attack or as evidence that we have failed to keep our children pure and good—then we are less likely to be successful in diverting this experimental flow of colorful language into the paths of acceptable, though possibly more drab, adult language.

If we scold or punish, make a child feel that *he* is bad, as well as the words, he is more likely to hold onto them. A sense of humor is more effective than a sense of grimness. And it doesn't injure him to let him know when you are really fed up. In fact he may profit from being informed before that stage arrives. It's possible to be firm and definite without being totally condemning. However, you can be sure that "stinker talk" at four does not indicate that your child is headed for delinquency. And you can also feel confident that the less direct attention is paid to objectionable language, the sooner it will be outgrown.

—By Evelyn Beyer

WHY PLAY IS IMPORTANT

THE primary job of children is to grow—strong and straight, skillful, friendly and competent. The three basic ways they go at it are by eating, sleeping and playing.

If a child doesn't eat or sleep well his parents always worry. They ought to be just as concerned about that "nice quiet" child who just sits around and doesn't seem interested in playing.

Next time you call your youngster and get scarcely a glance because he is busy with his toys, try to realize that he's busy playing—doing something that is important, not only because he enjoys it but because it helps him grow. When he's in the middle of it, it is as hard to accept interruption cheerfully as it would be if he were in the middle of a nap or a dish of ice cream.

The essential thing that distinguishes play from other activities is that it is self-directed, and as we watch children of different ages play it is interesting to see how a child's own impulses keep him busy learning what he needs to learn at his particular age.

Curiosity in Babyhood

The baby of a little more than a year trots around the house almost every waking moment. He's going places incessantly—not so much to get there as to practice the process of going—for locomotion is his current problem. He gets into everything, too. It will take several years to take the edge off his insatiable curiosity about the way things look, feel and taste, and whether they will roll or perhaps break with a lovely crash. He wasn't born knowing and he has to find out.

That is why so much of the play of the earliest years centers about learning what can be done with one's own body as well as about the surrounding world. Social play begins early, too, but doesn't usually occupy a large part of the child's time until he is three or four. At first, Johnny is going to investigate, manipulate and experiment, collecting a great store of information: balls bounce if you throw them, but teacups break, and mother doesn't like that!

A youngster is going to learn not only to walk but to run, climb and jump, swing and balance, hop on one foot, skip, throw and catch a ball and jump rope. Besides these big-muscle accomplishments, he will begin, toward the end of the preschool years, to get easy control of finger muscles so that he enjoys play that requires delicate, careful motions. He will tackle each of these stunts when nerves and muscles are ready, just as he started walking. He knows, and no one else can know quite as well as he, just which of his powers is crying out for exercise and development at any given time. This is one reason why it is important for the child to choose his own play activities. Gradually he learns to know what it is that he needs and wants and to have some idea of how to get it. That sounds simple, but it is one of the hard lessons of life. Only by trying for what we think we want can we learn whether it really satisfies our needs. How often we are wrong! Only with practice in free choice can a child learn to distinguish his real needs from his fleeting impulses.

Building Self-Respect

One has to learn about success and failure, too. Success in realizing his own purposes builds a child's self-respect and courage for further adventure as nothing else can. Praise and appreciation from others also increase self-confidence; but we sometimes stress this too much and make children overly dependent upon adult approval.

Bonnie is a look-what-I-did child. No picture that she paints, no success in climbing is complete for her until she has got an adult to admire it. Her faith in herself requires continual propping up. It has little inherent strength because she has been overdirected. She has not had enough experience in choosing her activities herself and enjoying her success simply because she has been able to do what she wanted to do.

Now look at Pat sitting back on his heels to admire his finished garage of blocks. For a moment he just looks, and then almost tenderly tries the door to see if it will open as he planned. It will, and he smiles. He doesn't need anyone's praise, though he may like to see his pleasure reflected. But his own sense of fulfillment has deep integrity. The child's own feeling about what he has done is the touchstone by which we must judge his success or failure; no external standard is valid.

Values in Failure

Success helps build strong character but so can failure, for it, too, is a part of the world that children have to learn to deal with. Sometimes people won't let you play the way you want to; sometimes there are limits set by the nature of things.

Parents can do much toward helping a child face such facts honestly but without undue discouragement. Of course, you may solve a problem for him by giving help or advice. That is fine as long as you don't cheat him into thinking he did it all himself. But sometimes there is no answer. Still, sympathy and starting on new enterprises take the bitterness out of defeat just as admiration adds a shine to success.

The relationship of play to social life is very close; the child must get acquainted with people as well as with things. Even a baby likes imitative and responsive play, although most of his play remains individual until he is about three. At that point he discovers the possibility of shared purpose, of planning with someone else, and real social play begins.

From then on it increases in importance until having "nobody to play with" is equivalent to having "nothing to do." That does not become an acute problem during the preschool years. There is still a lot of spontaneous, solitary play, the amount differing according to temperament as well as age.

Pretend Play

This being somebody (or something) other than himself is one of the most valuable and versatile kinds of play. In other forms of expression like talking, painting, singing or block-building a child is limited to one form of expression; but he throws his whole self into pretend play. He uses mind, voice, muscles and miscellaneous properties. He just *is* the part. That gives him complete freedom in working out his emotions, happy or unhappy.

Edith and Agnes have lined up the chairs and are going on a train trip with their dolls. Both have had that experience and loved it. They want to savor every detail again, to remember and enjoy. This time they will be the responsible mothers.

But what about the youngsters who insist on beating their children, punishing their pupils, extracting teeth, operating on their tummies, shooting each other and going to funerals? Not many sweet memories there, are there?

There may actually be, if the experiences they stem from were unreal enough to the child. A flurry of flying hoofs and barking guns across the television screen may be pleasantly exciting and carry very little sense of danger to some children, except in threatening voices. Those any child recognizes. But the men who fell down—well, they just fell down. Youngsters do that all the time. Similarly, a funeral procession may be just a parade dramatically headed by someone said to be "dead." If you watch children play, it is easy to see whether distressing scenes have any emotional meaning to them.

Emotional Release

Usually these scenes are chosen because they do. The child who has been scolded or punished would like to be on the other end of the deal. He could get rid of a lot of resentment that way. Almost every child feels bossed about and unfairly treated at times. That explains the ill-tempered and domineering teachers and parents who appear so persistently in children's play about school and home, as well as the ruthless doctors and dentists.

The aggressors in these scenes of violence are more easily understood than their victims. Sometimes, of course, children take turns with the roles, but not always. Some like to be the victims. Suppose that you really are afraid of the dentist. It could be rather fun to go to a pretend dentist who won't really hurt at all, to yell and carry on as much as you like, and to know that the whole thing is a joke. The familiarity gained by acting out frightening scenes as a game makes them a little less terrible. Repressed emotions are released, and escape from the mock danger gives a delightful thrill.

Besides, in play one is allowed complete freedom of expression. You can say and do all the things you dared not in reality. When the teacher screams, "Sit down and be quiet, Bobby Lowe," Bobby jumps up and yells, "No I won't you nasty ol' thing!"

The shrieks of laughter that follow represent both release of emotion and reassurance that it is all a joke. Often children feel deeply-hidden fear and guilt about their rages and hates of parents and teachers. Such feelings seem to threaten the basic relationship of love and protection that children know they need. In dramatic play, however, they can safely let it all out in clowning.

An Aid to Understanding

Pretending to be someone else is one of the best ways of understanding that person. Matilda who is putting her obstreperous friend to bed is learning how exasperating it can be to have her keep jumping up. Pretending is a way of testing the child's social hunches. He guesses, tries it out, and often learns something quite unexpected.

By the time they are four or five most children can "feel" themselves into a part and maintain it long enough for such learning. In almost all of these activities appropriate materials play a significant part and parents are the ones to supply them. (See articles on selecting toys in section on Home Management.)

If play is truly self-directed activity, as we have said, then freedom is of its very essence. When an adult organizes it, the real play spirit is lost and with it most of play's value. There have to be rules as to what may be used for play and where and, often, when or how.

However, within common-sense limits a child can still have much latitude for choosing his own activities and making his own decisions. Don't be distressed by the unconventional uses to which he puts things, unless they involve danger. Exploring, experimenting and investigating keep a child's mind active, alert and interested.

Encourage Social Play

Encourage social play, too, even if there is a lot of squabbling involved. Children have to find out for themselves how to get along together, and although we may help out with suggestions here as in other play situations, we must not try to solve all their problems for them.

Often a word of encouragement is all it takes to help a child persist in some difficult project he is about to abandon. But we must be careful not to push if he really wants to quit. If he struggles on merely to please us he isn't playing any more. The joy has gone out of it and he is working for fear of not meeting our standards.

If we give our children well chosen play materials, if they have companions their own age and are free to play in any way they choose, provided it is not dangerous, we can be fairly sure that their play experiences will contribute to their wholesome development. Their play will grow more and more diverse, ingenious and sociable, and they will grow with it. They will develop strong, capable muscles, ability to solve their own problems and delight in the company of friends. They will learn a lot about things and have endless fun.

—By Rhoda W. Bacmeister

CREATIVE PLAY
YOUR CHILD WILL ENJOY

SEASONED mothers know that the best answer to "What can I do now?" is to produce materials for creative play of one kind or another. Making things holds a preschooler's interest, helps him release that surging energy and gives him a great sense of achievement. There are always blocks, construction toys and materials, paints, crayons, scissors, pastes and cooking and water play. But beyond these standbys, mothers often run out of ideas for things to do.

In the following list of suggestions, each activity has been tested by a number of mothers and their preschoolers. Each requires only simple and inexpensive equipment. They should provide some of those shared experiences of work and pleasure that are such a rewarding part of family life. Moreover, some of them may result in delightful presents for your children's Christmas giving.

Mosaic pictures. Have your child fill in with mucilage a design he has drawn on cardboard or heavy paper. The design is "colored" by sprinkling rice, dried peas, lentil beans, sand, "glitter"—anything handy and stickable —over the mucilage, and shaking off the excess.

Dyeing. Dye easy-to-handle pieces of old sheets by dipping them into tints that do not require hot water. A flapping line of tinted strips to watch from the window will buoy the house-bound heart of any ailing youngster. Four and five-year-olds usually enjoy tie-dyeing. Tie bunched-up pieces of material with string before dyeing. When dry the cloth has an interesting pattern. Patterns can be varied by tying in different ways and using different types and thicknesses of string.

Mobiles. Keep a big box into which you can put all kinds of spare and suitable materials for mobiles—figures cut from magazines and pasted on cardboard, seashells, lobster claws, small tin cans and cookie cutters (with no sharp edges), giant paper clips, painted spools, wooden beads. Let your child choose from the box what he wants to hang up. A coat hanger is an easy thing from which to hang objects. Black thread in varying lengths to add variety to the designs can be used to tie the things to the hanger. You'll probably have to help out with the balancing. For Christmastime beautiful mobiles can be made by folding foil paper into fan shapes or let your child snip snowflake designs out of it, then tie and hang them from hangers.

Books. A child's drawings can be collected in a scrapbook. Cut-out pictures pasted on uniform sheets can be sewed or stapled into book form. Let your child select the theme and title for his book and dictate the text. He can design the cover, too—making his own drawings, cutting out his own pictures.

Potato printing. Cut a large potato in half and let your child outline a very simple design (a triangle or square, raindrop or leaf shape) on one of the flat surfaces. To a depth of about a quarter-inch, cut away the extraneous portions so the design is left as a raised surface—as in a rubber stamp. Fold a piece of absorbent cloth into a square and soak it with showcard color to make an ink pad. The design is then inked and stamped on paper with a soft surface. Tissue paper can be decorated and used for gift wrappings.

Book jackets. A five-year-old can make a book jacket as a present—maybe for his father. A montage of magazine illustrations glued onto heavy wrapping paper, then lightly varnished over for strength and durability, makes an attractive jacket.

Puzzles. Four and five-year-olds can paste magazine pictures, photographs, their own drawings on cardboard and then cut them into large jigsaw puzzle pieces.

Plaster of Paris. Plaster of Paris (a few cents a pound at your hardware store) begins to harden immediately when it is mixed with water, so have all your materials ready beforehand. The plaster should be mixed to about the consistency of pancake batter. Little children love to make plaques by pressing a hand or foot or some object into the hardening plaster. To prevent the plaster from sticking, oil the object whose impression you're making.

Bright-colored objects (beads, glass, broken plastic objects without sharp edges) can be arranged on the bottom of a paper plate and plaster poured over them. When the plate is pulled away, the design is fixed in the plaster. Hanger tabs can be glued to the back of the dried plaque and it can be painted or shellacked for permanence.

Table decorations. Holidays, parties and special family occasions provide a variety of themes for decorations. Children can make place cards, decorate paper napkins, arrange centerpieces, even make placemats. (See *Weaving*.) Little pipe-cleaner or toothpick-and-gumdrop figures add to the fun.

Stuffed toys. Young children enjoy stuffing an old silk stocking with snippets of rag—making snakes, dolls, animals—whatever fancy dictates.

Stringing. All kinds of materials can be strung on heavy thread, twine or fishing line—painted spools and seeds, pine cones, seed pods and acorns.

Weaving. Three and four-year-olds can weave on simple looms or chicken wire using strips of bright cloth. Since little children can't weave in and out in a uniform way, they achieve striking effects by their choice and placing of color.

Many five-year-olds can make paper placemats from construction paper. Cut construction paper into even one-half-inch strips and let your child choose his own color combinations. When he is through weaving help him give the mats two coats of clear shellac.

Decorative trees. All kinds of delightful trees can be made from branches tucked securely into pots filled with sand or stones. A cookie tree can be fixed for a child's party. A bird's Christmas tree decorated with suet, seeds and other bird treats can be put outdoors.

Papier mâché. Decorative animals, puppet heads, tunnels for a rack layout are among the things that preschool children can make out of papier mâché. Tear newspapers into tiny bits and soak for several days in water. When they're thoroughly wet and soggy, mix them with wallpaper paste according to directions on the package. The mixture should then have the consistency of soft modeling clay—easy for a child to spread over a basic mold.

"Rube Goldbergs." Taking an old clock apart is heaven for almost any child. Even some three-year-olds like to use a small screwdriver. Older children can carry the project further and nail the clock parts on a board. Strings and colored rubber bands can be used to connect the parts, or nails can be driven into a board and an intricate design made by connecting them with colored rubber bands.

Making a farm. If you have an old table in the cellar or attic or any other out-of-the-way place, your child can create a whole farm by covering the table with sand or mud, planting it with grass seed or different "crops," and shaping hills, valleys, streams, lakes. Little twigs make fine trees. Houses, barns and silos can be constructed out of cardboard.

Crystals. Put a piece of porous rock in a flat dish. The "rock" may be a piece of broken flower pot or brick or any unglazed earthenware. Make a solution of 3 tablespoons each of blueing, salt and water, plus 1 tablespoon of ammonia. Pour the solution into the dish, letting part of the rock stick up above the surface. Let stand overnight, and the next morning the unsubmerged portion of the "rock" will be covered with beautiful crystals.

Woodwork. A three-year-old can often begin to manage a saw and hammer. A soft board, very large nails and a mallet are good equipment to start with. Four-year-olds can build things. Spools make good wheels with dowels for axles. Old blocks are as useful as scraps from the lumberyard. Pine is the most versatile wood to begin with.

Most of the projects suggested above require a certain amount of parental preparation and supervision. For rushed hours, however, every mother needs a stock of ideas for independent play. Here are some ideas:

Indoor sandbox. Dump a large bag of salt on a table spread with newspaper, fetch a funnel and a sifter and you have an indoor sandbox to delight your preschooler for an hour or more.

Water play. Always engrossing, water play takes on added fascination when the water is tinted with vegetable dyes. A length of hose and some small plastic cups add to the fun.

Play dough. A child who wants to "cook like Mommy" when Mommy is too busy to supervise can be happily diverted to making cookies, pies, cakes or anything he wants to make—with play dough. For a smooth, malleable material, mix one cup of flour and one cup of salt with enough water to give it the texture of soft clay. His creation can be painted the next day, or the dough can be tinted in the making by adding vegetable dye.

Paper bags and cartons. The return home from a weekly shopping trip, often zero hour in a home with preschoolers, can be saved by paper bag play. Cut three snips for eyes and mouth in an inverted bag and your child has a mask he can decorate and wear. When he tires of that, let him hop around in a giant-size bag, as in a potato sack race. A carton large enough to hold a small child becomes a train, boat or airplane. Some small ones we know used to spend hours playing tiptop over. Procedure—rock your carton-boat until it dumps you out on the rug, shriek with laughter, climb back in and do it again.

Bath salts. Dump a large box of Epsom salts into your biggest mixing bowl or dishpan. Shake in a few drops of cologne and vegetable color. Then let your preschooler mix with his hands. The resulting product will be fragrant pastel bath salts which will make thoroughly acceptable Christmas or birthday presents. The mixing itself is fun, and once it's finished, a preschooler will enjoy filling small plastic bags with cupfuls of the mixture. Later, when you are less rushed, you can tie each bag with a ribbon.

—By Elizabeth F. Stonorov and Margaret H. Bacon

WATER PLAY

A GROUP of investigators made a three-year study of nursery school and kindergarten activities. Bent on discovering exactly how play helps children grow and develop, they found that the cheapest and most valuable medium of all—water—has an amazing versatility in the child's small world. Not only is it virtually unrivaled in keeping the youngster busy and occupied; it can also be used in a dozen different ways to help lay the foundation for a healthy personality in the years to come.

The young child frequently feels overwhelmed by a world that is big and perplexing. He needs to bolster his ego and prove that he can master something in his environment. The one medium that even the most helpless youngster can manage is water, provided his mother or teacher doesn't constantly restrain his urge to splash and spill. The beauty of water play is that it can be geared to varying levels of development. The toddler derives his sense of power from patting or stirring the water. The three or four-year-old gets a kick out of blowing a mountain of bubbles. At five the same child will see himself as a dauntless sea captain, steering his ship across the stormy sea of his tub or outdoor play pool.

Water to the Rescue

Susan, age five, grew furious because she couldn't put a simple jigsaw puzzle together. She swept the pieces to the floor and burst into tears.

"How about a tea party for your dolls?" her mother suggested. "I'll get the water for the teapot and you set the table."

After half an hour of pouring "tea" back and forth from pot to cups and filling a doll's nursing bottle for her "baby," Sue was happily relaxed and feeling sure of herself. Before dinnertime she had mastered the jigsaw puzzle and said proudly, "It's easy."

Water-power came to the rescue. It revived self-esteem and washed away feelings of frustration. It's good for removing more than dirt!

No child can go through the years of basic training without feeling angry at the people who hold him down and make him conform to the ways of civilization. Let him express his peeves and grudges in water play. Shooting water pistols, playing with a hose and wringing out clothes help drain off the natural destructive impulses in harmless ways. What is more, many a tense or hard-to-handle youngster will get so much out of his system in a half-hour of water play that he'll surprise you by suddenly wanting to cooperate. The timid child, too, benefits immensely. Water is so common and compliant that it holds no threat for him. As a consequence he may be enticed out of himself and his fears.

A Versatile Activity

Such is the versatility of water that it can tone down the tense child as well as stimulate the inhibited one. You've probably discovered yourself that a warm bath is a good answer to a child's convulsive crying, temper or extreme excitement. The best way to handle this problem is not simply to dump the child in the tub but to supply pieces of wood or boats or other bath toys or bubble-bath crystals. Then enter into the fun for awhile. Activities or things to do in the tub work better than plain soaking because they take the child's mind off his troubles.

A youngster does not need to be immersed in water to experience its healing effects. Pouring from pitcher to cup at the kitchen sink or in the sandbox, mixing interesting water colors, dabbing with finger paints on a piece of wet paper all have a relaxing influence on turbulent emotions.

Water play is soothing because it enables a growing youngster of four or five to recapture some of the former joys of infancy. When the struggle to become grownup gets too much for him, he welcomes the chance to be bathed with loving hands, to splash without being scolded, to play calmly without having anyone urge him to "hurry up now."

A Bridge to Creative Projects

Many a child who is too cramped in muscle or emotion to paint or model with clay can be eased into these projects through water play. Encouraged by his triumphs with bubble pipe and straw, such a child then feels more confident about undertaking more advanced forms of play. Sometimes a youngster who has been rushed into doing things that are too hard for him will betray a need to regress to water play by diluting his paint with huge quantities of water and will content himself with smearing the mixture about aimlessly. In these instances, it is usually wise to switch him over to water play for awhile, saving the so-called "creative" achievements for some later time.

The reverse is true of Ellen. This little girl constantly messes with her food or knocks over her milk. But after half an hour of unrestrained water play, her urge to turn everything topsy-turvy seems to be satisfied. At the next meal she eats more neatly.

Even children who are disorganized and restless are often able to spend as much as an hour at the sink or tub. In fact, for many this is a valuable first lesson in concentration. Because water play demands so little skill and puts so little pressure on the child, it is particularly valuable for children who are very young either in years or in development. Unlike the more demanding occupations such as modeling or building with blocks, it is not associated with practice and achievement. It doesn't put the child to the test and therefore won't keep him on edge.

All children feel the need to explore but this urge is constantly being curbed. Food is to be eaten, not messed with. Mud is to be avoided, not handled. Yet children must explore and experiment to their heart's content if they are to learn about the world and feel at home in it.

Satisfying Experimental Urge

A few minutes of water play every day will go far toward satisfying these young scientists, for it gives the intimate and enjoyable contact with one of the basic substances of life. Floating boats and rinsing clothes develops their sense of touch and teaches them how material things behave. When they bring clay, sand or soap into their water play they discover the nature of these materials as well.

Everything from soup pots to nut shells can be utilized in providing simple implements for indoor water play. Sponges for squeezing, bubble pipes and straws for blowing, an old coffee pot for pouring, rags for wiping—all these provide hours of fun and happy absorption with the magic fluid that flows from the water tap. Children like to "paint" their blackboards, the windows or the tile bathroom walls with two-inch paint brushes and water.

Some mothers complain of the mess this sort of play makes and others are disturbed because their children got too wet for comfort and their own peace of mind. But you can always drape the youngster in a plastic poncho or even a large bath towel. As for the floor, let the youngster help mop it up. It's less important than his healthy emotional development and if water is the worst thing that ever gets spilled on it, you're lucky.

If you're overinclined to worry about the mess, remember that the little girl who is allowed to wash the tile walls of the bathroom will be less likely later to daub your favorite Sheraton chair a gaudy green. And the boy who sails his boats in the bathtub won't be so eager to float them in the puddles on the street.

Giving your youngsters a splashing good time in the preschool years helps keep them joyous and enthusiastic about life.

—By Robert M. Goldenson, Ph.D., and Constance J. Foster

EASING THE ADJUSTMENT TO SCHOOL LIFE

GETTING a child ready for school is in good part getting him ready to start his life as an individual outside of the family. Many of the things you do to prepare him you would want to do even if he weren't going to school because they are part of his growing up. But school is a very clearly defined step, and one he needs help in taking. Letting him know what to expect and giving him certain experiences make the change smoother for him, for you and for the school.

To a youngster, probably the most disturbing aspect of starting school life is that he has to leave mother and stay with a stranger—moreover, a stranger who will not be devoting her attention entirely to him. The child who has been left with baby sitters, relatives or neighbors has learned that other adults can take good care of him. Just through casual talk about school, you can help your youngster understand that his teacher will be such a person, even though she will be taking care of many children at once.

Getting along with those other children is another big step for the beginner; so naturally your child is off to a better start if he's already had some group experience—in neighborhood play, at a library preschool story hour, nursery school or a day-care center. He'll know something about give-and-take, sharing and playing outdoors with other children.

Visit the School

It's a good idea to visit the school with your child sometime before register-ing. Let him get a good look around that big strange building. Introduce him to his teacher if you know who she will be.

Some youngsters are unhappy in their first school weeks simply because they can't play as well as the other children with the materials made available to them. A child who has never before wielded a paint brush, who doesn't know what to do with a handful of crayons or a chunk of clay, can feel pretty strange. So the variety of play materials and activities you give your boy or girl before school makes for that much more ease and comfort. Paints and crayons, clay, blocks and building sets, music, singing, playing toy in-struments, dancing—all these help.

By the time he is ready for school, a youngster should be able to take care of himself in certain ways. He should be familiar with safety rules, so he can get to school and home without being afraid and without worrying you. He should know about traffic signals, about cars turning corners, crossing lanes, police officers and safety patrolers. Emphasize to him the importance of crossing only at corners, of staying on the sidewalk in the city and, if necessary, walking against traffic on roads in the country. You may want to explain that he should never accept a ride with a stranger. Walk with him to school and back a few times, either before he starts or for the first couple of days. Either he or you will want to find out which other children in the neighbor-hood he might be able to go with, but be sure he knows himself what he's doing. He should be able to tell promptly, when asked, his name, address, telephone number and his father's first name. Some parents like to fasten identification cards to the inside of jackets or pockets.

Self-Sufficiency Needed

A school usually expects, reasonably, that your child will be able to go to the toilet unassisted, wash his hands properly, put on and take off his coat or jacket and hang it up where it belongs. Make sure he recognizes his own outer garments, but put name labels into his school clothes just in case. His clothes should be comfortable—with plenty of pockets—and simple to put on and fasten. No teacher has time to help every child with buttons, shoelaces, zippers. His rubber boots should be big enough so he can slip them on easily himself.

You want your child to be and stay healthy and so does the school. It is im-perative that he have a medical checkup before he enters school, so he'll be in shape to take on all the newness. Besides, in his first two years at school he'll be exposed to all the childhood diseases. Ask about the need for further immunization against smallpox, whooping cough and diphtheria. If he's never had the vaccination and shots, the school will require them before he enters. See, too, about polio shots.

You might start well before school opens to establish a bedtime and morning routine. A five or six-year-old needs ten to twelve hours of sleep a night and he may need a daytime nap, besides. Be fair about the morning rush. Many mothers don't call their youngsters early enough for them to wash, brush their teeth, dress, comb their hair—and have time left to eat and get to school unhurriedly.

You want your child to enjoy school. Just about one of the most important influences on whether he will or not is the family's attitude toward the school. When you talk about it in his presence, emphasize the pleasant aspects. Don't let his older brother's or sister's griping frighten him. Give your child the preparation he needs, give him confidence in himself and an encouraging picture of what is ahead and school will begin for him as the wonderful experience it should be.
—*By Merabe Marshall*

IS YOUR CHILD READY
FOR FIRST GRADE?

TIMMY S. was 4 years, 9 months old when he entered kindergarten—
a small, bright happy child. But he had a hard time. He couldn't draw
very well—it was hard for him to hold the crayons. He had a difficult time
with his clothes—he couldn't button his coat, he couldn't tell his right boot
from his left boot. He was used to having his mother do all these things for
him. Timmy wasn't interested in saying rhymes or poems with the group; he
talked baby talk all during the school year. Most of the time he liked being the
baby of the play family. He was absent for a long stretch when his mother had
her second baby and later he seemed to be sick a good deal. His test record on
readiness was low.

Toward the end of the school year, adding all these things up, his teacher
recommended that Timmy would benefit by spending additional time developing in kindergarten. His parents were incensed at the thought that their first-
born male child was not "bright" enough to "pass" kindergarten. So he
went on to first grade and ended that year definitely having to repeat.

Each spring, it is necessary to take stock of the development of each kinder-
gartner, to sort out those who can meet the challenge of first grade from the
ones like Timmy who need more time. Each spring parents are informed of
the school's recommendations. And each spring teachers face the realization
that too few parents know and understand what is meant by "not ready."

Aspects of "Readiness"

"Readiness" means ready socially, emotionally, physically and intellectually.
Development in these four areas does not always occur simultaneously. Each
child grows at his own rate and pattern. When this pattern shows these four
areas have begun to be fairly level, we can safely say, "This child is ready."

Billy will be 5 years and 1 month when he enters kindergarten. He is an
only child. He has played very little with children his own age, his mother
being his constant companion. She has spent a great deal of time reading to
Billy, stimulating his inherent curiosity, and she has kept him supplied with a
variety of play materials.

Larry, too, will be 5 years and 1 month when he enters kindergarten.
He is one of five children. His mother and father both work and Larry is cared
for during the day by neighbors and his older brother. He is independent,
self-reliant. His interests are primarily those stimulated by watching television
and going to the movies.

You can see that these two children, although the same chronological age, are at widely different levels in their own development. Broadly speaking, Billy will need particularly to develop in social and emotional areas and become independent of his mother, and Larry will most need help in developing interests in the real world about him to stimulate his intellectual growth. You cannot expect that these two children will develop at the same rate and you might find at the end of the kindergarten year that one of them has not developed enough in all areas to handle first grade requirements successfully. Placing that child in a situation for which he is not ready, not sufficiently mature, may result in harm that will hinder the rest of his scholastic life.

Assuring Success in Reading

First grade is a challenge to the child. It is in this grade that he makes his first attempt to put meanings to written symbols—in short, he begins to learn to read. It is of extreme importance that this first attempt be a conscious success for the child. Dr. Gertrude H. Hildreth, professor and author of many textbooks on education and readiness, and co-author of the Metropolitan Readiness Tests, states: "The first steps in learning reading or any other skills should be easy enough so that the child has a feeling of success from the very beginning." The unready child who is placed in first grade has two strikes against him.

Dr. Emmett A. Betts, author of many textbooks, estimates that from 8 to 40 per cent of the children in first grade fail to be promoted, the average being somewhere from 25 to 33 per cent.

Freddy was one of these casualties, but he need not have been. He was a bright little fellow, 4 years 10 months when he entered kindergarten, with interests on an older level. But Freddy didn't know how to play with children. He wanted their attention and resorted to the most eccentric ways of getting it. He spent much time talking to himself during story time, but in a gibberish only he could understand. He seemed systematically to do the opposite of any given direction. The children started to call him "Goofy Freddy." Toward the end of the school year he began to play actively with the children, but he was 6 months too late. Their playing was on their own pattern: fire truck, destroyer, Davy Crockett or Superman. Freddy's playing was to knock over everything that the other children had built and incur their righteous wrath.

What Can Happen

Freddy could not sit still; he was tense and jerky in his movements. In the spring, with these and more pertinent observation notes collected during the year showing the pattern of his behavior, his teacher recommended that more time in kindergarten would benefit Freddy. But his mother said he was too bright for that. What would their friends and relatives think if Freddy failed in kindergarten? So Freddy went on to first grade. Since he was not ready for it when he started, he had to repeat a year's work and by now is building up a dangerous resentment of the whole school system.

You ask, "What can I do about my child's readiness for first grade?"

1. You can see to it that your child is provided with kindergarten experience.

2. You can supplement this experience at home.

3. You can remember that waiting to be ready is no disgrace.

4. You can ask your school to provide a readiness test at the end of the kindergarten year.

5. You can respect your school's recommendation based on observation and your child's readiness score. The daily observations of the kindergarten teacher measure your child in his emotional and social growth. For kindergarten is just what its name implies: it is the garden for the small ones in which they learn about living with a group, learn to feel safe with an adult outside their own family, their new daytime mother-teacher, and learn to share this mother-teacher with twenty or more other children. The readiness tests measure a child's abilities in specific physical and mental areas. For instance, they measure his ability to see things and discriminate between and among different shapes; his ability to hear sounds and discriminate between them; his natural information about things with which he is acquainted; his ability to hold a crayon or pencil and make it do his bidding.

Consider Child's Development

If a child with normal eyesight cannot yet see the difference between and among shapes, it is not his fault and it is not poor teaching—it is simply because his eyes have not yet developed enough to handle this work. If a child with normal hearing cannot yet detect the difference between and among sounds, he is not stupid—he simply has not developed enough to concentrate on what he hears. If a child cannot yet hold a pencil or crayon in his small hand and make it do what he wants, his muscles have simply not developed enough to move with coordination.

A gardener does not transplant a seedling to the flower bed simply because the seedling has been in the flat a prescribed length of time. He transplants when the seedling is ready. And so it should be with the child. Sadly, in too many instances, the kindergarten child is transplanted too early to the mature flower bed.

—*By Margaret M. Hall*

LEARNING TO GET DRESSED

MOTHER tries to help the two-year-old put on shoes or coat, an operation far beyond the skill of the small child, yet Susie jerks away insisting, "Me! Me!" and resents mother's attempt to hasten the dressing process by doing it herself.

It is a hopeful sign, this strong urge for independence. Even while she laments the loss of time, the halfway results or perhaps the temper that Susie displays when she is thwarted, mother is pleased and proud that Susie wants to help herself.

This independence, which is so strong an instinct, is a delicate plant which needs encouragement and understanding to survive. Learning to dress oneself requires a great deal of mother's time. If she is in a hurry in the mornings, it may seem far easier to set Susie on her lap and shove her arms into each sleeve of her shirt or force the small legs into the proper openings in her training pants or overalls. Letting Susie experiment for herself takes just too much time and besides, the baby may get everything on wrong so the job will have to be done over, or she may get chilled working so slowly.

The difficulty is that soon Susie will take it for granted that mother helps her dress, and later on when mother decides that she is quite old enough to put on her own clothes Susie may bring them to her mother, complaining, "I can't! You help me!"

Encourage Self-Help

For this reason it is worth the time and patience it takes to give this desire for self-help every possible encouragement from the first moment it shows itself. It is hard for a parent to know just when and how much to help and how much freedom to give. Perhaps, for a time, Susie will be content to let mother get the heel of her sock in the right place after she has pulled it on as best she can. Or mother can show her how to loosen the laces of her shoe and pull out the tongue so that she can perch it on her toes, after which mother can give the final push that will get it on.

From the time the baby is nine or ten months old he will delight in pulling off his own socks, although mother may need to slip them down over the heel and show him where to put his hand to pull. When he tries to push his shoes off by rubbing one foot against the other, mother can show him where to put his spread hand at the back and help him to push, after loosening the laces as far as possible, and then she can hold the open shoes in front of him and show him how to tuck the socks inside before she places them neatly, side by side.

Later, instead of taking off her shirt or nightie top in one swift movement which the baby cannot follow, she can untie the strings or undo the buttons, slip her arms from the sleeves, and encourage her to pull it off over her own head. Gradually, Susie will be learning the technique of undressing and will want to try to help herself.

By the time Susie is a year old, she will enjoy shoving her own arms into the proper openings in her shirt or coat while mother holds it for her. About this time the way can be paved for Susie to help herself even further if mother dresses her while she is sitting down on a bed or bath table instead of holding her on her lap or slipping her overalls on while she is standing up.

Establish a Routine

Susie will become used to seeing her clothes laid out before her with the legs of training pants or overalls spread out ready to pull on. Mother can help her hold them at the proper place at the top while she shows her how to put first one leg and then the other into the leg holes, and then she can help Susie pull up the overall legs until her feet stick out before she stands to let mother pull them up.

It will help if, from the beginning, mother makes a point of going through the dressing routine always in the same order—putting on first the shirt (right arm and then left), then the panties, the dress and so forth. Every movement which will be needed in getting dressed should become so familiar to the child that there will be no confusion in Susie's mind as to what comes next when she gets ready to try it.

The two or three-year-old may be able to get most of his clothes on alone, except for buttoning and tying shoes, but he will still need mother's help in spreading everything out before him in the proper order. A polo shirt or pullover sweater should be laid face down with the bottom toward the child so he can hold it by the nearest edge and pull it over his head without getting it on backwards. Shoes should be placed alongside the proper feet. It may even help to mark one shoe with a spot of colored paint on the sole to help the youngster to know which shoe goes on which foot. A shoehorn, kept in a special place near the dressing corner, will help the older child get his shoes on more easily.

Simple Clothing Best

Clothing which is designed for self-help will make the dressing process simpler and will make it possible for the child to get most of his clothes on without running to mother for help. Shirts and dresses which have small buttons are almost impossible for the little child to manage alone. Short or long pants with elastic waistbands are possible for a child to put on alone, while overalls with straps must be fastened by mother.

Even when the child has learned all the skills that go into putting on each separate item of clothing, he still may not be old enough to carry through the entire process alone. When he has learned to button large buttons, he may want to do one or two and leave the rest for mother. Just because he can manage one with effort is no reason to insist that he take over the tedious task of doing them all. Or perhaps he can get practice putting on shoes by getting only one on by himself until he is so expert that he can handle both with ease.

When the child is still older, he will be able to manage the business of turning twisted clothes right side out and spreading them out for himself, but until he does, mother can help him learn by doing each thing slowly and deliberately in front of him, showing him how she puts her hand in and where to grasp the sleeve to turn it right side out, how to find the label which marks the inside of the shirt back so he can tell when it is right.

He will learn to lace his shoes and pull the laces tight, coming to mother only to have them tied. And, finally, he will be able to get his arm into the right sleeve of his coat and learn how to reach over his shoulder to hold it while he slips the other arm in—a difficult trick for a preschooler!

Patient Demonstration

Each step in the process of dressing requires patient demonstration, for what grownups do easily from long practice must be mastered slowly, a bit at a time, by the baby. Mother must move slowly and make sure the child understands each step. There is no instinct to tell him where to hold his overshoes so he can most easily shove his feet into them or how to hang up his pajamas, just behind the collar, so they will not slide off the hook.

After giving the child all the help and visual demonstration she can, mother must be willing to let him exert his independence in trying to dress by himself and she should not be too critical of the results. If his mother is too critical of the job he has done independently, the child may become discouraged. For the two-year-old to get his coat on at all, even if it is on backwards, is a real achievement of which he is justly proud. He will resent it if mother insists on undoing what he has done in order to redo it properly herself.

The child's clothes should be kept on hooks and in drawers that he can easily reach, and he should be given a certain amount of freedom in selecting his outfit for the day. Here again, when his choice of colors or combinations is not what mother would have selected, it will take discipline for mother to refrain from criticizing. She can avoid, to some extent, having to change the child's choice by keeping his good clothes in another place. Everyday play clothes, underwear and socks, however, should be in their own drawers, and even a very small child can get a sense of responsibility from selecting his clothes, putting dirty socks or underwear in the hamper at night and laying out clean ones for the next day, and even from helping mother put away the freshly ironed laundry that belongs to him.

It takes time and a great deal of patience to help Tommy or Susie acquire all the small skills of self-help. But the hours spent in encouraging self-reliance pay off richly in the end. —By Barbara Leonard Reynolds

MAKE LEARNING TO READ EASY

IN the controversy over teaching children to read, something fundamental is being overlooked. Some say the teaching methods are all wrong, others that standards for reading ability are lower than they used to be. Still others blame reading failures on crowded school conditions or on "the laziness of children these days." Then you come across an article that declares children are reading better than they ever have before.

One clear conclusion, though, is that some children learn to read well, while others do not. It is also clear that low intelligence is not the only reason for the failures. Another reason—the one being overlooked—is what kind of preparation a child has had for reading.

Reading is a skill, and a difficult one to acquire.

Is there anything parents can do to help their children acquire it? There are many things—and they do not involve home teaching or a course in pedagogy. Yet they are as essential to learning to read as proper diet and rest are to good health.

What Is Reading Aptitude?

An aptitude for reading is made up of capacities that fall within the bounds of normal ability. Thus, children with average intelligence, normal eyesight, hearing and speech have the native ability to learn to read very well. (Even those who are less well endowed can learn to read, but with greater effort on the part of the child and of his teachers.) Given these gifts, most children can be well prepared at home for learning to read at school.

Some capacities must simply be allowed to develop. One of them is eyesight. Babies are farsighted. Most children's eyes don't adjust to seeing large print until they are about six or seven years old. Mentality also has to develop, and a child needs a mental age of about six and a half years to learn much about reading. That is why it is probably unwise to try to teach the average preschool child to read. If he asks to learn, by all means oblige him, but never insist. He will probably be content to learn to read his name, the brand name on his cereal box, the name of his dog. He might enjoy some large printed labels in his room to designate "toys," "door," "window." That is enough reading instruction for most five-year-olds. To hold serious sessions for the purpose of teaching reading to a preschool child is an utterly unnecessary and wasteful thing to do. There are more important things to learn at this age.

Then what can you do to help your child be ready to learn to read when he goes to school? Reading stories to a little child contributes to his reading aptitude. Let him sit close to you to see the pictures and turn the pages. In these happy reading times with mother or daddy or an older child he associates pleasure and companionship with stories and books. His vocabulary grows and he learns to sit still and give attention to a story until it is finished.

Encourage Independence

Another trait important to reading aptitude is independence. The child who has learned to do things for himself has a great advantage in learning to read. If he has discovered the joy of dressing himself, the good feeling of taking his own bath, the fun of solving simple puzzles—all, of course, within the limits of safety and his ability—he is able to take an active part in the process of learning to read.

Another aspect of reading aptitude is the readiness to learn through listening. All the word-learning that a child acquires in his preschool days is from listening. If we adults speak slowly enough for him to understand us and in terms that he can interpret, he will acquire a great many ideas and learn a lot of words. What is more, he becomes willing to listen in order to learn. (See article "Do You Talk Too Much?")

The habit of listening develops vocabulary, too—which makes learning to read easier. Children learn to read words that they already use orally more readily than they learn entirely new words. So answer your youngster's questions—briefly and clearly. Leaf through a magazine, look at the pictures with him and tell him what he wants to know about them. When you read him stories, interpret strange words.

An important aspect of learning through listening is what teachers call "auditory discrimination." It means the ability to distinguish small differences in sounds. First-grade teachers spend long hours trying to help some pupils differentiate between the sounds of *bed* and *bad, sit* and *set, wrote* and *rode.*

Some children understand immediately, while others seem hopelessly unable to distinguish the sounds. Auditory discrimination is basic to learning to read by the phonics method, and it is helpful in learning by the sight method. It can be learned by almost any child with normal hearing, and the best place to learn it is at home.

Early Auditory Training

You can start auditory training or "careful listening" at a very early age, with the sounds that animals make: "What says 'Moo-oo'? What says, 'Baa-aa'?" A little later you can listen with your child to bird calls and teach him to identify a few. Share with him the pleasure of interesting sounds, different musical instruments, factory whistles, the hum of a well regulated motor.

When Bobby was four, his mother began to play listening games to pass the time while washing dishes or while driving in the family car. In the music game, they hummed simple tunes that Bobby tried to identify. Their favorite and most helpful game was making rhymes.

"What rhymes with dish?" Bobby would answer, "Fish." This game could go on for a long time and would gradually become harder. Bobby had to grope for words to rhyme with *butter* and *locker*.

When Bobby was five, they varied the game to listening for initial word sounds, "Which of these words start with the same sound: *big, boy, hat?*" They played this way with the sound of "B" for a while. Another day they played with the sound of "S", and later on with others. These games were played for fun, along with other games, and Bobby enjoyed them.

Learning the Alphabet

For a child to know the alphabet from memory is helpful and it presents no problem. Many children learn it from an alphabet song on a phonograph record. Or you can sing it yourself. It is very soothing when a three-year-old needs comforting.

Should children be taught to read by the sight or by the phonics method? Here we are back to the old controversy. Actually, a good reader uses both methods. The question is when each method should be introduced.

Probably your first-grader will learn his first lesson by sight. He comes home much excited, waving a mimeographed sheet, and from it reads impressively:

"Tim has a dog.
The dog is brown."

Then he colors the dog with his crayons. Most children can learn to read that lesson by sight in a few minutes. To read the same sentences by one of the systems of phonics now popular (there are many different systems) would require learning the following: four vowel sounds, one diphthong, twelve consonant sounds and one consonant blend, besides the difficult art of blending them into words. To many beginners, this is a bewildering and discouraging process. They are more encouraged by learning simply: "Tim has a dog."

Learning Phonics

Phonics, however, is a useful tool for attacking new words and every reader needs to learn it sometime. Many children acquire an understanding of sound symbols without direct teaching. Since learning phonics requires a capacity to remember rules and to apply generalizations, most schools introduce it after a child is launched in sight reading.

A child well prepared for learning to read has many advantages. He can readily profit from the good teaching he receives in school, and he can overcome many of the disadvantages he may have to face in our presently overcrowded schools. To succeed in reading from the beginning of his school experience gives him the confidence he needs to keep learning more. And the preparation you give him long before he goes to school is the first step toward that success. —*By Josephine Courtney Sisk*

HOW TO ENCOURAGE WRITING ABILITY

THE ability to express ideas in good, effective English is a priceless gift —one well worth cultivating from the earliest years of childhood.

There are a good many effective things we can do during the preschool years to foster natural expression and attitudes that will help our children grow naturally into writing. For instance, during the years that Meredith was of preschool age, her father did a considerable amount of traveling. In the interest of preserving family ties and fostering warm human relationships, Meredith was encouraged to dictate a few words of greeting to Daddy, added at the end of her mother's letters. She enjoyed thoroughly the experience of standing by the typewriter, assembling her thoughts, and finally coming out with some important message such as, "You know those red shoes I saw last week in Peter's Shoe Store—the ones with the little pieces cut out near the toes? Well, guess what? Mother bought them for me today." Always her recorded statements were read back to her and she signed underneath—at first with her mark and later with her name.

A Means of Communication

At four, she began to draw a simple picture to accompany her message. At five, she began to ask that her remarks be printed on a separate sheet of paper. Then she would painstakingly copy them on the typewriter. At this point, unlimited adult patience was called for. "What's this word?" she would ask again and again. "What's this letter? This letter? And this one?" Eventually she picked up the ability to recognize the letters on the keyboard by name. This, of course, was a mere by-product of the truly valuable outcomes of these "letter-writing" ventures. The really important thing she learned was that writing is a means of keeping in touch with those we love. She came to understand that family letters are written just as though you were talking to a person, and developed an ability to select from many possible items of news the ones most likely to be of interest to the recipient of the letter.

Also, at five, a series of birthday parties offered good opportunity for making simple birthday greetings to accompany the gifts. A more or less standard version—with a birthday cake, the requisite number of candles on it, and the words HAPPY BIRTHDAY—was used over and over.

Ability to Express Ideas

Children, even the very youngest, have fresh ways of expressing ideas.

We know that at all ages the most effective expression occurs when people talk or write in terms of what they themselves have seen or heard, touched, tasted, felt. Encourage your youngsters to put into words things they are experiencing.

The questions, "What is it like? How does it feel? What does it make you think of?" rarely fail to elicit some vivid response from children.

If we encourage our children to say in their own way how something makes them think or feel, the chances are that we may produce individuals who won't have to go through life describing their most moving experiences as "nice," "swell" or "terrific."

Once children get off to a good start in writing, they find the same satisfaction that they derive from any other creative effort. When they do, we can be pretty sure they will grow into the kind of competent writers who will not find writing dull and distasteful, who will not "freeze up" when they take pen or pencil or typewriter in hand. —*By Elenore Thomas Pounds*

SCHOOL-AGERS

DEVELOPING A CONSCIENCE • CONFORMITY • SHYNESS
FRIENDSHIPS • GOOD SPORTSMANSHIP
LEARNING TO BE TRUTHFUL • TEASING
DISCIPLINE AND PUNISHMENT • QUARRELING AND FIGHTING
MANNERS AND NEATNESS • FAILURE AT SCHOOL
HOME REFERENCE LIBRARY • MUSIC LESSONS
STEALING • THE RUNAWAY CHILD

HOW CHILDREN DEVELOP A CONSCIENCE

EVERYONE needs a conscience and the time to develop one is in childhood. A great part of what we describe as "proper upbringing" consists of developing in our children a sense of responsibility for their own conduct —in other words, conscience. There is a delicate balance between a healthy feeling of responsibility and an undesirable oversupply of conscience. It is just that nice balance we need to work for if our children are to grow into independent, courageous, considerate adults capable of working, playing, giving and receiving affection.

How does conscience develop? When mother or father frowns at the baby he feels something is amiss; perhaps he may cry. Even an infant catches the disapproval in mother's voice when she says, "No, no, mustn't touch," as he makes a lunge for the string of beads around her neck.

When the toddler goes to the grocery store with mother, she makes a dive for the cookie carton, only to be restrained by mother's "No, no." Mother may have to pick her up and carry her away from temptation. As children grow they become more keenly aware of what mother likes and doesn't like.

A year later Betsy, more experienced with the meaning of "no," walks up to the cookie display, solemnly says "no, no" to herself and takes a fig newton anyway. Her conscience is asserting itself, but her desire is stronger.

By the time Betsy is five or six, she will have experienced so many "no, no's" that a considerable number will have become a part of her very being. What mother and father like is "good"; what mother and father dislike is "bad." Betsy's conscience has grown to the point where she will not take a cookie if she thinks mother or the grocer is looking.

Gradual Growth of Conscience

It is probably not until Betsy is eight or nine that she will think of "right" or "wrong" apart from the standards set for her own behavior. Betsy will be very nearly adult before she can always resist temptation when there is no danger of being discovered.

So conscience grows, out of parental approval and disapproval, restrictions and demands. Its development tends to be most wholesome when approval is given generously; when commands are not too numerous or too severe but take account in a reasonable, consistent way of the child's ability to carry out directions.

An overdose of conscience often results when persistent parental disapproval, constant restriction and severity are a child's daily fare. The child then tends to doubt his own worthiness, and in one way or another tries to make up for what he feels are his shortcomings.

Parents are likely to become discouraged when Betsy or Jim takes the forbidden cookie even though she or he "knows better." "Knowing better" is conscience, but having the strength to live up to what is known to be right—that is maturity. Betsy at four, or eight or twelve, will not always heed that still, small voice when it is a question of coming home on time, doing arithmetic instead of reading the funnies or dusting behind the bureau when she wants to go out to play. If she always did, she would be one of those unfortunate youngsters we describe as a "regular little old woman." We would be saying she had a conscience more mature than normal or desirable for her years.

Overactive Conscience

Sometimes we may be quite sure that a child acts as he does because of "too much conscience." The second or third-grader's anxiety about being late for school is an example familiar to many parents. We often see, too, a child who is constantly asking for approval. "Is this all right?" or "Was I good?" Too much orderliness about possessions or continuous "model" behavior are also signs that conscience is overactive.

Often the results of the struggle between the child's desires and what he thinks he ought to do are not so easily spotted. Magic superstitions, nightmares or groundless fears may appear when a child is under particular tension because of a conflict between desire and conscience. Parents may be completely unaware of the real nature of the youngster's difficulty. The child himself probably couldn't tell what is bothering him, for such conflicts usually go on in the unconscious part of the mind.

Youngsters, even up to eight or nine years of age, may be bothered by their consciences because of something "bad" they thought about doing, or wished might happen. If Aunt Kate's visit has interfered with Mother's reading time after supper, it is hard to make the distinction between having wished Aunt Kate would go away or get sick, and having actually harmed her. To a young child, "bad" thoughts are likely to seem as dangerous as "bad" deeds, especially when he is given the feeling that he "should always tell mother or father all his secrets."

The Guilty Conscience

Many of the imaginary bears, lions and witches some children fear are invented by the children to satisfy a guilty conscience. Of course, the children themselves are unaware why "the goblins will get you if you don't watch out." It is as if conscience says, in effect, "You did wrong to have 'bad' thoughts, therefore these imaginary creatures have come to get even with you." When children won't step on a crack, or skip every other paving block in the sidewalk, conscience seems to be satisfied for "wrong thoughts" by the extra care in following "magic rules."

There is a kind of strain which usually appears when a child is in the second or third grade. Two different situations make life hard at this point. First the teacher, whether she be strict or lenient, is judging the youngster for what he can do rather than for what he is. For the first time in his life, a child does not get love and praise just for being sweet and cooperative.

On the other hand, the third-grader is exposed to the standards of neighborhood friends. He learns that unless your shirttails hang out, your speech is uncouth, your manners sketchy, you do not "belong"—a fate which may be considered somewhat worse than death. So the demands of the school and the gang, complicated by mother's and father's standards, make an eight-year-old aware of his inability to live up to his ideal of himself. Conscience tells him, though he could not put the feeling into words, that he is falling short.

This is one of the times that pressure on all sides may cause him to slip back into more babyish ways. The guilty conscience may show up in a return to thumb-sucking, bed-wetting or perhaps hair-twisting.

Signs of Disturbance

Would we still consider such behavior normal? Certainly frequent bed-wetting in a seven-year-old means help from a guidance clinic is advisable. But there are all the other signs of too much conscience that are not so clear-cut. Whether any given piece of behavior, such as skipping the cracks in the sidewalk, or fear of being late, is to be expected as a normal conscience develops, or whether it is a sign of real disturbance, depends not so much on the behavior itself, but rather on the degree to which it affects the child's daily life.

Any kind of fear, anxiety or "nervousness" that actually interferes with a child's eating heartily, making friends, playing vigorously or enjoying himself may well be regarded as a warning signal. On the other hand, a child who is full of questions about the world around him, alert and interested in his play, who shows a zest for living, need cause his parents no great concern on this score. Though he may still show some of the signs of too much conscience sometimes, there are ways parents can help him deal with his feelings of guilt before they become a burden.

It is an excellent plan to let the children know that mother and father are not and never were perfect. Eager to set a good example, parents may forget that to a six or nine-year-old they seem overwhelmingly powerful just because they are grown up. If father and his friends turned the street signs the wrong way in their early days, it will not be giving Sonny undesirable notions if such a tale is woven into daily conversation occasionally. As a matter of fact, Sonny will gain self-confidence and self-respect from knowing that in spite of one's shortcomings, one can grow up into so responsible and remarkable a person as dad.

Parents Can Relieve Tension

Sometimes the relief that comes from hearing that mother or father suffered from the same kind of "badness" is startlingly dramatic, as it was with Ellen. Ellen was boisterous and bossy. Her younger sister was quiet and retiring, but quite dependent on Ellen to look out for her interests in neighborhood affairs, and she often was the victim of the older child's bossiness.

When she was about nine, Ellen began to be afraid to go up to bed alone. She often cried out in her sleep something about "wanting to be good" or "not wanting to push." The waking Ellen was so different from the dreaming Ellen, that her parents decided to talk the matter over with the adjustment teacher at school.

After discussing the entire family situation, it was agreed that Ellen might be somewhat resentful of her rather goody-goody sister and feel a bit guilty over her resentment. So it might be wise to arrange to give Ellen more opportunity to play without having little sister tag along. The adjustment teacher also suggested that mother and father casually talk about some of their own feelings toward brothers and sisters when they were young.

The next evening mother remarked that she had had a letter from her sister. "It's certainly fun to hear from her these days, but when I remember how we squabbled when we were little! Why, one day I threw a shovel at her, and was I scared when it really hit her—"

Mother never finished the sentence, for Ellen threw her arms around her mother, "Did you really throw things at Aunt Orma? How funny! Well, I think I'll go upstairs now."

Ellen did not realize why she was able to go upstairs alone, but her parents saw that her guilty conscience had been relieved sufficiently, so that her fears, and eventually her nightmares, disappeared.

Of course, hearing about a parent's shortcomings does not always work magic, but it does help.

An overdeveloped conscience can often be prevented if standards are not set too high. Deeply rooted in the minds of many of us are such catchwords as "What's worth doing is worth doing well," or "There is a right way and a wrong way to do everything." Whether it is holding a fork, putting away toys or making a bed, the youngster may be doing it well for his own years, even though by adult standards the performance is pretty crude. It is not true that it's as "easy to learn the right way as the wrong." Minds and muscles at four or six or ten are just not sufficiently developed to draw a line or sew a seam or write a letter that would be a truly finished product. If children are made to feel that anything short of a perfect job is a disgrace, they will soon find even partial failure so painful that they are afraid to try anything. Letting a child feel that it is all right to try new ways of doing things, and then gradually raising standards as skill and understanding grow tends to keep conscience from discouraging new efforts. No good comes of forced competition with neighbors and cousins, but guilt and resentment are pretty sure to result.

Conscience, then, grows out of experience with parental approval or disapproval. The way in which it is developed counts for a great deal. As a rule, it is only if there is continually too much severity, if demands fail to take account of the child's ability or if parents are themselves too "perfect" that we see a persistent pattern of unfortunate behavior resulting from too much conscience. As a child grows, signs of too much conscience may show up from time to time, but with encouragement and support from warm, affectionate parents there need be no real disturbance. Conscience is part and parcel of the healthy personality. —*By Maria W. Piers, Ph.D., and Edith G. Neisser*

DOES YOUR CHILD FOLLOW THE CROWD?

A GROUP of schoolboys recently took part in a revealing experiment. Their teacher set up two square white cards against the blackboard. On the left card was a vertical black line about an inch long. The right card had an identical line, plus a shorter one and a longer one. The teacher announced that each boy was to call out which two lines were the same length but he wanted them all to give the wrong answer.

At that point, before they answered, a new boy was ushered into the room. He was told nothing of the experiment, simply asked to pick out the two matching lines when his turn came. After repeating the experiment a number of times with different groups, the teacher reported these findings: as the new boys scrutinized the lines and heard the other boys' answers, they furrowed their brows, stepped up to take a closer look at the cards, squirmed in their seats. Several interrupted to ask if they'd heard the instructions correctly, others turned in confusion to the boys who sat next to them.

How did they answer? Some went along with the group without hesitation. They automatically assumed that if all the other boys gave the same answer it must be correct. Some hemmed and hawed because they were sure the group was wrong, but finally agreed with the group because they didn't dare to be different. Only 1 in 5 stood up and said firmly, "This is what I see."

Parents everywhere are concerned about how far their children should go in conforming to other children's actions and goals and values. Too often this puts parents on the horns of a dilemma. Their child wants to do a certain thing because all the children are doing it. The parents may feel strongly that he should not do it but they are not sure how much he has to conform to be accepted and popular, so they're on the spot.

The Nonconforming Child

On the other hand, some parents are concerned about the child who stays outside the group and rarely goes along with what other children do or think. They fear he is missing out on an important part of growing up and they fear even more that he will have a tough time getting along with people when he grows up if he doesn't get along during childhood.

Lately psychologists and sociologists have been taking a closer look at children's social relationships. Their research shows that children who fit smoothly into the group and pattern their activities to match their friends' are generally more popular and admired. Some of these children are happy and secure, and their compatibility with the other children is for them a sign of sound development. But some children who seem outwardly the same are tortured by anxiety and deep emotional problems. For example, 10-year-old Joe is the most popular boy in his class. The other children always pick Joe first for a team, a committee, the lead in a class play. You might wish that your child was as popular as Joe and fitted as smoothly into his group. But a series of psychological tests showed Joe to be a gravely troubled boy, full of anxiety and fear of failure. He sees himself as unable to cope successfully with life. He doesn't know why he feels this way but thinks that somehow it is all his fault. He has strong feelings of aggression and hostility that he doesn't dare express. It is primarily to cover up his inner anger and guilt that he is friendly and conforms to the other children's expectations.

Dr. Mary Northway, of the Toronto Institute of Child Study, has come across many children like Joe. She summed up the findings of several hundred studies in the booklet "What Is Popularity?" published by Science Re-

search Associates: "The very popular youngster, in using his energy to conform to purposes valued by the group, frequently does so at considerable expense to himself. He is often filled with anxiety concerning his success or with apprehension that he may not be liked . . . He frequently shows fine adjustment to the group but may be lacking in inner security and peace of mind."

On the other side of the picture, research has shown that some children who don't bother much with what other kids think or do are happy and healthy. Others are gravely troubled and their nonconformity is an alarming sign of it.

With the child who wants to be just like his friends, the pattern often starts as soon as he is old enough to make friends with other children. He wants a gun because the other boys have guns. Or she wants cowboy boots because the other girls have them. As they grow older the words change but the chant sounds the same:

"All the kids stay up to watch that TV show and I want to stay up too."

Most children have a big need to feel that they are like other children, especially as they approach adolescence, and authorities on children say there are sound reasons for it. Dr. Sidney Green, child psychiatrist, put it this way:

"A child needs close and sustained relationships with other children. He needs to feel he belongs. He gets the same feeling of support and warmth from being part of the group that a baby gets when he is held by his mother."

Keys to Unhealthy Conformity

Since most children want to be like their friends, how do you spot the conformity that's not normal or healthy? You can get some idea by exploring these questions:

How much time does your youngster spend being like other children and conforming to their expectations?

Dr. Green suggests that the child who has healthy social relationships with other children recognizes when to forego them for other people or things. He also enjoys the hours he spends with his family. He is usually willing to pass a little of his time with a brother or sister. He likes the hours he spends alone working at a hobby, practicing a musical instrument or reading.

Next—does your child follow his friends' lead only in certain matters or in everything? Some youngsters buy without question all their friends' standards, prejudices, ideas of right and wrong. They take the group's word on everything from how high they should wear their socks to how honest they should be on school examinations. These children keep very busy with their friends and may seem to be happy and comfortable. But if you take a closer look you see they conform, not out of loyalty but because of too great a fear that the group will reject them if they don't.

Most children do not conform so indiscriminately. They are influenced on some things but not on others. One boy may yield readily to his friends' taste in clothes or slang or table manners, but not go along with the unkind things they say about the new boy who moved in down the block. Another may be fresh to his teacher because his friends are, but differ with them sharply on how to spend the money in the club treasury. A girl may want to wear lipstick because her friends do, but still help out with her baby sister though her friends tease her about it.

When To Be Firm

Once you have a picture of where your child follows his friends and where he doesn't, you can go on to estimate how healthy or unhealthy his conformity is. According to Dr. Green, you can size up the situation fairly well on the basis of three questions about what your child does with his friends: Is it humiliating to him or another person? Is it physically dangerous? Does it flout, far beyond the normal stages of rebellion against adults, the standards of right and wrong that he has learned at home?

Let's suppose your boy belongs to a school club and his friends urge him to take part in a ritual that involves sadistic hazing. Or suppose your daughter's friends are snubbing a new girl because of her religion and want your girl to do likewise. These are situations in which someone could be hurt, humiliated or treated unkindly. "The child who has healthy relationships with other children," says Dr. Green, "can recognize when the other children are going too far and can withdraw from the situation."

Many parents think that as their children grow older their friends have such an overriding impact on them that there's not much they can do about it. This is not so. If your child's friends lead him into some activity that is simply not acceptable you can start getting him back on the right track by telling him firmly where you stand and holding your ground.

Acceptance Based on Reason

In areas of deep concern to parents most children will accept their parents' standards if the parents' reasons are valid and clear. Children respond logically. They will accept your reasons why they shouldn't do something if the reasons make sense to them and are presented in terms they can understand.

There are times, however, when you can't handle overconformity just by being firm. You must first consider why the child is so anxious to conform. In trying to judge whether he conforms because he's a lot like Joe or because he is a healthy, comfortable child who is building sound relationships with other children, you can get valuable clues from his general behavior. For instance, Joe's mother reported to school psychologists that he wets his bed and continually bites his nails. Another child might reveal his inner troubles by being moody and withdrawn, by being cruel to a younger sister or brother, or by displaying some nervous habit. If he does these things not once in a while but continuously and intensely it might indicate that he's a child with problems that require expert help—no matter how well adjusted and well liked he appears when he is with his friends.

What about the child who doesn't conform, who rarely wants to do anything because the other kids are doing it? As we mentioned earlier, ample research shows that a boy or girl can have a satisfying childhood and grow into a successful adult even though he seems at odds with the group when he is growing up.

Individual Interests

How do you tell if the child who doesn't conform is making out happily or not? You can tell a lot by observing how he does spend his time. Maybe he is simply not interested in what the other kids choose to do and would rather make model airplanes, read or mount butterflies—and he is strong enough to stand up and say so without fearing he will lose status. Maybe he has a deep and important interest in music, invention or chemistry which should by no means be squelched merely to make him appear more like other children. If he enjoys what he is doing—seems generally contented and gets along well with you and the rest of his family—then you shouldn't worry about it. He will find friends and join more in their activities when he is ready. In the meantime, there is no point in making him feel he is odd or in pushing him to do more of the things other children do.

But some children aren't more like others chiefly because they don't know how to get the group to include them in its activities. At the start such a child is not actively disliked. It is more likely that he is a quiet, unassuming child who is simply overlooked. He may try to cover up his hurt feelings by taking no interest in what interests other children. Or he may ridicule them or disrupt their projects. Then the others stop overlooking him and start disliking him.

How Parents Can Help

What can you do about this kind of child? What he needs first is practice in taking part in a very small group. Maybe one or two other youngsters who share some interest of his could be invited over for a Saturday afternoon or maybe he could be encouraged to join a small club (but not pushed to participate). Keep in mind, too, that children don't overlook the child who can do things or has skills they admire. One study proving this involved all the ninth-grade boys and girls in a city in central New York State (696 children in all). Those who had some facility or talent—they told stories or danced or threw a good forward pass—were welcomed more warmly by the group than those with no skills. If your child wants to join more in the other children's pastimes and doesn't seem to know how to go about it, maybe you can help him develop a new ability or hobby that will rate with the other children and win his way into the group.

A final suggestion—and always a sound one—is: don't conclude too hastily that your youngster conforms too much or too little. It takes a bit of time and some clear thinking to see the total picture of why he is what he is and does what he does. If you do decide, though, after allowing time and considering the many factors that bear on his behavior, that he needs a hand, your own is one of the best hands in the world to help him find himself.

—By Amy Selwyn

IF YOUR CHILD IS SHY

WHEN you stop to think of it, mothers are confronted with as many problems as any business executive—and far more important problems since they concern the character of human beings. Of these, certainly one of the most baffling is shyness.

You can't, and you certainly shouldn't, take a timid child and say, "Now see here, there is no sense in this. Just because people are strangers is no reason for you to be afraid of them. So, stop it!"

Neither can you just ignore children's shyness, hoping they will outgrow it, because often they don't. What then? You can try to find out what's back of it. Usually the cause is complex.

At six Billy was an intelligent, presentable youngster. In the family sphere he was all right. But let a guest come to the house, and he would flee to the shelter of his room to remain until the coast was clear or until he was hauled forth to sit squirming, uncomfortable and agonizingly speechless.

His parents were hospitable, pleasant people and this attitude of Billy's was as much a trial to them as it was to their young son. A little sleuthing uncovered the fact that Billy's timidity had started about the time he entered first grade. But he was doing well in school, had a fine, understanding teacher and no more than normal friction with his schoolmates.

How Shyness May Develop

Then someone recalled Aunt Harriet's visit. An exquisite young woman with a roughshod sense of humor, she had delighted in teasing Billy about having feet that were too big for the rest of him. Could it be—? When Billy's mother thought of that she casually mentioned that when children are growing sometimes one part of them gets ahead of the others, but that they eventually all catch up with each other. Grandmother got out the family album one afternoon, and when they came to the picture of a decidedly bunchy young girl who bore only a faint resemblance to the slim and elegant Aunt Harriet, Grandma explained that when children are growing up they go through stages like that and nobody thinks anything of it. Billy seemed much interested, which served as a clue that they were on the right track. Then his mother coached the shoe salesman whom they regularly patronized to remark that Billy's feet were the usual size of most boys his age and height. Coming from an outside source, this bore authority. It wasn't long before Billy was acting in a normal manner again. Actually his shyness had been started by nothing more than acute self-consciousness about those feet of his.

Often shyness can be traced to just such thoughtless remarks made by adults who should know better, so look for something of this sort. It goes without saying that such sleuthing will have to be done with great tact and care or more harm than good may result.

Problem of the Only Child

The only child is particularly prone to shyness. Without the support and companionship, as well as the give-and-take that goes on between brothers and sisters, he usually gets too much attention. Sometimes he craves and demands it, and then we have the little smart aleck or show-off. In other cases he is embarrassed by the spotlight and longs to escape it.

There are times when a child may seem shy merely because he rightly resents the overwhelming advances made by adults. Most children like to look a stranger over before conferring the honor of friendship upon him.

Do a little observing and, if necessary, drop an aside to your friends to try ignoring your youngster after the first casual greeting instead of making a beeline for him and overwhelming him with attention. That may be sufficient to straighten things out.

However, if the trouble is not here, then you may be sure it is rooted in a feeling of insecurity. And overdiscipline may be the cause.

In many cases, the shy child is found to be the overdirected one. Constant reprimands, supervision even in little things, produce a hesitant fumbling personality, unsure of himself in any new situation as, for instance, in meeting a stranger. Has your child been led gradually to rely more and more on himself, so that the self-assurance which comes from expanding powers is his? It may seem a long stretch from knowing how to lace one's shoes to being at ease with others, but you'll be surprised to find how immediately one leads to the other. Has the precious faculty of thinking things out for himself, being permitted the right to make his own mistakes and learn thereby, been accorded your child? And is he made to feel that he has a definite place in the family, not as its center, but as one member, with his own rights, privileges and responsibilities?

Discuss Problem in Private

Never discuss his shyness, nor permit it to be discussed in his hearing. Children are not deaf. Even when they appear to be engrossed in play, snatches of adult conversation register in their minds. By talking about Junior's diffidence you lend importance to it and, paradoxical as it may seem, he is given a feeling of prominence through this possession of an undesirable trait outstanding enough to be commented upon. There's something rather pleasing, actually, in being thus singled out.

Are you really hospitable? Of course you have friends and entertain them from time to time. But if a neighbor runs in, or if guests drop in when your house is upset, as the best of houses are sometimes, particularly houses with children in them, are they really welcome, or do you privately hurl anathemas on them for coming? Children sense those things. Do you anticipate guests with genuine pleasure, or do you put yourself through an orgy of house-cleaning, grumbling and worrying, winding up by being too tense and weary to enjoy company? Rest assured, all this etches on an impressionable child's mind a picture of hospitality as an evil rather than the pleasure it should be.

Do you take your children visiting with you on occasion, so that they may have the opportunity to play the role of guest? Or do you always leave them behind? You are depriving them of rich social experiences if you always leave them at home. No child past the infant stage is too young to start learning how to be a welcome guest.

Home Environment Important

Consider the families you know, and think of those where the children possess that enviable quality, social poise. Invariably these are homes where visitors are coming and going, where membership in church and other organizations makes life richer and fuller, where the children neither monopolize the conversation and attention nor are ignored.

Having pried this far, let us go a little further. Are *you* shy? You can be, and not realize it. The symptoms are exaggerated concern with what other people may think, a tendency to avoid contacts with strangers rather than seek them, oversensitiveness. Do you, by comparing your family fortunes with those of others more prosperous, make your child feel that his family is inferior? Do you, by pointing out his defects continually, make him feel inferior?

Remember, your children reflect you in many ways. In their small worlds you loom big. Parental attitudes are molding influences. Parents who are timid and fumbling in their social relationships, a mother so concerned about such unimportant matters as well-worn furniture or a last year's dress that she cannot be a gracious hostess or an enjoyable guest, can hardly expect to rear sons and daughters who will not to some degree reflect these attitudes.

Perhaps in helping your child you will clear out some rag-tatters of social insecurity in yourself.   —*By Patricia Rayburn Olson*

IF YOUR CHILD
FAILS TO MAKE FRIENDS

MOST overaggressive youngsters have the same fundamental fear that they cannot live up to parental expectations. Parents want well mannered, good-natured boys and girls who get along well with others. Children do not always feel that way. As the pressure to conform to the parent's desires increases, so do fears of failure. It is this fear that generates the feelings which show up as quarrelsomeness with brothers, sisters, playmates. Only when a youngster can be helped to get rid of these uncomfortable inner feelings of fear will he be able to get along better with his friends.

Nature is asking him to stop being a baby and become a little boy, to move from being a tranquil five and turn into a well adjusted seven. The stress of transferring from one to the other of these ages is terrific and makes heavy demands on a child. When parents add additional demands that he can't fulfill, resentments may build up and increase aggressiveness.

Children want above all else to feel loved and approved of by their parents. It is amazing how often they get the idea that fathers and mothers don't love them as much as they want to be loved. Never assume that your child knows you love him just because you know that you do. It is when a young person feels unsure of himself in your affections or unworthy of your love that he is likely to become domineering, demanding and quarrelsome.

The Overconfident Child

If your child is given to throwing his weight around or trying to dominate his playmates, the way to help him is to build up his feeling of security. Don't let his exterior brashness fool you into thinking he is self-confident. He may seem to have all the assurance in the world. But this is often a false front for underlying anxieties about his real importance.

Ten-year-old Jimmy was so boastful that none of the children in the neighborhood liked him.

He was a good-looking, well built boy who fairly exuded self-confidence. It never occurred to his parents that he was anything but sure of himself. They even tried to take him down a peg and rub off some of his arrogance.

It came as a great shock to them when they learned that beneath all his bravado, their son was a troubled, unhappy little boy who felt that he belonged to no one. As the third of five children, Jimmy received neither the attention required by the two younger ones nor the approval reserved for his older sisters whose behavior was constantly being held up as an example to him.

Like many middle children, Jimmy was in danger of being overlooked and lost in the shuffle. His boasting and bullying were his ways of compensating for his feeling of being unloved and unwanted. It wasn't until his parents found ways of making him feel really important to them that he could stop insisting on a false importance in the eyes of others.

All youngsters have a way of misinterpreting parental good intentions. Mary's parents were anxious to have her do well in school because they couldn't afford to send her to college unless she earned a scholarship. As a result they were extremely concerned about her grades, so Mary got the impression that her achievements mattered more to them than she did.

Her hurt feelings came out in bold, flippant actions that were the talk of the neighborhood. Fortunately, her parents woke up in time to what was the matter. They had a frank talk with their daughter about their financial situation; then they put the choice up to her. Did she or didn't she want to go to college? Mary decided it was worth the extra effort to win the scholarship. Once they took the pressure off, Mary became her former pleasant self.

Larry's parents, too, had only his good in mind when they stressed the importance of taking care of his possessions. But without realizing it they overemphasized order and cleanliness. Larry became such a perfectionist that at school he hung back when the other children were playing games and refused to participate for fear of soiling or tearing his clothes. When his mother asked why he never invited any of his friends to the house after school, Larry said they might muss the rugs or break something. The boy next door stopped playing with him when Larry refused to let him ride his bike, read his comic books or fly his model airplane.

Attitudes of this kind are dangerous to a child's emotional health. He should feel that it is all right to get dirty and mussed up on occasion. He should feel that possessions are to be used and enjoyed.

Help from Parents

Larry's parents took him on camping trips and encouraged him to be a comfortable young savage for a change. His mother gave him some discarded flower pots to smash for drainage material in the bottom of pots for house plants. In these ways they helped to make him feel that he had their permission to break things and get dirty as a normal little boy should. When he was sure that they would love him even if he wasn't always clean and orderly, Larry could relax and be a real little boy who was friendly with his pals.

Sometimes overaggressiveness stems from refusing a child something that is very important to him. Thirteen-year-old Sharon had become highly critical of everything and everybody. She got along poorly with her schoolmates and held herself aloof. She was acting the way she felt—different from the others. No matter how much she pleaded, argued and cried, her mother still would not allow her to wear the jeans and sloppy-joe sweaters the rest of the gang delighted in.

Unfortunately, the very people who are most anxious to help a child who is aggressive and unpleasant often intensify his problem. Parents make matters worse when they get emotionally involved themselves and take sides with him against the friends he has alienated. Inevitably the overaggressive child does things to make other children dislike him. When they retaliate, some parents get angry and rush to his defense. This makes him more unpopular than ever.

Bruce bosses the neighborhood children and plays the young dictator. He orders them out of his yard or off the street in front of his house. Recently there have been several birthday parties to which he was not invited. He was hurt; his parents were annoyed with the other children for leaving him out.

These parents missed the important goal of helping their youngster get along better with his friends. To do so parents have to remain as objective as possible and control the impulse to make his battles theirs. A rebuff from a child who has taken enough from a bully is often more effective than many lectures from an adult.

Building Self-Confidence

As children grow older their way of expressing aggression changes. A six-year-old shows his rage by putting up a real fight. He hits, scratches, bites and throws. The same child at seven will often quietly leave the playground or the room when he is angry. When he is eight he is likely to respond with hurt feelings instead of with fists. He may argue, alibi or make disagreeable remarks. But on the whole he is more curious than aggressive. By the time he is nine he fights occasionally, especially if he is a boy. But it is mostly in the spirit of play and he is well aware that it is just a game. Now his aggression is chiefly verbal and he criticizes freely, often expressing indifference to commands or parental standards. The adolescent is inclined to sulk when he feels angry. Or he may express aggression by being stubborn, sullen, rebellious or hypercritical.

Some overaggressive children take it out on adults by constantly pestering and making excessive demands on them. Louise is the kind of youngster who always expects special favors and requires excessive help with her assignments. She pesters her classmates, too, and they are always telling her to go away.

At the bottom of Louise's demands on other people is a gnawing feeling of insecurity brought on by a series of events including a move to a new town, her grandmother's death and the fact that her father's new job keeps him away from home a great deal. Only when she is helped to feel more secure again will her need for so much attention disappear.

But whether your child fights with his fists or his tongue, bullies his friends, antagonizes others with his boasting or pesters you with constant demands for attention, the motivation for his conduct is the same and so is the treatment. There are a number of ways in which you can help him. One is to build up his self-esteem. Let him feel that you are proud of the things he does. Admire his genuine achievements such as learning to dress himself, building a model airplane, baking cookies, learning to swim, writing a good school theme.

One mother who is a meticulous housekeeper taped her daughter's drawings to the kitchen wall for special display. The little girl knew how fussy her mother was about those walls and felt she had really done something special to have her handiwork put up on them.

Learning New Skills

A youngster can often be helped to slough off an overaggressive manner by learning a new skill. At the age of twelve, Ruth was a big, awkward girl who was unable to shine at dancing, ice-skating or the other forms of recreation popular with her crowd. She felt left out of things and tried to gain attention through noisy clowning. Recognizing her problem, Ruth's parents encouraged her to join a class in ceramics. As she began to turn out lovely rings and lapel pins, her boisterous clowning subsided. She had a legitimate claim to attention.

No matter how fiercely they deny it, all children want to feel liked by their companions. The domineering youngster struggles with the knowledge that he has very few friends and is not popular. His parents can give him increased stature by inviting the neighborhood crowd in for simple get-togethers at which there are plenty of things to do and ample refreshments. Because he gives his friends a good time, he will feel more popular with them and be less demanding of them. His playmates will be quick to sense this new attitude and respond to it. They will begin to regard him more as good host than tough guy. As he gets return invitations to their homes, his morale is boosted to the point where he can get along better with them on a friendly give-and-take basis.

Children often get a special feeling of importance when they have a chance to share in something special that is going on at home. Let the eight-year-old show the guests where to leave their coats the next time you give a party. Planning a vacation trip and being entrusted with the money to buy the tickets for it will give an adolescent a feeling of importance.

All of us want and need to be loved and accepted just as we are. This is especially true of the child who is having difficulties in getting along with others. Don't predicate your approval of him on an improvement in his ways or reserve it for some future time when he has become less belligerent. Make an effort to let him know that he is important to you right now just the way he is. When he knows that, he won't need to push others around in order to prove his importance to himself.   —*By Helen Thomson*

IS YOUR CHILD A GOOD SPORT?

EVERY parent—especially every father—wants his children to be good sports. Of course, we like them to be winners, but we are determined that when necessary, they be good losers who can smile and shake hands with their opponents. We want them to be able to laugh when the joke is on them, and be at least moderately cheerful when their cherished plans fall through. We want them to take their bumps and bruises without too much complaining. Along with this kind of self-control, we want them to be able to stand up for their own rights.

This is an understandable and useful ideal. Good sportsmanship, expressed in many phases of living besides competitive games, is, we like to think, a part of our American way of life. But it is even more general than that. All over the world, in primitive tribes or the most urbane society, the ability to stand up under pain, loss and defeat is the mark of adulthood.

Usually it is not until a youngster is about six that we begin to worry over his ability to take setbacks gracefully.

But as children grow, we do notice that the third and fourth-graders have become sufficiently good sports so that they spend only 90 per cent of their time wrangling over who is "out" or "ahead." Somehow these eight and nine-year-olds do muddle through a game. Before they are ten, they gain some notion of how to take a defeat without much "beefing," and with only a reasonable amount of giving alibis.

Maturing Attitudes

If life has not been too hard for him, the same girl or boy who flew into a tantrum at not being able to go to the picnic at four, and who cheated in order to win at six, may by the time he is eleven or twelve, have gone far toward realizing the goal of good sportsmanship. He—or she—may, for instance, be able to help his cabinmates at camp pack up for a canoe trip even though he is barred because he has not passed the necessary swimming tests. We adults are sometimes so surprised at this sort of thing that we fail to give it recognition, but the children themselves usually give it due honor.

Our world puts a premium on successful achievement. It doesn't take a small person long to discover that no matter what else the adults around him permit or prohibit, failure meets with disapproval, spoken or unspoken. So losing out in any kind of situation may be more than a child can bear.

We can only take defeat or disappointment with a degree of calmness when we can look forward to tomorrow as another day, bringing with it a chance to make up what we have lost. To children—and the younger they are the more this is so—looking ahead is all but impossible.

It is then a parent's job to help his children understand that a disappointment or a failure is not the end of the world. Once they feel in their bones that it is not too dangerous to lose, they have started on the path to good sportsmanship. A solid backlog of satisfying experiences is necessary if you are to become a good loser. To a child, as to an adult, satisfying experiences come through achievement and through receiving warmth, love and encouragement from those around him. The persistently poor loser is almost certain to be the youngster who is emotionally undernourished. Real, spontaneous generosity must spring from a reservoir of emotional well-being. When you yourself have had plenty of success and recognition, you can more readily allow others to have a place in the sun.

Family Atmosphere Influences Child

Parents guide their children toward good sportsmanship through direct experiences as well as through the general atmosphere of family life. Family games offer the best opportunities for the first direct experiences. Wisely handled, animal lotto or hide the thimble can give a youngster an understanding of give-and-take.

For instance, at the A's house Grandpa plays dominoes with six-year-old Ellen every evening. Grandpa sees to it that Ellen always wins.

If Ellen were not keen enough to suspect she was being given an unfair advantage, she would be getting a false idea of her own skill.

On the other hand, in the B family, the older people play for all they are worth and the children never have the satisfaction of winning.

Between the overprotectiveness of the A's and the Spartan regime of the B's stand the humane and realistic practices of our friends, the C's.

When Mr. and Mrs. C play games with the children, the youngsters sometimes win and sometimes lose. In the latter case they have the chance to experience failure or disappointment in small doses in a friendly setting. When mother comes out ahead she takes the attitude, "Next time perhaps you'll win," and adds some pointers on how to improve their technique.

When father loses he says, "Tough luck, but it's fun to play anyway." The emphasis is on the game.

While children are learning how to be good sports, parents help them most by not belittling their efforts to gain victory and accept defeat.

Flexible Household Rules

What kind of an atmosphere at home fosters good sportsmanship? Perhaps there may not seem to be a very close relationship between a degree of easy-going flexibility and graceful losing. Yet it's hard to become a good sport in a household whose rules are rigid and whose schedules are never subject to change without notice.

If a tire blows on the family automobile trip, the delay may necessitate a complete revision of plans. But if everyone realizes that the unexpected sometimes happens, and that "to travel happily is better than to arrive," the children get the feeling that win, lose or draw, you can still have fun.

There is, too, the example mother and father set. If father suspects dirty work at the crossroads if his bowling team is defeated, or mother claims the boss is unfair to father children are likely to catch the alibi habit.

So parents, then, help their children toward the goal of good sportsmanship by giving them opportunities to win and to lose cheerfully; by not ridiculing their small victories; by being reasonably flexible and by setting at least a moderately good example. All this is not easy, for our own feelings and ambitions may influence our actions in subtle and surprising ways.

Provide Safety Valves

We all need safety valves. We cannot expect our children to keep a stiff upper lip all the time. Even if they grin and bear it publicly, children and grownups alike will admit, if they are honest, to feeling disappointment in their own hearts at times. Mothers and fathers provide the needed safety valve when they let a youngster spill his feelings and then help him build up his self-esteem, sandwiching constructive suggestions in between generous slices of encouragement.

One camp which did a splendid job of teaching sportsmanship painlessly used a certain song as an outlet for disappointments. It could always be sung with high good humor by the team that lost, the table that didn't get seconds on ice cream or the cabin that failed to rate honorable mention for neatness. To the tune of "Brother Jacques" they would chant:

> *We were swindled, we were swindled,*
> *We were hooked, we were hooked,*
> *Chiseled out of everything, chiseled out of everything,*
> *Gripe, gripe, gripe,*
> *Gripe, gripe, gripe.*

The very act of chanting together and gently ridiculing the griper drained off a good deal of resentment. Then they were ready to use their energy for more constructive things.

If we want our children to be good winners and gallant losers, we must understand how much—or perhaps how little—we can expect of them at each stage. We need to give them opportunities to win and lose in a friendly setting; we need to encourage self-confidence and flexibility and provide ways for spilling the resentment everyone feels when things go wrong. We need to understand, too, why we, their parents, may be a bit touchy if they show less self-control than we might hope. Then, perhaps in twelve years or so, we may find we have brought up a child who will be able, at times, without too much strain, to laugh when the tables are turned against him, and who does not feel that when he doesn't win he has been cheated.

—By Edith G. Neisser and Maria W. Piers, Ph.D.

HELP YOUR CHILD BE TRUTHFUL

WAS I a good boy today, Mommy?" Suddenly Johnny's bright, blue eyes were searching her face.

"Why, yes—" His mother thought back over the day. Came when called, no rude remarks, helped his little brother. "Yes, you were a good boy."

Thus reassured, Johnny's confession tumbled out. "I didn't mean to break one of your good goblets, but I opened the cupboard to get a glass and—well, it just sorta fell out. I'm sorry, Mom."

"My best crystal! Oh, Johnny!" his mother heard her voice rise. "They were so expensive. And what were you doing in that cupboard anyhow? You know perfectly well the everyday glasses . . ."

"But I cleaned up all the pieces and threw them away. I didn't cut myself either." He was sitting up in bed now, eyeing her hopefully.

No doubt about it: his mother was upset. Johnny could be so careless. Still, she was torn between her exasperation and a certain admiration for his admission. Breaking the goblet was an accident, of course, and yet Johnny realized he was responsible too—and felt he must square things before his mother found out.

His mother sat down on the edge of her son's bed. "Accidents do happen, Johnny," she admitted, "because sometimes we're not so careful as we should be. But I appreciate your telling me the truth. It's best to admit it when you've done something wrong, or broken something. No matter what happens, if you always tell me about it, I can trust you."

Because this was a wise mother, nothing more than a goblet was shattered and a small boy was set out on the path to truthfulness via a well developed conscience.

Duty of Conscience

"The conscience becomes that part of the personality which handles the matters of right and wrong, good and bad, proper and improper. The duty of the conscience is to give the child a workable set of values," says Dr. Harry Joseph in his book, "The Emotional Problems of Children."

And it seems logical to add, it is the duty of adults to help the child's developing conscience.

When it has nagged him into a confession, it is up to the parent in whom he confides to walk the thin line between reproach and forgiveness. The youngster must know he has done wrong, but also be assured it is over and done with and will not be held against him indefinitely.

Never punish a child for telling the truth. We adults know, of course, that the truth does not always lead to pleasantness; but until a child can understand the moral point involved, try to make truth-telling as painless as possible.

When Mr. Jones pounds on your front door to report that the neighborhood gang, playing ball in the vacant lot next to his house, have broken a window, and he's pretty sure your Jim was the batter—well, you will ask Jim about it, naturally. Mr. Jones could be mistaken; but if he is right, the wise parent will make sure that if punishment seems necessary, it is given for the crime, not the confession. Let Jim know you are grateful for his truthfulness, but, if need be, he can pay for the broken glass out of his allowance or perhaps by cutting the Jones' lawn.

Children accept fair punishment and actually prefer to be truthful. They find it easier than trying to get by with a misdeed and being nagged by a guilty conscience.

The ability to tell the truth, especially when it means admitting a wrong, is a vital part of good character. But it does not just happen. This desirable trait must be carefully nurtured from toddler days. And part of that nurturing is to remember the children want to tell the truth—if we will listen and understand.

—By Marjorie S. Hildebrand

HELP YOUR CHILD
BUILD COURAGE

BUILDING courage in children cannot be accomplished by mere talk. Precept is less effective than good example. A good example is less effective than the courage a child gains through his own competence. Courage, or its opposite, is an emotion and is not ruled by intellect. It will therefore do little good to tell the child that he should not be afraid, that he is too old to be a coward, or that there is nothing to be feared. The thing for you to do is to try to get at the cause of his fear, which is actually a symptom of his inability to face situations.

At the age of nine, Jimmy was a shy, lonesome boy. He was bright but lacked close friends. Although he was strong, quick, well coordinated, and large for his age, he took part in no athletic activities. His father was concerned. He felt disappointed at his son's lack of popularity as much as Jimmy did. His mother often wondered whether his timidity might not have resulted from an experience at the beach. Jimmy had been thrown into the water by some larger boys and badly frightened. From being afraid of water, he became fearful of people and situations and began to keep away from others and retire into himself.

How Parents Can Help

Jimmy's father wanted to help him. He took his son fishing and built up Jimmy's confidence, away from the observation of others. They went swimming, though the lad's fear was easily discernible. However, the father ignored it and by one slow step at a time, he taught the boy to swim. Lessons continued until the boy was a really competent swimmer. He began to go to the beach again and to take part in athletics. He made a few close friends. In this way, one father helped his son in very concrete ways to build courage— courage which kept him from being the lonesome lad he was beginning to be.

No child can be successful at everything. Neither should any child know nothing but failure. Both success and failure are important in the development of each one of us. The child who enjoys continual success, while protected by parents and teachers, is likely to find the failures he encounters outside the family and school unbearable. He will not have developed the courage to face life beyond his familiar circle, because he has not experienced the educational effect of an occasional failure.

Dr. W. C. Allee of the University of Chicago, has made some interesting experiments in the matter of building courage. His subjects were mice, but human beings might learn a lesson from his discoveries. According to Dr. Allee, there is nothing like an occasional victory to develop confidence. He took a meek little brown mouse and placed it in a situation where it would have to fight some even meeker white mice. The brown mouse was at first not anxious to fight, but after a few victories he not only fought white mice but would also engage stronger brown mice. Dr. Allee found the reverse situation to be equally instructive. That is, warlike mice became much less assertive after they had experienced a string of defeats. Like Dr. Allee's brown mouse, people in general acquire courage from their victories.

Confidence Through Ability

Planned experiments have been carried on which show that children, as well as mice, develop confidence through growth in skills. Dr. George D. Stoddard, while at the University of Iowa, described an experiment in which teachers were asked to select the most shy and retiring pupils from their classes. These shy children were paired with pupils considered by their teachers to be the most aggressive and dominant in the group. But before the two types of children were brought together, the shy children were taught skills in manipulating complicated toys. They were carefully instructed in the use of these toys until they became competent.

When the shy child had acquired skill, he was placed in a room with the sets of toys and in the company of the aggressive child. The latter at first dominated the scene—he pushed the child who knew how to manipulate the toys out of the way, but was unable to manage the toys himself. In the meantime, the shy child went to another table and played with another toy. The scene was repeated. But after a while the aggressive child would watch the other child before he "took over." Then he began to ask questions before assuming control. Presently the shy child was asserting himself rather firmly. Pretty soon, the children exchanged roles, the shy child becoming aggressive and the dominating child becoming more retiring. Moreover, the exchange in roles persisted even outside the experimental situation. The courage and confidence which the originally shy child acquired by learning to manipulate the toys helped to carry him through other situations. The experiment illustrates, among other things, the fact that courage is learned through experience and the development of abilities.

Special Training

Ability to hold his own in a fight, ability to operate toys—these help the child gain confidence. Other skills, other knowledge have the same effect. If a child is just average in everything, if he has no outstanding skill, then he receives no particular stimulation for developing courage. Parents can develop their children's self-confidence by giving them special training in some particular activity in which they show evidence of being above average.

In helping a child develop confidence, one thing must be constantly borne in mind. Independence of action is the goal sought. If the child learns to depend too much on his parents, special training will be relatively ineffective. Some time should be spent assisting the child but there should also be times when the child is left to his own resources.

The development of courage is of truly great importance. It is involved in simple acts and in projects of lasting significance from childhood to old age. It is needed in meeting people, going to the store alone, starting to school and college, asking for a job, tackling a new undertaking, working out the problems of everyday living. Because the habits of behavior that are acquired in childhood persist throughout life, helping a child to build confidence is of far-reaching importance.

—By Harold W. Bernard

WHAT YOU SHOULD KNOW ABOUT TEASING

VERY often one of the first topics parents want to discuss in study groups is the teasing that goes on among brothers and sisters. "After every meal, I'm ready to pack my bags!" one mother said. "The only time my seven and eight-year-olds don't tease each other is when they're with Grandma. Then they tease *her!*"

Though the immediate family is usually the storm center, your concern with teasing may not be bounded by the walls of your own home. Perhaps your heart aches for a sensitive, unhappy son or daughter who always seems to be the butt of teasing at school and doesn't know how to tease back. Or, on the other hand, perhaps you're worried about the growing unpopularity of your child who teases his playmates so unmercifully that it really comes under the name of bullying. Or you may wonder what you can possibly do, within the limits of politeness, to tell off some adult relative or friend who makes a practice of baiting your children.

Although teasing is so common, it has many complex causes, effects and ramifications, and obviously there is no easy answer as to what parents can do about all of them. However, a general grasp of the whys of teasing can enable you not only to take suitable measures in specific situations when you ought, but also to take teasing in your stride when it is harmless—or even desirable, as it sometimes is.

Understanding can begin, strange to say, simply with looking in the dictionary. It's immediately apparent that a wide range of attitudes, motives and behavior comes under the head of teasing. "The dictionary definition reflects the looseness and ambiguity of popular use of the verb 'to tease,'" writes Dr. Margaret Brenman, psychologist at the Austin Riggs Foundation in Stockbridge, Massachusetts. "While the accent is placed on the hostile, destructive component, accepted definition includes the more benevolent dimensions of affection and humor. Literally, 'to tease' . . . means 'to shred finely, to disentangle, to tear in pieces,' but more broadly, Webster tells us, 'to vex, harass or irritate by petty requests, or by jest or raillery.' Yet another definition is 'the awakening of expectation and then its frustration,' the extreme of which is 'to tantalize.'"

Varieties of Teasing

Dr. Samuel J. Sperling, psychiatrist of Beverly Hills, California, comments similarly that "the numerous synonyms for teasing . . . can be arranged in a series from the more hostile, such as tormenting, bullying, badgering and pestering, through tantalizing, jeering, getting a rise out of, pulling one's leg and ribbing, to the more friendly such as kidding, joshing and bantering." In the Laboratory of Child Research, National Institute of Mental Health, scientists have been working to classify accurately and to define all the kinds of teasing.

But for practical parental purposes the important thing to recognize about teasing among brothers and sisters is that it falls into two general kinds— the one normal and acceptable, the other requiring serious attention as a symptom of something fundamentally wrong.

Make up your mind to it, you are not going to bring up a family without teasing. Often so subtle that you can't do anything about it (like the innocent "But I don't *know* where his ball is," or the clucking noises which annoy the baby), it's a way that children in the same family express resentment against one another. Such resentment, according to Edith Neisser, author of the book, "Brothers and Sisters," may come from nothing more sinister than living under the same roof. Except in a penal institution, she points out, nowhere else do people have to live together so closely—even in the Army you can request a transfer! This enforced proximity and the inevitable competition within a family, add up to the reason most youngsters will take less from a sibling than from an outsider.

Expect, therefore, that occasionally or periodically you will have to endure spells of your children's teasing one another. One day, for instance, things will have gone wrong at school for Junior and, having to take out his bad humor on somebody, he may find the baby the handiest. Another time your youngest, disgruntled because he had to be left out of a family excursion, may "playfully" mess up sister's dressing table. Sometimes your children will tease each other unmercifully as a device for getting attention.

Allow Some Teasing

But don't make an issue of such teasing. You should allow a reasonable amount of it to go on, for no one is so secure that at times he doesn't want to set himself up and be funny at someone else's expense.

Persistent, chronic teasing among brothers and sisters is, however, something else. This is usually a signal that all is not fundamentally well in a family, that rivalries, jealousies and conflicts are a little too intense. Mrs. Neisser suggests a few ways to decide whether you need to give serious attention to the teasing that goes on among your children. The answer is yes if squabbling and pestering is the only way they pay attention to one another, if they never present a united front, if they do not defend a brother or sister against an outsider, if their bickering and disparagement don't lessen under favorable circumstances, if their tone towards one another is bitter, not just small boy-girl talk.

The solution might be as simple as a change in routines which would separate the children more. Or perhaps you need to revise your disciplinary ways. Generally, there seems to be more teasing among children who are strictly disciplined; they can indirectly take out on one another what they dare not directly take out on their parents. The more democratic the home, the better the children are likely to get along together. But too much permissiveness can set the stage for teasing, for some children will do it to provoke their parents into setting limits on how far they can go.

Family Influences

Another way to tackle the problem is to think about the way you manage the family. Are household chores fairly apportioned? Is each child getting his due share of attention? Do you provoke rivalry by holding up his brothers and sisters as examples of good behavior? Do you make sure that he gets the activities and companionship appropriate to his age?

If after honest self-questioning you still can't see why any of your children should be jealous of the others, or why they all get on one another's nerves, a third person may be able to give an objective opinion. Sometimes professional help is needed to unearth and correct deep-rooted resentments.

Perhaps you are not so much concerned with family teasing as with one child who tends to be a constant teaser with outsiders as well as with brothers and sisters. Often such behavior alters when a child is helped to understand why he behaves as he does. One mother, for instance, drew out of her ten-year-old Mary the fact that she had failed her spelling test for the first time and ruined her chance for getting a gold star; she had been too unhappy, Mary said, to tell about it yesterday, when it happened. Might her being upset, mother asked, have something to do with turning out her older brother's desk light three times while he was trying to study and making her younger sister cry by repeatedly pretending to throw her doll out of the window? Mary's teasing didn't end for all time, to be sure, as a result of that little talk. But with repeated similar interpretations that helped her see the connection between her moods and her expressing them by annoying others, she did begin to improve.

Teasing Due to Insecurity

Some youngsters, suffering from a continuous sense of incompetence and inferiority, build themselves up in the only way they know—by tearing down somebody else. They jeer at boys and girls who have physical defects, get poor marks or wear shabby clothes. Obviously the remedy is to help such teasers gain a greater sense of their own worth with praise, affection and attention, and to provide opportunities for them to excel.

Whether or not you have a real problem on your hands with a teaser is, as in family teasing, again a matter of degree. How frequently does he tease? How hard? How much does he hurt, physically or emotionally? If the answers are, you suspect, "too often" and "too much," don't dismiss the behavior as "just childish mischief" or attribute it apologetically to being "a born tease." Nor will you solve the problem by punishing him for what he does. What needs to be got at is not the symptom but the cause. Habitual, malicious teasing, especially when a child seems to delight in causing pain, is likely to be an indication of emotional disturbance requiring professional attention.

Since it is just as normal to be teased at times as to be teaser, and youngsters need to learn "to take it," it is, of course, a mistake for parents to make a practice of intervening every time they discover their child being heckled. Remember, that at times children much prefer being teased to being ignored!

If, however, your child is constantly a victim, you need to look into the reasons. Sometimes they're quite superficial and easily remedied. For instance, his clothing, all or a minor part of it, may not conform to what "they" are wearing at school; then all you need to do, in order to spare him torment, is stop making him wear the offending garments. Should he be teased about being a "baby" or "sissy" perhaps it's because you have not let him do enough for himself.

When Ignorance Causes Teasing

When youngsters make a butt of a handicapped child, it is usually out of ignorance rather than innate cruelty. If your teasee has a handicap, you can make life pleasanter for him by explaining his condition frankly to other children and their mothers.

Of course the more a child reacts to teasing, the more he is bound to be teased—after all, it's no fun to annoy unless you can evoke some reaction. So one thing that may help is advising your child to disregard the jibes whenever possible, to walk away, to try to avoid showing his feelings. Something else that works at times is suggesting how he can answer back. You might make a game of acting out together—"Now I'll say what the children say to you and you say what you'll answer."

Occasionally, children are harassed by a teasing adult. Some adults tease simply because they are essentially ill at ease with children and know no other way to make contact. Others tease as an expression of unconscious hostility. Without realizing it, they may identify a child with someone they disliked during their own childhood, and camouflaged by playfulness, give vent to what they then had to repress. Indeed, you yourself may tease a bit too often and relentlessly for some similar reason!

Any form of teasing that makes a child feel inferior or mean, confused, bewildered or fearful, ashamed of his family, his social status or anything about himself should be avoided lest his belief in himself be weakened. Using shame or sarcasm, threatening or frightening, laughing at a child or belittling him, as so many adults do under the guise of "having fun," can be destructive. When both polite and plain-spoken attempts to get a harmfully teasing adult to change his ways are unavailing, your only alternative is to keep your children out of his way.

Positive Aspects of Teasing

Happily, teasing has its positive as well as its negative aspects! Dr. Sperling calls attention to a number of social and psychological values of teasing. For one thing, he says, its playful nature enables children to test both their control of their own aggressive impulses and their tolerance of aggression; it helps them learn how to avoid unpleasant consequences, to meet what is disagreeable and accept it with good grace and humor, to hold their own in competition—in short, it is a way of acquiring social techniques. Also, teasing has its uses as an aid in establishing conformity to group standards without preaching or precept. Taking name-calling, ridicule and mockery on the playground with good humor, is part of developing into a cooperative member of society.

Between children equally matched teasing can be sheer, joyful play, like the play of puppies who feign and withdraw from attacks which never come. Children tease playfully to try out others' reactions, and this teasing is a healthful educational experience.

Teasing which is pure play is also a delightful part of adult-child relationships, beginning with the game of peekaboo with a baby, going on to "Where's Johnny?" at the run-around age, right on through parent-adolescent banter.

Despite some nerve-wracking periods, wouldn't your home be a duller place without the imagination and humor that go along with teasing? "Those who love each other tease each other," runs an old proverb. Run-of-the-mill teasing, in short, is a definite asset in family life; only when it gets out of hand need you tackle it as a liability. —*By Edith M. Stern*

IS YOUR CHILD A TATTLETALE?

CHILDREN still singsong the ditty that goes, "Tattletale tit, your tongue should be split." Adults say, "Don't be a tattletale!" Yet do we really have it straight in our minds just what a tattletale is? Can we discriminate between the child who is calling for help or giving necessary information and the child who is tattling?

First let's admit that some talebearing is necessary reporting, the bringing of important information, the bearing of reliable witness—and some is tattling.

How can we judge which is which? We can decide that it is not tattling if it is information on which one must act. For example, a child ran up to one of his teachers during recess, "Johnny hit Mary on the head with a rock!"

"Susan!" the teacher said reprovingly, "you know we don't tell tales on others. Where are they?"

"Over by the swings," said Susan.

The teacher hurried off, without noticing Susan's face—confused, perplexed, hurt. Johnny had thrown a rock without provocation. Mary had a huge, bleeding bump on her head. Johnny was threatening to throw more. It was a situation which called for more knowledge and skill than Susan possessed. She had gone for help to the nearest adult on whom she could depend. And she'd received a lecture on tattling!

If a child plays with matches or does similar dangerous things we must know, and quickly. Whoever tells is no tattler, but a helpful and sensible person—child or adult.

What is tattling? Tattling is the bearing of nonessential information for some personal motive. Such as getting attention: "Mother, Paula is sucking her thumb! You don't want me to suck my thumb, do you?"

Yes, this child is tattling, but what she needs is attention. Give it to her. You might say, "I'm glad you've stopped. But we mustn't make Paula unhappy about it. If we help her to have a good time at our house, perhaps she'll forget to suck her thumb."

A second common motive for tattling is revenge.

"Alvin hit Barbara!" A glance through the window shows Alvin and Barbara are playing happily again!

"Johnny took my gun!" Yet your talebearer has already got it back.

Let us then define tattling not as "the bearing of tales," but let us define it even more clearly: "Tattling is the telling of something that is over and done with or something that isn't apt to be repeated or something trivial, reported through motives of jealousy or revenge or through a desire to get attention."

When you recognize animosity, a desire for revenge at the bottom of tattling, it is a good idea to help the child face what he is doing. "You're cross with Alvin. Everyone gets cross with people now and then, but they must learn to get over it too."

What Parents Should Do

From there on, step warily, depending on the personality of the child. Perhaps, "Why don't you go kick that ball hard—kick your crossness out on it? Then you'll feel better." For this child may never have been allowed to express his feelings openly.

To another child, who has learned to express nothing but animosity, we can suggest a new way of acting. Perhaps you might say, "If we're always cross we don't enjoy playing. Here are cookies for everyone. Suppose you pass them out and see if you don't feel better?"

Mothering is an art. Rules aren't the whole answer when people, big or little, are concerned—though they help. So does clear thinking, such as seeking out the difference between tattling and necessary reporting and being guided by good sense. In the final analysis, it is the wise and understanding heart that helps most of all.

—*By Donna Geyer*

WHEN ARE CHILDREN READY FOR CAMP?

COMES the time of year to think about camp, probably a million parents ask themselves, "Is my child ready for camp? Is this the year to start him or should we wait until he is a little older? Will he profit more by staying home or visiting relatives in the country? How will the whole family be affected if he goes to camp?"

These are some things to think about in answering such questions:

Age

The age of a child is not a determining factor in itself, but it provides a convenient yardstick. For example, it is doubtful if children younger than six should go to a residential camp under ordinary circumstances. Most children of six are not far enough along socially and emotionally to profit by a camp experience and few camps are specifically suited for them.

But some children of six are as emotionally and socially mature as many other children of seven or eight. And there are a few camps that are designed especially for children four, five and six years old. In these camps, the groups are small and the program geared to the energy, interests and developmental needs of this age. In a camp not limited exclusively to young children, the youngsters usually play, swim, eat and sleep apart from the older campers.

Parents often ask if there is any "best age" at which children get the most out of camp. It's doubtful. One age may be better for learning certain skills, another for loosening the parental ties, another for developing friendships and so forth. The majority of children in camps are eight to twelve, with the eleven-year-olds probably the most common. Many camps operate with this age in mind, which may give the nine-to-twelves something of an edge over the other children in getting the most out of these camps. However, just as some camps concentrate on young children, others specialize in the high school boy or girl, or both.

Emotional Adjustment

To be ready for a camp experience a child must feel secure at home. He should also enjoy doing a number of things independently. A fair test in these respects is the ease with which the child stays overnight, for example, at Grandma's. Chances are, a child who welcomes opportunities to be away from his parents is secure and independent. His reactions to staying home with the baby sitter when you go out for the evening give further clues. A child who is not sure of his parents' love, for whatever reasons, is likely to be even more unsure and insecure if he is sent off to camp for the summer. The youngster who "clings to his mother's apron strings" is best separated gradually. A period at day camp might give him a start toward emancipation.

Social Adjustment

The ability to play well with children his own age is another sign of a child's readiness for camp. This is important, for camping is essentially a social experience. A child who plays happily with other children will enjoy camp more than the one who is left out or made a scapegoat because he doesn't know how to play with others. Though no child needs the camp experience more than he, to send him might boomerang.

The first year at camp presents a number of new and different types of social experience for children. Ideally, a child should be able to adjust quickly to this new environment and way of life and move through the varied camp adventures with ease and enjoyment. The extent to which a child is able to do this depends on his ability to meet different social situations skillfully. Obviously, a child who knows some of the other children who will be in camp has a head start in meeting the new situations.

Your child's social adaptability can be judged somewhat by looking at his reactions to various situations outside the home. How does he react to eating and sleeping in different places? How does he behave with strange adults or children? What does he do in situations where he must compete with others for attention and status? How did he react to the first few days of school or to similar new experiences?

Physical Condition

Good physical condition is highly important for most camping experiences. Camp is a very active place and some children even find it overstimulating. If there is any question about your child's health, consult your pediatrician. (A camp wants a medical report from him in any case.) Any special physical problems should be considered. Some that may make it difficult for children at camp are persistent headaches, allergies, serious deviations in eating or sleeping, persistent irrational fears and bed-wetting. A good camp has resources for dealing with such problems and a successful camping experience may be anticipated for the children if their particular needs are known.

Many children with more serious disabilities—diabetes, blindness, cardiac conditions, orthopedic handicaps—are also successful campers. Many camps operate with one particular handicap in mind. For example, there are camps for the blind, for diabetics and for cardiacs. There are also camps where youngsters with many different kinds of disability are brought together in the same cabin groups. Some camps have facilities for children who are confined to wheelchairs or who require frequent medical treatment.

The question of whether a child with any such difficulties should go to a regular camp or to one that specializes in handicapped children is important. It's a good idea to discuss it with other people who have some training and who know the child—his doctor and teacher, for instance.

How does your child feel about going to camp? If he initiated the camp idea and continually asks you about going, you can be pretty sure he is interested. It helps to talk with him about typical camp activities and see how he responds. It will also help if he can talk with children who have been to camp and see movies of camps. Seeing that some of his present interests can be satisfactorily followed up at camp is an additional incentive. The more the child can share in the decision about going to camp and in selecting the camp, the higher his "readiness quotient" is likely to be.

A child's saying he wants to go to camp, however, should not be confused with his real interest or readiness. Many children go through a stage where they talk with great enthusiasm and apparent determination about what they want to do. Paul, a five-year-old, would talk all week about sleeping outdoors over the weekend. When Saturday night arrived, he'd announce he was sleeping in the cabin but was sleeping out next week. Here again, it is chiefly a matter of knowing your own child.

The Family Situation

The needs and interests of the rest of the family are just as important in the long run as the needs and maturity of the child. For some special reason, such as ill health in the family, it may be essential for a child to go to camp for the summer. The working widow with a child often has no alternative. Or perhaps parents feel they need time together, away from the children.

A feeling that you need a break from your child may be the factor that tips the scale. There is no doubt the great "improvement" that parents often see in their child at the close of camp is partly a reflection of their own relaxed feelings because they've had a vacation, too.

Occasionally, one child's going to camp upsets the harmony in the home. Try to spot the possible complication before you make a decision. Often, complications do not relate directly to a child's readiness for camp, but to the family's readiness for a child to go to camp. And this is something to answer honestly, too—not just is the child ready, but is the family ready, are *you* ready?   —*By Hedley S. Dimock, Ph.D.*

WHY CHILDREN MISBEHAVE

WITH increased understanding of personality and how it develops, we have had to alter our ideas about misbehavior. We know that all human beings have feelings, needs, drives and impulses. When these are frustrated, the individual tends to react in ways that we label unsatisfactory.

Actually your child's troublesome behavior is a symptom of some deeper distress with which he needs your help. His misconduct is not a sign of natural depravity or plain cussedness. It is essentially an S.O.S. signal.

Andy carved his initials on the coffee table the other day. It was a rainy Saturday afternoon and he was trying to say, "I'm bored—what is there to do?" If his mother had taken the time to suggest some other project and get him started on it, trouble could have been forestalled. Children are trying to tell their parents important things when they misbehave.

Steve took a quarter from his mother's purse to buy candy for some pals. He was trying to say, "I'm old enough for an allowance of my own."

You should look on misbehavior as a means for discovering the reasons back of it and what can be done about them. Merely punishing or otherwise preventing undesirable conduct sometimes makes matters worse.

Understand Real Needs

The Blakes are worried about their young son's stuttering. Pete is supposed to play in his own back yard but he is an adventurous child who craves excitement. Several times he slipped away and crossed forbidden streets on his way to a corner sand-lot where the older boys play baseball after school. He was punished and the stutter has developed as a reaction to his conflict with authority. If the Blakes had understood Pete's real needs, they would have bought some new playground equipment and invited other children in to play.

Charles W. Leonard has made a penetrating study of some of these difficulties which parents encounter. Mr. Leonard, Superintendent of the Illinois State Training School for Boys, knows about children who misbehave from working with thousands who are emotionally disturbed. Yet he is far from being either a pessimist or an alarmist.

In his booklet, "Why Children Misbehave," published by Science Research Associates, he says reassuringly, "A child who was not guilty of some forms of misbehavior would, if he existed, be abnormal. Misbehavior is a normal part of growing up."

And if you think that your children are sometimes a little too normal in this respect, here's more encouragement. In a study of 6,000 families, Norma E. Cutts and Nicholas Moseley turned up 132 things children do that their parents disapprove of. If yours give you only a few causes for complaint, you can at least take comfort in the number of annoying things they don't do.

A Matter of Opinion

If we could all agree on exactly what misbehavior is it would be a less thorny problem. But what is wrongdoing to one parent is often just the natural exuberance of youth to another.

As Mr. Leonard puts it in his booklet, "A child misbehaves when he does not act the way a particular adult thinks he should under particular circumstances at a particular time."

Our individual standards of behavior vary widely, based on our differing backgrounds and past experiences. What we expect of our children often depends less on our reasoning than on our emotions. It pays a parent to take inventory of his ideas now and then, especially if the children frequently complain that certain requirements aren't fair.

Paul's mother had been expected to change her clothes after school every day when she was a child. Much to his disgust she insisted that her son do the same thing. Often he neglected to put on his old pants if she wasn't at home to remind him. Then his nice blue serge trousers with the sharp crease got soiled or torn.

"The other kids don't have to," he grumbled. "Why can't I wear dungarees to school the way they do?"

His mother realized that she had been living in her own little-girl past. Once she stopped imposing outmoded standards on her son, his defiance ended.

Why Misbehavior Occurs

Misbehavior will be less baffling if you understand why it occurs. Children misbehave because they aren't born with moral standards, ethical values, good manners, a conscience or the ability to distinguish between right and wrong. It's a long, slow struggle to acquire these ideas that call for so much self-denial and control.

It is the strenuous task of parents to help their children learn control and consideration for the rights of others. Yet, if you live close to children you can't help realizing how often all their impulses run counter to our rules and regulations.

Noises fascinate a child. He can't understand why yells, crashes and thumps disturb grownups. He loves to explore but there are a disheartening number of things he may not touch. His imagination is keen and his embroidery of the truth seems entirely credible to him. Yet adults caution him not to tell such whoppers. Dirt is pleasant and mud feels good when it is squished between the fingers or toes. Parents don't always see it that way, especially when the stuff gets tracked into the kitchen.

As the child gets older, he often has cause to be baffled by parental inconsistencies. When he is small he is told not to talk back. Later he is scolded for not having enough gumption to stand up for his own rights. Bruce used to be punished for snatching other children's toys. He gradually became quite unassertive. Now that he is 12, he is being taken to task by his father for letting the other fellows walk off with his new bicycle.

Many of the traits you find most troublesome in your child's early years are later of much value to him. Curiosity, imagination, aggressiveness, enthusiasm and competitiveness help to make him a more successful adult. It's a great mistake to punish them out of existence. You can guide these urges into safe channels without eradicating them or making your child feel guilty about them.

None of us can avoid frustration and disappointment as we go through life. We are constantly torn between what we want to do and what we must do. Children have not yet had much practice at coping with this conflict. They want to watch television but instead must do their homework. Rain calls off the picnic. The model airplane a boy is trying to make proves too difficult or cracks up on its first flight.

It is our job as parents to help our children learn that no human being, including ourselves, can have everything he wants. To say, "I know how you feel. The rain spoiled my plans, too," makes you partners in distress. Nothing is ever quite so hard to bear if it is shared.

What really matters most is not the misbehavior itself but the way you handle it. You are not likely to run into any serious difficulties if you take your child's position into account, consider his side of the story, impose only reasonable restraints and act consistently so that he knows what to expect.

—*By Constance J. Foster*

DISCIPLINE AND PUNISHMENT

MANY parents think of discipline as punishment, or in terms of "making" a child obey. But discipline and punishment are not the same. Neither is discipline concerned with "making" a child do something. The aim of discipline is to develop a self-reliant child who can become a self-controlled adult. If we think of discipline in this way, we will try to find methods of control and guidance which put the responsibility upon the child as he gradually becomes ready for it. In this way we help him to control himself.

It is our job as parents to show the way. How we do this is all-important. If we continue to think of discipline as the emergency handling of a situation, or of "making" a child behave in a certain way, we are apt to be severe and rigid, to hold the reins too tight. But if we think of it as helping the child learn to behave in ways that are acceptable, we can be more relaxed for we know that it takes time to teach. We shall also realize that we do not have to crowd all our teaching into the early years of a child's life. There is plenty of time before he is grown up.

Much of our discipline fails because we expect more of a child than he can give at his particular age. For instance, we sometimes punish or scold children of six or seven because they do not sit still. Yet children of this age cannot be expected to sit still for more than a few minutes at a time. Their very growth needs demand activity, not passive sitting. Yet a child is often made to feel that he is "bad" because he does not sit quietly at a desk in school or through the entire family meal at home. Many a meal at home is made miserable for both children and adults because of the emphasis on table manners. Children under ten, and many older than ten, rarely have good table manners from an adult's point of view. They may still knock over a glass, or hold a fork awkwardly. As they grow older and gain more control, they will develop good manners if an example has been set by their parents. But manners should not be a matter for nagging or punishment during the early school years.

Parents Must Set Example

If Billy is going to have good table manners by the time he is in his teens, he must want to copy mother and father more than to shovel food into his mouth the quickest way. If Mary is going to remember to put her bicycle in the garage instead of leaving it outdoors, she must want to take care of her things, rather than feel so rebellious against mother and father that she doesn't care whether she takes care of her belongings or not. If a battle of wills has developed between parents and child, the child will rebel against guidance and be less able to learn than he will be if he has a happy, relaxed relationship with his parents.

If a good relationship exists, a simple explanation of cause and effect usually gets results from the school-age child. "Bring your wagon in, Joe, because it is going to rain," or "Please put your roller skates in the closet or someone may fall over them." Instructions given with simple but adequate reasons are the most successful and lasting way of getting cooperation. Much depends upon the way in which the statement is made, of course. If it is made with obvious irritation, or with an attitude of "Well, he won't do it," the child is much less likely to do what has been suggested than if it is made in the tone of voice which says, "You are a reasonable person and will naturally do the right thing." Children sense very quickly whether we have faith in them or we do not trust them.

Children will not accept every reason. The reason must be as acceptable to the child as to the adult. "Study hard so that you can be a great man some day" means very little to a school child, but "Just as soon as your studying is done, we'll play the game you suggested," may be an incentive.

A request must also seem reasonable to the child if he is to accept it. If all the boys in the fourth grade wear blue jeans or corduroys to school, John is sure to protest if his mother insists on knee pants or shorts. If all the children on the block are playing out-of-doors after school, Mary cannot be expected to come in willingly to practice her piano lesson.

Give Children Reasons

Obedience based on the acceptance of a reason leads to self-direction and self-control. The child who is taught to listen to a reason will be much better able to take care of himself than one who has obeyed out of fear of punishment. Such a child is often too timid to take responsibility or make decisions for himself. Or he may rebel against authority and refuse to carry out even reasonable requests.

Too many "do's" and "don'ts," too much talking, nagging or threats of any kind are ineffective with school-age children. They soon learn to disregard much of what we say, and even develop a sort of "deafness" to our many directions and the threats we never carry out. Yet many of us keep on talking at our children, instead of waiting until there is something which we really want them to do and then giving them the instructions simply and directly after we are sure that we have their attention. Too much talk is one of the frequent mistakes parents make.

Praise gets better results than blame in teaching our children desirable behavior. Many of us praise our preschool children and forget that it is just as desirable a technique with our school-age youngsters. Sue's mother kept scolding her for forgetting to hang up her hat and coat after school. One day she looked up at her mother and said, "Mother, you always scold me when I leave my coat out, but last week I hung it up every day and you never even noticed." In the same way a word of praise for behaving nicely at a friend's dinner table will do more to develop good manners than many scoldings about bad manners at home.

No child can be expected to behave acceptably all the time, even where an excellent parent-child relationship exists, and teaching has been carried out well and patiently. All children have their unruly moments. There are times when we have to be firm and stand our ground. It would be unwise, for instance, to let a child with a very bad cold go out in the rain however much he might want to do so. When you are firm, be good-humored and friendly about it, avoid the "don'ts," "you musts" and "hurry ups." Often a humorous remark substituted for a commanding tone gets the child to accept the necessity for complying with a reasonable request.

When Punishment Is Necessary

There will be times also when our teaching has to be backed up forcibly by punishment. Punishment is used when other methods have failed and we feel the situation is sufficiently important to see the thing through even to the point of punishment. The trouble is that most of us back up our points too quickly and frequently with punishment, so that we come to rely upon it as our only method of control. This is neither good discipline nor good teaching, for it means that someone else is putting on the controls for the child when our aim is to teach him to put them on for himself. Punishment can occasionally be used effectively as a reminder if a child has known that he must not do something and has deliberately gone ahead and done it without an adequate reason.

Punishment is sometimes necessary as a reminder in situations in which a child has become careless or thoughtless. Jack had certain jobs to do about the house on Saturday mornings. His mother allowed him to choose what time he would do them, but Jack got in the habit of putting them off and then rushing through them, and leaving them half done in order to get to the Saturday matinee. His mother felt that he was not carrying his responsibility for a job which he had agreed to do, and after warning him she kept him home from the movie the next week until he had completed his job adequately.

If punishment is to be effective, it is important that the child feel sure that he is loved by his parents. He must realize that it is disapproval of a particular bit of behavior, not of his whole personality. It is not "I don't love you," but "I don't like what you have done."

Punishment must be accepted as fair. The child must accept the fact that he is being punished because he did something which he knew he should not do. Until a child can understand why he is punished and accept the reason, punishment is harmful rather than of any value. That is why we do not punish little children, nor do we punish school-age children for those things for which they could not be expected to take any responsibility.

Avoid Severity and Ridicule

Punishment should never be too severe, neither should it involve humiliation or ridicule. It should follow as closely as possible upon what has happened. Once the child has been punished, the issue should be closed and there should be no further nagging or reference to it. Neither should mother wait for father to punish the child, but do what she feels is necessary when the situation arises.

Spanking is not a desirable kind of punishment. It may sometimes seem effective, but too often it humiliates the child and breeds resentment. It is not a good teaching aid. Often showing disapproval is enough punishment for children without going any farther.

Sometimes it is desirable to let the child take the consequences of his action. This usually works very well if it is used with common sense. The consequences must not be more severe than the original situation warrants.

If Bill leaves his baseball bat out in the yard, he will have to be late for the game while he hunts for his bat. Or if the wagon is left outdoors and gets rusty, Phil may have to put in Saturday morning with some sandpaper getting rid of the rust. But you should not keep a child home from a long-anticipated birthday party because he has not done his Saturday tasks around the house.

Making amends is also an effective way of teaching the school-age child. If Dorothy and Betty have left the kitchen in disorder after making candy they may have to miss seeing the start of the basketball game and wash up the dishes instead.

Does Situation Justify Punishment?

Punishment should grow less and less necessary as a child grows older if we are succeeding in teaching him to become self-controlled. When we do punish we should be sure we know what we are punishing for, and that the situation justifies punishment. It is wise to listen to the child's reason for coming in late to supper before punishing him; he may have a good excuse.

Perhaps he stayed to help a friend clean up the mess they had made while working in the basement. Instead of punishment, he needs only a simple reminder to keep an eye on the clock and to start cleaning up a bit earlier.

If discipline has become a real problem in the family and the children are unwilling to comply with reasonable demands, are constantly rebellious so that punishments seem frequently in order, it is wise to stop and examine the situation. Is too much being expected of them? Are there too many rules? Is the household functioning on an authoritative rather than on a democratic level? The authoritative parent feels, "I know best; my children must do what I say because I say it." Children—like everyone else—resent this.

The democratic family thinks of each member as an individual with individual needs and individual rights. Each member is made to feel that his ideas and his opinions are of value. The child who is treated reasonably and who knows that his opinions are given consideration becomes self-disciplined more readily than the child who has been brought up under a more authoritarian regime.

WHEN CHILDREN TALK BACK

SHOULD my child be allowed to talk back? Such a question would never have been asked by a parent fifty or perhaps even fifteen years ago. If it had been asked, the answer would have been an emphatic "No!" for talking back was considered one of the most serious forms of disrespect which a child could show to an adult. If a child talked back, mother blushed, and frequently took out the hairbrush. The fact that now the question is asked so often is an indication of a different attitude toward the child, a questioning about his needs and rights.

There are times when most adults feel that something for which they were blamed was not fair. We do not criticize the adult who in such a situation says, "I don't think that was a fair statement. I was not late deliberately, but . . ." and the reason follows. But if a child who is scolded for coming home late starts, "But Mother, I don't think you are fair . . ." Mother without waiting to hear the explanation may say, "Don't talk back to me!"

We know that it is natural and normal at times to feel irritated with one another. As adults, we have learned or are learning to control expression of our feelings in some measure, but a child is not so far along. He also has a need to express his feelings of irritation toward us, his dislike of us for the moment, his dislike of what we have done, or his protest at the pressures we are putting on him.

Learn Causes of Anger

These expressions are not a sign for anger or indignation on our part, but for taking stock. What have we done to make the child feel the need of expressing his feelings so strongly? Have we been criticizing and scolding more than we realized? Was the thing we asked the child to do fair? Instead of scolding him for the words he used, perhaps you can honestly say, "Well, Bob, I can see why you may feel pretty mad at me about that." Then if the child is old enough, a chance to talk things over may follow. Mother and the child can exchange points of view.

This does not mean that parents should always "give in" to a child, but it does mean that they should take time to hear what he has to say, try to find out why he wants to do something, or listen to his explanations.

Often we issue commands or prohibitions without stopping to think about the child's point of view at all. Mrs. Stone wanted something from the store. She could see Timothy playing ball on the corner lot, so she called out of the window:

"Come home right away, Timothy, I need some sugar from the store."

Timothy's side was winning and he was up to bat. "Aw—mum—can't I do it later?" he shouted.

"Come at once. I can't wait," mother called back. Timothy threw down his bat, stamped into the house, and burst out:

"You're mean! I wish you weren't my mother. Why do I have to go to the old store just when we're winning?"

Baseball was as necessary and important to Timothy in his particular stage of growing up as was mother's need for sugar. A little more consideration on her part, a little more forethought to see that the errand was done before Timothy started his game or after he had finished it, could have avoided angry feelings.

Expression of Dissatisfaction

Then there is the talking back which expresses dissatisfaction with the way things are being done. Johnny came home late from school. Mother had made a rule that he must come straight home from school and check in before going out again to play. One afternoon Johnny came home an hour late. Mother had been worried and as soon as she saw him she scolded:

"Johnny, you are an hour late. Go to your room. You can't play with the other boys today."

"But Mom—it wasn't my fault—"

"Go to your room, Johnny. Don't talk back to me." Johnny went to his room feeling outraged.

It happened that this time Johnny had a right to talk back. His teacher had asked him to stay after school to help her clean the aquarium. Johnny had been proud of being asked and had done a good job. If his mother had been willing to listen, she would have been proud, too, instead of angry.

It is wise to let the child tell his story and offer his excuse. Why shouldn't he have the right to state his case and know that it will be listened to with an open mind?

There is a difference between talking things over, and an endless argument. The arguing, nagging child may use this technique in the hope that mother or father will relent and so alter his decision. Children should not get into the habit of talking back about everything. If the child has expressed his opinion and seems to want to argue, a parent may need to say, "I see your point of view, but I still feel that you must do what I asked because," and give the reason. The adult often has to close the argument, but it can be done good-humoredly.

Tending to Copy Habits

Children copy undesirable habits as well as those we should like them to cultivate. Often mother and father bicker back and forth about things more than they may realize and the child picks up the habit.

Many times, of course, bickering in the family is a sign of deeper tensions. If it is constant and intense, it is more than habit, and is a sign that something needs to be done. Sometimes it is wise to seek aid from a trained and understanding person who can help discover the basic causes for the strains.

Our American children cannot help getting the idea from radio, movies, television, even from some adults that the wisecrack is a highly desirable form of wit. The effect of this cannot be minimized. We cannot keep the children from being exposed to television and comics, nor should we be shocked when they turn up with a retort that we ourselves laughed at when our favorite comedian tossed it off. Children talk back because it seems to them a desirable and perhaps clever thing to do. This is an influence which children of the past did not feel. It may have considerable effect upon the talking back of our older children. It will be necessary to accept a certain amount of this type of retort, for no individual family can change the pattern.

Guidance Built on Understanding

We have heard many times that we must keep control of the situation. Talking back may seem to threaten our control. We are afraid that if the child gets away with it our authority will end; we will have lost face. We forget control built upon authority is in a shaky position anyway. It doesn't stand strains as well as guidance built upon affection and understanding.

"What will the neighbors say?" also makes it difficult for us to accept back talk from our children. It is still considered by many people a mark of great disrespect. Most of us were brought up to believe that children should show respect for their parents, that if they did not do so the parents had somehow failed. Children in the past did appear to treat their parents with greater outward respect than some of our youngsters seem to do today. Such conformity might and frequently did cover many tensions and strained relationships.

Today we are learning that a parent-child relationship based upon an enforced outward respect is not enough. Unless that respect has developed naturally from a deep, affectionate relationship between the parents and the child, it is neither desirable nor real. This does not mean that children should be encouraged to be ill-mannered toward their parents or toward other people. It does mean, however, that where this deep affectionate relationship exists it is possible to accept and to understand individual limitations. If we are realistic we must accept the fact that people cannot always show perfect love and respect for each other. There are other powerful emotions which must sometimes have release and expression. Where a warm relationship exists, occasional talking back can be accepted without a loss of respect or affection, whatever the neighbors may say.

Learning Self-Control

Talking back at home and talking back to grandma, a neighbor or a teacher are very different. Mother and father should have the capacity and maturity to understand and accept the need which a child has to express his normal feelings of anger, dislike and protest. But not all adults have the same tolerance and understanding. The mother who will stand calmly by while Jinny is rude to grandmother is not helping Jinny to become a very acceptable or accepted member of the community.

Jinny does have a need to express her feelings, but it is equally necessary for her to learn to live with other people. If she talks back to grandmother, mother can say to her later on, "You must not talk that way to grandmother, it hurts her feelings." She can then go on and let the child know that she understands how she feels about grandmother. By giving the child an opportunity to express her feelings about grandmother to her, she has begun to help the child inhibit and control herself when it is necessary to do so for the sake of other people, and at the same time she has given the child an opportunity to release her feelings instead of bottling them up inside herself. This is very different from simply saying to a child, "You must never say things like that about people." Within the family there should be freedom to express one's feelings about others. As one boy said, "If you can't talk like that to your own mother, whom can you talk to?" —*By Gladys Gardner Jenkins*

WHEN CHILDREN FIGHT

THERE is rarely a child study group at which sooner or later the problem of what-do-you-do-about-fights doesn't turn up. There are almost as many different kinds of fight as there are different kinds of children or situations in which they find themselves. Some of them may be good healthy outlets—others are very unhealthy.

Very often, when all we see is the on-the-spot battle, there is actually a long background of irritation, an issue between the two scrappers which had never been satisfactorily settled. Between two brothers, for example, there can be the issue of one taking liberties with the other's privacy and possessions —liberties that the parents don't know about. In such a case, the real issue isn't the fight at all, but the feud between them.

Sometimes the trouble starts as a justified defense on the part of a victim against something intolerable which another was doing to him. Such unwarranted attacks of one child against another occur frequently—sometimes viciously, as in the case of a bully who torments a weaker youngster for his own satisfaction, until the victim reaches the breaking point.

Playful Fighting

Still different is the case where two youngsters roughhouse with each other and both enjoy it—one or the other may even be "asking for it" playfully— until all of a sudden something goes wrong. One may hit harder in the excitement of the moment or go beyond the rules of the game, and what started out as good-humored roughhousing flares into a real fight. In such a case one who steps in to break it up or to umpire should be sure he knows the two partners began in good-natured play and the subsequent fight was actually accidental.

Sometimes it is a struggle over something that can be had by only one at a time—a window seat in a train or bus, the only screwdriver or hammer, an activity in which both want to be first.

When this type of fighting occurs with unwarranted frequency, as among youngsters in a camp cabin or among brothers and sisters, it is wise to help them by instituting routines which give a definite promise of fair turn-taking or, where it is possible, to supply enough of whatever it is that is being fought over to avoid conflict.

Often a youngster moving into a new neighborhood and challenged into fights, can take the challenge as rejection by the established neighborhood group. He needs help in understanding that this is not necessarily the case. It may rather be—in an unusual guise, admittedly—an offering of friendship. Such fights, however, must not be confused with cases of group persecution based on an evil desire to victimize a newcomer.

Fighting Prompted by Boredom

Much of the fighting and wrestling that children engage in on an overlong car ride or after a spell of rainy days at home or in camp, or even after a stretch in study hall or exposure to an overlong speech, is prompted by a need for heavy body movement or muscular exercise to relieve boredom.

While the individual characteristics must be taken into account in every case, there are a few general hints that may be helpful to you in handling a fight between children.

When you step in, keep calm. Watching, or even more interfering in a fight, automatically raises your blood pressure. However, it merely adds fuel to the fire when the one who tries to smooth things out injects his own anger. It may not only blind the combatants to any point he tries to make, but his own judgment may also be blurred as to what's best to be done.

How much talking should you do? There are two sides to this coin. One is that it is better to act, wasting no words—stop the fight, and let the consequences take care of themselves. The other is that so much lies back of the fight—the fight merely climaxing underlying issues—that a lot of verbal thrashing out is necessary to clear mixed-up feelings and confused thinking.

Both arguments have their justification, but each is applicable to different situations. There are some incidents where the issue is quite clear. All the youngsters need is help to smooth their ruffled feelings and a chance to find more reasonable ways to solve their problem. They can take over from there. Again, there are situations where stopping the fight is just a prelude to tackling the much more important job of working out the real issues.

When to Stop Fighting

It is well for all parents to remember that even with usually peaceful children, in fighting which starts out as a normal test of power, either of the opponents may be led to such a state of panic or fury that he needs help to get disentangled. Once fighting gets to that stage, it needs to be stopped, and fast. No matter who started it, or who is right or wrong, they both need to be taken off the hook. This is especially important for an adult to know because in such a situation one or both of the youngsters often would like to have an out, but neither dares stop for fear of losing face with an audience, or with himself.

It is a good idea to do a minimum of talking at the moment when you interfere. If there are any hangovers of ill feeling left, choose a better time. Argument or explanation can only take effect when the two partners are over their irritation and are ready to listen to reason.

With youngsters, particularly of school age, the question of losing face with the group or with themselves is of tremendous importance. In struggling to end the fight at all costs, the adult may become oblivious to this important issue.

To be on the safe side, avoid nagging, scolding or belittling at the time of intervening. It is enough to stop the fight. If anything critical has to be said to Bob or Jane, don't say it in front of others, but privately.

If you judge too quickly as to whether a fight was fair, justified, necessary, while the youngsters are still smoldering with excitement, you take too much of a chance. It is likely that your first impression is based on incomplete evidence—the real facts may not come out until you hear the full story. And even if your first hunch is right, a smoldering kid is not likely to understand what you say. You have a better chance after the combatants cool off.

Another thing to avoid is throwing adult standards at a youngster—"Nice boys don't fight," "You don't want to act like a bully." Children, especially in the heat of excitement, are much more likely to be under the influence of peer standards than those of adults. In the world of children, for instance, their fighting may be praiseworthy, impressive to their age mates, may even be demanded by the situation for the sake of prestige. If you want to argue with them against this, it's better to do it later. Admitting that one is wrong isn't pleasant for anyone, especially if an opponent is looking and listening.

How do you know whether they are fighting too much? There are two important clues. One is the question of how age-typical the fighting habits of a youngster are. We would expect some fights to be normal, in frequency and in form, for three-year-olds, while for a twelve-year-old the same circumstances would not lead to a fight at all, and certainly not to the same kind of kicking and screaming. On the other hand, we would expect the young adolescent to feel dared into a display of fighting spirit for no other reason than to demonstrate that he has outgrown the "little sissy" stage.

Note Degree of Excitement

The other clue to watch for is the extreme of excitement or behavior to which a child may be led in the course of a fight. The degree of excitement or fury should have some direct relationship to the issue involved and what led to the fight.

Make sure they get the point. Sometimes when you stop a fight, what you wish to convey to the fighters is not that they had no cause for the outbreak, but that they should have used other means for settling the dispute, or that they offended the code of what is fair and reasonable. Get the point across but don't confuse it with other issues.

Fortunately, children deliver into our hands so many opportunities to present our arguments about fighting that you are not likely to lose out in getting across your favorite point.

Just be sure to drive home the point that fits the case—don't leave the issue fuzzy so that the youngster is left feeling he's had a double dose of feeling misunderstood or has been handed an alibi that leaves him with an exaggerated sense of triumph. While children may need help in calling a halt to the brawl they got themselves into, they also need help in handling the feelings induced in the fight. This after-care is your job and may be just as important to a child's festering emotions as physical care is to a festering wound.

While at times the nature of after-care is to help a youngster come to grips with his own feelings about the incident and to understand your adult reaction, at other times the best method is to provide him with an opportunity to work out some of his anger, embarrassment, guilt or possibly lowered self-esteem, by providing him with some form of relaxing or sublimating activity. In other words, steer him away from moping by getting him as quickly as possible into some kind of constructive interest, preferably play with others, that soaks up some of his lingering emotion. Diversions of this kind can also serve as important preventive measures to avoid unnecessary fighting.

Prevent Unnecessary Fights

Some fights are unnecessary, the result of boredom, loneliness or reaction to overexciting gadgets or games; or they are outbursts due to feelings of impotence, or of being rejected or unloved. Such unnecessary fights can often be reduced by preventing such extreme situations from arising. For instance the parent who starts out on a long trip in good spirits, with enough toys, with something familiar for the younger children to hang on to en route or in that strange motel, with enough games to keep the older kids occupied and happy, will have done much more to reduce the number of scraps and feuds that arise than the family that does no advance planning.

Parents should not be fooled into thinking that all fights between brothers and sisters are just a form of sibling rivalry for not all fights between siblings stem from that source. Two brothers live in close communion in a small world of intensive family relationships, with many things to be shared, many facilities that must be used in common. Naturally conflicts arise and often lead to fights. Jealousy may not always be the primary issue, and it is well to find out what else may be the cause.

You may occasionally miss the real issue in a specific case. The main thing is that the youngsters know that you are not brushing off their conflicts as kid stuff. Most of them are quite able to sense whether you are genuinely concerned about getting at the real issues. They appreciate an attitude of fair dealing even if sometimes you lose your patience in the heat of a particular meleé.
                                    —*By Fritz Redl, Ph.D., as told to Katherine Glover*

HOW TO TEACH TABLE MANNERS

LET'S face it! Children have atrocious table manners. They eat with their fingers. They spill their milk. They either bolt their food or endlessly toy with it. They talk with their mouths full and use the backs of their hands as napkins. If all this sounds familiar to you, you have a child who is developing perfectly normally.

Why, then, should table manners be considered a child's problem? More truly, it is a parent's problem. All the child needs is time to develop the motor skills and tensional control necessary to conform to a more or less arbitrary set of conventions. It is not enough that he learn the rules of good behavior at table. He must be able to keep that body of his still for what seems to him an interminable time when his whole being is geared for action. He must develop a high degree of coordination if he is to manage silver, glass, food, mastication, speech and posture simultaneously and without mishap. And he must have practice, lots of practice.

Reports of group studies made of children, notably those of Dr. Gesell, show that, with few exceptions, all children follow certain predictable behavior patterns in eating. They go through various stages from the age of five, which is the earliest age at which any importance should be attached to table manners, to the age of ten, when most children have mastered the mechanics of eating and are acceptable dining companions both at home and in public.

Behavior Patterns in Eating

These stages must not be too closely connected with ages, however. While most books on child development find it convenient to classify by age there is considerable overlapping. In general, then:

Five still needs help with his eating. He tires soon and may wish to be fed the remainder of his meal. He likes to play with his food and spills a good part of it. He prefers his fingers to the silver although he will manfully try to manipulate his spoon or fork until he wearies. He finds it hard to sit still.

Six is a restless dynamo and appears to have less muscular control than he did at five. He is all elbows and seems unable to move without tipping over his milk or sending a plate crashing to the floor. He is apt to dive into his food like a hungry bull at a haystack only to slow down and stall once his initial craving is satisfied. He doesn't want to wear a bib, "like a baby," but has little skill with a napkin. He is determined to talk regardless of the amount of food in his mouth. He has developed strong likes and dislikes.

Seven can sit still for a longer period although he likes to jump up often and is impatient to resume his play. He handles knife, fork and spoon with greater skill but is not up to cutting his own meat. He is given to daydreaming at the table and is beginning to show interest in the conversation of others. Once in a while he remembers to use his napkin, if he can find it.

Eight eats with gusto, to say the least, amid a weird assortment of sound effects. He finishes his meal quickly and can hardly stand to wait until the other members of the family are finished and he can get back to his play. He continues to reach for whatever he wants but will surprise his parents occasionally with an unsolicited "thank you." He may eat in complete silence or burst into the conversation of others with a tale of the day's activities.

Growth of Good Manners

Nine is conscious of what is expected of him and is usually willing, if not eager, to conform but he still needs frequent reminders. His eating skill is of a high degree and accidents are rare. He continues to have decided likes and dislikes but more readily accepts the idea of eating small portions of food. Now and again he shows a glimmer of consideration for others such as passing food and being content with his fair share of dessert. He manages to coordinate eating and talking very well and usually awaits his turn at conversation. He may still prefer his napkin by his plate, rather than on his lap, but, oh, happy day! he uses it.

Ten is over the hurdle. Reminders are necessary from time to time but parents may expect to dine with their ten-year-old son or daughter (little girls follow the same behavior pattern) with ease and, sometimes, pride. Ten is capable of good table manners; he is ready to do an acceptable job. How well he does it depends in large measure on the treatment and training he has received during his apprenticeship.

Once we understand that Junior's difficulty with table manners is not a matter of perversity or backwardness but a matter of growth and maturity, and that he shares this difficulty with all other children, it becomes apparent that any attempt to hurry this growth process by pressure or punishment is both futile and unwise. It can do no good and it may do much harm. Many "problem eaters" are the result of a too strict insistence on table manners.

What Parents Can Do

What, then, can be done to ease a situation admittedly nerve-wracking?

1. Provide a chair that fits the child. A youth chair is excellent, or you can raise the seat of an ordinary chair by the addition of a booster seat or chair pads and foreshorten the seat with a back pillow.

2. During the worst of the spilling stage serve Junior's meal on a metal tray with a deep rim. The tablecloth is spared; mopping up is easy.

3. When adults choose tools, a paring knife or a golf club, they buy them to fit—size, balance, weight. Yet many parents expect their child to switch from baby spoon to man-sized silver when his hand is one-third the size of daddy's. Intermediate-sized silver is available or salad fork and butter spreader make a good substitute. A pusher will also make Junior's task easier and eliminate some of the handling of food that parents find so distressing.

4. Give the restless child a break, literally and figuratively. Let him flex his muscles between courses by running about or helping to carry dishes to the kitchen. If he is a speedy eater and finishes his meal long before the rest of the family, excuse him until dessert is served.

5. Most children under ten prefer plain foods. Their taste buds are sensitive and a mixture of flavors is confusing. Many seasonings and spices which adults consider mild are too penetrating for a child's taste. With this in mind, mothers can often arrange for an individual serving with little or no trouble. For example: if chicken à la king or chicken curry is on the menu, why not give Junior a drum stick and hot biscuit or plain buttered rice?

Additional Helps

6. Children like to eat with their fingers and they like foods they can gnaw on. Children also prefer their vegetables raw—carrots, turnips, parsnips, cauliflower. It is less work for mother and Junior profits two ways; raw vegetables are highly nutritious and he will eat more of them.

7. One of the most annoying traits children have is that of talking constantly at the table and interrupting adult conversation. It may be a bid for attention or it may be boredom. One method of dealing with this problem is for mother to start the conversation at table by saying, "Johnny, let's hear about your day and then we'll hear about Daddy's." Johnny will often recount his doings and be content to listen for the remainder of the meal. He has been recognized as an individual which, after all, is what we all desire at any age, and he has had his say.

8. Children who rebel at constant reminders to say "please" and "thank you" will delight in using the foreign language equivalents; the French "s'il vous plâit" and "merci beaucoup," the Spanish "gracias," the German "danke schön," the Danish "mange tak," and so on.

9. In training for good table manners, as in training for anything else, a word of praise is worth a hundred words of censure. "You behaved very nicely at the table tonight, Susan," will do more to improve Susan's table manners than repeatedly saying, "What a messy eater you are!"

10. Children are great little imitators. A parent who hopes to train a child to excellent table manners must unfailingly set a good example.

—By Helen S. Sharpe

HOW NEAT CAN YOUR CHILD BE?

GUM paper on the coffee table, jacks on the living room floor, coats on the couch, crackers on the bureau, ice skates in the front hall. When would she ever learn to put things back where they belonged?

Where, wondered Carol's mother, did I make my mistake? If I had been stricter with her when she was four would she be tidier now? Isn't there some way that you can train a child to be neat?

Perhaps the chronic disorderliness of the preadolescent would be less discouraging if you didn't still have a vivid memory of the tidy little three-year-old that he once was. You can still remember that little paragon of neatness who actually insisted on putting everything back in the proper drawers.

The three-year-old is a stickler for form. He puts the light out when he leaves the room. The cars go in the garage, the doll in her carriage, the gun in the holster, the coat on the hook. Actually, however, model behavior in this respect doesn't stem from any adult-like respect for the way a house looks or even from any desire to take good care of belongings. He seems to enjoy orderliness for its own sake.

Neatness Habit Short-Lived

Unfortunately we read into his tidiness motives that are not there so the letdown is great when at four or thereabouts all of his former "virtues" disappear. Now he doesn't need to hang his sweater on the hook. He learned how to do that ages ago! He has new worlds to conquer. And the very self-confidence that allows him to suffer a relaxation of his bedtime rituals or do without his mother for longer periods inures him to disorder about the house.

By the time he is going to school the young housewrecker may have calmed down appreciably. He takes a certain pride in his appearance and especially in his possessions. If, during the next years, he becomes an avid collector of baseball cards, match covers, shells, butterflies, mica and/or small white stones, he may even become so meticulous for a time that he is almost impossible to live with. And he cares enough about how he looks to slick down his hair with a quart of water each morning and start off to school combed.

This period of compulsive neatness is likely to be short-lived. By the time he is eight or nine he seems to have lost all interest in the state of his room, his appearance—and even in your estimation of him. His whole life is wrapped up in his contemporaries and if he stops in for a moment to get his catcher's mitt he would hardly notice if the house was upside down. He goes from one activity to another and although he has no principled objection to picking up his shirt on the way to his room, it would never occur to him unless you mentioned it. His dirty face and hands are a badge of his virility and even if he had time to tuck in his shirt he would scorn to do it. He could comfortably wear the same pair of dungarees for two weeks and he considers getting a haircut an unnecessary distraction.

Untidiness in Girls

The nine-year-old girl is no less exasperating—probably more so because you can't help feeling that a girl, at least, should by now be developing some standards of housewifely order and personal tidiness. She may, of course, have spurts of concern for the way she looks or the decor of her room. She may brush her hair for half an hour, experiment with six different hairdo's, and try on five combinations of skirts and blouses in rapid succession. But let her remember that it's time for her club meeting and she will fly out of the house, her dress half-buttoned, snatching her oldest sweater and a half-finished sandwich on the way.

The compelling needs, interests, motives which make children neat or sloppy, aware or unaware of disorder at different ages are deepseated and have a way of defying your best efforts to change them.

There is much that parents can do to preserve a modicum of order about the house. By making use of a child's interest in doing, his pride, his desire to please you or, at a later age, his matter-of-fact conformance with reasonable immediate requests, you can get a certain amount of help without making an issue of it. If you set your sights on the job to be done rather than the character to be molded the results will be less discouraging. The prospects of getting a nine-year-old girl to clean up the bathroom, merely by asking her to do it, are rather good. But the likelihood of transforming her into a child who really cares whether the bathroom has been cleaned up, is a slim one.

If, when your child comes home from school, you call from the kitchen, "Hello! After you hang up your coat come on in and have a brownie," you haven't really chalked up a major accomplishment in the way of teaching your child neatness. Her preoccupation with more important matters remains just as strong. But the coat is probably hung up. And at this stage parents must all be thankful for small favors!

What Parents Can Expect

You can, if you wish, declare the living room out of bounds for half an hour before your company arrives or decline to enter into a pie-making project ten minutes after you have mopped up the kitchen floor. You can limit clay and paint and water to a particular locale and keep an eagle eye out for the times when a well-placed wastebasket will save some later picking up. You can ask a child to wash his hands before dinner or comb his hair before school and expect him to do it. What you can't expect is that he will "care how he looks," "learn to be neat," "think what the neighbors will say," or realize how much work he is causing you. If he did, he wouldn't be the normal, happy, growing child he is.

Whatever success you have in enlisting your children to help you keep a semblance of order about the house the results will fall far short of that serene, well ordered, each-ashtray-in-place establishment that announces to you the moment you enter it, No Children Live Here. The hope that our home can maintain that childless-looking composure dies hard with many of us. Yet die it must, if we are to avoid the tension and sheer fatigue that come from trying to do the impossible. After all, there's no reason to keep our children a secret! Chances are that the guests who are coming to dinner or the neighbor who drops in for the afternoon have come in contact with a child before. The unfinished checker game in the living room, the dirty towel hung awry in the bathroom, or even the wad of clay on the chair will hardly astonish them. The lack of perfect order is no reflection on your housekeeping. It merely proclaims the happy fact that In This House There Are Children. —*By Jane Whitbread and Vivian Cadden*

HOW ATTITUDES TOWARD LEARNING ARE SHAPED

PERHAPS no other period of life is so full of listening, watching, mental pulling apart and putting together as the years of middle childhood—from ages six to ten or so. These are the learning years. Where he was previously content to note that balls bounce and airplanes fly, your child is now hungry to know how they are made and why they operate as they do. His concepts of time and space have broadened at the same time that his language ability has increased. He can begin to push out his thinking into distant times and places. He wants to know what goes on in the world of grownups and is ready to be taught whatever his culture considers essential.

Originally, of course, all the teaching of children was done at home. Then certain training and information was set aside as the business of special teachers who taught *all* the children. Home was to do the rest. But presently educators began to talk about "the whole child" and to realize that Bobby comes to school in one piece. He can't leave his toothache, his worry about moving or his interest in cowboys at home. No more, once his eager mind gets hold of them, can he leave school affairs at school. We have about come to the conclusion that the child's education must of necessity be a cooperative project of home and school. The basic emphases and responsibilities differ, to be sure, but we needn't be surprised or disturbed by overlapping. Bobby gets his teeth examined at school, and he brings into geography class items learned at home.

What Schools Can Do

Some things the school is better able to provide than the home. Here the child can function in "a small world" of other children, learning the give and take of social living. It is hard to do that at home, for even if there are several children they will be older or younger than he and have quite different interests and abilities. Then, too, at school the adult in charge is there solely to teach. She has special training for the job and can devote her time and energy to it.

The situation at school is more structured than at home. Certain definite things are expected, there is a time schedule, and limits for behavior have to be set more closely than at home. The authority to which a child must adapt is impersonal as compared with that of his own parents. This is his first experience of authority unweighted by emotional ties and the attitude he develops toward it may permanently color his feelings toward such authority.

Even the most comfortable classroom must be organized and businesslike, for the big adventure in exploring new knowledge must be systematic. It need not be dull; for the traditional "Three R's" are but tools which lead into all sorts of interesting fields as soon as the child begins to use them in a practical way.

Encourage Use of Skills

At home encourage your child to use these new skills in a variety of activities: to keep memos and lists, to exchange notes, jokes and so on—not as "homework practice" but for the fun and convenience of it. The tools themselves are challenging to a child. One youngster, for example, reduced the circumference of the earth (the biggest distance she could think of) from miles to yards, to feet, to inches, and came out triumphant with a number she had to write lengthwise on a sheet of paper. How she treasured that paper!

Wise teachers and parents realize the deep satisfaction and feelings of self-confidence that come from knowledge of one's own abilities. A good teacher lets every child know how she rejoices with him over each achievement that is progress for him. A wise parent shows interest in all his child's projects and products, the crude drawings, the improvised dramatics, as well as the report card. So often we're excited when our children show progress in reading, music or sports, but a clay horse that the child is excited about evokes just a glance or a nod. When work is done at home we can show that we consider it important by helping the child plan a good time for it and by supplying a quiet, properly lighted place to work. We can even help with it on occasion, so long as we give only the supportive kind of help that makes the child better able to tackle the next task independently. We show him how and where to find the answers—but do not patly solve the problems.

Opportunity for Responsibility

Nothing helps a child feel confident and capable more than being given an opportunity to take on various responsibilities suited to his growing powers. Both school and home can help, while being careful not to overburden him. For example, we should not expect him to live up to his greatest ability all the time. Nobody does. Although Elizabeth can make her room truly immaculate when she tries, she should not necessarily be expected to keep it so. Besides, if curiosity and eagerness to learn are to be kept alive and fresh, we must think not of what the child is able to do but of what he is interested in and wants to find out. We must try to help each one to develop his own unique bent so as to become more fully his own best self.

Aside from general health of body and mind the two most important parts of a child's equipment for school success are a good emotional attitude toward learning—that blessed curiosity and investigativeness—and an ability to understand and use language well. Being able to live comfortably in a group of children his own age is important, too.

The attitude of the home toward learning is basic. Do you take the time to answer your child's questions? Not to over-answer them and so choke off interest, but to tell enough to satisfy yet leave room for more wondering to develop. Do you take questions seriously enough to look up answers when you don't know them? A child picked up a barnacle on the beach and, before they were through, that child's family knew the whole life story of barnacles.

Attitude Set at Home

The child's attitude toward school and teachers is largely set at home. Most children are eager to start school, yet feel some natural apprehension about this new experience. Unfortunately, some have been threatened by older children or by parents with how good, quiet and obedient they will have to be in school. Some parents thoughtlessly make slurring remarks at one time or another about the local school system or modern methods; or they recount instances from their own youth of undue severity by teachers and of children's mischievous retaliation. There may be a few austere teachers around, but most are friendly and love children. Yet one has only to watch children "playing school" to see their hidden, lurking fear of a teacher's authority. The dictatorial tyrant that they usually portray is not a picture of what the teacher does but only a mockery of the things they half fear she might do if one were bad. Parents should make sure that their remarks about school and teachers do not encourage children to magnify these fantasies.

Any normally intelligent child can learn all the subjects of the elementary curriculum—unless he is afraid of them. That may make him helpless. Yet none of these subjects requires special aptitudes. The child may have to work harder or may need more help with some than with others, but don't let him develop that "I just can't do arithmetic" attitude. Especially make sure that he does not think of any subject as a bugaboo because father or mother (who both seem mighty wise and powerful) say it is too hard.

Share Your Interests

But aside from your duty to your children, how do you yourself feel about learning new things? Is it a necessary bore or half the fun of life? How do you react to discussion of a topic you know almost nothing about? Are you bored and indifferent or curious and eager to learn something new? Do you read both for pleasure and for information?

If parents themselves are mentally alert and have broad interests, they naturally talk about a wide variety of topics, read for pleasure, look up information as needed, organize family excursions to points of real interest and enjoy helping the children satisfy their many curiosities. All that involves using a lot of words, so the children develop good vocabularies. They know the right names for things and can say what they mean, not just roughly but with some precision. Think of the advantages they have in reading and writing because they do not have to learn the meanings of unfamiliar words at the same time that they are struggling with the written symbols for them. Think, too, how much more easily they can understand the many directions, explanations and items of information that come to them through words. If we realize these things we will not make the mistake of talking down to our children or keeping discussions of our own interests for times when they are not around. They understand a lot more than we think.

Your child can learn from you that acquiring knowledge is a bore—or something tremendously vital and exciting. —*By Rhoda W. Bacmeister*

WHEN A BRIGHT CHILD
FAILS AT SCHOOL

JIM BAILEY was an only child of rather ambitious, competitive parents who put a high value on his doing well and being a credit to them. In the first three grades he had measured up to their expectations. But it hadn't won him any friends among the other children who were a little jealous of the ease with which he learned. Now, at nine, Jim was simply finding more satisfaction in masking his brightness than in showing it. The approval of his classmates mattered more to him than the high marks he could report to his parents at dinnertime.

There are any number of reasons why bright children fail to learn as much or as fast as they are capable of doing. Sometimes, as in Jim's case, the trouble is temporary. Once he had found that there were ways of being both popular and bright, he stopped clowning. When Jim joined the other youngsters in working on a group project, they welcomed his brightness since it contributed to the success of what they were trying to do. He discovered that when his abilities served others, they were pleased with him.

In other instances the child is in need of considerable remedial help before he can get straightened out. The first thing to do if you have a bright child who still brings home unsatisfactory reports from school is to check with your doctor. A child can't learn properly if he doesn't hear well, has an eye defect, or is chronically fatigued.

If the trouble isn't physical, it may be psychological. This label can cover a multitude of difficulties, ranging from a left-right confusion that makes the child see "was" as "saw," to general nervousness and bewilderment because of some inner worries that make it hard for him to concentrate. Simple tests reveal the left-right confusion that makes reading so difficult, and it needs to be discovered early before the child develops a lasting hate for schoolwork or becomes a behavior problem at home. Unless he gets help, he's apt to decide that he isn't as bright as the others, whereas actually he may be only a naturally left-handed person who has been changed to right by training. More boys than girls seem to be affected by this difficulty. It is remedied by special teaching methods designed to overcome the handicap.

Detecting Emotional Conflicts

Emotional conflicts are more difficult to detect and sometimes call for expert help. But the run-of-the-mill kind, such as all children experience at times, are fairly close to the surface and yield rather easily to a good parent's detective work.

Linda had done well in school her first year. Then her mother had another baby. Unfavorable reports began to come home from the second-grade teacher. Linda was tense, distracted, unable to concentrate on her lessons. The answer wasn't hard to find. Linda was jealous of the new sister at home who occupied all mother's attention while she was at school. As soon as her parents realized this and began to give her more of their undivided time and interest, Linda was able to pay attention at school again and stop helping herself to the things with which she had tried to comfort herself for lack of exclusive parental affection.

Bright children are often especially sensitive and imaginative. Things bother them that don't even occur to less gifted children. It may seem silly to parents but youngsters in the lower grades often do poorer work at school than they are capable of for such slight reasons as fear of a barking dog they have to pass on their way to school, terror of some neighborhood bully who teases and taunts them, or shyness about having to ask permission to go to the bathroom. Self-consciousness on the part of a timid child can paralyze his thinking when he has to stand up and recite in front of others. Misunderstandings about sex often inhibit normal curiosity about other things and decrease enthusiasm for learning.

The Inhibited Child

When one big, important "Why?" fails to get answered, children are sometimes afraid to ask other "Why's," either because they have lost interest in asking questions or for fear they won't be answered. The inhibited child isn't free to learn. Too much of his energy is tied up in inner turmoil. It takes much of his time and strength just to keep the lid down tight on his feelings.

Whatever the cause, the child who is unwilling to learn is usually a troubled child. It's the job of parents and teachers to find out why. Scolding him only aggravates the trouble and complicates it still further. Children are not naturally lazy or incurious. Ordinarily they enjoy approval and love to excel. So if a bright youngster can't seem to make the grade at school or starts backsliding, it would be a good idea to ask yourself these questions:

Causes Contributing to Failure

1. Overmodesty. Is modesty or pride interfering with his desire to learn? The student who is embarrassed by public praise may try to hide his excellence. He doesn't like being the center of attention and he can't walk off with all the honors without attracting a lot of applause. So he clams up and acts dumb. The youngster who is too proud to admit that a specific skill is too difficult for him may comfort himself by pretending that it's not worth learning anyway.

2. Feelings of futility. Does he feel that it is futile to learn because he cannot possibly meet the standards set by his parents? If you push too hard or too soon, a youngster often becomes balky.

One boy in junior high school put it this way: "I quit. I can't win. If I get an A, my dad says it's because I'm a chip off the old block and inherited my brains from him. He just takes it for granted. If I don't get an A, he pulls a long face and asks me where is my family spirit? He doesn't think about *me*. It's all *him*."

3. Discouragement. Has your child accepted your discouragement about him and learned to regard himself as a failure? The parent or teacher who tells a youngster that he's a flop or is "poor" at arithmetic is not asking for any improvement. Only the feeling of success acts as an incentive to do better. Give a child a good reputation for something and he will work hard to deserve your good opinion of him. Let him feel that he's "no good" and there's danger that he will become worthless. A highly successful teacher once said, "I always find something to praise, no matter how small. I find it gives me more to praise a week later."

4. Boredom. Is he bored because the work is too easy? Where a school is rather rigid and each child does exactly the same lessons, the youngster who is brighter than the others may lose interest and actually drop behind because he gets in the habit of loafing or thinking about other things. The solution is sometimes to skip a grade, especially if he is large for his age. Often he can just be given some extra projects such as doing some outside reference work to help the others. On the whole it's better for a child to stay with his own age group and not feel "different."

5. Skills. Does he have a chance to use what he learns so that it seems real and important to him? To learn, a child must do more than just copy a list of words, practice scales, or do twenty examples. He must enter actively into what he is learning.

Joan found arithmetic easier after her mother let her put up a lemonade stand in front of the house and make change for her customers.

6. Understanding. Does your child understand what he is learning? We sometimes laugh at a youngster's classroom boners without realizing how hard it is for him to remember something that makes no sense to him.

If your child is having difficulty learning something new, talk it over with him and make sure he understands it and isn't just trying to memorize it. Drilling is of little use if what he is repeating has no real meaning for him. Many children get through the lower grades because they have good memories and can repeat like a parrot. But later these same children run into difficulty. See that your child grasps the basic idea of what he is trying to learn.

7. Overconscientious. Is your child overconscientious? Strange as it may seem, this trait of perfectionism often interferes with success at school. The youngster is so fearful of making a mistake that he goes over the work again and again, wasting much time. He checks and double-checks his problems for fear something is incorrect or unfinished. This fussing and fuming may put him behind the others and meantime he makes himself and everybody else miserable. Such a child isn't very sure of himself and needs a buildup. More love and affection may help him to think more of himself.

One thing is sure. We cannot develop interests or appreciation by demanding them. We cannot punish a child into liking anything. We cannot force him to do something he resents and expect him to relish it. The more we can help him enjoy what he is doing, the greater is the probability that he will learn to like it.

—By Constance J. Foster

IF YOUR CHILD
DISLIKES HIS TEACHER

JOAN has always done well at school. And she has been honest and candid in talking over her school problems at home. But suddenly she is failing in science and her explanations don't seem to make sense. Her parents are puzzled and troubled about what to do.

"I've told you a thousand times," Joan wails. "Mr. Scott and I just don't get along. That's the whole story—that's all there is to it."

Joan's parents are upset. There is enough earnest exasperation in their daughter's voice to leave them thoroughly disturbed. Suppose, they ask themselves, just suppose that Joan is right. She and her teacher simply do not get along. If so, what can they do about it—if anything?

The complaint is certainly admissible. What is so remarkable about this, when you stop to think about it? Aren't personality difficulties fairly common in practically all phases of life?

In such a case, the Smiths have a chance of a lifetime to make the most of a disturbing problem. Certainly, Joan's failing in science is serious. But there is opportunity here for education important to her future happiness: learning to get along and work successfully with people.

As adults, Joan's parents know the meaning of this principle from their experience in all kinds of activity—economic, social, religious, civic, recreational, and so on. They have learned how to keep peace with people who rub them the wrong way, because the reasons for their association with such people are bigger and more important than personal irritation. They are such reasons as supporting a family, building a church, working for the Red Cross or shaping up a successful bowling team. They are reasons that are important, dwarfing personal animosities and keeping them in check.

Developing Mature Insights

Joan's school career belongs to this type of task that is bigger than personalities. Somehow, her parents have to help her understand this. Not just by telling her and certainly not by scolding. They themselves must undertake the role of teacher (in the best parental tradition) and help their daughter think the matter through on her own. By asking thought-provoking questions, they may guide her to the insights which bring maturity and success not only in school work, but long after she is out of school. The important thing is that Joan herself should find the answers.

What are these questions? In part this depends on how the family confab works out spontaneously, but they should run something like this:

How many teachers do most people remember long after they've finished school? Why? This should lead to the idea that, like other people, teachers are not uniformly memorable, and that it is childish to expect them to be; that all teachers, regardless of personality, have valuable skills, knowledge, traditions and attitudes to impart; that teachers are not chosen as entertainers or superdiplomats, but as guides to learning.

Do you think everybody in Dad's place of business is lovable, attractive, understanding and friendly? If not, what enables him to go on living with some of his co-workers? Dad can point out the necessity for restraint where higher goals are involved.

Is it possible that what appears to be disagreeable in your teacher may be due to personal troubles? Teachers are human, too! There may be a sick person at home or loneliness. Joan will appreciate being invited to think in such adult terms. She is beginning at her age to feel broader sympathies for the woes of mankind. An appeal to largeness of spirit in human affairs has powerful urgency for children.

What do you stand to gain by making an issue of your dislike, and what do you stand to lose? This question calls for a practical appraisal of self-righteousness and its consequences.

How can one carry on successfully in class, even though there may be a lack of sympathy and liking between oneself and a particular teacher? This question should lead to a discussion of techniques of tact, diplomacy and humor in dealing with people who rub us the wrong way. Sarcasm of any kind, Joan will discover, is destructive and damaging. So are all forms of passive resistance. Her belligerent declaration against fawning and apple-polishing must be recognized as just. On the other hand, the Smiths will try their best to get her to discover the difference between hypocrisy and quiet, responsible, determined cooperation. Discreetly guided to insights like these, Joan is likely to reach new depths of understanding about certain realities of life.

—By Doris Pennant

HOW TO BUILD
A HOME REFERENCE LIBRARY

A GOOD reference library should be a basic part of every home. Such a library should include the following kinds of book and supplementary materials:

Dictionary. Children are in the fourth grade when the dictionary is commonly introduced at school. For your home reference library, a "beginner's" dictionary works best for young children. If you think word definitions are easy without a book, just try to describe a raft to a young child, or a cow.

In addition to the child's dictionary, every family should eventually invest in an unabridged dictionary. Here you can dig into the rich background of our language—where words come from, sample uses, and how words have taken on new meanings.

Encyclopedia. An encyclopedia serves a purpose entirely different from that of the dictionary. The dictionary describes *words;* the encyclopedia describes *subjects,* from aardvark to zygote.

We parents aren't nearly as well informed as our offspring think we are. We can't possibly know all the answers. Even a prize-winning Pop is likely to be stumped by a question as simple as "What makes it rain?" or "What do tadpoles eat?" or "Is a Bessemer furnace like our furnace, only bigger?"

The encyclopedia is a blessing, too, for parents who help their children with homework. Before you buy one, sample several and select the one that you and your children like best. There are a number of good ones, each with its own strong points and special features.

Don't worry too much about what educators call "levels of readability" in the encyclopedia you buy for your child. Some of the words may be beyond him, but you can help him form the habit of looking them up in the dictionary. Why miss the rewards of helping your child to understand what he reads? The ideal home learning situation is one in which child, encyclopedia and parent form a happy, comfortable triangle of knowledge-in-motion.

Children's literature. While reference books help you to extend your child's mental horizons, a professionally edited set of classic literature helps to mold not only his thinking, but his emotional growth. Who will his heroes be? How will he react to the responsibilities of adult life? Great literature, keyed to the child's interests, aids you in the all-important task of character formation.

"The right story at the right time" is a precept for graded series of literature for children. As you read to or with your children, you will meet some old friends. Many of the classic stories for children, such as *Alice in Wonderland* and *Water Babies,* have great appeal to adults.

A set of children's literature in the home stimulates the development of special interests in fiction and biography, leading a child into wider reading at the library and at home. Some sets include special activities for the younger children.

Is fiction part of a home reference library? Yes—if only because many of the allusions in your child's daily reading and talking take on true meaning if he knows their setting in fiction, from "Cinderella story" and "birds of a feather" to "much ado about nothing." Modern educators emphasize that the well rounded individual, no matter what his occupation, is one who has a good grounding in literature from childhood on.

Maps and globe. Maps are also a necessary addition. These include an atlas and, if possible, wall maps and a globe. An atlas has the great value of bringing one class of information together in a single easy-to-use reference work. Many atlases offer features which make them especially useful for planning a trip, tracing news events or doing homework.

The best kind of globe is one that can be taken off its stand and held in the lap, while you explain that there is actually no "up there" or "down here" on the earth, and that "where you are" can be thought of as the center of the world. With a piece of string stretching from point to point on the globe, you can show why the great circle route is shorter for airplanes than a route following east-west lines of latitude. This is difficult for children to understand even after it is demonstrated, but so fascinating that they usually want to try it again and again across various segments of the globe.

Wall maps are great attention-getters. Put one up in a room your children pass through frequently and you will find them stopping to "browse" over the earth's lands and waters, learning as they go. "Here is where we went on our vacation," "The new boy at school came from here," or "This is where bananas come from."

Religious books. The Book of your faith is an essential part of the reference library in a religious home. Your minister, priest or rabbi can suggest annotations or other supplementary reading to add to the historical background of your faith.

Yearbooks and almanacs. Yearbooks and almanacs are helpful. Most encyclopedia publishers issue yearbooks. Both yearbooks and almanacs summarize the news and trends of the past year. You really need both, however, because they serve your informational needs in different ways. The yearbook surveys the year's events in narrative form, and supplements the articles in the encyclopedia. It records the year's progress and trends in science and invention, vocational opportunities, politics and many other fields. The almanac provides summaries and tables of statistics on every conceivable subject, from the leading hitter in the National League to the number of television sets in Buffalo, New York.

Convenient Storage Place

This completes the list of your basic home reference works. Does it surprise you to learn that they take up only about four and a half cubic feet in your home—or one-fifth the space required for a clothes drier? It may take a little ingenuity, however, to decide where the best spot is to put these fact-hunting books. Some families have solved the problem of where to put reference books by stacking them on a library cart, or home bookmobile. This can be wheeled easily from room to room. It has space for your basic home reference library plus newspapers, magazines and new books. The bookmobile may be parked beside the table for question-answering at mealtime or near the television set for quiz shows or educational programs. It's a comfortable companion for mother in the afternoon before the children come

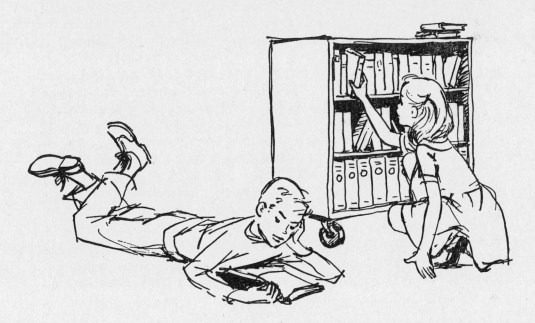

home from school. In the evening it rolls into the children's room for recreational reading or study. If you own a saw and hammer, you can make a
bookmobile which consists simply of two or three shelves mounted on large
casters. If not, your local librarian can tell you where she bought hers. An
old tea cart may serve the purpose.

Once you've acquired your basic reference library, special interests may
lead you to branch out in almost any direction—a book on baseball to help
father coach the Little League, a biography of Brahms for enlightenment
about a new symphony record. As children reach the "collections" stage,
there may be requests for books on any number of subjects, from rocks and
roses to bugs or battleships.

Public Library Can Help

The public library often prepares special reading lists for your guidance
on both book buying and borrowing. The librarian will help you find and
use published indexes to the available literature on any and every subject.

In expanding your reference library, don't overlook the type of publication
which librarians call "free and inexpensive materials." Your state university
probably issues free pamphlets on a variety of subject matter from raising
hamsters to raising the nap on a rug. Many manufacturers publish useful
booklets on subjects related to the wider distribution of their products, as
a little judicious coupon-clipping from magazines will demonstrate. Sometimes you can pick up useful free literature at the supermarket or drugstore.

A home library can mean enjoyment in acquiring learning together. It
keeps everyone on his toes—and as a side benefit to adults, it keeps us young.

—By Everette E. Sentman

TELEVISION
—AN AID TO LEARNING

THIS is a school composition by a ten-year-old. It sounds pretty average
—but there's a uniqueness connected with it. "About a week ago a little
girl from Clevelon was operated on. She was five years old. This case was a
very unusual one, because the girl was born with a hole in her heart. The
hole was in the center of the heart. Since the hole was just in between the left
and right side, when the blood was pumped by the heart, the new blood and
the old blood ran into each other. So they had to operate. They made the
operation by freezing the heart to a temperature of about 40 or 50 degrees.
You see by freezing the heart it slowed up sirculation of the heart and also

slowed up the heart, so when they operated they could take more time doing it. After they soed up the hole, they defrosted the girl and she was perfectly fine.

"So now you know what a blue baby is, they call it a blue baby because when the old and new blood mix, it forms a blue substance.—*by Ronald*"

What's unique about that? Just this—the composition was not based on material from a book or an article, but on a single sequence of a television program, lasting no more than five minutes. Yet, in spite of the fact that the material was entirely new to the boy, the details are highly accurate and the explanation substantially correct.

This brief essay, discovered by chance in a school notebook, instigated a number of provocative questions—and an extensive investigation to answer them. Are we parents doing a *constructive* job with the most intriguing medium in our children's lives? Can we do something more than guide our youngsters away from objectionable programs and see that they don't neglect their homework and other activities? Isn't it time for us to find an answer to the question: How can we use television to the best advantage for our children?

How to Promote Good Reading

In the early days of television, we frequently heard the comment, "Now they'll never read another book." Much to the surprise of parents, educators and librarians, this didn't happen. Certainly reading has been reduced in quantity and the peak period for reading has been pushed ahead by six months or a year. However, a survey conducted by the United Parents Association in New York City has come up with the interesting discovery that even though reading has diminished in quantity, it has increased in quality. And there lies one cue to our approach as parents.

We can improve reading by keeping track of the stories dramatized on the air—and then suggest reading other books by the same author.

To stimulate the transition from screen to book, put up a special Television Bookshelf (better yet, have your child make one at school or at home). The name itself will remind you and him to be on the lookout for books—and don't limit them to storybooks or even the classics. Science demonstrations, any one of the weather shows, circus, zoo and pet shows, as well as child-and-animal series can excite an interest in books.

Through these programs the child can get a provocative introduction to folk music and folkways, unusual occupations, various arts and crafts, faraway lands, as well as the inside of factories, laboratories and museums. The results are already showing: libraries and bookstores are reporting a far wider selection of books than ever before. This has occurred with relatively little cooperation from parents. What would happen if we all charted the way to the library and bookstore by going there with our children, by giving more books as presents, by dipping into new kinds of reading matter ourselves? Television can arouse many passing interests; we must be ready to feed those that merit cultivation.

Plan a Television Corner

In the average home today, children spend more time before the television screen than in any other single pursuit. We can, and should, cut down on the amount in most cases; but we must at the same time make the viewing productive. Here are a few concrete suggestions:

Place a low table near the set, with a dictionary and an atlas on it and nearby (if you have one) an encyclopedia. If your set is in a recreation room, a wall map of the world is a good addition to the atlas. Suggest looking up questions of fact.

For younger children, have a drawer or shelf at hand, containing a drawing board or clipboard, crayons, large pads, blunt scissors and other materials needed for participation in activity programs. Also, keep a chest or box in your child's room to be used for all kinds of odds and ends that will help him carry out his newly acquired ideas—bits of cloth, tape, string, wire, pipe cleaners, and so on.

Start Projects Through Programs

One of the constant cries against television is, "But it makes spectators of our children!" Actually children don't *have* to watch without reacting.

For instance, seven-year-old Johnny was fascinated by a time-lapse film he saw on a Saturday morning program; it dealt with the growth of plants from seeds. His father, who watched it with him suggested a simple experiment. Together, they placed beans in a saucer of water, and within a few days healthy sprouts began to appear. Delighted, Johnny gathered all the seeds he could find—grapefruit, orange, birdseed—and tried them all. The interest grew like the plants themselves, until at nine, the boy has a small window greenhouse in which he raises seedlings to be planted in the garden.

Any parent can find constructive projects via television. Does fifteen-year-old Jane admire a dress worn by a favorite actress? With some encouragement and assistance, she can make one for herself. Is twelve-year-old Andy intrigued by the easy way they make brownies on a commercial? Let him try it for himself—and learn that cooking can be fun for males, too. Is Andy's five-year-old sister entranced by the mobiles she saw on the nursery school program? See that she gets the materials and the necessary help—and hang her colorful handiwork near her window where it will dance in the breeze.

All you have to do is watch their faces, listen to their comments, be on the alert for budding interests, use your own imagination in finding materials! Your children will do the rest.

A Tip from Teachers

More and more teachers are recognizing television as a source of inspiration and information—and building on it. Some appoint, or have the pupils elect, committees to review the different types of program available during their viewing hours. Discussion of their reports helps to develop critical sense—and sometimes, happily, leads to *self*-criticism and revision of viewing patterns. Other teachers suggest putting reports in the form of a television script, or dramatizing historical events after the manner of a news program.

Parents can help children integrate television with school work. By keeping a close eye on programs to come, we can find shows that suggest subjects for research and reports. By watching outstanding programs *with* the children we can broaden their viewpoints and help them build a background for future academic work as well as life.

Many teachers are posting carefully selected television reviews on classroom bulletin boards, along with book notices and suggestions for out-of-school activities. On Sundays at home we might gather the family together and look over the presentations for the coming week, then post a tentative list. The mere idea of making up a schedule is a healthy reminder to explore programs and select judiciously. It also gets the child into the good habit of budgeting his time wisely. —*By Robert M. Goldenson, Ph.D.*

QUESTIONS AND ANSWERS ABOUT MUSIC LESSONS

HOW can I tell whether or not my child should have music lessons? Music is as vital a part of education as the three R's. It was considered so by the Greeks, centuries before Christianity. Its study is a long-term project which develops self-discipline, requires mental and physical agility, trains the memory, the imagination and the intelligence and gives indescribable joy. The rewards of this study consist not alone in the ability to play an instrument, but in the understanding and appreciation of the beauty contained in the orderly assembling of rhythm, melody and harmony known as music.

Any normal child can be taught to play an instrument and to become familiar with the materials of music. Music lessons are the form this instruction usually takes; if they follow or supplement some early experience of good music, such as singing and dancing, playing games, listening to radio and recordings, so much the better. When you allow your child to have lessons, you are setting his feet on the way to an endless source of pleasure and interest that he can make his own for life. Be glad if he wants them.

Are there tests that show natural aptitude for music? Yes, there are such tests. The Seashore and the Kwalwasser-Dykema tests, which are well known to educators, must be administered by a trained musician and take over an hour to complete. They are directed to children of nine or older.

A new pair of tests by Dr. Jacob Kwalwasser take ten minutes and can be answered orally by a child of six. They deal with the child's reaction to changes in pitch (high or low), in time (fast or slow), in intensity (loud or soft) and in rhythm (regular or irregular). They are intended for those with no previous training in music, and their object is to determine the extent of *natural* aptitude. The results are useful as a guide to the teacher and possibly as an aid in selecting the instrument the child will play.

Should only a child who shows talent take lessons? Even though a child doesn't seem to take to music, he should have his chance. There is no proven method of determining at an early age how much talent a child possesses. Aptitude can be appraised through tests but talent becomes apparent after lessons begin, not before.

Should a child under five who shows musical aptitude take lessons? It is a little early for formal teaching but not too early to develop a love and interest in music. If he really is exceptional, has heard a fair amount of music and is begging to be taught, you might try a few test lessons. Mozart was a performer on piano and violin at four, and many great men and women in music were boy or girl wonders. Watch carefully to see that the child is not forced. At this age, it is generally best to play and sing and dance with your child as much as you can; if you cannot, supply the need in some other way—through group play with friends or in nursery school.

If there are other small children in the neighborhood able to play musical games more advanced than those they learn in kindergarten, you might organize them into a pre-instrument class or a rhythm band and find an experienced teacher to guide them.

When should serious music study begin? The actual study of an instrument is generally best begun between the ages of six and ten.

How do I go about selecting a teacher? A recommendation by an impartial professional is more trustworthy than that of a nonprofessional friend or schoolmate. You need to know with whom a teacher has studied, how much he or she has taught and performed. He need not be a concert artist but he ought to be able to play well enough to illustrate how it should be done. His disposition is extremely important, too, for the teaching of music demands infinite patience. Make sure that he or she loves both music and children.

If you live in a large city where a music school is within reach, the school will recommend a teacher. You can attend a group lesson or a pupils' concert, and you can draw your own conclusions from this evidence as to his suitability for your child.

In small towns which may lack a good teacher, an enterprising and informed parent can benefit her entire community by bringing one into the town. A group or groups might meet once a week under guidance imported for the day. Then in time, as the need grows, the teacher might be invited to settle in the town, with a minimum guarantee of enough lessons to assure a living. Many foreign musicians have been successfully established countrywide in this fashion by the American Committee for Emigré Scholars, of New York. A teacher of music is as necessary to a community as a doctor and is to be chosen with the same care.

My thirteen-year-old has had lessons for five years. He is discouraged and wants to stop. Should he? He has come to a turning point. The first year his interest was fresh; the music, the teacher and the facts were a novelty; he could watch his own seemingly rapid progress. After several years there comes a time when his interest lags, as it does with many children. He is listless about going to his lessons, practices unwillingly, complains a lot, can't see why he has to spend time at his instrument when he'd rather be out with his friends.

This is the phase that tries parents' patience. Discuss it openly with his teacher. Suggest to her continuing lessons but relaxing practice discipline, while giving material that is connected in some way with his other studies and activities. You and she might find a new musical group for him, since he is at the sociable age when a musical team could bring as much satisfaction as a baseball team. You might give him a secondary instrument. Select a melodic one that he can play for fun. If his teacher doesn't cooperate with your efforts to hold his interest, try one who does.

He may not respond at all, and if not, you will probably have to discontinue lessons until the phase is past. If he has had moderately good instruction, then he has learned during his five years to read printed music, to sing at sight, to listen intelligently and to exercise some discrimination. Although he will never perform a concerto with orchestra he is not and never will be a musical ignoramus.

My child has had lessons for a year. How can I judge whether or not he is being well taught? Certainly not by the number of little pieces he can rattle through. One piece in which he knows what he is doing is worth a dozen mechanically learned and performed.

A child's way of practicing is revealing. If he goes willingly to his instrument, his teacher has scored a valuable point. If he seems interested, concentrates, plays well-selected music and improves, however slowly, he is on the right track. If he doesn't seem as advanced as someone you know who started at the same time he did, he may simply have less aptitude. Don't hold it against his teacher.

Listen to his own comments. "I like Mrs. X, she explains things." "Miss Y gave me a piece by Mozart and told me all about him. I love Mozart!" "Miss Z plays duets with me and the lesson is over before I know it!" Such comments are evidence that he is being well taught.

If a child doesn't like her teacher, should she change? The first thing to do is to find out why. The child may have good reasons or she may be rebelling on general principles. "Too strict," "dull," "too much to practice," "keeps me on the same old thing all the time," "talks too much," "makes fun of me when I make a mistake," "keeps telling me how much better others play than I do," are valid criticisms which should be taken up with the teacher. Intelligent discussion may clear the atmosphere. A personal antipathy which cannot be brought out into the open is harder to deal with.

If persuasion and discussion are useless, a change had better be made. It is true that a change of teacher usually entails a change of methods, which may slow progress for a time. This is a brief disadvantage. You want your child to like music, so you had better see to it that she likes her teacher.

Should a child have private lessons or is a class preferable? Both have their place. While learning to play an instrument, a child should at the same time be studying the construction of scales and chords, what makes a tune and what an accompaniment. He should have ear-training and sight-singing. These subjects are most enjoyably and successfully taught in classes.

In acquiring the technique of playing an instrument, on the other hand, a certain amount of individual instruction—say, one private lesson a week—is desirable. The teacher-child relationship becomes established, the child progresses at his own rate of speed, his difficulties are ironed out and his faults corrected before they become habits. In addition, at least once a month he should meet for a group lesson with three or four others who are studying the same instrument. Such meetings encourage friendly competition, dispel timidity and self-consciousness, provide an incentive for practice and instill the idea of ensemble playing.

Should my child join a class of beginners at school? After-school instrumental classes in the public schools are fairly new and there are not as yet enough teachers specially trained for this work, though among the few there are sure to be some inspired ones. In many schools classes are too large for individual attention. In New York City they are limited in size to four to six in piano, eight to ten in strings and winds; the public school owns and lends the instruments, and the charge per lesson is fifty cents.

In a public school class a child is in danger of acquiring bad habits in playing, especially in the vital beginning. On the other hand, if the classes are small, the teacher enterprising and not overworked, and if it is important to spare expense, public school lessons can be a test of the child's aptitude and liking. Whenever you consider it advisable, you can supplement the school lessons with outside instruction.

How can I help my child select an instrument to study? Don't be in too great a hurry to decide. Consider his natural aptitude, his likes and dislikes. If possible, let him be introduced to different instruments which he is free to handle while a trained observer is casually present. He may blow a wind instrument in such a way as to demonstrate a natural good embouchure (way of using the lips) and fingers that lend themselves well to the manipulation of the keys and valves on wind instruments. He may pick up a fiddle and approach it with relaxation and affection. He may gravitate to the piano, liking the feel of the keys, the agreeably stable sound. Or his baby devotion to drums may culminate in a preference for percussion. In certain music schools, several introductory weeks are spent in this informal supervised browsing.

The cost of the instrument chosen should not play too large a part in the decision, though it cannot be disregarded. Teacher or school can help to find a used instrument or one that can be rented. The recorder is an inexpensive melodic instrument, which sings pleasingly in solo and ensemble, and for which lovely music has been written. It is easy to play and has an agreeable sound. With its help, your child can learn to read written music and to play all the scales, while you and he are making up your minds what instrument he will ultimately study.

Should every child learn to play the piano first? You can be guided in this by the procedure of a well known music school like the Juilliard or the Mannes College of Music, in New York. Here, beginners on other instruments are not obliged to include the piano. They have one lesson a week on their chosen instrument and a weekly class lesson besides in the elements of music.

Often a small child is unwilling or unable to take the piano as a secondary instrument.

When they become more advanced, however (junior high school and up), they *must* include the piano, for only on the piano can the chord alphabet that spells harmony be fully revealed.

Aside from its practical value in music education, study of the piano offers many advantages. It is a preparation for learning other instruments. The tones of the piano are ready-made and even a beginner sounds pretty good. It possesses an enormous literature. It is a complete and self-sufficient instrument on the one hand, a glorious aid to ensemble on the other.

Not all children have an aptitude for it. Some find the task of coordinating eyes, brain, both hands and both feet too much for them. For the great majority, however, it is desirable, if not essential.

My eight-year-old sings out of tune but she wants to take violin lessons. Should she? A violin player is obliged to make each tone he plays by pressing his fingers down on the strings, the place and pressure determining the exact pitch. He must be acutely aware of his intonation if he is not to torture listeners. Singing out of tune doesn't necessarily mean that a person has no sense of pitch, it may merely signify that he can't sing.

Tests ought to indicate the pluses and minuses of hearing in your child's case. If her ear is not keen, all the more reason that it should be sharpened, whatever instrument she will play, but particularly in the case of the violin. She should have lessons in ear-training, which will enable you and her teacher to judge whether she seems likely to develop sensitivity to pitch.

If she does not respond well to these lessons she had better resign herself to an instrument with ready-made tones, like the piano or accordion. If she does show marked improvement, you might let her attempt the violin, having first discussed her difficulty with her teacher.

Do you believe in teaching saxophone, guitar, accordion and harmonica? These are popular instruments, comparatively easy to master, and on that account have been much associated with entertainment. The saxophone, star of the dance band, is occasionally heard in a symphony orchestra, where its tone resembles the cello. Any clarinet player can blow a sax, since the fingering of both is identical. The accordion is now handled on the higher professional level, besides being a jazz favorite. The guitar is a classical instrument. It is much used as a folk song instrument and for jazz.

However, if your child is to become interested in serious music, he had better plan on one of the major instruments for his primary activity.

My son is begging for jazz lessons. He plays the clarinet. Will jazz do him any harm? If his taste for music has been formed on the classics, it isn't likely to be ruined by an adolescent encounter with jazz. There is good jazz as well as bad, and it will do him no harm to learn the difference. His clarinet playing is bound to improve, for jazz affords endless opportunities for technical brilliance and encourages improvisation.

Can my child be taught how to practice? Yes, that is the most lasting service a teacher can render. The less the parent interferes except to listen and encourage, the better.

His teacher should have him clap the rhythm, sing the melody and play the scale in which a piece is written before he plays it. She should go over it with him, pointing out the spots which require special drill.

When he practices alone, he should start with a knotty point somewhere in the middle, playing it as an exercise. When he plays the piece through, he should stop to correct errors and to polish rough spots.

If he makes the same mistake in the same place at each repetition, you may be sure that he is not learning to hear himself. Teaching him to practice is teaching him to listen to his own performance with open ears, a kind of listening which makes practicing an adventure.

How long should I expect a nine-year-old to practice? You should discuss this with his teacher. Two fifteen-minute sessions a day are probably all that should be demanded of him now and for the next two years. Occasional duets with a friend or teacher can extend his practice time without strain. It isn't the time that counts but the duration of attention.

What if my nine-year-old refuses to practice regularly? If your child resists practicing, a talk with his teacher is in order. Perhaps she is stressing old-fashioned discipline. Remind her that your child is not headed toward a professional career but toward knowledge and enjoyment. Ask her to stress out-and-out pleasure in her teaching and her practice assignments. As the child grows older, he will have to realize that serious application and a certain amount of drill are inevitable, but that comes later. For the present, his cooperation *must* be enlisted, with the teacher's help.

A regular time should be set aside each day, in which your child is not interrupted, is always expected to be on the job. This establishes a rhythm which becomes a part of his daily life. Early morning, before school, is a practical time in many families.

Play for him occasionally or arrange for him to play simple duets, as a spur to ambition. Listen to his practice but don't volunteer criticism. Show him you believe in his talent and can see improvement when he practices. It is best not to resort to threats of punishments or rewards.

My children in high school never have time to practice. Should I keep after them or should I stop their lessons? If you have had to nag them in the past, you probably will have to do so now. But if they love music and have always practiced with reasonable regularity, they will get around to it in spite of high school distractions.

For pleasure-loving adolescents there is no more clinching argument than that they will miss a lot of fun if they don't continue. For the more serious the prospect of being eligible for a musical scholarship in college is appealing. Treat their apparent lack of interest as a passing phase.

Don't threaten to discontinue lessons unless you intend to do so. If you and their teacher can become reconciled to their practicing little or not at all for the time being, so long as they continue to have lessons they are assured of one supervised practice period a week, which will keep them from falling behind until they are ready to go ahead again.   —By Helen L. Kaufman

EVERY CHILD IS AN ARTIST

SOME parents seem to feel that as far as their children are concerned, art is a filler for odd moments between worthwhile activities: "Dinner isn't quite ready, so why don't you make a drawing?" or, "If you're only painting, you might take time to clean your desk."

Neither artists nor children can do creative work in the day's odd moments; they need time. If your child no longer sleeps during his naptime, he might use that period as a quiet drawing time. One mother lets her children draw while she reads to them. Children should have some regular, quiet, uninterrupted period in which artistic concentration is possible.

Children need to create. It is their way of interpreting and coming to understand the world in which they live. Through painting, coloring, drawing, finger painting and working with clay they find the release for strong feelings and the satisfaction that comes with creating something of their own.

But in order for children to be happy in such creative work, they need the right materials.

Provide Adequate Supplies

If children want to work with bright, strong color they should have a medium that produces brilliant color; if they are working for clear, firm outlines their medium should give direct crisp lines. For such children a good-quality wax crayon has excellent creative possibilities. If a child is primarily interested in the structural aspects of objects he needs a large soft-lead pencil. If movement and color variations excite a child he will respond to the freedom and flexibility of paint. To minimize mess, parents can encourage children to paint outdoors. Father's old shirt, put on backwards, makes a good smock.

Children shouldn't feel stinted on paper. If they want to start a picture a second time they have probably sensed a better artistic solution; if they want to work in the large they should have the opportunity. Stores keep standard and satisfactory drawing pads and there are also other inexpensive and appropriate papers. A roll of shelf paper, excellent for crayoning or finger painting, can be cut to any size. Newspaper printing presses cannot use the end of a roll of newsprint paper, and this leftover is usually free for the asking. Many stores give away large rolls of display paper that has become sunfaded. Children's art supplies need not be expensive, but they should be plentiful enough to encourage experimentation.

Let the Child Be Judge

Even the most prolific child can save his work until he has looked at it several times, finally selecting the few pictures he likes best. Many parents and children look over and talk about each new group of paintings. Which are his favorites? Are there any that he would like to do again? Comments should be voluntary; don't ask a child to defend or explain his pictures, because art is visual and not verbal. But if he has made a picture of a tree, and decides later that he doesn't like it, ask if he could do it better another time. Don't tell him how to make changes; ask if he would like to make them.

Give your child a display space. Children take greater pride in their art work if they see it treated with respect. Many parents put a bulletin board in a playroom or bedroom; the children pin up the work they like best. A large panel of wallboard makes an excellent backing, but even the side of a large cardboard carton, painted a solid color, will serve the purpose, or pictures can be fastened to a panel of cloth.

Develop your child's observation. Children recognize many objects—a cow, steamboat, traffic light—without being conscious of form or color.

Parents can help them to observe more carefully by saying, "Do you think you could draw a cowboy like that when we get home?" "Are all the windows in the house the same kind?" "Do you see how the fins fit on the fish's body?"

At most, try to focus his attention upon color and shape relationships, and let him, at his own pace, do the rest. Remember that you don't teach your child how to draw; you help him see more clearly and let the drawing take care of itself.

The Child's Viewpoint

Sally has two methods of drawing—the social and the creative. She indulges in social drawing with her friends. Each girl starts to draw with great verbal enthusiasm, announcing each idea as it appears. Every other girl immediately includes any items that her friends are including. After half an hour each child has filled a page with a conglomeration of symbols, haphazardly scattered over the page. Sally has never saved one of her social drawings; she discards them as a hostess discards leftover sandwiches and coffee.

Yet, when Sally draws by herself and for herself she chooses a subject she loves and with forethought and patience builds up a composition of selected, interrelated elements. This intentional quality in children's art work occurs when a child draws something that challenges and holds his deepest interest. If Sally is asked to draw trains or trucks she produces unplanned and, for her, immature stereotypes. But when she draws butterflies, flowers, her kitten, herself or children playing, the drawings are highly individual and carefully planned. Her sustained, intentional art expression appears when she feels a need to clarify or communicate some deeply felt personal experience.

There is logic behind a child's aesthetic selections and solutions if we understand his viewpoint. If a child paints a landscape with three suns in the sky, don't explain that there is really only one sun. One child, who made such a picture, explained: "See, there are three trees in this picture, so it looks better with a sun here and here and here."

Restrain Adult Criticism

Your adult judgment of size may be objective: nearer objects are larger than distant objects. Your child's judgments of size may be subjective: important objects and people are made larger, while unimportant elements are small or omitted altogether. Someone holding a jump rope needs big hands to indicate the important action of grasping; someone who is watching needs eyes, but no hands at all!

Your response to color may be objective: you like certain greens because you have seen them. Your child's use of color may be subjective: a disliked person may appear with a brilliant orange complexion because the child dislikes orange.

One boy, in drawing himself as a cowboy, worked over one hand for some time. First he drew five fingers, erased them, tried several solutions, and finally drew a hand with four fingers. His explanation was that in that place, four fingers looked better. There was some personal sense of aesthetic rightness that overcame his objective sense of numerical correctness.

If you, as a parent, provide your child with physical facilities—time, materials, display place—and with emotional support in respect and understanding, you have done your part. You will have a child who is learning to express what he sees and feels—the best possible guarantee of his mental and emotional health.

—*By John E. French*

CREATIVE DRAMATICS

D RAMATIC play and creative dramatics at home, in the early grades and through junior and senior high school are a much needed release for the tensions, worries, strains and problems from which boys and girls often suffer. What is creative dramatics? Simply stated, creative dramatics is the acting out of stories and the putting of activities in dramatic form using pantomime and dialogue.

The form should be informal, creative and original. The child should make up his own pantomime and dialogue under the guidance of an understanding person. He should be encouraged to use his own ideas and imagination. For example, given the story of Jack and Jill, beloved by the very youngest children, or The Three Bears, the children should tell the story, decide how the characters are to look and act, what the setting should be and what the characters say. In so doing, they act more or less as a group committee. They should hold tryouts and be given the opportunity to suggest and try out dialogue and set the stage.

The group should decide who is best for certain parts, whose lines are best and so forth. Mother or teacher should only guide, never dictate. A finished play is not the goal; the goal is a play which is the children's own with perhaps the exception of the skeleton story, although better yet, the children may originate their own stories. For example, when the children have decided how they want to dramatize Jack and Jill, then the dialogue can be recorded and learned if that seems desirable, although a more spontaneous result will come from ad-libbing. The play that results should be up to the standards of the age group, but should not be judged by adult standards.

Relieving Emotional Tension

It is amazing to observe how, through such simple creative expression, children find release. Having expressed much pent-up emotion through dramatization, the boy or girl achieves a sense of relaxation and is able to meet situations more capably without strain. In Pennsylvania a study with second-grade children showed that creative dramatics helps the child's vocabulary, his personality and voice. Personality and vocabulary tests were given at the beginning of the project and at the end of the year. Recordings were also made of the voices at the same time, and in one instance, five judges at a state university some thousands of miles away from the school rated the recordings. They found that a definite improvement had been made. But more than this, such creative expression helps free the child of cramping inhibitions, provides an emotional outlet, as well as a sense of comradeship and the feeling of being a cooperating member of a group. Each child is made to feel that he is of equal importance in the group. As such, he learns that he must consider his fellow schoolmates and sees that they realize the importance of the contributions he can make.

All the children should be given a chance to try out for parts, to give suggestions on how parts are to be played, to help tell the story, or to act as members of the stage crew. Stage terms should be used and the whole matter treated seriously. From such an experience, children learn to take responsibility. Order and organization also come out of such a group project. The teacher or the mother has a chance to study the children as she would study people in casting parts for an adult play. If she does this carefully, she can soon see whether children need to gain confidence or whether they are overaggressive. She can give the shy child the chance to play king or other prominent roles or to be stage manager—any responsible job that will give him a sense of importance. On the other hand, the potential bully can be given the part of a gentle person, a knight in armor, or a character who does kind deeds. He will learn a good deal from such a part. After such an experience, the boy who is called "sissy" on the playground may find he has regained his self-respect and the bully may begin to mend his ways—in most cases unconsciously.

The child who gets into fights can be given the part of the hero who wins the battle over the villain. In such a role he can act out his hostile tendencies and perhaps get rid of some of them. The boy or girl who pokes fun at the crippled child may play the part of a cripple and find out how it is to be the butt of such jokes. The overweight child should be allowed to play a normal-weight character, the small child can have a hero's role. Children who are shy with each other may work together. New friendships may develop and they will learn to share and cooperate.

Clue to Personality Types

Dramatic play makes it clear which children are natural leaders and organizers, which prefer to take direction, which are good workmen, which are restless and irresponsible, and which are good at working happily with others. The shy child should always be appreciated for his good qualities, and the teacher must be quick to give praise where it is due.

On what can rich dramatic play be built? Begin with Mother Goose rhymes, stories every child knows, such as The Three Bears, The Three Pigs, Little Red Riding Hood, Three Billy Goats Gruff, and many others. When the children are older, stories such as Robin Hood or scenes from Shakespeare will lend themselves to dramatic interpretations. The various dramatic incidents found in history or reading classes can be adapted. Original stories based on imagination or the child's experiences should be encouraged.

Dramatic play at home is also a happy and rewarding activity when carried on as suggested. One mother entertains her child's dramatic club weekly and finds it rewarding as well as good fun. Plays are put on for their families and friends and the whole project has become a delightful source of neighborhood get-togethers. At the same time, the children themselves have had endless good times and have profited much from the experience. Children never seem to get enough dramatic play and never tire of doing a story over and over. Try it and see for yourself. —*By Earl W. Blank*

WHAT DANCING CAN DO FOR YOUR CHILD

BEFORE men made sounds or discovered that they could draw they were using gesture and rhythmic movement to pass on to each other their needs, fears and dreams. Now as then, man's body is his contact with the world. It is the shrine in which his mind and soul are housed. And his instinct leads him to communicate by means of his body. Your child's desire to move about rhythmically is his happy birthright. His capacity to react to rhythm is as natural as the rhythm of his breathing, the pulse of his blood and the contraction of his muscles. The combination of rhythm and movement is a primitive delight natural to every child and too long forgotten by most adults.

If your child does *not* respond to music physically, if he *doesn't* like dancing about with or without music, *then* you have cause to take notice. If he does he is doing the simplest thing in the world—expressing himself in a language which he understands and uses more easily, more instinctively, than words.

You may be surprised at how well you can do in the attempt to encourage your child's natural love of rhythm.

Encourage Love of Rhythm

There are many songs that can be danced while you play them on the piano, sing or clap them out with your child. And there are many movement games without music in which you can stimulate and share this pleasure. One of the simplest is a relaxation game in which your child is a rag doll who has no bones, no muscles, nothing but sawdust—and there he lies, sprawled out out on the rug. You are the tester. When you lift his arm and then let it go, does it fall limply like a sawdust doll's? Can you shift his head from side to side, move his legs about, turn him over without any resistance? If not you must complain about the bones and see if the results can be better—more relaxed. They probably will be, for the learning can be very quick in a matter which may seem subtle to you but will be obvious to the child. So far you played only half the game. Now positions are changed and the child tests your arms, head and so forth for relaxation. This is much fun with one or with a number of children, boys and girls. (But it is important to control what is going on so that nobody gets rough.)

Another gratifying adventure in movement is "dandelion fluff." Your child may ordinarily sound like a herd of elephants as he goes upstairs. But if you explain that you will "blow" him upstairs, and you stand behind him at the foot of the stairs and puff a breath toward the middle of his back, he will miraculously be able to float up those steps so quietly that there will hardly be sound. He'll be delighted and you'll find it a happy game that may be reserved for bedtime, that may be kept for special treats or that's fun to play any time. You should keep in mind, however, that this works only going upstairs.

Charades

Another absorbing game is a sort of children's charades. This is also fine with a group. The rule of the game is that absolutely *no* words or props are allowed. You suggest the subject to be acted out, for instance, the answer to a question like "What did you do at school today?" or "What do you especially like to do?" or "How do you feel when you get up in the morning?" Remember, no words are permitted in the answer. A good part of the fun is the spectator's. He must guess what the performer is trying to tell him. If nobody understands, your little performer will happily repeat with added gestures and details, again and again, until somebody guesses correctly. Children love a secret and the combination of a secret and the use of movement to tell a story is unbeatable. There can be as many variations of this game as the imagination will permit. The general subject may range from going to see the animals at the zoo to what food is in the kitchen.

All such simple and childlike dance play is, of course, quite a different thing from sending a child to dance school. Unless your community has a dance teacher whose approach to children is sufficiently creative to make use of your child's imagination, you may be doing better not to send your child at all until he is seven or eight. But if you are fortunate enough to have a gifted and imaginative teacher nearby, by all means take advantage of it.

When to Begin Lessons

Eight is the age which, according to the consensus of the experts, is the best for beginning the study of ballet, the time considered most advantageous

for starting the disciplined and concentrated instruction which a precise study of that art demands. Ballet, a dance form codified in the court of Louis XIV, is a professional technique. Its study does wonderful things for grace and co-ordination but its achievement is not easily come by. Although your child may have no intention of becoming a professional, if she is studying ballet her training should be serious and careful.

This is as true for boys as for girls and, although a tinge of "sissy" is sometimes still connected with training for boys, if three or four go to class together the boys get a chance to discover that they will have to work as hard in ballet as in any form of athletics. They are not expected to behave or move in the same way as the girls, but rather they are given a definite masculine role in the classroom as well as in technique. There are numerous examples of dancers who were previously athletes. We can point to Igor Youskevitch, one of the greatest of ballet dancers. He was a prize-winning athlete before he became a famous dancer.

But we are not really talking of professional aims, but rather of the value of dance to your child. The renowned choreographer, George Balanchine, says that every child should study ballet "so that he or she may be able to walk into a room pleasantly."

Almost anything one says about dance must be tempered with "abouts" and "perhapses" since it is an art, practiced by human beings who have varying degrees of strength and talent. But, generally speaking, one can say that a child requires at least one class a week of careful ballet training for about two years before she is ready to wear the little hard-boxed slippers called toe shoes.

Use of Toe Shoes

Toe shoes, an extension of the pointed foot, were developed in the early nineteenth century, part of the romantic excursions into the realms of nymph-like beings then in literary fashion. Although the romantic era is no longer with us, *pointes,* as they are called in French (the language of ballet), remain part of ballet technique. One can understand that parents find their little daughter a visual delight in short fluffed out skirts (tutus) and tiny satin toe slippers. But from a larger point of view it is important that she learn the technique before she endangers the beauty of her legs and feet. The bunchy muscles that often result from getting on toe too soon are never seen in the topmost ballerinas.

Your child's teacher will appreciate knowing that you are not pushing her to put your child on toe or even in a recital, and that you respect her judgment as to when and if your child should have toe slippers. After all, especially if your child has no intention toward a professional career, the little leather ballet slippers are just as charming and much safer.

Ballet is becoming more and more a part of our normal cultural scene, and good training, even for a short time, brings with it a foundation of feeling and appreciation for beauty in music, as well as dance, that lasts a lifetime. But while ballet is generally accepted as a base for professional work, there are many kinds of dances that are not geared toward professional appearances. Modern dance, well taught, brings great pleasure, exercise and stimulation to those who participate. This is true for mothers as well as for children. Tap dancing, folk dances and ballroom dancing provide many happy hours for those who participate.

Select Your Teacher Carefully

In all cases it is important for parents to know something of the teacher to whom they entrust their children. Mass production is never satisfactory, yet classes in ballroom and folk dances may be excellent, though large, if the teacher has the skill to control and guide them. Technique should be acquired at the same time that the capacity to cooperate in group activity is being pleasantly developed. Tap dancing, although frequently misused in combination with inappropriate "sexy" songs, may be a happy kind of study when aimed at rhythmic awareness.

But do not misunderstand and confuse the word "grace" with any fancydancing stiff-fingered posturing. Grace is something else. It may be seen in a palace or in the slums, in a two-year-old or in a Pavlova. It is the true grace of spirit which is communicated through our common heritage, the language of movement. It is more than a form of entertainment, it is a living part of each of us, a part of you and of your child.   —By Lydia Joel

ENCOURAGE THE YOUNG MECHANIC

AN outstanding mechanical aptitude is a talent as definite and recognizable as musical talent. Often before he can talk a child will show a marked preference for things mechanical. And even though his talent does not show itself so early, if it is there, it will eventually become apparent and should thereafter be encouraged and appreciated, for it is valuable.

This age of radio and television needs technicians and this age of automobiles and aircraft needs skilled mechanics. Factories offer all manner of positions in maintenance and management. Mechanical aptitude is valuable to architects, plumbers, carpenters, electricians—to metal smiths and machinists. And there must be trained men to teach these skills to others. Perhaps the most outstanding profession open to the mechanically-inclined is engineering which in itself is a broad and varied field. Not only do engineers build great bridges, but they also design your car and your can opener—and the complex machinery that processes the quantities of canned food you consume. There must be men to design the machinery necessary to build other machines and tools. All the interlocking processes of manufacturing and production are in the hands of the engineers. Mechanical engineering is an expanding field.

Importance of Home Training

Mechanically minded children, like those who are musical or artistic, lay the foundation of their interests and training at home. Just as you seek to develop standards of character and habits of health in your children, so you can help develop their talents.

The mechanically inclined child will want to build, take apart and put together. His toys, ranging from the simplest construction pieces in his youngest years to elaborate construction sets later on, can fill this need and thus often save the family clock, toaster and electric mixer from his curious fingers. Model building also has its valued place in his education. And when he is old enough to handle tools reasonably well, he should have good ones and a place to keep them.

Be generous with your praise. When he comes in with shining pride in his eyes and a crude little object in his hands and says, "Look what I made—a wagon!" don't let him down. It looks like a wagon to him. Help him when he asks for it, but don't take over his job and do it for him. What he needs most from you at this stage is warm interest, encouragement and equipment.

In such fields as mechanics, machine work and engineering, it is of particular advantage to be neat, careful and methodical, so it is well to take special pains to encourage habits of orderliness whenever possible.

Ability to Accept Failure

There is also another trait that is of inestimable value to inventors or those engaged in experimental or development work. It is the ability to accept each failure as a lesson and a step—not a tragedy. So, during his formative years, when your youngster's projects fall short of expectations, as they will many times, be neither too critical nor too sympathetic. Just treat the matter casually and call the child's attention to the fact that in understanding why he did not succeed he has added something of value to his store of knowledge.

When he starts to school it may be well to help him a little with his arithmetic —not because he cannot do as well as his classmates, but because he needs to be outstanding in that field. If he does well in arithmetic, he will enjoy mathematics. It usually follows that what one likes one does well. A strong foundation of arithmetic is a necessary prerequisite to the higher mathematics and sciences that may come later. Number games at home, flash cards and other practice devices may help, but make your "homework" fun or the effect will be bad instead of good.

Do not feel that by encouraging your child's interest in mechanics you may be pushing him into a profession which he may not wish to follow. A man who is handy with tools is an asset to any business and any home.

—By Charles E. Marrow

WHEN YOU GIVE YOUR CHILD AN ALLOWANCE

CHILDREN learn very young that money plays an important role in everyone's life. But confused attitudes about money—how to spend, save and manage it—are common and children need their parents' help in learning to handle it wisely. Money management does have to be learned—just as writing and arithmetic are learned. The early learning must necessarily take place at home and it begins when parents give children a small regular allowance.

At what age should an allowance start? It is never too late to begin, but it is best to let children grow up with an allowance. Most children begin to have regular need for many little items—balloons, chalk, a whistle—by the time they are four or five. Ten cents a week gives a young child the chance to choose and buy one or two things each week. He probably has no genuine interest in the use of money at this age but his desire to imitate grownups makes him enjoy buying. The experience of possessing a few cents and parting with them for some desired object is step number one in learning to manage money.

How large should an allowance be? An allowance should match the child's age, abilities and regular financial needs just as a bicycle should match his size and skill. The actual amount of money needed can be decided after making a list of daily needs and wants. Starting with a nickel or a dime a week, it should be increased with time so that he can purchase more and more of his own things. As the child grows older his allowance should be large enough so that only part of it is for required expenses like carfare and the rest is for him to use as he wishes.

In families with several children, there is the problem of convincing each child that the amount of his allowance is fair. Some families plan allowances with each individual. Others call a conference every six months and plan all allowances at once.

With very young children, allowances may be given twice a week, then once a week. High school boys and girls who have grown up handling their own money may prefer receiving money once or twice a month. The important thing is that the allowance be regular.

Set the rules in advance. A child should know not only how much money he is going to receive and on what day it will be paid, but what items it must cover. He must know whether he can get more money if he runs out, and who will pay for unexpected items which may be required in school. The rules must be made clear and both the child who spends the allowance and the parents who give it must stand by the rules.

How much freedom with his allowance should a child be given? Most of us are guilty of a dictatorial attitude toward the way others spend money.

Similarly, we try to force our adult values on the beginner. We seem to expect him to spend with an inherited wisdom, whereas in reality it takes a long time and a lot of mistakes to learn to handle money wisely. It is important for a child to be free to make those mistakes and helped to learn from them.

A ten-year-old boy, for example, may spend everything on toy soldiers, forgetting that he wanted some fishing tackle. He may buy a cheap model airplane set to save money—and find it so flimsy that he is unable to build anything worthwhile. He won't be able to figure out how to get a haircut and have his skates sharpened all in the same week. He lends money to a friend only to discover that the friend doesn't return it. He makes a generous contribution to some good cause and is then embarrassed financially.

It is an agonizing process at times, but it is much better to learn from mistakes and start afresh with a new plan when one is still young, than it is to flounder through half one's life never having learned to use money to the best advantage.

Some children will save like misers for weeks only to spend all the money they have saved on some apparently worthless object. As long as children spend within their allowances, it is usually better for parents to shake their heads in private. Spending sprees may represent a temporary emotional need and usually amount to no more than amusing bits of history in a short while.

Should an allowance ever be withheld? Not for bad behavior, for poor grades in school or for any reason except lack of family income. Problems of discipline must be handled separately. To confuse punishment or bribes with an allowance is to confuse the child's thinking about money.

Suppose a child doesn't want an allowance? Children vary in their interest in using money and in their willingness to accept responsibility. Some children actually find it easier to get the things they want without having to be responsible for an allowance. If this is so, examine your way of handling money matters with your child. Do you tend to supervise his spending too strictly? Is it possible for him to get extra money by wheedling? Parents must find the right way to help these children face a reality which will be part of their world always.

Should Allowance Be Earned?

Some parents feel that a child has no right to spend until he can earn. But spending and earning are two different activities and the need for spending arises long before a child is really able or has the opportunity to earn. Parents sometimes pay children for everyday household jobs. This can defeat the spirit of cooperation which should characterize a family, where necessary jobs should be shared by everyone. Occasionally there is a job around the house which some outsider might be called in to do. If a boy or girl wants to undertake the job and can do it satisfactorily, he is entitled to the pay. But this work should have no connection with his regular allowance.

Should children be urged to save? Thrift has always been held up as a virtue and no one will deny that it is good to take care of one's property and to have something in reserve for a rainy day. But the abstract idea of saving for its own sake is outdated. The modern method is to plan one's spending for the present and for the future. Young children save for a trip to the circus, a new doll, a particular book or a wagon. Older boys and girls save for clothing, vacations, special education or parties. At first, parents will need to help children think about saving for future purchases. Boys and girls find it hard to plan ahead and control their spending. They will benefit by frequent and friendly discussions.

At times children may not spend an allowance after it is given. It is worth looking into the cause. Are they getting the things they want as gifts? Do they find it so difficult to choose between objects that they retreat and buy nothing? Perhaps they need to be encouraged by friendly parents who go into a store with them, discussing possible purchases and helping with decisions. Grown-ups have to make choices every day, and one reason for giving an allowance is to help a child learn to make satisfactory decisions while he is still young.

What if he spends all his money on candy? Candy is one of the first things children want to buy. Sometimes they buy more than seems good for them or they spend money which should have gone into something like a church collection. Keeping a little candy in the house may satisfy their craving and allow them to think of buying other things. Again, candy may be filling some special emotional need and wise parents will be aware of this possibility.

Should a child pay for things he breaks? Sometimes household objects are broken quite by accident, sometimes through carelessness or a refusal to heed warnings. Should a child be made to pay for the damage out of his allowance? If the broken lamp cost ten dollars, an allowance of twenty-five cents a week would be forfeited for forty weeks, almost a year. Meanwhile the child would be losing the educational value for which the allowance was created in the first place. Teaching children to heed warnings and respect property is a special training problem which has no logical connection with an allowance.

If a child breaks something belonging to a neighbor, however, somebody has to pay for the damage immediately. If the cost is moderate, an older child with a sufficiently large allowance might arrange for repairs himself. If the cost is too great for his allowance, you may have to help him out.

How about borrowing? Many emergencies arise in school or on the way home which cause a boy or girl to borrow money from friends. Parents may have to help children understand their responsibility for repaying loans promptly. Some children simply forget. Others borrow too much and can't seem to save enough to repay. Still others are confused in their reasoning, as was the girl who felt it unnecessary to repay a loan because, "Ethel's rich and can get all the money she wants." Parents can help children be proud of their ability to repay loans promptly.

Children sometimes want to borrow from parents for a large item. For example, if a child waits until he can save enough to buy a pair of ice skates, winter will have passed. If he borrows the money from his parents he can have the use of the skates while he is repaying the loan. The important thing is that lending should be kept within time limits. If the total cost is so great that it would require deductions from the allowance for too long a time, all training value in using an allowance is lost. In this case, parents may decide to make a gift of the object or pay part of the cost.

Frequently young children will spend all their money at once and find themselves without the necessary funds on Saturday when the rest of the crowd starts for the movies. Some parents believe in lending money at this point, at least once or twice until a child learns his lesson. Others feel that a lesson might as well be learned immediately and that missing a movie will not spoil an entire lifetime. They point out to the child that a choice was made earlier in the week when the money was spent. Now he must grin and bear it or find substitute pleasures. Perhaps they can suggest free entertainment.

School lunch money. Many parents fear that if lunch money is included in an allowance, it will be lost or used for other purposes. They know also that hot dogs and soft drinks at neighboring stores are often standard lunch fare for the crowd. Nevertheless, money has to be entrusted to boys and girls for lunches and the problem is one of teaching them to know the value of good food. Naturally, you plan family meals with a balanced diet in mind. Make a point of sharing your plans with the children. If they understand the relation between good food and health, they are more apt to cooperate.

Should an allowance cover clothing? Boys and girls need a good deal of experience in handling money before they assume the difficult problem of buying clothing. A twelve-year-old who has managed an allowance since the age of five or six may be ready to buy a few articles. Some parents suggest that children start with something simple like pajamas. "If they make a mistake, they can live with it in private," one mother says.

Allowances for high school boys and girls. By the time boys and girls reach high school, the urge for independence is very strong. They want to establish themselves as individuals and have a large share in taking care of their own affairs. But given a chance to handle their own money and to experiment in buying without having to explain or apologize, girls and boys suddenly realize that a dollar bill is not very elastic and many of them welcome advice and suggestions. Parents will be thanked for passing along all their knowledge of how to buy and for suggestions on how to economize and have fun on little money.

Teen-agers' acquaintance with money problems should slowly expand to include an understanding of a bank's services, of using traveler's checks and guarding receipts for important payments. They should occasionally help with family affairs, doing the marketing, paying bills, purchasing railroad tickets, taking the responsibility for tipping and paying cab drivers. They can pay hotel bills, arrange for tourist cabins, pay the check in restaurants. It takes a long time and plenty of practice to gain self-assurance in carrying out these everyday matters.

Parents who show patience and good humor during the long years when boys and girls are learning to handle money wisely, will be well rewarded by knowing these same boys and girls are competent when they are ready to leave home and manage their own affairs.   *—By Leone Ann Heuer*

IF YOUR CHILD HAS
A SPEECH DIFFICULTY

MOST parents know comparatively little about speech development and consequently are often worried when a child doesn't talk as early as a neighbor's child, lisps or hesitates in his speech. Peculiarities of pronunciation considered cunning in babyhood become a cause for worry if too long continued. When is a lisp or a stutter nothing to worry about? When does it become a speech defect which calls for treatment?

For instance, Susan, age five, is unable to say *s* or *z* clearly. Her tongue slips between her teeth and she pronounces her own name as if it were spelled *Thuthan;* she says *thlow* for *slow* and *ith* for *is.* Does Susan have a speech defect? The answer is no, and it is no because Susan is age five and not age eight. The small child should no more be expected to articulate perfectly than he should be expected to use grammatically perfect sentences when he starts to talk. Most children do not gain proficient control over all the sounds of American-English speech until they are almost eight years of age. Girls become proficient somewhat earlier than boys. Children who are late in beginning to talk sometimes require extra time to become proficient.

Although Susan should not be suspected of having a speech defect because she lisps at age five, she does have defective articulation if she is unable to make such sounds as: *b* in *bun, p* in *pen, h* in *hat, w* in *will, m* in *me, n* in *nose, g* in *get, k* in *key* or *cat, d* in *do, t* in *ten, ng* in *sing, y* in *yet.*

By six and a half years, Susan and most boys and girls of her age should add the following to their inventory of well articulated sounds: *f* as in *fun* and *enough; v* as in *vim* and *move* or *of; th* as in *the, father* or *bathe; zh* as in *pleasure; sh* as in *she* or *ash; l* as in *let* or *all; ch* as in *chew* or *match*.

By eight years of age, most children articulate as well as they are ever going to, except in the case of words which are long or contain unusually difficult sound combinations. Parents should not confuse errors of pronunciation with defects of articulation. Anyone, regardless of how well he may handle speech sounds, may mispronounce some words.

Faulty Articulation

There are three types of faulty articulation common in children. Sounds, especially difficult ones, are likely to be omitted, especially when they occur at the end of words. Thus a child may pronounce the word *glass* as *gla* or *dress* as *dre*. Sometimes a sound in the middle of a word may be omitted, and less frequently at the beginning of a word. Baby speech contains many such omissions.

Frequently little children substitute one sound for another, usually an easy one for one that is difficult. A child may say *wed* for *red*. Some children persist in calling their parents *muvver* and *favver* for a long time.

Children may also distort sounds. The most frequently distorted sounds are *s* and *z*. Small children find these sounds difficult because their correct pronunciation requires greater tension of the speech organs and greater precision than children can manage. If the child's front teeth are missing, he may not be able and should not be expected to produce the *s* and *z* sounds perfectly. To a lesser degree *sh* and *zh* also may be difficult. Next to these sounds, the *r* and *l* cause most trouble for English-speaking children as well as adults.

It is important to remember that omissions, substitutions and, to a lesser extent, distortions are frequent among small children. These faults only become defects when they persist as the child grows older. If faults in speech persist six months or more beyond the age when studies show that the average child can be expected to have established good speech, then they may be considered defects rather than faults.

Parents should also realize that a child does not become fluent all at once. He may say some new words better than he pronounces words he has always pronounced incorrectly. Unless parents, friends or relatives feel the child's mistakes are "cute" and encourage them, the youngster's speech, given time, will steadily improve. When he is eight or nine years old he should speak correctly and well. If he does not, it is important to have an examination to find out what is the cause of his difficulty—whether his hearing is impaired, his attention span unusually limited or his intellectual development not up to normal.

Of course a child must hear good speech if he is to develop it. If none of these causes for poor speech exists and yet a child does not speak clearly or well, the possibility of emotional disturbance must be considered. The latter is an occasional cause of persistent defective speech. In these cases speech therapy is needed and can be highly successful if parents are cooperative.

Defects Classified

Children with speech defects may be classified in four major groups. The largest group—including more than all the others together—suffer from defective sound production. The second largest is composed of stutterers. The third, a comparatively small one, is made up of those who have voice defects. The last group, also a small one, is composed of children who are retarded in language usage. These children are delayed in beginning to speak or in the general development of their ability to use language. Some, even at five years or older, may not yet have spoken their first real words.

Some children may have multiple defects. The child with a cleft palate is likely to have difficulty with sound production as well as voice. So may the child with impaired hearing. The child with cerebral palsy may be severely retarded in language development as well as in his sound production and control of his voice. Brain injury may also cause delayed speech.

In school, these children frequently have difficulty and do not do as good work as they are capable of doing. They do not do as well as their classmates and have more personality and adjustment problems.

Although stuttering is the speech problem about which most parents worry, seventy per cent or more of all speech disturbances are defects of articulation. About four schoolchildren out of every hundred have such defects. Fortunately such difficulties, if not due to physical causes, improve with help.

Few children have voice defects, but those who do should be given immediate attention. The child's voice, no less than that of the adult, is the mirror of his personality and his attitudes. Occasionally, voice defects are caused by physical conditions such as enlarged adenoids or a chronic rhinitis. These conditions call for medical attention. The child with a cleft palate will usually require surgical treatment before his voice can improve. But these causes account for only a small fraction of voice defects. By far the largest number of vocal difficulties are either due to imitation or are a reflection of a personality disturbance.

Learning by Ear

The child learns to use his voice by ear. He has no way of knowing whether what he hears is good or bad. If a parent or an older brother or sister or a favorite playmate speaks too loudly, so will the child. If he hears a nasal voice constantly, his voice will be nasal too. If the voices around him sound irritated and the speakers irritable, the child will copy this way of speaking.

A mother brought her nine-year-old daughter to a speech clinic to find out what could be done about the child's hoarseness. The child had previously been seen by a physician who found nothing wrong with her throat. The speech therapist excused the little girl and questioned the mother about her own voice, which was low-pitched, husky and excessively breathy. Was she aware of the quality of her voice? When did she begin to use so low a pitch? Did she care to correct it?

The mother, it developed, was not only aware of how her voice sounded, but occasionally embarrassed by it. She was frequently mistaken for her husband when she answered the telephone. Some years before, while in high school, she had begun to use a low, husky voice in imitation and admiration of a favorite actress. Yes, she would be interested to improve her voice, but couldn't we take care of the child first?

She was encouraged to come with her daughter on each visit to the clinic. The clinician worked with the mother and the child, but considerably more with the mother. The mother's pitch was raised to one appropriate for her, the huskiness and breathiness disappeared and she was delighted. The child's voice improved as her parent's improved.

Mothers have asked why their children spoke so that they could scarcely be heard. Frequently, the answer was to be found in an aggressive domination of the child. A timid child is apt to have a timid voice. If the child fights back, a loud and aggressive voice may be the result. Improvement is impossible unless the psychological problem basic to it is recognized and successfully treated.

Some Repetition Normal

The speech difficulty which worries parents most is stuttering. "Is my child going to stutter all his life?" asked Bobby's mother. Bobby, a four-year-old boy, handsome, bright-looking, was the son of intelligent young parents.

An interview revealed that Bobby had begun to speak at eighteen months of age, just five months after he took his first steps alone. Everyone was happy about Bobby's progress until about six months ago, when his mother noticed that he was repeating words and phrases, and was occasionally hesitating in the midst of a sentence. It worried her. Was Bobby stuttering? The boy next door, age nine, is a stutterer, and it all began with him just as it now seemed to be starting with Bobby—occasional hesitation in his speech.

Bobby was a sociable and talkative little fellow. He spoke easily and quickly, with only occasional repetitions of sounds or words, and he showed neither awareness nor anxiety about these. Twice Bobby's excitement in telling his story made him a little breathless, and he had to stop to catch his breath.

But Bobby was just a normal child speaking with a young child's normal repetitions and hesitations and sometimes breathlessness. All small children speak in this way at times, particularly between the ages of six or seven. Though children vary considerably in their tendency toward speech hesitations and repetitions, the average four-year-old is likely to repeat forty-five words out of every thousand. Furthermore, studies at the University of Iowa reveal that nothing in the speech behavior of nursery school children helps us to predict which among them may become stutterers at five, or older.

But if repetitions and a lack of fluency are not stuttering, what is stuttering?

When Repetition Becomes Stuttering

Such speech need not, and usually does not, become stuttering. But it may if the child becomes conscious of his repetitions and hesitations with the result that he is anxious and apprehensive about his speech. Usually, however, it is the child's parent who becomes anxious. If he shows his anxiety and speaks of the child as a stutterer, the child is on the road to becoming one. In this way, declares Professor Wendell Johnson, Director of the University of Iowa Speech Clinic, normal nonfluency is often transformed into stuttering.

But let's be realistic about the situation. Not all parents can be given the assurance that Bobby's mother was, that although their children do not speak fluently, they are not stutterers. And some children even as young as five, reveal unmistakably that they are aware of their repetitions and hesitations. They are tense and actually dread speaking instead of liking to talk as most children do. In such a case something must be done for the child.

About one in a hundred children—and the chances are four or five to one that the child will be a boy—is likely to become a stutterer. For this child, and for his parents, it is advisable that a program of therapy be carried out under the supervision of a well-trained speech clinician. (Names and addresses of such clinicians according to geographic area may be obtained from the Secretary of the American Speech and Hearing Association, Wayne University, Detroit, Michigan.)

Remedy for most defects. The outlook today for a child with defective speech is a good one. Most speech defects are remediable. Those which cannot be completely corrected can almost always be appreciably improved. Unlike the situation a generation ago, we have today a profession of speech correction. Trained speech clinicians in increasing numbers are graduating from our colleges and universities. Medical schools are showing awareness of the need to have physicians recognize speech defects in young children and to advise and refer parents for therapy. Many public and private schools employ speech correctionists as special teachers. Some schools now require their primary-grade teachers to learn how to handle relatively simple speech problems. Others are referring children to specialists. All things considered, the child of today has a much better chance of correcting his defects of speech or voice than did his parents. There is bright hope also that the personality maladjustments associated with speech and voice defects will be reduced.

—*By Jon Eisenson, Ph.D.*

STEALING IS A SYMPTOM

B URT and Nancy Hayes were terribly disturbed when a flashlight, reported missing at school, turned up among their young son's possessions. Another first-grader had left it on top of his desk and six-year-old Chris had appropriated it. "Is he going to be a juvenile delinquent?" his parents asked each other fearfully. "Should we punish him or just do nothing at all about it for fear of making things worse? Have we failed to teach him right from wrong? Is he unhappy? Insecure? What can we say to him? What can we do to make sure he never takes anything again?"

Parents are always deeply concerned when they discover that their child has stolen something. It may be surprising but it is certainly reassuring to know that stealing does not necessarily indicate a serious personality defect in a child. It can mean different things to different children and can stem from a wide variety of causes. When a child takes something that doesn't belong to him it is usually only a symptom of something else. And just as the doctor does in a case of illness, you have to look at the symptom before you can diagnose the condition.

Age Is a Gauge

Sometimes stealing is merely a symptom of your child's particular age. To label as "theft" the little "taking ways" of the nursery school set is pointless. Before the age of seven or eight, children have slight regard for property rights. The borderline between mine and thine is exceedingly thin and easily crossed without any sense of wrongdoing. The child simply sees something he fancies, helps himself to it and adds it to his collection of belongings. At the nursery school, kindergarten and first-grade ages almost all youngsters bring home from school or play a lot of things that don't belong to them. They are likely to pick up such things in full view of others, showing how little this pilfering can be considered "stealing."

Chris's parents are therefore quite needlessly alarmed about juvenile delinquency in the case of their six-year-old. Not that they should just do nothing about it. Chris should take the flashlight back to its rightful owner because he has to recognize the other child's prior claim to it. Perhaps, if he is a little upset, his mother should accompany him. Six-year-olds are often in need of a little moral support. His parents can have a talk with him about how other people have a right to their own things, just as Chris wouldn't like to have another child walk off with his bike. Gradually this idea sinks in and by the time he is eight or nine, the average child can distinguish between what belongs to him and to the other fellow.

Sometimes it helps the young child to keep things locked up or put away so that he isn't exposed to unnecessary temptation. An arrangement with the teacher might permit him to bring home certain cherished articles with the understanding that he will return the borrowed items later. Or he can be helped to handle his intense desire for things by learning to swap them. If he takes things that don't belong to him, it is wiser to avoid direct accusations. He responds better to an indirect approach such as, "Where did you find this shovel?" or, "How did you get so many marbles?"

Symptoms of Temporary Distress

In the case of the older child who knows the difference between what does and does not belong to him, theft is often a symptom of some underlying emotional need. A child's behavior is always an expression of some need of his personality. Socially undesirable behavior is no exception. Stealing is almost invariably the child's awkward attempt to resolve an emotional problem the real nature of which he himself is unaware. If he is upset about some unusual experience his stealing will probably be an isolated incident. But if the difficulty is of long standing, the stealing may be repeated.

Tom, age nine, took a dollar from the purse of his mother's best friend when she dropped in one day for a visit. Both women were terribly upset. Was Tom going to be a thief? Actually the reason was obvious. His mother and father had recently been divorced and Tom was all mixed up. He was considering running away from home and he took the money to finance his venture. When his mother found his partially packed suitcase, she was able to understand how troubled he was. She put her arms around him and he started to cry. Then she listened while he talked out all his disturbed feelings. Later, after supper together, Tom unpacked his bag and seemed to feel relieved. Gentle and understanding treatment helped him to get straightened out and stealing did not occur again.

David F.'s difficulty is more chronic but still not too deep-seated for his parents to help him solve it. He is an undersized boy of eight who at camp could not compete successfully with his bunkmates even in the relatively limited athletic activities of boys of his age. You can imagine how pleased and surprised David's parents were when he brought home a medal and said, "I won this for swimming."

Unfortunately it turned out that the medal belonged to another boy who had reported it missing from his trunk some days before. Obviously David's theft was rooted in his deep sense of inadequacy. He was convinced that he could never shine in competition with the other boys. Yet he yearned to win the good opinion of his parents and counselors. He badly wanted the admiration of the other fellows. Most of all, he needed to increase his own self-esteem. Having the medal in his possession where he could touch it and look at it made him feel more important.

There are untold numbers of Davids in the world. For one reason or another they have come to feel, as David did, that they are inferior or inadequate. Such children are usually inarticulate about their problems and need help in bringing them to the surface. Some of these children are painfully good, ingratiating and compliant. Others are perpetually tense, irritable, restless and perhaps rebellious. Or they may alternate between these two types of behavior. Only by observing how they get along with their playmates, what they say about themselves and the ways in which they react to adults can parents discover their real distresses.

The Wish To Be Punished

On the surface, at least, Leonard's stealing is very different from Tom's and David's. It has no apparent motive. He is a high-school sophomore who has always achieved top grades. He is well liked by his classmates and teachers. All know him as a boy who goes out of his way to be agreeable.

It was a great shock to Leonard's parents and teachers when they discovered that he had stolen a valuable art reference book from the library. He himself made the discovery inevitable for he carried the volume about with him conspicuously. Books which he had stolen from two teachers were also found on Leonard's desk at home.

The boy made no serious attempt to deny his thefts. He offered the flimsy excuse that the books were just lying around and he didn't think anyone would miss them. Here is a strange combination of character attributes in a young person. Leonard is an outstanding student, popular with his classmates—and a thief.

This kind of stealing seems more incomprehensible than Tom's and David's, each of whom had an obvious motive. Tom wanted money to run away from home. David wanted to succeed like other boys and please his parents. But why did Leonard steal?

Leonard is physically robust and even outstanding in competition with boys his own age. Yet in spite of his many fine accomplishments he obviously does not really think well of himself. Even his eagerness to be accommodating is based not on self-esteem but its opposite. He tries to be likable because he likes himself so little. Since he feels unworthy he needs to convince others that he has done wrong and should be punished for it. Then his guilty feelings are temporarily assuaged. Leonard's stealing is the expression of his desire to be punished—a more serious personality disturbance than Tom's or David's. It will require outside professional help to get at the roots of his guilty feelings and heal them.

Stealing has many important meanings for a child, varying from the trivial to the compulsive. He may steal to buy the love and affection of playmates, especially when he feels that no one in his home cares for him very deeply. Ann's father was lost in depression after his wife died and paid little attention to his little daughter. He was shocked into awareness of his neglect when Ann was caught taking money from the collection plate at Sunday school. She had been using it to buy treats for her friends and gain from them the affection her daddy failed to give her.

Delinquency and Stealing

Similarly, children will sometimes steal to acquire things that will impress others with a sense of their power and importance. Children are small and helpless. Even the cockiest of them have feelings of inferiority. These feelings become intolerable at times and they long to shine in the eyes of others. Bill, for example, fairly bristled with guns, all but two of which he had managed to pilfer from various stores. He swaggered about with them and won quite a "tough" reputation for himself.

If a child has some pals who are delinquent, he may steal in an attempt to be like them. Youngsters hate to be different, especially when they are going through the gang age. When a police officer brought Joe home after he had been seen taking a watch from a jewelry store, the twelve-year-old's first words to his mother were, "Chuck said I didn't have the nerve. I had to show him." It pays to know your children's friends.

Kleptomania

Finally, the act of stealing is sometimes a child's impulsive way of gaining release from tension. This is usually the basis of compulsive stealing, as in kleptomania. Kleptomania rarely occurs before adolescence and is characterized by an irresistible feeling on the part of the young person that he must take something to get relief from his internal pressures.

"I didn't need it," sobbed fifteen-year-old Carol. "I already have a dozen lipsticks. But I always feel better after I have taken something."

Actually kleptomania is not "stealing." It is the symptom of an emotional illness for which the child is no more to blame than for a fever. The psychiatrist who worked with Carol found that her desire to be loved and wanted had been badly thwarted in her early years. And instinctive needs, when hampered, take on curious disguises. Carol's stealing had two unconscious meanings for her. One was revenge on her parents who had rejected her. The other was an attempt to take things as a sort of symbolic substitute for the love she wanted so badly and never had.

Search for the Reason

Understanding these facts, what should be your attitude toward your own child if you find that he has stolen something? You can no longer accept the old belief that children steal simply because they are "bad," or haven't been taught the difference between right and wrong. Instead you will realize that stealing may have an unconscious meaning for a child of which he himself is totally unaware unless he has help from enlightened adults.

This new understanding of the problem gives you a sound basis for deciding how to handle any particular incident as it arises. Ridicule, sarcasm, scolding and corporal punishment serve no constructive ends. They simply humiliate a child and increase his resentments. Using force may unintentionally gratify a child's unhealthy need to be punished.

Under no circumstances should you do or say anything that would indicate to a child that you think he is a confirmed thief or will grow up to become a criminal. Children are provoking at times and parents are tempted to fly off the handle in dealing with them. But no matter how implausible your child's alibis or explanations may be, don't be contemptuous of them or tell him that you know he is lying. Even when you know his excuses are not the truth, try to remember that they may seem to be the truth to him. Since his real motives are often unconscious, he's as much in the dark as you are about why he acted as he did. Your job is to help him bring the real reasons out into the open. You can best do this by encouraging him to talk and by doing a lot of listening yourself. The conversation should be as friendly as possible. Avoid the mistake of using the police as a threat. Children need to view policemen as their protectors and not as their enemies.

A child must be treated with respect no matter what he has done. The deed he has committed may be reprehensible but the doer is still entitled to sympathetic understanding and consideration. He needs to have his motives and feelings taken into account. Emphatically this does not mean indulging wrongdoing.

You should always seek professional help for the child who steals if either or both of the two following conditions exist:

1. He has been disturbed by other behavior disorders in addition to stealing. These might include such things as persistent and needless lying; cruelty and bullying; apathy and indifference, accompanied by excessive daydreaming; nervous tics or stuttering; wanton destructiveness; the obsessive setting of fires; being too compliant and good.

2. He is past the age of six or seven and has stolen more than once, regardless of how long an interval elapses between thefts.

Adequate assistance in such cases is best rendered by a psychiatrist who is specially trained to work with children or by a child guidance clinic. Your family physician, clergyman, a family service agency or a children's court will help to refer you to such qualified personnel.

If it is hard for you to accept some of these facts about stealing, you can better understand why the child himself is confused and bewildered by his stealing. He often finds that he has taken something without knowing why he did it. You can help him grow into an emotionally healthy adult only if you take into consideration the fact that he really doesn't understand his own behavior. To help him get at the roots of his trouble is the way to handle his stealing; for stealing is a symptom.

IF A CHILD WALKS IN HIS SLEEP

IT was four A.M. when Freddie's mother awoke with a start and heard footsteps in the hall. They sounded like those of her ten-year-old son. When she turned on the light, she saw him trudging along slowly. Under his arm was bundled his blanket, one end dragging along on the floor behind him. "Freddie," she called. "Where are you going? Is something the matter?" He did not reply or show any change in facial expression and, even though his eyes were open, Freddie didn't seem to see her. He was walking in his sleep. His mother caught up with him, put her arm about him and spoke gently. In a moment he awoke. Then his mother led the drowsy boy back to bed, talking to him quietly and reassuringly until he was soon asleep again.

Sleep did not come as quickly to his mother. She tried to think back over the past days and weeks to see if she could find any possible explanation for Freddie's behavior. He had never walked in his sleep before. Something about the way he had carried his blanket recalled certain things that had happened the evening before and his mother wondered if they suggested the answer.

Just before bedtime Freddie had been excitedly discussing plans to go out

of town on a trip with his parents to see a football game. However, when his mother said that if the weather turned cold they might not be able to sit through the entire game unless they brought blankets with them, Freddie had seemed unduly disturbed. He had kept asking about it over and over again until finally his mother had laughed at his worries and hustled him off to bed.

Now, as his mother thought it over she guessed the reason for Freddie's sleepwalking. She was certain that he had gone to bed so keyed up about their trip that his eagerness to go to the game and his concern lest it be so cold that they couldn't sit through it had disturbed his sleep. Comforted by the thought that the sleepwalking was a passing worry, she breathed a sigh of relief.

In this case, Freddie's mother was right. She and his father assured Freddie that they would take plenty of blankets to the game and that they would stay till the end. They went to the game; everyone enjoyed it and they all kept warm.

But not all sleepwalking ends as quickly and satisfactorily as did Freddie's. Strange and frightening as it may have seemed to his mother, Freddie's behavior is re-enacted by innumerable children, and adults, every night. With many physically and emotionally healthy children, the somnambulism is a one-time affair due to marked emotional tension over something that happened prior to their bedtime. In some instances, even when it occurs only once, it may be a valuable clue to the existence of a state of chronic tension in the child. Somnambulism may occur in connection with certain physical illnesses as well. However, most sleepwalkers suffer from no physical disease which can be held responsible.

Consult a Doctor

It is essential to deal with sleepwalking with good judgment and a sensible avoidance of panic. Take your cue from the approach used by Freddie's mother and relieve your child of any acute apprehension he may show after you have gently awakened him. Remember that his somnambulism is caused by inner tension and that you can do a great deal toward alleviating or dissipating it if he is sufficiently awake to be aware of your reassuring presence. Then stay with your child until he has fallen asleep again. There is no reason to try to keep from him the fact that he walked in his sleep. You can explain that because he was distressed or worried about something his sleep was disturbed; this happens to lots of children.

He will have questions he wants to ask about his experience and finding you willing to listen and answer them, if you can, is the best evidence you can give that you are understanding and want to help. If you don't know all the answers tell him you will try to find out.

It is wise to consult your family physician or pediatrician in regard to any child who walks in his sleep. Not only will your doctor discover or rule out any possible physical cause, but you may become aware that your child has some particular emotional need which might otherwise have been overlooked. A thorough medical examination is mandatory for any child who walks in his sleep more than once. If this examination reveals no physical basis for repetitive sleepwalking, then it is best to consult a child guidance clinic or child psychiatrist.

Remember that sleepwalking arises as dreams do. Sometimes in dreams we try to fulfill the wishes we cannot satisfy in real life. Thus Freddie took his blanket and started for the game. Also there are times when we do not feel we should express our angry feelings. Probably Freddie felt angry because his parents suggested the possibility of not staying through the game, but he said nothing. His resulting anxiety and annoyance caused his sleepwalking.

Angry or exasperated feelings which are suppressed do not have to be of catastrophic proportions to result in sleep-disturbing activities such as sleepwalking or dreams. Dreams represent an expression of our suppressed wishes and associated feelings, somewhat disguised. Somnambulism usually represents an undercurrent of tension which a child cannot adequately get rid of by mere dreaming.

Let child know. It is important to emphasize one other point with regard to sleepwalking in children. In your desire to spare a child unnecessary concern, you may try to keep him from knowing that you are worried about it. This is unwise because if the reasons for *emotionally caused* sleepwalking are to be discovered the child must cooperate in trying to discover them. Parents and professional guidance experts *in combination* must be able to make him feel that they can help him only if he will help, too. Then together, they can face his difficulty and overcome it.

—*By Sidney L. Green, M.D., and Allan B. Rothenberg*

WHAT CHILDREN WORRY ABOUT

PARENTS have many things to worry about in these days of war threats, atom-bomb anxiety and the inflated cost of living. Often you may sigh for the unconcerned bliss of childhood when you hadn't a care in the world. If that's what you think, you're wrong. You have merely forgotten a lot. For children have their worries too, terribly important ones, to them.

Worse still, unlike you, they frequently feel they have no one with whom to share their anxieties. Adults tend to laugh off or minimize a child's worries. They may seem minor or downright silly to grownups. But not to *him*. Maybe they are small. But so is he!

Far from being the happy time we like to imagine, childhood is often a period of by no means vague alarms, attended by much uncertainty. Here, for instance, is what one nine-year-old reports as his reasons for finding life just one headache after another:

"I can't get along with my sister. I have to go to bed too early. I can't get done with my work book. My mother and father do not want me to play basketball. I never have anything to do. At school I have to sit by a girl I do not like. I can't get along with my teacher. I can't do arithmetic. I can't do geography. I do not like school. I can't understand girls. I can't draw. I lose my temper. I hit my sister. I get mad at my mother."

This sad recital of juvenile worries was uncovered when 500 nine to thirteen-year-olds were asked to write essays outlining their "problems." On the basis of the worries disclosed, Science Research Associates in Chicago published a Junior Inventory for elementary-school use. It consists of 223 problems that proved to be frequently faced by children in this age group. The check list falls into five categories: 1. My Health, 2. Getting Along with Other People, 3. About Me and My School, 4. About Myself, 5. About Me and My Home.

This study is the first systematic, country-wide survey of what girls and boys really worry about and consider to be their problems. Based on this sampling of 4,500 children from coast to coast, the findings are eye-openers for parents.

Concern About Health

We are accustomed, perhaps, to thinking that bodily aches and pains are primarily a concern only of the elderly or the hypochondriac. Not so. There are 45 items in the Inventory about physical symptoms and there wasn't a child who wasn't concerned about some of them, a quarter of them checking more than seven.

A sixth-grader reported: "I have a sore knee so I can't play football. I can't look at a show as my eyes hurt. I get headaches looking at shows. My father and mother say they can't afford buying me glasses." While few were in as bad a state as this youngster, still they had plenty of complaints. Mentioned frequently was: "My ears (or head, or teeth) hurt a lot." About one child in four worries because "sometimes I get real dizzy"; and almost half are disturbed because "I get out of breath when I run or play." Pimples bothered over a third of the pupils in grade eight, girls more than boys.

Younger children seemed to worry about problems in health more than older ones. This may be due to a lack of understanding about the workings of the body. Reassurance about its normality and more interpretation of the way in which it functions for your nine and ten-year-old would seem to be called for. Whatever these worries represent, they require attention from parents. Vague aches and pains, even if they prove not to be serious, are frequently indications that a child needs more love and attention than he is getting. Or perhaps he is receiving too much of the wrong, overanxious, fear-inducing kind.

The worries children have about getting along with other people show that they are eager to please. Only 2 per cent said, "I don't like people," or "I'm afraid of people." When your child hangs back or is reluctant about being social, the probabilities are that he is simply bashful and shy or painfully aware of what he considers his own shortcomings.

The results of the Junior Inventory are added proof that children of this age have strong feelings of inferiority and inadequacy. Many of those tested, for instance, worried because "I always say the wrong thing at the wrong time." Others labeled themselves as not strong enough, too fat, too thin or not attractive enough. (Nearly one in four believed that he was not good-looking!)

On the positive side, this cross-section of the nation's children proved to be eager to make more friends. They want to know more about girls if they are boys and boys if they are girls. Only 4 per cent said, "I wish people would leave me alone." But nearly a third either needed more friends or longed for a best friend. They feel the need, too, to increase their social skills. A large proportion want to learn how to dance and to take music lessons.

Social Adjustment Needed

Obviously, these elementary-school children need more help and encouragement in having fun with each other, getting along with adults and learning to feel at ease in company.

School comes off rather badly in the Inventory. One child in five just plain doesn't like it, though little blame goes to teachers. Arithmetic and geography seem to be the worst offenders. History and social studies are not much more popular.

Taking tests and getting poor grades disturb many children. Variety seems to be lacking, since so many complain, "I'd like to do more things in school." A quarter of the youngsters state that they can't read very well. Yet it is hopeful that an even larger percentage, 30 per cent to be exact, say that they'd like to find more good books to read.

Here parents should certainly be able to remedy matters by encouraging the library habit and seeing that there is no dearth of good reading material at home. The dread of taking tests suggests that mothers and fathers might exert their influence, through P.T.A. groups, toward having as few tests as possible given in the lower grades and confining them to the comparatively painless "true-false" variety.

More intelligent parental interest in homework, where there is any school difficulty, would at least relieve the child of feeling that he is struggling along alone without sympathy or understanding. According to the Inventory, one child in almost five feels that he isn't smart enough. In many cases this isn't true. Often such children merely believe what they have heard irate or discouraged parents say about them. The wiser way to relieve school worries is to encourage and lend a hand.

Plenty of opportunity for outdoor play and considerable freedom to do as they like after school hours might help to ease the burden of the 37 per cent who say, "I get tired of sitting." School is apparently physically too confining for most children and they need more chance to stretch, run and move about. Certainly long hours of practice at the piano after long hours at a desk would not seem desirable. And don't be concerned about a little boisterousness when the youngsters get home from school. It's a good way to blow off steam.

A child's great need for security and acceptance shows up with considerable clarity in the section of the Inventory on "About Myself." Almost a fourth of all fourth-graders worry for fear their mother or daddy might die. Other items that indicate feelings of insecurity included: "I'm afraid to be home alone at night," checked by a considerable proportion of nine-year-olds and about 10 per cent of eighth-graders, "I can't go to sleep at night," "I have bad dreams."

Interest in Future Career

One of the surprise findings of the Inventory was the large number of children who would like to know what they are going to be when they grow up. Even in the fourth grade this concern is already evident. Even the nine-year-old is not too young for some preliminary discussions at home about what sorts of different things people do to earn a living, what training is necessary and how the different occupations contribute to the welfare of others. This is the hero-worship stage when altruism can easily be encouraged.

When the Inventory dealt with home relationships, children recorded their worries about not having enough money, not being allowed to see enough movies, wanting a room of their own, having to take rests when the other kids were out playing, and wishing that daddy and mother would play with them more. There is more complaint about brothers and sisters being too bossy than about parents. Yet more children say they would like to have a brother or sister than wish they didn't have the ones they have.

If you think children aren't conscientious, it may surprise you to know that one in five worries a lot because he does things he shouldn't do, feels bad about it and wants to be good but feels he can't.

It may also be revealing to parents to know that over a quarter of the children long for a pet. This would seem to be one of the easier child worries to correct.

While these various problems belong only to individual children and not to all of them, the sum total of the amount of worry experienced by nine-to-thirteen-year-olds is rather staggering. It will pay parents to be alert to such anxiety and not just take it casually for granted that children are happy and untroubled merely because they are young.

Symptoms That Reflect Worries

Here are a few of the symptoms that indicate undue concern on the part of a youngster:

1. Frequent physical complaints for which the doctor can find no good reason, such as continued colds, upset stomachs, vomiting, headaches and even repeated accidents. Other danger signs of tension are chronic nail-biting, marked stuttering, facial twitching, insomnia and frequent nightmares or sleepwalking.

2. Rather timid children tend to try to escape their worries by doing a lot of fantasying and daydreaming. They may read continuously or be over-addicted to radio and television programs. These are the children who some-times even run away from home when anxieties become overpowering and cannot be avoided.

3. The more aggressive child is likely to attack his problems. He hits back at whatever happens to be in his way or defies figures of authority.

4. Many "too good" children adopt excessive conformity as a defense against their worries. By grimly controlling their natural impulses and con-forming to adult expectations, they are able to feel safer and better protected against anxiety.

5. The swaggering youngster uses denial to fortify himself against inner alarms. He tries to pretend to himself and others that he's not afraid of any-thing. Don't accept braggadocio at face value without doing a little investigat-ing.

6. Some children stave off their worries by adopting certain set ways of doing things and ritualistic patterns of arranging their belongings. Clothes must be placed just so at night or they must count lampposts or follow some other ritual. This is a rather serious indication of deep anxiety and calls for immediate help, often from a professional child guidance counselor.

While most childish worries pass in due time, it isn't necessarily true that the child outgrows anxiety. He is more likely to substitute new worries for the old ones. Solving simple worries early often prevents more complicated ones later.

What Parents Can Do

There are a few practical things that you can do to lessen worries:

1. Examine your own worries—often you expose your child to them un-knowingly by a process of emotional contagion.

2. Don't be an alarmist about every disturbing development in our modern world. Try to emphasize the positive all you can.

3. Keep the door wide open for your children to confide in you about their troubles. Encourage free and full discussion of problems.

4. Don't set up impossibly high standards of behavior for them, leading them to feel that "big boys don't ever cry" or keeps his troubles to himself.

5. Praise and approve of your child's strengths so that he feels better fortified against his weaknesses.

6. Avoid trying to make him a perfectionist. Don't expect too much in the way of performance until he is able to deliver the goods.

7. Do, however, give your child responsibilities geared to his abilities so that he gains the good feeling of competence and adequacy.

8. Never belittle or ridicule his worries.

9. Avoid comparing your child either favorably or unfavorably with others.

—*By Constance J. Foster*

IF YOUR CHILD
THREATENS TO RUN AWAY

MANY of us can remember the times when as children we felt angry enough at others and sorry enough for ourselves to think of "hitting the road." As parents we have learned that this is a normal part of growing up and unless running away becomes chronic and suggests some deeper problem, we are apt to feel we should treat it lightly. One of the ways parents try to seem nonchalant under such circumstances is in agreeing with their child that perhaps he does need a change. One mother reported that when her eight-year-old entered the living room carrying a packed suitcase, she offered to provide a picnic lunch and set about doing so. But while she was busy wrapping hard-boiled eggs in waxed paper, her small daughter burst into tears.

Another mother told of an experience with her ten-year-old son who was very angry at her for not getting him a dog. She said it seemed as if he just couldn't find a place in the house where he could get far enough away from her! One night after supper he came downstairs in his pajamas and announced he was leaving home. (It was snowing too!) Caught unprepared, his mother told him to go right ahead. When he did, she had to run after him, and was so confused, angry and frightened that it ended with her spanking him, which didn't solve anything.

One mother of an adopted boy who had previously lived in many homes and received little love described how much she and her husband had wanted to show Fred that they really cared about him. Once when he ran away from their home in anger, they were afraid to be too severe with him. In their uncertainty, they asked Fred what they should do. Without a moment's hesitation he said, "If you love me, you better not let me do that again!"

In other words, children want to know someone will set limits to what they may do. A story a New York policeman tells is a case in point. He was standing on a street corner and noticed that a small boy passed him at regular ten-minute intervals, so it seemed he must be walking around and around the same block. The officer finally asked the child what he was doing. "I'm running away from home," the boy explained. "But why do you keep going 'round and 'round the block?" the policeman inquired. The child replied with serious dignity, "Because I'm not allowed to cross the street alone."

Implication of Threat

Many parents, in trying to indicate that they do not take the threat of running away too seriously, play along with their children, helping them pack, saying in effect, "We're sorry to see you go, but if you feel you must, well there's nothing we can do about it." Some parents try to point out the hazards but find that this sometimes makes their children even more determined.

Perhaps parents misunderstand the challenge the child who threatens to run away is presenting to us. We know that usually anger—his or ours or both—is involved and has probably precipitated his wish to run away. "I'll show you," the child is saying. "I'll go away and never come back and then you'll be sorry." In other words, he hopes that after he is gone we'll find out we really care about him—find out how much we miss him. But threatening to run away may also be a way of asking, "If I got angry at you and felt like leaving you, would you let me go?" Children want desperately to believe that no unhappy feelings or anger on their part could ever persuade us to let them go. The child wants to feel that his parents, wiser than he and always loving, will let him know in no uncertain terms that while he may be angry, they will never let him go away from them until he is grown and ready.

Children are sometimes overcome by their own impulses and at such times they want to be able to count on us to help them control themselves. Children who are permitted to do just as they please become frightened and insecure. Perhaps when they threaten to run away they are really saying, "I feel like doing something I don't really want to do, so somebody please stop me!"

Looked at in this way, the running-away threat has much to say to parents. Besides representing anger and a wish for independence there is present, too, an equally strong wish to be loved, protected and to know for sure that these momentary feelings and impulses cannot really prove dangerous because one has parents who will see that things don't get out of hand.

What parents can do. Just how then should a parent handle the situation? He will try to understand and accept the child's anger or hurt feelings or wish to escape authority, or whatever else may have led to the crisis. He will try to make it quite clear to the child that these are natural feelings which can be comfortably handled within the family. Running away is not the answer. Under no circumstances will parents let him go away and stay away.

They will answer the unasked but present question, "Would you let me go?" with the firm and absolute "No!" That is really what the child wants to hear.

—By Eda J. LeShan

ADOLESCENTS

GETTING ALONG WITH TEEN-AGERS
GUIDING, NOT PUSHING • APPEARANCE AND PERSONALITY
WHAT TO TELL TEEN-AGERS ABOUT SEX
PHYSICAL FITNESS • CAREER TALENTS • KEYS TO COURTESY
GOING STEADY • CAMP OR SUMMER JOB
ALCOHOL AND ADOLESCENCE • THE GANG • SPORTS
DEALING WITH EMOTIONAL PROBLEMS

LIVING WITH YOUR TEEN-AGER

ALMOST before you know it your child has reached the teens and grows so big so fast—an adolescent! You can't pick him up any more and comfort him when he's hurt or frightened. But he still does get hurt and frightened. You can't kiss any bruises and tears. Yet, even though the bruises don't show and the tears are swallowed, he still gets his share of them.

At five, he could call the magic word, "Mother," any time of the day or night and have it answered with loving help for the small-child trouble. Hands soothed the injured knee, arms drove away the bad dream. But at fifteen! Left out of a party, failing to make the team—he doesn't cry and call "Mother!" He may look a bit pale, may not feel like eating, and may even tell you something of what happened—adding that he doesn't care a bit. But more than likely, your teen-ager won't say anything about his "hurt" at all, so you may be fooled. Some parents are—especially those who want to be particularly careful not to entangle their growing children in apron strings. "He doesn't need us any more," you might think. "He can handle it alone."

But don't be taken in by an indifference and confidence that is largely veneer. Maybe your teen-ager looks as though he can go it alone—and sometimes he can stand by himself—but more often than you think and surely more often than he'll say, he can't. Actually the adolescent needs many of the same things that made him feel secure when he was small—with three differences: the nature of the need is, of course, somewhat altered; he expresses it more hesitantly, more subtly; and the forms your reassurance and help can take must be different.

Your Presence Needed

What did your small son or daughter need at five? Most obviously, he needed you. Almost all the time, you had to be there. At fifteen he needs your presence, too. Not as much, of course, and not the same kind of care-taking. Yet remember the afternoon Jim found out his girl was going to the prom with someone else, and his friends ribbed him about it? The world was a gloomy place, but as he neared home his steps picked up just a little. Women were fickle—except possibly his mother. The guys had laughed—but his father wouldn't. Even if he didn't tell his parents what had happened, they'd be waiting at home with a good meal and the warmth of home.

Of course, parents can't always be right there. For one thing, no adolescent wants to feel his mother and father are in constant, solicitous attendance.

For another, one of the happy by-products reaped by parents whose youngsters are growing up is more personal freedom for themselves. It's far less complicated accepting dinner invitations when your child is fifteen than when he is five. Invitations, though, can load a social calendar before you know it, especially when it looks on the surface as though your son or daughter doesn't really need you at home. They may never say a word about missing you but, often, they still need the feeling that you're there.

Clearly, another factor in the security of the five-year-old was your affection. Hugs and kisses were freely given and received. "Well," you're thinking, "I'd give them freely now, too—but imagine what would happen if I put an arm around Tom when he's with his crowd!" What happens, if Tom is like most young people, is a rigid, uncomfortable, pink-faced squirming away, and later, "For Pete's sake, Mom, I'm not a child any more!"

Your Displays of Affection

Granted, you just can't be as demonstrative with a teen-ager as with a five-year-old. We who no longer have doubts about being grownups can embrace other grownups without a second thought. But to the almost-grownup, being the subject of such display can be humiliating. And yet, there was Carey. Long ago, he had given up kissing his father, in accordance with our society's custom that men do not show affection for each other in this way. Subsequently, he also eliminated quick pecks for his mother. Both parents were beginning to feel that if they even put a hand on him they'd be accused of "babying."

Then one night Carey came out of the shower briskly toweling his new-washed hair. "Your hair stands up just like mine when it's washed, son," smiled his father and reached over to tousle his son's head.

"Yeah, doesn't it?" remarked Carey, and to his father's amazement, leaned forward like a puppy to have his head rubbed again.

So if you can recognize the signs and sense the moments, there are still many times when your arm around a shoulder, your hand brushing a cheek, are welcome. For the other times, when you just simply can't tell, there are other ways. You can still let love warm your voice and let your eyes show pleasure in something they're saying or doing.

Listen, Don't Criticize

The five-year-old needed understanding support. Then, it often took the form of holding him and murmuring comforting sounds. The adolescent needs it, too—but now it has to be put into words. Jean's mother has a key phrase for those occasions (admittedly not too frequent) when her daughter will come to her with grief or gripe. "It certainly is a shame," she says quietly as

the hurt or confusion pours out. The words aren't always the same, but there's a definite I'm-all-for-you feeling behind them. She doesn't say much more. For the most part, this mother just listens, and perhaps being a good listener is one of the most welcome qualities a parent can offer a teen-ager. At times, it may be the only way you can give the support that's wanted.

Now and then, Jean's mother does find other ways. Jean is slow in doing homework, for instance. Comparing herself with her classmates, all she could think of for a while was how terribly slow she was—"and yet," her mother pointed out, "you remember and understand what you have studied. You do it so thoroughly, you get a lot out of it."

Jean knew this was so, and yet had overlooked it completely in her anxiety to be as speedy as the others. But heaven help the parent who hands out empty praises or comfort! Adolescents develop a sharp critical sense and adult approval has to be valid or they'll spot it as "phony."

Trust and Respect Needed

The adolescent needs your respect and trust. Wasn't your five-year-old's security strengthened, too, by your respect for his individuality, your trust in him? There's a lot more to respect and trust when he's in his teens. Take for instance, the seemingly peculiar fads and foibles of the younger generation. "Okay, so you think it's 'loud,'" your daughter says hotly if she catches your somewhat critical glance lingering on her latest idea of appropriate apparel. "Well, pictures of you in the family album look pretty silly to me."

And she has a point. Each generation looks—and sounds—pretty silly to the other at times. You have to find some tolerance for her "getup."

The continued respect and trust you give your adolescent can bring you satisfaction. Your child may open up and confide in you more than you expected. You may even have the thrill, as did one father, of overhearing his son remark to a friend, "Well, nobody can tell his parents everything. But I can talk to mine about some things. They're pretty good, all things considered." Coming from a teen-ager, *that's* pretty good—all things considered.

What else made your five-year-old secure? Your adult wisdom. Even if he howled at not being allowed to cross the street by himself, you didn't permit it. He complained noisily, but didn't he also feel somehow that here was proof of his being loved and valuable?

Adult Guidance Needed

Ten years later, though everything about him shouts "I know where I'm going," the same child still has frequent need for the same kind of fundamental guidance. For example, he knows he is big enough to drive the car. You may know he is not mature enough. He can be a man of purpose and responsibility as he backs it out and starts up the street, but after picking up a friend or two he may be a child with a dangerous mechanical toy. Now the howling is a storm of angry protest, but you say again, "When you're a little older. . . ."

He, too, can come to see that your denial is based on love and caring. It's rather nice to be that precious. And it's nice, if there are little doubts churning around in his stomach as to whether he really can handle the car, to have someone decide for him.

Sometimes it's hard to believe our adolescents still need us when their façades proclaim, "Come on, world!" But on occasion some of them drop the façade and confess (not to their own parents, of course), "Sometimes I feel lost." If you give them the chance, or just listen with your inner ear, you may hear your own teen-agers say it in so many words. They still want you standing by. It's when they are absolutely sure they can count on you that they dispense with the over-sure cockiness that shouts, "Come on!" to the world and instead step out into it with quiet certainty. —*By Dorothy Melrose*

DO YOU PUSH YOUR TEEN-AGER?

BILL'S father is a prominent lawyer. Addressing a judge and jury has long been second nature to him, so when his teen-age son said he didn't think he'd make the debating team at school, Bill's father was incredulous and felt all the boy needed were a few words of encouragement.

"You express yourself very well in talking to people," he assured Bill. "These doubts are all a state of mind. Just get up on your feet, open your mouth and let the words come out. You'll soon see how easy it is."

Bill's eyes were downcast and he shook his head. "It's no go," he insisted. "I hate to let you down, Dad, but I just know what I can't do."

Perhaps you've heard something like this from your own adolescent son or daughter. Mary knows that she can't possibly assume the chairmanship of the committee and John knows that he isn't good enough to make the track team. You've heard them say it. But are you aware of the edginess in their voices, the emphasis on the word "know," the defiant protest against being shoved or wheedled beyond what they consider to be their personal limitations?

Most of us feel it is our job as parents to reassure our young people when they express lack of confidence in themselves and their abilities. We tell ourselves, "He's just tired now or discouraged. Tomorrow he will be able to do it more easily. I'll just give him a pat on the shoulder and boost him over the hump."

When Encouragement Is Discouraging

This ready encouragement we give our children does sometimes help them. But at other times it closes us off from the teen-ager who is not asking for such glib help. He really does know what he can't do.

For example, by the time Dick reached junior high it was taken for granted that he was a superior student, since his grades has always been consistently high. But things were getting tougher for him as subjects became more difficult. Yet when he worried about a hard assignment, his mother and father would always smile and nod encouragingly. Of course he could do it, they told him. Hadn't he always sailed through with flying colors?

Dick sighed and went back to his room. Was there no way to make his parents realize he wasn't the ball of fire they thought he was? He felt guilty and ashamed because he was unable to uphold the fantasy they entertained about him. And inevitably, he felt resentful, too—because they wouldn't take him as he was. He showed his resentment by retiring within himself and retreating from their expectations. When he withdrew to his own room and shut the door, the door was closed in more ways than one.

At school his work began to slip but his wise teacher didn't try to build him up or give him a pep talk. Instead she suggested to his parents that perhaps Dick had already been given too much false encouragement. When they saw their mistake, took off the pressure and began to let their son be himself, matters improved and the boy's anxiety was relieved.

When Parents Push Too Hard

Often, parents—with the best intentions—seem to feel it a duty to talk young people into doing anything they feel they cannot tackle. Although it may make the parents feel better, young people do not want or need wholesale reassurance. When encouragement goes beyond the limits of what a child knows he can deliver, it often does more harm than good. He cannot then feel comfortable about failing occasionally because quite subtly his parents have managed to make him feel that he is letting them down if he does. He is unable to accept his failure because his parents have been unwilling or unable to accept it. Eventually, in some children, this can instill shame and fear of "weakness" where they should have come to know that failure is something all of us must experience at times.

Other children react differently. One becomes the daredevil who learns to hide his fear of inadequacy under a cover of bravado. We unwittingly develop the young person who is rashly "afraid of nothing." He hides his fears even from himself. But he hasn't lost them. Hidden, they haunt and plague him more than ever.

Another child may set up permanent housekeeping with childish ideas of omnipotence. Everybody begins life with the fantasy of being all-powerful. Many of us will not admit this but once we face the half-hidden dreams and images in our own minds, we discover how deeply the old wish for omnipotence is embedded. Telling a child he can do what he really can't do can perpetuate this infantile idea.

Still other children find a different way out. Betty was a highly talented little girl. Yet as she grew up she performed in a very mediocre way.

"It's safer that way," she once confided to a friend. "If you muddle along, folks won't expect you to be tops all the time."

Honest Self-Appraisal

To accept what one cannot do, to be realistically aware of one's own limitations is rather unusual in young people. We are talking about sober knowledge of one's own inabilities and incapacities. False modesty or plain discouragement is something else. But honest self-appraisal deserves support.

Perhaps you are wondering if this is the way to build self-confidence. But is it up to us to encourage or discourage feelings of limitation? Do we not have to respect the right of every human being, including our children, to accept their own instead of *our* feelings about themselves?

Listen closely and you will soon discover that sometimes they do not want to be encouraged. There is a big difference between a young girl who exclaims, "Gee, it sounds interesting. I sure would like to try but do you think I can do it?" and another who says, "That's not for me."

The first girl is asking for encouragement. There's no harm then, in saying, "Maybe you can. You could try—and find out." Very often the child discovers it's worth attempting something she feels a little afraid of.

But the second girl is *not* asking for encouragement. If we talk her into taking on the job, we have broken down her sales resistance and maybe her will and self-respect as well.

Respect Feelings of Others

Only respect for the other person's true feelings really works.

Larry is sixteen. He was allowed to grow at his own pace and his limitations were taken matter-of-factly. No premiums were placed on "acting like a big boy," walking or talking early, writing or reading sooner or better than the other children. On his first visit alone to the grocery he went only halfway and turned back. His mother didn't act disappointed.

"I'll be ready to go in another week," he said.

And he did go by himself with ease and comfort a few days later. Larry did not grow up with a need to prove anything about himself to other people.

Companions who dared him to do rash things never succeeded in bullying him. He told them he knew what he could and couldn't do.

"So why get all hot and bothered about it?" he asked them. His simple self-honesty floored the "wise guys" and they stopped picking on him.

Whatever the choice confronting a young person, the solid foundation of a human being who can accept himself *with his fears and limitations* is most important and must not be shaken.   —By Rudolph M. Wittenberg, Ph.D.

DISCIPLINE

GROWING up and becoming mature is something of a battle which continues until the youngster arrives at an armistice between the warring impulses within himself and the demands made on him by the society in which he lives. Certain controls appear during his earlier years. These are his developing conscience and his understanding of the world around him. He knows in general what is right and wrong, what is safe and what is dangerous. But his values don't always stay put. He is in a state of flux. Parents and teachers have a big part to play in what is to be the outcome during this stage of his development.

How can parents help? The problem is complicated by the fact that to do the job right they really have to be on both sides at the same time. They must sympathize with, understand and gratify certain of the young person's impulses. At other times they have to turn on some of the controls that will pull him up short. How can they do both?

Perhaps in the movies you have seen the commander of fighting forces standing on a distant hillock and peering through a pair of binoculars to watch the scene of battle. Parents can well take a tip from him and adjust their sights properly. Too often they seem to view youthful behavior through the wrong kind of glasses. Some use magnifying lenses only. What happens is exaggerated out of all proportion. Change, progress, a chance for improvement are all blotted out. Time marches on and other things get better. But not their Johnny, they decide. If he is untidy, tardy, given to putting things off or daydreaming, that's the way he will always be, they fear.

Don't Exaggerate Fears

Still others look through long-distance lenses that are trained on the day after tomorrow of a youngster's life. All they can see is what they expect Susie to be like when she is grown. If she shows tendencies to be wasteful and extravagant now, they are convinced that she will never be able to manage a budget. Or if she goes through a period of wanting to be alone a good deal, they decide that she is going to be friendless and withdrawn.

Such parents blast away at temporary behavior because they tend to see it as the finished product instead of just a step along the way. Nothing is wrong with the maturity model they have in mind for the young person. But they cannot focus on the child as he is right now—not yet quite grown.

The parent needs a bifocal approach that permits him to recognize temporary behavior as transient and passing. Instead of being blinded by present appearances, he should remember to look through the upper part of his glasses now and then to get a proper perspective on things. And he should remember that puberty and the teens bring new kinds of pressures and strains.

In leaving the relatively slow-moving world of early childhood, the young person has to acquire new and different controls in order to manage himself successfully. He is being bombarded as he gets older by many new sensations, impulses and strivings. He has to bring them into harmony with reality and his own inner standards.

Also, the boy-girl relationship has to be established. This calls for a surprising number of new techniques.

Impact of Society

Quite suddenly he has to rise out of the comfortable obscurity of being just one of the gang. Now he is hailed as a rising young citizen. For hardly a moment of his waking hours do radio, press or television ignore the adolescent. At one and the same time he is portrayed as "tomorrow's hope for a free world" and as "drug addict, vandal, delinquent."

Mayors form committees, deeply concerned about his needs. Simultaneously the local newspaper prints an alarming report about his breaking windows in the school district. An editorial in the same issue deplored "the growing crime wave of modern youth." At a time when he is trying to form a stable image of himself, he hangs suspended over the nation as a double symbol of good and evil. While he is still muddled about getting a clear picture of what he is really like, he also has to be making clear-cut decisions that call for judgments about the future. Will he take a college preparatory course? Or commercial studies, trade or mechanics?

At times he goes through phases of feeling like a displaced person. One day he may feel quite comfortable with close members of the family as he did during the serene years of early childhood. Again he swings far away from them and relies instead on his pals or on such parent substitutes as teachers and recreation leaders. Not infrequently he runs into a period when he doesn't seem to fit into any social niche. Then he crawls inside himself and seeks isolation.

These are some of the pressures and tensions of the teens. Most youngsters get through them wonderfully well, considering.

Preserving Existing Controls

It is helpful for parents to ask themselves what they are trying to help the young person achieve by way of self-control. As a first step toward this end, we have to help him preserve existing controls.

Frequently a young person is fighting an internal battle. He wants to go along with the crowd, perhaps. Yet he feels that the thing they plan to do isn't entirely acceptable. Maybe they are going to a roadhouse where liquor is sold.

But your son or daughter knows that it is dangerous to combine drinking and driving.

One father, suspecting that his son was in a somewhat similar conflict, ended his reading of the evening newspaper with a cheerful, "Thank heaven I can read about these crazy speed hoodlums and know that you have better sense, Bill. You're smart enough to want to live to grow up."

Much can be gained if we figure out ways to tip the balance in a positive direction rather than waging direct and heavy warfare against undesirable conduct. Here are some of them:

Stick to a minimum budget of "no's." This is the time of life when every "no" can become a challenge.

Give and Take Necessary

Cultivate an attitude of give and take. Suppose you want to have some chaperoning at your daughter's party. Then don't tell Ann whom to invite. Let her choose her own guests and she will be more willing to accept the casual chaperonage idea. If coming in late is a problem, let Joe have the family car on condition that he be in at a reasonable hour.

Make sure your young son or daughter knows that you like his friends— let's hope you do!—and that you believe in their wanting to have a sensible amount of freedom. If he knows that you are on his side fundamentally, he's apt to be on yours.

Remember that this is the time when it is hardest for a young person to take it straight from the shoulder. Something may be going on that you want to stop. Heavy-handed interference may only make matters worse. Gentle and understanding treatment is called for.

Humor often works miracles in moments of aggressive defiance. It shows that you are not angry or planning reprisal. Being able to laugh it off proves that you aren't hurt or shocked. Having found you loving and forgiving, the young person can quickly overcome the guilty feelings that may have been rising because of his uncontrolled outburst.

Help Him Avoid Temptation

Try to lessen, though you can't totally remove, the temptations in your teen-ager's life. Each parent knows the sort of situations that make special difficulties for his child. Obviously they are different for different youngsters. One has a hot temper and a tendency to lose it rather easily. Another may try to rationalize his way out of difficulties. You can often help to strengthen your youngster's controls by managing things in such a way that he isn't confronted with situations too difficult for him to handle easily.

Sometimes a young person seems to have weak control because he doesn't understand why he needs to exert any. There is potential control there all right. But he doesn't use it because he fails to see the need. In such instances the adult can help by explaining or interpreting matters.

Pete was teasing his sister unmercifully about her boy friend. It was more than she could comfortably take in her stride because of her own adolescent embarrassment about boy-girl relations. Their mother talked to Pete about this without making him feel guilty. Once his understanding and sympathy were enlisted, he was able to control his impulse to tease.

When wishes have to be denied for one reason or another, clear interpretation of the why is important. If a girl knows that she can't have the new formal because of some unexpected drain on the family purse, she's likely to be a good sport about it. Family rules and regulations are always accepted with much better grace if the youngster knows why.

Affection a Steady Influence

A display of parental affection can sometimes come to the rescue and save the day when controls threaten to break down. Don't be overimpressed by the adolescent's contention that he wants to be entirely on his own. He still has many dependency needs, just as we all have. There are moments when emotional closeness and strong ties of affection help to steady him. Often they give him just the little extra confidence he needs in order to control himself better. A spontaneous but diplomatic hug or kiss (in private, not in public!) may restore his sense of security in trying moments. Don't let your child's need for independence make you aloof at times when he needs your support.

It isn't always simple or easy to handle young people while they are trying to put childhood behind them. Children differ so much that what works with one may prove ineffective with another. Even with the same child, an approach that gets results one day can fail the next. That's because identical behavior has different underlying causes on different occasions. What proves effective when Andy wants to get out of going to Sunday school may not work when he plays hooky from junior high.

It is good to know that it takes a tremendous amount of mishandling over a long period of years to do a child much harm. The parent who loves his children and wants to be understanding and fair can usually recognize his own mistakes and find a way to correct them—often with the help of his children.

—*By David Wineman*

HOW APPEARANCE
AFFECTS PERSONALITY

PERSONAL appearance is tremendously important to Americans. Our interest in looks is attested by the time and money we devote to the care, modification, adornment and camouflage of our bodies. In the immense and diversified field of clothing the emphasis upon appearance values is so great that comfort, economy and functional suitability are often overlooked or even deliberately sacrificed. Our children cannot avoid the effect of this pervasive pressure and in varying degree and in different ways each child's personality is significantly molded by it. It is something that parents should recognize, understand and direct.

Every normal person wants to be significant—to count as an individual, to be thought of, remembered and talked about. Also, every person wants to think of himself with some degree of satisfaction, and the satisfactions of personal appearance are peculiarly supporting.

After all, the body is the simplest and most obvious symbol of the self. Although we realize that physical appearance is but one aspect of personality, we get our first impressions of a person from it and then relate what the person thinks, does and feels to this visual image.

It is no wonder, then, that to boys and girls growing up their looks are very important, and it is obvious that in the America of our time personal appearance has very real significance as a factor in developing personality.

A Common Problem

During adolescence there are few youngsters who do not have some difficulties in coming to terms with themselves in the matter of personal appearance. As the child approaches adult stature the family group becomes more critical of everything about him and less apt to make allowances for deviations from the adult culture standards. The desire to look like the other girls or the other boys is strong in every adolescent and is both enhanced and complicated by a new desire to look well in the eyes of the opposite sex. Moreover, on every side—at the movies, in his reading, and from the adults about him—he becomes aware of the importance placed upon beauty and physique as the fundamental ingredients of romance.

Also immensely important is the fact that during this period the young person compares himself not only with his friends but also with his ideal of himself. His ideal at this stage may resemble a well-known movie star or a champion athlete. The adolescent persuades himself that a certain kind of body is the symbol of the self he wants to be, and so the blemishes and shortcomings of the body his looking-glass shows him become threats to the realization of his most cherished yearnings.

In the questions boys and girls of this age ask and the concern they show about themselves, there is unmistakable evidence of the peculiar importance they attach to appearance as a means of achieving a personality they can accept.

In the case of over-sensitive adolescents, extreme dissatisfaction with personal appearance may contribute to symptoms of mental illness. Others, who show no symptoms to the casual observer, may pass through a period of months or years during which they are constantly preoccupied with such dissatisfactions.

Acne Causes Difficulties

Acne is more common during pubescence and early adolescence than it is at any other period of life and because of it a very considerable number of boys and girls suffer tortures of self-consciousness which may affect their personality development for years. For girls skin blemishes are particularly hard to forget. (See article on "Acne" for further discussion of this problem.)

And pity the girl in her early teens who tends to be fat. These girls are caught between a natural biological tendency toward increased plumpness during the puberal cycle of development and a strong desire to be slender. Fortunately for many of them, the plumpness of pubescence is succeeded by the tendency toward more streamlined contours of later adolescence. When fatness does not decrease, or when it actually increases, the girl faces a difficult personality problem in reconciling her real self and her ideal self. Her disturbance is often reinforced by the brutally frank jests of classmates and the obvious refusal of boys to be seen with a fat girl. Even when her excess weight is transient and not particularly obvious to her parents, her own disturbance may cause physical ills due to fasting, and psychological maladjustment due to self-consciousness.

Obesity in Boys

Among pubescent boys fatness is also both common and disturbing. In extreme cases it interferes with success in athletics. In perhaps one-third of the boys who are distinctly fat there are other physical appearance differences which, combined with fatness, seem to threaten their progress toward appropriate male development. The puberal spurt of growth in height and shoulder breadth is delayed, the secondary sex characteristics are slow in appearing, the hips are too wide and there is a noticeable increase of fat about the nipples. Boys are painfully aware of these sex-inappropriate differences.

A study of such boys over a period of seven years seems to prove that the

popular generalization that fat boys are happy and good-natured is not correct. On the contrary, these boys are unhappy, suspicious, and retarded in social adjustments. They resent having to undress before other boys in preparation for physical education. They dislike medical examinations. Although their sex-inappropriate development was not noticeable when they were in ordinary street clothing, the consciousness of it made them uncomfortable in the company of girls. Their personalities were significantly affected.

Realizing the significance that personal appearance has for boys and girls and the really damaging effect that unattractive characteristics may have on developing personality, what can parents, teachers, and others do to mitigate such bad effects?

First of all, we must try to understand how these youngsters are feeling and why they feel as strongly as they do. If we are to help our youngsters we must not shut off their confidences by ridiculing their concern over appearance and their attempts to make themselves more attractive. We may have forgotten how we felt at their age. After all, very few of us are satisfied with our looks, but as we live and learn we realize that self-respect springs from many other sources besides personal appearance. We forget our childish fears of "looking queer" and our adolescent preoccupation with short cuts to beauty.

Correct Serious Handicaps

If a young person has a definite physical handicap, it is extremely important to do whatever we can to correct it. Obviously, it is our responsibility to enlist the help of physicians and dentists to try to efface any disfiguring blemishes and distortions as early in life as possible so that the child may accept his physical appearance as bearable and pass on to play, work and social satisfactions.

When a child is distressed about a physical variation, such as acne, fatness or retarded growth, which has been shown by experience to disappear entirely or become less obvious in many children as they grow up, we should take pains to explain to him the prospect for improvement.

Most important of all, we must make every effort to help our youngsters find friends, happiness, and satisfactions that do not depend upon personal appearance. This is particularly important for two types of adolescent: those whose appearance is least attractive and those who are particularly well favored in face and figure. Among children who are deformed or crippled, there are many examples of how the handicap can be balanced by success in other things. One girl whose misshapen body forced her to spend her days in a wheelchair played an accordion with such skill that she made a significant place for herself in a large circle of friends. If a boy can play baseball well, no one thinks much about his big ears.

Parents and teachers must be alert in sensing when a boy or girl is disturbed about his appearance and help him find other ways to achieve satisfying significance as a person. —*By Herbert R. Stolz, M.D.*

WHAT A MAN SHOULD TELL HIS SON

IF your son is between eleven and thirteen, you—his father—have a chance now to offer him something only you can give: a man's hand in his struggle to become a man. By now he knows that being a man doesn't mean "doing whatever you want." He has seen for himself that what seemed to be a Shangri-La of adulthood has responsibilities along with its privileges, worries along with its pleasures. What he thinks and feels at this time of his life come to: "I'm growing up. I have to be able to handle grown-up problems. I have to be able to do it by myself. Will I succeed?"

He wants to be a man, yet there are times when he would just as soon forget it and remain the cared-for boy. But his body won't let him forget. His body begins to show signs of that mental-physical-emotional upheaval we sum up as "puberty." The emergence of his sexual function is an unavoidable reminder of the fact that all his other functions as a man are developing, too. So these days, "What's happening to me?" is his query. Is there anyone in a better position than you to give him the answers?

At this point perhaps you're veering off uneasily and skeptically because you think a suggestion for a man-to-man talk is coming up. It seems most of us who had these cooked-up sessions with our own fathers didn't get much out of them, however well-intentioned. Some of the failure, it would seem, lay in the aim of those times to "be a pal to your boy." That doesn't really work. Your son can't possibly have the adult qualities you require of a friend, and you can't retrogress twenty years to be his bosom chum. "Dad's always trying to act buddy-buddy," one teen-ager remarked. "First I feel sort of sorry for him and embarrassed and then I get pretty mad. It comes across so phony! If he'd just act his age . . ."

Act Your Age

There's the point: acting your age, you give your boy not a man-to-man, but a father-to-son talk. For many reasons, almost any father gets a little uncomfortable at that suggestion and counters with "How?" The only honest answer, of course, is according to your particular knowledge of your son, yourself, and the kind of relationship you have. However, some things apply to all fathers and sons, and with this in mind here is a general four-point plan for giving your boy the answers he is after:

Choose a suitable time. Some men get an uneasy feeling because they envision a delicate, lengthy, explanatory discourse—the kind foreshadowed in your own teens by a clearing of the throat and a "Son, there are Some Things You Ought to Know."

It doesn't have to be that way between you and your boy. Actually, you've been answering his questions about sex and his sex role for some time now. His education doesn't begin at twelve noon on his twelfth birthday, or the first time you see him eyeing a cheesecake photo. Maybe you will have only one conversation, but it's more likely to be several. Whichever it is, you can choose the right times by being alert to your opportunities. Perhaps, looking up from your newspaper some evening, you'll find he's been watching you. Your responding grin or "How you doing, son?" may open the floodgates on a torrent of questions, ideas, uncertainties, wishes—or just one concern.

Make an Opportunity

But don't count on his warming up immediately and speaking openly. Since boys at this age are fighting just as hard to be independent of their fathers as to be like them, your son may offer no clear opportunity at all. You may have to make one. You cannot assume he "knows everything now."

In making the opportunity, you've won half the battle with any discomfort you and he may feel if you take advantage of a moment when a special closeness already prevails. You've just watched a shut-out game on TV . . . or you've settled that he can drive the car when he's old enough for a license . . . or you're refinishing a table together. Now is the time, when your companionship is deepest, for words like, "Bob, you're growing up so fast—I wonder how much you know about what goes on with all this growing?"

Find out what your son knows. Some of us get so eager to put across all information we think necessary that what is supposed to be an exchange of ideas becomes a one-way street with us doing all the driving. The result? You can get some idea from the remarks of several teen-agers who had been buffaloed by just this kind of behavior on the part of parents:

"What does he think I am—a dope?"

"Some things my father mentioned I never even heard of—and he acted like I *ought* to know."

"Dad meant well—I could feel that. But I didn't have a chance to get in a word about what I really wanted to know . . ."

"You know what? I felt like telling him to go hire a hall!"

Don't Talk Too Much

In any discussion at any age, a child should have the chance to bring out his own information and his own ideas. A few simple questions are usually all that's necessary for a starter. Maybe your son thinks "puberty" means a changing voice; maybe he has a minutely detailed scientific knowledge of his endocrine interworkings—and no knowledge of his emotional interworkings. How can you know unless you give him a chance to talk? It may take time for him to get to it; many boys don't talk easily about what's on their minds. But you can't lose if you let him carry the ball most of the time.

Another thing about talking too much: every one of us has some hangover from the days when all these things were only whispered. Some fathers are only too aware of such feelings in themselves and, trying to be outspoken and honest, are almost too determined to reassure their sons that "It's okay—don't worry." But saying "don't worry" too many times doesn't really accomplish anything—except that it may make a boy who wasn't worried in the first place think that there *is* something to worry about.

Correct distorted ideas. Don't be surprised if he comes up with some vague notion that nocturnal emissions in a boy are comparable to menstruation in a girl; or thinks pimples are caused by masturbation. He may have picked up a lot of peculiar ideas. Even your own teachings—since you first answered his "Where did I come from?"—when they reappear now may be almost unrecognizable. Or you may see a yawning gap in his information.

You'll find yourself going over lots of ground you've covered before. But remember that now your son sees and feels the information you gave him in a new way, more personally, with a more mature concept of his functions and of man-woman relationships. Having a date is different now than when he played pick-up-sticks with the pretty little girl next door. So is kissing a girl.

Don't Use Ridicule

Incidentally, an effective way to cross up all your own good intentions and efforts is to poke fun at the boy or his friends. Not that you'll be dealing his emotional stability a death blow if a couple of his ideas are so outlandish you just can't help smiling. But if you act as though he just said a howler—he'll freeze. No one at any age likes to be laughed at and this age of puberty is particularly sensitive.

What is he likely to want to know? One of the questions in his mind is probably, "Why do I have wet dreams?" He may not know the term—but the occurrence bothers him. There's a good reason why he has them, starting with the simple fact that now his body is secreting semen. It accumulates and has to be discharged. In a sort of reflex action, the discharge happens at night, sometimes accompanied by an erotic dream that is also normal.

Not only what causes nocturnal emissions, but what causes his erections at any time, is likely to be a big question mark for your son. Erections on wakening, in boy or man, are often due to the full bladder pressing against the seminal vesicles, located right next to it, that store seminal fluid. A boy who has an erection during a bowel movement may be relieved to find out that his full rectum can cause this by pressing directly against the very sensitive prostate gland. Erections can result from local stimulation or irritation, too—for the head of the penis is also extremely sensitive. Of course, they can also come from erotic thoughts and feelings induced by movies or books or conversation. But boys who lead active lives, intent on school work and sports, are not apt to be bothered by this.

Masturbation

Another concern is masturbation. Remember when it was linked with acne, cancer, impotence, sterility, insanity, perversion? It may still be defined in your family dictionary as "self-abuse." Maybe you can't rid yourself completely of these old attitudes, but the fact is that any normal teen-ager mastur-bates occasionally. The pleasurable sensation it brings need be no source of shame. One reason he masturbates is to be sure his penis can do what he knows it is supposed to be capable of.

Many boys worry about the size of their genitals. The fact is that size varies considerably from one individual to another. Also, in most men one testicle —like one foot or one hand or one eye—is larger and at a slightly different level in the scrotum than the other. Even more important for a boy to know, the size of his genitals has nothing to do with his "manhood." Nor is the presence or absence of erections any measure of maturity.

Boys sometimes fret over lack or delay of other physical signs, too—for instance, beard and pubic or axillary hair. The secretion of testosterone, the male hormone that is the major factor in bringing about the appearance of the hair, doesn't begin at precisely the same time in every boy. This is the hormone, produced by the testicles, that promotes the growth of the sex organs and also gives a boy the other masculine characteristics that he keeps looking for—broader shoulders, longer limbs, stronger muscles, deeper voice. If he seems to be worried because he isn't developing these characteristics as soon as some of his friends, you ought to let your boy know that this, too, is a matter of individual growth. Another common source of concern is height —especially when the girls he knows have suddenly and inconsiderately zoomed to where he has to look up at them. He has to live with this situation for a couple of years until he catches up.

Something else that troubles boys is that they are apt to think the urethra may carry urine along with semen in an ejaculation. They should know that one of those astonishing automatic devices the human body has makes this impossible. When semen is about to leave the seminal ducts, the opening from the bladder is completely closed off.

Tell Boys About Girls

A boy is curious about what's going on with girls at this age. Maybe all you ascertained from your own father was that you "ought to have considera-tion for them." But boys ought to know that girls also undergo body changes. And unlike the impression of awe or mystery or pain that boys of our genera-tion got, they should know that menstruation is neither harmful nor mys-terious nor awesome. It is part of the function of child-bearing.

Stick to the facts. That doesn't mean giving your boy mechanical, unfeeling replies to his questions. On the contrary, the way you talk to him is essentially the something only you can give him. His mother could furnish him with scientific data, but she can't give him the feel of being a man. She can't put across the view of things as a man sees them. Your attitude and manner are much more meaningful to your boy than anything his mother could tell him about you in words.

However good your own attitude, however much you want to help, you can't possibly eliminate every source of worry that a boy has. Even a boy with "perfect" parents and a "perfect" environment would inevitably have certain anxieties at this age—if only as a result of the shifting body balances due to endocrinological changes. Some conflict is inevitable—and necessary. In order to become the man he wants to be, he has to work his own way through his conflicts and problems. The best thing you can do for your son is to arm him with simple facts in simple language, let him know he can always come and talk things over with you if he wants to. And above all give him the feeling that what he is working out is what every boy has to work out— that it's all right—nothing wrong, nothing nasty about it—just the natural business of growing up, finding out things and becoming a man.

—By Sidney L. Green, M.D., and Margaret Albrecht Gillmor

WHAT TO TELL YOUR DAUGHTER

DO you remember when you first learned about menstruation? Was it from some of the girls your age or a little older? Did your mother announce that she wished to have a little talk with you? Did she leave a book lying about? Many of us have painful recollections of embarrassed mothers and embarrassed selves, or of downright nervous mothers and nervous selves. In others the effort to remember evokes a feeling of anxiety and loneliness since their mothers gave them no preparation whatsoever for the coming of menstruation. For these were still the times of hush-hush for such things. And this pretense that an ordinary function of womanhood didn't exist twisted that function, for our mothers, into something embarrassing, uncomfortable and often painful. So just as they handed down family heirlooms, they inevitably passed on to their daughters something of their own feelings about menstruating. Is your daughter going to be troubled by similar memories and reactions?

Changing Attitudes

She doesn't have to be. Things have been changing, and with your help your daughter can share in this changing attitude. Where young women once dreaded the coming of "the monthlies," today's teen-agers are becoming more matter-of-fact about their periods. "Falling off the roof," "being unwell," "the curse," clearly revealed the reactions of an older generation. You don't hear such evasive phrases as often nowadays. "My period's due" or "I'm menstruating" many a teen-ager says quite frankly. Where young ladies once sat about pale and wan, headachy and useless, for three or four days out of a month, a good proportion of today's daughters make those 40 or 50 days out of the year as productive as any others.

Today we are getting away from age-old shackles of fear, scorn, taboo and superstition about this natural function. The child is rare these days who doesn't pick up or ask for some information about menstruation at an early age. She may see drugstore displays and ask, "What's that, Mommy?" She may come across newspaper or magazine articles and advertisements. Or come home with some biological smatterings from school or curious half-knowledge from her friends and want you to clear up her confusion. So you will probably have repeated occasion to weave facts about menstruation into the fabric of your daughter's total knowledge as it expands year by year. It sometimes happens, of course, that a girl gets to be nine or ten without ever evincing such curiosity. If this is so, since menstruation can begin that early, it is none too soon to bring the matter up yourself. But the modern mother isn't setting up any strained heart-to-heart talk. She takes advantage of a natural occasion, or she waits for a moment when she and her daughter are for some reason especially close.

Not merely the fact that we can now talk about menstruation more normally, but how we are talking to our daughters is another factor in the increasingly healthy attitude of today's teen-agers. Just as we took from our own mothers feelings as well as words, so do our daughters absorb something of our own outlook. Those of us who acquired a fairly natural attitude in our own childhoods are lucky—we need make no special effort. Those not quite so fortunate, unable to erase entirely the years of concealment and whispering, are doing their best—and that best is proving worthwhile.

Physiology of Menstruation

Ovaries are almond-shaped glands attached to the uterus by ligaments. A newborn baby girl has in those ovaries egg cells by the thousand. Beginning at puberty, one ovum grows big enough about every four weeks (and even then it's just a watery-looking speck) to ease through the thin membrane that has kept it embedded in the ovary. This part of the cycle, ovulation, occurs roughly two weeks before menstruation. The ovum is drawn within a few hours into one of the Fallopian tubes.

Fallopian tubes or oviducts are two muscular, convoluted tubes about four inches long and roughly the diameter of a pencil. Ordinarily, the fringed, funnel-shaped mouth of a tube is less than an inch away from its neighboring ovary. At ovulation it moves still closer, one of the waving, tentacle-like fringes curving over the ovary. This, along with the motion of microscopic hairlike projections and mucous secretion lining the tube, attracts the expelled ovum. The egg is then moved slowly along toward the uterus.

The uterus or womb looks somewhat like an upside-down pear and lies approximately between the bladder and the rectum. The mucous membrane and glandular tissue which line the womb are called the endometrium. Right after a menstrual period the endometrium begins to re-form and for a while is very thin. Then day by day, it grows steadily thicker, swelling with more blood and glandular secretion. Finally it is ready to nourish a fertilized ovum. If fertilization does not take place, the endometrium disintegrates. The soft bed of tissue passes through the vagina. This—in quantity about two to five ounces—is the menstrual flow.

The Menstrual Flow

How long does the flow last? Usually about three to five days. But some women have a light flow for six to seven days, some a heavy flow for only two days, without discomfort.

Is the normal menstrual cycle 28 days? This seems to be the mean but there are wide variations within the range of normal. There are cases where women menstruate regularly every 21 days, some every 35 days. For the first few months after she begins menstruating, your daughter's cycle may vary until her own individual balance is established.

Are there any signs that a girl is about to menstruate for the first time? Look at your daughter. If she's about eleven to fourteen, probably her hips are rounding and she's beginning to have a waistline. Perhaps her armpits and pubic area are showing a light down. Her breasts may be two diminutive mounds. As her first period begins, it may be preceded by a heavy, thick vaginal discharge.

Whether your daughter has learned about menstruation gradually over the years, or whether you had occasional talks with her, or whether you are just wondering about bringing the subject up, chances are she'll pop out with some questions that will stump you. No one can answer all the questions alert young minds evolve. But the more information you have the more directly you can answer her, or the more directly you can say, "I don't know." Some of her more obvious queries may be among the following. For example:

What is menstruation? Maybe you know a lot less than you realize about the remarkably complicated interworkings that go steadily on in the circle of your pelvic bones. Your answer to "What is menstruation?" can't be satisfactory unless you have a pretty good picture of it as a cycle, so here's a brief review.

The Menstrual Cycle

Should menstruation normally begin between eleven and fourteen? Not necessarily. Some girls start at nine or ten, some as late as eighteen. Beginning in the late teens is often simply part of a particular girl's own normal body function, but sometimes it can be due to poor health or other factors. If your daughter is over fourteen and has not had her first period, it's advisable to mention it to your family doctor.

What brings about these changes—what causes puberty? That, of course, is somewhat like asking what makes us grow. However it is primarily glandular action that changes child into woman. The special release of hormones at this time helps genital maturing, gives your daughter the rounded contours of womanhood and initiates the menstrual cycle.

Is it better to use pads or tampons to absorb the menstrual flow? Although opinion varies, and your doctor may especially recommend one or the other for your daughter for specific reasons, the general rule is: use whatever is most comfortable. Here you can give some practical advice. A sanitary belt, for instance, may be narrow or wide; it should be of comfortable size, with a secure fastening. Both tampons and pads are available in different sizes, with different absorbent capacities. Choosing the right type and size avoids chafing and discomfort. Manufacturers know their own products and following their instructions gives maximum benefit.

How often should pads or tampons be changed? That's a matter of common sense and whether the menstrual flow is heavy or light. Most women change every few hours for the first two days. A tampon used too long can lose its absorbent capacity. A pad used too long can chafe. It is interesting to know that while the menstrual flow itself has no odor, an odor can develop as the discharged substance is exposed to the air. It is important that your daughter learn to keep a good supply of pads or tampons in her pocketbook and school locker. Most ladies' rooms have dispensing machines.

Cleanliness Is Essential

Should extra attention be paid to cleanliness during menstruation? Your young lady, thanks largely to you, isn't likely to be as concerned with cleanliness as you may have been—since she hasn't been imbued with insidious suggestions of uncleanliness attached to menstruating. The sweat glands seem to be more active during menstruation, so she may want to take an extra bath or shower. No "nice hot tub" or "brisk cold shower," though. The one can speed up menstrual flow, the other can stop it.

Some of the major manufacturers of sanitary protective items offer excellent free material helpful in informing a girl about menstruation and hygiene.

What about physical activity—shouldn't a woman take it easy? Not today's generation. Normal exercise is part of good health. Lack of it can contribute to congestion of the menstrual flow, just as it can be a factor in constipation which can also cause menstrual discomfort. Some schools have found special instruction in how to relax completely, or exercises for toning up the whole abdominal cavity, to be beneficial. Your daughter can do what she feels like doing. Of course, if her normal exercise is walking, it wouldn't be common sense to make her body adjust to a fast game of volley ball just as her period is beginning. But if she has always played volley ball regularly, her usual game isn't likely to have any particular effect. Many women even go swimming during the last few days of their period and there's no harm in it if the water isn't too cold.

But don't women feel a little "different" while menstruating? Maybe your daughter will and maybe she won't, once her cycle is established. Common premenstrual sensations are a heaviness in the pelvis, lower back and thighs; swelling and slight tenderness of the breasts; twinges of slight cramps. "Nervousness," "touchiness," "the blues"—these usually come under the more scientific heading of premenstrual tension, and it has been found that much of this is rooted in emotional attitudes toward menstruating.

Good Health Prevents Discomfort

How can menstrual discomfort be avoided? You are already helping your daughter avoid it by establishing the feeling that menstruation is part of her function as a woman, part of a rather exciting yet quite ordinary cycle. You can also help her by encouraging attention to sensible diet, sufficient sleep, adequate exercise—in other words, general good physical health. If she's on a nonstop merry-go-round of activity, try to slow her down. Doctors have found that today's fast pace can be a factor in menstrual tension and the attendant discomfort.

Supposing there is menstrual pain? If your daughter has considerable pain or if her periods are extremely irregular, if she has a discharge between periods, if the flow seems too scant or much too heavy—it is no longer considered something she has to go through or something she'll outgrow. Take her to a doctor. Maybe she's in poor health. Maybe her posture is poor and stooping is crowding her organs. Perhaps she has some physical disturbance, some glandular dysfunction, or just something on her mind, that he can diagnose and take measures to alleviate.

Is it a good idea to take her to a gynecologist? That depends on your daughter, the doctor and the circumstances of her visit. If you have established a practice of regular medical checkups, your family doctor may recognize during one of them the signs of approaching menstruation, and this is helpful.

Some girls like to continue with the family doctor. Some family doctors themselves recommend a gynecological examination at times. If you visit a gynecologist, your daughter may like the adult, womanly feeling of doing the same thing you do.

Boys Need to Know

Remember that someone else in your family may have some unanswered questions. Don't leave out your son. If over the years he hasn't been told about menstruation he, too, has certainly seen advertisements, overheard parts of conversations, possibly acquired some one-sided concepts from his friends. He deserves a frank explanation.

Attitudes and feelings in explaining menstruation to a young man are just as important as they are in talking to daughters. Men, too, have been affected by the lack of knowledge and outlandish notions once attached to this important, not at all mysterious function. If your husband's mother was strangely "ill" several days out of each month, he could easily have had some peculiar childhood impressions. Your son, possessed of honest and accurate information, can have a much more realistic and less embarrassed attitude.

When talking to either your daughter or your son, what you say is, of course, important and you need to be sure of the basic facts. But don't forget that how you say it is of equal importance and this depends on how you feel about all this. Have you ever stopped to think how you do feel? It is interesting and also important to find out.　　　　　—*By Margaret Albrecht Gillmor*

TEEN-AGERS NEED PLENTY OF SLEEP

THE purpose of Saturday mornings—and Sunday mornings, too—is plain and simple: surely they come around just so teen-agers can catch up on sleep! Have you ever tried to pry your own young man or lady out of bed on a week-end morn? Most times the effort is doomed to fail. If it does succeed, you have a leaden-eyed somnambulist stumbling around the house. If they can't sleep lying down, they'll sleep standing up—for teen-agers decidedly need that extra rest.

They are growing—fast and furiously. It is important to remember that although children grow gradually and constantly from birth, there are two periods in life when growth is particularly rapid. The first is in the child's first year, after which time he slows down and enters a long period of slow but steady growth. By the time a child reaches his early teens, a new and intense phase of growth begins to be apparent. A gain of twenty pounds in a year is not at all unusual. With the pounds come the inches, too—as much as six inches in a year for a boy. Girls seldom soar quite this much but they, too, grow rapidly in height. However, it isn't just the addition of pounds and inches that creates the need for adequate sleep. Nerves, muscles, bones—all the tissues of the intricate human body are involved in this growth. The heightened glandular activity that comes with puberty makes heavy demands on body change and development. The system is temporarily out of balance, and working steadily to achieve a new goal.

Growth in All Directions

Physical growth isn't the whole story, either. Remember how much more easily you tire when there's something on your mind, some mental knot to untie? As you've seen for yourself, your teen-ager is in an almost constant state of trying to "find the answers." On top of all this, he's probably studying hard, working on a hobby, perhaps taking music or art lessons, participating in club and sports activities and just generally keeping up with the crowd. He's growing upward, outward, inward and sideways. In order to do this, he has to have enough of the restorative balm of sleep.

Of course, the methods you use to make sure he gets the sleep he needs can crash head-on into another adolescent necessity: Independence. The golden proof of being grown up is staying up late. Actually a boy or girl of 14 or so needs more sleep than one of 10. However, if you try to make the 14-year-old go to bed before his younger brother or sister you are certainly going to clash with the older child. But if you know he's going to have several extra hours of rest come Saturday and Sunday, you won't feel so great a need to push him.

Naturally, this won't mean he can stay up till all hours on weekdays. You can be sympathetic but frank: "You may go out Friday and Saturday nights as much as you want, but you do have to go to school, and school begins at nine o'clock. That's why you should get to bed in good time on school nights so that you can get up rested in the mornings. Week-end nights you can afford to sit up because you can sleep as late as you want next day." You can even explain—not all in one sitting, maybe, but as the occasions come up—why he needs more sleep now than he did earlier or will later on.

Ability to Take Responsibility

Adolescents can often take a lot more responsibility than parents give them credit for. To some mothers and fathers, the transition from child to adolescent seems to happen almost overnight—too fast for them to adjust to. They see no warnings of the change. They haven't changed and so they continue to act as they did a few years back (or sometimes it seems like only a few weeks!). The result, all too often, seems to be an endless struggle between the growing maturity of the child and the virtually unchanged habit pattern of the parents.

So, once you have altered the pattern toward week-end catching-up, don't unwittingly hang on to the times when you had to watch over things. Let your teen-ager go out week-end nights and come home at a time that seems reasonable to everyone. Even on week nights, there's no need to get upset if he dawdles around and doesn't get to bed when you think he should. If he is tired enough in the morning to make getting to school on time difficult, you might comment that "going to bed earlier makes getting up easier." Then stop. He will probably realize it himself even without comment. When you set rigid curfews ("You *must* be in by eleven on Fridays and Saturdays. You have to be in bed by nine on school nights.") you usually accomplish very little. Rigid curfews often serve to make the adolescent more rebellious.

Let the Chores Wait

A busy mother can easily feel abused when a great husky son or daughter lies in bed until noon on week-end mornings. She feels that she deserves some help. Mary could at least scrub the kitchen floor for her, or Johnny could get out and cut the grass. But the kitchen floor can be scrubbed or the grass cut later by a well-rested, peppy young man or lady. Scheduling chores to be done *sometime* on Saturday makes more sense than keeping a time-clock on them.

When the adolescent has reached his full adult size, his need for sleep will be like that of an adult. Just as he will no longer want four helpings at dinner, an ordinary night's sleep of about eight hours will suffice. He settles down, and is not apt to need the Saturday slumber of his teens.

—*By Dorothy V. Whipple, M.D.*

HELP YOUR CHILD DEVELOP CAREER TALENTS

YOU probably wonder sometimes, if you are like most parents, what your child will be when he grows up. You dream of your son, perhaps, as a brilliant surgeon or famous lawyer. Or you picture your young daughter as an artist, schoolteacher or nurse. Naturally you always think of them as being happy and successful in their future careers.

But just hoping that your child will succeed isn't enough. You have a definite responsibility as a parent to help him prepare for that success. With over 40,000 different jobs in our present economic structure, you can't just leave the important responsibility of vocational planning to chance. It is unrealistic to expect that upon graduation, on the basis of limited information, Robert or Ruth will have had just the right school training for the best careers or that they will even be placeable. Further, you can't turn this vital matter over to Robert's or Ruth's teachers. With all their academic duties they can't be expected to carry your share of the load.

You Know Your Child Best

No outsider—teacher, counselor or psychologist—can possibly know your child as well as you know him. His personality is so complex and so full of interesting potentialities that nobody—no matter how expert—could discover all of them from a few limited contacts. Here's where you have the advantage. Living with your child, observing him in dozens of different situations, weighing his development over the years, you can spot special evidence of vocational aptitude and interest.

Johnny, for instance, has always loved to take things apart and put them together again. It's as much a part of him as his eyes and nose. Or Mary has a gentle way with sick people and likes to take care of them. Valuable insights of this sort can be used in perfectly natural ways to help your child organize a plan for successful career development.

Since there is no divining rod to locate latent vocational abilities, it is up to a parent to supply the magnet that will lure them to the surface. He must provide both the particular environment and the special motivation that encourage a child's personality to grow and unfold to the best of his particular abilities. This means that such a parent will work with his child's school to help the youngster gather information about new and expanding occupational fields, and then help his child to a better understanding of his own abilities, interests and aptitudes in relation to these fields.

Such an educational process grows along with your child. It can be initiated before he enters high school or college. Encouraged but not dominated by a parent, the child will become increasingly aware of the world of work and his own capacities in relation to it. Such knowledge will eventually help him to choose a career more wisely and make him a better student.

It's Your Child's Future

A child's career should, of course, be *his*—not his parents'. Mr. A., dissatisfied with his progress as a lawyer, should not expect his son to be a better one and make up for his own frustrated hopes. Mr. B., proud of his success as a newspaperman, should not expect his child to have just the same kind of success. Both parents A. and B. have to accept the fact that their children are individuals with talents, interests and capabilities of their own. They need to work with their children, not against them, in choosing a future career.

If you could sit in on professional vocational guidance sessions and read the case histories of job applicants, you would soon realize that there is no such thing as one perfect niche for each individual. People are not especially "cut out" for particular jobs. But within the more than 40,000 different jobs in our economic structure, there are probably many that will offer a real challenge and provide healthy satisfaction for your child.

Further, you would promptly discover that all jobs are important whether they are classified as professional, administrative, clerical, sales, skilled, semi-skilled or unskilled. Building up a job-snobbish attitude in children limits their opportunities. Also, no magic formula for success has ever been invented. Hard work is still an essential ingredient. Finally, from their study of occu- pational trends, professional vocational counselors tell us that there are still frontiers to crack not only in Alaska but right on New York's Fifth Avenue, Los Angeles' Wilshire Boulevard and probably even in your own home town. A careful study of actual case histories shows that most people fail in their jobs and are "let go" not because of a lack of intelligence or training but because of some flaw in their personalities. Perhaps they are churlish, lacking confidence in themselves, bombastic or carry a chip on the shoulder. Person- ality is molded in early childhood, long before John decides to be an engineer or Jane picks stenography as a career. Much depends, both consciously and unconsciously, on parental interests, aspirations and sense of values. Since personality traits are relatively stable over the years, parents will want to be sure that they themselves have the right vocational attitude before trying to develop it in their children.

Widen Career Horizon

Begin by helping your child gain some knowledge of many different kinds of job. Perhaps you could suggest to the teachers in your local high school that they arrange a job forum each year with representatives of the various professions and occupations in your community agreeing to talk to interested students about the demands, requirements and rewards of their particular fields. Dick had never thought of being a veterinarian until he attended such a forum and heard one speak. Now he has an animal hospital of his own in his home town and loves his work.

Interested parents should not rely on the school alone. Most schools have limited guidance facilities that are sometimes incapable of handling large numbers of students individually. Nor do they always have the amount of timely occupational material needed for enriching purposes. If your child's school does have a guidance program, consult the director for advice and work with him. If the school doesn't have a special guidance program, it may be a good idea to discuss with your child's teachers the possibility of carrying out some of the following suggestions on your own.

What Parents Can Do

You can help your child a great deal at home by giving him interesting career books for birthday, Christmas or graduation gifts. Excellent books are now available covering many fields and designed for all age levels, from story books for young readers to well-documented career monographs for college students. Ask your local librarian for help in their selection. She will also be glad to show you such bibliographical sources as the "Occupational Index," published by Personnel Services, and "Guidance Index," published by Science Research Associates. These list, classify and evaluate current guidance literature.

While you are consulting the librarian, find out about the many free or inexpensive leaflets and periodicals published by the state and federal governments. These cover a variety of fields and topics related to vocational guidance.

If you and your son or daughter want a good idea of how and where America works, leaf through the Dictionary of Occupational Titles, published by the United States Employment Service of the Department of Labor. The Decennial Census Reports are an additional excellent source of information about jobs. Copies of both are generally available in your local library or may be obtained by it.

Where to Find Help

Census reports mentioned earlier provide a wealth of information about trends in population, housing, farming, factories and mines, retail services and wholesale trades, foreign trade, and city, state and federal government. For purposes of career enlightenment they can be a source of much relevant information for the interested, thoughtful parent and the older teen-ager, preparing for college training.

Information about special fields may be obtained by writing directly to professional, trade, commercial and industrial groups and to labor unions. Get the addresses from your telephone book, classified directory, library or school. The local office of your state employment service is a gold mine of valuable information on current trends and occupational research. Suggest that your child start a scrapbook of job information. Daily newspapers, magazine articles, radio and television programs all have pertinent information to help fill it. Contact Chambers of Commerce in towns you visit to learn what factories, mills, business and professional offices are open to the public for inspection.

Jobs Keep Changing

Occupational fields are not static. They are responsive to national and international conditions, political and economic developments and technological changes. A new process hitting the labor market today may considerably alter tomorrow's work picture. In vocational planning with our children we and they have to be concerned about the future effects of occupational trends on their chosen fields at the time of their choice. We also have to take into consideration the delay our sons must face because of military service.

For some boys this is a period of marking time. If your son has a general idea of the various occupations where he will be best fitted, he can better describe his interests and qualifications during the classification interview at the time of his induction into the service.

Young men who must plan for military service and young women interested in enlisting, would do well to thumb through the appropriate section of the Dictionary of Occupational Titles. It shows how military jobs are related to civilian ones. There are military counterparts of many civilian occupations. And military classification officers, like civilian personnel officers, are impressed by people who know how they can best serve an organization. In making assignments, they are more likely to give preference to this type of candidate. The young person who has informed himself in advance about his own interest and aptitudes is sometimes in a better position to get a more rewarding military assignment. He will then get some vocational experience in a field where he belongs.

Long-Range Vocational Trends

Leafing through the United States Department of Labor report, "Occupational Outlook Studies," one is reminded that 80 years ago over half of our workers were farmers. Today less than 15 per cent are. Agriculture employed fewer workers as industrialization increased. Sons and daughters of farmers flocked to the cities to work in the many new occupations created by industrial expansion and specialization. Soon their purchasing power increased and with it the demand for goods and services.

The effect of all this on our economy shows up in the following trends which are likely to continue:

1. Expansion in manufacturing of durable goods (especially in metal working) and of nondurable goods (especially in the textile, clothing and food industries).

2. Chemical, printing and publishing areas up.

3. Encouraging outlook in finance and distributive service areas and in the construction industry (especially electrical, sheet metal work, plumbing and pipefitting).

4. Much additional personnel needed for retail and wholesale trade, aircraft, electronics, machine tool, industrial chemicals and petroleum industries.

5. Upward trend in the communications area with the exception of television and radio, which are relatively small industries providing too few jobs for the keen competition that exists.

6. Sharply increased employment opportunities for technicians, draftsmen, electronic technicians, laboratory technicians, tool and die designers, design engineering draftsmen, engineering aides, physical science aides, inspectors, estimators, time study analysts, medical and dental assistants.

7. Fewer workers needed in basic extractive, commodity-producing and transportation industries.

8. Downward trends in farming and legal employment.

9. Discouraging outlook for certain professional careers.

Professional Opportunities

In the past 80 years, professional and semiprofessional workers have increased fourfold. The professional field is still growing but not at a sufficiently great rate to absorb all the young people who want to work in it. Many more youngsters would do well to consider the semiskilled areas which have shown considerable expansion and promise to keep right on expanding.

To meet with success in the professional field, future candidates must be prepared to meet higher educational requirements than in the past. Graduate training beyond the bachelor's degree will be requisite for better jobs.

These professional fields will offer opportunities: education, engineering, medical care, social work, library service, home economics (especially for nutritionists and dietitians), government, physics, chemistry, accounting (private rather than public), and earth science as related to defense interests, especially for geologists, geophysicists, meteorologists, geographers and oceanographers.

Because our social progress has not kept pace with our technological advances, long-range trends point to rising employment in the social sciences. There will be a slow but fairly steady growth in the number of jobs available for sociologists, economists, and statisticians. There is an increased demand for statisticians in business administration, market research, advertising, engineering, the social sciences. There are also good opportunities for them as teachers of statistics in colleges and universities. In general, college teaching will provide increased opportunities.

Your Child's Personality

To choose a career wisely certain technical knowledge about your youngster's personality is essential. The degree of success a worker achieves in any field depends not only on what opportunities it affords but also upon the particular attitude and temperament he brings to that field.

What is this distinguishing thing that we label "personality"? How do we measure, evaluate and rate it against job requirements? Since this is the factor that is largely responsible for getting a better job and succeeding in it, we must help the young person get specialized information about himself.

First, since different jobs demand different types of intelligence, it is important that your child know about the kind of intelligence he has. It isn't just all-of-a-piece. It consists, instead, of several different mental abilities such as word fluency, verbal meaning, numerical ability, spatial relations and reasoning faculty. How much or how little your child possesses of each of these special abilities may spell the difference between success and failure in certain jobs.

Of course, Tom's high score in word fluency doesn't necessarily mean that he will make a good editorial assistant, although it's a job requiring that type of talent. He may be better as a salesman—a job which also uses this kind of intelligence. Perhaps he likes people and enjoys steady contact with them. The editorial job might not furnish enough of such contact to satisfy him.

Interests and Social Intelligence

In addition to determining abilities we therefore have to help a child examine his interests.

We also have to be concerned about such other factors as the amount of his social intelligence. This includes his ability to do the right thing at the right time, get along with people, like them and be liked. And then there is the important matter of his emotional stability—ability to meet and solve problems, profit from mistakes, keep on an even level.

Psychological tests have been developed to measure many of these traits. They are usually grouped into the following four categories:

1. General intelligence tests which measure general learning ability and potential for handling situations in which ideas, rather than things, are most important.

2. Aptitude tests which measure potential for learning a specific skill.

3. Skill tests which measure current efficiency in performing a specific task or function.

4. Personality tests which measure general attitudes, interests and habits. Your child is different from any other child and tests of this sort detect some of his uniqueness. The knowledge obtained is then used for prediction and diagnosis. Prediction is based on the ability to carry on some future activity. Diagnosis, the second function of testing, helps to identify both strengths and weaknesses and shows how they are interrelated.

Don't Depend on Tests Alone

While such tests can be of real value in helping you and your child to understand his traits and abilities, you should not expect to get the whole career answer from them. At the present time much of this testing is still in a highly experimental stage, requiring professionally trained experts to administer, score and interpret. No one test can accurately predict success in any field.

Success depends on intelligence plus many other related factors such as his drive, skills, perseverance, interests, health and appearance. If you want your child to benefit by this type of measurement, you need the help of not one but a battery of tests. Aptitude tests are usually a part of such a battery. Some parents, misinformed about aptitudes, think of them as special innate powers. But the tests reveal only how easy or difficult it would be for the individual to pick up specialized training along certain lines. To be successful he would still have to get that necessary training and he would still have to learn how to apply it on a specific job.

Don't fall for advertisements of so-called guidance services which pretend to be able to predict your child's future. Get help instead from people who are qualified. Find out if your child's school has a testing program. If it has, seek advice and information from the counselor in charge. If it hasn't, consult principal or teachers as to where you and your child can safely go. Additional information on vocational testing programs can be obtained from your local branch of the American Psychological Association or the American Personnel and Guidance Association. The latter organization has published a directory which lists approved agencies offering such services.

Share what you know. Even after a professionally trained counselor administers and scores a full-scale battery of tests on your child, it would be a mistake to expect him to tell both of you which of the possible 40,000 jobs is best. By himself he can't do that. All that he can do is assemble a lot of pertinent data obtained from objective measurements. Then comes the most important part—the interpretation of these facts in the light of your child's unique personality and behavior pattern. From your daily contact over the years, you know what evidences he shows of leadership, dependability and self-reliance. You also know to what extent there has been a lack of initiative, cooperation and responsibility. To understand the true and full significance of test results in relation to job requirements, a counselor or teacher needs the help of your observation and insight.

Parents' Check List

Here are twenty important questions that will yield many needed insights about your child's social and emotional development.

1. Does your child prefer dealing with people rather than with things?

2. Can he make a quick, good impression on people?

3. Does he prefer to work alone?

4. If he likes to work alone, is it because he wants to get away from people, rather than because he finds challenging things to do by himself?

5. Does he mix easily in a group?

6. Is he a leader rather than a "second-the-motioner"?

7. Is he basically an organizer rather than a developer?

8. Does he prefer routine activities to variety and change?

9. Does he like to find out what makes things "tick"?

10. Does he prefer to read about things rather than to *do* them?

11. Can he say what he means?

12. Can he work under pressure?

13. Is he generally relaxed rather than constantly "on the go"?

14. Is he the devil-may-care rather than the cautious type?

15. Does he shoulder responsibility without having to be told to do so?

16. Can he sustain interest in a project until it is completed?

17. Does he take chances rather than follow the tried and true?

18. Is his work during a school term better than on examinations?

19. Can he generalize so that each experience is not necessarily new?

20. Does he tire easily?

Important questions like these have all kinds of significance for future personal and career adjustments. They require well thought out answers. To avoid judging too quickly, you need to observe your child's behavior in response to many different situations. So give your youngster all the scope he needs. One way is to encourage him to participate in a variety of vocational learning experiences. These encounters can serve as a kind of laboratory for a child. Various try-out experiences in fields that he enjoys will give him the chance to demonstrate many of his latent career talents.

Job Experiences

Vocational counselors believe that a child has to learn how to work by *working*. Two important vocational learning experiences your child can have are the part-time job after school and the summer-work job. You as a parent will best know when it is time for him to start getting some actual work experience and how heavy a load he can carry.

If in your judgment and the school's, your child is ready, encourage him to get a job in a field he likes. Never mind what it is as long as it doesn't have any adverse effect on his health, morals or scholarship. Don't worry about the salary he earns at first. A $1.50 per hour rate may be paid for a job whose dead-end nature makes it unrewarding. A 75¢ per hour job may, on the other hand, be a real stepping stone to a career. Nor is a job a more desirable one just because it will keep your child close to home. A job down the block or around the corner may be just marking time for your child, whereas one in the next town could represent a real learning experience. Job selection should always be related to the long-range career plan.

A parent and child might reject all types of paid-work experience in favor of another type of vocational learning—the school's extracurricular program. A boy or girl who wants to be a reporter on a newspaper might get much more valuable training working on the school newspaper than as a paid file clerk in the "morgue" of your town's daily. The would-be accountant who handles the financial accounts of a production by the school's dramatic society will probably have no salary. But he might gain more experience than he would running an adding machine as paid assistant in an accountant's office.

Hobbies. Even in a large school not all the embryonic actors, artists, musicians, reporters, chemists and journalists can be given significant opportunities to find themselves. Other types of vocational learning experience which may prove valuable are the development of hobbies and participation in community service. A careful examination of the long list of hobbies, from building model airplanes to raising African violets, will reveal valuable applications to broad occupational fields. Participation in community affairs has both direct and indirect vocational value. The potential social worker, for example, gains valuable experience through her tie-up with the Community Chest Fund or the Christmas Empty Stocking Drive. She also meets and learns to get along with many different people engaged in a variety of occupations.

Do's and Don'ts

If you want to help your child find and develop his career talents:

1. *Don't* set a given time limit ahead such as graduation from junior high when you expect to start thinking about it. To ask your child out of the blue, "What do you want to be when you grow up?" at a time when it becomes necessary to choose an elective subject or a major field of concentration is unrealistic. That's a big answer to expect any young person to give! How does he know what there is for him to *want* to do unless you have encouraged him all along the way to find out?

2. *Don't* hope to find a store of well developed occupational interests and aptitudes *inside* him. No child has locked up within himself a job title such as "lawyer" or "librarian" to indicate his life's career. Our occupational interests do not come from within but from without. We are not born with them. We learn them.

3. *Do* help your child to become vocationally mature while he is maturing physically, mentally, socially and emotionally. During his growing-up years, encourage him to grow occupationally and to reveal some of his rich potential through home-school cooperation, use of occupational information, psychological testing techniques, tryout work experiences, participation in the school's extracurricular program and in community activities.

—By George Davenel

SUMMER JOBS

IF someone in your family is going-on-fourteen (or even less), it may seize him any day now—the work urge. Perhaps you'll have some forewarning. When he eases the want-ad section out of the Sunday paper, it isn't to make paper hats. "What's going on at your office, Dad?" can turn out to be not just a flattering question, but a leading one. Another common symptom is, "But I really *need* a bigger allowance!"

On the other hand, you may have no inkling of what's up until the unheralded announcement, "Guess I'll look for a job this summer." If you ask why, chances are the answer will be: money. Money to spend on hobbies or girls or a bike or gas for the jalopy if he's old enough and lucky enough to have one; money to save for college clothes or tuition; money to help out with the family bills that your growing-up teen-ager has seen coming in. In some cases, the answer may be, "I want to get some job experience." In others, the reason is, "Heck, I was the only one on the block who didn't work last year. What'll I do with myself all summer long?"

There is another answer, unspoken, that probably underlies all of these: a job equals independence. Working for a few months is a discreet way to try out one's wings. It's a way of saying, "I'm old enough now to work and make my own way—I think."

Work Benefits Character

But you, being older and having taken care of this boy or girl for so long, may wonder just how good summer work would be. You know, of course, that there is good, first of all, in letting those wings have their trial flight. This is your child's time for discovering more fully the true satisfactions and genuine rewards of proving his own abilities, making his own decisions and feeling himself a part of the grown-up workaday world. More important, perhaps, is the good of discovering that his mounting urge for independence requires a solid understructure built of responsibility, courage, initiative, self-discipline, cooperation. Nor will these lessons be absorbed in the abstract. On the job the teen-ager will find he has to be on time, carry out orders, get along with co-workers. He has to give a day's work for a day's pay.

In addition, the work experience is advantageous in later years. It need not even be directly connected with the teen-ager's chosen field. Any good job he fills responsibly will give him the background and the proof to show future employers that he is alert, ambitious, energetic, that he could hold a job. "I just got out of the Army," a college graduate said ruefully to a vocational guidance counselor, "and I've no experience—no real work background." He forgot about his teen-age summer work. But the counselor unearthed the following: the young man had started to work in his early teens with a newspaper route; he had next built a magazine route from 10 customers to 250; in his later teens he worked a 4 A.M. milk route steadily. To the counselor and a prospective employer, this added up to the character requirements mentioned above—plus a clear ability for customer contact.

How Parents Can Help

So this summer, you may join the millions of other parents who are saying, "It's okay with us if you want to work for a while." But some of those millions, too anxious not to be interfering parents, follow up their okay with a hands-off policy. This leaves boys and girls standing in the middle of the wilderness road to "Job." And young job hunters not only need a map, they need an adult to interpret it. You can't plan the whole journey, of course, but you can point out the grade-A highways. Here are some ways to guide your boy or girl past detours, ditches and dead ends.

Promote practical planning. The young job seeker needs to:

Give himself plenty of time to look. Investigate the possibilities among his friends' parents, school advisers, church connections, neighborhood trades-people. There are many advantages in working near home, or for someone the family knows.

Try local companies and organizations, get leads from newspaper want ads, apply at a reliable employment agency, consult the state employment service.

Consider organized summer work—federal and state apprenticeship programs for trade training; agricultural projects; work camps.

Using Initiative

One year two boys in an area hit by a hurricane saw a chance literally in their own back yard. With a power saw, they spent some profitable weeks disposing of their neighbors' fallen trees. Some boys and girls in their early teens have expanded the baby-sitting field to dog and cat-sitting for families away week ends or all summer.

Help your child be realistic. Very often, the adolescent work-wish is more zeal than real. For some, the sign of the dollar or just the allure of the adult working world is so dazzling, they lose sight of the basic fact that so many dollars equal so many hours of labor. "We like boys and girls," one employer said, "and they can fill a definite need during the summer months. But some are just too flip. They come in late, overdo the coffee breaks and only perk up when payday rolls around."

Even the teen-agers who are more interested in experience than money are sometimes so taken with what a job can do for them, they never think of what they can do for it. How can you bring about a more realistic viewpoint? Perhaps you can:

Call attention to facts that may be overlooked. One young lady was aglow with the thought of being receptionist in the plush offices of a high-fashion magazine. But a friend of her mother who had had experience in this field passed on information as to how she would be expected to dress. Pencil, paper, some unglamorous arithmetic—and the glow dimmed considerably. The girl did take a receptionist's job, but in an office where the wardrobe she already had was adequate.

Talk About the Job

Talk over the job with your boy or girl. Don't confuse this with a talking to or a talking down. Make sure it's a talking *with*. One wise and honest father who saw that his son's idea of a job was "the most money for the least work" had a back porch council one evening. "Tim," he said, "when I worked summers I wanted money, too—lots of money, like you. Wherever the money was—I was. Even for a couple of years after school, it was the same. It took five years for me to realize I felt empty about my work. There was never the feeling, that I have now, of getting somewhere or doing something I wanted to do. Believe me, son, that feeling is worth more than money. Think it over, will you?"

Work satisfaction may be a vague concept for an inexperienced teen-ager to grasp. But, partly because of his father's trust, which denoted respect, and partly because the facts appeared worth considering, Tim did think. He was interested in mechanical engineering, and took a summer job helping an automobile mechanic that gave him a feeling of achievement and learning.

Unveil the mysteries of your own paycheck. Its stub may be a revelation in itself—showing what comes out for taxes, social security, hospitalization, insurance and so forth. And the family budget breakdown, the costs of your transportation and lunch, can well bring out a streak of practicality in your teen-ager.

Employer-Employee Relationship

Help him understand his value to an employer. Some boys and girls underestimate and undersell themselves. The beginner often knows literally nothing about how to get a job, or may be bashful about ascertaining specific pay and working conditions. A prospective employer is not impressed by apparent lack of self-esteem. Even worse, such young people are open to exploitation, as in the case of an employer who got a summer's typing done by taking one girl after another "on trial." Either way, early disillusionment and discouragement may result for your child.

Bolster that wobbly ego a bit. See to it that your teen-ager understands people don't pay salaries for nothing. The packing or delivering he may consider trivial is obviously of value to his employer, and he has the right to know what he will get in return.

Try home rehearsals of employer-employee interviews with questions like, "What are your best subjects in school? . . . What are your extra-curricular activities? . . . Can you be on time? . . . Do you intend to go to college? . . . How much do you think you should get for this work?" In turn, your boy or girl should be able to ask with self-assurance, "What are the hours of work? . . . How long is the lunch hour? . . . Is heavy lifting involved? . . . That monthly pay—it comes out to so much weekly, doesn't it?"

Show your boy or girl how to make up a standard resumé of fundamental information—full name, age, address, parents' names, schools attended, references, work they feel qualified for.

Guard Against Overwork

Make sure you know what kind of work your child is undertaking. His eagerness may outweigh his real capacities. Overwork can creep up before either one of you is aware of it, whether it is physical overwork or the burden of biting off too large a chunk of responsibility. Adolescents do need some vacation. Physically, they are in an important phase of growth. Depending on his build and general health, a boy may benefit from the exercise he gets in car-washing, but suffer if he takes a stock-room job. And, as you know only too well, adolescence is also a time for social growth. A few weeks after she took a salesgirl's job young Jean found herself saying, "Golly, Bob, I guess I'm just too worn out for the party tomorrow night."

Get as many facts as possible about the prospective job from the teen-ager himself. Provided you don't fall into stuffy or bulldozing approaches, he's likely to welcome the interest of someone with a little know-how about this business of going to work.

If you don't have personal knowledge of the reputation of a particular firm or employment agency, check with your chamber of commerce or local union, with an organization like the Better Business Bureau, with a business-man in the same field.

Jobs Away from Home

If the job involves living away from home, make doubly sure you really know what it's like. For instance, there is good opportunity for boys in summer resorts. But in some cases the hours are long, the work hard, the living conditions poor and earnings inadequate—especially if there is some vague understanding that part of the pay lies in customers' tips.

Investigate carefully any job potentiality for your teen-age daughter that seems off the beaten track or suspicious to you. Young girls have found them-selves in embarrassing and unfortunate situations.

Some parents go too far in their checking-up—both irritating the employers and creating resentment in their children. There's no need to go on a crusade, for most employers are as anxious as you that there be unquestioned fair play. But some, unhappily, are not—and you do have the right to know what kind of venture your adolescent is taking on.

See to it that you and your son or daughter don't unwittingly break the law. Children, when jobs are hard to find in ordinary channels, may end up shopping around and taking work that is unsupervised, hazardous or in violation of child labor laws. Do you know about employment certificates, age certificates, working papers, working permits? In different areas, such terms mean different things.

There can also be some unwritten laws you will not want your child unknowingly to break. Union organization and rulings differ, for example, from location to location, store to store, job to job. A call to your local union branch can settle any doubts.

Whatever the laws, you will also profit by finding out about the recommendations of the National Child Labor Committee, 419 Fourth Ave., New York 16, N.Y.

If He Wants to Drop Out of School

In the thrill of new-found independence, it is easy for some young workers to think, "School is kid-stuff. Look, I'm taking care of myself!"

The thought may never enter your own child's head, but if there are any such signs, be prepared to bring all your tact and firmness and influence to bear. It may be that just a word or two will turn the trick. It may take more persuasion, more explanation of the practical aspects of education when it comes to being a genuine success later on, financially as well as in other ways. A school guidance counselor can, of course, be most helpful. Perhaps your child will also want to talk to your minister or a favorite uncle whom he respects. It may also be that your particular son or daughter will have to feel the iron hand beneath your velvet glove. Should it be unavoidable, don't feel that you will ruin their lives by saying, "Absolutely not!" This is one of those situations where adults *do* know best.

Communities Can Help

The community can also be of assistance. In Colorado, for example, the Denver Boys, Inc., sponsored by the public schools, State Employment Service, City Recreation Department and Rotary Club, has helped boys find suitable jobs. In Berkeley, California, with city cooperation, youths have been kept busy with such work as public landscaping, suitable construction labor, and trail widening. Under the Berkeley program, mornings are for work, afternoons for organized recreation. The Iowa City Woman's Club came up several years ago with a Teen-Age Employment Service and Work Experience Program. If businessmen, trade unionists, counselors, educators, and parents —everyone in your community—help, the community as well as your young people will benefit.

Here is a general list of suitable work opportunities. For the most part, sixteen seems to be the minimum age when boys and girls can for various reasons more easily get work. There may be regulations, but on the whole there are fewer limitations. The greatest opportunity for under-sixteens lies clearly in making their own opportunity in their neighborhoods.

Job List

For young teens: errand runner, delivery boy, dog-walker, car-washer, lawn-mower, newspaper carrier, floor-waxer, Venetian-blind cleaner, pet caretaker, door-to-door sales (seeds, subscriptions, greeting cards, stationery), doll's seamstress, minor repairman, home fruit canner, clam-digger and seller, truck farmer, berry-picker, inside window-washer.

Possible for 14–16-year-olds: tree nursery helper, gardener, veterinarian's helper, kennel worker, harvester, movie extra, library checker, book-mender, page, photographer's assistant, office boy, minor household repairs handyman, mail opener, envelope stuffer, baby sitter, counter clerk (candy, drug, variety, gift stores), small boat handyman, boat-yard or yacht club helper, stable boy, model, club handyman, caddy.

For boys or girls who are over 16: hospital aide, runner, messenger, page, typist, stenographer, clerk, farm hand, summer resort worker, telephone operator, bellhop, junior camp counselor, day camp assistant, life guard, waiter, bus boy, trade apprentice, commercial art assistant, bakery worker, cashier-wrapper, dude ranch-hand, fishing boat hand, forestry worker, service station or garage helper, stock clerk, packer, concessionaire's helper, usher, beach or park attendant, laboratory assistant, construction worker.

—By Margaret Albrecht Gillmor

TWELVE KEYS TO COURTESY

I'M glad my son has begun to date," says the understanding mother. "I can see, now, that all the things I've been trying to teach him about manners and social poise have begun to seem important to him. He's learning because, for the first time, he *wants* to learn."

In every home, of course, children learn by imitation and from family attitudes. In many homes they learn that courtesy is really thoughtfulness for someone else. The "Good morning" that is traditional courtesy is also a way to start the day off well for others, no matter how we feel ourselves. The youngster who is thanked for his efforts and asked politely to do something instead of being peremptorily ordered to do so, is going to grow into a "thank you" and "please" sort of child.

But when the teens hit the household the whole subject of manners grows more complex. The teen-ager is on his own, socially speaking, often in emotion-packed situations that shake his confidence in his own behavior, no matter what his background.

"I don't see Joe around any more," mother will comment to her son.

"What a drip," replies his erstwhile best pal. "You should see him at parties. He doesn't know how to talk and he can't dance. So his idea of a good time is to try to get a girl into a dark corner to neck."

Up to the age of about thirteen, Joe was popular with the other boys. Independent, self-sufficient, tough and wiry, he had qualities his all-male group admired. But now see what has happened. Joe had not been prepared at home for the change in behavior that was expected of him once dating began. He's smart and he'll learn. But in the meantime, he is miserable.

Home Influence

There is no doubt that a teen-ager who has been privileged to live in a family in which courtesy is second nature and where social situations are handled easily and properly has an enormous advantage when manners become important to him. But any boy or girl can get the help he needs if he knows where to look for it. Many junior and senior high schools help pupils with matters of social behavior. Often an extracurricular class of this kind is the result of pupils' own request for it. Young people's groups often plan their own programs and find teachers, adults and books of great help in learning the ways of the social world.

How can we help our children pass this big social test of first-dating? Their preparation must begin years earlier, and we are their models. We all know our manners but do we save them for our friends and abridge them to extinction at home?

We must face the fact that children absorb our manners and mannerisms. Our tensions make tensions for them. Sharp orders, unreasonable behavior on the part of parents are reflected in our children. Likewise, if we show considerate behavior toward them we are preparing our boys and girls to enter the social world of the adolescent and the adult with poise and pleasure.

We must find time for courtesy and consideration and companionship within our own homes. That word "time" is often the key to courtesy. Taking time enough for what we must do lessens tensions and encourages proper social procedures.

Let's look particularly at the teen-ager's needs when first he enters the social world and begins dating. What are the requirements for social success at this age?

Aids to Social Success

1. Appearance. Because it makes the primary impression, appearance comes first. Not every girl is pretty nor is every boy handsome, but all can be neatly dressed and carefully groomed before a date. At this age, parents' taste can guide but must not dictate how the young person should dress.

2. Accepting invitations. Girls and boys should know how to give and accept invitations. A boy does not lay traps for a girl by saying, "Are you doing anything Saturday night?" Instead, he makes his intentions quite clear by saying, "Would you like to go to the club dance with me Saturday night?" A girl needs to know she can always refuse an invitation from a boy but that she should do so without hurting his feelings.

3. Refusing invitations. The same rule of courtesy holds true for the boy who refuses an invitation from a girl. "I'm sorry, Janey," he says with a sincere note of regret in his voice, "but I'm not free that night." Girls can be very insistent with a popular boy and it takes grace to keep from being pinned down to something one doesn't want to do. "Thanks, though, and I'll call you sometime," is a way out and makes a girl feel better. Detailed explanations are never necessary but courtesy protects the sensitive ego—and this is very important.

4. Be on time. A girl should not keep her escort waiting when he calls to take her on a date. And a boy needs to know that in the few minutes he is expected to exchange social amenities with a girl's parents, he needs to do no more—if he is suffering from embarrassment—than be attentive and look interested. It is the parents' job as host and hostess to lead the conversation and make him feel comfortable. They expect some reticence on his part.

5. Introductions. When introductions are being made, a young man shakes hands with the women if they make the move first, not otherwise. If they do not offer to shake hands, he bows slightly, on introduction, and looks pleasant. A backward jerk of the head in response to an introduction is crass. Boys and girls are introduced to mothers, not the other way around. It is, "Mother, this is Joan Mathews, my friend at school." Not, "Joan, this is my mother." Every boy should know that he must rise when a girl or an older person enters the room. Girls, too, rise when an older person approaches.

6. Dining out. A teen-ager going to a restaurant or to a home where there is formal service at the dining table needs to know what to expect and how to behave. For example, he makes no attempt to serve others at the table unless, in a home, he is asked to do so by the hostess. He never gathers his dishes together to help the servant or waiter, nor does he carry on a conversation with the person serving him. These rules are, of course, for the more formal home and for the well-staffed restaurant. Often in simpler homes a servant may wait at table but the family and guests do assist in the service, family style. In this case, what the family does is the proper guide for the guest. In simpler restaurants, too, some service may be performed by the guest, as in the case of a buffet arrangement of the salad or dessert courses. The boy may offer to fetch food or they may both go to the buffet, the girl serving herself first.

7. Courtesy at the table. Teen-agers should know how to enter and seat themselves in a restaurant or in a home. A boy leads the way to a restaurant table if there is no headwaiter to perform this function. The hostess approaches the dining table first and indicates where the others are to sit. The boy holds the chair for the girl nearest him and waits until the girls are seated before sitting down himself. The guests take up their napkins after the hostess takes up hers and place them, opened, lengthwise across their laps, not shaken out. They should know, too, that the napkin is left loosely folded at the left of the place setting when one leaves the table and it is the hostess or a boy's girl guest who gives the signal to rise.

8. Table manners. There is much more nervousness than necessary among young people concerning the use of silverware. Children should be taught early that one works from the outside in on both sides in a line-up of silver. The water glass is always at the point of the knife—and should be returned there. Nothing should be drunk when one's mouth is full. The lips should be wiped—rather dabbed—with the napkin before drinking.

9. Table conversation. The things teen-agers say to each other are some-times offensive, and they should be restrained from such topics of conversation at the table, even among themselves, as a necessary social discipline. As parents, we may get so used to teen-agers' laxity in this regard that we may not remember to impress on them that the dinner table is no place to mention such things as accidents, illness, catastrophe of any kind, bodily functions, or unpleasant gossip. Bitter debate of all kinds should also be avoided; it may even interfere with digestion.

10. Pleasing adults. It is rather hopeless for parents to insist that teen-agers use good manners toward others of their own age because there seems to be a certain camaraderie in the well-placed insult—even toward the opposite sex sometimes—and boys and girls usually know just how far to go along these lines. But there is nothing more impressive to a girl than to hear from her elders that the boy who at the moment is her true "heart-throb" has really good manners. To earn this accolade a boy needn't spend all his time buttering up the grownups, but a really friendly manner plus a few well placed "sirs" may boost his reputation amazingly. It is good, too, for a child to realize he has the ability to make a good impression, make people like him. And it is good for him to know that he is welcome to come back.

11. Thank-you notes. Some parents seem to feel that once a child is in his teens, he can't be made to write such notes and that it is no longer the responsibility of parents to stand over him in this regard. The habit should be taught early so that it is well ingrained by the teens. Certainly if we can teach our child to express appreciation, without fail, we have taught him an important thing. He must learn that if he receives a gift for which he cannot give an oral thank you, he writes a thank-you note. He must learn that every time he is entertained overnight he writes a note to the hostess—in his case the boy's or girl's mother. And we must see that he does this promptly, within a week. These are things every well mannered person must do.

What is written in a thank-you note is perhaps less important than their prompt dispatch. We develop our own style of letter-writing as we grow in grace and experience. No one expects a literary masterpiece in a thank-you note, and not every boy or girl is gifted with the ability to express himself with originality.

12. Car manners. A teen-ager permitted to use the family car for his dates or to have his own car should understand that this is a privilege that must not be abused—and that if he does abuse it, prompt action will result. Teen-agers—like all children—need rules and they prefer them to be made clearly from the beginning, not subject to spur-of-the-moment whims on the part of their parents.

No teen-ager should be permitted to use his car in an arrogant manner. One of the most unpleasant habits is that of honking outside a girl's door instead of going in. It is also bad manners to litter a car floor with gum wrappers and other debris or leave it full of wet bathing suits or sports equipment. The least a young person can do for the right to use the family car on occasion is to keep it clean and always in gas. And of course, like an adult, he must obey all rules of the road or lose the right to drive.

Resistance to Rules

These are some of the rules parents have come to understand as necessary in the guidance of adolescents. Even when they have the full accord of their children on such matters, it is still very difficult for most parents to accept a certain innate resistance that teen-agers have toward rules and regulations. Even delicate suggestions are likely to be anathema to them, even when they know that once necessary rules are imposed, everyone is more secure.

Parents need to understand what causes this resistance—a battle between the desire to be grown up and an unconscious wish to be babied.

When a child shoots up in height and in many ways seems grown up, it is very easy to forget that this period of resistance is even more acute than is the negative stage of the three-year-old. His very size makes him look adult and he is likely, at times, to imagine himself supremely competent in everything from manners to morals. We are all apt to expect too much of him because we see him so nearly a man.

Overcoming resistance. Parents can cope with teen-age resistance if they believe in their own strength of purpose and of mind. What they must remember is that the teen-ager needs much recognition, some necessary rules and a minimum of restraint in matters that are not of vital importance.

Perhaps the most important key to courtesy is to convince our children that manners are necessary, but it is more effective to arouse our children's interest in them than to impose them haphazardly.

Let us show our children that good manners are a passport to many interesting activities. They are not something to be put on like a hat when one goes out, but need to be truly a part of us. What we don't know, we can learn, and if we make a mistake once in a while, it is not important. The general impression that a person is courteous and considerate is what really counts.

—*By Amy Vanderbilt*

GOING STEADY

THIS is the younger generation speaking—teen-agers explaining why they "go steady": "The whole gang is doing it. I don't want to be left out." "Well, this way I know I always have a date." "I like my 'steady'—we have a lot in common."

These reasons seem sincere and harmless enough, but we—the older generation—don't appear to be accepting without question either the sincerity or the harmlessness. Some of us are silently worried, some openly suspicious. Our fears show up in long talks after the door closes behind son or daughter gone off on a date. They are likely to show up too in "tell us about your evening, dear" checkups next morning.

Nevertheless, the signs indicate that going steady is here to stay, and there's nothing to be gained by playing ostrich. Those of us who treat it as a fad, or as a forerunner of early ill-considered marriage or even as an indication that the race is headed for moral ruination need to take a closer look at the custom, at what it signifies to parents who grow grooves in their brows over it, and at what it means to the young people themselves.

When Trend Began

Looking back, it seems to have started—this trend toward selecting one steady partner—with youngsters who grew up during the last war. Now it is an undeniable part of teen-age culture. Girls begin dating at twelve or thirteen and go steady at about fifteen or sixteen. Boys as a rule begin both the dating and going steady a year or so later. What brought it about?

Step into the teen-ager's shoes for a moment. It's a reasonable expectation that he wants to grow up as soon as he can. In a way, going steady seems to be related, for him, to a need to get this earlier start on living, and also to a need to cling to something or someone.

Another factor seems to be the generally increased independence of adolescents in these times. They make many important decisions, have more freedom socially, get work experience earlier—and in many cases for more mature reasons than most of us did. However, independence can't be restricted to just certain areas of growing up. It is to be expected that besides maturing faster in other ways, they will also reach out earlier for boy and girl relationships.

What Worries Parents

What is it about going steady that worries fathers and mothers? In our youth, "going steady" at least approached and in many cases was the same thing as being engaged. And a vestige of this lurks somewhere in our minds. No wonder parents ask each other, "What of our son's career? If he gets tied up this early, what chance will he have to prepare for his trade or profession? All he seems to think of is this girl—wait till he has to support her!"

Those parents who have daughters, even though they are not as a rule quite so concerned about career, ask, "What is she getting herself into? Is she going to marry before she is really grown? Why, she might be a mother at nineteen or twenty!"

The matter of sexual relationships makes many parents fret, too. Do the young people know where to draw the line? Will Jim or Jane get into some kind of sexual involvement?

These are reasonable worries because we want our children to have a chance at complete lives; we don't want them snared by responsibilities they aren't ready to cope with.

But step back a few paces for a different view of all this—a view from where your teen-ager is standing. Startlingly, the new perspective brings the whole thing into a different focus: *to the boys and girls, going steady doesn't mean anything like being engaged.* Jane is certainly not thinking of herself as engaged when she goes steady with Sam this month, Joe the next, and settles on Herman for the spring season. At the end of the year, her "steadies" add up to a baker's dozen. Or perhaps her particular crowd has it worked out that one has a steady, acknowledged by all, but is still free to date others.

Relationship Usually Brief

In some cases, of course, the relationships do go on for a year or more. And some have ended in marriage—apparently about 15 per cent of them. But most such boy-girl affairs come to an end because of geographical separation—going away to a job or to college—because of dissatisfaction on the part of one or both partners, because a more attractive new interest comes on the scene.

What does going steady mean to your son and daughter? Apparently, it means just what they say. Where we read marital implications, they read popularity and security. "Everybody does it"—you've seen signs of this urge to be like the rest of the crowd long before going steady came into the picture. Mary just had to have a certain style of skirt. John wouldn't be seen in a jacket, or he had to have *that* kind of jacket. Because the crowd is doing it. Because you have to be sure you are basically the same as the rest of human-kind of your age, before developing the courage and maturity to be truly independent. This applies to having a steady as much as to having a pony tail or a crew cut.

They mean it, too, when they tell us, "This way, I know I always have a date." They probably mean more than they are aware of or will admit. "This way," your young lady is saying, "I'll always be out like the rest on Saturday night, and I know I'll have an escort for the prom. This is my social security." Status as a young man or woman, the capacity to get and hold a girl or boy friend, is there for the world to behold.

Extending Social Experience

And they mean it quite literally, too, when they say they just plain like their steadies. In just this attitude lies something we can be particularly happy about. We know that social experience with the opposite sex is an important requisite later when it comes to selecting a marriage partner. The girl "protected" from working out a good relationship with boys might, for instance, believe herself in love with the first man who pays attention to her in her twenties, or might be so uncertain and apprehensive that she might never develop a close relationship with any man. Or a boy might marry out of some peculiar sense of obligation that makes him feel any relationship must be permanent, or he might marry a girl because he feels "safe" with her. The undesirable possibilities are many.

Our young "steadies" are getting to know each other—and not just as good mambo partners, either, or as generous spenders or a lot of laughs to be with. Even Jane—her flitting the only steady thing about her—benefits from knowing Sam, Joe and Herman. She absorbs from them the awareness that different men see things differently, have their own characteristic attitudes, problems and goals. Kay and Bob, on the other hand, who have been steadies for almost two years, have an even more valuable experience. The phone rings and Bob blurts out, "Hey, I got that part-time job. Come on over!"

"That's wonderful! But I'm staying with the baby—you come over here."

"Gotta brush up for trig. You feel all right? You sound funny."

"Just kind of blue. Had a fight with Dad. Bring the trig book—I'll help."

Maturing Relationships

At the age of sixteen, Kay meditates: "Bob is a wonderful guy. Of course, he makes me mad sometimes, but we get along pretty well together, everything considered . . . I wish he could dance better, but he's shy about that the way I'm shy about reciting in Assembly. I guess we'll both get over it . . . We've got to watch the clock tonight if he's going to be good on that exam tomorrow. Gee, I'm glad he got the job! Maybe he can save almost all of his pay. It takes an awful lot of education to be a doctor . . . Maybe he'll forget me when he goes away next year. But I'll never forget him. Not ever."

Bob at seventeen isn't much given to the kind of moonbeam idealization we were inclined to attach to our own teen-age crushes. "What does she have to wear that droopy hairdo for? Oh well, it's *her* hair . . . I better get her to talk about her fight with her father—she keeps things bottled up too much."

This isn't the thinking of children.

The fact is, so many of us still do see our adolescents as children. Parents are perhaps the last people to realize that their boys and girls are growing up. And when a relationship is termed "going steady" there's a double shock.

Think Before Interfering

If in your concern you decide you're going to "put an end to this silly business," you had better take pause. You have first to consider natural adolescent rebellion. The more parents hammer, the more teen-agers refuse to budge. The more you take the attitude that it's something they do just to spite you, the more likely it is to turn into just that.

Further food for thought: are your fears real? Outlooks change sometimes when a mother and father devote one of those evening confabs of theirs to airing their own deeper feelings. Sometimes they can hear the whispered truth that their child's friend is to them an intruder—that of course they want their teen-ager to grow up, *but not that fast!*

Some parents who have felt uncomfortable have found relief in inviting their child's "steady" to the house more frequently. They begin to realize as they hear other young people talk about friends that their son or daughter is no different from the others. And they see for themselves the casualness of going steady and the good to be found in it. One father's attitude about his daughter's steady was: "He wants to be a lawyer? Tell him to stop by at the office sometime—I'll show him around." In that household, adults and children feel at ease with each other and a normal boy-girl friendship will not be forced into something it never started out to be.

If Father Is Upset

On the other hand, it is very often fathers who get most upset and who interfere with young friendships. One father was so completely blinded by his anxiety about his boy's future as to shout at a guidance counselor, "You can't tell me a thing! That boy of mine was just born that way!" "That way" meant that the boy's determination to keep his girl friend was a deliberate attempt to hurt his parents.

If your chief concern is about sexual involvement, remember that you have this to rely on: boys and girls who have good relationships with their parents through all their childhood years are likely to go along with their family's standards. If you are worried, nevertheless, it may be wise to ask yourself whether you are offering your son or daughter the trust that enables them to trust you and themselves. Sometimes, too, parents who remember, perhaps, experiences they had of "spooning" or "necking" are particularly worried about their teen-age children. In this case there's only one thing to do—re-examine your own experiences with honesty. From such a looking-back may come new understanding and the ability to talk with your boy or girl in a way that is convincing and realistic.

When Adults Should Interfere

If adolescents have been helped to develop good judgment, the times when adult interference is necessary are rare. But here and there it is possible that a child, for whatever reason, may become fascinated with another whose bad influence is a reality. And sometimes, also, in much less serious situations, a little support may be welcomed. One fifteen-year-old didn't like her steady at all, but feared to give him up because there was no other boy friend in sight. Sensing her plight, her parents encouraged week-end hosteling trips and within a month the young lady's problem was to decide between two new steadies. What you really have to do is be sure the circumstances are actually what you see, not something your anxiety has created. Perhaps talking with other mothers and fathers or with someone like a Y leader or your child's school counselor can help pin down the truth.

Our teen-agers are saying to us, "All the people we know—*our* people—are going steady. So we are, too. It's here and we're part of it and we're going to keep right on this way." If we have difficulty in accepting this, the constructive thing to do is find out why. It is hard to see things from a different point of view when our own life experience makes our particular way of seeing them an inherent part of our thinking. But those parents who can work it out, who realize that going steady—like television or vitamin-consciousness—is part of the web of their children's lives, are fortunate. Young people come and go in such homes, frankly, without fear of condemnation or ridicule. If, occasionally, either generation does slam a door on the other, it swings wide again to a friendly knock. There are no hurtful, ice-fettered silences. A freeze is impossible in the warmth of increasing trust and friendship between parent and child. —*By Goldie Ruth Kaback, Ph.D., and Margaret Albrecht Gillmor*

SUMMER CAMPS FOR OLDER CHILDREN

MARK had happily spent several of his fourteen summers at camp. Yet, when his parents raised the subject last year, he objected, "I don't know if I want to go. It's getting sort of boring."

Is your own youngster singing a variation on this theme? If so, there is encouraging news that some camp directors have come up with exciting, rewarding—and educational—programs that will change the tune. Although there still aren't very many, they do satisfy a wide variety of interests. More and more teen-agers are now finding fun and a sense of fulfillment too at regular recreational camps, as well as at special interest, study, work or travel camps.

If a youngster says, "We never do anything *interesting* any more," he is really telling you that he has reached the stage where it isn't enough just to be entertained. He wants to do something useful.

Boys and girls of this age respond most enthusiastically to a program that has a real purpose. A spokesman for the National Recreation Association put it this way: "Parents should look for a program that will challenge their boys and girls to put forth more than they have before. These kids need to learn resourcefulness and they want new, tougher things to do."

Purposes of Different Camps

In a recreational camp, the focus may be on physical fitness. A work camp may try to build good working habits in general, while introducing youngsters to the world of labor. Additionally, a good teen-age program encourages responsibility, independence and self-reliance; offers constructive activity that stimulates campers and makes them feel they're doing something worthwhile; and challenges campers' minds and muscles.

"You know why I like our camp?" 15-year-old Paul asked rhetorically. "They let you do things yourself. For instance, you can't just snap a picture and leave it to be developed. Our photography counselor will show you how, but he expects you to do it for yourself."

Most teen-agers do get tremendous satisfaction out of working with tools, learning new skills and polishing old ones. They need a program with lots to choose from, to try themselves out in varied activities. And they also need the chance to "dig in" for more thorough mastery of some particular field— leadership training, farming or construction work, crafts, dance, music, sports and others. Goals should always be realistic and worth aiming for—building a camp bulletin board, clearing a nature trail, passing a junior life-saving test or creating a ceramic vase.

Some camps lure youngsters back with broader versions of earlier programs spiced with plenty of privileges based on age. But no camp has much of a teen program if older campers are considered "big shots" just because they're seniors! On the other hand, when teen-agers use the new barbecue pit first because they built it themselves, that special privilege makes sense.

Offering New Experiences

Exposing teens to new and different experiences—longer trips away from camp, designing and building sets for the show in which they've only acted before—is another well rounded program. As one camper earnestly and accurately put it: "Trips broaden our perspective and put us in touch with things we don't naturally come in contact with. They help us grow."

Boys and girls also grow when they accept personal and social responsibility—taking care of themselves, their belongings and quarters, learning the give and take of group living. Youngsters who channel some of their taste for talk about anything and everything into thoughtful group discussions can take an intelligent part in shaping their camp program.

Teen-age responsibility also includes working out their own values and goals. Camps encourage this by letting campers select most of their own program. "When I had to choose from a bunch of things to do," one boy explained, "I had to think about what each one really offered. So camp taught me to use my own judgment."

In a good teen-age camp, counselors play an especially important role because in some ways, teen-agers need more supervision and guidance than other age groups.

"I look harder for my counselors than for my campers," one camp director said. "It's not easy to find someone who works well with teen-agers."

Qualities of a Good Counselor

The good counselor understands teens but doesn't identify with them completely. He is patient with their moody spells without taking them too seriously. Armed with patience, warmth and a flexible sense of humor, he's got plenty of imagination and enthusiasm and he always finds time to listen to problems or just talk. Basically, he "cares"—and the kids know it!

Teen-agers, like adults, respect someone who really knows his stuff—whatever his specialty—so a highly skilled counselor has no trouble leading and controlling his youngsters. They want to please him and they really want to learn because they know he's not just "watching" but is helping them to develop their own skills.

A counselor who maintains friendly discipline by setting a good personal example usually ends up with a bunk of teen-agers who can and do control themselves.

As to supervision, it works best when campers have a voice, either through a camp council or a "town meeting" setup. Just as they should have a say in planning their program, they need to have partial self-government too. You can't shove rules and regulations or a rigidly scheduled program down a teen-ager's throat without asking for trouble! "We announce our own rules and standards at the beginning of camp," one director explained. "But we don't just say 'don't' and leave it at that. We explain *why* certain things just aren't done. And given the chance, teen-agers can really show grown-up good sense." When a couple of girls started carrying on after lights-out in one camp, their bunkmates showed them the door. "If you want to make noise, do it outside," they said. "We're tired and want to get some sleep!"

Skillful Guidance Necessary

At a coed work camp the council was asked if boys and girls might go off in pairs for a few minutes in the evening. After some discussion, skillfully guided by adult advisers, a decision was announced. "We feel it isn't a good idea," the council chairman said. "If some people go off together, others might feel like wallflowers because they haven't been chosen. And things might get to the point where we couldn't control our emotions. Anyway," he added, "it's not as if we don't have a chance to be together during the day. If a guy and girl want to be alone, they can sit together during an activity-break and no one will bother them."

As these youngsters showed, a coed camp gives them a chance—particularly when there is constructive activity in the program—to size each other up as complete individuals and not just as possible dates. Working toward a common goal takes the tension out of boy-girl relationships and gives them more than dating to think of. Sharing the same concerns and triumphs, they learn to respect each other for what they've accomplished. It's fine to be a good dancer, but it's just as admirable to be able to clear underbrush or lay a good campfire—for girls as well as boys.

Whether or not you want a coed camp, your boy or girl should definitely go to one that's *exclusively* teen-age or that clearly separates older and younger campers. Mingling with younger children once in a while, as "big brother" or "big sister," is fun, but it shouldn't happen too often.

Of course you'll also want to check on the physical setup of any camp you're considering. Obviously, the best way to judge is to visit them in session. If you can't do this, try to talk with parents of campers.

Safety First

Look for arrangements that ensure the safety and well-being of your child and don't be dazzled by luxury features. A camp with a guarded, safe waterfront and toilets in only a couple of outbuildings may be better than one which has toilets in every cabin but leaves its waterfront unguarded. A good deal of health, safety and sanitation depends on a camp director's attitude toward "housekeeping." In a well kept camp, for example, there are no piles of lumber lying around inviting accidents or fire.

Which kind of camp—special interest, recreational, work, study or travel —will suit your youngster most? Except for travel camps, most have varied programs, offering a little of everything.

Recreational camps are the most numerous. Mainly, they hold a teen-ager's interest by calling for previously learned skills to be applied in new situations and more demanding ways. Campers who already know how to clear a campsite, set up camp, make several kinds of fire and cook over them, can make trips into wilderness areas. Youngsters who know the rudiments of riflery are ready for trap and skeet shooting. Swim enthusiasts can concentrate on perfecting their style and stroke. In one western camp, young naturalists used their skills to serve others, exploring a national forest and collecting molds for an antibiotic research project.

CIT Programs

A CIT (Counselor-in-Training) program may be the answer for the sixteen to seventeen-year-old who would like to help younger children enjoy camping. He spends part of his time polishing up his basic skills—majoring in one activity and minoring in a couple of others—and in addition, he'll get actual leadership training. A good CIT program really turns out future counselors. Experienced and skilled leaders help trainees put theory into practice and are always ready to sit down and discuss problems, successes and failures. "Lab work" varies. A CIT may live in a regular cabin where he can study the counselor's techniques and learn how a program is tailored to fit individual campers. He'll probably also sit in on staff meetings to see another side of leadership and administration in action.

A CIT program is strictly educational and should cover at least two sessions. Most camps offer no reduction in tuition the first season but if the CIT can really help during the second season a reduction is proper.

In study camps academic subjects are stressed for part of the day. Campers may brush up or work ahead in many fields or take school courses to improve their grades.

At a special interest camp, a youngster may specialize in natural science—archeology or geology, for example—in one of the fine or performing arts, or in a sport, such as riding or sailing.

Both special interest and study camps can offer a well-rounded program, leaving part of the day free for other activities and workshops. They're good bets if your youngster has a specific academic or vocational goal or hobby interest.

Constructive Activity

Constructive activity is especially emphasized in work camps. Devoting part of the day to actual work experience, such camps set high, long-term goals. Campers on a construction crew may erect new camp buildings. The farm crew weeds the garden, gathers the harvest, milks the cows. Forestry crew members put up overnight shelters or work on conservation projects. After chores, campers take part in regular camp activities, sports and workshops. When they offer work with a realistic purpose—not just "busy work"—these camps are very worthwhile. One 16-year-old city-bred camper proudly demonstrated her milking technique and spoke knowingly of varying butter-fat contents. Another camper gave pointers on constructing cement block piers and rubble foundation walls. "It's great to think some of my rocks are holding up the new dorm!" she observed with satisfaction.

Travel camps include canoe and/or wilderness camps, caravan camps and straight tours. Several commercial organizations, together with the American Youth Hostels, specialize in sightseeing tours for teens in this country and abroad.

Caravan camping emphasizes *doing* as much as seeing. Youngsters travel by station wagon or bus to different parts of the country and really camp. They may visit the magnificent Rockies to fish in mountain streams or scale a peak. They may go on pack trips to areas still untouched by civilization.

Canoe tripping and wilderness camping also offer lots of outdoor living in wild country, and make use of all previously learned camp skills. Trippers know the common sense safety rules of land and water, and can settle down in comfort just about anywhere. Properly guided, they can sustain themselves in the wilderness.

For some older boys and girls, canoe or wilderness camping is the "last word" in camping experience. Appealing to a taste for adventure and exploration, such programs show campers the pleasure and satisfactions of simple living minus the gadgets and gimmicks of civilization. And canoe campers often get a chance to relive history by following the same watery trails used by our early pioneers.

Teen-agers don't have to be bored at all by camp—especially when they take part in selecting one (usually they're mature enough to do so). Talk things over with your boy or girl. Describe the different camp programs to them and when you've settled on the kind of camp that seems best, show them the catalogues of several that meet with your approval. Let them sit in and ask questions when you interview directors.

With this kind of send-off for a happy and exciting summer, your camper may return at the end of the season with that reverse twist on the classic camp disease, homesickness—"You know, I'm glad to be back—but I'm a little camp-sick too."

—By Dorothy Siegel

ALCOHOL AND ADOLESCENCE DON'T MIX

LET'S face the fact: teen-age drinking is prevalent. Communities throughout the nation have been experiencing a variety of incidents involving that fact. Typical was one in Chappaqua, New York, when the high school seniors made a bombshell proposal that their parents serve them beer and cocktails at their graduation party. As it turned out—after much headlining and a good deal of confusion among the parents—a rousing party, without alcohol but with a "name" band, was served instead.

A study of 1,000 students at 12 high schools in rural-urban Racine County, Wisconsin, revealed that two out of three adolescents drink beer, wine or whiskey "at one time or another." Tragic highway accidents, moral lapses and other excesses are not uncommon as a result of such teen-age drinking. A similar survey in suburban Nassau County, New York, showed that 88 per cent of the students over 16 "use" alcoholic beverages. Researchers agree that while the various religious, social and "folk-ways" factors among different families and areas of the country must be taken into account, all children need guidance in making a sensible decision about drinking.

As a matter of fact, they're getting one type of "guidance" long before parents are aware they're giving it. "Most parents," states Yvelin Gardner, associate director of the National Committee on Alcoholism, "don't realize how much their own drinking affects the habits of their children. This does not mean that all fathers must go on the wagon to teach their youngsters total abstinence. But fathers and mothers can set a pattern of moderation which their children are more than likely to follow."

Influence of Parents

The most significant conclusion of the Racine study was that the drinking habits of most young people are related to those of their parents. Only about one-third of the children of abstemious fathers ever had a drink. But in homes where the father takes a drink once a week or oftener, about three-fourths of the youngsters drink at least occasionally.

Whatever the family pattern, it is as their children approach teen age that parents look for answers to certain questions about drinking. One is: just when is a child old enough for drinking to be discussed with him? Generally, in the freshman or sophomore year of high school. Before then, you can't expect much understanding, though there will be curiosity and questions to be answered even when he is very young. But the subject has no direct connection with himself. From his freshman year on, he is more personally interested and asks amazingly astute questions. While he may have preconceived notions about liquor, they're usually easily disposed of with sensible explanations. The young people want facts, though—not emotional dramatics. Says Arnold E. Henderson, well known Canadian educator, "Their decisions should be based on facts, presented in an unemotional, unbiased manner to clear up misconceptions and ignorance."

When is it safe to permit your child a glass of beer or sherry, or something strong in the punch at a teen-age party? The prevailing custom today is for many children to have their first drink by the time they are sixteen. If your religion permits it, eighteen is the minimal age on the basis of physical and emotional stability, according to a consensus of doctors and other experts. It takes emotional control and maturity to avoid the danger of alcohol becoming too meaningful.

Extent of Consumption

Will your child drink more or less if you permit him to take alcohol "on some occasions"? The Wisconsin survey showed that those students drank most who were permitted to drink occasionally both at home and away from home. They drank twice as much outside as they did with the family. So it's probably best to restrict your "some occasions" rule to at-home drinking. The assumption is that you take the glamour, mystery and daring out of drinking by having your child's liquor debut in the ordinary home situation. If you take the liberal view and permit outside drinking, it helps if the child sticks to beer, which has only 4 per cent alcohol and fills him up. Wine, which may have as much as 20 per cent alcohol, should be considered as hard liquor; it can make physical inroads on the adolescent that beer can't.

If you strictly forbid your child to drink at all, is he likely to be defiant and hostile? A large majority of high school students in the Wisconsin study who were not permitted to drink on any occasion showed a fairly high respect for the parental "forbidden" law. Those who did break the law, however, drank much more than the others. Much depends on the family's religious beliefs and the example set by the parents. If you drink, a rigid ban may strike your child as inconsistent and arouse conflict. In general, rules should be fixed as a matter of advice, not law. Of course, reasonable safeguards must be set up. But restrictions can be elastic—adapted to the individual child and to the occasion. And they must be carefully applied and enforced.

Set a Moderate Course

Clearly, in some things teen-agers need not only helpful supervision but also firmness. They can be made to recognize there are things they can do and things they should not do. It shouldn't be hard for a parent to set a moderate course between being too permissive and too demanding.

You can't deter your child from drinking, contends Yvelin Gardner—you can only guide him. You can emphasize that *abuse* of liquor, rather than use, is dangerous; that it's as true for adults as it is for teen-agers.

Except for religious groups which teach that drinking is immoral, mere moralizing is not likely to work, several surveys have shown. When youngsters are told liquor is bad or poisonous, they skeptically look around and see people who drink but don't deteriorate; they just can't believe it's deadly. They should know the physiological facts about consuming alcohol.

For instance: alcohol is *not* a stimulant, as most people believe. It's actually a depressant, reducing sensitivity and bringing on a progressive depression of the central nervous system, like an anesthetic such as ether. Reflexes are slowed down, alertness dulled and there's a loss of mental controls over behavior. That's where the danger in liquored-up driving comes in.

Physiological Effects of Alcohol

Unlike other foods, alcohol is absorbed into the blood immediately. Most of the alcohol is oxidized or burned up in a series of chemical changes. But when the consumption of alcohol is faster than the rate of oxidation, the percentage of alcohol rises in the blood and throughout the body. Depending on the degree of alcoholic concentration in the body, a person becomes giddy, intoxicated or passes out.

Even when certain teen-agers understand the physiological impact of liquor, they're still apt to drink. For some of them, a different kind of logical approach may work. For example, one night Bill Wallace received a phone call from the police.

"Your son Jimmy is here at the station, Mr. Wallace. He's drunk. You'd better come and get him."

At the police station, the sight of Jimmy was a violent shock to Wallace. The boy had vomited all over his clothes, his face was white, he kept muttering incoherently and cursed the policeman who had found him staggering along a street.

Drinking "On a Dare"

As Wallace pieced out the story later, Jimmy had met four of his friends near the school grounds. One of the boys had a bottle of whiskey which he had filched from the family cupboard. Jimmy had been dared to drink "all you can take."

At home, Wallace put his son to bed. In the morning, he sat down for a talk. "Look, son, I'm not going to bawl you out or give you a lecture. I'll just give you some facts. You've been awfully sick from the whiskey you drank. That should tell you that your body can't handle the stuff. You understand that, don't you?"

Jimmy nodded, his face miserable at the memory of his experience.

"All right," his father continued. "You tackled too much when you weren't able to handle it. If you want to try it again four or five years from now, you'll be able to decide whether or not you're going to drink. Meanwhile, think about something else.

"In a few months you'll be eligible for your driver's license. If you'd been driving when you were that drunk you probably wouldn't be alive this moment. Now, if you ever want your mother and me to consent to your having a license and using our car, you'll have to prove you can be trusted in a car— that you'll stay away from liquor."

Jimmy, his father is certain, hasn't touched liquor since. The "fun" of drinking was gone for him.

Other parents would probably have handled the situation differently. The point is that Wallace's approach worked for his own child. As psychologists put it, a strongly motivated drive—such as Jimmy's intense desire for a driver's license—can create a conditioned pattern that can last for several years. If a school athlete can observe training rules to stay on a team, then any boy or girl should be able to keep from drinking when the goal is important.

Perhaps the most important thing in your attitude toward your child's drinking, though, is not to lose sight of the person because you're concentrating on the problem.

"It is unfortunate," says Professor Raymond G. McCarthy of the Yale Center of Alcohol Studies, "that we single out drinking as an isolated bit of behavior. Drinking should be handled the way parents approach such problems as going steady or staying out late. They should be consistent in their attitudes on *all* these questions, including drinking."

The drink-or-not question hits our young people just at the time when they are most determined to kick over the traces and declare their independence from adult authority. So they may get too little sleep, flout health rules, smoke—and drink.

The Eagerness to "Belong"

Drinking is but one of the things—both wise and foolish—the adolescent tries. It's part of the complicated growing-up process, just as he experiments with boy-girl relationships.

Also, adolescence is the time when the opinions of friends are elevated to new heights and the adolescent's need to be a "regular guy" like the others in the group reigns supreme. It's the stage when a boy wants to impress a girl by taking her to a gin mill and the girl is desperately anxious to be popular. In their eagerness to "belong," they merge their identity with that of their friends. Hence, they learn to dress like the "rest of the crowd," to use the lingo and follow the crazes. Drinking, when the time comes for it, is sometimes part of that group belonging.

It may be a cover-up for shyness or timidity, too, just as it is with some adults. Joan, a very attractive 16-year-old, confronted her mother with this poser:

"Look, Mother," she said, "I know a cocktail or two will make me peppier at the party tomorrow night. If I'm more lively, I'll be more popular and get more dates, won't I? So why shouldn't I drink?"

Another youngster asked his father: "Everyone else in my crowd drinks, and if I don't the guys will say I'm chicken, so why shouldn't I?"

Be Realistic

The answers are not easy. Adolescents resent being "treated like children." Joan's mother put her answer this way: "Sure, Joan, a couple of drinks remove tension and make some people relax at a party. But would you know when to stop? Alcohol affects your judgment. And when girls get drunk, they're often sick and messy—you certainly wouldn't be appealing to the boys that way. You're bright and pretty enough not to need a crutch to make the boys like you."

To the boy who fears the label "chicken," the thoughtful parent can point out that no doubt the star athletes at school don't drink and they're not called sissies. "If some members of the crowd," the parent might say, "want to jump off a roof, would you do it, too? If you'd rather not drink, you don't have to follow the herd."

Many parents find it effective to talk over the drinking question frankly with the young folks and recruit their help in deciding upon rules. The value of this technique is that it helps teen-agers understand the purpose of protection. If the regulations are realistic teen-agers are likely to agree to them. After all, children do look to their parents for instruction in the arts of living, as they would in vocational guidance to the choice of a college.

Above all, child guidance authorities agree, to protect your teen-ager from the excesses of drinking you should give him the kind of home and family life in which he'll feel secure.

—*By Theodore Irwin*

WHY CHILDREN NEED A GANG

YOU don't like that word "gang"? Maybe it even makes you flinch, because it has been associated with juvenile delinquency. It wasn't always that way. "Our Gang" comedies symbolized misbehavior, yes—but laughter, too. And if a writer used the word in the 20's, it didn't necessarily mean something undesirable. When Paul Furfey wrote "The Gang Age" in 1929, he was simply studying the tendency of preadolescents to group together. Your parents sentimentally humming "That Old Gang of Mine" had quite a different feeling about "gang" from the one you may have now, what with the past years' concern about gangs and delinquent behavior. A concern, to be honest, that has sometimes smacked of hysteria.

It's certainly true that a percentage of our children have violated the law, and that we ought to do something constructive about it. But what we seem to be losing sight of is that these are a very small per cent of the juvenile population. The millions of young people who don't break laws don't receive equal publicity. We hear much more about gangs acting outside the law than we do about the fact that gangs of teen-agers organize help in national emergencies; set up community projects; help our hospital staffs; form United Nations clubs; come through with all sorts of constructive and admirable achievements.

Once, the phrase "gang of kids" brought smiles to people's faces. It sounded like fun, good fellowship. It still means just that to your child entering the "gang phase."

What a Gang Teaches

Actually, it means more than he as a child can understand. For the gang has a great deal more than fun to give and teach your boy or girl. For instance, the gang teaches cooperation. Or call it democracy, or even wise compromise—any word that suggests to you the living, and not just the mouthing, of give-and-take.

Ten-year-old Gloria, for example, wants the Jolly Jills to adopt a clarion shade of red for the kerchiefs all eight of them will wear. Laura proposes blue—and blue it is, five to three. A bitter pill for Gloria, because she was also outvoted about taking Laura into the Jolly Jills in the first place, so the red-versus-blue issue stirs up the residue of an old grudge. But her personal feelings have to be subjugated to the wish of the group (and without griping). This may seem a mere bowing to superior forces. From such a seemingly trivial start, though, a gang can gradually foster the awareness that you have to expect to make concessions if you want to live with other people.

We can say a gang teaches a child morality, too.

If you could sit in on a meeting of those same Jolly Jills three or four years hence, you might not believe your ears. Now they are dissecting the "why's" of rules and values—their own, their parents', society's. Together they have learned to judge, and to judge by moral standards of justice and tolerance that many grownups have allowed to tarnish.

Something else his gang gives your child is a different picture of himself. To you, Bobby may be a Quiet, Well-Behaved Boy. To the Tigers, he's something of a sissy, and he's Bob—not Bob-bee! To the school staff Jean is a glowing star in the intellectual sky. When the Secret Sisters meet—well, it's nice to get 98 in math, but more important by far is whether she's a snob or "regular."

Different View of Himself

Sometimes this new look at himself, this being judged by his peers, can be of special value to a child. At eleven, for instance, Peter had become rather inclined to expect obeisance when his influential father's name was mentioned. It slipped out at his introductory meeting with the Daredevils— "My father's Sheldon Dawes." Silence. Then, "A joker," pronounced Don, deadpan.

"Yeah—a joker," Tim picked up. "Oh, how do you *do!*" he twittered. "My father's Timothy Costello, the third."

It snowballed to that "silly stage"—"My old man's Wyatt Earp"—"Mine's Superman!"

While the group stoned the idea to its death with laughter, Peter sat red-faced. Happily for him he finally joined in—even outdoing the others in the use of some quaint language as a sort of compensation. But whenever he made a similar slip, he was awarded the "stone-face treatment."

A gang also helps a child learn more about the roles and the relations of the sexes. The first signs of this are deceiving, for in our culture they look like complete abhorrence of the opposite sex. Your daughter may sum it up, if she's somewhere from nine to twelve, in a single word: "Boys!" She says it as though she's talking about bugs. The standard observation from her brother is a bit more picturesque: "Go with a girl? I'd rather cut my throat!"

Reinforcement of Sex Roles

What they're doing is reinforcing their own femininity and masculinity. The boys stride in the paths of maleness by emphasizing physical courage. The black eye that symbolizes "that bunch of roughnecks" to you is a badge of honor to your son. Activities like football, baseball, airplane modeling, carpentry, boxing, take first place. Also swaggering, speaking *basso profundo* and offering noisy commentary (not necessarily displeasing) on any passing girl or girls. The feminine retaliation for this traditionally takes the form of nose tilted in air.

In the girls' crowd, similarly, the emphasis is on feminine pursuits and interests. Never again in their lives will "What are you going to wear?" be uttered as often. As a club project they may take up the creation of jewelry that is unquestionably colorful, or advertise the club as available for afternoon baby-sitting.

Having proved to themselves that they can be man among men, woman among women, boy and girl are ready at puberty for a new look at each other. "Drop dead" becomes miraculously "Wanna' walk home together?"

Perhaps the biggest thing his gang offers your child is a toehold on independence. Somewhere around nine or ten, our boys and girls begin looking forward to being free of us. What they can't escape is the obvious fact that they are still children and parents are still home and love, reassurance and guidance. When a child needs these things so much, where will he find courage to break with them—to take the freedom he wants?

Gang Becomes Second Home

He'll find a good deal of it with his gang, which becomes a sort of second family to him. He finds another home (literally in some cases, though it may only be a clubhouse they all built together or an old packing crate set up in the back yard). His own home becomes a place to eat and sleep. He finds love of a different sort in the emphasis—and it's a passionate emphasis—that the group places on loyalty. He finds reassurance in the large sense in simply being accepted, in belonging. He finds it in minor things when the group commiserates with him on flunking an exam. And he finds guidance in the Code.

You could almost say "the Code" is synonymous with "gang" and of this phenomenon William H. Wattenberg, Professor of Educational Psychology at Wayne University, observes in his book "The Adolescent Years": "Each gang has its own code, a collection of unwritten rules and regulations. These define how to dress, how to act in many situations and what attitudes to take toward adults. Such a code reduces uncertainties. It gives the gang member a feeling of assurance. Although it may bring him into conflict with adults, while he is with pals he knows what is expected of him."

Much of the guidance a youngster gets from his gang and its code is not, to put it mildly, in accordance with adult standards. Remember, the very thing the children are struggling toward is independence from adult authority. They can't strike for freedom maturely as yet, so they resort to characteristic excessiveness. This means getting away with as much as they can in flouting adult rules.

Code Requirements

The Code takes care of the details. Some of its requirements strike grown-ups only as peculiar, like shearing your hair to within a quarter-inch of your scalp. Or the eerie jingling that invades a home because "We voted all the girls have to wear bells on their shoes—I *have* to!"

Other parts of the Code are downright objectionable to us. Toothbrushes and combs, washcloths and towels are apparently destined to be museum pieces. Soap, you would think, was lethal, especially to the male. "Please" and "thank you" die a sudden death. The Code may demand a contribution of dirty stories to its repertoire. It is also likely to demand, when something very important to the gang is at stake, that a member lie—even, or particularly, to his own parents.

There's no denying that all this can make for uneasy moments for mothers and fathers. What can be done is to line up things it's important for you to keep in mind for your own sake and your child's:

Remember—these years aren't easy for him, either. Although the omnipotent "They"—the gang—seem to outweigh by far your own importance to your boy or girl, your children are still very much tied to you, too. Dr. Fritz Redl, Director of the Children's Unit at the National Institute for Mental Health at Bethesda, Maryland, puts it this way: "The change from adult-code to peer-code is not an easy process for a youngster, but full of conflict and often painful. For, while he would like to be admired by his pals on a peer-code basis, he still loves his parents personally and hates to see them misunderstand him or have them get unhappy about what he does. And, while he would love to please his family and be again accepted by them and have them proud of him, he couldn't face being called a sissy or be suspected of being a coward or a teacher's pet by his friends."

Inevitable Conflict

The conflict is inevitable—and necessary—but it can become much worse for your child if he feels that he must choose not merely between two codes, but between your love and the gang's love. It can be easier if he knows you are fundamentally for him, no matter what.

Let go. Perhaps what parents suffer from most at this time is a sense of loss—"We hardly see anything of you any more." Everyone feels a twinge of sadness as a beloved child turns more and more away. But if that sense of loss is exorbitant, if you feel over-sorrowful or deprived or empty, you can act in ways that can only be harmful. There's the father, for instance, whose attitude is "All right, do it your own way if you're so smart. Only don't expect me to help you out if you get into trouble."

There's the mother who binds her daughter so close that she will never really have the child's love. One thing we know for certain: only if a child is free to spread his love out wherever he will—in this case, to the gang—does he come full circle and return to his parents with genuine affection.

Be a parent. Letting go doesn't mean giving up your responsibility for guidance. The mothers and fathers who take the road of "mustn't meddle" have stopped being parents. Your child still needs your adult experience and judgment. He may not be aware of it, but when a few years have passed he will have worked his way around to some of the very things he scorns right now—adult standards. And if you don't stick to such standards, how is he going to know what they are? For his sake, to say nothing of your own rights and peace of mind, he still has to know you don't feel the same as the gang about fibbing or bad language; about filching candy from the store on the corner or trying to sneak through a subway turnstile; that you don't relish rudeness, that you want him to do his share of the family chores, that you expect him to be reasonably on time for meals. Even more important, that you're always available if the going gets just too rough—for instance, if the gang should vote him out.

He'll need you, too, if the gang's rebellious activities take a genuinely destructive turn. This is in the realm of possibility, not of probability. As Mr. R. Clendenen, who was Executive Director of a Senate Sub-Committee on

Juvenile Delinquency, has pointed out, "A kid is not, suddenly and without warning, going to go 'bad' if his behavior has been relatively normal in the past."

He also concluded, though, when a child does fall in with the wrong gang, "What is needed is to find out just why a kid got into trouble, what he needs to get out of it, and then to provide the required help."

It usually works out better if you don't undertake your child's redirection all by yourself. A parent and teacher, together, for instance, can more effectively figure out just why a boy has chosen this sort of group, or remains with it. Why does he line up with a destructive gang? What needs does it fulfill?

But suppose you wean your boy from the gang—is that the whole answer? Have you and your neighbors played no part in whatever made the gang destructive? A good deal of oversimplification has gone on as to the causes of juvenile delinquency and the remedies. The factors that make up the picture are myriad. Maybe among your boy's "bad companions" you can see the effects of slum environment or racial discrimination, of an unhappy home, of learning difficulties, of physical disability that has taken an emotional toll.

Community Action

Yes, the causes are many and there is no one answer—except perhaps this: community action. It's wonderful to think what could be accomplished if all parental concern, instead of focusing solely on one's own children, were expanded into organized, understanding, practical help for all children. Mr. Bertram Beck who was the director of the Special Juvenile Delinquency Project of the United States Children's Bureau, pinpointed it when he said, ". . . when people manifest concern one for the other . . . this is in itself the major contribution to curbing delinquency."

Keep a clear head about what's important. What really matters and what doesn't, what's worth arguing about and what isn't, differs from family to family, from one community to the next. Maybe it really is important that Sue wear a dress to go downtown, instead of those shabby jeans her club has decided to wear. Then again, maybe your embarrassment over the neighbors' seeing her that way magnifies its importance. Certainly it's necessary that Jimmy get adequate rest—but perhaps you should review your concept of how much rest is adequate, and also find out what bedtime is set for the other members of his gang.

Try to have some fun. Sometimes we can get so immersed in the meanings and the sub-surface churnings of both our children's growth and our own that we can't see the fun for the dust. The gang is having fun. With all its bickering and its earnestness, in the long run it's enjoying itself tremendously. You've heard them laugh—or is bray a better word? You've seen their flushed faces radiating friendship and enjoyment of life.

Perhaps there can be enjoyment here for you, too. You can get a new look, for instance, at a part of life you've forgotten. Your boy and girl are building some of the same memories. They're growing up, and the gang is helping them do it. —*By Margaret Albrecht Gillmor*

SHOULD YOUR BOY PLAY FOOTBALL?

THE football season is a time of year dreaded by mothers who may be faced with a tough decision. Junior may come home from school and say, "I'm going out for football this year, Mom." His mother's reaction may not be all that a boy could wish. For years she has been constantly on guard to insure his welfare. After protecting him against a multitude of hazards, she may well be uneasy at the thought of football. And yet he cannot play without her consent.

I have been a football coach for eight years. I am thoroughly sold on football as a great sport, which can contribute much to the mental and physical growth of the right type of boy. Perhaps my knowledge of the game will help you decide whether or not your boy is capable of participating safely in football.

Many times pressure is put on a boy to go out for football when it really is not his type of game. Often this pressure comes from the boy's own social group—his classmates or neighborhood buddies. High school boys and girls are extremely sensitive to this kind of persuasion. Or the pressure may come from adults. Many a well-meaning, but overzealous father, who himself gained a glimmer of stardom at Podunk High in the late thirties, wants his son to follow in his footsteps. Or the athletically frustrated father, who feels he missed a great deal in high school by not being on the football team, wants his boy to be a star athlete. Sometimes the football coach himself is responsible. Each fall many coaches stroll about the school halls with their portable scales looking for candidates. More than once I have seen a school principal call in a likely candidate and try to sell him on the game.

Beware of Football "Salesmen"

Many of these well meaning salesmen know little about the product they are trying to sell. Just because a boy looks like a football player does not necessarily mean he is fit for the game. There are too many factors in football of which the unfamiliar are not aware.

As parents, it is your responsibility to see that your boy is not exposed to unfair tactics. Don't let him be "buffaloed" into playing football. The decision should rest solely with you and your son for, after all, you know him better than anyone else.

The first thing to consider is your boy's age. In recent years there has been a radical increase in programs sponsoring organized football contests for younger boys and girls. They call it Small Fry Football. In my opinion, it has no place in a program for boys from nine to twelve. They are still betwixt and between—they like to play cowboys one day and throw a football around the next. Granted, some are more mature than others, but we cannot base a program on the highest level of maturity if we are to include all.

From a physiological standpoint, the boy of this age is still in the process of growing. His bones retain much of the cartilage growth areas that will disappear by the time he is fourteen or fifteen. An injury to such an area can have far-reaching effects on the normal growth of the child. Because of this it is my opinion that the most satisfactory minimum age for football is fourteen. Even then there are boys who have not matured enough, so their parents should have the last say in the matter.

Informal Games for Younger Boys

In speaking of football for younger boys I refer only to organized tackle football with a regular schedule. (Touch football, played by many schoolboys, affords practice in all phases of the game except tackling.) Small Fry Football supporters will argue that the boys are going to injure themselves by playing tackle football without equipment if there are no organized programs. But in informal games if Junior is tired he will quit. If the weather is bad he may stay home. In Small Fry Football he must attend practice two or three nights a week. He may play in all types of weather. In certain Small Fry Football leagues, the schedule calls for ten games, with additional games in case of a tie and one for the championship.

Do you know how many football games are considered sufficient for a high school team? Most people agree that eight or nine should be the maximum number. Even colleges rarely play over ten games per season. Several state athletic associations set a strict limit on the number of games high school teams may play, but the Small Fry League is not under the control of any educational system and has no limitations.

Aside from age, what makes a boy fit to play football? The essential thing is that he indicate some ruggedness. For example, does your child like the type of game which includes physical contact? Does he enjoy good-natured wrestling?

Of course, parents can help a child overcome fear of being pushed around —this is a part of education. But some boys just naturally take to rough play with more enthusiasm than others, and this is the kind of boy who will really enjoy football.

Physical Examination Is Necessary

Then, of course, there is the matter of health. The only way you can be certain that your boy is physically fit to play football is through a complete physical examination. The normal school checkup is not enough. In most states a physical examination is required of each football candidate before he may participate, but even if this law applies in your state it doesn't guarantee that the examination will be adequate. So make very sure your boy gets a really complete physical checkup before you allow him to play football.

Now let's assume that your boy is healthy and has passed his fourteenth birthday. He is the type of boy who likes a bit of rough and tumble in his play and enjoys competition. So you and he decide in favor of football. This is not the end of your responsibility. There are other important factors to be considered.

First, what about insurance? Does your school have insurance for football injuries or do you have to shoulder this responsibility yourself? If you have to do the job, make sure that you have a health insurance policy that covers football injuries to your son. Many schools do have insurance policies covering player injuries. Some policies set a maximum limit for each type of injury. See that this maximum is not a foolishly low one, as is too often the case. A better type of insurance has a maximum amount payable for any injury. This type takes complications into account, to a point. Find out what kind of policy your school has.

Equipment

Second, what type of equipment is your son going to be issued? Manufacturers have spent a great deal of time and money to insure proper protection for football players. This is one reason that injuries have taken such a downward trend in recent years. But many schools are still using equipment that should have been discarded a decade ago. Of course, each parent can't be an expert on football equipment. The only guide I can give you is the approximate price of acceptable equipment.

It requires over one hundred dollars to outfit a football player in a safe manner. Don't think your school is spending too much money for equipment if they go over this minimum—more power to them.

It's a good idea to take a look at the school's practice field, if they have a separate one. Is it free from rock piles, post holes and other hazards? At the Saturday game you may see Junior cavorting about on beautiful firm turf. Just make sure that the practice field is also safe.

Get to Know the Coach

And last, but not least, get acquainted with the local football coach. Find out what kind of man he is. Unfortunately, some coaches are out primarily to enhance their own reputations as trainers of winning teams. This kind of ambition tends to make them plan too heavy a schedule, long practice hours, unequal competition in games and even the use of an injured player if he happens to be the star performer. A good coach—and this is most of them—is truly interested in the welfare of his players. After-school practice does not last into the evening. During the pre-season sessions, practice may last up to two hours, possibly slightly longer, but once the season is underway the time should be considerably shorter. Games are scheduled only with other teams of comparable age and skill. Equipment is at least up to minimum standards and the football field is in good condition. Perhaps most important of all, a good coach thinks of football as a game—not a grim contest or a business venture—and gets this idea across to his boys. Coaching football is an important undertaking which should be placed in the hands of a competent individual.

A boy will experience situations in football not possible in most other sports. Under the proper conditions, football can contribute a great deal to his mental, physical and emotional development. —*By Andrew W. Grieve*

IF YOUR CHILD HAS ACNE

LOOKING across my desk at the young girl who had just seated herself opposite me, I said to myself, "Why do they always wait so long!" What I saw could have been a pretty teen-ager, but her face had pox-like scars and many active lesions of acne. She sat there looking at the floor as her mother talked away about how she kept after Mary to stop eating sweets and to scrub her face with strong soap—"but she just won't listen to anyone!"

I had heard the story many times before and my sympathies were with this miserable youngster. I had learned a long time ago that some teen-agers' compulsive eating of sweets and uncooperativeness about personal hygiene may be a kind of rebellion against their parents.

As soon as the mother had calmed down, I asked her daughter some general questions about how she felt physically. She summed up by replying, "I'm tired all the time." It also turned out that her appetite was practically non-existent. On the few occasions when she did get hungry, she nibbled at whatever was handy. She slept restlessly and it was a struggle to get herself out of bed in the morning. Usually there was barely enough time to grab a piece of toast as she ran out the door for school. She told me that she had only one or two friends at school and these, I sensed, she hung onto for dear life. She spent most of her time after school at home by herself, much of it alone in front of her mirror, squeezing the lesions on her face. Her face usually ended up looking worse, because squeezing acne lesions damages the tiny blood vessels of the skin and causes bleeding into the tissues.

Overactive Oil Glands

I sent the patient out of my office into the examination room so that I could speak alone with her mother. I explained that for a while it would be better if she left Mary's management to me. I told her the basic trouble with Mary's skin was that the oil glands were overactive—a condition not uncommon right after puberty—and many of the oil gland openings to the skin were plugged. I explained that the treatment I was going to outline was designed to reduce the oiliness of the skin and make it peel slightly, to open the plugged oil gland openings.

There are many misconceptions and half-truths about acne. Parents have said to me, "My boy must have bad blood," or "I had my boy's tonsils taken out and he still has acne." Teen-agers themselves often have the notion—sometimes implanted by adults—that their acne is caused by too much or too little sexual activity. It is not uncommon in the privacy of my office to have young people voluntarily confess that they masturbate, as though they're explaining to me why they have acne. This is one of the biggest "old wives' tales" of them all, and one which engenders crippling feelings of guilt. Another misconception about acne one often hears is, "Leave it alone, they'll grow out of it." Yes, eventually they will, but very likely not for many years—and in the meantime acne can leave as much of a scar on the personality as on the skin. Acne is common in the twenties and is even seen in the early thirties. Because one cannot predict which case will persist and which will not, acne should not be neglected.

I went into the examination room where my nurse had helped Mary remove her blouse and saw that the patient had a typical eruption. Her skin was very oily and, as usual, though there were also lesions on her chest and back, the eruption was worse on her face where there are a great number of oil glands. There were many blackheads—which are oil gland openings plugged with dried oil. They are black not because of dirt, as is commonly thought, but rather from chemical changes (oxidation) which take place in the dried oil after exposure to the air. There were also many lesions which started as blackheads but had become infected and now were greatly enlarged, inflamed and contained pus—"pimples" in the language of laymen. A few oil glands which had been plugged up for a long time, causing the oil to back up and enlarge the glands, had formed cysts. Sometimes such cysts get infected and become red and acutely painful.

Mary mustered her courage and meekly asked, "How long will it take till I won't have these awful pimples?"

"That depends on many things," I said. "One is how well you follow orders and take care of your skin at home. To do that, there are some things about your skin trouble that you should understand." I explained the cause of acne to her as I had to her mother. She wanted to know why her oil glands were "acting up like this." I told her that the hormones which made her body develop from a little girl's to a young woman's, when she was around 11 or 12, overstimulated the oil glands of the skin. "As you get older," I told Mary, "they will quiet down and resume a normal balance." Unfortunately we do not know too well yet how to keep these hormones in check during this period of growth. Therefore we must do the best we can with the tools we have to work with. Some of the new antibiotics seem to have a favorable effect on the infected form of acne lesions. In moderate doses, some dermatologists like to use these drugs, at least until infection has quieted down. Naturally, they must be taken only under a physician's supervision.

Good Nutrition Essential

I went on to tell Mary that one of the most important things she could do to help herself was to eat three nourishing meals each day—with foods particularly rich in proteins, minerals and vitamins. While she should not eliminate starches and fats from her diet entirely, especially since she was not overweight, she should eat less of them and more meats, green vegetables and dairy products, less starches and fats. I also gave her some capsules of vitamin B-complex to supplement her diet and stimulate her appetite.

There has been a lot of talk about acne being caused by certain foods, particularly "sweets." It is true that an occasional patient will be made worse by chocolate or some specific food, such as milk or nuts. But actually the most important role foods play in acne is that so many young people don't eat well. There always seem to be more important things to do than to sit down and calmly eat three good meals a day. Breakfast is likely to be caught on the fly and lunch is sketchy. Often, dinner is the only complete meal. As a result, youngsters, and indeed many of their parents, get by on so-called "nervous energy." Sooner or later, something has to give and with today's pace, many of us become snared in a vicious cycle of tension, loss of appetite and inadequate nutrition. To break this chain we have to discipline ourselves and our children into better eating habits.

Cleanliness

Next I explained to Mary that she must wash affected areas of her skin thoroughly with soap and water, using a clean washcloth or soft brush, three or four times a day. After each washing she was to apply the drying lotion I prescribed for her. I warned her, however, that she should not become so overenthusiastic in her home treatment as to irritate the skin. Scrubbing violently, using water that is too hot and applying the lotion too frequently are not necessary. Finally, since dandruff is a common companion of acne, I recommended a weekly shampoo with a non-oily preparation. I also told her that plenty of rest and sensible amounts of outdoor recreation are principles of good general health which help in treating acne. Similarly, regular elimination and about four glasses of water a day are important. Sun bathing in moderation is fine, but there is no benefit to be obtained by "following the sun" to the point of getting sunburned.

Before Mary left I had my nurse expose her face, chest and back to a few minutes of ultraviolet light. Ultraviolet rays cause a mild sunburn which in a few days turns into a slight scaling of the skin. This very light peeling effect removes some of the dead, topmost cells of the skin which are soaked with dried oil and at the same time it frees many plugged oil gland openings, and prevents new blackheads from forming.

Something else I told Mary was, "You know, your complexion isn't going to clear up overnight. You might as well have some fun while it improves. Don't think of yourself as only a face—there is much more to you than that. Don't look at yourself with a magnifying glass—no one ever sees you that close. What people think of you doesn't depend on the looks of your skin. They like you for your whole self. The less you think about your skin, the busier you keep yourself and the happier you are, the quicker your skin will clear."

Removal of Blackheads

The next time Mary came she was given another ultraviolet treatment, this time, as in each succeeding treatment, of a slightly longer duration. When it was finished, I took a small rod-like instrument with a tiny hole at one end, placed the hole over a blackhead and, by pressing down firmly, forced the blackhead out. I did this to several large blackheads, explaining what I was doing as I went along. Then I told her, "I want you to do the same thing each night for a few minutes. However, first compress your face with a steam towel, like they do in a barber shop, for about 20 minutes to get your skin soft. This will make it much easier to get the blackheads out. When you are finished, wash with soap and water and apply your lotion."

I had to tell her, too, that the greasy cosmetics she used to cover her acne tended to plug up the oil gland openings. However, there was no objection to her using a dry powder.

Recently a group of doctors studying the effect of emotional upsets on acne had their patients keep what I call an "anger diary." Every time new acne lesions appeared, the patients recorded in their diaries what they had been doing or thinking about the previous day. With surprising consistency, it was found that each new crop of lesions was associated with something upsetting.

For example, one young boy in the study, who at one time had very bad acne, remembered that each time he had an argument with his father, a not infrequent occurrence, his acne flared up.

Emotional Aspects

Mary and her mother had gotten themselves in a position where a U.N. mediator was necessary! At the moment no matter what the mother said or tried to do to help, it was the wrong thing as far as Mary was concerned. And there was nothing for me to do except try to arrange a "cease fire." From time to time, on Mary's office visits she and I would sit down and chat about her "problems." Being misunderstood by her mother and feeling inferior were her favorite subjects. When such feelings are aired by patients in the presence of a sympathetic but neutral listener, the air becomes strangely cleared, perspective is gained and things don't look so black. Counsel of this sort by a physician, minister, counselor or even an older acquaintance, when parents are too enmeshed emotionally in a child's conflicts, can be very helpful.

When most of the activity of Mary's acne had left, her mother came in with her one day to ask if anything could be done about the scars. I told her that in time many of the scars would flatten out and be almost invisible. However, a few were so deep that I thought their appearance would be helped by the new planing technique. In some cases the scarring of acne can be benefited by anesthetizing the skin and actually planing off the superficial skin layers with a fine, power-driven brush. In a few weeks the skin heals and the depressions and ridges which formed the scars are leveled. While this procedure is not necessary in most acne cases, some patients who have had severe acne scarring feel that they are improved in appearance.

The precise causes and an infallible treatment of acne are still among the unknowns of medicine. But knowledge is progressing by such leaps and bounds that it is exciting to visualize how much more will be known 10 or even 5 years from this writing. In the meantime, no child need suffer from the ravages, both physical and emotional, of acne. The simple principles of treatment I have outlined here, if applied early, will prevent your child from suffering what Mary did.　　　　　　　　　*—By Herbert Lawrence, M.D.*

EMOTIONAL PROBLEMS OF TEEN-AGERS

AS a psychologist who has had experience in private practice as well as in connection with a large city high school, I have been consulted by hundreds of boys and girls about their problems. I am forced to conclude that youth is both the happiest and at the same time the unhappiest time of life. The troubles boys and girls undergo are those experienced by young people in every generation—a shift of emphasis here, a new stress there, perhaps, but still basically the same. "How can I get along better with my parents?"; "How can I be more popular?"; "Why am I shy?"; "What is real love?"; "What's the reason for living?"

And today another problem is causing many young people a good deal of anxiety. They seriously question whether at some future date they will be alive at all. Who is not worried about the atom bomb, the H-bomb, and any other superbombs that might be devised as the years go on? This major concern of our Age of Anxiety hits the young with a special impact. "You have lived your lives," they tell us adults bitterly, "but we're just starting out. We have a right to live. It's not fair that we should be so threatened before we've even grown up." As one boy put it: "What's the use of planning for the future? The H-bomb will end all our worries anyway." And a girl said, "Whenever I hear an ambulance dashing through the night with its siren going, I imagine it's an air-raid warning, and my heart starts to pound."

But we can say to youth that throughout the ages, despite war and tragedy and suffering, somehow life goes on; that the healthy person does not experience panic in advance of a real situation; or that since the future is unpredictable, worrying is pointless. This world of ours has never been a safe or sure place. There can be no guarantee that anyone's private ambitions will be fulfilled, but likewise there is no guarantee that they will not be fulfilled.

It may seem strange to jump from fear of bombs to the problem of shyness. But while fear of external happenings is often agonizing, inner fear can also be devastating. Who but another shy person knows the agony a shy boy or girl can experience? Tom described it this way: "When I have to get up and say something with people around, I begin to stammer and tremble and feel all jittery inside. I wish I could run away and be alone in my room at home. The funny thing is that once I do get home, I become a totally different person. I'm terrific then. But that's when I'm alone."

Tom wasn't born shy. Tom was made shy by circumstances in his earliest childhood. Something has made Tom afraid of being critically appraised by other people. He feels he is constantly under a test, and he feels so unsure of himself and his abilities that he cannot stand up to this test. Like all shy people, Tom really has an exaggerated view of his importance in the scheme of things. He imagines that all eyes are on him and on everything he says and does. Contrary to the general opinion, the shy person is not a modest, diffident, unassuming fellow. Actually, he is self-centered. Privately, he has built up an image of himself in which he is a pretty extraordinary individual. But this picture, so dear and necessary to him, is in danger of being shattered by other people, and this is what he dreads.

To get over his shyness Tom has to give up this false image and learn to accept himself as he really is, with all his faults and limitations. If he can do that, he will be on the way to a cure. The shy youngster and the brash one are brothers under the skin. Both are suffering from the natural uncertainties of youth.

Moodiness

Mary came to me one day in distress over her moods. "Some days I get up feeling on top of the world," she said. "Everything seems wonderful and I am as happy as a lark. Then, suddenly, for no good reason that I can see, I feel awful. I can hardly drag myself around, and I am irritated by everything anyone says."

What are moods and why do so many young people have them? Moods are essentially an escape from the real world. When we are confronted by a task or a problem of which we are afraid or which we feel we cannot handle, it is easier to have a mood about it than to tackle it. We can feel bitter, or full of self-pity, or blame everyone else; or we can indulge in gorgeous daydreams of becoming great and famous and all-powerful and of getting even with everybody. But when this emotional spree is over, we find ourselves just where we were before.

We all have moody moments, but young people have them often. In the course of growing up, they encounter many new experiences and responsibilities. How can they be expected to act with wisdom and dispatch when they are still in the process of learning what they can and cannot do? At such times they will often take refuge in moods. Extreme gaiety may be just as much a sign of an attempt to escape from a problem as is extreme dejection.

The adolescent goes blundering on, backing and filling, falling in love, falling out of love, questioning and frightened, impelled by powerful needs he is trying to understand and to control. While young people are in the throes of these conflicts, their feelings are deeply involved and their bewilderment is very real. If they feel free to talk things over with their parents, it will help. Otherwise, fortunate is the boy or girl who can take these worries and problems to a well-qualified counselor.

Hints to Popularity

If you should ask the average teen-ager what he wants most in his relations with other people, he would probably answer "to be popular." What makes one boy or girl sought after, and another neglected? There is no magic formula for achieving popularity, but there are some definite "don'ts" that can be pointed out. An important one is not to monopolize the conversation in a group or with a companion. Common courtesy should make us realize that the other fellow has joys and troubles as interesting as our own. Once we get our companion to talk, we must know how to listen. Listening is an active, sharing kind of response. The art of small talk is more essential to social success than big talk is. Through small talk people can make a sort of reconnaissance to the unknown territory of each other's personality.

Young people are constantly torturing themselves with doubts about whether they are as good as their companions. They often capitulate to this sense of inadequacy by withdrawing from social contacts. Thus competition and comparisons with others can be avoided. Another way in which they try to compensate for this feeling of inadequacy is by criticizing others. By making others appear weak, small or silly they hope to feel powerful and command admiration. Both these methods defeat their purpose, which is to get people to like them. Withdrawal brings only isolation and loneliness. As for the overaggressive person—who likes a bully?

Boys and girls who are concerned about their ability to attract friends might consider one fact: very few persons are universally liked—and even fewer are universally disliked. There exist somewhere for every person several individuals who would approve of him exactly as he is if they could really get to know him. It takes years of practice to develop flexibility in dealing with people—learning when to talk, when to listen; when to ask questions, when to answer them; when and how to be agreeable, or, should the occasion arise, when to be otherwise.

High on the list of troubles is tension between teen-agers and their parents. The teen years are a period in which a human being stops being a child and starts becoming a grownup. In the process of discovering himself, working out his own standards, his own choices and goals, the ex-child will rebel at parental attitudes and discipline. He will do this even if there is actually little to rebel against. In this way he develops emotional "muscles."

Satisfying Needs of Teen-Agers

There is a great need on the part of children to love and admire their parents. This need is so great that they are willing to forgive them again and again for some blunder or hurt they have inflicted. In a sense parents are lucky, because for a good many years their children will let them start each day with a fresh slate. Suppose, however, as time goes on, the child goes to sleep night after night feeling unloved, not understood, a stranger in his own home, a kind of psychological orphan. He may want to forgive but he will no longer be able to forget. A deep hurt and anger develop from which he cannot shake himself loose. He generally concludes that "It must have been something in me, some fault or weakness of mine." This is one way in which a feeling of inadequacy often begins.

There are several basic "musts" which, if honestly carried out by parents, can help young people become well-adjusted and happier. These have been chosen from among the wishes and hopes expressed by adolescents themselves: Make us feel we are loved and wanted. Stand *by* us, not *over* us. Don't make us feel inferior because we are young. Praise us when we deserve it. When you must say no, explain your reasons; don't just hand out commands. Show respect for our wishes even if you disagree with them. Treat us fairly. Show interest in our activities. Give us a right to participate in decisions that affect our lives. Let us make our own mistakes and learn from them. Teach us gradually to be independent of you—don't hold us back by overprotection.
                                                            —*By George Lawton, Ph.D.*

Section Five

FAMILY RELATIONS

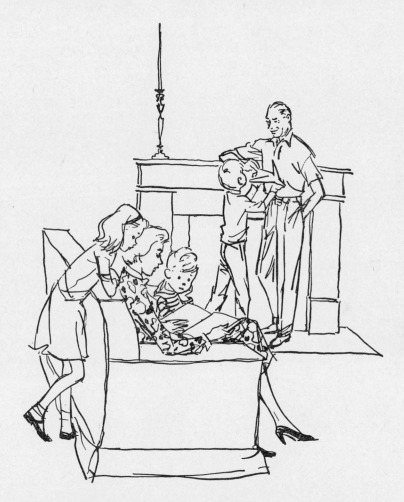

MARRIED LOVE • QUARRELING, GOOD OR BAD?
TALKING OUT PROBLEMS • EMOTIONAL DEVELOPMENT
MAKING CHOICES • LOVE AND HATE • FOOD FOR MENTAL HEALTH
SEX EDUCATION • WHAT TO TELL CHILDREN ABOUT DEATH
ONE'S PLACE IN THE FAMILY • THREE GENERATION FAMILIES
DEMOCRACY AND RELIGION • HEREDITY AND ENVIRONMENT
TWINS • COLOR BLINDNESS • LEFT-HANDEDNESS • ADOPTION

THE TRUTH ABOUT MARRIED LOVE

MEN, more than women, are apt to take the acts of love as proof of love. Talking about it seems unnecessary to them. This is difficult for many wives to understand or accept, especially if they have a real need for reassurance that they are loved and approved.

Courtship is full of delightful evidences of affection. Even the most undemonstrative man makes every effort to woo his woman. Before marriage the ardent suitor cannot bear to be in the same room with her without wanting to be close to her, touch her, hold her hand. Yet so often does all this change after the wooed has become the won that we have a common expression which we apply to all sorts of situations where the humdrum or ordinary has taken the place of ecstasy—"Well, the honeymoon is over."

Comes the time when a woman is keenly aware of her need for a little more romance and glamour than domesticity seems likely to afford. Cleaning, washing, doing dishes, cooking, ironing and tending babies present a deadly monotony at times. Her husband's life in the outside world of affairs may seem exciting by contrast. So she is all the more eager for him to make up to her for her sense of being something of a household drudge by telling her how much she means to him.

Be Realistic

Actually, however, if a woman stops to think about it, a man's life in an office or shop isn't any easier than a woman's. In many ways it is far more demanding. To expect him to come home and act the dashing lover is unrealistic. Far from feeling like a young Lochinvar, dismounting from a white charger, he is apt to be tired, and is often discouraged. Wives would get many more spontaneous expressions of affection from their men if they would just wait for the psychological moment instead of expecting them at the wrong time. Just as you wouldn't ignore the law of gravity by parking on a hill without your brakes on, so you can't expect a husband to express undying affection when he is worried over a business problem or is dog-tired and hungry.

Love puts itself in the other person's place and senses his feelings and problems. Ten to one if you offer your man a smile instead of a gripe, pour him a cool drink or a cup of fresh coffee, tell him the bathroom is empty so he can have a shower and take his time about it because dinner will wait, later that psychological moment will come. Clean, rested, relaxed, a good dinner under his belt and appreciative of your understanding, he is pretty likely of his own accord to come out with one of those remarks that warm a woman's heart.

Emotional Development Differs

A good deal of the difficulty between the two sexes is due to a fundamental difference in their emotional development. Both boy and girl start life with a stronger dependence on the mother than on the father. Their original emotional attachment to her is greater since she is with them more and takes care of them. In return they give her the larger share of their love. For the boy this emotional situation remains unchanged. Later he merely transfers his adult affections from one woman to another—mother to wife.

The girl, however, must make a profound shift in her psychosexual development from mother love to father love if she is ever to accept husband love. Often she may encounter obstacles or experience difficulties in making this transfer of her affections. Perhaps she fails to get enough interest and attention from her father when she is attempting, around the age of three or four, to be good friends with him. He either does not understand her needs or is too busy and doesn't take the time to show his interest and affection for her and to accept her approaches. Later, when she grows up and marries, she may never be quite able to feel confident and secure in a man's love, but needs constantly to be assured that he cares for her.

Father-Daughter Relationships

If a woman has had an unsatisfactory father-daughter relationship which has resulted in an emotional problem of this sort, it will help to discuss it with someone who is understanding and wise and who can help her recognize her dependence and try to do something about it.

Steve Evans showed that he understood his wife's problem when he said, "Ruth's father deserted the family soon after she was born. No wonder she needs a lot of affection from her husband. But that's all right with me. Who wants to be married to a cold fish?"

But it isn't always "too little father" that makes a woman eager to have her husband show her more attention. Sometimes it is too much of the wrong sort of paternal affection. Having been set up by an adoring father in childhood as a little Princess, she now demands continued enthronement. She wants her husband to fetch and carry for her, keep her ego built up and dance constant attendance on her. Here the need is obviously for a little more growing up. Such wives must acquire more emotional maturity which sees love is not just a matter of getting, but also of giving and sharing.

The whole subject of love is one which has been much misunderstood and as yet hardly explored or scientifically studied. Do all individuals have the same capacity to love? As more work is done in the field of genetics we shall know better. But already we know that each person is unique, different from all others with traits and attributes all his own. So it may be, if your husband isn't as demonstrative as you would like, that he is still showing as much feeling as he has to give. It is well to consider this possibility and not make demands he may be unable to meet. Such a man may make up in other ways for his lack of warmth. He may be an exceptionally honest, loyal, responsible human being.

Again, apparent coldness or undemonstrativeness may be a false front for timidity or not really knowing how to express feelings. A man may feel love but find it difficult to show it because he fears it will be ignored, ridiculed, not received and returned in kind. Or he may fear that love will make him too dependent, or expose him to more obligations than he can tolerate.

Such a man has usually been unable in childhood to count on a dependable love from his mother. For one reason or another he has met with rejective treatment and now he no longer dares to trust or hope for understanding. If he marries, his wife will have to make every effort, perhaps over a period of years, to prove that love can be not only warm and happy but safe and sure.

There is another reason why men are loath to show their feelings. Our culture has extolled control of the emotions. Because of all this "sitting on" our emotions, both sexes as they grow to manhood and womanhood often find it hard to know whether they really feel love for another person or not. The engagement period is frequently filled with these worries and doubts.

When we do think of ourselves as "in love," it is often a state of fantasy in which we endow the loved one with all the virtues and all the romance which we hope and expect to find in love. This "rose-colored spectacle" stage is intense and is usually accompanied by a strong sexual urge. After marriage, disappointment sets in for it has been a psuedo-love, actuated largely by self-love and the desire to see what we want in the loved one, not what is there.

Where a person truly loves, however, he or she is fully aware of the defects and idiosyncrasies of the beloved person as well as his or her assets and charms.

Fluctuating Love

Many people are on speaking terms with a love that is like a water tap; it can be turned on and off at will. It is withdrawn when something about the loved one fails to please. A young man recently consulted me about his marriage. I asked him whether he loved the girl.

"When she's good I do," he said. "But when she acts up I don't."

Undoubtedly this is the sort of love he received in childhood from his own mother, and so he knew no other kind. Many of us suffer from doubt and fear because we have grown up feeling that far from being dependable, love is something to be bought for favors or received only for good behavior.

The pathological forms of love are numerous and all too frequent in our society. They include self-love, using love to undermine the partner, and withdrawing from love for fear of becoming too dependent on the other or hurt by him or her. Those who have been forced to turn inward on themselves usually feel isolated and lonely even in the intimate relationship of marriage. And isolationism, as we are beginning to know only too well, can extend beyond the individual to groups, states and nations, causing hostility, fear, intolerance, misunderstanding, even war.

Many problems challenge men and women in this period of transition from the old, patriarchal family system to the new, slowly evolving democratic ideal. But we are becoming more and more aware of the child's need for love. As this understanding of basic emotional needs becomes more generally accepted, it is reasonable to expect that a generation will grow up which finds it natural to love freely and without awkward embarrassments or restraints. Such men will not find it necessary deliberately to change their ways or make special efforts to give women reassurance of their love. Nor will such wives need to make unreasonable demands on their husbands for emotional security.

Education for marriage. Much help is being given to men and women to educate them for their roles in marriage and family life. Premarital and marriage counseling in both preventive and curative aspects is available. More and more young people are coming to experts for psychological help and premarital consulations. Should they or should they not marry this particular choice of partner? These problems of choice were, for many years, brought to doctors but they were usually related to physical defects or eugenics. Now they are likely to involve more subtle questions such as "Do I really love him or her?" or "Is he too attached to his mother?" or "What makes him behave in such a peculiar way—does he love me or doesn't he?" or "Is she too immature?" These matters are considered very carefully and analyzed thoroughly. Sometimes the decision is not to marry. But many times it is found that there is sufficient basis for marriage and that together the young couple can face these problems and work them out.

Today more than ever we need to love and be loved. This need does not end with childhood. Men and women need love, too, for their emotional security. And emotional security is essential for the establishment and maintenance of a good marital relationship. Love gives a feeling of trust, respect, comfort and assurance. Shared, it makes for good living together. It creates the atmosphere in which children can thrive and grow so that they, in their turn, learn how to express love, give it freely, and receive it.

—By Lena Levine, M.D.

QUARRELING CAN CLEAR THE AIR

"WE'VE been married for thirty-five years and there's never been a cross word between us," remarked my host the other evening. His wife nodded affirmation, as she was expected to do. Later on she took some delight in regaling the company, made up of her husband's faculty associates, with the details of his fainting spells. We were all rather embarrassed for him, since only women are supposed to faint. When he remonstrated, his wife developed a headache and excused herself. These two never quarrel, but was this a happy relationship? No, there was tension between them, so apparent that strangers could feel it!

Undercover conflict of this type is a form of mutual destructiveness which is seldom faced or clearly understood by either party. It is often the product of bearing and forebearing. The emphasis which has been placed on peace and harmony has given people the idea that marital conflict is detrimental and harmful. According to this view any expression of conflict in the family is wrong. The partners attempt to maintain an appearance of perfect peace and happiness, but behind the false front there is built up a multitude of un-resolved tensions.

Thirty-five years is too long to go without a quarrel. The husband and wife already mentioned are resorting to covert conflict which is destructive be-cause it is deceitful and elusive. This same model wife jabbed again at her husband's vanity the following rainy morning: "Darling, you must put on your rubbers. You aren't as young as you were." There's much more to the art of getting along in marriage than the mere avoidance of quarrels!

A much healthier mode of handling differences is open and aboveboard conflict. The cards are on the table, and each knows what the other thinks. There isn't much chance for longtime misunderstandings, because the troubles are taken up periodically and settled on the spot. Happy is the couple able to deal with their differences so openly.

All growing families have differences. It's part of the price we pay for the privilege of living in intimate association and being entrusted with family responsibilities. Coupled together as we are in marriage, all decisions reached provoke some disagreement in the initial stages. Yet it is only recently that overt conflict has been admitted to polite society. To quarrel was regarded as vulgar, unseemly, a sure evidence of faulty upbringing. Polite, restrained discussion or passive assent was preferred to quarreling, even if we came out of it with a splitting headache. What we overlooked was that conflict was conflict, whether the weapons were soft words or clubs!

Influence of Patriarchal Family

The customs which forbade quarreling in the home grew up to support the absolute power of the father in the patriarchal family. Out of this period came our hundreds of maxims glorifying marital bliss and family harmony at all costs. We use some of them today: "Forgive and Forget," "Speak When Spoken To," "The Soft Answer Turneth Away Wrath," "It Takes Two To Make a Quarrel."

A different school of thought and behavior has resulted as the wife and children have been liberated, and the father transformed from a dominating figure to a companionable partner in family life. This change is the result of psychiatry and social science and is best represented by the family life education and child study movements in America. Parent education has fostered the democratic, equalitarian family in which children and mother join with the father in shaping family plans. Conflict in the family is regarded as having a functional value. It is through conflicts and their solution that a family sets up and achieves goals, works out a division of labor, and develops cooperative action.

While many of us would like to adopt this new and compelling philosophy of democracy and freedom of discussion in family life, few of us are sufficiently out of the woods of transition to accept discord and quarreling as evidences of growth. Because we were reared in homes which insisted that we count to ten before sounding off, we are conscience-stricken after indulging in a marital spat. It may take another generation to rid family members of the vestiges of the earlier self-righteous sweetness-and-light mode of thinking. The least we can do is to give our children assurance that quarreling is not something to fear or condemn, but to understand.

In every marriage, husband and wife bring to the relation different philosophies of life, different wants and ideas of what's funny and what's important. Their ideas of what marriage is all about often differ, just because courtship in America brings together people of widely varied backgrounds. Every time a decision is reached in the early years of marriage, some of these differences are likely to come to light. Only after a bit of grinding of gears do the parts seem to mesh correctly. Consensus of opinion can only follow exchange of opposing views.

Difference in Backgrounds

Susan married when she was just out of high school, and was eager to make her marriage a success. Her husband, Jim, was a pleasant chap two years older than she. He had been reared with four brothers by his widowed father, with no memory of the needs and wants of women in a family. He had never been exposed to the orderliness, neatness and regularity of meals prized by the good housewife. He feigned ignorance of the cost of permanents, silk stockings and household articles and made his financial plans accordingly. Jim had been reared, moreover, to feel that the man should be the head of the house and control the purse strings.

Susan appears to have overlooked these differences in their backgrounds during the engagement, and early marriage found her ill-prepared to cope with the situation. Instead of forthrightly battling out the issue when he came late for meals, or sometimes didn't eat at all, as had been his pattern in his parental home, Susan adapted herself to her husband's unorthodox tastes. After the children arrived, it became increasingly difficult to manage financially with what Jim gave her. Susan made no moves to battle for joint handling of the family finances. She held back the angry words with the misguided intention of preserving harmony. Tensions built up and, as so often happens, spilled over into the couple's sex relations which heretofore had been mutually enjoyable. Jim admitted that his marriage had gone sour, but didn't know why. After all, they had had only one or two serious squabbles in six years of marriage!

A couple with more insight would have recognized that the differences in backgrounds would need to be ironed out and a way of life agreeable to both worked out. In the process there might be conflict. For it is in the nature of growing, changing families that conflict will be present. Especially is this true of the parent-child relationship where the healthy, growing child is constantly challenging the decisions concerning his privileges and responsibilities which were reached when he was younger. When conflict ceases it may only mean that the family has ceased growing.

The family is a sort of funnel or bottleneck through which flows the everyday life of its members. Every member brings to his family his hopes, disappointments, unsolved problems and accumulated frustrations from the work-a-day world. It is the one place of security and intimacy where people are free to behave like human beings with the normal variety of emotions. From the interchange of both views and blows, the family members attain the spiritual resilience which enables them to do the world's work.

Emotional Release Necessary

The individual must often act like something more than human to get along in our complex industrial society. If he flies off the handle at his boss he risks losing his job. If he shows his irritation to his associates at the office or factory, they may make it painfully difficult for him. There needs to be some place where the individual can give vent to his annoyances and be himself. The only reasonably safe place is at home.

This burden is often a difficult one for families to carry, but if there are clashes and emotional outbursts in a home, parents may comfort themselves with the thought that their marriage is performing one of its most important functions, providing a place to let off steam and reestablish emotional balance. Dr. Richard Brickner, psychiatrist, once declared that marriages which are so fragile that they have to be maintained by the same kind of artificial manners that keep an office force functioning are pretty precariously based.

Conflict has been termed the collision of wishes, and collision is inevitable wherever more than one person are gathered together. When the reconciliation of wishes fails (or is not attempted) tensions result. These tensions may be expressed openly; when they are repressed, added emotional force accumulates. Consistently repressed tensions are unusually hard on the relationship and on the personalities of the participants. In a marriage they tend to circumscribe and narrow the topics of conversation, the areas of activity. In the case of Jim and Susan, family entertainment, family finances and sex relationships were rarely discussed because of the strain both felt when these matters came up. Tensions disturb the normal functioning of living because they accumulate and spread.

A healthy family is one in which family members are not circumscribed and limited in their discussion. There is no fear that a coolness will fill the room or that someone will say, "Now, we won't talk about that. You know it makes your mother nervous." Such inhibitions are the real family skeletons.

Having taken the position that much of conflict is normal and desirable, it is still necessary to distinguish between that which is productive and that which is destructive. We know full well that certain types of conflict become progressively more bitter and disruptive as marriage goes on. Destructive quarreling is most often directed at the mate personally, or someone dear to him. It attacks the ego of the other in belittling and punishing fashion, destroying the illusions which kept the marital relationship intact.

Productive Quarrels

Productive quarrels, on the other hand, are more frequently limited and directed at issues, conditions, problems. The strengthening factors of a productive quarrel are that the wishes of each member are made known, problems threshed out, and a new and more complete understanding achieved. Concentrating on problems and conditions which are frustrating the couple rather than on their personal deficiencies, the productive conflict tends to be less disruptive and less fraught with emotional tensions.

As children are added to the family, most of the conflict they engender may well be productive. With changing family needs, the family must change to meet them. Children who rebel against things as they are are concentrating on conditions. If the young fry are accepted as worthy of combat by democratic parents, a productive solution to the conflict may ensue. Moreover, children who are allowed to fight for their rights are being given valuable preparation for handling conflict productively in homes of their own making.

Only persons of sound emotions can quarrel successfully. Emotionally infantile individuals resort to substitute activity to keep their marriage on an even keel. Daydreaming, rationalization, depreciation, martyrdom, neurotic illness and idealization are some of the mental mechanisms employed to escape from the reality of marriage. The obvious difficulty with running away from the differences which make for conflict is that the marriage may become structured permanently on a substitutive basis.

Another requirement for successful quarreling in marriage is previous successful experience with conflict in one's parental family or with one's peers. There needs to be a conviction that problems can be solved and that consensus is possible. The habit of expecting a successful outcome is mighty compelling! A happy by-product of successful quarreling in the parental family is the absence of fear when conflict looms in one's own home. People who are afraid of combat are often the first to get hurt.

Finally, a primary requirement for productive quarreling is the ability to focus on the problem, steering clear of the pitfalls which entrap those who slip over into a discussion of personalities. Thin-skinned, sensitive people are ineligible for this very reason. They take everything personally, and are easily wounded in the rough and tumble of marital combat. Proud should be the family which rears its children to be tough-minded, invulnerable to the glancing blows of inept opponents.

Strong Marital Relationship

Successful quarreling requires a strong marital tie. A firm relationship built during courtship and engagement is needed to survive conflicts of this order. A factor which gives temper to the relationship is the expectation of success in the marriage. Those couples are very fortunate who can differ strongly and openly without getting panicky about the future of their marriage. One couple said, "We think the fights we had helped our marriage because they taught us that we cared more for our relationship than we did about winning the argument, and we soon found a workable compromise we could both accept." They went on to say that they felt no marriage was a strong marriage until it was tested by crisis, conflict and adversity.

There are techniques for constructive quarreling. Evelyn Millis Duvall, in a Public Affairs Pamphlet, makes some valuable suggestions:

"Accept the fact of conflict without shame or pretending it isn't there. Remember that conflict is normal. Face the fact that you and your spouse are human beings. Don't be alarmed when differences arise from time to time.

"Try to find out what the whole thing means to your mate. What's 'eating' him? Or her? How does he feel about it and why? Keep as calm as you can yourself while you encourage him to talk it out.

"What does it matter to you? Why are you annoyed or irritated by it? Ask yourself honestly why it is that you are so excited about it.

"Adopt a problem-solving approach to the situation, but keep remembering that many situations need not really become problems. On the basis of your mutual acceptance and understanding, try to see what can be done to work things out comfortably. Don't let tensions pile up day after day. Work them out as they come along.

"Try to agree on some next step for taking care of the situation. Get busy on it together as soon as possible.

"Do what you can to help the other to save face, feel stronger, to feel your love, no matter what. Avoid sniping at each other. Keep your energy focused on the problem as much as you can—rather than on the other's faults.

"Be patient. Be willing to take a little time for the solving of your difficulties. Don't expect miracles.

"When the whole situation gets beyond you, get some competent counseling help."

Remove unresolved tensions. Lest the point of view expressed here be misunderstood, let us emphasize the fact that we believe marriage is the source of the deepest companionship, respect and devotion. But genuine and free interplay of emotions in marriage and the home paves the way for more honesty in the husband-wife relationship. Husband and wife must face issues squarely and master the arts of conflict in this democratic free-for-all if they are to indulge successfully. It is not so much conflict in families which is to be deplored as the inability to recognize differences and battle them through. Unresolved tensions are the real family skeletons which should be removed from the closet and put through the mill of family discussion. Conflict has two functions—the solution of issues and the release of resentment and tensions which arise in every relationship. —By *Reuben Hill, Ph.D.*

TALK CAN SAVE YOUR MARRIAGE

EVERY husband and wife brings to marriage a background of experiences, expectations, tastes, ways of reacting *to* men and women and *as* men and women, which stem in large part from influences in their own childhood. Only a small part of what they feel, what motivates their feelings, is visible on the surface. The rest is hidden—even from themselves.

A husband may, for example, unconsciously expect his wife to be just like his mother was—gentle, all-accepting, all-forgiving. Or he may, having loved but felt smothered by this kind of mother, gravitate unconsciously toward an opposite kind of woman for his wife, a more independent and less dominating one. These are rather pat examples, of course—the possible combinations of what we all seek in a marriage partner are manifold. In any case, since such a man hasn't learned to know himself, since he's still reacting primarily to his mother and not to his wife, he's bound to be communicating more with what he *feels* his wife is rather than with what she *really* is.

For his wife—bringing with her the emotional effects of her own past childhood experiences—is most decidedly *not* his mother, no matter how much she may resemble (or be the opposite of) her in superficial ways, and no matter how much she herself may be driven to fit a mothering role because of her own past, her own needs. Thus, when her husband unconsciously expects her to be invariably understanding, tender and forgiving with him because his mother was, or to stand aside and not "fuss" over him because he's had too much of that from his mother—he is cutting off the possibility of genuine communication.

Women, of course, do the same thing. When a husband asks his wife to make sure the garage door is kept closed in cold weather, she may find herself resisting because she will *not* be ordered around by a man—as she herself was or as her mother was by her father. If she's in thrall to her past, she doesn't stop to think, "But my husband isn't my father. It does make sense to keep the door shut."

Suppression of Emotions

A further answer to the question, "Why can't we talk to each other?" is that most Americans have been raised and educated to suppress emotional expression. (This, of course, is fear, too, in another form.) We can see it in the way we still raise our own children. Most of us have come far enough not to say, "It doesn't really hurt" to a child who's in pain, but don't we still feel somewhere they really *ought* to be a little braver and not raise such a fuss? And although most of us now recognize a child's "right" to be angry—doesn't it still somewhere, somehow, seem "wrong?" We don't like our children to show anger or hostility, or any of the other unpleasant emotions. As a matter of fact, even the lovelier emotions—liking, loving, enjoying—cause many of us to draw back when they are deeply felt, deeply lived, directly expressed.

We want our boys especially to be "tough," with poker faces and poker feelings. "Boys don't cry," we say to them—or if we don't say it we still feel it's not as natural in a son as in a daughter. So in our society men in particular grow up clamping down on their feelings. If a man shows that he can be or is hurt, troubled, or indeed tender, he's apt to be considered a softy.

One unfortunate result of this kind of childhood training is that men and women enter marriage with different capacities to accept their own feelings and to say frankly what they are. As a rule, a wife can discuss emotional problems more easily than her husband. He may either not respond at all, or say that he sees no point in "digging into all that stuff—it gets you nowhere." To a wife, her husband's silence usually implies a shutting out, a rejection, though he may not be rejecting her at all. On the contrary, most of us—when we allow ourselves to feel beneath the anger and the hurt—really want to reach out to our partners.

This misinterpretation of silence is substantially what happened in the marriage of Harry and Phyllis. Harry rebuffed with silence all the attempts Phyllis made to discuss the difficulties they were having together. With the channels of communication blocked, the difficulties loomed larger and multiplied. In a last, desperate try to reach her husband, Phyllis wrote him a long letter while she was away on a trip, baring her hurts and fears, asking him to make a fresh start in their troubled marriage by talking things over with her when she returned. When she got back, Harry never even mentioned that he'd gotten the letter. Bitterly disappointed, she brought herself to ask him if he'd read it. "Uh-huh," he answered—and that was it, the beginning and end of the discussion.

Overwhelming Fears

Even years later, as Phyllis talked about this to a marriage counselor, she still felt the pain of rejection, especially since she had made such an effort to overcome her own fears and reach Harry. Fortunately, their feeling for each other was strong in spite of their difficulties, so that they did eventually seek outside help. It was only then that Phyllis discovered Harry's lack of response didn't mean he didn't love her—he did very much in his own way—but that his upbringing had made it impossible for him to talk freely to any woman, especially about his feelings of love, anger, hurt, fear or helplessness. How could he admit to such feelings, Harry asked the marriage counselor? Through counseling he learned not only that he could, but that the resulting love between him and his wife was all the more genuine, all the richer.

Is outside help such as marriage counseling always necessary? Can other ways be tried first? Take the case of Dick and Ellen. Suppose, instead of assuming that Ellen deliberately treated him like a child, Dick asked her what she was feeling. Or suppose, to take an even greater "risk"—we always feel such a great risk in acknowledging the "awful" truth about ourselves—he chose one of their companionable, affectionate moments to give his wife as honest a picture of his real self as he could manage.

Or suppose Ellen could stop wanting Dick to be the "manly" man she thinks her father was—the man whose standards she had to meet in order to be loved. She might abandon the pretense that she's perfect and consistently does what she should, that she's a responsible person and Dick isn't. This would lift the iron curtain on the hurt little girl still lingering on in the woman, seeking approval or fighting with a disdainful father for her right to be a person.

What might happen? For each of them a revelation of their humanness with all its weaknesses and limitations, and so, less fear of each other; an arousing of compassion for the other's needs; an inevitable feeling of greater closeness because of their honest attempt to break down the wall between them.

In many marriages, because of similarity of personalities or backgrounds, husbands and wives manage to understand each other quite well. Even if they've started out by speaking foreign emotional languages, as it were, they've learned to listen and understand. When a husband and a wife are this comfortable with each other, whether they chat, talk seriously—or indeed, are silent—they have no problem in communication. Their acceptance and understanding of each other doesn't depend on a flow of words.

Keys to Communication

It depends on what underlies the words. In an address before the National Council of Family Relations, Dr. Robert Harper, Secretary of the American Association of Marriage Counselors, pointed out that "The spouse . . . must feel it is safe to indicate how he or she really feels . . . convinced that no real harm will come from his expression of how he actually feels."

Next, "a sensitive empathy is needed . . ." a response from husband or wife that amounts to saying, "I *understand* your feelings—no matter how childish, stupid or bizarre you may think them."

And beyond that, Dr. Harper suggested, must come the communication: "I find you lovable." In other words, Dick might convey, "Sure I get annoyed and irritated with you when I feel you're neglecting the house—or me. But never mind that. The point is, I'm no more perfect than you. I can flare up and tell you off. And you can too. But that doesn't destroy what we have together—for I love you, and I know you love me."

Perhaps most important was Dr. Harper's statement that "Couples must learn to feel that *you and I* matter as persons—not the words we say, not the principle of the thing, not what my mother or your friends or our neighbors think, not what the book or the marriage counselor says. If each of us learns to deal respectfully and lovingly with the you, me, and us of this relationship, meanings will somehow get communicated, marriage will be enjoyable much of the time, and problems will somehow get handled, if not solved."

Then, "Why can't we talk to each other?" becomes a question that is not raised so often. And when it is, it can be answered.

—By Priscilla Rosten and Ida Davidoff, Ed.D.

IS YOUR HUSBAND A GOOD FAMILY MAN?

GRANDFATHER'S only domestic service used to consist of carving the roast and winding the clocks. Anything else he considered beneath his masculine dignity. But today's young husband isn't ashamed to be caught wearing an apron. He can sizzle a steak, burp a baby and mix a formula.

Labor shortages, high wages, the vanishing domestic servant and inflation have made it necessary for today's young marrieds to do things for themselves, or go without. As a consequence there is no longer any sharp dividing line between man's work and woman's. Mom still has the babies and Pop does most of the supporting. Otherwise it has become a fairly fifty-fifty design for living. He bathes the kids, perhaps, and puts them to bed while she does the supper dishes. It gives them a longer evening together.

Not all men, of course, have taken readily to the new ways. Some still go on the principle that housework and raising the youngsters are exclusively in the woman's department. If your husband falls into this category, perhaps you can do something about it. But first you had better make sure that it isn't, at least partly, your attitude that's at fault.

Consciously, you may wish that your husband were more like the man next door who putters around with a screwdriver and is handy with the kids. But unconsciously, you may really prefer that he stick to making money, keep out from under your heels and leave the child-raising to you. Men have a way of obliging by doing what their wives expect of them. So if you aren't pleased with what you're getting, take another look at what you've been asking for.

Alicia, for example, consulted a family counselor because she wanted him to straighten Steve out for her.

"He doesn't take the least interest in the children," she complained. "I can't get him to go to PTA meetings with me or plan for any family fun the way other people do. When I worry about some problem I have with one of the children, he just says to settle it any way I like because they're my business, not his."

When Alicia was asked about her own feeling about children and family living, she glowed.

Husband Kept in Background

"Even when I was a little girl I used to fall asleep at night picking out names for the dozen children I wanted," she said. "I couldn't pass a baby carriage without stopping to peek under the hood. Everyone said what a wonderful mother I would make some day. I never wanted a career—just marriage. I'd daydream by the hour about the big church wedding I was going to have. I could see everything so clearly—me in floating tulle and a long train, the candles, flowers, and bridesmaids . . ."

"And the groom?" the counselor asked. "What did he look like?"

Alicia looked startled.

"I never thought much about him," she admitted. "He was just a sort of shadow there beside me . . ."

"I'm afraid he still is," the counselor told her. "I suspect that's the root of your difficulty. You've kept Steve a part of the background—sort of incidental to things you regarded as more important, such as acquiring a 'Mrs.' in front of your name and having babies to fuss over."

Marriage has and probably always will have more prestige value for women than for men. Bearing children is, after all, a woman's biological destiny and nature has written it deep in her body and emotions.

Sometimes the ego-satisfaction she gets out of homemaking and motherhood makes her reluctant to share her importance in these provinces with her mate. She may even be a little competitive toward her husband where the affections of the children are concerned. Without being conscious of it, she sometimes wants to matter more to them than he does.

She tends to hover over her young ones like a mother hen, cackling with cautions when their father approaches.

"Look out, you'll drop him! Here, give him to me."

"Don't play with him now. It's his bedtime and you'll get him too excited to go to sleep."

Then later, when her husband has lost interest or failed to develop any because he wasn't encouraged to early enough, this steal-the-act mother frets and complains that "Bill just never was much of a family man."

If you have a Bill, it will pay you to do a little soul-searching and see whether, without realizing it, you have been doing some of the things that make a man retire behind his newspaper or play golf instead of enjoying his youngsters and taking a sharp interest in his home and all its doings. Try answering the following questions as honestly as you can, even if this process of self-examination is a little painful.

Why Fathers Lack Interest

1. Do you feel that you must try to keep the children from "bothering" their father or getting on his nerves, as shown by such remarks as "Don't pester poor Daddy, he's tired," or "Let Mommie tie your shoelaces, Daddy's reading his paper"? Often this apparent "sparing" of a man isn't the kindness it appears to be. It is sometimes a form of rivalry for the children's affections and as such indicates considerable jealousy of the other parent's rights and claims. Or it may represent a transference of old, childish fears a woman has had toward her own father. A mother should not act as a buffer state between her husband and children. Rather, she should be a bridge across which they pass freely to each other.

2. Do you fairly frequently refer to the children as "my" son, or "my" daughter? This may be a dead giveaway of an unconscious desire not to share the credit or responsibility for them with your mate. You exclude him from the family group in doing so. And an excluded husband is seldom a good family man. Remember that he can't be a better father than you permit or encourage him to be.

3. Do you ever confide things in the children which they are not supposed to tell their father? Often these little confidences are innocent enough in themselves—a new hat which a woman fears her husband will consider a foolish purchase, the dime she slips a child for some "extra" when Dad is, she feels, too stern in trying to teach the youngster to get along on his allowance, the dancing lessons she is paying for out of the household budget. But secrets from Father are unfortunate. (Birthday and Christmas "surprises" aren't, of course, included in this category.) If you represent him as some sort of an ogre who has to be disarmed by keeping him in the dark, the children come to regard him with suspicion and distrust. This isn't conducive to the warmth and closeness he needs to feel if he is to be a good family man.

4. Do you make a "big stick" out of him with such threats as "Just wait until your father gets home," or "I'll tell Daddy if you don't stop that right away"? Turning father into a policeman is bound to make the children look on him with an awe that discourages the friendly feelings necessary between them. He is usually away from home all day, and the few hours he is able to

have with his family should be ones that the youngsters can look forward to and enjoy. It is not doing yourself, your husband or the children any favor to make his return at night associated with the fear of retribution.

Avoid Disparaging Father

5. Do you ever depreciate your husband in the presence of the children? It's a great mistake to belittle a man in the eyes of his youngsters. He can't be a good family man unless he has their admiration and respect. Some of the cowboy hero worship is undoubtedly a substitute for fathers whom children haven't been allowed to make into heroes.

"Other people seem to be able to afford new cars. But your father says we'll have to make do with the old one. Why doesn't he get up enough gumption to ask for a raise? He'll never get anywhere . . ."

Disparagements of this sort lower a man's stock with his children. And when he isn't permitted to matter enough to them, they seldom come to matter much to him.

6. Do you stand between the children and your husband when he tries to discipline them? It's a mistake for a woman to represent herself to a child as his best friend who can always be counted on to protect or defend him even from the consequences of his own misdeeds. No male has much incentive to be a good family man when his youngsters are encouraged to look on him as cruel, unkind or unfair. Never take sides against him or gang up on him with the kids. It erects barriers and alienates a man. In a good family there are no fences between members.

7. Do you tend to be "all mother" and not enough wife? When a woman spends all her time fussing over the children, her husband gets the idea that she hasn't much interest left over for him. The mother who "lives" for her children hasn't much life to invest in her man. It's bad for the youngsters and it isn't good for the husband-wife relationship. It's true that youngsters need a lot of attention and a strong sense of mattering a great deal to you. But so do husbands. And yours will be a fonder father if you aren't so fond a mother that all he gets are the tag ends of your frazzled energies. He'll like his children better if they aren't permitted to devour you.

Perhaps you commit none of these seven sins of maternity, yet still have occasion to complain that your husband is all wrapped up in business or golf and seems indifferent to his home and family. Then the probabilities are strong that he has a low aptitude for playing the role of family man. If he isn't a "natural" at it, you may as well accept the fact and start with him "as is" instead of deploring his inadequacies, nagging at him or wishing he were different.

Classification of Failures

It may help to classify him in terms of his problems and limitations; then perhaps you can help him improve his performance. In general the males who flop as family men have had a poor experience themselves in early childhood with their own fathers. Depending on how emotionally scarred it has left them, they fall into two main categories:

1. The man who would like to do better but doesn't know how. He's the easier of the two kinds of husband to cope with. At least he's willing to try. This man tends to feel that exacting discipline and obedience from the children is his chief paternal function. It's difficult for him to relax and just have fun with his kids. He can't put himself in their place. He thinks that the money he earns is his most important contribution to family life.

If your husband falls into this class you will have to be pretty forceful about combating the notion that making a living is the be-all and end-all of existence. It's essential to convince this man that it's equally important to learn how to live. You will have to make a special effort to see that he enters into the family activities and finds them rewarding.

Maybe he forgets birthdays and family anniversaries, so remind him in advance and even cast pretty broad hints. Suggest something suitable for him to bring home as a gift from a trip. He doesn't mind being told. In fact, he appreciates it. His intentions are good but he just has no feeling for these family matters.

You'd much rather he didn't require coaching, of course. But if that's the way he is, you may just as well play the role of prompter rather than wait for him to do things of his own accord and then be disappointed or resentful when he fails to remember. Perhaps you'll always have to coax him along a little by making it easy for him to do what's expected of him and putting up plenty of signs to point the way.

2. A more difficult, but by no means hopeless, proposition is the husband who not only has no feeling for family life but doesn't want to cultivate any because it involves assuming obligations that distress him. Even when reminded that one of the children has a piano or dance recital coming up, he ducks out of attending on the grounds that he has a big deal on and can't take the time.

If you have a husband of this sort, you may have to make a special plea for him to do certain things as a personal favor to you. Admittedly, this isn't ideal, but if you are willing to ask on a "just to please me" basis, he often develops an acquired taste for domesticity.

Try Realistic Approach

If your husband is indifferent to the plans and problems involved in raising the children, you can often reach him on his own ground by saying, "You believe in training your employees, don't you? How can you expect the youngsters to be successful or get along well unless you're willing to put in a little time and effort helping to train them, too?"

If he plays golf every weekend or otherwise seeks his diversions independently of his family, appeal to his good sportsmanship to give you and the children every other weekend. Then see that he enjoys himself. Unless he gets some pleasure from family associations and activities, he can't take pleasure in them. So, don't plan a picnic if he hates flies and food out of a basket. Make sure it's something he enjoys doing.

Just keep getting this type of husband into things one way or another and he may get the hang of it after a while. Not having had enough warming family experiences in his own childhood, he is lacking in certain feeling-memories just as some people are tone-deaf. So be patient with him and don't feel that he is being stubborn or resistant.

Above all, don't reproach him for his inadequacies and shortcomings. He needs plenty of approval for even his smallest efforts. By being understanding, resourceful and appreciative you'll win him over in the end though he will probably never be a sentimentalist.

Why bother to turn a lone wolf into a domesticated animal when it takes so much effort? The answer is—you don't know what you're missing until you do. Children need two parents right from the start. They want a father who is concerned about scraped knees, hurt feelings, refusal to eat vegetables, measles, mumps and trouble with multiplication tables.

When they reach the teens you need a man on the job. Often dad has more influence with young people after puberty than mother has. In a survey of Harvard and Radcliffe students, over 25 per cent reported that they were more influenced by their fathers than by their mothers during their teens.

If a man has participated in the homely routines of early childhood, from reading a bedtime story to pulling down training panties for the toddler, he has paid his initiation dues to the fraternity of fatherhood and earned his right to be warmly regarded by his growing sons and daughters. Having comforted a colicky baby on the night stretch, he is likely to find that he has an eager rhumba partner on the dance floor in his middle age or an opponent to be reckoned with on the tennis court.

The mother who has encouraged closeness, warmth, friendship and understanding between her youngsters and their father now reaps her reward, too. More and more she finds herself saying happily, "Just ask your father. He's sure to know."

Absorbing and delightful as children are, they aren't yours for keeps. Sooner than you think, they must be released to their own destinies. Then you and your husband will find that you are going to need each other more than ever before. —By O. Spurgeon English, M.D., and Constance J. Foster

GROWING UP EMOTIONALLY

EMOTIONAL growth, far more difficult to understand than physical growth, often alarms and confuses parents. We hear them say, "I don't know what has got into him; he used to be such an affectionate child!" We see mothers worried when a child begins to run to his father instead of preferring her as he used to. We feel the anxiety of parents of both sexes as children begin to take their loves outside the family to others for the first time. Yet all of these are part of the normal pattern of emotional development in healthy human beings.

Baby's first love is himself. He starts with so little experience and sensitivity. It takes him some time even to be aware that there are other persons to love. First he discovers himself. He finds his fingers and toes and enjoys them lustily. He kicks and sucks and jabbers and laughs with himself as only a baby can. He gets hungry and yells for food. If attention does not come at once, he becomes angry and red in the face. It does not occur to him that there may be reasons why his meal is delayed. He is pleased when his demands are met and angry when his needs must wait. It is as simple as that—at first.

All of us slip back to this first stage from time to time. A sick child or a convalescing husband may act like a petulant infant. A young adolescent girl just coming to terms with her rapidly changing body may spend hours before the mirror in an orgy of self-interest that harks back to her baby days. During any personal crisis preoccupation with self is normal. It is only when this love of self continues over a long period of time that it becomes cause for alarm.

Mother is the child's next love. He learns to associate her with pleasure and satisfaction. She brings food and warmth and cuddling when he is hungry and cold and lonely. As the baby nurses at his mother's breast his hands fondle her and his fingers hold tight to hers. At this stage the baby smiles and welcomes his mother with his first efforts of outgoing love. But when his mother does not come at once he scolds in his own way and acts as though he does not love her any more.

Untying Mother's Apron Strings

Some mothers keep on loving their growing children as if they were still babies. It is hard for a child to grow up if he feels that by doing so he will hurt his mother. So he remains tied to his mother because he doesn't dare break away. But with a little encouragement the normal youngster goes on to other stages in his development.

A child is not very big when he first becomes aware that someone besides himself loves his mother. Right then the child has his first experience with "the eternal triangle" in family life. He loves his mother. His father loves her, too. So the child is jealous and tries to rival his father for his mother's attention.

This early hostility is normally outgrown as soon as the boy tries to be like his father. He struts around the house with his daddy's hat on. He "reads" the paper in the same chair, with the identical posture he has seen his father use. He acts out his father's role so feelingly that he *is* his daddy. Years later he may still be following in his father's footsteps as he chooses a vocation or looks for a girl "Just Like the Girl That Married Dear Old Dad."

Girls outgrow their earliest jealousy by identifying themselves with their mothers and acting out being married to their fathers. The preschool girl plays house, cuddles and scolds her dolls, cooks make-believe meals and welcomes her daddy home very much as she sees her mother do. When she feels the part intensely she may say to her mother, "Go away, I will take care of Daddy myself." Father is her favorite now, and her first model of the kind of man she wants to marry. Many girls do eventually choose husbands very much like their fathers.

Feelings of brotherhood arise in early childhood enjoyment of brothers and sisters. But there are times in the best of families when children do not enjoy one another at all. An older child may look upon a younger brother or sister as a pest, and often he is. Siblings, whether brothers or sisters, are not only "pests" but also keen rivals for the attention and affection of their parents, for belongings, privileges and in the never-ending struggle of competition to achieve. Thus, squabbling, bickering and teasing among children in the family is a normal part of growing up. As each child is helped to feel secure in himself, he becomes increasingly able to tolerate and enjoy his brothers and sisters. As he grows up emotionally he is able to overcome this early rivalry, but it does not happen all at once. It is not banished by pleading or scolding. The child grows to love his brothers and sisters as his capacity to appreciate others develops.

Enjoying New Attachments

When kindergartners embrace each other adoringly, the humor of the situation is usually far more apparent than its real value. Feelings of affection and love for other children in childhood help wean the child away from attachments within the family that might become too binding. Loves outside the family give him faith that others can be trusted. If parents realize that it is very important for the child to care for others outside the family, that it is a part of normal love development, later in life the child will be able to turn to others with full confidence that it is safe to love them.

About halfway through elementary school it is usual for youngsters to have close friends of their own age and sex to whom they are devoted. These early loves may be marked by expressions of intense loyalty, by inseparable devotion to the same interests, activities, clothing and behavior, and by the intimate sharing of secrets and confidences. This is a normal stage. It helps the girl to feel her way into womanhood by association with other girls at a time when she is still unprepared for a closer association with boys. Also, boys gang together at this age in overt masculinity-striving in which no girl has a chance.

Late in childhood or very early in the teens comes the crush on an older person of one's own sex. It is then that the boy worships the coach, or the girl adores a favorite teacher with an intensity and preoccupation that may bewilder and frighten parents. These attachments help wean the child from too close dependence upon father and mother and provide experience in loving adults outside the family. Intense though such love may be, it does not last too long with the normal young adolescent. It serves to prepare the child for the next, even more exciting stage in love development.

The schoolgirl infatuation for the man old enough to be her father is something more than fodder for the cartoonist. It is a very real stage in the process of growing up emotionally. Although ordinarily less obvious, it is not unusual for the young teen-age boy to fall in love with a much older woman, and to suffer in silence or let himself in for an agony of ridicule until he gets over his infatuation. The girl or boy often feels safe and secure with the older person of the other sex. In a way, this person is a stepping-stone to the boy-girl relationships that lie just ahead.

Boy Meets Girl

At last, somewhere in the teens comes the stage at which boy meets girl and they find they love each other. Now comes dating, going steady, becoming engaged and getting married. Into it go all the unfinished loves of earlier years, some self-love, a portion of mother-dependence, some father-figure, a bit of this or that crush, all in a complex weave of feeling that should be appreciated for the exquisite tapestry it is. Parents can endanger the emerging patterns of heterosexual involvement by too much pressure for social success, or too great anxiety or too much interference. They help most if they set an example of happiness in marriage, accepting with understanding and appreciation the happiness of being young and in love.

With some success in the earlier stages comes the readiness for a more generalized outpouring of tender love and kindness. The maturing human finds his spirit welling up in surges of sympathy for others. He develops a love for children. He grows up and *out* until his love encompasses all mankind. This is the hope of the world. This is the creative power upon which all great religions rest and upon which our human destiny depends.

Just as parents help children grow up physically by giving them food and encouragement, so may they help, rather than hinder, emotional development. Ridiculing a child's "puppy loves" is like making fun of his efforts to walk. Expressing fear and anxiety over a youngster's temporary attachment to another may cause him to freeze at that spot, much as a tree-climbing boy is frozen by his mother's shriek of terror. Wise parents stand by and let, as well as help, their children grow up. They accept each stage of growth as the rich, fascinating new experience it is. They love their child for being himself. They are there to help if he needs them. They have faith in life, in growth, in their children and in themselves.   —*By Evelyn Millis Duvall, Ph.D.*

SHOULD CHILDREN
BE GIVEN A CHOICE?

NOWADAYS we don't order our children around, as was once the custom. We're more apt to give them choices rather than commands. This is fine. It respects the child's preferences, recognizes his individuality and helps him to learn how to make his own decisions rather than having them made for him. If used wisely, choices can be one of the most effective and painless ways of avoiding friction in home relationships.

"Would you rather have me read a story to you before you go to bed or would you rather watch television for another fifteen minutes?" has a magical way of dissolving conflict about going to bed.

Even adults succumb to the choice technique and all good salesmen know it. Haven't you often found yourself signing on the dotted line after one of them asks, "Which of the two do you prefer?" or, "Shall I have it delivered this week or next?" So it's pretty natural for children to be won over rather easily when you offer them a pleasant "Would you like to wear the blue dress or the yellow one?" or "Which doll do you want to take to bed with you tonight?"

This method is likely to work like a charm at certain ages, in certain situations and with some children. But there are other ages which find choice-making extremely difficult and even painful. And there are some situations in which no child should be expected to make a wise or happy choice. Parents need to know what to expect at these times and be prepared to cope with the problems realistically. They have to have a sort of yardstick of what their youngsters can decide and when they should make decisions for them.

Gesell Institute Discoveries

We are indebted to Dr. Arnold Gesell and his associates for some of these discoveries about what relationship a child's age has to the ease or difficulty with which he finds it possible to make a choice. Dr. Gesell explains that the average youngster of three, five, seven or ten can usually choose between two alternatives with relative comfort and benefit.

These are ages of comparative stability. The pressures of previous growth challenges have been absorbed and assimilated. The child is more or less in equilibrium with his environment and the demands it makes on him. He is under less inner stress and strain. The general feeling he has of being equal to things makes him able to face choices without too much emotional conflict. He even enjoys having some choices to make.

Mary, age three, was always cranky after her nap and uncooperative about getting dressed to go out. Then her mother hit on the happy idea of suggesting that she choose between whether she would like to wear her pink socks or her red ones to the park. This started her on the business of getting dressed and they had a half-hour longer in the sunshine instead of spending the time in a hassle at home.

But there are other ages when the offer of a choice may do more harm than good. It is frustrating and even frightening to a child when he is asked to make decisions for which he is unprepared. The two-and-a-half-year-old, for example, is temperamentally unable to choose easily or wisely between two alternatives. Whichever he picks, the other immediately becomes more desirable.

As Dr. Gesell puts it: "Life is charged with double alternatives. Every pathway has become a two-way street. He has a great deal of intermediating to do between contrary impulses, and yet he has to become acquainted with both alternatives. Being inexperienced as well as immature, he often makes two choices where he should make one; or he makes the wrong choice; or he makes none at all."

Steer the toddler to choose. Obviously parents must do everything they can to steer a two-and-a-half-year-old gently but firmly in the direction it is best for him to go. Don't confuse him by offering him any more choices than necessary. Especially don't offer him choices that can be answered by "no," such as "Would you like to?" or "Do you want to?" "No" is already his favorite word at this age and sometimes he doesn't even mean it. It is much safer to say, "Now it's time to eat," than, "Are you ready for lunch?"

A nursery school teacher says she has found that the magic words for this age group are: "You *need* to wash your hands," "*First* we'll put the toys away," "*When you're finished* we'll have juice," "You *forgot* to eat your carrots," "*It's time* for rest." She also recommends, "You *have to have* a bath." Such phrases help the child to organize himself and avoid resistance. They spark him to proceed in a forward direction instead of getting stalled in the grip of opposing choices.

Helping the four-year-old. Four is another age when choices are poorly handled. The typical four-year-old is not so much vacillating, like the two-and-a-half-year-old, as expansive. His ebullience knows no bounds. Since he wants all of everything and knows no reasonable limits, choices are apt to get sadly out of hand. Since he does nothing by halves, he may use choices to lead you on a merry chase. Anyone who has listened to the tall tales of the four-year-old knows how adept he is at elaborating. It is because he can think of so many things he wants to do that he finds it hard to narrow down to one choice.

Susie's mother had told her that she could ask anyone she liked to go on a trip to the beach with them. When they were ready to start, her parents were dismayed to find eight children waiting to get into the car.

"But you said anyone I liked and I like all of them," wailed Susie.

In dealing with the four-year-old, unless you want to get in over your head, it's wise to outline plans rather carefully in advance. Make your own rules, set your own limits and then stick to them. Otherwise he may get you into situations you never dreamed existed. Don't rein him in. But do tell him what you expect and be pretty specific about it.

Say something like this: "We're going on a picnic and you will sit on the back seat next to Grandma. When we get to the beach you'll play in the sand but not go in the water because it's still too cold. We won't buy anything to eat at the stand. But after our picnic lunch you may have a nickel for a candy bar."

Six-year-olds are uncertain. Six-year-olds are among the world's worst choosers. Their trouble is that they want both of two alternatives. Having made a choice, the child then regrets it and wants the opposite. He'll hold you up indefinitely while he tries to decide between caramels and an almond bar. Whichever he picks, he is likely to cry on leaving the store because he didn't

take the other. It is hard for him to be decisive or make up his mind about any choice and stick to it.

Like the two-and-a-half-year-old, six is painfully aware of all the opposites. He fluctuates wildly between "I will" and "I won't." He is troubled by more alternatives than he can manage. All of this is merely because he is now growing out of the inexperience and placidity of being five. But in the meantime he is hard pressed by new emotional tensions and this makes him temporarily uncertain. Edna St. Vincent Millay pictures the conflict graphically in her poem.

> Come along in then, little girl!
> Or else stay out!
> But in the open door she stands
> And bites her lips and twists her hands
> And stares upon me trouble-eyed:
> "Mother," she says, "I can't decide!"

For the time being the six-year-old needs to have as many as possible of his choices made for him. Don't overload him with decisions. Say, "I'd take the strawberry ice cream if I were you—you had vanilla yesterday," or "This is a good book. You'll like it." Present him quietly with what you want him to do, or eat, or wear and you'll really be doing him a big favor as well as sparing yourself a lot of unnecessary agony. Otherwise he's likely to see-saw back and forth between this and that, keeping the whole family in a dither.

Eight-year-olds vacillate. Again at eight there is a period of marked vacillation between choices. Strangely enough it is now usually about unimportant little things—the choice of a Valentine, whether he will take puffed rice or puffed wheat for breakfast, a decision about a second helping. The proprietor of a hobby shop said he hated to see an eight-year-old come into the store. It recently took one of them two hours to decide between two airplane construction models costing twenty-five cents apiece!

But parents had better make sure that all choices offered him are acceptable because once the eight-year-old has made up his mind, it's hard to budge him. He's reasonable, though, and often says, "You decide for me" when he is having trouble in choosing. He has often matured enough by this time to recognize his own shortcomings and difficulties. He even has good sense enough to turn off a radio or television program if it scares him. One mother of an eight-year-old was surprised when he walked out of a movie and came home in the middle of the show.

"I was afraid I'd dream about it," he explained.

Eleven-year-olds need direct motivation. Choices are often worthless around the age of eleven because the child frequently uses them to defy or inconvenience his parents, like the boy who refused to go to school one morning because of an examination he dreaded. When he was told, "You'll go to school or else spend the whole day in bed," he quickly snatched off his clothes and jumped into bed. He insisted on holding his mother to the choice she had inadvertently offered. Some more direct method of motivating a child's behavior usually proves more effective at this age period. Just outline what you want him to do and take it for granted (keeping your fingers crossed!) that he will comply. Or try using a little bargaining such as "You dry the dishes for me while I dress the puppet for your show." The eleven-year-old is interested in "swapping" and "making a deal." He wants to know "What do I get out of it?" Make anything you ask of him attractive enough and he will "buy" it.

Troubling situations. Besides certain ages at which free choices are risky business, there are also certain situations where they are likely to cause trouble. A tired or convalescent child is a poor candidate for choices. He needs to have things made rather easy and simple for him.

Jean was at an age when choices are usually effective. But she was over-tired after an exciting birthday party. Her mother made the mistake of telling her that she could choose her favorite new gift to take to bed with her. The little girl couldn't decide among all the dolls, games and story books she had received. She ended up in a tantrum that could have been avoided if her mother had simply put the weary child to bed.

Another situation in which choices are likely to work out disastrously is the new or unusual one. The first time the Clarks took Billy to a restaurant, they told him he could choose his own meal from the menu. He was already overstimulated by the novel surroundings. He ended by hurling his fruit cup to the floor because by that time he wanted tomato juice instead. Unless a child is experienced enough to handle the situation, by all means order for him and don't raise the issue of too much choice.

Finally, don't risk offering a choice where it is important that a child act in a certain way and the choice of the alternative would be unfortunate.

"You can choose between taking your nap like a good girl or else missing the drive-in movie with the rest of us tonight," three-year-old Barbara was informed. The child was too excited by the prospect of the movie to go to sleep. As a consequence the whole family had to stay home and the older children blamed Barbara for their disappointment.

A great deal depends, too, on the personality of the youngster to whom you offer choices. Some children seem to be just naturally clear-cut and decisive. They exult in the freedom of choices and make them easily. You can safely count on them to stick to their decisions without undue confusion or later regrets.

Other children, even at ages ordinarily favorable to choices, are rebellious and obstinate. They are inclined to argue a lot and be on the off side of everything. Or else they never make a choice without wishing they had chosen its alternative.

Be Fair and Flexible

Giving a child freedom of choice makes good sense only if it is appropriate for his age. Otherwise you may be saddling him with decisions that are too much for him. This leads only to despair and frustration. Especially is this true if you imply that you leave so much up to him because you love him. Then your love becomes an extra burden because he must justify it by his choices.

Parents need to be very sure, too, that they are not unconsciously using choices to manipulate a child and get their own way. The Stantons are divorced and each is a little jealous of the time their son spends with the other. They asked whether he wouldn't prefer to go to boarding school and listed all the advantages of the school they had selected as the best one for him. Then they said, "Now it's up to you. We'll abide by what you decide." Twelve-year-old Peter really wanted to stay at home near his pals. But he didn't dare say so because he knew that each of his parents was uncomfortable when he was living with the other one. So he let himself be influenced into "choosing" a school. Later he was unhappy there and tried to get out of having to stay. But his mother and father reminded him, "You chose it of your own free will. Now you'll have to stick by your decision."

We have to be fair and flexible while children are learning to choose. Choices are a happy, democratic way of family living. But they can backfire badly if you count too much on them when your child's age and temperament or the circumstances themselves are all against a favorable outcome. Then youngsters are better handled in more positive ways.

—*By Constance J. Foster*

LOVE AND HATE GO HAND IN HAND

A^T a discussion group meeting, a pretty mother described the post card her young daughter had sent from summer camp to the four-year-old in the family. "Dear Ronny," it said. "I am having a fine time. How are you? Love and hate. Karen."

Of course, everyone laughed understandingly. But do we truly realize what a tremendous revolution lies behind Karen's ability to communicate her own plus and minus feelings? Today we say that love and hate go hand in hand.

We go even further: we say that we cannot genuinely and fully love someone unless we can accept as normal our own sometime anger and hatred toward him—and his sometime anger and hatred toward us.

But when we were children, anger and hatred were almost always considered evil character traits. "Nice" people didn't experience such feelings or, if they did, they were careful to hide them so that other "nice" people were not aware of this secret depravity. As a matter of fact, human beings throughout the ages have felt ashamed and guilty of any sign that they might be less than filled with feelings of brotherly love (meanwhile behaving in far-from-brotherly fashion).

If the research into mental health during the past twenty-five years had made no other contribution than to assure us that all human beings naturally experience feelings of anger and hostility, it would have justified itself as of immeasurable value to parents. Slowly but definitely it will bring about some exciting changes in our relationships.

Because our new understanding is so recent, however, parents are often caught between the old attitudes built into us and our new understanding. As a result, many of us still feel uncertain about our handling of hostile feelings. And someone may ask, "Well, what was wrong with the old way? It never occurred to me as a child that I could or did hate my parents or brothers and sisters—and I grew up all right."

Did we grow up "all right"?

Repressed Hostility

We are learning now that human beings have often paid a high price for believing that "good people" always love and only "bad people" hate. The price we paid was damage inflicted sometimes upon ourselves, sometimes upon others. Children were taught that if you were a nice, decent sort of person, you loved and respected your family—no ifs, ands or buts. When, for a moment, normal, healthy, growing youngsters did think something mean about someone else, their own feelings frightened them. If they blurted their thoughts out loud they were severely punished, so hate became a secret thing—it went "underground." Sometimes the burden of keeping the secret was so great that all kinds of fears and anxieties occurred. Often the angry feelings that had no outlet turned inward on the individual himself. A little girl who was angry and jealous of her baby sister could be so ashamed and guilty that she would begin to feel she was not worthy, no one could love her, no one *did* love her.

Or take the case of a little boy who was constantly angry because his parents demanded that he compete scholastically with a cousin who happened to have unusual gifts as a student. This little boy was not only anxious because he could not fulfill what his parents demanded of him, he also was struggling constantly to control and hide his resentment over the unfair, ever-present demand. He had to use up so much energy hiding his anger from his parents and from himself that he could not concentrate on learning to read in school. He became a problem reader.

Some children who learned to control their angry feelings around those whom they feared hit out later at other people's property or at targets weaker than themselves, such as younger children in another neighborhood. Sometimes as these children grew older their anger came out publicly and openly in the form of hating groups of people, encouraging irrational prejudices and suspicions of others different from themselves.

We have learned that many people grew up still feeling so frightened and guilty about their less-than-lovely thoughts that they got sick rather than ever get angry. Headaches, digestive upsets, respiratory difficulties, circulatory complications, all might in some way be connected with mounting tension because the victims felt themselves to be less than perfect human beings.

Capacity for Many Feelings

And we have learned at the same time that we are all many-sided; that we have wonderful potentialities for love and compassion and sensitivity—and for feelings of rivalry, competitiveness and anger. What a relief! Understanding our many-sidedness, we can free ourselves and our children from the ravages of guilt when we do have negative reactions. We can save ourselves and our children from the emotional process in which anger is turned against the self and the human being attempts inwardly to tear himself to pieces rather than allow himself to feel an unacceptable emotion. Psychiatrists know only too well how vicious and self-damaging the process can be.

Freed, we can enjoy the vigor of our feelings and use our healthy drives to develop the best that's in us. After all, pride and courage, belief in our own worth as individuals, start very often with our capacity to want things for ourselves and to put up a fight, if necessary, to let the world know each of us matters. A young mother told how her five-year-old son confessed that he really liked himself better than anybody else. "Good!" she replied. "Liking yourself first will help you to like other people."

We know that we do make it more possible for children to like themselves as we come more and more to accept their human, hostile feelings. But if we say that it is normal to hate sometimes, will we encourage children to become cruel or even delinquent? How will children learn to respect their parents and teachers if we let them express freely what they feel? As one father put it, "So maybe my kids won't get ulcers—but don't they have to learn to behave decently to other people?"

Of course they do! Understanding the many-sidedness of human nature doesn't mean encouraging children—or adults—to *act* on their unsocial impulses. While his mother was entertaining guests on the back terrace, a little boy of four decided it would be fun to pour sugar in the mustard, was told he shouldn't—and ran down to the garden and began to tear up a flower bed he knew was particularly cherished. The mother stood by helplessly, perhaps afraid to act with decision before her visitors. Then she said with a nervous laugh, "Well, experts say it's normal for him to be angry!" What she could have done was to stop the destruction immediately! Not only to protect the flowers but, much more important, her son, who was asking for help. It must be terrifying to be little and at the mercy of strong impulses that make you feel guilty and anxious—and not have your parents help you to control yourself. There is a world of difference between understanding that a feeling is normal and permitting that feeling to take the form of destructive action. It is true that once this little child would have been punished severely and told he was a very bad boy. But knowing that kind of handling was harmful doesn't mean we should do the opposite.

Feelings must be channeled. We can accept an angry child's feelings but not necessarily his behavior. Instead of destroying, he can put it into words, if possible, or he can hit his doll, he can stamp his feet or hammer his pegs for a while if that will help—or perhaps he needs some time alone. In other words he is *not* a naughty boy and beyond understanding or forgiveness. But his feelings must be channeled by older and wiser people toward mature ways of handling them. Children want to feel comfortable about getting angry but they don't want to be carried away so that they do or say things they are sorry for.

Interestingly, children who turn against society, in one form of delinquency or another, are rarely if ever those who had help in handling their feelings. Children who are aware of their natural feelings, who have felt free to express them, are better able to translate them into acceptable behavior. The little girl who signed her postcard with "love and hate" is not only comfortable with her mixed feelings, she seems to enjoy her brother more, for being able to accept both of these feelings.

Today children learn that even the most devoted and loving parents get angry at each other and their offspring once in a while. They learn that they are also subject to such feelings. They learn that even the very "nicest" people can have mean thoughts and say cruel things to each other. Why isn't this frightening? Because the strong bond of family love can withstand the letting-off of steam that might prove far more dangerous if expressed outside the safety of home.

Love and hate go hand in hand. We start with that truth. We don't shy away from it. And then we move on from there to work toward greater maturity, understanding, compassion, sensitivity—toward greater love.

—By Eda J. LeShan

DO YOU PUT A PRICE ON LOVE?

MANY of us bring children into this world joyfully and hopefully, only to find that by the time they reach teen age, they have become sullen, resentful strangers. Such an attitude of resentment toward parents is often the result of using emotion to keep children under control. Both love and anger can be used in this way with disastrous results. For what the parent is saying is, "Be a good boy or I will be angry."

John, a lively, active child, was already being exposed to anger at the age of two. Since John's mother and father were determined that there would be no spoiled children in their family, they set high standards for his behavior. When John didn't settle down quietly at naptime, he was scolded or spanked. When he staged tantrums over small difficulties in an effort to get more of his mother's time and attention, he had cold water thrown in his face.

Shortly after John was two, he had a baby sister. His parents gave happy attention to her but frequently gave disapproving attention to John. Soon John's resentment of the situation began to show up in asthma attacks. His mother and father were up with him night after night. At the same time, they became stricter with him because they felt he was "a big boy now" and should be made to behave. When he didn't, they became quite angry and punished him for even the slightest infraction of their many, many rules.

What happened to John? By the time he was five, he was a "good" boy, but his resentment showed in nail-biting, bed-wetting, attacks of asthma, and timidity in the presence of other children.

There are many Johns in the world. Not all of them have asthma. Not all of them bed-wet. Some of them become difficult, rebellious, instead of extra "good" children, but all of them are resentful and insecure because of the angry treatment they received from parents. In adolescence their bottled-up resentment often pops out to astound their parents who are used to submission. Their bewildered parents don't know what has happened. They were looking forward to having children. They disciplined them, they explained, only for their own good. But now, in spite of their efforts, they find in their son or daughter many undesirable personality traits.

Love as a Weapon

In contrast to the parents who use anger to get obedience from their children are the parents who use love as a weapon of discipline. What they say, in one way or another, to their children is, "If you behave the way I ask you to, I will love you. Otherwise, I won't."

An example of the effect of this method is Peter. Peter's mother, who had found that physical punishment failed to keep her lively intelligent boy from being what she considered "naughty," tried using reason insidiously mixed with emotion. Since she was a widow, she buttressed her appeals by frequent mention of the fact that she was all alone. Actually she didn't say, "Be good for mother." She did say, "Why can't you be a good boy? Why must you fight with other boys? Why don't you come home when mother wants you to?"—always with the implication that a boy who loved his mother would naturally do or not do these things.

As time went on, Peter's mother started the custom of talking to him at night after he was in bed, when he was especially defenseless, discussing why he should be a good boy—mother worked so hard for Peter—mother tried so hard to help Peter—mother did special things and went without things just for Peter. These sessions often deteriorated into a handkerchief-wringing time for both. Poor Peter didn't know what was the matter! The more his mother cried over his trivial offenses, the more convinced he became that there was something terribly wrong with him.

Why does such use of emotion—either love or anger—disturb a child? He feels guilty because he is afraid he doesn't love his parents enough, yet he senses there is something wrong somewhere which is not his fault. So he feels resentment toward them along with his guilt feelings. It is a vicious circle, resulting in the conviction on the part of the young person that he is not good enough since his parents obviously don't think he is.

If parents show constant anger over little things, it makes the child feel that he is "bad"—not good enough to have anyone like him. So he develops a sense of resentment, of insecurity and of unworthiness.

Is your child resentful of authority, rebellious, confused about many aspects of his life, discontented or easily discouraged? Does he feel inferior to others, persecuted, inadequate or insecure? Does he bite his nails, stammer or bed-wet? Does he have trouble with arithmetic? Your answers to these questions are a good indication of whether you are handling him wisely.

Direct Irritation Against Act

Suppose you feel that you should change your way of dealing with your children. Perhaps you admit that you become too irritated with your child over trifles. You find it hard to keep calm, even though you may want to. Keeping quiet when you are angry won't do any good because irritation will show itself in tenseness and in facial expression. Admit your irritation but direct it against the act, not the child. And it is important to ask yourself, for instance, how important it is when a five-year-old always says "stinky." Is the teen-age daughter who complains about doing the dishes really reprehensible or only behaving as a girl will sometimes? Should the seven-year-old who wets his bed be looked upon as "bad" on purpose? Viewed objectively, most people can see that none of these things should anger a mature person.

Does the fact that there is danger in ruling by emotion mean that children should live their lives in a sterile, unemotional environment? No. Emotions, even occasional anger, do have their place in our relationships with our children, but it is the positive use of positive emotions—love, approval and so forth—which should be stressed. We should assure our children that we love them no matter what they do. They need to be certain of this. At the same time, we should help them to enjoy behaving in socially acceptable ways.

Sometimes a guidance clinic can help both parents and children to straighten out their ideas and emotions. John, who was ruled by anger, was taken to a guidance clinic at six years of age. Both he and his parents were able to get rid of their resentments, bringing about a definite improvement in family morale. At the end of a year, with the end of "rule by anger" by his parents, John's bed-wetting, asthma and nail-biting were lessened and visits to the clinic stopped. Six months after that, John was like other boys in his occasional resentments and angers, but his timidity in the presence of other children had vanished, as had his nail-biting.

More and more, the influence of emotional environment on children is coming to be recognized as a strong force in their mental, physical, personality and emotional development. Do not be afraid of strong emotion, but learn to use it constructively to give fire, vigor and happiness to living.

—By Elizabeth Lee Schweiger

FOOD FOR MENTAL HEALTH

WHEN she's worried and anxious, one woman eats more than when she's not. Once, when one of her boys caught his foot in his bike and she nervously awaited the doctor, she ate a pound of cookies without even realizing what she was doing. This woman is fat. Another is slender to the point of skinniness—she reaches for cigarettes more often than she does for food. One little boy has never eaten a bite of meat in his life, while a young girl appears to live on soft drinks and quantities of milk. Another child after his parents were divorced ate constantly, and gained ten pounds in a month.

All of us know people like these who periodically or habitually seem to eat as much out of emotional hunger as out of physical. (Or refuse to eat not because they lack appetite, but to fulfill some emotional need.) Yes, food and eating for all of us are tied up with emotional gratification. For all of us, food means security and comfort as well as an end to physical hunger. For infants and children especially, food means love and to be fed means to be loved. ("What is a mother?" psychiatrists asked disturbed children in the course of working with them. "She gives you food," said most of the children.)

Trouble—in the shape of eating disturbances—brews when the emotional needs of eating come to outweigh the physical, not once in a while (which is true of all of us), but continuously.

The number of children who suffer from more or less severe eating disorders is disturbingly large. Twenty-four per cent of all pediatric cases, say two well known authorities, Doctors O. Spurgeon English and Gerald H. Pearson, consist of the emotional disorders of eating and appetite. "Many pediatricians consider," they say, "that nearly every child has had some more or less marked disturbance in eating by the time he attains seven years."

What goes wrong? What contributes to this widespread picture of eating disorder? To find out, first take a look at the way eating and food habits normally develop.

No parent has to be reminded that an infant, new as he is, is an old conservative. He gets used to a set routine—even if he's on a self-demand routine. If the nipple is changed, if he's changed from breast to bottle or cup, if his banana is lumpier than usual, he's likely to express his displeasure in no uncertain terms.

Development of Eating Habits

When he's between six months and a year old, he begins to find pleasure in messing with his food, feeling its texture, poking it with experimental fingers, bringing it weavingly to his elusive mouth, batting merrily at the bottle or the breast. Babies do this instinctively because their fingers are growing more dexterous. Inexpert finger feeding is a necessary preliminary step to accomplish self-feeding, just as crawling is to walking. Troublesome as is the mess a baby makes in this preparation to feed himself, dislike as we may to mop the baby, mop the floor and wash his clothes—the mess is part and parcel of the development stage he is in. If we interfere with it too much, if we wholly prevent the baby from wallowing in his normal spilling, smearing and pouring, we are setting up a roadblock on his way to healthy eating habits.

When he's about a year and a half, a baby's appetite is apt to decrease—and stay decreased through his second and third years. Again, this is part of a developmental process—the rapid growth that characterized infancy has come to an end. Fussiness about food often comes in the wake of this slowing up. Emphatic preferences develop, preferences that baffle, irritate and mystify mothers. "Take away those weak peaches," screams a two-year-old, confronted with peaches whose consistency is softer than usual. "It's too red," "It's too round," "It's too smelly!" object other moppets who a short while before happily guzzled everything put before them.

The color, form and consistency of food are vital considerations to a child of this age. Still worse from our point of view, his eating habits are riddled by rituals, taboos and compulsions. (All common to his age.) He may, forsaking all other menus, demand that the same dish be served over and over again daily without end; he may become mystically attached to one spoon, or one cup, or one plate, and eat from no other.

At three, our little friend goes off on food jags and food strikes. But at five, the first glimmering of civilized behavior flickers through the jungle of his primitive antics. The five-year-old is a budding social personality—he has his eye on his peers and is likely to be influenced by what they eat and how they eat it. At six, the appetite of infancy is likely to return with a bang but, "He spills, stuffs his mouth, chews with his mouth open," say those specialists in child development, Drs. Gesell and Ilg. "He grabs for food,

knocks things over, teeters in his chair, kicks table legs and criticizes the behavior of others."

Throughout this period of early childhood—again as no parent needs to be reminded—most children prefer plain foods. They suspect sauces, view stews and casseroles with alarm.

This, then, is the normal eating behavior pattern of most young children. Of course, the pattern varies from child to child. And it varies, too, with the emotional climate of the household—for feelings are a great conditioner of appetite. All children are likely to eat less when they are temporarily unhappy, afraid, angry, excited or anxious.

Common Eating Pattern

Vary as the normal eating pattern does from child to child, and vary as it may with the emotional climate of each family, its broad outlines are common to all. Most pediatricians, psychiatrists and parents who have been through the mill are convinced that nothing but trouble comes from ignoring the pattern or trying to force a child out of its normal stages.

Certainly, our children need to have an adequate diet. (But they don't necessarily need to have it at every meal. Nor even during the course of any given week.) And certainly, we as parents neither can nor should ignore the demands of society that we civilize our children; they need to be reasonably unfussy eaters, and they need to have table manners or they will be headed for trouble in another direction.

However—and this is a big however—we aren't likely to achieve these goals by failing to understand or ignoring the children's attitudes toward food —or by putting too much pressure on them to conform to our own adult tastes and ways of eating.

As a matter of fact, the more we can reduce the pressures that surround our children's eating, the less trouble they—and we—will have.

The biggest of these pressures is the one that haunts too many of us from our own childhoods: the moral pressure of "You should eat" and "You ought to eat." Dr. Margaret Mead, the well known anthropologist, declares that food in our culture is "part of a moral plot" enforced by mothers. It's true that "should" and "ought" sometimes become more important to us than the pleasure of eating, or how our children feel. Morality, ethics and the stern voice of duty are somehow still mixed up with eating for us, just as are religious totem and taboo in the food rituals of more primitive societies.

Our investment of food with "You should eat it," "You ought to eat it," "Eat it—it's good for you," "Eat it—it's shameful to waste all that good food," builds interior attitudes in our children which, if expressed, might be phrased like this:

"There are two kinds of food. First, there's the kind *I* like, the 'good' kind—ice cream, frankfurters, sausages, doughnuts, pickles, candy, cake, pie. Yum, they're good. And I never get enough of them. Then there's the kind Mommy says is good for me. But I don't like a lot of them—I think they're bad. How can they be good if they taste so bad?"

Many children, says Dr. Mead, have unconsciously summed up this dilemma this way: "If you eat enough of the food that's good for you, you can eat a little of the food that is good, but not good for you."

Conflict at Mealtime

As one of the outcomes of this "moral plot," mealtime often becomes the scene of a battle of wills. When it does, many children, say pediatricians and psychiatrists, choose to refuse food in order to prove their independence. Other children give in completely and overeat in a wholesale effort to win the approval that is synonymous with love for all of us. Some feel an almost constant need for comfort that expresses itself in eating constantly between meals. Something—love? tolerance? sympathy?—is missing in their relationships. They substitute for this lack, they comfort themselves, by eating. Food comes to stand for the love, security and satisfaction they get in no other way. Alan, a thirteen-year-old boy under psychiatric treatment, showed this. For many months during the course of his treatment, every time he talked about his feeling of being unloved by his mother, he said he wished he had two malted milks—right away. Doctors studying refugee children have reported their universal tendency to gorge themselves upon first arriving in the United States. Not hunger, say the doctors, but the need for comfort, motivates these children.

Because eating, more than any other function of the body, is central to a child's whole emotional life, children who've been subjected to too much moral pressure often develop queer fantasies about things that realistically have nothing to do with eating. A few years ago, a woman psychiatrist working with children hospitalized with tuberculosis, reported that most of them thought food was the cause of their illness.

To come down to our own specific problems: What do we do that's so bad when we press our children to eat? (After all, they should eat, they have to eat.) Put very simply, we impair and may begin to destroy their pleasure in eating. Whenever the tensions, the dissatisfactions and the frustrations connected with eating are too intense or too severe, they outweigh the pleasure connected with eating. When a child's gratification in food has been reduced this way, he is apt to become a feeding problem. "Bad eaters," says Anna Freud, "become so because of loss of pleasure in the function."

Again—because eating is central to a child's whole emotional life, neurotic personality traits arise more easily when this loss of pleasure in eating has prepared the ground for them. Since this is so, we have much to learn about our own children's eating needs and wants from the treatment of neurotic children. (For the needs of neurotic children are after all, no different from the needs of all children. They are simply more intense.)

Food as Therapy

At the University of Michigan's Neuropsychiatric Institute, there is a 25-bed Children's Unit where disturbed children live and are treated. In describing the different therapeutic approaches to these children, two staff doctors say that food is the denominator common to all kinds of treatment. "Our children always seem hungry, and if they are to feel gratified, food must be available."

It is—in plenty. In the occupational therapy room, a large bowl of potato chips appears in mid-morning, with the children free to dip into it as they want. They can prepare popcorn or fudge, too, during this period. During the evening programs after dinner, the same kind of thing goes on—with a cake baking in one room, popcorn popping in another, fudge bubbling in a third. The most important thing to the children about their weekly parties is that the food is plentiful and attractive.

And eating away from the ward is considered a wonderfully special treat by the children. So, staff members often invite them to the coffee shop or to outside restaurants—particularly just before they are ready to leave for home. Food is used, too, in direct psychiatric interviews. "Every child psychiatrist," say the doctors, "knows the importance of the candy bar at the right time." And, they conclude, "In all of this treatment, the symbolic significance of the food is of much greater importance than the food itself."

How does this information help us with our own children? For one thing, it's clear that the pleasure and gratification connected with eating are as important as food itself. Equally important are: the recognition of what a child needs and wants; permitting him a comfortable amount of self-decision; providing him with an atmosphere of understanding and consideration.

Simple as this sounds, none of it is possible if we bring our own anxiety to the experience of feeding our children. For many of us, anxiety is the uninvited guest at the dinner table. Just as food stands for mother in the child's mind, so many mothers unconsciously believe their success as mothers depends on their children's acceptance of the food they offer. All of us have seen mothers depressed over their inability to nurse. We've seen, too, this feeling of failure show itself as anxiety, overprotection, or exaggerated concern over a "balanced diet," the amount of food eaten, or the number of calories consumed. Where this kind of anxiety surrounds a child's eating, it's almost always reflected in his own emotional discomfort about food.

How to overcome anxiety. Fortunately, there are ways of overcoming this anxiety. There is much help to be gotten from the discoveries and observations of modern pediatrics. Dr. Clara Davis's famous studies have shown that children tend to eat what's best for them over a period of time, if they are given an abundant choice of good foods. She and other doctors have demonstrated, too, that children don't care much whether food is hot or cold—and that the younger the child, the less he likes decidedly hot food. We know that children prefer plain food served *au naturel,* with vegetables served in the simplest way possible, often raw, and foods always recognizable instead of disguised in mixtures and with sauces. We know finally that children who are allowed to omit foods at will don't develop lasting dislikes the way they do when food is forced on them.

For many of us, of course, our children's eating presents no problem. For others—for those children reported to be fussy eaters at home who adapt themselves easily and gustily to eating away from home—the problem is slight.

Almost all of these upsets and disorders can be prevented through discussion and guidance from a good pediatrician beginning at a child's birth or before; and through better insight into the nature of our own unconscious attitudes toward food. This takes time and effort. But even a partial realization of the goal can mean improved eating habits among our children.

But we need to bear in mind these three points: no pressure—or at least as little as is humanly possible; the recognition that eating is as much an emotional experience as it is a nutritional one; and the fact that if we are patient and willing to make haste slowly, guiding rather than forcing, waiting rather than "ought"ing, our children are capable of finding their own best way toward healthy eating habits.

—*By Helen Puner*

THE SEX EDUCATION OF CHILDREN

A GREAT deal has been said about what and what not, and when and when not, to tell children the so-called "facts of life." Because not many people talk comfortably to their children about sex, something very simple has been made into something very complex.

Yet, this generation of young parents is better equipped than any other generation to handle the sex education of its children naturally and without embarrassment. It is not merely a matter of telling—though telling is important. It is a matter of feeling, of passing on attitudes, of realizing that sex has many manifestations and that it colors our lives from babyhood on. Parents' attitudes and conduct toward their children's sexual behavior are as important as what they tell them, because the ultimate goal of sex education is one of conduct as well as knowledge. When our children reach adulthood, we hope they will feel deeply, be able to express well, yet be able to control, the sexual side of their natures. With that goal in mind, we should go about the business of guiding and teaching them accepting attitudes toward sex from babyhood up.

If we seem to be talking mainly to mother here, it is because mothers are on the spot most of the time. But father should be aware and ready to do his share in sex education, too. On walks, when he is putting a child to bed or baby sitting, he will have his turn to answer questions. It is important that he and mother talk over sex education and agree on what should be said.

Beginnings of Sex Education

Here are suggestions to help in the process, starting in infancy. As you read you may ask at times, "What has that to do with sex?" and add, "That's just being a good parent." The more you feel that way, the better job you probably are doing.

Because children learn about sex and acquire attitudes toward it from the time they are born, let us see how it enters into our daily experience with a baby.

In nursing your baby or holding him close while you give him his bottle, you are introducing him to love while he is doing something pleasurable. Some day, some of these same warm pleasant feelings of personal contact will be relived on a sexual level. So it is important that you make feeding a pleasant, secure experience for him.

Talk to your baby and look pleasant while you are changing him, no matter how messy the job, because you want him to know that all of him is acceptable to you and there is nothing dirty or distasteful about any part of him.

All babies discover that their genitals are pleasant to handle. Your attitude should be one of acceptance. Simply to pay no attention is not enough. To remove his hand or distract him, is too much. You need show no disapproval; just continue good-naturedly with whatever you were doing for him.

How to Tell the Story of Birth

If you try to make the story of birth a colorless, factual, biological lecture, you get into trouble because you just don't feel that way about it. Anyway it isn't very interesting when told that way. But if you remember some of the nice things about your pregnancy—things people said, things people gave you or interesting speculations about the sex of the child, you can probably recapture some of the happiness of that time and you will enjoy telling the story that is one of the most exciting ones you know. You will be telling it to the one other person in the whole world who is most interested in it, because he was as much a part of it as you were. Of course, in telling your child about his birth, you leave out all "blood, sweat and tears." Accuracy here isn't as important as climate, which should be warm and sunny.

When to tell. The "tell-them-when-they-ask" theory is an admirable advancement over *not* telling them when they ask, but it implies that you never bring up the subject of birth until the child does. It also implies that maybe you won't have to tell him anything at all, because some children never ask. It is better to begin the story yourself, at a time when you and your child are feeling particularly close and happy and at a time when you feel emotionally prepared to talk about it.

It is amazing how early you can start this story and how comfortable you can feel when telling it to a little child; much more comfortable than you would if your five-year-old, in the middle of a company dinner, suddenly asked, "Where do babies come from?"

What to tell the 2 to 3-year-old. The story of birth is one good for dozens of retellings. Begin it something like this for the two-and-a-half-year-old, preferably at bedtime, while your youngster is sitting on your lap. Say to him with your voice full of love and excitement, "Do you know where Daddy and I got you?" Being two, he probably will not answer but will just grin because you are talking lovingly about him. Pat your tummy and say, "Right in there you grew! Oh my, but we were happy when the doctor told us you were growing inside there. I could feel you. You kicked. It made me happy! When you got this big (show with your hands how long), the doctor helped you get out. Then we could see you, and hold you and love you."

That is enough for the first time. Maybe your youngster won't even understand all you have said. That's all right, too. You will have had practice in saying a few happy simple words about his beginning. Maybe you thought it would be hard and it is a relief to find it wasn't! In a few days you can tell this story to him again. You can add anything that will interest him—what grandma said, what kind of a little bed you fixed for him. Every time he wants to hear about how he "got born" you can embellish the original story. The more you talk about it, the easier it will be, and you will have started a bedtime story that can grow as fast as your child's understanding grows.

But this is not just a good bedtime story. It is one that reaffirms your love for your child; and it is one providing a sound foundation on which the whole of life can be built. Unlike the "stork" or "little black bag" stories, it will never have to be discarded later in favor of truth when the child's reasoning catches up with you.

What to tell the 3 to 4-year-old. The child between three and four can understand a few more details such as how big he was at various periods before he was born. Your accurate knowledge of the facts isn't as important as your perfect willingness to talk about them. A conversation might go like this:

Child: "How big was I when I was inside of you?"

Mother: "You started out about the size of a tiny little seed, and you grew and grew until you got this big (illustrate) and weighed seven pounds."

Child: "Was I as big as my kitty?"

Mother: "Yes, after a few months you were that big. That was about when people began to notice the lump on the front of me and knew I was going to have a baby."

Questions a Child May Ask

Child: (who sometimes enjoys pursuing an idea into what seems like absurdity) "Was I as big as a mouse? . . . . a Teddy bear? . . . my big doll?" This is the way he experiments with the ideas you have given him. His own size in relation to the world around him is very important to a child. Also,

you may give a very good answer to a very good question and have him demonstrate two minutes later that he didn't hear a word you said. Children can
ask questions and then suddenly get involved in thinking out the answer for
themselves and just not hear your carefully worded reply. This is why it is
impossible to tell you exactly what you should say, and what your child will
reply. Just be ready for anything he might ask, and realize that this conversation represents some pretty abstract thinking for him, which will mean
that the harder and faster he is thinking, the more ridiculous some of his
questions may sound.

He may continue, "Could the doctor see me before I was born?"
Mother: "No, none of us could see you. You were very well hidden."
Child: "Were my eyes open?"
Mother: "I don't really know."
(It's all right not to know about some things. You don't have to be an
obstetrical authority—just a friendly person willing to talk.)

Your answers. You can explain the place where the baby grew something
like this: "You lived in a little round sac made especially for holding babies
until they are big enough to live outside their mother. The name of the sac
is 'uterus' but you don't have to remember it. It's a cozy little pouch (or sac
or bag or whatever your child seems to understand best) that acts as though
it were made of rubber. It stretches as the baby grows. It is full of warm water
so the baby is protected from bumps and light and noises that would bother
him." Again it is important that you talk the language that *your* child understands. You can gesture and point and draw pictures. You can show him how
he was all curled up before he was born, by pulling his knees up and clasping
his arms around them, and tipping his head over on his chest. He will laugh
at that and probably think it was quite a relief to get out.

A small child is much more interested in the importance of his birth than
in the physical details. He will love to hear over and over again how much
you wanted him, and how happy his coming made all his relatives and friends;
how you named him, and what people brought him. He is not at all shocked
to hear how he got out, although it isn't of as much importance to him now
as it will be later when the marvel of it all strikes him. Better tell him now, as
a part of the story though, because it gives you good practice and seems
perfectly logical to him.

What Happened at the Hospital

You can tell about the actual birth somewhat like this. "We knew it was
about time for you to come because the doctor had told us when to expect
you. We had everything ready. Your new clothes had been washed and put
into your chest, and my suitcase was packed with things I would need at

the hospital and things for you to wear home. Most mothers go to a hospital when their babies are born because the doctor can take good care of them there. One night I noticed that the rubbery bag you were living in was squeezing into a hard lump every once in a while and I knew it must be a sign you were getting ready to be born."

At this point when you have just geared yourself to tell about the physical details of birth, your child may show interest in how you got to the hospital, what the nurses looked like, or something else that to you seems irrelevant. Answer his questions as they come. If your child tires of the story or shows interest in something else, forget the whole thing for a while. There is no rush about it. However, if he is enjoying your account you can continue. "After we got to the hospital, the nurse showed Daddy where he could wait, then put me to bed and got me ready to have my baby. The doctor came in and examined me and said it would be just a few hours until you would come. The little bag you were in squeezed harder and longer and harder and longer until finally you were squeezed right out—head first into the doctor's big strong hands. There you were—all pink and shiny and new! You opened your mouth and took in some air and let it come out in a loud cry. That was the first time you ever breathed, but you knew just how to do it."

Go into as much detail as you both enjoy over how happy everyone was, how you sent telegrams and called people, and how Daddy passed cigars and so forth. Be sure you express satisfaction over the sex of the child, even if he makes four of a kind.

The facts about cutting the cord are of very little interest to a child under seven or eight. Most young children don't question how they ate and breathed before they were born. If they do, you can say to a child old enough to understand, "You got nourishment and oxygen through a long tube called the cord that goes from the mother to the baby. It is fastened onto the baby where your belly button is. You didn't need to breathe through your nose or eat through your mouth until you were born. So right after you were born the doctor tied a piece of string around the cord and cut it, but that didn't hurt either of us. In a few days the little bit of the cord that was left on your tummy dried up and fell off, leaving just your little belly button."

After-birth details. Any information on the placenta or after-care of the mother is lost on a child; not because it's difficult to understand, but because children are too wrapped up in themselves to be interested. They want to hear just about themselves.

Your child will enjoy knowing about the identification beads he wore in the hospital, and how friends and relatives looked at him through the nursery glass and laughed at the faces he made and how everyone tried to make out whether he looked like his mommy or his daddy. You can tell him that one of the few things he was born knowing was how to suck on anything that came close to his mouth, which was a very good thing for him to know, and that when milk came into your breasts he knew just how to drink it.

Then tell about his trip home, how you weighed him, how he gained; how you fed and burped him, how he liked his first solid food and so forth— these are all fascinating topics of conversation to a child of any age.

By making good conversational material out of his prenatal life, and by continuing the story well into his babyhood, you relate his birth to your own lives.

Father's Part in Reproduction

The fact that people are embarrassed to talk about the sexual side of reproduction frequently makes them unwilling to talk about any of it. If you and your child become so familiar with the story of his birth that no part of it makes you uncomfortable, then you are both pretty well prepared for the next step. Fortunately your child's interest and understanding have to grow up a little before he is ready for information about insemination. You have two or three years to prepare for that story. In the meantime small children are interested in seeing and commenting on the genitals of children of their own and the opposite sex.

What to tell the 4 to 9-year-old. Be ready to reassure the child that his genitals are the right kind for his particular sex.

Say it in your own words but say it so that the child understands that both boys and girls are made "right" for them. Be ready to talk about it whenever your child wishes to do so and this may be many times, because although this difference in boys and girls is very interesting to them, it is frequently a source of worry. It makes them feel better to know that children are supposed to be the way they are, rather than that something "happened" to the girl's genitals.

If it is a little girl you are dealing with, she may look a little wistful at the more elaborate equipment of her male playmate. If you pass it off with "Yes, boys have penises and girls don't," you leave her feeling very poorly equipped. It is better to say, "You don't have the same kind of genitals that boys do. Boys have a penis, and you have a vagina, which is just as important. It is inside and can't be seen as well as a boy's penis." At this time, if you want to say, "That's where your babies will come out when you get big," that's all right, too. This conversation won't completely convince her that the boy's body isn't trimmed up a little fancier than hers, but basically she will know that somehow the design of her body fits into the whole scheme of things as well as the boy's does.

And another point which has an importance of which mothers are often unaware: convenient as it is to have a child stay clean, the truth is that over-cleanliness in children is not a sign of emotional health. It may seem strange, but frequently children make an association between parents' dislike of dirt and their possible displeasure over sex play, the idea being that both are dirty. To guard against any such feeling try to understand your child's pleasure in playing with dirt and to approve of his delight in dirt and squishy things.

Between four and eight, observation of animal mating and reproduction may be of help not only to the child but to the parent. Feelings of modesty, nastiness and the invasion of our privacy are not so apt to trouble us when we talk about animal mating, because we know they are doing what nature intended them to and we can accept it. Our healthy feelings about animals can aid us in giving sex education. We must be sure, however, that we make this material an aid and not an end. Some parents have talked a lot about birds and bees in order not to talk about human reproduction.

Knowledge of Animal Mating

If we recognize them, opportunities will arise to help us with the story of mating and many of them will be furnished by animals. The cat has kittens. The fact that only one kitten resembles the mother would cause you to speculate with your child on the color of the father. Perhaps your child picks up your remark and says, "I didn't know kittens had fathers." Then you can explain, "All living things have fathers as well as mothers. To make babies of any kind it takes two parents, one male and one female. The father cat plants the male seeds inside the mother cat; mother and father seeds join inside the mother cat and grow into kittens. They are born when they are old and strong enough to live outside of the mother cat's body."

Parents usually expect the children to ask next about their own father's part in reproduction, but they seldom do. It takes time for a child to grasp an idea well enough to draw a general conclusion.

At another time you may be with your child and see dogs acting as though they were going to mate. Instead of walking faster, try saying, "I believe those dogs are getting ready to mate." The child will be curious, of course, and you can continue, "The brown dog is a male and the black one is a female. The male wants to put seeds into the female which will make her have puppies." Any one of a number of different questions may follow, such as, "Where is he going to put his seeds?" or "Where does he keep his seeds?" Answer as simply and clearly as possible. "He keeps them stored in little bags of flesh called testicles between his hind legs. They come out through his penis into the female dog's vagina, which is under her tail."

The child may ask, "Does he want her to have puppies?" or, "How does he know that will make her have puppies?" He may ask nothing that shows he is thinking along this line, but it will help you both to feel natural about the whole thing if you say something like this: "The dog doesn't know that what he wants to do is going to make puppies. He just knows that he wants to do it. Nature makes sure there will be puppies by making the dogs feel this way."

Nature's ways. Here the concept of nature's insurance that species do not become extinct is well worth some thoughtful consideration. The flight of the bumblebee, the urgent trip of the salmon upstream, the vicious competition of the bucks in the forest for the right to sire the young, are all striking evidences of the remarkable plan to make sure that life goes on.

If you are dealing with a five or six-year-old, this last idea will give him enough to think about for a while. If on the other hand you are dealing with an eight or nine-year-old, who by now is old enough to know about the mating of human beings, you could go immediately to what logically follows, that human beings are moved by the same force of nature and mate similarly. You might say it this way, "Nature commands human beings to mate too, but our mating is different from the animal's. Men and women come to love each other, they get married, build homes and make plans for their children. Most animals mate and leave each other, and mate with others the next season. They do not understand what they are doing, but human beings do, and must plan for their children."

Explaining the Act of Mating

During this discussion, or later when your child has thought more deeply about it, he will want to know exactly how human beings mate. Perhaps you are dealing with a child over eight who has never seen mating animals and whose curiosity for some reason has never goaded him into wondering "how that baby got in there in the first place." If he doesn't ask directly about fertilization, it would be well to bring up the subject sometime when you are alone.

You might begin by saying, "You must have wondered how babies get started growing in their mothers' bodies. Let's talk about it because I am sure you would be interested." Listen first to what he has to say. Maybe he has heard something about sex relations and needs a little straightening out, or he may have some very erroneous information that needs to be discarded with dignity before you get into what is true.

If you review the names and descriptions of the genitals of the male and female, you can proceed more easily. You might say to your child, "You remember that a woman has a vagina which is a long narrow opening leading to the uterus where the growing baby lives before he is born. A man has a penis which is also long and narrow. The penis becomes stiff and hard and fits right into the vagina where it deposits fluid. That fluid is called semen, and although there is only about a teaspoon or so of it, it contains millions of sperm cells, which is the name of the father or male cells. The sperm are very active and can move rapidly in every direction. Some find their way through the mouth of the uterus and into the Fallopian tubes." (It would be better for you to sketch these organs on paper, at the time you are talking to your child, than to try to find a magazine or a book showing them. Keep the drawings simple and you should have no trouble.)

"At a certain time each month the female cell called the ovum comes slowly down one of these tubes from either ovary. If one of the many sperm meets and enters the ovum, fertilization has occurred and there will be a new life. The newly fertilized ovum travels on down the tube and imbeds itself in the wall of the uterus where it grows and grows until it becomes a baby— old enough and strong enough to be born.

"If no fertilization takes place, the ovum drifts on out of the body. Since it is tinier than the point of a pin, it is not noticed when it is discharged. The other thing that happens when no fertilization takes place is that the lining of the uterus which is very rich in blood to nourish the new little life, sloughs off and goes out of the vagina. This is called menstruation, or the menstrual flow."

Telling about menstruation. The subject of menstruation can be handled very naturally for both boys and girls as part of the explanation of fertilization. Most boys stumble on half truths about menstruation without having any idea of its purpose. Girls, of course, need more detailed information about what to expect at the time of menstruation and how to deal with it, but certainly both sexes need to know the biological reasons for it and to have their curiosity satisfied. Both will have seen advertising dealing with sanitary merchandise. Girls should be provided with the necessary equipment well before they need it, and be reassured with the fact that menstruation is not an illness and that during the menstrual period life goes on as usual. You can explain to both your daughter and your son: "Women wear a pad or a tampon when they menstruate to protect their clothing. You have probably seen these pads and tampons advertised in magazines. The menstrual flow lasts three or four days, and then the body begins to build up another supply of blood in the walls of the uterus in anticipation of nourishing a baby, should one be started."

Explaining seminal emissions. A question boys and girls frequently ask after hearing about the menstrual cycle is, "Do boys have anything like this?" You can answer that they don't menstruate because their bodies are not preparing to house and nourish a baby, but they do have a frequent discharge from the penis called the seminal emission, meaning an emission of semen. This signifies the boy has reached sexual maturity. It happens usually while he is asleep and is often accompanied by a dream of a sexual nature.

You can go into more detail with the boy because he needs to be assured that the seminal emission is a natural phenomenon to be accepted just as his changing voice and growing beard. If you have been understanding with him on the subject of masturbation when he was little, he will have no particular reason for anxiety about this new event. If he can feel that when you find a spot on his pajamas or sheet you will know what it is and it is all right, you will be giving your son the reassurance that he now needs. An attitude of acceptance and understanding on your part can relieve him of one of the heavy burdens of his age, which is guilt over masturbation or seminal emission. The seminal emission is an involuntary thing and not necessarily accompanied by masturbation.

It would be hard to anticipate the emotional reaction of a boy or girl to information regarding insemination. Don't talk too fast. Sometimes, feeling embarrassed, parents get too eager to be through with the explanation and race along at a pace that doesn't give the child a chance to assimilate what he is being told. The biological facts are a little hard to understand and, regardless of how you handle it, the material is charged with emotion. Children deal with that emotion in different ways. One child might just sit looking at his feet, while another might whistle through his teeth and mutter "My gosh!" Some children grin foolishly and others may even stifle a snicker. There is nothing wrong with any of these reactions; all they are showing is that the child has come upon something surprising and terribly important. Children also show by their reactions how well you have prepared them for this material.

Help Your Child Feel Comfortable

You will have to use your intuitive knowledge of your child to know how to help him in this situation. Don't make the mistake of observing his reaction and then saying, "You mustn't feel that way." If he feels "that way" he needs help with it. You don't want him to feel ashamed of how he acted when you talked with him. This added to his emotional reaction to the information might be too upsetting. And remember, if you are thinking about the comfort of your child rather than your own conduct and words, you will do a better job with less self-consciousness.

If your youngster just looks down and can't meet your eyes, be reassuring. Say gently, "That surprises you, doesn't it? I guess it surprises most of us when we first hear it. It does make sense though, doesn't it? Just think how much you look like Daddy, because part of you came from him. You think it over all you want to and ask either Daddy or me about anything you don't understand."

Or, if your child stifles a giggle, you can laugh with him and say, "This whole thing strikes you funny, doesn't it? That's the way it strikes lots of people. The world has been laughing at sex as long as anyone can remember. Laughing helps people handle their more serious feelings. People are apt to make jokes about the things in life that are most serious to them." Then go on and finish what you were telling him. Getting pencil and paper out for some drawings helps give you something to do, and if your drawing is as poor as most people's, the child will have a legitimate excuse to explode with the laughter he has been trying to control. You have shared with him the fact that sex itself is a serious matter, but that the tense feelings generated by talking about it sometimes find release in laughter.

Examine Your Own Attitude

If your child is approaching adolescence and you have kept putting off sex education, try some honest introspection. See if you can find answers to questions like: Why do I freeze up every time I think one of the children is going to ask something about sex? How do I feel my parents could have done a better job on my own sex education? Why do I still react so strongly to certain incidents that happened way back when I was a child, like being jerked away and reprimanded for looking at dogs mating, or seeing an adult naked for the first time and feeling guilty about it, or finding out the meaning of a four-letter word written on a fence?

Discuss with your husband the matter of giving sex information to your child. Perhaps you'll find that he can talk about it more easily than you can, or vice versa. But no matter who does the talking, mother and father should agree on how it should be done and each should be ready to back the other and to answer any questions which the child may ask.

If you try out with each other various ways of giving sex information you will find where the difficult spots are and maybe better ways of expressing what you have to say. Read aloud to your husband or friend the parts of this article that are in direct quotation, and see how they sound coming from you. If you feel awkward when it comes to saying some of the necessary words, say them so many times that they become meaningless. You will probably get to laughing hard, which will be a great help. However, if no matter what you do, you still feel embarrassed, upset and unequal to the situation try to get help, if possible, from a psychiatric or mental hygiene counselor.

In this article it has been assumed that the job of telling the child about sex belongs to the parent rather than to the minister, doctor, teacher or other professional person. It is very easy to imagine that someone else might do it better than you feel you can, especially after reading articles like this that may sound glib when they try to show how easy it is if you only know how. Yet, nothing could more completely convince a child that sex is unmentionable and unacceptable than your assigning the task of telling him about it to someone else. Also, this job of sex education can't be done in a set number of appointments. Information should be given the child only as he can mentally and emotionally assimilate it, which means it will be given piecemeal all through his childhood. It may happen in the privacy of his own room just before bedtime or it may take place in broad daylight in the zoo or the street. Your own willingness and readiness to discuss birth, growth and development, love, marriage and conception with your child will do more to relate sex to life than will even the best-worded talks by your doctor or minister. This is not to say that sex education stops with the parent. Doctor, school, minister make their own special contributions.

Take the long view. At some point you may say to yourself, "My mother almost died of embarrassment trying to tell me about birth and sex and I can't see that I am any better off for it. Why should I suffer and do an awkward job with the whole matter of sex education when probably my child won't appreciate it either?" The answer is that those of us whose parents did a sincere though embarrassed job of trying to help us with the sexual side of our lives, at least know that they thought sex should be an acceptable part of life, even if their feelings weren't quite as advanced as their thinking. As a result, we are better prepared today to talk to our children about sex than we would have been had our parents found the subject completely unmentionable.

Your child will benefit by your attitude of honesty and your sincere attempt, even though he may not show his appreciation any more than you did. You will have helped him to realize that sex is a happy and acceptable part of life and by so doing will have increased his chances of happiness in marriage. Also you will have made it easier for him to tell his children the facts when the time comes. Each generation helps to push forward toward a time when all the passion, wonder and beauty of life and love and childbearing will be honestly and gladly accepted.

—*By Helen Reid*

WHEN CHILDREN
ASK ABOUT DEATH

PEOPLE sometimes say, "Children should be protected from the harsh realities." They may be thinking that the birth of every living thing is a complex and often painful business, and that death is a great sadness. But the two great facts of birth and death are also universal, inescapable and true. Birth is the beginning of a life, death is its end. These are the facts. This is the reality we must accept ourselves if our children's personalities are to be sturdy and their lives happy.

Some people find in their religion a hope or conviction that the human spirit transcends its body and exists beyond the limits of death. If this is a vital part of your philosophy, it will certainly be part of the truth-as-you-see-it which you will try to communicate to your child. Significant and comforting as this belief is, it does not necessarily deny our immediate experience of reality—and we must not try to make it seem to do so for our children. Whatever our religious beliefs, we have to recognize that we cannot know a human being except as he exists bodily and that when he dies it is not "just" a body that dies—but the whole person whom we knew.

If it were possible to bring up our children ideally, we would present them from their earliest years with the story of life of which birth and death are parts. We would tell them very simply the biological sequence of conception, birth and growth; and we would convey, along with all these facts, that the birth of a new being is, above all, always a miracle. Just as simply, we would tell them the facts of death: that barring accident, each life runs its course and then is done; but life itself goes on with new and always different beings taking the place of the old. And we would say as we did of birth, that here too, is mystery.

Adults are sometimes ashamed of their ignorance and afraid to admit it, so they pretend a brash knowledge of all the answers. Although loving and well-meaning, such a parent might say, "God took the little bird because he wanted it in Heaven," and think that this was a satisfactory version of the truth for a small child. Often, however, the comfort a small child derives from such an answer comes more from the warm and tender way it is expressed than from what is said.

Give Satisfactory Answers

The words themselves raise even more questions for a child—and usually ones that are harder to formulate. For instance, "If God wanted that particular bird who is He going to want next? Me?" Or, "What does she mean? Nobody took the bird. The bird is there but it's broken. Somebody ought to fix it."

When a pet dies there are likely to be even more anxieties for a small child. Going-on-six Judy for example, was a capable and responsible caretaker for the kindergarten's best white mouse, Jimmy. During Christmas vacation when she had it at home, it died. This was a tragedy to Judy. Her grief, of course, wore off with time—but something else didn't wear off so soon—a feeling that it was all her fault. Originally, it had been mother's voice that said, "Judy, you forgot Jimmy's water again!" Now it was a voice inside Judy clamoring, "You forgot. You forgot . . . and he died."

Judy's mother might have made things worse for her daughter. She might have said, "This'll teach you a lesson! This is what happens when people are careless." But her mother was wiser than that and more honest. She knew that while it was important to teach Judy not to be careless, it was far more important to teach her the facts of life, to reassure her about the natural limits of her own responsibility. So she found opportunities to say in different ways that Judy had been a good caretaker, that Jimmy had been a dear little mouse, and that it was always sad when something dies—but that was the way it was. After a while, Judy stopped being haunted by the fear that *she* was a bad girl who had caused her mouse's death.

David followed his own eight-year-old logic when told that his step-uncle, a man he had seen only once or twice, had "passed away." It didn't take long for David to discover that this was a way to say "died." Perhaps grown-ups used the phrase because it seemed to them more respectful of death. David, however, was only a little boy who had occasionally been told that there were things he shouldn't say because nice people didn't use words like that! So this dressed-up "passed away" they breathed in hushed voices, looking at each other over his head, conveyed to him that death and dying were bad words that nice little boys didn't say.

Death Not a Punishment

If the word alone was bad, what of death itself? To David it seemed that death must be very bad indeed—and that it had taken something very bad to produce it. He thought of the worst thing he could: "I guess he passed away," said David, "because he didn't eat his vegetables."

A conclusion, logical for him, but twisted because the idea was planted in his mind that death is a punishment. Even for many adults this false idea lingers, causing additional and unnecessary pain when someone dies.

In answering a young child's questions about death we must try to understand what his words mean to *him*. "Are you going to die?" may mean, "Are you going to leave *me* all alone?" Your answer can be truthful and casual: "Sure, I'll die sometime. Everybody does. But not for ages and ages—not until you're a great big grownup yourself."

Similarly, when a child asks if *he* is going to die we must think what he may mean by his question. He might mean: "Does it hurt?" Or, "Where will I go when I'm not here? Will it be a good place?" (questions that are really about living, not about death at all). While the answer must be truthful:—"Everyone does sometime."—it can also be reassuring:—"Nothing hurts you after you're dead." For the most part, children are satisfied with simple and casual answers if they trust the person who gives them.

When a child becomes preoccupied with questions about death and dying, it usually means he is really quite worried about some aspect of living. In some cases, it takes help to understand the infinite channels into which children's anxieties sometimes run.

Grief, of course, is something else again, something that can't be eliminated or even very much alleviated. But, facing the fact of the death of people we love, we can live with our grief in a more bearable way.

When death strikes, it is best for the whole family if we can recognize and acknowledge our grief and, in whatever form it appears, our children's. Parents sometimes try to conceal all evidence of grief from children, feeling mistakenly that they should be shielded from pain. But a household in which there is grief must of necessity be sad. A child can cope with this sadness if he is permitted some chance to understand it. He cannot cope with a mysterious miasma of gloom. Not knowing its source, feeling the phoniness of adults' abstracted smiles, aware of their altered voices and manner, a child must try, like little David, to explain the gloom for himself. With his limited experience of life, and with the truth in hiding in his house, he is likely to believe that it is he who is somehow to blame.

Have Faith in Children

We must have enough faith in our children to believe that they can tolerate the truth of grief if it is presented with decency and kindness. Grief for the loss of someone loved is normal, natural and inevitable. It is a fact just as the death of that person is a fact and children have a right to the truth.

They shouldn't, however, be subjected to a parade, a flood of grief. Unwittingly, grief is paraded in many families. Adults are very likely to underplay their possible relief at a person's death and to overemphasize their regret, when their feelings were mixed about the person.

When a cantankerous, unlovable old person dies, children in a household shouldn't be expected to understand or share in the sadness of the adults. Adults can recall the days of the old lady's youth, the many years when she was strong and useful. They can sorrow as they could not when she was alive and cranky. But the children didn't know her in her prime—and a parade of grief for someone whom everybody clearly disliked is to them untruthful and therefore confusing and worrying.

Children show their own grief in ways that are not always recognizable to adults and may even seem grotesque to us. One child may grow sullen and unmanageable, rude to those who are trying to help him. Another may appear to have shrugged off the whole event, refusing to talk or to listen to others talk about it—and then seem "monstrous" to the rest of the family by playing boisterously until he falls asleep exhausted. Some children worry their parents or other adults by playing death games—acting out such details as they know of funerals, burials, last illnesses. Others may nag and cling, become afraid of the dark or revert to babyish ways like thumb-sucking or bed-wetting. Older children may either refuse to eat or stuff themselves at every opportunity.

One little girl of about nine worked out her feelings when her father died suddenly, through an intense preoccupation with breeding and raising kittens. In the time left over from her work with birth and life she proved a most responsible and sympathetic companion to her mother. Another, in very similar circumstances, took her own feelings out on her mother: "You didn't love him! He was afraid of you! Everybody in this whole world is afraid of you! And he loved *me* and you're just an old witch!"

Accept Child's Feelings

It's difficult for a parent suffering under a heavy load of grief and loss herself to be patient and understanding of some of these seemingly bizarre reactions to death. But a child faced with death needs more than ever to be accepted as he is for whatever he is. If he's able to be courteous, kind, and a source of comfort to the adults who are left—splendid. If not, though, he needs somehow to be made to feel that whatever feelings he has, he's not a bad person for having them.

Of course, this is far easier said than done. For—it bears repeating—to help our children accept these facts of life, *we* must be able to accept them and to accept *ourselves,* with all our own conflicting, supposedly ugly feelings. In our best relationships with our most loved people, there are at times feelings of irritation, dislike and sometimes hatred mixed in with our love and tenderness. Along with honest deep sorrow at the death of a loved one, may go relief—relief that the irritations and the angers have died too. Even dimly aware of such feelings, many people push them away deep out of sight, and are conscious only of a sense of guilt that they were not more patient or less critical. Those who can face themselves as people who are *both* glad and sorry, *both* loving and hating, evading neither of these admissions—will be better able to help their children do the same.

As for particular answers to particular questions, like—:

"Should young children be taken to funeral services?"

"Should they watch a casket being lowered into the ground?"

"Should they see the dead body of a parent or other relative?"

"Should they stay home from school for a time?"

"Should they be taken on memorial visits to the cemetery?"

"Should mementos be cherished and recollections of the dead person be encouraged?"

Be honest. The answers will be different for every family—for the questions have different meanings for different people. In general, nothing is to be gained either by enforcing any of these actions or by preventing them. If any seem natural and right to you and to your child, then carry them out. If they don't, then don't.

In other words, be honest. Be honest with children about the facts of life, the facts of birth and of death. Help them to be honest about their own feelings, their curiosities, their worries. Help them to accept themselves as they are—human beings limited in many ways and bound to experience a good deal of frustration and probably pain in the course of living—but capable also of a great deal of effort and a great deal of joy.

In his book "Childhood and Society" Erik Eriksen wrote, "Children will not be afraid of life if their parents are not afraid of death." The converse is equally true: children will not be afraid of death—if their parents are not afraid of life.

—By Helen Steers Burgess

IF YOU HAVE AN ONLY CHILD

AS the mother of an only child and as a teacher who has worked with only children I am doubly aware of the special problems parents face when they are bringing up just one child.

It's still fairly common these days to hear the words "spoiled," "demanding," "pampered" linked with an only child. Too often he is found to be unpopular and unreasonable with other children. There's also a prevalent belief that such a child is apt to incur psychological scars due to overprotection and the pressures of a too-adult atmosphere at home.

There's no doubt that these criticisms and fears concerning the only child may have a logical basis. What can parents do about them?

Let's first face the fact that an only child does miss certain things in life— he is bound to. He misses the protective aid that children in the same family give to each other in their natural war with adults. He misses the loyalties that brothers and sisters can have for each other. If he is with adults too much, he misses a child's world of whimsy and fantasy, the sights and sounds and games of make-believe that adults could never provide as tirelessly as playmates of his own age.

The result? He lives in a world that is far too big for him, often far too demanding. He is apt to develop tastes and interests that are beyond his years for, being forced to make his own way in a world peopled by adults, he soon learns to imitate that world.

Parents, on the other hand, often try to make up to the only child for what he may lack by giving him too much of the wrong thing. An overdose of parental attention can be as bad as an underdose.

For example, there is the case of Alice Jackson and her son, Johnny, an only child of five. When he finally fell asleep the other night, long past his bedtime, his mother walked into the living room, a tired and exasperated woman. One painful thought was circling about in her brain, "Johnny is our only child, and yet I can't cope with him!"

Actually, because Alice realized that one child in a family can be lonely, she had set herself the superhuman task of feeding Johnny's insatiable hunger for attention.

When, finally, on that particular night, Alice heard herself asking resentfully, "Aren't you ever going to go to sleep?" she knew with a pang that she sounded as if she wanted to get rid of Johnny and his nagging. Thus the vicious cycle began again: Johnny, feeling more unsure than ever of his mother's love, continued to test her out, until finally, when both were equally exhausted, he fell asleep—a lonely sleep.

Who would ever dream that so much self-doubt and energy could go into the rearing of one little boy?

Strain on Parents and Child

As the mother of an only child, I know only too well how Alice was led to try to give more than was humanly possible to her child. That wasn't what our son, Steve, needed, either. Whenever Steve ran into trouble, his path was smoothed by adoring parents. Because he was our only one, we had perhaps a deep-seated need to make him a model child, to urge into premature focus all the signs of brightness in our boy. Stevie, as a result, was overstimulated, pushed a little too hard. The strain showed both in him and in us.

It was natural enough. An only child inevitably occupies the center of the stage. From his first days on, he sees his parents, grandparents, relatives concerned with him and him alone. He hears his name mentioned constantly on the telephone. When he's sick, he is the subject of innumerable conversations and the center of much concern. He loses his sense of proportion. He won't give up the spotlight easily. And why should he? He's learned to live by it, drawing his definition of love from the amount of sheltering and indulgence that have been showered on him.

I have observed only children in the junior high school where I am a teacher. I found that over and over again these children showed, in more or less degree, certain traits in common, among these a marked inability to share attention—and even more poignant, to take defeat.

Paul is a case in point. When Paul became a serious problem at school,

I asked his mother to come and talk things over. Paul, then 12, was having a bitter struggle with the rest of the group. Everything was fine as long as Paul could be chairman, group leader, exercise some form of control over his classmates. Ordinarily, this would be a good sign of initiative and leadership. Not so with Paul. His was a constant clamor for recognition, a total inability to see himself in a proper relationship to the group. When inevitable moments of failure came to him, Paul could not cope with them. When he wasn't in the limelight, he became disruptive, insolent or defiant.

How could such a claim as Paul's to unqualified approval and prominence be wisely handled? The answer is that his parents should have helped him from earliest childhood find his place in the family group as one who shares attention and enjoys privileges but who also respects the rights of others. The child who learns give-and-take at home carries over his ability to get along happily with others into his life away from home.

Feelings of Insecurity

Parents have to recognize the particular problems that an only child faces. He may have the feeling that he is a "fifth wheel," almost an intruder in his parents' lives. No matter how devoted his parents may be to him, he tends to see his existence as a "two-against-one" affair. When his parents are celebrating an anniversary or when they go out to supper together, he is apt to feel rejected. He feels that bedtime excludes him from the scene which his parents now share together. He has a haunting fear that his parents love each other more than they do him.

How many times has our son asked us if we would sleep in his room. When we explained that mommies and daddies sleep in their own room and that it wasn't time for grownups to go to bed, he was unconsoled. He bitterly accused me of loving Daddy more than I did him.

It was amazing how a few simple remedies helped to ease his anxieties: eating supper out with us on a few "special" evenings, for example, or waking him up as we had promised, to meet the guests at our party. We even permitted him to go to bed and leave his door open. It was a revelation to learn that the sounds of dishes and talk and movement, made him less lonely. In time, these sounds were his familiar lullabies and sleep was reduced to a predictable routine.

One thing is inevitable in bringing up an only child. His real problem is one of heightened intensities in a close-knit situation. His inner conflicts, his guilt and jealousies are intensified by anything he sees around him. He is always on guard. The job, then, is to *de-concentrate* some of these feelings, to neutralize them with the best ingredients we can find. These should include other children for him to play with. If possible, attendance at nursery school. His playmates and a genuine world in miniature, more than all the formulas in the world, will help him find the feeling of well being he needs.

Suppose we parents admit that an only child does face loneliness. Suppose we make that very human mistake of overindulging our only child to the point where there is an unceasing clamor for attention. Suppose we recognize that this can be an obstacle to building self-reliance in our child.

What definite suggestions can be of help to us and to our child?

I believe the key word to help us is BALANCE: moderation—and a certain easy-going attitude which cushions and pads the problem. Certainly an only child can be a lonely child. But only if the parents are themselves lonely. A family of three can seem like a bristling household full of life and energy if the spirit of fun and cooperation is there.

Love Balanced with Discipline

Then, too, proper balance of love and discipline sets up a kind of equilibrium so that when the child goes out into the world of school and children he can take what comes.

When the household is brimming with the parents' affection for one another, and for him, with a sense of mutual loyalty the only child can go outside the home and still feel safe.

And very early in life a little child needs other children to play with. A mother should encourage her child's playmates to come to his house. She should take every opportunity possible to give him the benefits of substitute brothers and sisters.

A nursery school or play group is ideal for a preschool child, for it gives him a chance at a very early age to learn group give-and-take and group responsibility, to develop many of his talents with the help and stimulation of other little children.

Very often an only child finds it hard to develop self-confidence because his overprotective mother or father has made it impossible for him to act independently. He should be given responsibilities to remind him that he is one of three; he must also be made to feel that he is worth consulting and that his opinion is important. He should be helped to enjoy doing things as part of a family rather than as the center of it. He must learn to take defeat without its being an altogether devastating blow. He should be helped to recognize limits, gradually and as he is able to cope with them. Neither too much nor too little should be expected of him.

What some mothers of an only child tend to forget is that only children do need correction and discipline—and that it can be given in a way that shows the child that he is loved. —By Betty Thayer Miller

MIDDLE CHILD IN A FAMILY

I HAD to admit it. Our four-year-old Chris had definitely changed. By noon, I was nagging at him and he had progressed from misdemeanor to worse misdemeanor, had responded to my constructive suggestions with whining negatives, cried if I asked him twice to do anything and every contact with his seven-year-old brother ended in his screaming, "No, it's mine!" or "I don't want to!"

And it wasn't just today. I had had three phone calls the previous week from neighbors about his toy-snatching and repeated violations of their play and yard rules. Any attempts I made to delve into these matters were met with sullen and evasive "I don't know's."

Four years old was a difficult age, all the books assured me, and I kept telling myself this through gritted teeth. I remember how Nicky, the oldest, had reacted when Chris was born and I realized Chris might be reacting in a similar fashion to the baby, although I hadn't thought a child who had always been used to another child in the family would feel it so intensely. But the baby was over a year old now and Chris was getting worse instead of better.

It was a kindergarten-teacher friend, visiting one particularly bad day, who gave me a clue.

"Poor Chris," she smiled. "It's tough to be a middle child. I know, I was one. The oldest can always do things better, faster, and sooner and the youngest always gets more attention. And it's always that way, you can never catch up to the big one and grownups scold when you try to regress to the baby's level."

Immediately I got a bigger view of the situation. Poor Chris indeed! Here he was in the throes of four-year-oldness, a difficult period in a child's development, and he was beginning also to realize that he was a middle child. Nicky was in school, could read, ride a two-wheeler, swim, run errands, eat more, run faster, throw better, and so on ad infinitum.

Baby Colleen was cute, curly-haired and demanding. Visitors exclaimed over her, played with her. I fed her, bathed her, dressed her, pushed her carriage and we exclaimed often at her accomplishments.

Chris, I realized, was getting a lot of "When you're bigger (or older) you can, too." Or else "Oh, you're too big (or old) for that!"

And this part of the problem wouldn't resolve itself by the time Chris was five. He would be a middle child all his life.

Bids for Attention

The fibbing, sneaking and whining Chris had developed were pitiful little defenses set up by a small, bewildered, but determined little fighter—determined to get his share of attention, no matter how.

Now that I understood, I was chagrined to find in how many ways I had thwarted him every day. "It's your turn to feed the dog, but let me open the can, it's too hard for you."

"Will you boys go and get some eggs for me? Nicky, you'd better carry the money and the eggs."

"Nicky answer the phone—Nicky watch the baby—Nicky get the mail—"

But now we have had major policy changes. Chris no longer takes a nap. He goes to his room for a "rest period" after lunch on school days only. I read him a story at this time, which makes an extra one for him that Nicky doesn't get. He may take books or a coloring book to bed, and occasionally he falls asleep over them.

We bought him a wallet like Nicky's and he is sent with the money to fetch eggs. He hasn't yet dropped a coin or an egg. He is referred to as Big Brother Chris when we are talking to Colleen and is allowed to push her carriage all by himself.

Chris receives his own allowance. I have allowed him a wider play range, explaining that when he is out of calling distance he must tell me where he's going, and he is getting much more reliable on this score.

I have spent several sessions with him on telephone usage and allow him to answer and call his own friends. He pushes the cart at the grocery store, selecting items I point out to him on the shelves. Sometimes he prefers to ride on the carts with baby-seats attached. I make no comment. Chris is now the one to tell me when the stop lights change. He brings in the mail.

I let Chris choose his own clothes from his play-clothes drawer and, incidentally, have cut all bibs and shoulder straps from his overalls and dungarees. Usually he dresses himself, but sometimes he says, "You dress me." When he does I dress him. And when he says, "Look!" I look, even if it's not too convenient.

I often go afield conversationally to bring in comments on Chris' ability and trustworthiness, and go out of my way for a hug and a kiss.

Grown-up treatment. The results of these efforts were not sudden, but they are now noticeable. We have had no neighbor trouble about Chris for months, he does his work and runs errands faithfully and as well as he can. (I don't expect him to do them as efficiently as his older brother.) Because I have given him more responsibility, Nicky seems to regard Chris as less of a baby, and there is less teasing and goading, fewer whines and screams from Chris.

When he starts school it will help a lot, but it will never solve the situation of the middle child, who gets the short end on both ends. But by being given more grown-up treatment and more sheer loving and attention, the middle child can be helped to come into his own. —*By Jane Lynott Carroll*

WHEN THREE GENERATIONS LIVE TOGETHER

IT is a paradox, indeed, that what we all dread we do our best to attain— old age.

Of course there is no set time when old age begins. Many people are eager and irrepressible at eighty, still ready to try their hands at new projects. Others at sixty or seventy feel that having managed thus long to survive the perils of modern bathtubs, synthetic foods and reckless motorists, they had better let well enough alone and rest on their laurels.

It's a moot question which kind of older person is preferred by the younger set; but with both kinds there is often some friction, especially when several generations have to live together. Some of it is unnecessary, and is due simply to a lack of understanding.

Old folks seem set on living longer and longer, thus daily becoming more of a problem, and so any increase in understanding should be a blessing.

There is a general complaint that old people make a great to-do about their age, even adding on a bit sometimes in a bragging sort of way. Old folks feel they are due a little recognition—but how can anyone *ask* for such a thing? So instead of saying "See how smart I am," as children do, or "Notice how straight my back still is," they try the more indirect way of drawing attention to themselves. You see, at their age there is no fond mother to do it for them and most young people are too taken up with their own accomplishments. So old people trot out their most striking achievement in an effort to keep themselves on the map. It is really a sort of humility. A person who felt quite sure of his importance, someone engaged in a great and recognized work, would never bother to mention his age, except perhaps in deploring the little time left him to get on with it.

Someone else, however, may feel the need to justify himself, and by dwelling on his age hope to suggest that, however unqualified he may be in every other respect, his years do give him the right to speak as an authority.

With another, it may be that he is conscious of his lack of alertness and speaks of his age in a plea for patience and understanding. Or it may be a cry for gentleness. Gentleness means so much to old people. But often in these cases something quite sad occurs; they unconsciously use such a querulous tone that they only irritate others and thus defeat the very end they would achieve. Or perhaps the gentleness does come, but the old person's reactions are so slow that the moment for reciprocation passes and is gone before he can respond. He has asked for gentleness and then seemed to rebuff it. Nevertheless he has responded; inside he feels a glow of comfort.

Slowed-Down Reactions

This slowing down of reactions is one of the old person's fundamental problems. It is part of nature's plan. And a very sobering one it is, too! But like most things in life it has compensations. While physical prowess lessens, perception and reasoning and, let us hope, a wiser set of values increase.

Young people would do well to understand this phenomenon. It is no one's fault. The old person's tentacles, so to speak, have been shortened and have become less sensitive. And, at the same time, whatever part of his physical makeup works at all does so more slowly.

As to the charge that old folks are hypercritical of young ones—well, sometimes they are. They were young themselves and made mistakes, and they would like to save others from doing likewise. This is a case when instead of asking for patience they would do better to practice it.

One hears that old folks are fussy about trifles. But now that they are out of the bustling life, these trifles are their life, and they turn them over and over in their minds till they become really important. And, indeed, they may be at least as important as some of the questions young folks worry about.

Some old folks hoard, there's no denying it. They are too old to earn their own living and are terrified of being left with nothing. This is surely not hard to understand. Of course, the real misers are different; they are definitely unbalanced. But it's just possible that the old body who has been found starving to death with $80,000 sewed into the hem of her dress was queer all her life, and it wasn't old age that did it.

On the whole, old age is easier for women. They may be more pliable than men, their years as wives having accustomed them to adapting to strange conditions, and they may be more patient. But how annoying they can be!

Take an old body who has an unconscious habit of, say, humming or letting out little grunts as she moves about the house. She has no wish to irritate, but if she doesn't know when she does it she will find it difficult to stop. In such a case a frank discussion might help; but its whole effectiveness will depend on the open and kindly spirit employed.

Forgetfulness is one of the most common crosses an old lady and her family have to bear. That part of her brain that remembers has worn itself out; and so, forgetting that she has made a certain remark, she repeats it over and over. Someone she loves might tell her so, very gently, trusting she will ask to be told when she does it. And if her feelings are spared in the process she probably will.

Forgive Forgetfulness

Or she may forget something someone else has told her, and ask questions that call forth an irritated "I've told you that before." But telling her again would take little more time than reproaching her, and wouldn't have the effect of making her wish she could turn herself inside out like a stocking.

Sometimes her mind goes suddenly quite blank. In the midst of a conversation she may run down and come to a dead stop like a toy rabbit that needs rewinding. It is a little trying to be left waiting in mid-air, but she hates this helpless run-down feeling more than you do. A gentle "You were saying so-and-so" will generally wind her up again and set her trotting merrily on her way.

On the other hand, some old chatterboxes cannot be stopped. With them the victim would do well to cultivate a "tin ear" and a look of moderate intelligence, giving an occasional grunt as long as he can stand it. After that it is up to him. But don't get impatient; think what a good time the old lady is having. And who knows, she may be alone so much that when she does get a chance she goes on a talking spree.

Among the more serious difficulties of old ladies, one of the commonest is being forced by circumstances to live with someone who does not want her.

Never fear, she knows she is not wanted, and she spends her days in silent fortitude going about the house doing whatever chores she can find to compensate for being there at all. The sad thing is that this poor old creature, being perpetually under a strain, makes many more mistakes than the average person.

Even the old lady who feels fairly relaxed may behave peculiarly at times. She may "take a notion," as the saying goes, to do some rather odd thing that upsets the household routine. But after all, why shouldn't she? Didn't she spend many years of her life satisfying her family's whims?

And her moods may change without apparent reason. There probably is a reason, a feeling, perhaps, that an injustice has been done, too trifling to protest but not quite trifling enough to forget immediately. Just wait. Likely the mood will pass.

It is not uncommon for quite contented old ladies to be found quietly crying. Try, without prying, to find out the cause, lest it be something serious, but if there seems to be nothing the matter, just let her cry. She may have remembered some touching incident in her past or have felt a wave of gratitude or pleasure, and that sort of crying does her good. Or it may be just a vague unaccountable mood, and if you press for an explanation you won't get the truth, for probably she doesn't know it herself.

Avoid Change of Habits

If an old lady has her own way of doing things let her go on that way. She operates so much on habit that a change confuses and worries her. When the change is really necessary, suggest, rather than tell. And, since old folks forget, be definite. She will do her best to conform—unless, of course, she's a stubborn soul, in which case she'll do as she likes anyway.

Sometimes, when an old lady's friends give her a present her response disappoints them, for she tucks it away in a drawer instead of using it and they think she doesn't like it. But that's not it. The gift as a rule is an article of clothing, and habit being so strong she is just putting off the effort of changing her routine. Furthermore, she may be loyal. Using the new things means casting aside the old, and I think there are few old folks who don't have a preference for their tried and trusted friends. It is sad that the impression is one of ingratitude. For she is very grateful. She likes having something new in reserve. But better still is the reassurance that she has been remembered. Old people are very grateful for attentions, especially from the young, and this attention is taken out and mulled over and enjoyed, even though the gift itself never again sees the light of day. She may be responding in the wrong way, but she is certainly responding.

Aside from the things I've mentioned, chiefly patience and consideration, the things old people want are simple and few. Also, the things they don't want are many and expensive. They don't want to be given new clothes often, or a large wardrobe ever, finding them just a bother. They don't want rich food. They don't want to go to large parties, since cross-currents of conversation confuse them. They don't even want physical luxuries they aren't accustomed to (though comfort is very important) because getting acclimatized is an effort. A shabby home in which every scratch is familiar and dear may be preferred to the slick modern apartment some loving son wants to move them into. And in pressing for the move this son should ask himself whether he is perhaps being influenced by public opinion, and if he finds the shabby place is really preferred he should give in.

The things old folks do want are elementary. Simple nourishing food, not much at once but in four or five dabs a day. Plenty of undisturbed rest at frequent intervals. Freedom to do things in their own way, even if a new way is better. Some spending money in pocket. And forbearance for failing memory and slow reactions.

Remembrances cherished. But all those wants are nothing beside the one great want—to be remembered. The attentions that cost nothing but time, the telephone call, the drop-in visit, the message sent through a friend, these are more important than all the food or comfort. I know one lucky old lady whose bureau top is bright the year round with greeting cards. The Mother's Day cards stay till her birthday in the fall, which brings one or two along with gifts. These remain till the Christmas ones come, and they in turn till St. Valentine's Day. And the circle is completed on Mother's Day again. They remind her that she is remembered, the greatest of her compensations.

—By Mrs. A. W. Stirling and Nora Stirling

DO YOU HAVE GRANDMOTHER PROBLEMS?

WHEN my first child, Timothy, was born, I remember lying in my neat, impersonal hospital bed with Mother's gift of roses on the table beside me, waiting anxiously for her first visit. Why was I anxious? Why not just relaxed and happy? Looking back I know that subconsciously I felt the moment in which my mother and my son were introduced would symbolize the beginning of a new relationship between me and my mother—one that would have deep meaning for all three of us.

Mother came in and I remember noticing how smart and young she looked —not "grandmotherly" at all. She kissed me lightly and said she had seen the baby through the nursery window and thought he was beautiful. Her manner was light and airy and I knew from it that the moment was strongly emotional for her, too.

The incident may seem a trivial one. Something like it happens to almost every new mother these days. But a generation ago when a grandmother's role was as well-defined and almost as important as that of the doctor who delivered the child, it would have been unheard of. Today the age-old relationship of grandmother-mother-child is on a new basis. The gray-haired granny of yesterday, with her automatic and unquestioned right to shelter, assist and supervise her daughter's new family has gone.

In her place there is apt to be someone like Timmy's grandmother—youthful, independent, with a full life apart from her children—who is, nonetheless, truly eager to assume her role of grandmother. Nowadays, however, she can assume it only to the extent that her children permit and the extent to which she takes part in the rearing of her daughter's family is determined, not by custom, but by the love, understanding and loyalty between her and her daughter.

Unless human nature has changed this mother-daughter-child triangle has always been one of the trickiest of human relationships. No matter how well mother and daughter get on, with the arrival of a baby—particularly the first —all sorts of tensions and troubles, some perhaps unrealized before, come to full bloom. The daughter of today, with more leeway in handling the problem and more understanding of the causes underlying it, can do a lot to smooth out these inevitable rough spots.

Until Timmy was born I worked as a psychiatric social worker in a child guidance clinic. Analyzing the troubles of young mothers and their children, I had found what at first seemed surprising: in fully half the cases the "grandmother problem" loomed significantly large. This was expressed in various ways. Sometimes a woman still clung to her mother, running back to her whenever things got rough in her own household so that a grown-up married life was never achieved and a stable home for the children was impossible. Sometimes a young wife would be dependent on her mother's help with the children for practical reasons and find that inexplicably she and her mother now quarreled and disagreed so constantly that her home was a battlefield. Occasionally a grandmother had taken over so fully that only she could do anything with a child, and the mother found herself a helpless bystander.

Problem of Dependency

Technically, I knew that the explanation for all these situations revolved in one way or another around the problem of dependency. But technical knowledge doesn't make one immune to personal problems, and I was shocked to see that when my baby was born, my relationship with my mother was a source of very real tension and difficulty. I had turned away, years before, from relying on her, but under the strain and newness of having my first baby there was a strong temptation to go back to the little girl role. For some months this didn't come out clearly, but took the form of turning to her for help and then, to her hurt, turning away.

It came out directly with the problem of toilet training. She insisted that this must take place at six months. We had long, serious talks about it and these sessions, even though the subject was comparatively slight, were somehow emotionally grueling. I can remember her saying, "Oh darling, I can train him so easily in a week if you'll just let me take care of it." Although I knew her method was outdated and impractical, I felt a strong pull to let her take over. In the end we were all relieved, even Mother, when I made it clear that Timmy would not be trained for another year at least, and then by me. In other words, I did at long last what I should have been able to do in the first place: just cheerfully announce what would be done and not discuss it at all.

What we were wordlessly struggling over was this problem of dependency. Because my independence had been pretty well established and accepted by Mother long before, there was a minimum of resentment in this particular situation. But this is not always the case. The more dependent a daughter has been in the past, the harder her struggle to cast it off and the touchier she is about any new threat of domination.

Dependency, however, is not the only basic cause for conflict. Competition and rivalry between you and your mother can be even more troublesome. If such rivalry exists it will come out most clearly when both of you are fulfilling your major role of mothering.

Marion Rogers, a patient at the clinic, considers herself a truly modern parent. She told me with satisfaction that her mother hadn't been allowed to come near the baby until she had read Drs. Spock and Gesell from cover to cover and been quizzed on them. Imagine how that grandmother felt! How humiliated and how unhappy by the implication that she couldn't be trusted with a baby unless she followed the books explicitly! Yet it was a long time before her daughter realized how clearly her very satisfaction with this story showed her own competitiveness and insecurity about her mother.

I remember a little girl of seven who had been sent to visit her grandmother. When, on her return, her mother met her at the train, the child's first words were: "Granny says to tell you that I am coming home very much improved."

The Possessive Mother

On the other hand, some new mothers are so possessive that they suspect rivalry where a grandmother is simply indulging the human desire to earn a little praise. I recall that sometimes when Timmy had been left in my mother's care, she'd tell me proudly how much longer than usual he'd slept, how much better he'd eaten and so on. It irritated me until I gradually realized this was her way of proving to me that it was all right to leave him with her.

When your mother becomes a grandmother perhaps the most basic step toward making a happy relationship for all three of you is for you to be aware, first, of your own feelings about her, and then try to understand what the new situation means to her—how it makes her feel. One of the most helpful things Mother and I did before Timmy was born was to have a long, honest talk about how we felt. For instance, her misgivings about relinquishing her youth came out and this is quite a typical reaction nowadays when many grandmothers are attractive, worldly women who look younger than their years. My baby "dated" my mother in a way she couldn't deny.

Later, when Timmy was born, the very fact of his presence was emotionally disturbing to her. Anxieties and conflicts she had felt as a new mother years before were revived now. She worried about handling the baby, was fearful of doing the wrong thing, anxious about his response to her. She didn't know how much she was giving him in the way of grandmother love. After a little while, during which, thank heaven, I held my peace and my distance, the fears wore off and she was entranced by her success with him.

A baby evokes the most profound and complicated emotions in a woman and while you are experiencing them yourself, don't forget that your mother, if she is on the scene, will be feeling some of them too. The baby will remind her of what may have been the happiest period of her life.

Knowing well that Mother gave my baby a great deal helped me refrain from insisting that she do things exactly my way. When she was handling the baby she was free to do it her way and, rather than confusing the child, I felt it added a new dimension to his experience. (After all, when he grows older, all the world isn't going to treat him "my way" by any means.) As the months go by, some of the aspects of your mother's treatment of your child may disturb you—you may disapprove of them. But, by the same token, the good things about her as a mother, the things you think of lovingly, will still be there too. I remember my surprise at first recognizing in Mother's handling of Timmy things I recalled from my own childhood: cleaning the plate, clocklike routine, scrupulous washing and so on. But I also remember how strong my pleasure was when Mother took Tim for a bird walk in the woods for the first time. My own memories of doing that were so lovely.

Avoid "Retraining"

If you try to "retrain" your mother you will only hurt her. To her, it will imply that what she did with you was wrong, that she was a bad parent, and this is your way of showing her how it should have been done. Her resulting defensiveness will harm her relationship with the baby. And besides, you may not be willing to see that there are many helpful tricks about baby care she can show you.

Have you ever seen someone struggling with a puzzle when you knew exactly how to do it? Didn't your fingers itch to pick up the pieces and quickly fit them together? Your mother is quite likely to have the same impulse when she sees you floundering over some problem she feels sure she could solve. If she is wise, however, she won't interfere. It may be true that her way of doing things would be as practical as yours. But yours is the best for you—just because it is your own.

Suppose that, in spite of all your efforts, a time comes when you just have to ask your mother to keep hands off. Don't feel too badly about it, because it is done for the welfare of the child. On the other hand, a competitive or defensive daughter who takes such an opportunity to get back at her mother will, of course, only bring about more unhappiness. But if you are a mature woman, honestly trying only to protect your child, you will be able to put your point across in a gentle way.

Actually, many grandmothers are so sensitive about "interfering" that there is often more need to draw them in than to curb them. When Grandma comes to your house, the more quickly you establish that you are in complete charge and that "Granny" has nothing to worry about, no responsibility to take, the sooner everyone will settle down. You can do this and still share the fun of playtimes, letting yourself enjoy how much these two, grandmother and child, love and give to each other. For your own part, when you do leave the baby alone with your mother for a time, don't burden her with voluminous instructions on every detail, or check up constantly as if you were just waiting for her to make a wrong move. A few casual tips on how things usually go best, a brief account of the baby's routine, should be enough.

If, when you go to visit, you have your child on a regular routine, you should accept the fact that it is going to be disrupted. Even a young child is bound to be excited and stimulated by new surroundings, new faces and doting attention. When you get home it will only take a day or two to straighten things out again and the importance to the baby of being grandmothered is worth it.

When relations are strained. Most of what I've said is, of course, predicated on your having a basically affectionate and mutually loyal relationship with your mother. If this is not the case, if, unhappily, you never really get on even at the best of times, then the time of your own new motherhood is not the best moment to undertake to reconstruct the relationship. Under the powerful stimulus of this new situation all the old troubles may come out in full force when you are least able to cope with them. In this case, face the facts before the child is born and decide how you will handle the situation— and then stick to it.

Though my relationship with my mother in no sense reflected the situation described above, it took some experience of trial and error, with tense times, for Mother and me to find a very simple rule that has turned our sharing of Timmy into a smoothly working relationship. The rule is, simply, that when we are together the responsibility is mine although the fun belongs to both of us. But when Mother takes care of Timmy, the full responsibility is hers.

When things can be worked out this way it is one of the nicest experiences in the world. For you it means sharing a deep happiness with someone very close. For the baby it is a unique and precious part of his introduction to an expanding world. For Grandmother it is the fun of having another child without the daily burden of responsibility.

—*By Tinka D. Engel*

TEACHING CHILDREN RELIGIOUS TOLERANCE

YOUNG children are attracted by intriguing differences in the ways they and their playmates do things. They are interested in what can be seen. In religion, they are concerned with what is done in worship, rather than in questions of belief. Why does Jonathan have holidays when the rest of the children go to school? Why is Latin used in the Catholic church? Why is it that the cross in the Protestant church does not have the figure of Christ upon it?

Parents and teachers who wish to teach their children religious tolerance have a double problem: to give each child a wholesome, intelligent pride in his own heritage, and at the same time to teach him that the more intensely we care for our own convictions and love our own religious forms, the more we should respect the convictions and try to understand the practices of others. This is the only true tolerance. The need for such understanding is seen in the story of the Protestant child who went with her Catholic friend to church and waited outside while her friend went in for confession. The priest, seeing her, asked if she wanted to come to confession too. "No," she replied, "I'm a Presbyterian; we don't sin."

We must teach our children that while we all reverence the same God, there are many ways to worship Him. Each person seeks the way which makes him most conscious of God's presence. We must teach our children that in all churches there is the same outreach toward God, and that contempt for any creed or ritual is contrary to the spirit of true religion. To do this we need to give our children some understanding of the various faiths in America, especially the three largest religious groups, Jewish, Catholic and Protestant.

Few Christians realize how much our Western civilization owes to the Hebrew people and their religion and morals. Christian children should be taught about this heritage. The Hebrews were the first people to believe that there is only one God. They were the first to set aside one day in the week regularly for rest and worship. Moses gave them and the world the Ten Commandments. He first spoke the benediction most frequently used in many Christian churches:

"The Lord bless thee and keep thee;
The Lord make His face to shine upon thee;
The Lord lift up His countenance upon thee and give thee peace."

Hebrew leaders taught the social and ethical ideals which are basic in our Western world and developed the custom of democratic worship in which all the people share. Congregational worship is found only in religions which have learned from Judaism. The sacred scriptures of the Jews are also used in Christian churches; they are known as the Old Testament.

Even the general arrangement of church buildings goes back to the Jewish synagogue, with its pews for the worshipers and its platform at the front with a reading desk and a worship center. This center in the synagogue is called the Sacred Ark. It is a cabinet in which are kept the scrolls of the Law. Before it hangs the Eternal Light, symbolic of the undying light of faith.

Christian children should understand, too, certain Jewish observances that differ from Christian ways.

With the Jews, more than any other people, religion centers in the home. Every religious festival has its special home observance. The mother gives great care to the observance of dietary laws, even though the reason for them may be lost in the changed conditions of modern life. The faithful Jew loves these observances because they are a part of his heritage. Great care is taken as to how any animal to be used for food is slaughtered; pork and some other meats are not eaten; and meat and milk products are not mixed. Of course, many modern Jews feel that they can keep the spirit of their religion without observing all these provisions.

The Sabbath. The Jews gave the world the blessing of one day of rest after six days of work. They called it the "Sabbath," which means seventh. When people told time by the sun, each day ended when the sun set. So the Sabbath begins with the coming of evening on Friday and ends at sunset Saturday. Many Jews interpret strictly the commandment that they should not do any work on the Sabbath. The dinner Friday night is the Sabbath meal and is observed in each home with old, familiar ceremonies. Saturday morning the family attends the synagogue.

Although American Jews observe the first day of January as other Americans do, their much older New Year comes in the fall, determined by the old agricultural customs of Palestine. But because, like many other ancient peoples, the Jews reckoned time by the moon, it does not always come on the same date of our calendar year. Their Rosh Hashanah is the day when God inscribes in the Book of Life His judgment upon each person. Ten Days of Penitence follow, days of grace during which the judgment may be changed for the better. The tenth day is Yom Kippur, the Day of Atonement, a solemn day of fasting from sunset to sunset. The final impressive service takes place toward sunset, closing with a long, loud blast of the trumpet, to mark the sealing of the Book.

(Continued after picture section)

When a BABY joins the family

THERE'S a new baby at the Potters', another little girl, Peggy. The other children are Chrissie, who at seventeen months is barely more than a baby herself, and Howie, three and a half. What the arrival of a new baby, whether it is the first or the third, means to a family, is the theme of the unusual documentary pictures that follow.

ALL PHOTOGRAPHS IN THIS SECTION BY SUZANNE SZASZ

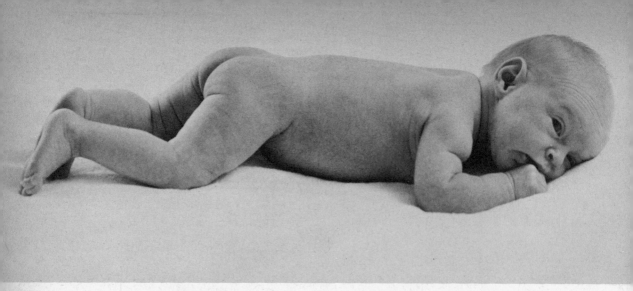

Still redfaced at ten days, Peggy contemplates the world.
Though she sees light her eyes do not actually focus yet.

ABOVE—Chrissie's mother
knows that now is not the time
to try to wean her from
the bottle when so much
of Mother's attention must
be given to the baby.

LEFT ABOVE—But more independent
Howie, watches the baby-tending
with interest. Mother makes
both youngsters welcome, tries
to divide her time among all.

LEFT—Mother picks up baby,
supporting head and back.

The First Month

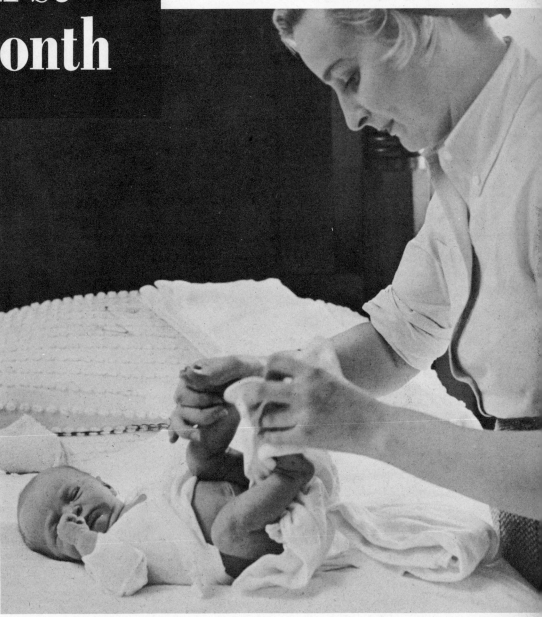

Peggy's wardrobe is plain, loose enough for easy dressing.

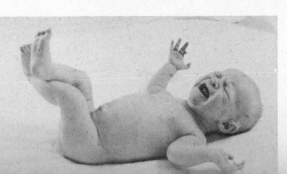

Something startled her and like all new babies her response is total. She cries without tears and kicks with no control.

At this age babies sometimes cry for no understandable reason. Here Mother tries to comfort Peggy.

The Second Month

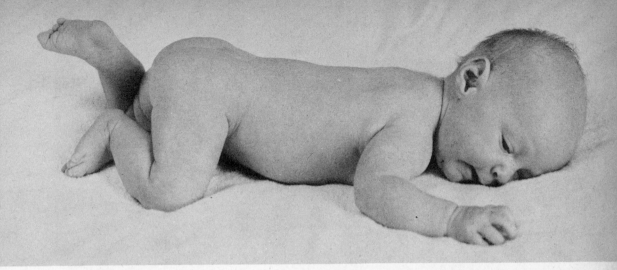

Peggy shows a preference for her right side when she turns her head and contemplates her outthrust hand. She is not yet able to raise her head.

Peggy gets prescribed vitamin drops strategically squirted on the back of her tongue.

Continued on next page ⟶

Peggy is now one month old and has a regular bath while Chrissie looks on with interest.

Though Peggy is a breast fed baby a freedom bottle gives Mother a breather and puts Peggy in an accepting mood for later weaning.

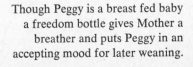

THE SECOND MONTH
continued

Peggy lies snuggly sleeping,
getting her airing
while Mother drives to market.

Home again and awake she lies
on Mother's big bed absorbed in
the light from the window.

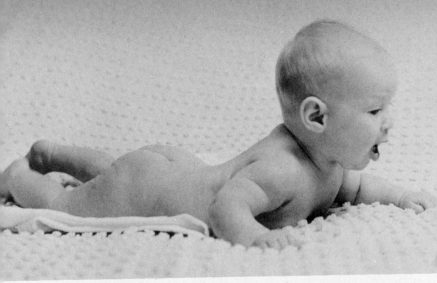

The Third Month

In nine weeks Peggy has gained several pounds; she is strong enough to lift and hold her head up.

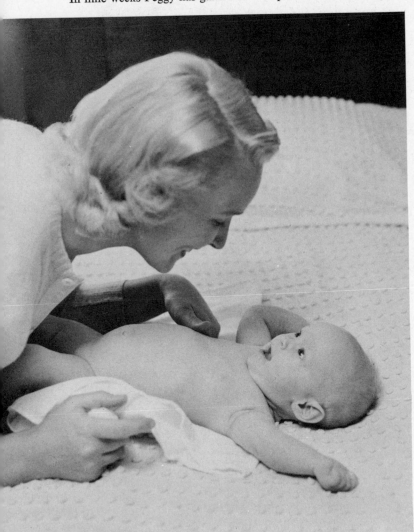

Mother talks to Peggy who happily babbles back—first practice for later speech.

Peggy can now grasp a rattle between thumb and fingers and hold on to it.

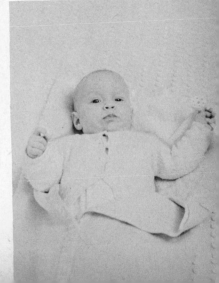

Continued on next page ⟶

Real tears now. Peggy doesn't want to miss anything and has learned that crying gets sympathy.

Expect dribbling from that first solid food; some babies like strained fruit better than cereal.

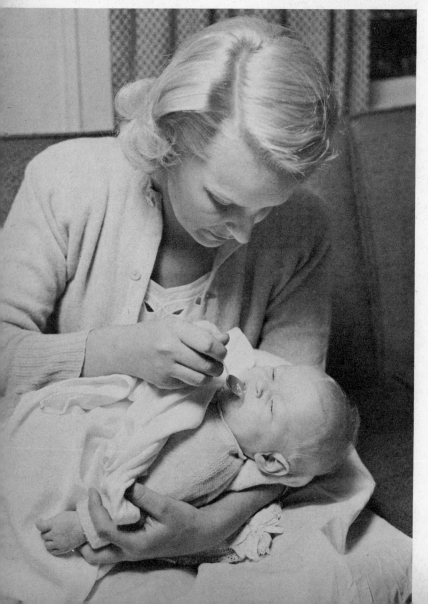

Above and Right—Sister Chrissie stands by watchful, not yet won over, as her friendly older brother is, by Peggy's coos and gurgles.

The Fourth Month

Triumph of a four-month-old—supporting herself on her hands.

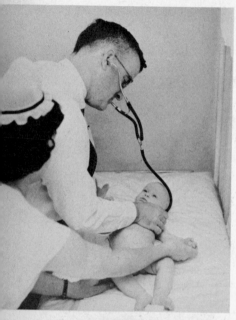

At check-up time in her doctor's office, Peggy gets her immunization shots.

Curiosity gets the better of two-year-old Chrissie, who has been keeping her distance till now.

Play exercise like this with Mother is Peggy's delight. It helps to strengthen growing muscles, too.

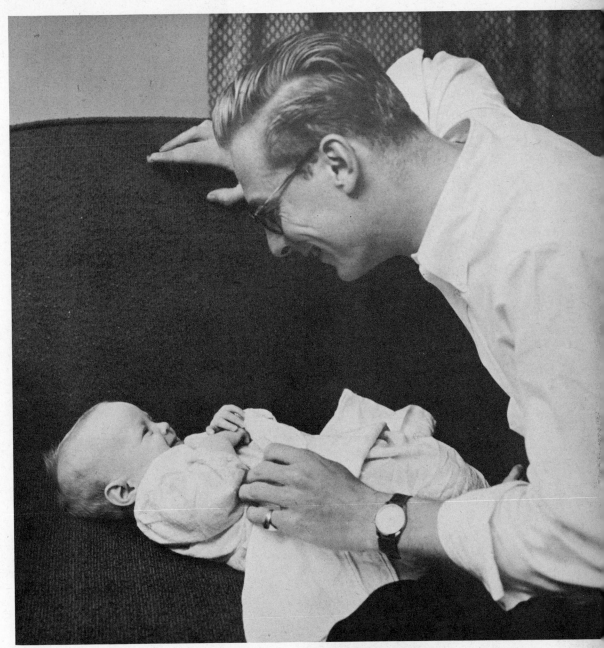

Peggy's at her best in
the afternoons, after her nap.
If Daddy is home early, they
have a delightful social hour.

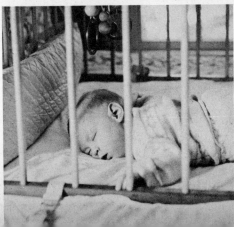

Peggy has settled down
to an ordered routine of meals,
naps and nighttime sleep.

At five months Peggy has doubled her birth weight; she's up on her haunches now for the first time.

The Fifth Month

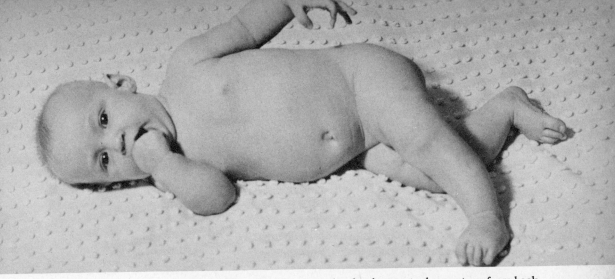

Another proof of Peggy's muscular development: she can turn from back
to side, but doesn't roll over yet. Fist in mouth may be teething sign.

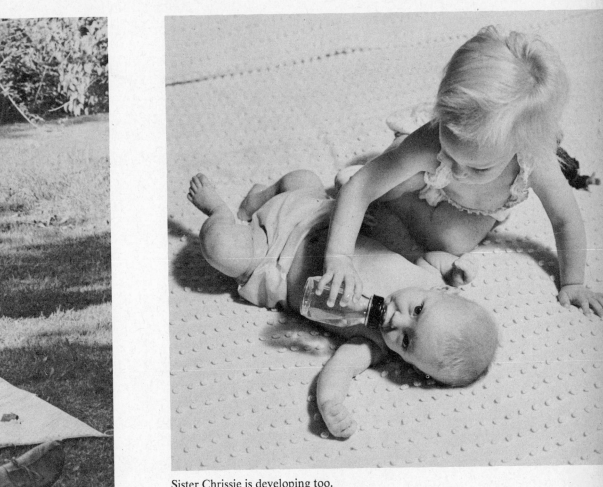

Sister Chrissie is developing too.
She's become interested in helping with the baby,
gives her a drink of cooled, boiled water.

Peggy enjoys her airing
outdoors with the family.

The Sixth Month

Peggy at six months is set on getting ahead; better coordination of her legs shows she'll soon be creeping.

Peggy doesn't mind her Mother's absence when Grandma sits for her.

Solemn stare for a stranger is a sign she's beginning to discriminate between family and outsiders.

Peggy has graduated from the startle reaction of early infancy. She now shows anger and fear when she comes up against unfamiliar objects.

Howie is unconcerned but Chrissie is disconcerted about baby's perch on Mommy.

Continued on next page ⟶

Peggy meets a friendly puppy.
She's cautious at first
but soon shows a decided interest.

Try to take the pot lid away
from Peggy and see how she'll cry!
She can amuse herself now
and is less dependent on Mother.

The Seventh Month

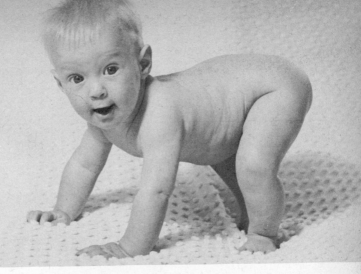

Not all babies learn new skills at the same time or in the same way; here's Peggy getting ready to creep.

Peggy's teething now; when her gums hurt at night she wakes and cries and Mother comforts her.

Peggy is proud of her ability to switch a toy from hand to hand, or handle more than one at a time.

Continued on next page ⟶

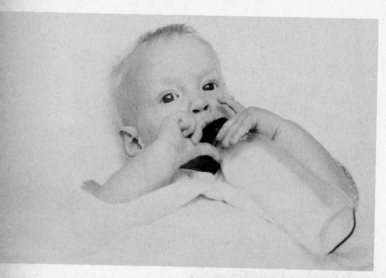

Tucked in with her bedtime bottle
Peggy can now hold it herself;
she uses her thumb, tilts
her hand when grasping,
unmistakable signs of her rapidly
developing muscular control.

An outing with sister Chrissie
finds Peggy enjoying graduation
from big carriage to stroller.

Peggy, sitting up by herself now, goes along to the supermarket.

A piece of toast or zwieback
starts finger feeding, is relished by
a teether who likes chewy food.

The Eighth Month

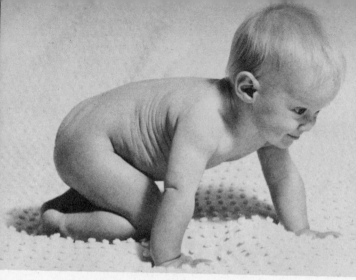

If it's within crawling distance Peggy goes for whatever she sees. She wants to touch and taste everything.

"No, no, musn't touch."
Peggy learns the heater is off limits.
Dangerous objects and
breakables are put out of range now.

Daddy becomes increasingly important
to Peggy, but it's hard
to stay awake for fun with him.

Mornings Peggy now joins Howie
and Chrissie at dress parade.
"Ma-ma" is her enthusiastic
greeting to her family.

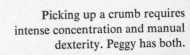

Picking up a crumb requires
intense concentration and manual
dexterity. Peggy has both.

Although Peggy is moving on toward independence, she still requires lots of Mother's time and love.

The Ninth Month

Milk comes mostly from a cup now, except for the bedtime bottle.

Peggy prefers her hand to the spoon, so lunch is a slow affair when she goes it alone.

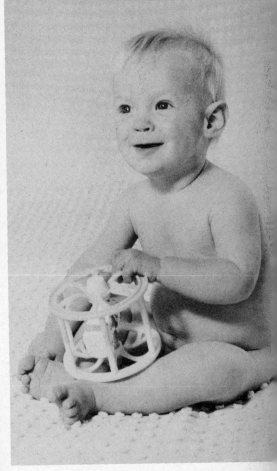

You can get her attention now—she recognizes her name. "Peggy!" Mother called—thus a portrait of a bright-eyed nine-month-old.

Continued on next page ⟶

Peggy is beginning to feel jealous. She's standing! But Mother is busy with Chrissie and doesn't see.

Peggy tests the size and feel of everything;
she likes company near by as
she plays and delights Howie when she
laughs at the funny faces he makes at her.

Peggy can get around now by holding onto the furniture. She is growing more daring all the time—even tries to climb stairs—under Mother's watchful eye.

Daddy gets a big bye-bye as he leaves for work in the morning.

The Tenth Month

After her afternoon nap, Peggy enjoys playtime. She especially likes a bit of roughhousing.

Continued on next page →

Peggy's first Christmas is coming. Gift
wrapping is so fascinating to watch
that Peggy forgets to object to being dressed!

Mother has a pre-bedtime "talk"
with Peggy. Peggy imitates
Mother's tone and inflection so
her chatter almost
sounds like real conversation.

Chrissie knows better but
Peggy goes in for some
pre-Christmas unwrapping.
For her the box is as
fascinating as the contents.

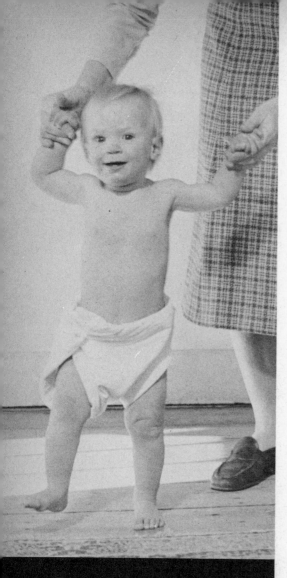

Peggy has now tripled her
birth weight. She's not
ready to step out on her own
yet but with Mommy holding
her she feels safe.

Peggy holds her own toy while
watching Howie and Chrissie
"divvy up" some lemon drops.

Resistance to parting with a toy, being diapered
or going to bed may bring on tears.
Mother comforts her here but often diversion works.

The Eleventh Month

Peggy takes part in two-way nursery games, her favorite, peek-a-boo.

Peggy consciously uses her ability to let go of things. Howie plays retriever but isn't fooled by that abashed look.

ONE YEAR OLD

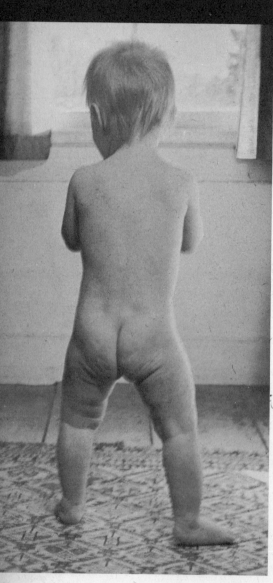

Peggy uses wide stance to balance herself; she stands alone but won't budge without something to hang onto.

Sister Chrissie gives
Peggy a great big birthday hug.

The yearling understands and carries
out simple commands. "Put the small cup
into the big one," says
Mother and Peggy thoughtfully obeys.

"Happy Birthday to you!"
says Peggy's family. While Peggy
looks as though she's
getting ready to blow out the candle.

Continued on next page⟶

Shoes are fascinating objects. Mother knows that taking them off comes before learning to put them on.

This birthday is full of firsts. Peggy's enjoying her first haircut because Mother's quick snipping doesn't require too much restraint.

(*Continued from page 480*)

Festival of Passover. The foremost of Jewish festivals is the Passover. When most of the Jews lived in Palestine, all who could went to Jerusalem to celebrate this feast. Now it is observed in Jewish homes around the world with much the same ceremonies. Everything is made clean and fresh for spring. The most wonderful meal of the year is the dinner on Passover Eve. As family and friends gather at the table, they follow a regular order of services. The story is told afresh year after year of how God delivered His people from bondage in Egypt, delivered them that they might bear witness to His power and righteousness, and that they might help to free all nations not only from bondage to men but also from sin and evil. The Passover is the Festival of Freedom, when Jews pray for freedom for all.

Jesus and the first Christians were Jews. The last meal that Jesus ate with His friends was the Passover. He took the bread and then the cup and blessed them, as does every Jewish host at the Passover. But He also said: "This is my body. This is my blood," and He asked His disciples to remember Him whenever they ate the bread and wine. This Christians do in the service called "The Lord's Supper," "Communion," "The Eucharist" or "The Mass."

Meaning of the Mass

Children who are not Catholics will be interested to learn the meaning of the Mass. For Catholics it is more than a re-enacting of the Last Supper. They believe that the substance of the bread and wine is changed into the substance of the body and blood of Christ, so that whoever receives the sacrament, receives Christ Himself. Some of the bread of the Sacrament is kept in the beautiful box, called the tabernacle, which occupies the central place on the altar. The ever-burning lamp, reminiscent of the Eternal Light before the Ark in a synagogue, symbolizes the real presence of the Lord's Body. When, therefore, one bows before the altar, one bows in the presence of Christ Himself.

Protestants observe the sacrament more simply, as a symbol of the spiritual presence of their Lord. The forms vary somewhat in different churches but all alike find in it the occasion for a closer communion with Him.

Perhaps no other single fact has caused so much ill will between Jews and Christians as the death of Jesus. "Did the Jews kill Jesus?" a seventh-grade boy asked. "Is it true that whenever Christians look at the cross of Christ, they are thinking, 'Those dreadful Jews'?" a Jewish boy inquired.

Rome was the ruling power in Palestine at the time of Christ; the death sentence was passed by a Roman ruler. But those who accused Jesus and delivered Him to the Roman soldiers were Jews. Always when a foreign nation has overrun and subdued a country, there have been some people who for personal gain collaborated with the conquering power. But it is as unreasonable to say, "The Jews killed Jesus" as it would be to say, "A Virginian killed Lincoln; therefore we will hate Virginians." Jews delivered Jesus to death, not "The Jews." Jews also watched beside His cross, gave Him burial, and later risked their lives in loyalty to Him.

Significance of the Cross

He might have escaped death but He did not. He believed that it was God's will for Him. From the cross, He prayed, "Father, forgive them; they know not what they do." Through the centuries His followers have thought of the cross as a symbol of love stronger than sin and death.

The Christian festival of Easter celebrates the resurrection of Jesus. It is the festival of life triumphant. Like the Jewish Passover, with which it coincides in time, it is a festival of freedom from bondage and fear.

The first Christians, being Jews, observed the Sabbath as they always had, but they also met on Sunday to celebrate their joy in Jesus' resurrection. When Christianity spread among non-Jews, Sunday became their holy day and they carried over into it many of the Jewish customs.

We need to make clear to children that Catholics and Protestants are both Christians. The many Christian denominations are confusing, but however great the variations, all are different branches of the one church which gives its allegiance to one Lord.

Papal authority. Catholics believe that Christ Himself appointed Peter to be the head of the Church and gave him all authority; he was the first Pope and he passed on his authority to his successor. Every Pope has done the same and has delegated power to the bishops, who in turn ordain the priests. Catholics believe that their doctrines and their ritual and all the organization of the Church have direct divine sanction and thus are authoritative.

Protestants believe that every individual has the right and responsibility to think for himself, to study the Bible, and to try to do God's will.

What Protestants Believe

The Pilgrim Fathers were Protestants. They came to America that they might be free to worship God and to serve Him according to their own consciences. The American idea of democracy began in religion. The largest number of people in the United States are associated with the Protestant churches. Because there are so many Protestant denominations, there are many differences of opinion as to beliefs, forms of church organization and the ritual of their services. Despite these differences, there is a growing spirit of cooperation; many of the denominations are united in the Federal Council of the Churches of Christ in America. There is also a National Conference of Christians and Jews, which is making all groups more conscious of what they have in common and the work they can do together.

Religious heritage of America. When one thinks of the ancient traditions and ceremonies of the Jews, of the way in which their home life throughout the long centuries has been permeated with the consciousness of God's concern for His people, a Christian might well be envious and ask, "How can we give our children such a sense of the unity and continuity of life?" When one considers the closely knit Catholic Church, its authority, its at-homeness in all lands and among all peoples, the richness of its ritual, one covets for all children the awe and reverence it inspires, the sense of security it gives. When one notes the directness and spontaneity of Protestantism at its best, its simplicity, its freedom, one would like to bring to every child the challenge to make his individual life noble and to do his part in building the world-wide Kingdom of God. These all belong to our Jewish-Christian heritage. American religious life at its best is a symphony requiring all the varied forms to bring out the richness and beauty of the whole.

Let us tell our children the stories of the saints, heroes and leaders who have a place in all our traditions. Let us encourage them to visit synagogues and churches other than their own. Let us invite children of other faiths to our homes. Then when they are ready to make the religion of their parents their own, as the vast majority of them will, they will do it with more intelligent loyalty and with sympathetic appreciation of the ways in which others worship.
—*By Florence Mary Fitch*

DEMOCRACY BEGINS AT HOME

MANY a school in America is doing an excellent job of teaching democracy in the classroom. Learning today is associated with doing, and comes through group activities and group discussions in which each child plays a part. Questions of "right and wrong" are no longer handed down as dicta from the teacher. They are the subject of group discussion, and are decided on the basis of whether they are innocent or harmful to the group. Even in these discussions the democratic method plays a part. No child is expected to monopolize the conversation, but each is encouraged to make his contribution to the whole.

These fine examples of working together provide the boy and girl with a splendid technique for democratic living. In a deeper sense, however, democracy is more than a technique. It is a matter of thinking and feeling, and the foundations of our emotions and thinking are laid in the home. Unless the home is tolerant, moderate and democratic the child will hardly be able to absorb a real democracy.

The foundation of our American way of life, as defined by Thomas Jefferson, is a government which exists "by consent of the governed." On this principle also our home government must be established or fail in true democracy.

At first blush it may seem stretching a point to say that the government of children exists by consent of the governed. Yet anyone who has seen a two-year-old in a temper tantrum is likely to have watched a rebellion against a government which, to the child, seemed unsatisfactory. He has also been afforded, incidentally, a striking demonstration of the difficulty of governing a child who does not want to be governed. Eventually the two-year-old learns that some government is inevitable and desirable, and becomes able to adjust to it. But if his government is really unsatisfactory to the deep-seated, although inarticulate, standards within him, his rebellion may continue by devious means through many long years.

Children want and need government, and they know it. They will respond happily to discipline, provided only that it is sound and just. Every child recognizes his own weakness and the superior strength of the adult. He needs and is reassured by authority so long as that authority is moderate, kind and reasonable, and so long as it respects his dignity as an individual. He wants and needs fair, impartial and scrupulous good government in his home, as much as the adult wants it in his nation—a courteous and considerate good government which will respect his dignity as an integral part of the whole.

Respect Child's Dignity

We can begin this respect for our child as an individual in his cradle. We can be attentive to his wishes and his needs, instead of expecting him to conform wholeheartedly to a plan we have conceived for him. As he grows older we can continue this respectful consideration of his needs and desires. This does not mean that we will turn over to him responsibility for which he is not ready. In the last analysis, authority is the parent's and must rest with the parent, just as in government it rests with the executive body. The responsibility for the child's sound development is placed by law, as well as by nature, upon the home and the parent cannot escape this responsibility. He will exercise it most wisely, however, if he exercises it moderately.

For the establishment of a true democracy in our homes we can do no better than to take as our ideals the passionate principles upon which this country was founded. The very Preamble to our Constitution sets the pace, as any fifth-grader can quote you. Any home attempting "to form a more perfect union, establish justice, insure domestic tranquillity, promote the general welfare and secure the blessings of liberty for ourselves and our posterity" has a sound foundation for an enduring democracy.

Most children are good enough sports to realize that if legal responsibility rests with the parent, his also should be the final authority. If they have been treated with respect from their earliest babyhood they will in turn respect the rights of adults. Government by consent of the governed is, after all, government. But often it takes skillful sailing, particularly as the child grows older, to steer so reasonably and so fairly that you win his consent to this government even if it be in violation of his own desires.

There are times, of course, when the decision must be made without the child's psychological consent. If the parent's general democracy is recognized, however, his authority will be accepted whether it is relished or not. Daughter may have her preference in preparatory schools, but it is mother and father who must decide whether catalogs with enticing photographs of students boating should be allowed to outweigh such more serious considerations as credits, school standards, and the extent of the curriculum. Son may be allowed the freedom of the family car, yet still have to accept the decision of his father that it may not be taken, for instance, on a motoring trip to far-off Florida. The father, who pays the car's insurance and is legally responsible for the safe driving of anyone chauffeuring it, may also decide that it shall not be driven by youths who have had a drink, or who have stayed out so late that they may be considered a group of reckless-driving joy riders.

Designating Responsibility

Responsibility goes with every activity. It must be judiciously decided what responsibilities may be the parent's and what are the son's. And a parent must often plumb deeply his own reactions as well as his offspring's—recognizing both the drive of the growing youth to act like an adult and the instinctive, often jealous, desire of the adult to keep him still a child.

Perhaps we ought to have, every so often, a self-administered Democracy Test for Parents. How do you rate on Life, Liberty and the Pursuit of Happiness? Do you set an example of tolerance and broadmindedness where other people are concerned? Do you believe that all people are born with an equal right to be respectfully treated, or do you subtly look down your nose at the Smaller-House Block around the corner? Can you "take it" when the nice-mannered son of the Italian cornetist comes around with the gang—or when the not-so-nice son of the striving contractor becomes a shining model for your hitherto polite little boy?

How do you meet that perennial problem of "Why can't we have a new car like the Palmers?" or "My bike is just an old crate, and all the other children have big new ones." Or "Every girl in my class has nice-looking clothes except me." and "Why don't we live in a nicer neighborhood?" Do you, in your turn, prod Dorothy to excel at the skating club because ice-skating is now "the thing to do?" If you can't teach your children that there are other standards than money standards, and that even though it hurts we must face the fact that few of us have equal possessions or equal abilities and our chance in life comes from enjoying and making the best of what we have—then your democracy may not get so high a rating after all.

One of the first principles of true democracy is violated by intolerance. The housewife who is "high hat" with the grocer, and the grocer who is indifferent and autocratic in the mistaken idea that this spells independence, are alike undemocratic and will pass this idea on to their children. Democracy is founded on respect for the dignity of the individual.

In our Democracy Test let's just run through the Bill of Rights, and see how we check up against the specifications which our founding fathers made for us, for the preservation of human liberties. What about Article I, which provides for religious freedom, and forbids abridgment of freedom of speech or of the press? Do we react intolerantly if our high-school son disagrees with our politics? How far does "freedom of speech" go in our household when twelve-year-old is critical of father's management? Can we "take it" when daughter—no offense intended—moans despairingly over our hair-do, our practical shoes, and the style of our last year's suit?

Family Maintenance

Article II takes us back to the homely problems of family maintenance. The right of the people to bear arms may not come into the family picture, but the right of each individual to contribute to the daily maintenance of the family does. Shall Shirley be expected to dry the dishes? Of course she shall. And not as a special employment for which she receives compensation, but as her contribution to the routine running of the family. Allowance is a separate matter—such part of the family income as can be fairly divided for her spending. She should be free to do with it as she likes—provided it is given her for her enjoyment and not for necessary purchases—but it should not be regarded as pay for performing a duty. It should be just another part of the family democracy.

Article III might make us, now and again, feel a bit uncomfortable if we followed it to its logical implications. "No soldier shall in time of peace be quartered in any house without consent of the owner, nor in time of war but in a manner prescribed by law." A child's room is his castle; his bicycle is his exclusive domain. Do we insist that he let small brother come in to listen

to his radio or read his books, or that he give sister a turn on his bike? Of course we don't want our children to be either selfish or exclusive, but perhaps parental proclamation is not the best way to encourage unselfishness. Possibly a respect for the child's own possessions might give him in time enough security to branch out in generosity of his own.

Article IV continues with the same safeguards of the individual's security. "The right of the people to be secure in their persons, houses, papers and effects against unreasonable searches and seizures shall not be violated." It makes one uncomfortable to think of it, but there are mothers who feel justified in trying to keep up with their children by peeping in their diaries. Some parents take it as a matter of course that they may read their children's mail.

A child has also a right to a reasonable physical privacy. If it is at all possible he should have a room of his own; at least a corner of a room should be his without question in which his belongings may be cherished. Even the youngest toddler appreciates this respect for his individuality. When daughter reaches the age of ultra modesty she should be protected and provided for in that modesty.

A child has the same need for a place of retreat as has an adult. The "hide-outs," the "shacks," the "forts," the "club houses" which children construct are potent testimonial to this. They gain spiritual solace and comfort, just as do their elders, from a retreat of their own in which they can quietly take stock, and in which they can find refuge from the problems of the world.

Avoid Snap Judgments

"No person shall be held to answer for a crime except under indictment, nor be deprived of life, liberty or property without due process of law." That hits the parent who is given to making snap judgments or blanket indictments where he lives. Do we treat our children with due deliberation when we feel called upon to protest some misbehavior? If Tommy keeps the car out far after the time prescribed we should not let him "get away with it" for half a dozen times, then suddenly clamp down on all his privileges.

Article VI says "The accused shall enjoy the right to a speedy trial." That word *enjoy* was perhaps not used without reason. This provision should be a great relief to children who are burdened with the threat of punishment "when father gets home," or with vague warnings of denials or of parental disfavor. This article guarantees to all of us "the right to be informed of the nature and cause of the accusation." A child who has behaved unsatisfactorily is entitled to a clear, concise and logical complaint against his misbehavior. Then remedies to secure better behavior may also be arrived at in a judicial and friendly manner.

Article VIII forbids the infliction of "cruel or unnatural punishments." There are other forms of punishment besides retaliation for a misdemeanor. It may be a cruel and unnatural punishment to compel a fifth-grader to wear high-waisted dresses when "all the other girls" are wearing low-waisted ones; to dress Bob in short pants when all the other boys are wearing long ones.

But here again democracy does not mean that the child is old enough to make all decisions, merely that his point of view must be considered. Just what shall Jennie take to camp when the prospectus says five pairs of slacks and shorts, and Jennie wants to take all white ones while mother knows the dark practical garments are the ones needed? Surely a concession to Jennie's wishes should be made if possible, in the way of including at least one white garment, but mother is the practical leader of the family, and hers is the decision that the dark garments are what will be wanted and needed.

"The powers not delegated by the constitution to the government . . . are reserved to the people." "The right of citizens to vote shall not be denied or abridged." The voice of the child in his own affairs will not be denied in a democratic home.

The home founded on the ideas of mutual service and mutual respect for the individual, the home which maintains a tolerant and broadminded belief that one should live and let live, is the truly democratic home needed in our world today.

—*By Evelyn Emig Mellon*

WHAT WE KNOW ABOUT HEREDITY

SOME years ago, in the interest of science, a man and his wife "adopted" a newborn chimpanzee named Gua and raised it with their own son, Donald. They wanted to see how a human environment would affect a chimpanzee's heredity.

Gua and Donald had the same sort of home life, ate the same food, slept in similar beds and wore the same kind of clothing. Gua's adoptive "parents" showed him love and affection just as they did their own son, even toilet trained him and taught him to "kiss and make up."

On that treatment, Donald developed into a normal healthy boy. Gua developed into a normal, healthy chimpanzee.

As may be presumed, the first thing heredity determines is that your child will belong to the human race, but it goes far beyond that. If geneticists could breed people as they do fruit flies, they might in the course of a dozen or so generations deliver up on order one human infant, blue eyes, long lashes, wavy blond hair, type O positive blood, a pug nose, dimples and the ability to wiggle his ears.

To see just how much heredity might determine, consider the case of one set of identical twin boys, separated in childhood and reared in different homes without any knowledge of each other's existence. Developing from a single egg fertilized by a single sperm, these two boys had exactly the same inheritance. But growing up in different homes, their environments differed. When they were reunited in their twenties, the two had strikingly similar features, intelligence and personalities. Both had married, in the same year, women of the same age and type. Both were engaged in the same work—telephone repairmen. They were even working for the same company, a thousand miles apart, and each had a baby son.

This authentic case history may suggest that your child's entire future is predetermined from the moment of birth. Yet stubborn facts leave no doubt that many differences among people, even between identical twins, depend directly upon their environment. People change through their lifetimes, developing and growing according to inherited predisposition. They become more or less wise in some things, more or less foolish in others. They cultivate some of their abilities and let many others lie fallow.

Chromosomes Influence Heredity

What then does a child inherit from his parents and other ancestors and what comes to him from the example and personal influence of his parents? Just how much can you do to help mold your child's character and talents?

The earliest notions about heredity arose from the obvious physical similarities between parents and children and those that sometimes run through a family for generations. It was explained as "something in the blood." We now know that the connection between one generation and the next is through tiny particles of matter called chromosomes, found in every cell of the human body. Each human cell contains 24 pairs of these chromosomes, 48 chromosomes in all. One of each pair in the father, separated at random, goes into every sperm cell. One of each pair in the mother enters the nucleus of the egg cell. When egg and sperm unite, starting a new individual, the fertilized egg and all the millions of cells that make up the body contain the 24 pairs of chromosomes. One in each pair is supplied by the mother and one by the father. The child's inheritance is determined at conception.

Making up each chromosome are still smaller structures, the genes, complex molecules that act like certain drugs, hormones or ferments. They act upon one another. They may interfere with each other or they may reinforce each other. By their interaction, the chromosomes with their genes make it possible for the fertilized egg to develop into an individual with all the infinite detail of a human being and his unique combination of characteristics and potentialities.

How Recessive Genes Work

When two parents have contrasting characteristics such as light eyes and dark eyes, straight hair and curly hair and so on, the genes related to one contrasting trait from one parent may cancel the effect of its opposite from the other parent. Curliness of hair for example, would be "dominant" over straightness; light eyes are "recessive" to dark.

If a "pure" dark-eyed person married a light-eyed mate, all the children will have dark eyes. But each of the children will carry a hidden recessive gene the effect of which does not show. If two persons with such hidden qualities marry, they are likely to have one light-eyed child among dark-eyed brothers and sisters. The effects of recessive genes thus skip a generation or result in throwbacks after several generations. This explains the often mystifying appearance of a blue-eyed child in an otherwise dark-eyed family.

The role of the genes in shaping our features is most dramatically illustrated by identical twins, two distinct human beings possessing identical genetic makeup. The structure of their body cells is so much alike that skin from one can be permanently grafted onto the other. In appearance, identical twins are so close that often their mother has difficulty distinguishing them. Fraternal twins, conceived of two sperms and two eggs, may be of different sex. They generally look no more alike than brothers or sisters who are not twins.

Height and Weight

Height and weight depend greatly upon heredity. Tall parents tend to have tall children and short parents short children. Several different genes are related to height, as this depends upon the relative lengths of the head, trunk, thighs and forelegs—which all develop under the action of different sets of genes. In mixed families it is impossible to predict how tall any given child will grow. Improved nutrition and medical care in recent years result in children being taller, on the average, than their parents were at the same age.

Degrees of slimness or obesity also may run through a family because of heredity. But a lusty appetite, developed at the family dinner table, can make a substantial contribution to the waistline.

If face and form are largely fixed by the chromosomes, what can you do to pass a more "beautiful" set on to your children? Nothing! The chromosomes in your body were present in the egg and sperm at your own conception and will remain constant throughout your life. Though mother may bleach her hair for a lifetime, the genes do not change. And father's body-building exercises won't put the slightest bulge in his son's biceps. Nothing you do to yourself or for yourself during life can affect your child's heredity.

How intelligent will your child be? To determine the relation of heredity to intelligence we must first define and measure "intelligence." Our best yardstick, the IQ test, may be a rough index of a group of mental capacities, but it fails completely to reflect ambition, leadership or common sense.

Development of Intelligence

The processes of our minds are very complex; they are influenced by a great many dominant and recessive genes. We all carry both "smart" genes and "dumb" genes. Their interaction may result in widely varying intelligence in children, superior or inferior to either of their parents in some particulars. Ordinary brothers and sisters differ by an average of about 15 points on the IQ scale.

Heredity never fixes a child's IQ. At most, it determines his potentials for various kinds of future development. Which of these he develops, and how far, depend upon a multitude of chances and circumstances. Educators have repeatedly shown that a child's IQ can go up or down, depending on his education, motivation, home life and the stimulation and challenges that affect him.

For example, there is the case of identical twin girls separated at infancy by adoption. One girl graduated from college and became a schoolteacher. The other never went beyond the third grade. The college graduate was found to have an IQ 26 points higher than her sister.

Influence of Home Life

A large group of New York City children who rated "100 IQ" in intelligence tests given to 8th-graders, were followed up 20 years later. Some had had no further schooling after the 8th grade. Others had graduated from high school, some from college and a few were Doctors of Philosophy. There was great variation in the whole group; the Ph.D.'s averaged 20 IQ points higher than those who had not gone beyond the 8th grade. How much influence did home life play in inducing some of these young people to continue their education and develop their capacities while others, with the same capacities, did not?

For the most part, the same is true of special talents like music, art or mechanical aptitude. A study of some of the nation's most gifted musicians conducted by Amram Scheinfeld, author of "You and Heredity," showed that where both parents had musical talent, more than 70 per cent of the children were also talented. Where only one parent was talented, about 60 per cent of the children had musical talents. Where neither parent had musical talents, only 15 per cent of the children were talented.

What is inherited is not the talent itself but special traits and capacities, such as superior muscular coordination, dexterity or color sensitivity. The patterns into which those traits develop depend on inclinations of the individual and the atmosphere in which he lives. In one environment, inherited artistic abilities might lead a child to become a skilled engraver. In another environment it might lead him to be an equally skilled counterfeiter. Without the inherited abilities, he could become neither.

A child must be given a chance to show whatever natural talents he has through opportunities to explore, experiment, and dream. Then his talents need to be cultivated or they may be wasted. Sometimes, though, an individual of original creative ability also has the drive and self-assurance to overcome circumstances that would destroy another.

Fortunately no injury or disease acquired by you through environment can be passed on to your child! But this is not to say that diseases and abnormalities which the parents themselves inherited cannot be transmitted. They can. Hemophilia, the "bleeding sickness," is hereditary, generally confined to males and transmitted through the daughters of affected males.

As for the more prevalent causes of illness in children, the findings of geneticists are all on the encouraging side. No matter what the state of your own health, no common ailment is "predestined" to strike your child.

Most Illnesses Not Hereditary

Tuberculosis was once thought of as hereditary because it appeared to be more concentrated among certain families. We now know, however, that it is caused by a germ which people living in slum conditions are less able to resist. If the disease ran in certain families, it was because the members shared unsanitary living conditions.

There is even less possibility of your child inheriting pneumonia, influenza or polio. The so-called "communicable" diseases are caused solely by known external agents and can't possibly be transmitted by inheritance. But individuals differ greatly in their inherited ability to resist the invasion of particular bacteria.

Heredity does appear to be the direct cause of a few rare types of cancer. But of the forms particularly affecting young children, including cancer of the blood (leukemia), bone cancer and cancers of the skin, eyes and kidneys, the origin remains a puzzle. If cancer has appeared in your family it is no cause for alarm but routine precautions are always desirable in that case.

Diabetes is definitely inherited in many families, through a pair of simple recessive genes. It is transmitted from *both* parents, neither of whom necessarily has the disease, in much the same way that a blue-eyed child is born to parents with brown eyes. The evidence indicates that one does not inherit diabetes but rather a "predisposition" for the disease—a capacity to develop it under conditions of exceptional stress or unsuitable diet. If the doctor suspects this predisposition from the family history or the results of certain tests, he can prescribe a way of life and diet that will enable a child to get along without developing the disease.

The potential for rheumatic heart disease can also be inherited, like diabetes, through the action of two recessive genes. But the capacity develops into the disease only under certain conditions. Climate and nutrition seem to be contributing factors. Where rheumatic heart disease has appeared in a family, parents should be watchful for suspicious symptoms.

Heredity is also thought to be a factor in hypertension and some other forms of heart and arterial disease. There is no conclusive proof that epilepsy is inherited, but the evidence suggests a predisposition to it, that may develop in special circumstances.

Mental Illness

Science is now finding some truth in age-old fears about mental illness. No common type is clearly due only to heredity, although in almost every case predisposition plays a role. If mental illness could be explained entirely in terms of heredity, identical twins would both be either sane or insane. The case has been reported of identical twin girls who were separated while still children and reared in different homes. Both girls had about the same intelligence and nervous and physical makeup. Clara was loved and cared for as a child, and led a secure and comfortable married life. Doris was one of four in a strife-torn family and later married a neurotic war veteran. Clara was nervous and high-strung because of her heredity, but otherwise showed no ill effects. Doris wound up in a mental institution. Heredity loaded the gun against both girls, but unhappy circumstances pointed it at Doris and pulled the trigger.

Specialists are learning to recognize certain inherited physical and mental conditions at an early stage and to stop their further development. In some cases they are able to compensate for a deficiency, as in diabetes—which cannot be cured but can be lived with. Other inherited conditions can be remedied by special treatment.

Heredity plays a fundamental role in shaping your child's body and the working of its parts. Yet the ways in which that body and temper develop into attitudes and prejudices, into beliefs and purposes, into social values and responsibilities, will depend on his "environment." That means his home, his companions, his community and its institutions, its customs and its ideals. In short, aside from ability, vigor and forcefulness, much of one's behavior is learned, not inherited. The son of a criminal may stand a better than average chance of becoming a criminal himself, but only because he has been exposed to the same influences that made his father a criminal before him. But, like the proverbial minister's son, he may also rebel and grow up to be a different kind of person from his father.

A child's heredity may be fixed at conception, but his potentialities can become realities only in an environment that we largely control. Today we know better ways to feed, train and care for our children than our ancestors did. When we use our knowledge, children show better physical development, have better health and make fuller use of their native abilities. More of them attend school longer and rise to the highly skilled professions and crafts. They discover a great variety of ways for enriching life and for enjoying their social and cultural heritage.

—By Benjamin C. Gruenberg, Ph.D., and Joel Berg

TWINS IN THE FAMILY

PROSPECTIVE parents have a habit of stumping their doctor with questions about twins. Their curiosity regarding duplicate offspring is evidence of a universal fascination. It prompts strange old maids to stop and lovingly chuck Tweedledum and Tweedledee under their respective chins. With mingled feelings of anxiety and awe, parents pose questions which reveal so many strange rumors and old wives' tales abounding even in this enlightened age that considerable confusion exists between fact and fiction.

Typical queries run something like this: Isn't it true that twins are often subnormal mentally and physically? Twins are awfully rare, aren't they? Is their birth dangerous to mother or babies? What do you think about dressing twins alike? Do twins really read each other's minds? I have heard that one twin is sterile; is it true?

Confronted with questions such as these, it is a good idea for the doctor to discuss briefly some of the main facts parents should know about twins. A clear understanding of these known facts will give them a sound basis for guiding and enjoying their unusual offspring and, incidentally, help to stave off misdirection by the alarmist, the sentimentalist and the overoptimistic.

First of all, let us consider the magnitude of the twin problem. There are enough twins in the United States to populate a city the size of Philadelphia, our third largest. When you realize that most twins have a mother and father, brothers and sisters, as well as numerous relatives and friends, the number of persons who regularly come into close contact with twins is staggering.

A trifle over one in a hundred births in one year are twins. But this is just an average and the possibilities of having twins in any given family vary according to a number of factors. Parents can easily judge whether their chances are better or poorer than this average by applying each of these factors to their own case.

We have not yet found out exactly what causes twins, but it is well known that they are hereditary; that is, twins occur more commonly in families which have had them than in those which have not. For example, if anyone in the immediate family of the husband or wife has had twins, the chances that the couple will bear twins are about four times the average. If twins have occurred on the wife's side of the family, the event is even more likely. If a sister of the wife has had twins, the chances are eight times greater than the average, or about one in a dozen. Of course, the marriage of twins, or of persons who both have a family history of twins, increases these possibilities still further.

Occurrence of Twins

In addition, twins are born more frequently to older men and women and occur more often in the country than in the city.

If there have been previous children (especially twins), multiple pregnancy is more likely. The rate of twin births is significantly higher among the Northern European peoples than it is among the Southern Europeans and it is higher in the white race than in the others.

Having estimated from these rather formidable statistics the odds on their having twins, the next parental query will probably be: "How can we know we are expecting twins, once the baby (or babies!) is on the way?" This is a matter of no little concern. Many an unsuspecting family has suddenly found itself with only half enough diapers, cribs, blankets, sacques and yes— even names!

When twins are definitely expected, both the parents and doctor have time to make necessary preparations for the new arrivals.

By the fifth month, when the baby is beginning to let loose with some pretty powerful kicks, its tiny bones can be made out by means of X-ray. If two fetuses are seen, the diagnosis is readily established. This is by far the most certain diagnostic method but if this technical procedure is not available, usually the doctor's careful examination will be reliable.

The most important reason for ascertaining as early as possible the presence of twins is to provide for maximum protection of the mother and her babies. Carrying two little ones is hard work and results in more aches and pains than are usually expected. In addition, complications are more common and careful watch must be made to detect the first signs of trouble. If she knows twins are coming, a woman can conserve her strength and enhance her comfort by following closely her doctor's orders. Improved general hygiene, especially plenty of rest, will make her confinement safer and pleasanter. Frequently a well-constructed maternity corset will ease her extra heavy load. With care and regular medical attention, the strain should not be excessive. Certainly it is not much more difficult and in many ways is easier than carrying two babies at different times.

While it is true that complications during delivery are more common with twins, the knowledge of the diagnosis will alert the doctor to any deviation from normal—"forewarned is forearmed." With the constant advances in obstetrical knowledge, this danger factor is gradually being eliminated.

Prematurity and Twins

Because more than half of all twins are born prematurely, the diagnosis before delivery is important. The death rate among newborn twins is higher than that of full-term single babies, although not much greater than that of the single premature infant. Their initial handicap is prematurity; they are in no other way abnormal. Medical science is continually finding new methods of giving these tiny ones strength until they can get along on their own. Twins who pass the age of infancy have just as good a chance of surviving as do any other children. Adequate diagnosis, coupled with expert care of mother and babies, is making it possible for more twins every year to survive the early, difficult months.

Are twins who manage to get through this somewhat more strenuous period at all subnormal or backward? Numerous and exacting studies record an emphatic "No!" to this question; twins of school age, as well as adults, are of normal intelligence, are not physically handicapped, and have the same potentialities as do average people. Nor is the superstition that twins may be sterile true. This is a faulty and unconfirmed assumption from an anomaly which occurs in cattle.

If two babies are coming, special preparations must be made at home. Most of the supplies must be collected in duplicate—diapers, bottles, cribs, clothing, bedding, formula, and so on. Baby services will usually give a reduced rate for a large number of items and this is an excellent way to save wear and tear on mother, if the family can afford the service.

Some department stores are prepared for such a contingency through a form of "twin insurance," and the second child may receive layette, clothes and various other articles free of charge. Pediatricians will frequently arrange to care for twins at less than the regular fees. People generally become more cooperative when they hear that such an unusual and exciting event is forthcoming—sort of a bargain day with two for the price of one.

Squeezing the amount of work required for two into the time available for one may at first appear to be an impossible task. But, as a well-known humorist once put it, the time is not spent in washing, dressing and feeding the baby, but in getting ready to wash, dress and feed the baby. Once you have gotten ready, it takes only a little extra time to handle one more—production line fashion.

Twins Need Affection

One item on which parents must never under any circumstances economize is affection for their babies.

Here, too, twins have a distinct advantage over many single children. No one can resist them and they are a constant center of much attention, fondling and playing. In addition, they quickly learn to amuse themselves and become close companions. Many people who work with twins feel that this security and successful cooperative effort developed early in life yields profits in better emotional adjustments later, and point out that twins are usually happy, extraverted persons.

Although the first year is filled with a multitude of problems, compensations begin to appear as the twins grow older. Having learned to get along with each other, they are soon able to look after themselves. Their mutual loyalty gives them confidence in assuming new responsibilities quickly. Child training is often easier than expected—when one twin begins eating certain foods which mother thinks would be good for him the other will follow suit. And so it goes in learning toilet habits, in developing sleep and rest routines and in growing mentally and emotionally. The fundamental tenets of child psychology are unchanged and applying them is often only half as hard as anticipated; twins give each other a boost toward becoming useful members of society.

Because of their constant association, they frequently evolve their own methods of communication, practically unintelligible to adults. This habit may lead to speech retardation and can easily be avoided by teaching them songs, stories and word games, and by refusing to indulge in baby talk or imitation. Once twins have reached school, they are apt to make up quickly for any backwardness they may have developed.

It is important for parents to realize that twins are constantly in the limelight. They are natural attention-getters—that is why so many are successful in show business. By the same token, they are apt to be criticized more severely for their occasional misdoings. They tend to depend too heavily upon each other and their twinship. This dependency may give them a distorted view of life and prove to be a disadvantage if separation comes later, as it is apt to do.

When twins begin to develop individual personalities—and they do earlier than one might think—this problem of maintaining balance between dependence and independence becomes paramount. Dress them alike or not? Same toys or different? Keep them together or let them find their own companions?

Fraternal and Identical Twins

It is over these problems that much controversy has raged. The fact that a difference of opinion exists between parents as well as others interested in child guidance shows that they fail to recognize the significance of the fact that there are two distinct and separate kinds of twins! The facts we have discussed so far refer to twins in general. But it is important to know something about the two types of twins if we are to understand their problems.

You will recall twins who did not look at all alike and who often had very different personalities. They are not really true twins at all, but come from the fertilization of two separate eggs by two different sperms at about the same time. They are commonly called fraternal twins, and actually are no more closely related than brothers and sisters. They may, of course, be of either sex, and in rare instances have not had the same father.

On the other hand, we all know of twins who look so much alike that they are frequently confused with each other. In many ways they are so similar that they are almost identical; from this outstanding characteristic they receive their common name, identical (true) twins. They have developed from the fertilization of a single egg and are often called one-egg twins. They not only look alike, but are of the same build and sex, act in the same ways and have strikingly similar personalities. Even their fingerprints and the shape of their ears are nearly identical, supplying the best methods of telling that they are one-egg twins. About one-fourth of all twins are identical.

Careful comparison of the builds, facial contours, ears, fingerprints, hair whorls, complexions, eye shades, hand contours, teeth and mental capacities will easily tell whether two children of the same sex are identical or fraternal. Fraternal twins have many differences in traits, whereas identical twins show an amazing resemblance in all of them. This important diagnosis of twin type can usually be made by parents of ordinary intelligence and observation.

The significance of making this distinction is that each of the types develops in entirely different ways. For parents to understand their twins and deal with them intelligently, they must know how the personalities of these types of twins grow and differ.

Fraternal twins, as emphasized, have the same hereditary relationship as siblings. This means that they also have the same inherent and potential differences. Careful studies have shown that not only are fraternal twins quite unlike each other in many ways, but they also tend to become more and more different as they grow older.

Development of Antagonisms

It is common knowledge that strong antagonisms, even feuds and hatreds, sometimes arise between brothers or sisters; the same possibilities exist for fraternal twins, who are no more closely related.

In general, fraternal twins will discover their differences early and will begin to expand them of their own accord. Since they bear no closer relationship than brothers and sisters, how ridiculous to force them into rigid lines of similarity! Dressing them identically, while cute for a year or so, will soon have its drawbacks. What self-respecting boy wants to be dressed like his sister? Just because she happens to be his twin will not impress a budding cowboy. And once the twin girls—not identical—begin to show their individuality in taste for clothes, the duplicate garments become hated symbols of uniformity.

Since fraternal twins have different capacities and talents—just as do siblings—they are going to develop their own interests. Forcing Jack, who is absolutely without a sense of rhythm, to do his daily stint at the piano "because Jill is taking" is illogical. If he is not musically inclined, give him a chance to become proficient at sports or woodwork or whatever interests him rather than emphasizing Jill's superiority. Let their interests complement each other, rather than create a one-sided scramble for preference and privilege.

Unfortunately, many parents attempt to exploit the similarities between twins, and drag the youngsters out for performances, antics and the general amusement of any and all visitors. The idea that twins are public property to be displayed and sentimentalized over is one of most twins' pet peeves.

Fraternal twins are going to be as different as brothers and sisters, so why fight against it? The answer is simplicity itself; let them choose for themselves when they begin to recognize their differences; give them a chance to develop their individual personalities.

Identical twins, however, present an entirely different problem. They are similar from birth and early begin to mimic each other in many details.

This similarity remains quite constant as they grow older. Even identical twins separated in infancy and reunited in adult life show remarkable similarities in the many traits we have mentioned.

Strong Mutual Feelings

Identical twins have a strong mutual feeling which is lacking between any other pair of individuals. They react physically and emotionally in the same way; and their personalities are closely similar. Frequently they say the same things simultaneously and spontaneously or write identical answers to examination questions—much to the teacher's and their own embarrassment. Interdependency is the outstanding characteristic of these twins, in contrast to the rivalry and lack of strong mutual affection often evidenced by fraternal twins.

Identical twins, therefore, are going to be very much like each other no matter what happens. The problem of how much interdependence should be allowed them is a question pretty much solved for the parents. You cannot force any child to be someone or something he really is not and expect him to be a normal, well-adjusted member of society.

This does not mean, however, that an attempt to guide identical twins is of no avail. On the contrary, a great deal can be done. The most important contribution parents can make is to foster twins' slightest differences. (And there will be differences. Even their pet puppy will soon learn to distinguish between them.) Too strong an interdependence has a tendency to lessen each one's ability to adjust quickly to new situations without the aid of the other twin. They must be prepared for the eventuality of their separation.

Such small things as separate rooms, different books and some individual toys will help develop their originality. Training of one twin's particular talents may also aid in establishing a sense of independence. However, by and large, identical twins are content to submerge their personalities into one "twin personality"; many a twin has remarked that when his partner is away, it is as though half of him were gone, too.

Developing individuality. Much can be done by friends and outsiders to counter some of the headaches peculiar to twins. Certainly repeating the same stale jokes about them year after year should be outlawed. Constantly confusing their names gets to be pretty tiresome, too. One prominent set of twins solved many of their problems and straightened out a lot of their friends; one of them grew a mustache. Girls can change their hair styles or types of hats and dresses to accentuate their differences.

With a little sympathy on the part of their friends and some well deserved consideration from strangers, twins' lives can easily be twice as interesting as those of ordinary people. With a clear understanding of the pitfalls and their compensatory pleasures and fascinations, parents can truly enjoy the double lives of their twins.   —By C. H. Kramer, M.D.

COLOR BLINDNESS

MY first child was born color blind but I didn't know it until almost nine years later! When Tim was a toddler, my husband and I sometimes said jokingly, of his mistakes in naming colors, "He must be color blind," but we didn't really mean it. He did name many colors correctly. He called grass green, fire engines red, tree trunks brown, and recognized many other familiar one-color objects.

During his first years at school, his mistakes seemed to occur more often. He mismated his socks, picked green berries, overlooked dirt on his hands and face—but isn't that the way of little boys? However, when he was almost nine and still thought all tan cars were the same color as our green one, that dark red and black were identical, that the pink, gray and green threads he had so patiently wound onto one spool were all the same color, I had to face it—maybe Tim really was color blind!

During an eye examination I asked the doctor to test Tim's color vision. A few flips through the Pseudo-Isochromatic Plates for testing color perception replaced suspicion with fact. Tim *was* color blind. To my question, could it be cured, the answer was no. I learned that although acquired color blindness may sometimes be corrected, for the inherited kind as Tim's was, there is no cure.

But I had to know more about it. What caused it? How many people had it? What would it mean to Tim? What could he see—and not see? How could I help him?

According to Webster's dictionary, color is "a sensation evoked as a response to the stimulation of the eye and its attached nervous mechanisms by radiant energy of certain wave lengths and intensities." Color blindness is defined as "total or partial inability to recognize or distinguish chromatic colors."

While color blindness can be acquired through injury, disease or excessive use of certain medications, it is usually inherited. Congenital or inherited color blindness is a sex-linked condition chiefly affecting males which usually skips a generation as it is transmitted from the maternal grandfather to grandson through the female who is not herself usually affected. Girls can be color blind, too, but only if both parents carry this condition. In the United States about one out of every ten boys and one out of every hundred girls is born with some color perception deficiency. We realized that my father, whom I never knew, must have been color blind and that although I'm not, I'd passed it on to Tim and to Nicky, too, our second son. Our third boy, Kerry, however, has normal color vision.

How We See Color

We see colors by means of three mechanisms in the eye, which reflect red, yellow and blue from which all other colors are blended. If one or more of these mechanisms is defective, color perception will be affected. But color perception is not related to visual acuity nor will it show up on ordinary eye tests. A man may be color blind although his vision is "twenty-twenty" and his eyes appear perfect even to the doctor. Only professional testing for color perception can give the complete picture.

Color perception is classified in four groups. The vast majority of people are trichromats—those who can distinguish the three primary colors and therefore all other colors, although we may confuse some shades. Dichromats who see two primary colors form the second-largest group. The color most often indistinguishable to them is green, or frequently red. A third group, the monochromats, see only one color. Achromats are rare individuals who apparently see no color at all. No classification exists for the very rare individual who is color blind in one eye and not in the other.

At first I was ashamed that it took me almost nine years to recognize Tim's color vision deficiency. Then I read that World War II service induction examinations uncovered many previously undetected cases. Sometimes even the color blind persons themselves were unaware of their condition. And of course hopeful inductees sometimes tried to conceal their color blindness, but modern testing methods are foolproof.

My curiosity about the facts of color blindness was fairly well satisfied but I couldn't find any books about how others had adjusted to the situation so I decided to start by first trying to see the world as it looked to my sons. I learned that they are both weak in red-green perception, although they see clear yellows and blues.

First I tried to develop what I call "c.b. consciousness." When I looked out at the garden I mentally subtracted all colors except yellow and blue, imagining the others as shades of gray. No wonder the boys couldn't see red berries among the green foliage! In addition to missing nature's display of colors, my children spent quite a few years in a house that didn't appeal to them. When I became c.b. conscious, I re-evaluated our home and its furnishings. Everywhere I saw reds, greens, browns, tans, corals or gold. Rarely a clear yellow and never a blue. There really wasn't much a color blind child could enjoy in our house. Of course we couldn't immediately discard what we had, but every replacement or change now fits into my new concept of c.b. interior decoration, using accent colors our boys can see, and many bold, black line prints on varied textures that please their eyes.

Clothes Problems

One day Tim asked me why I always wore such drab clothes. Then I understood I always chose colors they couldn't see, never including blue, which I dislike, and seldom clear yellow. Tim's remark changed my clothes buying policy for him and Nicky. If they're not along to make their own choices, I now choose plaids with lots of blue and yellow or a very distinct pattern created by lines. And I buy everything color-keyed to go well together so that they can't put on clashing colors by mistake. But in spite of my color-key formula I have to supervise, when a white shirt is a must, since the boys can't tell the difference between white, pale yellow and pale pink.

Before I learned the boys were color blind, I was puzzled that they couldn't see dirt on their clothes or hands and faces unless it was distinctly marked.

Tim's inability to see dirt led to a series of infections as he grew beyond daily bath supervision and attention to minor cuts. Since he didn't see the dirt, he often didn't know when a scrape or cut needed to be soaked and cleansed with soap. Then he couldn't see if redness appeared around a wound until it had become painful and serious. Twice he had the warning red lines of blood poisoning creeping up his arm before he heeded the pain enough to tell me about it. Now both boys and I are on guard, and they come to me for consultation whenever there is any possibility of infection.

Color perception is important in hobbies and games. We never choose games that rely on normal color vision, and in all hobbies that require color recognition the boys remember to use another member of the family as the advisory committee before buying equipment.

Art in school was a problem until they learned how to read the names of the colors on the crayons and the positions of the colors in the paint box, then learned the rules of complementary colors. But since I've told the art teachers about the boys' condition, their instructors have given Tim and Nicky extra understanding help.

Informing teachers of a child's color perception difficulty is important in other ways. She then won't inadvertently frustrate the child by forcing him into games that rely on color recognition and she will avoid using colored chalk on blackboards or flash cards that use color as a cue. Most important, she'll understand the child better. I've often wished that my children's color perception had been automatically tested along with their routine vision tests when they entered school. Then I would have known sooner how I could help them.

Traffic Sign Problems

Traffic signs and signals were a problem, too, until we explained that the lighter shade is green, the darker red, and the signals always have the red stop-light on the top, the warning light in the middle, and the go light below. A slow growth in realization of the needs of color blind people has gradually brought about changes in traffic lights. More blue has been added to the green and more orange to the red, thus increasing the difference between them. In one city, a stripe has been added through the signal that shows clearly even to the totally color blind.

My sons don't have difficulty with traffic lights, but there are other traffic uses of color that are not as easy to recognize. For example, they don't see the color of a red cloth used as a warning signal on projecting items carried on trucks, so I have taught them always to suspect that any waving cloth on a truck or car may mean danger.

Another problem arises on multiple-lane roads where traffic direction is switched to accommodate rush-hour loads. On one avenue temporary traffic cones were set out, broken red lines were painted on the cement, and signs warned motorists to stay out of converted lanes marked by red lines. The plan was a good one, except that for those who couldn't see red, there were no broken lines on the pavement. The red didn't show up against the dark cement. Even those of us with normal color vision are color blind in the dark, so that the red lines were really invisible to everyone on dark rainy winter mornings and late afternoons.

I suggested a change—perhaps using white marks with the red to form some different pattern—and some changes were made. But in general, many improvements are still necessary to accommodate color blind persons.

As the population increases so does the number of people with some color deficiency. Since it would hardly be justifiable to deny them the right to drive because of warnings based on color alone, I believe that in the very near future all traffic signs (air, rail and marine, too) will use shape or design in addition to color.

Vocations closed to color blind. It is to be hoped that industry also will change its ways. Tim, a junior in high school, is now ready to think about a vocation. He has had many ideas of what he'd like to do, but his color perception deficiency has already closed a number of avenues. The Navy and Coast Guard, for example, have customarily refused admission to the color blind. Scientists, astronomers, physicists, physicians, submariners, artists and countless others depend on color in their jobs.

By the time I've finished my study of color blindness, perhaps I'll have enough material to write an instruction book myself for my future daughters-in-law to help them understand my sons' color blind world and to teach their children about the possible color blind world of my sons' grandchildren.

—*By Bee Wyndham*

IF YOUR CHILD IS LEFT-HANDED

A GROUP of mothers were discussing their problems. One brought the subject of handedness up. She was worried. "My husband thinks it's cute for the baby to be a southpaw," she said. "But I wonder if it isn't going to make a lot of trouble for him later on."

"At the clinic they told me that some of my boy's difficulties in school come from his left-handedness," another woman contributed. "They call him double left-handed, whatever that means. All I know is that he can't read a thing and he's in fourth grade."

"They say you can tell from the side a baby seems to want to lie on whether he's going to be right or left-handed," a third member of the group volunteered. "Do you suppose that's so?"

Most children grow up without having anyone pay much attention to their preference for the right or left hand. The popular feeling is that you can't do anything about it anyway. If a youngster seems not to have made up his mind which hand he prefers by the time he starts school, or if he favors the left, the question may arise as to which one he shall be taught to write with. Once that is disposed of the matter is usually dropped unless, or until, trouble develops.

There ought to be more understanding of handedness than that. Experts now tell us that it is a part of understanding the whole of a child's development. Some go so far as to insist that every clinical examination should include a test for handedness. Others believe that all kindergartners should be screened for it.

True, the experts themselves are far from seeing eye to eye. How handedness comes about in the first place, what develops in the child's personality as a result of it, and what can or should be done about it are unsettled questions. Differences of opinion on the subject grow violent. More research is needed, but one thing is clear. Handedness is important.

Once the individual is used to it, it may not make much difference to him whether he is left or right-handed. It doesn't make much difference to other people either, provided they don't mind being bumped a little. But what does getting used to handedness involve? And what if, deep down underneath, you never do get quite used to your choice? The business is not simple. Moreover, not only is there handedness to be considered. There is also, surprisingly enough, eyedness and footedness. Even the possibility of earedness is now being looked into. Jawedness, too—on which side you chew.

Children are not born "handed." They grow that way. As the nerve fibers develop and the motor apparatus matures, the two hands come by degrees to work together, and with the eyes and ideas. Then later one hand gradually takes over the leadership. This is a specialization on which civilization depends. It was only when man started selecting one hand and concentrating on its training that he began to develop skills as a tool-using animal. It was with the emergence of handedness that speech evolved, too. So it is with each child.

Heredity vs. Environment

Just how this development takes place is not clearly understood. One group holds that as one side of the brain gains control in the normal course of growth, the corresponding hand assumes precedence also. The two parts then reinforce each other in action. Another group contends that handedness is more or less a matter of coincidence—the child just happens to use one hand by accident and then circumstances stamp in the habit.

The controversy here is pretty much the old one between heredity and environment. Neither has been wholly ruled out but some experts stress one point of view more than the other. Others add a third factor—temperament. They believe that much of what happens depends upon how rigid the personality is. Whatever the explanation may be, children show many degrees of rightness and leftness, achieving their individual patterns to different extents at different times.

What Dr. Arnold Gesell of the Gesell Institute of Child Development calls the "fencing attitude" of early infancy is probably the first indication of the child's individual preference. This is the sleeping position assumed by infants from the fourth to the sixteenth week after birth. One arm is extended and the other crooked behind the exposed ear. While this is thought to be connected with later hand choice, more study is needed before it can be affirmed that the extended hand is "the" hand.

Sidedness is only part of a whole action system that is developing and shaping itself. One trend abates while another speeds up, as if the very young could attend to only one thing at a time. Thus while the baby is learning to reach, grasp and pick up objects, he may let his hand choice ride for a while, returning to concentrate on it later when babbling begins. Or again, the development of handedness may either take a spurt or a relapse when he is learning to walk. Later, starting school with its tough new adjustments may upset what before had seemed a definite decision about which hand to use. There are even rather common two-handed phases, noted in the research laboratory, at the seventh and ninth months, again at the ages of two-and-a-half, three-and-a-half, and seven.

If when all is said and done, you find yourself with a right-hander, the going is likely to be smoother both for you and for him. But your child may be a "leftie." Five per cent of people in general are, and probably twice as many young children.

Many troubles beset the left-handed person. Can openers, scissors and salad forks fail to work smoothly for him. Screws and handles turn in the wrong direction. He is aware that derivatives of the word "left" in any language have uncomplimentary connotations—gawky and sinister, for instance. Even in his own language the word implies insult—"left-handed deal" and so forth.

No Handicap to Reading

In school it would appear that left-handedness has no particular disadvantage insofar as the mental act of reading is concerned. Several investigations have shown that there are just as many good readers among left-handed children as poor readers. The Reading Institute at New York University is attended by the most serious cases of reading retardation. All are of average intelligence or above. This Institute reports that out of 160 full-time retarded readers only 17 are left-handed and only two have mixed dominance.

So you need not worry about your child having difficulty with reading *just* because he is left-handed. When it comes to writing there may be trouble.

The body naturally tends to move from the center out. For the left-handed child this means going contrary to the way writing is done in English. It's up to the leftie to switch the inside control buttons. This he can do. But seemingly small things loom large when one is just learning to write.

For instance, the left-hander has to push when he writes instead of pulling, and it's easier to pull. Also his hand gets in the way of his seeing when he writes. This interferes with the teamwork of seeing and feeling. It may be, too, that the teacher demonstrates only in right-handed fashion. And she may never get around to showing every child in a crowded classroom how to slant his paper in the best way for him. Leftie stumbles along the best he can, often picking up bad habits that must be painfully unlearned or else continue to dog him. Although it is estimated that a quarter of a million left-handers enter first grade every year, most classrooms make no special provision for them.

In some up-to-the-minute schools, of course, teachers are alert to all sorts of special needs and meet them without overstressing them. That's the way it should be. But even this may not work. Your left-handed son may be a wow at sports and the head of his class. If so he is an exception.

Researchers have found left-handed children in general inept in all forms of finer muscular coordination as compared with the right-handed youngsters. Typically they are more clumsy at games and at doing all kinds of sports. As previously stated they usually have some difficulty in writing, also. By the way, more boys than girls turn out to be left-handed.

Some Special Problems

The child is not so badly off if he is definitely and consistently left-handed, especially when he is also bright and even-keeled. He will probably make and maintain the necessary adjustments without too much difficulty. But many left-handers are actually in-betweens. Perhaps they have altered their natural tendency to use the left hand in response to their right-handed environment or through copying what they see others doing. If the transfer is incomplete "double-left-handedness" results.

"Look! I can do it just as good with the other hand!"

That's a boast that always sends a chill down my spine. Parents sometimes take this so-called ambidexterity for prowess and even encourage it, little knowing what they are doing. It is true that Leonardo da Vinci painted now with one hand, now with the other. A few modern surgeons have the reputation of using the scalpel equally well with either. But genuine ambidexterity is extremely rare, if indeed upon close examination it is found to exist at all. The "either-handed" usually turns out to be "neither-handed."

Some people have identified reversal tendencies with left-handedness. These people have observed that beginners often start at the wrong end of words and read them backwards. They may see "b" for "d," "slat" for "salt," "was" for "saw." Most children who do this at first show only a mild degree of the tendency and soon grow out of it. In some, however, it is frequent and persistent, a rare few even reversing completely as in a mirrored reflection. These reversal tendencies usually have nothing to do with left-handedness. If the difficulty is severe the parent would do well to have a scientific diagnosis made.

Many children are so-called "multiple dominants" who may be either of the "mixed" or "cross" type. That is, they may be impartially handed or eyed, or both. Or they may be right-handed and left-eyed, or vice versa. When you test large numbers of children for sidedness, as I have, you find that some very good readers show such patterns and that some very poor ones do not. Recent investigation is inconclusive in showing a definite relationship between mixed dominance and reading.

Since handedness and eyedness are helpful guides to a child in finding his way about among symbols, lack of clear-cut sidedness may throw him into confusion. It sometimes indicates a peculiar, though not necessarily defective, brain organization that interferes with his recalling symbols and requires special teaching methods.

What to do about left-handedness, on the contrary, is widely argued. Approved practice has swung this way and that. There was a time when schoolchildren were required to use the right hand for writing, regardless of preference. Then psychologists started warning: "Leave left-handedness alone." But this idea, too, can be overdone. Left-handedness may be fastened on a child unnecessarily.

Don't Impose Left-Handedness

This has happened to Stanley, a bright youngster who changed schools when he was in sixth grade. He used his left hand in most situations but so poorly that his new teacher thought of trying him out on the other. From the first he wrote with it more legibly. He claimed, too, that he liked it better. Thorough testing then revealed that he actually was more right than left-sided.

A number of case studies show that children even at this age have changed over successfully. The whole personality of the child and his previous history must be taken into account in making the decision. Retraining has to proceed with consistency and skill. But under such conditions, it may solve a problem.

The advantages to be gained from changing handedness are thought by many, however, to be offset by the risks. In the past, stuttering has been held to be the particular bugbear. But as more work has been done on both stuttering and sidedness, the danger of instigating the one handicap while trying to correct the other has tended to be discounted.

Speech disorders run high in left-handed children, regardless of any attempt to change them to the other hand. Youngsters with unestablished handedness also have more than their share of them. Any transition or strain may touch off stuttering. Why pick just on hand change? In many cases stuttering has lessened as handedness has become more firmly established. Where it has developed during a transfer it often disappears when the change is fully effected. Stuttering may not be caused by the switch itself so much as by the indecision that is apt to precede it.

First grade is considered a good time at which to change handedness if the teacher has the time and interest, and the parents are willing to do their share. Where the child is cooperative and first trials succeed, the outlook is favorable, particularly if he is healthy, bright and steady—and the teaching is good.

The truly Golden Age for counteracting leftness, however, is from three to five. This is the stage when the least effort goes furthest. Handedness has then hardly begun and in most children is still "unjelled." Left-handedness tends to assert itself a little later than right-handedness. Even when fairly apparent, it appears less stable at the start. In this early period when the child engages only in simple motor activities and his controls are still crude, the matter of handedness can be managed rather easily if tact and gentleness are used.

A still better move is to avoid leftness where possible. Nothing is gained by attempting training too early. After the first year is time enough and early self-feeding helps. The baby's spoon should be placed in his right hand, casually, good-humoredly, repeatedly. Put his toys where he will naturally reach for them with his right hand. Encourage him to wave and kiss goodbye with it, too.

Gentle Training Helps

Such training should go gently forward through the nursery years. Say nothing yet about right or left. Even at six a child may need a colored ribbon to distinguish one from the other. Make it a game, a pleasure to use the right hand. Never force in the face of resistance.

Most children's inclinations lie somewhere between the extremes of right-ness and leftness at first and are relatively easy to deflect. Yet some are so positive in their choice of the left hand that pressure to the contrary will either work havoc or fail utterly. An indication of the strength of the baby's preference is how insistent he is and also how he manages his two hands together. With which does he perform the important part of any act?

"When we saw that our baby kicked his ball with his left foot," remarked one observant father, "we decided left must be his type and we ought to help him be the best leftie he could. By tests and performance he turned out to be

100 per cent left and he doesn't suffer from it."

If you want to discover your own child's pattern, you can watch him carefully and try him out. If you have a puzzling decision to make about sidedness or a real problem in which it is a factor, you will be wise to consult a specialist.

You may feel quite safe on your own, though, in doing your baby the favor of helping him choose to be right-handed if you can. You will probably be surprised at the simplicity of the process. But if he is determined to be a leftie, or if a left-handed stand has already been taken in the case of an older child, waste no time on regrets.

The chief challenge is the child who puts off deciding between hands. He needs assistance in making up his mind and learning to specialize. The tendency that appears unmistakable should be encouraged. If none such appears spontaneously, the hand of most promise should be cultivated. The most important thing of all is for each person to be surely, skillfully and wholeheartedly one or the other—right-handed or left-handed. Handedness is no place for divided loyalties. —*By Francis Drewry McMullen*

IF YOU'RE THINKING OF ADOPTION

MY husband is a businessman and I am a child psychologist. We have four very good reasons for being deeply interested in adoption: our two sons and two daughters who showed us what fun it is to be an adopted family. For twenty-five years we've made it our hobby to learn all we can about adoption and to share our enthusiasm and ideas with others who want to adopt their families.

From Atlantic to Pacific in the U.S.A., and from Ireland to Italy in Europe, we've visited children's institutions and talked with social workers and adopting parents about adoption.

"How do you find a child to adopt? How long will it take?" are the first questions couples ask us. We always answer, "Go to an agency. But first think hard about the kind of child you want."

Adoption to most people means a tiny baby, helpless and cuddly. Many couples are afraid to adopt older children. It's true that they're not as easy to handle at first as babies, but love does wonders for unruly, which means unhappy, kids. Once a child settles down in a real family of his own, he's no more difficult to manage than children who have lived with their own parents all their lives.

That's the way it was with our four. Three of our youngsters came to us when they were six, with front teeth missing, shirt tails hanging out. The fourth was eleven years old, on the brink of adolescence. We found that the satisfactions of adopting older children far outweigh the difficulties.

Consult an Agency

Whether you are looking for a baby or an older child, the best way to find a child is through an agency. The services it performs are threefold: selecting a child who will fit into your home and whom you can love as your own; making sure he will be yours for good, that the birth mother will not claim the child some day; and seeing that all legal papers are in order. All this involves handling psychological problems with many overtones, and requires the special training and skills social workers have.

Ideally, you should select an adoption agency with the same care you would an obstetrician. (The Department of Social Welfare at your state capital has the names of licensed agencies.) It is easiest, but not mandatory, to work with one near your home. As we see it, rapport with the social worker is more important than geographical location—if you possibly can, select an agency where you and the social workers are "simpatico." Find out all you can about several agencies—in other states, if necessary. Discuss your plans and hopes with any agency that will see you. Some are so swamped with local applications that they won't take couples who live outside their district.

Pick the agency with which you have the most rapport, and resolve to co-operate with it for at least a year. Don't pin all your hopes there, however. Keep a weather eye out for another agency which you could turn to if and when you feel that you're not getting anywhere with the first.

Parent qualifications. "What will an agency look for in us? When will we know if we pass the 'good parent' test? How long will we have to wait for a child?" are other questions couples ask us. There are no general answers. Your progress in your search for a child will depend on 1) whether that agency has a child available who meets your specifications, and 2) how you stack up against other people who want that child.

Children, remember, are people, not commodities. What is an agency to do when ten, even twenty, couples clamor for a child? Choose those they consider the best parents, of course. However, since agencies are made up of human beings too, they don't all agree on what constitutes "the best parents." So if you fail to pass with one agency, don't be depressed. Look around for another. (One word of advice. You won't make a hit with any agency if you state your requirements too precisely. "We would like a blue-eyed, curly-headed girl from college parents" gives the impression that you don't love children as children.)

Laws and rules. Ask the agencies you approach about fees—how they're arrived at and when you will have to pay. There is no general rule about adoption fees. Agencies only recently began to charge for their services and many of them are still feeling their way.

Find out, too, what the laws and rules are about matching a child's religion with that of the adopting parents. There are very definite rules about religion. Most state laws require that a child be adopted into a family of the same religious faith. And even where this is not written into the law, it is difficult to get court approval nowadays for an interreligious adoption.

One point of agency procedure that couples find hard to understand is why one couple gets a child much sooner than other couples who applied earlier. This is because once your home has been approved, it is placed in a pool, not on a numbered waiting list. As each child is ready for adoption, the agency selects from this pool the parents they feel offer the best home for this particular child.

Independent Adoptions

We are convinced that most adopting couples would rather work through agencies, that they turn to independent adoptions and the black market in babies only when the agency system fails them.

If, after trying to work through agencies for a year or more, you get no place, then you can consider an independent adoption. Many people think that all independent adoptions—those made without agency supervision—are illegal. Not at all. In some states and under certain circumstances, the law permits a couple to obtain a child directly from the mother or legal guardian. Obstetricians, lawyers, ministers and others sometimes help unwed mothers give their babies directly to childless couples for adoption.

An independent adoption through the black market is not only illegal but immoral as well. Unwed mothers and their babies are often cruelly treated by money-hungry schemers.

Finding the child. How do you find a child for independent adoption? Through the grapevine among parents who have adopted independently. Let it be known you are looking for a child to adopt and you'll be surprised how helpful people will be. When you do hear of a child whose mother is reported ready to have him adopted, first make sure that the person serving as go-between is reputable and honorable, that he is placing the child out of the goodness of his heart and not for financial gain. Next, be wary of exorbitant fees. You can expect to pay something to adopt any child today, whether through an agency or independently but when the fees seem out of line, watch out.

Consult a lawyer. Make haste slowly. Beware of high-pressure methods, document forgeries, "hush-hush deals." *Consult your lawyer at every step.* Be very sure that the mother or legal guardian has signed all the proper papers. The adoption wrangles you read about in the newspapers usually arise because the legal formalities were not properly completed in the first place.

From the moment the child comes into your home, you and you alone are responsible for his happiness, even before the court adoption proceedings take place. With an agency placement, there is a "living together" period before the final adoption, during which the agency can remove the child (it almost never does) and you can return the child to the agency (an idea that never occurs to most adopting parents). In an independent adoption, the child comes to you for better or for worse, with no return privileges. Every child has a right to parental love and affection, so before you take a child, make sure that you are ready to love him whatever he turns out to be; cross-eyed, genius or mentally retarded.

Adopting a Foreign Child

This is a possibility, but think hard and long and honestly about the kind of foreign child you can love. Then tell your plans to the local agency, ask them to study your home. Once you pass their good parent test, they will ask the International Social Service to bring over a child for you. When the child arrives, the local agency will supervise the placement as it would if you were adopting an American child.

Keep away from proxy adoptions—in which you authorize a stand-in to act for you in the adoption proceedings in a foreign country—as you do from the black market. Too many unscrupulous people, ignorant of our laws and of human feelings, are operating there.

Twenty years ago, when we were looking for our family, we believed that somewhere in the world there were children who needed us as we needed them and that it was up to us to find them, through adoption agencies if possible—on our own, if that didn't work out. But find them we would! We traveled far and wide in the U.S.A. Wartime restrictions kept us from going overseas. We were turned down by several agencies, for various reasons. It took us eight long years to complete our family with two sons and two daughters, who came to us from three different agencies.

Now, many years and five grandchildren later, when people ask "Has it been a successful adoption?" all six of us answer a most enthusiastic "Yes." Our hope is that you too, will find the children you want to adopt, and savor, as we have, the joy of being an adopted family.

—*By May Reynolds Sherwin, Ph.D.*

HOBBIES AND FAMILY FUN

STAMP COLLECTING • PHOTOGRAPHY • MOVIE MAKING
HAM RADIO • WEATHER FORECASTING • GENEOLOGY
STORY HOUR • LEARNING TO SWIM, SKATE, SKI
HIKING AND FISHING • LEARNING TO HUNT
FAMILY TRAVEL AND CAMPING • ASTRONOMY • SHELL COLLECTING
GARDENING WITH CHILDREN • EXPLORING NATURE IN SUMMER,
AUTUMN AND WINTER • PARTIES AND GAMES

HOBBIES ARE FOR ENJOYMENT

WHEN a music teacher came to give the six-year-olds their music lesson, she saw on the blackboard, scrawled in immature letters, B-A-K. The proud class informed her that the word was "Bach." In their enthusiasm they had been writing out the master's name.

No one could be around this particular teacher without catching her enthusiasm, absorbing her delight. She stood at the opposite pole from a conscientious mother who decided her little girl ought to learn tennis. The lady had never done anything more athletic than meet her husband at the train every evening, but she stood patiently at one end of a court for half an hour every morning, tossing balls to a sulky child who made passes with her racket. Many years later this same mother was still mourning the fact that her daughter had never learned the game.

The obvious conclusion from these companion pieces is that if parents want to put a subject across, they should, like a fine teacher, be enthusiasts themselves. Otherwise they have little to offer but their conscientiousness, which is never very inspiring. Most children, in fact, tend to be highly allergic to it.

Many parents feel that what they really enjoy is too trivial to be worth passing on. But there is not a hobby, a subject or a relaxation that cannot be made a fruitful source of interest to share.

Take the case of one mother who never was happier than when she applied grease paint and stood behind the footlights on an amateur stage, with dishwashing, darning and kindred occupations forgotten. She was successively the girl with the camera eye in a murder mystery, a romantic schoolteacher in a farce, and a middle-aged shrew in a drama. Actually she was an escapist who played at being these creatures much as a child plays cowboys and Indians. It may not seem like a promising avocation to share with an eight-year-old boy, but it was this mother's passion—so much so that she began to write one-act plays. And such was her fondness for the stage that she absorbed enough technique to win a prize and have her work produced in a little theater.

Enthusiasm Is Catching

By this time, eight-year-old Ted was clamoring to be taken to his mother's Players Club, for, being a shrewd psychologist like so many children, he judged from his mother's shining eyes that exciting things were happening there. His mother looked doubtful. The club was definitely an adult affair.

"Well, I could use you as an offstage noise in my play," she volunteered dubiously. "There's a boy chasing a cat down the street. You don't see him. You just hear him."

So at a series of rehearsals, Ted's shrill voice was heard whooping on the trail of an imaginary cat. He enjoyed it. He got a certain ego-satisfaction, too. At this point it occurred to him that writing must be rather fun.

The final result was not a play, for individualistic Ted never thought of copying his mother. But he turned up with a fairy story he had dictated, called "The Unicorn That Wanted To Be Mothered." He takes the keenest interest in his mother's writing and even suggests fresh and charming titles for her work.

Wherever children find excitement and delight, they are drawn as flies to honey. But they can tell the real from the imitation in a split second. To offer them make-believe enthusiasm is not only a waste of time, it bores them to the point of restlessness and may turn them against any subject so unfortunately presented. For this reason, parents would do well to introduce children to their own true enjoyments—the ones that bear their personal stamp. Other fields are better left to other guides.

Enthusiasms, however, bring their dangers. Hobbyhorses have a way of taking the bit in their teeth; everybody knows how difficult it has been on some occasion to break away from collectors who must show one more specimen, or gardeners who exhibit one more flower, and one more . . . and one more. Here again parents can learn from teachers.

Teachers realize that a child's span of attention is brief. They do not attempt to carry on even the most delightful activity for any considerable time, but like the skillful serial writer, they break off when people long for more. Unless mothers and fathers keep this point in mind, they may find they are not initiating their children into delightful experiences, but only exploiting a helpless audience which cannot escape. When Sally or Tommy are hopelessly bored with baked potatoes, they will not willingly eat them again for months and months, and any occupation—fly-fishing, stargazing or listening to the patterns of music—may suffer the sad fate of the baked potato.

Let Child Make Discoveries

A skilled teacher is psychologist enough to realize that one of the major pleasures of life is finding things out for oneself. So she lets the class make discoveries. It takes longer than telling the children herself, but they get a great deal more out of the subject. A well known architect, keen to make his son an architect too, took a tip from teacher. When he came home from work, he'd sit down for a few minutes and play with his small boy's building blocks. He always made the most fascinating structures, lighthouses with bridges attached, towers a yard high with setbacks every few inches. Of course the boy was enthralled. Presently his father began to leave very simple plans around—very simple indeed. But they showed how to construct the massive foundations of a suspension bridge. A few nights later the father did not have to build bridge foundations for his son; his son built one for him.

After a few such sessions a more difficult plan appeared—for a railway station. The child was challenged. Not long after, he showed his father the station completed. Step by step the child progressed until one day the architect asked, "Son, how would you and your gang like to build a shack? If you draw up some simple plans, I'll get you the lumber." All the boys in the neighborhood enjoyed building that shack. And there is every indication that this man's son will choose architecture as his profession.

Another trump card that teachers play—a trump since Socrates taught young Athenians to think for themselves—is to begin at a point where the learners' interests are involved.

Most successful parents proceed on the same lines. If Susie has a faint hankering to cook like her expert mother, then mother lets her bake a batch of cookies rather than stir the cream sauce. If Sammy wants to carpenter like his father, his dad shows him how to build a simple doghouse for his pet.

Start with child's interests. A generation ago parents often overlooked this principle of starting with the child's interests. Perhaps a mother who was an expert needlewoman decided that Jennie ought by now to be sewing. It is ten to one she made Jennie hem petticoats for the poor, because the hems were simple work suitable for a beginner and the ultimate end a worthy one. It is equally probable that Jennie found all sorts of excuses for avoiding her sewing lesson, excuses she would never have trumped up had her mother produced some scraps of flowered material and suggested that since the dolls served mud pies, they needed aprons.

But the parent who is pursuing his own hobby while sharing it with his son or daughter is likely, through his very pleasure, to avoid the pitfalls mentioned above. Masefield once wrote that the days that make us happy, make us wise; an instinctive wisdom is likely to be the portion of the father or mother who, like a teacher instructing in a deeply loved subject, is simply passing on to his children the delights he has abundantly received. Since a happy teacher is invariably a good teacher, why not copy her, stop worrying about advantages or accomplishments your children should have, and offer instead your personal enjoyments? —*By Doris P. Buck*

STAMP COLLECTING

I NEVER seem to do anything with the boys in winter," one father used to complain. "When I come home it's too dark to go out and have a catch, I'm too tired for anything energetic and too busy for those long-drawn-out games they like. I wish there was something we liked to do together that wouldn't take up too much time or energy."

A friend who lives in the city insisted he was even worse off. "At least you get out and play with your boys most of the year," he would say, "but what can I do in a city apartment miles from a park?"

Saddest of all was a father whose son is in a wheel chair. "We read and play games," our friend said, "but I wish I could find something that would keep building up an interest for both of us year after year."

Now all three of these fathers have found an answer. They're capitalizing on a growing boy's instinctive love of collecting things and directing it into a field which many fathers enjoy. They've started collecting stamps with their sons, and they're building up a satisfying mutual interest which can take up a little time or a lot, where there are no skills involved to make an unequal contest that's no fun for the loser.

Stamps have opened up whole new fields of common interest for my husband and our boys, all because Steven came home one day and said, "Neil collects stamps. Look at the ones he gave me from South Africa. Can I collect stamps, too?"

Paul had collected stamps as a boy. He was sure that Steven and Denis would both enjoy it, but he didn't expect to join them. He'd outgrown stamps —he thought! But he did want to get the boys off to a good start.

"Let's go to the library and get out some books on how to start a stamp collection," he said. "And we'll send to some dealers for their catalogues."

Naturally, he read the books to the boys and went over the catalogues with them. To his surprise, he discovered that his interest in stamps wasn't dead, only dormant.

"Tell you what," he said, "until you get really under way, I'll match you penny for penny and you can get twice as many stamps as you could afford yourselves. And I'd better give you an album, too, so your stamps won't lie around loose."

I think few things have equaled the excitement those boys got when their stamps came, unless it was the thrill of finding that their father was just as excited as they were. For the rest of the week I had a hard time getting them to come to dinner. As soon as Paul set foot inside the door, two little boys descended on him, and three heads were bent over the stamps, sorting, hinging them in the album, admiring.

Finally all the stamps were neatly in place. They'd bought all they could afford for a while, and there was an inevitable falling off of interest.

We looked into stamp clubs, but found none locally for six and nine-year-olds, and weren't able to interest the boys' friends in organizing one. Then Paul had his wonderful idea.

Family Project

"We'll have our own stamp club. Denis and Steven and I. And Joanne and Mother, too," he added.

The boys were a little dubious. "But what would we do? We've all seen our own stamps lots of times."

"How much do we know about them, though?" Paul asked. He flipped open the pages of the album. "For instance, here's a stamp celebrating the Texas centennial. How much do we know about that stamp and about Texas? And here's one from the Congo. Some of us don't even know where that is. A stamp club will give us a good chance to learn things together."

That was the beginning of our family stamp club, which has just concluded its first successful year.

Because youngsters love ritual, our meetings, every Thursday after dinner, follow a regular pattern. The treasurer (elected by secret ballot as are all officers) collects our ten-cents-a-week dues from each of us, and reads his treasurer's report. If there's a balance of a couple of dollars, we vote on how to spend it: a subscription to a stamp magazine, perhaps, or a trip to a stamp exhibit, or a choice stamp for the family collection. (In addition to that first album, each child now has a looseleaf notebook for his own special stamps—animals, sports and military subjects respectively.)

Then come the projects. We each tell about some stamp and the state or country it comes from. This, of course, has meant much scurrying to encyclopedias and atlases during the week, with side trips to the library to ask for "A book on California, please," or "Do you have something about animals in Malaya?"

Paul and I are continually amazed at how much we learn from these projects. We're absorbing geography painlessly, and history and economics too. We're learning how people live in different parts of the world, and what they look like. The projects suggest excursions, too: a trip to Washington's headquarters nearby, or up the Hudson. The Famous American series of stamps started a lively curiosity about our literary and musical heritage, and the Austrian castle series led to visits to two American "castles" we'd otherwise have overlooked.

Stimulating Interest

Once a month we have a "quiz show" about the various projects and every child who does well gets a prize—a stamp for his special collection. The questions are carefully gauged to each child's ability, so there's no chance of not doing well!

We usually take time to discuss the stamp news of the week as gleaned from newspapers and magazines, and we have a general showing of albums, with comments on any new stamps.

It isn't just on Thursdays that Paul and the boys get together over stamps. Because Steven is just learning to read, Paul helps him with his projects, and they all pore over stamp catalogues between meetings. There's the business of hinging in new stamps and soaking old ones off envelopes, and the occasional, very welcome gifts from friends.

Naturally, all this stamp activity falls off in summer. We have our meetings once a week, but that's about all.

So far our collecting has been the haphazard sort. We buy stamps according to the pictures, and we stick to inexpensive stamps, of which there are thousands. We make no attempt to build up a valuable collection because we're not interested in stamps as an investment, but as a family hobby from which we expect no more return than from skating or reading. We buy each new American stamp at the post office the day it's issued, but most of our other stamps are used ones—much cheaper and, if lightly canceled, just as satisfactory.

We go also to stamp stores, where we find dealers taking a real interest in children no matter how little they have to spend.

We're glad to find that our theories about stamps for families find support from the manager of a large stamp store who tells us that our family stamp club isn't at all unusual. He has some very definite do's for families who want to have fun with stamps:

1. Read a book or two, if you're a novice, and ask a dealer for advice before you start a collection.
2. Start with single stamps, and inexpensive ones.
3. Buy an inexpensive album so the youngster can have the fun of seeing a special place for each stamp.
4. Encourage any special interests—trains, ships, animals, and so on—by collecting stamps which depict them.
5. Keep an atlas handy, and an encyclopedia if you can.
6. Go shopping together, but let the children do the actual buying.

—*By Katherine Clifford*

STARTING CHILDREN ON PHOTOGRAPHY

BOYS and girls like to take pictures because it gives them a feeling of accomplishment, and it also is a fascinating hobby. Moreover, it gives them something to look back on—a means that is a little more concrete than memory alone of recalling pleasant, carefree moments when they had a lot of fun.

When 10-year-old Nancy and 12-year-old Jimmy went to camp, we thought that only Jimmy would do much in the way of picture-taking—because, like so many people, we had the impression that girls were not interested in photography. We found that not only did Nancy take more snapshots than

Jimmy, but that on a national scale there are just as many girls who enjoy snap-shooting as boys.

Then we discovered that the hobby we had started had a definite and beneficial carry-over. We had thought that after the summer's picture-taking the children would put their cameras away and forget them. But we found that their summer's fun had welded them to a new and engrossing pastime which they followed through the remainder of the year. They were always eager to comply when called upon for snapshots on special occasions.

Preparing a child for a summer's picture-taking is, however, more than a matter of giving him a camera and several rolls of film. We took Nancy and Jimmy to our camera dealer's and let them help in the selection of their cameras. We chose reflex-type cameras which are basically box-type cameras dressed up. Thus we made certain that no lack of technical knowledge would hamper the children's fun or limit their abilities. And by deciding on cameras for which simple and inexpensive flash attachments were available, we were able to provide the youngsters with equipment which would enable them to make snapshots indoors or at night with the same ease with which they took pictures during the day.

Lessons in Photography

Then the whole family joined in a few simple lessons in picture-taking. The first session covered the proper manner of opening and loading the camera, advancing the film, and releasing the shutter, and also included picture-taking. We had the pictures developed and printed as rapidly as possible so the children could see what they had accomplished.

Then we took the children on "camera tours" around town and to local parks to give them more of a "feel" for their cameras, and to show them what they could do with them. The results were so satisfactory that by the time Nancy and Jimmy left for camp, they handled their cameras with ease and certainty. By pointing out good pictures in various publications, and outdoor scenes in books, we also were able to give them ideas for good pictures.

As far as film and supplies were concerned, we purposely kept things at a modest level. Each child, when he left for camp, was provided with three rolls of film, and a half-dozen flash bulbs for his camera—enough to keep him clicking happily through the first weeks—and then at regular intervals throughout the following weeks an additional roll of film and more flash bulbs were either mailed to them or delivered during our visits.

We also supplied each youngster with a bright and attractive snapshot album, plus some picture-corners so that snapshots could be mounted and preserved as each saw fit. Jimmy divided his into groups of "People," "Places," and "Things," which reflected his direct and forthright personality, while

Nancy preferred to keep hers more or less in sequence—pasting each picture, and titling it, in about the order her pictures were taken. However, both took great pleasure in their albums and delighted not only in showing us what they had done, but also how they had done it.

It was a source of deep satisfaction to us to see how interested and appreciative were the counselors and other camp personnel. The counselors told us that our preliminary training was of great value in getting our children started properly. They carried on by suggesting likely picture possibilities and a camera club developed as a result. —*By N. C. Ferguson*

HOME MOVIES CAN BE WONDERFUL

A HOME movie camera and projector, no matter how inexpensive, are a wonderful acquisition for any family. That year-by-year pictorial record of the growth of your offspring, especially if it is in color, is something you can't fully appreciate until five, ten or fifteen years later. By then you wouldn't take a thousand dollars for a $10 strip of film, no matter how bad it may be photographically. Naturally, the better it is from a technical standpoint, the greater the enjoyment is; so a few tips from an old hand may not be amiss.

First of all, don't be afraid of a movie camera. There are remarkable automatic controls used in the processing of home movie film—electric eyes and such which take care of your exposure errors as no human being ever could. In other words, you can grossly under or over-expose with black-and-white film and still get a presentable result. This is less true with color where your exposure judgment has to be pretty nearly right. But the answer to that is to use a reliable exposure chart or meter—just as professionals do. You'll save the price in wasted film many times over. Far more important, you'll save lost shots which you may never be able to get again.

Another wise thing to do, especially with child pictures which you especially want to preserve, is to have them "vaporated" after they have been developed. This is a process of impregnating the film with moisture so that it doesn't become brittle and dried out in a few years and thus subject to being chewed up by the projector.

Beginners' Mistakes

In making movies six simple mistakes are almost always made by beginners:

1. Scenes too short. Any picture worth taking should be on the screen at least six seconds—and you'll find that nine or ten aren't too much. This means that when you shoot your film you should count off each shot: Not 1, 2, 3, but 101, 102, 103. If you count in single digits you're counting half-seconds or less; adding the 100 takes up just about a full second.

2. Excessive panning. Too many amateurs confuse a movie camera with a garden hose and spray their scenes up and down, back and forth. This is more prevalent in travel pictures, but you see it often in family group shots where it would be far better to make an individual portrait of each person than to swing down the line, not getting enough of anybody.

Panning is very hard on the eyes of those viewing the picture on the screen, and while there are occasions where the technique is useful, a little goes a long way. It is preferable to pan from left to right when possible, which is the way your eyes travel when they read. The camera should be moved very slowly. And at the beginning and end of each panorama it should be held still for at least three seconds.

3. Jumpy pictures. The unsteady camera—or, rather, the unsteady camera-man—is one of the greatest curses of amateur movies. Very few people can shoot at less than 1/50 of a second without getting movement. So when you stop to think that movie film is normally exposed at 1/30—and in addition you have a spring-drive action operating to increase the tremors—you realize why so many amateur films bounce all over the screen at a sickening rate.

When starting a scene, it helps to take a deep breath and hold it as long as you can, for even normal breathing can give you a great deal of camera movement. The real answer, however, is to use a tripod for every shot you make.

4. Not enough close-ups. A consistent failure in home movies is the lack of sufficient close-up shots. Probably the safest answer to the question, "How many should you have?" is the flat statement that nobody ever had too many! Next time you see a professional film in the theater, notice how many times it breaks into an action with a close-up, giving welcome variety and spice to a sequence. You can do the same thing to good advantage when you're filming Junior. You can open up with a long shot showing him in his high chair. But after six to ten seconds of that, stop your camera; move in close enough to get a head and shoulders shot that will almost fill the finder; then you can, if you like, back off and get a three-quarter-length shot from a different angle. It's always better to have the long shot first, then the close-up, rather than vice versa. But the vital thing to remember is that when you move in close, you've got to be mighty accurate in estimating the focal distance at which to set your lens, especially when the light is weak and your lens is pretty wide open. At five or six feet a slight miscalculation can give you a fuzzy picture that is worthless, so measure the distance and be safe.

5. Subjects mugging the camera. One of the most tiresome ordeals in life is to sit through a couple of reels of a family movie in which the various characters appear in turn and outdo each other in making snoots at the camera. This has led to the misconception that the best pictures are those taken with their subjects unaware.

Undeniably, some of these spontaneous shots are honeys. But when you stop to think that professional movies are posed—or rehearsed, if you prefer —a dozen times before a shutter is opened, you get a cue that can help you greatly in your home operations. That cue is, Plan Your Shots Ahead.

Obviously, you can't write a scenario and rehearse it with an infant, although you definitely can with children old enough to understand—and they love it. For the babies you just have to content yourself with striving for variety. Why shoot 35 feet of the Heir Apparent being bathed and forget about his wolfing down his formula, being jiggled on grandpa's knee or sleeping peacefully in his crib?

If the average parent would simply watch his offspring closely for a week, making pencil notes of the fascinating things the youngster does, he would have a wealth of material which couldn't possibly be equaled by "shooting from the hip."

This doesn't mean that spontaneous shots aren't the best: it simply means that if you rely entirely on them for a pictorial record of your children's development, you won't get enough.

The best way is to stage them. Children, as you well know, love to play make-believe. So if you will take the pains to outline a number of typical situations—getting dressed in the morning or undressed for bed at night; getting their rain togs on and catching the school bus; taking a shower or a tub bath—(with bubbles!); helping Mommie mix a cake in the kitchen; saying their prayers at night; coasting in their snow suits—you will kill two birds with one stone. That is, you will have the pictorial record you want at different ages; and you will have enlivened the whole film with variety.

The sequences in these little scenarios should be jotted down roughly; they should be rehearsed once or twice before the actual shooting, to iron out the rough spots, eliminate awkward lags and aimless action which too often spoil the "unaware" shots. In the end, this studied spontaneity will pay off handsomely with a movie that keeps moving.

6. Soft-hearted editing—if any. A sort of sadistic editing policy will make your friends honestly enthusiastic to see your pictures again. Your pictures may not be any better than any other halfway decent photographer's; but by just cutting out all the bad shots, they seem better!

Another aspect of editing is titling: that is, adding type captions at reasonable intervals which offer some explanatory comment on the film. Especially useful for establishing dates which you may forget later, these titles also add to the "relief" from continuous long shots. If you don't care to make them yourself, your camera store can have them done for you from your script. But you can have more fun making titles than in shooting the actual film: this is where your Hollywood flair can really come out! Using stand-up or stick-on letters, available in all camera supply houses, you can add all kinds of props, from baby shoes to the high chair and cuddle dolls for atmosphere. Thus your titles can be amusing, informative and individual.

Of course, the thing that spoils more film than any other is improper exposure. But with the reams of literature to be had at your camera store on this subject, there is no point in trying to go into it here.

In black-and-white photography all the elementary literature will tell you to shoot with the sun behind you. This is the safest way—but not the most pictorial. The sun at your left or right will give you much more striking effects. You get more sparkle; better modeling of features and definition of detail; greater contrast.

When you start working with color film, however, you've got to reverse all this. For the best color effects you want a flat, soft light rather than a strong, contrasting one. Actually, you get the best color films on an overcast or hazy day with no direct sun. This doesn't mean that you can't get shots in the sunlight; it simply means that when the sun is out, you should keep your back to it when you're shooting color film.

If you are going to exhibit your film to large groups, the 16-mm. size is none too big: if you're just going to show them to intimate gatherings of friends in your living room, the 8-mm. size is big enough—and cuts your costs quite considerably.

The main thing, however, is the priceless asset you will have in these permanent records of your youngsters as they grow up. Memories dim, no matter how vivid they may be at the moment. But when you put them on film, you have them for keeps.

—By Paul W. Kearney

HAM RADIO

ONLY recently has ham radio come into its own as a hobby the entire family can share. The popularity of amateur radio is snowballing as thousands of parents and teen-agers discover this most fascinating and democratic of pastimes. Its devotees are young and old of both sexes, the rich and the poor, the rural as well as the city dweller.

What better way to feel close to people the world around than by speaking together? Voices flashing around the globe in an instant, scorning distance, vaulting political borders. This is actually putting the "One World" concept into everyday use. Here is a fraternity you can join.

"Hamming" is as old as radio. But the stimulus that lifted it from the little-known hobby of the few to the pleasure of the average family was the authorization, in July 1951, of the "Novice" apprentice license by the Federal Communications Commission.

This beginner's license was intended to encourage the younger generation to become interested in electronics. In an atomic age, our national survival may well depend upon having a reservoir of trained technicians in peace and war. Most governments recognize this need.

The new Novice license brought a deluge of applications to FCC (Federal Communications Commission) from every corner of this country. Teen-agers who had been frittering away their leisure time began to crowd the rooms where the examinations were given. FCC officials were delighted. But an unexpected trend manifested itself early. Half of these newcomers were grown-ups! Fathers who hadn't known enough about electricity to fix a lamp cord found themselves relaying amateur message traffic and having the time of their lives. Mothers found bridge clubs rather dull after picking up a microphone and swapping recipes and ideas on bringing up children with another housewife a thousand miles away.

What is this universal appeal of ham radio? The answers are as varied as individual temperaments.

Bobby Fiske, who had a ham friend in Liberia, enjoys most "working DX (distance)"—chatting with fellow amateurs around the globe from the privacy of his own home, day or night, the year 'round. His inability to speak anything but English proved to be no handicap at all; ham radio long ago discovered how to topple the Tower of Babel.

International Code

For there is a magic key which unlocks the doors of international understanding and fellowship. It is the "international Q-Code"—a list of simple three-letter symbols with universal meanings. For instance, "QTH" means "Where do you live?" to Hottentot or Hungarian, Arab or Eskimo, Zulu or Japanese; "QRT," "I must stop now"; "QRX," "Please wait a moment."

Americans use a dot-and-dash slang all our own. Every male operator is an OM (Old Man) regardless of age. A YL is a young lady operator, who becomes an XYL when she marries. HI is the Morse code chuckle, HI HI is a resounding guffaw. FB means "fine business!" The numerals 73 mean "best regards" while 88 is translated "love and kisses." BCNU could only be hamese for "I'll be seein' you!"

Many people are just natural-born collectors—they treasure stamps, coins, insects or autographs. This type of person enjoys the ham custom of swapping "QSL cards." When two hams contact each other over the air, they usually confirm this by exchanging postcards bearing their call letters and other information. Visit any ham's "shack" (the name given his radio room, be it in a cold-water flat or a millionaire's penthouse) and you will probably find the walls papered with QSL cards. The same hobby is enjoyed by thousands of SWL's, or Short-Wave Listeners.

The fascination of ham radio to those of mechanical or inventive bent is obvious. Most hams build their own sending sets. The gadget-lover is in seventh heaven while hamming. Radar and television owe their rapid growth to early pioneering by amateur experimenters. Short-wave communication is a ham product. How do you go about taking up amateur radio as a family hobby?

Bobby Fiske's case is typical. He was exposed to the radio "bug" when a neighbor boy won his Boy Scout radio merit badge. Bobby at once clamored for a station of his own. But Mr. and Mrs. Fiske, well aware of Bobby's fickle enthusiasms, were dubious. They compromised by renting a "communications receiver." (Your ordinary home radio will not tune in the amateur wave lengths between 200 and 10 meters). Bobby was now a Short-Wave Listener.

Out of idle curiosity, Bobby's parents listened too. They heard the southern drawl of a Georgia tobacco grower arguing baseball with a Boston fan with a Back Bay accent. A Kansas wheat farmer was bringing an Idaho lumberjack up to date on Dick Tracy. And then the Fiskes heard their next door neighbor in a round-table chat with amateurs in Cairo, London and Buenos Aires!

Facts About Ham Radio

It didn't take many evenings of this for the whole Fiske family to succumb to an irresistible urge to join the fun. But Mrs. Fiske had to be practical. This hobby seemed too good to be true. Before investing time and money on ham radio, Mrs. Fiske had a few questions she wanted answered in advance:

How much does ham radio cost? A basic station—receiver, transmitter and antenna—sells from about $45 up in build-yourself kits. Factory equipment is priced from $100 to $3,000. The average ham has an investment of around $100. Repair costs are negligible on a year-to-year basis. As for boosting the light bill, an amateur radio station draws less current than your electric iron.

How much space is required? A writing desk or bridge table is more than ample room for even an advanced station. In city apartments, whip antennas similar to those on car radios can be installed on a window ledge. On the farm or suburban lot, single-wire roof antennas from 33 to 135 feet are used.

Is ham radio dangerous for children? Any electrical device is potentially lethal if you touch a live wire. High-voltage circuits in ham equipment are inaccessible when the set is in operation. Ham radio gear is as safe as TV.

Can a ham station be taken on trips? Your license specifies a "fixed" location. However, by signing your call "portable," you can legally operate your station while traveling, on vacation, at school or in a friend's house. By signing "mobile" you can send and receive messages while in an automobile, airplane or boat.

Local Civil Defense, Red Cross, Boy Scouts or Police Department will be happy to sign you up for emergency duty—especially if you have a miniature transmitter and receiver in your car. FCC records are replete with heroic tales of the roles played by hams during floods, earthquakes, fires.

With these thoughts in mind, Bobby Fiske's mother decided ham radio was worthwhile. So Bobby took the next step: he sent away for a copy of the booklet, "How To Become a Radio Amateur." This booklet and other literature on ham radio may be obtained from the American Radio Relay League, West Hartford 7, Connecticut. Special questions submitted by mail are answered by their Technical Information Service. The booklet Bobby received explains in the simplest terms what makes radio work; it shows how to build a receiver and a transmitter. It also told Bobby that ham radio requires a federal license to practice—and explained the Novice Class.

Requirements for Novice License

The Fiskes learned that all you have to do to get a Novice license is to be able to send and receive International Morse code at the rate of five words a minute, and pass a very elementary written exam on radio theory and federal regulations.

The boy next door taught Bobby and his parents how to send and receive code in about two weeks' time. Other beginners have rented code-practice machines utilizing punched tapes, or Morse code phonograph records. It was not long before Bobby wrote to his nearest FCC district office for application forms and examination papers.

Since June 10, 1954, federal law requires that Novice tests be taken at home, in the presence of a licensed amateur. The notarized papers are mailed back to the District FCC office. Those who flunk can try again in 30 days. There are no fees in connection with obtaining an amateur radio operator's license, but only American citizens qualify.

While impatiently waiting for their licenses and station calls to arrive—it took three weeks—Bobby and his father built a transmitter from the illustrated directions in their ARRL beginner's booklet.

Do-It-Yourself Equipment

Few experiences in life can equal for thrills and suspense the moment when the mailman brings your "ticket" and you switch in your key or microphone to put your first CQ (calling all stations!) on the air. Who will answer? It may be a movie star in Hollywood or a cowboy on an isolated Arizona ranch.

Fortunately for families on modest incomes, long-distance radio contacts do not depend on high power or fancy equipment. A homemade 20-watt "rig" circles the world as does a deluxe 1,000 watter. The relative unimportance of power, per se, is one of radio's happy paradoxes.

The Novice license intended only as a means of giving you on-the-air experience, expires in one year and cannot be renewed. By that time, however, most hams have absorbed enough advanced theory and built their code speed up to 13 words per minute so they can pass the "General Class" examination. A General license is good for life, if renewed by mail every five years.

Eight-year-old boys and girls frequently win their General licenses, but the ages between 10 and 16 appear to be average. Adults have made the grade after their 80th birthday.

Most cities have Amateur Radio Clubs where local enthusiasts get together. More and more high schools are giving radio courses, graduating pupils as licensed hams.

Therapeutic benefits. Doctors recognize ham radio's therapeutic benefits and it is being encouraged in Veterans Hospitals. For the spastic, blind or otherwise handicapped person, radio is a godsend, since it literally brings the whole world to the shut-in. Polio victims have even operated radio stations from iron lungs! As a deterrent to juvenile delinquency, amateur radio has the enthusiastic endorsement of PTA, churches, social service groups and law-enforcement agencies.

Hamming has long-range benefits. For the young student facing Selective Service, a radio license gives him a tremendous jump over non-hams, since the armed forces are hard-pressed to find trained communications personnel. And in this scientific age, radio, television, radar and allied fields offer unlimited opportunities.

There is unexpected drama at your fingertips, too. Don Wherry, a schoolboy living on a farm near Churdan, Iowa, was idly tuning his homemade set one night when his earphones picked up an SOS from a Norwegian whaling ship, sinking in icy seas north of the Arctic Circle.

When no one answered the distress call, Don relayed the ship's position to a fellow ham in New Jersey. Within the hour the U. S. Coast Guard had contacted another whaler in the vicinity of the doomed vessel, whose wireless operator, due to a freak of atmospherics, had not heard the Norwegian's feeble signal. All hands were rescued—and a hero's medal went to Don Wherry!

Just one word of warning: if you expose yourself to ham radio you are lost! Once a ham, always a ham. Good luck—BCNU and very 73!

—*By Walker A. Tompkins*

WEATHER FORECASTING

EVERYBODY knows it is important for fathers and sons to be good friends and to work out a real companionship. One way is by doing things together. In this modern age youngsters seem to take to science like ducks to water. Not all fathers are scientific, but if they don't know too much about the subject, so much the better. There are very simple scientific experiments which can be fascinating to both fathers and sons, and if both are learning as they go along it's more fun for the child.

No experiments are more fascinating than those having to do with the prediction of weather. A visit to your local weather bureau is an interesting trip if you can arrange it.

Here is a simple weather instrument that any boy and his father can make together: a hair hygrometer (hi-grom'e-ter). Don't let this word frighten you. It is simply the scientific name for a gadget which measures the moisture in the air. It is one of the instruments used in forecasting the approach of a warm front, which brings its days of drizzle, and a cold front with its quick showers followed by clear, cool weather.

Materials needed—A clean, empty milk carton (or a box of about that size), a needle, a broom straw, cellophane tape, nail polish or glue, a human hair at least nine inches long, three pins or thumbtacks, a sharp knife or razor blade, a blank card, a paper clip and a penny.

How it works—Humid air causes the hair to stretch, while dry air makes it shrink. This change in length is very slight—you'd have a hard time measuring it with a ruler. But if this slight change is magnified, we can see it and make use of it. And that's what the needle and broom straw do. When the hair shrinks a hundredth of an inch, the tip of the broom straw moves about 1¼ inches. That's a magnification of 125 to 1.

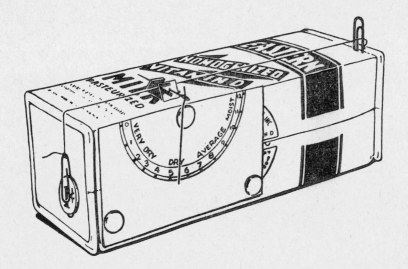

How to Build It

1. Wash the hair with soapy water or alcohol and rinse it in clear water. Put it aside to dry. **2.** Cut an **H** at one side of the carton. **3.** Bend up the two tabs in the **H** and punch a hole in each with your needle. Twist the needle around a bit, so the needle will turn freely. **4.** Split off a piece of broom straw about three inches long, with one end just thick enough to push into the eye of the needle. Put a dab of nail polish or glue to fasten it there and let it dry. **5.** Cut a narrow slit at the far end of the carton, then push the paper clip halfway in. **6.** With compass or a drinking glass as a guide, draw a half-circle on the card and print the words *dry* and *moist*, as shown, and numbers 1 to 12 along the half-circle. **7.** With three pins or thumbtacks, fasten the card to the carton. **8.** With cellophane tape, fasten one end of the hair to the penny. Try not to touch the rest of the hair, because the grease of your skin prevents the hair from absorbing moisture. **9.** Place the needle and straw into the holes in the **H** tab. **10.** Wind the hair one turn over and around the needle. Slip the free end of the hair into the paper clip and fasten it with a dab of glue or nail polish. The penny should hang about an inch over the end of the carton.

Now you're ready, except for adjusting your hygrometer. The broom straw must be set to show the right humidity. There are two ways of doing this:

1. Set the hygrometer on a level surface in your bathroom. Turn on the shower and let it run until the mirror and windows cloud up. Now the air is 100 per cent humid. You will see the broom straw turn slowly as the hair stretches. It will finally come to a stop when the hair has stretched as far as it will. Turn the broom straw so it points to number 12. Then carefully carry your instrument to a shaded, protected place where you plan to keep it.

2. Another way of setting your hygrometer is to place it in a large metal container, such as a bucket, with a damp washcloth next to it, and cover the bucket with a damp towel. After fifteen minutes, take off the towel and immediately set the pointer to number 12.

How to use the hygrometer—Your hygrometer shows the humidity of the air immediately around it. In seasons when the windows are open, the air in your house will be about as moist as the outdoor air in a shaded place, so you can keep your hygrometer indoors and yet be able to find out the humidity of the outside air. But when the windows are closed, you'll have to keep your hygrometer outdoors, in a protected place, out of the sunlight. Before taking a reading, tap the carton gently two or three times.

In order to use your hygrometer as a weather-forecasting instrument, you should take readings at the same time every day. In general you will find that the humidity of the air increases before a rain and decreases afterward. When a front is approaching, the humidity will change as follows:

	BEFORE FRONT	DURING FRONT	AFTER FRONT
WARM FRONT	INCREASING	VERY MOIST	SLIGHT DECREASE
COLD FRONT	STEADY	VERY MOIST	RAPID DECREASE

With your hygrometer and several other simple instruments which you can build yourself, you can try your own weather forecasting. Your results will not be as accurate as the weatherman's but they will be plenty of fun for you and your son.

—By Herman Schneider

WHY NOT MAKE A FAMILY TREE?

WHAT was the maiden name of your great-grandmother? (One-eighth of your life's blood comes from this worthy lady, as well as your blue eyes, perhaps, and, for all we know, your keen sense of humor.) You've forgotten? Well, you have lots of company. Very few Americans could answer the question. In the process of cleaning out the attic, I came upon a rather ancient and dusty family album. The red plush cover was faded but the pictures inside were still clear. Leafing through the pages, I suddenly realized that these were the people responsible for my own existence and that I knew very little about them.

My children knew even less, and I decided to do something about it.

When I came down from the attic and announced my intention to draw up a family tree, I was greeted with complete indifference from my two children and mild amazement from my husband, who warned me to watch out for the proverbial "skeleton." Undaunted, I sketched out a rough draft, filling in as many spaces as possible.

It seemed such a simple undertaking at the time. One year and four months later, I was carrying on a lively correspondence with at least a dozen formerly unknown relatives. Our son's grades in American history improved. A chance bit of house cleaning, then, has sparked my entire family into a brand-new hobby—ancestor-hunting.

Many types of chart can be used in constructing a family tree. If you want to become a member of the D.A.R., it will have to be a long, elaborate one. However, a simple one showing four to five generations seems adequate for most families.

Merely sketch it on a sheet of paper, and build it out as far as you care to continue your research. There are only a few simple rules to follow:

1. Every name should be in full—no nicknames—unless you want to add them in parentheses.

2. Always include the maiden name of a married woman.

3. Date and place of birth, marriage and death should be listed after each name.

Some clans are blessed with self-appointed historians from whom all the vital statistics can be obtained. Fortunately this was not true in our family. Though it would have saved a lot of work, we would have missed the fun of doing our own research.

Seeking New Information

Before long, even the youngest member of our family began to enjoy watching the tree grow. By that time, I had exhausted my own resources and had turned to the family patriarchs for more information. They loved recalling the good old days. A single question would inspire the telling of half a dozen stories chock-full of family history.

I always carried a small notebook with me and jotted down everything I heard. Later I would sort fact from fiction; for any story is apt to become distorted through re-tellings.

No data was too small or trivial to escape my notebook—even the curious fact that my Uncle John is related somehow to Cousin Wilbur's third wife, Sarah. Someday a great-granddaughter of mine may want to continue the research. A clue like this may supply her with a vital link.

Soon I had made the rounds of all relatives in our immediate vicinity. Grandfather then suggested that I get in touch with those at a distance and supplied me with several names and addresses. It was a wonderful excuse for picking up the threads of a long-dropped correspondence, or for starting a new one. We gained a lot of information for our history. More important, however, were the new friendships we enjoyed, for whenever possible we exchanged week-end visits with these new cousins.

We were not fortunate enough to locate an old family Bible, though a thorough search was made for one. They do yield the most intriguing things sometimes—even the written record of important events.

I have been told that town records are usually more reliable than Bible records, should there be a disagreement. Nevertheless, lacking any other reliable source, a Bible record is accepted as proof of eligibility for membership by most patriotic societies and, in some cases, has been accepted for passport purposes.

At one point I came to an impasse. Our family tree was still lacking many items. My husband suggested that I consult the town records, as well as those of the probate court. I was delighted with the information to be gleaned there, and pass the suggestion on as a source which must be tapped by the would-be ancestor hunter.

Ancestor-hunting. Each year our family makes a Memorial Day pilgrimage to the cemetery and it had special meaning this year. With Great-Aunt Fanny for a guide, we located several family markers which we did not know existed. The inscriptions, faded almost beyond recognition, gave us several more names for our tree.

A fitting climax to the year-long search was our trip through the New England states. Historical settings meant more to the children when they realized that their great-grandparents had once lived in this area. Also, our tour had the aspect of an adventure, since we were seeking information about the birthplace of my husband's maternal grandfather—the last record needed to complete our family tree. We found what we were looking for in the records of a little town in Connecticut. It might be a little town in the Alps for your family. That's another exciting aspect of ancestor-hunting, especially for Americans. The "typical American" usually doesn't have to look back very far to find his family coming from across the seas.

An interesting and rewarding hobby, this business of collecting ancestors. So why not dig out that family album and get to work? —*By Bea Renaud*

READING ALOUD

R EADING is an important part of your child's mental and emotional life. Reading aloud is one of the easiest and happiest ways in which a family can have fun together. Once you have chosen your books, make up your mind to give the listeners all that the text holds in the way of excitement, suspense, humor and drama. Get into the spirit of the thing, relax, let yourself go. Almost all public libraries have a list of "Books to Read Aloud" or your librarian will be glad to recommend books for this purpose.

When it comes to the mechanics of reading aloud, three things are important: stress, modulation and tempo. Stress consists in putting varying degrees of emphasis on action verbs and designating nouns and pronouns. It will take a little application on your part before you remember to pronounce important verbs with special distinctness so that you carry your hearers along with you when *Garvi runs* downstairs, *crashes* through the screen door and *tips over a flower-pot* on his way to meet his *father*. Here the stress is important lest you leave your audience's attention still in the upstairs hall. Incidentally, you want to be sure it is clear that father is home; he may be important in the next paragraph.

In our adult reading we are used to the author's stratagem of switching from one set of characters to another, or from one place to another in order to round out the details of a plot. It doesn't bother us very much to be whisked from Milwaukee in 1912 to Monte Carlo just before the war, but this bit of business will often confuse the less sophisticated audience. Make sure that the children understand this new aspect of the story before you continue reading. It will prevent future misunderstandings. If a character has just put in a reappearance after an absence of three chapters, find out if he is a definite picture in your listeners' minds. You'll be surprised and delighted after a while to note just how much they absorb if you carry them along carefully and definitely.

Now we come to the part that takes the boredom out of the pastime of reading aloud. This is where you have your fun, after a little practice.

Employ Varied Voice Levels

You have several different voice levels which you employ during the day without ever noticing the difference. The way you converse with your husband is really quite different from the manner in which you talk to your old friend over the telephone. Gaiety and good spirits make your voice rich and vibrant. Anger or annoyance sharpen it, sadness tones it down. The variations are probably greater than you ever realized, and you can put them to good use when you have to interpret the many characters found in most books. To the

hero or heroine, give your voice with the beautiful modulation and let the villain take the sharp, querulous or bitter tones. The advantage of that system is that you will be using your best voice on the part that is likely to have the most conversational space in the book.

There will be minor characters whose number would tax the ability of a professional mimic. You needn't give each an entirely individual voice, but get in little gradations, a brogue, an accent, a speech eccentricity of some sort. Use your imagination freely.

As a starter I shall pass on to you some of my own tricks. I read to my children a good deal when their mother is busy, and notice that she keeps one ear in on the entertainment when she can, so my system must have some merit. For instance, I decided quite early that I couldn't keep up a strained alto for Mary Poppins, so, since Mary Poppins invariably snapped out her words, I didn't bother to try, but simply snapped, sniffed and snipped my way through a very satisfying characterization. It went so well after a while that I just dropped most of the author's "Mary Poppins snapped, Mary Poppins said with a sniff" and it seemed to lift the words right out of the book and into the room. I was sorry that there was not more of Admiral Boom in this book because I really let myself go with the decibels when he had anything to say. I grew quite fond of the Scarecrow in the Wizard of Oz, because I found that he came from my heart in a sort of husky tenor.

I came across one character in a book whom I did not care for. She seemed shallow and rather poorly done, and I found myself rushing through her lines with almost unintelligible haste, and then I realized that that was probably the way she talked anyway, after which I got along with her all right.

Release from tension. There are enough similar ideas that will occur to you as you go along to keep you content with your evening's hour of reading to the children. You'll find in it a form of release from routine tensions and a genuine outlet for everyone's innate wish to be an actor or actress. Try it when you begin that next book. The children will love it and you will too. Reading aloud often suffers from being monotonous. When this happens children lose interest and their attention wanders. But if you will throw self-consciousness to the wind and let your voice really portray your characters you will have a group of enchanted listeners.

The books you read will often serve as a source of conversation at the dinner table and also provide food for humor. Many children who have been read aloud to through their early years, after they learn to read, become avid readers themselves. It's natural for them to develop good vocabularies and so they learn to express themselves interestingly and aptly.

—*By John Thomas Urwin*

LET'S VISIT A MUSEUM

ARE your family outings fun or a headache? If you want one where there is something of interest for each member, where you are not harassed by crowds and where the temperature is right regardless of season, go to the nearest museum.

Plan to arrive by the time the museum opens in the morning as children are freshest then and most eager for new experiences. Wear comfortable shoes, check all unnecessary parcels at the desk. Set a leisurely pace, take each gallery in turn and look thoroughly.

Perhaps you will invite other youngsters to enjoy the trip, and if you have a group of four or more, the interests will be varied. It is best not to try to keep them together and try to see everything each person is interested in, but let them separate in groups of twos or threes and proceed to galleries of their choice. Then collect them all in about a half-hour for reorganization.

Technique of looking is important in the assimilation and appreciation of museum fare. For general effect, stand off at a distance and study the picture or exhibit, then go close and study details more minutely. Decide whether the exhibit belongs to the scientific, cultural or ethical contributions of the past or whether, as one adult suggested to some children in a gallery of impressionistic art, it belongs to tomorrow.

No matter how great your personal interest may be, try not to force your ideas on the youngsters. For some reason, few children care about Oriental art, and it is a rare child who will take a second look at religious paintings.

A little dramatization will make exhibits come to life for the very young child. Read explanatory material aloud or talk about an exhibit that seems to interest him. Perhaps the habitat group of deer suggest the story of "Bambi," or the other animals will be reminders of nursery stories and rhymes. Most children are thrilled with familiar objects and when they see them in a museum, they want to hear more about them.

Proper behavior. Previous briefing on museum decorum is a moot question. However, proper conduct can be taken for granted with most children unless, in their interest and excitement, they forget and lean on glass cases or shout across galleries. The average child is not likely to be tempted to skate on polished floors or swing on rope barriers unless he is tired and bored. Then it is time to get outside into the daylight, rest the eyes in fresh air, and perhaps eat a snack.

Not the least important part of such a trip is talking it over afterwards. Going over booklets, museum guides and photographs purchased at the desk impress what has been seen upon the mind, and are an aid in organizing reports that may be given at school or club meetings.

Museums may range in size from small historical shrines to large institutions maintained by municipalities or private organizations, but all perform the same function; they provide an opportunity for an interested public to study the development of anything from the history of man himself to his cultural and economic endeavors. They preserve significant objects of the past, explain the wonders of the contemporary world of science, nature and the arts, and occasionally even indulge in brief speculations about life in the future.

Museum visiting can further personal interests and hobbies of a wide-awake child, supplement and broaden his understanding of school subjects and teach him to be observing. But most of all, it develops in him an awareness of the world about him and a deeper appreciation of the great American heritage that is his.

—By Katherine Peavy

HOW TO TEACH
YOUR CHILD TO SWIM

THERE are many things a child doesn't have to know in order to live safely—but if he's anywhere near water, swimming isn't one of them. "The ability to handle normal water hazards is in the same class as learning to wait for the red light and looking both ways before crossing the street," is the way one crack swimming coach puts it.

Another top swimming instructor observes, "There are only two choices where water is concerned: a child either has to know how to swim or else wear a life-jacket at all times!"

There are two other important advantages to learning to swim besides its survival value. Swimming ranks high as a recreational sport and hobby, and it's one of the best over-all body exercises in the world. So getting your youngster off to a good start in learning to handle himself in the water rates more thought and preparation, probably, than you've realized.

Naturally you are not just going to throw Johnny and Jane into the water and expect them to take off like young ducks. A child has to be ready for this new adventure—and so do you. Actually, your own attitude is probably most important because your child will sense it and react to it whether you say anything or not.

Though youngsters should know that water is a force to be respected, parents can do a lot of harm by harping on its dangers while a child is learning to swim. One Red Cross instructor told about a little boy who refused to go near the water one day though he had previously gone in willingly. She tried to find what was troubling him, without success. Then the bus driver let the cat out of the bag.

"I can tell you what's eating him," he volunteered. "This morning when his mother put him on the bus she said, 'Now you be careful out there. I wouldn't want you to drown.'"

Are you inclined in general to be nervous, apprehensive, fearful? Overprotective? Timid about allowing a youngster enough physical freedom to be curious and explore? Get yourself in hand first, and when your youngster's ready for swimming you will be, too.

There are three general qualifications by which a child's readiness to learn to swim may be judged. First, can he take directions? Amos Smith, a Florida instructor who has made swimmers out of hundreds of people from 18 months to 80 years, says that the youngster who learns fastest is the one who pays attention and accepts instruction. You can easily spot those who can't. Given some simple command, they wander off into, "I got a truck for my birthday" or "We're going to have a picnic," probably because they aren't interested.

Fear of Water

The second factor is whether the child is unafraid. "Fear" of the water is often just unfamiliarity with it. If exposure is long and pleasant enough, the fear soon vanishes.

Never, never force a child into the water before he is willing to go, advise all these experts. Don't shame him for cowardice or label him a "sissie." No one can teach a tense, fearful, shivering, unwilling child how to swim. To "dunk" a child who is genuinely frightened of water is to run the risk of stamping him with a lifetime fear.

Finally, the "ready" child shows good muscular coordination. Some children are just naturally better at this than others. Even in the same family it varies a great deal so that a five-year-old may be better coordinated than his seven-year-old brother.

There is no one age at which a child is ready, but there is much parents can do to assure that his natural readiness is allowed to develop, even helped along. Long before he is old enough to venture into pool or ocean, a youngster is acquiring pleasant or unpleasant feelings about water. The very first baths of infancy are a preparation for later introduction to larger bodies of water. They should be arranged so that the baby enjoys them; he should always feel well supported and in no danger of slipping out of your grasp. Even so small an incident as water uncomfortably hot or cold, or soap in the eyes can put a damper on his enthusiasm for his bath.

Later you can play water games in the tub or basin or the kitchen sink— and let him splash! Children who aren't used to splashing take longer to learn to swim. Little boats, plastic cups or pitchers, washcloths to squeeze out, are some of the things that will serve to show further that water play is fun.

Robert Zubrod, developer of the game method of learning to swim, says that the child who is able to put his face down in the water and open his eyes is already far on the road to learning to swim. He suggested that parents could teach this skill at home by playing various games with the child. Have him pretend that the water in the tub is a big bowl of soup that he has to cool off a bit by blowing on it, gradually bringing his face closer to the surface of the water. Next he can play motor boat. He takes a deep breath and places his face in the water up to his mouth, blowing the air out through his mouth to make a "putt-putt" noise.

To get him to open his eyes under water, try dropping some pennies or small bright objects to the bottom of the tub and have him play diver, hunting for buried treasure. A child who doesn't like the feel of opening his eyes under water is sometimes helped by a pair of goggles or a mask.

Never Leave Child Alone

At this point, a word of warning is in order. "Be sure," cautions one Red Cross Water Safety Director, "that you never leave your child alone while he is playing these games. Many drownings have occurred in even the shallow water of home bathtubs."

She has another word of good advice for parents. "Many children associate only pleasant warmth with water when they come for their first swimming lessons. It's a shock to them when they enter a pool or the ocean. It's a good idea to accustom them gradually to cooler water as they are growing out of babyhood."

Many swimming experts agree that much of the groundwork for learning to swim can be laid right on dry land. You don't need to wait until you get to the beach. It's a great advantage if your youngster already knows the proper body positions and has practiced the motions needed for swimming before he actually goes in the water. At home use your bed or the floor to go through the motions with him. Or the two of you can practice them on the sand once you are at the beach. Having a best pal or two along when you're off to a lake or the beach adds to the fun and is always a spur. Seeing another child swimming or diving usually inspires the envious gasp, "I wish I could do that!" When other children are enjoying an activity, your child is apt to develop an ambition to do the same thing.

Here's a starter on training your child. Stretch out face down on bed or floor and go through the following with him: stretch the arms and hands forward as far as they will go. (Place some small object a little farther than he can reach and he'll stretch even more.) Now lift both legs and do a gentle little flutter kick. Easy does it. This is the prone flat position in which all swimming on the front is done. Once it has become second nature, the rest is fairly easy. You can later add the hand stroke and the proper breathing.

A child who sees a large body of water for the first time may be a little in awe of it. One small boy I saw on the beach couldn't be persuaded even to try wading, because "there are too many bumps"—referring to the little ripples the wind was making on the water. By all means give your child time to get used to the vastness of the scene while he digs in the sand, gathers shells or plays ball with you. Subsequently, he might like to "mudcrawl" in shallow water. Hold a colored plastic clothesline between your outstretched hands under water while he ducks under, head and all, to attach varicolored pins to the line. Or they may already be attached and he must remove one of a particular color. This requires him to open his eyes under water.

Group Water Play

Gather several children together and play relay games to get youngsters used to the water. With the group standing still near the water's edge, have them pass some object such as a beach ball over their heads, beneath their legs and then to the person behind them. Gradually move the group to shallow water as soon as they have become interested in the game being played. Next move them to water slightly above the knees, using the same walking and running games. The youngsters are usually so keen about having their team win that they will not be concerned about the coolness of the water or even having it splashed in their faces. A child who falls quickly scrambles to his feet again and meantime he is getting the feel of the water.

Once your child is accustomed to moving about freely in the water, you are ready to start on breathing skills. All breathing in swimming should be done through the mouth. If your youngster is concerned about water in his nose or ears, throw into the water a small can that was emptied by hole-punching and let him see that as the small holes let the water in it sinks. But plug up the holes (chewing gum will do it) and it floats indefinitely on top of the water. Breathing out through the mouth under water similarly "puts a cork" in the child's nose and ears so that no water can get in.

Now you are ready to teach the prone float which is a real life-saver because it requires so little effort to maintain for long periods of time—merely the energy needed to lift the head and breathe when necessary.

Have the child stand waist-deep in the water and tell him to reach for some object on the bottom a short distance away from his feet—a bright pebble, perhaps. At this depth his arms will not be able to touch it but his body, as he reaches out and down, will automatically assume a face-down floating position. Support his hands at arm's length in front of him. At first he may clutch tightly to you, but as he acquires more confidence he'll gradually be willing to relax his grip and trust to his own buoyancy.

To teach the back float, have him pretend that he is a steamboat which has run out of steam. "Now you'll have to float down the river like this." Demonstrate the back float yourself. In waist-deep water have him squat down as if he were going to sit on a chair. When his shoulders are below the surface he should stretch his hands out to the side with palms up. Tell him to lay his head back on his "pillow" just as if he were in bed at home. Have him keep his body as close to the surface as possible by explaining that a steamboat has to keep its passengers dry, "So keep your chest above the water." If he finds the position a little difficult at first, you can stand in back of him and support him at the shoulders until he gets the hang of it.

Safety precautions. There are several safety precautions you should teach your child and observe yourself at all times.

1. Never swim alone. "Always go in the water with a buddy" is a safety slogan of the Red Cross.

2. Always swim in shallow water until you become an expert swimmer. While the child is learning there should always be an adult between him and deep water.

3. Don't play practical jokes in the water, such as grabbing someone by the feet and pulling him under.

4. Don't swim during an electrical storm.

5. Wait at least an hour after eating before going in the water.

6. Never stay in when you begin to feel chilled.

7. Unless thoroughly trained in lifesaving techniques, never undertake a rescue. Look around you, instead, for something to extend to the victim— a rope, oar, paddle, inflated tire-tube or even a towel.

8. Swim or wade only in supervised areas, preferably where there are lifeguards on duty or other people.

9. Don't take chances. About 80 per cent of all drownings occur within 30 feet of safety. Keep an eye on your child at all times.

10. Above all, no matter what happens, don't panic. If a wave knocks a child off his feet or he finds himself in water beyond his depth, tell him to float—preferably in the prone position—keep air in his lungs and kick or paddle gently toward shore.

Are flotation devices safe? The answer is "yes" only to the small child-size lifejacket that is approved by the U. S. Coast Guard. Children can be dumped out of tire-tubes by a heavy wave or leaks may cause the tubes to become deflated. And far from being of any help in teaching a child to swim, many flotation devices hold the child too far above the surface of the water for him to assume the correct swimming or floating position.

To waterproof your child takes your imaginative, enthusiastic, patient guidance and encouragement. But it's one of the most important safeguards you can give him.

—By Constance J. Foster

ICE SKATING

ICE skaters are not born. They are taught. I never wore a pair of ice skates until I was sixteen, but your child can start to ice skate at the age of four. I have seen younger children on ice skates but they are the exceptions. Children from the ages of four to six years should begin to skate on a single-runner blade which is low-built, one-half the height of the usual skating blade and not as heavy. This gives the child the sensation of actual skating while at the same time it does not strain the ankles and legs. You should not buy double-runner skates for your child. These do not help him skate; as a matter of fact, the child walks or runs on them. The muscles in the legs which are used in skating are developed by the single-blade skate.

Be sure to get a shoe that fits perfectly. It is the main support for your child's ice-skate balance. Don't make the mistake of anticipating the growth of your child's foot and getting him a shoe that is too large. Buy the shoe that fits him today. Have him wear a light wool sock both for warmth and to help the shoe fit snugly.

Ankle supports and straps are entirely unnecessary if the shoe fits well and only serve to hinder the circulation of the blood by binding the ankles. There is no such thing as a weak ankle in child or adult unless there has been an injury. Wobbly, aching ankles are caused by little-used muscles which are called into play by ice skating. A few times on the ice, and ankle strength will develop and discomfort vanish.

Proper clothing is most essential for the ice skater. Kind rather than amount of clothing is the important thing. Dress your child in warm, comfortable togs and be sure that they are not bulky. Freedom of body motion is important and bulky clothes hinder such action. Rely on activity rather than heavy clothing to keep your child warm. Be sure that the youngster always wears a hat and gloves when he skates, not so much for warmth but as a protection in case of falls. He will instinctively lean forward and use his arms and hands extended to cushion his body in case of a fall. This, incidentally, is the correct way to fall on the ice. The gloves protect the hands from what might result in a minor skin burn from the ice. The hat will render good protection in case of the very remote possibility that the child falls and hits his head.

First Lesson

When it comes to your child's first steps on the ice, perhaps mother and daddy or big sister and brother will be there, walking or skating by the side of the child, to hold him under each armpit. If there is only one person to help him, see that the child is held underneath the armpit of the *left* arm as in that way the child's arm is not strained should he slip. Impress upon him

the need of keeping his knees close together and bent and of looking ahead and not directly down at the ice in front of him. This will help him to relax. The proper posture and form for ice skating is as follows: Lean forward, knees together and always bent, left shoulder bent forward as left foot is extended forward, and the right shoulder forward as the right foot relieves weight of left foot. Allow the arms to swing and hang naturally like a pendulum of a clock for proper rhythm. The motion is one of leaning forward and gliding, or pushing the ice with the rear leg as the weight is thrust forward on the forward leg.

Remember that your child must learn to fall before he will be able to avoid a fall. Once a would-be skater overcomes the fear of falling he has conquered ninety-nine per cent of the sport. When teaching adults to skate, my first lesson to them is how to fall. It is the tenseness, conscious or unconscious, that causes the beginning skater to stiffen and lose the coordination that is natural to a relaxed body. The result is apt to be awkward falls. Most children are naturally relaxed. So let your child fall down on the ice, instructing him to lean forward, in a natural way and to use his arms outstretched forward to break the fall. Make him feel that it is all a game rather than a serious business. After the child becomes used to the sensation of falling on the ice he will not fear it, and will seldom fall.

Encourage your child to take it slowly the first two or three times on the ice. Have him sit down and relax every few minutes to allow the body to become accustomed to the exercise. The child should not be allowed to skate more than half an hour the first time. This can be increased to three-quarters of an hour the second time, the third time about an hour—and from that point on, if these three times have occurred within a week or ten days, the child should be allowed to skate without any fear of exertion or strain because muscles will be fairly well developed. Do not let your child become dependent on you or on a professional instructor, since in this case he will not develop the necessary ability and will be afraid to try skating alone.

Don't push instruction. When your child has skated more than three times, if you have allowed him to follow his natural instincts, you will see that he shows steady improvement and imitates the better skaters as it is natural for children to do. This is the best instruction he can have.

Don't try to teach your child more than the fundamentals during the first year. Let him pick up his own tricks by playing games with other children on the ice. The first year is the kindergarten period in skating. Your child should go through the developing and play stages only.

The second year you can buy him the regulation skates for any phase of ice skating he prefers and have him instructed in it. If he is not interested in a specialized field of skating, such as figure, hockey, or speed, buy him the all-around skate which is the hockey model. He can have more fun on this skate than any of the others.

Last, but far from least, be careful about outdoor ice. Make sure that the ice is at least three inches thick before your child ventures out. Don't let him skate on ponds or lakes unless an adult is around for protection.

Once the art of ice skating is acquired it is never forgotten. Persons from the ages of four to seventy years find it both exhilarating and healthful.

—By Irving Jaffee

SKIING FAMILY STYLE

TEMPERATURES and snowfall totals haven't changed significantly since John Greenleaf Whittier wrote "Snowbound," but costumes and customs are definitely being restyled for winter. Families no longer hibernate around suburban hearth or apartment house radiators.

Look at your neighbors stuffing skis, skates, sleds and kids into their station wagon. They're not setting out over the meadow and through the woods to grandmother's house—unless grandma happens to operate a snow-sport resort half-a-hundred miles from home. In an hour or two they'll be swinging downhill on skis, skating hand in hand on a blue-black, snowbanked pond, or zipping down a toboggan run.

More and more, such winter breathers are being taken in mountain region resorts, with federal statisticians estimating that 12,000,000 Americans can now be classified as winter sportsmen.

According to resort operators in the high, cold country between New England and the Cascades, this growing army of snow-season weekenders and vacationists contains a mounting percentage of family funseekers. Family rates are established components of "Learn-to-Ski Weeks" at such geographically diverse spots as Stowe in Vermont, and Alta in Utah, and middle-income families can now find accommodations tailored to their needs at Sun Valley, Idaho, as well as near state parks in New York's Adirondacks or Catskills.

Moreover, parents in increasing numbers are learning that "winter sports" can provide a very real opportunity for a family's "coming together." Speaking both professionally and as a parent, Dr. C. H. Hardin Branch, Chairman of the Department of Psychiatry at the University of Utah College of Medicine, finds that "in most winter sports the parent is not the fifth wheel."

With his wife and two teen-age sons, Dr. Branch skis at Brighton, Utah, a forty-five minute drive from his home, nearly every winter weekend. The Branches took lessons en masse and Dr. Branch feels "such lessons make an excellent joint enterprise. You not only achieve with the kids—but in most cases they can out-achieve you." To this expert on family affairs, "identification as a family group comes about even more strongly when parents who are experienced skiers start their kids on skis as tykes."

Age for Ski Instruction

In many winter resort areas visitors look with wide-eyed wonderment at three and four-year-olds nonchalantly schussing down steep slopes. But a spot check of western ski instructors indicates seven seems the median age for starting all but the most awkward youngsters on a dozen or so lessons. Most ski resorts have at least one or two lodges which—perhaps due to the character of their operators, become known as "family establishments." However, parents with sizable broods and modest budgets will probably discover that "package ski weeks" are their best bargains, because such rates include ski-school lessons and lift-line passes as well as meals.

At the most popular winter spas, prospective guests should check schedules carefully, since in the main, package plans are not operative over the Christmas-New Year's and college holiday seasons.

Ski schools, a "must" with non-skiing parents who want a proper start both for themselves and their youngsters in a sport that can and should provide years of pleasure, go largely unsupervised in most states. However, it is pretty much rule-of-thumb that reputable ski areas have reputable schools and certificate-holding, top-grade instructors.

Your best bet—barring private lessons—will be classes in which a dozen or so youngsters of all ages "imitate" teacher in time-honored fashion, clumping through simple control maneuvers, getting skis parallel, bending the knees, running gentle slopes, and learning to latch on to rope tows in proper fashion. The prices are roughly $3 for two hours in a class—about $15 for an eight-lesson book and somewhere around $8 an hour for private lessons.

If those prices "throw" you momentarily, it will help to know that the average adult can learn to manage skis fairly well with perhaps five two-hour classes and children may head for the tows on their own in somewhat less time. Most youngsters, and a good many adults, learn to ski adequately more readily than they learn to ice skate. By the way, despite horrendous reports, skiing injuries are relatively few. In the main, broken bones are caused by too much derring-do, by over-skiing (skiing when fatigued, attempting expert slopes when you're a novice) and such patent foolishness as skiing in dangerous terrain.

Know the Rules

A few rules which parents can readily drum into skiing small fry and teen-agers, as well as themselves include: never ski cross-country alone; stay strictly away from hazard areas marked as such; no horseplay on runs, lifts or tows (there are perhaps as many injuries on lifts and tows as on the slopes); don't ski when bone-tired, in fog or heavily falling snow; don't fail to fill those sitzmarks! (For stay-at-homes: a sitzmark is the depression left when a skier flops—"sits"—in soft snow.)

In purchasing skiing equipment, as in buying golf clubs, tennis racquets, fishing tackle or any sports gear, the price range is extremely wide. Your "compleat skier" wants goggles, mittens, downhill pants, sweater and windproof parka. However, most parents and their offspring preparing to give snow-sports a whirl have windbreakers, sweaters and other serviceable wearing apparel in various closets, clothing adequate for an early season trial spin on the ski slopes. Most snow country resorts and sports shops in major northern cities will rent you the other necessities: skis, boots, bindings and poles. Such rentals are in the $3.50 to $5.00 range for a week end's use of an outfit.

If, after a weekend's sport, you decide skiing is not for you, your loss is small.

You will find general agreement among winter sportsmen that proper ski bindings—the gadgets that hold your boots to the skis—are the most important single factor in ski gear.

Once you've determined to ski, you can, as the saying goes, "spread the cost over the years." Good boots, bindings and skis should last your entire skiing lifetime; those you buy the children can be handed down and traded 'round.

Learning to ski properly requires old-style persistence. After a winter or two of ski-slope weekending or vacationing, the day will come when each member of the family group is skiing with assurance and ease.

—By Jack Goodman

HIKING AS A FAMILY HOBBY

THE most exciting discovery our children ever made was to find that their own feet were a wonderful means of transportation! They learned one enchanted spring that their feet could carry them to nests of wild birds, or to sweet, yellow violets in hidden woodsy banks—places that had never existed for them before. Why not? Because they could never be seen from the family automobile.

Like millions of other American families, we had come to rely on our car to go places. A Saturday or Sunday found us piling our four children into the car to whirl ourselves—amid the noise of bored and bickering youngsters—as far and fast as possible.

Then came a sudden shock. My husband's work took us for a few months to a tiny New England town. Since his job there was to be within walking distance, and since our car had reached the age of retirement, we decided to turn it in on a new one to be picked up when we returned to the city.

In spite of the novelty and fun of our new life in this town, the first few week-ends after the car was put to pasture were really pretty dismal. We missed our week-ends of being out, of seeing and going places. The months ahead before we could have another car seemed terribly long.

Then, one week-end, when the children were at loose ends and we were regretting our decision to give up the car, the little girl from across the street ran our doorbell.

"My mommy sent me to ask if you'd like to take a walk in the woods with us. She's got sandwiches all packed, and the wild apple trees are in bloom. Will you come?"

We went. What a wonderful day it was—a day that opened doors to many months of adventure for us! We walked before we stopped for lunch, for nearly two hours—a feat we'd believed impossible for our youngest. He loved it! So did the rest of the children. They all jammed their pockets with "rare" stones and "magic" birds' feathers and learned at once some of the rewards of hiking.

Each week-end brought new rewards. The children saw the gentle unfolding of spring as they never could have through a car window. June came, and with it the wild berries we found along the trails. October found our four kicking joyfully at the heaps of maple and birch leaves in the forest as they began to feel in the sharp wind, the approach of winter. December gave them the satisfying scrunch of snow underfoot while they searched for Christmas pine cones.

Rewards of a Shared Interest

In these months Sherry learned from her dad to make an Indian trail—a Boy Scout skill he hadn't called up for twenty years. Kris, a great reader of make-believe tales, taught me where to look for a fairy glen. Scott and Susan, like two puppies, just ran around, gathering sticks, leaves and weeds and other objects hard to catalogue. We all took home pink cheeks and appetites that threatened to break the family budget.

But best of all, we learned that year the simple joys of hiking as a family. Swinging through the woods arm in arm, the children singing the songs they'd learned at school, we felt very close to each other.

In the years since we lived in that town, my husband's work has taken us to cities like Philadelphia and Los Angeles and to other small towns in Florida, Maryland and California. In each place we've lived, we've tried to remember the things we learned in that New England town. For a time, we lived in a city so crowded that it was impossible to find a house or even an apartment, and we were forced to live with our children in a hotel. Like many people who live in hotels or apartments in big cities, we had to rely on public parks for our children's playground. Here again, we learned what fun walking can be for a family.

When we began to feel that we knew nearly every blade of grass in a certain park, we toured the city streets, peeking into pet shops, or looking in the window of the big 5 and 10. Many things I would never ordinarily have given a second glance became interesting and alive for me because the children were along! The construction of a city office building was—with Scott's hand gripping mine in excitement as we neared that special corner—a fascinating daily excursion. For Susan, the city square where she fed the pigeons, was a favorite spot, while Kris liked the outdoor flower stands best. She loved to go there, she used to say, to "smell the colors" and listen to the wheedling cries of the old flower women.

Now, on our long drives across the country, when we're tempted to "drive straight through," we try to stop whenever we can to let the children do some exploring. (Often of course, when we have to make time, it's downright impossible.)

Our children have each had a chance to look a real live cow in the eye, to pick cotton growing on the plant, to feel the wool on a "baahing" lamb—to put their noses right up to a sage bush. We've taken them for a walk after bedtime hours in New York City, and we've shared their delight in the wondrous lights that shed a magic glow. We've walked with them in little western towns with the sun so hot that it made shimmering vapors along the streets. Our children have had desert and ocean beach sand in their shoes, and they've tracked the red clay of Georgia right back into the car with them.

Wherever we go now, we walk. We know now that no matter how fast or far the family station wagon can take us—our children must leave the car to see and touch and "smell the colors."   —*By Margaret L. Lane*

FISHERMEN ARE MADE, NOT BORN

ASK several people how they happen to like fishing.

"My grandfather visited us every summer, and to me it was the biggest event of the year because he took me fishing," says one man.

"No one in my family fished, but our hired man took me when I was so little he had to carry me home, and I've loved it ever since," adds a middle-aged woman.

"The happiest memories of my childhood are the days when my father took me with him when he fished in the millpond dam," continues another.

And so it goes. In each case someone was interested enough, and liked the child enough, to bother with letting him tag along.

Little girls like to fish just as much as boys, and sex has absolutely nothing to do with proficiency or enjoyment.

Look at the world's records for prize catches, and compare weights in the men's and women's divisions. You'll see that the gals can hold their own.

Four is a fine age for beginning to fish. A four-year-old, however, is not a miniature adult. He is going to act four years old. Because of this, there are certain ways of establishing and holding his interest. Tell the child he can go with you only a day ahead. More than one day is an eternity. Too much anticipation builds up excitement to the point where the actuality becomes an anticlimax. Once promised, let nothing short of a broken leg keep you from going. Even if your young daughter gives your three best lures to the trash man the day before, don't punish her by not letting her go after she has been promised the trip.

For the youngest beginner the best method is pole and line with plain old worms for bait. No matter what you think privately of this practice, keep it to yourself. There is plenty of time later to be initiated into the more complicated forms. Right now the primary aim should be fun with no difficult skills to acquire. Let the child help in digging the bait. This gives him as much pleasure as the actual fishing if it is done leisurely, so that there is plenty of time for questions.

Stay Near Home

If you are one of those privileged souls who has a place to fish on your own land, Heaven is indeed yours. If like most people you are not so blessed, do pick a place near enough home so that your pride and joy is not already tired by the time he arrives. Take along a straw hat to shade his eyes, some sandwiches or fruit just for fun, and a thermos of water so that the "I'm thirsty" business can be solved promptly. Young children are often extremely sensitive about hurting anything. Assure him that it does not hurt the worm (we don't know that it does) and that the fish is not injured if removed from the hook carefully. As a precautionary measure let him feel the sharp end of the hook with the tip of his finger, then guide his arm a time or two until he gets the hang of throwing the line into the water.

Start fishing and pray that this is the day they will bite.

Young children cannot sit still for over five minutes at a time. Nature was wise in this respect, for if they led the same sort of sedentary life that adults do, how would they ever explore and learn about the millions of things they need to know? Their energy and their curiosity are two of their most charming characteristics. To try to curb either of them is both undesirable and impossible. When squirming starts, as it will in a short time if the fish aren't biting, do something to prevent boredom. Hand out a piece of chewing gum, pour a drink of water, or best of all start a story about "When I was just your age." If there are still no bites, the perfect medium for play is right at hand— mud and water. No toy maker has ever been ingenious enough to design a toy that can compete with this means of amusing small fry. Do insist, however, that they carry the water away from the bank to make their pies. It is a mistake to let children wade in the water where they are fishing. Once a precedent is started, it is difficult to stop, and too many times wading would be dangerous.

Boat fishing is definitely less desirable than bank fishing because activity is too restricted. If you do go out in a boat, a life jacket of some sort is essential for the child. No child who is afraid of boat riding should ever be taken out fishing in one. Fear of one particular thing often becomes a fear and dislike of all associated things.

If you happen to catch fish, and the child doesn't, subterfuge is in order. Send him on a short errand, and put one of your fish on his hook. Call him back by saying, "I think there is a fish on your line," which is certainly no lie. Of course, if the opposite happens, and little Barbara, who weighs fifty pounds, hauls out one bigger than you have ever dreamed of getting there are two or three things you can do. (1) You can throw Barbara in the lake. (2) You can let her fish slip back into the water, or (3) you can congratulate her, say you are pleased, and hope that God will forgive you for lying.

Insure Happy Memories

Always leave before your young guest is quite ready to go home, and if no fish have been caught, stop by the drug store and buy him the biggest ice cream cone in town. It may ruin his appetite for dinner, but that is of little consequence. The important thing is for the child to have a happy memory of his first fishing trip.

Your own children will enjoy fishing more if they are occasionally allowed to invite their friends along. Under ten, two is generally enough responsibility for one adult. Don't be a stern taskmaster, and don't make it too serious. Fishing is fun, but it ceases to be fun when shrouded in reverential solemnity. Children will giggle, push and shove, wrestle a little, and resort to sharp verbal disagreements. They act that way all the time, and just because they are fishing is no reason to expect a radical change. Keep your sense of humor by holding on to the fact that they won't act at eighteen the way they do at eight. (But neither will they think you are the best fisherman in the world at eighteen.)

The age when a child can use a rod and reel depends on his muscular coordination, his previous interest in fishing and his desire to imitate his father. Some can begin at eight, others at six. Usually when daddy starts practicing in the back yard, the child also wants to try. Use a dummy plug (no hooks), and take turns of five casts each. Perfection doesn't inspire confidence in a beginner. He feels more at ease if he sees an adult make some of the same mistakes he does. Do show him the correct form of casting, but don't insist on exact conformity to your instructions. His unorthodox approach may suit his grasp better, and in the long run be the best method for him. Again, stop before he is quite ready. After a few practice sessions in the yard, let him try casting in the water with a dummy plug until he gets the feel of it.

Your choice of the child's own rod and reel should be made only after careful consideration. Certainly he should not have a piece of worn-out, discarded equipment. All beginners should start with an anti-backlash reel.

Untangling a line is discouraging for an adult, and for a child it destroys the incentive to continue.

Fly casting. The age of beginning fly casting depends on the same factors as those for rod and reel, but ten is about the average age for the novice. If you feel that fly casting is an art, or if you feel that it requires an inordinate amount of skill to master, don't let the child know about your feelings. Stripped to essentials, a fly rod is nothing but a stick with a string on it, which is cast by pumping it up and down like a buggy whip. Start the beginner with a seven and one-half foot creek rod with a line only as long as the rod. For the first few practice times use a dummy lure, or cut the hooks from a brightly colored old one. Explain the necessity for keeping the upper arm close to the side. Show that the movement is from the elbow down, and then let the child try. His adroitness and skill may surprise you. As he becomes more adept, lengthen his line very gradually, about a foot at a time. The fine points of technique should not be brought out until he has mastered these essential beginnings.

The whole process of teaching children to fish should be a gradual one. There will be spurts of interest followed by periods of complete lack of interest. With patient training however, you will find yourself one fine day with a fishing partner who is your equal in skill, dexterity and sportsmanship. Who could ask for more?
—*By Carmen Stone Allen*

IF YOUR YOUNGSTER WANTS A GUN

BOYS climb trees, naturally. They catch frogs and bring them home in dungaree pockets, naturally. And at some time in their growing up boys set up a clamor for the ownership of a gun, a real rifle that shoots. That is an equally natural event. When the cast-metal or plastic six-guns with which they have harmlessly slain the redskins and routed the rustlers like movie heroes, become passé, a boy wants either an air gun or a real .22. Then, all too many parents throw up their hands in confused horror and squelch the issue with a firm "No."

That parental fear probably doesn't exist in families where dad spends winter evenings happily oiling his own rifles or shotguns. There the responsibility that weighs on parents when Johnny touches his first rifle has long been anticipated as a labor of love. The shooter-father has been awaiting the day when he can share his own pleasure with the boy. But it is a very real concern in families where guns are unknown quantities, perhaps terrifyingly and often wrongly associated with overblown tales of tragedy born of ignorance. Hundreds of parents have written, ostensibly about the problem of a perfectly normal gun-craving boy, but actually for a solution to their own problem of meeting that craving in a way that will be best for the boy, a way which will best develop his sense of responsibility.

And always they have two basic questions: How old should a youngster be before he should have a rifle? How can we, as parents, be sure that he will handle it safely?

Chronological age serves as no yardstick. One of my friends started his lad with a small-gauge shotgun at eight, and the boy brought home his first cock pheasant at eleven. My son has cared for his own .22 rifle since he turned ten. Both rather exceptional, yes, because of our personal devotion to shooting sports. But for most lads, the beginning age should be as late as twelve or fourteen. There's a simple rule of thumb, based on the youngster's own ability to handle responsibility as measured by these homely questions: Would you send him to the grocery store with a shopping list and a ten dollar bill? If you feel that he is capable of such trust, a boy is old enough to own a gun—*for use only under proper supervision*.

In that last phrase lies the implied answer to the second question. Accidents and dangerous or damaging use of guns arise from ignorance, from lack of properly supervised training. Since 1926, millions of boys and girls have been trained with firearms under the Junior NRA program, yet very few accidents have ever been traced to graduates of such supervised riflery.

Proper Training

Properly trained in handling guns, youngsters neither have accidents nor get into dangerous mischief. It would be easy for any father who likes to shoot to demonstrate what havoc even a .22 can wreak by bursting a can of water with a bullet or, in the safety of the local gravel pit, by punching a .22 lead bullet through eight or nine inches of pine plank. Those are sufficient object lessons to teach complete respect for a .22. For a shooting father, with range facilities near at hand, it's no trouble at all to give a boy a full course in both marksmanship and safe and sane gun manners. But how does the son of a non-shooting father ever find such training?

One answer would be to enlist the aid of that shooting-minded chap in your neighborhood. He might be willing to stand *in loco parentis* and take over your son's—or daughter's—training in rifle skill and safety. Even if he has neither time nor mind to take on this responsibility, the outdoor-minded neighbor very likely knows where and when your boy can step into a supervised shooting program.

Scattered over the country are over 3,000 Junior NRA clubs, often affiliated with the more than 8,000 adult National Rifle Association groups whose members, completely qualified, instruct boys of a Tuesday evening or Saturday afternoon. Many of these have club-owned rifles your lad can use for the price of his ammunition and targets. Is there any reason why your youngster shouldn't be one of the more than 110,000 having fun and developing a keener sense of personal responsibility at the same time?

No fly-by-night operations these, any more than is the insertion of systematic riflery instruction into the Boy Scout merit badge program. They are backed by local police groups, by the American Legion, by Kiwanis and Rotary, by 4-H clubs and high school authorities. In one town, a move for a rifle range in the basement of the new grammar school was sparked by the local police chief. In central Connecticut, on a public shooting area near Wooster Mountain, a state policeman was the mainspring of a shooter-training program that drew hundreds of youngsters to a range busy day and night.

But what answer is there for a family whose community doesn't happen to have any sort of Junior NRA activity? No sloughing off of the parental onus here—it will be up to dad. But he has an oak to lean on in the Sporting Arms and Ammunition Manufacturers' Institute, familiarly known as Sammy, and its Ranger Program. It's ready to supply him with something resembling a correspondence course, an armload of very detailed and graphic handbooks, even cleverly instructive comic books, and a batch of official targets. With their help dad can go along with his boy in a course of shooting sprouts. The only equipment needed is 50 feet of safe shooting range, a .22 rifle and common sense. And the chances are pretty good that Billy will qualify as a Ranger before dad does!

Equipment Needed

Of course some families will be stymied by that need for fifty feet of safe, properly back-stopped range, and by the financial outlay for a .22 bolt-action rifle, anywhere from fifteen to fifty dollars, and its ammunition, about sixty-five cents for fifty shots. But where powder burning is impractical there's always compressed air to fall back on. The air rifle once had a black eye because kids of our own generation never got beyond the sparrow-shooting and lightbulb-popping stage, but there is now in existence a complete training program for the air gun. Any youngster from eight to eighteen can collect for himself a hatful of pins, diplomas and badges for all the stages of skill, from Pro-Marksman to Sharpshooter, *down cellar!* I don't think there's a father in this country who doesn't feel he can teach his boy to handle a BB gun sensibly. Beyond that assurance all he needs is 15 feet of cellar space for the spring-powered guns—made so nonlethal they won't break glass—or 25 feet for the more potent CO_2-powered rifles and pistols.

There are facilities enough so it is pretty hard for any family, even in a big city, to deny a teen-ager opportunity to shoot. But is there anything in a shooting program that goes beyond the gratification of a lad's whim, however natural? Can it do anything for the boy or girl?

Rifle Programs at Camp

When he went to camp for the first time, one lad was slender and handicapped physically. He was no whiz in mountain climbing, no seal in the water, out of a lot of normal boy activities. But as one of the more than 50,000 youngsters who have access to a rifle range and good sound training in over 1,000 of the better summer camps, he shot his way through the first four stages of the Junior NRA program. With pins in his cap and brassards bright on his jacket, he came home a man among men, able to do something as well as any and better than most.

There's basic value in the fact that any boy who is a member of an organized shooting group very soon learns he must follow the range procedures set for the safety of all that group, that he is given a tool, a rifle, which must be kept clean and mechanically perfect if it is to shoot badge-winning scores for him. Those are vital parts of riflery training.

And in shooting, even a handicapped youngster can succeed. With the macula of his right eye scarred by a pre-birth injury, my youngster has at least one strike on him when it comes to moving-ball games. A matter of depth perception. Though he does his sums and skips pebbles right-handed, he very quickly learned to shoot from his left shoulder, well enough to make his stouter friend's two sound eyes bug in respect.

Therapeutic benefits. Many years ago I was an English instructor in a large private school. We had a skeet and trapshooting club there, which I inherited as the only master, seemingly, who enjoyed freezing in a duck blind. One frail and difficult lad, on the ragged edge of scholastic, athletic and social failure, was discovered to be absorbingly interested in tying trout flies. That indicated a liking for outdoor sports; we eased him into the shooting club where he would be with boys who talked the same outdoor language. With a new and compelling interest in life this youngster graduated with grades good enough to get him into Yale.

Is there any reward to the man who undertakes either the responsibility of introducing his own son to the marvels of shooting or of settling him into a group where better qualified teachers can take over?

There is—a million dollars' worth. For the non-shooting father it lies in the realization that his son—or daughter—is learning self-control, a respect for the safety of others that goes far beyond mere gun manners, and a proudly personal sort of lifetime skill.

—*By Warren Page*

FAMILY TRAVEL CAN BE FUN

THE happiest families are the ones who do things and go places together. If you're planning to travel with big or little children, here's helpful advice on *how to, when to, where to.*

Children barely out of babyhood have, on special occasions, traveled alone across the continent and across the ocean. Labeled with large name-and-destination tags, and handled with great care by the stewardess or conductors, these solitary young tourists arrive right side up and in good condition.

School-age children sometimes travel in packs to points of interest. Every year, nearly half a million of them happily descend on the nation's capital in tremendous groups, shepherded by brave schoolteachers and travel representatives.

But the most fun of all, according to children as well as parents who have tried it, is traveling with your own family. There are exciting sessions to decide where to go. The sooner that's settled, the longer you have to look forward to the trip. As for the trip itself—children triumphantly point out that even school teachers admit travel is educational and stimulating. It's an unusual family—or a poorly planned trip—if everybody doesn't come home happier and closer after sharing all these wonderful adventures.

Family-style travel has money-saving advantages, too. Domestic airlines offer special "family rates" to encourage mid-week travel. Father pays full fare, but mother and all the children under 21 may go along for half price. A baby under two can travel free if mother will hold him on her lap. This would be possible only on short trips, of course. The larger the family, the greater the saving—for a change!

A few eastern railroads have been experimenting with a similar money-saving "family plan" effective seven days a week. Many hotels also offer price reductions for family groups.

Planning the Trip

A fat pocketbook is not essential to a fine trip. But what is important, whether your accommodations are plain or fancy, is careful planning. With well-laid plans, plus a little ingenuity, even the most inexpensive types of travel can be fun.

The first step in getting organized is to call the family together and explain the facts: how much time and how much money are available. Then lean back and let everybody have his say on where and how to go. The debate will be spirited, but you'll notice a good-natured tone even in brother-sister arguments.

When you've narrowed the field down to the places that meet your time-and-money requirements, start collecting travel folders, travel literature and maps. Even your youngest child will catch the contagious excitement as the family discusses different vacation spots.

It's a problem—but what a pleasant one—to decide which of the tantalizing trips to take. The National Parks, New England or New York? Florida with its new summer popularity and persuasive out-of-season rates? Bermuda, Hawaii, Canada or California? Or even Europe, which can be visited for less than you may think.

Means of Transportation

Once you've settled on where to go, you'll want to take a very close look at how. Planes are thrilling and time-saving; meals are included in the fare (except tourist fare) and there is no tipping. A train is more leisurely and less confining, allows you an eye-level look at the countryside, and the schedules don't depend on the weatherman's whims. A ship is restful, often a vacation in itself as well as a means of getting somewhere. Travel by bus is inexpensive, gives you a good close-up as you go and is available almost anywhere. The family car, if you like to drive, allows great flexibility. You can stop and go as you please, and it's equally convenient whether you're doing your sleeping in hotels, motels or a tent.

You can get more detailed information on these modes of travel from the companies, from your automobile club or state tourist bureau.

If there's a baby in the family, you'll naturally face special travel problems, but you may decide to take a deep breath and tackle the trip anyway! With a very young baby, why not compromise: go somewhere and stay put, don't vagabond to a new spot every day unless it's really necessary.

You'll find, however, that transportation lines and hotels have gone to imaginative and surprising lengths to make traveling with a baby quite a comfortable business.

Before you start, be sure to find out what special services are available. Be sure, too, to let your transportation company know there'll be a baby aboard.

Many airlines provide on-the-house menus of strained baby foods. Baby's formula—the only thing mother must bring—is kept cool, then warmed at feeding time. Some airliners even carry a supply of baby powder, baby oil, diaper bags and disposable diapers in case mother underestimated.

Trains which carry a diner will be happy to keep the baby's formula under refrigeration and warm it at your request. Certain trains serve baby food à la carte, or will stock it, with advance notice. On some trains there are registered nurses who will help mother make up formula or do anything they can to add to the baby's comfort. At least one ultramodern train thoughtfully includes a playroom complete with tiny tables and chairs, a padded playpen, toys, a blackboard and a special children's lavatory! Many ocean liners have attended playrooms, too, and Punch-and-Judy shows and parties to keep small fry amused.

Train Travel

You'll naturally buy the best travel accommodations you can afford. If you're going by train with several children, a drawing room costs very little more than other Pullman accommodations, and gives you great privacy and convenience. But if your budget indicates a day coach you can, with careful planning, enjoy your trip and not just endure it—even with a baby along.

If possible, do your family traveling in the middle of the week instead of on week ends. There's less crowding and confusion, and the hostess or conductor can devote more time to your baby's needs.

Besides, when the train or airliner isn't crowded, the baby can occupy an empty seat beside you—an arrangement that's considerably more restful than having your little friend wiggle and climb on your lap for several hours!

It's a good idea to take along one or two of the baby's old favorite toys. Include a few new ones, too, for times when the going gets tearful and a distraction is strongly indicated.

Take the baby's favorite foods—nothing new, nothing he doesn't digest easily. (And don't forget the can opener and a spoon!) Expect the baby to eat less than he usually does—too much excitement.

If you use fresh milk in the baby's formula, your doctor may suggest a switch from fresh to evaporated or dried whole milk when the baby is traveling. With these, the formula can be made up as needed—if you take along sterilized nipples and bottles and boiled water. Change to the new type milk a few weeks before you leave, to accustom your baby to it.

If you make up formula for the trip, don't plan to carry more than a 24-hour supply, even under refrigeration. Never keep bottles at feeding temperature in an insulated bag, bacteria thrive in warm milk.

Happily, it's no longer necessary to try to look nonchalant strolling down the aisle carrying the baby's toilet seat wrapped in a blanket or protruding from a paper bag. Toilet seats can now be bought complete with their own carrying case.

On Pullmans, with advance notice, they'll provide a "baby guard"—a web-like side fixture that keeps the baby from tumbling out of the berth.

It's simple to pack the baby's clothes and belongings in a separate suitcase. Include disposable diapers or liners, disposable bibs, a waterproof sheet. An outfit suitable for impressing grandma can be carefully stashed away, then put on—crisp and clean—just before arrival.

Keep Children Amused

Keeping toddlers and young children amused on a trip requires careful planning, too. If you're traveling by train, a personally conducted tour of a few coaches gets the trip off to a good start and satisfies young curiosities— for the moment, at least! "Sit still, now, and be a good girl" is a large order to a little one seething with excitement. On the other hand, it's not necessary to let children tear up and down the aisle, making life miserable for others.

The solution lies in finding ways to keep children busy at their seats, with strolls down the aisle limited to a reasonable minimum. A seventh-inning stretch on the station platform when the train stops for five or ten minutes is a good way to see interesting sights and let off pent-up steam.

If each child carries a little suitcase of his own, he'll spend considerable time packing and unpacking his small toys and treasures. Plastic or rubber cars, small dolls and animals, cards and picture books are fun for a while. A kaleidoscope amuses children from around age four to seven or eight. Hand puppets are popular—the older children manipulate them mysteriously while the younger ones, wide-eyed with wonder, make a most satisfactory audience. Paper and crayons should be included, or one of those small imitation blackboards which can be wiped clean merely by lifting the transparent plastic cover.

As a final surprise when the fidgets set in, mother can produce a small magnet. This magic instrument will pull a paper boat or animal, folded for the occasion and fastened at the end with pins.

Before boredom becomes too desperate, it's generally time to eat. A picnic lunch is fun, a trek to the diner even more exciting. Many trains offer special children's menus—smaller portions and smaller prices. Most trains, at no extra cost, will supply silver and china and let a child share an adult's food.

On airliners, the hostess brings meals on a tray to your seat. When you're traveling by bus, there'll be frequent stops for a meal or a snack.

Car travel with children also has its special problems and compensations. The local service station will supply complete information on routes, including how to avoid those disposition-spoiling detours. Your automobile club will not only plan your route but will also supply a list of recommended restaurants, auto camps, motels or hotels with their telephone numbers so you can call ahead for reservations.

Safety Measures

Before you start, and at frequent intervals en route, a thorough safety checkup of your car is in order: brakes, tires, lights, windshield wipers. Special safety locks for car doors are not expensive, and can save a child's life! A well constructed car seat lets him see the scenery, keeps him safe.

Long Trips

On a long trip, it helps to have a small surprise package for each child, each day—a toy or picture book or big beads to string. Besides the games we've already discussed, car trips can include "number" games for the older children: the first three cars "belong" to Susie, the next three to Bill, then Susie, and so on. Whose cars will have the highest and the lowest number license plates? Whose will come from the most distant state?

The little fellows who can't count can keep a sharp eye out for the next red barn or black and white cow.

The privacy of car travel permits boisterous song fests—the more and sillier verses a song has, the better.

Frequent stops forestall boredom, lessen fatigue and increase safety. Picnic lunches give the children a chance to run around. They soon learn to form eagle-eyed clean-up squads and leave the picnic grounds uncluttered.

There are two all-important rules for family car travel: don't try to break mileage records. And never leave the baby alone in the car.

It's easy these days, thanks to the new synthetic fabrics, to keep travel luggage to a minimum. Such clothing can be washed and dried in short order and needs no ironing. (Take your own soap if you're going overseas.) Jersey and seersucker are good travelers; so are rayons, cottons and wools.

Don't forget a warm wrap for everyone, whether you're heading south or north. Tuck in plastic raincoats—the kind that fold into envelope size. Carry the biggest handbag you own, you'll always wish you had a bigger one.

And see that every member of the family wears shoes that are tested friends. The world's finest scenery is no good if your feet hurt!

Take your best camera and, preferably, color film. Movies or snapshots of your trip will keep it alive for many years.

One of the nicest parts of any trip is getting home again, admiring the pictures you took and telling everybody about the good times you had. But don't be surprised if you soon find yourselves down on all fours on the living room floor—peering at travel folders and planning next year's trip!

—*By Ruth Newburn Sedam*

WHEN THE FAMILY GOES CAMPING

A LOOK at the camping map on our kitchen wall brings back the smell of wood smoke, the ring of hammers pounding tent pegs, the taste of pancakes cooked over an open fire, the miraculous blue of mountain gentians and all the thousand sights, smells, sounds and tastes of outdoor life.

Some ten years ago, my husband and I bought a tent and headed for the mountains with our four-year-old Peggy and our sixteen-month-old Robert. The vacation turned out to be so much fun that we've taken others like it every year since—adding equipment, experience and children. Dorothy was only six weeks old when we packed her baby carriage into the back seat of the car and took her camping high in the San Juan Mountains of western Colorado. Two years later, Cathy was the carriage camper. Stars on our kitchen map show that we've tented from Yellowstone to Washington, D.C., from Ontario to the Great Smokies.

Visitors peer at our map and ask questions. "What's camping like?" "What does it cost, and what do you take with you on these trips?" "Isn't it a lot of work?" "What happens when it rains?" "How do you decide where to go?" "Is it really a lot of fun?" "Is it hard to manage with kids?"

What's camping like? It's telling stories over a fire on a chilly, starlit night; watching the sun break through the clouds above a mountain top; following a mossy trail through the woods to a waterfall; sharing an evening Ranger program with campers from nearly every state. And far more.

What does it cost? Tents, bedding, air mattresses and other things needed for camping cost less than a couple of weeks at a resort hotel. Besides, once you try camping you'll go many times and use the equipment over and over again. Many campgrounds charge nothing for the use of camping sites. Where there is a fee, it's about twenty-five cents to a dollar for a night for a family. Most campers do all their own cooking, so this costs no more than at home.

What do we take? We take a lot of things—at least it seems so when we pack. After some trying omissions like a can opener or warm sweater (discovered miles from a store where they could be bought) we've gotten up a master list which we check before leaving.

Camping gear available at mail-order houses, sporting goods stores and many department stores is, of course, the prime necessity and the only one requiring an initial investment. Gear needn't be bought all at once. For our first trip we invested in a tent and sleeping bag only. When one tent wouldn't hold our growing family we added another. Gradually, we accumulated additional sleeping bags, air mattresses, a stove and a small icebox.

For a first trip a tent is the one real necessity, even though some hardy campers with small families use a station wagon as their only shelter. We're not that rugged. A tent large enough for two adults and several small children costs about $65. Umbrella-type tents are much the easiest to put up. Air mattresses, at about five dollars each, make sleeping more comfortable. Most families already have usable bedding, a water bucket and an axe. (Keep that axe sheathed when you're traveling with children!)

Of course, you can go in for a lot more elaborate gear. If you do, though, remember that you're going to have to pack and carry all you buy. This is a not inconsiderable consideration—as we found the summer we invested in a small trailer. Because we had all that extra room, we took things we didn't need. Our lesson learned, we now pack bedding and tents into a top carrier and stow everything else inside.

Clothing? For six, it takes space and planning, since we must prepare for rain, shine, heat and cold. As we shop during the year we look for simple sports clothes that won't need ironing. So at camping time, we seldom need to buy more than a few pairs of jeans and socks to make up for the winter's decimation. Dress-up clothes are seldom needed. I include a drip-dry dress for each of the girls and myself, just in case.

Cooking Equipment

Cooking equipment has to be thought out, too. We assemble our own kit, despite the many attractive ones on the market, for ready-made kits don't include four essentials: a heavy iron skillet, a pressure cooker, a double boiler and a big pot for heating water. A pressure cooker, desirable anywhere, is particularly important in the mountains where it's almost impossible to cook beans and potatoes without one. An oblong dishpan and a folding plastic dish drainer simplify packing and dishwashing.

It's also a wise idea to lay in a supply of essentials like aluminum foil and emergency powdered foods. The foil has innumerable uses. You can line your pots and pans with it and save dishwashing. You can wrap a whole meal in it for cooking over an open fire. You can use it as a divider for a large pot and cook two or three vegetables at once. Powdered foods like milk, pancake mixes, instant coffee and so forth, always come in handy at run-out-times.

Books and toys, although less essential help to make traveling happier and rainy spells easier. Crayons, dolls, a deck of cards, notebooks and paper avert backseat squabbles that begin when games and scenery pall. Books are particularly good for layovers. We carry nature guides and books about the locality we plan to visit. *Tom Sawyer* and *Huckleberry Finn* were read on the way to Mark Twain State Park. Tales of adventure seem particularly enthralling on a camping trip. The children will never forget the summer we followed the exploits of *Swiss Family Robinson*.

Of course, if you're good at storytelling, you can cut down on the books you pack. With us, storytelling is a regular campfire pastime. Years ago I began the remarkable saga of a certain Snodgrass family and this tribe has grown with ours each summer. Now the children take turns with me and often spin their own tall tales. Far from TV, we have the glorious opportunity to use our own imaginations.

Do Camp Chores Together

What about the cooking and laundry? Camping does involve more chores than staying at tourist courts. But that's part of the fun. For we all work together and enjoy it. Gathering firewood and cooking outdoors aren't ordinary all-year-long activities. Even dishwashing can be an event when you have a mountain to look at and chipmunks for company. When the children were little, the camp housekeeping took longer but to me seemed lighter than at home because my husband had more time to help. What needed to be done we did together and as the children grew, they lent willing hands.

Now Robert saws wood and helps take down and put up tents. The little girls fetch and carry and help our eldest, Peggy, cook. Perhaps because my outdoor chefs give me a real vacation from pots and pans, and because food cooked outdoors tastes better, I find camp-cooking a joy, not a chore.

With several pairs of hands to wash and hang out clothes, laundry doesn't take much time, either. And there are sometimes automatic laundries nearby.

What if it rains? Well, unless it pours every day for a week, rain, too, can be fun and adventure. When it thunders, we sit inside our tent telling stories and playing games. With a tarp above our picnic table we can even eat outside in a shower. Seeing a rainbow over a mountain top after the storm is one of the thrills of a camping trip.

How do we plan our trip? This is part of the anticipatory enjoyment of the trip. Kitchen-table conferences begin before the snow leaves the ground. First of all, we make a general plan trying to set up a route which allows for overnight stops about two hundred miles apart. We've found that about two and a half hours must be allowed for getting breakfast and breaking camp, and the same amount of time for getting dinner and making camp for the night. Therefore, we don't plan a long day on the road. And we make sure to stop early enough to set up camp before dark.

Good maps for all routes are available from the oil companies, the United States Department of the Interior, Rand McNally and state information services. *The Campground Guide,* published by Campgrounds Unlimited, Blue Rapids, Kansas, is indispensable and low in cost. It lists all the state and national campgrounds, a few private ones and a description of their facilities as well. "Facilities" means whether or not there's swimming, fishing or boating; how large the campground is; whether there are showers.

Any camper soon discovers that there are facilities and more facilities. Outdoor fireplaces and a pure water supply are usually standard for all. A few campgrounds have screened-in cooking shelters. Potomac Park in Washington, D.C., is equipped with a large automatic laundry. Mesa Verde, a popular Colorado park, has hot showers, clean flush toilets and even laundry tubs. These attractions bring crowds of people, so while we enjoy Mesa Verde and climbing up and down the ladders to its ruins for a day or so, for a longer stay we prefer a more primitive but less crowded campground. Among these, one of our favorites is above Aspen, Colorado. There, we draw our own water from the Roaring Fork River and use an outhouse. Nights are cold at 8,000 feet, but we love the sunny days, the cliffs and forests.

Recreational facilities, too, vary. Most campsites are on a river or lake and generally have marked trails for hiking. At many, we've had the delight of coming across bubbling hot springs, strange rock formations, wild animals, ruins of vanished Indian villages, fossil remains. Above Aspen, our mountain retreat, we hike, fish, take trips up the Aspen chair lift. Other camps offer more formal facilities. Mammoth Cave National Park in Kentucky, for example, has complete Ranger service with guided tours, illustrated campfire talks, an interesting museum and a nature trail. Most national parks offer much the same kind of thing. Campers who want to go on excursions can choose from a wide variety. There are strenuous all-day climbs, overnight pack trips, short easy strolls and motorcade tours. There are even special trips under Ranger supervision for teen-agers. When any fee is charged the amount is small.

BASIC EQUIPMENT
recommended by National Campers and Hikers Association

9 × 11 umbrella tent with sewed floor
Sleeping bags
Air mattresses and pump
Blankets (small pillow, if desired)
2 or 3-burner stove and stand
Lantern; 2 flashlights
Rope
Ax; shovel
2-gal. thermos jug
Whisk broom
Tarp 10 × 12 (optional)
First aid kit
Insect repellent; bug bomb
Portable icebox

Nest of pots; coffee pot
1 heavy frying pan
Pressure cooker, Dutch oven
Knives, forks, spoons
Plastic and paper plates and cups
1 carving knife; spatula
Can opener
Aluminum foil
Paper towels
Soap; matches
Toilet paper
Scouring pads (soap impregnated)
Sponge
Plastic basin

(You may wish to add other items which you feel necessary for comfort. We advocate taking as little as you can get along with!)

Membership in the National Campers and Hikers Association is open to all families who participate in camping or hiking activities. For more information write to N.C.H.A., 1507 National Newark Bldg., Newark 2, N.J.

—By Harriet D. Pennington

THE ENCHANTED WORLD
OF OUT OF DOORS

THE out of doors is a world of wonder to children. Everywhere lie possibilities for discovery and adventure; and to a child whose parents explore with him, these possibilities may be richly fulfilled. Happily, nature exploring does not necessitate a trek to Mongolian deserts or to African jungles; it can take place in your own back yard or in a city park. It can add zest to a hike in the country and provide endless activity during vacations near woodland, lake or seashore. Nature's ways are as remarkable at home as they are in remote lands!

Children look at their surroundings with constant wonder. They are curious as to why stars disappear in the daytime and what makes rain. They wonder how birds fly and how fish can breathe in water. They want to know why tree foliage changes color and how flowers make seeds. Their inquisitive and eager minds are always ready to investigate the ways of animals and the wonders of plants that adults often take for granted. In time, school studies will answer many of their questions, but the parent who does not guide his own child along nature's ways misses a priceless opportunity. Shared adventures of discovery bring parents and children closer together, and they can develop a bond that will remain strong throughout a lifetime. As your child gains in knowledge and understanding of this world, you find yourself growing with him.

There is no set pattern to be followed for nature exploring. Children are individual in their approach to nature's activities. Basically, however, a sure way to further a child's love of nature is for parents themselves to be aware of natural wonders, to encourage youthful inquisitiveness as to why animals, plants and the elements behave as they do, and to provide some opportunity for the child to satisfy his curiosity as it is aroused.

"Exploring" may consist of as simple a pastime as watching a spider manufacture its silken trap or a squirrel hoard a nut by burying it underground. On the other hand, it may lead into absorbing hobbies such as butterfly collecting and mounting which require both patience and skill. But whether the explorations are merely observations shared and talked over or extensive activities, they provide a lively and very real basis for companionship between you and your children.

One delightful, yet extremely simple hobby is attracting birds to your home. In winter, the most effective lure for them is a feeding station. The exceptionally high body temperature of a bird prevents its suffering from the cold so long as it has sufficient food to keep this temperature up to normal. Therefore when usual food supplies are scarce, your feeding station may not only be a source of pleasure to your family, but may actually help a number of birds to survive.

Bird Watching

Even very young children can take part in Operation: Bird Rescue. If you have a yard, they can trample down the snow at some suitable spot (where the surroundings will not permit a cat to carry out a surprise attack) and on the packed snow they can sprinkle crumbs and seeds. Then they may tie pieces of suet to a tree or post to tempt downy woodpeckers and others that enjoy this kind of food. If there is a young carpenter in the family he may enjoy constructing a covered platform attached to a post. This is an excellent type of feeding station, for the covering keeps the food dry and the elevation gives the birds protection from enemies while they are feeding. Another efficient plan is to fasten a tray to a window sill. This not only is safe for the birds, but it gives your family frequent opportunities to watch them.

In warm weather when food-finding is no problem, a bird bath placed close to your home is a real inducement for birds to be your neighbors. Songbirds are especially attracted by water. Not only do they need it for drinking, but they enjoy bathing in it as well. Although parents may have to supply the bird bath, youngsters love to assume the responsibility of keeping it filled.

If you and your children watch cardinals, robins, bluejays, juncos, chickadees and others appear and disappear through the changing seasons, you will have an unending source of interest. You may enjoy keeping a calendar on which to note the comings and goings of migrators. You may record which birds eat seeds and which the suet and compare these choices to those they made under natural conditions.

Once boys and girls have become interested in watching birds near home, they are often eager to go farther afield to observe them in orchards, meadows and woods. Here fathers and mothers can really shine as guides if they will do some research on the birds of the particular area. To know what kinds may be expected in various types of localities simplifies identifying them. The

ability to recognize the various calls and songs adds immeasurably to the pleasure of a "bird walk" in spring and early summer; and listening to phonograph recordings (obtainable at many libraries as well as at music shops) is pleasant tutoring for this particular study. As you become thoroughly familiar with the distinctive notes of various birds, you may wish to go a step further and imitate them. Later in the year when their voices are stilled and leaves have fallen, you can search for deserted nests, enjoying the detective work of deciding what kinds of birds made the various types that you discover.

The equipment needed for a bird-discovery walk is simple. An interested pair of eyes is actually the one essential. However, field glasses are valuable in identifying species and a pair is well worth taking along with a child of eight or more who is old enough to use them. Also helpful is a pocket guide of birds for reference; and you will be glad of a notebook in which to jot down the color, size and characteristics of birds that you cannot identify immediately, as well as the names of those you recognize. By far the best time to go on such a walk is early morning; soon after sunrise bird activities slow down.

Many children are fascinated by insects. Of all these six-legged creatures perhaps top place of interest is held by ants. There is almost never a problem in finding them during mild seasons of the year—they flourish about city pavements as well as in pastures and forests. You may come upon them in gardens, on lawns and dirt roadways. They vary in size from the big black carpenter ants which construct their homes in trees, posts or other wooden objects, to the little brown fellows widely known as cornfield ants.

A lively experience in nature study started when one little girl noticed swarms of cornfield ants not far from her doorstep. She rushed to report her discovery and to see whether anything should be done about them.

"Would you like to see how large a piece of food an ant can carry?" her mother asked.

She threw down a cube of bread, and they had the fun of seeing one of the ants quickly seize the prize, swing it above his head and start to march away. Almost immediately, however, other ants rushed toward him. Soon a full-scale battle was under way! The child was fascinated to think they could tell friend from foe when they all looked identical to her, and by the fact that ants sometimes carry on "slave raids," attacking a nest and robbing it of its immature members which develop in the nest of the captors to spend their lives in slavery.

Many of the remarkable habits of ants cannot be observed out of doors, since examining the interior of a nest is extremely difficult. However a child who becomes more than casually interested can quite easily have an observation nest indoors. There are several ways in which suitable quarters can be made. One is to construct an ant house that is, in effect, a glass "sandwich." This requires two pieces of window glass about twelve inches square. One serves as a base, the other as a top. Quarter-inch strips of wood must be glued around the edges of the base. In one of them should be made two small holes, to be used for feeding and watering the ants. A piece of sponge (to be kept moist with a medicine dropper) may be placed inside the water hole. Both openings when not in use are kept plugged with cotton.

Ant House Interests Children

With the base and side strips ready, it is time to collect ant tenants. To do so, it is necessary to dig around a nest carefully with a small trowel, lifting dirt and insects into a carton. When this (tightly closed) has been carried home, both dirt and ants are transferred to the glass house. Very quickly, then, the second piece of glass must be glued on the top, and all edges sealed with adhesive tape. Since ants thrive in darkness, the final construction work on their home should be to attach a cardboard cover to the top. It may be attached with two hinges of adhesive tape so that it can be lifted easily when anyone wishes to observe the ants below.

Thus it is possible to watch the industrious creatures excavating a system of tunnels, constructing a central hall, grooming themselves with tongue and front legs and even lying down to sleep. The ant home should never be left in bright sunlight or near a radiator. Inserting water through the sponge hole at least once a week provides the insects with sufficient water. Morsels of solid food—apples, bananas, bits of dead insects, as well as a drop or two of honey—should be inserted through the food hole every few days.

Tracking animals is a perfect hobby to enjoy with a child whose sleuthing instincts are strong. When a walk takes you near marshy mud or soft river banks or you hike across snowy fields, you will discover tracks of animals that were in those places before you. What kind were they? Were they hunting for food or running for their lives? A knowledge of tracks makes it possible to play Sherlock Holmes concerning the habits of many wild creatures.

You may begin a study of tracks at home, observing the differences in form and size of the tracks of various domesticated animals. A dog's tracks are almost identical with those of a wolf except for being somewhat smaller. A cat's tracks are like those of a mountain lion—again, except for size. Also in your own back yard you may find the tracks of squirrels or rabbits. Going farther afield with the aid of a guidebook, you can learn to know and interpret the traces of deer, fox, woodchucks and other wild animals.

Tracks may be "collected" in several ways: a simple sketch will record them graphically, or you may photograph or make plaster casts of them. A little research at the library on types of track and the habits of the creatures that make them, may soon transform a casual interest into a family hobby and open a new world for exploration.

Identifying Wild Flowers

Plants offer endless possibilities for pleasant companionship with your children. A simple walk in the country takes on the glamor of exploration if you plan to look for and identify wild flowers. Some that are both plentiful and hardy, such as daisies, Queen Anne's lace and buttercups, may be picked to be enjoyed as home decorations. Others that wilt quickly after being plucked may be chosen for pressing and mounting. (Since many wild plants have become rare, it is vital to check with local authorities regarding which flowers are protected by conservation laws.)

When your plans for an expedition include collecting flowers for pressing, it is well to take with you a few damp newspapers. The plants, carried between the pages, will not dry out. The papers may be loosely rolled for ease in carrying. Some kinds, such as a violet, usually look more natural when pressed in profile; and a few buds and leaves add to the interest of the composition.

The "press" is made simply by placing a piece of newspaper about twelve by eighteen inches on the floor. Flowers and leaves are arranged on this, with no parts overlapping. This arrangement is then covered with a layer of newspaper equal in thickness to the thickest part of the plant or plants below. More layers of paper and plants may be added until the entire wildflower collection is taken care of. A board or other flat object must be placed over the completed pile, and rocks, books or other heavy weights put on top of it.

For at least four times, the plants should be changed daily to a dry place on the papers or the papers should be changed. Then, during the next week or ten days, this process of shifting to dry paper should continue with longer intervals between shifts. The more rapidly a plant is dried, the better its delicate colors are preserved.

A child will feel a happy sense of accomplishment if his flower specimens can actually adorn your home. To prepare them for exhibition, you need a sheet of glass as large as the floral arrangement. Cover this with a thin coating of glue diluted with a drop or two of vinegar. Place the dried plant on the glue for an instant, then quickly transfer it, glue side down, to a piece of mounting paper. Now it is ready for framing. Very delicate plants may curl when picked up from the glue. These may be mounted by placing thin strips of gummed paper at intervals across the stem.

Growth of security. Pressing flowers, feeding birds, tracking animals and a vast variety of other nature exploring activities may seem no more than pleasant pastimes, but they serve a far deeper purpose. As a child becomes acquainted with the ways of nature—with the harmony that exists between all living things so long as man does not disturb them—he gains a sense of inner security. As he matures, something of this understanding may give him perspective and faith when he comes to face the problems of this anxious world. Parents who give their children a love of nature as a precious heritage find themselves enriched in the process. —*By Dorothy Edwards Shuttlesworth*

STUDYING THE STARS

THE stars that stud the sky in early evening change with the months. Just as surely as your garden starts its bloom in the spring with the crocus and the daffodil, continues with the summer lilies and the phlox, and ends with asters and chrysanthemums, so the stars that look down each evening change with the changing seasons. The identification of the stars above your garden is intrinsically no more difficult than the identification of the flowers in it. Star study is a fascinating and rewarding hobby which you and your children can share.

The stars are giant suns, similar to but larger than the sun around which our earth revolves, and which gives us our heat and light. They appear tiny, and can be seen only when our side of the earth is turned away from the sun's bright light, because they are so very far away. They are not all of the same size, nor are they at the same distance, but are scattered through space at incredible distances from each other and from us. They are giving out tremendous amounts of energy which we see as light. As we look out into space from the earth, these giant suns appear as tiny points of light on the inverted dark blue bowl of the sky. Long before men knew anything about astronomy, the shepherd on the hill, the sailor on the sea, the soldier on the march, wondered about the stars, and looked at the sky, night after long night, until the stars seemed to form patterns of dippers and kites, crowns, crosses, triangles, birds, warriors, and heroines. They did this in much the same way that a convalescent staring up at the same wallpaper day after day will see the likenesses of familiar objects in the patterns. Some of the designs are easier to see than others, and these have been handed down as the constellations, or star designs. As primitive peoples looked at the stars again and again, and made out the same star figures, they began to weave stories to account for their presence in the sky, or they used the constellations as illustrations of existing legends or religious beliefs; in time, the sky, a more intimate companion to them than to us, became a sort of historical and religious picture book.

Stargazing Stimulates Interests

Modern astronomers use these constellation or star group names as a convenient way of finding and describing the location of individual stars. Thus, when we and our children study the stars, we find a combination of history, folklore, literature and scientific facts about the structure of our universe. Almost every member of the family can find an interest in star study. If one likes science, science at its most majestic is revealed in astronomy. Another may be interested in logical thinking and reasoning; rarely has it been displayed to better advantage than in the hypotheses and theories developed from what we, isolated on earth, have found out and deduced about the universe beyond us. One may be interested in poetry; many are the poems written about the stars, and these become more enjoyable when you know the stars they mention. If you are interested in fanciful and adventurous tales, you will find that many of them concern heroes immortalized in the constellations. Failing these interests, one may look up at the heavens merely to enjoy the color and beauty and the mystery of the stars.

It is a happy combination of circumstances that during the months when your family is most likely to be together in the garden or back yard after dark, the star groups are especially easy to see and to identify and form especially interesting groups. Here are brief introductions to each of the constellations to show you how, having found one, it will logically lead on to the next. After you learn to find the stars in the sky and want to know more about them, you may consult some of the many interesting books on stargazing and astronomy to be found in your public library.

Locating Constellations

Let us start with the Big Dipper, a constellation you have probably known since childhood. During the summer months it is standing almost upright in the sky, not far above the northwestern horizon, with its bowl downward, just as if it were a dipper hanging in your pantry. The Big Dipper will give you a measuring scale, or yardstick of the sky. In the curved bowl of the sky, distances between stars cannot be measured in terms of inches or feet or miles, and degrees are the unit of measurement. The two stars forming the side of the Big Dipper's bowl opposite the handle are about five degrees apart, and furnish a convenient measuring scale.

Facing north, and leaning backward, continue the curve formed by the stars of the Big Dipper's handle high overhead toward the southwest. Along this curve, about 30 degrees from the end of the dipper's handle, you will see a large star, brighter than any in the Big Dipper. You should have no trouble finding it if you remember that 30 degrees is six times the distance between the "yardstick stars" of the Big Dipper.

This star is named Arcturus, and it is the sixth brightest star in the sky. Arcturus is so far away that its light, traveling at the enormous speed of 186,000 miles per second, takes about forty years to reach our eyes, or as the astronomers say, the star is about forty light years away.

Do you notice that Arcturus, besides appearing larger than any of the stars of the Dipper, also differs from them in having a tinge of red in its gleam? Look at the heavens and you will see that the stars present quite a range of color differences. These tints vary according to the heat given off by the star, and are determined by the "age" or stage of development of the star. Red stars are fairly cool and "young," orange stars are warmer and "older," yellow ones still more so, and white and blue-white stars are brightest and hottest.

Just after dark in the summertime the part of the sky directly overhead is the most interesting. Turn around and face the south, lean back—lawn chairs are a help—and look above you, or at the zenith, as the point in the sky directly overhead is called. First of all, from your changed position, pick out Arcturus again, looking back at the Big Dipper, if necessary, to find it. Up from Arcturus toward the zenith you will see four stars forming the outline of a kite about twelve degrees in height, with Arcturus looking like a reddish button near the end of the kite string. To the ancient Greeks these stars that we see in the shape of a kite formed the constellation of Boötes, the Bear Driver, so called because as the night advances it seems to be chasing the Big Dipper, which is part of the constellation of the Great Bear.

To the left of Boötes, and just to the south of the zenith, is a semicircle of stars, one brighter than the others. This is the constellation Corona Borealis, the Northern Crown. According to legend, it belonged to Ariadne, wife of Bacchus, and he enshrined it in the sky after her death.

Just east of the zenith you will see four stars arranged in the shape of a wastebasket, about eight degrees to a side. This is part of the constellation Hercules. Notice the nearby stars that form his arms, legs and head, and the club in his right hand. The chief interest in Hercules is its celebrated star cluster. It cannot be seen with the naked eye, and a pair of opera or field glasses shows it only as a faint speck. But powerful telescopes have found over 40,000 stars in it, and it is so huge that it would take light over 200 years to travel from one side of it to the other, the light still traveling, of course, at its enormous speed of 186,000 miles per second.

Looking down toward the eastern horizon from Hercules, you will see three bright stars forming a huge triangle through which runs the pearly glow of the Milky Way. These three stars, Vega, Deneb and Altair, form the Summer Triangle. Vega, the star nearest Hercules, has a faint bluish tinge to its light. It is truly "Queen of the Summer Sky," brightest in the summer heavens. If you watch the sky when it is just beginning to get dark, you will see that Vega and Arcturus are the first stars to appear.

Summer triangle. All three of the stars forming the outline of the Summer Triangle are first-magnitude stars, which means that they are among the twenty brightest in the sky. Each of them has a constellation as its protegé. Vega has the Lyre, Altair the Eagle and Deneb the Swan.

Stargazing together has rewards for all the family, even the very young, who delight in stories you can tell as your knowledge of the heavens grows.

—*By Lou Williams*

SHELL COLLECTING

AMERICANS by the thousands, in groups or by families, are busy combing the beaches of the Atlantic, Pacific and Gulf coasts for sea shells. They ferry to Sanibel Island, a shell-hunter's paradise, from Fort Myers, Florida. (It's second only, it is said, to Australia's Great Barrier Reef.) They gather at Beaufort, South Carolina, where specimens of both northern and southern origin are in splendid plethora since this is the juncture where the northern and southern tides meet. They scrutinize the New England waterfront, and in town and cities far from the seaboard, many are discovering happily that their local hills, marshes, ponds, brooks, lakes, river banks and stretches of woodland offer just as good pickings as the seashore.

Shell-hunting is the kind of interest that can begin little—just a second glance at a pretty shell on the shore—and end big with an incredibly beautiful, treasured collection.

As a beginner, you will have to know only a few things about shells. One is that in your search you will most likely be concerned at first with just two classes of mollusk. Most shells found in the sea or on land are snail shells. At a conservative figure, three thousand different species of land and fresh-water snails may be found under logs, leaves, at the edges of streams and ponds, and even in trees.

The second group are the bivalves, the tribe made up of clams, oysters, scallops and mussels. All of these can be tracked down at the shore or wherever fresh water runs.

Moreover, the tracking down sometimes goes on right in your own neighborhood—and not outdoors, but in. Collectors have unearthed yields in barns, old shops, a cluttered attic. Not that the snails have crawled into ancient boxes and barrels to put hunters off the scent. Their shells have been brought back from far places. Captains of whaling ships were great ones for carting home shells as mementos of their voyages; world travelers of every era have found shells interesting enough to warrant precious luggage space.

Many museums throughout the country have wonderful collections and some families even plan trips with a certain museum as the target. In the National Museum in Washington, D.C., over 9,000,000 shells are on display. There are breathtaking collections at Harvard and Yale; the Museum of Natural Sciences in Philadelphia; the one at Rollins College in Winter Park, Florida; the Chicago Museum of Sciences; the Museum of Zoology at Ann Arbor, Michigan; the California Academy of Sciences in Golden Gate Park, San Francisco; and in other collections in San Diego; Berkeley; Boston; Mystic, Connecticut; and Fort Myers, Florida. Many museums have trays full of specimens for sale.

Nomenclature

Almost every beginning shell collector—children especially—is given to thinking of the shells in his own hoard by their local descriptive names, such as cat's paw, bleeding tooth, lion's paw, angel wing, turkey wing, Scotch bonnet, nutmeg, Venus' comb and jewel box. But Latin is the universal scientific language and the names of shells are easy to learn. Once you know them, it's easy to explain to another collector anywhere in the world what shell you want to trade, what shell you want from him.

And that's just what you'll be doing when you join a shell club—for that's what usually happens when the shell-hunting bug bites you. Generally the clubs hold forth somewhere around the local museum or university. Children are invited to join and often become accredited members. At the monthly meetings of New York's Shell Club in the Museum of Natural History, for instance, you'll find members of all ages.

In all shell clubs you can find out about the supporting "literature" you should read—books, magazines, leaflets; about shell dealers and how to make exchanges and purchases.

Shell clubs have another lively function. They take the entire family on expertly led field trips to stalk both the living and fossil shells. At some meetings special motion pictures are shown, problems discussed and significant items of news announced.

At a shell club meeting you have the stimulation of talking with experts and others who are on their way to becoming experts. Shell collectors are a generous breed and when someone just back from a foreign safari brings in a carton of shells for free distribution, children often stagger away from these meetings weighted down, but in ecstasy.

It doesn't happen often, but it's possible that a young amateur hunter will take an honored place among the professional specialists. Several years ago, a New York boy discovered a species of land snail never previously reported in that vicinity. Eddie's lecture on his find, complete with an automobile map to pinpoint its location and a homemade map to bring the location into close-up, wound up as a scientific paper which appeared in one of the field's leading journals.

Stimulates Other Interests

But youngsters don't have to aim for outstanding discoveries to get a lot out of this hobby. The clambering over pilings or rocks, the poking into cracks and crevices, trying to distinguish between static stone and a living shell, is a part of its thrill. So is crawling around on the beach to poke into seaweed and rubble when a storm has left behind a dazzling shell deposit.

A child learns all the while. Through trading his shells, classifying them, reading and hobnobbing with other collectors by mail or in person, he comes into an awareness of world geography and the ways of the people living in countries he never dreams he'll see. He also brushes with geophysics, though maybe he has never heard the word, when he learns about tides. All collectors watch tide-tables since tides determine the best time to bag the best shells.

Collections, as you might suppose, have infinite variety. There are cones, spirals, spindles, globules; shells that look like stars, trumpets, Christmas tree ornaments, boats, hats, fans, turbans, chessmen, fools-caps; one is precisely like a pure white sugared valentine heart; another an almost perfect replica of a strawberry—even to the tiny black seed spots dotting it. And still another is like a sundial with minute markings on its face which might be numerals.

Words can give a fair idea of the shape of shells. But the colors are description-defying. Their shadings can be either so gentle or dramatically vivid most of them have to be seen to be believed.

As if it were not enough for the shells to be flamboyant in coloring, they have markings and textures that make you stop, look and wonder at what nature has been up to. They come complete with stripes, Morse code dots and dashes, pin-head polka dots in reds, gigantic polka dots in maroon, black and brown. They go giddy with swirls of pastel interweaving lines in pink, rose, mauve and blue-green; some branch off into checkerboards in tones of brown against pristine white enamel, or delicate Scotch plaids in blue, yellow and light red or look charmingly feminine with lacework traceries of tapestry-like design in deep cardinal red and purple.

One of the biggest satisfactions in family shell collecting is sitting down together to mount finds. One family group of collectors uses an old dish closet for showing off fine shells against some left-over grass-mat wallpaper and a series of discarded bamboo placemats for the background. When they snap on the inexpensively contrived lighting, the display is breathtaking.

Displaying shell collections. There are other ways to set up a display, of course. Another collector has arranged his shells in a large glass-topped table in his living room. Units of a collection might also be cemented against a sea-blue paper background set in white shadow-box frames and hung on the walls.

Orange crates from the grocery store house the finds of a youngster who has made miniature beaches of sandpaper with light-blue craftpaper sky behind them. Another child used sectional plastic boxes, to his mother's delight, for these boxes are tidy and not too space-consuming. Plastic shoe and hat boxes which can be stacked are practical, too.

Nothing about shell collecting is static. It is constantly expanding, continuously opening opportunities for learning, forever bringing in new and delightful surprises for all the family to share. The lure of the shell is as endless and intriguing as why the sea rumbles on forever in the heart of an empty conch.   *—By Bernard Katz with Lola Pergament*

GARDENING WITH CHILDREN

CHILDREN love to dig. They dig in the sandbox from the time they are two years old. They dig in the dirt if they haven't a sandbox. Digging seems a natural activity of childhood—plenty of grownups love to dig, too.

Whether or not you are a digging parent, let your children dig with you this year. Perhaps it will be only a few pansy plants that you've been lured into buying by the promise of spring. Let the children help you plant them. Better still, buy each of them a box of pansies and give them gardens of their own.

If you are an experienced gardener you will not need to be told how to set in the pansies, or forget-me-nots, or whatever it might be. On the other hand maybe your mind needs refreshing, or perhaps you've never had a garden.

Ground will have to be turned over and chopped fine for young plants or seeds of annuals planted where they are to grow. The soil should be of good tilth, preferably a sandy loam. If it is very poor it should be thoroughly mixed with several shovelfuls of compost or manure per square yard. Here's where dad and the boys can take over. Boys of eight and nine are wonderful diggers but with poor soil they might need additional help.

Shopping for Plants

After the soil is dug and raked smoothly, it's time for young gardeners to go on a shopping expedition. At planting time, florists, hardware stores and even groceries display seedlings. It's fun for the children to pick out their own boxes of plants. Let them buy their own trowels, too. Incidentally, a good trowel, preferably one with blade and handle in one piece, is no more expensive than many less useful toys. Within reason, give the children as many choices in this project as possible, even to selecting the planting locations.

Try to choose a cool, cloudy day for setting out the young plants. If a rain is due, so much the better. Teach the children to dig a hole large enough to hold a young plant without crowding it. Then they can carefully dig the plant from its container, disturbing the roots as little as possible, and set it in the hole so the neck of the plant comes even with the top soil. The next step is to show the children how to press the soil gently but firmly into place, smoothing the surplus soil around the stem by hand or trowel.

After a recent rain or if the ground is evenly damp, the earth only needs one watering after the plants are set in the ground. If the ground is at all dry, the holes for the plants should be watered *before* planting as well as afterwards. How children of all ages love to use the watering can! Up to about nine years old, a one-quart can is satisfactory and one they can easily handle. After that, boys in particular will begin to look around for something bigger. Don't let the children over-water! You can explain to them that plants, like people, need water to live but if watered too much or too often are apt to drown.

Planting Time

If planting is done in hot, sunny weather, the children can protect their plants by covering them with berry baskets which are light and easily handled. Pots, large enough to be airy, can also be used. Three or four days' protection should be enough for pansies and other plants which have a good-sized ball of earth around their roots. Seedlings, transplanted from the original box so that the roots might have been exposed in moving them, should be covered for about a week. If it happens to be cloudy or rainy the covering can be removed.

Three to six-year-olds prefer to work with plants already in bloom. They can learn a further lesson by being taught how to pick flowers correctly. Children are naturally attracted to the bright blossoms but they need to be shown how to pick them without yanking up the plant. Give them a pair of blunt scissors or small garden clippers and suggest that they treat the flowers gently. Explain that it is good for most plants to have their flowers picked as this inspires the plant to produce more flowers instead of sending its strength to making seeds.

Children six years old and up enjoy planting seeds as well as plants. They will delight in hearing about the miracle of the seed: how it contains within it the beginning of a plant's life and how a seed is a resting period in the life-cycle of a plant. Other explanations can follow. Very few seeds sprout as soon as they mature. They lie dormant for awhile, sometimes for several years. When you buy seeds, such as those of annuals or vegetables, they are dry and cool and should be kept that way until planted.

Success with planting begins with buying seeds or plants from a reliable source, thus assuring that they have been well harvested and cared for. The rest depends on the buyer following directions on the packages.

You'll probably find it more satisfactory for the children to experiment with large seeds such as sunflowers, dahlias, zinnias, marigolds, nasturtiums, tomatoes and others that they can handle and see easily. Children from six to twelve find cherry tomatoes especially interesting. They grow easily and rapidly and, since they are really vines, will have to be securely staked or fastened to wire supports. Cherry tomatoes bloom early followed shortly by the round red fruits resembling good-sized cherries, usually in clusters of eight. Delicious to the taste, they are fun to pick and pop into the mouth straight from the vines.

All of the seeds mentioned before germinate within a week or so. The seed leaves, or cotyledons, are large and unmistakable. These seedlings are also more easily handled than the young plants of such things as petunias and snapdragons which are very delicate. If you have a sunny window it's fascinating for the children to start the seeds indoors in pots, seed flats or even large cans. Marigolds, zinnias, dahlias and so forth can be separated and transplanted to the garden when they are a few inches high and when the danger of frost is over. Other annuals, like sweet alyssum, Nigella, and nasturtiums, are best planted out of doors in the places where they are to grow. This is usually stated on the package along with the time of planting.

As a child's interest develops, he can work into planning a whole flower or vegetable garden. Studying the catalogues together and learning the names of different plants, their colors and habits are fun for both parents and children. Fascinating questions will come up. How high does a plant grow or is it a climbing vine? Is it tall or a little round bush?

Some children take to gardening more than others but most children at one age or another are interested in the planting of a seed. In winter, indoor experiments with seeds are fun. Try sprinkling grass seed on a plate of water or wait for an avocado pit to split open and send up leaves. Gardens, wherever they are, are sure to be fun for children.　　　　—By Emily S. Parcher

EXPLORING NATURE
IN THE SUMMER

THE summer months provide many opportunities for investigating and exploring by the child whose explorations may go no farther than the back yard. They may be as simple and natural as making mud pies. Water added to dry, powdery dust changes the texture to a slushy, oozy mass. To demonstrate the different types of soil, make some of the pies from loam, others from sand and a third group from clay. Let them dry in the sunshine, then test to find which are easiest to crumble and which disintegrate first in water. Discuss the types of soil best adapted to different plants in dry weather and in wet weather.

Summer mornings before the sun is high are the best times to examine the dew. It does not fall, but is formed when the earth cools and the moisture from the warm air condenses on cooler objects. Let the child make dew by adding a little cake coloring to a glass of ice water placed in a warm room. Drops of clear moisture will form on the surface of the glass. Warm air likes moisture, but when the air gets cold, it can no longer carry the moisture, and in this case deposits it on the glass. Some children think that the moisture comes from water inside the glass, but using colored water proves this false.

Clouds, Hail, Heat and Rain

Observe the clouds on a summer day. Children will soon notice that there are different kinds: some are fluffy like balls of cotton, others are thin and wispy, some are in even layers, while the thunderstorm type are tall, towering and black. Pick out imaginary pictures formed by the clouds. They change so rapidly that a rabbit becomes a dragon in the space of five minutes, and in another five the whole thing may disappear. Most children express a desire to walk in the clouds. They can have their wish by walking in a heavy fog; fog is a cloud resting on the ground.

If hail falls during the summer, collect some stones, and split them open. Notice how they are made up of layers much like an onion. The hail started toward the earth as a drop of water, but it was caught up in an upsurge of air, and carried so high in the atmosphere that it froze. Again it fell, and again it was carried upward, adding another layer of ice. This process was repeated as many times as there are layers of ice. Speak of the force of such air currents powerful enough to carry anything so far, and discuss the reasons pilots avoid thunderstorms.

Watch the thermometer reading on the hottest days. The older child will be interested in an instrument that gives both the temperature and the humidity. He will soon see that his comfort really depends as much on the amount of moisture in the air as on the temperature. No one can become intimately acquainted with rain except by staying out in it; yet too many children are herded inside during warm summer showers. Water play with a hose is always a merry occasion. Cover part of the nozzle to show the force water has when under pressure. Turn the hose on a grass-covered slope, then on a bare slope, and contrast the amount of soil loosened. What is happening to our soil in areas where erosion is not checked?

Too many city children never see a sunrise. It is well worth getting up a few hours early for this experience. Discuss the methods of telling time before clocks were invented. Study the shadow of a tall pole, noticing how its position changes during the morning, noon, afternoon. Let the child make a simple sundial. Drive a nail in the center of a piece of wood about a foot square. Set it where the sun can strike it all day, and mark the places where the shadow from the nail falls at nine, twelve, three and six o'clock. Make shadow pictures with a flashlight or candle in a dark room. Notice that if one stands behind the candle, the shadow will not form on the same surface. Watch for unusual sunsets and try reproducing some of them with crayon or water colors.

All children should have the delightful experience of fishing. Digging the bait is pleasant if it is done leisurely. Dig with a spade and examine all forms of life that are brought to the surface. Notice where the moisture is and how much harder worms are to find in dry weather. Earthworms are valuable— so valuable that some farmers buy them for their land. They enrich the soil, make it more porous, and their burrows form drainage canals so that the rain soaks into the earth instead of running off.

During an extremely dry period, examine the plants to see what effect lack of moisture has upon them. Notice that some leaves wilt, others curl and, if the drought continues, the whole plant dies. A picnic spoiled because of rain is less a tragedy if the disastrous results of drought to the farmers' living and to our own food supply are understood.

Visit a farm to see food growing in all its stages of maturity. Power machinery has taken away much of the charm of wheat harvesting, but it may be possible to find a farm that still uses a binder and a thresher. Let the child help with as many of the processes as possible. Have him chew some of the wheat grains to get the taste and try grinding some wheat into flour.

Watch the growing corn and explain what a contribution the Indians gave our new civilization when they introduced corn to the early settlers. Many people think that the colonies could not have survived if it had not been for corn. Play a game with one person naming a common domestic food and the other telling how it grows: underground, on vines, trees, stalks or bushes.

Benefits of Vacation Trips

Many new concepts can be learned during vacation trips. The usual danger is in pointing out too much when the child is overstimulated. Adult conversation will often prompt questions from children. A young child can soon identify lakes, rivers and streams. The contour of the land should be given its correct name: hill, mountain, valley, plain or swamp. When vacation is over, make a contour map in the sandbox of some well remembered spot. To add realism, use the stage properties that were brought home—rocks, shells, wood and sticks. Glass dishes filled with colored water make authentic-looking lakes. Reliving the experience helps the child to assimilate his new adventures.

The Collecting Urge

The collecting urge begins around six and consists of any and everything that catches the child's fancy. The house will stay a little less cluttered if containers are provided for the treasures. Cigar boxes are perfect for the young collector. The outside paper may be removed with steel wool and the boxes painted, but they are loved just as much if left natural. Limit the number of boxes to the amount of space in the house because all of them will be filled. The amateur collector of any age is indiscriminate. His emphasis is on quantity, not quality. This is a normal process of growth and he should be allowed to treasure his accumulations even though they look suspiciously like trash to adults.

The collections are among the child's most cherished possessions and they should never be thrown away without his permission. As he grows and matures, he will discard. One ten-year-old had thirteen collections all active at the same time. Her wise parents interfered with none of them. Later, in a surge of room cleaning, she sniffed disdainfully at box after box wondering aloud why in the world she had wanted that "old junk."

Rock collecting. Rocks make interesting and instructive collections. Even the two-year-old picks up pretty pebbles and carries them around. Smooth rounded stones can be found along the banks of a swift stream. Visit a rock quarry and, besides watching the method of mining, notice the difference in the newly-mined fragments and those that have been exposed to weathering. Examine tilts and seams in the steep banks along the highway. Were they caused by the earth's tilting or by being folded under great pressure? Leaf prints are often found in coal and fossils of shells in limestone. Nothing proves to the child so conclusively as these fossils that parts of the earth were once under water. Rocks are often grouped according to hardness. Test to see which ones will scratch others. Slate will write and was used for that purpose before pencils were thought of. Mica can be split into thinner and thinner sheets. Sandstone will crumble. Soapstone can be shaved with a knife into powder, then mixed with water to make marbles. Make lists of things man uses from the earth. Would our kind of civilization have been possible without them?

Making cages for insect collections develops ingenuity and resourcefulness. A lemon crate covered with mosquito netting or screen wire is effective for many kinds of specimens. Shoe box containers are convenient and fun to use because they are like miniature houses. Remove the cardboard from the lid, leaving an inch of margin. Replace the cardboard with cellophane held in place in the sides with transparent tape. Punch holes for ventilation. The simplest cage for small insects is a lamp chimney placed in a flower pot filled with damp soil. A small square of netting held in place with a rubber band makes the cover. This is a superb place for lightning bugs because they can be used as a bedside lamp with no danger of escape. For a large outdoor cage, roll a yard of screen wire into a cylinder, sew or wire the long side and cover the top with netting. Sink the cage in loose dirt in a shady place. This will accommodate several specimens and, if some of them eat the others, explain the struggle for existence all living forms must take.

Insects can be kept for days in such cages, if green foliage, food and water are supplied. Grasshoppers eat fruit, lettuce and clover. Crickets and katydids like pulpy fruits and lettuce. Spiders eat flies and insects. A solution of sugar and water tempts butterflies and moths. Any kind of caterpillar should be given the same kind of leaf upon which it was found. There are books that tell how to feed and care for any kind of specimen, but they are expensive; getting the information at the library offers good training in note-taking and independent research.

Observing Insects

It is diverting to observe many insects in their natural habitat. Break open the nest of a dirt dauber to see all stages of its development. The female makes her nest from mud, then seals food in the passages so there will be an ample supply close at hand when the young hatch.

Because of their incredible skill in web building, spiders are fun to watch. Very few are poisonous, but the child should be taught to look and not touch. Find one building or repairing a web to appreciate the amount of work and perseverance required. Drop a live fly into the web and see what happens. Notice the victims left under the web. The spider does not eat his prey but merely sucks the juices from it.

Some children are oversentimental about killing anything. When the garden is filled with pests, point out the offenders, show what damage they are doing and explain what would happen to all gardens if these insects were allowed to go unchecked. A matter-of-fact voice and careful explanation of why killing is necessary will allay most prejudices. Do point out the good things about different forms of life. The bumblebee fertilizes the red clover and, without its help, we would not have this food for our horses and cows. Spiders destroy flies that carry disease germs. Wasps eat mosquitoes and thus help to prevent malaria. Birds eat thousands of harmful insects. Find out what kinds of snake in the locality are poisonous and protect the others. They contribute to man by eating insects.

Watch toads on warm summer evenings. They are harmless, they do not cause warts and they are of untold benefit to man because of insects they destroy. Keep one for a few days in a box with damp earth in the bottom.

Provide a small dish of water and add live flies. The toad catches them with his long tongue, but the motion is too fast to follow. Notice how well the toad's coloring blends with his surroundings. Try to find other examples of protective coloring.

While young children do not like killing, the older ones may want to start a collection of butterflies and insects. A butterfly net is a necessity. Seam a yard of netting down the side and bottom, run a wire hoop through the top and attach it to a broom handle. A fruit jar with a tight lid and a rubber makes an effective killing jar. Put a spoonful of carbontetrachloride on a piece of cotton, covering the cotton with paper to prevent the specimen's tangling in it. Leave the insect in the killing jar overnight. Cigar boxes lined with corrugated paper in the bottom make good display cases. If the child's interest continues, get a good book on preparing and mounting.

A summer science program should be as casual and natural as any form of play. It should be a pleasant part of everyday living, with no definite hours or time allotted to it. If all plans are based on the wants and desires of the child, the program will give much enjoyment and much satisfaction during the summer months.

NATURE ACTIVITIES IN AUTUMN

AUTUMN is a season of warmth and color. It is loved by all ages but to children, especially, it is a season of enchantment. Autumn is a preparation for winter. Man's preparation, caused by past experiences, is a deliberate effort made to survive the coming winter. The preparation of birds, insects and animals, caused by instinct, is also a method of survival. Some of this preparation is noisy and bustling; some is so quiet and unobtrusive that it escapes unnoticed, but all of it is a rewarding occasion for children.

Man's preparation for winter is best observed on a farm. Digging potatoes, picking apples and gathering corn are all tangible operations that children understand. They should help with as many of these processes as possible. Take apples that the child has picked to a cider mill to learn how they are squeezed into cider. Keep some of the cider in a closed jar until it turns into vinegar. Cane is a spectacular example of a food plant. If it grows in the neighborhood, let the children examine it, chew it, and visit a mill to see how the juice is extracted from the stalks and boiled to make syrup. A small mill is preferable because the mechanical processes are more obvious.

After children have seen others prepare for the coming months, they like to make their own preparations. Let them make corn meal with some of the corn they gathered, using a mortar and pestle, or a food grinder. After this experiment, try to visit a small mill to watch modern methods of grinding, and understand how machines are time saving.

Our pioneer ancestors relied on drying as a means of preserving much of their food for winter. Dried apples are easy for children to prepare. Firm apples are peeled, quartered and placed on drying trays in direct sunshine until all the water has evaporated. The trays can be of wire mesh, of slatted wood or any other material that allows free circulation of air. The apples should be turned every day and, of course, brought inside at night and at the first drop of rain. Peaches, pumpkins, berries and persimmons were all dried in bygone days, but to our palates, unfamiliar to their textures, they leave much to be desired. The child should understand that in most homes of today canning and freezing have taken the place of drying. He should also understand that it is the farmer who supplies us with most of our food. He harvests his crops in the fall, not only for all of us, but also for the domestic animals, who through the centuries have lost their power of survival without man's help.

All children like the bright leaves of fall, and even the youngest likes to pick up and carry the crimson ones. Do not stress names, but do notice the difference in sizes, shapes and colors. Some have smooth edges, others are toothed and still others lobed. The brightest colors occur when heavy frosts are followed by sunshiny days. Pick a number of the prettiest leaves to mount. Press them in a weighted book for two or three days, then iron under waxpaper with a warm iron. Mount them on paper with transparent tape.

Autumn Flowers

Fall flowers are gaudy and gay and, unlike the spring ones, they are plentiful enough to pick. Goldenrod, black-eyed Susans and asters are all favorites of children. These can be pressed between blotters under weights and mounted in a scrapbook, but the colors fade to a dull brown. This is the time to collect grasses and everlasting flowers for winter bouquets. Hang them upside down in a warm place to dry. Pine cones of varying sizes can be dried and saved for Christmas decorations. Dried cattails last longer if given a thin coat of shellac. Contrast the growing places of goldenrod and cattails. Plants, like people, are selective in the places they like to live.

Nature has wisely given seeds many kinds of locomotion. Some, like ash, elm, birch, maple and linden, sail through the air with their wings. The balloon-type seeds are extremely light, and a puff of breeze starts them on their journey. Dandelion, milkweed, thistle, wild lettuce and cattail seeds are all shaped like miniature balloons. Others, like those of the pea family and the garden touch-me-not, shoot out their seeds at the slightest touch. Some like the cocklebur, beggar-lice and stick-tights, are hitchhikers. These seeds have barbs or hooks that catch to our clothing and to the fur of animals, getting rides far from the parent plant. Other plants have seeds in edible fruits or berries. When we toss cherry seeds away, we are helping those seeds find new homes.

A collection of different types of seed is the best way of insuring the interest of a child. To display the seeds, put them in cellophane wrappers from cigarettes, and tack them on the bulletin board. Most teachers would be delighted with the gift of such a collection. Even though the selected seeds from a good nursery are better, some seeds from domestic plants should be saved. The Halloween pumpkin seeds can be washed, dried and planted the next spring. Nothing shows a child the continuation of the species more than this method.

Even domestic animals who do not gather their own food prepare for winter by growing thicker and heavier hair or fur. Both squirrels and chipmunks store nuts for winter. Watch to see if they use the same routes on each trip, and let the children discover how they carry their treasures. Many animals make no attempt to store supplies, but instead eat large amounts of food during the late summer and fall until they develop a thick layer of fat. Then they find a sheltered spot and sleep until spring. Their bodies use up the accumulated fat, so they can go months without food or water. Frogs, turtles and numerous fish hibernate in the mud at the bottom of the water.

Migratory Birds

Because of the scarcity of food supplies during the cold months, many birds migrate to a warmer climate where food is more plentiful. They use regular paths of migration, and some have a definite schedule of leaving and returning. Secure a map of bird routes to see if any of them pass near you. Most birds fly by night so they can find food during the day. Any large group of birds staying together are probably visitors who have stopped to eat before continuing their journey. Geese and ducks fly by day, and are often seen flying in perfect formation toward their winter home.

When the migratory birds have all gone, it is a good time to study some of those who stay in one vicinity the whole year. Hawks, owls, buzzards are all interesting because they are predatory and eat other animals as well as insects. Mice, snakes, frogs, fish and carrion are their favorite foods. Their feet and bills are shaped differently from those of other birds. They have claws for catching, and curved bills for clasping and tearing their prey.

With the coming of frost, most insects die, but not without leaving some means of survival for the coming year. Many lay their eggs in sheltered spots where they stay all winter, and hatch in the warm days of spring. The queen of other species finds a protected place and clings there dormant until spring when she lays her eggs. Caterpillars spin webs of silk around their bodies and live on as a pupa in the cocoon. Open one of these cocoons with sharp scissors, and explain that from this kind of brown, lifeless pupa a gaily colored moth will come in the spring. The monarch butterfly is one of the few insects that migrates to a warmer climate. The monarch caterpillar eats only milkweed. He is a bright, showy fellow, and it is worth while to bring the plant with the caterpillar indoors for a few days' observation. Keep the plant in water and bring in fresh leaves when necessary.

Bees store their honey during the warm months and live throughout the winter on their own accumulated food. If the beekeeper took all their honey he would have no bees for the coming year because they would all starve. Let children examine the honeycomb, call their attention to the shape of the individual cells, and tell them that man with all of his learning and skill has never been able to duplicate the feat of the bee.

Plant Study

Gather one stalk of goldenrod or Spanish needle, spread it on a piece of paper or a sheet and count how many insects were using it for a home. Notice the bulge on the stems of goldenrod. Each bulge is a gall used by an insect who lives inside. Split some of them open to see the inhabitants. Bring some of them home, put them in a glass jar with a net top to observe for a period of several days. Split stalks of sumac lengthwise to see if some of them have been used as apartment houses by bees and wasps. Each room in the stalk was once the home of a young insect.

In early fall gather several curled leaves, take them home and uncurl them very gently to see the leaf-roller inside. It curled the leaf over like a tent so it could eat and grow, hidden from enemies. Pull the silk that holds the leaf together to test its strength.

Children enjoy walks more when they can find some kind of booty to bring back. Gathering wood to keep us warm in winter is a starkly simple process that many children never experience. Picking up nuts is another simple pleasure that every child should have. If a small paper bag is taken on every walk, there will soon be enough nuts to divide with the squirrels during snowy weather. The watery taste of the nuts disappears after they have dried.

Autumn actually begins on September 21st. On that date the day and night are equal in length. From that day until three months later, the days shorten and the nights lengthen. Check the time of the sun's setting one day each week for a period of a month to show that the days are getting shorter. Watch the thermometer readings, especially noticing the contrast between those of early morning and those at noon on a sunshiny day.

The first frost. Watch for the first appearance of frost to see what effect it has on plants. Cover some of the plants with paper bags to see if they are also killed. Watch for frost crystals on windowpanes and roof tops. Show that frost on the coils of the refrigerator is made in the same way as the frost outside. Both are caused by condensation and freezing of moisture in the air.

The trees drop their leaves as part of their preparation for winter. During the summer they evaporate the excess water that has been brought up through the roots. If the leaves continued this evaporation in winter when moisture is scarce, the tree would die. What happens to all the leaves that fall, to the vegetation killed by the frost and to all the animals and insects that die? Explain that new soil is being made constantly by the action of wind, rain, sun and bacteria on the decaying particles of plants and of animals. We all help make new soil every time we step on a dried leaf.

These plans for introducing science to the child should be carried on with variations, and with the addition of new materials from year to year. Children like the continuity of the same activities during the seasons. When new plans are introduced that the child does not like, they should be dropped immediately and introduced again at another time. A year later they may be of absorbing interest. By the time a child is ten, let us hope he has some concept of climate, soil and food supply. He should sense the interdependency between man, animals and plants. He should appreciate, however vaguely, the complexity and completeness of the world. He should be trained to demand evidence, and to reject some of the more childish superstitions. Let up hope he grasps some of the never changing natural laws, but most of all, let us hope he has had fun, and has shown a spontaneous delight in his experience.

DISCOVER WINTER
WITH YOUR CHILD

FIRSTHAND experiences provide the easiest and the true scientific method of learning, and give to all of us an enrichment of our everyday life.

Winter is an exciting and exhilarating time to children. The weather is stimulating and dramatic. Begin reading the daily weather forecast aloud, watching especially for snow predictions. Buy a good magnifying glass. When the first snowflakes come, let some fall on black cloth or paper to show the beauty of their miraculous designs. Put a small pan of snow on the stove to show how heat causes it to melt and evaporate. When the snow melts and evaporates outside, explain that the heat from the sun is causing it.

Hang an outdoor thermometer with easy-to-read numbers outside a window. Watch the temperature changes from day to day. Instead of an adult's arbitrary judgment, why not let the thermometer settle the question of when mittens and leggings should be worn? Children may begin keeping a record of the daily temperature, but it will probably not continue long. The young child has intense but fleeting enthusiasms. He has so much to learn, he cannot settle down to specialization.

When the temperature drops below freezing, suggest filling a narrow-necked bottle with water and leaving it outside overnight. Say "Let's see what happens." The next morning, after the cracked bottle has been thoroughly examined, guide their thinking to understand that water does get bigger when it freezes. Discuss what a force water can produce; wonder aloud about cracks in the sidewalks and in rocks. Why are seams left in streets and walks?

Walks on pleasant winter days can be a source of much pleasure and information. Call attention to the size and shape of trees. Point out the difference in the texture and color of bark. Do not stress identification beyond citing instances of how trees differ. Too much factual information often kills interest. If the child wants names, buy a tree book and help him look them up. A dime store one is sufficient if it contains the names of the fifteen trees most familiar in your locality.

Nature Walks

Search for cocoons on shrubs and black oak trees. Investigate when you see some brown leaves curled together. The cocoon is in the center, and the leaves serve as effective camouflage. Take the cocoons home and put away in a safe place until spring. Collect old birds' nests to compare construction, size, shape and kind of nesting materials used; collect a hornet's nest and cut it through the center to show its intricate design. Watch for squirrels and chipmunks. If the children take some hard nuts for them each time, they will often become quite tame.

Scales are interesting and instructive. The balance kind are superior, but unfortunately they are expensive. Substitute some discarded baby scales. They will keep children constructively occupied for hours while they weigh many things in the house. Let them check a five-pound bag of sugar, a bag of coffee or ten pounds of potatoes to confirm the accuracy of the weights. Play a game to see who can pick the lightest, the heaviest and equal weights of several objects. Verify the answers by weighing each.

A magnet is a source of much satisfaction. Searching throughout the house for articles made of iron and steel develops independent investigations. One group of children put paper clips on their valentines, and dumped them all down the stairway. Using short lengths of string, they tied the magnets to small sticks and spent the afternoon "fishing" for the valentines.

Allow the children to use a siphon to empty the goldfish bowl or the sink. Submerge a three-foot piece of rubber tubing in the water to be emptied. When the tube is completely filled, pinch one end of it together tightly, place it in the pan below, and the water will run out. Demonstrate that it will not flow if the water levels are of equal heights.

For sheer enjoyment, every child should own a prism. Some of the salvage companies of war surplus goods sell a slightly chipped one for two dollars that is worth several times that amount. Any age, including parents, will enjoy the rainbows that can be made with it.

Plant Experiments

Winter is a good time for experimenting with plants. Paper narcissus bulbs are a good choice for inside growth. Let the child go to the store to buy them, allow him to examine them leisurely and call his attention to the resemblance between bulbs and onions. Surround the bulbs with an inch of pebbles in a shallow bowl, and cover the pebbles with water. Store the bulbs in a dark closet until they begin to sprout—about a week or ten days—then bring them out and watch the developments carefully.

The sprouted onion from your vegetable bin also has possibilities. Wedge it in a narrow-necked bottle filled with water. The root system develops rapidly and illustrates how much of the plant is below the surface. Sweet potatoes and avocado seeds also make interesting plants but they are much slower to begin growing.

Lima beans, because of their large size, are good for experimentation. Soak them in water from twelve to sixteen hours, then let the children split some of them open. With a magnifying glass, the tiny baby plant inside can be seen very clearly. Place two of the soaked beans in each of several glasses filled with pebbles and add just enough water to touch the beans. (If they are covered they will rot, but to prove this fact, submerge some entirely.) Leave another glass with no water to demonstrate that the beans will not sprout. After the roots and leaves have begun to grow, allow the young botanist to examine and experiment upon some of them. Transplant a few to a flower pot with good soil. Postpone final judgments on such questions as "Which will grow better?" by saying, "Let's wait and see." Keep the plants long enough for the experimental evidence to demonstrate that plants do need soil.

When the bean plants have developed a good root system, put one in a glass cup with water to which a little red ink has been added. Say again, "Watch what happens." When the red color seeps up to the top, it will illustrate how the plant gets its food through the roots and carries it up to the leaves.

Calendar study. Get a calendar that has the moon phases, the time of sunrise and sunsets, and all the holidays. Name the days and count them to prove that seven days do make a week. Make no attempt to teach the names, because most children are so intrigued they pick them up rapidly. The next calendar time, name the months and count to see how many there are in a year. Watch for the new moon and the full moon. Check the dates to see if the calendar is accurate. Check the time of sunsets also. Show the day when spring officially comes.

Because the clear objectivity of science helps to develop logical thinking and accurate perceptions, a parent should use every opportunity to stimulate the inquiring mind.
                                                        —*By Carmen Stone Allen*

WHEN CHILDREN PLAY HOST

IT was one of those days when parents perspire and wonder what to do with a group of youngsters who have become irritable and crabby because it is so hot. They refuse to expend even a little of their boundless energy in active play, but choose rather to sulk or squabble among themselves.

I called to Peter, my eleven-year-old, and suggested a croquet tournament. This caught his fancy and he set out to organize it. Gretchen and Paul, seven and eight years old respectively, were invited to help, with the result that the three of them, with five neighbor children, held a tournament. This was topped off with cookies and lemonade, served picnic style on the lawn.

The average child delights in playing host or hostess. He likes to entertain just as grownups do and when he learns how, parties become surprisingly easy for a mother. Last year my two smaller children collaborated on a cookie-baking party. The dough was prepared in advance and eight young "bakers," wearing aprons, proceeded to cut out gingerbread men, stars and elephants to be popped into the oven. By the shiny brilliance of their eyes, as they busily decorated the cookies with red and green sugar and candles, anyone could tell that this party was a great success. Everyone was given a gay box in which to carry home all the cookies that he did not eat.

When they finished baking, I spread a lunchcloth on the living room floor in front of the radio-phonograph. With music as a background, my two young hosts served sandwiches that they had made earlier and chocolate milk.

Well, that was the party given by the seven to ten-year-olds. Our twelve-year-old, Peter, takes the job of being host for granted now.

After asking permission, he invited four of his pals to the house for a party. Long before his guests arrived he had everything ready, from the candy thermometer to the popcorn and the popper, for a popcorn ball and taffy party. It didn't really take much supervision. The host knew that when his party was over, things in the kitchen had to be shipshape. They were, too.

Child's Sewing Bee

Several of my friends and I have initiated sewing bees, and Gretchen, my eight-year-old, has followed our example. After an afternoon spent making doll dresses, the young hostess went to the kitchen to collect cookies and milk and so put a party touch to the gathering.

Our party idea has spread and now these social gatherings are taking place in other homes as well. I don't want to give the impression that our home is the scene of a continuous round of parties. Parties are for special occasions, but I have found that a child would rather give a party than be given one. Often one of my children asks to give a birthday party for the other, and my young son entertained for a neighbor lad on the latter's birthday.

With three children in a home thrilling to the experience of entertaining, it would be quite false to maintain that these events are staged in an atmosphere of tranquillity and quiet. Sometimes it seems to a mother that there are a lot of little people cavorting around in a very small house. Be that as it may, there's a lot of happiness too.

But there's more to letting a child give a party than happiness, even if the party is not an elaborate one. It gradually gives him a social sense of responsibility and manners. Even a wiener roast in the backyard places the responsibility of being host or hostess upon the child who does the entertaining. He begins to realize what is necessary in the way of preparation, such as gathering wood for the fire and seeing that there is enough food for everyone.

Good social training. You will also find that a child host or hostess is different from a child who is a guest. Children are discerning and never for the world would the host grab the first piece of cake and lose face before his guests. They learn little niceties too, such as arrangement of candles or table decorations if the party is in the home; and impressed upon their minds are the social requisites of welcoming guests, helping with caps and coats, and saying a gracious good-by.

When a child has had the experience of being host or hostess you will find he acquires a new self-assurance. It is most noticeable when the parents entertain. There is less tongue-tied reticence on the one hand or show-off tendencies on the other. From the youngsters' own experience with entertaining people of their own ages they know how it feels to be host and hostess and they have consideration for their parents in that role. They are often so polite and well mannered that I am secretly astounded. Parties are fun, yes, but they are also good social training.

—By Margaret Ione Etzell

BIRTHDAY PARTIES FOR CHILDREN

TO any child a birthday party is particularly his personal possession, and he gains more pleasure from this celebration of His Own Day than he does from the more general family holidays. Since it comes but once a year, a celebration should never be considered too much trouble. But birthday parties which fall on dates between September and May present problems to parents.

This is partly because too many mothers have come to think of a birthday party for younger members of the family as an occasion requiring elaborate preparations, an affair including all the children of the neighborhood in spite of their age range. (It is next to impossible to make a party including four-year-olds, ten-year-olds and teen-agers a success.) They also think it should be a meeting of fond mothers who are apt to take over the party, and a chance to pay back social debts.

But remember, it is not mother's party but that of the birthday child. If you remember that, a much more simple entertainment is possible.

Here are some tried and true birthday parties, all put to the test of actual enjoyment by children in the stated age groups. None involves much expense, although they do demand some time and thought in planning.

Rules for Successful Parties

(1) The birthday child must be the center of the party and should enjoy it.

(2) The guests should all be within a year of the age of the child giving the party. (Older guests tend to dominate the party and rob the young host or hostess of his or her right of being as important and as adept at the games as are the guests.)

(3) No matter how many party invitations your child owes, do not pay them back by inviting a collection of uncongenial guests to his birthday party. Limit the number of mothers invited to two who can help you.

(4) If it is necessary for adults to accompany the children to the party, provide some entertainment for them in another room.

(5) Prizes should be inexpensive. Try to select something which will give the child something to do with his or her hands, such as: pencils, plain and colored, crayons, coloring books, paper doll books, small packages of construction paper in variegated colors (very popular), beads to string. Be liberal in your prize-giving. Each guest will love to carry home a souvenir.

(6) Timing of games depends entirely upon the popularity of any one game. Drop at once any game which does not hold the children's attention, and prolong one which does.

(7) Children have no sense of time. It is best for the adult hostess to announce firmly that the party is over, and she must have no qualms about speeding parting guests. No feelings will be hurt and other mothers will thank her for getting their children home on time.

For a Two-Year-Old

This party begins at about eleven in the morning with two or three guests present. Afternoon naps are still necessary and the regular routine should not be too disturbed by any social gathering.

Entertainment: Clear a large space in the living or dining room and place suitable toys around to attract attention. Borrow freely in order to have several identical ones. This duplication will prevent unhappiness. Have blocks, pull toys, soft toys, pegboards and big soft balls. Let the children play at will individually. Social, cooperative playing together and taking turns do not begin until about five years of age. Be prepared for some conflicts, and perhaps even tears. Do not take such reactions too seriously. Offer the distraction of another toy.

Luncheon should be served at noon, preferably in the kitchen at the hostess' own little table. Have a very small amount of milk in a little glass and a small pitcher of milk to pour oneself. This is a very popular, if somewhat sloppy, occupation.

Pull down the blinds or curtains before you bring in the small sponge cake with the two lighted candles. Invite the birthday child to blow out the candles while the others sing "Happy Birthday."

When the guests are through eating, the party is officially over and it will be time to go home.

Menu: Baked potato, carrots, egg or boiled minced meat, gelatine, birthday cake.

For a Three-Year-Old

Make this a morning party also. It may begin about ten-thirty with the arrival of three or four guests. At this hour they are all apt to be at their brightest and best, and are ready to enjoy such a gathering.

Entertainment: Again clear space in one of your larger rooms and bring out toys. Blocks, trucks, wooden trains, pegboards, hammer and peg sets, and if you are lucky, a rocking horse—perhaps you can borrow another such steed. Let host and guests play at will for about thirty minutes and then some social games can be tried.

Marching. (Three to five minutes.) Equipped with paper hats, Jackie and his friends can march around the room in preparation for the next game which is the old, well-loved ring-around-a-rosy (six minutes). Join hands to form a circle and march slowly around singing: "Ring-around-a-rosy, ring-around-a-rosy, all fall down!" You will discover this to be considered a gem of wit and the attendant action will send three-year-olds into gales of laughter. Not too much of this or they will become overexcited.

Instead, pass along to train or automobile. Use grocery store pasteboard cartons—one for each child. They must be low enough and large enough so that the child can crawl in and kneel down. Let them then push themselves with their hands around the floor as trains or automobiles.

At twelve o'clock, luncheon can be served at low tables or on boxes put together. "Let's pour milk from small pitchers into our own glasses" is still great fun. Perhaps this meal should be served in the kitchen where the linoleum-covered floor can simplify the problem of the too-enthusiastic pourer.

When the birthday cake is served in the glory of its lighted candles, the singing of "Happy Birthday" is again on the program. And then it will be time to see the guests on their way home at one o'clock.

Menu: Baked potato, spinach, minced meat, sliced banana, birthday cake.

For a Four-Year-Old

Ask four or five guests to come at ten-thirty on the birthday morning. Since four-year-olds are much more active, it might be well to move to the recreation room if you are lucky enough to have one.

Entertainment: This is the year that you start the perennial Pin-the-Tail-on-the-Donkey game. Buy a good one—it will have to last a long time and stand a lot of hard usage. A blindfolded child pins the tail where he thinks it ought to be—this charms the four-year-olds completely. Be liberal with prizes for good efforts.

Then comes Farmer in the Dell. Form a circle, hand in hand, and march around, one child in the center according to the song.

Singing games will be new to some of the children, so they will move slowly but they will enjoy them. So you may also add London Bridge. Two children facing each other clasp hands to form a bridge. The others line up to pass under, all singing. Each prisoner in turn chooses one side or other of the bridge and a gentle tug of war ends the game.

A quiet game should now follow these two active ones, so here are two finger plays which the children will like to play several times each:

> Jack-in-the-box, (Hands closed with thumb inside)
> Sits so still,
> Won't you come out?
> Yes! I will. (Thumb jumps out)
> Here's the church. (Fingers interlocked, palms down)
> And here's the steeple, (Index fingers rise to a point)
> Open the door, (Keep fingers interlocked but turn palms up)
> And see all the people (Wiggle fingers).

Another active game. Now the children will be ready for another active game. Remember that it is hard to hold attention for quiet games at this age.

So try playing Train. Choose a child to be the engine. Tie the center of a fifteen-foot light rope around his waist; line the other children up behind him as passengers inside the rope, and have the last child hold the rope ends. He is the caboose. Another is the conductor who marches beside the engine and calls the station stops. The train then moves around the room with the engine saying "chug-chug" to a sign that says "Station." At each station the rope is dropped and the passengers get off. Everyone, of course, must have a turn as engine, conductor and caboose. It is even more fun for the conductor to wear a special paper hat and collect paper money fares. The stations may be named for the streets where the children live.

After this try Animal Chase. Pig (a bean bag) is passed around a circle of children seated on the floor. The pig is closely pursued by a wolf in the form of a block. Both can be passed either way and the children try to keep the wolf from catching the pig.

At luncheon there are fancy paper hats and napkins and candy baskets to take home. Inexpensive favors may now make their appearance along with the ice cream and cake.

Menu: Creamed potatoes, broiled bacon, buttered green beans, milk, birthday cake and ice cream.

For a Five-Year-Old

Have this party for six or seven guests early in the afternoon before the schoolchildren come home. And this is the year when special entertainment can be offered. So we have three different parties to suggest, two unusual ones and one of the ordinary party-game sort.

Cookie party: When the guests arrive they are provided with gay improvised aprons, and their hands washed before they are sent to the kitchen. (The aprons might also be the party favors, or each guest might bring one from home.) In the kitchen a simple cookie dough is ready.

Each child rolls out a small amount of dough on a play board or bread board and then cuts his own cookies with small, fancy cutters. (Well-washed pint milk bottles make good rolling pins.) Cookies may be decorated according to the guests' desire with raisins, nuts and colored sugar. The work may be done on small tables and boxes as well as at the big table. The high point of the party may be the fashioning of a cookie man with raisin features. Songs while cookies bake.

Menu: Sandwiches, cookies, ice cream, birthday cake.

Construction party: This is an especially nice party for little girls. Each guest will be furnished with a set of toy furniture—the cardboard sort. With scissors, each child cuts out her set and puts together a roomful which is displayed with all the others on a table. The furniture set is the party favor and goes home with the guest.

Menu: Ice cream, birthday cake, simple candy to be taken home.

Game party: Five-year-olds ready for kindergarten are more cooperative in play. Start with last year's singing games; they are more familiar now with London Bridge and The Farmer in the Dell. To these add Drop the Handkerchief and Charlie over the Water.

> Charlie over the water
> Charlie over the sea
> Charlie can't catch a blackbird
> And he can't catch me!

Again the players form a circle with one of their number as Charlie in the center of the ring. The circle moves to the left, chanting the song. As the last word is sung, all players squat. Charlie must try to tag one before he is fully down. If successfully tagged, that child becomes Charlie in turn.

For a sitting game repeat the Animal Chase of last year, but add another animal—the Dog. So that now Dog chases Wolf as Wolf pursues Pig around the seated circle.

Pin-the-Tail-on-the-Donkey must not be forgotten either. You may start with this one again if you wish, or use it to conclude the afternoon's fun.

The third new game will be an action one, but without singing. It is Airport: Cut eye, nose and mouth holes in brown paper bags and put them over the children's heads. One child is the airport manager who directs traffic in and out on the runway. The "planes" squat until the airport manager sends them off to fly to California or New York or to some other destination. Wing banking and engine noises are part of the fun. The children will add such details themselves. Be sure that the manager does not forget to give the planes gas or start their engines properly.

Menu: Ice cream, birthday cake, candy in baskets.

For a Six-Year-Old

Your six or seven guests are now bound by school hours, so the party time will be from three-forty-five to five-thirty or thereabouts, since busy mothers cannot plan dinner parties. Do not postpone the birthday party until Saturday just because the proper date falls upon a school day. The birthday is one certain date and that is the best time for the party. Children are apt to feel that it is not truly a birthday party when it is a postponed one. Because of the lateness of the hour and because children coming home from school are unusually hungry children, it is well to start the party with the refreshments.

Menu: Small peanut butter and jelly sandwiches, birthday cake, ice cream.

Entertainment: The six-year-old is learning to read and is much better at following instructions, but he is not too old for the favorite singing games, so play them again this year. Add Here We Go 'Round the Mulberry Bush, which is familiar to most parents and children.

Bean bag toss: Toss bean bags into a narrow wastebasket at a suitable distance. You may score this game for a prize.

Another active game requiring some room to play it in is Statues. Put down on the floor at one end of the room a rope or tape measure, its end secured with weights. Set a starting line at the other end of the room. In the center of the rope, with his back to the players at the starting line, stands "It." He counts aloud to ten and then swings around. The players must be motionless, posed as statues, when he sights them. If "It" sees anyone move, that child must get safely to the finish line without "It" catching him on the move. The one who does so successfully wins.

Heel and toe race: Use the same start and finish lines as the ones put down for Statues. Players start off with the right foot and must place the left heel in front of the right toe, touching it, then the right foot in front of the left in the same manner, and so on until one reaches the goal line.

Bean bag race: Again your starting line and goal marks are used. But this time bean bags are placed on the contestants' heads. If, while the child is moving at a fast walk, the bag falls off, he must return to the starting line and start again. No steadying hands allowed, of course.

Charades. After so many active games it might be well at this point to introduce a quiet one, such as Charades.

Mother Goose charades are best, since all the guests will be familiar with the rhymes. Divide the children into two groups. Give one group some simple properties to work with and let them dramatize a rhyme of their choice. The audience group will then guess the proper verse. Good rhymes to suggest for use are: Old King Cole (requiring pipe, bowl, and one child making the motions of violin playing), Jack-Be-Nimble (candlestick with a boy jumping over it), Little Boy Blue (horn), Little Jack Horner (a pie tin), Jack and Jill (a pail). After each scene the audience and acting group change places.

Pin-the-Tail-on-the-Donkey appears again to end the party. Since the refreshments have come first, it may be somewhat difficult to bring the party to a close. A tactful and pleasant way might be to bring out little crepe paper candy baskets on a tray and pass them around with the suggestion that they are to be taken home.

Parties for Seven to Twelve-Year-Olds

We've put the dividing line of children's parties at seven years of age because boys and girls over seven can usually read and spell and this makes possible a number of activities which are out of the question for younger children. When a party is being given for one child, there is generally little difference in the ages of the guests. Children tend to seek their own age level in their friends. However, when there are two children in the family, one of seven and one of eleven or twelve, it is still possible to combine their friends at a party and have games and entertainment suitable to both groups.

Any child over seven should have a voice in the arrangement of his own party. He can write, or help write, the invitations, make suggestions as to games, and be consulted as to who is to come.

Pirate Party

Children who have learned to read love the thrill of receiving mail so it's a good idea to send written invitations. An invitation which gives the approaching party a definite flavor is always more exciting than a mere letter. One mother invited a dozen boys and girls to a pirate party. The invitations were in the form of pirate's hats, cut from heavy black paper and decorated with red paper cockades. On each hat was written, in white ink:

"Tommy Jones invites you to join his Pirate Band next Wednesday afternoon from 4 until 7 o'clock. Don't forget the password. It is 'Captain Kidd' and you will be asked for it. Come promptly."

At four o'clock on the day of the party, Tommy stood at the door, a pirate hat on his head, and around his neck a bright scarlet bandanna. Each guest was asked for the password and then led to a chest in the hall from which he was told to select a hat like his host's and a colored bandanna. There were three colors to choose from, blue, scarlet, and green.

When the guests were assembled, a treasure hunt was announced. The four children who had chosen green bandannas were grouped into one pirate band, those who had chosen scarlet, in another, and those who had blue ones, in a third. The leader of each band was given the first "clue" to the whereabouts of the treasure. The clue, printed on a piece of torn paper, directed the pirates to

"Look for something red next to something blue.
"In between those colors, you'll find another clue."

Each band was told to keep together. The leader of each was to decide which part of the house to search first. His men must stay in the same room with him, although each might look for the clue in a different part of the room. The first one to find the clue was to tell the leader quietly and let him read it. Then the clue was to be put back in its place and left for the other groups to discover.

The clue was on a bookshelf—a small piece of white paper sticking out from between a red book and a blue one. It directed the treasure-hunters to "Go 25 steps uphill and keep your eyes on the ground." The twenty-five steps were the stairs to the second floor and the third clue was found under the corner of a rug.

There were six clues in all. They were just mystifying enough to make the search exciting, but not so obscure as to make the discovery of the treasure too difficult. Tommy had helped lay the trail himself. The final clue was a key to the locked door of the hall closet. The leader of the band which found it first opened the door and the treasure turned out to be a wooden box, decorated to look like a sea chest. In it were prizes for each of the members of the successful band.

A variation of the treasure hunt idea is a game called "Cobweb" or "Follow the String." Start in one room, allowing about half a ball of string to each person and proceed by as circuitous and difficult a route as possible until you find a good hiding place for a small gift to be tied to the end of each string. Each guest is told to take the end of a string, roll it up slowly, and follow it until it reaches the prize to which it is tied.

"Magic Music" is a good party game for seven-to-twelves. To play it, one child is sent out of the room, and the others choose some object in the room which he must touch when he comes in. The music becomes loud when he nears the right object and soft when he is far from it. If he fails to touch the article within a certain time, he pays a forfeit.

"I Packed My Trunk for China" is an excellent sit-down game. The leader announces, "I packed my trunk for China and in it I put an——," and points to a child who must mention some article beginning with the letter "A". He repeats "I packed my trunk for China and in it I put a——," and the child pointed to must name something beginning with "B". Forfeits are collected from those who fail to name something beginning with the correct letter, and are redeemed later through stunts.

For Older Children

Children from eight to twelve enjoy simple progressive games such as tiddlywinks, jackstraws, various games of lotto, easy card games, parchesi and ring toss. When these are played, scores are kept for each group and, after each child has played every game, the scores are added to determine the winner.

At outdoor parties or parties held in large houses, there is more chance for active games, such as hide-and-seek and treasure hunts—both lots of fun. If your space is very limited, a party consisting mainly of entertainment will solve your problem. A good amateur magician can keep children amused for hours. If you haven't one among your acquaintances there are entertainment bureaus in most cities through which one may be hired reasonably. Many department stores have party departments which will furnish information about professional entertainers such as magicians and puppeteers and clowns who specialize in entertaining children. These party bureaus, as well as camera supply stores can also tell you where you may rent motion picture projectors and films suitable for children's parties.

One city mother solved the problem of a birthday party for her ten-year-old son by inviting five of his friends for lunch and taking them to a big league baseball game afterwards. Another woman took a group of six boys and girls to a children's matinee and then back to her apartment for supper. Before starting out to the theater, the girls were given nosegays as souvenirs and the boys tiny blue ragged sailors for their buttonholes.

Take-a-trip party. For a take-a-trip party try a train ride. Many children even in this age group have never had the thrill of a train ride in this age of automobile travel. There is little preparation beyond the baking of the cake and a talk with the station agent, who will help choose a nearby destination where the waiting period for a return train will be brief. Such an expedition would not, of course, prove practical during crowded commuter hours. The party is less expensive than one might think, as children up to the age of twelve ride for half fare.

Consult the railroad conductor immediately on boarding the train so that he can direct you to the least occupied coach. Dining car stewards prove sympathetic and helpful when informed of the circumstances. Railroads know all about children. Out of consideration for other travelers, do not take noise makers, party hats or favors. The children are invariably so deeply filled with joy that they strive to remain decorous. Of course there are innumerable trips to water cooler and lavatory.

Take the cake along in a picnic hamper. Make it a large two-tiered square. Frost with vanilla butter icing. Across the top of the cake form a chocolate railroad track and ties on which a little toy engine pulls its string of four cars. Birthday candles serve as telegraph poles. The return trip is a good time to have the feast. Go at once to the diner. It's an exciting moment when the lighted cake is brought to the birthday child.

The more studious young travelers will enjoy following the trip to its destination on a map, so tuck a few into your hamper.

Curiosity about every detail of the ride is boundless. If you put your party on rails, be prepared to answer questions ranging from the workings of internal combustion engines to the reason for the numbers on the chairs. If the party group is large, invite a second mother to aid in the constant escort the children need.

—Adapted from material by
Margaret S. Young and Andre Norton,
Margaret Mochrie, Dolly Connelly

GAMES CHILDREN LIKE

THERE'S nothing quite like a good game to bring all the members of the family together for fun and excitement. At first it may take more self-control than most youngsters have to watch others win, but gradually they can learn to be good losers as well as enthusiastic winners. They can develop through games, too, that sense of fair play and the give-and-take so necessary in living. As children grow, games can get more difficult so that they challenge the child's resourcefulness and his ability to adjust quickly to the new situation which each throw of the dice or move by an opponent creates.

The four or five-year-old is just beginning to enjoy simple games, and likes playing with a grownup. Children of this age like to whirl spinners and to draw cards from a central pack to match colors or pictured objects. Soon they are ready for games based on familiar stories, and there are many of these. As children begin to acquire skills in reading and arithmetic and then in spelling, they enjoy games which use their new knowledge. Such games hold interest all through elementary school years, and geography and history games can be added as those subjects come along in school. Simple card games involving scientific calculations of interplanetary space hold high interest for today's children.

Games of skill preferred. Boys and girls have pretty much the same interests when it comes to games. Both enjoy the fast action of target games and other games of skill. The whole family can have fun playing geography games or whatever the favorites happen to be.

In order to hold a child's interest, a game should be within his ability so that he can win often enough to feel satisfied. Simple, clearly written instructions are a big help and, of course, the game should be fun. Action, suspense, chance, all add to the need for skill. Colorful design always makes a game more attractive.

And don't forget that children need a variety of both indoor and outdoor games for seasonal activity.

For a child to enjoy the fun of a good game whether or not he comes out ahead, is the basis for good sportsmanship and a contribution to emotional stability since it helps him learn to get along and to like and be liked in a group. Happy is the child who has a chance to learn to enjoy games—and if the family plays together so much the better. —*By Grace Langdon, Ph.D.*

HEALTH
AND SAFETY

ACCIDENT PREVENTION • BICYCLE SAFETY • FIRST AID
SURVIVAL SKILLS • COMMON SENSE AND SICKNESS
NURSING CARE • PREVENTIVE INOCULATIONS
COMMUNICABLE DISEASES • ALLERGIES
NUTRITION FOR GOOD HEALTH • GROWTH • FOOT HEALTH
POSTURE • HEARING AND VISION • ORTHODONTIA
HANDICAPPED CHILDREN • PREPARING A CHILD FOR SURGERY

ACCIDENTS
DON'T NEED TO HAPPEN

IF you have a son between the ages of one and sixteen, he's more likely to have an accident than a daughter of the same age . . . children are more likely to have accidents during the summer . . . falls are children's most common accidents . . . an overtired child is more likely to have an accident than a rested one.

These are a few of the facts uncovered by a group of medical personnel and civic-minded citizens of Greater New Bedford, Massachusetts, who several years ago formed the Greater New Bedford Children's Accident Prevention Program, to study the child accident problem in the community and develop a program aimed at reducing accidents to zero.

Child accidents in this country constitute the chief cause of death of children more than a year old. In a recent year, accidents killed more children between one and fourteen than the seven deadliest diseases combined. And they cripple three or four more times as many children as they kill. Yet nine out of ten accidents can be prevented, says Dr. George W. Starbuck, who served as chairman of the New Bedford program.

Age a Guide to Prevention

Happily, New Bedford has now set up signposts to guide parents along the way to prevention. Among these is their uncovering of the fact that different ages are prone to different kinds of accident. Says Dr. Pauline G. Stitt, Assistant Professor of Maternal and Child Health at the Harvard University School of Public Health, a speaker in the New Bedford Program, "At a given age an infant will roll over; at another he will explore with his fingers and find the electric light socket irresistible. Although each child has his own timetable, we know approximately when he will enter another era of performance."

Under a year is the "helpless age." The leading cause of accidental death at this age appears to be suffocation by pillows or bedclothes. (However, studies indicate that many of these deaths actually result from acute respiratory infections or other "overwhelming" disease.) Next is accidental strangulation caused by choking on food or other objects taken into the mouth, followed by death due to burns (mostly conflagrations), motor vehicles, falls and drowning.

One to Four-Year-Olds

From one to four years is a period of great danger from accidents. The average toddler, still unsteady on his feet, can get into untold trouble through his normal drive to explore everything about his surroundings.

Falls cause almost half of all injuries among one to four-year-olds. Blows and other impact injuries run second. A surprising number of these injuries are inflicted (sometimes accidentally, other times deliberately) by brothers, sisters or playmates. Motor vehicles, too, cause their share of injuries and fatalities.

Too many poisonings in one and two-year-olds result from eating aspirin, particularly sweetened "baby" aspirin unthinkingly left within easy reach. Other New Bedford children swallowed such diverse items as rubbing alcohol, kerosene, mothballs, nail polish, perfume, turpentine, furniture polish, shoe polish and rat poison. Poisoning from chewing or sucking toys, furniture or painted objects containing lead, caused nine per cent of the deaths. Burns too, cause a great many injuries. Children's clothes catch fire. One toddler was scalded when he got into a pail of boiling water his mother left on the floor. Another tried to remove an electric plug with his mouth.

Then there are drownings—second as a cause of death in New Bedford—22.7 per cent of the total. Dr. Starbuck emphasizes that more drownings occur among one-year-olds than at any other single age, and that a major cause is lack of supervision of youngsters who wander away unnoticed from their parents. Still, one New Bedford four-year-old with parents nearby, slipped from a creek bank and drowned. But it needn't be creeks or rivers; bathtubs and back yard pools present dangers, too.

The Reckless Age

Kindergarten and primary school children are in "the reckless age." In New Bedford these youngsters suffered more accidents from being hit by motor vehicles while playing or running into the street, from playing recklessly or in unsafe surroundings, from cutting and piercing instruments and from dog bites than any other age group.

Bicycles are a primary source of accidents. Some children did tricks, ignored traffic regulations, carried things that were too heavy or used bikes too small or too big for them.

Rough play caused injuries from baseball bats, rocks, pipes. One child was hit by another with the sharp end of a stick. Some children, going barefoot, stepped on broken toys and pieces of glass. Cutting and piercing accidents occur at all ages and some are the fault of careless grownups.

Falls cut across all age lines. In New Bedford they caused over one-third of all injuries to children from birth to sixteen and produced 13.7 per cent of the deaths recorded in a six-year period. Many reports came in about babies momentarily unattended who fell off the bed or bath table.

But most falls occur among the one-to-four's who often fall downstairs or trip or run too fast. One New Bedford child fell out of a market basket; a two-year-old climbed on a chair by an open window and fell three floors to his death. Five to sixteen-year-olds also fell often.

Traffic Accidents

Second only to falls in causing injuries are motor vehicle accidents. A New Bedford four-year-old ran in front of a parked car into the fender of a moving one and was killed. There was the seven-year-old playing tag, who dashed into the side of a moving bus and was killed. Traffic mishaps caused the greatest number of New Bedford deaths—40.9 per cent.

As youngsters enter their teens, accidents begin to decline. But boys over ten sustained twice as many accidental injuries as girls! Your son at all ages except early babyhood is likely to suffer more injuries than your daughter. More than four-fifths of those children who died by accident in New Bedford were boys.

Now that you know what accidents are likely to happen, what do you do? The answer: during the first year of life, protect a child completely. Never leave him alone in the house. Then, as he grows, cut down on protectiveness —and increase safety training.

This involves much more than saying "No." Dr. Starbuck suggests these constructive methods: teach as you discipline. That is, say "It's hot," rather than "Don't touch." Use "No" sparingly and when you say it, MEAN it. Never give a command you can't enforce. See that both parents agree in the demands that are made.

Action Program

Here are points New Bedford stresses in its action program:

1. Make your home safer. New Bedford calls this "baby-proofing" the house. This means, for babies, never rely on straps and never leave them unattended on a flat unenclosed surface. For toddlers, it means safety gates at stair headings; locked basement and driveway doors; tight window screens; a back yard free of glass and debris; backyard pools fenced in; fireplace guarded by a fire screen. Also—aspirin, medicines, household cleaners stored out of reach or under lock and key; tools, garden equipment, knives, matches kept out of reach, too; floors free of marbles, buttons, pins, beads; open light sockets covered; firm mattresses, light, loose coverings, no pillows on baby beds; crib

sides kept up; only safe toys provided; a playpen in use at suitable times; pot handles turned so they can't be grabbed by children.

2. Make it safer inside your car. This means a car seat, crib or belt for the youngster under two; keeping older children occupied and sitting down; locking car doors.

Danger from cars in the street can be avoided only one way. *Keep your child out of the street.*

3. Make it safer near water. See that your child learns to swim—the earlier the better. About seventy per cent who drown are non-swimmers. All non-swimmers in boats should wear life jackets. Boats should carry safety equipment. Never overload.

4. Stress bike safety rules. Many accidents occur because of violations of traffic regulations or lack of nighttime safeguards.

"Be sure you follow safety rules yourself," warns Alice B. Miller, R.N., New Bedford program director.

Do you cross streets at corners; look both ways; obey traffic signals; walk, instead of run; face coming traffic when walking on roads; refrain from crossing around parked cars?

In your car, do you keep arms and head inside; drive with your safety belt fastened; drive carefully?

Around water, do you swim only in patrolled areas with lifeguards; refrain from standing up in a small boat; know that you shouldn't swim away from a capsized boat?

As for fire, do you close the flap on a match book before striking; never carry single matches loose in your pocket; break a match in half before throwing it away; burn rubbish in a metal container; refuse to leave an outdoor fire unattended?

Do you watch to see that poisonous household substances aren't stored in food or beverage containers?

Do you choose your baby sitters with care; make sure they understand what to do in an emergency?

Outside your home, you can make safety your business, too—you can be safety-conscious wherever you go. If you see rubbish blocking a theater exit, you can report it. If you find lifeguards not regularly on duty at the swimming pool, you can look into it. Enlisting the interest of other parents, you can take steps to improve your community's safety.

Community Safety Measures

New Bedford has used a variety of approaches to make parents safety-conscious. When parents bring their youngsters to the doctor, the physician calls attention to specific hazards that threaten a child's safety at the particular stage of that child's development. Community public health nurses incorporate accident prevention information in their routine home visits to families. Accident program officials speak to parent groups, P.T.A.'s, mothers' clubs, service clubs, Girl Scouts—anyone who will listen. Specific parent groups are reached through special projects such as the Accident Log, in which 300 New Bedford families recorded every accident to a family member during a period of three months, analyzing it for cause and methods of preventing a repetition. The Greater New Bedford Retail Druggists Association and the schools were also involved, waging an educational campaign against accidental poisoning. The program has supplied over 150,000 copies of child safety suggestions for distribution by physicians and nurses, and has prepared teaching materials such as flip charts and special exhibits. A seven-session course was held on child growth and development with emphasis on accident prevention to help nurses do a more effective safety education job. Press and radio are used constantly. Methods of keeping baby safe are taught in different Red Cross courses for expectant parents and baby sitters.

Advisory Committee

A citizens advisory committee meets regularly and acts as a forum in which the general problems of accident causation in the community are discussed. It has initiated activities resulting in:

- An improved plan for referral of children injured at school.
- New and more adequate material on the treatment of burns for the Fire Department.
- A part-time safety officer in the Police Department.
- A poison information center at the hospital.
- Educational work with children to warn about dog bites.
- A bicycle safety program.
- A stepped-up program of teaching children to swim.
- Training in first aid for summer playground supervisors and municipal beach employees.

This focusing of attention on accidents through one central agency is tremendously important, New Bedford believes. Dr. Starbuck points out that, unfortunately, in most communities there is no single responsible group aware of the total problem. "One of the biggest things we have to combat," he says, "is the resulting lack of awareness of the size and importance of the child accident problem. Also, unfortunately, a feeling of resignation exists in the thought that accidents are bound to happen and you can't do much about them —so why bother? This misconception must be replaced by positive attitudes that accidents can and must be prevented if we are to shoulder our responsibility to our children."   —*By Mary Margaret Kern*

12 RULES FOR BICYCLE SAFETY

CHILDREN love bicycles. They enjoy the exhilarating feeling of going places with speed and dispatch, the feeling of freedom and independence, the feeling of power that comes with their evergrowing skill in making a bicycle do their bidding. All this is as it should be, but it is important for parents to make sure that the youngsters know and observe the rules of the road that will insure safe riding. These can be pretty well summed up in the 12 rules given below.

Naturally parents have a lot to say about the selection of a child's bicycle in the first place. Proper fit affects safety as well as comfort and enjoyment. Adjustable handle bars, seat and pedals allow for growing. Steering apparatus should be firm, brakes even; horn or bell audible at 100 feet; headlight visible at 500 feet and rear light at 300 feet.

In the matter of keeping their bicycles in good riding condition children need to learn what to do, how to do it, then to remember to do it. The what-to-do includes keeping bolts tightened, brakes even, worn or broken parts replaced, bearings cleaned, chain lubricated, horn (or bell) in working order and lights likewise. For safety's sake parents had better keep an eye out to be sure these things are done.

Rules for Safe Riding

1. Ride singly, no passengers, in single file and where cars and pedestrians are not likely to be encountered. The matter of riding singly is a hard rule for children to observe. It is such a temptation to take a friend on the handle bars "just this once." But it is not safe for either passenger or cyclist. Children can learn to use judgment about the single-file riding. Crowded streets are no place for riding two or three abreast but on unused country roads it is a different matter, of course.

2. Use hand signals to indicate turns and keep both hands on the handle bars except when signaling. Signals are made with the left arm. The commonly used signals are forearm up to indicate right turn; arm horizontal for left turn; arm dropped for stop or slow. If other signals are used locally the child should know and use them.

3. Always ride on the right side of the road, near the curb, with no zigzagging in and out of traffic. Weaving in and out of traffic is poor business any time and any driver of an automobile dreads the uncertain swerving that invites trouble. The safe passing of parked cars calls for a lookout for oncoming cars and care that the passing shall not be a split-second race to avoid being side cut.

4. Never ride holding to another vehicle and keep far enough away from

trucks, buses and cars not to be affected by their sudden stops. The temptation is a big one to get over the ground fast and with little effort by holding to a moving vehicle but it is a temptation that in the interest of safety the youngster must learn to resist. Learning at the same time to keep a respectful distance away is a safety detail for which children do not always realize the necessity. They assume that the car will keep moving but it does not always, of course.

5. Carry packages only in a carrier fastened to the bicycle and carry only packages that are small enough not to require taking hands off handle bars to hold them. It is easy enough for children to see the necessity for such a rule as this. Incidentally, grownups may have to watch themselves lest inadvertently they ask that some too-big package be transported.

6. Ride at such a speed that the bicycle is always so well under control that a short emergency stop could be made. This ever-readiness to stop in short distance is a vastly important safety detail. It is a good idea for youngsters to practice doing it so that they have a sure feeling of what they can do. Of course, it means always having brakes in good condition.

7. Always give right of way to cars and pedestrians unless there is a signal from them that they intend to wait. Children often resent being expected to do this. However, arguing over the right of way is unprofitable business and children can learn that there's no need to be always in a hurry.

8. Look in all directions to be sure that intersections are clear before crossing. If cars are approaching be sure there is ample clearance for crossing at normal speed. Here again is a good chance for learning not to go tearing through life on the split second but to take time to be safe. Sometimes children get great fun out of seeing if they can beat the car—but it is not safe fun.

9. Know the local traffic regulations and observe them. This includes noting and observing all traffic signs and signals. It is one thing to know—and another to observe—traffic regulations. It does sometimes seem to be a sort of game to beat the signal. Perhaps seeing grownups do it has its influence!

10. If sidewalk riding is permitted by local ordinance or custom, always give horn or bell signal before passing a pedestrian, and give it in time so that it will not be startling. This is a matter of common courtesy as well as safety. Often youngsters do not think about doing it until they are almost upon the pedestrian.

11. Keep close watch for cars pulling out into traffic, for cars making sudden stops or unsignaled turns; pedestrians also are often unpredictable. One would never want to make children fearful—only watchful—but they do have to learn that you can't always count on the other person in traffic doing what you think he is going to do.

12. In making turns do so only at a speed at which the bicycle is under full control. If there is not a full view of what is around the turn slow down until turn is made and view is clear. In the same way children should get the habit of never coasting down a hill unless they can see what is at the bottom.

—By Grace Langdon, Ph.D.

FIRST AID FOR ACCIDENTS AND ILLNESS

DO you know what to do in case of accident or illness at your home? Your knowledge of how to handle an emergency may mean the difference between unnecessary distress and rapid recovery. We cannot stress too strongly that this knowledge should never be used as a substitute for the expert help your family doctor can give. Remember that you can often avoid serious trouble by calling your doctor promptly at the first sign of illness.

Your Medicine Chest

The items listed below are recommended as basic drugs and first-aid equipment. You may wish to add others or substitute some which your doctor suggests. You will need one roll each of 1-inch and 2-inch sterile gauze; six 1-inch and six 4-inch sterile gauze pads; a roll of 1-inch adhesive tape; aromatic spirits of ammonia; a clinical thermometer; rubbing alcohol (70%); and bicarbonate of soda.

You should also purchase an antiseptic solution, sterile applicators, a remedy for burns, petroleum jelly, aspirin, absorbent cotton, a vaporizer, ice bag, hot-water bottle, eye cup, a diarrhea remedy, and a first-aid manual.

The following questions are those you are most likely to ask in the event of a home emergency:

When should you call a doctor? If your child is acting unlike his usual self he may not be feeling well. Let the doctor decide whether he should see your child. A youngster coming down with an illness may show any of the following symptoms: lack of appetite, running eyes or nose, diarrhea, vomiting, rash, fever.

What symptoms should you report to the doctor? Describe the child's symptoms and behavior and report temperature, character of stools or vomiting and any other unusual condition, such as a rash or swelling. (See article, "If Your Child Has A Fever.")

How do you prepare a hot-water bag for a child? Mix the water in a container and test; if it is comfortably warm on the inside of your wrist, it will be safe for a baby. Fill the bag about half-full and expel the air. Test the bag for leaks and cover it with a towel or other soft material. Refill as needed to keep the water in the bag warm.

How do you treat a small cut? Wash the area thoroughly with soap and water. Dry with sterile gauze or cotton, apply an antiseptic and cover with a piece of sterile gauze or adhesive bandage.

How do you treat a bruise? A bruise is an injury caused by a fall or a blow. A black eye is a bruise. Apply an ice bag or cold compresses to relieve the pain and swelling. If the blow was severe, have the doctor examine the child.

How can you control bleeding? The first and most important thing to do when dealing with an external wound is to stop severe bleeding. Blood flowing in quick spurts means that an artery has been cut; a steady flow means that a vein has been cut. Most bleeding can usually be checked by applying a pressure bandage made up of several layers of gauze. The arm, leg or foot should be elevated. If the bleeding continues even with applied pressure, a tourniquet (bandage twisted tight with stick) should be applied. It *must* be loosened every few minutes to let blood circulate in the limb below the tourniquet. If a doctor is not immediately available, rush child to the hospital.

How do you treat a simple nosebleed? Have the child lie down and apply cold packs to the forehead and nasal areas. If the bleeding continues or is profuse, consult your doctor.

How do you treat frostbite? Signs of frostbite are whiteness and numbness of the flesh. Thaw out the frozen parts slowly by bathing them in cold water. Keep away from heat, fire or hot water and do not rub the parts.

What should you do when a child swallows a poison? Call your doctor at once! Or rush the child to the nearest hospital. Keep a small supply of universal antidote on hand. It can be bought at the drugstore. If the child swallowed a known household preparation, read the label on the container; it may give instructions for the antidote. If you are not sure what caused the poisoning and do not have the universal antidote, give an emetic to induce vomiting. This can be large quantities of warm salt water or soapy solution. Repeat induced vomiting until the fluid comes out clear and then give a soothing drink, like milk or thin starch in water or the raw white of an egg in a little water.

What should you do if the poison is an acid or an alkali? There are two exceptions to the induced vomiting treatment—if the child has swallowed an acid or alkali poison. Acid and alkali poisons leave burns and stains on the victim's lips, tongue and mouth. The antidote for an alkali poison, like lye or ammonia, is a mild acid, such as vinegar or lemon juice. To neutralize acids like oxalic, nitric, sulfuric, give two glassfuls of diluted milk of magnesia or two tablespoonfuls of baking soda in a pint of water or finely powdered chalk in water. Follow treatment for acid and alkali poisoning with a soothing drink of milk or thin starch in water.

How do you handle choking due to a foreign body in the windpipe? Hold the child upside down and slap him on the back. Reach into his mouth and try to grasp the object that is causing the choking. If this does not dislodge the object, rush the child to the hospital.

What do you do if a foreign body is pushed into the nose or ears? Do not try to remove it with homemade instruments and methods. You may push it farther in or cause more damage. Let your doctor remove it.

How should an enema be prepared and given? Your doctor will prescribe the kind of enema and the amount to give. For an older child, you may use an enema bag, raising it gradually to a few feet above him. For infants it is advisable to use a small hand syringe, being careful to force the water in very gently. Let the child lie on his back or side across your lap. Lubricate the nozzle well. The fluid should flow in slowly under moderate pressure.

What do you do when a child is bitten by a dog? It is important that the dog be caught and kept under observation for signs of illness. Your doctor will know whether the Pasteur treatment for prevention of rabies is needed. First wash the wound under *running water,* using soap to remove the animal's saliva. Then see a doctor immediately for further treatment.

What do you do if a child is overcome by carbon monoxide? This is an odorless deadly gas which causes asphyxiation. Break open windows and door before entering any gas-filled room. Do not light a match. Pull the victim into fresh air. If he rallies immediately, keep him quiet and warm until he regains his strength. If breathing has stopped or comes in gasps, start artificial respiration and continue until natural breathing is restored. Administering oxygen through an inhalator helps to restore breathing.

How do you revive a child who has fainted? Loosen all tight clothes. Lay him flat on his back, with head lowered. See that he gets plenty of fresh, cool air. Hold smelling salts or a handkerchief containing a few drops of aromatic spirits of ammonia under his nose every minute or so. When consciousness returns, keep the child lying down and call a doctor.

What do you do about fractures? All fractures need the attention of a doctor. Careless first aid may cause unnecessary distress. When in doubt, handle the injury as a fracture. Keep the child lying down and warm to combat shock. Stop severe bleeding if it is present and then cover the wound with a sterile dressing. If it is necessary to move the child, the limb must be splinted to keep the broken ends of the bone from moving about and doing more serious damage.

How do you treat burns? Small burns. Phone your doctor at once and ask what to do. He may say: cut loose clothing away from burn with scissors; soak, do not pull anything which sticks. Cleanse by pouring quantities of comfortably warm water and soapsuds (bland) over wound. If possible use water that has been boiled. Do not scrub. Do not drain or break blisters. Apply bland burn ointment such as petroleum jelly or mineral oil or whatever your doctor advises; or gauze already impregnated with it. Then sterile elastic bandage, not too tight or swelling may cut off circulation.

Do not apply any harsh antiseptic. Unless doctor advises it, do not use tannic acid, picric acid, boric acid or silver nitrate.

Do not let breath, tears or anything unsterile touch burn. For burn on face use no dressing.

If even a tiny burn becomes hot and red or swollen consult your doctor at once.

Extensive burns. Deadliest dangers are shock and infection. Get medical help fast.

Keep child lying flat or with feet up on pillow even while carried. Calm his fears. Stay with him. Show no panic.

Keep child comfortable but cool rather than warm. Do not take time to give local treatment if you can get doctor. If he is delayed cover burn with clean sheet or pillowcase and take child to nearest hospital.

If it is absolutely necessary for you to give local treatment, dress it as described in the foregoing section on small burns.

Know Your Doctors

The general practitioner or internist is a physician whose training and experience qualify him to diagnose and treat most diseases. He calls in a specialist when he is unable to establish a diagnosis or treat certain illnesses.

The pediatrician deals with children through adolescence—he is their general practitioner. He is concerned with emotional and physical development and care and treatment of children's diseases.

The obstetrician or gynecologist cares for women during pregnancy, childbirth and the period immediately following. He treats women's diseases, especially of the genital and urinary organs and the rectal tract.

The dermatologist is an expert in diseases of the skin, such as acne, hives, skin tumors, ringworm and skin infections.

The allergist devotes his practice to conditions of sensitivity which cause various reactions in the body such as hay fever, asthma and various skin ailments. Substances producing sensitivity include drugs, fungi, pollens, animal hair and foods.

The orthopedist treats diseases, injuries and deformities of the bones and joints. Orthopedics is a branch of surgery.

The ear, nose and throat specialist diagnoses and treats disorders of the ear, nose and throat. He carries out any necessary surgery, such as removing tonsils and adenoids.

The ophthalmologist (oculist) diagnoses and treats eye diseases and conditions dealing with the function of the eyes.

The psychiatrist is concerned with treating persons who are mentally and emotionally disturbed.
—*By Barbara V. Hertz*

DOES YOUR FAMILY HAVE SURVIVAL SKILLS?

SUMMER is the time of happy, carefree days with children exploring and having fun in the out-of-doors. Although we want our youngsters to enjoy the sense of freedom and initiative they get from camping out, fishing, swimming and exploring the neighboring countryside, we must be sure they are safe. And the best safeguard is to prepare them to meet emergencies.

Hiking and Camping Out

Be sure to wear sturdy shoes and sensible comfortable clothing when hiking. In rocky terrain or dense undergrowth wear leather boots, long heavy pants, and a long-sleeved shirt. These are a protection against insects, snakes, brambles and poisonous plants. Under a blazing sun, be sure to wear a hat.

The following items are considered essential for an overnight camping trip: a compass, matches in a waterproof container, knife, flashlight, first-aid kit, whistle for signaling, food rations, cooking utensils, a sleeping bag or bed roll, mosquito repellent, strong soap (in case of poison ivy), water purification tablets, and a map of the area.

If you build a fire at your campsite, you must first have a permit from your local fire warden or conservation officer. Then follow these rules: scrape the fire site bare of burnable material; cut away all overhanging branches; circle the fireplace with stones. Before leaving the campsite, douse the fire with water. In rain, snow or wind, some natural shelter—such as a cliff or a clump of trees—will keep a fire from going out.

Hiking in unfamiliar places. When you hike through unfamiliar territory, look out for such pitfalls as protruding and loose rocks untested for footing, abandoned pits and wells camouflaged by vines and brush. Be extremely careful when venturing into swamps and bogs—don't pull a disappearing act!

Insect bites. Serious situations can develop from the bites of some kinds of insect:

The tick. A flat brownish bug less than ¼ inch long that burrows into the skin. It is deadly when infected with "spotted fever." When camping or hiking, inspect your entire body each night. If you find a tick embedded, *never* try to pull it out. It will let go and back out if you touch it with a drop of kerosene or scorch its rear with a lighted match. The latter sounds drastic, but better this than tick fever.

Black widow spider. Common throughout the United States. Up to ⅝ of an inch long, it has a crimson hourglass marking on the abdomen. Give it a wide berth. If bitten, send for a doctor. Stay quiet and keep warm until he comes.

The tarantula. Prevalent in the South and West. It has velvety body and legs. Is the largest of all spiders. Is not likely to bite unless you deliberately tease it.

Poisonous snakes. Find out if poisonous snakes are common in your locality. If they are, it's safest to wear high boots, carry a snake-bite kit and be wary where you step when you go hiking. There are two types of poisonous snakes in this country. Pit vipers, with long, movable fangs, have flat heads and a pit below and behind the nostril which is situated at the end of the snout. Rattlesnakes, copperheads and water moccasins belong to this group. The other group, coral snakes, have short, fixed fangs.

Rattlesnake. Found across the country, its tail ends in a series of horny, loosely connected rings which clash together with a buzzing sound. There are 15 species.

Copperhead. Also exists in most parts of the country. Colored golden brown with Y-shaped darker blotches on the back, the top of the head is pure copper-red.

Water moccasin. Found in the South and Southwest, it loses its marking as it ages. Becomes dark brown or black, dark gray or olive with light marks on each side of the head.

Coral snake. Found along coast and lowlands of the South. It is marked with broad bands of red and black, separated by narrow yellow stripes. The front of the head is black, the back part yellow.

Poisonous plants. An irritating, itchy rash can follow contact with certain plants. Be able to identify and avoid them.

Poison ivy. A climbing or crawling plant found on tree trunks and poles or close to the ground, along roadsides and at the edge of woods. Its shiny, dark green leaves always grow in groups of three and turn red in the fall. Has white berries.

Poison oak. Similar to ivy but the edges of the three leaves are notched more deeply and the tips are more rounded.

Poison sumac. A shrub with white stalks and drooping clusters of white berries. Poison sumac is found in swampy areas. If you suspect that you have been in contact with one of these, wash exposed areas with warm water and a strong soap lather half a dozen times. Follow with an application of rubbing alcohol.

If You Get Lost

Stay calm and try to get your bearings by one of the following methods: Check your compass. If you have none, a watch can substitute. Point the hour hand to the sun. Halfway between that and twelve o'clock is the south. Climb a nearby hill or a tree and take a look around. At night, look for the North Star. In mountainous country, locate a stream and follow it down, not up. You're bound to find a settlement eventually.

If darkness is less than two hours away, stay put and seek shelter. If possible find a windbreak—a rock, ledge, or log—and place yourself between this and a fire which will provide warmth and a signal for searchers. Even in summertime, the nights in hills and woods can be cold. Lacking a fire, you might find shelter in a natural cave or on a ledge against which sticks and brush may be leaned, or beneath a fallen tree trunk with branches piled over it. As a last resort, grass, pine needles or leaves piled under and on top of you will offer some warmth.

Mother Nature supplies a generous variety of edible foods, such as dandelions, water cress, milkweed flowers, palatable nuts, wild plums, strawberries, raspberries, blackberries, and blueberries. However, unless you know your botany well, be careful of what you eat out-of-doors. In any case, beware of the following highly poisonous plants:

Water hemlock. One of the commonest and most deadly brookside plants, it has a hollow stem with smooth, celery-like leaves and white flowers. Any part of this plant is poisonous to eat.

Pokeweed. Stay away from the root and berries of this common flowering branch with greenish white blossoms, red stalks, and fleshy, dark purple fruit.

Mountain laurel. The leaves are evergreen, the flowers pink. The very young plants are highly poisonous.

Mushrooms. It's a wise idea to avoid all wild mushrooms, but be especially wary of one called Death Cup, practically pure white with white gills and so named because the lower end of the stem rests in a cup-like envelope. Fly-Amanita, almost as fatal, is distinguished by a bulbous and scaly lower stem.

First Aid for Injuries

If you're off in the woods or the hills, by yourself or with friends, it's not always possible to get a doctor in a hurry in case of injury. Know how to help yourself until help arrives. (To control bleeding see article, First Aid For Accidents And Illness.)

Treating snake bite. If you are bitten by a poisonous snake, stay quiet, and proceed immediately with the following steps:

• Tie a constricting band two inches above the fang marks just firm enough to make the surface veins stand out.

• Sterilize a sharp penknife or razor blade.

• Apply iodine to bites.

• Avoiding veins, make an X-shaped cut a quarter inch long and deep in each of the two fang marks.

• Use suction over each wound alternately for an hour.

• Lacking a suction cup, suck venom by mouth, spitting out blood and poison.

• If help has not come in an hour, move the band up two inches, make a ring of cuts around the first ones and continue suction until doctor arrives.

• Never run for help yourself, since such motion may speed the poison's course through your system.

In case of shock. Shock often follows injuries. The symptoms are faintness and nausea. If a companion shows these signs of distress, proceed as follows:

• Make him lie down on his back.
• Elevate his lower extremities six to twelve inches.
• Keep him warm.

Water Safety

The ability to swim is itself a survival skill. It is also a favorite summer pastime and has its own rules for safety:

Never enter cold water when overheated.

In unknown waters, enter feet first before diving, to determine depth and locate submerged objects.

Stay reasonably close to shore.

Swim within hailing distance of another person, especially if you're not an expert swimmer.

If you find yourself exhausted, too far from shore for comfort, don't get panicky. Rest awhile by floating, sculling or one of the other survival swimming skills.

Cramps are painful and frightening. They usually occur in chilled, tired muscles. If you get one:

Inflate lungs.

Roll into face-down position.

Apply pressure to the cramped area with one or both hands.

Lifesaving. If a fellow swimmer is floundering you will, of course, want to help, but there is one unbreakable rule if you are not a trained lifesaver. *Keep out of his reach.* A drowning person will seize anything. If he clings to you, both of you may drown. If you find that you cannot manage to bring him safely back to shore at least save yourself.

When a victim is near shore, take a firm grip on dock, tree or other solid object and extend to him: your hand, your leg, a pole, stick or oar, an article of clothing. Pull victim to shore.

In deep water, wade or swim to victim. Approach him from behind so he can't grab you. Grasp him by the back of his wrist, a bathing suit strap or his hair and pull him in.

If you're over your depth the hair carry is best. With one hand grasping his hair, turn on your side and stroke hard with both legs and your free hand until you reach the shore.

In order to keep a greater distance from the victim, swim a plank or pole ahead of you and offer the free end to the victim. If he doesn't grab it at once, press it firmly against his chest and he'll almost surely respond if he's conscious. Then tow him in.

Artificial respiration. If you do not know the standard method, the Red Cross recommends these instructions for the mouth-to-mouth method:

Remove foreign matter from victim's mouth.

Tilt victim's head back so chin is pointing upward. Pull or push the jaw into a jutting-out position to move the base of the tongue away from the back of the throat.

Place your mouth, opened wide, tightly over victim's mouth. Pinch the victim's nostrils shut and blow into his mouth.

Remove your mouth, turn your head to the side and listen for the return rush of air. Repeat blowing effort. For an adult, blow hard at rate of about twelve breaths a minute, for a child take more shallow breaths, about twenty a minute.

If you do not get air exchange, recheck the head and jaw position. If you still do not get air exchange turn victim on his side and give him a few sharp blows between his shoulder blades to dislodge foreign matter.

Boating

Regardless of the type of boat you have, there are certain safety rules you should observe:

Be sure you can handle your craft.

Check coastal weather reports and stay home if storm warnings are out.

Wear a life preserver if you can't swim.

Never overload a boat.

Take along a bailing receptacle.

Stay reasonably close to shore.

Be sure to keep track of time and tide.

Avoid stunting and recklessness.

Head for shore fast if electrical storm is brewing.

Rowboats and canoes. Both are easily tipped over, so it's important to balance the load whether it's people, fishing tackle or bed rolls and camping equipment. Always step in the center when getting in. Be careful to keep the balance if you change seats with another person.

If a storm comes up: Head your boat into the wind and waves.

Keep your body weight and cargo low.

If storm is extreme, lie in bottom of boat and ride it out.

If you're caught in a strong current, the trick is to work off diagonally toward shore.

Motor boats. One of the most common mistakes people make is to put a powerful outboard motor on a small rowboat. This can lead to disaster. Be sure that motor power is proportionate to boat size. Avoid the temptation to make fast, sharp turns. Before you take off, check to see that you have the following on board:

A life preserver for each person, a fire extinguisher, oars, reserve container of gasoline.

What to Do if Boat Capsizes

How to right a canoe. A canoe is the easiest craft to handle. If it capsizes, you can turn it right side up again without help.

Proceed as follows:

- Pull easily and steadily on keel.
- Grasp the near gunwale and continue pulling until canoe is upright.
- Hold near gunwale between two thwarts with one hand. Reach across with other hand and grasp far gunwale.
- Lie prone on water.
- Kick your feet.

• Draw water-filled canoe under you. Once in, spread your legs and push back against the midship thwart to keep canoe steady. Now you're ready to paddle home. If paddles are lost, slow progress can be made by paddling with both your hands.

Staying afloat. It's better to hang on to any available flotation and await rescue than to risk drowning by trying to swim ashore. A boat, whether water-filled or capsized, will stay afloat. If you become separated from your boat, cling to boat seat, cushion, paddle or oar, or water wings made from clothing.

To make water wings, tie knots in the legs of slacks. Hold them aloft by the waist and throw them as if opening a paper bag. A combination of air and water is forced into the opening and the slacks become water wings. You can do the same thing with a buttoned shirt.

Survival Swimming

If you lack flotation, remove shoes and cumbersome clothing and resort to these survival swimming methods which will help you conserve your energy:

Dog paddle. Arms move as in crawling. Legs kick up and down.

Floating. Lie on your back, ears in water, arms extended to the sides with your palms up and breathe deeply.

Backstroke. Lie on your back, arms at sides. Move hands up to armpits. Then stretch arms outward in line with shoulders and sweep them in an arc to starting position. Legs go through a similar motion to arms, both in unison.

Sculling. In a floating position move your legs up and down, your hands back and forth as if smoothing sand.

Treading water. With body upright, chin at surface, make the arms scull water while your legs go in a walking motion.

Fishing

Fish hooks can be dangerous when handled carelessly. One morning a boy was fishing alone off a dock. When a hook became imbedded in his hand, he wisely stepped back from the edge. Seconds later he fainted, falling on the dock, instead of in the water. He could have avoided all this if only he had followed these safety rules:

• Pick up hooks by their shafts only.
• Never leave hooks lying around.

• Keep extras in a covered box or with points stuck in a cork.

• Look before you cast to make sure no one is in range of your line.

• Take a firm grip on both fish and hook when removing the latter—a slip can mean a hook in your finger.

If you do get hooked, cut your line and go to a doctor. *Never* try to pull out an imbedded fish hook.

Many a boat has overturned because of uncontrolled excitement over a hooked fish or by feet becoming tangled in the anchor rope. Watch out for these hazards.

Fish to avoid. The following fish can inflict painful wounds. If you catch one, cut your line and let him go.

Sting ray. It's found from Chesapeake Bay southward, shaped like a disk with a long whip-like tail.

Scorpionfish. Found in both Atlantic and Pacific oceans. Mottled red and brown.   —*By Arnold A. Fenton, D.D.*

TAKE HIM— OR PHONE THE DOCTOR?

WHEN a child seems ill or feverish many a mother wonders what to do. Should she take her child to the doctor's office, ask the doctor to come to the house or just telephone? These questions and others like them, common to most parents' experience, were put to a number of representative pediatricians. Here are their answers.

When is it reasonable to phone the doctor? Phoning is justified if any *one* of the following conditions exists.

1. Fever of more than a degree and a half—that is, temperature over 101.5 (by rectum). Or low-grade fever, under 101.5, that persists (about 100, rectally, is normal).

2. Dramatic change from a youngster's usual behavior or attitudes—for instance, a pepless and draggy siege when he is usually full of energy.

3. Sore throat, runny nose or cough.

4. Total loss of appetite (if he is not "snacking" it away).

5. Nausea or vomiting.

6. Persistent pain, including severe headache.

7. Diarrhea.

8. Anything out of the ordinary in the appearance of the skin, like blotches, rash, pustules or excessive redness or paleness.

The tiny baby cannot communicate in words how he feels. You should call the doctor if, in addition to any of the above symptoms, he—

9. Cries when he urinates or defecates.

10. Pulls repeatedly at his ear or slaps at it or turns and shakes his head violently.

11. Is unusually fussy.

12. Doesn't sleep—or sleeps markedly more than usual.

13. Loses weight progressively.

A very good reason for phoning, when you're really concerned, is just for reassurance.

If you do decide to call the doctor, don't panic. Few illnesses hinge on an hour or two. If, however, you feel there's a real emergency—if the child seems very ill or is in great pain—insist on talking to the doctor at once or as soon as he can be located.

Never underestimate the common childhood diseases. If measles are going around, for example, and you suspect your child has been exposed, by all means call the doctor promptly.

What sort of information does the doctor need? Before you start dialing, have well in mind—you might even jot down—the symptoms that are out of the ordinary. All the doctor has to go on in a telephone diagnosis is what you report to him, so be thorough. Specifically, you should be able to report:

1. Temperature, preferably rectal, how long it's been going on, when it was last taken. By mouth or by rectum?

2. Any condition that isn't present in health, such as the symptoms indicated above.

Should you wait until morning to phone? The question implies, of course, that an illness bobs up or gets worse at night. Most parents are aware that their doctor is a human being with a life of his own outside of his profession. We naturally hate to break into his home life unnecessarily.

Doctors themselves prefer to be called at night *if the parent is in doubt.* Health, after all, is the doctor's business, and if it is endangered he wants to know about it so he can treat the ailment early. On the other hand, doctors understandably feel irritated if parents get concerned in the night about an illness which has been running all day, and about which they have neglected to seek help during office hours.

In short, do what you can to relieve the child. If he gets worse, instead of better, call the doctor. No thinking parent will rout out the doctor for a toe-ache which could be endured till morning. But if the child can't stand the toe-ache, or if you can't stand the child's suffering, pick up the telephone.

Should the child be taken to the doctor's office? Most doctors agree that if a child is not too sick to be moved comfortably he can be taken to the office with no ill effects. Most doctors prefer their patients to come to them. More thorough examination and treatment are possible at the office than at home. A trained nurse and diagnostic equipment are available—and the doctor can usually see the child sooner, too, than by making a house call. Caution: dress the child adequately, see that he keeps warm and comfortable during the journey, and suffers no undue fatigue.

A child suspected of having a contagious disease should be seen at home unless the doctor has a separate entrance and waiting room for such cases. Also, in case of serious accident or acute infection, it is better for the child to be examined at home.

If you have any misgivings about whether it is safe to take your child down to the office or not, tell your fears and reasons to the doctor over the telephone. He will advise you.

Is telephone diagnosis reliable? Some doctors will not diagnose over the telephone. Most do. Some pediatricians treat more than half their cases over the wire. However, these are patients whom they know, whom they have examined personally in the past, and whose parents know and trust their doctor.

Usually, the doctor knows what diseases are "going around" at the time and is able to pinpoint an ailment accurately if he has a good report of symptoms. The pediatrician invariably asks for a report back if the patient is not better in a day's time, and may then recommend an examination.

"To be technical," said one pediatrician, "a doctor should *always* see his patient when called. We don't—because we can't. If we made house calls on all patients, or even saw them in the office, we'd never get done."

When should you ask for a house visit? Doctors generally recommend the house call:

1. When it is better for a child not to be moved, as in acute infection, fracture, severe head injury or a serious accident where the injury is obscure.

2. When the parents find it much more comfortable.

A doctor usually says frankly that he can do a better job at the office, that he can see the patient sooner if he is brought in, and that the cost will be less. If the parents still want him, he'll come.

"It's worthwhile," one doctor said, "if it makes the parents feel easier. Mental anguish is just as real as physical pain. And being willing to make house visits helps a doctor's relations with the parents of his patients, too."

Is telephoning an imposition, since the advice is often not charged for? Most doctors like and expect to use the telephone a great deal. It enables them to keep in touch with their patients. By its intelligent use they can treat an illness earlier and more effectively.

But here are a few considerations to prevent running the privilege into the ground:

1. Find out if your doctor has preferred hours for incoming calls. If not, write down his office hours and try to make your calls within them.

2. Except in emergency, call as early during office hours as possible. Not only does the doctor appreciate it, but you will get better and more un-hurried advice by avoiding end-of-the-day calls, and better service from the pharmacy if prescriptions are needed.

3. Make your report complete, but brief.

4. In calling for an office or house appointment, don't insist on talking to the doctor. Let the office nurse make the arrangements.

What about pay for telephone calls? Pay for telephone advice varies with doctors. Many charge nothing, even in these days of the high cost of illness. If your doctor is new, and you are wondering whether he charges for phone calls, ask him. Most of those who do charge, make the fee nominal. One doctor charged a dollar if he ordered a prescription, nothing if he didn't.

So if in doubt—TELEPHONE! Let your doctor decide whether your child needs his attention or not.

—By Fletcher D. Slater

COMMON SENSE
IN THE SICKROOM

EVERY mother knows that taking care of a sick child at home requires all the patience, buoyancy and ingenuity that she can muster. There are certain ways of handling the situation that make it easier for the child and the mother.

Be sure the child understands the temporary nature of his illness. The limitations of a young child's knowledge are hard to realize sometimes—one four-year-old actually thought the rash he had accompanying measles would be permanent, if he survived the illness at all! Reassurance with such vague generalities as "There, there, you'll be all right," are inadequate for a child. He should be told in simple terms the reasons for prescribed treatment and bed rest. A description of the body fighting germs appeals to his imagination and may help him to be more reasonable about following instructions.

Don't forget the patient in your concern about the germs. If you are too preoccupied with the fear that other members of the family may contract a highly infectious illness, it may appear to the child that you have forgotten him completely! Naturally, throwing caution to the winds in the matter of isolation and sterilization is not recommended, but reasonable precautions can be observed without making your patient feel unimportant and neglected. All children need mothers who, in spite of the extra job of nursing, still have time just to be with the invalid.

Don't make sickness more attractive than health. If the young invalid is pampered and generally spoiled while ill, he may draw the conclusion that he likes to be sick because it pays off so well!

Teaching Hospital Techniques

Use this opportunity to familiarize the child with hospital techniques just in case. Do you change an invalid's bedding in the accepted hospital style? Do you arrange a bell or other simple call system with which your youngster can summon you? Each hospital procedure you can make familiar to him will make the hospital that much less strange should he ever need to stay there.

Naturally, when your child is ill and prone to exaggerate all fears anyhow, it would be extremely unwise to label such practice as hospital technique. Such information can be mentioned in casual conversation later, when the child is well.

Do not permit thoughtless visitors. When a child is ill he needs security and reassurance more than ever. Think of the confusion created in his mind by visitors who doubt the doctor's course of treatment openly; who ridicule the appearance of patient (rash, swelling and so forth); or who say, "What a shame you have to miss Nancy's party," or otherwise bring up the dismal fact of isolation. Be sure that your visitor will not behave in this way before you let him see your child. Briefing may be in order.

Convalescent Activities

As his convalescence begins, a child may sometimes feel that while ages of misery may be past, eons of boredom stretch ahead. Start him on a project that will emphasize his return to normal activities. A mother used one January convalescence to make Valentines. Spring, favorite time for many childhood diseases to strike, is ideal for a leisurely planning for summer vacation. Camp brochures, bulletins on local crafts classes, travel folders relative to a possible family jaunt, are all available from various sources and provide hours of fascinating study and speculation.

In one local school system, students in the lower grades are not required to do actual class assignments while convalescing—authorities wisely feel that the child should recover completely first and then make up any work he has missed. However, one sick second-grader was so interested in his class study of local history that his mother obtained some library books from the children's section for him to dip into while recovering from an illness. During his convalescence he learned considerably more than he would have had time to absorb while carrying on normal classwork.

Or perhaps you can encourage your invalid to plan a party around a theme that interests him, perhaps a cowboy party or for a girl a paper doll party. Let him put his ingenuity to work making favors and decorations, planning games and menu.

Seek Outside Help

Draw on outside assistance. As soon as a childhood disease crops up, drop postcards notifying a dozen good friends and relatives, "Bruce just came down with measles. Expecting period of boredom two and one-half weeks. Will you send a card to break the monotony?" The appeal was successful for one mother. One relative sent a surprise package of little puzzles, another offered to lend her child's anthill under glass (*what* a hit that made!) and an especially gifted friend sent an original story with sketches.

Try to keep the most important engagements on your social calendar. It is not necessary or wise to stay by the bedside day in and day out when recovery is proceeding normally. If the child is left in competent hands, he usually enjoys the company of someone else after such an unavoidably large dose of Mother. A change gives your spirits a lift, and your child knows that when you begin to go out again he's getting well.   —*By Anne Barnes*

IF YOUR CHILD HAS A FEVER

MANY people have an exaggerated fear of fever. Fever is not a disease but a symptom, as is a headache or vomiting. Although we don't go to bed every time we develop a slight headache or tuck Junior between covers when he throws up, we do regard both as warnings that something is not quite right and we try to find out what it is.

The same is true of fever. It may be a mild symptom of some minor upset or a danger signal of serious illness, depending not on the degree of fever as much as on its frequency and persistence. In other words, a low-grade mouth temperature of 99.8 or 100 degrees that returns persistently every afternoon can be a warning of something far more serious than a fever which suddenly shoots to 104 degrees and is gone the next day.

Fever is an elevation in body temperature that usually indicates nature is attempting to fight an alien invader. The invader may be the common cold or an army of troublesome measles germs. Nature may be battling a germ that has set up an infection in the throat or in a cut finger, or it may be waging war against some hidden source of infection such as a diseased appendix or tonsils.

Fever a Warning Signal

Whatever it is, it has no business being there and Nature's protest is shown by fever. As such, it is good. Not only is it battling against the enemy but also it is flying a distress signal asking your help. Fever does have its good points. In certain conditions, doctors induce artificial fever to help fight disease.

Though the presence of fever in a child should not send a mother into a frenzy of futile worry, this doesn't mean that she should be unconcerned about it. Fever is a warning which should be heeded.

The medicine chest of every home should contain at least one reliable clinical thermometer, mouth or rectal. One of each would be better, the rectal or stubby bulb thermometer for babies and young children, the mouth thermometer for older youngsters and adults. Moreover, every mother should know how to use a thermometer correctly and judiciously. Even the most experienced nurse cannot gauge a high fever accurately by simply feeling the patient's forehead. If it is hot and dry, she may conclude there is a fever. But exactly how high that fever is she cannot judge with accuracy, and the insidious low fever she would miss altogether. There is no sure way to determine body temperature except by means of a good clinical thermometer.

Temperature

But even the clinical thermometer can be of little value unless the mother understands something about its use, about fever in general and about so-called normal temperatures.

The "average-normal" temperature is about 98.6 degrees Fahrenheit by mouth. This means approximately 99.6 degrees by rectum, since the rectal temperature usually runs about one degree higher than the mouth. Since there is no absolute normal in body temperature any more than there is in any other body function, a variation of one full degree above or below the so-called normal should not be considered evidence of illness unless it is accompanied by definite body disturbance.

Even the healthiest of us would probably be surprised were we to take our temperatures every two hours some day when we were feeling at our best, to see the fluctuation which often occurs throughout the day.

Most doctors agree, however, that a mouth temperature of around 100 degrees, with or without other symptoms, should be an indication that something is going on and the patient should be watched.

Using a Thermometer

What about thermometers themselves? Perhaps you know that when buying a thermometer you should be sure to get one that is made by a reputable manufacturer and guaranteed for accuracy in registration. Poor thermometers are worse than none at all.

Learn how to read it. Your druggist will be glad to show you how. It is a good idea to stand with your back to the light, holding the thermometer horizontally in your right hand and on a level with your eyes. A slight rolling motion with the thumb and forefinger brings the column of mercury into view as a silver streak.

Learn how to shake it down after using, and why this is necessary. The mercury in a good clinical thermometer will always remain where it registers until it is shaken down. It is made that way for accuracy's sake. A constriction in the mercury path keeps it at the degree registered.

When shaking it down, it is a good idea to do it over the bed just in case you drop it. Hold the thermometer firmly between thumb and fingers by its top, not its bulb end. Flick it with a quick, jerking motion of the wrist until you have shaken the mercury down to at least 96 degrees. Do this each time you take a temperature.

Cleansing a Thermometer

To cleanse any thermometer before and after using, wipe it first with a piece of tissue or cotton, and rinse under cold water. Then, with your fingers or a piece of cotton, soap the bulb carefully and rinse in cold water again. Wipe with cotton dipped in alcohol and rinse off. If it is to be used regularly in the sickroom, keep it in a small glass of antiseptic solution (alcohol or other kind). A light layer of cotton placed in the bottom of the glass will provide a protective bed against breakage. Rinse the antiseptic off the thermometer with cold water before using.

A thoroughly cleansed rectal or stubby bulb thermometer may be used to take a mouth temperature if necessary. The rectal thermometer has a short, rounded bulb; the mouth, a slim, somewhat pointed one. It is unwise to use the mouth thermometer for the rectum because of this slim, pointed bulb. It may cause discomfort when inserted and it breaks more readily.

When taking either a mouth or rectal temperature, and particularly when reporting the readings to your doctor, be sure to tell him which type of temperature it is, keeping in mind that the rectal temperature registers one degree higher than the mouth.

Taking a Temperature

To take a mouth temperature, first, be sure that the thermometer is shaken down to at least 96 degrees. Place the bulb end under the patient's tongue, instructing him to keep his tongue over the thermometer and his lips, not his teeth, tightly closed. Leave it in at least three minutes. Supporting the thermometer with the hand does not alter the reading as so many people think. Remove after three minutes and read in degrees and tenths. Each degree is marked off in fifths, each fifth equals two tenths—as 98 degrees and 6 tenths. No matter how long the thermometer is left in, it will not register more than the body temperature. But if it is not left in long enough, you may not get an accurate fever reading.

Never take a mouth temperature directly after eating or drinking, after brushing the teeth or gargling or coughing or smoking. Any of these things may temporarily prevent accurate registration of the body temperature.

Few children under six years are capable of holding the mouth thermometer safely under the tongue without dropping or biting it. For these children, for young babies, for any patient who for some reason is unable to keep his mouth closed over the thermometer or to follow directions, the rectal temperature is advisable.

Rectal Thermometers

When taking the rectal temperature, follow the same precaution in seeing that the thermometer is shaken down to 96 degrees. Cover the tip with some kind of lubrication, gently separate the buttocks with one hand and insert the thermometer with the other, about 1 to 1½ inches. Let go of the thermometer but keep your hand ready to replace it if it starts to slip out. Holding the thermometer rigidly is not wise, for a sudden movement from the child may cause it to break. Leave the thermometer in at least four minutes. Remove, cover your patient and wipe the thermometer with a tissue. If necessary, place it in a safe spot until you have made the patient comfortable.

Then read it, cleanse and replace in case or jar.

Though the clinical thermometer should unquestionably be in every household medicine chest, it should be used as judiciously as the bandages and antiseptics. Here is a list of conditions which may or may not be accompanied by fever. But if they are, you certainly want to know about it. Pain—abdominal, ear, legs or joints, chest; sore throat; rashes; vomiting or retching; body aches as in grippe, symptoms of head or chest colds; chills, sudden changes in feeling, hot then cold; injuries; unusual quietness or drowsiness in otherwise active child; unusual restlessness in sleep; shooting leg pains, especially if accompanied by frequent nosebleed; extreme thirst; refusal to eat by usually hungry child; extreme pallor or flushed appearance or other "sick look." If even slight fever accompanies any of these symptoms, you should put your youngster to bed and consult your doctor.

Don't give medicine for reducing fever unless your doctor has ordered it. Your doctor is the one to take steps to lower a fever and bring relief. Your job is to know how to handle it intelligently.   —By Adeline Bullock, R.N.

WHEN MOTHER IS NURSE

EVERY doctor knows that the nursing care a sick child gets determines to a large extent how soon he will recover. Usually mother is nurse, and added to her household duties is the additional one of caring for the young patient. It is not an easy task, but it can be handled with greater efficiency and ease if the setting is right. Then, too, there are certain simple but fundamental rules which a mother should observe for the well-being of the patient and for the safety of the rest of the family.

For his own protection as well as to safeguard other members of the family, the patient should be in a room by himself. A southeastern exposure, because it provides more sunshine and for longer periods each day, is better than other exposures. Next, see that his bed is a good one. The mattress should be smooth, firm, free from lumps. One or two pillows will be useful for support of the patient's body, with several smaller ones to tuck in here and there. The covers should always be light in weight and right for the season. Too heavy covers can easily cause overheating, with an increase in temperature.

Place the bed in such a way that the patient will not be forced to face a bright light, either natural or artificial. Allow fresh air to circulate in the room continuously, but keep draughts from the patient as they tend to cause chills. Open windows at top and bottom for ventilation. Sixty-eight to seventy degrees is the best temperature for a sickroom. Avoid sudden changes in room temperature. These are especially undesirable when the patient has a cold or influenza, as such changes irritate bronchial mucosa and induce coughing. If it is necessary to place the bed between two windows, the patient may be protected from a draught by putting a blanket over a chair or placing a screen in front of one or both windows.

Daily bath. A daily bath for the patient in bed is essential for several reasons. Chief among them is the fact that it stimulates his circulation. In bed he is deprived of normal exercise and as a result there is decreased elimination from the skin. The bath with its accompanying massage serves as a form of exercise and improves circulation. Good circulation, especially for a patient with fever, is needed to bring the wastes of metabolism to the surface of the skin and to rid the body of toxins. The bath has definite therapeutic value. The skin can destroy any bacteria on its surface; the cleaner the skin, the greater its power. Oils from sebaceous glands have a tendency to coat the microorganisms on an unwashed skin, preventing actual contact with the skin.

A third important reason for the daily bath is that it raises the patient's self-respect. Feeling clean and looking clean, plus fresh linen on his bed, gives him a lift, a sense of well-being. It helps to overcome depression and, feeling relaxed and comfortable, the patient often falls into a peaceful, restful sleep as a result.

When bathing the patient, expose no more of his body than is necessary, to guard against chilling. Wrap the washcloth around the hand like a mitt, thus preventing dangling of ends which feel cold and wet to the patient. Change the water frequently enough to keep it at a uniform temperature between 105 and 110 degrees F. The patient will enjoy putting his hands and feet in the water. Follow the bath with an alcohol rub and powder. Use long, firm, even strokes, proceeding in an orderly manner, and stop before the patient gets too tired.

Mouth care. Oral hygiene is important because it raises resistance to infections—most organisms enter the body through the nose and mouth.

If the patient is very ill, applicators moistened with any good mouth wash or dentifrice may be more acceptable than a brush for teeth cleaning. One teaspoon each of salt and baking soda in a glass of water is excellent. Cleanse or rinse the mouth several times a day and before and after each meal. Gargles of salt and soda solution often relieve an irritated throat.

To prevent cracking of the lips, which often occurs with fever, apply cold cream or oil.

Diet in the acute state of illness is liquid. This is necessary because whenever fever is present the water balance of the body is disturbed due to sweating. Increasing the liquid in the diet helps to replace the water lost. Liquids also help eliminate toxins, thereby reducing body temperature. Strained fruit juices are excellent.

Don't Force Food

Don't try to force food on a child with a lagging appetite at this time. His appetite will return when he feels better. The doctor will suggest a suitable diet.

As the fever subsides, the patient's appetite and desires are a fairly safe guide in convalescence, provided he doesn't overeat. To do so might cause an upset in digestion and elimination, thus retarding his recovery.

The doctor may order steam inhalations to relieve a cough. Antiseptics such as tincture of benzoin—one teaspoon to a pint of water—help loosen and increase secretions. There is excellent equipment for such treatment on the market, but lacking it, a teakettle and electric plate may be used.

If the patient suffers from headache, an ice bag may relieve it, and eyes will feel more comfortable with cold or warm moist boric acid compresses of gauze. Frequent back rubs with rubbing alcohol relieve aching and general discomfort. Tepid baths will help reduce temperature. Follow your doctor's orders in regard to them.

Prevent contagion. Every precaution should be taken to prevent spread of the illness to others. Paper handkerchiefs or absorbent cotton should be used for secretions of the nose and throat and these should then be collected in paper bags. Fill the bags only two-thirds full and close before removing them from the bedside to be burned. The person who takes care of the patient should wear a mask over the nose and mouth. Excellent masks are on the market, or they can be made from two or three thicknesses of gauze cut six by four or five inches. Tapes at each corner should be long enough to tie at the back of the head.

Often a child may have a light attack of a disease but suffer serious after-effects. This is particularly true in the case of influenza and the common cold. Middle ear infections, pneumonia, acute sinus, pleurisy are some possible complications. Often, they can be avoided by good care.

—*By Elinor Neal, R.N.*

PREVENTIVE INOCULATIONS

TYPE OF INJECTION	FIRST INOCULATIONS	BOOSTER DOSES
DIPHTHERIA TOXOID	Series of 2 or 3 monthly shots begun at age 1 to 6 months.	Booster 1 year later; Schick test for immunity at age 4 years; booster just before entering school.
TETANUS TOXOID	Series of 2 or 3 monthly shots begun anytime between 1 month and 3 years of age.	Booster shot within a year after first shots and every 3 years thereafter.
WHOOPING COUGH VACCINE	Series of 3 monthly shots begun as early as age 1 month.	Immunity develops 3 to 5 months after shots. Booster doses 1 and 2 years later, and every 3 years thereafter.
ABOVE THREE COMBINED * (D.P.T. SHOTS)	Series of 3 monthly shots begun at age 1 month.	Booster dose 6 months later and again at age 3 years.
POLIO VACCINE (SALK)	May be begun as early as 2 months. Older children and adults under 40 (including pregnant women) should also be inoculated. Series of 3 shots, 4–6 weeks between 1st and 2nd, 3rd 7 months later.	A 4th shot, 1 year or more later, is now recommended by many doctors.
SMALLPOX VACCINE	A single shot, given preferably by age 6–12 months, no later than age 3 years; consult doctor.	Repeated upon entering school and every 5 years thereafter.
TYPHOID VACCINE	Series of 3 shots, 2–4 weeks apart, usually not given to infants unless they travel or live under unsanitary conditions. Recommended at age 2 and older where water supply is not purified, and for those who travel and those in the armed services.	Repeat booster doses yearly while danger persists.

* Many doctors use this 3-in-1 combination instead of the 3 separate injections. If there is a polio epidemic in the community, doctors may advise postponing inoculations (other than Salk). A new vaccine has been developed adding polio vaccine to the 3-in-1 combination, making a 4-in-1 shot.

REFERENCE CHART OF

DISEASE	SYMPTOMS	INCUBATION PERIOD
MEASLES	Fever; runny eyes; eruption in mouth followed by rash on face.	From 7 to 12 days before onset of fever (rash appears as late as 7 days after fever).
GERMAN MEASLES	Slight cold followed by red rash on face and body; slight fever; sore throat; glands in neck swollen.	Usually about 18 days, varies plus or minus 6 days.
CHICKEN POX	Small reddish blisters, usually more abundant on trunk than limbs, face; slight fever.	From 14 to 16 days, occasionally as long as 21 days.
WHOOPING COUGH	Tight, dry cough that becomes steadily worse for 2 weeks until "whooping," noise of in-rushing breath, begins. Vomiting often follows coughing spasms.	From 5 to 8 days; occasionally as long as 21 days.
MUMPS	Fever; swelling of salivary glands in cheeks, under tongue. Many mild cases go unrecognized, yet spread infection.	From 12 to 28 days, usually 18 days.
STREP THROAT (including Scarlet Fever)	Sore, inflamed throat; fever; nausea; followed (in the case of scarlet fever) within 24 hours by a red rash on neck and upper chest. Rheumatic fever is always preceded by a strep infection.	From 2 to 5 days.
DIPHTHERIA	Inflammation of the tonsils, throat and nose with grayish-white patches; fever.	Usually 2 to 5 days.
INFLUENZA	Sudden onset; fever, aching limbs and back, runny nose, sore throat, cough.	24 to 48 hours.
POLIO (Infantile Paralysis)	Sudden fever; pain on flexing neck; headache; vomiting. Later, one or more muscle groups may be weakened and possibly paralyzed.	From 8 to 10 days.
HEPATITIS	Fever; lowered appetite; darkened urine; eventual jaundice of eyes and skin.	From 10 to 40 days, average 25 days; or from 2 to 6 months after a transfusion of virus-carrying blood.

COMMUNICABLE DISEASES

COMMUNICABILITY	HOME CARE	PREVENTIVE MEASURES
Most contagious for 4 days preceding rash and first 5 days of rash.	Isolation (in dimmed light if eyes become sensitive). Calamine lotion for itching.	No immunization. Consult physician about gamma globulin for young children.
For 4 days before rash appears and 2 days afterward.	Isolation. Avoid chilling the patient.	No immunization. Second attacks rare. Gamma globulin for a woman during first 3 months of pregnancy. Some doctors advise *not* preventing girls from contracting German measles while young.
Highly infectious for 7 days, beginning the day before rash appears.	Isolation. Calamine lotion or a paste of baking soda and water to relieve itching.	No immunization. First attack usually immunizes against recurrence of the disease.
During initial coughing and for about 3 weeks after "whooping" begins.	Isolation. Avoid sudden temperature changes that bring on coughing. Eating lightly frequently helps to allay vomiting.	Immunization prevents or lightens first attack. Second attack rare. (See Preventive Inoculations.)
From a few days before fever until swelling of the glands disappears.	Isolation. Cold or hot applications may ease pain.	No immunization. Second attacks rare.
Apparently runs the course of a strep throat attack, from first appearance of symptoms until complete recovery; scarlet fever can be caught from someone with strep throat but no scarlet fever symptoms.	Isolation in bed for rest; guard against chilling. Consult doctor.	Penicillin aids the body's resistance during exposure to strep infection. Consult doctor.
Until bacilli disappear completely (as shown by test), usually in 2 weeks or less, rarely more than 4.	Isolation. Soft or liquid foods.	Immunization. (See Preventive Inoculations.)
Uncertain—very contagious, especially during first few days.	Bed rest; keep room temperature moderately high; consult doctor.	Ask your doctor about immunization; there are vaccines for some types of influenza.
Until a week after onset, maybe longer; communicable by food, water, etc. and probably by carriers.	Isolation. A doctor's care is imperative. (Hospitalization is common.)	During the polio season avoid fatigue, postpone inoculations, (other than Salk), tonsillectomies. Consult physician for a vaccination schedule.
Just before onset and for a variable number of days following.	Rest. A doctor's care is imperative.	No immunization. Gamma globulin may prevent infection by contact.

IF THERE'S AN ALLERGY
IN THE FAMILY

LIKE the witch in the fairy tale, allergy can appear in a variety of forms. In the skin it may take the form of eczema, hives or some other rash; in the eyes, conjunctivitis or iritis; in passages of the nose, hay fever or allergic head colds often complicated by sinus trouble; in the throat, allergic laryngitis or pharyngitis; and in the respiratory tract, allergic bronchitis or asthma. Some stomach upsets which in infants may appear as vomiting, colic or gas, and intestinal disturbances in the form of diarrhea or constipation can be due to allergic reactions. Nor are blood vessels, kidneys, liver or any other organs exempt. Yet, actually, allergy of these types can be thought of as a single disease. It is a constitutional disorder that makes an individual, otherwise seemingly as healthy as anyone, burst forth in distressing symptoms on encountering some substance which to other persons is harmless or even beneficial. Such substances, whether breathed, swallowed or otherwise introduced are called "allergens." Different ones annoy different individuals and often the same individual at different ages. What are the strains which favor the outbreak of an allergic illness and how can they be avoided? Many of them are physical, such as too great a concentration of pollen, spores of molds, house dust, animal danders and certain foods.

Some of the strains that produce symptoms in the sensitized child are emotional—among them repressed resentments, a sense of frustration and fear—especially fear of losing the protection and approval of those powerful beings, the parents. Sometimes physical allergens are chiefly responsible for an attack, sometimes emotional strains. Usually, perhaps always, both figure. Here special emphasis is given to emotional factors because over them parents have more control than the physician.

The earlier in your children's lives you set about protecting them from serious allergic manifestations the better. According to one study, 60 per cent of adult allergies started in childhood, and many of them before the fifth year.

Allergy in Infants

As to preventive measures, pediatricians, for many reasons, are placing increasing emphasis on mothers nursing their babies when possible. Breast milk rarely causes an allergic upset. A breast-fed infant has several times as much chance of escaping eczema as a bottle-fed one, according to one study. Emotionally perhaps even more than physically is nursing valuable. It seems to strengthen love between mother and baby and give the baby a special sense of security in the warm, cherishing tenderness of the mother.

If your doctor has reason to think your baby has an allergic constitution he may advise that the weaning be especially gradual with new foods, particularly those to which children often become sensitive, added one at a time and in the forms least likely to cause trouble. For example, common allergens are egg, wheat and milk. Yet so valuable are they, especially milk, that no trouble should be thought too great to guard a child from developing such sensitivity to any of them that it must be omitted from the diet. The better cooked foods are, the less likely are they to cause allergic reactions. Your physician may prescribe that milk be evaporated or boiled or, in case of trouble, both, and that when egg is first given, the white be omitted because it causes far more allergic upsets, and that just a crumb of hard-cooked yolk be tried at the start, with amounts increased day by day. Cereals, soups, and other foods he may prefer not to have given in mixed forms until each ingredient has been tried separately. This may save you and your small fry endless trouble later on by enabling the doctor, in case of an upset, to detect and eliminate the right food culprit at once.

As for drugs, only on the advice of a physician should even the most seemingly harmless ones be given to any child. For youngsters of allergic tendency this is doubly important for some of the most valuable medicines,

such as penicillin, aspirin and sulfa drugs, can produce violent allergic reactions.

Dust a troublemaker. Of the allergens that are breathed, dust—not outdoor dirt but house dust—is generally believed to be the chief troublemaker in infants and preschool children. Such inhalants, as they are called, can add just enough strain to make an allergic constitution unable to stand some food which alone would cause no reaction. Do not clean a room while a baby or toddler is in it, and clean with a wet mop and a damp cloth rather than a broom and brush. Keep the room where small children sleep as free as possible from dust-makers, dust-catchers and insecticides. Allergists prefer rather bare nurseries with washable draperies and a minimum of wool rugs, upholstered furniture, pictures and ornaments. It is good to avoid fuzzy toys.

Other allergens. In older children, as well as in adults, pollen grains are the greatest cause of allergies of the breathing apparatus. To prevent hay fever in youngsters of allergic tendency, do not take them driving in open cars in the midst of the pollen season, and be cautious about using electric fans that may blow more pollen and dust on them, besides increasing symptoms through rapid temperature changes. If such changes do not bother your child, air conditioners may be useful to decrease the pollen count indoors. Iced drinks set up reflexes in nose and throat which may produce asthma in the pollen season or all year round. Fresh paints also should be avoided.

Usually it is true that no one thing, but a combination of substances, is responsible for symptoms. Animal danders and feather pillows are extremely important allergens. In children, especially, foods—notably chocolate, spices, wheat, milk, citrus juices and fish—may be the primary causes of hay fever, asthma, eczema, hives and other allergic manifestations including upsets of the stomach and bowels. Your doctor may advise the elimination of any troublesome foods.

Psychosomatic Aspects

When you know something about that vast, intricate network, the nervous system, which stems from your brain touching and influencing every tissue of the body, it is not surprising that the emotional impulses it carries have physical effects. In weeping, blushing, gagging at a disgusting sight, flushing with anger, fainting from shock and so forth, we are all familiar with such effects. In less familiar ways, too, they affect the body's functioning. Emotions which are not frankly recognized and expressed are especially likely to cause physical troubles. This happens especially often in patients of allergic tendency for they, even more often than most of us, have a temperament which, for full health, needs to feel sure of being wanted, loved and cared for. Many specialists agree on this and on the fact that allergy patients—especially in childhood—usually have clinging natures which are peculiarly dependent on mother love.

The effect of mothering—and the lack of it—on health was brought out in a report of the Children's Aid Society. Children who, for lack of a foster home, had been forced to live in hospitals for their first two years, may be "abnormally fearful and subject to more skin, asthmatic and nervous conditions than children who began life in normal surroundings." Even children in good homes may fear being not loved, especially when they sense trouble or coldness between father and mother. In sensitive youngsters, a death in the family, jealousy of a new baby, over-strict toilet training, over-severe punishment or threats by the mother that she can't love a child who does so-and-so are a few other frequent causes of emotions that can injure health. Even attention, when it is so excessive that it makes a youngster feel smothered, can result in such feelings.

Case history. One patient, age eight, had asthma caused by summer pollen, as far as physical tests showed. Yet even in seasons when there was no pollen he often had such severe attacks that he had to be sent to the hospital and kept under an oxygen tent. When the doctor went into possible psychological causes with the mother, he learned she had been somewhat neglecting the boy, not because she did not love him but out of fear arising from guilt feelings. She had divorced his father to marry another man and although the stepfather provided a good home for her child, she was afraid she might be punished by losing her new husband's love. This fear was the greater because the boy's asthma was expensive and demanded so much of her attention that a stepfather might well be resentful. After the physician persuaded her to unburden herself to him, she gained full realization of her own motives, and what she was doing to her son.

She began reading to him at bedtime and in other ways giving more expression to her affection for him. Immediately the asthma began to respond to drugs that had had little effect before. Never, from that time on, was any attack severe enough to need hospital treatment. It is possible that allergens other than those found in the tests could have played a part in the child's illness, but the fact remains that his symptoms did not disappear until after the emotional strains were relieved.

Eczema, too, is strongly influenced by emotions. Again and again patients say, "Whenever anything upsetting happens I begin to itch."

Four women who were still emotionally involved with their mothers in immature, harmful ways suffered from the kind of eczema usually confined to babies. In three of these patients there was strong hostility between them and their mothers. The fourth had an overprotective mother who made the young woman feel smothered by continuing to interfere in her concerns as if she were a child.

Sensitive children. These are just a few examples of attitudes by which, in all innocence, mothers sometimes awaken fears in sensitive children of the clinging type and increase their sufferings from allergic illnesses. Such youngsters are often amazingly intuitive about feelings that their parents think are hidden. For instance, if a mother's overconscientiousness drives her to make such a heavy burden of her maternal duties that she cannot help feeling resentful, her child may sense it. Far better would it be if she found ways to enjoy her children and play with them even though that meant not keeping their clothes spotless all the time. A small person's emotional climate depends to a great extent on the moods of the parents.

Try to appreciate your child for the kind of person he or she really is regardless of whether that is what you would prefer. Many a child feels unloved because of being pushed to develop talents different from those with which nature equipped him. Find out, too, from your pediatrician what to expect in the way of behavior at various ages. Do not demand more than the child can give. If you have an allergic child, talk to your doctor about possible emotional as well as physiological causes. Sometimes just a few such talks bring so much better insight to the parent that the child's symptoms are greatly improved.

When symptoms persist in spite of your own and the doctor's best efforts, it may be that psychological treatment should be considered. Nowadays it is recognized that all doctors must use psychotherapy. Your allergist may do so. Or he may refer the patient or his mother or father or all three to a psychiatrist interested in allergy. Parents, too, may be perplexed by unhappy feelings that they cannot get rid of alone. More than once a stubbornly allergic child has improved after a psychologically trained physician had given the mother insight into her own troubles.

This does not mean that physical treatment may be neglected. Whether or not emotional strains are partly to blame, physical diagnosis and treatment may be prolonged. No detective in a murder mystery has to track down more clues than an allergist. The history alone takes time for it is all-important. Be patient about answering endless seemingly silly questions such as, "Have you a cat, dog or rabbit?"

Skin Tests

Skin tests, too, are usually needed except in infants. By whatever method your doctor prefers, he will introduce a number of suspected allergens under the skin in separate spots and watch to see which produces a hive-like bump indicating, perhaps, that that particular allergen could be guilty. Sometimes dozens, even hundreds, of suspects must be tested before the criminals are detected.

If they prove to be inhalants that are inconvenient or impossible to avoid, like pollens and dusts, injections of them in minute amounts may be increased to build up a tolerance to them in the patient. Such treatments always take months, usually years.

If some food is guilty, allergen shots are usually not needed, for the food can be eliminated or reduced to a point where it causes no trouble. The same is true of things like feather pillows and the dander of pets. In the case of a beloved cat or dog, however, the emotional factor involved in getting rid of the pet may do more harm than good and a compromise like not letting the animal indoors may seem the wisest solution.

The allergic child always needs both treatment and understanding. Hence, the management of allergic illness is often a proving ground for the parent's love and insight. —*By Harold A. Abramson, M.D., and Louise Fox Connell*

WHAT YOU SHOULD KNOW ABOUT NUTRITION

MEDICAL research is constantly adding to our already considerable store of knowledge about vitamins. One survey turned up no fewer than 3,000 nutritional research projects under way at university, industrial and government laboratories, each one seeking to shed more light on the nutritional content of foodstuffs and the role of each nutrient in maintaining growth and health. Such research has in recent years added the three vitamins —B_6, B_{12} and folic acid—to the list of "essential nutrients" recognized by the U. S. Food and Drug Administration, and investigators have been recommending that still another—pantothenic acid—be added.

Research Studies

While animal nutrition findings cannot be applied directly to humans, they often open up new lines of study. Thus animal researchers have reported that when young rats are fed inadequate amounts of a common nutrient, choline, damage to the kidneys results, and this leads to high blood pressure much later in the lives of the rats. This and several other findings of this sort—especially findings in connection with the effects of diet on hardening of the arteries in humans—have aroused a rapidly growing interest in the role of nutrition during human maturity and old age. Nutritionists know, for example, that elderly people cut down on the amount of meat they eat and generally favor soft foods that require a minimum of chewing. They also eat smaller quantities of all foods, for their energy requirements are lower. Is it possible that some of the infirmities we associate with old age are in fact due to vitamin and protein deficiencies which arise as food habits change? "I believe we can expect substantial progress in this field as a result of research programs now under way," says Dr. R. S. Goodhart of the National Vitamin Foundation.

How to Plan a Family Diet

Among the newer vitamins are some which are so widely distributed in common foods that it would be almost impossible to select a full diet lacking them. Others are important only to physicians in treating specific diseases and abnormalities. The average parent need pay attention to only a relatively limited list of essential nutrients:

Vitamins A, C, D and three or four of the B vitamins.

Proteins, which contain the "building blocks" of human tissue and are also a source of energy.

Carbohydrates and fats, the chief sources of energy.

Calcium, iron and perhaps a few other minerals.

Despite many recent discoveries, the best and cheapest source of vitamins and almost all the other food essentials required by the normal human being at ordinary times is still a well-balanced diet, including the many vitamin-enriched and mineral-enriched foods that are now standard in American homes. Keeping your family's meals in balance is readily assured by including in your menus foods from the Basic Four Plan.

Basic Four Plan

To make it easier for mothers to plan a family diet that is both adequate and satisfying, the United States Department of Agriculture has sponsored a new daily food plan. This plan streamlines the Basic Seven food grouping which was developing during World War II to a Basic Four. To follow this four-point plan, pattern your meals to include foods from each of the following categories in the amounts recommended and supplement the "must" foods with others such as fats and sugars.

I—Milk. Recommended: For children, 3 to 4 cups daily; teen-agers, 4 or more; adults, 2 or more; pregnant women, 4 or more; nursing mothers, 6 or more. This group is the chief source of calcium. Milk and milk products, such as cheese and ice cream, are also rich in protein and riboflavin. Whole milk and butter provide vitamin A. The vitamin D added to some milk helps calcium to do its work in building strong teeth and bones.

II—Meats. Recommended: Two or more servings of meat, poultry, fish or eggs every day; beans, peas and nuts as an occasional substitute. This group is relied on to supply about half the daily protein requirements and is valuable for iron and other minerals and the B vitamins.

III—Vegetables and fruits. Recommended: Four or more servings every day. Remember to include at least one dark green or deep yellow vegetable rich in vitamin A and minerals and one citrus fruit or other fruit or vegetable rich in vitamin C. Some of the foods which contain vitamin C (although not so much as the citrus fruits) are cabbage, cantaloupe, broccoli, green peppers, potatoes, strawberries and tomatoes.

IV—Bread and cereals. Recommended: Four or more servings each day of bread or cereals made from enriched, restored or whole grains. These provide carbohydrates, some protein and other nutrients.

Essential Food Factors

Although scores of "essential food factors" are known to science, nutrition authorities stress the following nine as most important. Here they are listed with their primary sources.

1. Vitamin A—Liver; yellow, and dark green leafy vegetables; whole milk; cream; butter; egg yolk; fortified margarine; fortified skim milk.

Fish-liver oils rich in vitamins A and D are usually prescribed during pregnancy, nursing, infancy and throughout childhood. A deficiency of vitamin A produces night blindness and skin troubles, and increases vulnerability to some kinds of infections. Serious deficiencies are rare in the U.S.; but, says the National Research Council, "There is evidence that dividends in health . . . may accrue when quantities of vitamin A are allowed which are in excess of those required to prevent signs of deficiency."

2. Thiamine (Vitamin B_1)—Pork; whole-grain breads, cereals; enriched breads, cereals; beans, dry kidney or lima; peas, split; milk; peanuts.

Essential for the body's production of energy from starches and sugars. Pregnant women and nursing mothers require more than the usual amounts. A serious deficiency produces the nerve disease, beriberi, rare in U.S.

3. Riboflavin (Vitamin B_2)—Milk; liver; green leafy vegetables; whole-grain breads and cereals; enriched breads and cereals.

Essential to the body's utilization of other foodstuffs. Pregnant women and nursing mothers require more than the usual amounts. A serious deficiency causes soreness of the lips, tongue, mouth and eyes; rare in U.S.

4. Niacin (a B vitamin)—Liver; lean meats; legumes, peas and beans; whole-grain breads and cereals; enriched breads and cereals; peanuts and peanut butter.

Necessary for proper functioning of the digestive and nervous systems. A serious deficiency produces pellagra, now rare in this country; lesser deficiencies common among alcoholics and others who fail to eat well-balanced diets. Pregnant women and nursing mothers require more than the usual amounts.

5. Vitamin C (ascorbic acid)—Citrus fruits; broccoli; green leafy vegetables; strawberries; cauliflower; cantaloupe; tomatoes; apples; potatoes; raw cabbage.

Essential for connective tissue, tooth formation and various body functions. Orange juice or other sources of vitamin C are therefore required from second week of life through adolescence; also throughout adulthood. Not stored by the body. A serious deficiency produces scurvy.

Recommended amounts high (8 ounces of orange juice or the equivalent) in pregnancy; higher still (12 ounces) when nursing baby. Contained in standard multiple-vitamin preparations.

6. Vitamin D—This is the only major vitamin not adequately supplied in a well-balanced diet. (Some D is manufactured in human skin exposed to normal amounts of sunlight.) It is supplied by salmon, fortified margarine, vitamin-D-enriched milk, eggs.

Essential for bone and tooth growth, it is contained in cod-liver oil and other fish-liver oil products; also available in non-oily form. Some milk is enriched with vitamin D. A serious deficiency in this vitamin produces rickets, still common in children not given fish-liver oils or some other form of D. Pregnant women and nursing mothers require D supplements. Children should get D in some form from second week of life or so throughout growing years. D is contained in standard multiple-vitamin preparations.

7. Protein—Found in meat, milk, eggs, fish, poultry, cheese, dried peas and beans, nuts.

Protein is made up of amino acids, the building blocks of human tissue. Vegetable proteins are valuable, but should be accompanied by proteins of animal origin. Requirements are high throughout growing years, pregnancy, higher still for nursing mothers.

8. Calcium—Milk, cheese, greens like kale, mustard greens, egg yolk. Essential for bone and tooth formation. Skim milk or non-fat dry milk is sometimes recommended to hold down weight.

9. Iron—Liver, lean meat, molasses, egg yolk, enriched and whole-grain breads and cereals, peas, beans, green leafy vegetables. Essential for formation of red blood cells. Increased amounts recommended for pregnant women and nursing mothers.   —*By Ruth and Edward Brecher*

HOW A CHILD GROWS

GROWTH is a useful word. It must be a key word in any philosophy of child rearing. We cannot understand children unless we understand something of the ways of growth. We can scarcely understand ourselves in relation to our children unless we appreciate the ever present fact and the fatefulness of growth. The concept of growth helps us to see the processes of life in perspective.

Plants grow. We place a seed in the earth; it puts forth leaves; it bears fruit. "First the blade, then the ear, after that the full corn in the ear."

The human body grows. And in much the same manner. First the microscopic beginnings of germ cells; then the body cells which multiply, organize and undergo continuous transformation throughout the whole life span. Germ, embryo, fetus, infant, child, youth, adult—these are the seven successive stages in the biology of development.

The human mind likewise grows but not as a thing apart. It is inseparably bound up with the growing body and therefore undergoes continuous transformations, from embryonic beginnings to adult maturity.

We may picture the mind as being a kind of organism which, to be sure, is intangible but which assumes characteristic shapes as it matures. In a sense, the mind is the sum total of all the reactions and the behavior patterns of the individual. Mental growth is, in fact, a patterning process very much like the process which molds the shape of physical structures. We come by our minds in much the same way that we come by our bodies.

The early growth of the mind is prodigiously swift. Four months before birth the future infant is already in possession of some twelve billion nerve cells, all that he will ever have. They are subject to great modification through education and experience but the major lines and sequences of their growth are inherent. Therefore all members of the human species pass through comparable stages in the cycle of mental growth.

No one needs to teach a baby the most fundamental ways of growth. He naturally follows a ground plan which is characteristic of the species. But he is also an individual. He was born with traits and tendencies inherited from father, mother, grand and great-grandparents. These traits, physical and mental, give individuality to his body type, his body chemistry, his temperament and the make-up of his action system. Moreover, the baby is born into a household and into a culture which influence him. The result is that he displays a distinctive variation of the basic ground plan of growth. He has ways of growth which are peculiar to him. They are the key to his individuality.

The wise parent learns to recognize these individual traits and interprets them in terms of the over-all cycle of psychological growth. It is a long cycle, which extends into the teens and the twenties. If all parents had a basic acquaintance with the general sequences of development, they would see the day-to-day behavior of the child in truer perspective.

Here in sketchy outline are some of the age trends for the first three years of life:

From Birth to Three Years

As early as the age of four weeks an infant quiets when he is picked up, held, warmly wrapped or given calm and assured handling; at eight weeks he smiles; at twelve weeks he both makes sounds and smiles in response to others. At sixteen weeks he smiles at others on his own initiative and he shows signs of recognizing his mother. At twenty-four weeks he begins to realize who are strangers to him and at thirty-two weeks he may withdraw from them. He soon exhibits a remarkable perceptiveness when it comes to interpreting facial expressions. Toward the end of the first year, he takes part increasingly in two-way nursery games.

At two years of age the child calls himself by his own name and shows a new sense of possessiveness. At two-and-a-half years he uses the pronoun "I" with imperiousness. He does not have himself well in hand and has difficulty in distinguishing between mine and thine. He is discovering opposites. Life is no longer a one-way street as it was at eighteen months but is charged with double alternatives and he finds it hard to make simple choices and decisions. This is essentially due to his immaturity, for at the age of three years he will take pleasure in making voluntary choices which lie within the range of his ability. Meanwhile, because of what scientists call his bipolar confusions, the two-and-a-half-year-old tends to be impetuous, hesitant, "contrary," dawdling, defiant or ritualistic. He needs skillful guidance.

The Older Child

Similar growth phenomena occur throughout childhood and youth and actually into maturity. The adolescent is sometimes more aware of these growth forces than are his elders. Adolescents—and adults alike—may well cultivate a sense of growth in a way of life, an attitude toward life that has important implications for mental health. Life becomes more meaningful to a youth if he can be helped to understand the orderly process of growth. Such realization may help him as it helps the adults who watch his personality development.   *—By Arnold Gesell, Ph.D., M.D.*

FAST AND SLOW GROWERS

BIOLOGICAL maturing does not take place in all children at the same age. There may be a difference of as much as six or seven years in the age at which perfectly healthy youngsters go through the changes of puberty. The average American boy matures at about fourteen, but some boys start the changes of puberty as early as twelve, while others show no signs until eighteen. For girls the average is about 13, but a few mature as early as 10 and a few as late as 17. These early and late maturers often have problems.

One example is Tony, whose troubles started long before adolescence. At eight, he was as big as most boys of eleven. But his coordination was that of an eight-year-old, not that of boys three years ahead of him in muscular development. The biggest in his class, he was often taunted, "Whatsamatter, you get left back a couple of times?"

At twelve, Tony's shoulders are broad, his voice deepening and he's added five inches to his already big frame—physically a man, but socially far from being adult.

Late Maturing

Uncomfortable as early maturing may be, late maturing is even harder for boys. Andy was born healthy, wiry, bursting with energy—and smaller than average. His size didn't matter too much through grade school, but at thirteen—the age when puberty changes occur in most American boys—

Andy's troubles began. He barely stood five feet tall and weighed about 100 pounds, his voice was still firmly high-pitched. The boys began tagging him "runt" and finally settled on "Peewee." He had experienced none of the glandular changes that now impelled them to whistle at and gab about girls. His feelings about girls hadn't changed a bit—and it didn't help that they too teased him about his size. When it came to the school teams, he wasn't big enough or strong enough to join in. The boys found good sport in making sly remarks about the size of his genitals, and Andy slunk home desperately, thinking "I'm abnormal."

Still worse, attitudes at home began to confirm this. His mother mentioned fretfully and frequently that she ought to take him to a doctor. His father's conversation bristled more and more with the brusque admonition "For land's sake, act like a man!" Andy's feelings that he was and always would be inferior deepened.

It would probably have been a good idea if, instead of just talking about it, Andy's mother had taken him to the family doctor. He might have told Andy that the change of voice and change of muscles, growth of hair, seminal emissions, and glandular changes that go along with interest in girls—all the changes of puberty—don't take place for some boys until they are 16 or even 18.

Understanding from Parents

You can't eliminate all the inner struggle of these "fringe" youngsters, but being loved and understood at home at least helps mitigate their deepest fears. Thus, they can live through the bad times without having to find an out-of-bounds place for themselves.

Andy had no such help, however. He is 14 now, terribly worried, terribly alone. His school grades have slid down to a run of C's and D's, and he has joined a "gang of toughs"—boys just as disturbed as Andy, for other reasons—but Andy feels he has found a place for himself, somewhere to belong.

Girls, too, may have their problems when they do not mature at the average age. Most of Deborah's girl friends crossed the threshold into womanhood during junior high school days. By the time Deborah was ready for senior high at the age of 15, her difference began to be conspicuous. The other girls were interested in clothes, hairdo's and dates, but Deborah scorned these frills. To her dismay she found her erstwhile friends didn't enjoy their old games and activities any more, and worst of all, they didn't enjoy *her*. Deborah felt she wasn't wanted by her old group of friends. She became lonely and withdrawn, retreating into daydreaming.

Deborah was worried about her "normalcy," too. However, her mother and father had nothing against postponing for a time the social-sexual problems they saw Deborah's friends growing into. They reassured her that she would catch up.

When Girls Mature Early

Although Deborah had her troubles, on the whole it is early maturing that is most difficult for girls. Alice was born with qualities ahead of most children's developmental schedules. Throughout her childhood she grew more rapidly than most youngsters, so that she was at once one of the youngest as well as one of the biggest in her class. She *was* a little more mature than the average for her years—but not as mature as the world expected her to be. Fortunately, neither home nor school pushed Alice, but she did have to put up throughout her childhood with remarks from other children and casual acquaintance adults.

Fortunately for Alice, both her parents and the school understood her problem. She wasn't pushed by the truly important people in her life, and because she felt comfortable in the vital phases of her life, she grew up without the sense of inadequacy that being pushed so often gives a child.

When she was nine, things became complicated. The doctor confirmed that Alice was showing signs of pubertal change, and toward the end of her tenth year, she began to menstruate. At home, thanks to her parents' attitude, she was comfortable and happy with this sign of womanhood, but among her friends she found no one with whom to share her pride.

At eleven Alice was a woman. The world thrust her into boy-girl relationships, but she was willing and anxious to act the part the world expected of her. Even though Mrs. Bishop had always understood Alice's precocious growth and the accompanying complications, she was a bit taken aback by her daughter's interest in boy-girl relationships in a too-early adolescence.

Sex Education

She talked the matter over with her husband and did a lot of thinking about how "sex education" must include whatever information a parent can convey about feelings, not just body functions. She realized that because Alice's body had rushed her into a too-early maturity, she had by-passed the usual social apprenticeship of preadolescence: the chance to be casually acquainted with many boys. Subsequently, she and Alice talked a long time about kissing, necking and petting, and the feelings they aroused. Mrs. Bishop didn't try to talk Alice out of feelings that were perfectly normal, but she did help her to understand them.

Parents of "fringe" youngsters have no easy job in helping their children accept themselves happily. The first step is always to understand that there *is* a problem. Most important of all, your child needs to feel he is all right with you, that you love him and respect him no matter what his size or shape.

What parents can do. If you have a small boy, let him know you feel he is old enough to cross the street alone even if other people think he looks too little for such responsibility. Your faith in him builds up his faith in himself. If your child is too big for his years, don't push him beyond his capacities. When it comes to the adolescent problems, reassure him if he's slow.

For the rapid maturer, rigid restrictions and prohibitions can send him underground to find the experience he craves in quite undesirable ways. You can guide with a loose and gentle rein, but you cannot drive with a whip.

Your "fringe" child is bound to be hurt—you can't do much about that, but you can do a lot about whether the hurt is slight and passes by, or deep enough to leave a scar.
—*By Dorothy V. Whipple, M.D.*

TAKE CARE OF YOUR CHILD'S FEET

ALTHOUGH you may not realize it, feet are highly specialized organs —as specialized as eyes or ears. Moreover, their extraordinary abilities are already present as your baby snuggles contentedly in your arms.

Just consider these remarkable facts. Let's say your child, at five years, weighs 50 pounds. It would take a superman with the muscular strength of a Samson to toss a solid iron ball weighing fifty pounds to and fro from one hand to the other, and the effort required would be very apparent. But when your child comes running toward you, his feet toss his fifty pounds of body weight from one to the other, as lightly and effortlessly as we might juggle a baseball. This extraordinary power possessed by your youngster's feet is not explained by massive muscles and bones, but by a mechanical perfection in their working and design. For instance, as soon as your child's body weight is put upon his ankle, the weight is immediately broken up into small shares and distributed among the delicate and slender bones of his foot. Under normal conditions, each segment of the foot receives only as much weight as it is designed to carry; and the effortless tossing of your child's fifty pounds of weight signifies how capably each segment of his feet handles its small share of the load. When for some reason the distribution of weight becomes faulty, foot function is impaired and opens the way to painful disorders.

The internal structures of the foot constitute a highly complicated mechanism. The care of children's feet is therefore chiefly concerned with protecting this delicate internal mechanism in order to insure full and unhampered usefulness in adult life.

The prevailing idea that muscles support the arches and the weight of the body is a fallacy. This is the function of the bones which lie beneath the muscles.

The function of the muscles is merely to move that weight. Of course, when we climb stairs our weight is lifted, but for that motion the powerful muscles of the hips, thighs and legs come into play.

Every mother can take comfort in realizing that in working for foot health nature is on her side. Common types of foot trouble are avoidable if we understand their causes.

The only force which is capable of causing injurious stresses and strains on our feet is the force of gravity represented in the weight of our bodies. Consequently, a mother need not worry at all about her baby's feet during the first few months of his life. During this time, the actively kicking legs are steadily gaining muscular strength, and the feet bear no weight.

Feet Begin Bearing Weight

Pretty soon, however, the baby begins to creep and before many months have passed, he develops the ability to stand upright. Now for the first time the entire weight of his body is concentrated upon the immature structures of his feet. But still, there is no cause for worry because this is a normal developmental stage which infants are equipped to handle successfully. But it is at this point that we should be aware of conditions which may threaten foot health.

Cribs and playpens, for instance, help the child to stand. But combined with the child's pride in his new accomplishment, they may invite too lengthy periods of standing with the child's body acting as a dead weight on the immature, plastic structures of his feet. Standing for brief periods is quite all right, but standing for long periods should be discouraged.

At about one year of age or soon after, the baby's feet take over the burden of body weight with increasing effectiveness as the child learns to walk.

It is remarkable to see how, during the second year, the child's increasing body weight is carried constantly and comfortably by his small legs and feet. This is the time when the important internal mechanisms of his feet are being put to their first real test, and the best proof that they are developing normally is the eagerness with which the child engages in active play. A mother should have no worries about the child's feet at this time, but should trust to the doctor's examination to be sure that all is as it should be. Her main concern should be general foot care.

Cleanliness

First of all, cleanliness. The child's feet should be kept just as clean as his face, hands and body. Toenails should be trimmed straight across, not curved. The mother's special responsibility is to protect her child's toes. This responsibility is her major one because the most dreaded and frequent types of trouble are with bunions, crumpled toes, ingrown toenails and corns. If uncared for, these may be magnified in later life and hammer toes, overlapping toes and other toe distortions may also develop. All these ailments are limited to the toes and are directly caused by badly designed or badly fitted shoes. The parent can prevent any such difficulties if she will take the proper care in selecting shoes. Women are the most prevalent victims of foot disorders. Only by convincing the teen and pre-teen girl that it is smart to be comfortable in well fitted shoes can she be saved from painful foot troubles later on.

If a mother will take care of her children's toes, by seeing that their shoes are long enough and do not press anywhere, nature will take care of the arches. In case any arch trouble is suspected, professional advice should be sought. This group of ailments is directly concerned with the complicated weight-bearing mechanism of the feet. For that reason they lie beyond the range of ordinary parental care. It is important to get efficient professional help with such ailments. Feet must last a lifetime.

Arch Disorders

Except where a conspicuous degree of weakness in the feet has already been observed by the doctor, arch disorders develop slowly and the time to overcome them most effectively and quickly is during early childhood. Because the tissues are pliable in youth, this is the period when disabling tendencies and conditions are hastened by neglect, whereas corrective changes are easily made.

It is especially important to clear up the confusion about foot disorders which are caused by what are called "flat feet." All foot specialists know that there are countless individuals with extremely low arches who have never experienced any foot trouble; and that many of the most severe cases of painful disability occur in feet which have well-formed arches. Arch contours may be inherited.

If we realize that the efficiency of adult feet is dependent upon the proper distribution of weight stresses and not upon the height of the arches, one may disregard the popular bugbear of "flat feet" and realize that arch height has no more to do with foot function than different heights in the bridge of the nose have to do with the function of smell.

Weak Ankles

Rather than being worried about "flat feet" or "falling arches," mothers should be able to recognize weak ankle position when feet tilt or roll inward. This is the earliest sign of arch weakness. It is a condition which should immediately be brought to the doctor's attention—especially if the growing child shows a persistent reluctance to walk or to play actively or if he complains of muscle cramps in his legs at night.

Before the child walks, he can go barelegged if he is warm enough. Socks that allow his toes plenty of room can be slipped on if he needs warmth. At the creeping or playpen age, the child's increased activity indicates the need for soft-soled leather shoes to protect feet from accidental bruises.

The heavier heel and sole portion of adult shoes is designed to give greater protection to the bottoms of our feet. The baby also should advance to the more substantial leather sole when he begins to play actively indoors and out. Not only do the soles protect the bottom of his feet, but, because they are stiffer and extend beyond the toes, they save the toes from many painful bumps. *—By Dudley J. Morton, M.D.*

DEVELOPING GOOD POSTURE

"JOHNNY, can't you stand up straight?" . . . "Sue, do you have to lie all over the table when you eat?" . . . "Throw your shoulders back, Bob, and *please* pull in your stomach." . . . "Now what's the use of getting you a new formal, Nina? If you stand like that nothing will look well on you."

The sad thing about this kind of nagging, which goes on in so many homes, is that it never does any good. No youngster willfully has poor posture. So even if your child responds promptly to a command or scolding, the next minute, you may be sure, he will unconsciously relapse into his usual position.

Indeed, parental harping on posture only tends to make matters worse. Subjected to constant criticism, the child may lose self-confidence and slump all the more. Or he may become antagonistic. Or he may develop such self-consciousness about his body that he is completely ill at ease with himself.

Posture isn't usually the serious issue many of us make of it. Unless a child has a structural deformity—which, of course, should have medically prescribed correction—the way he carries himself is so tied in with his natural anatomy, his general physical health and his emotional well-being, that posture can't be viewed as a separate problem. In other words, if your child's general needs are met, the chances are that posture will take care of itself.

Treat Structural Defects

In order to be so comfortably casual, however, you have to be certain that anything that seems wrong to you has no structural cause. The earlier a structural defect is caught and treated, the better. Observe your child periodically when he is undressed for such warning signals as one hip obviously higher than the other and one shoulder held constantly higher than the other. Also, check with your doctor if your child seems to have a sunken chest and is exceptionally subject to colds and other respiratory ailments. This may mean that a caved-in rib structure prevents his lungs from working properly.

Dr. Robert T. McElrenney, Wesley Memorial Hospital, Chicago, advises that mothers examine their children's spines every six months. The youngster, stripped to the waist, should bend over from the hips, arms dangling. If one shoulder is higher than the other, he may need treatment for scoliosis—one type of spinal curvature. This condition usually begins before the age of eleven, but with the loose clothing of childhood often goes unnoticed until it has progressively proceeded to a marked deformity. Then, perhaps when a girl puts on her first formal, it does not fit properly because it is tight around one hip, and correction is more arduous than it would have been if begun sooner. Consult your doctor immediately if you have any reason to suspect that a structural defect is affecting your child's posture. Happily, the great majority of so-called postural faults that worry parents are neither structural nor serious. They are functional—a result of the way the body is used.

According to a joint statement by a committee of the American Medical Association and the National Education Association, with which experts are agreed, posture is not simply a matter of how a child stands or sits, but also of how he holds himself and moves when lying down, walking, running, dancing, working and playing.

Strengthen Muscles First

Dance therapist Marian Chace, who has won an award for her work at St. Elizabeth's Hospital, Washington, D.C., has stated that when children were sent to her for posture correction she never worked directly on posture as such. "You can tell a child to 'stand tall' indefinitely," she said, "but unless his muscles are built and strengthened he won't be able to do it. When bodies are conditioned for the dance, through leaping, running, walking to music, and especially through rhythmic stretching exercises done on the floor, good muscle action results. A child is able to use his body in a coordinated, efficient way and achieves good posture without thinking especially about it."

But what can you do to help your boy or girl acquire better posture? One of the best things is to provide the opportunity for a variety of enjoyable

activities that help all-around muscular development and coordination. Since these should be appropriate to a child's age, probably all you need to do is to let your youngster be himself. During infancy, for instance, don't hold him in with tight covers, but give him every chance to squirm, wriggle, kick and reach. When he is at the creeper stage, encourage him to creep to his heart's content, for he has found the ideal way to develop his abdominal, shoulder, back and thigh muscles. Don't try to hurry him past this phase into standing and walking.

As a preschooler, a child's natural activities like climbing and hopping are excellent "posture exercises." So, too, are balancing and hanging from parallel bars, for such play develops the muscles of the chest, shoulders, arms and trunk. At school age, bicycling and skating and games that involve ball throwing, running and kicking are all valuable for stretching, which is technically known as "extension." Extension is involved, too, in many normal teen-age pursuits—among them swimming, basketball and certain forms of dance.

Beware of Fatigue

This doesn't mean, of course, that a youngster should wear himself out with physical activity, for fatigue is even more bound to make him slump than are flabby muscles. Try to see that he alternates periods of rest with periods of play or sports, especially during adolescence when he is growing rapidly and tends to overestimate his endurance. Fatigue may also be the result of poor nutrition or a chronic illness or a too-quick return to regular activities after convalescence from an illness. In any case, a tired child is going to droop and slouch. What needs to be corrected is not the position he assumes but the basic cause of his fatigue.

Although there is no scientific evidence that certain types and heights of furniture make for better posture than others, it stands to reason that a child is likely to sit straighter and more comfortably if the chairs, tables and desks he uses are proportioned to his size. See that he has properly fitted shoes, too, with the heels always in repair so that his body isn't thrown out of alignment. Provide him with a firm mattress.

"Head high, chin in" is an emotional as well as a physical attitude. No one who feels depressed and inferior is going to face the world proud and erect, unless he is disciplined in a military setting. Many a youngster, suddenly taller than his friends, slumps in an effort to appear smaller. Other boys and girls, markedly shorter than their contemporaries, are often literally bowed down with embarrassment. Teen-age girls who do not have a healthy attitude towards their femininity tend to carry themselves with their chests hollowed so that their growing breasts will be less evident. The more you can make boys and girls with problems like these feel that they are as attractive and desirable as anyone else, the more likely they are to straighten up.

Lack of Scientific Evidence

Because of a dearth of true scientific evidence on what constitutes ideal posture, many doctors, physical therapists and physical education teachers have simply proceeded on the assumption that "correct" posture means a straight line can be drawn from the ear through the shoulder, center of the hip and ankle when a person is in standing position. Because there is no evidence contrary to this ideal and because parents naturally want the children to make the best possible appearance, most of us go along with it.

But you should not hold your child to absolute standards, because posture is a highly individual matter. "These differences (in posture)," states the American Medical Association and National Education Association Joint Committee, "are of such a nature that it is impossible for all persons to stand exactly alike, walk exactly alike, or sit in precisely the same position . . . Attitudes toward posture should not be different from those which are held toward other individual traits and abilities."

There is no proof that, as you may have heard, poor posture endangers health or cramps the abdominal organs so that they cannot work properly, and the like. "When children's home life, nutrition, general health and adjustment to school and community are good," one authority says, "they seem to get along in the world all right, even if by commonly held ideas their posture leaves much to be desired."

Age Affects Posture Changes

On firmer scientific ground, studies have shown that posture is normally different at different ages. Preschoolers quite normally have a protruding abdomen and hollow back. A pre-adolescent sometimes seem to have a hollow back, but actually this is because the upper part of the trunk sways backward. During adolescence, with its uneven spurts of growth, almost anything may happen. But muscles are developing and becoming stronger, and among young people in the later teens there are fewer hollow chests and round shoulders.

A series of photographs of healthy, normal children, from birth to twenty-five, which were made in the course of a long study of children's posture, proved impressively that what may be "good" posture at one age is not necessarily so at another. As they grew, for example, the youngsters seemed positively to zigzag from bowlegs to knock-knees and back again—but they all came out adequately straight-limbed in the end. Tummies, too, seemed to move out and in, until the subjects of the study attained the straight body profiles of young adults.

None had any corrective treatment during the many years they were measured and photographed. They just grew up!   *—By Edith M. Stern*

IF YOUR CHILD DOESN'T HEAR WELL

THREE million U.S. children have defective hearing—even though their parents frequently do not realize it, warns the American Hearing Society. The majority can be kept from becoming deaf adults—if their hearing difficulties are detected and treated early enough. Impaired hearing can either be "cured" or prevented from becoming worse. Today science has developed many new techniques to save children's hearing.

Because of ignorance, neglect and apathy, the growing deafness of tens of thousands of children escapes notice every year. Of course, a profoundly deaf child is easily recognized, but the child with a partial hearing loss is frequently overlooked.

"But aren't the schools taking care of this?" you may ask. Unfortunately, not as well as they might if they had better testing equipment and more personnel. Only 11 per cent of America's schoolchildren get regular scientific hearing checkups, a recent survey reveals. Schools generally do not test pupils' hearing until the third grade—too late to correct many defects.

Parents are therefore the ones who should discover hearing difficulties in infants and children up to eight years old. Dr. Adam Sortini, director of the hearing clinic, Children's Medical Center, Boston, states, "It is important to know if a child has a hearing loss *before he enters school*. The critical speech learning years are two to six."

Psychologists have traced countless cases of lying, stealing, truancy, delinquency and other antisocial behavior in children to poor hearing. Many children who are considered "dull," "inattentive," "shy," "aggressive" or "slow talkers" are suffering merely from impaired hearing—which can often be cleared up by proper medical attention.

Needless Maladjustment

The tragedy is that so much of this maladjustment is needless. Living in a world of guessing is a great burden to a hard of hearing child. Because he must strain to hear what his teacher says, he gets tired. When he doesn't do as well in school as his normally hearing classmates, he begins to feel inferior. To escape, he often cuts classes and gets into trouble.

Children with hearing difficulties repeat their grades four times as often as those with normal hearing, studies reveal. The annual national cost of these grade repetitions for hard of hearing children was about $20,000,000 in 1956.

No figures are available on how many so-called "mentally retarded" children are merely hard of hearing. Some children—who have only had impaired hearing—have been committed to institutions for the feeble-minded! "Today there are many children in residential schools for the deaf who could be living with their families if adequate measures had been taken early enough," says Dr. Arthur J. Lesser, U. S. Children's Bureau director of health services.

Unfortunately, children don't complain about poor hearing as they do about other ailments. That's why you should be especially alert to the following warning signals in your child: inattention, excessive fatigue, awkward listening posture, voice peculiarities, mispronouncing, mistakes in carrying out simple instructions, not hearing the telephone or doorbell, not noticing people who enter the room, earache, a frequent weary, tense or exhausted expression, slowness in learning, avoidance of playmates. Some children's impaired hearing is even more obvious with their constant use of "What?" and "Who?"; their falling into the "uh-huh" habit, and frequently asking to have things repeated. Marked changes in a child's voice and a tendency to leave off *s* sounds may also indicate a beginning hearing loss.

Despite these telltale signs, many parents foolishly say, "My child will outgrow his ear trouble." But a child *never* outgrows a hearing loss. On the contrary, it usually gets worse.

Why Defects Go Unnoticed

Dr. Edmund Prince Fowler, Sr., dean of America's ear specialists, has pointed out the following main reasons why parents may fail to detect early hearing defects in their children:

Parents are usually near the child during most of the day and night, and when they are not, they are less apt to expect the child to hear them unless they raise their voices.

Parents are apt to speak loudly when they wish the child to hear them, especially if they demand obedience, and even a severely deafened child can hear a loud voice.

Therefore, parents may not notice or may not admit that their child shows any sign of deafness, even though they may have had evidence of it for several years.

"When there is a loss in the higher frequencies," explains Rose V. Feilbach, an Arlington, Virginia, hearing conservation specialist, "the sounds often missed are *s, z, sh, ch, j,* soft *g, f, th.*" With a loss in the lower frequencies one may not hear the vowel sounds sharply. *Say* may sound like *see; wet* may sound like *wade.* Hearing loss in the middle of the range may cause difficulty in hearing the liquids and the nasals such as *l, m, n, r* and *w.* We speak by imitating what we hear; therefore, if something sounds like *"Ow muh it oo ay or at?"* that's what the hard of hearing person may say, instead of "How much did you pay for that?"

Sounds Taken for Granted

It is difficult for a normally hearing adult to understand the problems of a child with impaired hearing because every waking moment of our lives is identified with sound. We take for granted the familiar sounds of automobile horns, alarm clocks, doorbells, telephones and typewriters.

Too many of us think only in terms of normal hearing and total deafness, forgetting that children may have only partial hearing. Such children also often have speech defects. They may have trouble pronouncing *sh, ch,* and *j* sounds, and hearing high-pitched *s-s-s* and low frequency *o-o-o* sounds. For example, "The noon sun is shining" may sound like *"E nn e ining"* to them. The youngster who says *"burfday"* when he already has had eight of his own may be unable to hear the difference between the *th* and *f.* He may pronounce "five cents" as *"fi shent"* and "speech hospital" as *"peash hopital."*

Yet few children, comparatively, are born deaf. Most lose their hearing, suddenly or gradually, as a result of repeated colds and infections in the ears, nose and throat. Loss of hearing often follows measles, mumps, scarlet fever, influenza and meningitis. The common cold is one of the biggest threats. Germs from a head cold or sore throat can travel from the back of the nose into the middle ear where an inflammation is the major cause of a hearing loss. It is even worse when the infection spreads to the mastoid bone behind the ear. Abscessed ears, inflamed tonsils and adenoids, blows on the ears and head, also may bring on deafness.

Audiometric Testing Programs

When most grownups were in school, hearing was tested—if at all—with dollar watches, whispers, tuning forks, coin clicks, bells, clickers, snappers and other unscientific devices. Experts agree that they have no place in a modern school testing program. "An audiometric testing program finds thirteen times as many children with hearing defects as the old watch tick, whisper and other methods," reveals Western Reserve University's Dr. Warren H. Gardner, former chairman of the American Hearing Society's Committee on Hard of Hearing Children.

Today the only reliable method of detecting early hearing losses is with an audiometer which measures how much hearing is lost at different tone levels. The result of the test—a child's audiogram—reveals his threshold of hearing.

Nevertheless, only 11 per cent of America's 35,000,000 school-age children now receive audiometric tests. Less than 300 cities and merely 21 states require them in public schools. Even in some of these 21 states, the compulsory hearing conservation laws aren't being enforced.

In communities where boards of education don't own audiometers, children are often tested by traveling technicians from the state health or education departments.

In some schools, children only have audiometric tests every three years—at the fourth, seventh and tenth grades—and often none before fourth grade. Ideally, children should have their hearing scientifically tested even before they enter school, and at regular yearly intervals afterwards.

Hearing Test for Infants

A new hearing test for infants as young as two months, developed at Johns Hopkins University, is now being used at many children's clinics throughout the U.S. Known as the galvanic skin-resistance test, it involves the use of a standard audiometer, which produces sound of measured intensity, and another instrument, the psycho-galvanometer, which gives the child a slight shock. The responses of his sympathetic nervous system to the test signals are amplified and charted. Through this method, doctors can tell what sounds the young child has heard.

Whatever testing method is used, the need to follow up children with hearing loss can't be emphasized too strongly. The American Academy of Ophthalmology and Otolaryngology recommends that county and local medical societies furnish a "school examining otologist." This ear specialist, who would hold a clinic at school on a specified day which parents could attend, can recommend what treatment a hard of hearing child needs. Where done, following up children with hearing losses has achieved remarkable results.

Poor hearing in children, ironically, is often discovered haphazardly. A five-year-old California boy's bad hearing was brought to light only when an angry truck driver—who had to apply his screeching brakes to avoid an accident—shouted at the youngster's frantic mother in the doorway, "Lady, can't your kid hear my horn?"

When hard of hearing children become more deaf, many bewildered parents breast-beat, "Why did this happen to me?" This may result in an overprotective attitude which brings on emotional difficulties in their children. Parents should encourage their hard of hearing children to develop the same capacities as other children, not an attitude of dependence. One seventeen-year-old boy revealed, "My father always answers for me because he thinks I might not hear and then I'll look dumb."

Parental Attitudes

Besides oversolicitude, parents' wrong attitudes may also take the form of rejection, inconsiderate treatment, giving the child impossible educational goals and refusal to accept the hearing disability realistically. A New York couple were on the verge of eviction from their apartment because Marvin, their hard of hearing ten-year-old son, played the radio full blast and disturbed the neighbors. The family kept the apartment only when an understanding social worker had an earphone attachment put on the radio for Marvin.

Parents should encourage their children to wear a hearing aid if an ear specialist recommends one. Though considered impractical for children until recent years, today most children can begin wearing a hearing aid even in babyhood. An unself-conscious six-year-old who did so, explained, "I got glasses for my ear."

Learning to hear can be a poignant experience. Howard, a hard of hearing nine-year-old, felt that he didn't "belong" in school. Patiently, he learned to recite with his classmates the Oath of Allegiance to the flag. Several months later, after he had been taught to use a hearing aid, he excitedly rushed up to his teacher exclaiming, "Did you know when we pledge allegiance to the flag, the other kids say it out loud?"

Children with hearing aids are better adjusted than hard of hearing youngsters who refuse to wear them, a Columbia University study revealed.

Improved Hearing Aids

Hearing aids have improved tremendously since grandpa's time. During the past decade or so, the size and weight of hearing aids have been remarkably reduced, while their general efficiency has increased enormously.

Besides being furnished with a hearing aid, a child with an average loss of 20 decibels or more in his better ear, should be trained in lip-reading which can be learned in 20 to 30 lessons. The sounds which are the hardest to hear (*th* and *s*) are the easiest to see.

Far too little money is being spent in medical hearing research, though deafness strikes twice the number of persons suffering from tuberculosis, polio, heart disease and cancer combined—the four most publicized diseases.

If your child's school doesn't have an audiometer to test hearing, the American Hearing Society, 817 14th Street, N.W., Washington 5, D.C., can help you find one. Its 119 local chapters usually offer audiometer tests, lip-reading instruction, speech correction, auditory training, hearing aid advice, employment guidance, recreational activities. Most of these services are free, or fees are based on ability to pay. Your State Department of Education can also steer you to an audiometer.

What Parents Can Do

If your child's school doesn't have a regular hearing program, work through your PTA to start one. State departments of health and education are now teaming up in many places to buy audiometers and to train persons to operate them in schools.

If your child's school reports that he has a hearing loss, make sure that he gets a prompt follow-up examination by an ear specialist or in an ear clinic. You can write to the American Hearing Society (address above) for information about the availability of specialized hearing services in its local chapters in the various states, or in universities, hospitals and hearing centers.

The John Tracy Clinic, 924 West 37th St., Los Angeles, has an excellent correspondence course for parents of children who are severely hard of hearing or deaf. For information about oral schools for the deaf, write to The Volta Bureau, 1537 35th St., N.W., Washington 7, D.C.

—By Jack Harrison Pollack

SAFEGUARD
YOUR CHILD'S VISION

TO an amazing degree, the kind of person your child is depends on his type of eyesight. Bill, whose nearsightedness makes him a dub at sports, turns into a bookworm. Farsighted Phyllis finds sewing, reading, even playing with paper dolls hard but shines at baseball and becomes a tomboy. With Pete, whose nerves are frayed from unsuspected double vision, temper tantrums become a habit, while Nonie, worn out from eyestrain due to astigmatism (blurred vision), becomes a chronic whiner.

A case was reported of five teen-age criminals who were brought to Juvenile Court for violation of parole. All had failed at school before it was discovered they were "hopelessly visually inefficient." When eye tests revealed this handicap and it was corrected, four of the five became satisfactory, law-abiding pupils and now are on their way to being good citizens. School surveys have shown that many pupils fail to be promoted simply because of unsuspected seeing difficulties.

Dr. Arnold Gesell and his associates in "Vision: Its Development in Infant and Child" show how the way a youngster holds and uses arms, legs and head, his skill with his hands, the unfolding of his intelligence and even his personality are profoundly influenced by the kind of vision he has. All this makes it clearer than ever how vital it is to notice the way young eyes are working, guard them from injury, see that tasks expected of them are not beyond their stage of development and correct any defects.

Mature Vision Develops Gradually

It takes between sixteen and twenty-one years for eyes to acquire full maturity. Until the tenth, they grow in size, while the lens grows throughout life. At birth an infant is almost as blind as a newborn kitten though he can see light. Soon afterward he learns to hold his eyes steady long enough to stare at something, but they do not stop being free-wheeling, nor work together as a team for at least three months; while six months are required for the part of the eye which gives sharpest sight to work efficiently. Dr. Gesell noted marked changes in vision every few weeks in infancy, every few months between one and four years and every year between five and ten.

A mother may help her child even before birth to develop the best vision in the whole animal kingdom—that of normal man.

By eating and living as your doctor prescribes you can do much. Avoid exposure to infection if you can, and if you can't, report at once to your physician. He may be able to give you an injection such as gamma globulin used against measles, which will keep you from catching it or, if you do, lessen its severity. German measles, especially, can do serious injury to an unborn child's eyes.

Take whatever precautions your doctor advises against premature birth. Although one of the modern achievements of medicine is that the lives of many mites born at seven and even six months are saved, their eyes are not fully developed then and sometimes sight is lost. Report at once to your doctor any reason you have for fearing early labor.

Prevent Glare

After your baby comes, do not expose his eyes to glare. Glare is so bad for mature eyes that after every eclipse of the sun there are some cases of partial blindness from gazing at it, even through sunglasses. Baby eyes should not stare at a light bulb. Outdoors, the carriage should head away from the sun with the hood up. In a bright climate the hood should be lined with something dark.

Nature ordinarily takes care of washing a baby's eyes by a continuous film of tears and secretion. Only when there is white matter or the lids stick together from some trouble such as a plugged tear duct (a common but not serious disorder of infancy) will eye drops or sterile compresses be needed and only as prescribed by the pediatrician.

Some contagious diseases, such as diphtheria and smallpox, can damage eyes. Have your child given all the immunizations your doctor advises. Remember, too, that the eyes are a part of the body and are temporarily weakened during and after any illness. Guard them against fatigue.

Cross-eyes

Infants often appear cross-eyed. That is no cause for worry during their first three months of life. Even at two months, eyes may look too close together simply because the bridge of the nose is undeveloped. Just the same, tell the doctor any time you think your child's eyes look queer. This is a must after the age of six months. Early treatment of crossed, wall or up-turned eyes (lumped under the name squint or strabismus) usually saves the wandering eye from losing its sight, which often happens by the age of six if untreated. Treatment, even when given too late to save the eye's vision may correct its appearance. The strabismus operation is no more serious than a tonsillectomy and should not be postponed longer than the doctor advises.

Eye Examinations

Your children's eyes should be examined every year from the time the child is three (some specialists say one) and whenever any signs of trouble appear. Only nineteen states have laws requiring school eye tests, and many of these are not made every year. Valuable though school tests are, they seldom go beyond the reading of an eye chart at a distance of twenty feet, which leaves much to be learned about close vision.

Some reasons for having eyes examined (including your own) are: frequent frowning, blinking or rubbing of eyes; peering through half-closed lids; holding small things or books too close or far (for reading, 14 to 16 inches is right); tilting head forward or sideways; shutting one eye or seeming oversensitive to light; when eyes look red or watery, have frequent sties or red, encrusted or swollen lids; when a child has unusual trouble with schoolwork, tires easily, complains of headaches or eyesight, is dizzy or nauseous after close work; when he is poor at sports (which may mean defective distant vision) or if he often stumbles.

Bill, a New York boy of fifteen, was so awkward about bumping into things that his father took him to have his legs examined. The doctor sent Bill to an eye specialist. No wonder Bill was awkward; he could hardly see anything farther than a few feet away. Glasses corrected this.

For preschool children farsightedness is normal. They should not be expected to read or do close work. When they enter school many are still farsighted and some, even at nine, are found with vision too immature to read without strain. Most such youngsters will eventually develop closer vision without glasses if their eyes are not abused.

When Glasses Are Needed

One out of every four school children ought to have special eye care, many need glasses. So great are the advances in their design that no longer does a boy or girl hesitate to join in sports because he wears spectacles. He can get them with frames reinforced with wire and extra durable lenses, either the "nonshatterable," laminated kind made into two layers with cellophane between or the case-hardened "unbreakable" kind which can be hit with a hammer without injury. For extra rough sports, plastic lenses are often prescribed. These have been improved so that the chance of their scratching too easily is greatly decreased. They are more expensive than glass but not unreasonably so. Because plastic is thin it is often preferred to the thick glass lenses for extreme nearsightedness.

Prescription glasses can be tinted to prevent glare, but colored glasses (and it makes no difference what color they are) ought not to be worn except when there is unusual glare, as on the water or the beach or when driving on light roads in the sun.

In the past two or three years an improved type of contact lens has been developed, the corneal lens. The previous lenses touched a larger area of the eye and caused discomfort, and they necessitated the use of fluid dropped into the eye between it and the lens. With the corneal lens, tears are used for the fluid, the lens does not rest against so much eye surface and it is easier for the user to put on.

However, the greatest care is necessary when inserting contact lenses, and it requires the highest skill to make and fit them properly. For patients with the type of eyes that make contact lenses more effective than ordinary glasses and for professional people such as actors, rodeo riders and others, contact lenses are proving a boon. The corneal lens when it is well made, can be worn for quite a number of hours at a time. All aspects considered, unless contact lenses are prescribed by an ethical and highly skilled eye specialist, their use should not be considered.

Eye Exercises

Sight depends only partly on good eye machinery. Equally important is the proper use of that machinery. And this can be improved by training, according to Walter B. Lancaster, M.D., whose review of the merits of eye exercises was published by the National Society for the Prevention of Blindness. The eye's problems are much like those affecting feet. All the exercises in the world will not cure a club foot, though they may help a person to make better use of it. On the other hand, a clumsy individual who has no deformity may become an expert dancer by means of good teaching. Dr. Lancaster tells of a young man who had been wearing glasses for nearsightedness (myopia) whose vision became normal after a course of exercises. His was not a case of true myopia but of poor habits in using his eye muscles. Many persons with reading difficulties have become expert, fast readers through eye exercises given by qualified specialists.

Before considering a visual training course for yourself or your child, however, have a specialist make sure there is no organic eye disease. Dr. Lancaster says, "Eye exercises do a great deal of good," but adds that, indirectly they can do harm if a patient with an eye disease which needs treatment neglects to consult a competent ophthalmologist, thinking that exercises are sufficient.

Every year 85,000 children suffer eye injuries, though laws restricting the use of firecrackers have greatly decreased the many tragedies that once occurred every Fourth of July. Forbid young children explosives, sharp scissors, knives, darts, air guns, slingshots and bows and arrows. Train older children to use such dangerous things safely. Three times as many boys as girls injure their eyes and 40 per cent of such injuries come from blows on the eye. Teach children care in throwing hard balls. If a child's eye is hit hard or pierced, waste no time on home remedies, but consult an eye doctor. When a cinder gets in the eye do not touch the eyeball. If it is necessary, take the child to an eye doctor. But often after pulling the lid down over the eye, tears will wash away the speck or it will stick to the lid from which, after washing your hands, you may remove it with a *clean* bit of fabric or swab. Sometimes using an eye cup and an eye wash will remove the speck.

Proper Lighting

Good lighting and good posture are important to protect vision. At home and at school, rooms where reading or close work is done should have pale walls and ceilings and plenty of light without glare. No part of a room should be less than one-fourth as light as its brightest part. This may call for artificial light in dark corners even in the daytime. Do not be afraid to mix electric light and daylight. The idea that this is harmful is an old wives' tale. The custom of keeping window shades half drawn in the daytime when rooms are in use is senseless except when there is too much direct sunlight. See that children have light over the shoulder, not in front of them when they use their eyes. After dark, have not only the work area lighted, but the whole room. Looking from brightness to dark while using the eyes is a source of strain. Do not let children read in direct sun or when strong shadows are on the book. Before children are five give them big, not small, things to play and work with, for example, crayons and sheets of wrapping paper for drawing, and discourage work or play with tiny objects.

Prevent Eyestrain

In moderation, television does not strain eyes if there is other light in the room so that it is neither too dark nor too bright, and the child sits a comfortable distance from the screen.

When children do close work see that their posture is good and that every half-hour or so they rest their eyes by closing them or looking into the distance. Teach them not to rub their eyes with unwashed hands. If your child wears glasses, teach him to keep them clean and be sure that every few months they are taken back for readjustment of the frames which may become crooked. This is done without additional charge.

In a Denver survey it was found that youngsters above fourth-grade level are intensely interested in how their eyes work and how to take care of them.

Teach them the rules of eye hygiene and safety, and obey these rules yourself. It is also important to realize that a well balanced diet contributes to eye health.

Almost every day some wonderful new discovery is announced for the treatment of serious eye diseases and even some forms of blindness. Yet it is still true that an ounce of prevention is worth a pound of cure.

—By Louise Fox Connell

QUESTIONS AND ANSWERS ABOUT ORTHODONTIA

HOW **can you tell if your child needs orthodontic treatment?** A child needs orthodontic treatment when he suffers from malocclusion or faulty bite —a failure of many or all upper and lower teeth to meet properly when the jaws are closed. Orthodontists recognize three main classes of malocclusion. First, individual teeth are in poor relationship to each other. Appearance is normal when the mouth is closed, but a smile reveals a mouthful of bunched-together teeth.

Secondly, a lower jaw that recedes in relation to the rest of the head. The back teeth are at variance with each other and the uppers may be as much as one full tooth forward. The result is protruding teeth.

A third classification is the reverse of the second. The lower jaw juts forward and the lower incisors cover corresponding upper teeth.

How does orthodontic treatment work? Orthodontics is a method of gradually moving teeth through alternate periods of pressure and rest. The teeth are held in place by periodontal membranes and tissues which, although bony, are not inflexible. Under pressure, these bony supports are broken down. At rest, deposits of bony tissue develop around the base of the teeth in their new positions. The orthodontist's skill and experience guide him in determining the rate at which treatment can proceed without risk to root, tooth or gum health.

Why correct an improper bite? Failure of the teeth to meet properly reduces chewing efficiency, which forces the stomach to assume an extra burden and impairs functioning of the digestive system. A child may also avoid essential but hard-to-chew foods. There is always the chance, too, that what begins as a few charmingly crooked teeth may change into deformity. Defective bite sometimes starts as a slight deviation from normal which may right itself. All too often, though, the first crooked teeth set in motion a series of imperfect adjustments that end as malocclusion.

It is in later years that the benefits of orthodontic care are fully realized. Straight teeth are easier to keep clean and less prone to cavity formation. Chances are they'll last longer, for gums are healthier and more resistant to periodontal diseases such as pyorrhea and gingivitis which, more than decay, account for loss of teeth in middle age.

Is malocclusion inherited? Although it is a family trait, heredity is not its sole cause. The only cases of improper bite due to heredity alone are those arising from too few or too many permanent teeth.

In general, malocclusion is the result of heredity and environmental factors acting on and reinforcing each other. According to dental theory, not "crooked teeth" but patterns of growth for various parts of the face are inherited. Irregular development during the critical period of second tooth eruption upsets the delicate balance of the mouth (sometimes the jaw has not enlarged sufficiently to house the increased number of permanent teeth) and produces other structural imbalances.

Actually, defective bite is a complex and interrelated condition, so that orthodontists hesitate to attribute its cause to any single factor.

Can thumb-sucking or other habits affect teeth? Some habits such as sucking a pacifier, the fingers, or chewing a blanket may bring about dental difficulty if they are continued beyond the time when first or deciduous teeth are being shed. Pressure does move teeth and upsets the balanced interplay of muscles that maintain the shape of the dental arch. Sucking, however, is normal, instinctive and universal. Most children abandon the practice by the time they are five or six and teeth then resume their proper positions in the jawbone. Although prolonged thumb-sucking is very likely to favor malocclusion in a child with an inherited tendency to imperfect bite, some orthodontists believe that a strong bony structure will counteract the harmful after-effects of even prolonged sucking and chewing.

But sucking is only one of many pressure-producing activities that can cause faulty tooth placement. Sleeping constantly on the face or side of the face, constant resting of chin or cheek on the hand, mouth-breathing, unusual swallowing habits, abnormal speech habits and improper action of the tongue all may take their toll of dental health if carried on beyond early childhood and there is a tendency to malocclusion.

Are there other causes for malocclusion? High on the list are premature loss of baby teeth or their prolonged retention. Apart from chewing, baby teeth have several important functions. They guide the permanent teeth into place in the mouth, maintain the shape of the dental arches and insure the correct relationship of upper and lower jaws. When one baby tooth is lost, its neighbor will shift to fill the space. Room that should be left for a permanent tooth is taken. The permanent tooth may then fail to erupt or may emerge in an undesirable position, pushing adjoining teeth. The end result is the same when baby teeth are retained too long, and permanents cannot break through.

Consequences are most serious when first teeth are lost in the region of the first permanent or six-year molar. The "keystone" of the dental arch, this tooth must meet firmly and accurately with its opposite number. If it fails to do so, the form of the arch and relationship of the jaws become distorted.

Emotional conditions may also lead to malocclusion. A habitually tense mouth, for instance, may form a rigid muscular band on the dental arches and prevent them from molding correctly. The consequently underdeveloped jaw provides insufficient room for second teeth which then crowd together or protrude.

Poor facial muscle tone, sometimes seen in listless children, can have an equally harmful result. The form of the dental arch is maintained by a balance of forces exerted by the muscles of the tongue, cheeks, and lips. Weak lips do not provide an adequate counterbalance to the force of the tongue. Thus, the upper front teeth protrude and a chain reaction of faulty muscular activity and facial growth sets in.

Can malocclusion be prevented or minimized? Care of the teeth, beginning with regular visits to the dentist at the age of 2½ or 3 is a good preventive measure against malocclusion. Cleaning and filling baby teeth will help them last until permanent teeth come in. If a deciduous tooth is lost through accident, the dentist can install a removable artificial tooth or space maintainer if he thinks it necessary to leave room for the permanent tooth by preventing adjacent baby teeth from drifting.

The dentist can also check to make sure first teeth are loosening on schedule and seconds erupting in good alignment. He may even pull teeth that are not being eliminated on time.

A good diet is another safeguard. Certain foods, especially those containing vitamins A, C, D and B complex, are essential to the health of facial tissues, bony and dental structure and also foster tooth eruption.

A third precaution is exercise. Strenuous chewing stimulates growth of the jaws, helps them expand to receive the more numerous second teeth.

Playing a wind instrument is also a form of exercise. Dr. Edward R. Strayer, an orthodontist whose avocation is music, favors different instruments for different "bite" conditions. The oboe, for instance, may help children with poor muscle tone or flabby lips. All in all, however, this is a complicated subject and a controversial one among orthodontists.

When is malocclusion most likely to occur? Malocclusion may occur at any time. Current opinion holds that the nature of the case rather than the age of the child determines whether or not treatment should be started. Improper bite in the early period when both first and second teeth are present, for example, may indicate prior defects in facial growth. But if the causes interfering with growth can be overcome, the child may catch up quickly and future development can proceed normally.

There are also phases in the maturing of the jaw that resemble malocclusion but are actually signs of normal development. Between the ages of 6 and 9, for example, the jaw widens to make room for the permanent upper front teeth. The resultant spaces may look like faulty tooth alignment. Actually they are merely symptoms of oral growth.

When is the best time to treat malocclusion? Most orthodontists give Nature every chance to make adjustments in growth before recommending treatment. Between 10 and 14 most permanent teeth are in and the jaws have reached near maximum development. But bony tissue is still growing and moving teeth is fairly easy. Thus, while orthodontists no longer adhere to a hard-and-fast rule of delay until most of the second teeth are in, most orthodontic treatment takes place among children in this age group.

Can bands and braces hurt the teeth? Under the supervision of a competent orthodontist—no. Actually, bands protect the portions of the teeth they cover. And although braces do favor retention of food particles, precautions can be taken to avoid decay.

It is routine orthodontic procedure to clean teeth and fill all cavities before an appliance is installed. At each visit, the arch wires holding the bands are removed and teeth are given a thorough cleaning. Orthodontists take care to instruct their young patients on how to brush their teeth.

Are there reasons for postponing treatment? The case of a child unable to wear braces and bands for physical reasons is relatively rare, particularly if he enjoys good health and has had proper dental care. Only in case of a bony jaw that is too spongy to support pressure of the bands may orthodontic treatment be inadvisable. This condition may occur temporarily during convalescence from a recent serious illness in which case dentists advise postponing orthodontia until recovery is complete. It is possible, too, that during an emotional upset, the presence of a cumbersome mouth appliance could cause undue psychological strain.

How can parents help make treatment successful? A matter-of-fact emphasis on the advantages in health and attractiveness of straight teeth generally appeals to youngsters. The wearing of braces can be seen, after all, as a stage through which many adults have had to pass.

Since some pain and soreness for several days are common after the appliance has been fitted, mother should serve easy-to-chew foods (perhaps even some favorites). This is also the time to work toward establishing routines of brushing. Parents must see to it that a child retains the rubber bands, adheres to the brushing routines and performs prescribed exercises. Setting aside the same time every day when mother and child can go through the exercises together might be a good idea.

Many youngsters respond when they are given responsibility. Putting a child on his own as far as office visits are concerned often works. Children are more cooperative when they come alone, say many orthodontists. Care of the teeth becomes the child's own concern rather than something he has to do for his parents. Children even find it easier to give up chewy candy and gum when the need for these restrictions has been thrashed out with their orthodontists, rather than their parents.

How long does treatment take? Active treatment lasts, usually, for two or three years, followed by a period of about eighteen months during which time a child wears a retainer to consolidate the new position of his teeth. Naturally, timing varies according to the nature and severity of the case.

How much does it cost? As more dentists enter this specialized field, costs of treatment have decreased. Today the range is between about $600 and $1200, depending on the complexity of the case and the part of the country in which the patient lives.

Some orthodontists work on a monthly-payment basis. Others prefer the flat fee, ensuring them of seeing a case through the retainer stage, which is a favorite time for some parents to break off treatment because the teeth "look all right."

The flat fee is generally pro-rated in monthly installments for convenience. In most cases an initial sum is required to cover the orthodontist's services for X-ray, plaster impressions, diagnosis, as well as the fitting and cost of the appliance.

—By Ruth C. Fredericks

HELP FOR HANDICAPPED CHILDREN

ANY attempt to get Bobby to a doctor threw him into such tantrums that his worried parents kept putting it off. At eight, he could neither read nor write and his efforts to speak were painful to see. When guests came he hid in a closet—for Bobby knew how uncomfortable his mother felt about his ugly harelip.

At New York's Mount Sinai Hospital, though, the gentle psychiatrist invited Bobby to play a game with her. He soon had a dozen new friends, all specialists. And in a while they held a conference about him.

It was a long, lively conference, for the Mount Sinai Cleft Palate Group is one of the therapy teams in which psychologist, social worker and teacher have joined hands with doctors to provide all-out help for the handicapped child. Team therapy today is speeding thousands of handicapped children all over the country toward a normal, gregarious life—the kind of life from which they were once "protected," often in institutions and special classes that nursed crippled attitudes. Team centers for all types of handicap are now springing up throughout the nation.

Treatment for cleft palate. Bobby's program included individual psychiatric treatment for both himself and his mother; a prolonged stay in the children's ward to prepare him emotionally for an operation; repair of the cleft lip by plastic surgery; individual tutoring, speech therapy and regular checkups at the clinic. Hospitalization costs were borne by the Department of Health. The doctors donated their skills. Teachers were supplied without charge by the Board of Education. Other expenses were paid by the hospital and private agencies.

Because care like this is beyond the reach of most families, it is usually underwritten by the community—and in the end it pays. At nine, thanks to team therapy, Bobby is an alert, fine-looking boy who makes friends easily and is catching up on his school work.

Team therapy was a novel idea when Dr. J. A. Salzmann first organized the Cleft Palate Group. An orthodontist, Dr. Salzmann had observed that facial deformities are usually accompanied by social handicaps and emotional problems. Correction of the deformity, he found, creates new complications, for it deprives the child of his claim to special privileges. "We now recognize," Dr. Salzmann said, "that treating the physical handicap is only part of our responsibility. Rehabilitating the child is the real job. This calls for pooling many skills."

Program of bureau for handicapped. In New York, the Health Department's Bureau for Handicapped Children invited leaders in all fields of child care to draw up a set of standards. It dispatched teams of specialists to survey all hospitals and convalescent homes that wished to get on, or remain on, its approved list. It conducted a case-by-case review of the children who had been in these institutions a year or more; of children in public school classes for the handicapped; and of those who were getting instruction from visiting teachers at home.

Here is what the Bureau found:

1. New York actually had a vast surplus of institutional facilities for the handicapped.

2. Some of these facilities were among the most advanced in the world, but many were obsolete.

3. There was a serious shortage of clinics for children who needed treatment but not hospitalization.

4. Some of the best medical staffs failed at teamwork. If a child was seen only by orthopedists, his general health and family problems were often inadequately met.

5. Institutions tended to become "wastebaskets" for forgotten children.

6. A good third of all these children were kept in hospitals when they should have been home; home when they should have been at school; in special classes when they could attend regular ones.

For example, Michael, a heart case, stayed in a hospital three years because of the stairs at home. Peggy, born with a dislocated hip, was in the hospital four years later because her widowed mother had to work.

Now, since the Bureau's contact with a private agency, Peggy is living with foster parents who love her. Michael went back home when a housing project agreed to reserve a bloc of ground-floor apartments for the handicapped.

Periodic revaluation of children in special classes, on home instruction or in institutions has resulted in a steady migration of handicapped youngsters away from special placement toward the world of the normal.

Institutions have cooperated, not only because Bureau approval is desirable but because Bureau teams talked sense. Out of these talks have come dramatic improvements in medical and social services, conversion of hospitals to team therapy and the growth of sorely needed outpatient facilities. For these, too, the Bureau has set high standards. To assure their fulfillment it is now surveying all clinics to which it sends children.

A most important development has been the enlistment of teachers and parents in the child's treatment program. Those children whose parents join in do best by far.

New York's specially trained teachers, always among the closest friends of the homebound or hospitalized child, have welcomed team therapy. With a teacher on his team, each child is now assured continuous education that is geared to his needs.

School aid for the program. Team therapy is by no means confined to medical institutions. A joint effort by the Departments of Health and Education, United Cerebral Palsy of New York and other agencies has brought the team into the schools.

Entering one of the city's special orthopedic school units, you may find a distinguished pediatrician harnessed like a horse to an overturned table. It is a "covered wagon," packed with pioneers and trailed by whooping Indians. Susan, four, who hasn't learned to sit, walk or talk, is strapped into the wagon.

Her eyes are shining, for she is playing a game. Everywhere there is activity.

These are all severely disabled children—victims of brain damage, polio, muscular dystrophy—for whom, a few years ago, school was unthinkable. Meeting their extraordinary needs calls not only for elaborate equipment but for an unusually large on-the-spot team, including a medical director, co-ordinator, pediatrician, several therapists, two teachers, psychologist, social worker, public health nurse, attendants and—to the greatest extent possible —the mothers.

Every mother who can, accompanies her child to school about once a week in a special bus equipped with a hydraulic lift for wheelchairs, and stays to help. She learns how to lay out clothes so her child can put them on; she gains new understanding of his emotional needs; she finds she isn't alone. Often she is able to contribute valuable insights to the team.

Every child who is able to, spends part of each day in a regular class, and nearly 20 per cent eventually move out of the special unit altogether. Some go into conventional classes for the handicapped which, though they don't provide treatment, do work closely with therapy teams to keep up the "push" toward normalcy. Some children even go on to regular classes. Most of them are being trained for dignified work. All are gaining the experience of a meaningful community life.

Nursery school for blind children. The Lighthouse, one of the many private agencies which have embraced team concepts, opened the nation's first nursery for the blind in a public school. The principal, eager to try the experiment, nonetheless looked alarmed when the equipment began to arrive— jungle gyms, sliding boards, tricycles and rocking horses.

His doubts melted in amazement when the sightless tots came in and took over under watchful team eyes. And trotting out to the park or the soda fountain, they soon won the hearts of neighbors and tradespeople whose helpfulness has contributed to the project's success. Parents, too, join in. "They've found it's good medicine," says the executive director of the Lighthouse. "Working with our team or meeting in groups, they stop pitying their children and begin to enjoy them."

Freeing children from the fear that surrounds heart disease has been the main task for several years of the director of a cardiac diagnosis and guidance team at New York's lower East Side Health Center. Many of her patients have no organic ailment—only fear. "It will be a great day for the cardiac child," she says, "when grownups stop frightening him half to death."

Therapy for cardiacs. The American Heart Association has recently published national standards for cardiac team therapy. The same has already been done for many other types of handicap.

In smaller communities with limited facilities, a minimum team consisting of a doctor, a public health nurse and a social worker, working with new techniques and the assistance of national agencies, can provide high-quality care for most handicapped children.

Even in isolated rural areas, machinery now exists to bring team therapy to your child. An itinerant team clinic will, on request, make periodic visits to your community to evaluate your child's needs and prescribe treatment, which can then be administered by your local doctor.

Your state and local health agencies are prepared to help you set up team therapy in your community, not only for treatment, but for the early detection of handicapping conditions.

Most handicapped children will some day take part in community life. Programs to help them toward self-sufficiency, started for humanitarian reasons, are paying off in cash. The high cost of sending a child to a special public orthopedic school unit looks modest when compared to the alternate expense of keeping him in a hospital. Equipping the handicapped to earn a living is far less costly than supporting them for life.

But turning out "producers" is not the major goal of team therapy. Today's programs balance vocational training with cultural interests, recreation, sports and group activities, with all the human interchange that helps to make the handicapped person's life a worthwhile adventure—one that he can share with all of us.
—By Garrett Oppenheim

HELP FOR RETARDED CHILDREN

ALL in all, Charlotte and Clarence Bogert, Jr., consider themselves lucky. Lucky seems a fantastically inappropriate word to apply to a young couple burdened with that saddest of misfortunes, the birth of a mentally defective child. But lucky is the word they use for themselves because they have succeeded in finding an institution to take care of their child—a clean, bright, cheerful, modernly designed, scientifically managed place—and they are keenly aware of how few such places there are for children like theirs.

Today the Bogerts can relax, secure in the knowledge that their little girl will get the expert care she requires and which they would have been incapable of giving. They know she will have a better chance for happiness, living with children of her own mental level. And they know they will be better able to give a normal upbringing to their other two daughters, now that the family no longer need struggle with the manifold problems of caring for a child severely handicapped in body and brain.

The solution these parents have found is denied to thousands of other parents in many parts of the country. No door opens for them, no skilled hands take their problem from them. They are shackled with it; trapped within their four walls. They must fight it out alone, with all the hazards of emotional wreckage for themselves, other members of the family and the unfortunate child himself.

Such parents find a bitter irony in the situation. Around them they see a society that is finally facing up to the facts of mental deficiency. People at last are learning to speak without shame or revulsion of babies born with microcephaly, hydrocephaly, Mongolism and other forms of idiocy and imbecilism. They are recognizing the fact that these aren't visitations of the devil, aren't things to be concealed or spoken of in whispers, but are practical problems in physical health and psychology that should be approached in the same rational manner as are polio and rheumatic fever.

A Lack of Public Facilities

Yet in spite of this saner attitude, in many places nothing whatever is being done to provide facilities for babies born with mental defects. The story of overcrowding in state institutions is a familiar one. But crowded as they are, at least there are institutions all over the country for the feeble-minded who are of school age or older.

For those who are younger, the story is strikingly less favorable: there is a glaring shortage of facilities for the care of mentally deficient children between birth and the ages of five or six.

Of course, in many cases children need not and should not be institutionalized. They can be cared for at home. The parents, though, often need help—and the community can do a lot to help them, says the National Association for Retarded Children. It urges the establishment of out-patient clinics for the diagnosis of retardation and the guidance of parents, and a system of home visitors to train parents in the proper care of the retarded—a system in which New Jersey has pioneered. The Association is also pressing for the establishment of nursery classes where retarded children can learn to socialize; day-care centers to look after the children of working mothers; and short-term residential centers within the community where the children can be placed for limited periods when the parents are unable to take care of them because of business trips, illness or vacations.

But there remain many cases in which complete and permanent institutional care is necessary. Divorce or death may make home care impossible. There may be chronic illness or emotional difficulties among other members of the family group. Or else the retarded children may be so severely handicapped in body as well as in brain that they need constant medical care and in some cases must be bed patients as long as they live.

Working to call attention to the appalling shortage of facilities are organizations like the National Association for Retarded Children and state and local societies made up of parents of the mentally retarded. However, they feel the matter should be of concern to others, too, for the grimly simple reason that one can never know when his own family might be caught up in the same problem.

Case History

It happened to Bud and Charlotte Bogert. By the time their second child, Valory, was five months old, Charlotte began to wonder why the baby didn't sit up—hadn't even tried. When Valory reached eight months Charlotte could no longer ignore the plain signs that something was wrong, and pressed her pediatrician for an explanation. He asked her to take the baby to a specialist for consultation.

The specialist's examination didn't take long. He faced the young parents across his desk, and said, "I know of only one way of telling you this—I'll give it to you straight. Your child is Mongoloid. It isn't anything you can blame yourselves for. The medical profession isn't sure of the cause, but heredity, at least, has been almost completely ruled out as a determining factor. All I can advise you to do is to find a better home for Valory than you can provide. Have another child as soon as possible—and try to live as best you can with one of the greatest tragedies that can strike a family." During the following days Charlotte lived in a state of shock, but in time came to realize that she could not let herself go to pieces. She had to think about her older child and her husband. Charlotte then determined to learn everything she could about her daughter's affliction. She learned that Mongolism is a form of mental deficiency associated with certain physical characteristics, such as slant eyes and flattened features, that give a superficial resemblance to the Mongolian race. Mongoloid children are children as long as they live; they rarely reach the mental age of six. They are extremely susceptible to disease, particularly respiratory infections, but many more are living to adulthood because of new drugs.

Nature is kindly in one respect: Mongoloid children are usually docile and good-natured, and play contentedly with their toys. They are particularly happy with children of their own mental level. In an institution, they are free of the frustrations of having to compete with normal children or to deal with situations beyond their capacity. It was this consideration that convinced Bud to follow the doctor's advice about finding another home for Valory. The thought of letting her little girl go was intolerable to Charlotte; but she eventually gave in as she saw how much she was neglecting Susan to take care of

Valory's manifold needs; and the birth of a third child, which she was now awaiting, would, she knew, create an impossible situation in the home.

Private care costly. Having reached a decision, the Bogerts began to look into the possibility of placing Valory in a private institution. They discovered what so many families in the same situation have discovered—that good private care is expensive—beyond reach of their income. They then made anxious inquiry about public institutions, where fees are graded according to ability to pay. They learned that the State of New Jersey, where they lived, operates a nursery-hospital—the first institution in the United States specifically designed for mentally retarded babies.

Shortly after this nursery was opened, the babies' mothers were called to a meeting. Standing before them, the superintendent, Dr. Alfred H. Meese, gave an extraordinary talk which abolished the iron curtain that stands between so many public institutions and the public.

"I am going to open wide the doors of this nursery to you parents," Dr. Meese said. "You are going to be permitted—in fact, urged—to come here any hour of the day or night—three o'clock in the morning if you want to. You'll always be welcome. You won't have to stop at the office and register. You may drive directly to the nursery—stay as long as you please. I'll provide the sandwiches."

By this unorthodox approach, Dr. Meese completely transformed the role of "relatives."

Parents' Association Organized

Looked upon as nuisances and snoopers by many public institutions, here they became loyal, enthusiastic supporters. Organized as the Totowa Nursery Parents' Association, the fathers and mothers of the children have been rendering important aid to the institution.

At each meeting, held in the basement classroom at the Nursery, the parents find at the door highchairs and other furniture in need of repair, and many regularly take a piece with them as homework. At a cost of $2,000, the parents installed a public address system used for paging staff members and providing music.

"A state institution doesn't have to be a 'snake pit'—provided everybody connected with it is determined that it won't be," Dr. Meese says.

"One mother told me that when she informed a friend that she was going to bring her baby here, the friend looked at her in horror, and exclaimed, 'You'd put your child in one of those awful state institutions!'

"That's an all too common reaction," comments Dr. Meese. "Before parents bring their children here, I always invite them to come see the place, to attend a meeting of the Parents' Association and see what goes on. They quickly see that their fears are unfounded.

"Attending the meeting also has another good effect: they see they're not alone in their trouble. Looking around the room they see all kinds of parents —a minister, a schoolteacher, a physician, a newspaperman—all parents of children similarly afflicted—and the newcomers realize that this thing happens regardless of education, social status or any other consideration, and the realization gives them the reassurance they badly need."

Dr. Meese tells of a private-school teacher who was dead set against sending his new daughter, born pathetically malformed in body and brain, to a state institution. But there was another daughter in the family.

How Parents Are Helped

"My wife and I were able to stand this new situation," the teacher said, "but it knocked our ten-year-old daughter right off her rocker. She had always been a happy, high-spirited girl. Now she moped around the house all day. She had a burden. It completely changed her personality.

"My wife and I realized that there was nothing we could do for our new baby. If we could arrange to have her special needs taken care of elsewhere, perhaps we could win our other daughter back. That was why we decided to bring our baby here."

What this teacher subsequently found was that taking the child to the To- towa Nursery did not mean as marked a separation as he had feared. The Nursery's liberal policy on visits, and the many activities by which parents can contribute to its successful operation, preserve a feeling of closeness and pro- vide an outlet for parental love and concern. Some of the mothers periodically come to the Nursery to work; they join the nurses and attendants in dressing, bathing, feeding and playing with the children. Bud Bogert, who has served as president of the Parents' Association, and Charlotte, who has served as chairman of the Mothers' Committee, testify to the great feeling of release they have found in being able to work with other parents for the welfare not only of their own child but of many children with similar afflictions. They and the other parents feel a proprietary interest in the new Nursery; they believe that its success will encourage the establishment of similar institu- tions elsewhere. They are deeply happy when they hear of progress in that direction, such as the news that the State of Wisconsin had dedicated four new buildings at Union Grove especially planned for the care of young children with severe mental handicaps.

Four years after Valory was placed in the Nursery, her mother said, "She is still part of our family, though she may not sleep and eat with us. We have not hidden her from our lives, and we are not ashamed of her. Our children, Suzy and Paula, visit Valory with us frequently. Our friends and neighbors and the new people we meet are told about her. We know that she is happier in her own circle, where she doesn't have to compete with normal children for comfort, affection and enjoyment. We also know that whatever might hap- pen to us, Valory will always be provided with good food and someone to look after her."

There are parents' groups throughout the country working to bring about help and understanding for the retarded child. They also support medical re- search to aid the retarded and to prevent mental retardation in the future.

For information about state chapters or organizations, or for help in form- ing one, write to the National Association for Retarded Children, 99 Uni- versity Place, New York 3, N.Y.   *—By Joseph Shallit*

WHEN THERE'S TROUBLE IN THE FAMILY

I CAN'T imagine what's wrong with Johnny," the third-grade teacher said to the principal. "This is the third time this week I've had to keep him in after school. There he goes now . . ." she looked out of the window at a small boy with lowered head and bent shoulders who was trudging along the road.

"That's not how Johnny used to walk. It's not that he has done anything really bad these past weeks; he just doesn't do anything at all. He always used to be a pretty steady worker. Now he goes around with a sunk, desperate look and the boys can't even get him to participate in games."

"Why don't you call his mother for a conference?" the principal suggested. "She might give us a clue."

When Johnny's mother came to school, it was clear enough what was troubling him. His grandmother, who lived with the family, had become seriously ill, was dying. She couldn't be moved to a hospital and she needed constant care. The family couldn't afford private nurses. Johnny's mother was deeply attached to the dying woman and when her physical energy wasn't being drained in sickroom attendance, she was running her house and trying to see to her children's and her husband's needs. In her few free moments she was overcome with grief at the imminent death of her mother. To make matters worse, she was upset because she knew her children were suffering.

"I try to be cheerful," she told Johnny's teacher. "I try not to show how anxious I am, but they seem to know. Why, yesterday I was sitting in the living room crying when Johnny came home. Most times, I could have stopped, but nowadays I'm so tired I can't seem to keep myself under control. My mother called downstairs for something and I was afraid to let her see me so upset. Johnny said he'd go up. I thought he might tell her I'd been crying but when he got upstairs, I heard him saying, 'Ma's resting, Grandma, she can't come now. Can I get you something?' Now, that's real tact for an eight-year-old. He's a good boy, Johnny. I know I haven't given him any time lately. Whatever I can spare I give to Rita; she's only four and there's so much to do for her."

"Does Johnny know your mother is dying?" the principal asked.

"Oh, no," Johnny's mother answered, shocked. "I keep saying Grandma will be better if we take good enough care of her. I don't want to frighten him."

Don't Overprotect the Child

"I know you don't want to frighten him," said the principal, "but I wonder if it isn't more frightening for Johnny this way. He sees that his grandmother isn't getting better. And you've implied that if you could give her better care she'd get well. Perhaps he feels that just by being around, he is taking you away from her and so he's helping to make her worse. Of course that isn't true. With the disease she has, she'd be failing no matter how much care she got. But it's bad for Johnny to feel in any way responsible for the progress of her illness."

"I wonder," put in Johnny's teacher, "if the thought of your mother's death isn't so frightening to you that you find it impossible to admit it to yourself. It's a dreadful thing to face and it's a hard situation for your husband and your children to live through. But it just might be a little easier if Johnny knew his grandmother was going to die and that all of you were working to make her last days as comfortable as possible. That's pretty hard to do, but it would keep Johnny from thinking that he was in the way and it would keep him from feeling in any way responsible when your mother dies."

Difficult though it was, Johnny's mother saw the point and did what she could to be honest with her young son about his grandmother's condition. And though this was a trying period at best, and Johnny's work and play fell below his capacities, the terrible desperation left his face and he began to be like himself again.

Face Calamity Openly

Death, sickness and calamity are a part of living and are never easy to grapple with. They have lasting effects upon a child, but if they are faced openly and accepted these need not be disastrous.

When trouble comes we are sometimes so overwhelmed by it, so unwilling to accept it ourselves that we may actually transfer to our children our own bewilderment and terror, our own feelings of inadequacy and helplessness. In times of stress it is a good idea to examine our own conflicts first and see whether things have to be as bad as they seem to be. Even though there is pain and grief and anxiety we can, by awareness and effort, make it possible for our children to live through the black periods without permanent damage and with some sense of balance. If we succeed in this, sorrow, bitter though it is, may ultimately prove a constructive force in our children's lives. For it is important to learn that pain is as much a part of living as pleasure, and that the fairy-story life in which everyone lives happily ever after is pure fantasy. It is even more important to learn that pain can be endured and that sorrow passes. As impossible as it may seem at the time, one can survive without being inwardly destroyed.

Sickness causes particularly acute trouble. In addition to the worry, it means that mother cannot be with the child as much as she has been. Moreover, if a brother or sister becomes ill, there are subtle conflicts to complicate things further for a child: there is his pity and sympathy on the one hand, his rivalry and jealousy on the other. If it is father, an economic anxiety may be added to the sorrow over father's illness. When mother herself falls ill, this is perhaps the hardest of all for a child to handle. In such a case it is particularly important to find some warm, understanding friend, relative, teacher or maid who can serve as a genuine mother-substitute during the crisis.

We don't like to think about these things, but they do happen and it is at least some comfort to know that if they are honestly faced, if the child's position and conflicts are understood and if he is allowed to know the truth so far as his age permits, he can accept his deprivations, live through the situation and still maintain a healthy attitude.

Economic Troubles

There are other adult troubles besides sickness and accident that disturb a child's balance. Economic instability can play havoc with a home in any stratum of society. At such a time father may be depressed, panicstricken or in a helpless rage. Mother feels the strain and the children are the victims of a deep anxiety which is often harder to meet than are the actual economic privations. Worry over money and job can throw anyone off his base and make life anything but rosy. Of course one cannot burden children with economic problems that they won't understand, but there is much in the situation they can and do understand. It is far healthier for them to know the real cause of their parents' strange behavior than to have their parents try to keep up the myth that "everything's all right" when they well know that something is wrong.

Mother is worried about father's job. She punctuates the day by screaming at Suzy. Suzy begins to feel that she must be a terribly bad girl and that mother no longer loves her. Father comes home from a bad day at the office depressed and fearful. He lets loose his rage at the state of affairs on Stevey, who has just broken an ashtray. Stevey is frightened, becomes convinced that his father hates him and that he must be terrible.

If mother could say, "Look, Suzy, I screamed at you because I'm worried. Daddy's having trouble. He doesn't know where he can find work and it's Daddy's work that buys us what we need. I'm worried these days so try not to mind if I scream at you sometimes. I'm not really angry with you. I'm just worried." That would not be precisely joyous news for Suzy, but she would be able to cope with it more easily than she would with the thought that mother doesn't love her any more or that she herself has done something to cause mother's anger.

If father could say to Stevey, "Stevey, I'm sorry I lost my temper. It really wasn't you or anything you did. It's just that things have gone badly downtown and I'm all upset. Everything will probably work out but right now don't pay too much attention to me if I blow up. It's not you, it's the way I'm feeling these days." Stevey would be apt to feel pretty grown-up if his father talked to him like that and would undoubtedly be careful to keep out of dad's way when he sees a storm coming on.

The times in which we live are not conducive to peace of mind. The relationships we work hard to maintain are often fraught with tension and strain. Whether it is a function of the times or of our own inner conflicts, we are likely to run into emotional upheavals in our family relationships that affect our children deeply. For instance, we might as well accept the fact that mothers and fathers don't always get along happily all of the time. There are bound to be some storms, but they pass.

During emotionally anxious times, just as in times of sickness or financial stress, there is no use in trying to act out a role. To pretend that everything is sweetness and light when you feel like throwing things or crying just doesn't work. It's true, you can't throw things or cry all day, especially if you are the mother of children, but you can let them learn the profound truth that even when people love each other and live together, they sometimes get angry, hurt or confused; that life doesn't always offer smooth sailing.

Parental Quarreling

"Pete," said his mother one day when her husband had stalked out of the house after an angry quarrel, "you must think your father and I have gone crazy. Well, in a kind of way we have. Dad and I just don't seem to be hitting it off right just now. I'm angry at him and he's angry at me. It's hard on us and it's hard on you, I know. But we'll get over it so don't worry too much. And remember, we both love you and you are in no way responsible for this mess we're living through."

As uncomfortable as living with mother and father can be during such a time, Pete will be able to weather it more easily after his mother's honest admission that she is not the perfect wife or mother, that dad is not the perfect husband or father and that their relationship is not storybook stuff. Pete will come out better in the long run than Mary, who comes home every day to find her mother with red eyes and swollen face. "What's the matter, Mother?" Mary used to ask sympathetically. "Nothing, darling," her mother would sob. "I just got to thinking about things." "Things" has got to be a terrifying word in Mary's mind. "Things" explain why her father comes home glum these nights if he comes home at all; why the family eats meals in dreadful silence; why, when dad begins to say something, mother nods a warning in Mary's direction; why, after she's in bed, she can hear sobs and angry voices downstairs and sometimes a door slamming. Mary is frightened, just as frightened as her mother, and Mary doesn't know what it is all about or what is going to happen. She knows everyone is dreadfully unhappy at home and she is afraid that something even worse is going to happen, but no one tells her anything. She gets upset stomachs whenever she eats nowadays. She has developed a nervous twitch in her face. Her school marks are getting worse. Everything looks about as black as it can for Mary.

It is easy enough to say that adults should not act this way. But sometimes they do. And when this happens it is best for parents to try to be honest with their children. For children must learn sooner or later that human beings have trouble, that trouble is painful but it can be lived through and it can end. The child whose parents are honest with him realizes that they respect him and feel he has a share in their joint life. He won't be too afraid to grow up nor will he be so afraid of trouble that he will avoid any real living in order to avoid any possible unhappiness. He is learning that trouble tends to be doubled or squared or cubed if it isn't faced. He is learning that, hard as it is, it is best to look his troubles in the face and find a way to overcome them. This is a lesson we all should learn.

—By Ruth Newman

PREPARING A CHILD
FOR THE HOSPITAL

IF your child faces an operation you will want to do everything you can to build up his courage and relieve him of his doubts and anxieties. The unprepared child approaches such an experience with great apprehension. Taking the anesthetic may be an ordeal for him and awakening a time of great upset with refusal to cooperate in any way and excessive crying. When this happens, his convalescence often is difficult and his return to normal routine may be delayed. The child is apt to remember the whole distressing terror-filled experience for a long time and will show after-effects that are upsetting to him and to his family.

As one precocious five-year-old said in telling of her night terrors following an operation: "You know, I had my tonsils out. And now when I go to sleep at night my imagination bites me and I have bad dreams." Other children may make greater than usual demands on their mother for attention. Some go back to long discarded fears of darkness or of being alone. Other temporary reactions may include a distrust of doctors, nurses or strangers, or resentment against parents or teachers. This may be shown by disobedience, destructiveness or temper tantrums. Rarely, an even more serious disturbance of behavior may occur. However, it is comforting to know that these upsets do not necessarily follow every operation, nor do they usually last very long. But it is important for parents, and doctors as well, to realize that they may occur and to exercise every care and precaution to avoid them.

Careful preparation of the child who faces an unfamiliar experience with definite physical discomfort and psychological anxiety will lessen or avoid undesirable emotional after-effects of surgery and hospitalization.

Parents play an important part in the psychological preparation of a child for surgery. The anxieties that they may unintentionally pass on to a child can overload him with frightening emotions that he cannot easily handle. Thus he is handicapped by a double load, his own quite natural fears and those he has caught from his parents.

Parental Anxiety

When your child is facing an operation you naturally are concerned. You begin to remember the alarming stories told by friends and relatives. Or, perhaps you recall distressing experiences of your own. We all remember only too well our own childhood fears and anxieties and the pain-filled incidents in our early lives. And just as we relive our joys through our children, we also relive our worries through them. So we must expect some degree of fear or resentment on our own part. If unchecked, this will affect our attitude toward our child's forthcoming operation. Without wishing to, we thus pass on our own anxieties to our children. Remember that your child reacts like a barometer to the emotional pressures of your internal climate. When your dark feelings and thoughts are hidden by a forced smile or unfelt gaiety, you may succeed in fooling yourself but you don't fool him.

Then how can you steer a course between your own fears, open or hidden, and your children's fears, which you so strongly influence?

Face disturbing thoughts. Force yourself to face your disturbing thoughts. Try to trace them to their sources. Analyze them realistically. As you think through your own past experience, isolate the disturbing incidents and determine to prevent repeating them with your child.

Did Aunt Sara's frightened whispers that stopped when you entered the room scare you?

Or was it grandmother's oversolicitous, "And how are you now?" Or did mother look at you and cry?

Or what probably was the most alarming—did no one ever mention the coming operation as though it were too dreadful to talk about? Did the conspiracy of tight-lipped silence freeze the natural questions you wanted to ask, so that simple facts became shadowy, unknown demons, living in your vivid imagination? Were you ignored pointedly? Did oversolicitude, excess caution, timidity, worry you? Did the phony pretense that "it was nothing" terrify you?

Coming to terms with the past will relieve you of much of your tension. Also it will help you to recognize and accept the fact that things are different today. Medical methods have improved tremendously. Since you were a child, hospitals are better equipped, personnel better trained. The dangers of tonsillectomy, for example, have been reduced to almost zero. Also, most doctors are well aware of the psychologic needs of their patients. With your cooperation in calmly preparing your child, in terms of the present-day realities of operative procedures, there is no reason for excessive worry.

To reassure your youngster, first reassure yourself that all will go well. If you have doubts or worries or you want specific information, speak to your surgeon. At his first contact with the child, your surgeon will want to take definite steps to establish himself as the child's good friend—as a trustworthy person who is kind, sympathetic and interested in making him better.

Explain About the Operation

A child will show his anxiety either directly through changes in behavior or more openly in words. A frightened child may become restless, disobedient, aggressive, uncontrolled or unnaturally reserved. He may lose his appetite, grow cranky, cry out in his sleep and generally seem not himself. His biggest fear is the operation itself.

To combat this basic fear give him a full explanation of what to expect —the smell of antiseptic, the bed on wheels that will take him to the operating room, the white face masks and rubber gloves that the doctor and nurses will wear. Patiently repeat the details of your explanation as often as the child asks for them and in words with which the child is familiar. Be sure that the words themselves aren't frightening.

Tell why the operation is necessary. Convince him of the benefits. The success of "talking out" the anxieties depends on the child's confidence in you, his parent, and your ability to explain about the operation and how it will help him in a way that he will understand. Don't become impatient if he asks you to explain again and again. Remember how often a young child enjoys hearing the same story or nursery rhyme. Also, by letting the child know how you expect him to act, how the brave child acts, you tip him off on how to win your approval. Your approval is what your child depends on most urgently to carry him through this and other difficult situations, so help him to win plenty of it.

Don't say it won't hurt. To answer reassuringly a child's direct or indirect questions about how much the operation is going to hurt is of major importance. The child's response to pain will depend both on its intensity and on how well prepared he is for it. Surprise intensifies all reactions, particularly unpleasant ones. So tell your child frankly, yet casually, that he will be uncomfortable after the operation. If it is a tonsil operation, for example, tell him that he will have a sore throat—but after all, he has had them before, hasn't he? Sure, they were unpleasant but he took them bravely. And this one won't be much worse than the others and, at least, it will keep him from having bad ones in the future. The child who is unprepared for the postoperative discomfort will feel deceived and resentful. Consequently, his anger will actually add to his pain by exaggerating his reactions.

It is most important to tell your child that he will feel absolutely no pain during the operation, as he will be sound asleep. Knowing that he will feel nothing will reassure him. As for the after-pain, tell him that the doctor and nurses have medicine which will help. Children have such faith in their parents that this sincere reassurance from you will allay much apprehension. Most children are responsive to an honest discussion of their difficulties. They probably have learned already that some pain is unavoidable in life and that they can depend on their parents to help them bear it. Except for those too young to reason, most children will accept logical explanations from a trusted parent and feel greatly relieved by them.

Length of hospital stay. Some hospitals allow parents to stay overnight with their children, most do not. Usually the child shares a large room or ward with several other children. Nurses are always on duty, either in the ward or within easy hearing range, and frequent checkups are made. You should find out the details of the particular arrangements being made for your child. Ask in advance the routine of the hospital, whether the child enters the night before the operation or in the morning, when he can reasonably expect to go home. These decisions depend on the judgment of the surgeon and should be discussed with him. Under proper safeguards, there is considerable advantage in returning the child to his own familiar bed as soon as possible.

Help Child Be Courageous

Mention, if possible, good examples of courage on the part of children in similar situations. Obviously your child must know and like the children mentioned and they must be about his same age and level of emotional maturity. Make him feel that all of you—daddy, mommy, the doctor, nurses— are somewhat like actors in a movie, that each has a part to play. But that he is the main actor and all the rest are only assistants to help him play his part as well as he can. The feeling that he has the important part will appeal to his natural sense of the dramatic.

Tell about the anesthetic. If possible make a preliminary visit to the hospital. Comment on the doctor as a helpful, friendly person; mention pleasant facts such as visitors, gifts and ice cream when he is well enough. Don't give any details about the operation itself, since your child will have no memory of it. However, mention the anesthetic, even though the child under sedation remembers very little of that. Focus the conversation on the novel aspects of the experience ahead: the hospital room he will occupy, the bed that can go up and down, the dressings cart, the food tray, and so forth.

The younger the child, the greater is his need for help in undergoing a new experience. Many doctors feel it is best, if possible, to postpone surgery on a child too young to understand your explanations and reassurance until he is a bit older—over four if possible.

In addition to his normal curiosity about what is going to happen to him, a child has many fears and uncertainties. Though some of these may not be expressed, all of them have to be anticipated and satisfactory assurance given for each. Don't underestimate or disregard childhood anxieties and don't assume that the child has no fears just because he doesn't express any. A general preview of what's going to happen and how it will happen greatly diminishes his natural worry about the unknown. The knowledge of an approaching event—even of an unpleasant one—makes it much less terrifying to a child. We all know that it's easier to look forward to something that has been explained than to live with an exaggerated dread of expected but unfamiliar harm, danger or pain.

Common Fears

Parents will want to allay any fears their child may have about the operation or his stay in the hospital. One of the commonest anxieties children have is fear of separation from their parents. Any threat of danger intensifies the child's need for the parents' sympathetic and watchful presence. To lessen the anxiety brought on by the expected separation assure your child that you will be with him constantly, except for the time in the operating room. Here, his friend, the doctor, will be waiting to take care of him. It's important for this friendship to have been established—for here the surgeon temporarily takes over for the parent as the source of security and comfort.

Fear of change. Children often fear change. A child is less certain of himself and of his ability to gain the approval of those around him when he is away from his customary routine and familiar environment. To help set him at ease, try to turn his attention to the interesting surroundings. You might encourage a laugh about the funny hospital gown he puts on with strings tied in the back, unlike his usual pajamas. You can tell him about the room furnishings unlike those at home—the high bed with the elevating back rest, the bedside cabinet, the signal button to summon the nurse, and so forth. Although these are taken for granted by adults, they often disturb a child. When explained they become objects of interest rather than of fear. To a very young child the doctor's mask may be presented as like those worn on Hallowe'en. An older child will be impressed by its importance for cleanliness.

A favorite toy or book brought to the hospital provides a link with home.

A familiar object affords comfort, particularly to a younger child.

Nurses, internes and hospital attendants, with special skill in handling children, contribute greatly to a child's peace of mind by being cheerful and patient. A moment taken to answer a question kindly or a friendly compliment heartens the youngster considerably and makes him feel important as an individual.

Fear of bodily loss. Fear of the loss of a part of his body may trouble a child deeply. A child may learn suddenly that his appendix or his tonsils and adenoids are to be taken out. He understands only imperfectly what they are and how the removal takes place. Unless the what and the how are carefully explained, the child may brood over the loss of something that is a part of him and so is important to him. This disturbing notion may be distorted to a dread of mutilation and of change in appearance.

Even after you have discussed in general the fact that the tonsils or appendix are now useless, that they have become troublemakers, that many people have them removed, your child may actually ask some strange questions, such as "Will I have a big hole in me?" or "Will I be able to talk again?" To dispel such fears, assure him that there will be no loss of any of his abilities and no deformities whatsoever. Also, that no other parts of the body will be removed. You might mention playmates of his who have been operated on.

Fear of death. This is a less common fear in children than it is in adults. It usually is based on having known of someone's death or perhaps on having lost a pet. This fear is influenced largely by the child's observations of the attitudes of parents or friends toward death. (For a further discussion of this subject see article, "When Children Ask About Death.")

Imaginary fears. Phantom fears may arise from distorted tales told by other children or by tactless adults or from the child's own imagination and misconceptions. These distortions are due to his immaturity and inexperience. However foolish and illogical such fears are to the adult, to the child they are terrifying. Do not pooh-pooh them.

Imaginary fears are common. To deal with them, one must understand what they mean and how they threaten a child's self-confidence and security. Try to explain them away in words the child understands. When possible, compare them with the realities of the child's own experiences. Be casual and confident, and keep reassuring the frightened child of your support and love. But guard against increasing his fears by overemphasis. Listen to your child carefully. He'll let you know when he understands what you are saying, when his fears have quieted—not always in words, perhaps, but by changing the subject, running away to play, snuggling up to you, or even by eating his supper with a suddenly regained appetite.

Convalescence

Stable children intelligently informed of what to expect will undergo an operation and bounce back rapidly with the customary resilience of childhood. "Operation" even becomes their favorite game for a while. Your child may be the surgeon. His playmates are nurses and assistants. The Teddy bear will have to grow repeated crops of tonsils or appendixes or what not to enable the young medico to act out his recent experiences. By becoming the doctor, the child becomes the one who "dishes it out" instead of "taking it." In acting it out he gets even, so to speak, and finally digests the experience so that it ceases to be a troublesome memory.

Most children respond very well to good handling because they have the security of their parents' love and help. They trust their parents and those whom their parents endorse—including doctors and nurses. Guided successfully through an operative procedure the child will have the great satisfaction of having faced and controlled his fears. *—By Jack Allan Weiss, M.D.*

IF YOUR CHILD
HAS A MUSCULAR TIC

MUSCULAR tics are fairly common in children; you probably know at least one child who has a batting, twitching, or squinting of the eye, a contortion of the neck or face muscles, a wrinkling of the nose or some other involuntary habit, frequently repeated.

Not only do habitual coughs, grunts and throat clearings constitute tics, but many experts include stammering, too. Certainly stammering is habitual, repetitious, and wholly beyond conscious control, while it serves no useful purpose.

It is one thing, however, to know somebody who has a muscular tic. It is quite another when your own child has one.

This is how W. R. F. Collis, editor of a well known "Textbook of Pediatrics," defines muscular tic.

"By tics," says Collis, "we mean peculiar twitchings which often take the form of sudden sharp spasms either in the face, blinking, wrinkling the brows, grimacing, gnashing the teeth, or in the region of the body muscles, shaking the head, shrugging the shoulders, grasping or dancing movements, which repeat themselves persistently in the same manner at irregular intervals . . . When the patient thinks he is being watched, or if he has other feelings of discomfort, or becomes angry, the tic spasms grow worse. They cannot be suppressed by exercising will power."

So the diagnosis is usually not difficult. In mercurial, always-on-the-go children, their motor unrest may express itself in the form of jerkings and twitchings which, however, do not exist, as authorities point out, when the child's attention is held.

Most authorities testify that muscular tics are both harmless and useless. As one authority puts it "However violent the motor tic may be . . . it never results in any physical hurt to the patient or damage to his surroundings. Its inconvenience consists mainly in making him conspicuous and self-conscious."

Vulnerable Age Group

According to some doctors who have made a study of these nervous manifestations, "Children with tics often are restless and lively. Their thought flow is very fast and intelligence considerably above average." . . . "Tics are found in children of high-strung nervous organization. They are often diminished by rest and diversion, are accentuated by self-consciousness or excitement, disappear during sleep." Is there a close connection, then, between personality and tics? It would seem that there is.

All authorities agree that tics occur most frequently in children, and the early-school age seems to be the "ripest" time—between five and seven. 71 per cent of all tics appear by the age of 10. Tics do not occur in infants, and often they disappear in adolescence.

Tension a Cause

Many pediatricians freely admit to knowing little about muscular tics. To them, they are a harmless symptom in a child, pointing to emotional imbalance. The comment of Dr. Charles A. Tompkins, well known pediatrician, is to the point.

"I think you cure tics when you eliminate tension. Yet I'm sure that long-standing tics hang on long after the underlying reason has been cleared. A habit of years' standing doesn't just drop off suddenly.

"I knew one boy who for several years had an eye-squint tic. It was caused, basically, by emotional conflicts at home which he couldn't cope with—he was very competitive with his sister and brother. He couldn't allow himself to blow off his tenseness and anger directly; instead, it worked itself out in this odd habit, which may have started because he got some foreign object in his eye.

"After the object was out, though, the blinking and squinting continued as an automatic, unconscious act—a muscular tic. It made his parents notice him, show concern over him, even get angry at him. At least he got attention.

"When the parents understood the underlying cause of the habit and changed conditions at home so that Bill's needs were met directly, he didn't have to resort to this device, and gradually, some months later, it dropped away completely. In a word, when the tension left, the tic eventually left."

"All of us," says Dr. H. H. Humphreys, Chief Psychologist of the Children's Division of the Nebraska Psychiatric Institute, "when pressure is great, or exhaustion is near (and emotional exhaustion causes bodily exhaustion), tend to express the tension in less-controlled muscular activity."

The school beginner. "A child is less able than an adult to curb impulses successfully, and yet, as he starts school, he is going to have a strong need, through new social pressures, to curb them. If this results in failure, the groundwork is laid for a tic to develop. The tic may represent a compromise between the need to act and a fear of acting.

"There is more pressure during this period of starting school, to hold back his own natural impulses to act. That's possibly why tics are much more frequent in children; though even some adults, with their greater ability to clamp a lid on their impulses, can't help jumping if a book is closed suddenly. And the jumping will be exaggerated if the adult is harried, anxious, tired, or high-strung."

Don't Make the Child Self-Conscious

Parents are often irritated or made anxious by a tic in their child. Maybe this feeling is due to the child's inability to control the tic; to many of us, lack of control is upsetting. The parents' sense of embarrassment is sometimes very strong, because they often identify closely with their children.

Be reassured: the tic is absolutely harmless. And focusing on it, even with loving concern, is the surest way to entrench it. Most children are not bothered by their tics, unless someone keeps calling attention to them. After all, it is the child and his environment that need study, not the tic.

"Children almost never come in to the Nebraska Psychiatric Institute for treatment of a tic, as such," says Dr. Humphreys. "The tic is regarded as an annoying symptom, suggesting deeper emotional tension and conflict which is working out in this motor, involuntary way."

Relief of tension causes cure. One girl not yet in her teens, Dr. Humphreys recalled, came to see him with a violent arm tic. Mary would also break off a sentence simultaneously with a sharp head twist. Neurologists ruled out neurological causes—brain damage, nerve damage, and the like—with a thorough physical examination. That is routine procedure, always.

Mary was okay, physically. But then he began finding out other things— she was being ostracized by the other children at school; her father and mother were separated; her grandmother was severe with her and was worried about having money to get along.

The treatment given Mary was general, permissive, accepting. There was no focusing on the tic at all. She was allowed to just talk, at first, about her doings. Gradually, though, as she talked, she got to her feelings.

Asked, "How did you feel over this thing?" she became more and more able to tell how she felt. She became more comfortable with herself. Soon her multiple tic had disappeared.

Why? First, she was better able to handle her problems. Second, her problems were whittled down. Her mother, also coming in to discuss family problems, became more understanding. They moved to another town, a different school, where Mary made new friends. They got a TV set and shared an enjoyment of programs. They talked together at home, where before it had been a silent house. She learned some of the reasons behind her parents' inability to get along. All these things helped.

Much bottled-up hostility is present in some children. And such children are more apt to have tics. These children with much hidden anger often appear passive, until there is a break-out somewhere; then they over-react.

Release of energy important. Children who have grown up in institutions are very apt to develop habit mannerisms or tics like "rocking," rhythmic movements that have no real meaning except that they are the child's instinctive way of creating motor response to release energy which has no other way out. Sometimes such tics appear in children from good homes who have been fenced off and not given enough to do.

"I think," says Dr. Humphreys, "it is better to give young children plenty of motor activities—doing things, but not focusing on how they shall be done. Some parents, for example, constantly try to make a three-year-old perfect in speech, instead of just letting him talk. This kind of thing, it seems to me, makes a fertile ground for the formation of a tic. Also, a child needs to exercise his big body muscles, to romp, climb, swing, run and play."

Cure Cause, Not Symptom

Most authorities hold out no hope for corrective muscular treatment and control of tics unless the inner emotional cause has been dealt with. If tension has been diminished, then perhaps exercises which voluntarily call the self-same tic muscles into strenuous play, may shorten the time the habit hangs on. But exercises should never be imposed on the child; they should never even be thought of unless he insists on them. Then your pediatrician may be called on for help in working out such exercises.

Operations to correct tics are ill-advised. All forms of retention dressings and appliances, too, are worse than useless; at first apparently helpful, they soon become irksome, unbearable, and harmful.

By themselves, changes of environment also seem to have little effect on tics. Probably the reason is that, in a sense, the child carries with him his own environment. His parents' restrictive conscience and standards usually have become his own.

Nor is there any magic treatment, any drug, that will banish the tic, though some of the drugs prescribed for seriously disturbed, unhappy people, may ease the tic temporarily.

As one authority puts it, "The treatment of tics is a difficult task. It is a matter of common experience that the more the patient's attention is directed toward the movements, the less they are likely to disappear. This is why parental admonitions, nagging, and warnings do not usually result in improvement. This is also why such measures as massage, electrotherapy, exercises before a mirror, and suggestions centering on the tic only too often prove unsuccessful. It is the child, not the tic that should be treated."

What Parents Can Do

First, know what tics are—what they mean and what they don't mean. Overconcern in parents is common, and is always complicating.

Second, if the tic is of long standing, and if it seems to be one symptom among others—trouble at school, unusual passivity, poor social relationships, conflict in the home, poor health, persistent loss of weight, lack of appetite, and so on—probably the parents should discuss the whole problem with some understanding, capable person.

Perhaps your pediatrician can give you help, or knows where you can get it. Maybe a child psychiatrist is available. Maybe you can relieve tensions in the child yourself just by making an effort to be more understanding. Maybe what he needs most is acceptance of himself as he is; maybe he needs to feel that you like him with tic or bad grades or eating problem or whatever.

Look at the child's relationships in the home and at school. There's a reason or reasons for tension always, if we can only find them. You may need skilled help. It will help you to talk to somebody who can give that help.

Third, it is common sense for parents and friends to focus as little on the tic itself as possible, unless the child insists. Then the nature of the movement, the part it plays in helping him to relieve his inner tension, may be explained to him.

If your child is really bothered by his tic—if he feels it is keeping him from making friends, or is making his parents dislike him—encourage him to talk with you about his troubles. Talking things out together is often helpful.

—By Fletcher D. Slater

HOW SOUND ARE YOUR VALUES ABOUT MONEY?

IS there any parent who hasn't been somewhat taken aback the first time a child asks, "How rich are we, Mommy?"—or "Daddy, do you make more money than Jimmy's father?" Questions about money and status can start popping when a child is only two or three. And they can be among the hardest of children's questions to answer.

For how we answer reveals our most personal, often unconscious attitudes about ourselves and others. We may suddenly be brought face to face, for example, with hidden wishes or fears we never fully knew we had. What we say tells our children, too, how much and in what way and why we value this thing of coins and paper we call money.

If one part of us secretly or enviously yearns for lots of money while another part of us believes that money isn't everything—then what? We can tell our children what sounds good, without fully believing it ourselves, or we can tell them what we really believe, feeling the belief to be shameful.

It's true that in concrete matters like family budgeting most of us find our way to some kind of balance. Most of us don't find it too troublesome to decide where to stop between giving our children "too much" or "too little." When, for example, three-year-old Janie wants to buy twelve packages of cupcakes in the supermarket, it's not difficult to say, "No, we can't. If we spend that much money on cupcakes we won't have enough money left to buy you a hoop."

An answer like this usually works. Janie will usually prefer a toy she's been wanting. Even if she still prefers the twelve packages, she's been exposed to the idea that there are limits: we can have this or that, not both. In a pinch, it's you who makes this choice.

When Janie gets to be eight years old, she may take it into her head to ask for a cabin cruiser. That's easy too: "It costs too much." We can elaborate: "If we bought a cabin cruiser, we'd have no money for food, or dresses, or to pay for our house." Here we've made another distinction for Janie, the one between necessity and luxury.

Competitive Values

But questions that center about money become more complicated when they involve us in comparisons with other families. For one thing, it's then that we have to face the bugaboos of competitive feelings—not only our children's and their playmates' but, more important, our own.

The three-year-old son of one of my neighbors refused one day to play with his friend, Arthur. When his mother asked him why, all he said was, "I don't like him." But then he blurted out, "All he wants to play is *biggerness.* He always says everything he has is bigger than mine!"

In Arthur's case, a blatant competitiveness has been taught him by parents who keep trying to prove their own superiority by "biggerness" in everything they do and have. Usually, most of us strongly disapprove of this kind of competitiveness. Because we find it unlovely, we tend to bury our own competitiveness even when we keep on comparing ourselves with close friends, neighbors and relatives, so when our children ask us questions about money we may be troubled about what to say.

We may find ourselves trying to pretend that there *are* no economic differences when, as our children can see, there are. This doesn't mean that we should always be pointing out economic differences. It does mean that we need to know clearly ourselves why there are differences and what these differences are before we can set our children straight.

Suppose for example, your answer to "But aren't 'they' richer than us?" is "No, not really." In thinking about it, you realize that "they" must be roughly comparable in income to you—but "they" spend their money differently. Then your answer makes plain the fact that different parents decide for themselves what expenditures seem best for their family.

You may buy more ballet tickets and less expensive clothes, while Judy's parents buy better clothes and fewer tickets. Your family may drive a ten-year-old car and take farther-flung, more expensive summer vacations, while Judy's family has a new car every year but stays home in the summer. What you are saying is: It is our family's decision to spend our money this way, and the decision of Judy's family to spend it their way. What seems "richer" isn't money—it's choice and difference.

Material vs. "Real" Values

But something else is involved when "they" *are* in fact richer. Sometimes because we have hidden competitive feelings ourselves, or perhaps feel envious or guilty for not having done as well financially as another family—we may try to pretend that the other family isn't really better off. We may, for example, go so far as to admit they have more money—but rush to offset that admission by detailing "how much better off we are really." When five-year-old Helene told her mother that a little friend had "more things" than they did, Helene's mother answered, "Yes, but you have a grandma and grandpa who love you, and she has no grandparents at all. You have a sister and brother to play with and *her* sister is away at college."

Isn't it ourselves, more than our children, whom we reassure by answering in effect, "But we really are better off!" Our Helenes are by and large simply seeking matter-of-fact information and all we need answer is, "Yes, the Smiths do have more money." We needn't allow our guilt, anxiety, competitiveness or unsorted feelings about money to force us into trying to prove that we are "as well off" or "better off" when the question raised is one of *money*. We do our children the greater service of keeping them in touch with reality when we admit to them that there are some things other families have that we simply cannot afford.

Prestige and Earning Power

If Bob comes in with the announcement that Henry has a brand-new two-wheeler we can say, "How nice for him." If he goes on to say that he wants a new two-wheeler, too, then we can tell him whether we can afford it or not. If we can, fine. But if we can't, "We don't have enough money." When Bob asks why we don't have enough money while Henry's family does, we can say: "Because Daddy's job doesn't pay as much as Henry's father's job."

This needn't mean, as it unhappily does to many people in our times,

"Because your father isn't as good as Henry's father." It means this only if we feel this way and only when our previous answers to "How rich are we?" have been coverups, begging the real question.

Suppose Bob goes on to ask: *"Why* doesn't Dad make as much money as Henry's father?"

The truth usually is: "Because different kinds of work pay differently."

Of course, sometimes there's more to it than this simple statement. Sometimes, because of discrimination in jobs and for other reasons, people can't get the kind of well paid work their abilities entitle them to. If you feel this unfairness exists in finding or getting good jobs, you can say so. Just a bare statement with young children—not waxing bitter or emotional about it. It's never good to burden very young children with too intense feelings of our own. It *is* good, though, to give honest answers.

What should we tell the youngsters who ask, "How much does daddy make?" Many parents who'd like to be honest with their children but don't want their income broadcast to the neighbors, don't know what to say. Some just say in a friendly, reasonable way that they don't want to answer that question now—and sometimes get away with it.

But if you feel there's really no reason for you *not* to tell, it certainly does your child no harm to be given an answer. He won't be able to do much with the information anyway—and the figure will be satisfying.

Keeping Up with the Joneses

What happens to our children when we pretend to be richer than we are —either by word or the deed of "keeping up appearances?" First, we tell them in effect that we feel inferior because we aren't as rich as others, or perhaps that we feel others won't accept us if we aren't as rich or richer than they. We imply then that our relations with other people hinge largely on the matter of money.

A child may react to this in one of two ways: He may adopt the technique of pretense—thus carrying on our confusions, dubious values and distorted way of relating to others. Or as he becomes aware of our bluffing, he may reject our way of relating—with contempt and in rebellion—which seriously mars our *own* relation with him.

None of this is meant to imply that we should give our children the idea money isn't important. On the contrary, we need to teach them to recognize its full value. So it's vital that our children be taught how to get good value for money. And we also want them to understand that our value as people— our human resources—can't be measured just by money. *—By Sara Welles*

EDUCATION

CHOOSING A NURSERY SCHOOL • PRIVATE SCHOOLS
SPECIAL SCHOOLS • GETTING INTO COLLEGE
PARENT-TEACHER COOPERATION • HOME HELP WITH SCHOOL WORK
LEARNING TO STUDY • GIFTED CHILDREN • ALL ABOUT TESTS
SCHOOL HEALTH CHECKUPS • SCHOOL LUNCH PROGRAM
ARE WE WASTING MONEY ON SCHOOL BUILDINGS?
WHAT DO YOU KNOW ABOUT YOUR CHILD'S SCHOOL?

NURSERY SCHOOLS

YOUR first step in choosing a nursery school is to make a list of all the schools in your area—provided, of course, that you are lucky enough to live in a town with more than one nursery school. This may comprise your whole section of the city or your whole town, depending on size, because many nursery schools provide transportation. If there is a central licensing or registering agency in your city—the Board of Education or some other municipal agency should be able to tell you whether there is—you may be able to get a list from them. Some nursery schools are listed in the telephone directory under "Schools," "Nursery Schools" or "Day Nurseries." Some may have small announcements in the classified advertisements of the newspaper, under "Schools," "Instruction," "Business Personals" or "Special Services." Your friends may give you the names of still others. When your list is complete, it may contain names ranging from the impressive State University Nursery School or First Presbyterian Church Nursery School down to the quaint "Jack and Jill" or "Henderson's Happy Haven for Little Folk." Don't let the name make your decision for you. You'll want to consider them all. It is wise to start your inquiries early as some schools have waiting lists. You may want to follow these suggestions:

Get Factual Information

Telephone all the schools on your list and ask them three factual questions: 1. Are there any openings in the youngest group this fall? 2. What are the fees? 3. Is transportation provided? The first question alone may cut down your list considerably, perhaps to your disappointment. The other two questions will eliminate schools that are too expensive for your budget or too far away if you haven't the use of a car.

When you are ready to visit one of the schools on your list, telephone ahead of time and ask the director when it is most convenient for you to come. If you can, try to see the school in action.

The first thing you notice about the physical setup of the school may predispose you to like or dislike it, depending on whether the school seems bright, pretty and roomy, or dim and unattractive. After your initial glance around, go over these details: Is there plenty of light and air? Enough windows, artificial light in dark corners? Is some of the children's work displayed? Is the playroom large enough for many activities to be going on at once?

Observe the furniture and play equipment. Are tables and chairs sturdy-looking? Are shelves low enough for any child to reach? Is there a wide variety of play equipment in evidence? Look for things to push, to pull, to pound, to build with and to put together. Look for simple doll equipment: dolls, a bed, a rocker or two. Look for books, wooden picture puzzles, formboards and pegboards. Material for creative activity may not be in use at the moment, but look around for pictures or objects made with paints, crayons, scissors, paste, clay and wood. A piano or phonograph will be evidence of music play—although music and rhythms may be held in a separate room. None of this equipment need be elaborate or expensive-looking. The simplest material for play stimulates the most varied activity among children.

Don't be too easily pleased by an appearance of perfect neatness. A certain amount of clutter is one of the good signs you will want to look for, because it tells you that this is a place with genuine freedom to develop. However, the clutter should not be messy and trashy. Something between perfect order and complete chaos characterizes a good school.

Perhaps you entered the school by way of the playground. The important thing here is size: it should be large, because outdoor play needs plenty of space. In a good school you'll see stationary equipment, like swings, slides, climbers and sandbox, and a variety of movable equipment. For warm weather, there should be some provision for water play.

You will want to go all through the school to note safety and convenience of arrangement. Are there at least two exits from each room? Is it possible for the children to open the doors? Is first aid equipment readily available? Is the bathroom accessible to all rooms and to the playground? Are bathroom fixtures child-size or provided with platforms?

There should be provision for a staff nurse to examine the children each morning for colds and contagious diseases and a doctor should be available. The kitchen should meet sanitation requirements and luncheon menus should measure up to the nutritional needs of preschool children.

Basic Program

Next to consider are the school's activities. Make a note of how many children there are to one teacher and what age span is grouped in one room. Ideally—but for many reasons the ideal rarely exists—there should be seven to ten children per teacher, depending on age, and the children in each group should be close in age. An intelligent and understanding teacher should always be on hand to guide, suggest and help when needed, but the children's free play will remain essentially unorganized and undirected. It cannot go on too long without variation, however. Watch to see if the teacher occasionally sits down with a story book or sets out clay or fingerpaints on the table to lure the children to a period of much-needed relaxation. This alternation of free play with organized activity constitutes the basic program of a good nursery school.

Organized activity in a good school will not be rigidly organized, with quietness and fixed attention demanded, because very young children are not capable of either. There will be a freedom of choice, a freedom of method that encourage expression of the child's own interests. Cutting on lines, coloring in spaces, singing on key, and so on, are not emphasized in a good nursery school. The children are not being taught skills but are being introduced to mediums of self-expression. Skill will develop later on. You will hear a good teacher praising and commenting on results, but not in a critical manner. She will encourage questions and comments from the children themselves, even during singing or storytelling, knowing this is an excellent way for them to test their knowledge and to become adept at expressing themselves.

Teacher Qualifications

What kind of person is the teacher herself? How should she qualify when it comes to knowledge, personality and technique? Each of these things is important, but not by itself.

You will be aware of the teacher's personality, because it subtly pervades the atmosphere of the whole room. Look for evidence of the warmth of personality which is so desirable. A teacher's technique is partly a natural expression of her personality and partly a result of training. Education in child psychology and specific training in nursery school technique are necessary. On the other hand, not all the training in the world will make a good teacher out of one who really has no fondness for or understanding of young children. Find out about her training; it is important. But don't be overawed by degrees and certificates.

You can judge a teacher's technique by her words and actions. Does she direct activity in a firm, friendly way, without resorting to commands or threats? Does she answer the children's questions thoughtfully and simply? Does she correct the children in positive, helpful ways, instead of with "Don't"? The words of a good teacher are quiet, helpful words.

The teacher's reactions and her manner are as important as her words. Does she offer help only when it is needed, instead of doing for the children what they can do for themselves? Is she firm and consistent? Is she calm and decisive in manner? When two children start fighting, a good teacher doesn't rush in to coddle the injured and scold the aggressor, but gives them a chance to work out the situation between themselves, and if they can't, gets them interested in something else. She studies and understands her children.

Does the teacher seem interested in having your child join the group? If you talk to her about entering your child in the school, notice whether after asking questions about age, date of entrance and so on she seems to show a personal interest in your child. A good teacher will ask about his brothers and sisters, his playmates, his eating, sleeping and toilet habits, his medical history and his particular interests and problems. You may in turn ask her leading questions. This is clearly your privilege, so don't be shy about it. A good question to ask is, "What do you consider the purpose of a nursery school?" The answer of a good teacher will go straight to the point of developmental guidance—the promotion of a child's physical, mental, social and emotional development. She may speak of adjusting to group activity, encouraging creative expression, stimulating motor coordination and other things, but her answer will include the important idea of guiding a child's all-around development.

If the school you have visited measures up on most of these points you are fortunate. It is an excellent place to enroll your child. —*By Louise Ellison*

IF YOU WANT YOUR CHILD TO GO TO A PRIVATE SCHOOL

"SHOULD I send my child to an independent school? If so, how can I get him into one?" More and more parents are mulling over those two questions. The demand today for independent schooling was unheard of twenty years ago, and competition for admission to independent secondary schools stiffens by the year. Why? Every family has its own combination of reasons, of course, but some are pretty universal.

Perhaps you, for instance, feel your local school is inadequate. You may be among those seeking a school that will give more individual consideration to your child's academic needs. Perhaps you're looking for a school that is free to teach without regard for politics or prejudice. Perhaps you want a church school. Or you may be especially in search of high scholastic standards, a well balanced curriculum and opportunities for advanced courses in the liberal arts or sciences—especially if you're looking ahead and are concerned about the competition for college admission. Although the number of top public school graduates admitted is increasing, your Jane or John may be more successful in one of the independent schools because of the particular emphasis they can place on preparation for college admission. The term "private" or "independent" refers to secondary boarding or day schools that specialize in college preparation.

Some people still labor under the false belief that the word "private" connotes "problem" and therefore a private school is a haven for problem children. In point of fact, there is no school, public or private, that doesn't have children who have problems. The primary mission of independent secondary education, however, is with excellence rather than with eccentricity.

The Child's Special Needs

Does your child have special needs which the public school cannot satisfy? Sometimes, for example, where there is serious illness, divorce, or painful stresses of any kind in the family, a parent may feel that a particular child will find more harmony in an independent boarding school. There are special schools for the mentally retarded, schools for the handicapped, schools that offer special training in remedial reading. Especially gifted youngsters, too, may need special attention.

It cannot be denied that the question of associates may be a deciding factor for some families. While one of the great advantages of public schools is the opportunity they offer to meet with people of many different backgrounds, ideas and values and standards of behavior do vary widely from one public school to another. For instance, parents who find their child succumbing to a barrage of bad conduct in his community too strong for the home to combat may have no other choice but to give him a change of environment. To send a child to a private school as a form of social climbing is, of course, the worst possible reason. Besides, it's virtually impossible to find an independent school these days that condones "snob" appeal. On the contrary, most of them are working hard to get students of varying economic, social and religious backgrounds.

Certainly a primary consideration in thinking about an independent school is your child's own wishes, especially if a boarding school is contemplated. If you do not know how your son or daughter feels about going away to school, now is the time to find out. At first, you may encounter some reluctance or possibly strong resistance. The comforts of home life, the companionship of close friends, the loyalty of school teams—give all these up—in exchange for what? In exchange for an opportunity to share an educational experience with contemporaries from many parts of the country and diversified social backgrounds, in a school community where all are working toward a common objective—success in college and professional life.

Looking for the Right School

Once you both are convinced of the desirability of an independent secondary school, how should you begin looking for the right one? If your teen-ager will be seeking admission to a first-rate college preparatory school, start your search in plenty of time. In your own community you may know some friends or business associates who are graduates of private schools or who have children enrolled in them. Ask them about the schools they know. Inquire about their location, the size of the faculty, the kind of student body, the educational program and what it costs. If one or more appeals to you, write directly to the schools for their catalogues and other descriptive literature.

Should you prefer to read descriptive summaries about a variety of schools before requesting catalogues, you will find a wealth of valuable information in "Private Independent Schools, a Directory," by James E. Bunting, or "Private Schools, a Handbook," by Porter Sargent. Another source of descriptive information are the education departments of magazines and newspapers. For a step-by-step account of the best procedure to follow in selecting a school, you will find the pamphlet "Choosing an Independent School for Your Child," published by the Secondary Education Board, Public Relations Committee, a most enlightening source of practical advice.

More than likely your child has never seen a college preparatory boarding school. So it would be well at this point to plan to visit several schools which seem most desirable from what you have heard or read about them. You may want to look at a large school of some 600 or 700 students, a medium-sized one of 350 or 450, or one limited to 150 or 200. You may consider schools in New England, or because your child plans to attend a New England college, you may be interested in the advantages of his attending a school in another locality.

The cost. Your pocketbook may govern your selection, too. You will discover tuition rates as low as $950 in a few church-supported schools. Others range from $2,000 to $2,500. There are some that offer full scholarships to worthy applicants for four or five years. In one of the leading secondary schools, more than 40 per cent of the students have received scholarship aid during the past five years. In the same school, a fund of $250,000 from a single donor is awarded, on the basis of a candidate's merit and parents' need, to "boys of extraordinary ability whose parents cannot provide an adequate secondary education." Other parents in more affluent circumstances not only pay the full tuition but contribute generously to the scholarship funds. In most schools, tuition is far below what it costs the school to educate the students.

Visit the school. Whatever kind of school you feel your child needs, a church school, military or coeducational school, a boarding or day school, a boys' or a girls' school—there is a school to fill that need. The main objective is to find one where your child is reasonably assured of enjoying and benefiting from the experience. And only by visiting each school and meeting the people there can you evaluate this.

For your own convenience, write in advance for an appointment with the director of admissions or headmaster. Don't be disappointed when you arrive on campus to find that the head is not immediately available to welcome you. This is not a sign of apathy on his part. In one boarding school of 450, the headmaster teaches English, coaches two sports, advises the student governing committee, leads chapel services and knows personally every boy on campus. His first responsibility is to care for the individual needs of the boys in school. He delegates to others the responsibility of representing the school to prospective students and their parents, although he always finds time to meet each one.

Judging the School

Students often show candidates the campus, make friends with them and even evaluate them. There are all kinds of candidates! I know of one 14-year-old applicant who was interested primarily in opportunities for scientific research. During the interview he presented his own 350-page typewritten manuscript in which he had carefully drawn individual sketches of all the insects in his collection, with Latin identifications. He left quite an impression. On the other hand, there was the anxious father of a 210-pound high school senior who drove 150 miles solely to inquire about the quality of the football field and the seating capacity of the grandstands.

Parents should be alert for significant features that distinguish a good school from a mediocre one. Not all independent schools maintain the same standards. You may therefore want to consider first the people who will be closely associated with your boy or girl, namely, the faculty and students. What is the ratio of students to classroom teacher? Does the school have frequent turnover in faculty? Have most of the faculty been at the school five years, ten years or more? Does the school provide teachers with opportunities for professional advancement, sabbaticals, pension plans? Is there a good cross-section in age and experience? Are most of the faculty married and living in dormitories along with the students? These are some of the questions that may not be answered in the catalogues and should be considered during your visit.

As to the students themselves—on campus, you may be immediately impressed by their friendliness, manners or dress. Are they the kind of associates you want your child to have in the classroom, dormitory and on the playing field? Are they all from well-to-do families or is there a sizable representation of various economic levels? Do most students come from one section of the country or is there a broad geographic distribution? Does any religious persuasion predominate or is the school strictly nondenominational? Where do most graduates attend college? What percentage of those who enter college earn a diploma? You are entitled to the answers before you entrust to a professional educator the responsibility of caring for your child.

Academic Standards

One question a parent has difficulty answering for himself is, "Will my child be able to meet the academic competition?" A grade of "A" in one school may be equivalent to a "C" in another. A student in the first quarter of a given grade may find himself in the last quarter in the same grade in another school. It would be harmful, if not frustrating, to place a child in a scholastic situation that proves too demanding of his talents. Equally disastrous, from the academic standpoint, would it be to place an able child in a situation which offered little challenge to his scholastic potential.

The solution may be suggested during the interview with the admissions officer. It is customary for parents to be present at the time of the interview. In a few schools, officials prefer to talk to the boy or girl alone. He or she will be asked about academic background, course of studies, the quality and quantity of reading. It is well on such occasions to have an unofficial transcript and the most recent report cards available for discussion. The interviewer will also inquire about interests outside the school, community activities, favorite hobbies and summer camp experiences. Inevitably, the questioning culminates in an expression of choice of college (if known) and the reason why the school under consideration has attracted the candidate's interest. All during the conference the interviewer is mentally sizing up the prospect in comparison with several other candidates vying for the same place. The poise, bearing, friendliness and personal appearance of the individual will definitely impress the interviewer one way or another. Usually the interview results in placing the candidate's name in one of the following classifications: A—acceptable; B—borderline; or C—cannot make it.

Like boarding schools, day schools have limitations on enrollment and the advantages of small classes. Unfortunately, there are not enough independent secondary schools of high quality, either boarding or day, to meet the needs of the increasing school-age population. Most of these schools are reluctant to increase their enrollments lest they risk the "watered-down quality of basic learning" that might result. They give careful and sympathetic consideration to the qualifications of every applicant. Yet while the applicant's parents are asking: "What school will do the most for my child?" the admissions officer must ask: "What will this boy or girl contribute to the school?" It is his grave obligation to maintain the integrity of his own school's particular aims and functions.

In view of this, sometimes the parent who gets the biggest shock of disappointment is the one who claims his child has "real ability," but has failed to show much academic achievement. This is the kind of parent who is seeking an educational garage to repair a defective academic chassis. For these students, no entrance tests yet devised can predict their willingness to work up to capacity. As a result, the "bright" candidates with mediocre scholastic records who have loafed through previous schools are rejected in favor of the youngsters who have done their best with the talents which may look, on test results, less impressive.

Admissions Tests

Because parents are becoming increasingly aware of the stiffening competition for admission to independent secondary schools, they are now filing applications in as many as five or six schools. Until fairly recently, a candidate might take as many as five or six different sets of examinations—sometimes a duplicate set for entrance to two different schools. Now, most schools are participating in the Secondary School Admissions Testing Program which enables a candidate to take one battery of objective tests for all schools. The results are sent to as many schools as the candidate requests. To be sure of first consideration for an available vacancy, it is advisable to place a candidate's application on file a year in advance of his prospective date of entrance. The custom of filing an application at the time of birth no longer has the significance it had some decades ago. Today, most admissions decisions are made no earlier than nine months and no later than five months before the opening of school in September.

Because more parents are receiving sympathetic letters of rejection than congratulatory messages of acceptance, one might get the false impression that many of the leading independent schools are considering *only* those students with extremely high I.Q.'s and straight "A" records. Granted that private schools are designed to offer gifted students an opportunity to exercise their specific talents and abilities, this does not mean that the independent school does not have a place for the well-rounded "B" or even "C" student whose record of achievement and qualities of character show promise that he will contribute not only to the academic life but also to the extracurricular life of the school.

Each school aims, in its own way and with its own material, at the concept of excellence rather than mediocrity which is best described in the following excerpt from a "Statement of Faith" published by the National Council of Independent Schools:

"We believe that education resting on freedom of inquiry and freedom of faith is a basic guarantee of cultural continuity and of liberty itself. We hold it the duty of our schools to teach how to meet and manage difficult intellectual tasks. We believe that all good teaching is rooted and grounded in character carefully cultivated and based on religion and ethics. From such teaching learning will grow into a lifelong strength on which a person may draw in all the private, economic, political and spiritual stresses, strains and joys which he will encounter." —*By James V. Moffatt*

IF YOUR CHILD
NEEDS A SPECIAL SCHOOL

IF you have a mentally retarded child who has reached school age, you are probably faced now with more poignant and compelling problems than ever before. You want to give him the experience of school, the opportunity to learn as much as he can, the benefits of being with other children. But where is he going to get these things?

You don't have to grope in the dark without help in order to find a school —and a school that's right for your child. Investigate systematically, and you'll be heartened by the number of guide lines and helping hands you will find!

Public School Classes

First explore what the public schools have to offer. All but two states have some kind of special education program for the retarded. By 1953, the latest year for which figures are available, there were nearly 109,000 slow-learning boys and girls with I.Q.'s roughly from 50 to 80 (usually called "educable") in special classes both in large and small communities. Ultimately with good teaching, most of these youngsters become self-supporting. Public school classes for children with I.Q.'s of 30 to 50 (usually called "trainable"), who aren't expected to master academic skills, but who can learn self-care, how to get along with others and very simple routine work under close supervision, are a more recent development. Although the number of these latter classes is growing, it isn't yet nearly big enough to meet the need. Even in 1953, however, more than 5,000 trainable children were in special public school classes.

If your public schools have no place for your child, try to work with your Board of Education toward getting special classes started, says Dr. Gunnar Dybwad, Executive Director of the National Association for Retarded Children. Your child, like every other taxpayer's, is entitled to schooling. Nearly all states have funds to help pay local schools' extra costs for special education. Indeed, your state laws may not only permit or enable the formation of special classes—but require that wherever there are a certain number of educable retarded children who cannot benefit by regular classes, a special class must be formed. A few states have similar mandatory legislation for trainables. But local school people, beset by many pressures, may understandably let matters rest unless parents request action.

National Association for Retarded Children

Legislative provisions for special education in your state may be obsolete. Then, says Dr. Dybwad, the local school board may need the support parents can give by joining together and taking the issue to the state capital.

At present, there are more than 500 local associations of parents of retarded children affiliated with the National Association for Retarded Children (NARC). The easiest way for you to locate the one nearest you is by writing to NARC, 99 University Place, New York 3, New York.

Some of the associations have a parent-counseling service. Others delegate an individual to give information on special schools in the vicinity. Money is raised through drives, bazaars, raffles, membership in the Community Chest. Often, equipment is donated and a school or church provides rent-free quarters. Mothers help to dress the children, serve fruit juice, assist the teacher and do janitor work so that tuition is usually kept within most parents' means. Many groups run their own day schools. (There are a number of privately operated day schools for the retarded. Your State Department of Education may or may not have any control over them, but it should definitely be able to direct you to the ones that may exist in your community.)

The kind of school depends on the degree of your child's retardation, his physical condition, his age, his behavior, the state and community in which you live, your finances, the needs of other members of your family, and your own feelings. A school that's good for one retarded child and his family may be bad for another. Again, a school may be good at one time of a child's life, and wrong at another.

Residential Schools

Although it's felt today that it's good to keep a retarded child at home and send him to a day school, in many cases for many reasons, twenty-four-hour-a-day residential school care is preferable. A mother may be ill, or have to work. A brain-damaged youngster may need the kind of routine and surroundings impossible to achieve in a family. A child who has become disturbed because he feels so "different" from the rest of the family may, temporarily at least, be better off in a world of his peers. Similarly, if a retarded child is so difficult to manage that other children are being deprived of attention, residential care may preserve everyone's well-being. And you will probably want your child in a residential school if that is the alternative to no schooling or companionship at all.

The first step in finding a residential school is to study a directory of special schools. The American Association on Mental Deficiency puts out a paperbound one called "Listings of Public and Private Schools and Homes for the Retarded." If this isn't available at a local parents' association, you can get it for $1.00 from NARC. Grouped by states, practically every residential facility for the retarded is listed—plus a few day schools. Under each listing is information like the size of the school, types and ages accepted, fees, number of staff members and their qualifications. The "Directory for Exceptional Children," published by Porter Sargent, 11 Beacon Street, Boston, Massachusetts, should be available in your local library. In it, there is usually some information not in the AAMD directory about curriculum, program or activities.

Factors to Consider

Let's assume that you're using the AAMD directory. You'll rule out any school into whose categories "types accepted" and "ages" your child doesn't fit. If your child has particular health needs, look for "resident physician." "Attending physician" is adequate only for the regular medical supervision desirable even for children in the best of health. "Physician on call" means that a doctor comes only when someone who is not a doctor decides he might be needed.

Look to see how long a school has been in existence. Although a new school may be excellent, or an older one's former high standards may have deteriorated, by and large the fact of a school's existence over a long period is evidence that it must satisfy many parents. "Licensed" may mean much, little or nothing. There may be a fine, unlicensed school in a state which doesn't require licensing. Some states give licenses if nothing more than sanitary and fire requirements are met. In other states, where several agencies are empowered to license, a license may have been obtained from the one whose requirements were easiest.

Don't be discouraged if you're beset by ifs, ands and buts while you're trying to make even a preliminary selection. You may have to make a choice between an excellent school too far away for you to visit often, and a possibly inferior one nearer home. You may want achingly to have your child in a small, homelike place, yet realize that only a larger school can afford a staff psychiatrist and other trained personnel. There is no generally "right" or "wrong" choice—there *is* a school which best meets your and your child's particular needs.

Should the school be state or private? Again, "it all depends." Some state schools have much better psychological, psychiatric, teaching, training and medical programs than the great majority of residential private schools. Many, on the other hand, are so underfinanced, understaffed and overcrowded that they are schools in name only and offer little but kindly care to herded, idle youngsters.

Calculate Costs

Nearly all state schools have long waiting lists. And court procedure is still necessary in most states for admission. A few states charge nothing—the rest, from $20 to $150 a month, depending on parents' ability to pay. In one state, at least, the state schools don't accept children of high-income families.

What tuition can you afford? Well, "afford" is a relative term—families with identical incomes spend money quite differently. One always buys a big new car yet lives in a small house, another makes the opposite choice. You must decide for yourself how much of a sacrifice in your scale of living you're prepared to make—always taking into account the possibly different feelings of your husband or wife. The needs of your other children, the cost of their education, present and future, ought also to be taken into account. Some mothers find it worthwhile to go to work in order to give their retarded children the best possible schooling. Others feel that their place is at home.

In any case, keep certain practical points in mind when you calculate costs of a residential school. Where "extra charges" are listed, get the school to tell you what these are likely to amount to. You may find that another school, whose tuition seems formidably high but is all-inclusive, is no more expensive. Subtract from the total charges what you would spend on food, medical care, toilet articles, recreation and perhaps day school for your child at home. The cost of special schooling for mentally handicapped children is deductible from income tax as a medical expense. A few states contribute to tuition when public education or public residential care isn't available.

Make Inquiries About the School

Having made tentative choices from the Directory, make it your business to talk with someone who knows about the school or schools you're considering. A social worker in your local Family Service Agency or Welfare Department should have the training and experience to give you a professional evaluation. In some communities, public health nurses know about facilities for the retarded. Perhaps someone connected with your local schools and certainly someone in the State Department of Education can give you information.

But for an inside, intimate picture, talk with parents who have children in the school. The local parents' association will be able to put you in touch with other mothers. Some associations have regular visiting teams of parents to state schools. Don't be ashamed of asking what you think may be considered silly, trivial questions, such as "My little girl has such lovely hair—do they take good care of the children's hair?" Every mother knows how much such little things worry other mothers about to experience the pang of giving over a child to someone else's care.

Visit the School

When you're ready to visit, make an appointment in advance, so that a staff member can give you sufficient time. Take someone experienced with you—preferably a knowledgeable parent. You may, for instance, be aghast at seeing severely handicapped little children lying on the floor instead of in their cribs. Actually, this is good practice, for it gives the youngsters a chance to use and strengthen their muscles.

Unless you're different from most parents, you'll be upset by your first visit. The initial shock of seeing a large group of children who neither look nor act normal, is deep—even for parents who have a retarded child. For nearly every parent feels "But my child isn't like these! He doesn't belong here!" So don't make only one visit. On a second, your judgment will be better.

During any visit, don't harass or confuse yourself by going to every part of the school. Restrict yourself to the classroom, unit or ward where you're told your child is likely to be. There, try to see as much of the activity and staff as possible.

Guard against being overly impressed by buildings. They are not nearly as important as staff or program. Although surroundings should be cheerful, decent and comfortable, remember that many little niceties you'd want for yourself mean nothing to children. The school should be clean but not too neat. If toys and equipment are rigidly in place, there's probably regimentation.

Assess What the School Offers

Try to meet and get some impression of the head of the school, for he generally sets its tone. He should not only be willing to answer all your questions frankly, but also ask plenty himself. He may, after talking with you, advise you to apply elsewhere, for his school may not be set up to meet your youngster's particular needs. If you aren't asked anything, you may be sure that other parents aren't either. Then, if you're encouraged to enroll your child, you can assume that the school is more interested in getting pupils than in properly selecting them. Retarded children do best in a group with others similar in mental capacity and social development. Indeed, every good special school, day or residential, insists upon a psychological evaluation as a prerequisite to admission.

At a residential school, find out what arrangements for substitutes are made when staff members are on vacation. Is there always someone on hand at night if a child wakes up and cries? At any school, note whether too many youngsters are doing the same thing at the same time. Ideally, there shouldn't be more than eight pupils to a classroom. A group of children shouldn't act so dulled or inhibited that they show no interest in visitors. On the other hand, if they seize your hands, pat you repeatedly or cling to you, this may be a sign that they don't get enough individual attention and affection. Look to see if the children seem to feel easy with the staff. As a whole, do they appear to be enjoying themselves? They ought also to look as if they were kept busy, stimulated and alive—but don't assume they aren't if you visit immediately before a mealtime. Then, as at home, everyone is likely to be just sitting and waiting.

Warning Signs

Avoid the school whose spokesmen are too free with the word "never." Since no one really yet knows how far which children can go with what kind of teaching, it is defeatist to predict absolute limits to accomplishment. Even more, though, beware of those who promise too much, who assure you that in their school your child will definitely reach this or that point. Some are unscrupulous individuals capitalizing on parents' desperation. Others, although sincere, reveal inexperience and ignorance. Classes for trainables are still so new that teachers use trial and error, adapt nursery school practices and continually experiment with hopeful techniques. Your best bet is the school with an attitude something like: "We think we can help your child here . . . we'll try our best . . . and we'll see how far he can go."

Listen not only with your ears but also with an open mind, to what the school you finally select tells you it aims to do for and with your child. This may be quite different from what you had originally wanted. Perhaps you had hoped that your youngster would get "vocational" education, in the usual sense of learning a trade. Experts in special education, however, feel that even educable youngsters should be taught the elementary academic skills and good habits that will enable them to fit into a wide variety of unskilled jobs, rather than a specific technique which might leave them unemployable in a pinch.

Whether you send your child to a day or residential school, face the fact that however wise you think your choice has been, you will be bound to have some qualms and regrets. Give yourself and your child adequate time to adjust to the school. Don't snatch him out if he doesn't seem happy and improving in the first few months. But afterwards, base the next step on the next situation. He may have reached the age limit of the school. He may have changed for better or for worse. No decision you ever make for your child need be irrevocable. If you honestly and conscientiously make the one you think best at the time you make it, that is all any human being can do.

—By Edith M. Stern

HOW TO GET YOUR BOY OR GIRL INTO COLLEGE

EACH year, for the past several years, more than 3,000,000 young Americans have enrolled in the country's more than 1,800 colleges and universities. And future years will see the hurdles that students must surmount to get into college grow ever higher. The colleges of the years ahead (and most of them today) will be expecting sound preparation and good grades. How can you help see to it that your sons and daughters get into a college of their choice?

Start early, around the time your boy or girl starts seventh or eighth grade. It's an important time in the development of good or bad study habits and also a time when foundations are laid for many of the most important subjects which will top the list of college requirements more and more— English, mathematics, the sciences, foreign languages and history. Of course, a bright student can sometimes make up for lost time, but it isn't easy. And the average student frequently finds it impossible to catch up once the earlier opportunity has been lost.

It is also around seventh and eighth grade that many schools offer youngsters some fairly wide choices as to their curriculum. The best schools offer this choice with considerable guidance, frequently amounting to a firmly mapped out program of study. But there are, unfortunately, still many schools which leave too much of the choice to the student, and if this is the case, you ought to take a hand in the matter and insist that your son or daughter pick some of the more demanding subjects, even if it means extra-hard work. Specifically, a child should take certain subjects for an adequate number of years, instead of dabbling in too many directions, without getting any firm grounding in anything. Colleges will increasingly demand a real working knowledge, not just a smattering, of at least one foreign language, a sequence of mathematics leading at least up to solid geometry, and a meaningful understanding of history. (To give you an idea, within the past three years some 15 colleges, at least, have reinstituted the foreign language requirement for admission.)

Types of Schools

None of this should be taken to mean that colleges expect every freshman to be a budding genius. Besides, while the relatively few "name colleges" may be pretty hard to get into, there are several hundred good schools which, though not widely known, offer your child a very good education. What's more, far from overcrowded, they are looking for students.

You might also consider one of a number of very small colleges, some of them not yet accredited, but on the way to becoming big, wealthy and sound enough for accreditation in the near future. These schools (including a number of small but fully accredited colleges) are grouped together in an organization called the Association of Small Colleges, Inc., 726 Jackson Place, N.W., Washington 6, D.C. You can get their listings and literature by writing to them.

When should you begin actively to aim at college admission? It's wise to start giving some thought to the choice of a college toward the middle or end of a boy's or a girl's sophomore year in high school, or tenth grade. It is too early to make any real choice, but you should have in mind a number —perhaps as many as 20—different types of college and junior college as a basis for the process of elimination and final choice of about four. It isn't too early to read through some of the routine literature—the catalogs and the view books—which most schools provide. As some of the names become familiar, you will probably begin to be aware of people who have direct knowledge of some of those schools, perhaps alumni or parents of students now attending.

By the middle of eleventh grade, the choice should narrow down considerably. The time has come to think seriously about specific schools, to have a look at some campuses if this can be done conveniently and without too much expense. You should start—with the help of your child's teachers and advisers—to get the list closer to the three or four colleges to which application will have to be made within a year.

Consider These "Don'ts"

At this point, there are a few things that should *not* influence your choice.

Don't think the college mother or father went to is necessarily the right one for son or daughter or would make special efforts to admit him or her.

Don't be guided by the college choice of your friends, or your children's friends. Your children are different.

Don't select the college by name. There are many schools relatively unknown outside education circles which are high up in the category of excellent. If you do pick one of the name schools as a possible choice, be sure that at least one, possibly two, of the total of three to which you will want to send applications are in a somewhat different category. In other words, you may want to aim high (and keep your fingers crossed) with one application; you ought to shoot straight (and hope for the best) with another; and you ought to send a third to a college which is likely to admit your child, as a sort of life insurance. (If your son or daughter happens to be turned down by the first two and accepted by the third, don't let that dampen your child's enthusiasm. Chances are the school will be the right one and the student will get a good education there.)

Large or Small College?

Think about the college in terms of the personality of your son or daughter. A relatively shy boy or girl, for instance, would probably do better at a fairly small college where the individual doesn't run the risk of being left too much to his own devices. On the other hand, an independent type who has little difficulty in getting into the stream of things fairly quickly might do quite well at a large institution such as a state university.

Special Interests

With a little personal research and intelligent listening to alumni reports, you can also tell whether a certain college is particularly strong in a field that coincides with some of the interests your child has. Not that you want to limit his education to those particular fields. On the contrary, you unquestionably will be doing him a favor by furthering his general education. But you do want to select a school where, for example, a youngster with an ear for music will be certain to find some first-rate faculty members in that field or where a student with promise in science is sure to be offered not only adequate laboratory facilities but also the inspiration of great science teachers.

Careers in Science and Engineering

Today, of course, many parents wish that their children might make great careers in science and engineering. These are fields which, for quite some time to come, promise job security and good salaries. But don't let this alone permit you to push your child into a field for which he may not be suited. Fortunately, you have a good compromise solution—or delaying action— offered you which may be just the way for you to deal with the uncertainty. A considerable number of liberal arts colleges have entered into special agreements with some of the country's leading engineering schools. Under this agreement, a student takes the first three years in the liberal arts college and then finishes the last two years at the cooperating engineering school. As you can see, the total course adds up to five instead of four years, but the reward, in addition to a broader education plus the special training, is the receipt of two degrees—a Bachelor of Arts from the liberal arts college and a Bachelor of Science from the engineering school. There are now 47 liberal arts colleges cooperating with this scheme. You can get a list from the registrar of the Massachusetts Institute of Technology or the Columbia University School of Engineering, or any of the other participating engineering colleges.

Junior College

Don't overlook the possibilities of a junior or two-year college. In fact, for any student who is not certain he wants a full four-year course of studies (and that includes many girls who are impatient to change from study to marriage) the junior college often is the better bet. It attempts to offer an educational package of some sort of completeness within two years, while the four-year college more often uses the first two years mainly as a sort of setting-up exercise for the really important higher education experience during junior and senior years. Furthermore, many four-year colleges reserve the cream of their faculty for the upper classes while the junior college uses its entire staff for all its students. There is, of course, always the hope that the student will change his mind and want to continue his education. That's no problem: it is quite easy to transfer from any good two-year college to a four-year institution without loss of credit provided the student's marks are satisfactory.

Entrance Requirements

One of the questions on every student's and parent's mind is: what counts most for college admission? Alumni connections? College board examination score? Extracurricular activities? The college interview?

Everything counts, including the number of students who may be applying for a certain college from your child's school or geographic area. But the most important factor remains the student's record. High grades ARE important and it is equally important that the grades have been going up rather than down. The boy or girl with a fair record which has been steadily improving may have a better chance than a student with a better final average but with a curve that has been going downhill.

College board examinations. Of course, every effort should be made to present a good college board examination score. But in most instances this is not the most vital factor. Many colleges use these grades mainly to resolve ties or near-ties. The most important thing about these exams is for a youngster not to be panicky about them. Colleges know that some people do better on exams than others and that this is not necessarily an indication of relative ability.

Extracurricular activity. Much the same is true about extracurricular activities. A normal and intelligent interest in a selected few activities is a fairly good yardstick for measuring an interesting and lively personality, but it is important that the activities be *selected,* not simply piled on top of each without discrimination. A dean of admissions is more interested in knowing that an applicant has participated constructively in one or two activities than dabbled aimlessly in a dozen.

Nor does a college look exclusively for "wheels" or campus politicians. Sure, every campus needs potential student-government leaders, but it doesn't need—or want—too many. Chances are, too, that the college interviewer will give full credit—and some admiring extra recognition—to the boy or girl who has not had much time for extracurricular fun because the family fortune required some measure of after-school work, whether it be baby sitting, delivering groceries or walking the neighborhood dogs. Independence is not the worst quality to take to a dean's office for credit.

College Interview

This brings us to the interview. The college will tell you in most instances whether a personal interview is required and if so, whether a parent is expected or invited. Either way—and this goes for parents as well as their sons and daughters—the interviewer should be approached with honesty. The men and women who are doing this important job can see through pretense. They don't expect you or your boy or girl to sing the praises of their school. They are not likely to be taken in by a recital of highbrow, scholarly interests. An applicant who happens to like Plato or modern languages or math shouldn't make a secret of it, but one can also like jazz or stamp collecting.

The point is: help your son or daughter to be natural, honest, polite and sensible—and give the interviewer credit for intelligence and competence. As a parent, remember that this is your child's interview, not yours. Don't dominate the scene.

The Application Form

Almost exactly the same advice holds true for filing the actual application. An applicant should describe himself as accurately as he can and leave the rest to his record, which is his strongest or weakest asset, anyway. Reasons for selecting a particular school (asked in most application forms) ought to be sound and honest ones, and the same attitude should hold in answering whether a particular college is first, second, third or fourth choice. Few schools are offended to be low on the list. If an applicant's record and personality appeals to them, they are even likely to try to snatch him away from the school of first choice.

The women's colleges. For girls with high academic records in their junior year in high school who want to try for Barnard, Bryn Mawr, Mount Holyoke, Radcliffe, Smith, Vassar or Wellesley, a new scheme has been started. They may apply to one of these colleges in their junior year, and if their high school certifies that they have applied only to this one institution, these students will be judged on the basis of a three-year high school record, the Scholastic Aptitude Test and the Achievement Tests. If the student is not accepted she will be reconsidered at application time the next year.

Scholarships

There still remains that question: how can we afford the mounting expense of a college education? If it's a big problem, you'll want to find out about the many low-cost public institutions—the state and municipal colleges and universities (with some of them actually offering free education). But you should also keep in mind that a great many scholarships are available. Your local high school can give you details about the Scholarship Qualifying Test offered under the auspices of the College Entrance Examination Board, as well as about the tougher and highly selective National Merit Scholarship Qualifying Test. All together, it is estimated, there are about 300,000 scholarships available today. You can get a booklet with a fairly comprehensive listing of scholarships from the U. S. Office of Education, Washington, D.C., or the more detailed *College Scholarship Guide* by Clarence C. Lovejoy and Theodore S. Jones ($3.95), published by Simon & Schuster, with specific information on the type of grant that may be available.

Loans and Installment Plans

There are extensive loan funds open to students at many colleges. And if you are interested in installment paying, such organizations as the Tuition Plan, Inc. and others operated under the auspices of banks and insurance companies are worth investigating. Harvard has just begun to permit students to pay for their education in monthly installments, and it's a safe bet that some other colleges are following.

Does "Influence" Work?

One final note: Can you (or should you) use "pull"? The answer is relatively simple: it's almost impossible to get anywhere with "connections" in the college admission business.

That doesn't mean that you should not ask relatives or close friends who know the college or are alumni to send honest letters of recommendation. This is not wire pulling; it's another addition to the important dossier the college is building around your child's personality. The more information there is, the better—and the views and testimony of people whom the college trusts are obviously of value. They won't get an applicant in unless he is otherwise qualified, but they are among the many items which help. If you think about it dispassionately, that's the way it should be.

Listening to Advice

In much the same way, you ought to use the opinions of alumnae and alumni wisely and intelligently. Don't listen to the rah-rah boys (and girls) who have never grown out of the cheerleader stage of juvenile judgment. But if you know mature people whose opinions you value, get their advice and their counsel. Frequently the college will make such persons available by setting up local or regional informal get-togethers—sometimes even preliminary interviews—with former students who happen to live in your area. Take advantage of this additional chance to know more about the college to which your sons or daughters may eventually be going.

This may all sound frighteningly complicated. Read it over again and you will find that the main requirements from you are some foresight, some research and a little objectivity toward your children. Even though college admission will be constantly tougher, with this kind of help from you—they'll get in.

—*By Fred M. Hechinger*

PARENT-TEACHER COOPERATION

YOU know, you're really not a bit like a schoolteacher," my next-door neighbor said to me one day. I smiled gratefully, for this remark is always meant as a compliment. It would only have puzzled my neighbor if I had replied, as I might have, "But I am a schoolteacher; why shouldn't I look like one?" How does a teacher look, anyway? Fat, slender, young, middle-aged? Schoolteachers look like most men and women. We spend our lives helping to bring up children, worrying over their problems, seeing them through infant shyness and adolescent storms just as you, their parents, do.

Underneath this compliment lies a deep distrust. Since that time I have become a school principal and that is even worse!

Popular prejudice is hard to combat. Like mothers-in-law, teachers are the victims of widespread censure, some of which we deserve because we are human and sometimes make mistakes, but most of which is unmerited. Many parents who have become friendly can laugh at their former skepticism. As soon as they see us as people, they accept us as having the usual mixture of virtues and failings. Some parents even learn to respect rather than to distrust us. There are even some who, after a day's visit in the modern school, ask the teacher, "How do you do it?"

With many parents, however, this distrust, unfortunately, remains. The wariness and misunderstanding that separate parents from teachers are, at the worst uncomfortable for the teacher, but for the child the division may be disastrous. It is hard enough for a child to grow up under present conditions, without our making it harder by allowing a division between the two forces which, along with the churches, are primarily responsible for his upbringing. Children, after all, rely on us to set their feet on the right path. How confusing it must be to have guides at home and guides at school, and to feel that one set of guides resents and dislikes the other.

Teach Democracy

We urge children, if we are good parents and teachers, to tell the truth, to live together as friends without disliking one another's race and religion. We tell them that money isn't everything, that honesty and hard work will bring happiness and fulfillment. We show them that violence is wrong and senseless, that a quarrel is best settled by reasonable discussion and compromise.

And what does life tell them? Our greatest rivals as guides to the young are the movies, radio, television, the comic books and current events! Mother and Miss Jones agree that children should tell the truth—but our newspapers are full of stories about corruption in high places.

Dad and the school principal advise that hard work is the way to success —but how about the newsreel picture of the gangster retired to luxury in Florida, while dad toils toward a modest social security? The principal is not getting rich either.

Fighting is wrong, we tell our child, but Superman, Dick Tracy and the others win glory in a trail of corpses and blondes. It is an enticing world we advise him to reject, and obscure and toilsome paths which we urge him to follow.

This younger generation is influenced by our anxieties: the possibility of war, of more burdensome taxation, of economic insecurity. We cannot protect them from these things. We can only hope to train them to be strong, to be just, to be kind and loving, to trust in God and goodness, to fight for what is right.

Young Americans are faced with the enormous job of building, improving, defending democracy. Our job—the parents' job and the teachers'—is to give them the strength to face and to succeed in the task. If we in their homes and in their schools learn to trust one another, to put up with each other's peculiarities patiently, we can do more for young people. They deserve our best.

Perhaps you feel that I am indulging in the principal's dangerous habit of exercising authority. "Now she's telling us what to do. She wants to rule parents as well as children."

Don't Condemn

Well—I shall try to avoid that. Don't take the school on faith. But give it a chance. Find out before you condemn. Here's an example:

One of our younger teachers consulted me about Fanny, a meek, gentle child who refused to take any part in school life. She made no friends and resisted the teacher's efforts to interest her in art, music, clubs, anything at all. It would have been easy enough for us to let the problem go. Fanny was never troublesome, except to herself, for it was plain that she was unhappy. She looked pale and seemed listless, so the school did what some parents regard as interfering. I asked our school nurse to visit the child's mother and to try to persuade her to come to school to talk over Fanny's problems. Our nurse is used to a variety of receptions, but this one nearly ended in blows. Fanny's mother indulged in a tirade on the school system in general and our school in particular. Yet Fanny had been with us only two months and her mother had never come to school; during Open School Week or to Parents' Association meetings or to grade conferences.

"That school is no good," Fanny's mother fumed. "When a school is no good, it's usually the principal's fault. The principal ought to be fired." One develops a certain armor against this kind of thing. We are, as I have said, accustomed to being scapegoats for variously frustrated people. But Fanny's problem was still unsolved, although we were now able to understand it better. Fanny, a nice child, felt in her heart that she would be disloyal to her mother if she took part in school activities. If she let herself like and enjoy school she would be denying her mother's authority. She solved the problem in a dangerous way; she withdrew, resisted friendship, rejected the opportunity to develop.

This particular case had a happy ending, because Fanny's mother finally did come up to school. I did not discuss my professional qualifications with her but I did talk to her about Fanny. Immediately it was clear that this mother, like other mothers, loved her daughter and wanted her to be happy. She was aware of the girl's shyness and anxious to help her. She began to see that our concern was the same as her own; we talked things over understandingly and made plans to encourage Fanny to join a singing group. Her mother promised to welcome Fanny's friends to her home. The bugaboo of the school that was no good faded away. Fanny was finally free to be happy because she didn't have to choose between her mother and school.

Parent on the Defensive

Another story had an unhappy ending. The incident occurred years ago when I was a very young new teacher. No doubt it could have been handled better. In those days, I was a second-grade teacher, and the second grade was a more formal place than it is now. At any rate, Frederick, a big, handsome, dreamy lad, was my big problem. Frederick's problem was a profound and impenetrable self-absorption which showed itself in a vague, faraway look which gently resisted my efforts to have him learn to read and write. I remember that I was particularly anxious that he learn how to add and subtract 2's. That was part of the second-grade course of study in those days, and I was convinced that Frederick could learn it.

I did what I should probably not do now; I insisted. Frederick decided to indulge my arithmetic mania, finally, and he began to hand in perfect papers. He found it easier to copy the paper of the boy sitting next to him than to learn the 2's, however, and this added another item to my worries about Frederick. He remained patient with my flutterings, drawing deeper into his private dream world. I was convinced that Frederick, who was healthy and intelligent, nevertheless had a serious problem which needed further help than I could give him. His father was a lawyer, big and handsome like his son, and very successful. He made it plain that he considered the teacher a social inferior. When I mentioned to him the fact that Frederick preferred to copy his arithmetic, I shall always remember the arrogance with which his father answered me: "I copied my way all through school, and I've done all right in life."

This father refused to see his child's problem and he resented the school's effort to help. Perhaps his own pride in himself would have been injured if he had admitted that his son had a problem. It was more comfortable to shut his eyes and mutter about the meddling teacher. Years later I heard that Frederick was rejected by the army because of emotional instability. I felt that somehow it was my failure as well as his parents. If the father had been less blind and if I had been more persuasive, Frederick might have been helped.

Teacher Learns from Parents

When parents and teachers fall out, the child is left in the middle, confused and unhappy. Sometimes they have sense enough to help each other to help the child. In the days before I became a parent myself, I had much to learn from good mothers and wise fathers. I still have, of course, because there is a great deal for all of us to learn about how to bring up children. I always remember one parent with gratitude because she said something which gave me a nasty turn, but which did me a great deal of good. "Marilyn is afraid of you," she said. She had spoken appreciatively of her child's improvement in English composition and in the addition of fractions, but still—Marilyn was afraid of me! It was a blow, but a salutary one. It made me sit down and study myself as a teacher.

I realized that I was so intensely determined that Marilyn learn everything perfectly that I was driving her too hard. Because of her sensible mother I found out in time. I have been, I believe, a more humane teacher ever since.

Learning goes on in the world at an uneven rate. How I wish that everyone who has children knew that and accepted it. Have you ever listened to women in a grocery store boasting about their children's accomplishments? John won the history medal; Elaine had all A's on her card; Sheila has been on the honor roll since birth or nearly. Then there are those parents who are grinding their teeth because Bertha had only B plus and Harry fell off the honor roll this month. These mamas descend on the principal with wrath to fight for their young. What is the answer? How often I have said, but not always have I been listened to: "You have a healthy, happy child. She is doing well. Don't drive her or make her unhappy. No one can win top honors in everything all the time. Let her find that out now."

There is always a deeper meaning in these cases of parents who show unreasonable anger at the school and the teachers. The school is often the whipping boy for various discontents. It is more socially acceptable to blame the school, which is an outside agency, than the real sources of personal unhappiness. Perhaps a parent is disappointed with marriage, resents the confinement and monotony of housework and bringing up children, envies others who are more fortunate. But it is important not to take out our jaundiced feelings on other people—least of all on an institution like the public school.

Let us, in justice to our children, put our foolish differences aside. Together, we just may manage to do our best for them. Together, we can find some of the answers to our problems. Teachers and parents are much better friends now than they were a generation ago and that is very pleasant and very helpful. We have quite a way to go before we fully understand and trust one another, but every step we take will help us to help the children.

—By Elizabeth C. O'Daly

SHOULD PARENTS HELP WITH HOMEWORK?

A CHILD is responsible to his teacher, not to his parents, for the accomplishment of his homework. A good teacher tries to kindle a child's interest in the work assigned and to impress on him the importance of accomplishing that work on time.

But don't think this lets us parents out! We are responsible for seeing that he has the means and opportunity to do this work. Parents and children should plan together a schedule for activities which includes time for preparation of school assignments as well as time for favorite TV programs, play, visits with friends and even the opportunity to do nothing at times. Parents and children must also agree upon the place where homework is to be done. It should be a place, undisturbed by loud television or little sister or brother, with adequate space and light, where the student can work in quiet and peace.

Providing the necessary tools is also a parental responsibility. Time is saved if there's no need to search for a pencil, paper, and so forth. Reference books are necessities for independent study. (See article on "How To Build A Home Reference Library.") Magazines are good resource texts also, and if an agreement has been arrived at ahead of time, you are less likely to find that the most exciting part of your continued story has been torn out of this month's issue (unfortunately, it had a picture of an Indian on the back).

In spite of adequate time in which to do homework and all the facilities needed for it, sometimes a child still doesn't do his spelling. What then? This, of course, is the big problem. The advice of teachers is that at this point the issue should revert to the classroom. One of the primary goals in assigning homework is to increase a child's sense of responsibility. If parents take over and force, cajole, bribe or punish, we may see to it that the studying is done, but hardly in a way that suggests learning can be an interesting occupation, and certainly without helping our child grow in his ability to assume his own responsibilities.

Refusal to Work

Let the child who refuses to take responsibility find out for himself what happens at school when he arrives unprepared. If this isn't enough to make him change his ways, then talk the situation over with his teacher. The two of you, working together, should be able to discover the blocks that are keeping your child from working to his best capacity.

There is one more essential part the parent plays in getting homework done and that is in developing attitudes about it. When Jane comes home and says that tomorrow she has to bring an apron to school, when six-year-old Johnny says he needs to find a picture of a train to show the class, do you help your child meet these assignments? These are the beginnings of homework. The importance you give to these simple requests, your attitude about fulfilling them, will directly affect your child's attitudes about homework in the upper grades.

If you select the apron for Janie without consulting her as to size or color, or find John's train picture for him after he has gone to bed, you may find that you will have to take quite a part in helping Jane and John with their assignments when they reach the upper grades.

How much help is really legitimate? Should you correct spelling, check long and tiresome lists of arithmetic problems, try to explain the science problem if Susie doesn't understand? Usually, when your child comes to you for help, you want him to feel that he can count on you and your support. You wouldn't want to flatly refuse all assistance. But, obviously, the teaching of process and method is the job of the classroom teacher. However, if your child needs a little more explanation and asks for it, by all means give it to him unless you find that your method conflicts with what the teacher said or, equally important, what your child thinks she said. The moment your explanation seems to confuse the child, stop! Refer your child to his teacher. It is essential that his loyalties should not become confused.

Should Parents Check Answers?

As far as checking and correcting answers is concerned, many teachers agree that some children need the security of knowing in advance that most of their work is correct. It is not too difficult to check a paper to make sure that the process is right. On the other hand, there is usually no valid reason for parents to check every computation for careless slips or errors.

When homework is of a research variety—"What can you find out about the kinds of food we need every day?" for instance—parents can be very helpful. Obviously, however, the finding and selection of answers is the child's task. In general there are things which we parents should do if a child needs help in completing a research assignment. We should make sure he really understands the assignment. We should, if necessary, help him find the resource materials he needs, and we should make sure that he can understand them. But the final selection of pertinent facts and the manner in which these facts are expressed are the sole responsibility of your child.

Often a child can do the work assigned but needs an opportunity to talk over what he is learning in order to clarify it in his own mind. Here, of course, parents can help immeasurably and learn too. In today's world we often find our lives and the lives of our children running in separate channels. Homework can serve as a bridge to bring us closer together, to provide mutual in-

terests and topics for discussion. But when you work with your child in this way, remember that you do not want to impose your ideas upon him. Encourage him to do his own thinking and express his findings in his own way.

Set Realistic Standards

A word of warning about standards you set for your child. It is important that you be realistic about what he can do. Parents who demand more than a child can achieve, may cause more harm than if they had ignored his homework altogether.

What is homework all about? What is it supposed to accomplish? Do we really believe it is vital that a child in the fifth grade be able to name and spell all the capitals of the middle Atlantic states or that a sixth-grader know exactly how many gallons of paint will be required to paint a mythical room? Isn't it rather to accomplish the following: give practice in skills; help a child learn how to follow directions; help him learn how to organize his time; give a child experience in independently attacking a problem and working it through; acquaint a child with some of the resources of his home and his community; develop a feeling of responsibility; give a feeling of accomplishment and success.

If we accept these reasons for homework, we can use them as guides for our own behavior. When we answer, or refuse to answer, remind, nag or ignore, are we helping or hindering the purposes listed above? The importance of homework lies not so much in completing the assignment itself as in what our children gain from fulfilling such assignments.   —*By Estelle R. Roddy*

HOW TO HELP WITH READING

JOHNNY returned home from school with a note saying he is going to fail. He can't go into third grade with his friends because Johnny can't read.

As a remedial reading tutor for elementary grades, my contact with Johnny and his mother usually begins here. Why can't Johnny learn to read? Will he progress in reading if he repeats the work in the same grade? These are questions to which Johnny's parents—and the parents of many other Johnnies —urgently want an answer.

There is practically never anything wrong with Johnny. His eyesight has been examined and his hearing and general physical condition checked by the school nurse. If there had been a physical handicap, he would have been sent to the clinic for special help long before this. Most children with reading problems are normal youngsters in average to excellent health. What is the matter then?

Has Johnny been sent to school regularly every day? Has he been to kindergarten or nursery school? Has he learned to accept school routine and companionship with other children? Has he been out of school a great deal because of illness? Or worse, has he been out of school repeatedly because sending him interfered with some private plans of mother or father? Unfortunately, some parents still have the idea that the first and second grades, as well as kindergarten or nursery school, are not important. "They just fool around half the time," some parents say. This is an entirely wrong notion. The first and second grades are important years of your child's school life, and every day in a good school is planned with definite steps in mind for the educational progress of your child.

Repeating a Grade

Let us suppose that this particular Johnny has been out of school for only two short periods—once with measles, and once with a cold. His social adjustment to the other children is average, his health normal. Is he a behavior problem? Can he control his actions and his talking long enough to be able to listen? Also, has he been treated with fairness and respect at home? If not, can one blame him for violent reactions and resistance which may include rebellion against learning?

Repeating a grade can be either a great blessing or a tragedy—depending on the parents' attitude. If a child is immature for his age group, it is a fine thing for him to be able to take the work again, so that he may be "comfortable" in his progress from then on, instead of striving and struggling at the tail end of a group beyond him in development. This has nothing to do with whether he is younger in years—he may be older chronologically. It happens often, especially in boys, that a child is immature for his age in the first grades. It is for this reason that some Boards of Education rule that no child is to be held back until the last half of third grade, since many times a child overcomes the immaturity lag completely. Not all seeds that we plant blossom on the same day.

Some parents, and consequently their children, suffer unnecessarily over the fact that Johnny will leave all his friends if he does not pass. Rejoice that he has made good friends, but consider this a priceless opportunity to teach him the important fact that there are just as fine friendships to be made in the new group—perhaps even better ones.

It is not a coincidence that 90 per cent of my remedial reading cases are boys. It might be a good thing if boys could enter first grade a year later than girls. Much of their difficulty as readers stems from the first year of school when they are apt to compare unfavorably with girls of the same age, who are, by a simple process of growth, ready for reading. Obviously, however, failure to be promoted is sometimes the worst possible way to handle nonreading pupils.

How Tension Causes Failure

Normal in health, above average in intelligence, Stanley was physically present almost every day in first grade, although the strain and tension of his home life made it impossible for him to concentrate on school work. By the time he reached second grade, he was in the lowest reading group. Continually scolded by members of his family, particularly his mother, he was compared unfavorably with his cousin of the same age.

Stanley's parents, who knew he was a bright boy, believed that stirring the boy's competitive spirit was the only stimulus he needed to make him work harder at school. Stanley, however, felt he was failing his parents completely, and by the third grade alternated between two escape devices—recurrent stomach upsets that kept him out of school, and retreat into a smart-alec, don't-care attitude that made him a discipline problem.

The school recommended special help for Stanley. Since it was summertime when he registered with me, he was placed in a group with five other boys and their mothers who were interested in learning how to help them at home. He puzzled me because, with superior mental equipment, he did the poorest work in the group. He had an almost complete insulation of cockiness and nothing "took." One morning I said to him quite suddenly: "Stanley, has someone made you ashamed at school?"

His eyes grew very dark and large. "I mean," I continued, "did someone hurt your feelings?" He started to nod his head in assent, and with that it went down on the table and the storm broke.

Never have I experienced anything quite so moving and so heartbreaking as the little boy's sobs. It is terrible enough to see the exposed soul of a grownup, but to fling aside the curtain of a little boy's inner consciousness and find such stored up misery (and to have been the unwitting cause of its being torn aside!)—I can never think of it without tears coming to my eyes even now.

Changing Criticism to Understanding

Yet it was this quick and unconsciously brutal incision which seemed necessary to expose and cure. The problem became clear to all concerned with the boy. Fortunately his mother now saw the situation as it was and took over the job of helping. She helped Stanley in every way until he was not only on a par with his age group, but until a quiet, real confidence had replaced his cockiness.

Something wonderful happened between that mother and boy, the same wonderful something that always happens when criticism changes to understanding. Failing a grade would definitely not have helped in this case. "But what a lot of difference," the mother later said, "a little wise counsel in the first grade would have made." When are we going to become humane enough, and practical enough, to put our finest, best-paid, most experienced and loving teachers into the first grade? When are we going to see that there is an expert, full-time counselor in every school to get in touch with every home where there is a child with a problem in first grade? This would not be an expense, but a saving, economically and socially.

Every child, unless he is subnormal, can learn to read. I have seen, over and over again, a child restored to happiness and competency when the stigma of being a nonreader has been lifted. If the particular child is well-adjusted and happy, but hasn't learned to read, it is likely that he has not grasped all the reading fundamentals he needs.

The tools of reading include the teaching of phonics—the sounds that make up words. About 60 per cent of the children learn phonic fundamentals by induction. That is, by unconsciously putting 2 and 2 together. Some of the 60 per cent are not sure enough to carry the principles over into their spelling, however.

But 40 per cent of the children will never master reading skill unless they grasp the simple phonetic principles—directly and definitely. Such children have the logical type of mind that produces the Thomas Edisons of our society. They simply have to know why and how the puzzle fits together.

Instruction in Phonics

These children, given a good dose of phonics and shown how to use the simple rules, are quickly helped—usually in ten to twenty half-hours, unless confusion already is very great.

Briefly, if your child has missed the reading fundamentals he needs, he may be the type of youngster who can learn only by logic, rather than by context or memory process. Just more of the same will not help him, and he never will become a good student unless someone helps him over the hump. That someone is the mother of the child. Now, if ever, is the time for mothers to come to the aid of their children, for the public schools are in a real state of emergency. Mothers can and need to help in every way possible.

Public school teachers under the present system are working under difficult conditions, a system overcrowded and underpaid, a supervisory staff that can get around to the individual elementary teacher only occasionally (in some counties about once in two years), a "tenure of office" law plus the teacher shortage, which makes it practically impossible to oust a poor teacher. Working under these conditions, the sincere and able teacher is already doing a Herculean job (and getting little credit for it) without taking on the individual teaching your Johnny requires if he is failing.

If Johnny is failing, he needs help now to learn to read, before he gets confused, before he believes himself to be mentally inferior.

"But I don't know how to help him!" or "I might get him confused," many mothers say at this point. To the second argument I say: "Nonsense!" He's already confused if he's failing. There is no magic, secret formula imparted only to first-grade teachers. All you have to do is find out what fundamentals he has missed and see that he gets them, in whatever way he can learn them. Find out where your child stands in his need and understanding, and help him from there. The idea that all children must learn in one way, and if they won't or can't, then they are failures, is one you can prove a fallacy from the first day. If you attack the problem with the understanding that Johnny needs your help, whether he knows it or not, dozens of different ways to help him will occur to you.

A Method to Follow

As to the first argument, "I don't know how," here is a method easy enough for any mother to follow.

Begin by checking the 15 easy consonants. B, D, F, H, J, K, L, M, N, P, R, S, T, V, W. Does Johnny know the sounds of these 15, in or out of a word? Now, that doesn't mean their alphabet *names*, though it's handy to know these too, but their *sounds*, for that is what you use in learning to read. These 15 consonants always have only one sound, and it's always the same in every position in the word. Anchors for the confused child to tie to! Then check the "Y." It says "Yuh" at the beginning of a word (consonant). Inside a word it says "ih" or "I" (vowel) but this fact can be taught later when the need for it comes up. The 3 "unusual" consonants—Z, X (ks) and Q—it's really qu (kw) can be taught next.

G and C are two little troublemakers. They each have 2 sounds. When an E or I or Y follows either one, its sound changes. G (guh) usually changes to J (g) and C (K) changes to S (C). That's 21 definite sounds he must know by the written or printed symbol. Does he? And if he knows them, does he look for them as a clue to what the new word is?

Next, does he know ch, sh, th and wh?—these 4 digraphs are "idiomatic," and are not to be taken apart. You may be surprised, at this point in your checking, that there are only a few of these letters that Johnny cannot sound.

But think how many words you as an adult would miss if you had no clue to three or four letters in one language! Ever try to read Russian?

Let us assume that Johnny knows all these sounds so far, including the 4 digraphs. There are still the most important ones, the vowels, A, E, I, O, U (and sometimes Y). These can be taught simply and directly. Show him that when there is *one* of these in a word or syllable, it has the short sound. *At, egg, in* and *up* contain the correct sounds of these letters.

Then show him that when there are *two* vowels, the first one says its own (alphabet) name, and the second is silent (*ate, ear, like, coat, tune*).

Exceptions Can Be Learned

"But that rule isn't always true—what about *love, have* and *bear*, for instance?" You are right, there are exceptions. At the present stage of our language development, 14 per cent of our words violate the phonetic rules, and these words have to be learned as exceptions. But is that any reason why the rules governing the 86 per cent cannot be learned?

Then fix what the child has learned by obtaining pleasant, easy reading books, until he uses his "tools" (phonetic knowledge) unconsciously, which he may need to do very slowly at first if he has been a chronic "guesser" or a "picture" reader. Once he experiences the delight of mastering a new word himself, progress will amaze you.

Establish a regular daily time for lessons. Human nature being what it is, Johnny is not going to be too enthusiastic at first, but help him stay with it. Your first aim is to help him perfect the use of the "tools of reading"; then work for smoothness and speed. By that stage, he will be reading for understanding and pleasure.
—By Margaret McEathron

HOW TO HELP WITH SPELLING

A SCHOOL child may do well in other subjects, but his inability to spell pulls down his grades, worries his parents and is the despair of all his teachers.

If spelling is a bugaboo for your child, you don't need special training to help him. Simply use this four-step way of learning to spell. The youngster trains his sight, sound, touch, and gets the very feel of the word in his muscles. There is no chance for mind-wandering. A high order of concentration is given to the work at hand. For this reason, many teachers comment that this way of teaching spelling is especially valuable for those children who seem to have difficulty in concentrating.

Dr. Grace Fernald who helped originate this method, explained its success by saying that individuals differ in the way in which they learn to spell. Many children after looking at a word can picture it. These are the youngsters who are usually good spellers. They possess in generous measure the ability to form visual images and to remember them.

Other children remember words more easily in terms of sound; they form what are called auditory images. Other boys and girls learn to spell by the sense of touch. They can remember words by recalling how their finger felt as it traced the words. Still other youngsters remember by means of motor experiences—the movements of the hand in tracing or writing words. Many children learn best through a chance to combine these various types of image. That is why the steps suggested here are often so helpful, for they provide a way for the child to see a word, hear it, feel it with a finger and actually with his muscles by tracing and writing it.

Formation of Visual Images

Since the forming of visual images is extremely important in learning to spell, you might well work toward strengthening this all-important ability.

Select five or six words which the child is expected to learn to spell and try one of the following experiments. Each encourages the youngster to form sharp, accurate images of the words being learned.

Write on a blackboard or sheet of paper the words to be studied. Pronounce each word and use it in a sentence. Then have your youngster say each word and use it correctly in a sentence. If he can think of sentences that illustrate various meanings of the word, so much the better. Obviously it is important to emphasize the meaning as well as the correct spelling of words; spelling words is of little value if their meanings are not known. Then have the child look at each word carefully, cover the word and try to "see" it in his mind. Finally let him look again to compare his mental image with the word.

While your child closes his eyes, erase several of the key letters in each word on the list—but take care to leave enough of the general framework of each word to suggest its total form. For example, if the words *today, come, house, school* are being studied, you might leave these skeleton forms:

t–day   c–m–   h—se   s–h—l

Ask the child to pronounce each word, to try to see in his mind the word as it looks when complete and then to write in the missing letters.

Puzzle Aids to Spelling

Boys and girls also enjoy the puzzle element offered by configurations—and these too can help them with their spelling. For example, using the four words mentioned above, draw the following configurations. Notice that they indicate the tall and half-space letters in a word and they suggest the general word form.

Then say to your child, "Which form makes you think of the word **h o u s e ?** Look at this form carefully. Try to see the word. What letter do you see in each block? Now write in the letters that spell the word 'house.'" Then do the same with each of the other configurations.

After you have given plenty of attention to helping your child improve his ability to visualize words, you might try some other interesting ways to clinch his mastery of the words. If you are working with a primary-age child, remember that children of this age learn best when they are manipulating, doing, moving about instead of sitting still. These children enjoy writing the words that they are learning to spell on smooth surfaces covered with finger paints, "painting" them on a blackboard with a finger or brush dipped in water, or writing in sand or on plasticine with a finger or stick.

Use of Rhythmic Chants

Young children also enjoy rhythmical activities and chants. You can build upon this with primary-age youngsters by suggesting that they bounce a ball or skip rope to a chant: **s-c-h-o-o-l** spells **school**
In doing this, the child should bounce the ball (or skip rope) once for each letter and once for each word.

Afterward, the youngster can write the word, softly saying each letter to himself as he writes; for example,

t-o-d-a-y spells **today**

Many of us, in our school days, learned the spelling of such demon words as *Mississippi* by means of rhythmic chants.

After the boy or girl is making progress with his spelling he will enjoy going over a list of words to note errors and to correct them. But, of course, he isn't ready for this until after you have used the other methods suggested to help him form sharp images of the correctly spelled words. Then he might enjoy correcting a list:

Todoy (today) coné (come)
houes (house) scool (school)

Spotting errors has particular value because it encourages the habit of checking for correctness and helps develop sensitivity to incorrect spelling.

Besides the words in his spelling lessons at school every child needs to learn to spell the names of relatives, pets, friends and classmates, the names of streets, towns and states frequently needed in addressing envelopes. Hobbies, too, develop needs for spelling specialized words. Since your youngster has plenty of reasons for learning to spell these words, you might encourage him to keep a notebook in which he can write them. You can use the methods suggested to help him learn to spell them.

Learning Made Pleasant

As you work along with your child, try to make learning to spell a pleasant experience. Don't push too hard. Be patient and relaxed. You naturally come to know what words are most difficult for him and can give more time to these. Time after time, of course, you'll be asked by your child to spell words that stump him. And, incidentally, when your child does ask, "How do you spell *penicillin?*" or whatever word he has in mind, it's a good plan to write the word for him instead of spelling it aloud. When you spell it aloud, it often becomes a meaningless jumble of letters. When you write it, you make it possible for your child to get a visual image of the word before he copies it.

No one expects to be able to spell every word perfectly. Most adults like to have at hand a good dictionary to which they can turn. And the dictionary habit is an essential one for children to form in the upper elementary grades, in high school and in college. While his school will do its part to help teach a child to use the dictionary, parents can do a lot too. Starting with the primary-age child, you can make available one of the picture dictionaries. Then when your youngster asks you how to spell a word, you can say, "Let's look in the picture dictionary and see if we can find it."

Before long, the child himself will take great satisfaction in using these simple dictionaries as an aid in spelling. When he reaches this point, he is well on his way to forming the dictionary habit. For the older child, a dictionary of his own is a good investment, helping him form a "dictionary habit" that will be helpful to him all his life.

If you will encourage your youngster to carry on a lively correspondence with friends or relatives, saying yes when he wants to write for box-top premiums, encouraging his interest in keeping diaries or making scrapbooks, your boy or girl is bound to discover by first-hand experience the importance of spelling. He will have strong reasons for wanting to learn to spell.

Four-Step Spelling Method

1. Write the word your youngster is to learn as large as you can on a blackboard or on a sheet of paper. Use the form of writing your child is using at school. (Generally, manuscript writing, like printing, is used in grades one

and two and regular writing, cursive, from grade three on.) Then say the word and have your child look at it and pronounce it.

2. Have your child trace this large model of the word to be studied with a forefinger, while he slowly says the word, not the individual letters within the word. Take care that the youngster does not distort the sound of the word as he slowly pronounces it while tracing it.

3. Have the youngster continue to trace the word while slowly saying it. This will help him get the feel of the word in his muscles and the sound of it, as well as help him form a visual image. He should do this until he thinks he can write the word on his own.

4. Let the child cover the model and try to write the word independently. Next have him compare his word with the large one. If he has written correctly, have him cover the model and rewrite the word. He should do this until he has written the word independently several times.

If the youngster writes the word incorrectly, he should start all over again.

—By Elenore Thomas Pounds

THIRD GRADE
—A CRUCIAL SCHOOL YEAR

NO year at school is more crucial for your child than his year in third grade. This is the year he changes from printing to writing in most schools, begins to learn the multiplication tables, makes his start in independent work. And perhaps most important of all, this is the year he must learn to utilize fully the reading skills acquired in the first and second grades. This, too, is the year when he becomes either a happy, accepted member of his group or a shy and retiring child going his lonely way.

By this time, you have become accustomed to having a schoolchild. His mastery of a new word is no longer a novelty. The fact that he can print a few phrases no longer is something to be proudly displayed to friends. Probably his pictures seldom get pinned up at home any more. School work is taken for granted and often forgotten in the after-school routine of play, music, dancing lessons and TV programs that fill his life.

It is especially important for a parent to be aware of the development in his child as he progresses from grade to grade during his first three years in school. Here, in the critical third grade, parents have perhaps the greatest chance to be of real help in their child's school growth.

Overcoming Arithmetic Difficulties

Third grade arithmetic has meaning to the child only if it is related to his experiences. He needs to know, and so is interested to learn, how to tell time to the hour and half hour. He often goes to the store for his mother and wants to know how to make change for a quarter, a half-dollar or a dollar. He keeps score in games, divides candy bars, cuts a cake. He knows the ages of his brothers and sisters and is interested to figure out how much older or younger he is than they. By means of such everyday problems he learns addition, subtraction, simple division and multiplication.

While third-graders range in ability from those youngsters still using fingers to count by to boys and girls who can add columns of four digits across and ten down with ease and accuracy, parents and teachers need not be too much disturbed by this variance.

If your child seems slow with numbers you can help him by playing number games at home. A homemade set of cards with combinations such as 7 plus 4 on one side and the answer 11 on the other will offer many opportunities for drill that can be fun. He can also set the alarm clock, tell you when it is time to start to school, watch the clock for his favorite radio program. Checking lunchtime and watching for the recess hour become important procedures.

One tendency many children have at this age is to reverse numbers. The seven will point the wrong way; the curve at the bottom of the six will be on the same side as the loop of the nine. Parents can watch and ask the child to correct this each time.

Independent Work Habits

The third year is critical, too, when it comes to the development of independent working habits. In the first two grades the child has worked with a group all doing the same thing. He copied sentences directly from the board or recited with his class in a group. Third-graders are expected to work more on their own and because of the range of individual ability, their speed in finishing any assigned task varies greatly. It is often up to the brightest children to think of ways to keep themselves profitably occupied. The question of "What can I do now?" they must often answer for themselves. Teachers often encourage these children to write about anything that interests them, taking care of any spelling difficulties as best they can by sounding their words to themselves.

Independent work of this kind is much prized by teachers. Parents who encourage this at home, praising originality of thought and expression, showing interest in the story and providing plenty of writing materials (while overlooking the peculiarities of spelling at this age) are doing their child a real favor.

A home supply of working materials is important to the third-grader. Nowadays his school probably supplies his in-school needs and parents are apt to take it for granted that that is enough. But a roll of blank paper on which the child can make big pictures is useful. The more he writes, draws, paints, works in clay or enjoys handcrafts the better. It is an age when he needs to express his feelings and develop his skills. Through them he gets a sense of accomplishment which helps build confidence. Third grade is the time, too, when a child should be making friends. His social attitudes are becoming established at this age. James, for example, is a shy, intelligent child who is still finding it difficult to make contacts with other children his age. He will soon recede into his quiet shell unless his parents and teacher can help him. Just eight, he is still willing to be gently shoved in the direction of friendships and fellow eight-year-olds are still willing to be persuaded to accept him. This is the time to give him encouragement and help in making friends.

How Parents Can Help

Raymond's friends began leaving him out of ball games when he couldn't catch the ball often enough or struck out too often in their contests with teams from the other third grades. Raymond's father happened by the playground one noontime and saw his son looking wistfully on from the sidelines. "Why don't you get into the game, son?" he asked. Shamefacedly Raymond answered, "They won't let me, I'm no good at baseball." That evening Raymond's father began a game of catch with his son. Soon this became an every-evening routine neither father nor son would miss. Before school closed Raymond had gained a place on the team.

It is important for a parent to see his child on the playground when he is eight and nine. At this age he can still be helped from the sidelines. Each year that passes makes this harder.

In school and out, your third-grader is at an important stage of development. And this at a time when the pressure of sheer numbers on lower elementary grades is great. In many schools the third-grade teacher averages less than ten minutes per day per pupil in actual teaching time. Most work must be group work.

Never was help from parents more needed. It is important that they supplement classroom teaching with help for their child at home. A parent can do this intelligently only if he is aware of what his child should learn in this grade, how he gets along with other children his age and what his individual problems and needs are.

Parent-teacher conferences. Individual parent-teacher conferences present a wonderful opportunity for getting just this information. No parent of a third-grader should miss even one of these conferences. Here he can ask searching questions and be assured of a fair, confidential answer. He can see his child's work as it compares with that of his classmates, he can ask for specific suggestions to guide him at home.

But no parent of a third-grader should stop here. He should visit his child's room and observe the whole class at work. He should drop by while the children are at play and observe his child on the playground. He should discuss with his child's teacher how he can help his child at home. In that crucial year, third grade, see that these two strong sources of interest and love—parents and teacher—join forces to make it the best possible year for your child.   —*By Janet Jackson*

HOW TO HELP
YOUR CHILD TO STUDY

MANY children, who seem bright enough, have a difficult time in learning a particular subject or subjects. Sometimes they plug away with dogged frenzy, as if by sheer hard reading they will conquer it. Sometimes such failures in one subject turn children against school in general and they become behavior problems. Sometimes they withdraw into themselves, become discouraged, unhappy and apathetic. All have one thing in common. They need help. Some may need sympathy, encouragement or prodding, but in addition they all need help in learning how to study.

Few schools teach children how to study. They teach children how to do arithmetic, how to use encyclopedias, how to read, how to set up and run a simple scientific experiment, but few teach them how to learn quickly and effectively from the printed page. And skill in learning doesn't, like Topsy, "just grow." The ability to study well is developed through careful guidance and systematic practice in good habits and techniques of study.

When your child begs, "Mother, please help me. I just CAN'T learn this old stuff!" do you feel helpless or confused? Most parents do. Many teachers do, too!

"Well," you answer, "you read, and pay close attention to what you are reading."

A Study Plan That Works

Now isn't that a helpful thing to tell a child who has done just that but is now weeping in angry frustration and declaring, "I just can't learn that old stuff?" Reading is necessary, and paying close attention is necessary, too. But there are special steps in studying which, if carefully followed, will help your child or anyone, for that matter, learn faster and better. They are simple steps which almost any parent can follow and which you can teach your child. Here is a plan of study that has been tested in hundreds of elementary schools, high schools and colleges, and reports state that it really works.

It is called the PQRST method. These five consecutive letters of the alphabet make it easy for even a young child to remember the five steps in the method: Preview, Question, Read, State, Test. When your child needs help in learning any reading-type lesson, go over his lesson with him, using the PQRST plan, and see if his face doesn't brighten with a feeling of really learning what he is studying! This is the way to do it:

Preview. When you first look at the lesson with your child, simply leaf through the assigned pages with him. Have him read the first sentence in each paragraph and the topic headings if there are any. As you go along, ask him what the lesson seems to be about. Don't expect him to give you all the details of it, just the general drift. Explain to him that this preview step, just like the preview of a motion picture, is supposed to give him an idea of what the lesson covers. You know how much easier it is for you to put together a jig-saw puzzle if you have some idea of what the finished picture is going to look like. Having an idea of what the lesson is about will be just as helpful to your child in learning and understanding it. This preview step should seldom take more than two or three minutes. But be sure you explain to your child that he is to watch for the "plot" of the lesson as he turns through the pages.

Question. After getting the general plot of the lesson, help your child formulate some questions he might expect to find answered in the lesson. If it is a geography lesson about South America, for instance, a fifth-grade child might be expected to find answers to such questions as: Where is it? What kind of country is it? How thickly settled is it? What do the people there do for a living? What are some of the things it is noted for? What is its largest city? Other questions may have been suggested by the Preview, too. Help your child formulate several such questions. It will probably pay you to write these questions down at first, although with practice you—and your child, when he is able to use the PQRST plan by himself—may be able to remember the questions without writing them down. Don't slight this step. You will probably need to take longer on it than you did on the Preview step because here you start your child really thinking about what he is to learn from this lesson.

Read. Now your child is ready to read his lesson. Because he has been through the Preview and Question steps, he will not be reading with dogged, blind aimlessness. He already has a general idea about what he is going to read which makes things seem somewhat familiar to him as he reads. Perhaps even more important, he has questions he wants answered, so he is reading with a purpose in mind. He is examining everything he reads, trying to find the answers to his questions. This usually helps a student in three ways: First, it helps him concentrate, because it is easier for him to hold his attention on what he is reading if he is looking for something special, than if he is just plowing through a lot of words. Second, it helps to stimulate and sustain his interest, because he gets a little sense of triumph and achievement every time he finds the answer to a question. Third, it is teaching him to hunt for ideas in his reading, to analyze and deduce meanings from the words he sees.

State. As soon as your child finishes reading his lesson, have him turn back and glance at the first paragraph, then look up and tell you what was in it— the main thoughts or facts. If the Preview and Questions steps were successfully accomplished the child shouldn't have much trouble in summing up the points, especially after a little practice. If he doesn't quite remember, drop him a hint. If he still can't remember, let him read the paragraph again, looking for the answers to a couple of questions you can quickly formulate about its contents. Then proceed to the next paragraph and repeat the process.

All this isn't as time-consuming as it sounds, especially as your child gets the knack of it. As he begins to use the PQRST plan without help, he should State the paragraphs aloud to himself.

This State step is an important one in determining how much your child will remember about his lesson. Many studies have been made to determine how a person should spend his study time in order to remember most; and these studies indicate that a person is likely to remember most if he spends *at least* as much time in trying to recall (stating, we call it) what he has read as he spent in reading it. Spending ten minutes reading a lesson and ten minutes recalling what he has read is likely to result in your child's remembering more of the lesson than he gets from reading it a second time.

Test. After two or three days of studying lessons by the PQRST steps, take five minutes or so at the beginning of each study period and test your child's memory of day-before-yesterday's lesson. To do this, use the State step quickly on that lesson. Of course, your child will not remember as many details as he did when he had just finished reading the lesson, but he can look quickly at a paragraph and so refresh his memory on important items that may have slipped his mind. This is a review exercise that will do an amazing lot to refresh his memory for a test. If you test on the previous lesson each day you will probably be surprised at what your child will remember.

How Parents Can Help

Admittedly, the PQRST method takes time. But do remember this—whether you plan for your child to spend ten minutes or half an hour on a lesson, he will probably learn most from it if you will divide that time among all of the PQRST steps, instead of spending all the time on one or two of the steps. Be especially sure not to slight the Question and State steps. They are the ones requiring most thought and understanding. If they are done thoroughly, the others should pretty well take care of themselves, provided, of course, the child spends time on them.

Younger children will have to receive help from you on several lessons before they can follow the PQRST steps by themselves. A high school pupil, on the other hand, should be able to handle it alone.

It will take time to help your youngster learn to use the method, and develop the habit of using it. But once this PQRST habit of study is firmly entrenched your child has an asset which will serve him through school.

All this isn't just somebody's theory. Every point in the procedure has been tested and has proved itself in use. So try it when your child pleads, "Mother, I just CAN'T learn this old stuff!" You may be surprised at how good a teacher you are, if you watch your PQRST's!　　　　　　—By Thomas F. Staton

GUIDING THE GIFTED

WHEN Einstein first went to Princeton, the story goes, a little girl used to drop by regularly to see him at his home in the afternoons. Reporters grew interested—was she some kind of scientific prodigy? The friendship had a very simple explanation, Dr. Einstein told them: the little girl brought him cookies her mother had baked. In return, he helped her with her arithmetic.

Unfortunately for the parents of bright children, there aren't enough Einsteins (nor maybe even cookies) to go around. Few youngsters can enjoy the privilege of being guided by genius. Indeed, the whole problem of giving our nation's brightest children an education commensurate with their abilities isn't easy to solve. If your boy or girl is among the five to ten per cent ordinarily referred to as "gifted"—those with an I.Q. of a hundred and twenty-five or more, or those with a pronounced talent—you'll probably find that their upbringing in general and their schooling in particular call for some extra effort on your part.

Gifted children have always tended to find special favor with the best teachers. Thousands of dedicated teachers in school systems that don't as yet offer any special program for talented youngsters, are doing a job that few specially designed programs could do better. Many school systems today have special programs—at least for the academically gifted—and more are being started all the time. If you know something about them—where some of the best are operating, along what lines they're set up—you'll be in a better position to evaluate just what's being done for the gifted in your own community. Along with other interested parents, you may be able to get a special program started in your local school system. Or you may find it possible to move to a community where a program is already operating successfully.

Special Programs

The special programs are of two general types: those aimed at acceleration, which get the gifted youngster through school at an earlier than average age; and those with enrichment as their goal, which offer highly endowed boys and girls a curriculum expanded in scope and depth. Obviously, enrichment is a term considerably more difficult to pinpoint than acceleration. The "enriched curriculum" may be one peppered with extra foreign language study, advanced mathematics and science courses or, sadly, simply the drabbest kind of "busy work." You may have to do some sleuthing to discover exactly what enrichment constitutes in a given school system and whether or not it's worthy of the name. Your best bet is probably to visit classes and talk to teachers and recent graduates, preferably graduates whose interests are similar to those of your own youngster.

Each type of program has many variants. And the two aren't necessarily mutually exclusive. "What's all this nonsense about acceleration versus enrichment?" demanded the mother of a twelve-year-old recently. "My son is getting both. He's in a class that's going through junior high school in two years instead of three. At the same time, the class is doing more advanced work in most subjects, especially social studies." Her son is in one of the Special Progress Classes in the New York City school system.

Acceleration. Some parents are unnecessarily leery of acceleration. Perhaps they themselves were "skipped" as children and feel that in the process they missed some significant elementary material—spelling, maybe, or fractions. Or their fears spring from having been skipped so often that they felt too young or immature for their classmates.

There's certainly some risk involved in shoving a child ahead of his age group, but probably less than is generally thought. Present-day educators are so aware of the importance of healthy social adjustment and so sensitive about past mistakes in this area that you can be pretty sure acceleration won't be suggested for your child unless he's able to handle it emotionally and physically, as well as intellectually.

But youngsters rarely skip a grade today. Acceleration is accomplished differently. In some cities, children can enter first grade early—at five rather than the standard age of six—if their scores on intelligence tests warrant it. This has been tried successfully for a number of years in Brookline, Massachusetts, to mention one example. Or gifted youngsters may be placed in special classes which progress at a faster pace. A number of cities have such classes at the junior high level. Canada is trying them at the elementary level. There's also the practice of giving bright youngsters tougher courses in high school so that they can enter college early, after finishing the eleventh grade, or be admitted to college with advanced standing and graduate in three and a half or even three years. Both these practices are currently being tested, with financial backing from the Ford Foundation, in a number of our high schools and colleges.

Enrichment. Parents are often taken with the idea of enrichment because it appears at first to pose fewer adjustment problems for bright children than acceleration. Enrichment *can* be effected in any classroom, provided the teacher is gifted and has funds at her disposal for purchasing supplementary materials—an unabridged dictionary, a young people's encyclopedia, collections of myths and legends, art and music histories, folders or books of mathematical puzzles—to name a few possibilities. The trick is to spare fast learners the boredom of drill sessions necessary for their slower fellows, by assigning them interesting research projects keyed to their individual abilities.

Jeannie, who's in the sixth grade, has a flair for drawing. When her class is being drilled in grammatical and arithmetical skills she's already mastered, Jeannie spends the time making greeting cards. She's become so proficient that she sells all she makes and expects to earn enough money by the time she graduates from high school to pay for art lessons. Her classmate, Donald, who's especially good at math, is encouraged to work simple algebra problems when the rest of the class is having arithmetic sessions. "Why, that's nothing new," you say, "it was done in my time." You're right—there's nothing new about this kind of enrichment. What's new is that it has more official encouragement and supervision today.

Special Classes

Generally speaking, though, enrichment today, like acceleration, involves some segregation of the gifted into special classes—"grouping" it's called. You may find yourself drawn into the battle of the educators over To Group or Not To Group—and if so, for how much of the time. A vocal band of professionals opposes grouping as undemocratic and inimical to the social development of the gifted. But, so far as democracy is concerned, a growing body of evidence points to the fact that the caliber of teaching tends to im-

prove all along the line when a program for gifted children is inaugurated in a school.

Some cities, which have a few special classes or seminars for the gifted, segregate their youngsters only for part of the teaching day. The rest of the time, fast, average and slow learners are together in regular classrooms. Others maintain full-time special classes but house these classes in regular school buildings and encourage the pupils to participate in all intra-school activities. The most extreme form of grouping is to be found in schools which enroll only gifted pupils—Hunter Elementary School in New York City, for one.

The artistically gifted. What's being done for children who are artistically gifted? Most schools with special programs for academically superior youngsters make a stab at trying to meet the needs of children with other gifts as well, although it's admittedly difficult to measure these talents. And frequently it takes real professional training to develop the potential skills and interests of artistically talented youngsters. Community organizations, especially the professionally staffed urban museums and libraries, often have special classes and lectures in music and painting, providing better artistic training than one school can offer. That's why every program for the gifted should be community-wide.

Guidance for Your Child

How can a parent find out which cities offer what special educational opportunities to gifted children? Or how to get the ball rolling in his own community? To start with, see what material your local library has on the subject. Two national organizations which also may be of help are the American Association for Gifted Children, 15 Gramercy Park, New York 3, N.Y., and the National Association for Gifted Children, 409 Clinton Springs Ave., Cincinnati 17, Ohio.

One of the knottiest problems about the gifted child is how to identify him correctly. Experts agree that this is the school's rather than the parents' job and that, inevitably, some errors will be made—mostly ones of omission. The child whose gifts mature late may be passed over. A good program should include frequent retesting of all pupils and be flexible enough to admit "late bloomers."

Testing your child. Unfortunately, this is an ideal easier to state than to live up to. If you honestly believe your child's potential has been incorrectly evaluated and school authorities are unsympathetic to a tactful protest, you may want to have him tested at a reputable psychological testing center. It's always possible that the school *has* made a mistake or that your child has significant learning blocks with which he and you need trained help. However, be sure to weigh, against any possible advantage, the more tangible harm you can do your youngster by making him aware of your dissatisfaction with the school's decision.

As every parent knows, native endowment and educational opportunity aren't the only factors that determine achievement. As significant, possibly more, are your child's motivation, the effort he makes and standards of achievement set at home.

We don't yet know all the factors that condition motivation and effort, but we do know that fundamentally they spring from a child's natural curiosity, his love of activity and the pleasure he gets from accomplishment. Anything parents can do to encourage and satisfy children's native curiosity contributes vitally to the learning process in later years.

Your Child's Achievement

When it comes to setting standards of achievement, parents are faced with the problem of finding a happy medium between two extremes. We must demand neither too much nor too little—and learn when to press, when to relax.

Two couples were discussing their children's progress in school. Both the youngsters were in a special class for gifted children and both sets of parents had been told by the teacher that their child wasn't doing as well as his ability warranted. "I've wondered," said Matthew's mother, "if it's because we've pushed the boy too much, criticized his homework too severely, nagged too often about how hard he must study to get into M.I.T. like his father."

"Nonsense," said Susan's mother. "If that were true then Susan should be going like a house afire. Because we've never pushed her a bit." What these two sets of parents failed to realize was that the two extremes of standard-setting they represent tend to produce the same disability.

What about parents who set different standards of academic achievement for girls and for boys? And what about parents who, consciously or unconsciously, *don't* want their children to develop into "brains"? Some parents, like Susan's mother, actually try to hold their bright children back, perhaps under the erroneous impression that too much emphasis on learning may make them maladjusted, unhappy. This stereotype should be dead by now, but isn't. Some years ago, Dr. Lewis M. Terman, whose long-term studies of gifted children are well known, demonstrated that academically talented children tend statistically to be socially gifted, too. His research and clinical findings of other psychologists indicate that bright boys and girls have a better than average chance of developing confidence without self-conceit, of growing into likable, successful, personally fulfilled adults.

What it all adds up to is this: with a bit of extra awareness, of extra doing on your part, your gifted youngster can have his chance—even without an Einstein on the next block.   —*By Mary B. Hoover*

TESTS AND WHAT THEY TELL YOU

AS part of their regular program, almost all schools nowadays give tests which furnish good estimates of a student's ability and achievement in school work—estimates not dependent on the grading standards of the school he attends. With the current national interest in identifying students with high-level ability, chances are your own youngster will be taking an increasing number of such tests. Can you find out how he stands? Probably. In more and more schools, teachers and counselors now discuss the results of such tests with students and parents.

The tests in question are "standardized" or "objective"—that is, procedures for giving questions and scoring them are standard. Several different publishers compete in offering tests to the various school systems, so tests may vary from one school system to the next. But they are enough alike that the same general principles of interpretation apply.

What Tests Are Given?

The two kinds of test most commonly given are: *achievement tests* and *scholastic aptitude tests*.

Achievement tests may be given in spelling, arithmetic, science, English, history, foreign languages or any other area of study. Scores tell how much a student has learned—how much he has achieved—in particular school subjects. They attempt to measure how much he knows *after* completing a given course of work.

In many schools, achievement tests are given every year from the fourth through the seventh or eighth grades, only once or twice at high school.

The scholastic aptitude tests are usually given about every third year from the third or fourth grade through the twelfth. They differ from achievement tests primarily with respect to their purpose, which is to estimate how well youngsters *can* do, not how well they *have* done. In other words, these tests are designed to measure capacity or potential for *future* achievement in school. The scholastic aptitude test may be called by a variety of names such as school ability test, mental maturity test, general classification test, mental abilities test, I.Q. test. These all measure ability to do school work.

The I.Q. Tests

Special mention should be made of the I.Q. test because its significance has been so widely misunderstood. I.Q. stands for "Intelligence Quotient," which is usually computed by dividing a child's mental age (derived from his test score) by his chronological age, and multiplying by 100.

Generally speaking, there are two kinds of I.Q. test—the *individual* I.Q. test, usually given by a trained psychologist to one child at a time, and the *group* I.Q. test, a paper and pencil test given to many youngsters at once. This is probably the kind your child has taken.

A number of different group I.Q. tests are published. Scores on these tests are only roughly comparable. This means that your youngster's I.Q. score may vary 10 or 15 points, or even more, depending on which test he took. Perhaps the most erroneous concept about an I.Q. test is that it measures "intelligence" in a broad sense. Despite its name, it measures, strictly speaking, only certain *kinds* of intelligence. Studies have shown that persons who do well on I.Q. tests do tend to do well in school.

On the other hand, scores on I.Q. tests are not closely related to other kinds of intelligence such as persistence, ability to get along with others, artistic creativity. These qualities may be crucial to success in many endeavors. Parents might use the term "scholastic aptitude" or "scholastic ability" in their conversation and in their thinking instead of "I.Q." because this is what the test measures most of all.

Measurements of a child's personal and social qualities are also often called "tests," but they are more in the nature of questionnaires or inventories or records. There are no right or wrong answers to them.

What Do Test Scores Mean?

The number of questions your child gets right on a particular test doesn't mean very much in itself. A perfect score on an easy test may not indicate as much ability as getting only half the answers right on a hard test. What you need to know is how he did in comparison with other children at his level. Systems for reporting scores to indicate this have been set up.

Perhaps the most common is the system whereby the score representing the number of right answers is converted to a percentile. Percentile scores range from 1 to 99. A score at any given percentile indicates the child's standing within a particular group. If your child scored at the 61st percentile, he did better than 61 per cent of a certain group and 39 per cent did better than he. If he scored at the 30th percentile, he did better than 30 per cent. At the 99th percentile, he's in the top 1 per cent.

Since percentile scores permit you to compare your child with a specific group of children, you have to know the nature of the group before you really know what the percentile means. The most common group used in developing percentile scores is the so-called "national norm group," representing children selected from all over the country. When your child takes an achievement test and scores at the 90th percentile on the basis of a national norm group, this means he did better than 90 per cent of a cross-section of children from the same grade level on a nation-wide basis.

Sometimes local norms are used. In this case, the percentile tells how well your child is doing compared with the other children in your school system. Although test scores are not always given in percentiles, statistical tables have been set up to change almost any kind of score to a percentile.

A kind of score that is commonly used for achievement tests is the *grade-placement score*, which represents how well a child has done compared with other children at various grade levels. For example, a grade-placement score of 5.4 on an arithmetic achievement test is typical of a fifth-grader who is four-tenths of the way through his grade. Here, too, there are statistical tables a teacher or counselor may use for converting the grade-placement scores to percentiles, which will probably give you the clearest picture of your child in comparison with other children.

What to Ask Teachers About Tests

Make an appointment in advance with the school counselor or your child's teacher so he or she can have his scores ready to discuss with you.

For most parents, the first visit to discuss test scores should be made when the child is in the middle elementary grades (grades 4–6), the next visit at the junior high school level (grades 7–9) and the last visit at the high school level (grades 10–12).

You should realize that your child's test scores are a good general indication of his scholastic aptitude and achievement, but not an exact one. For example, the difference between a percentile score of 45 and 55 cannot ordinarily be considered important. What you need to ask the teacher to tell you is not the score itself, but the general level of the score. Ask:

Which standardized tests has my child taken? With what norm group is he being compared on the test score? What was the general level of my child's score on each test?

You will probably want to know whether your child was in the "high" group (scoring above the 75th percentile), the "average" group (the 25th to the 75th percentile) or the "low" group (below the 25th percentile) in each test. These questions are legitimate and the teacher or counselor should be willing to answer them.

What Special Tests Should Be Taken?

If your youngster is doing good work in school and his scores on the tests regularly given are at least average based on national norms, he may want to take special nation-wide tests. These are the tests sometimes required for admission to secondary schools and colleges and for the granting of scholarship awards. A small fee is charged for taking them and it is necessary to register in advance. The tests are given in designated testing centers located throughout the United States and other countries. In many schools, counselors or other qualified persons are available to provide students with information about these tests.

Detailed information may be obtained by writing to Educational Testing Service, Princeton, New Jersey. For information about the National Merit Scholarship Qualifying Test, write to National Merit Scholarship Corporation, 1580 Sherman Avenue, Evanston, Illinois.

The Secondary School Admission Test. Designed for use in selecting students to be admitted to grades seven through twelve. If your youngster is planning to enter a private school, he may be required to take it. About 200 independent schools now require scores on this test and more than 12,000 students take it each school year.

The Scholastic Aptitude Test and the Achievement Tests of the College Entrance Examination Board. "College Boards"—required by hundreds of colleges and universities. Each year more than 400,000 candidates for admission now take these tests. They may be taken in the eleventh grade to provide information for the guidance counselor. However, most colleges require students to take them in the twelfth grade for admission.

The Scholastic Aptitude Test (SAT) and the Achievement Tests are administered in two separate sessions on the same day. Students taking both may, if they wish, take the SAT on one administration date and the Achievement Tests on another. Students should check with the colleges to which they are applying for advice on which test to take.

Advanced Placement Examinations. These are offered by the College Entrance Examination Board for able high school students who wish to receive advanced standing for college-level courses *taken in high school*. These courses include English, Latin, French, German, Spanish, mathematics, biology, chemistry, physics, American history and European history. A student who does well in his college-level course and the examination may be excused from taking the same course in college and may even receive college credit for it. However, each case is considered on its own merit and colleges vary widely in their policies relating to advanced placement.

If your youngster has high ability, you may want to check whether the secondary school he is attending is offering special courses requiring college-level ability.

The Scholarship Qualifying Test. Used to help select winners in many different scholarship programs. One of the tests offered by the College Entrance Examination Board, it should be taken in the twelfth grade by those applying for scholarships, but may be taken in the eleventh grade to provide information for educational and vocational guidance. Each year more than 150,000 students take the test.

The National Merit Scholarship Qualifying Test. Used not only for scholarship selection but also for purposes of educational and vocational counseling. The cash stipend granted depends on need and cost of education in the college selected. At present, it varies from $100 to $2,400 a year for four years.

What About Testing in the Future?

Very likely, tests will play an increasingly important part in educational and vocational planning. The Federal and state governments will probably give greater support to large-scale testing programs. This should mean not only wider identification of the talented but also that all youngsters will be more likely to receive training appropriate to their abilities.

With the increasing use of tests, however, there is danger that decisions may be made on the basis of test scores alone. Other evidence about the individual's abilities may not be considered, and his own hopes and ambitions may be ignored. Parents and their children should become informed about the meaning of test scores so they can evaluate the evidence presented by tests *and* all other evidence, to choose the line of action that is best for the individual child. —*By Quentin C. Stodola*

SCHOOL CHECKUPS
SAFEGUARD HEALTH

TO most families "school health" means the occasional reminders calling for special examinations that come from the school medical team. But a school health program does more than that. It follows three main avenues:

1. Health teaching. 2. The provision of a healthful social and physical environment. 3. Health services.

Health services include the periodic examination of your child by doctors, dentists and specialists; testing, observation and screening by teachers and nurses; if necessary or appropriate, the following-up of recommendations by the school health team to see that they're understood and carried out.

The job of a school doctor is to spot conditions which may cause difficulty now or later. From his knowledge of a child, he suggests what should be done—including, if necessary, a visit to a private doctor or specialist. Basically, the school doctor examines, recommends and refers. The private or family doctor also examines—but prescribes and treats as well.

An entry examination and similar checkups throughout your child's school career are required by all school health systems. Many cities have a spring or summer roundup to encourage advance examinations. Some school systems call for annual medical and dental reviews. Others specify three or four medical examinations at strategic intervals—at entry and perhaps at the sixth, ninth and twelfth grades.

All too often, because a child has no obvious defect or complaint, these periodic scheduled checkups are considered "routine"—and ignored. Since five to fourteen-year-olds are healthier than any other age group in our population, it's not surprising that parental indifference to the school's reminders is widespread. But no parent can rest secure in the belief that his child will always be well. It's your job as a parent to take care that both the periodic checkups and the referrals are met promptly and completely.

How to Cooperate

For Jon about to enter first grade or for Sue set for kindergarten, much of the school health way can be paved beforehand—with your help. Practically all schools try to give each child a head start in health by getting medical information early—if possible before admission.

At spring registration, Jon's mother had been asked to have the family doctor examine her boy several weeks before classes started. She did this, and made sure that Jon's medical report got to the school nurse. Thus, when school began, the nurse had already set up Jon's permanent, confidential health record with his doctor's findings and instructions, and a record of Jon's immunizations completed and due. So prepared, the nurse could tell Jon's teacher at their first meeting that Jon could take part in all activities—but should be watched for signs of eyestrain.

Sue wasn't examined by her family doctor but waited for the school doctor, who was able to see her about a month after school began. He asked that Sue's mother come to the examination, held in the school's health room. She watched him examine Sue's eyes, ears, nose and throat; check her heart, lungs, glands and posture; observe her skin, her general appearance and her muscular coordination.

The Nurse and the Teacher

While the nurse measured her height and weight and began to draw up her health record, the doctor commented on what he found, filled in her immunization record and asked Sue's mother about her child's illnesses, diet, sleep habits, special likes and dislikes. Since Sue needed her final polio shot, he got her mother's permission and gave it to Sue then and there. The nurse summarized the doctor's suggestions for keeping Sue in trim and set a date for her next immunization.

As a member of the school health team, your child's teacher is trained to watch for signs and symptoms of ill health and deviations from developmental norms. Most teacher training institutions include courses on health observation. And active school programs provide refresher courses for teachers and health counselors.

Your child's teacher is often the person who hangs the familiar Snellen or "E Chart" on the wall once a year on Health Day, to test the vision of her pupils. This simple vision test is obviously not a complete eye examination, but when carefully conducted by trained teachers it can and does identify those children who can't see well enough for school work. You should not, however, be lulled into security because your child "passes" this common test. Screenings like this are intended to discriminate only within a fairly wide range between the well and the unwell.

Health Day is the time, too, when teachers weigh and measure their pupils and conduct hearing tests. Like the vision screening, hearing tests are only an indication of possible loss. The observant teacher and parent should continue to watch for problems and signs of change.

The school nurse and your child's teacher confer at least once a year and hold special meetings whenever necessary to review the health of each child. Between them, nurse and teacher decide which children appear to need medical care.

In many ways, the nurse is the most important member of the school health team. As the link between doctor and teacher, she interprets medical recommendations and gives advice about classroom problems.

Her main job, however, is maintaining contact with your child and his family. Her knowledge of home, school and community is applied both in planning a total school health program and in formulating a very specific health plan for your child. She may be able to spend only two or three half-days a week in any given school. She is, nevertheless, in charge of your school's health room, prepares for and assists the doctor, cooperates with the principal and teachers and confers with parents at school examinations. All this adds up to the fact that she's kept pretty busy.

Because of this, and to cover all contingencies, many schools require that trained teachers take on the job of handling first aid. First aid and the responsibility for safety, hygiene and health education have been successfully assumed by teachers and made part of their regular classroom work. The teacher refers special health problems relating to behavior, guidance and social adjustment to psychologists, counselors and social workers. The nurse keeps in touch with these specialists and brings to the doctor suggestions which may help his diagnosis and treatment.

It's discouraging to report that conscientious nurses have made as many as seven and eight home visits a year to get a mother to bring her child to a cardiac clinic. It's equally discouraging to report that a twenty to thirty per cent rate of broken appointments exists in some free clinics. It's up to you as a parent to help overcome this. Don't make your school nurse make unnecessary visits to your home.

Programs for Parents

No perfect school health program exists in the United States. All are in need of constant study and improvement. Fortunately, our educators and public health officials are aware of the need and trying to answer it.

How can you, as parents, help? By thinking of yourselves as school aides as well as mothers and fathers. The most successful health programs are those in which parents take an active part.

In many cities, permanent parent committees assist at Health Day in the transportation of handicapped children, in monitoring groups referred to dental clinics.

The organization of parents in Prince Georges County, Maryland, which started with testing hearing and vision at the schools, was eventually able to initiate an over-all health program for children in town and rural schools.

Associations of parents have also contributed to *building* school health. The health council at Central Elementary School in Mamaroneck, New York, was instrumental in getting a safe school driveway, improving lunch-room facilities, getting funds for a health counselor, instituting sanitary inspections and approving fluoridation of water.

Where public health assistants aren't available, responsible parents may set up, but of course not maintain, health records. Records are confidential and open for authorized use only. Volunteers issue standard notices, act as receptionists or escorts.

Not only parents but other members of the community have pitched in and helped. Men's and women's service clubs have contributed to the purchase of equipment for the early detection of hearing loss, for the education and rehabilitation of the deaf, the partially sighted, the crippled and the mentally defective.

In all aspects of the school program, there is an interplay of responsibility between the home, the school and the community. But nowhere is this interplay more vital than in the school health program. Its effectiveness—and the health of your child—depends on your taking responsibility and cooperating.

—*By Irving Ladimer, S.J.D.*

THE SCHOOL LUNCH PROGRAM

DOES your child rush to the refrigerator, as if half-starved, when he gets home from school? And if you ask him what he had for lunch does he say something like, "Gee, Mom, I don't remember—but I didn't like it!"

It's not unusual if he does. But it does not mean he was not served a good lunch at school. It probably was a very good lunch and the chances, by big odds, are that your child ate every bite of it and liked it, too. There will be days, of course, when a child will not like his school lunch. But he doesn't always like everything his mother cooks, either.

If you have never done it, you ought to go to your child's school for lunch some day. Don't tell him or anyone else you plan to do it—just go. School lunch managers like to show mothers what they are doing. But don't judge the program by a single lunch. You may hit the meat substitute menu day. Schools, like mothers, cannot always serve beef or chicken.

One of our PTA members was asked to give a talk about school lunches. She had eaten lunch at her child's school and found it good, but she wondered if perhaps it was served specially for her and the other mothers who were invited that day. So for several days she dropped in for lunch at nearby elementary, junior high and senior high schools, without telling anyone she was coming.

Later she reported to her PTA that she was pleasantly surprised by the meals she had at all the schools. Each one was nutritious and balanced and appetizing, but what amazed her most was that the lunches could be prepared and sold for so little. She could not match the low cost at home, she said, nor could she buy a comparable lunch in any restaurant at the school lunch price.

This mother watched the plates as the children took them to the counter after eating, knowing that how well the children eat what is served them is the real test of a school lunch program. She noted that almost all the food served was eaten. The few trays with some food left on them were returned mostly by girls who, she learned, were dieting.

Good school lunch managers are just as interested as mothers in what the children eat. And if a child does not eat well they try to do something about

it. They know that the better-nourished child is mentally more alert, shows greater zest at work and play, and has a happier outlook on life. Their goal is threefold: to provide a lunch that is nutritious and balanced and that supplies at least one-third of the daily food requirements, to teach the child to eat and enjoy a variety of healthful foods and to set the stage for social development during the lunch period.

Low-Budget Lunches

How schools can serve the good lunches they do at the prices they charge is a miracle in this high-cost era. Each school's lunch program is nonprofit—which means it cannot *make* money and at the same time it should not *lose* money.

You may have read that the federal government buys and gives to schools such surplus farm products as flour, corn meal, butter, dried eggs and dried milk. Sometimes schools get meats, canned fruits and canned vegetables, too. Some schools get more than others, depending upon their need which is determined mostly by the number of their pupils whose parents cannot pay for meals.

The federal government also gives a per-plate "cash reimbursement" to schools. This, too, varies greatly, depending upon individual school needs. At best, however, the food and cash reimbursement that schools get from the federal government represent a small percentage of their total food and serving costs. In most schools, the federal cash reimbursement is less than two cents per plate.

Most schools accept the surplus foods and cash reimbursement. To get the full amount they must serve a "Type A" lunch consisting of, as a minimum:

1. One-half pint of fluid whole milk to drink.

2. Two ounces (edible portion as served) of lean meat, poultry or fish; or two ounces of cheese; or one egg; or one-half cup of cooked dry beans or peas; or four tablespoons of peanut butter; or an equivalent quantity of any combination of these foods, served in a main dish or in a main dish and one other menu item.

3. A three-fourth cup serving of two or more vegetables or fruits, or serving of one vegetable and one fruit.

4. One slice of whole-grain or enriched bread; or a serving of corn bread, biscuits, rolls, or muffins made of whole-grain or enriched meal or flour.

5. Two teaspoons of butter or fortified margarine.

A typical Type A lunch might be: ½ cup orange juice, ¾ cup chicken on ¼ cup rice, ¼ cup green peas, muffin with butter or margarine, oatmeal raisin cookies and ½ pint milk.

No mother's food budget was ever so complicated! The school lunch manager, in planning her menus, must not only figure out what she will serve to make the lunch nutritious and balanced by these standards, but also what she can afford to serve and what the children will like best. She must also estimate closely how many children will buy lunches each day, so there will be no wasted food. Every penny has to count.

Good Food Habits Encouraged

Some schools publish menus in advance to help mothers avoid serving the same foods at night that the children get at noon. However, on days when the menus include something the children do not much like, they may, knowing what's coming, spend their lunch money for a soft drink and candy at a store down the street. This is not good for the children and badly disrupts the school lunch program. Consequently, some schools now are radio-broadcasting their menus after school starts for the benefit of mothers only. Schools serving the best lunches day after day are those whose children eat them every day.

It takes a lot of people to feed all the hungry schoolchildren in the country. More and more workers each year are being trained for this in special workshops on the problems of preparing and serving foods. These workshops teach school lunch managers and workers how to prepare appetizing, nutritious, balanced meals within the limits of their plate charges; how to buy foods most economically; how to prepare and serve just the right quantities; how to follow proper sanitation procedures and bookkeeping methods.

Parents should understand that the school lunch program is not just providing the child with a good noonday meal, important as that is. The program is a part of the total school curriculum.

In this complex, rapidly changing world, the child who will be the man or woman of tomorrow should be able to eat and enjoy all kinds of nourishing and wholesome food. That's why the schools encourage children to eat a wider variety of foods than they may be accustomed to at home. It is an important part of every child's learning. Guidance in building good food habits starts in the home rooms where the teachers explain the importance of good diet and the part played by various nutrients. The children are shown pictures of well-balanced foods and encouraged to try new ones that are served in the school lunchroom.

The experience of eating with other children is good for your child. It promotes social growth, encourages friendship. It helps him solve some of the problems of getting along well with others. So do your child a favor. Take a real interest in his school lunches and encourage him to look forward to the lunch period as one of the bright spots of his school day.

—*By Helen Macomber Walker*

CHEAP SCHOOLS COST THE MOST

WHENEVER some bewildered citizen, beset by tales of "costly palaces" in school building, asks someone in my profession, "Couldn't you have built that school for less?" the truthful answer, of course, is "Sure." Anything can be had cheaper. You can buy a used car for less; you can buy a shoddy suit for less. And you can throw the shapeless suit away after a year.

Still, that's too simple a comparison and could be misleading—like a lot of too simple comparisons that are being made in the attacks on school construction. Explanations would be easy if we could classify building schools the way mail-order catalogues list articles under quality headings of good-better-best. But when your school board talks with their architect about a school building, they should keep three different categories in mind—three M's: Money (the budget you allow), Mass (the area and volume of enrollment it must accommodate) and Materials (quality). If you put them down as a triangle, making each M a side, your architectural job is in balance when all three sides maintain that triangle. But if one of the sides has to be stretched or lopped shorter without another side changing proportionately, the job's out of shape. If your school board wants, say, more area than the budget allows, we can reduce quality. If your board fixes the standards of quality, we can reduce the size of the building. There's another and better alternative in both cases, of course—more money. Sometimes people seem to think there's a magic formula that can stretch that money leg of the triangle when one or both of the others are lengthened—but you can't change hard facts.

Nevertheless, as the taxpayer who foots the bill, you may ask, "Since we have to look after our buildings anyway and have a budget for that purpose, why not keep the first cost low?"

The answer, as with the car and the suit, is that you pay more in the long run. In a few short years the costs of keeping up a cheap building add up to a lot more than the cost of quality construction in the first place.

Maintenance Costs

Take for example, *minor* repairs. If you are a homeowner then you're familiar with the "minor" item of caulking. (For those who aren't—caulking is used to seal against the weather those little joints and corners where water may enter around windows and doors.) About every five years caulking has to be renewed or it dries out, cracks and lets in rain and snow.

What happens when you put off renewing it for a year or two? For a while it's just a minor repair—applying some new caulking wherever the old falls out. But one day you find some of that rain has seeped into the walls around the doors and windows, water stains show up on your walls. Does it make sense to ask an architect to specify an inferior caulking compound and set off this chain of disintegration and expense that much sooner? Multiply this one example by the hundreds of items in any school building and you get some idea of the magnitude of the problem.

Years ago good architects foresaw that the expanding education program and the expanding crop of babies would demand more space—more of everything. So off came the gables, cupolas and columns of the old-time schoolhouse; in came the clean, straight lines of our new schools, with built-in color, sunshine and vitality. Children liked it; their parents accepted it. Of course, there were—and still are—many with a nostalgic longing for the way a school used to look—even though the traditional building was an obstacle to teaching, a problem to maintain and expensive to build at present-day prices.

Unit Schools

Today, architects are still trying to look ahead. What are some of the things we think of?

Just the increasing enrollment in itself will influence the pattern of future school buildings—especially high schools. With more and more young people knocking at the school door, we can build either mammoth high school "plants" or more and more individual high schools with costly duplication of expensive laboratories, shop facilities and physical education areas.

Or we can think along new lines. Foresighted educators and their architects have come up with the concept of the "little school" or "schools-within-a-school." This means subdividing the very large high school into a group of 3 or 4 small, more manageable units, each a small high school within itself. Facilities such as the library, gymnasium, auditorium and vocational arts shops are constructed separately and serve all of the unit schools. In some cases a large central kitchen prepares the food for the entire operation and then transports it to the "little" school dining areas where only a small serving kitchen is needed.

This concept holds great promise for getting the most out of specialized facilities and equipment usually too expensive to duplicate in several schools. Besides—or perhaps foremost—pupils and teachers working together in the unit schools get to know each other much better than in our overlarge schools. Another advantage of the "little" school is that it can be planned to grow with increasing enrollment.

Flexible arrangements. Another gauge of the future: our present pre-occupation with science will surely mean immediate changes in high school facilities. Science departments will have to be expanded to provide more small research areas. We know we will have to have a more *flexible* arrangement of interior spaces to change both size and shape of rooms as the demand requires.

The entire Hillsdale High School building near San Francisco, California, designed with this flexibility in mind, is under one roof and subdivided with removable metal partitions which can be arranged and rearranged. Fortunately, most present-day schools, while perhaps not having this high degree of flexibility, have been designed with complete structural steel or concrete frames.

Educational television. Thinking ahead, we must surely take educational television into account, too. Early in 1956, my firm had the good fortune to be connected with the largest single experiment in the field of closed circuit educational television at Hagerstown, Maryland. From this experience and subsequent observation of the program in action, we have concluded that, if it becomes a working part of education on a widespread basis, we will not only have to make provision for television laboratories and broadcasting facilities, but revise our thinking about the size and shape of instruction areas, daylight and electric lighting sources and controls, among many other modern concepts. These changes could affect both elementary and secondary school planning.

Changes like these, changes in education itself, are the most important ones to foresee, but we can't overlook another vital influence—some of the techniques and materials now being developed within the building industry. With automation growing apace, for instance, it's likely that more and more of the products used in building will be fabricated in the factory. This will lead to prefabrication of a wider range of building elements or component parts.

Based on the ever-increasing knowledge we're acquiring about materials both new and old, it seems that what we need in the field of school design is more, not less, experimentation with new forms. It's only by using new materials and techniques that we can hope to achieve the benefits of mass production and automation. If we continue to use only that with which we are familiar, we are consigning to the back shelves some of the very things we sorely need to give us beauty, economy and durability in our new school buildings. The only way to find out whether a new product is the answer to a long-felt need is to use it.　　　　　*—By John W. McLeod, A.I.A.*

HOW GOOD
IS YOUR CHILD'S SCHOOL?

IF you want to find out how good the schools in your town really are you will have to ask a lot of specific questions. Following is a list of 10 key questions to ask your school board. The answers should help you determine whether your school system has the money, personnel and equipment to pursue the great task which has been set for it, and how well it is using what it has.

Of course, a Mothers' Club, a PTA or a representative citizens' committee is far better equipped to evaluate a school system and to help improve it than any individual. If every individual in your community started asking the school superintendent all these questions, he would have no time for the children. Form a committee and arrange to have the questions asked once for everyone. And when you have the answers, ask the school superintendent what you can do to help. The National Citizens Council for Better Schools at 9 East 40th Street, New York 16, New York, will be glad to supply you with additional information and advice.

Questions to Ask About Your School

1. What is the average expenditure per year per child?

2. How does that compare with the $275.47 which was the national average for 1955–1956?

3. How does it compare with the average for your state? (Your school superintendent or chief state school officer can supply state figures.)

4. How do your school expenditures compare with other neighboring communities?

5. How many pupils does your school system have per teacher? (25 is considered ideal, with 30 acceptable. A smaller number makes for an inefficient school system and a larger one for poorer teaching.)

6. How does the pay your teachers get compare with the average for your state, the national average ($4,000 a year in 1955–1956) and with neighboring communities?

7. How many pupils are in your school? The Committee for the White House Conference on Education concluded in 1956 that "The minimum size of an elementary school should be 175 pupils and 7 teachers for a 6-grade school. There should be at least one teacher per grade in any school. There are improvements in efficiency and economy up to 300 pupils and 12 teachers. Each high school should have a minimum of 300 pupils or 75 pupils in each age group, and 12 full-time teachers. There are gains in economy and efficiency until the enrollment reaches 700 pupils. Such a standard is applicable regardless of the type of internal organization. There is little or no evidence that anything is gained by having an enrollment of more than 1,000 pupils in any school."

8. What percentage of your teachers have doctor degrees? Master degrees? Bachelor degrees? No college degrees? What percentage have only "emergency certificates" rather than full licenses to teach? How does this compare with neighboring communities?

9. What percentage of those who enter your high school drop out before graduation? The national average is just over half. How does your community compare in this respect with the average for your state and with neighboring communities? The fewer who drop out the better.

10. What percentage of those who graduate from your high school go on to some form of higher education? The national average is 35 per cent.

—*By Maxine Livingston*

HOME MANAGEMENT

MAKING A HOUSE A HOME • HOUSEHOLD EFFICIENCY
KEEPING HOME RECORDS • AVOIDING OUTSIDE PRESSURES
HOT WEATHER COMFORT • FIRE SAFETY
WHEN YOU NEED A BABY SITTER • BUYING CLOTHING
CHOOSING AND REPAIRING TOYS • FOOLPROOF WILLS
INSURANCE FOR SECURITY • CHILDREN AND CHORES
SECOND BABY • FATHERLESS FAMILIES • THE WORKING MOTHER

A HOME IS TO LIVE IN

THERE is more to the problem of neatness than there is to that of manners. We agree at least fairly well on what good manners are and most of us would like to see our children have them. But what *good* neatness might be, we do not know. Each person has his own ideas about neatness and order and he even changes these to fit his moods or the immediate situation. That makes it all pretty complicated and sends us back to first principles, and we discover that the same principles that apply to manners apply to neatness. See that our youngsters are happy, then look to our own patterns of neatness —these serve as models for the children. Next, be tolerant of other people's ways of doing things, our children's as well as our neighbor's. And then, relax—don't take it all so seriously. Neatness is not an end in itself, it is just one means to a more comfortable as well as richer, fuller life.

There is one thing that we homemakers forget often—that things are to be used, homes are to be lived in. It's the people who count, not the neatness. If you are a very neat person yourself—the kind who has to have everything in its place all the time—stop and think a minute. What is a home for anyway? To look neat or to be used and enjoyed, a place where your family can be themselves, even the disorderly ones? If you go about all the time picking up here, fussing there because something is out of place, then aren't you paying too much attention to things and too little to people? A little disorder is necessary where people are doing things.

In our hurry to get things done, we often lose sight of our real function as homemakers. Ours is a big job—to help the personalities in our family develop, all the personalities including our own. We can't do this big job well if we're too tired from all the little jobs, like cleaning and picking up. We often forget this fact. We are driven to spend our energies on the trivial things, losing sight of the importance of the job we can and must do as counselor, helper, general manager, supervisor, financial planner, purchasing agent, fixer-upper and healer of heartaches. The list is endless of the things that make up our real job. In comparison, cleaning, tidying and putting things in order seem insignificant, once we give the matter a little thought.

Tolerate patterns of others. Tolerance of other people's patterns of neatness is also important in teaching neatness to our children. Did you ever think over how many ways there are to "clean" a room, for instance? No two women do the job in quite the same way. Give three people the same job. One would put everything in its place, even the sewing materials you need to finish the skirt you are making. Another might carefully dust around the "work centers" so as not to disturb anything you might need later. And the third might tear the room apart—wash windows (perhaps even wash the curtains) and leave the room looking as impersonal as a hotel room when the bellboy ushers you into it. To each of these women the room is neat when she has finished with it, but there is certainly a great difference in the results. Who, then, is to say which is the right way?

Neatness and manners boil right down to this. They are ways of smoothing the rough places in life for yourself, as well as for others. They are not ends in themselves. As parents our first responsibility is to make our children happy. Our second, to develop in ourselves the kind of models we want our children to follow. And last, to take it easy. It's really not neatness and manners as such that we want our youngsters to have when they grow up but an understanding of where these fit into our scheme of living.

—*By May Reynolds Sherwin, Ph.D.*

MAKE EVERY MOTION COUNT

HAVE you really tried to find easier ways of doing your housework? Have you thought about ways to save steps? Have you done anything beyond complaining of being tired? Are you dissipating your time and energy by not gathering together in advance all the tools to be used; by failing to eliminate unnecessary tasks and details—washing breakfast and luncheon dishes after each meal instead of all at one time; by not keeping equipment nearest to the place where it is most frequently used—storing utensils, serving dishes and platters closest to the range; by not providing a place in the dinette or near the kitchen where the youngest can play and keep his toys? Far too many homeworkers work the hard way, whereas the easier way is not only more efficient but more pleasant and far less exacting.

It is the *way* you do things rather than *what* you do that is so important. Housework is much less arduous when the homemaker makes every motion count.

Using your body properly is one of the easiest ways to save energy. Distribute the work over several sets of muscles and use the stronger ones. If you do this, you will feel fresher and happier at the end of the day. When climbing stairs, keep your body erect and raise yourself by leg action and a vigorous thrust with your toes. When lifting anything, bend your knees and get your body, as much as you can, underneath whatever you are lifting —then lift with the leg muscles, not your back muscles. You will accomplish more, have fewer accidents and spend less energy if you adopt a moderate pace and find a rhythmic relaxed way of doing things.

Certain principles which have improved methods in business and industrial jobs can be used in simplifying housework. The first step toward simplifying housework is analyzing the job, listing all the details exactly as you are presently doing them—getting ready (collecting all tools and equipment), motions used in doing the job, and then putting away the equipment. The second step toward doing better work with less effort is to question whether the job is really necessary. Does it pay for the time you spend doing it? Does it contribute to the physical or emotional well-being of your family? Where should the job be done—why iron in the basement or laundry when you could iron in the living or dining room, meanwhile enjoying your husband's company? When should a task be done and who should do it? Are you using the most convenient equipment or appliances, including long-handled brooms and dustpans that eliminate stooping and squatting? Is the equipment in good working condition?

Call a Family Conference

After you have answered these questions, the third step is to call a family conference and, in the belief that homemaking is creative and worthwhile, together develop a method that eliminates unnecessary details and simplifies all the necessary ones. Whenever possible, combine two jobs, such as setting the table for breakfast while the dinner dishes are being washed, and let each member of the family share in the homemaking.

Improper storage spaces and incorrect work heights are serious wasters of time and energy. You can save space as well as eliminate lifting stacks of things if shelves are different distances apart—bowls need much more space than cups—and you can easily build shelves between those you already have (or buy narrow ones to place between wider shelves). Revolving shelves make for easier accessibility and can make use of corner spaces that might be wasted otherwise. Vertical dividers, like those used in phonograph record storage cabinets, place at one's fingertips tall platters, trays, lids, shallow pans and so forth. Deep drawers can have smaller trays built in the top section to make small things more easily obtainable, and you will save stooping and other unnecessary motions (besides being safer) when knives are kept in a rack which hangs on the wall. Storage cabinets that open to the eating area as well as to the kitchen save dozens of steps when you set the table, as well as when you return the clean dishes to the cabinets. Convenience racks, attached to the inside of cupboard doors, make condiment jars and other small packages immediately available. You might be amazed how much energy is saved when there is no reaching around and over for hidden items.

Height of work counters. Even the best kitchen equipment and utensils will not keep you from getting overly tired if the work counters are either too high or too low. The height should make it possible for you to stand in a relaxed position and work without stooping or raising your hand above the level of the elbow. Even when you sit to work—and you should sit whenever possible—the relation of your elbow to the work surface should be the same as when you stand to work. Therefore, it is desirable that the kitchen be equipped with work surfaces of two different heights or with work surfaces that can be adjusted in height. For the average woman, jobs such as vegetable preparation, where short-handled tools are used, require the work surface to be 36 inches high; when using long-handled tools such as egg beaters and long-handled spoons, the lower height of 32 inches is better. Even a pull-out lap board or a portable table can provide the two work heights.

Once you become aware of ways and means to simplify your work, developing improved methods will become a game at which the entire family can play. It may take a short while to establish the new habit, but you will soon become accustomed to the new method and be amply rewarded by having more time to spend with your family and in leisure pursuits.

—*By Maxine Livingston*

WHAT A GOOD HOME FILE
CAN DO FOR YOU

IT certainly is true that the steady pressing of the business world toward greater efficiency has simplified work processes with elaborate systems and handy "tools" for smoother, easier operation.

For example, there is that marvel of efficiency—a good filing system. But even though many homemakers are familiar with office procedures they still follow the age-old method of chucking useful bits of household information into desk drawers, cupboards, between book pages, or in the old cracked teapot. Have you ever tried to find the guarantee tag from your electric clock, or Aunt Sophy's "hints" for removing stains after tucking them away for safekeeping in one of these hideouts?

No business office would dispose of the plans of its engineers and experts merely by stacking them in a basement or attic. All such items would be carefully classified and filed for future reference. This indispensable tool of business can become equally important to every well organized home.

Don't let the file run you. This is the most important thing to remember. Start mildly, not wildly, with a basic file and expand only as needed. Don't stuff the file with clippings just for the joy of filing something. Periodically, probably semiannually, weed out obsolete material.

Arrive at a Logical Sequence

Alphabetical filing is out. It is as bad as no filing system at all. You could file an article on meat cuts under "M," along with articles on music or mud packs. Your file would be meaningless. Instead, organize your basic file by subject matter. Ours is like the outline for a simple story that would run like this: "We are a family. We live in a house. Three times a day meals must be planned and prepared. All the family must be tastefully and economically clothed. There is housework to do—cleaning, laundry, mending, repairing. We try to keep healthy, but occasionally there is illness, and the sick member must be cared for and made comfortable with a degree of skill. The family makes financial transactions and occasionally requires legal assistance. We enjoy our recreation and hobbies. We are active in church, school, civic and political activities." Thus, my basic file is set up in this manner:

Family—Newspaper clippings about members of the family. Birth and baptismal certificates, diplomas, etc. Miscellaneous memos of interest to particular members of the family.

House—Guarantee tags for home appliances. Names and telephone numbers of recommended carpenters, plumbers, other tradesmen. Pictures and articles containing useful ideas in home planning, decoration, remodeling, or furnishing. Dealers' circulars describing paints, wallpapers, cement, heating equipment, etc. Flower arrangements, bulletins on home safety.

Foods, nutrition—Do not file recipes in this file. A card index system is better for recipes. Here file nutrition charts, calorie data, gardening guides (cross-index with "hobbies"), special information such as notes on outdoor or camp cooking, government booklets on nutrition, articles on food selection such as economical meat cuts. This is an excellent place to file menus.

Clothing—Patterns. Printed sewing instructions. Tips on speedier, more professional sewing. Clippings giving ideas for remodeling old clothes. Dealers' pamphlets on clothing or fabrics. "Where to get it" information.

Housework—Household hints clipped from booklets or magazines. "How to" articles on general home repairs. Work schedules for the family, name and phone number of recommended outside help for spring housecleaning.

Health, physical care—Booklets, pamphlets, bulletins and articles dealing with this subject. Information on infant care and feeding. Children's immunization records. Record of childhood diseases and serious illnesses. Articles on hair grooming, cosmetics, that are useful for later reference.

Financial and legal—You will probably want to keep valuable papers in your safety-deposit box. Here file check stubs, cancelled checks, budgets, records of expenditures, correspondence dealing with financial or legal matters, household goods inventory.

Recreation and hobbies—Pamphlets and booklets on games and party fun. Material on hobbies for family, travel information.

Social and service—Correspondence, notes, literature dealing with church, school, civic, patriotic or political activities of members of family.

Setting up the File

There is little or no expense involved in setting up a file like this. You will need a carton, wooden case, or deep desk drawer which will accommodate file folders standing upright. The carton or case may be painted or wallpapered to fit in attractively with your decorative scheme. Use flat manila envelopes or, preferably, file folders measuring approximately 9″ × 11¾″. If you intend to use large envelopes which you have on hand, seal the flap and slit one side. Stand the envelopes broadside in your filing case, with the opening at the top.

Make labels for your folders with colored art-paper, or use colored, gummed

labels made to fit the tabs on your folders. Use a different color for each basic file. Later, when folders become bulky, break-down or expansion folders should be labeled in the same color as the original basic file folder. A Recreation and Hobbies file might include these headings for example:

1. Recreation and Hobbies (general, difficult-to-classify)
2. Book catalogs, lists, reviews
3. Family Fun and Party Ideas
4. Home Workshop
5. Music—Record catalogs
6. Photography

Occasionally you will want to do some cross-indexing. For instance, a valuable article on gardening may appeal to your hobby interest and your nutrition interest as well. File the article under one of the headings and write out a cross-index slip; indicating title, publication, date of issue, and heading of file folder which will hold the article. Place the slip in the secondary file folder.

Let the family enjoy the file. Children will gain interest and knowledge in home activities by contributing items of genuine interest. Older children will want their own folders on hobbies, social and service, or other headings of particular interest to them.

If you are ill or called away from home, you will be surprised and gratified at how much more efficiently the family carries on in your absence, with this library of practical, helpful information at their finger tips.

—*By Jean A. Lyons*

DO YOU TRY TO DO TOO MUCH?

THERE has been a lot of talk in recent years about the amount of time modern household equipment and prepared foods have saved women. When you go down the list of items like the automatic washing machine and its companion drier, modern self-timing stoves, the vacuum cleaner, refrigerators and freezers—and add to that the modern grocery store that has relieved most women from baking, canning and many other culinary tasks—it is obvious that a clean, healthful and well-stocked home costs a modern housewife far fewer hours of work than it did her grandmother. Add to this the fact that many of our grandmothers had larger families than we do, and the modern housewife emerges almost as a lady of leisure—in theory, that is.

As a matter of fact, most women with young children lead incredibly hectic lives. Their working day often starts at six or seven in the morning and lasts until the last child is persuaded into bed, sometimes as late as nine-thirty or ten in the evening. This, of course, goes on seven days a week, and for most women there's no annual vacation.

The paradox of the modern housewife who is frantically busy in spite of all her labor-saving devices is easily explained. A lot of attention has been given the work modern woman no longer has to do, but little notice has been taken of her new responsibilities.

A woman in the old days did not feel under any obligation to be more than a good housekeeper—her house was almost her entire business in life. Nowadays, many a woman feels that in addition to maintaining a comfortable home, she should take an active part in community activities, be well rounded culturally and add something to the family income. The rearing of children has become more than it used to be, because more is known about it. A conscientious young mother today reads a lot about child care, and makes deliberate decisions about methods of feeding, discipline and training which her grandmother, blindly following folklore and tradition, rarely had to make.

Food is easier to prepare, but much greater variety is expected now than in the past. The same goes for clothes—few children of fifty or sixty years ago had anything like the wardrobes most modern children have today.

Standards of personal hygiene and household cleanliness are infinitely higher now than they have ever been before. Grandmother didn't have a washing machine, but neither was she expected to maintain clean sheets on all the beds, snowy towels in the bathroom and spotless clothes for everyone in the family every day.

Less Help for Modern Mothers

And, of course, most of our grandmothers had much more help than modern women do. An astonishing number of our mothers and grandmothers had hired girls. Even those who could not afford paid help often had an unmarried sister or aunt in the household to lend a hand. There were few outside jobs an unmarried woman could get in those days. Fewer old people had pensions or savings large enough to maintain their own homes and they moved in with their sons or daughters. The word "sitter" had never even been heard of—Grandma or Aunty Bess did the sitting. The housewife did not face her duties alone.

All these factors are minor compared to the greatly increased demands women place upon themselves nowadays. Many a woman consciously or unconsciously strives to:

1. Keep her home not only spotless, but attractively decorated and furnished. This often means that she paints walls, re-covers furniture and does other such tasks herself.

2. Serve economical but really attractive meals. Though bread and canned foods are more available than in former days, fancy dishes still take time, especially if they are made from inexpensive ingredients. Shopping for bargains also takes more time than simply telephoning an order.

3. Foster not only the physical, but the emotional well-being of her children—and that takes time, too.

4. Make clothes for the children because ready-made clothes are more expensive and often less original than clothes made at home.

5. Help improve the schools—and she cannot turn down a request for work from the Parent-Teacher Association.

6. Help raise money for efforts to combat polio, heart trouble, and so on.

7. Become more active in the League of Women Voters and various citizens' committees because good government is a concern of any intelligent woman. She feels she should study the newspaper and news magazines more, and become better informed about what's going on.

8. Learn more about the United Nations—also Africa, Asia, India, the Middle East, Europe—for, with the world as it is today, only a ninny is ignorant of international events.

9. Be a glamorous wife. This means that she is on a diet to take off fifteen pounds, gives herself regular permanent waves, has pasted a schedule of exercises on the inside of the closet door, and is learning to rhumba.

10. Be more conscientious in getting the children to Sunday school and her husband and herself to church regularly. It's wrong to be just a passive member of a church, she feels, and hopes to find more time to help with fund-raising, young people's activities and so on.

11. Be a den mother, since her son has become a Cub Scout.

12. Create a proper cultural atmosphere for the children and do more herself to cultivate the mind. She's taken out a library card and joined a book club and tells herself that, since she's bought them, she's got to read all those books that come in the mail. She hopes to save enough to buy a good high fidelity phonograph and some classical records. When there is a concert or a good play in town, she feels the family should go.

13. Add something to the family income, especially in case of an emergency. She feels that she should learn shorthand or take a course in retailing at night at the local high school. When she meets a career woman with a really good job, she somehow believes that she has been a failure. When asked her occupation, she thinks it's dismal to reply simply "housewife."

Too Many Goals

This list could go on much longer, but already it may seem a farce. It is quite a pathetic list, for obviously no one can achieve so many different goals, and a woman who aspires to them all is doomed to eternal conflict and frustration. If she succeeds at half of them, she will brood about failing at the others. This list is the reason why so many women feel inhumanly rushed, everlastingly inadequate to cope with life's problems.

The solution for these worried women is, of course, obvious. They must achieve enough maturity to realize that no one can do everything well, not even all the important things. What items on the list are really *most* important to her family and herself, and what items can be, without any strain on the conscience, reduced to a minimum? Different women will, of course, choose different items, but somewhere along the line, a choice must be made.

The women who have made such a choice consciously do not seem harried or hurried. One mother, for instance, is a really omnivorous reader and one of the best-informed people, but meals in her house are simple to the point of monotony and there are almost no decorations. Cleanliness is maintained to the degree health makes it necessary, but it is not made a fetish. Her husband does not complain, nor do the children and life is relatively serene.

Another woman took the opposite tack—her meals are elaborate and her house is considered a model of distinction by interior decorators, but she cheerfully admits that she doesn't have time to read anything, nor for any but the most important community activities. She and her family, too, seem happy and at peace.

Naturally, it isn't necessary for most people to go to such extremes, but it would be helpful, I think, if more people sat down and did a thoughtful job of budgeting their time. We all have an income of only 24 hours a day, 365 days a year, and it's as silly to try to buy everything with it as it would be to try to buy everything in a department store with a monthly paycheck. This doesn't mean that people should try to live according to rigorous schedules, but when the telephone rings with a new demand upon an already busy woman, a good answer—if only to oneself—is, "I simply can't afford that. I would have to take precious hours from something else, and I've made my choice."

Make a choice. Everyone is driven to make some sort of choice on how to spend time, simply because the days can't be stretched, but too often decisions are made haphazardly and depend more on the insistence of those asking us than on what we really should do. This is one of the causes of a gnawing sense of guilt: not so much the feeling that we haven't been able to do everything well but that inconsequential things have somehow been allowed to take precedence over those of fundamental importance.

The decision on how to budget one's time involves all the basic values in life. It can be a fruitful and enjoyable subject for a family conference. No choice is permanent, of course—a woman will probably want to spend her time entirely differently at different periods in her life. When the children are young, the home may need almost all her time. When they are grown, a career and community activities may take precedence. But no matter what decisions are made, a firm choice can relieve what may be the most painful disease women suffer from today: the feeling of being pulled in a dozen different directions at once. —By Sloan Wilson

HOW TO KEEP COOL WHEN IT'S HOT

WHEN a heat wave hits, instead of resigning ourselves to sit and suffer, we can take certain scientifically approved steps to improve matters.

First understand and cooperate with your body's built-in cooling system. The body's private air conditioner operates in a number of remarkably efficient ways, but for best results it can use a little help from you.

Take the matter of perspiring. Called by any name, this process comes in for considerable derision and apology rather than the encouragement it deserves. Actually, a good if unfashionable sweat is the body's greatest contribution to helping both adults and children cool off when a heat wave is on.

Here's how it works: on a signal that things are getting too hot for comfort, the blood rises to the surface of the skin. There, through blood vessels especially dilated for the occasion, it radiates some of its excess heat into the air. For further help, millions of little capillaries also expand and carry the blood to tiny skin-surface sweat glands. These obligingly produce perspiration which, as it evaporates, cools not only the skin but the blood underneath. As a result, our bodies feel cooler and more comfortable.

The only time this efficient system won't work is when the humidity is so high that the sweat can't evaporate and cool the skin.

How can we encourage evaporation and help ourselves and our families cool off?

Clothing. We can, as a starter, choose our hot weather clothing wisely. A practical policy is to adopt clothes that are loose in fit, light in weight and porous in texture. The loose-in-fit part is a little hard for Father to achieve especially so long as men remain unemancipated from neckties, but the other two comfort specifications present no serious problems.

Whether you choose cotton or one of the cool synthetic fabrics for yours and the children's clothes, pay special heed to having the armholes, neck and leg openings loose enough. At the rate children grow, their clothes can get tight and uncomfortable almost overnight if you don't watch carefully that they're the right size to begin with—and then remember to check fit frequently.

For anyone who is going to be out in the sun, here's another clothing tip to keep in mind: heat rays bounce off light colors, cling to dark colors. You may feel cooler in dark clothes, but actually you're not.

A good rule for health and comfort in hot weather that applies to parents as well as children is: take hot sun in small doses—with the skin well protected by an oil or lotion.

Indoors, a fan is an effective aid in encouraging evaporation and making the family more comfortable. But don't forget to keep electric fans well out of the reach of young children. Also, don't sit in a fan's steady blast for too long at a time.

Hot Weather Foods

What about food during summer days? Should it be hot or cold, smaller in quantity, special in any way? Nutritional studies show that our bodies need normal well-balanced meals to keep up strength, produce energy and help cope with the heat. Hot or cold—take some of each—protein, carbohydrates and even some fats have their place in the diet.

A wise mother will not declare a moratorium on hot food when the temperature soars nor will she ask her family to live on nothing but salads. In hot weather she'll make extra use of quick-cooking helps such as frozen foods and quick mixes. If there's a back yard grill she'll plan menus with it in mind. If meals must be cooked indoors, they'll be quick-broiled—not slow-baked.

As for hot food versus cold: it apparently isn't the temperature but the number of calories food contains that causes body heat. So it's wise to cut down on all heavy sweet desserts.

Iced drinks, too, have a paradoxical effect on body chemistry. What those delightfully tinkling ice cubes do is dull the central nervous system and momentarily impair the body's temperature controls. This makes us conclude we're cooler when we really aren't. And if there's alcohol among the ice cubes, we're just adding more fuel to the fire. Try drinking your soft drinks cold but not ice cold.

Taking liquids is a wise habit in hot weather because the body loses a great deal of needed moisture through perspiration. And, of course, drink cool (but not necessarily iced) water—and plenty of it. Most children just naturally drink more in hot weather, but sometimes they get too busy to stop for a drink unless mother remembers to offer it.

On hot days remember that salt, like water, gets washed away in perspiration and needs replacing. In most cases, a little extra salt sprinkled on food will do the trick. When you work or exercise strenuously in the sun it may be wise to ask your doctor about taking salt in water or in the form of salt tablets. But don't self-dose with salt tablets.

How Much Exercise?

Too much exercise in hot weather is frowned on by health experts. Weekend athletes who are not as young as they used to be are particularly warned of its dangers. Moderate exercise, in small doses, can help take your mind off the weather. But if you feel you must play tennis or otherwise dash around, say medical men, you'd better do so in the cooler parts of the day.

See if you can get the children to slow down to a walk during the heat of the day, at least. A reading hour right after lunch helps relax those members of the family who have graduated from taking naps.

When you're feeling hot and muggy, don't you often wish you could take a lovely cold bath? Experts agree, however, that in hot weather extremes of any kind are best avoided—and that, they say, includes cold baths. Whether by tub or by shower, lukewarm water leaves you more refreshed and cool than cold or hot water does. You can also get quick if temporary relief from splashing water on your temples and holding your hands and forearms in cool water. (For special care for infants see "Summer Care For Babies.")

Air circulation. Experts of all kinds have studied hot weather problems and come up with all sorts of practical help. One suggestion is that it is a good idea to place furniture at right angles to the wall and so take advantage of every bit of air circulation. It is also pointed out that naturally whatever makes Mother work less keeps her cooler, so try such mother-saving hot weather practices as shopping for food once a week, leaving the dishes to dry by themselves.

The Cooperative Extension Service at the University of New Hampshire suggests another cool-living hint: keep the windows closed and shielded with curtains during the day; if you do, the temperature inside the house will be about ten degrees cooler than it is outdoors.

Unless a strong breeze is blowing, experts of the Texas Agricultural and Mechanical College recommend opening just one window on the side of the house where the air is stirring. Then, by opening all the windows on the side where the air exits, you'll encourage a stronger flow.

Heat and Fatigue

In the middle of one summer's record-smashing heat wave, the American Psychological Association held its 61st annual meeting. The psychologists discussed human reactions to heat and concluded that during a hot spell our "forgettery" goes up, our efficiency and ability to make decisions hit a low point. Heat saps energy, makes us cross and tired, and inclined to scold our children (who are cross and tired too!).

Fatigue, however, is more than just a physical condition, it was pointed out by Dr. Paul Torrence who directed some psychological research at Snead Air Base near Reno, Nevada, site of the Strategic Air Command's Advanced Survival School. Mental attitude is an important factor in fatigue as well as in facing extremes of heat or cold. So in a heat wave, Dr. Torrence suggested, it probably would help a family to "think of something that's fun to do and not just sit still and sweat."

What seems like fun to one family may make another family hot to even think about! Some people like to pile in the car and descend on the nearest beach—no matter how crowded the sands, how bumper-to-bumper the trip coming home. Others much prefer to have fun in their own back yard.

Being without a back yard—a condition common to many of us—can be compensated for during leisure hours by lying on the floor (warm air inevitably rises to the ceiling) and beating the heat by doing absolutely nothing for a while. Sit-down games can be fun, too, and even hot and wiggly children will usually be still for a while in order to participate. The public library is often cooler than most places in town, and books can become good friends during hot summer days.

One reassuring fact: summer's first hot spell is the hardest to take. Your body—if you follow the rules—gets adjusted to the heat and more able to cope with it as summer goes on.   —By Ruth Newburn Sedam

DEPEND ON YOURSELF
FOR FIRE SAFETY

IT'S a wise homeowner who takes all the precautions he can to keep fires from occurring, and to protect his family and property against them if they do. This applies to city dwellers as well as to residents of small towns and rural areas. While it is true that cities have large, fully manned fire departments, and outlying areas only small volunteer units, a city fireman would be the first to tell you that, no matter where you live, prevention is your best defense against fires. And contrary to what many homeowners think, it is possible to make a country or suburban home as fire-safe as a house or apartment in a metropolitan area.

Most fires spring from conditions which can be reduced to a minimum or eliminated entirely by taking simple precautions. Improperly used electricity and carelessly handled petroleum products cause a large percentage of fires, both urban and rural. Efficient, safe wiring practices have been established cooperatively by manufacturers and utility companies; it is vital to your family's safety to follow them in your home. Your local utility company will be glad to help you see that they are. Use great care in handling or storing oil, gasoline, kerosene or other petroleum products. If your garage or tool shed is attached directly to the house, you can reduce the gasoline and oil hazard by using a masonry partition for the adjoining wall, cement plaster on other walls and on ceiling.

Faulty chimneys, flues and stacks cause many fires; so also do stoves, furnaces, boilers and their pipes. If your home meets the requirements of an average modern city building code, you have little to fear from fires caused by these conditions. Should you be unsure whether your house is up to par in these respects, it is wise to have it checked. Usually minor improvements or some remodeling will raise a below-par house to safe standards.

A majority of house fires start in the basement, most of them caused by the heating plant and its accessories. It is sensible, therefore, to put such units in fire-safe enclosures. Such an enclosure is just as wise for a heating unit located above grade. Fire-safe doors are a practical addition, either metal, or plywood with a core of fire-resistant material.

Protection Against Roof Fires

Roofs of metal, asbestos-cement, slate, concrete or clay tile and the better grades of asphalt shingles offer the greatest protection against roof fires, according to the National Board of Fire Underwriters. Good-quality wood shingles, properly laid and maintained, have been widely and safely used as roofing for American homes for nearly three centuries. Wooden shingles that are broken, loose or curled, however, are a fire menace—keep them in good condition or, should that become impossible, replace them.

Lightning, though a greater danger in rural areas than in cities and towns, is a possible hazard anywhere. It is easily and almost completely eliminated as a danger by the use of approved types of lightning rod. Standards for them are set by the Underwriters' Laboratories; they can be installed by any reputable dealer. Whether or not they are necessary for your home depends on the climate and the frequency and severity of electrical storms.

As for the material of which a house is constructed, this is less of a fire factor than many homeowners realize. All the conventional building materials are more or less equally safe from exposure fires (those due to outside causes such as grass fires). If a house has an exterior surface of masonry—stucco, brick or stone veneer, asbestos-cement shingles or siding on frame construction, or all-masonry walls of stone, brick, concrete block or other types of concrete wall—this will, of course, give additional protection against outside fires.

The danger of even violent exposure fires, such as forest fires, is more to the *inside* than to the outside of a house; the exterior—brick, stone, wood or otherwise—might withstand the searing heat, but it will quickly break the windows, thus reaching the highly combustible interior. As protection against exposure fires, it's better to rely on fire prevention and good housekeeping and maintenance practices than solely upon structural materials.

If Fire Breaks Out

Interior construction differs little from one house to another; the average family home has about the same amounts of wood trim, doors and floors, the same combustible furniture, rugs, draperies and so forth. Filled as houses are with combustibles, it is only common sense to provide equipment to detect fire and to extinguish or control it efficiently. There are on the market several approved fire-detecting devices, many not at all expensive, that will automatically ring an alarm and keep it ringing if a fire starts. A telephone is a must, because it will bring help promptly. Telephone wires should run through steel conduits so the service will not be cut off by fire just when it's needed most. For a reserve water supply, a storage cistern may be advisable. Other excellent precautionary equipment: fire pails with water and sand, fire extinguishers of at least two types (one for electrical and oil fires, one for other kinds of fire), ladders, ropes and fire tools.

Means of escape from a burning room or house should be planned in advance, not left to chance. Remember that if a fire starts, the first five minutes are more decisive than the next five hours. Study your home's floor plan for the safest, fastest exits from any room and, if you have two or more floors, down and out of the house. Flat-roofed porches which are accessible to bedrooms far removed from stairs, may be practical means of escape. A large house requires two stairways, well separated from each other; it may be necessary, in case of fire, to shut doors in hallways or at the head or foot of the stairs to cut off the rush of super-heated air that often precedes flame, and dual stairways will assure that this can be done without barring the only means of escape. Be sure that stairways, hallways or other "escape" areas are free from obstacles such as furniture or slippery rugs. Check to be certain all doors are easy to open, not just for adults but for children too. For their own sakes, children should be taught where these escape areas are and, as much as is possible depending on their ages, how to avoid fires and deal with them if they occur.

Confining a fire. If a fire can be confined to one room for a time, it may take long enough to "burn its way out" that everyone can escape or be taken out. In modern open-plan houses, with a few doors and large interconnecting areas, it is all but impossible to confine a fire this way. Single-story houses in general, however, have many compensating advantages—no stairs, no dangerous updrafts, no hazards if it should be necessary to escape a fire by stepping out a window.

You can't begin a moment too soon to take fire safety precautions, to plan ways to prevent, fight and escape from fires. No matter how you measure their value—in peace of mind or in protection of your home and family— they're well worth any cost in time or money. —*By Maxine Livingston*

HOW DO YOU RATE
WITH YOUR BABY SITTER?

THERE are two sides to this baby-sitting business. Usually we are only concerned with the qualifications of the sitter we plan to hire. Is she honest, capable, dependable, and does she really like children? Often we have to use the trial-and-error method to find just the right one for our particular brood.

But the sitter has her standards, too, as indicated by a teen-age panel discussion held sometime ago. According to them, it is important that you, the parents who employ them, meet certain qualifications, too. And since teen-agers represent the majority of today's sitters, let's look at their specifications for a good employer. How do you rate?

Is the situation well in hand when you leave? Children need to be prepared ahead of time for your departure—especially if the sitter is coming to your home for the first time. You will want to set the stage for her entrance as carefully as for a grandmother or an aunt. Talk about her anticipated visit in a happy, friendly manner. Use her name until it is as familiar as a family name. If the baby is old enough, you can mention some things he and his new friend will do together, like putting the dolly to bed or having a tea party—routine play that will ease the newcomer into your child's life. Through your own actions and anticipations let your child sense the importance of the new guest.

Be sure the child understands that you will be leaving soon after the sitter arrives. Even a small baby can be talked to, soothed by your voice, prepared for a new experience that might otherwise upset him.

Much of the routine of feeding and going to bed is better done by you in advance. For if you leave chaos, chances are the sitter will have more than she can handle successfully. The child will resent the upset of his schedule and he may take it out on the sitter. It is wise to let your sitter be responsible for only a few of the family routines at first until you know how much she can handle effectively on her own.

In fact, the ideal arrangement is to have the young lady spend an hour or two with you in advance of the day you will be leaving her in full charge. She can get to know the baby, see how you handle him, notice what he likes or doesn't like. Sometimes even the way the spoon is held will determine whether or not a baby will eat his food. The sitter can see—or you should tell her— that he has to have that old sweater in bed with him, adores being bounced on someone's knee, hates being lifted up if he's trying to get somewhere by himself. Letting her in on such seemingly trivial details can give her a head start toward friendship with him.

Very often, a rushed leave-taking will upset a sensitive child. A schedule planned so that the child has a few minutes to admire mommie's pretty dress or sparkling necklace or fragrant perfume can make parting a more pleasant experience. It's a matter of timing.

But what to do when the child does cry because you are leaving? If you have prepared him adequately ahead of time for the experience and have looked after his routine yourself—go anyway. Chances are he will stop crying when you are out of sight. Check with the baby sitter when you return to make certain it was a passing demonstration. If it wasn't, and the baby continues in prolonged crying whenever you go out, you may have to cut down on your dates for a while. Spending a little more time with him during the day and having the sitter over for a few afternoon visits—all three of you together—can help smooth things out.

Do you leave instructions and emergency information? There are now on sale blackboards that are made especially for this purpose. Space is headed for feeding information, bedtime hour, doctor's name and telephone number, fire and police numbers. Most important of all is a space for your itinerary.

Do you leave a phone number? It is only fair that you let the sitter know the details of your whereabouts, in case something out of the ordinary should come up. If you will not be near a phone, then leave the name and number of a close relative or neighbor willing to be called.

Do you return when you promise? Just as you have every right to expect the sitter to arrive at your home on time, she has the right to expect that you will return very close to the hour you have set. This is especially important for schoolgirls on week nights. Many of them are reluctant, for obvious reasons, to take jobs that will keep them out after ten o'clock.

Most teen-agers are good baby sitters because they have parents who feel the responsibility of their daughters' jobs as much as the young ladies do themselves. Therefore, if you do not return when you promise, your sitter's mother worries. And when this happens too often, you have lost your baby sitter.

Do you show appreciation? This is partially determined by what you pay for services rendered. Not that you need to pay above the accepted rate of your particular neighborhood in order to show appreciation. But do check with other mothers and with the sitter herself. What is the usual fee? What does the girl expect? If she gets sixty cents an hour from Mrs. Jackson and you give her only fifty cents, the other lady will have preference over you if you both want the sitter on the same night.

When you are paying by the hour, it won't usually break the bank if you give the girl a full hour's pay for the fifteen minutes or half hour beyond the even hours. Yet that little extra bonus gives the sitter a satisfaction that is important in public relations. Also, if you are out after midnight, you should pay more.

Over and beyond the monetary value of baby sitting, young people also like the feeling of importance that goes with the responsibility. If the job is well done, your expression of approval will be as heartwarming as the money you put in the girl's purse. She likes acceptance and praise. If you offer it honestly, she will come again.

Do you escort your baby sitter home? This is a must. Yet, surprisingly, even the best-intentioned parents fail in this courtesy and safety measure. One couple sent their sitter home alone at two o'clock in the morning because she lived only a block away. Her mother was furious. Needless to say, they lost their sitter.

Do you leave refreshments for your sitter? This does sound like a teen-ager's concern, doesn't it? But if we are going to employ them, we should recognize their needs. Why not make a habit of telling your sitter there's soda in the refrigerator for her or candy on the table?

If you've been having "sitter blues," maybe you ought to look over this list of qualifications once more. It just might be that somewhere you don't measure up as a sitter employer. —*By Shirley Pollock*

WHEN YOU BUY
CHILDREN'S CLOTHING

EACH child in a family should have a balanced wardrobe. He needs school clothes, play clothes and at least one outfit for parties and Sunday school.

Even though time for shopping may be limited, it's a good idea to take each child on a separate buying trip. Anyone who has ever tried to drag several small children through a crowded department store will see the wisdom of this. If you limit your shopping trips to about two a year for each child, you save hit-or-miss buying, avoid spur-of-the-moment purchases and so-called bargains that don't fit in with your all-over plan.

As to the practical aspects of wise buying, you should of course deal only with stores having a good reputation. While you may be able to find some genuine bargains offered because of limited size range, slight soil or other legitimate reasons, be wary of the store that always advertises drastic reductions. Shop around and see just where you can get the most quality and service for your money. Never buy clothes without trying them on the child (or being sure of a return privilege), for age and size standards in children's clothes, alas, vary enormously.

As to the items to be purchased:

Sox. Plain cotton and/or nylon sox are the most useful and suitable for children—white or beige for girls, brown or dark blue for boys. Nylon toe and heel reinforcements more than double the wear of cotton sox. All white sox can be worn with anything. They wash well, without running or fading, and odd sox can be mated with others to make a pair. If you do buy other colors, get two or more pairs, just as you do with your nylons. Sox to match boys' cotton knit shirts are inexpensive and give a nice touch of coordination.

Shoes. Don't be penny-wise about shoes. But even the most expensive shoe is harmful if it isn't correctly fitted. Find an experienced shoe salesman, and be guided by his judgment as to size and fit. Have both feet measured for length and width, with each foot bearing weight. Measurement is taken of the longest toe (frequently the same person's feet differ a little in size) and correct size should fit the larger foot, leaving a space of three-quarters to an inch between the end of the toe and the end of the shoe. The correct width allows the leather to be drawn slightly together between the fingers. Shoes should not press or hurt when new, should not slip at heels or pinch either toes or heels. A well designed shoe is straight along the inner border; wide and roomy through the ball and toes; narrow at the top of the heel, yet wide enough at the base to provide plenty of pivoting room for the broad base of the heel bone, and ample height in the toe box. Watch out for wrinkled linings, heavy seams and similar things that may chafe the foot. The tops of shoes should be soft and pliable, the soles firm and flexible.

You can make shoes wear longer by using a good polish on them before the first wearing and keeping them polished thereafter to soften and preserve the leather. See that the children wear overshoes when it rains. If their shoes should get wet, stuff them with crumpled newspaper and let them dry slowly away from direct heat or sunlight.

Have minor repairs made on shoes as soon as you see that they are necessary, but question the advisability of major repairs in view of the rate at which a child's foot grows.

Underwear. White is the most practical color. Nylon tricot is widely used in girls' underwear. Although a bit more expensive than cotton or rayon, it washes and wears beautifully. Cotton knit is practical for boys.

Be sure that your children's underwear allows plenty of room to sit, bend or stoop and that the seams are well made and "give" with the garment as it stretches. Elastic which runs through a hem at the top of the pantie can easily be replaced whereas an attached elastic waistband cannot.

Training panties and plain undershirts can be passed on from girls to boys and vice versa; but after the toddler stage, each sex is on its own.

Nightwear. Gowns of crinkle crepe for summer and flannelette for winter (no ironing necessary in either case) are practical for girls. The life of a good-quality nightgown can be extended almost indefinitely by adding a wide band or ruffles on the bottom, whereas pajamas soon begin to bind in the crotch. A small print or polka dot on a light ground is attractive. It's a good idea to keep several yards of plain color crepe and flannelette on hand for additional ruffles or wide bands as needed. But for summer camping trips, girls do need pajamas.

Don't be too proud to accept good used clothing from relatives or friends. As a matter of fact, in some neighborhoods groups work out very practical programs for the informal exchange of children's clothing. The Woman's Club or PTA might sponsor such a project.

School clothes. Up to about age seven, little schoolgirls wear just about the same kind of clothes as their younger stay-at-home sisters. This means simple cotton dresses. Many nursery schools and kindergartens like to have little girls wear overalls, as many of the games and activities take place on the floor, and the children stay warmer and are more comfortable in overalls.

For little girls jumpers are much more practical than waistband or suspender style skirts. Blouses do not pull out of jumpers as they do with most skirts.

Jumpers are a boon to the amateur seamstress who feels unsure of her skill when it comes to fitting sleeves and collars. A simple white or pastel dress, too short for regular wear, can sometimes lead a second life as the blouse for a jumper. Just cut the skirt off at the waist with your pinking shears, and presto, an attractive blouse!

Cotton jumpers, without their blouses, double as sun-dresses for warm weather wear.

For girls of eight and up who like to dress like big girls you can assemble a wardrobe of "separates" built on the principle that the more separate, yet harmonizing, garments available, the better. Go-together skirts and sweaters, blouses, jackets, corduroy jumpers, scarves, leather belts, all have many and varying parts to play in a schoolgirl's wardrobe. Clothes of this sort chosen with due regard to color harmony, and properly cared for, will always look well and give the impression of a much more extensive wardrobe than is actually the case.

Denim or corduroy overalls, and gabardine shorts, worn with knitted cotton shirts, will meet the playtime needs of most boys and girls. Probably all you will need to add are a bathing suit for summer and a snow suit for winter. For the very young child who goes to nursery school, play clothes and school clothes are synonymous.

Party and Sunday school clothes. Party clothes are influenced somewhat by local custom, but you can hardly go wrong on simple dresses of fine cotton (cotton can look like faille or taffeta these days), plain silk crepe or pastel linen.

Coats and hats. You can save money by selecting a coat of plain wool or monotone tweed that can be worn with both school and party clothes. A light-weight jacket with a zip front is useful for mid-season wear in place of a coat or a sweater. For coats with a longer lifeline there are those with zip-out linings for both mild and cold weather. These are available for both boys and girls.

Simple hats of matching fabric are sometimes available with girls' coats, or you may choose a felt of matching color for winter and a straw with simple trimming for summer.

Finally, here are a few tricks of the trade when it comes to caring for children's clothes. A stitch in time *does* save nine. This means that you should see that buttons are securely anchored, that pocket corners or plackets are not ripping, that attached belts or sashes aren't pulling loose from the seams. Darn back and forth over the thin spots in socks before a hole actually appears, and mend small holes at once.

See that dresses, whether made at home or bought ready-made, have wide seams and adequate hems which you can let down. The life of a favorite dress may be extended by adding a band of plain material to the bottom and then cutting the gathered skirt off a few inches below the waist and inserting another matching plain band so that the dress will look as if it had been designed that way.

When the threads in sweaters get caught, always pull them to the underside and weave them in. Thin elbows in boys' sweaters can be patched with oval pieces of soft leather. Blue jeans which wear at the knees can be made into shorts.

Examine the labels on any garments or yardage you may buy. Is the material preshrunk and fast color? Be sure to follow any washing instructions that are given. Never hang colored garments in the sun.

Keep clothes that are only worn occasionally in garment bags to protect them from dust. Small children's clothes should be hung on children's-size hangers. Teach the children to keep their sweaters flat in drawers—clothes hooks may stretch and tear them. See that woolen clothes are aired frequently and that they are never put away for the summer without being protected from moths.

"Quite a job!" you say? Yes, but it will pay off in the satisfaction of seeing your children well dressed even though you may not have a mint of money to spend on their clothes.

—*By Betty Cunkle*

LONGER LIFE FOR TOYS

FROM the day the first rattle comes into the house until the last bicycle is scrapped, toys and mothers seem to be at odds. Where to store them, how to protect them, how to keep track of them!

A poll of a toy-shop owner, a nursery school teacher, a mother-pediatrician and some just-plain parents, for enlightenment on these problems, produced these general rules:

Buy the right toy. A successful start means buying toys of good quality which are suitable for the child. A toy too advanced may be misused. A toy outgrown may be abused. A six-year-old can ruin a push-toy built for two.

Look over toys before you buy them with an eye to reparability. Bolts are replaceable. Rivets are not. Wooden toys can be glued but shattered plastic cannot. Some wagons have inherent weaknesses in the tongue. Some wheelbarrows are rickety on their stands from the beginning.

Using such a yardstick for toy-buying may eliminate those spur-of-the-moment purchases to satisfy a child's teasing which can lead to tremendous junk collections. Only you can decide whether or not a little buyer-resistance then would have been wiser than giving in.

Having bought the right toy, a toy suitable, sturdy and well made, how can you help your child keep it in good condition?

Quite apart from the benefits of teaching children to be orderly, the play-room which is ready for today's new play will be more fun than the one which is the aftermath of yesterday's game. This isn't unlike the living room scattered with newspapers, glasses and overflowing ashtrays which a house-wife cleans up before it's used for the same purpose the next night.

A daily pick-up time—which with preschool children at least should have mother as helper—is the time when missing wheels will be discovered and broken toys put aside for mending. This is the time when blocks go back into their box and puzzles are reassembled.

Of course, a daily pick-up isn't going to rout every colored peg out from under the bed or stretch out long enough to find every wooden bead. Those come to light on cleaning day and a smart mother keeps a small box on the dresser top into which she can drop such items before the vacuum devours them.

Out-of-Door Toys

Out-of-door toys should have the same daily attention. Wagons, wheel-barrows, trikes and tractors should certainly be in the stable by dark. Even the most expensive pieces of model truck equipment will rust if they spend all their time outside. They do better under cover every night. If you've no outdoor shelter, they can be taken to the garage or house. One family leaves out all the plastic trucks, buckets and sand toys, but puts all the metal things into the barbecue shelter or toolshed at sundown.

Toy storage is something for every architect, housebuilder and furniture-maker to chew over, but usually each household has to come up with its own custom-designed storage.

Many families use open shelves for trucks and cars, dolls and stuffed animals and books. Some families have removed bedroom closet doors and fitted shelves into the recess. Ambitious fathers sometimes build complete storage walls into play space. But stowing toys means more than just shelving.

Some households add peg-boards for items like scissors and jump ropes; closet hooks for paint-smocks and bows-and-arrows. They save small boxes to use, well labeled, for trading cards and "collections." (A picture is a good label for the child too young to read.) They hoard shoe boxes for crayons, chalk, erasers; plastic bags for jacks and marbles; big baskets for assorted balls, bats and mitts; mesh vegetable sacks for wooden beads. They fit orange crates and apple boxes with casters for blocks and train equipment. They prefer vertical storage for records, a rack that holds records on edge to prevent warping and to keep them from being stepped on. They put art supplies—crayons, paste, activity books, construction paper and water colors—all on one open shelf. Young children's powder paints belong way up high. For very young children, in fact, it also seems best to keep the games of many parts (wooden beads, peg-boards and puzzles) on an out-of-reach shelf to be brought down upon request. This minimizes the under-foot problems and keeps the games safe from exploratory dumping by visitors.

In spite of all this, of course, toys get broken. A place in which broken toys can be kept, out of play, until they're mended, removes the temptation to misuse toys with the excuse, "It was wrecked anyhow."

There's more than just "saving a toy" to be got out of repair work. Usually an ordinary screw or bolt, friction tape and household tools (wrench, pliers, screwdriver) is all the repair takes, and a father and son tightening bolts on trikes together or reattaching chains to steam shovels are sharing fun, too.

Mother's Role

Mother's place in the fix-it-department more usually involves the sewing-basket-cellophane-tape-household-cement routine. Heads come off toy monkeys, buttons come off clown suits; doll clothes are ripped.

Washing and ironing doll clothes occasionally is a good joint project for mothers and daughters. A clean doll wardrobe can stimulate days of play with an almost forgotten doll.

Dolls sometimes need new wigs or arms or legs. Doll hospitals restore such maimed creatures if you can't, and a trip to a doll hospital is a wonderful excursion.

While broken records belong nowhere but in the trash can, torn books are quite a different thing. A torn page makes additional damage likely and may encourage a very young child to do more tearing. Get the proper book-mending equipment and fix up all the books some rainy day. Use transparent book-mending tape. You can also buy a stitched linen-tape, used for mending musical scores, to reattach covers. Often, stitching through the center break in a paper-bound book with a darning needle and string will add years to its use. Your library can advise you on book-mending and, in addition, has reference material on bookbinding if your children have damaged books you want to keep for their permanent collections.

When toys are outgrown or unmendable, get them out of the way. You might store outgrown toys somewhere for young guests to use or a younger child to grow into; you might give them away to suitably aged children. But don't clutter up the daily-use storage space with toys that are no longer used or usable. There are organizations which accept used toys for children and various institutions in many communities welcome them.

—By Ronnie Welch

CHOOSE TOYS FOR STAGES, NOT AGES

YOU can take your cue from your child where toys and play equipment are concerned. For a child is his own best expert on what toy he wants, what interests him, what gives him pleasure, what provides an outlet—either for his stupendous physical energy or for those feelings that need ways and means to be acted out.

Since they all go through similar stages of growth and development, large areas of toys and equipment spell a common pleasure and interest to most youngsters at various stages of childhood. Still, all children are different, and keeping an eye alert to hints from your own child can show you pretty clearly what kind of play equipment he wants or needs or would profit from at a particular time.

Most tiny infants, for example, are learning to use their eyes, their ears; through random, apparently aimless movements, they will soon be able to guide, direct and control their hands; their teeth will soon erupt. So from *roughly three months to roughly a year,* the dangling crib toys offer practice to the eye and hand; wind-harps make pleasant sounds for ears to hear and vocal chords to try to imitate. Rattles of all kinds, of course; rubber, bone, or plastic things to chew, toys to squeeze and bath toys to bob and duck— all these are not only traditional, but right for this stage of growth.

From 1 to 5. *Beginning at about a year and a half,* when greater mobility makes for greater curiosity, when drawers get opened and shut, when things

get taken out and put back, when objects that can be touched, poked, matched, fitted into, exert an irresistible pull—at this time push-and-pull toys, toys with openings to receive objects of different shapes, large "ride-'em" toys, hollow blocks, beads to string, if the string has rigid tips, blunt scissors, large unpainted blocks in two or three simple shapes, a toy telephone, wooden puzzles graded according to age, sand toys, sandbox, interlocking block train, wristbells, drum and a hundred other good toys on the market that offer opportunities for exploration and accomplishment are useful and pleasurable.

After age 6. *From six or so,* the children's interests and bents begin to differ more markedly, more visibly from one another's. True, large areas of toys and equipment remain commonly pleasurable to most children: playyard equipment, clay, crayons, paints, easels, records, books, bigger and better blocks, bats, balls, bikes, things to climb, scale, jump on, toss, slide on, things to tend and keep house for—dolls, doll-houses, doll baths, brooms, lawnmowers, play-tents and houses; things to make—to sew, or build, or cook, or put together; puzzles to puzzle out and magic tricks to perform; things to collect and learn about (shells, coins, bugs, butterflies, stamps, rocks); roller-skating, skiing, rope-jumping; games of skill and chance. This is the equipment for mind, for body, for the fulfillment of curiosity and the need to achieve, for the growth of large muscles and small grey cells, of dexterity and assorted skills.

But beneath the interest and needs that are common to most children, breathes the child who is also uniquely Billy or Sue. Billy Jones, it's plain to those who've known him since first he took apart a wristwatch, is bent on finding out how things work. His parents have fed his interest as he's grown with put-together kits, construction sets, model assemblies, simple books detailing simple scientific experiments. Billy Smith, it's equally plain to his parents and family, has loved to make things of another nature from the time he was first given clay, play-dough, blocks, stick-'em paper, scissors and paint. Now at 12, this Billy has long since graduated from his toy workbench and works along with his father at his father's bench. Sue Black has never lost her interest in the dramatic play so dear to preschool children. Now at 11, she's been given a stage and marionettes (some of the marionettes she made herself) and she's preparing a show for Christmas to which she's already invited her friends and family. Sue White? Well, she's a whiz at sewing, baking, cooking—and has come up through toy baking sets, sewing kits, braiding-craft materials, collar and cuff and belt-making kits, miniature sewing machine—to the point where her parents plan to give her a real sewing machine for Christmas.

Your guides to buying. To take your cue from your child's interests and stages of development doesn't mean to flood your youngster. Nor does it mean to narrow his horizon exclusively to what he likes best. It doesn't mean to neglect the fact that interests change, may go underground for a while to re-emerge later. It doesn't mean that all children develop one special interest at an early age and stick to it without changing.

It does mean that money for toys and equipment can be spent most effectively when the cues from Sue or Billy—what *they* like, what *they* need, what interests *them* today or will be of potential interest to them tomorrow—are kept firmly in mind. —*By Helen Puner*

WHAT YOU NEED
IS A FOOLPROOF WILL

LET'S put the question squarely. Who would get your money and property if you died tonight? Maybe not the people you think, and maybe not the way you think.

Harvey Freeman, a 33-year-old restaurant owner, was killed in an automobile accident, leaving a wife and two small children. The legal machinery began to grind. Since he left no will, the probate court appointed Mrs. Freeman guardian of the children and, with her permission, named an administrator to handle the business details.

Mrs. Freeman confidently expected to raise her children on the earnings of her husband's thriving business. The administrator set her straight. "My job is to turn the business and real estate into cash as soon as possible," he explained. "I can't sign a contract, borrow money or make an investment, except as ordered by the court to help wind up the estate. If I did try to continue the business indefinitely, I could be sued and held personally liable for any losses, even if they weren't my fault."

All bills owed by the estate became payable immediately, including a few Mrs. Freeman didn't expect. The administrator's fee, set by law, came to $520. The attorney charged $1,500. She was required to post a bond, to protect the children's inheritance, at a cost of $150 a year for each year until they become 21.

To meet urgent expenses, the restaurant was thrown on the market to the highest bidder. The good will and reputation of a going business were cheap commodities in a forced sale, Mrs. Freeman found. After the bills were paid and all personal property turned into cash, what was left of the estate was distributed according to the inheritance laws of the state. That's when Mrs. Freeman got the biggest shock. She received only one-third. The rest was divided between the children and will remain in a special trust account until they come of age. Out of her small share of the estate, Mrs. Freeman is now expected to maintain herself *and also meet the ordinary expenses of raising the children.*

The children's money can be used only for exceptional costs like heavy medical bills or a college education and the probate judge has final say as to what is and is not "exceptional." Each year she must appear in court and account for how it is spent. When her oldest child began school last fall and needed new clothing, she asked the court for permission to use some of his money. The petition was denied.

The two-thirds of her husband's estate tied up in the children's trust fund would have been enough to start the restaurant up again, but the money was beyond reach. The children couldn't give or lend it to their own mother if they wanted to. With her own inheritance rapidly shrinking, Mrs. Freeman placed the children in a day nursery and went back to work—in someone else's restaurant.

Failure to Leave Will

In an average year, more than half the people with property who die leave no will behind them. They work a lifetime to gather an estate and then, by default, leave the state the job of giving it away. Paradoxically, the proportion without wills is even greater among the very group that needs them most —young married couples with growing children. When a man of 60 or 70 dies, his children are old enough to support themselves and the widow can usually stretch her inheritance over the remaining years. If a parent of young children dies without a will, half or more of his estate is put in a legal deep freeze during the critical years of their growth and education. And the less money there is, the more important it is that it should be directed carefully— not on the hit or miss chance of what state a family happens to live in.

Each state has its own distribution and inheritance laws for people who die without leaving a will. The surviving husband or wife usually gets between one-third and one-half of the estate, and the children divide the rest. No exceptions permitted.

Rigid and arbitrary as the state laws may appear, they are the only way the courts can deal with a man (or woman) who declined to say how his worldly goods should be distributed after his death. The administrator, the guardian, the bonding, the trust fund for children and the annual accountings are all part of the elaborate legal network designed to protect creditors, beneficiaries and, particularly, young children. For a man who expects his widow to plunder his children's legacy, the will the state writes can't be beat. If you harbor no such fears, you can write a better one.

A few lines in a will could have empowered Mrs. Freeman to continue the restaurant after her husband's death. The bond could have been dispensed with, saving the estate a dead waste which will mount to $3,000 by the time the youngest of her children reaches age 21. Even more important, all the money could have been left to Mrs. Freeman to use as her best judgment dictated in raising the children.

Through a will you can name your own executor instead of forcing the probate court to appoint one. You can specify the precise powers the executor shall have in continuing or disposing of your business interests and investments and, if desired, dispense with the need for a bond.

If the estate is small and the business interests not complex, you can save money simply by naming your husband or wife to serve as executor. You can appoint a relative, friend, business associate or practically any adult, as long as he's willing to take the job and you have confidence that he can handle it. Banks often serve as executors, and for very good reasons. They don't get sick, die or move away. Fees are set by law, and are the same whether Uncle Charlie or the Umpteenth National Bank serves.

A will can pinpoint the way you want your property distributed. A father can leave his own son the golf clubs he's cherished and a mother can give her daughter her wedding gown.

Conditions for Beneficiary

You can also set up certain conditions which must be met for the beneficiary to receive the bequest. Patrick Henry ordered that his wife's legacy be cut off if she remarried. The Revolutionary statesman, Gouverneur Morris, left a sizable fortune to his wife—to be doubled if she married again.

The conditions in a will should be reasonable and as clear as you can make them. Some years ago a father willed property to his son on condition he didn't become "a drunkard and a vagabond." The courts held that the son could become either a drunkard *or* a vagabond. The bequest was his as long as he didn't become both.

There's nothing simpler than a will. It's a statement of what you want done with your property after you die. The late Edward H. Harriman passed an $80,000,000 railroad empire over to his wife with less verbiage than you'll find on the back of an average laundry ticket.

The courts want the will to show you knew what you were doing when you wrote it and that you didn't have a gun at your head at the time. The "I, being of sound and disposing mind" phrase and the rest of the legalese is not strictly necessary. A will written in your own handwriting can be as good as a formal legal document—even better since in some states it doesn't require any witnesses. However, such wills are not recommended. The late Charles Tressler Lark, a famous lawyer and authority on wills, wrote one of these "holographic" wills (one written wholly in the handwriting of the person making it) for himself. Throughout his many years of practice he never had a will broken by contest. But his own will was worthless. New Jersey, the state he lived in, is one of those that does not recognize holographic wills.

The cost of drawing up a will by a lawyer ranges between $15 and $50, depending on the size of the estate and any special problems raised. If you feel moved at this point to save a few dollars in legal fees by writing your own will, sit on the urge long enough to read a little further. When the unwary start putting words to paper, surprising results sometimes follow.

A frugal midwestern shopkeeper did a painstaking job of drafting his own will. To be on the safe side, he called in a notary public to serve as a witness with one of the clerks. "That document will stand up in any court in the land," he proudly told his friends. He was wrong. The notary who signed the will attested to the fact it was the shopkeeper who signed it. Notarization did not signify that the man knew it was a will he signed—a primary job of a witness. The will was thrown out of court and the man's property distributed as if he had never made one.

Misleading Form Wills

You can buy a form will in almost any stationery store. With it may come an impressive guarantee—for whatever good that will do after a man's dead —and the assurance that it is "valid in all states." The New York County Lawyers' Association recently attacked these five-and-dime wills for inducing a false sense of security that is "wholly misleading."

Just as foolhardy as writing a will by yourself is trying to change one. Adding a few lines to the end—and, of course, initialing the change to give it the proper legal flavor—is wasted motion. Unless witnessed and executed with the same formality as the original will, the changes are void. The will is read as if they had never been made.

The number of witnesses required varies from state to state; some require two, others three. Pick them carefully. It may be necessary to find them whether or not the will is contested. Don't make the mistake of having a beneficiary serve as a witness. The will is generally good, but the witness may be barred from receiving anything under it.

Wills must be reviewed periodically to make sure they've kept pace with events since drawn. An alert eastern businessman dusted off his eight-page, deluxe edition and found that it accomplished exactly the opposite of what he intended. After he wrote the will he and his wife had another child. With its first whimper the baby was entitled to the same share of the estate as he would have received if there had been no will.

Moving from one state to another can also invalidate a will. Even more dangerous are the events that *don't* invalidate one. A second will, for example, doesn't automatically nullify the first. Unless you specify otherwise, the second will is treated as an addition to the first and part of your property will be distributed in accordance with the first will.

Divorce doesn't necessarily nullify a will either. A Pennsylvania man left his entire estate "to my loving wife." After he wrote the will he was divorced and a few years later married again. His "loving wife," decided the court, was the woman he was married to at the time the will was drawn—the woman he later divorced.

Apart from changes in residence and family status that might affect your will, it should be reviewed periodically in line with the ups and downs of the family exchequer. The $5,000 pittance you bequeathed in prosperous days to Old Jed for teaching you how to bait a hook may be most of the present family fortune. Or, you may want to change the executor to a man capable of managing your newly acquired chain of newspapers, timber lands and the uranium strike.

Joint Ownership

To avoid the need for a will, many married couples resort to a joint ownership scheme. All stocks, bonds, property titles and bank accounts are put in the names of the two owners. If one dies, the other becomes the sole owner. It can be that simple and automatic. The red tape, executor, bonding and fees are neatly short-circuited. Before you wander into the arrangement, though, there is something you should consider.

Contrary to popular belief, the joint ownership device won't save estate taxes; if anything, it will increase them. A New York couple held $40,000 in a joint savings account, mostly the man's money. The wife died, leaving everything to her husband. To his great surprise, before the man's own money could come back to him it had to pass through the estate tax strainer. The share of jointly held property paid for by the one who died is taxed exactly the same as if it weren't jointly held. And unless you can prove otherwise, the law presumes the one dying first paid for *all* of it.

For estates that run into sizable figures, taxes present some special problems. The Federal law allows a specific exemption of $60,000, but up to 50 per cent of an estate left to a surviving husband or wife can be exempt under the "marital deduction." The requirements you must meet to obtain the marital deduction are quite involved, but a consultation with your lawyer can save a considerable amount in estate taxes. This deduction was written into the law only ten years ago, so any wills written before then are likely to be dangerously deficient. The states also impose estate taxes, and these vary widely. Ask a lawyer in your community for advice on how to hold the tax to a minimum.

Courts sometimes go to great lengths to help a man achieve what he wanted through his will. To clear the muddy waters, they have disregarded certain words and punctuation, and even shifted sentences. But the courts can't write a new will for you.

Your will must be clear and explicit. When questions are raised about it, you won't be around to answer them.

— *By Joel Berg*

WHAT YOU SHOULD KNOW ABOUT LIFE INSURANCE

LIFE insurance has become such an integral part of American thinking that people of all ages and incomes now consider it a vital factor in their financial planning for present peace of mind and future security. Here are questions and answers on this subject for parents who want to get the most for their insurance dollar and build an adequate backlog of family savings and family protection.

How does a particular family go about mapping out a Life Insurance Program? How much protection should they have? How much can they afford? There are four main needs to be considered in working out a basic life insurance program:

1. Enough cash on hand to cover death expenses (doctor bills, funeral, and so forth) and outstanding accounts. This is a Must.

2. Some additional cash or income for a limited period—say six months to a year—during which a widow can readjust to what is probably going to be a smaller budget than she has been used to. This also is a Must.

3. A steady basic income which, together with Social Security, can take care of the family until the children are grown (usually until they have reached the age of 18). This is highly desirable.

4. If possible, some continuing income to make a widow self-sufficient after her children have become self-supporting.

Then, of course—if your budget can stand additional premiums—policies for the education of the children, mortgage on the home, for self-retirement or for outside bequests. These will round out an excellent financial plan for the family.

As to how much you can afford for a basic program, you can best answer this question by asking yourself another. How important to you is security for your family and how many present adjustments are you willing to make for these future benefits? Only you and your wife can decide this.

Is there any percentage of income which determines the amount a family should put into life insurance premiums? Is there a real danger of overloading and losing all protection eventually? There is no definite percentage of income which any given family should set aside for life insurance. Each individual case is different. The number of children, their ages, whether or not the husband or wife has inherited any wealth or outside income, whether either or both parents qualify for Social Security, whether the insurance is to be used just as life insurance or as a combination of protection and savings—all these things have bearing on the amount and kind of insurance which should or could be bought. So all these needs and situations must be taken into consideration in arriving at the amount of insurance each family should have.

As to the dangers of overloading—the companies themselves check against this. Before a company issues insurance, in addition to requiring a satisfactory physical report it makes a careful check of your financial picture. They want to know, for instance, the specific purposes for which you are buying your insurance and for whom protection is intended. According to general rule, if reports indicate that more than 20 per cent of a man's income is going toward premiums, the company will curtail or limit his purchase. In a well planned financial program about 8 to 10 per cent of a young couple's income should be invested in life insurance. This takes quite a bit of doing for the first year or so, but the strain eases fairly rapidly as dividends reduce premium costs and increased earning power reduces the difficulty of meeting them when they come due. This early sacrifice pays off handsomely later on when the children have grown up and cash values of policies have grown up with them.

Should a family have extra protection while the children are young? Unless a young man and/or his wife have inherited money, it is highly unlikely that

they will be able to accumulate sufficient means to guarantee any reasonable continuing income for a widow and children in case the wage earner dies. Life insurance seems to be the only possible way to create an estate quickly. So, extra protection while the children are young and dependent stands out as a clear and definite need and it is advisable to buy as much insurance as you possibly can as early as you can. If there is not sufficient money in the till to buy the necessary permanent insurance, it is a good idea to eke out the difference with term insurance.

What is term insurance and how does it give protection? Term insurance is solely insurance for a specified length of time. Usually it has neither cash nor savings value. At age 30, the ten-year term rate is $7 per $1,000 of insurance. It pays off only in case of death, just as fire insurance protects you against loss from fire but pays off only if a fire breaks out. However, most of these policies have a clause permitting them to be changed over to a permanent form of life insurance within a certain number of years without requiring the insured to be physically re-examined. A competent agent will usually set up a schedule for you, so that you will convert a small portion of your term insurance each year until you have it all in a permanent form which will benefit you as well as protect your family. Term insurance can be very useful to young families during the child-rearing period while family responsibilities are heavy. It also provides valuable temporary protection for loans and mortgages, for partners in a new business and for the man or woman who wants adequate life insurance but cannot immediately afford a permanent form.

What makes term insurance so much less expensive than other kinds of insurance? In life insurance, as in everything else, you get what you pay for. The premium rate on term insurance is less because the company accepts a risk for a limited time only, and your policy is redeemable only in the event of your death and carries no cash values or other flexible privileges such as are contained in permanent forms of life insurance.

Why is Ordinary Life the least expensive type of permanent life insurance? Does the premium rate always remain the same? All policies and premiums are figured according to standard basic mathematical formulas. Ordinary Life is cheaper than other permanent forms because the policy holder is going to pay premiums throughout his lifetime, instead of over a specified number of years.

Actually, at age sixty-five or sometime thereafter, when the need for protection has decreased or ceased to exist altogether, many policy holders use the cash values of their Ordinary Life policies to provide income for themselves. Others who still desire protection, but want to discontinue paying premiums, take advantage of what is known as the Paid Up Option in their contracts. For example, a $1,000 Ordinary Life policy, taken out at age 30, will have a cash value of approximately $600 at age 65. The company, if you wish it, will cancel out all further premiums, and exchange your present policy for a fully paid up one with a face value of $770. You will notice, of course, that while you have eliminated premium paying, you have at the same time reduced your amount of protection from $1,000 to $770. However, you still own the same cash value equity ($600) plus dividends and small annual increases and this continues to be available to you at any time you may want it.

Is Ordinary Life the best kind of all-round protection for a family? Are there other kinds which might be better? The Ordinary Life policy is a fine basic, permanent policy. Many people take it not only for protection but also for the backlog of savings it can provide, in accumulated cash values, for their old age. Others prefer to have their premium-paying period out of the way by early middle age and to this end are willing to buy more expensive types of insurance. For example, if at age 25 you are able to pay an extra $10 per thousand for your insurance, you might wish to purchase a Twenty Payment Life policy and thus be through paying premiums by the time you are 45. The extra $10 a year does not increase the amount of death protection, but is reflected in additional and faster increasing cash values, always available if you should need them for an emergency, children's education, paying off a mortgage, and so forth. Every family's individual needs, budget and pocketbook are the deciding factors in determining what kind of insurance is best for them.

Is it a sensible plan to insure the children themselves, as they are born? Only when the wage earner is adequately covered. With young marrieds life insurance should be on the life of the father and/or the mother, rather than on the children. If parents want to accumulate money for their children, through insurance, they can buy endowments or other policies with high cash values, on their own lives. These will provide cash for the children whether the wage earner lives or dies. Sometimes a policy is bought on a child's life with the idea of starting his life insurance program at an early age and to encourage development of thrift.

Should a wife be insured? Again the best answer to this question is to ask yourself another one. If my wife should have an extended illness and die, would the costs entailed seriously affect our family's financial picture? Would there be extra money problems to face in running the household and taking care of the children? If so, then at least a minimum of life insurance coverage should be considered.

Why are endowment and annuity policies popular?
1. People are living longer than they used to and each advance in medical

science and methods of protective sanitation increases the average life span still further. Therefore, there is a natural, sensible tendency for the insurance buyer to think of himself, as well as his family, in providing security in future years.

2. Before Social Security most families could not hope to accumulate enough to provide anything like a reasonably adequate income for retirement and old age. But now Social Security gives a firm base and beginning for this kind of later financial independence, and has caused many people to think of making provisions for their non-earning years.

3. The fact that many private pension plans use life insurance and annuities to accumulate their trust funds accounts for the sale of many millions of dollars' worth of this type of policy.

4. Professional men and women who are not in line for pensions and do not qualify for Social Security benefits have turned to endowments and annuities as the only type of investment which guarantees a specific income when it is needed.

How does Social Security affect my life insurance plans? Although Social Security was originally intended to provide a minimum pension at old age, it also provides death benefits. For example—if a man with growing children (under 18 years of age) dies, Social Security benefits can provide an income to his widow and the children until the youngest child reaches 18. You should also know about old age benefits at age 65 for you and your wife.

Caution—There are certain conditions to be met in securing all Social Security benefits. You should become familiar with them. Your life insurance man can help you get this information or you can write direct to the Federal Security Administration in Washington, D.C., or its local office in your town or community.

How long should I hold on to my GI insurance? What's the best way to convert it? What is commonly known as GI insurance is, in effect, Government Life Insurance. This government protection is divided into two categories —National Service Life Insurance (N.S.L.I.) and Servicemen's Indemnity Insurance.

For those veterans whose policies were issued before April 25, 1951, there is a dividend-paying Term Policy (National Service Life Insurance) with no cash values, which was the kind of contract originally issued.

If you have this type of insurance, it can be renewed every five years on a term plan (at a higher premium rate at each renewal). These term policies also may be converted to a permanent insurance policy at any time. They can be converted into an Ordinary Life Policy, a Twenty or Thirty Payment Life Policy, Endowments at Age 60 or Endowments at Age 65.

N.S.L.I. is the cheapest insurance you can own because all costs of operation are absorbed by the government. Hold on to this insurance, by all means, and convert it to a permanent form as soon as possible.

For those entering the service after April 25, 1951, the government provides, without cost, automatic insurance (Servicemen's Indemnity Insurance) for $10,000 against death for all persons in active service in the armed forces. Within 120 days after separation from the service, these veterans are given the right to continue the $10,000 or any part of insurance on a term basis at a low premium. No dividends will be paid on these policies and the insurance *cannot be converted to a permanent plan.* The premium on such insurance is increased every five years.

If there are any changes in the rules you can always get information from the Veterans Administration.

If I should die, will my wife have to pay income tax on the money she receives from my life insurance policy?

1. If the policy is paid to your wife in a lump sum, she will pay no income tax on it.

2. If the principal is left on deposit with the company, the income your wife received will be subject to income taxes.

3. If your wife uses up the proceeds by accepting a fixed number of installments, the principal received in each installment will not be subject to income taxes, but the interest portion will be to the extent that the total interest received in a year exceeds $1,000.

4. If your wife receives a life annuity income in lieu of a lump sum, then some part of each installment is subject to income taxes. Life insurance companies will furnish figures so that you will know what this amount is.

Policies on your life will be included in your total estate and if that estate is large enough, it will be subject to federal estate tax and to state inheritance taxes. But there is an exception to this under the federal estate tax. It is now possible for a husband to buy an insurance policy which will not be included in his estate at death. An illustration of this would be a policy which he had previously given irrevocably to his wife.

The omnibus tax bill that was passed by the 83rd Congress in August, 1954, has brought about many significant changes in the taxation of life insurance and annuity policies which are believed to be more equitable than under the old law. These have been outlined above, but you will want the advice and guidance of an agent to help you give them careful consideration in the planning of your estate.

Should I leave my life insurance to be paid in one lump? As indicated in the previous answer, life insurance should be bought for specific purposes and some of these purposes require ready cash. For instance, the cash to liquidate a loan or a partner's interest in a business or expenses incurred by illness or at death would call for lump sum payment. But basically, life insurance is simply income translated into principal, which may be translated back into income again for the family when the earning power of the breadwinner is taken away. One of the great privileges of life insurance policies is your option to have the money paid out as income.

What are settlement options in a policy and how can they be used? All policies contain a list of privileges called settlement options. These options provide that instead of having a death claim paid in one lump sum the company will, at your request, arrange to pay out the money as income in a number of different ways.

1. You can leave the cash at interest with the company. The principal and a minimum amount of interest is guaranteed, but if more interest than the guaranteed amount is earned, that will be paid, too.

2. You can arrange for a guaranteed income for life for your wife or your children. The amount of return depends upon the age of the beneficiary at the time the income starts.

3. You can arrange to have the policy paid out in even installments over a specific length of time. There's a schedule in the policy which indicates the amount of income each $1,000 will provide for a specific number of years.

4. Or you can arrange that the money be paid out in a combination of any of these options. All income settlements can be paid annually, semi-annually, quarterly or monthly. Usually people have their income paid each month.

While these options are primarily for beneficiaries in the case of your death, they may also be applied to your own retirement if you live. These privileges are included in all present-day contracts but even where they are not included in older policies, most companies will consider a similar arrangement although under a slightly different rate of return.

These options can be the most valuable clauses in your life insurance contracts. They give you a chance to plan the amount and manner of your life insurance estate—they often provide tax advantages—they guarantee principal, interest and performance.

What is the cost of life insurance and what part of the cost goes toward protection and what remains as equity if the policy is paid up or discontinued? Life insurance premiums are based on scientific, mathematical formulas approved by all states, and their operation is supervised and administered by an Insurance Department within each state. A premium is divided into two parts:

1. To build a fund from which all current and future death claims will be paid.

2. To defray operational expenses. Originally, life insurance was written for only twelve months at a time and the policy holder paid an increased rate every year. As men grew older, the cost of their policies became prohibitive and many were forced to give up their insurance just when they needed it most. To correct this situation, a new system was devised called the Level Premium method, whereby the insured pays the same premium each year. The cash value of your policy is your *equity*. In the early years of your policy, your equity is naturally small, but it increases each year you own your insurance. For example, if you were to cash in an Ordinary Life policy at the end of twenty years, you would under today's average costs receive very close to— perhaps slightly more than—the amount you had deposited over those years, and you would also have had full protection over the whole period of time.

What is the best way to pay premiums? Premium rate is based on the fact that a premium is due and payable at the beginning of the insurance year and will earn interest for the life insurance company from that date. If you pay your premium quarterly, semi-annually or monthly, you will be asked to pay an extra charge to cover the costs of collecting 2, 4 or 12 installments instead of one lump sum, and to make up for the difference in the amount of interest your total premium would earn if it were in the hands of the company. So if you have enough money it is best to pay premiums annually.

However, if you find it difficult to manage this, don't let the payment of a few additional cents per thousand dollars stop you from buying as much protection as you need. You can always change your method of paying premiums by notifying the company of your wishes in the matter. One convenient way to put premium paying on a simple basis is to arrange for your bank to pay your premium annually and allow you to pay back one-twelfth of the amount each month. Many banks provide this kind of service at a reasonably small charge.

What would happen if I were to lose my life insurance policy? You should always keep any important papers in a safe and handy spot, but even if you were to lose your life insurance policy the insurance coverage would still hold. Companies keep very complete records and will at your request send you a loss form to fill out and then they will send you duplicates of any policies you have lost.

Why are policies written in such technical and hard-to-understand language? State Insurance departments insist that all the rights and privileges to which you are entitled must be set down in black and white. Actually the reason for using technical language in life insurance forms is to make them legal contracts. Contrary to popular belief most of the language is designed to protect the rights of the policy holder rather than the company.

How can one determine whether an insurance company is reliable? Every insurance company is regulated by state law. Some state requirements are stricter than others, but in every case full information is available to you from your State Insurance Department which regulates and supervises all the companies licensed in your state.

To what extent can one rely on an insurance broker to handle one's insurance problems? That's very much like asking how you know whether you can rely on your lawyer or your doctor or your accountant. The agencies through which life insurance is placed are headed by carefully selected men, who in turn choose their salesmen or brokers with the greatest care.

When a man comes into the life insurance business today, it is necessary in most states for him to pass an examination. In addition, most companies insist upon a comprehensive training course before the underwriter is allowed to call on prospects. Then too, there are additional training courses available to all life insurance men. One intensive course of study qualifies a successful candidate for the degree of Chartered Life Underwriter. Salesmen who have earned this distinction may use the initials C.L.U. after their names, just as a Certified Public Accountant displays C.P.A. after his.

By and large, you can expect competent advice and service from the great majority of life insurance men. Just as you judge the ability, enthusiasm and interest of any other person with whom you deal, you should be able to determine from the manner of an individual underwriter his understanding of your problems, the clarity of his recommendations and whether or not he is a reliable, well-qualified person. You must find a man compatible with your disposition and interests to whom you are willing to give all the personal information he needs to help you evaluate your life insurance situation.

A word of advice to everyone who owns life insurance:

Give yourself a life insurance checkup once a year. When you have worked out a satisfactory life insurance program you are apt to find that you are putting into premiums an amount equal to from one to four weeks' earnings. This being the case, you should surely be willing to spend two or three hours a year in checking over your life insurance investment—to make sure that you are getting the most for your money.   —*By Ralph G. Engelsman*

DOES YOUR INSURANCE
COVER YOUR BABY SITTER?

BABY sitters rarely came a second time to the D'Angelo home in Los Angeles, California. Five-year-old Sal made a game of ramming into them—head down, full-tilt. One uninitiated sitter, spending her first night with Sal, hit the floor and came up with two broken wrists. The state court awarded the woman damages. Since Sal's parents knew of his playful tendencies they should have warned the woman. Because they failed to do so they were guilty of negligence.

Next time you welcome a baby sitter into your home or let your own child sit for someone else, consider these questions. What if the sitter should be injured in your home? Are you liable, and if so, would your insurance policies cover you? What protection do you have against any damage your sitter may do to your home? What if your child is injured while sitting in someone else's house?

No matter how informal and friendly the arrangement, baby sitting is employment. The same labor laws that protect children from the cruelest form of exploitation may apply equally to the young person watching television in your parlor while you enjoy an evening out. So may the same tax, social security and workmen's compensation laws. Countless parents and children unwittingly violate them. By doing so, they invite legal trouble.

Labor Statutes Regulating Minors

Though everyone baby-sits, from registered nurses to college fullbacks, high school and college girls remain the backbone of the "industry." More than a dozen states technically outlaw evening work by minors. Under the laws of some states, minors under 16 may not sit after 6:00 or 7:00 P.M. Some require minors to have an employment permit for every person for whom they work. A few states go further and regulate the hours of work until the age of eighteen.

Though labor statutes are speckled with special provisions for youthful tightrope walkers, contortionists and musicians, only two jurisdictions make any mention of the most common occupation of all. In Alaska, the law contains a special amendment exempting baby sitting. In California, the attorney general ruled that the state's 10:00 P.M. curfew on child labor doesn't apply to sitting if the sitter is escorted home. Elsewhere, if domestic service is restricted by child labor laws, so is baby sitting.

State labor authorities, the police and school officials watch with concern the nightly procession of sitters going to work, but they haven't the slightest intention of charging into your home to check employment permits. A New York State Department of Labor report admitted that while baby sitting is covered by the state's child labor law, "this theoretical legal protection is completely absent in practice." But before laughing off the idea, consider what might result if your sitter were injured while "illegally employed."

Anybody hurt while on your property might sue you, but if the person happens to be employed illegally your legal defenses slide down around your knees. Courts have held homeowners guilty of negligence for that reason alone. In upstate New York, a youth burglarized the place where he was employed illegally. The owner was found guilty of contributing to the delinquency of a minor. Illegal employment also jeopardizes your chances of recovering if the sitter damages your home, on the theory that you contributed to the accident.

Workmen's Compensation

In some states, the workmen's compensation law covers sitters. A sitter injured in New Jersey is entitled to the fixed scale of compensation benefits, regardless of whether the homeowner was responsible. At the same time you lose the protection of your insurance. All personal liability policies specifically exclude workmen's compensation cases.

Not long ago in New Jersey, a middle-aged sitter fell down a flight of stairs. The state workmen's compensation court awarded her $275. Though she was employed for only a few hours once a week, the court said she was entitled to the same form of benefits as an industrial worker.

The workmen's compensation and child labor laws can react on one another in interesting ways. Watch closely as the legal wheels grind:

If a baby sitter in New Jersey is employed illegally—in violation of the state's child labor law, for example—the sitter is entitled to double compensation if injured. Even if you bought a special workmen's compensation policy it would cover only half the amount. The punitive half, the part for having employed the child illegally, cannot be insured against!

Most other states exclude domestics from workmen's compensation. New York's law generally requires coverage for domestics only if you live in a city of 40,000 or over and if they work for you at least 48 hours a week; in California if they work 52 hours. Baby sitters will not ordinarily pass these limits, but a practical nurse, hired full-time to care for a newborn, should be covered. In a few states the compensation law applies only if you hire the minimum or more number of employees. If a Connecticut resident hires two or more people in his office or shop, for example, the baby sitter he hires is covered, too.

Where the workmen's compensation laws don't apply, the sitter always has the right to sue under common law for injuries, claiming they were caused by your negligence. One elderly baby sitter fell through a hole on the porch that parents failed to warn her about. She injured her leg and later won her suit for damages. In Connecticut, a toddler playfully jumped on the sitter's back and knocked her down. With back and hip injuries, she sued for $15,000.

Even the growing practice of neighbors' baby sitting for each other can be a source of conflict. One woman agreed to care for a neighbor's six-year-old. The boy tried to scale her woodpile. He pulled the wood down upon himself and was badly injured. The mother settled for hospital bills.

When baby sitting breaks into the headlines it is usually because of some accident or injury to the child. More commonplace are the damages baby sitters may do to the home.

Responsibility for Damages

Baby sitters, like anyone else, are responsible for any damage they do. How much good that will do you in recovering small losses is another question. Some states have passed laws making parents responsible for damage done by their children, but in most a parent does not have to answer for his child's sins unless in some way he contributed to them. You could sue the young sitter and get a judgment against her. If the child has no assets, the judgment can be kept alive until she does. But outside of that, you will have to depend on the fairmindedness of your sitter.

However, if the sitter was sent by an employment agency, with the agency setting the rates of pay, the agency will be held as the employer and must answer for any damage.

The Social Security law may apply to baby sitting. It is possible that with as little as one and a half years of covered employment, a sitter 62 years of age or older may be eligible to receive monthly benefits for life.

Sitters are covered by the law for any calendar quarter-year in which they earn $50 or more from any one employer. A sitter earning $2 a night twice a week from one family would go over the top. If the sitter divides her work among several families, so that she doesn't earn $50 a quarter from any one employer, she would not be covered. Agencies supplying sitters to different households are the sitters' "one employer."

There is a special rule for baby sitting and other domestic work done on a farm operated for profit. The sitter is covered if she earns $150 a calendar year or works at least 20 days a year for any one employer.

If the sitter meets the tests for coverage, you must file a quarterly report with the Internal Revenue Service enclosing the Social Security tax.

Some people have realized that they can help older relatives win Social Security benefits by employing them as domestic servants. The Internal Revenue Service realizes it also and studies these intrafamily arrangements carefully. A father or mother hired as a domestic servant is not covered and neither is a child under 21. Brothers, sisters, in-laws and other relatives are covered only if there is a true employment relation.

If your own child sits regularly, she may have to pay a federal income tax. A child under 19 or still attending school full-time for at least five months of the year may earn any amount and still be claimed by his parents as a dependent, provided only that the parents contribute more than half his support. But the child must file a return and pay any tax due if he earns more than $600 a year.

Avoiding legal complications. What can you do about possible legal complications of baby sitting? The first line of defense against monetary loss is the insurance policy. Comprehensive personal liability policies will protect you against most suits within stated limits. Almost as important, the insurance company will take over the job of dealing with the claim, sparing you much time and legal expense. Your automobile liability policy will guard you against any injuries suffered by the sitter while you are driving her to and from her work, except if workmen's compensation applies. Auto policies, like homeowners' liability policies, do not apply in compensation cases. In states where workmen's compensation laws might apply—New Jersey in particular—a special compensation policy is a "must."

The second line of defense is your choice of baby sitter.

"Experience has shown that the welfare of young baby sitters is better safeguarded when they work in their own neighborhoods and for families known to their parents," warns Paul E. Gurske, director of the U. S. Labor Department's Bureau of Labor Standards. The National Child Labor Committee, devoted to raising the labor standards for children, recommends a 16-year minimum age for evening baby sitting and a 14-year minimum for afternoon work.

Baby sitters bear one of the greatest responsibilities, the protection of a child's life. Choose carefully. —*By Joel Berg*

HOW TO FINANCE YOUR CHILD'S COLLEGE EDUCATION

ALL colleges and universities are facing mounting overhead and deficits, and consequently have had to step up undergraduate charges, though there is considerable variation in fees, depending on the type of institution and kind of capital funds on which it draws.

For purposes of planning, we'll assume $1,800 as a median outlay, each year, for four college years. Frankly, we think it is logical to assume, also, that to scoop that $1,800, all of a sudden, out of an average annual income would require the mathematical wizardry of an Einstein.

If your income is a moderate one, you are already tugging at its corners to make it lap over food, rent, clothing, taxes, property upkeep, insurance, doctor and dentist bills. Your higher-bracket neighbor is not much better off. He has scaled his living standard upward to where most of these items are costing him more than they cost you. His taxes are taking a bigger bite. His budget is stretched to capacity, too.

So—rich, poor or medium—parents in general find paying for education a problem. Here, then, are suggestions of very definite plans for financing or helping to finance your children's education.

Deferred payments. A good many colleges, with the aid of private financing companies, will arrange for board and tuition to be paid on a monthly basis. Though this system involves interest charges, many parents find it less painful than meeting large payments in September and February at the request of the bursar's office.

Scholarships. If your child has a better than average school record, he has a good chance to qualify for a scholarship award which will take care of part of his expenses. Increased enrollment has sharpened the always keen edge of competition, and administrators sift scholarship applicants with a careful eye. But there are millions of dollars' worth of state and municipal grants to be parceled out, and more millions from endowments provided by alumni. (For information on scholarships see article, "How to Get Your Boy or Girl into College.")

Student loans. Most colleges and a good many educational and church foundations maintain rotating loan funds for undergraduates in good standing. Use of such money, of course, imposes a later burden of repayment, but it certainly helps to cushion college years. Here again, competition is keen and funds are carefully administered to reach young people who would have no chance of continuing their education without this sort of help.

Self-help. A lot of independent youngsters are eager to pay their own way, or part of it, by taking on extracurricular jobs, and a good many of them manage the double assignment successfully. Educators, however, often advise against outside work unless it is a strong financial necessity. College, they point out, is in itself a full-time job and can be handled better if the student puts all of his energy into it.

Still, in spite of all these chances of help, the fact remains that the majority of parents who want their children to have that coveted college education are going to pay for a large portion of it. Fortunately, the average young family does have the invaluable asset of time! There are precious years ahead in which to build your child's education fund via any of a number of practical installment plans.

Savings banks. If you start an educational savings account as soon as your child is born, regular deposits of $315 each year for eighteen years will, with accruing interest, reach the $7,200 mark we have spoken of to cover four college years. If your child is five years old when you begin his savings account, annual deposits would have to be raised to $465 per year to reach the desired total. And if you wait until he is ten, the yearly lay away should be $804 to meet the same goal.

It takes will power to make voluntary deposits and to keep on making them. There's always temptation to skip a deposit here and there in favor of a vacation, a household emergency or just to ease that old budgetary pressure. But, if you follow through you'll have the amount you need, when you need it, and you'll have it at a discount, thanks to the magic of compound interest.

U. S. Savings Bonds. You can discount your total even more by buying the new Series E Savings Bonds. The most efficient way to do this is via the Payroll Savings Plan, whereby your firm makes an authorized weekly or monthly deduction from your salary and buys the bonds for you. If you are self-employed, or if your firm has no Payroll Plan, you can make arrangements with your bank to have the purchase money for bonds deducted from your monthly balance.

In either case, weekly deductions of only $5.75 per week would net college costs by the end of eighteen years. Of course, as with the savings bank plan, the later you start, the larger your deductions will have to be to catch up with requirements.

Life insurance. One direct and absolutely sure way to prepare yourself for your child's college costs is by buying a life insurance endowment policy designed to mature when he reaches the age of 18. The policy is usually placed on the life of the father with the child as beneficiary and there are several advantages to the plan. First, it guarantees that the necessary money for college will be on hand whether or not the family wage earner remains alive to accumulate it. Second, the life insurance company will administer the funds during college years, in regular allowance form if desired. Third, you receive premium notices, on schedule, from the company to remind you that payments are due and that they must be made or your insurance plan will lapse.

To provide $1,800 per college year, this kind of policy, bought at a child's birth, would cost a 30-year-old father about $375 a year. Here again, delay costs money and the premium rate goes up with the ages of parent and child.

When dividends are paid on your policy, they may be used to reduce premiums, to speed up the maturity of the endowment or, perhaps, set aside as a bulwark against emergencies, as a sinking fund for postgraduate courses or spare cash for a larger allowance for campus days.

Mutual funds, savings and loan plans, investment trusts. There are a number of mutual funds, investment trusts or savings and loan plans which may give you a more liberal return on your put-away-for-college dollar than any of the conservative savings systems we have outlined. In funds like these, you join forces with thousands of other shareholders. Your money, plus theirs, is spread over a broad field of investment in many different companies, industries and developments. Thus, there is less gamble involved than there would be if you decided to take a flyer on your own in any one—or even several—common stocks. Securities fluctuate, as we all know, so it's difficult to estimate just what your mutual fund savings would be worth after any given number of years. At a guess, investment of between $200 and $300 a year should build the amount you need in time for college—if you are lucky. Mutual fund results have been good over recent years, but there is an element of speculation and neither your original investment nor a liberal return on it is guaranteed. So if you choose this kind of savings plan, pick yourself a wise investment counselor and take a careful look at the background and reputation of the fund you select.

Partial savings. Even if, right now, you're not in a position to adopt any of these programs in full, don't just shove them aside in the hope that you'll swing them later. Start some saving, perhaps with a goal of meeting just tuition fees for the present. You may be able to round out a complete plan later, and in any case you'll find that even partial savings make it easier to eke the difference out of income.

Self-completing coverage. You'll notice that the endowment policy we mentioned is the only plan which makes it absolutely sure that your $7,200 will be on hand for Jane or Junior's campus costs, whether or not you live to build their college fund yourself. If then, you have chosen some other savings system, you'll be wise to supplement it with a low-cost term insurance policy. (See article, "What You Should Know About Life Insurance" for further discussion of term insurance.)

Most important of all, decide now on some form of financial action and start it at once! Remember that the longer you put it off, the larger chunks you'll have to lay aside in order to be ready for freshman year.

—*By Ralph G. and Naomi L. Engelsman*

BEWARE THE
ATTRACTIVE NUISANCE

DO you know the meaning of the term "attractive nuisance"? It may sound like a description of your youngest offspring, but all too often it is a synonym for tragedy.

In the interpretation of the courts, an "attractive nuisance" is something on your premises which can harm children but which inevitably tempts children to play with it. As parents, you realize that just about everything under, on and above the ground falls into this category. Having children of your own means you play host, willingly or not, to everybody else's youngsters, so it is important to do immediate battle with the attractive nuisance.

The most innocent-looking objects can cause a mishap—a mole hole in your lawn, even the family car standing in your own driveway.

Are you wondering what you can do to safeguard the trusting kids who play in your yard? There are three basic phases in the war against the attractive nuisance.

The House and Yard

The first is an open-eyed survey of your house and grounds. Naturally, you've been vigilant all along against electric socket booby traps, the skidding rug and lurking toy ambushes, so we'll emphasize the outdoor angles of a practical safety campaign. Lest you forget, however, the law reminds you that as owners of a dwelling, it is your responsibility to keep every part of your property in such condition that anyone who has a right to be on your premises and who exercises due care will not be hurt. At the same time, the lawyers say that guests in a house are under no legal obligation to guard against accidents, so don't think Jane Jones' fall down your stairs was her own fault for not looking where she was going. She had a perfect right to plunge floorward—considering that Junior's skates on the landing accelerated her progress. But getting outside again, where children are most likely to congregate, it isn't enough that the tools are locked away, the poison ivy killed.

Look sharp. Is your fence simple and sturdy, or are there challenging pickets which might impale young climbers? Make sure your lawn is reasonably smooth, free of unexpected holes which might snap small running legs. Are there tempting low-hanging branches to lure children off the ground?

You can't stop the kids from climbing but you can make sure that those alluring limbs are sound enough to bear a child's weight. Use your imagination and try to visualize your yard with a child's eyes.

Daily Checkup of Yard

And one grand cleanup isn't enough. A thorough course in the do-nots of a back yard should be given your own children, with strict penalties imposed for the infringement of rules. You might enlist Junior's aid for a day-to-day checkup, just to make sure the hose is coiled safely out of the way or that no hammers and saws are left lying around.

Next in your campaign for peace of mind and protection of your pocketbook from damage suits is supervision. Remember you are responsible for the well-being of every little guest on your premises including the ones you've never seen before in your life. A child not of the age of reason is legally *non-suis-juris* and a court may refuse to consider a young child a trespasser even though he's been warned not to appear on your premises. When there are children on your property, your place is near them—near enough to foil foolish projects before they get under way. When you are indoors, keep windows open and one ear cocked so that you can hear what is going on at all times.

Personal liability insurance. Third, and this is basic to the problem of the attractive nuisance, is insurance. For an insurance-minded people, most of us are surprisingly ignorant of comprehensive personal liability insurance, which protects you against the financial thunderbolts hurtled by suing neighbors hurt on your property. Insurance executives reveal that only ten per cent of the insured population carries a personal liability policy, and that insurance agents usually have to exert a good deal of salesmanship to convince even the most cautious citizen that it isn't just an "extra." Yet it is very inexpensive to maintain. Play safe and check with your agent. Then, if your survey and supervision fail and an accident does occur on your premises, you'll have financial help to see you through the legal storm.

Incidentally, since children and pets are pretty inseparable, this is the time to regard the family dog with an unprejudiced eye. Loyal he may be—to members of your family—but are an outsider's bones his meat? There are countless thousands of dog bite cases handled through the courts and they are truly the bane of the insurance company's existence. The pup's owner always pays. It doesn't matter if the dog has never bared a fang before, and the fact that a child's relentless teasing incurred Fido's righteous wrath does not placate a jury. When young children are on the grounds, do Fido a favor; lock him up.

Other common cases involving children—and most of them revolve around the most simple situations—are neighbor's children breaking arms and legs falling off or over your children's toys or any handy shrubs, trees and fences, or sustaining more serious injuries in forbidden contacts with your car, gas tanks, work implements and animal traps.

Combating the Attractive Nuisance

The homeowning parent, if he is wise, takes to heart these rules for dealing with the attractive nuisance:

So long as there is a child, he will probably be followed by a crash. Be prepared to prevent an accident, but also be prepared to sustain its repercussions if one occurs.

Make regular inspections of house and grounds for needed repairs.

Promptly repair broken fences, gates, windows—anything within reach of children.

Lock away garden and carpentry tools immediately after each use.

Keep dogs muzzled or away from children.

Remove bicycles, toys from yard.

Make lawn reasonably smooth and fill up holes and cracks.

Keep sidewalk and paths repaired.

Remove exposed tree roots, rotting limbs and low-hanging branches.

Repair loose bricks, cornices and so forth that might fall and hurt someone.

Keep sidewalks and steps cleared of snow and ice.

Remove clothesline or portable hangers after use.

Make sure garage door is kept closed.

Keep all insecticides and combustibles out of reach.

Make the children aware of the problems.

Keep a watchful eye and ear on the children.

—By Virginia and Morton Edwards

IF YOU PLAN TO BUY A HOUSE

YOU should get the answers to the following questions before you buy:
1. Does seller have valid title to the property which he can transfer? (A lawyer or title company should make title search.)

2. Has the seller given anyone other than yourself the option to buy the property? If so, the third party could subsequently claim from you (the purchaser) any loss which resulted from his inability to exercise his option. This should be determined before signing sales contract and is one reason for obtaining affidavit.

3. Has the property been carefully surveyed to determine whether the buildings on it encroach on another property, or if adjoining buildings encroach on the property you contemplate buying?

4. Are there any mechanics' liens against the property? In some states they may be valid even if unrecorded.

5. Are there unpaid taxes, special assessments, other liens? Title search should reveal how much.

6. What mortgages are there against the property? Will they be paid off before you take title? If not, what are the mortgage provisions? Can mortgage be paid off without penalties before maturity?

7. Are there chattel mortgages against personal property (range, refrigerator) included in purchase?

8. Are there restrictions in the deed against the use of the property? These may restrict fencing, also renting out part of the house.

You should secure the services of an attorney before you sign the contract. You should obtain the following list of documents when you buy a house or property. These are all matters which the attorney should handle for you. The extent, however, will vary with local custom, but none should be entirely omitted.

Get These Documents

1. Deed. Require seller to produce the deed by which he acquired title as a protection against forgery or impersonation.

2. Abstract of title (or other evidence of title, depending on local practice).

3. Bill of sale itemizing all personal property included in sale price (range, rugs, draperies).

4. Receipt for purchase price paid to seller.

5. Survey.

6. All paid notes or other evidences of payment made by the seller on any mortgages you assume at time of buying. Also request from mortgagor a statement showing balance due. This prevents future claim for a greater amount than indicated at time of purchase.

7. Insurance policies and assignments thereof.

8. Copies of any leases, if property is occupied by tenant.

9. Last receipts for taxes, special assessments, gas, electricity, water.

10. Affidavit from seller which states there are no judgments, no repairs or improvements which are still unpaid, no unrecorded deeds or contracts, no known defects of title, no other claims such as would arise from divorce or bankruptcy; that seller has undisputed possession of premises you are buying.

—By Maxine Livingston

CHILDREN LIKE TO HELP

WE hear a lot of laments these days about the bad effects of push-button living on our children. Where are the opportunities for character-building and self-reliance that the good old days used to offer, people ask. No wood box to keep filled, no cow to be milked and put to pasture, no need to trudge long miles to school and back. Without hardships—or at least a heavy quota of daily chores—it is implied that modern children are deprived of acquiring a sense of responsibility.

It is also generally assumed that our streamlined living and modern appliances have so lightened the burden of housekeeping that help from the children is not really needed at all, and so must be "invented" for the sake of their character-building. We need to dispose of this notion or we're off to a bad start with the kids.

Many modern mothers need help as much as, if not more than, our grandmothers did. Many of us work at a job outside the home—and a very small percentage of these so-called "working mothers" employ household help. Among the mothers making a career of homemaking, how many can find much leisure, after donating the extra time and work expected of them in the endless community, church, school and welfare projects? And now there's the do-it-yourself movement to eat up spare hours; with paint, hammer and saw, as well as needle and thread, mother pitches in to help dad save family money on everything from a converted attic to new slipcovers.

How to Get Cooperation

In all this humming activity of the average American home, how can the kids be considered fifth wheels? We *need* their help (partly to save time for some fun with them!) and to feel needed is important to anyone's spirit of cooperation. Some children usually—and all children occasionally—like to help around home. What's the secret behind this cheerful kind of help? There is no over-all answer, of course. Each child is different from his brother or sister or neighbor, and each child is different at various ages. But there are certain rules of thumb that will give any parent and child a sound basis for good on-the-job relations.

No child likes—and he can always sense—the idea that chores are delegated to him "for his own good." He resents being reminded that his father, as a boy, carried a two-hour paper route, rain or shine, every night before supper. He'll like you and the chore much better for any simple reason that makes sense to him: you're late with dinner and need a helping hand, or, if this is his established job, table-setting can hardly be put off till *after* dinner.

Express Your Appreciation

When I say to our five-year-old, "Thanks for putting all those groceries away—that was a big help!" he fairly sparkles with pleasure and pride. A little necessary rearranging—unjumbling the canned goods, moving cottage cheese from cupboard to refrigerator—is small trouble after the bright-eyed way he asks, "What can I do now to help?"

As children grow older we not only tend to take their help more for granted, but to be more critical of their efforts. And this is really unfair. Husbands or mothers-in-law don't always do things quite *our* way, yet we try to be appreciative and tactful about their help. Why shouldn't the same etiquette apply to the children?

There is always something worthy of praise in even a sketchy job. If we comment on that, instead of the flaws, it inspires a child to be more self-critical. I've seen this happen over and over again.

"My room's all done, Mom." Well, it may be far from my own standards of "done" but I react favorably: "My, what a difference!" And as I look all around: "You really cleaned out those shelves—that's a nice arrangement you've made!" "I spent a lot of time on that!" he says proudly, but after a moment, "I guess the closet could be a little better." And he's off to add some finishing touches.

Let him help plan his work. If a child can help decide what jobs at what times of day suit him best, he'll tackle them much more willingly than work arbitrarily assigned.

Turning over entire projects to the children, with only the most necessary sideline supervision by a grownup, pays off in teamwork that's usually a model of cooperation and as good as a picnic for fun.

A meeting will help clear the air when the children get lax about routine chores, or begin to squabble over who's doing more or less than his share. If you have a born organizer in the family, don't discourage him. The other children are more apt to welcome him as a leader than to resent him as a boss.

Our oldest child, now twelve, has always shown a real flair for putting fun as well as order into her own and her brothers' house-help. For one of her frequent meetings, she whips up individual invitations, chore charts and refreshments. Since she loves the "paper work" of her organizing, the chairmanship usually falls to a brother. Everyone volunteers for duties; names are duly listed and our household chores are clicked off in a businesslike way.

You'll find that any written directives have some sort of magical effect. They are far more authoritative than verbal instruction and seldom, if ever, resented!

Let him have fun while he works. If you harbor some notion that work should be only work, you're imposing a handicap that operates against you.

In our family, playing "restaurant" and "laundry" and "ranch house" make lively new fun of mealtime, washday and indoor or outdoor cleaning projects. Everyone changes character, along with names. The role of a cook named Old Gertie once fell to my lot; the kids liked her crotchety ways so well that she's still in demand—though I'm sometimes a little fed up with her! When dad gets into the act, he's invariably Slippery Slim, and his "ranch-hands" all work like eager beavers.

We make no distinction between girls' and boys' work. Our boys find fun in ironing, cooking, dishwashing; our girl likes lawnmowing and snow shoveling as well as baking a cake.

Out-of-the-ordinary jobs never go begging. Relining kitchen drawers with their interesting paraphernalia, going after cobwebs with a long-handled mop —anything that's not humdrum is fun.

But the very tops in pleasure at our house is work involving wet rags and scrubbing! From two years old to twelve, there are always enthusiastic volunteers for woodwork or floor or window washing. True, someone has to mop up the puddles and slick over the streaks left by the littler helpers—and change them into dry clothes after! But nothing else surpasses it in sheer delight and pride of accomplishment.

If a child is not much good at helping except when he's "in the mood" that's your cue to show interest in the jobs he thinks up himself, and to have a few suggestions on hand that are not run-of-the-mill. If he's a "spotty" helper, and frequently wants to shift chores, he's the child for short jobs, well timed according to his play plans. Small services of the moment—whether done voluntarily or by request—should be counted in his favor. If regular jobs begin to be really disliked, a child is probably ready for more responsible work. When table-setting becomes too dull, he may have fun feeding the baby.

Avoid bossy attitude. Easy cooperation, at any age, never fares well under a big-boss attitude. Barked-out orders, curt demands, may stimulate action, but not enthusiasm. And it's so easy to kindle interest in children! Call for someone to carry out the garbage pail and chances are no one will "hear" you; but announce that you need an arm full of muscle and you'll have several on hand in a jiffy! Even terse commands set well with children if there's a spirit of fun about them. "All hands on deck!" is more inviting than "Time to help with dishes." "Operation Clean-up—three minutes to go—on your mark . . ." gets a room put to rights in double-quick time.

One aspect of helping that each of our children enjoys is the chance it sometimes gives us to talk over things together. It's somehow easier for a child to bring out problems when his hands are busy instead of idle. Working in a twosome over dinner dishes or some outdoor job, I hear all sorts of ins and outs concerning school or friends, and lend a sympathetic ear or word of advice.

There is more real reward in all the intangible satisfactions that grow out of helping than a concrete reward system can offer. Some parents find merit in a chore-by-chore payment arrangement; others worry over whether monetary matters should or should not come into the picture but one way or the other chores should carry other satisfactions, too.

When I hear that "Martha's mother pays her fifteen cents every time she does the dishes" and that "Billy Roberts gets fifty cents a week for burning their trash every day" my answer is simply: "In our family we don't do it that way." We do give special treats on occasion, but the principle is well established by now that the children's help has no connection with their regular spending money, which is never used as a bribe or a threat in relation to chores.

Children have busy lives of their own, besides a real need for leisure time to use as they wish. I find that the help I can reasonably expect varies a great deal depending on the time of year, the child's age and his personality. "Playing it by ear" is the best bet in making requests. But it's understood that some help from the children is always needed—and appreciated. And a good part of the time, they donate their services as a matter of course.

—*By Maja Bernath*

WHEN IS IT SAFE
TO LEAVE CHILDREN ALONE?

D O you ever leave your children home alone in the evening? We asked this far-from-simple question of a hundred families. They all gave the same sound, practical answer: "It depends."

It depends on the child: on his maturity, on his experience—not just on how old he is. One parent reports that she and her husband leave their daughter of eight alone. "She doesn't mind. In fact, she's proud of her independence."

A mother of eleven-year-old twin boys says, "One twin can be left alone. The other, no. He's too insecure."

Of the families we questioned, more than half had left children alone at some time before they were twelve. Four-fifths had done so before the children reached fifteen, and practically all by the time their children were fifteen.

These were responsible families, living in good neighborhoods in a city, a suburb and a semi-rural town. Difficulty in getting a baby sitter, or the hardship of paying one, or a yen for a good time no matter what, are not the reasons back of their leaving their children alone. They believe the benefits are mutual when parents and children can be independent of one another now and then. The time must come. The question is when.

It is natural for parents who have never left children alone to wonder: Why take a chance?

The answer is that under the right circumstances no undue chance is taken. And what are the right circumstances? There are many individual opinions about that. But in spite of their differences, we found in the comments of these one hundred families common standards and safeguards that we feel are a valuable guide for all parents.

First and most important: leaving a child alone is not a matter for sudden and drastic action. Security grows from experience, which is best acquired gradually. A few minutes at a time is enough to start with. That way, his parents return before a child has a chance to miss them, before he has time to feel abandoned. Gradually, instead, he discovers for himself that there is nothing frightening about being alone. He begins on his own to develop a feeling of security and self-sufficiency, by a process that can be as painless and slow as a well-managed weaning, with as successful results.

Preschoolers Need Supervision

Certainly we would all agree that a child under six needs an adult nearby most of the time. He shouldn't be left even in another room or in a yard, no matter how safe, unless he has a responsible person within call. But almost all parents who report that their eleven and twelve-year-olds seem happy alone, say that from the age of seven their children were accustomed to being left by themselves for brief intervals, perhaps while their mothers chatted with neighbors or posted a letter. Only gradually, as the children grew older and seemed ready for it, were those few minutes stretched to an hour or two, and sometimes shifted to the evening. ("An hour is long enough," advises one mother of a ten-year-old whom we consulted.) Even then, parents of eleven and twelve-year-olds were prompt to add, they do this "very occasionally" and "never after ten-thirty," eight-thirty the latest for one eleven-year-old.

Nearness is a factor in making a good beginning, too, and one that should be continued even when the time away has increased. One couple is in a position to achieve it very easily. "In the summer we go next door to play bridge," says the mother. "When it begins to get dark our eleven-year-old boy quits play and goes to bed himself. We're usually out on the neighbor's screened porch and he can see us and call to us."

Some parents use the telephone for this close touch. Those who ask the child to do the phoning say it gives him a project that makes him feel self-sufficient and able.

Friendly neighbors in next-door apartments, or where single houses are close together, are frequently called on to bolster a child's feeling of security (and his parents' peace of mind) by keeping an eye on him and being on call. One family has a fisherman's conch on which the children, ages thirteen, eleven and six, can sound a call to a relative who lives only a few hundred yards away. They know it works because they've tried it out. But they've never had to use it or the phone.

If several children are left. Our reporting parents have quite different tales to tell on the question of leaving several children together. Most of them like the idea because the children are company for one another. Some parents of only children even invite a friend to spend the night. On the other hand, some have tried once and regretted it—too much excitement and damage.

A mother of three (two boys of nine and eleven, a girl of six) writes, "I never leave the three of them alone for any length of time because of rough-housing and fighting."

Yet we have a number of reports of six-year-olds being left peaceably with eleven-year-olds. Our youngest successful combination is two brothers, six and eight. So, once again, it very definitely "depends." From our considerable observation it seems to us that there is less chance of serious fighting among children who have been gradually trained to responsibility by being left alone occasionally than among children who have always been supervised.

One couple is content to leave their daughter of a year and a half with their fifteen-year-old son, and another considers their ten-year-old girl mature enough to "sit" with their six-year-old. They pay her a fee for her service, and bolster her confidence by staying within a fifteen-minute ride of the house.

Is the child responsible? How do you decide when a child is mature enough to take such responsibilities, or simply the responsibility of staying by himself? Here are useful points for judging, mentioned in our reports:

"The ability of the child to cope with situations." (You can observe that every day.)

"If the child has been taught to read and enjoys it," writes one mother, "to use the phone intelligently and to open a can and fix a meal, I think he is probably ready to be left by himself—twelve seems a safe age to me."

A widow who earns needed money by going out occasionally to cook dinners leaves her boys, ages nine and thirteen, alone until ten or so on such evenings. She counts on their appreciation of her problem. "They understand and are good about it."

In another family, a twelve-year-old took the initiative one evening. He had chronic asthma, so his parents were particularly reassured by the fact that his regular sitter was a retired trained nurse. But one night she couldn't come and they couldn't find anyone else. "Dad, did you have a sitter until you were twenty-one?" asked twelve-year-old Jack.

"But your asthma?" countered dad.

"I always start the croup kettle for myself," said the boy, "and I could ring the elevator bell or telephone you or the doctor."

So they left him alone and have been doing so ever since. "He's really happier," reports his mother.

And that is certainly one test of when a child can be left alone.

Take Necessary Precautions

The headlines, and our own records, are full of disasters that haunt parents. How, in the face of them, can we even suggest leaving children alone? It's true a thirteen-year-old girl burned to death with her German shepherd dog while her parents were out watching her brother play basketball. It's true that a baby was killed by an exploding oil stove when his mother "went to the corner store for just a minute." Boys do burn themselves playing with chemistry sets.

It is also true that parents are burned to death at home, along with their children. Children break arms and legs, cut themselves, even drown—with their parents there.

It's risky to be alive, and to have children. It's risky to cross the street, but that doesn't stop us. We simply take precautions and go ahead.

Against the physical danger of accident, if we leave children alone, we have to weigh the psychological injuries from babying and overprotection if we never leave them alone. Neither one is sure to happen because children are pretty able and sensible. But generally the physical dangers, when reasonable precautions are taken, are less of a threat than the psychological.

Fire prevention. Fire is the greatest danger. Every house should be as fire-safe as possible. Your insurance agent will be glad to give you booklets that will tell you what the danger spots are, and how to correct them. He may be able to arrange for a free inspection of your house by a safety expert.

Make your house as accident-proof as possible. But still you must consider your child's maturity and experience. How does he react to accidents? If he cuts his finger does he take it calmly enough and ask for help if he needs it?

Of course you won't leave your child alone if he is sick, and there is little chance of serious sickness developing in the short time you are away. But can you count on his good judgment to tell you if he doesn't feel well before you leave? Can you be sure he will call you or the doctor if trouble should develop while you are away? The parents of the boy with chronic asthma were sure. They knew from experience he could provide first aid himself.

Headlines about rape and kidnapping frighten many parents. Actually both are exceedingly rare, in spite of the news stories. And we have found no records of either happening when children are left alone; when they do occur the child is usually on the way home from school.

Burglary. We have no records, either, of burglaries happening while children are left alone. But we do have an account of two girls, thirteen and eleven, having a bad fright. They had been left alone with strict instructions not to answer the doorbell if it should ring. At ten o'clock it rang, and rang. Then they heard a window being forced. They peered, shivering, down the stairwell to see a man's leg thrusting its way over the hall windowsill. Suddenly a light flashed on, revealing their older brother, home from college unexpectedly and taking the only way in.

Our parents are divided on how to protect their children against fright and mishaps. Some think children are safer awake: "I do not feel that children should be left alone when asleep. Even at fourteen or fifteen they sleep too soundly," writes one parent.

From the other point of view comes this comment: "We leave our boys, who are twelve and ten, alone after dinner on their honor to go to bed at eight-thirty. This is the first year."

We feel ourselves that if children are accustomed to getting themselves to bed there is no gain in interfering with their regular bedtime. They should leave some lights burning, to discourage burglars. A phone within easy reach is a wise precaution.

Insurance against fear. There are adults who are afraid to be alone. Every creak is a stealthy footstep, boding no good. Certainly you do not want to subject your children to such fears. A good insurance against them is a slow initiation into the business of being alone for brief, casual periods with you nearby. Bit by bit, they learn there is nothing terrible about being alone. They learn, instead, to like it.

Every twelve or thirteen-year-old craves independence. He wants to be on his own—but he wants his family back of him, too. If he can be treated to small doses of independence, with assurance all the time that his parents are going to return on schedule, he can have his self-reliance and his family security, too. The combination will help him grow into an adult who will not shiver when the night shadows dance.

—By Norma E. Cutts, Ph.D., and Nicholas Moseley, Ph.D.

HOW TO GET READY FOR A SECOND BABY

WHEN you already have one child, perhaps more, many of the preparations for a new baby will seem like second nature to you, but you are bound to find, perhaps to your surprise, that you face certain new problems. For one thing, your forthcoming hospital visit may be the first real separation between you and your child. You must prepare him for your absence, and you must also prepare him for the newcomer.

When should you tell your child? This is up to you. What is important is that he should know long enough in advance to live with the idea, and that he be made to feel part and parcel of the welcoming committee. It is important to him that he is about to become a big brother or a big sister. Father and mother should both be in on the telling. With a child old enough to get any feeling of what this means you might slant your telling this way: "Our family has some good news. We're going to have a new baby. You are going to be a big brother (or sister)."

Notice that this is not "mother's baby" but the family's. Later on your child will realize that mother has a very special relation to the newcomer, but if both you and father are wise and generous you will spread the ownership all you can. As to the question of where babies come from, a little child should know that the baby is growing in a special place in mother's body, and that daddy helped it start to grow. He will want to put his hand against mother's tummy and feel the baby inside. Tell him that he was once there, too.

Let child help with preparations. He will love to help get the new things for the baby. By asking his cooperation you do all you can to keep him from feeling left out. Show him the little shirts and diapers, the blankets and towels, as you buy them. If some of these are hold-overs from his own infancy, be sure to tell him this. Let him help you prepare the bassinet. If he is to be moved into a new bed or a new room, do this some time in advance of the great event, so your little first one won't have a strange unhappy feeling that the baby has taken his place.

Your child may not know what a new baby looks like. It's a good idea to prepare him by telling him how little he was when he was a baby. Show him with your hands how small the new baby will be. Tell him that new babies can't walk or talk at first—they can only cry; that they don't eat the things he does but only drink milk, just as he did. Make him understand that it will be quite a while before the baby will be old enough to play with him. Let him look forward to ways he will be able to help when the new baby comes, bringing diapers when the baby needs one, washing the baby's feet very carefully when mother gives him a bath, helping push the carriage when he and you and the baby all go out for a walk.

Gift for older child. It's an excellent idea to plan in advance for something happy to happen for the older child to mark the day of the new baby's arrival.

With all the gifts and excitement centering around the newcomer, be sure there is a gift for the older child to celebrate his becoming a big brother or sister. Plan so he will be the one to spread the glad tidings of the baby's arrival by telephone and personal calls, to grandmother, to neighbors and friends.

Daddy can take over some of the child's routine care. Perhaps he is already a partner in these activities. Perhaps he can be the one to help with undressing, to give the evening bath, to tell the good-night story. It will help a great deal if your child feels daddy knows just how to care for him when mother leaves for the hospital.

Ready for nursery school? If your child is over three, you might consider starting him in nursery school some months before the baby's arrival. Nursery school doesn't always work out successfully for young children, but it will be a great help if your child adjusts happily, for nursery school will give him an outside interest to help tide him over the days when you are away from home. He will also feel less threatened by the new baby if school has become a happy part of his life.

Prepare child for your absence. Your absence from home is going to be a serious experience for your small child. You and his father should try to make this time as easy and pleasant as possible for him. Generally a child is happier and better adjusted if he can stay in his own home during this time instead of going to visit a relative or friend. The exception would be if he were going with a person or to a place that he knows very well and it had the aspects of a treat.

Choosing a caretaker. However, if he is to remain at home there must be a housekeeper or a grandmother or a friend, who can come to live at your house and take care of him. This brings up the question of cost and of the type of person to select. If possible, choose the person the child likes most to be with. Select a loving and companionable person rather than a spit-and-polish housekeeper. Choose a woman who seems to have insight into your child's feelings and understands that your child's happiness at this time is more important than anything else.

Many a mother is surprised when the time comes to leave her child for the hospital, to find how deep is her feeling of anxiety over his welfare. Prepare for this in advance by choosing the kind of person with whom you will feel safe in leaving your youngster.

Let your child get used, well in advance, to the idea that someone is going to come and take care of him while you go off to the hospital, where the doctor will help the baby to be born. If the housekeeper will be a grandmother or a friend, your child can be making plans with her and talking all this over for some time before she actually comes to stay. If you are employing a professional housekeeper have her come at least a week before you go, if this is possible. Certainly ask her to stop in for a few good visits with your child ahead of time, so that they can get acquainted.

If, on the other hand, he is to go away, make a game of pretending that he is taking the trip. Let him pack his bag and make believe he is leaving. Talk about who will take him and what he will see on his journey. Tell him where you will be while he is gone. If you can manage it, it is a good idea to walk or drive past the hospital and point out to him the building where you will be staying. He will not feel so deserted if he can visualize the place. Tell him you will phone or write often.

In packing his belongings for the trip include his favorite toy, so he will have something familiar and beloved to hold on to.

Prepare housekeeper in advance. When the housekeeper or the grand-mother arrives, take her on a tour of your home and show her—as well as tell her—where the various household supplies are kept. Orally given information is sometimes only partly heard while the listener is mulling over other questions; seeing a thing usually makes a definite impression. Talk to her about your child and what he is like and give her an idea how you handle him, so she can carry on in the familiar way.

You will add greatly to your child's comfort during this experience if you will write down for the person who is to care for him a list of the things he is accustomed to in his daily life. Start in a couple of months ahead of time, and take notes for a day or two of everything you do with him and for him. Write down what he likes for breakfast and how he eats it, what he wears, what he plays with and how. List his favorite dishes, the routine of his bath, what toy, if any, he sleeps with, how he goes to bed.

When you have jotted down every item you can think of, prepare two information sheets to leave with the housekeeper. One will be the Household Schedule. The other will be a collection of notes on the habits of your family, the things they like and the things they don't. These guidance sheets will be of invaluable help to the relative or housekeeper who is going to fill your place and who will want to keep your household running smoothly. They will be even more important to the security of your child during your absence.

Household schedule sheet. On the Household Schedule include: What time your husband gets up and what time your child rises. The usual time of meals. What time husband usually leaves for work, plus anything which must be done for him before he goes, such as packing his lunch, calling a taxi. What time your child leaves for school, how he gets there and whether he must be taken to the bus. What he wears if the weather is normal and what if it gets colder or hot. What time your child gets out of school, and approximately when and how he gets home.

What your child usually does, and plays with, at various times of the day: outdoors with his tricycle, indoors with blocks, blowing soapbubbles. What activities are forbidden and how you handle such situations. How far the older child is allowed to range around the neighborhood. What friends come and play with him (their telephone numbers). Bathtime and bedtime for your child. What deliveries are made on what days and at what times.

List family habits. Under the listing of Family Habits you will want to jot down the following: What your family eats for breakfast. The kind of meals you usually have (dinner at noon or night). Add a few sample menus. The things your family particularly likes to eat; things they balk at.

The special cup from which your child likes to drink his milk, the particular toy he likes to take to bed; all the little things your child is used to having around him.

Routine of going to bed—whether child gets a story, which one he likes, how long and when.

Do you leave him a night light? Which one and where. Do you open or close the window, open or close the bedroom door?

Does your child get up at night, and when; what do you do about it, if anything, if he wets his bed.

With details like this your housekeeper will be saved many an innocent misstep. She will also have a ready answer for many of the questions which may come to her.

List telephone numbers. This is one more list you will want to have ready. A housekeeper must know how to get in touch with your husband's office, how to direct friends to you, how she can get in touch with the children's grandparents, or a friend or neighbor of yours in case she wants to turn for advice to someone who knows the family well. A list like the following right beside the telephone will be a big help:

Your husband's telephone number, and the name and address of his firm.

The name of your hospital, number and address.

Your doctor's name, numbers and addresses.

Child's doctor's name, numbers and addresses.

Grandparents' numbers and addresses.

Name, number and address of a neighbor or a friend whom the housekeeper may call.

Name of drugstore, address and telephone number. Grocery where you shop by phone. Name of laundry and phone number. Child's school.

Ask a friend to help. An arrangement which a lot of mothers have found gives them comfort is to ask a trusted friend or neighbor to drop in at the house once in a while, to see how things are going and to ask whether they can be of help. This can be of real assistance to the person you have left in charge, who may have a question or two about some of your accustomed ways with which she won't want to trouble your husband. Even a grandmother who is familiar with your household may be glad to have someone to discuss things with occasionally.

Also this gives you an additional channel to news from home. You will welcome every tidbit of news which your friend reports, particularly since most hospitals have become so strict about allowing children to visit. It will be cheering and reassuring to have your friend drop you a daily line, call up, or come to report the family's doings.

Keep in touch with your child. If you are to have a private or semiprivate room, you will probably have a telephone by your bed and can call your child every day at a certain time. This will help very much to bridge the gap of your absence. If this is not possible (or even if it is) take a collection of picture postcards to the hospital and send him one every day. The postman's visit will become an important event in your child's day. Lay up a collection of simple toys, preferably toys that require activity: a coloring book, a puzzle, a pull-toy, a boat to float in the bathtub. Daddy can bring one of these home after his visit at the hospital. They can be, in turn, a present from mother, a present from the new baby, a present from daddy.

Daddy can also tell the child what mother is doing and what the baby is doing—how he cries, how he sleeps, how he squeezes up his little face and yawns, how he drinks—just the way big brother used to drink when he was little and in the hospital. But don't expect too much interest from your child or devote too much conversation to the newcomer. What your child wants most is to have his mother come home and take care of him again.

Plan for new experiences for your child while you are away. Perhaps a friend or neighbor would invite him for lunch. Perhaps he can visit the zoo, or a movie long enough to see the animated cartoon, or take a ride on a bus or streetcar. New experiences will help him compensate for the lack of his mother. In addition, he can draw pictures for her, write letters to her, send messages by daddy. He can help get things ready at home for the day when she will be back.

Stage set your homecoming. Plan in advance that when you come home from the hospital daddy or the practical nurse will carry the baby into the house. Keep your arms free for your older child. Pay no attention to the baby, even if he cries, unless your child directs your attention to him. It's a good idea not to offer to show him the baby until he asks to see him. Then show him how to be gentle, do not grab his hand away if he wants to touch the infant. Guide it gently instead.

Introduce the baby to your older child. "Here is your big brother. Isn't he a nice boy?" (But don't overdo the "big" angle. Your child may be undecided at the moment whether he really wants to be big.)

Ask relatives and friends in advance to greet the older child when they come before asking to see the baby. Then ask Big Brother to show the baby to them.

How your child meets the baby, and how you feel toward your first child after the new baby comes are important to the future relationship. Plan your homecoming carefully, well in advance, so you can give your older child what he desperately needs at this time—the sense that he is very near and dear to you and though it's wonderful to have a new baby, no other child could ever take his place.

When you and your firstborn are together again, remember from time to time to talk about his trip, or his stay at home, and your trip when you went to the hospital to have the new baby. This will help him to accept the experience even if at the time it was a shock. It is a mistake to conclude that a child has forgotten an experience just because he does not talk about it. Always be careful to explain the reason you had to go, and to say that you missed him and were so glad to see him when you got back. To a small child a parent's illness often feels like rejection and death like a desertion. Make sure that your child is told very clearly that you regretted the separation.

—By Evelyn Emig Mellon

THE FATHERLESS FAMILY

HOW can I run a house and bring up the children without a husband to help?" Many mothers are asking this question today as widowhood comes to many women and as divorce statistics rise.

How can a mother left alone be reasonably happy herself and help her children grow up without their father? The chances are that if she can make a fairly satisfying life for herself, they will survive pretty well too. But where does she begin?

Before a woman can face the responsibility for making a home without a husband's help, she must face her grief. Some women have the gift of tears, and cry unashamedly through the first weeks or even months of separation. Others need to think and talk to friends, or work feverishly on house or garden. Spilling out troubles makes most of us feel better—friends' shoulders were made to cry on.

One young widow learned that keeping up a brave front for the sake of the children was doing the family more harm than good. Children have an uncanny knack of absorbing the serenity or distress of their mothers, no matter what words we may use to disguise our true feelings. The children in this case copied their mother and bottled up their feelings, too. Instead of setting loose their misery so it could be squarely acknowledged, they threw rocks at the dog, battled with each other, teased the baby and grew sullen with their mother. When the little girl finally asked, "Don't you *care* if Daddy is gone?" the mother saw her mistake. If children know why mothers weep and are reassured that they are not responsible for daddy's departure, they are not likely to be hurt by their mother's tears. In fact, they may be helped to let out their own natural grief.

Any woman feels shaken and miserable when she loses a husband, but she must pull herself together eventually and face a few practical facts. Often the first question must be—can she continue to live in the same house or must she move into a smaller place or share her parents' home? The eventual decision may be based entirely on finances, but usually it is influenced by that first feeling of fright or inadequacy about running a house and bringing up children all alone. The desire to go home to mama is strong in all of us, no matter how grown-up we may be.

Living with Parents

During the last war, many mothers did live with their parents and many of them found it very pleasant. It was cheaper and grandma was there to help with the children. But the majority of mothers whose husbands are gone say that keeping a separate home is very important for the children, even if it means economizing on rent or extras. Children are often confused by discrepancies between parents' and grandparents' standards. Your own young family seems to lose its identity when merged with an older household. Unless you are certain that you, your parents and your children understand each other and get along well, or unless the financial picture looks impossibly black, it is usually better to wait a bit before deciding to give up your own diggings.

It's a good idea to wait a while, too, about taking a job. One of the troubles in a fatherless household always seems to be lack of money. Insurance or alimony rarely covers more than the barest essentials. So a mother's first reaction may be: "I've got to get out and earn."

If the children are small, however, a job outside the home poses many problems. It is very tempting to visualize the leeway that extra income would mean in the family budget. But before a mother rushes off to work, she must stop and ask herself, "Will that income really be extra?" What about income tax, the wages and food for the woman who takes her place at home, the laundry which may have to be sent out, transportation and lunches, not to mention extra clothes?

You can now deduct for expenses for care of your dependent children "if such care is to enable the taxpayer to be gainfully employed." But you should find an expert to check on your actual income tax situation before you count on many luxuries from your new income. Even more important in the long run is the question: What effect will mother's working have on the children? Some little children are disturbed when they have their mother for only a short time in the evening; some older children are sensitive to their mother's absence when their father is gone. They are angry when you cannot attend the school play or chauffeur them to afternoon meetings and parties. They want to be very sure that at least *one* parent is ever-present and dependable, otherwise they may feel that their whole world has gone to pieces about their ears.

The Working Mother

Also, a question to ask oneself is, "How will the job affect the kind of mother I am when I get home? And how can the housekeeping get done without wearing me to a frazzle?"

If her job is a tough one, demanding patience, tact and imperviousness to tension and noise, it may be too much for a woman alone to also handle the children's end-of-the-day turbulence when she gets home. Another thing to keep in mind is, if the job does not pay well enough for much household help and the children are not old enough to handle bedmaking, vacuuming, and dishwashing efficiently, mother's health may suffer. (See article, "Should A Mother Work?")

Some women have found that they can make the extra money the family needs through part-time jobs: nursing, typing, specialty baking or dressmaking, substitute teaching, nursery school work, tutoring, or giving music or art lessons. Some skill you have may produce just enough income to balance the budget and still not take you away from home all day long.

Sometimes it helps to rearrange small habits of daily living to make the whole family more comfortable. This is not easy to do. Some women hesitate to change the old ways because of loyalty to absent husbands. Some of us still go on having dinner at seven, even though dinner at five-thirty may mean more time with the children after dinner, time for games, music or reading aloud. But whatever the course we chart, we must all realize that nothing is gained by becoming a martyr.

Some women who have lived alone with their children for many years report that it was helpful when they decided not to eat every meal with the children. As one mother put it, "The children were distracting, the food was pretty simple and I never sat down long enough to eat a decent meal." She found her whole day improved by looking forward to her own special tray by the fire after the little ones were in bed and the older boy was doing homework. And she didn't just warm up the left-overs of the children's meal. She prepared food that she especially liked.

How to avoid self-pity. But try as a woman will, the private tiger of lonely women—self-pity—lurks in the living room waiting to appear after the last child is kissed goodnight, and it takes a resolute campaign to rout him. We all know that evenings are the lonely times. Yet two hours per evening amount to sixty hours a month—enough to produce satisfying results in almost anything you want to do. Some of those hours always go for tasks like ironing and mending, but it's lethal to fritter away all of that precious time on chores. Evenings alone at home offer wonderful opportunity for learning new skills or pursuing old hobbies: learning to play a musical instrument, to make clothes, learning a new language with phonograph records, sculpturing, developing films, decorating furniture or china, making jewelry. But perhaps most important is going out one or two evenings a week. It makes a tremendous difference in the morale of the whole family and is well worth the price of a sitter. Even the smallest towns offer movies, church clubs, hospital work and perhaps a dramatic or singing group. The larger towns often have adult evening classes in the high schools, where you can learn all sorts of things. Also, the PTA, the League of Women Voters and other worthwhile groups would be delighted to have your active support.

Social Life

Some evenings will, of course, be social. Adult friends are never so dear as when one spends the whole day with children. Human affection is the best thing that grows, wherever you find it, and the interest and support of friends often bucks you up when life looks too difficult. Of course, the social life of the lone woman presents problems in most towns. Fortunately, formal dinners are becoming rare, so your fifth-wheel status is usually less conspicuous than you at first expect. And though it seems inconceivable at first, the time will come eventually, if you are widowed or divorced, when you may not be without an escort. The healthy need for the affection and companionship of a mate may reassert itself. Meanwhile, keep yourself and your home interesting enough so that your friends will want to keep in touch with you and include you in mixed parties. It is fun to have a few friends in for a buffet supper and let the children help, too.

Each woman has her own ways of keeping busy and filling her life with interesting things to do and with interesting companions. As soon as we can begin to add a little fun to living, we find that our new way of life becomes less burdensome. We feel more cheerful and so do the children.

But there remains the second part of our two-fold problem: how can we help our children grow up without their father?

Whatever the cause of a father's absence, his departure is a real shock to any child, and he needs time to think it through and react in his own way. One little boy, whose father was killed in an accident, went through the neighborhood like a whirlwind, beating up every boy who crossed his path. (His mother discovered that he was trying to prove to himself that he didn't need his daddy to protect him but could protect himself.) A big girl of nine returned to playing with toys she had long scorned as "babyish" while she got used to her father's absence in the Navy. Many children between ten and adolescence seem to abhor the expression of emotion in any form. They, too, are suffering, even if they betray themselves only by slamming doors and yelling insults at their friends. After the dust has settled and mother can talk about it, the children can be helped to talk about it too, and so together they will learn to face the inevitable without self-pity or resentment.

Divorce in the Family

In the case of divorce, many children are not only wounded by their father's seemingly unreasonable disappearance, but feel that they thus become unique objects of scorn and amazement to their friends. Occasionally, some wrathful playmate—wanting to hit where it will be sure to hurt—may yell, "Well, *you* haven't got a father!" All you can do is soothe your own child through whatever pain this may cause him. It won't last. If other fatherless children can be brought into the picture, their matter-of-fact acceptance of their lot may be reassuring, too.

On the other hand, the natural callousness of children, although shocking at times, can even be beneficial. One girl of twelve was heard to say to a friend, "My father and mother are divorced now. What do you think of that?" Fists clenched, mouth tense, she waited for the reply. Her friend shrugged her shoulders and remarked, "So what?" Thousands of families in America are living without fathers, and often children seem to accept this kind of family much more casually than their parents do.

Children also accept a new order of household responsibilities more cheerfully than we might expect. As far as physical work goes, distributing some of father's household jobs probably does no harm, if the children can carry them without undue strain. Many boys and girls love the extra responsibility of a really important grown-up job. Marketing, home repairs, hanging up and sorting laundry, simple ironing, vacuuming, gardening, taking down screens and car-washing can all be satisfying chores if the boy or girl is capable of them.

But when we approach the reassignment of father's responsibilities and relationships we are on dangerous ground. It is so easy to say to a boy of eight, "You're the man of the house now. You must take your father's place." A boy that age has enough to do trying to keep moderately clean, do his homework, get to school on time and keep up with his friends. To ask him to play an adult role, too, to keep his mother happy and be a father to his baby sister—that is an impossible burden.

It is easy, too, to bask in a son's devotion without reckoning with the day when he must be free to give his whole love to the girl he wants to marry. We all know men who never married because they "couldn't find a girl as wonderful as mother." American women are often accused of stifling their sons with "smother love." The temptation is great for those who have no other man in their lives.

Child's Reactions to Divorce

When divorce is the reason for a father's leaving, children are often unreasonably angry with their mothers and blame them for his departure. If a little girl is at an age of great closeness to her father, she particularly may feel rejected and often suffer more acutely than her brothers. Girls do not

usually gain family stature by their fathers' absence as boys may. Nevertheless, some girls seem to grow in understanding and kindliness as they take more responsibility for cooking, ironing or helping care for the younger children.

But no matter how cheerfully our children take on new jobs, they still remain children, beset by the usual assortment of growing pains. It seems to take more deliberate effort to be as firm with them when they need discipline as we were before our husbands left. As many of us learned during the last war, there are real hazards for both mother and child in the increased need each feels for the other when daddy is gone. We catch ourselves thinking, "My children are all I have left," and at those moments, carelessness, disobedience and back-talk are easy to overlook. Without knowing it, we may be bargaining for their all-important love by too much doting and too little discipline.

A lone mother who loved her children deeply realized that they were getting away with murder because she was too anxious to have a "happy, peaceful home." Her daughter, for example, had not made her bed for months and her son had borrowed six weeks ahead on his allowance. The atmosphere became much healthier after she began to firmly insist that the bed be made before breakfast and refused to be touched by anguished pleas for "just one quarter—I'll pay it back, honest." She found that children do not stop loving mama because she is firm.

In spite of the well meaning advice of friends who say, "Now you must be both mother and father to your children," a mother cannot possibly be a father. The best she can hope for is to be as good a mother as she can and help her children meet friendly men who can occasionally do for them what a father might do. Grandfathers, uncles, friends, scoutmasters all help to fill this need.

Child's Preparation for Adulthood

Often the woman without a husband asks, "What kind of preparation are my fatherless children getting for future marriage?" We know that to a great degree children pattern their ideas of family life on their own early experiences. And there are unpleasant figures showing that children from broken homes are less successful in their marriages than children who grew up in normal families. But statistics have no magic power over us. Common sense tells us that happy, mature men and women, who know how to live comfortably in a group, are likely to be happy husbands and wives. If our children feel that they are a cherished and important part of an affectionate and cooperative family, the chances are they will be well prepared for adult responsibilities and perhaps even more eager to make their own families happy and normal than children who have always taken these things for granted.

No matter how well a woman comes to operate a fatherless family, holidays and family emergencies may from time to time upset the balance. She may sit down at the breakfast table on her birthday, rejoicing in the cheerful clamor of the children and their homemade presents, and suddenly the bottom drops out and she finds herself choking on the coffee. She fills stockings alone at Christmas and feels pathetic and a little bitter. When the children all have chicken pox at once, the furnace breaks down and the car keeps developing mysterious complaints, she feels as if her load were too heavy to bear.

There is no pat solution for these recurrent crises or for the melodramas which are a part of every normal household. One big help is to fall back on friends and relatives and plan to be with them when you foresee the need of their friendly support. Many people hesitate to offer help, but are delighted to have you say, "Tomorrow is my birthday and I wish you'd come and help celebrate." Or, "My bureau drawers are sticking and the pole in the coat closet keeps falling down. Would you come over some Saturday and fix them?"

After the first months of confusion and discouragement, you will notice one day that things are going a little better than you thought they could. Allowing for days of backsliding, when you feel like weeping and the children ask, "Why can't we have a daddy like other kids?" there are more and more days when life is full of interesting things to do and the children seem contented and pleasant people.

You are amazed at the inner strength you seem to develop in the difficult process of steering your family's fortunes alone. Even the young shoulders seem to broaden to carry their part of the extra load. When you see that you and your children are surviving as healthy, comfortable people in spite of your loss, you can be very proud.   —By Martha Collins Johnson

SHOULD A MOTHER WORK?

THE question, "Should wives work?" always fires discussion. My work brings me in daily contact with many mothers—some who are working outside their homes, others who are considering such work, and many more who come to our social welfare agency for financial assistance so that they may stay at home with their children. From my familiarity with the problem, I believe that the decision to work must be made by each mother in the light of her own situation.

A mother must ask herself whether her working will result in a happy child, a satisfied husband, a companionable home life, a better community.

Or will her working cause her youngster to feel deprived of a normal, happy childhood, her husband to feel he is an inadequate mate and provider? Will her home become a schedule-ridden household? Because of her decision to work, will the community eventually have to deal with a broken home or a potentially delinquent child?

Even if a mother decides to work, she must continue to review the correctness of her decision. Her child's feelings, her husband's attitude and her own desires may change, and what once seemed a wise plan may later become a questionable one.

The first question a mother should ask herself when she is considering going to work is "Why?" A mother may see working as the only way to get Johnny a bicycle so that he'll be like all the other children on the block. She may see her going to work as the only means of setting aside a fund for Johnny to go to college. She may wish to have Johnny go to the summer camp which other youngsters in the neighborhood attend. But the questions we must ask this mother are: Are you interested in Johnny or are you trying to keep up with the Joneses? Are you trying to make up to Johnny in material ways for something you feel you are not giving him in your mother-child relationship? Are you seeking some emotional outlet outside your home because you are not happy and satisfied and yet know the true reason wouldn't be acceptable to your family and friends? Or will you be a happier person and better mother if you work?

Some Mothers Need to Work

I am reminded of Joe and Martha Smith. Joe insisted that Martha give up her job when they married because his family and friends would think he was not doing well if she continued. Monty was born 13 months later. Martha's home routines were excellently organized. She divided her time so minutely that to the horror of her friends, even Monty's "play and hug" time had an hour in the morning and afternoon. She did not enjoy the long periods alone with Monty when he sought her undivided attention. Since there were no children in their immediate neighborhood, when he was three she made arrangements with high-school girls to take Monty to the park in the afternoon for an hour or two. She found both Monty and she were happier when they were separated for this time each day. Later she felt she would be a better mother if she were away regularly for a brief period during the day and Monty could attend nursery school with children his own age.

Some mothers are unable to be good mothers over long periods of time, but like Martha, they are better mothers if they do not spend 24 hours a day straining to be mothers according to the book. Part-time employment may be the answer for this type of mother.

There are some mothers who consider working because they are not satisfied with being mothers only. They believe that to be good mothers they must have work away from home, as well as contacts which are not available to them through social clubs and community activities. In such cases these women may actually be better mothers because they have this outside job satisfaction. They return from their work eager for their hours of companionship with their children. Such women, happy in their responsibilities, are able to transfer these positive feelings to their children. This is especially true of the woman who has trained herself in a career or has a chosen field. She may enjoy being a mother but gets satisfaction in her work too. Combining these two achievements, she may be an ideal mother for her child. Even giving her child some of the additional material things may add to her satisfaction in motherhood.

Butch was ready to enter first grade when his mother decided to return to her job in the personnel office of a large department store. She had been on leave since he was born. Butch wanted his mother all to himself. He didn't like sharing his mother with his father. The best meal of the day was at noon when he was alone with her.

When It's a Mistake to Work

When Alice walked Butch to school the morning he started on a full day, she told him that soon someone else would be taking care of him during the day as she was going back to work. She described Arnee, the woman who was going to come each morning to take care of him, but he seemed uninterested. She told him she expected him to be a good boy so Mommy wouldn't have to worry about him while she was away. She'd try to bring him a little present every day from the store where she was to work and in detail described the wondrous things that were there. His only reply was, "Are you going to work with Dad?" Each noon Butch came home breathless, saying, "Oh, I was afraid you wouldn't be here when I got back."

The morning that Arnee failed to appear, Butch waited to go to school while Alice called several friends to see if he could come for lunch and stay after school. Her husband had no suggestions. He had not been in favor of Alice's returning to work, but had not told her, because he knew she wanted many things he could not provide and that she missed her many friends.

When Alice couldn't make any satisfactory arrangements, she called her office to explain her absence and walked Butch to school. She talked to Butch's teacher about his problems and his progress. In this talk and a later one with the school counselor, Alice became aware that she should not be a working mother. It was important for her to stay at home for the time being if she wanted a happy Butch and a happy husband. She realized, too, that she was not happy in her work as she was in a state of conflict about it. Moral: some mothers should work and some shouldn't.

Public disapproval. Even mothers who do not work are not with their children every hour of the day. Our community encourages mothers to join clubs, social and educational in nature, for it recognizes that outside interests create happier mothers and in turn happier children. However, the mother who is thinking about working must realize that, although she may not be away from her home as many hours as her neighbor who is participating in a club or social activity, the censure of leaving children is reserved for the mother who earns money. This censure is less severe toward the woman who helps her husband in his work or business than toward the one who earns money. The criticism is often reflected in the attitude of relatives, neighbors and friends by setting for the children of working mothers higher standards of behavior in play, speech and dress than for the children of non-working mothers. A mother must carefully consider the environment in which she leaves her child, for the hostility felt by a family, neighborhood or community toward a working mother may be turned upon the child. A well-adjusted, happy offspring of a working mother reared by a warm, outgoing person whom he knows as his nurse and housekeeper may be completely offset by an experience in which his mother's love for him is questioned. He may suddenly reason that if he were loved, his mother would not leave him to go to work. Other mothers stay at home. Bob's mother stays home and she says that if his mother were a good mother she would stay home too.

Arrangements for Child Care

It is obvious that no mother can work unless she can arrange for adequate care for her child during her absence. Adequate care means that a child is loved, protected, enjoyed and wanted by some person or some group while the mother is away from home. It is not parking service or custodial care. It is an extension of the home life the child enjoys when the parents are at home. It is an arrangement which to the mother's satisfaction (and with the father's sanction) protects her relationship with her children and makes it possible for her to perform one job at a time, although it may never relieve her of the responsibility of the others.

Such care may be available in a good nursery school where physical, cultural and social standards are compatible with the family's own standards and the child is an accepted member of the group. It may be present in his own home with a carefully selected homemaker who teaches the child through example what constitutes good, happy living. Such a homemaker must understand and accept the reasons for the mother's working or she can, in subtle ways, undermine the relationship between parent and child. Or arrangements for care may be in the home of a foster mother who can give the child the warm companionship of a capable and outgoing adult. Or he may be cared for by a grandmother or other relative or friend living in his home. But whatever the kind of care, it can only be considered adequate if it makes the child feel that he is wanted and loved, that his mother is working part of the day but is coming back to him. And it is adequate care only if it relieves the mother of the tensions and strains that are too apt to be a part of this "double life" that she is leading.

Adequate care is usually expensive so that a large part of the mother's earnings may be spent in wages for an exceptionally good person to care for the child. This expenditure is important for both husband and wife to consider in evaluating the advisability of the mother's working. It may be that the costs of arranging for substitute care, delegating responsibility for household management, purchasing foods which may be more expensive but which can be quickly prepared, buying additional clothing suitable for work, lunch and transportation costs and other necessary work expenses will offset any financial benefit derived from the mother's working. It should be economically as well as socially sound for the mother to work unless her employment is solely for emotionally therapeutic purposes.

Strains of "Double Life"

The emotional and physical strain of leading "a double life" should be carefully reviewed by any mother who is considering working. If she is unable to pay for service to do the heavy housework, she must consider whether she is physically able to carry two jobs. Her ability to do two jobs is tempered by her own personality characteristics and standards. If she is a worrier about punctuality, she may develop insomnia, fretting about getting to work on time. If she is an inveterate schedule maker and keeper, she will upset her family by too complex an organization of her life and theirs. If she is a "dig in the corners" cleaner or a snow-white laundry producer, her problems in carrying the two jobs will be more difficult than those of the easygoing mother who is satisfied with a "lick and a promise" for the house, but who realizes it is important to have time for companionship with her children.

The working mother who feels guilty or uneasy about the plans she has made for her children is doing a disservice to her children, her husband, her employer and herself. She will receive none of the satisfaction of working except the salary and then, because she is feeling guilty, she may use the money extravagantly to buy useless gifts for her family.

Any experienced working mother can testify to the tensions created in arranging for adequate care and to the guilt brought about by compromises that are sometimes necessary to retain a job. Working mothers interested in their children's welfare realize that there must be continuity in the arrangements they make for their care if they are to keep the children from becoming upset.

A mother must also consider what she will do if her child becomes ill. Is the care she has arranged adequate so that she can go to work or must she remain at home if her child is ill? If she stays home, will she be fearful lest she lose her job and thus make the child feel guilty because he is sick? Will she be so disturbed that the child is ill that she will shower him with such abundant attention that the child will see in being sick a way to keep his mother at home?

Effects on the child. The mother must consider other possible effects on her child if she works, all related to the kind of mother she is. One has been mentioned earlier—the child's feeling he is different from other children because his mother works. Such a child may have his activity circumscribed because the mother is fearful of his safety while she is away from home. She may be the kind of mother who insists that the child should not play outdoors after school until she returns from work, for fear that he may do something that may cause people to be critical. She may make demands on the child to carry many household chores. This may require that he sacrifice playtime with his friends whose mothers are home and he will be resentful. She may tell the child that the reason why she is working is that she wishes him to have more material things even though her work is exhausting. The child may not accept these reasons and may create his own fantastic alternative reasons. He may, when faced with a trying school situation, use the absence of his mother to excuse undesirable behavior, because he feels it would be an acceptable reason for his unacceptable behavior.

However, these same problems may crop up if the mother is home, for they are closely related to the kind of person she is. She may be stifling the children's development by not permitting them freedom and latitude in growing up. She may throw all her energies into her home and the bringing up of her children and not participate in community activity.

Husband's Attitude

How does your husband feel about his wife's decision to work? This must be considered in deciding for or against working. Is the mother thinking about working because she wishes to punish her husband and knows he will be embarrassed by her employment? Does she believe that by working or threatening to work she can inspire him to increase his income so that he can insist that she remain at home? Does she wish to prove to her husband, perhaps, that she has ability which others can recognize even if he does not? If so, there is something wrong in the basic husband-wife relationship.

The decision to work should only result from mutual agreement between husband and wife. Then together they must plan for their child's security. Together they must plan their budget. Together they must evaluate what working will mean to their relationship; they must know how each feels about it. Unless the husband concurs in the advisability of his wife's working because it is for his, her and their best interests, he will have continuous conflict, especially when questions are raised by his family, friends and business associates. Even under the best circumstances there are times when he may question his adequacy as a husband and wage earner.

Unless husband and wife are secure with each other, there may be competition between them for job recognition. The wise wife will be aware that her work must not be a threat but rather a treat and it must be a tool for building her relationship with her husband, not destroying it.

The mother with a job will have many adjustments to consider: for example, if her child is not to feel deprived, she should try to make some arrangement with her employer so that she can attend those school functions in which mothers and schoolchildren jointly participate. Her vacations and weekends must be free for the family. A mother who contemplates working must carefully consider what a satisfactory balance between home and job involves and how each has the right to expect the best the mother has to give.

—*By Ruth Schley Goldman*

IF YOUR FAMILY MOVES

MILLIONS of American families are on the move these days. Added to the tribulations and trials of moving is the need to adjust to a new house, a new neighborhood. This may be somewhat difficult for everyone, especially for the children.

"Mother, I don't like the kids around here. Why did we have to move?"

A remark of that kind is common enough at such a time, but it is particularly hard for a mother to bear. Perhaps you have been up to your neck in work all day, pushing boxes and crates around. The rug that you thought you had measured so carefully doesn't seem to fit as it should. The refrigerator sticks out just far enough for you to bump your funny bone each time you pass it.

At that point you, too, have begun to wonder, "Why did we have to move?" It will not be particularly helpful, however, to give in to depression. The chances are that the house will begin to look homelike after a few days. But what about your son or daughter? Helping the child in his adjustment to a new home, school and neighborhood is an important job for his parents.

Some of it begins long before moving day. It is not likely that the child has had any voice in the decision to move. Property values change, daddy gets a new job, an expected baby makes a roomier place necessary. These are adult matters; but whatever the reason, the child needs to be told about it, to help him feel that he is in on the planning. Tell him as much as you can about his new home. Be explicit about where it is. If he's old enough and you're moving quite a distance he'll enjoy looking up the location on a map. What kind of a house will you have? Describe it to him in detail. If you are building your own home, he'll probably be interested from the first blue-print stage to the hanging of the last strip of wallpaper. If it is an apartment, give him a picture of its size and layout. If possible take him to see it, but warn him in advance if the place is unfurnished so that the emptiness will not startle him. Remember you can visualize the new curtains and just where each piece of furniture will go, but he sees only bare rooms and floors gritty with plaster dust. You might make a rough drawing of how his room will look in the future, and decide together where his furniture will be placed.

When you discuss the move, make the advantages clear to your youngster. He'll have an opportunity to make new friends, or perhaps he'll have his own room for the first time or he'll be near a favorite cousin. Give him a happy picture of the future, but be sure it's realistic. Include the disadvantages if you foresee any. When he finds that you, too, will be sorry to leave friends and a familiar atmosphere he won't be so worried about his own misgivings.

Allow Time for Child

When it's time to start packing, set aside a morning to go through his toys with him. Remember these are his prized possessions, so let him decide which he wants to discard, which to give away, which to take. In the excitement he may part with an old battered Teddy bear, but if you know it's one of his favorites, rescue it from the give-away pile—your child will be happy to see this old friend in his new room.

Don't worry about keeping your youngster amused while you pack; let him help wherever he can. Even a toddler can hand you books to put into cartons. The busier he is with the actual business of moving the more co-operative he's apt to be. This will be especially true if you create a general atmosphere of anticipation rather than strain and drudgery.

Moving day. On moving day you're all packed and ready. Relax and take it in your stride. Your child will take his cue from you so don't look as though the end of the world had come. Of course you'll have lots to do, but don't forget to be reassuring. If it will be difficult to prepare a meal that first evening in your new home, take along a casserole or cold dish favorite.

Chances are you won't have time to do much about arranging furniture the first day, but straighten out your child's room even if you haven't time for anything else. It won't matter if you go to bed in a disorderly room, but it will make a big difference to him if his belongings are in place. Before you tuck him in, be sure he knows where the bathroom is, where lights are and where your room is in relation to his. Tell him you'll be in the minute he calls in the morning—and keep your promise!

First Day at New School

His first day at the new school is a big experience. An older child may consider it a great indignity for you to take him to school—not so the younger child. But at least give the older child a paper with his teacher's name and room number so that he will have exact information. The new child at school is often subjected to a great deal of questioning by his playmates, so a little briefing on family data may come in handy. Does your eight-year-old know his father's occupation and the ages of his brothers and sisters? Questions about nationality or religion can be embarrassing if he does not know the answers.

If your child has not wanted you to take him to school that first day, then make an early visit to the school. It is important for you to get acquainted with his teacher. Be active in the community and join the Parent-Teacher Association. You will make friends, and will also learn what kinds of community interests and problems are shared by other parents in the neighborhood. The more you know about his school, the better chance you have of helping your youngster adjust to it.

As every parent knows, children have an amazing capacity to make acquaintances. Perhaps even the first day when he comes home from school he will bring two or three extra playmates. Never mind the messy house, never mind the fact that you are as busy as can be—they won't notice if you welcome them with a smile and cookies and milk. If you are cordial to his new friends, it will help your child become a part of the group.

Your youngster may acquire some brand-new mannerisms and expressions or make requests for things he or she would like to have. Keeping up with neighborhood fashions gives children the feeling that they belong, that they are like their friends. Don't be too surprised if Sister suddenly decides she wants bangs, or if your son engages in a new game that seems senseless to you. These surface conformities help the child feel a part of the new group.

Longing for old friends. It is natural for a child to miss some of his old friends. Parents would have cause for worry if their youngster showed no regrets at not seeing his old pals. The child whose affections were that fickle would not be building a very sound base for satisfying relationships in adult life. Son and Sister need to be given the opportunity to express their homesickness and their longing for Sally and Buster and Buddy and Mary with whom they used to play. If the distances are not too great, try to visit these friends. If you've moved to another state, postcards will help fill in the gap and give the child a sense of continuity. As he is finding his place in the new setting, the return cards from his old buddies will be comforting to him.

Moving time is hard for all members of the family. The adults are busy and preoccupied with all their own concerns. Some of the old routines which have given solidarity to your child's experience may be lost in the shuffle. Some of them may really not be geared to the new setting. But it is important to try to continue some of the old family behavior patterns so that the youngster can see that this is the same old family that does things in the same old way. If he is used to going to his grandma's for lunch on Saturdays, even if it's inconvenient, now it is important to take him there. Or if you usually have ice cream in town on Friday evenings, try your best not to skip this Friday. These are the simple things which cause the person in later life to say, "In *our* family we *always* . . ." Perhaps it was not *always,* but the great positiveness with which adults recall such small things indicates how important they are. It is these little practices which contribute to the child's sense of the solidarity and constancy of the family unit.

Inconsistencies in Behavior

In the new setting the youngster may show sudden changes or inconsistencies in his behavior. He may surprise you with his grown-upness among the other children, and at other times return to childish habits you thought were outgrown. The strain of living up to the gang outside may make it necessary for him to be a little more of a baby within the family circle. There he knows he is loved, both when he feels like being big and when he feels like being a baby. Be patient with crying spells or outbursts of anger or aggression. They will disappear when he feels safer. Impatience, punishment and insistence that he's "a big boy now" will only increase the strain on him.

These outbursts will grow less frequent and intense if parents are understanding. By realizing that he is going through a difficult time and by helping him adjust to the new school, the new playmates, the new teacher, they can see that rough spots are smoothed and he is helped to find himself and enjoy his new home.
                                                        —*By Elizabeth G. Meier*

COMMUNITY LIVING

TIME OFF FOR MOTHER • CHILDREN IN HOSPITALS
HOW GOOD IS YOUR TOWN? • COMMUNITY SPIRIT
CHILDREN'S CONCERTS • FLUORIDATION FACTS
NEIGHBORHOOD SITTERS' EXCHANGE • SUMMER DAY CAMP
STARTING A PARENTS GROUP • BETTER SCHOOLS
PARENTAL HELP FOR HIGH SCHOOLS
JUNIOR HIGH SCHOOL PROJECT • ADULT FRIENDS OF CHILDREN

HOW TO GET A
DAY OFF FOR MOTHER

SUFFERING from an overdose of house and children? Tired and irritable from doing the job single-handed? Feeling generally inadequate? There's not much consolation in knowing that others feel that way too. But there is cheer in the thought that a nation-wide organization has recognized your need for time off.

If you're the mother we're talking about—with a preschooler or two keeping you housebound seven days a week, get in touch with your nearest YWCA. Ask about a "day-out-for-mothers" program. If they have none, there's a good chance that they'll get one started if you and your friends ask for it. But if their clubs already include one called "Ladies' Day Out," "Holiday from Apron Strings," "Our Day Out" or "YW Wives Nursery Group," that's your cue. Hie yourself and children there without delay. If there's no YW within reach see if you can't start a day-off-for-mother project in your neighborhood. Naturally it will have to be much simpler than that sponsored by the YW, but it can still offer a chance for young mothers to get together for recreation and sociability while their children are cared for. It's a worthwhile project for a PTA, women's club or a church group to undertake. It can offer recreation, adult companionship, intellectual stimulation, various activities guaranteed to take you out of the doldrums.

Varied Program Offered

If, on the other hand, you are fortunate enough to be near a YW you can probably have your pick of classes in arts and crafts, sewing, dancing, gym or swimming. You may find a weight-control class or a charm clinic; a skilled instructor to teach you dressmaking, millinery, furniture repair or bridge and canasta. Or a lively discussion group will help brush the cobwebs from your brain. In fact, here's your chance to do some of the things you've been wanting to "if you only had the time." The YWCA will do this for you and take care of your children too! At the end of the day you'll be delighted to see your children again and share tales of the day's doings. When dad comes home he'll find the tension gone, a cheerful home and a buoyant wife.

Maybe this reads more like fiction than fact, but it's a real event in the lives of thousands of mothers all over the country. Since the YWCA started the "day-out" program, it has been spreading rapidly in cities, small towns and rural areas from Maine to California. Several hundred local YW's now have programs that give mothers and their preschoolers a day apart and send them home happier, more relaxed and more companionable wives and mothers.

How the program works. There is no set pattern because local conditions vary. Each YW branch arranges the day to suit the needs and interests of its particular group of mothers. Here, for example, is how one mother spends her holiday and this is the way her day-out club functions. Helen, who now lives in Michigan, had moved three times in six years because of her husband's work. Each time their roots were pulled up they were farther from friends and family. With two children under four years, it was hard going for Helen until she heard about "Ladies' Day Out." Now Wednesday is a red-letter day for the whole family. Every week on that day, she gathers up her brood and heads for the YW. Once inside the door, with the small fry delivered to the nursery, their mother has six hours to do whatever she wants to do. She can spend her day at painting, ceramics, dressmaking, photography, or gym. Helen picks "Slimnastics" for her morning activity because as she puts it, "You exercise muscles you don't use in housework and you go home feeling perked up, especially after a dip in the pool."

After her swim, Helen dresses and joins the other day-outers at lunch. They have a wonderful time. But there's no discussion of home problems. This club has declared home and children a taboo subject at lunchtime. "We're here to think of other things," they explain. Perhaps they discuss current books with one of the members giving a book review. Occasionally there is a luncheon speaker. Sometimes one of the group reads aloud.

In the afternoon, Helen works with a small group in ceramics. She finds this relaxing after her morning workout and it gives her a sense of accomplishment. At 3:30, the holiday ends and Helen collects the children.

Child Care Arrangements

What kind of day do the children have? Usually just as exhilarating as Mother's. Arrangements for child care vary at the different Associations, depending on the number of children, their ages, the amount of time mothers spend at the YW, facilities and personnel available. The branch described above had space for a nursery and found in the community a former nursery educator who was available for one day a week. Three volunteer students from a nearby college helped care for the forty children.

Equipment for the nursery was collected by parents from families whose children had outgrown items like playpens, small tables and chairs, sandboxes and a variety of toys. The Junior Chamber of Commerce contributed a record player and a radio. A piano was moved into the nursery. The children's day runs somewhat like this: time for drawing, painting or modeling in clay; play period including singing games and the use of records; storytelling periods;

luncheon; free play period; nap or rest time; rhythms and a rhythm band. At the end of the day, there's usually a newly learned jingle to sing for mother and dad or a tangible product like a finger painting or clay object to take home. Helen's pottery and the children's clay animals now have equal billing on the family bookshelves.

You will find day-out programs as appealing as this one at other YWCA branches, with variations. The club setup may be duplicated in some but in others activities are likely to be as different as the interests of the day-outers.

In many Associations the program is naturally affected by the local facilities. Not all branches have swimming pools or gyms. Some have a roof or garden for children's outdoor play. In one branch a whole floor is set aside for nursery groups two days a week. Another uses a building next door with adequate space, kitchen and toilet facilities. In some communities, especially where the day-out program is new, only the simplest arrangements are possible.

Different Localities, Different Programs

Provision for the children depends upon the ingenuity of both local Y staffs and the mothers who assist in the operation of the nurseries. In one Association you may find the children playing in a corner of the recreation hall; in others an attic crafts room or residence room may be used. Some YWCA's are decentralized with a mobile staff reaching out from their base to smaller communities and often to outlying rural areas. Somehow they manage to find room for mothers' activities and child care in a housing project, in a church or other meeting place.

However simple the facilities may be at first, if the day-out project takes hold and fills a permanent need, the Association stands ready to help.

Have the mothers a voice in the kind of care their children get at the YW? "Try and stop them," said one director of women's programs. Since the groups are self-governing, the wives plan their own programs. The quality of the project, as well as its cost, are related to the amount of volunteer work the mothers will and can do in connection with the program activities. Whether they mean to or not, mothers—and fathers too—get involved when they see the gratifying results of their own and their children's group experiences.

One of the best examples of this is a Philadelphia YW group which decided to launch a cooperative nursery. The nursery is directed by a nursery educator and an advisory board of professionals. Mothers alternate as volunteer assistants, working one day and attending their own classes the next day. This project has developed into a family affair. In the evenings husbands join their wives and all work together on making equipment and props for the nursery.

Expenses Are Small

What does it all cost? Very little when you compare it with rates for hourly baby sitting or other hired help. This is a deliberate policy of all the Associations so that the group can be democratic. Mothers and children come from low, middle and high income brackets, representing a cross-section of the country. In most cases the Association assumes overhead costs including maintenance help. Charges for child care are kept low. At some YW's mothers bring lunch for their children and the Association provides milk and mid-morning juice and crackers. The only other charge is the small annual YWCA membership fee.

Who is eligible for membership? Anyone regardless of race, creed, color or economic status. The YWCA is an international movement committed to nonsectarian principles. For those who take part in the day-out project, the only requirement is that they join a YW Wives Club and attend one class a week. If there is no YWCA branch near your home, write for information to the National Board YWCA, 600 Lexington Avenue, New York 22, New York.   —*By Stella Applebaum*

HOSPITALS THAT LIKE MOTHERS AND HOW TO ENCOURAGE THEM

AT ten-thirty in the morning, in one ward of the Mount Sinai Hospital, New York City, a young mother dressed in a white gown is bathing her baby. Nearby a thirteen-month-old, just admitted, is getting acquainted with his new surroundings in his mother's arms. She hugs him reassuringly while the nurse takes his pulse. Beside a glass-enclosed crib with an oxygen tank attached, another mother sits silently watching a critically ill infant. Her presence may not help her baby—but it helps *her* to be there.

On another floor a father is playing checkers with a ten-year-old boy in a wheel chair. A mother is braiding her daughter's hair.

What has happened to make all this possible?

Several years ago, Mount Sinai Hospital began an experiment in its pediatric department. It lifted restrictions on visiting hours and invited parents to stay with their children as much of the day as they liked. Mothers come after breakfast and stay to tuck a child in for his after-lunch nap or rest. They may come back again at two in the afternoon and remain until after supper. The results of this experiment, and others like it at such places as Children's Hospital in Cincinnati and Syracuse Memorial Hospital, may well bring about a revolution in child care in hospitals throughout the country.

Visiting Arrangements

Unrestricted visiting does not mean that hospital wards will be crowded with parents all day long. In a ward of 24 beds, there are likely to be no more than six or seven parents at any given time. A mother may stay all day for the first day or two that her child is in the hospital—until the strangeness wears off—but after that the time she spends there with him will naturally be limited by the job she has to do at home. Liberal visiting hours allow her to see her child at times that are most convenient for her.

When an infant is hospitalized, the liberal visiting hours are especially helpful. Instead of visiting at 3 o'clock and spending an hour sitting beside a sleeping baby, a mother may come when it is time to feed her child.

The nurses at Cincinnati Children's Hospital tell how important this was to Mike who came to the ward a few hours after his birth for a serious bronchial operation. He weighed less than four pounds when he was operated upon. For weeks he needed constant medical and nursing supervision. Then he had a second operation, so that for six months he was under almost constant nursing care. His progress was slow and uphill and his care such that it was impossible to pick him up and give him much mothering. His doctors and nurses realized that Mike was being deprived of the fondling, caressing and physical contact he would normally have with his mother, so as soon as his condition permitted, Mike's mother was asked to come in and help take care of her baby in the hospital. She would come in at nine in the morning and stay until Mike's evening feeding at five. Besides giving him care in the ward, with the nurses' help, she carried him into the playroom in the afternoon where she rocked and talked to him. On sunny days she took him out into the yard under the trees. At first Mike did not smile at his mother as he did at the nurses he knew but by the end of the second week his broadest and sweetest smiles were for her. To the staff of the pediatric ward it was wonderfully exciting and rewarding to watch Mike and his mother getting acquainted.

Parents' Anxiety Eased

The parent who has spent several days in the ward quickly loses her anxiety about what is happening to her child in her absence. Far from increasing the work of the hospital, visiting mothers can and do actually help. At Mount Sinai mothers bathe and feed their children, carry trays back to the pantry, smooth the beds, fetch a glass of water, help a child into his slippers. Simply by being there, by playing with the children and helping to keep them amused and contented, they transform the ward into a happier place.

At Mount Sinai, mothers may go along to the X-ray room with their children or stay at the bedside while many of the medical procedures are taking place. Often a father comes to hold his child's hand during a treatment.

The staffs at both Cincinnati Children's Hospital and Mount Sinai feel strongly that parents should be with their children before and after surgery, whether it is a tonsillectomy or a major operation. At Cincinnati Children's Hospital all the private rooms are equipped with cots so that a parent can stay overnight. Nurses will also make a mother comfortable in the ward.

There are, to be sure, times when a hard-working hospital staff finds mothers somewhat trying. But Marion Steven, who for many years worked in the pediatric section of Syracuse Memorial Hospital, feels that the answer to this is *more*, not less contact between nurses and mothers.

Several years ago, an eight-year-old girl was rushed to a Milwaukee hospital gravely ill with pneumonia. Her parents were told to phone the hospital for information on their child's condition and to return in five days to see her, as visiting day was on Friday, from 2 to 3.

When the child was well enough to be moved her parents took her to a hospital in a nearby city to convalesce—a hospital where they could be with her several hours a day.

Returning home, the mother vowed that this would not happen again—to her child or any other in the city. She and a group of her friends talked the problem over with the hospital administrators. In Milwaukee, as in other communities, women are the most devoted supporters of voluntary hospitals. They are the driving force behind the Community Chests that provide funds for hospitals. Their voices, raised on behalf of more humane visiting hours, could not be ignored. Within a short time most Milwaukee hospitals responded by lifting their rigid restrictions.

Some of the changes that will improve our hospitals for children will take time, patience, money. More nurses, more doctors, newer buildings, increased medical knowledge all come slowly. But the experiments at Mount Sinai, Cincinnati Children's Hospital and other pathfinding hospitals throughout the country show that there is no hospital that cannot improve the quality of its care of children *today* by adding parents to its list of curative agents.

—*By Vivian Cadden*

MAKE YOUR TOWN
A GOOD PLACE TO LIVE

AT ten o'clock one sunny morning a boy walked out of a music store in a New Jersey town. The boy carried a glossy new violin case under his arm and there was a grin on his face.

A commonplace incident, you say, that could have happened in many towns? Yes. But also an incident that revealed a lot about this town—that in some ways it was a good place to live.

First, the presence of a music store is a healthy sign that there are worthwhile cultural interests in a community. Then, the parent buying a violin for his child is a sign that some people of the community are spending their money for the fine things in life and people who do that are apt to be good people to live among. The boy's grin suggested that there was, in that town, a spirit that encouraged children to take part in music—and probably other worthwhile activities as well. This would be likely to mean happy, busy young people.

Do you think this is jumping to conclusions that this town was a good place to live? If so, you are mistaken. It's the little everyday things, what people do, how they look, what they are interested in that are often the most important clues to how they live. No community is perfect, but some are better than others and it is interesting to know how yours stacks up. On the strength of interviews with national experts on community affairs, there are clues for you to look for in your town. Most of these can be seen simply by keeping your eyes open or by asking yourself and others questions.

Schools

Nothing is more vital in a community than its schools. You need not be an educator to know about them; there are clues you can pick up by visiting them and you can get many answers to your questions at a PTA meeting. If there is no strong, active PTA in your town that in itself is a bad sign. It suggests weak schools, but worse, it suggests lack of interest on the part of parents.

Look at the school grounds. It is desirable to have at least five acres around a grade school with one more acre for every 100 students. A high school, if possible, should have at least 10 acres of land plus one more acre for every 100 students. Look at the streets near the schools. They should be quiet and safe. If a school must be built along a busy road, there should be an overpass or underpass. One town bought land for six new schools and then discovered that five of the sites were on busy truck routes. Fortunately, the discovery was made before the schools were built. They were placed elsewhere.

Look at the classes in your schools: According to current professional opinion, there should be one teacher to 25 or 30 pupils. Even in crowded schools there should be no more than 35 pupils per teacher. Look at the schools' physical condition: Are buildings in good repair? Safe? Are classrooms well lighted, airy, clean, well arranged and equipped? Are desks adjustable to fit the individual child? Are washrooms modern and clean?

Keep in mind some clues that may tell you a lot about the quality of teaching: If teachers' salaries are at least slightly above the state average, if teachers are welcomed into the social life of their neighborhood and if they are free to take an interest and initiative in community affairs, the chances are your town will attract the best teachers.

Are your schools free of political pressure? Is the school board independent, elected by the citizens and responsible to them? It should be.

Look at the children: Do a large proportion of those who can afford it go on to college (a sign of strong teaching)? Are they free of tendencies to juvenile delinquency and snobbishness? Is the U. S. Supreme Court decision abolishing segregation in schools accepted and are Negro boys and girls going to school safely and happily in your town?

Is there a nursery school in your town? Is there a program of adult education? More and more schools offer such a program.

Churches and Cultural Centers

One town (pop. 38,000) is building or has built, fourteen new churches since the war. Your first clue: Is the church of your denomination alive? It is, if it is in good repair or perhaps building a new church or addition. It is, if it has a busy Sunday school. It is, if it is well filled every Sunday.

Your second clue: Are the churches of other denominations alive? The answer tells you whether or not people of all faiths have an opportunity to worship in your town. When they have, healthier community morale results.

Dr. Chester Rapkin of Columbia University's Institute for Urban Land Use gave those clues on churches, and also pointed out that the presence of a music store in town was a healthy sign of cultural activity. "Is there a music shop in town? A book store?" he asked. "These are two important indexes. People have an opportunity to buy records and musical instruments, and have a chance to browse—the fact that the stores are right there gives people a chance to be familiar with good music and books."

There are other indications of a town's cultural opportunities: a good library with plenty of cardholders (one per family is a good average), and with many of the latest books. A local symphony. A local little theater. A good museum. Don't let anyone tell you small towns don't have these things. Many do. The spread of orchestras, theaters and museums in America's small towns is one of the big developments of our time.

One of the nation's outstanding museums, to take just one example, is that of St. Joseph, Missouri. It has built fine collections on Indian relics, local and natural history, but the museum provides more than exhibits. There are art and pottery-making classes, and science clubs for children and adults. Like many museums today, it is fitting its programs to the community, and is making the town a better one to live in.

Homes

In Milwaukee even the low-cost homes with postage-stamp lawns have the lawns lined with flower beds. This is one detail that gives Milwaukee attractive homes where there would be slums in some towns.

The presence of slums—any slums—is a bad sign in a town, and you are paying for them with higher crime, juvenile delinquency, disease and accident rates than you would have without them. Conversely, owner-occupied, neat, clean homes are the best signs that people care about their town.

Other clues: Are homes reasonably spaced to provide both room for child play and privacy for the family? Sixty-foot-wide lots are a desirable minimum. Are there numerous healthy trees in home sections? Does everyone have a place to live? There should be no "Young family, desperate" ads in the local papers.

Neighbors Are Important

Are there enough children of similar ages in your neighborhood so that yours have plenty of playtime companions? Are your neighbors congenial when it comes to income and interests? Are newcomers greeted and quickly made part of the town? Look for a Welcome Wagon or a similar service performed by a community organization as well as individual friendliness.

And you may not have thought of this: Do your neighbors have hobbies? An expert ceramics man or a fly fisherman next door is a good neighbor and may be an indication of a lively town.

Job Opportunities

Ideally a community should provide jobs for all, with a wide range of kinds of jobs and a wide range of salaries.

Clues: Are jobs in your area varied enough to hold young people of different talents, training and ambitions? If most high school graduates stay in town, the answer is probably "Yes." Will there be jobs in the future? If industries are growing, there are likely to be. Are there many people on relief rolls? Is it simple to get a loan for a sound business venture? Do people of different races, religions and nationalities have a full chance of employment? If they have, the lack of discrimination and injustice will make your town happier.

Town Planning

The Timbercrest and River Oaks sections of Houston, Texas, are splendid examples of good zoning. Here for blocks and blocks are homes, and only homes, on ample grounds, with shady, winding streets.

Your clues are simple: Are there gas stations, cemeteries, laundries encroaching on home neighborhoods? Is there an airfield so near that planes fly low overhead? All are undesirable.

Is there an over-all town plan? Ask at City Hall. It should provide for the town's development, screen undesirable places out of home areas, and put factories where they belong—probably on one side of the town.

Is the town solving its problems, whatever they are—blighted areas, low-flying planes, grade crossings? If committees or commissions of citizens are at work on them, it probably is. City Hall or your local newspaper can tell you. Do not give up on a town because it has problems. The time for discouragement comes only if the citizens don't care and nothing is done.

Recreation

Madison, Wisconsin, which is located on two lakes, has boating, fishing and swimming right at hand, and thirty parks. Looking around Madison, you would see at once that it is a city that scores high on recreation. So are many towns on Long Island, New York, an island that has a dozen state parks, and provides water sports, games of all kinds, golf courses, picnicking facilities. There is even, in one Long Island park, Belmont Lake, a playground restricted to adults only (the children have a bigger playground of their own right next to it).

There are certain standard clues that can tell you how good your recreational facilities are: Are recreational areas big enough and properly located? Is there enough supervision at playgrounds? There should be a supervisor for every 25 or 30 children who use a playground regularly.

Are there enough adult volunteer leaders for Boy and Girl Scout troops? Is there a teen-age recreation center which the teen-agers help to direct? Are there organized athletics for teen-agers? Are these directed with the physical well-being and the group needs of teen-agers more in mind than fierce competition? But your most important clue on recreation is this one: Is there recreation for both children and adults?

Health

Both local pride and the existence of a hospital in or near your town are signs of a good community. America has learned a good deal over the years about what constitutes good provision for health.

The number of hospital beds is one clue: There should be about five beds to every 1,000 citizens. Is your town adequately staffed with doctors and with up-and-coming young doctors? One doctor to 1,000 or fewer citizens is a good ratio. Another clue on the question of health comes from Wesley J. Hennessey,

Associate Dean of the Faculty of Engineering at Columbia University. Each year Dean Hennessey's students survey many towns and suggest improvements. One thing they investigate is sewage disposal. A municipal system is best; individual cesspools are not as good; and plants dumping their sewage into a creek or river are unsanitary.

Dean Hennessey's students ride the garbage trucks to find out how good a garbage collection is, but you can evaluate it by simpler clues: Collection several times a week is good, once a week fair and no collection should, of course, not be tolerated. The best systems of collection pick up garbage right from the basement or back door—you don't have to lug garbage out to the curb.

Does your town provide for emergencies? In part as an outgrowth of wartime and present civilian defense, there is a spreading movement toward preparedness in emergencies. For example, ambulances should be on call and should be swift. For another example, many towns are adding what are called rescue squads—which may be composed of firemen—to do things like administering oxygen, artificial respiration, cutting through wrecked cars or rescuing swimmers from the river or boys—sometimes girls—from treetops.

There should be adequate health examinations given in the schools, and many towns are providing clinics for expectant mothers and young children. These have been a great help in reducing infant deaths and detecting conditions which should be corrected in childhood.

Related to the health question is that of the water supply. A public water supply with the mains in place is to be desired; individual wells are a poor solution.

Mental Health

Not so easily observed as are health facilities, but also important to your well-being, are a number of social services. A town with enough smooth-functioning social services is likely to be a happy town.

Does your town, county or state provide marriage counseling services, offering pre and postmarital advice? Does it have available doctors, psychologists, psychiatrists, religious leaders—a cross-section of capable advisers with varied training? Is there a family service clinic? This can provide advice not only on marriage but also on such problems as bringing up children and living with elderly members of the family.

Check also on other facilities that can solve problems in your town by asking yourself questions like: Are foster homes for children licensed in your state, and are standards in your community adequately high? Do your courts, especially in the case of youthful offenders, take into account the influence of environmental and emotional conflicts? Are informal hearings held for juvenile offenders? And are all social agencies staffed by professional workers?

Local Government

Suppose you live in Milwaukee. You read the papers and observe there are no reports of organized crime. There has been none in Milwaukee for two generations (almost 60 years). This is a clue that your local government is a good one, of course. Organized crime cannot exist, says the executive director of the National Municipal League in Milwaukee, unless it ties in with City Hall.

If you are in Kansas City, you observe a system of community councils that regularly sound out public opinion, and you see a weekly TV show that reports to citizens what the local government is doing. These clues also indicate good government. They show Kansas City is anxious to translate citizens' needs into action, and that the city is anxious to keep its people informed.

If you live in Seattle, you have, in the Municipal League of Seattle and King County, what the National Municipal League calls the strongest organization of citizens interested in local affairs. In another town, the watch-dog citizens' group may be the Chamber of Commerce or the League of Women Voters or the American Association of University Women. Any strong citizens' group taking an interest in government is an indication of a healthy town.

Clues to watch for. Some clues to watch for, then, are these: Are there, in your town, ways to get desired changes into effect—ways like Kansas City's community councils or the more common town council meetings, open to the public? Are citizens kept informed, not necessarily by a TV show but by regular reports to the people?

Other clues as to local government include: Do capable townsfolk hold office? Who runs your town? A politicians' paradise is bad, of course; a combination of mayor, local editor, town banker is healthy. Do you yourself take part in local affairs by doing more than voting?

Are there experts in charge of the town's nonpolitical services like street-cleaning, the police and tree care? Are there college graduates in local government? You need them, not only as engineers, where most towns have them, but also in the police, fire and other departments. And the payoff clue on fire protection is the obvious one: Is your fire insurance rate low?

Streets and Traffic

Can you drive around town easily? There should be few blocks where you have to slow down below 15 m.p.h. Are residential streets curved to cut speed? Are trucks kept off residential streets? Where two through streets run parallel, it is wise to allow trucks on one only.

Are there well-stocked, modern shopping centers? If you rarely go to the next town for shopping, the answer is probably "Yes." Are they convenient?

They should be within one mile of your home for groceries, drug stores, and so forth, within four miles for major shopping centers. Are there off-street parking lots? Is local bus or other public transportation good? Clue: it should take less than 30 minutes, including waiting time, to get to work.

And is your town safe for you and your children? What is the accident rate? There are U.S. towns as big as 40,000 where no pedestrians—adults or children —are killed in a year, and the same conditions could prevail everywhere. Are streets clearly marked? Do local speeders pay the same fines as out-of-towners? Do volunteer guards help police at school crossings?

If your town measures up well, you can be happy that you live there.

What Can Be Done

If not—what? It comes back to you. If you will do something about it, your town can be better to live in. Here are a few examples of what other communities throughout the country have done.

In Richmond, Virginia, a couple of businessmen noticed that citizens took little part in government. They stirred things up, and got out 35,000 voters in city elections instead of 3,000.

In a New Jersey town, a homemaker found the library was inadequate, so she campaigned via car and phone for funds and books. She got them.

In Hartford, Connecticut, a group of high school students got together and made thoughtful recommendations to the city council on recreation, juvenile delinquency, traffic. These were welcomed and have been acted upon.

Over the nation, citizens like yourself have installed the council-manager plan which provides a trained expert as municipal manager and a council of elected citizens to advise with him.

In countless towns and cities throughout the country citizens' committees, after studying their local public schools, have pushed through bond issues for new buildings, campaigned to improve community-school relations, obtained much-needed state aid for local schools.

When you need help, whether it's reforming a government or getting a new park, you can get help on how to go about it by writing the National Municipal League, 47 East 68th Street, New York City, New York. The league is non-partisan, its information and advice are free, and membership is open to all. The league's single job is to help citizens act. In the same way, if you need help in improving your school situation you can get it from the National Citizens Council for Better Schools, 9 East 40th Street, New York, N.Y.

This is what is bringing about the betterment of America's towns—people like yourself are caring enough to work for the improvements they need. Is your town a good place to live in? It can be as good as you are interested to make it.   —By Gardner Soule

COMMUNITY SPIRIT, U.S.A.

IT DIDN'T look like a classroom. A group of teen-agers swarmed over a couple of tired chairs whose upholstery had been stripped off. A girl studiously measured strips of webbing for a divan. A tall man with a low voice and clever hands shuttled back and forth among the pupils, explaining and demonstrating.

This was the home-economics class of the Great Neck High School in Great Neck, Long Island. The man was teaching, but he was not a teacher. He was Jerry Arvine, owner of an upholstery store on Main Street. And he was part of a program that is making educational history.

The idea grew out of a paradox. Every community has scores of men and women who are experts in their own line—salesmen, store managers, gardeners, artists. Yet almost everywhere this vast reservoir of practical knowledge is untapped by the schools.

That anomaly was a challenge to John L. Miller, superintendent of Great Neck's schools. Why, he wanted to know, couldn't these local experts be brought right into the classrooms as part-time teachers? Screening the town directory, a list of some 2,000 residents who had useful skills was prepared. Each "specialist" was informed that his skills might be drafted for the good of the community. The response was terrific.

The program has been operating successfully for several years. Great Neck is fortunate in having many unusual and talented people among its citizens. Artists speak to art classes; a stamp dealer brings geography to life via philatelic exhibits.

Vocational Guidance Given

Most of Great Neck's experts, however, are the kind you might find anywhere. Insurance men, lawyers, engineers and business executives. Periodically these professional folk take a day off from their busy office routines to give expert vocational guidance to the youngsters. The youngsters are happy to have their parents come into the classroom and exhibit some special skill.

This volunteer teaching project is typical of a self-bootstrap-raising movement that is very American. From remote backwoods areas to large metropolises, the goal is the same: enrichment of the lives of our children, closer participation of parents in the life of our schools.

Take the case of another exciting educational project already pioneered and proved by the people of Battle Creek, Michigan. At St. Mary's Lake, a few miles out of Battle Creek, exists a year-round public school—the first of its kind in the country.

Every two weeks a group of grammar-school children leave their classrooms, accompanied by teachers, to spend two weeks camping. As soon as one group goes back, another takes its place.

Since 1944, when the residents of Battle Creek put the program into action, hardly a week has passed without a representative of some other school system visiting the camp. (See "How To Start A School Camp")

Safety in Athletics

Safeguarding athletic programs is another serious responsibility of every community. It is a fact that one out of every ten American youths active in scholastic sports will get hurt before the end of the year. Your child may be among these statistics—unless you act the way the folks in Marietta, Wisconsin, did.

When a wave of athletic injuries sent many of their children into hospitals, the parents got together with the Wisconsin Interscholastic Athletic Association. As a result, the boys and girls themselves were invited to make a survey of all accidents and suggest how they could have been avoided.

Their findings made history in safety circles. For example, it was found that many of the injuries suffered by boys playing football were the result of being tackled by opponents wearing hard pigskin helmets. These armor-plate helmets snapped ribs, knocked out teeth and broke jaws. Promptly they were outlawed in Wisconsin and fourteen other states and replaced by the air-foam-padded crash helmet, of the type worn by aviation pilots.

Metal cleats on athletes' shoes turned out to be another contributor to school-boy injuries on the field. These spurlike accessories reap a cruel harvest of severed tendons and infected limbs when boys accidentally "spike" each other. So Marietta ordered cleats of hard rubber for its young athletes.

Improved Athletic Equipment

The bamboo pole used for pole vaulting was found to be dangerous; too often it broke under stress while a boy was eleven feet in the air. So a foolproof aluminum pole was substituted for this sport.

To eliminate baseball "beanings" to junior Joe DiMaggios, a baseball cap padded with cellular rubber was devised. When the kids reported that too many of them tripped on the high hurdles, the barriers were lowered six inches and mishaps practically disappeared.

When one mother reported that her son always caught cold after a football game because he took a shower in the gymnasium and then went outdoors with his scalp still wet, hair-dryers were made standard equipment in the locker room. The girls did their part too. They observed that in basketball games between girl teams accidents frequently resulted because of sharp pins and bracelets with sharp edges worn by the players. Nowadays, the referee forbids players to wear costume jewelry while in action, even sees to it that long fingernails are clipped before the game so that accidents will be prevented.

The Marietta athletic reforms swept the state. Today, Wisconsin ranks lowest on the national scoresheet of scholastic injuries. Truly this is a pattern for survival that should be supported by every parent and child in every community in the nation.

Bank Loans for Schoolboys

Rural communities the nation over would do well to borrow a leaf from the citizens of Phoenix, Arizona, who recognized the fact that nowadays youngsters need money as well as morale when starting out on their careers. As a result, they got one of their banks to institute a special department for schoolboy loans. Known as The Saturday Morning Bank, this is a unique project which finances boys and girls who want to raise dairy animals, bees, poultry, alfalfa, vegetables or anything else they can grow or sell.

Saturday mornings the bank manager chats with a procession of students who have traveled to Phoenix to borrow money.

"We usually start by lending a boy the money to buy one dairy cow," the manager explains. "He earns enough by selling its milk to pay us back in a year. Then we finance a second one for him. With the milk of two cows paying for one, he cleans up the loan in about eight months. By the time he's finished high school he owns a herd of ten cattle."

The Saturday Morning Bank keeps in touch with the youngsters, tells them what to do if an animal takes sick or the crop doesn't flourish. And—hardheaded bankers take note—the bank manager claims his bank has never lost a dime!

City Clean-Up Project

If you live in a big city, you might be interested in hearing about this adult-inspired project. In New York a woman wrote to a large daily newspaper commenting about the untidy conditions of the tenement streets and suggesting that the paper gets its readers to do something about it.

As a result, the newspaper conducted a neighborhood contest in which every family on the winning block was offered a choice of nineteen prizes ranging from radios to electric grills.

Almost before the campaign had started, the children of the tenement area had taken over. Girls swept sidewalks, boys gathered refuse. Garbage-littered lots were picked clean and even streets were washed down. The younger children worked before school and again at night, while older ones patrolled areas so that passers-by were ashamed to toss even a cigarette butt in the gutter.

But the fact which most impressed the judges was this: not once did any child express interest in the prizes. All really wanted a clean neighborhood—

they just needed the push that set them to cleaning up. Incidentally, the success of this project kindled similar sparks in Philadelphia, Detroit and other cities.

Religious Activity

Now what about religion? When certain critics of our teen-agers charged that our young people are quite literally going to the devil, it catapulted the churchgoers of Portage, Pennsylvania, into dramatic action. As a regular part of its program, the Bethany Evangelical United Brethren Church there organized a "junior church."

This "junior church" holds weekly basement services for its congregation, ranging in age from six to thirteen. Besides its own vested choir, church treasurer and organist, the congregation has its own teen-age pastor. Clergy leaders who have observed this young religion-in-action project recommend its sponsorship in every community.

And so there you have them—a cross-section of worthy projects which any community can duplicate right in its own back yard. "Syndicate" rights to these ideas are free; use them to help yourself and your children.

—*By Mort Weisinger*

CONCERTS FOR CHILDREN

"WOULD you like to go to a Children's Symphony?" That question put more than ten years ago to the boy-on-the-street in Cincinnati, Ohio, would have been answered by: "What's that? Heck no!" But today, due to the efforts of the Cincinnati Symphony Orchestra, the Women's Committee, and the cooperation of the parents and teachers of all the schools of the city, the answer to that question is likely to be: "I do go. I have a season ticket."

Boys and girls by the thousands flock to the popular Young People's Concerts. Dismissed from school and chaperoned by music teachers, mothers, devoted aunts or just neighbors, the children happily arrive at historic Music Hall on foot, in buses, station wagons and automobiles. As they jam the entrances and push down the corridors and aisles of the large building, the very rafters echo. But after they've settled in their seats a hush falls on the auditorium.

The children who come represent a cross-section of the city. Newsboys who rush out after the last chord in order not to be late for their paper routes; young men in military uniforms; children from the basin districts who have been given tickets by philanthropic organizations; carefully coiffed young ladies from hilltop academies; toddlers, too young to keep seated, who peer over the railing of the boxes; and, in predominance, the rank and file of children from the city schools.

Music as Therapy

Teachers and parents alike have felt the benefits to the children who attend. There is the example of the boy described by his teacher as "unmanageable," given to playing hooky, almost delinquent, but who turned up on Symphony days washed and scrubbed, with thirty cents for his ticket neatly tied in his handkerchief.

Then, there is the story told by one of the members of the Women's Committee, who had gone to a school to address the parent-teachers' meeting on the subject of the Children's Concerts.

"Understand me," said the principal, "I don't mind if you talk to the group. I just want to warn you that it won't do any good. This is a tenement district. The parents of these children are in no position to buy tickets and what's more they are only interested in juke boxes."

But the representative went into the meeting undaunted. She told the mothers that the Symphony was an opportunity for their children. Just as they wouldn't go to the zoo and not look at the animals or to an amusement park and not ride on the roller coaster, why live in Cincinnati and not go to the Symphony? She explained that the concerts were fun for the children; that they played musical guessing games; that different sections of the orchestra were featured and the whole youthful audience often joined in singing; that an appreciation of music could be a safeguard for the leisure of their teen-agers; that a ticket to one concert costs a few cents more than a double-dip ice cream cone or a large comic book! The mothers in that auditorium saw the Symphony in a new light. They had thought of the Symphony as dull, highbrow, and out of their reach. From that school alone that year, a block of seats was sold to a group of enthusiastic children.

Enthusiasm for Concerts Grows

But talks to parent-teachers' meetings alone could never have produced the astounding enthusiasm for music that now exists among the young people of Cincinnati. This was a gradual growth. The Children's Symphonies had a backlog of musical interest that has always been a part of the cultural and social life of this midwestern city. Music is as much a background of Cincinnati as the hills on which it is built. Cincinnati, by its very topography, attracted many German settlers who continued the musical traditions of their homeland. As early as a hundred years ago, the first Music May Festival was held in Cincinnati and since then fine music schools, musical clubs, choral societies and, in 1895, the Cincinnati Symphony Orchestra followed in logical order.

The remarkable success of the Young People's Concerts is due largely to the youngsters' recognition that music can be fun as well as instructive. How has this been accomplished? First of all, by introducing musical games and novelties and by featuring members of the orchestra and their instruments. Whole sections of the orchestra are brought out in front and the children are given the opportunity to hear and compare the range, tone and quality of each instrument. At one concert a red ribbon was stretched for thirteen feet across the stage to show how long the French horn would be, if unwound. Could any child forget that? These demonstrations are followed later in the program by guessing games or "Unscrambling of Instruments." As many instruments as possible are featured. Thus, the children who have been regular subscribers for a few years have had the opportunity to hear solos by almost every instrument.

Often featured is musical material written by present-day composers especially for children and on subjects directly appealing to them. Many modern composers are now old favorites to Cincinnati children. To list a few: George Kleinsinger, whose "Once upon an Orchestra" was given a world première in Cincinnati in 1950; Nicholas Slonimsky, whose "My Toy Balloon" was played to the popping of real colorful balloons; Julius Levine, whose "Timid Tim, the Trumpeter" was a great success one season; Arcady Dubinsky, whose "Overture on Children's Names" was followed by a new game called "There's Rhythm in Your Name"; Aaron Copland, whose "A Lincoln Portrait" was given with one of the members of the orchestra serving as narrator.

Classical Music Included

The introduction of new and modern music does not mean that the wealth of classical fare is neglected. It is the real basis of the concerts.

There have been unusual series such as The Famous Composers Series, in which one composer was featured at each of three concerts (a large picture of the composer whose music was being played was drawn on an easel on the stage); The Famous Americans Series consisting of the "Paul Bunyan Suite" by William Bergsma, "The Overture to Rip Van Winkle" by Chadwick and "The Legend of John Henry" by Lamar Stringfield; and one called Instruments Your Great Grandparents Knew, featuring the viola d'amore, harpsichord and posthorn.

The central idea around one entire program (for the junior high group) was A Musical History of the Early Days of Our Country, tracing our heritage musically from Indian days ("Dagger Dance" from Victor Herbert's opera "Natoma") until Civil War days ("Battle Hymn of the Republic"). Another time, Music from the Mediterranean Countries was played against a background of a large map and at another concert, Music from the British Isles.

Another unusual musical classification was: Transportation in Music, using compositions representing a donkey, a boat, a train, an automobile and an airplane; another, Insects in Music.

To stimulate musical creativity, a contest was sponsored for an original melody for an instrument of the orchestra, by either a child or group of children working together in class. The winning melody in each grade from the fourth to the ninth was orchestrated and played at Children's Concerts.

Parents who chaperone their children to the concerts have been impressed by the musical knowledge their children are acquiring. They find that children can be interested in the best music if the approach is right.

—By Katherine Earls Gerwin

DO YOU KNOW THE FACTS ABOUT FLUORIDATION?

"GOOD news, Mrs. Jones. Not a single cavity in Mary's mouth. I've told her if she keeps brushing her teeth the way she's been and takes it easy on sweets, she'll grow up looking like a toothpaste ad. See you in six months!"

Until a few years ago, a scene like this in a dentist's office could have been dreamed up only by a writer of fiction. Today it is happening in city after city and town after town. The reason: water fluoridation, the first really effective public health measure for preventing tooth decay.

Next to the common cold, tooth decay is probably the most universal disease suffered by mankind. It affects 95 per cent of the population—19 out of 20 Americans. It is so widespread, in fact, most people don't think of it as a disease at all, but rather as an unavoidable nuisance.

This, unfortunately, is far from true. Protracted neglect of teeth can lead to many problems, both physical and psychological. Missing or deformed teeth mar facial appearance, distort speech and can even undermine an adolescent's self-confidence. Missing teeth, especially among older people, make chewing difficult and often lead to nutritional deficiency. Abscessed gums, at any age, can result in serious infection.

From an economic point of view, too, there's nothing minor about dental disease. Dr. Howard A. Rusk, chairman of the President's Committee on Health Manpower Resources, reported that dental defects were the largest single cause of rejections among the first 2,000,000 men examined for military service in World War II. In terms of the family budget, the Health Information Foundation reports one dollar out of every six that we spend today for family health goes for dental care. In addition, each family pays a share of the expense of tax-supported school, military and veterans' dental programs and dental programs for indigent families.

Dental Care Inadequate

The city of New York alone spends $1,500,000 a year on dental care for 40,000 children between the ages of 6 and 14. Its studies show that well over 300,000 boys and girls in this age group do not get the dental care they need. Five times as much money is needed to treat them all. Even if it were available, there would not be enough dentists to do the work.

All in all, a dental bill of a billion and a half dollars is met each year by American family budgets. Despite this expenditure, far fewer than half of the American people receive adequate dental treatment. The most extensive dental neglect occurs among low-income families.

Prevention of decay is the obvious answer and twelve years of concentrated study by outstanding authorities in this country and abroad have proved that water fluoridation is a safe, practical means of decay prevention on a community-wide scale.

Tooth enamel containing the right amount of fluoride resists decay far better than enamel which is fluoride-deficient. The typical modern diet leaves enamel fluoride-deficient, unless there is enough fluoride in drinking water to make up that lack. Water fluoridation is the process of adjusting the fluoride content of community water supplies to the level of one part per million. Research has repeatedly verified the fact that nourishment from conception and birth with fluoridated water will prevent one-half to two-thirds of new tooth decay.

Benefits of Fluoridation Program

In 1945, Newburgh, New York, Grand Rapids, Michigan, and Brantford, Ontario, each began a fluoridation program. Controlled studies were begun, checking dental health in these places as compared to a cooperating community which was not correcting the fluoride deficiency in its drinking water. Other programs and studies were begun in Sheboygan, Wisconsin, in 1946, in Evanston, Illinois, in 1947 and in Madison, Wisconsin, in 1948. The results after nine years of fluoridation:

1. Grand Rapids' six-year-olds had 54 per cent less decay in baby teeth and 60 per cent less in permanent teeth.

2. Newburgh children drinking fluoridated water from birth showed 58 per cent less tooth decay and had one-eighth as many permanent molars missing as did youngsters in the nonfluoridated city of Kingston.

3. Brantford children from 6 to 16 had 54 per cent less decay.

4. Evanston children from 6 to 8 who drank fluoridated water from birth had 64 per cent less tooth decay in permanent teeth.

5. No adverse health effects, despite thorough medical examinations.

Since then, an international committee of scientists of the World Health Organization has unanimously recommended the use of fluoridated water whenever and wherever possible, noting that studies of fluoridation programs in 17 countries show "remarkable uniformity" in their good results. And late in 1957, after a year-long study of all scientific data, the AMA gave its approval.

With such conclusive proof on hand as to the effectiveness of this method of preventing a serious, costly, extremely widespread disease, it would seem worth adopting at almost any price. And no matter where you live, you will pay less for water fluoridation during your entire lifetime than you would for having one tooth filled or pulled.

Endorsed by Scientists

These are the facts that have led to widespread endorsement of water fluoridation by scientific bodies throughout the country. In more and more cities and towns, local medical and dental societies are joining with parents' groups and other civic organizations in urging adoption of water fluoridation. By July of 1957, fluoridation had been adopted by 1,522 cities and towns in the United States, with a total population of 31,664,474. This includes Chicago, Philadelphia, San Francisco, Pittsburgh, St. Louis, Cleveland, Washington, Baltimore, St. Paul, Buffalo, Milwaukee, Providence, Miami and Rochester. But many cities and towns still lag in adopting fluoridation and some have even dropped it after adoption. As a result, for every American being given the benefits of fluoridation, three others are being denied these benefits. The reason is that in recent years a curious resistance or skepticism has arisen over fluoridation in many places where physicians and dentists have recommended it.

Sifting out the purely emotional arguments that have beclouded the fluoridation question, here are the key questions and factual answers to them.

Fluoridation Is Safe

The safety of fluoridation has been confirmed by many studies, conducted independently by outstanding scientists. The staff of the Kettering Laboratory at the University of Cincinnati, under the direction of Dr. Robert A. Kehoe, has collected and appraised more than 8,500 scientific reports on this subject. Dr. Kehoe's conclusion is that "the question of public safety of fluoridation is nonexistent from the viewpoint of medical science."

The loudest opposition word is "poison." In Atlantic City and East Orange, New Jersey, in the final days before referenda on fluoridation, opponents mailed thousands of leaflets stating that "fluoride is rat poison." In Yonkers, New York, and Seattle, Washington, they used the skull-and-crossbones as their symbol. In New York City, they placed newspaper advertisements and mailed postcards with the illustrated slogan: "Don't Be A Fluoridation Guinea Pig."

Those who seriously make the charge of poison seem to have forgotten that most substances necessary to sustain life are poisons when taken in excess. Drinking water fluoridated at the ratio of one part fluoride per one million parts of water is safe. To absorb a lethal amount would require drinking fifty bathtubsful at a sitting. To produce even the mildest symptoms of fluoride poisoning would require drinking two and a half bathtubsful during a single day.

Water consumption does vary from individual to individual. But fluoridation is not based on people all drinking the same amount of water. We know that among persons drinking the greatest amounts of fluoridated water and those drinking the least, tooth decay is reduced without harm.

Is It Compulsory Medicine?

This charge tends to take the fluoridation question out of the realm of science and into the no-holds-barred arena of politics. Yet every time a claim against water fluoridation has been brought to court it has been rejected. The United States Supreme Court twice has refused to review lower court decisions and twice has dismissed appeals because no constitutional issue is involved.

The practice of preventing disease through nutrition is nothing new or radical. In 1795, the British Navy began requiring sailors to drink lime juice for protection against scurvy. Today, the irradiation of milk and addition of vitamins to bakery flour for general health are accepted as normal, sensible health measures.

Water fluoridation, as a measure for the common good, is no more compulsory than such community measures as fire protection, public education and highways. It is clearly within the rights of a community to fluoridate its water supply.

Is it socialized medicine? If fluoridation were "socialized medicine," it hardly would be endorsed by the American Medical Association and the American Dental Association. In practical terms, it is a move away from government medical services. It cuts down the amount of dental work needed, so families are more capable of paying for their own care.

Are there harmful cumulative effects? Some 4,000,000 Americans now live in good health in areas of the country where drinking water naturally contains fluorides in proportions equal to or greater than the recommended one part per million. Long and painstaking research reveals no harmful cumulative effect. Even older people suffering from chronic ailments, including diabetes, arthritis, kidney disease or heart disease, are not harmed by fluoridated water, according to a report of a special committee appointed by the Commission on Chronic Illness.

Is fluoridation still experimental? Actually, nature has conducted the largest experiment conceivable. Fluoridation programs imitate natural conditions.

Dental Care Necessary Too

If your town now has fluoridation, those children young enough to have been drinking fluoridated water all their lives are getting the full benefit. But remember, fluoridation is not a substitute for a well-balanced diet, for keeping teeth clean or for periodic care by a good dentist. With proper dental hygiene and regular care, you can expect your children to have only a third as much tooth decay as they would without fluoridation.

If your town doesn't have fluoridation, you might ask your dentist about local applications of a fluoride solution for your children's teeth. A series of four applications at age 3 will provide protection to first teeth, and additional series at 7, 10 and 13 years of age will protect permanent teeth coming in. But as a community health measure, benefiting all children alike, topical application is not a substitute for water fluoridation.

Whether or not your town has fluoridation, you can do a real service to your family's health and your community's health by learning all you can about it and building interest and understanding among your friends, your neighbors, the groups to which you belong. This is one public health measure you can't just take for granted.

What Parents Can Do

In Peoria, Illinois, for example, even though the local dental and medical societies and the board of health were on record for fluoridation, the city council tabled the matter for several years in the face of rather vocal opposition by a small minority. Nothing really happened until the parents got on the job. Once PTA groups and mothers' clubs began to demand fluoridation, other community organizations took up the cry. The public health committee of the Association of Commerce decided to help. Along with the dental society, they formed a speakers' bureau to talk to groups all over the city and to distribute pamphlets of the American Dental Association. Soon people all over Peoria began to learn the facts. In the face of intelligent understanding, opposition simply never got a foothold. When the City Council held a referendum to sound out public opinion on the issue, fluoridation was backed by a large majority and subsequently adopted.

This can happen anywhere, if parents band together and demand this protection for their children.   *—By Louis I. Dublin, Ph.D.*

HOW TO ORGANIZE
A SITTERS' EXCHANGE

JUST a few years ago a modest ad appeared in a village newspaper: MOTHERS—Are you interested in a Sitters' Exchange? The ad was placed by an energetic young mother of five children, all under seven years. The night before, as she and her husband sat peacefully watching television, their six-year-old son fell out of bed and set up a wail; their three-month-old baby vomited her last bottle; and the dog yelped urgently to go out—all at the same time. When the household had settled down again, the mother of the family turned to her husband and asked, "Now what would a teen-age baby sitter have done in that mixed-up situation—even the most responsible teen-ager? Really, the only kind of sitter for a house full of children is another mother or father!"

An idea was born, and starting next afternoon the response to her brief ad kept this mother's phone ringing for days. One applicant said uncertainly, "I'd love to be in on this, but who'd ever sit for me? I have five kids."

"Me!" chortled the mother on the other end of the phone. "I have five of my own!" The calls totaled thirty-six. But the initial enthusiasm, as so often happens, was dimmed in some cases by difficulties of transportation, a husband's working hours, and unwillingness to work cooperatively with others. Some women who applied even seemed puzzled by the plain fact that in order to get something out of the Exchange you had to put something into it. Finally, just seven mothers formed the nucleus of the Exchange.

No Obstacle Too Great

They wanted to make it work, and no obstacle was too great. They were convinced that the best sitter in the world was another mother who could call on her own knowledge and experience should emergencies arise. These mothers also felt that just knowing the youngsters were in such dependable hands would free them for even greater enjoyment on evenings out. Budget-conscious, too, they knew that such mutual exchange of time would be of real financial benefit to each family. Why, if they wanted to, they could afford even more nights out—thanks to the saving on sitters' fees.

The first step, though, before undertaking to put the idea to work was to confer with seven husbands. Every one of them was for the idea and not a bit displeased at the prospect of "sitting" with his own children when his wife was out sitting with others. That very important point settled, the next step was taken. Believing a certain degree of formality to be necessary, the mothers set up a Code as a guide. It has been altered and expanded many times since then, but has proved invaluable.

What most people are first interested in is the Code's provisions for keeping track of hours spent sitting—when, by whom, for whom. This is how it works: Mrs. X calls the group's elected bookkeeper for the name of an available sitter-mother for a specific night. When the evening is over, the sitter has hours to her credit, or "on deposit," and Mrs. X has used up or "withdrawn" the same number of hours. She is therefore in debt to the exchange "bank" and must make herself available as a sitter for an equal number of hours to fulfill her obligation. That's all there is to it—in black and white. In actual practice, of course, many ramifications and questions may arise. The exchange settles each new problem as it comes along.

For example, it proved sensible to have each member inform the bookkeeper of her personal specialties—whether or not she drives, whether she minds late hours or short-notice calls, is agreeable to daytime sitting, the days or nights that she is unavailable (such as husband's bowling night), whether she expects to be out of town, and so forth.

Keep a Membership Chart

The bookkeeper has on her wall a chart showing all information of this nature for each member and also the sitting status of each member—hours' credit in black, debit in red. She can tell at a glance who owes the most hours and is available, and suggests that Mrs. X call Mrs. "In Debt" or Mrs. "Next-In-Debt." (The Sitters' Telephone Directory lists the names, addresses and phone numbers of the members, as well as the names and ages of their children.) Mrs. X calls the sitters herself and then reports back which mother she has engaged.

If Mrs. X calls someone more than a week ahead of time, the Code states she must call the sitter again the day before the date and confirm the time. If Mrs. X has a change of plans, she must notify the sitter twelve hours before the scheduled date. Any cancellation given less than twelve hours before the time the sitter was asked to arrive automatically gives the disengaged sitter three hours' credit.

If, on the other hand, the sitter can't keep the engagement, she is duty-bound to provide a substitute—always, of course, to be approved by the mother who is going out. It sometimes happens that husbands have gone out to sit when their wives could not keep appointments. The children love it when a father appears. Should an engaged sitter be unable to locate a substitute, she is docked three hours even though she tried. The mothers agreed that such a penalty system is fair.

Late Hours

A minimum sitting time of two hours was established. Sitter and sittee determine the official time spent sitting before the sitter leaves to forestall any disagreements over hours in the future. In order to avoid hair-splitting, any time under fifteen minutes is not counted, and any time over fifteen minutes is booked as half an hour. Recognizing that tomorrow will be a sleepy day if a sitter keeps late hours, the Code notes explicitly that any time spent sitting after 2 A.M. is credited as double time for the sitter, and double time owed for the mother who is out.

The Code provides that a member may not owe more than fifteen hours. This prevents anyone from getting too heavily in debt. Should a member have to leave the Exchange for any reason, while she has hours banked to her credit, the Exchange will make up the hours she has earned before she is obliged to leave. If, however, a member resigns from the Exchange while still in debt to the bank, she must either make up the hours she owes, or compensate at the going neighborhood sitting rate.

To be admitted to the group is not easy, as they are careful to be certain a new member will live up to her responsibilities. At present there is a waiting list of mothers anxious to join, and in discussing the subject of prospective members, the president remarked, "Some of the mothers just want to come to the meetings for social reasons."

Expansion into Discussion Group

Meetings? Who mentioned meetings? Well, they started because each woman is required to keep track of her own hours, and as a result, they started meeting once a month to check the accuracy of their bookkeeping. Then quite naturally the members of the group began discussing problems of child rearing. Eventually, they began to call in competent speakers on the subject of child care. Today, the member who is hostess for the evening selects the topic for the meeting's discussion and states it in personal and specific terms. Then the mothers all talk it over and relate their own methods of handling similar problems or situations. One mother learned that what her Johnny did was perfectly normal, while another mother saw that her child may need special help with a problem not common to other children. Sometimes professional help is needed.

An initiation fee of 25 cents was established and, each month, ten cents in dues are collected from each member to cover the Exchange's few expenses. Auditing of the little money involved is the duty of the elected treasurer. In a group which has no physical plant, hires no help, buys no supplies, it might seem that no money was needed, but there's a good outlet for those extra dimes. When a member has a new baby, she is presented with a small gift from the women who will be sitting with that baby in the months to come.

Little wrinkles in organizing numbers of women to sit for each other still arise, and it is at the monthly meetings that they are ironed out. It was over a period of several meetings that the safety precaution rules of the Code were developed to safeguard sitters and the children. In the first place, if the engaged sitter is fifteen minutes late in arriving for the evening, the member who is expecting her must call her house to be certain she has not run into trouble on the way over. Secondly, the member who is going out must be certain to fill out the Family Guardian Pad. This includes the phone number where she can be reached, as well as that of the doctor, police and fire departments and neighbors. Any specific information, TV rules and children's bedtimes must also be written here.

Follow Parents' Instructions

The sitters like to have, too, as much information as possible about parents' own ways of handling their children. One couple left very explicit directions about the care of the family dog. No sooner had the young couple left the house than the six-month-old baby woke up crying frantically. As the sitter attempted to calm the howling child, she wondered, "Should I pick him up or let him cry? I've got instructions for the dog but not a word about the baby!"

When the sitter is ready to leave, it is the sittee's responsibility to know the make of the sitter's car, her license number and the route she plans to drive in going home. The sitter must call back when she does arrive home to indicate a safe return. If she does not call within a reasonable time, the sittee's husband follows the sitter's route to see whether she has had car trouble. If a member who goes out returns home after 2 A.M., her husband must follow the sitter home in his own car.

The Sitters' Exchange has grown into a real project, a real community service. And it's the spirit existing among the members, which you can't put a dollar value on, that has made it all something special. One Christmas Eve, for example, a Catholic member of the group wanted to attend Mass. A Jewish mother volunteered to sit for her. That's the sort of neighborliness which finds expression through this group. —*By Susan Stampfer Heller*

PARENTS ORGANIZE A SUMMER DAY CAMP

ON a hot August afternoon several years ago, Alice Barsky, housewife, sprinted out of her new housing-project apartment to rescue her daughter Peri. She fended off the mass of shrieking, sweating children milling on the narrow sidewalk between the two-story brick building and the chained-off grass plot. She dodged the bike riders, stepped over the toddlers, pushed her way through the mothers yelling about whose kid poked who with the shovel first, snatched up her yellow-haired 3-year-old just as the first rock broke a window.

"Mommy, I don't want to play out any more," Peri started to cry.

Alice Barsky felt like crying herself. They'd moved way out here to Bell Park Manor Terrace, an hour away from Manhattan, so their kids could play in the fresh air and sunshine and green grass—the Barskys and 849 other ex-GI couples who'd once played in the streets of New York themselves. The trouble was that among them they had a thousand kids who were to play.

All Bell Park's 50 low white-shuttered brick buildings had the same grassy lawns—chained off. The cement-paved drying yards were always full of laundry. The black asphalt driveways just led to garages. So many kids had already cracked their heads in the miniscule playgrounds, the swings had to be taken down. There wasn't even a "Y" or a library out here—just miles of new little houses and raw developments equally overflowing with youngsters. "Is it any wonder they throw rocks?" a harassed neighbor shrugged.

Varied Camp Activities

There are more kids than ever in Bell Park today. But now they are swimming the backstroke, pitching fast ones, blazing forest trails, dancing to a guitar, and exploring decks of an ocean liner. For out of the bare asphalt driveways behind the housing project, their mothers created their own "Bell Park Manor Terrace Summer Day Camp."

It's a parental do-it-yourself story that parents in any project or raw new suburb might adopt to solve "the summer problem." For when the Bell Park mothers got together to solve theirs, they had no training or experience, no funds or facilities; most of them had never even been to a "real camp" themselves for that matter.

In fact, Pat Berkowitz, the young optometrist's wife who first had the camp idea, was told by experts it was "impossible." She reported to the mothers' meeting: "Day camps are either supported by big agencies with thousands of dollars from charities, or they charge $200 to $300 a child. You need indoor facilities for hot lunches, rests and toilets, fenced-in grounds and all kinds of equipment. And they say you can't run a decent day camp with 800 children."

"But we've *got* 800 children," said Alice, volunteering to work on equipment herself. Then eight women were talking at once. "We'll use our own grounds . . . the kids can go home for lunch and rest . . . and to the toilet . . . and when it rains." About costs, they decided that $25 for one child, $35 for two, and the third for free, was all they could afford.

Organizing Work Begun

First, they had to persuade the housing company to let them use the grounds. "It'll protect the stockholders' investment because the kids won't destroy so much property," argued Camp Chairman Pat Berkowitz in her sixth call to the Bell Park Chairman of the Board. The Board finally agreed—but only *behind* the buildings, and *off* the grass, which left—driveways! and un-rented garages. Scattered over 43 acres. At once tenants started objecting: "Not behind *my* apartment."

The mothers divided up the project and went from door to door through a rainy March registering each child in person, and educating the parent objec-tors. Each night they brought their paper bags full of dollar bills to Dornee Robinson's apartment. Her husband Henry, an accountant, got used to finding them under his pillow.

Alice's husband, Sid, watched the kids while she went into town Saturdays, going from jobber to jobber, pricing wagons, bats and wading pools by the dozen. It wasn't too different from comparing cans of tomatoes at the super-market. She got carpenter-fathers to build work tables and benches that would collapse (they couldn't be left up on driveways when the men would be com-ing home from work). And tenants were asked to leave old toys and pots on the sidewalk, instead of in the garbage can, for a camp pickup squad to collect and rejuvenate.

Professional Help Needed

The Bell Park mothers agreed that they could do all the spade work for the camp, but only "outside experts" should handle the children. They them-selves didn't have the time, didn't know enough, and "it'd be hard to fire each other." But it seemed even harder for nine "ignorant housewives" to hire an expert. The few who answered their ad just shook their heads when they heard "800 kids . . . driveways." A tweedy, pipe-smoking Ph.D. looked around the apartment living room at the nine women in slacks and cotton skirts, knitting, and politely inquired for whom he would be working. "Us," said Pat, timidly. He gulped and left. They gratefully hired the first man with degrees willing to take the job, and promised not to "interfere" in the running of the camp.

Somehow, the Bell Park camp survived that first summer. The counselors spent hours blowing up the wading pools, which kept springing leaks and collapsing to flood the driveways. With the children grouped behind their own buildings, there were, as Alice puts it, "850 supervisors peering out from behind the Venetian blinds." If Miss Jones scolded the wrong child, a second-story blind would yank up, and the irate mother would scold Miss Jones.

First Year Troubles

The counselors, who'd been hired in a college placement office remote from housing project reality, began to arrive for work later and later. They really didn't know what to do when they got there. The director had 19 years' experience but never in a camp like this. "The kids aren't *doing* anything at camp," the mothers would complain to Pat or Alice, in the laundry room or the market. They finally recruited the 50 worst complainers into the committee. "We've got to stop expecting somebody to hand us all the answers," Alice said. "Use your own brains—it's a chance to be more than nosewipers and diaper-changers." So they canvassed all "850 supervisors behind the Venetian blinds" and found out what *they wanted* for their kids' camp. It was the blueprint they needed, all right. Alice learned of it at one of their frequent unplanned "committee meetings" in front of the supermarket. "We'd need space platforms," she groaned. Then she saw the bus coming down Hillside Avenue. The others stared, too, and the idea struck five brains simultaneously. "If we hired a bus for the whole summer . . ."

Now the whole world was theirs to give their kids. They wrote to a bread factory, a bottling plant, a forestry nursery, the captain of a sailing schooner, museums, zoos and a farm with real cows and pigs. Anytime one of them read in a paper or heard over TV anything that sounded interesting, the Bell Park camp activities grew. "I never knew there were such places around New York before," Pat said.

Planning for Second Year

Winter saw more practical preparation for the next summer. Mothers with young babies that kept them from working on camp committees themselves would watch Pat's or Alice's kids anytime, as their contribution to the camp. But husbands complained they could never reach home by phone. "And at dinner, six people are lined up on our couch waiting to talk to Pat about budget or personnel," said Fred, the chairman's husband. "It makes me nervous, people watching me chew." In the interests of home life, the women decided nobody should be chairman more than two years at a stretch. "Besides, it's such an exciting responsibility, we've got to pass it around," said Pat, as the job was turned over to Alice.

"Next summer, we've got to have music and dancing," pronounced Dornee Robinson one day. "We can't move a piano around," Alice said, "and we can't buy 43 pianos." They hired a guitarist to stroll from driveway to driveway and make Bell Park ring with children singing. They hired a modern dancer and a folk dancer, and bought them portable record players—plugged with extra long extension cords through the windows of mothers living over the driveways.

"Next summer our kids should learn to swim, and the public pool's too crowded, and they can't in the ocean," Alice remarked. Mrs. Dornee Robinson besieged the Board of Education with a call every day for three months until she got the use of a high school swimming pool.

The Bell Park mothers *knew* what they wanted now in the way of a director, too—thanks to solid advice and assistance from the New York City Health

Department's Day Camp Unit. They started advertising in October for a director, writing most explicitly to colleges and social agencies. They broke into teams of four to weed out the applicants. Degrees—that was just the beginning, they had learned. They pounced on their well-educated prospects with questions that left them gasping. And if an applicant didn't ask *them* questions— they'd signal each other with their eyebrows, cut the interview short and rush to the next apartment where another team was interviewing. A man who passed the first team had to come back and be interviewed by the full 21 top brass. "Never went through such a trial in my life," said Harry Janoson, a New York public school principal. "A whole roomful of dames knitting, looking me up and down, exchanging those significant smiles. Such questions! I said their setup was impossible. They told *me* how it could be done." He took the job—and kept turning down fancier ones to come back to it.

Budgetary Plans

The full committee of 58 mothers spent three winter months analyzing what was wrong with the summer before. They'd noticed 13-year-olds hanging around, making nuisances of themselves. Conferences were held with teen-age experts, and with the teen-agers themselves, to work out camping trips, high-diving instruction, trips into town for restaurant dinners and live TV shows.

The mothers also made up, over coffee, their $40,000 budget—fees had to be raised to $58, three buses cost $3,600. On a January weekend, they registered 870 of Bell Park's thousand children over three (the others go away summers). Registration is no longer conducted door-to-door, but in a basement room, like registration to vote. Then the mothers broke the 870 into groups of 10 to 15, by age and development now instead of by location— better if they're not near their own "mommies." Easter week the basement room was draped with sheets and the 870 children were brought in for medical exams. Bell Park mothers who were once nurses got out their white uniforms, weighed the kids, filled out the forms as the doctors dictated and made themselves generally useful.

Interviewing Counselors

In that basement room, every Sunday since January some of the mothers have sat beside the camp director interviewing counselors. Under the bare hot-water pipes, a crew-cut psychology major was asked bluntly: "Can you catch a fast ball?" A college athlete was hit with "What's the Einstein theory?" and "Why do you want to be a counselor?"

A mother explained: "Muscles aren't enough for our teen-agers. Got to excite them about the world."

They turned down an art teacher who relied too much on tracing, hired a young scientist who stared out at the asphalt driveway and talked about bird-watching, snake-catching, star-gazing. And they ascertained how each applicant felt about the fact that "our kids are all races and religions."

From the past years' experience and planning, this is a typical day in Bell Park after school ends in June. At 9:25 in the morning Alice looks out her window and prays it won't rain (camp must still adjourn rainy days for lack of indoor space). At 9:30 her own little girls dash to one of the "pickup posts" at half-block intervals throughout the project, wearing the red and blue tags of their group, and then march behind their counselors across the project streets singing "On Top of Old Smoky" and "Skip to My Lou."

At 9:32 there's not a child at loose ends in the housing project. Alice gets her housework done by 11 now. Her two-year stretch as chairman served, she's free to stroll through Bell Park, and simply exult at what she sees.

Youngsters Enjoy Full Program

Ten three-year-olds are painting pictures on easels tacked over the chicken-wire fences of the drying yards, the wash of thirty families blowing a white backdrop. In an angle where two garages make a square of shade on the drive-way, five-year-olds are making model airplanes and wire jewelry. On the hill behind Building 24 the four-year-olds on the grass are singing to the guitar. (The landlords have now relented on grass *behind* the buildings.) On the next long driveway, six-year-olds, who won't be bus-ing to the beach till afternoon, are playing volleyball over a net strung between two garages. Saucy nines are "climbing Mt. Everest"—the 3-way high-climbing bars the Health Department social worker advised them to buy.

On the ball diamond, painted in red on a driveway, where the tens usually practice, a dozen little girls are "swaying like trees in the wind" to Débussy. More five-year-olds are planting radish seeds on the triangle of mud behind the pottery kiln—the landlords agree that on bare spots where nothing else will grow, they can plant. Up the driveway, still more five-year-olds are poster-painting green garage doors watermelon red—it'll wash off in the next rain.

By noon, the littlest children have the grounds to themselves, for the three buses have been shuttling back and forth on a split-second schedule all morning. They've ferried one group of the older children to a beach, another to Cunningham Woods for berry-picking, another to Kissena Pond for fishing, another to a railroad roundhouse.

As the sun gets higher, the little children and their counselors "follow the shade" of the building walls. Oversized yellow and red beach umbrellas sprout on pipes sunk into the ground, wading pools are dragged out, shower hoses turned on. Children run in and out of the cool water, float toy boats in the pools, play "thumbkin" under the umbrellas.

The End of the Day

At 4:30 all the buses are back and the children pile out and run to tell their mothers, sunning in the peaceful apartment courts, what they did that day. "I saw a blackbird, and it's really black," yelps one little girl. "I swam all the way across the pool," cries another enthusiastic child to his admiring mother who is too scared of water ever to have taught him to swim herself.

"I hit the ball, I hit it!" yells "Skinnylegs," who used to yell only when the other kids slapped him, and never ran because he couldn't run fast. His counselor had the training and experience in "group psychology" Bell Park requires, knew after two weeks of camp how each child in his group needed to develop. Skinny learned that it's fun to run, even when you're last. The bully who used to order Skinnylegs to "stay out of our ball game" now has the responsibility of keeping count of the boys on the bus. He feels so important he doesn't have to bully. "Good stuff," he shouts when Skinny hits the ball.

The children are home. Camp's over for the day.

Parents from other projects and professional workers with children began coming to Bell Park to take guided tours through the camp, and cooperative day camps like Bell Park's are being organized in many places now. What pleased Bell Park most is that the Fresh Air Fund sent 30 underprivileged children to stay with *them* during one summer. It was the first time in 75 years that "Fresh Air" children were located within the city limits. In the eyes of the experts, Bell Park's barren asphalt now has as much to offer children as the country itself.
—*By Betty Friedan*

HOW TO START A PARENTS GROUP

TAKE two parents and eventually you have a conversation about children. Take a group of parents and what happens could be called an "organized conversation." But when you want to have this kind of organized conversation regularly, with whom do you talk—where and about what? Just how *do* you get a parents group started?

Maybe you live in an intimate neighborhood where you already do some morning coffee visiting. Six or seven of you can decide to start getting together more regularly and make up a list of topics you'd like to discuss. This type of group needs very little organizing. In some other neighborhood, one or two of you might take the responsibility of getting things started. You can make up a list of people you think would be interested. Call them on the telephone and invite them to come over next Thursday night to talk it over. A parents group that is still going after nine years started in just that way.

One PTA decided they would like to have a parents group that met informally in members' homes, quite separately from the regular PTA meeting. The program chairman, one of the teachers and two room mothers formed the committee and arranged two groups: one for parents of younger children, the other for parents of adolescents.

If you groan at the idea of more meetings in your community, feeling you're already overorganized, maybe an extension of an already established meeting is the answer. You can have a small parents group meeting for an hour before the regular PTA meeting. One parents group even includes high school students. At a meeting they discussed the use of the family car. Those parents certainly gained insight from the practical suggestions their teen-agers made for avoiding clashes in that area.

Informality is essential to a free exchange of ideas in a parents group. A meeting held in someone's house is always a good idea. The comfortable chairs and easy arrangement of the living room are better settings for frank and easy talking than the rigid rows of a schoolroom or church.

Serving refreshments can serve a very real purpose as an icebreaker. One parent group divides responsibility by having a refreshment committee to help the host and hostess, who can concentrate on getting the house clean and the kids to bed early while the committee takes care of the food. That group also own a set of divided glass plates which moves from meeting to meeting and relieves any worry of crockery shortages.

Icebreakers

This may sound like a lot of fuss, so why not just skip the refreshments? In the first place, food encourages sociability. Sometimes the most important thinking takes place after the regular discussion has ended and people are sitting around talking casually over coffee. For example, Janet asked one night, "Should you allow children their dessert when they haven't cleaned up their plates?"

Elaine asked, "What do you serve for dessert?"

"Oh, we usually have pie or cake because that's what John likes," Janet said. "But look at my figure. I've got to reduce. So I eat fruit. That gives the kids the idea they ought to be allowed to choose, too—and they're not thinking of fruit."

Mary joined in. "I try to make dessert part of the plan for the whole day. I figure that if it's part of what I want the children to eat anyway, it doesn't matter so much when they eat it."

So the group explored this subject, quite far removed from "Toys for Christmas," the scheduled topic for the evening. And they scheduled the whole subject of "Food for Families" for their next meeting.

Yes, as an icebreaker, refreshments are well worth the trouble. One group tried having dessert and coffee at the beginning of their discussion. A member said, "With something to hold I didn't feel nearly so shy about talking up."

There are other icebreakers. A discussion gets off to a good start when everybody is asked to introduce himself. In a neighborhood where parents already knew each other, they once started with each one trying to remember an outstanding incident from his childhood. They began to realize that no one could remember how often mother mopped the floor, or whether the bathroom fixtures sparkled. What tended to be remembered most often were feelings about things—such as whether they were welcome to bring friends home from school, whether parents listened when they had something to say. It showed fairly clearly where the emphasis should be put for children in their own homes.

What about topics? They almost grow on trees—it's just a question of picking the one that suits your group best. Often the topic for the next meeting grows very naturally out of something brought up at the present one.

One group had a wonderful discussion based on one of a series of pamphlets, "Some Special Problems of Children Two to Five," published by the National Association for Mental Health. Ruth, Jerry and Ida had read the pamphlet, so they presented the material to the group and they served as leaders for the discussion. Jerry introduced the material on toilet training, which he felt had some very good suggestions. Ruth felt that the experts quoted were trying to tell her not to worry if her child wasn't toilet trained, but that they weren't the ones who had to deal with the dirty laundry or the shocked grandparents. Ida, who had somewhat the same reaction, had gone on to read what some other authorities had to say and could report a slightly different approach. Some of the parents with large families had practical ideas and suggestions, and lively discussion resulted.

Several People Lead Discussion

In some groups two or three persons may lead the discussion. This is a useful way of helping nonprofessional leaders feel more comfortable. You may have heard that a group must have a professional leader but in many places professional leaders are not available. Yet in these same places there are excellent parents groups.

Leading a parents group isn't too difficult because you are always drawing on a reservoir of common experience among the members. It is not the job of the leader to be a teacher, so it is often easier for the nonprofessional leader to turn the question back to the group. The expert is expected to have a ready answer. The psychiatrist, social worker, doctor or other professional person is trained for his own profession, but not necessarily as a discussion leader. Often he can be used best as a source person—one who will sit in as a member of the group, bringing in specific material or experience.

One group invited a psychiatrist to sit in on a meeting about children's fears. During the discussion someone cited the example of a child who was frightened of thunderstorms, but not nearly as frightened as his mother. This seemed a dramatic possibility for role playing, so a scene was set up with the mother, father, child, his older brother and the paternal grandmother who lived with the family. The psychiatrist volunteered to play the part of the grandmother. The cast then began acting out what happened on a stormy night in this home, making up their lines as they went along. The role playing was cut off by the leader while it was going strong—a good technique—and a dynamic discussion followed. At the end the psychiatrist thanked the parents and said, "Not only have I had a barrel of fun, but I've learned a lot too."

Use of "Buzz Sessions"

This working together of parents and professional people is developing a whole new field of parent education. We can all experiment in it by trying some of the techniques that have been developed for group participation. Use has been made of a "buzz session," dividing the people into groups and asking them to take about six minutes to think out one question on a topic, such as discipline. Each buzz group has a reporter. The very first one asked for her group, "Does a mother have a right to correct her neighbors' children when they're playing at her home?" As the discussion continued, it became obvious that this was a problem in that particular community. Without this query—and the questions of three other reporters—the discussion leader might have talked for an hour about discipline without ever hitting on the aspects that interested these people most.

Working through the "neighbors' children" problem, the members began to find out that each one of them had to deal with it and they all did it in different ways. Parents group members are always emphasizing the comfort they get from finding that other people are living through family situations similar to their own. There is fun and humor suddenly in the very things that were such hair-raising incidents at home.

At one parents group meeting, Marion, a young mother, asked: "Listen, people, will you please tell me how I'm supposed to get my kitchen floor mopped? All four kids can be perfectly happy playing outside until I get out the mop and pail. Then suddenly they're all in the kitchen together." She went home that night with five workable suggestions, and an area of tension in her family was reduced.

Growth of Positive Attitudes

Jim said one night, "You know, I never seem to say anything but 'don't' to our boys." He voiced a general feeling among the men. So all that month, each member actually kept score of the number of times he or she said "don't" to the children. A much more positive attitude resulted in these families as the scores piled up.

Parents really *can* educate one another. Elaine, who had been active in a parents group for four years, often recalls, "I still remember when you phoned to invite me to join. I talked to Eddie about it that night. He said, 'What do you want to do something like that for? We're doing okay with the kids.' You know, he wouldn't miss a meeting now any more than I would. What if I'd listened to him!" *—By Corinne Weil Mattuck*

COMMUNITIES WORK FOR BETTER SCHOOLS

ARE your school problems piling up faster than your school board can deal with them? Maybe they need help. Across the country, thousands of citizens groups have sprung up—many of them assisted by the National Citizens Council for Better Schools—to deal with such problems as lack of classrooms, lack of teachers, supplies, half-day classes, overcrowded classes, long bus trips for small children to schools far from home and many other school matters. It takes the cooperative effort of the entire community to better some conditions. Are people in your neighborhood really interested? Will they work together to get things changed? Groups interested in their public schools have been sparked by one individual or by a small group of individuals who have cared enough to inform themselves and to give time to work for better schools.

Crowded Classrooms

The second grade in our school was so crowded that classes were put on half-day sessions. Many mothers felt as I did that our children would miss a great deal with the loss of half a day. The school principal agreed with us but could do nothing. Her only hope was that a new school being built in the next school district would relieve part of the load—in a year. But we who were mothers of the children in the second grade didn't want to wait that year. I invited the class parents to meet at my house to discuss the situation. Out of a potential of fifty families, twenty were interested enough to come and five were eager to help in any way possible.

In Detroit our schools are placed centrally in square mile areas. In our area the rapid building of homes had brought many new children into the school and although the area next to ours had long been largely vacant, new building was now going on there at a rapid pace. In order to be armed with facts our first step was to make a survey to find out whether the new school in this neighboring area could be expected to relieve the overcrowding in ours.

Locality Surveyed

A committee of five counted new homes and vacant property in our own area, then we went into the next area and counted new homes, houses occupied and lots recently sold where homes would probably be built within a year. When we met again the conclusion was clear: not only would the new school be inadequate to relieve us, it would hardly be able to take care of the pupils in its own area.

Armed with this information I made an appointment to see the superintendent of schools. He was concerned and considerate but he told me flatly that all the schools in the newer parts of town were overcrowded, that there was only so much money to be spent and that nothing could be done.

The more we found out about the problem the more complicated it seemed, but we were determined to see what we could do and not to be easily discouraged. So we drew up petitions, had them signed by as many parents and other interested persons as possible, and sent them to the Board of Education. After hearing nothing for several weeks, we called to find out the result. Our petitions had gone into the wastebasket!

Firmly believing that the schools belong to the citizens and that petitioning by citizens is a basic democratic process which warrants attention, our group was incensed and demanded an appointment to appear before the Board. After much discouragement we were granted an opportunity.

Facts Support Argument

In preparation we worked hard to get specific data together. We made a population survey, a survey of the number of preschool children who would be entering our school in the next four years and marshalled facts to prove that our building was violating the plumbing code because almost double the prescribed number of children were having to use toilets, lavatories and drinking fountains. On the appointed day we appeared before the Board and pointed out that the situation would grow graver each year, backing our argument strongly with facts and figures. We also tried to make it clear that the new school in the next area would not relieve our problem.

Our hard work, our sincerity and determination paid off. Doubtless these were not the only factors involved but we knew what we had done had been effective. In about six weeks we learned that our school would get an addition!

This was a solution for one school, and we were happy about it. At the same time the situation in the other city schools was poor. Depression years, followed by war with its combination of restricted building programs and high birth rate, plus a school board which had become complacent with its average tenure of twenty years, all combined to create overcrowding, understaffing, lack of supplies and other disadvantages.

Help for City Schools

So we decided to form a local citizens committee to see how we could help the city schools. We realized, of course, that much of our school trouble stemmed from lack of funds. (Our local school tax was limited by state constitution to 15 mills which we shared with the library and parks, and any change would have to be approved by two-thirds of the electorate.)

Millage is one of the mysteries we had to penetrate in order to understand tax-supported institutions. We discovered that millage is based on property valuation assessments—15 mills of each assessment dollar making up the school tax. Thus a property owner with a home assessed at $5,000 pays $75 a year school tax. If an additional 5 mills is asked and approved by the voters it means that the owner would have to pay an additional $5 per thousand, or $25 a year more school tax.

At the next November election there appeared on the ballot a proposed constitutional amendment which would allow a simple majority to pass a millage increase. And that increase could be asked for a period up to 20 years instead of being limited to five years as in the past. Our citizens group added its efforts to the work of teacher groups, the Board of Education and many other groups throughout the state to help pass this amendment which was a necessary first step toward solving our school dilemma.

The whole community became interested. Our radio stations were most cooperative in giving public service time to explain what the passage of the amendment would mean to our children and the schools. One station, with its clear channel reaching throughout the entire state, was generous in presenting three half-hour documentaries explaining our school needs and the proposed tax amendment. Two other major stations gave time for short announcements. The press was immensely helpful too. Everyone worked together and the campaign accomplished wonders. The amendment passed! While our city schools may not be perfect, they are improving every year because they now have more money to meet their needs. We have learned that intelligent, hard work really pays off and, best of all, that the whole city is really interested in the welfare of its schools.

Citizen Responsibility to the Schools

This report of what happened in one community is beginning to be typical of what is going on the country over. Actually there is today a nation-wide movement toward better schools. Sparked by individuals and communities, it is important to have every segment of the population represented. In Tippecanoe County, Indiana, for instance, where there are small towns, a major university and large areas of rural country, townspeople, farmers and university personnel got together to talk over common school problems.

The men and women who met agreed that they wanted their schools to offer sound teaching of basic subjects such as reading, writing, arithmetic and history. They also agreed that the schools needed a planned guidance program for boys and girls. Teaching of good citizenship was a must, but there must also be an emphasis on teaching students *to think* and at the same time develop a "curiosity to learn." They agreed that, since not all the children would go to college, the schools should offer training which would help them to earn a living as well as the standard college preparatory classes. They agreed, too, that along with a sense of good citizenship, the schools should try to develop the children's individual abilities to the fullest.

As for what this group could do as citizens to further these aims, they decided that one of the first steps was to help other citizens in the county realize their responsibility to the schools. Then, they felt, each individual could help to develop a closer cooperation and understanding between parents and teachers. This would help, they pointed out, to make teaching more attractive and so interest more young people in it as a profession and also help keep their present teachers happy in their profession. They pledged themselves to work through their local organizations to develop closer, friendlier relations between schools and community. In the dairy, timber and agriculture lands of Wisconsin is an outstanding example of how citizens helped improve their schools with the aid of a map, some sound thinking and continued interest.

School Merger Leads to Improvement

Joint School District No. 8, Shawano, Wisconsin, now operates its rural, elementary and high schools under one administration. After the merger took place the school board acted to form a Citizens Advisory Committee to study the schools and serve as a unifying force. That Committee was representative of all the former districts and all segments of the community as a whole. With the help of the school board, it established the need for an up-dating building program for certain schoolhouses and the need for new classrooms in the high school and elementary grades.

A campaign to educate voters was launched. Everything from radio time to citizens committee speakers' time was contributed free. Result? The vote for school improvement carried.

A new senior high school has been built. The administration of the schools has improved and with it the quality of the teaching. Better teachers have been attracted. New and broadly cultural courses—such as music and art instruction—are being offered.

Rural schools have been improved with better lighting, better heating and interior decorating. The tax rate has been equalized for the whole area. A shift in grades within the various rural schools has helped lighten the teaching load. A lunch program has been established in some schools. And there is a large group of persons with an active interest in schools from which good school board members can be drawn.

In Richmond, Virginia, action was taken when it was learned that the salaries paid to teachers were slipping down the scale as compared with other towns.

Teachers' Salaries Increased

In the early fall of 1954, the Richmond City School Board appointed a Special Citizens' Committee on Teachers' Salaries—twelve prominent citizens, representing various areas and business and civic groups.

The committee was asked to ascertain salaries being paid by business and industry in Richmond for positions of comparable training, as well as to look at the local economic situation in relation to the state, region, and nation. They were also asked to make detailed recommendations concerning teachers' salaries. The committee met again and again. Their findings revealed that both starting and maximum salaries for the classroom teacher did not make teaching an attractive career for two reasons: it was less than an individual with the same qualifications and experience could earn in private industry and after 11 years there was no further financial incentive.

The Committee came up with its recommendations, and the School Board promptly seconded them. As a result, Richmond teachers received an increase in salary.

Literally thousands of communities are now taking time off to look at their schools, as did Detroit, Shawano and Richmond. Whether the problem is getting enough good teachers and keeping them, enlarging the schools or building new ones, consolidating schools now in existence, providing for vocational education, or more specialized local problems, they're all awake and aware of the fact that the public schools are their schools and that they need the help and backing of every citizen in the community.

National Citizens Committee

However, interest and willingness are not enough. Enthusiasm and good intentions have to be harnessed and organized. Have you heard about the National Citizens Council for Better Schools? It is a nonprofit corporation founded by businessmen, educators, parents, people from all walks of life who are awake to the fact that our public schools lack funds, buildings, teachers and many other essentials. The Council doesn't pretend it has all the answers to the school situation but it believes American communities the country over can come to grips with their problems and work them out, given the sort of help and backing that the Council is prepared to give.

The Council's function is to serve as a clearing house. It keeps in touch with local communities, keeps records of what is being accomplished in the school field the country over—how groups organize, how they spread the word, how they work together for better schools. Then when other communities want to know how to get started, how to carry on, what pitfalls to look out for, what difficulties they may meet—there is data based on actual experience all ready for them in printed form, free for the asking. With it goes sound advice and suggestions offered by the National Citizens Council itself. There is something inspiring in the way this makes it natural for communities across the country to get in touch with each other, pool ideas and experiences, and help one another work for better schools.

Information may be obtained from the headquarters of the National Citizens Council for Better Schools at 9 East 40th Street, New York, New York.

Is your community aware of its school needs? Is it planning to hold a conference on education? Does it know of the help to be had for the asking? These are important questions. Can your community answer them with "Yes"?

—By Edith Harwin Goodman

HOW TO START A SCHOOL CAMP

IF you've heard or read something about classes of schoolchildren going off to spend a few days camping together—and this is happening more and more as the School Camping Program catches on all over the country—you've probably thought, "That's a wonderful idea. Wish our school could do it." But then—"Must be expensive, though," or "Our town's too small," or "Our city's too big."

In Croton-on-Hudson, some forty miles from New York City, the residents feel that their town isn't too small or too big, or too poor, but that just as they are, they do a good job with their school camping program. About seven years ago, the supervising principal of schools suggested to the seventh-grade social studies teacher that he work out such a program. After a trial run, the community's help was sought.

As a result, seventh-graders in the early fall and late spring scramble into a school bus to head for a five-day school week by the side of a lake ten minutes away. The camp is a regular summer camp for children which has been made available to local groups during the ten months of the year when it is not in use. The average five-day school encampment costs about $7.00 for each child, including food and a nominal $1.00 per camper for the use of the camp. If a child cannot afford the expense, the school, without revealing the child's name, asks the PTA to pay for him. The school bus is used for field trips so there is no other cost. To see how the camp is managed, you need only look in at any time.

Camp Activities

Here's Jane rubbing a round stone in a well worn stone vessel. The manager of a nearby estate who happens to be an amateur archeologist is teaching Jane how the Indians ground corn. He has been digging up ancient samples of Indian workmanship in the area for many years. He shows the children his private museum and teaches them to watch for arrowheads and other treasures still to be found.

Some of the children are clambering over stone foundations that hint of things gone before—an old wire mill. Under the guidance of the Village Historian, they discover that history may be read in ruins as well as in books. To contribute to the historian's continuing research, the youngsters make rubbings of ancient gravestones in the local cemetery.

Here's another group no longer taking the length and height of a hill for granted. An electrical contractor, who has maintained his interest in surveying since his engineering-student days, helps the youngsters in actual earth-measurement problems—an experience which not only makes maps more meaningful, but later will give reality to many mathematical problems.

At night the boys and girls turn their eyes to the stars above them. The director of Camp Rainbow, an amateur astronomer, shows them how to look through a 6-inch telescope and find the rings of Saturn, cloud belts of Jupiter, ring nebula in Lyra.

How Parents Help

You can see that the answer to the problems of setting up a school camping program in this community lay in recruiting the special interests and talents, the enthusiasm and good will of residents. The school has a file on "community resources" which was compiled by the PTA. Parents and others were asked what they have to contribute, either from their vocational backgrounds or from hobbies and leisure-time activities.

A great many parents and other volunteers are directly involved in the school camping program. Besides serving as leaders, they help in the operation of the encampment. Some mothers teach cooking and supervise the kitchen police assignments. Fathers supervise the children on painting jobs or setting fence posts or other tasks undertaken as the children's sign of appreciation to their hosts. They also participate in such sports as baseball or horseshoe pitching.

Over the years, a backlog of experienced volunteers has grown. Although there are newcomers and changes among the adult participants each year, the fact that an increasingly larger group has had experience makes for smooth functioning.

Values of Camping

This school camp also helps to highlight the great value to children of going to camp. Some youngsters go to full summer camp, too. To those who don't, this project gives a taste of what camping experience can mean. Having to live together from morning to night, the children begin to take a new look at each other. They are helped toward a better understanding of themselves and each other. They become closely acquainted with a wide and varied cross-section of the adults in their community, too.

The adults gain as much as the children from all this. Better understanding between school and community, for one thing. Before an encampment, the volunteers are briefed by the staff on the objectives of the program and their part in it. After the week's session, volunteers and school people meet again. Many a mother has new insight into a teacher's problems. Similarly, living with their charges twenty-four hours a day has given the teachers new insights into the problems parents face.

If you want such a program for your children, perhaps you can adopt this solution. Even the big problem of where to set up your camp isn't as impossible as it may look at first glance. A farmhouse that has several bedrooms or a big comfortable barn, an estate emptily waiting for owners, a county or state park, a private camp or a "Y" or Scout camp that stands unused for ten months out of the year—any of these can serve. It's highly probable that one of them isn't very far from you. Even if you live in one of our biggest cities, some place for a group of children to eat and sleep is within a few dollars' worth of travel cost.

Every school can have a camping program, if it wants one. You only need people who realize the benefits enough to plan and work for it.

—By Jennie H. Allen

HOW A PARENTS GROUP CAN HELP ITS HIGH SCHOOL

A UNIQUE and refreshing experiment in public high school education has quietly been gaining momentum in the village of Pleasantville, a middle-income community 31 miles north of New York City. Those who have seen it in operation feel strongly that in these days of lamentations over juvenile delinquency and the breakdown of teen-age ethics it points the way to vast improvement. It is, quite simply, the inclusion of high school parents in their sons' and daughters' classroom and social activities.

The students of Pleasantville High School think it's wonderful, the teachers are asking themselves how they ever got along without it and the parents are making sure it's there to stay. What's more, interested queries from many other communities indicate that in time it may become an accepted high school pattern.

The experiment began several years ago, the brain child of the high school's principal, Ronald McCreary, who had become increasingly disturbed over what he chose to call the "High School Iron Curtain."

Year after year he had seen parents flounder on the shoals that divide elementary school from the mysterious new world of high school. The realization that they were no longer wanted when the big league training started came as a bewildering shock to them.

"Their little boy or girl was suddenly a first-year high school student, undergoing matriculation in self-reliance and independence, developing in a matter of weeks an undisguised scorn for the apron strings just shed," McCreary said.

Symbols of the Past

"He—or she—was wheeling into the wild blue yonder, as proud as punch and big as all Texas, and Mother and Father overnight became symbols of a callow past. A query about academic or social progress brought a noncommittal nod or shoulder shrug. And a freshman who was forced to share conversation with a parent publicly and conspicuously at a function designed primarily for his own pleasure became flushed of cheek, furtive and all but denied his relationship.

"It was a situation of nobody's making and to nobody's liking. The kids followed the trend because they thought it was the thing to do. The parents accepted it because they thought both the school and the kids wanted it that way. And the teachers—who longed for some kind of help—thought they were expected to carry on alone with the task of keeping junior in line."

Principal McCreary felt that the banished parents could be a potent force for educational betterment. "They'd approach me as if they had no right to at all," he recalled. "The usual entering wedge was: 'It's none of my business, of course . . .' or: 'My daughter would kill me if she saw me here, but I just had to know . . .' I'd tell them it was decidedly their business and they had not only a right to know, but a duty to know what was going on. I kept planting this seed and finally it sprouted.

Organization of the Class

"One day a mother with more than usual determination marched into my office and put it right on the line. 'How would it be if we parents organized into a kind of freshman class society?' she asked. 'That would be wonderful,' I said. 'Go right ahead.'"

That was how the first Parents Class was born. It didn't start off with a bang. As a matter of fact, you might say it whispered its way into existence. One weekday night a group of 32 mothers and fathers of freshman students gathered in the high school cafeteria like a band of conspirators. The optimistic McCreary was present to allay their fears and they managed to elect officers and draw up bylaws. They didn't quite know what they were going to do, but they had exercised the great American right to organize and it was a beginning.

McCreary carefully felt the pulse of the students, from freshmen to seniors. Had they heard that a freshman parents group had been formed? One that would be devoted entirely to the problems of a single class made up of children of its members. He was prepared for revolution, but curiosity—as he suspected it would—won out. A parents class? That was a new one! What in the world could the parents do?

Orientation to School Procedures

The Parents Class set to work. A Freshman Night, designed to acquaint parents with school procedure, was arranged. Oldsters squeezed into desks normally occupied by their offspring and got the lowdown straight from the class instructors. At 15-minute intervals, they moved on to another class and another period of revelation and orientation. It was the first organized contact between parent and teacher and an eye-opener for both.

Mothers and fathers discovered that things were somewhat different and maybe a little tougher than in the good old days, that junior was not nearly the scatterbrain they'd thought him and that teacher generally was a warm-hearted, considerate human being whose strength and patience could be sorely taxed by 40-odd lively youngsters groping for emotional and social stability. Over coffee and doughnuts in the basement cafeteria understanding and friendship grew apace.

Before the year was out Parents Classes had been formed by the mothers and fathers of the sophomores and juniors, too. The seniors, only a term away from graduation, escaped the parental fever that year.

The freshman Parents Class had its first chance to make good at the freshman dance. Daniel could have faced no more frightening a prospect, lions and all. Freshman boys, brave as all get out in their masculine bailiwick, wilt like heated lilies when a mixed social looms. The day before the dance it looked as if the orchestra would play a recital for chaperones and janitors. The boys were in hiding. But a 24-hour telephone campaign by mothers turned up a sizable portion of the unwilling males. It was later conceded that promises of fancy door prizes and super-duper refreshments were what had turned the trick.

Students Ask for Guidance

As the next school year got under way the Parents Class took stock of themselves. An orientation night and a class dance rescue were little enough to show for the past season. What did the group plan to do?

Perhaps the students themselves could offer a clue. At the first parent meeting of the term the new sophomores, special guests, sat attentively while their teachers and parents expatiated on the merits of good marks, good fellowship and goodness knows what else. In the midst of the wandering speeches an earnest sophomore marched to the improvised rostrum.

"We appreciate what you folks are trying to do," he said, "but it's like we were being led around by the nose. Honest, we get enough of that in school. If you'd sort of help us make up our minds, kind of guide us . . ."

The intrepid spokesman had provided a warning, a yardstick and a rallying word: guidance. Well, what sort of guidance? What did they need and want? A parents committee worked out plans for a survey of student likes and dislikes, criticisms, opinions, suggestions for improvements. Each student in the class was interviewed at length by a sophomore parent other than his or her own. The interview was set up at a time convenient to the student in his or her own home. The results were carefully recorded and included—without student identification—in a summary.

Children Air Complaints

The axe fell indiscriminately.

Teachers, while praised in the main, were taken over the coals for overloading on homework, failure to give individual attention where necessary, unfair marking, favoritism and even—such is the brashness of youth—for being inadequately prepared to dispense the daily lesson.

Parents came in for an unmerciful lambasting.

"We don't think we're the smartest people in the world," one girl told an interviewer, "but sometimes our parents treat us as if we're dopes."

"They forget," a boy pointed out, "that we're not going to school in 1930. Courses are different now and schedules are heavier. They won't bother to find out what the changes are. It's always, 'Now when I went to high school . . .' And I'm sick of hearing how we don't learn the fundamental three R's. I bet Pop's face would be awful red if he took a look, today, at some of *his* high school compositions."

"They worry about what we do at night," explained a boy. "Boys hang out on the corner or at the diner. Girls stay out too late. Most times there's nothing wrong. We're just looking for something to do. No one's helped us have organized fun outside school hours."

Girls were indignant over the romantic immaturity of the sophomore males. "We thought that this year they'd be anxious to date us for dances," one commented, "but they still have to be coaxed!"

And the "going steady" custom—indulged in by the comparatively few sophomore girls lucky enough to catch the eye of more mature juniors and seniors, and accepted as indispensable by all upperclassmen—got some unexpected slaps.

The response was not all criticism. Gentle quizzing evoked some soul-searching, too. Students who had been classed as uninterested in extracurricular activities revealed deep-seated yearnings to participate and the reasons that kept them from doing so.

Some, because they had not gotten into service clubs like the Tri Hi Y, a YMCA-sponsored organization, before membership quotas were filled, or failed to make elective groups, felt unwanted and inferior. Others labored under the delusion that personal effort was useless in the face of imagined antipathy. And still a third group displayed a shyness which actually was ignorance of the value of healthy competition.

A sophomore boy disclosed the disconcerting fact that he stayed out late nights in spite of his father's orders because his friends would think him "chicken" if he knuckled under. Another who had achieved straight A's in elementary school blandly admitted he intentionally got barely passing grades so that his confreres would not brand him a "brain."

Girls wanted a charm club, driving lessons, a costume club, skating parties, noon hour dance lessons, singing groups—and less homework. Boys wanted a ski club, hunting and trapping, a rifle club, skating, target shooting, swimming, less homework.

Parents Take Stock

The parents, a bit alarmed by the shock waves of their self-made explosions, took stock, and a quiet behind-the-scenes campaign was begun to salve bruised egos, iron out misunderstandings and supply some of the requested activities.

Before the end of the school term three more Tri Hi Y's were added to take care of burgeoning membership; a rifle club was organized; the gym was opened after school for dancing practice; the groundwork for an auto driving class was laid; a doctor-parent donated space in an office building basement and other parents furnished it, complete with juke box and TV, for evening student get-togethers; extracurricular activity went up 25 per cent.

The Parents Class did not clear up all the problems presented them by any means. They let time—as they knew it would—take care of the male sophomores' social unawareness. They wisely left the "going steady" custom strictly alone. And their reluctance to usurp school authority was an excellent excuse to do absolutely nothing about the homework situation.

Teachers did some housecleaning in their own precincts, too—a move the students were quick to recognize and appreciate.

When the next school year rolled around everybody was in the groove. Each class group set up liaison committees to keep in touch with the class ahead and the class behind.

Scholastic Projects

This was the year the original Parents Class devoted mainly to scholastic projects. One mother, an expert in education, made an exhaustive study of the juniors' outside needs and set up a detailed bibliography to help them in their summer reading.

Though they would not face college board entrance exams until the following year, it was arranged for them to take the aptitude portion of the test to acquaint them with the procedure and prepare them for the real thing twelve months hence. A "prep rally" was held the night before the quiz at which teachers and recent graduates explained what to expect and parents lent moral support.

Teachers and parents also set up a coaching service for those falling behind, and there were two other achievements: the voting of funds for an auto driving class in the school budget and the inauguration of an annual graduation tea given by the juniors for the seniors.

"But the real progress," McCreary pointed out, "was in the intangibles, the things that don't show on the record. I think that for the first time the new upperclassmen felt completely at ease with the parents group arrangement. They'd been afraid of losing their independence and realized now that this would not happen.

"Parent-teacher-student relations had reached an informal, friendly stage where individual difficulties were straightened out amicably and sensibly. Now whatever complaints parents had sprang from a desire to criticize constructively and not—as had been the case in the past and still is in many high school communities—from hysteria induced by ignorance. Most agreed home relations with their kids had improved, too."

Career Plans Discussed

The first Parents Class sailed through the final term as if they were going to graduate themselves. They worked up a Career Night that included college educators, trade union officials and even representatives of the armed forces to spell out the prospects of the college, workaday or service world.

They held panel discussions on test procedure, English and history to prepare the seniors for the college board exams on which they'd already had a practice run. They made guidance available in other subjects on an individual basis.

But perhaps their greatest success that final year lay in the purely social area. For years it had been the custom of the graduating class to make the senior prom a stay-awake marathon. After the dance's end at one A.M. senior couples usually repaired to neighboring nightclubs until four A.M. closing, then drove in the first flush of dawn to distant Jones Beach on Long Island, where they stayed until late afternoon.

Young drivers a bit high on a few brave drinks, young drivers sleepy at the wheel after 24 hours awake—these frightening thoughts had kept many a senior parent sleepless on other prom nights.

This time the parents quietly arranged a prom program of their own and put it before the seniors: the municipal swimming pool would be theirs from one A.M. to three A.M.; after a refreshing swim they would be served a steak dinner; then a couple of hours' sleep at chaperoned homes, picked out in advance, and buses would take them to and from Jones Beach. The plan was offered simply, without urging or pressure, and the parents sat back with their fingers crossed. All but a few students went along with it.

What had the years of experimentation accomplished? "It was a good deal," a senior spokesman said. "If the parents had shoved us around I think it would have flopped, but they treated us like equals and that means a lot to high school kids. At first it seemed strange, sort of going to school with Mom and Dad, but after a while we got to like it."

"We're not looking for miracles," a teacher summed it up. "However, we all know that the parents have made our school a happier place to work. I used to brace myself when I saw a parent coming. 'Oh-oh . . . what've I done?' I'd ask myself in panic. Now I throw open my arms and cry, 'Welcome, friend!' "

—By Jack Stone

DANCE PROJECT FOR THE YOUNGER SET

ONE day the telephone rang and a neighbor said, "We're thinking of organizing a seventh-grade dancing class. What do you think of the idea and do you think your daughter would like to be a member of the group?"

It sounded simple enough but back of that invitation was an important purpose that some of us had been talking about for some time.

Most parents in the community had the same problem. The budding adolescents of twelve, thirteen and fourteen were determined to depart from childish ways. They needed physical and social outlets, they needed to be their own age. They didn't want, on the one hand, hovering parents, but on the other, they weren't quite equal to managing social affairs all by themselves. After consulting with high-school counselors and mothers of eighth-graders, forty mothers agreed that a dancing class might be the answer.

What was wanted was wholesome, supervised recreation for boys and girls. They would learn dancing and good social behavior. Friendly boy-and-girl relationships, so important at that age, would be encouraged and the youngsters would have a lot of fun.

Preparatory Arrangements

All the parents agreed to keep expenses down. The girls would wear simple dresses. Refreshments would be light. Parents would assist unobtrusively, for adolescent children tend to draw away from us yet need guidance.

The group of boys and girls represented each elementary school in a town of about 20,000. It was felt that twenty boys and twenty girls were all that could be accommodated in one group, but as interest spread other groups were organized.

The class met three Friday evenings in the month from 7:00 to 8:30 with a party on the fourth Saturday from 7:30 to 9:30. Those early hours were a blessing and were never once protested against because they were set from the beginning. There was ballroom dancing, square dancing, folk dancing and a monthly party.

Of course there were problems. These included finding a place large and sturdy enough to survive the energy released by forty youngsters and the selection of a teacher whom they liked and respected. Fortunately, the use of a college recreation hall was offered for Friday evenings. There were two provisions: that a small fee be paid to cover utilities and janitor service and that the classes be over early. If you do not live in a college town, see if you can make arrangements to use the armory, school gymnasium, church recreation center or a respectable dancing spot. Since 7:00 P.M. to 8:30 P.M. is a slack hour, such an arrangement may be possible.

Finding a Teacher

Through the Girl Scout Association a local girl was contacted who had taught dancing in summer camps and was experienced in directing groups of young people. Since the early hours did not interfere with her secretarial work or evening engagements, she was willing to take on the assignment at a reasonable fee.

Neighborhood car pools provided safe, sociable transportation. Parents who were chauffeurs for the evening agreed also to be unobtrusive chaperones, to assist the teacher and to bring a portable radio when possible. To minimize telephoning regarding transportation arrangements it was agreed to rotate turns. Since each car could carry five or six children, these responsibilities would recur only every five or six weeks. This saved endless hours of telephoning and worry.

Details which arose from time to time were handled by an elected planning committee consisting of four mothers, four fathers, four boys and four girls. On matters of dress and behavior, they were the supreme court.

Expenses were kept down to a nominal figure. Parties were held in private homes that had sufficiently large recreation rooms, and party expenses were evenly divided among four host families.

Party Policy

"Uniform policy of simplicity in dress," the rules read, so the planning committee very sensibly ruled that the accepted dress would be blouses or sweaters with skirts for girls, casual clothes for boys. On festive party nights, the girls would wear simple party dresses and the boys would appear in suits with shirts and ties. Most of the parents heaved a tremendous sigh of relief when the dress problem was settled.

When the party night came around the fourth Saturday of each month, eight hosts were allotted for each affair, two boys and two girls, and four parents. This was a master stroke for it resulted in excellent cooperation between children and adults.

The hosts decided the type of party. It might be seasonal, such as Thanksgiving, Christmas, Valentine's Day, an outdoor party including wiener roast, rides or hikes, or it might be planned around sports, such as ice-skating or swimming. It might be a costume party, hobo, pet peeve or any other type. Dancing was optional.

One family offered the use of its basement recreation room for a costume party. Guests were asked to come in utterly ridiculous costumes. "Nothing your mother makes or buys," they were told, "just any old thing you can rig up out of stuff in the attic." There were prizes for the "craziest."

The whole group of young people responded enthusiastically to this wholesome, supervised recreation. At the same time, they have developed poise and better relationships with other boys and girls. Parents, too, have joined in the fun, thereby getting to know better their children's friends as well as other parents. —*By Gladys Toler Burris*

IS YOUR CHILD A POOR SPORT?

AFTER a bitter Kentucky high school football game, pop bottles and fists flew. Because local police were unable to quell the disturbance, the state highway patrol had to be called in. So enraged were youthful spectators that the referees, coaches and players had to be escorted home by police.

In New Jersey when the home team lost a basketball game by one point, its hysterical teen-age rooters beat up the opposing coach.

During a riot after a Tennessee high school game, a girl was stabbed.

In Texas, a principal who suspended several members of his high school's football team for playing hooky was threatened with physical violence. One night after his school lost an important game, the windows of the principal's home were stoned by adolescent hoodlums who hadn't yet learned that sports are only a part of education.

Isolated incidents? Not really. These are shocking but typical examples of a wave of poor sportsmanship that seems to be increasing in the high schools of America.

The situation has gotten so far out of hand that some high schools have even cancelled their traditional games. Where turbulent games have ended unresolved in juvenile riots, authorities have often been afraid to re-schedule them.

Need for Good Sportsmanship

Never before in U.S. history has there been a greater need for teaching good sportsmanship. Obviously a child who isn't a good sport can hardly grow up into a good citizen. What he learns on the playing field and in the grandstand is influential in shaping his character.

Educators and athletic officials are the first to point this out. But across the country thousands of well meaning principals, coaches, teachers are now asking themselves and each other: "What can we do to stop the booing, fighting and bad behavior?"

Let's face it: the teaching of good sportsmanship begins at home. Children also develop their sportsmanship standards by observing the behavior of grownups at athletic contests. But adults don't help matters when they try to control teen-age games through high pressure Alumni Athletic Councils and Booster Clubs.

One immature father was so enraged by a high school referee's decision that he dashed onto the basketball floor and began jostling the official. Who was this overzealous spectator? An eminently respectable local businessman—and a member of the county school board!

Parents' Attitude Important

In another community sport slap-happy parents during the football season refused to talk to parents whose children attended a rival school. Small wonder youngsters get false ideas about winning and losing!

Children—whether players or spectators—also take their sportsmanship cues from their coaches. An undignified, ill-tempered coach who curses, boos, jumps up and down, protestingly storms out onto the floor, or throws up his hands after losing a game is hardly setting an admirable example. A wiser coach or parent recognizes achievement and applauds good play of *both* teams.

One high school coach tells this story on himself: "In an important football game my 130-pound center was taking an awful beating from a 195-pound opposing guard. He had a split lip, skin off his nose and a closed eye. I kept getting angrier and angrier, especially because the referee couldn't catch the offending guard in the act. I called my boy to the bench and told him, 'Go after that roughneck!' He made me feel like two cents when he said, 'No, coach, you never taught me to play that way.'"

America's school sports would be in a far better state if more coaches and players had such insight. Players generally are not as unsportsmanlike as spectators even though there have been instances where high school athletes scratched, kicked and even bit each other.

Fortunately, some alert schools are coming up with constructive sportsmanship programs which could easily be emulated elsewhere.

Model Sportsmanship Program

Outstanding is the plan of Clifford Scott High School in East Orange, New Jersey. It has quietly launched a unique sportsmanship program which insiders are now hailing as a model—a simple yet practical idea that any school could adopt.

There is much more to Scott High's new style sportsmanship than such perfunctory gestures as exchanging cheerleaders at intermission or having one school band play the other's school song. Far from being a lip-service, occasional thing, the school's students, players, coaches and teachers have fun working at sportsmanship the year round—before, during and after their games.

Like most high schools, Scott had its share of booing, soreheads, and roughnecking. Scott High wisely never let it get out of hand. Convinced that such win-at-any-cost antics were self-defeating, it administered some preventive therapy: a heavy dosage of the good, old-fashioned win-or-lose courtesies.

After home games, the visiting players, coaches, cheerleaders and officials are invited for soft drinks and cookies. These friendly post-game get-togethers help wipe out hard feelings after a close game. Scott's gay recreation center used to be a dingy storeroom near the gym. However, paint furnished by the Board of Education and elbow grease furnished by the students transformed it into a cheerful Red and Gray party room. The young people built partitions and plastered pennants and pictures over the walls to decorate it. They coaxed old rugs, chairs, sofas, lamps, a radio, record player and even a television set out of parents. Amid such surroundings everyone present makes a sincere effort to be a good loser and a gracious winner. Visitors rarely depart without the friendliest of feelings.

How It Functions

You may see a visiting basketball player jitterbug with a Scott High girl cheerleader while the record player beats out a rhythm as the encircling onlookers applaud. During the football season, visiting teams find a big basket of apples on their bus for the ride home. During home baseball and track contests, Scott players trot out pails of sliced oranges packed in chopped ice for both sides. "The oranges made a hit even though we didn't," wisecracked one baseball player.

If an opponent is injured in a game, Scott players take up a collection to send him a gift. To cheer his convalescence, they also visit him at home or at the hospital. A football foe who sprained his back and was visited by Scott's co-captain remarked, "I was sure surprised to get a basket of fruit from the *other* team."

Unlike many schools which only play teams of similar outlook, Scott deliberately tries to let its boys meet youngsters of different faiths and backgrounds in friendly rivalry. To break down barriers, Scott schedules games with parochial, private and vocational schools.

At Scott assemblies, before every sports season, coaches and players show actual game situations to the students through films and talks. In this spectator education, legal and illegal plays are illustrated and common rule infractions explained. Recently, for example, students were shown new basketball rules on foul-shooting.

A question period follows to clear up anything the kids still don't understand. "When is it blocking and when is it charging?" a 15-year-old boy wanted to know. A girl of 16 asked, "Why are so darn many officials needed?" Even the most elementary questions are welcomed. Surprisingly, most booing, referee-baiting, spectator squabbling—and other displays of poor sportsmanship—stem from ignorance. Fans often don't understand the rules, officials' signals or the plays they're watching.

If a Scott player ever cusses a referee he is immediately benched.

Of course, sportsmanship Scott-style doesn't work 100 per cent. Once a disgruntled football player threw his helmet on the ground only to have the coach make him apologize to the helmet! Another time, after losing a basketball game on a last-second shot, a few Scott fans went wild. At the start of the next game, the Scott captain made a brief speech saying, "Good sportsmanship isn't confined to players. It applies to you spectators, too." He then told the home crowd what his teammates and Scott expected of them. It worked fine.

Scott's sportsmanship philosophy has had even more far-reaching effects. One result is that locks are no longer used on lockers. Compare this honor system to that of some surrounding schools which lose up to $2,000 worth of equipment annually—even with locks!

Texas Program

Down in southeast Texas, high school sportsmanship is also getting a shot in the arm. They used to have uproarious rows but happily, a newly-formed Good Sportsmanship League in Beaumont, Orange, Port Arthur and Port Neches is changing that. Not overnight, naturally, but the progress has been steady. A constitution and a code were drawn up. Each school has three representatives—a faculty member, a girl and a boy junior elected for a two-year term. Among activities are: Visitation Days when students are invited to spend the day at the host school; meeting the visiting football team at the 50-yard line and giving it a token of friendship for its trophy case. The Good Sportsmanship League also stages a Good Sportsmanship Week before the district championship game with posters, buttons and tags displayed throughout the schools.

The Southeastern West Virginia Sportsmanship Code was also adopted in December 1952 to "further sportsmanship at athletic contests" at the high schools in the five-county area of Wyoming, Summers, Fayette, Mercer and Raleigh. "We believe our over-all Sportsmanship Code will become as much a part of the athletic program in high schools as the game itself," explains the Sportsmanship Council secretary.

The Code consists of a code of ethics for coaches, students, players and officials; acceptance by principals and athletic directors of recommendations on playing fields and game administration; a unique Rating Plan whereby the officials and two selected students of each school after each game put, in sealed envelopes, their ratings (excellent, good, fair or poor) of the other's sportsmanship performance, based on spectator booing, coaches' harassment of officials, rough antics of players and cheerleaders.

Student Rating Program

Similarly, the West Suburban Conference—composed of high schools outside Chicago—has a student rating program. At the end of the season, the ratings are tabulated and the sportsmanship winner announced. The New York State Public High School Athletic Association is working out new sportsmanship principles.

In addition, a national Babe Ruth Sportsmanship Program was launched several years ago. Administered by the American Association for Health, Physical Education and Recreation and endorsed by many leading sports editors and columnists, it gives awards for good sportsmanship.

What does all this add up to? Simply that progress is being made, even though not fast enough. Many schools are squeamish about reporting acts of poor sportsmanship to their high school athletic associations for fear of giving a school a black mark. Hence, only the most publicized unsportsmanlike acts come to official attention. The National Federation of State High School Athletic Associations chiefly, lays down rules rather than punishment for unsportsmanlike demonstrations.

Probably what is needed most today is teaching our boys and girls the old Jeffersonian concept of the "Aristocracy of Virtue." Our children must be taught how to lose gracefully. A true sportsman not only wins without gloating but loses without rancor. Children must learn they can't win all the time —there are just so many first places. Defeat must be taken in stride.

British Team Spirit

Americans sometimes pooh-pooh British sportsmanship. But England's attitude towards sportsmanship has been far more mature than ours.

The thought of criticizing a visiting player for missing a shot would shame the youngest British child. On the contrary, at a cricket, football or any other match, applause for the opposing team is louder than for the home players. The onlookers shout impartially, "Well played!" "Well done!" "Good shot!" Or groan sympathetically "Bad luck!" or "Oh, well tried!"

Opposing captains hasten to shake hands immediately after a game. The loser congratulates the winner; the winner murmurs something tactful like "You put up a grand fight," or "Stiffest game we've had this season."

If the losing captain feels his team did very badly, he usually apologizes for giving his opponents such a poor game. The winning team must, in politeness, be prepared to deny this or to find a ready excuse: "It was bad luck not having Harold today." Or: "You were a bit off your game today, but you'll beat us next time."

If, as is customary, the visiting team is then entertained at tea, the teams pair off with their opposing numbers, making polite conversation. The hosts take great pains to show neither triumph nor mortification.

Teams are allowed only one "reserve" (substitute) in Britain. If for any reason a player drops out and can't be replaced, it is customary for the captain of the opposing team to withdraw one of his own men from the game to keep numbers even.

No British child would, in his wildest moment, question a referee's decision. If he did, he would be considered an outcast—a "bad sport"—by everyone, including his own side and would instantly be sent from the game. This applies even to the most hesitant decision on the part of the youngest and least experienced player who may be acting as umpire for the first time in his life. British philosophy is that the umpire is an impartial observer— if his decision isn't final, the game can't be played.

Occasionally tennis players argue over a point. But the chances are that each is insisting the point belongs to the *other!*

Team spirit is particularly stressed in British sport. A player who "hogs" the ball, no matter how brilliantly, is sharply reprimanded. "This is a team game, you know," he is apt to be told.

Our own sportsmanship code undoubtedly derives from Britain's. What has happened to it? Has it grown rusty through disuse—and too much stress on winning?

Example of Sportsmanship

Way back in 1940, through an honest blunder of the referee, Cornell defeated Dartmouth 3–0 in an important football game. Today such an error would probably cause a spectator riot. But not then; in the ancient days of 1940 Dartmouth waited patiently. Soon afterward photographs of the game revealed the error and the verdict was reversed. Cornell gracefully relinquished claim to victory and congratulated Dartmouth. The Dartmouth coach voiced "regret over the disappointment which the great Cornell team must have experienced." The incident rang through the sports world like a clean breeze.

"If we were Cornell," the *New York Times* said, "we wouldn't trade that telegram of the Cornell coach's for all the team's victories."

A game isn't a battle. It should be played for fun—not for bitterness or sorrow.

Sportsmanship, after all, is only an application of the Golden Rule. It is an inherent part of democracy.

Today everywhere we need more sportsmanship—and fewer "sports."

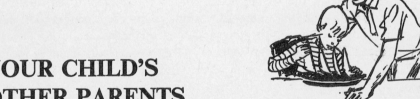

YOUR CHILD'S
OTHER PARENTS

Did it ever occur to you that other adults in your community can frequently help your adolescent son or daughter in ways that you cannot? It may be a sympathetic youth leader, teacher, clergyman, social worker, athlete, employer, family friend, neighbor up the street, cop on the beat. Responsible grownups can be extremely valuable in your teen-ager's life—more so than you perhaps realize—giving your youngster priceless educational, vocational and personal guidance. When they are wise counselors, they help meet special needs, smooth over rough spots and offer democratic learning experiences that an adolescent often does not get at home. So don't assume that you are failing as a parent or shirking your responsibility if your youngster confides more in a favorite away-from-home grownup than in you. The "other parents" are supplementing your work—not replacing you.

A teen-ager frequently needs outside advice on anything from choosing a career to a minor dating problem. An adolescent girl may get helpful tips on her hairdo from a friendly girls' organization leader which her own mother couldn't give. A growing boy may find in a gym teacher, male guidance that he doesn't receive or can't accept from his own father. Occasionally, an adolescent desperately needs to talk to an outside grownup about a family problem. It may be a mother's illness, a father's long absences from home, parents' feuding or troublesome younger brothers or sisters. Some adolescents ask outside adults they trust, "Should I quit school?" "Should I marry?" "Shall I leave home?" These "other parents" often straighten out your child's thinking without your ever knowing it. But it's even better if you do know how important other adult influence can be and encourage it.

Help from Youth Worker

Listen to this perceptive father: "Our 14-year-old Fred was very shy and got pushed around easily. If he got a scratch, he howled! Because he was a city boy, my wife and I thought camping would be helpful to him. But I knew that I wasn't the person to introduce him to this world of adventure. I'd never even loaded a pack. So we decided that Fred needed a good camp counselor who would make a special effort with him. Fortunately, he landed one when we sent him to a YMCA camp last summer. Fred was taken on overnight hikes and loved it. By the end of the summer, he was taking some of the younger kids on overnight hikes himself. Frankly, my wife and I were amazed at the change in him. We always tried to give him love and security but this wonderful counselor gave him something else."

America's great youth organizations, many of which are supported by your local Community Chest or United Fund, have countless unsung, dedicated "other parents." They show your child how to get along with others, encourage his special abilities, instill a sense of belonging, teach self-reliance and the art of becoming a responsible citizen. Adolescents often remain in these groups mainly because they admire their leaders.

Prominent People Cite Experiences

Numerous successful men and women have been helped by wise "other parents" in these youth organizations. Connecticut Governor Abraham Ribicoff recalls that in his New Britain Boys' Club "the supervision and program were of invaluable benefit to me in my formative years." Freedom Foundation President Kenneth D. Wells can never forget the influence of an Akron, Ohio, scoutmaster on him. Actresses Debbie Reynolds and Celeste Holm were encouraged by sympathetic Girl Scout leaders. Playwright Moss Hart and movie executive Dore Schary as youngsters were encouraged by a dramatics director at the Newark, N.J., Jewish Community Center. Retired heavyweight boxing champion Rocky Marciano revealed that the Catholic Youth Organization in his native Brockton, Mass., helped him keep on the right path.

Thousands of other boys and girls have been guided by proxy parents in youth-serving organizations which are, as one of them puts it, "places for growing." For example, Doris at 16 was an ugly duckling—until she joined the YWCA. "I was fat, unattractive and unhappy," she recalls. "But I didn't want to worry my family about it. My mother was sick and my father had too much on his mind. But after I joined the 'Y,' a woman there showed me how to dress and use makeup and how to lose 20 pounds. That 'Y' woman did things for me my own parents could not have done in a thousand years."

How Children Are Helped

Margie, a neglected 13-year-old southern girl, felt lost in her family of six sisters and brothers. Margie's parents gave her no sense of personal worth. Trying to feel important, she started running around with a tough gang of boys and girls who were destroying school property and disrupting classes. One day, a Girl Scout leader talked her into joining a troop. Margie was warmed by the way the leader made her feel at home, giving her responsibility, encouragement and affection. Margie was extremely proud of her green uniform because it belonged to her—it wasn't one of her older sister's hand-me-downs. It wasn't long before Margie left the vandalous gang—because a wise outside adult believed in her at the right time.

Similarly, in boys' organizations, "other parents" have helped—quietly, casually and undramatically. Consider 12-year-old Tommy whose parents just didn't have time for him. His father was a traveling salesman and his mother a tense, overworked woman with five children. Feeling rejected at home, Tommy became a bully and troublemaker outside—until a leader of a neighborhood center, who understood boys, took an interest in him, praising Tommy whenever possible, making him feel wanted. Instead of becoming a delinquent, Tommy is now a good-citizen-in-the-making.

In Hollywood, California, a unique counseling service for socially uneasy boys 8 to 18 is sponsored by the local Rotary and Kiwanis clubs through the YMCA. Two friendly, full-time counselors help boys with their problems—many of them family ones—parents who are too strict, not strict enough, uninformed, disinterested and so on. The counselor is always ready to "shoot the breeze" with a troubled boy day or night, take him to ball games, act as a friend, confidant and even a substitute father.

Proxy Parents

Children from broken homes or with working mothers are often helped enormously by proxy parents in youth organizations like the Big Brothers.

Typical is the boy without a father who is helped through school by a Big Brother volunteer. After becoming a successful adult, he in turn gratefully acts as a Big Brother to another fatherless boy. As one 12-year-old put it, "A Big Brother is a guy who knows all about you and likes you just the same."

The Travelers Aid also acts as proxy parent to children who must take trains, planes or buses alone. Nearly every day at some Travelers Aid booth, a passing adult remarks, "Years ago when I was a kid, you helped me."

It isn't only organizations, though, that give this kind of help to young people. Favorite teachers act as "other parents" all over America every school day in the year. More objective about children than most parents, teachers help them not only in formal guidance interviews but in casual remarks before and after class, during lunch—anywhere they meet.

Clergymen as Counselors

Clergymen, likewise, can have a profound influence as "other parents." Not long ago a father with a mixed-up 17-year-old boy asked a friend in the National Council of Churches to write to the local minister in the town where his son was going away to school. "I was never sure how it was accomplished," the father recently told me, "but in a remarkably short time this minister whom I never met helped our son straighten out a difficult situation."

The priests of New York City's famous Trinity Church have been very successful in persuading warring teen-age gangs to settle their disputes in church quarters. "Constructive guidance was what these young people needed," observed one of the priests.

Adults who aren't parents themselves frequently help get youngsters out of trouble. Recently when a gang of teen-age Chicago boys were picked up by the police for card-playing on the sidewalk, the adult who bailed one boy out was the friendly owner of the hamburger joint where the gang hung out. Today this grownup is treasurer of a new Youth Council which is starting a neighborhood center for these boys.

Some years ago a kindly, little-known, small-town Kansas newspaper editor was talking to a local high school graduate who didn't know what he wanted to do next.

"Why don't you take the exam for Annapolis or West Point?" the editor suggested.

Though the boy's pacifist parents weren't overjoyed at this idea, he did— and that was the beginning of Dwight D. Eisenhower's career.

Athletes Aid Youth Programs

Many ex-athletes are now sparking programs for youngsters, inspiring them, helping to develop their personalities and teaching them to become good citizens as well as good ball players. Jesse Owens, former Olympic track star, is now running Junior Olympic Games for 1,800 boys between 12 and 17 as a member of the Illinois Youth Commission. In Chicago also, former baseball star Rogers Hornsby is showing hundreds of 8 to 11-year-old boys how to play the national game.

The transition from child to responsible adult is a difficult one but it can be easier for us and the teen-agers if we accept such outside help and, moreover, take steps to see that it is available to our young people. Many communities could do far more in furnishing additional "other parents" in well-staffed school guidance programs, recreation centers, child care clinics and so on. But typical of how short-sighted some communities are, when a new playground is planned, owners of nearby properties are likely to gang up to knife the proposal. In some towns, city fathers will quickly vote money for a new city hall but flatly deny it for a social worker to aid the juvenile courts. Yet youth services are cheap—compared to other community costs.

What You Can Do

And what about you? Can you lend a helping hand to the children of other parents by being a den mother, scout leader, Sunday school teacher, recreation worker? Today good volunteer leaders are desperately needed in most of the youth programs mentioned in this article. Too many children are being deprived of the priceless experience of belonging to an effective youth group simply because adult leaders aren't available. The organization of your choice, your town's volunteer bureau, your community welfare council, Community Chest or United Fund can tell you where you are most needed.

By volunteering as an "other parent," you do something good for yourself, too. The experience will give you new insight and understanding in living with your own child.   —By *Jack Harrison Pollack*

A CODE FOR TEEN-AGERS

ONE mother in our town grew upset when her teen-age daughter told her, "There's so much necking going on now, that parties aren't fun any more."

Then she began hearing about teen-age codes springing up all over the country—in Teaneck, New Jersey, in Vicksburg, Mississippi, in Arlington, Virginia. Finally, she read about the famous Minnesota Teen-age Code. Being a woman of action she wrote to St. Louis Park, the first Minnesota town to adopt their statewide code, for a copy of it. Then she talked to other parents who agreed that even our small town of Brookfield, Connecticut, with a school population of 650, could do with a similar code to youthful conduct.

So a group of interested parents and church representatives got together to discuss the Minnesota Code. After much talk—pro and con—a father finally said, "How about the young people? What do they think of a code?"

On this sound note, it was agreed that copies of the Minnesota Code be distributed to our town's eight youth organizations. At their club meetings the young people would be asked to consider the idea of a teen-age code, then send representatives to meet with interested adults to decide what, if anything, to do next. The pastor of one of the churches agreed to act as moderator at the next discussion.

Adults and Teen-agers Meet Together

The next meeting was a joint one, of adults and young people—about a dozen of each. The attitude of some of the youngsters seemed to be, "Who's going to tell us we can't do this and we can't do that? We don't need any code in Brookfield." But when the moderator explained that the idea was for them to develop their own code, which would simply be a guide and not a law and that no one was trying to force anything on them, they decided to form a working group to develop their own Code.

Now the project was turned over to the young people, with two adult advisers to be chosen by them. "No parents of teen-agers," they insisted, and chose instead the Reverend Mr. Walker and the Reverend Father Dennis. (Both men, incidentally, are gentle and fair-minded, ready to listen and counsel but not to push.)

Teen-agers Evaluate Problems

The committee of twenty-two young people began to meet, almost weekly, for two months, each member reporting back regularly to his own organization. They stuck to the Minnesota Code, simplifying wherever possible. "We skipped over going steady as we didn't think there was too much of that here," said a senior girl on the committee . . .

The big problem, it turned out, was *hours*. There was a good deal of arguing about them, not so much about the time for parties to end as about the reasonable amount of time to allow for arrival at home. But finally, after much heated discussion, clubs and committee had agreed on a code and a title: Tips for Teen-Age Thinking. "We mean this to be suggestions, not rules," said the youngsters. " 'Code' sounds too strict."

A few weeks later, copies were mailed to all parents of youngsters from seventh grade through high school, along with a letter from the Reverend Mr. Walker and the Reverend Father Dennis, which said in part: "These suggestions are intended as a basis for developing local standards similar to codes of conduct that are working successfully in other parts of the country. Please read them well and discuss them thoroughly with the young people in your family . . . The next step will be a meeting of parents and teen-agers to which you are urged to bring your questions, your suggestions and your willingness to help complete a mutually agreeable guide for the parents and youth of Brookfield."

Final Evaluations

The next meeting was peaceful and congenial. Three teen-agers representing the committee, joined by two who were "just interested," served as a panel, with three fathers, one of whom acted as moderator. Parents and teachers sat informally before them and raised their questions. Naturally, the big question, *hours,* popped up first. Other questions discussed were party crashing and parental supervision of young people's parties. Finally they all agreed that the Minnesota wording was pretty good and reasonable; that a committee of parents and teen-agers should be set up to arrive at a suitable code for Brookfield.

Two weeks later, the committee, consisting of four teen-agers and four adults, met. With all that time to think about it, the youngsters had swung full circle on the question of party crashing, and the party crashing paragraph finally inserted in the code was a good deal stronger than the parents had first suggested.

The changes made, the conversation turned to parent, not teen-age behavior. "Often as not," said one mother, "it's the parents who are at fault. They're afraid to be thought old-fashioned—and so help to encourage an 'anything goes' atmosphere." A teen-ager chimed in, "Some parents just don't seem to care about their children. They don't pick them up after parties and they don't care when they get home."

Thus, a final emendation in Brookfield's code was made: Its title was changed to *Guide for Teen-Agers and Parents.* Everyone now felt that parents should be included in the title, because the guide was as much for them as for their teen-agers.

Final questions were: Would Brookfield's *Guide for Teen-Agers and Parents* be followed? Would it do any good? Probably not for those who needed it most, the committee members thought, though general acceptance of the code would put pressure on them to behave, too. The following year Brookfield would have its own junior high, instead of grades seven through nine having to go to Danbury, seven miles away. The Guide, backed by PTA and Student Council, would naturally take hold in the new junior high.

But how about the sophomores, juniors and seniors still going to Danbury where there is no code? "Danbury's been eyeing us—and the possibility of their own code," said one of the adults. "Why only the other day, a Danbury school official said: 'We need a code more than we need a new school.' Not a mild statement from a school on double sessions! Maybe Brookfield has started something that will spread."

But meantime, how would the other Danbury students take Brookfield's attitude? "They'll just have to understand," said one of the teen-agers, "that this is the way we do things here." —*By Ruth Carson*

AGENCIES

AGENCIES

These agencies may be able to give you further counsel

Many agencies offer information or help with family problems. Consult the services in your own community first. The following organizations serve all parts of the country, in many instances through local branches. Here they are listed under the following headings: Family Relations, Hobbies and Recreation, Home Management, Health, Education, Community Living.

FAMILY RELATIONS

The following agencies offer services such as welfare aid and counseling in family problems:

AMERICAN INSTITUTE OF FAMILY RELATIONS, 5287 Sunset Boulevard, Los Angeles 27, California

AMERICAN NATIONAL RED CROSS, 17th and D Streets, N.W., Washington 6, D.C.

AMERICAN PUBLIC WELFARE ASSOCIATION, 1313 East 60th Street, Chicago 37, Illinois

ASSOCIATION FOR FAMILY LIVING (regional), 32 West Randolph Square, Chicago, Illinois

COUNCIL OF JEWISH FEDERATIONS AND WELFARE FUNDS, 729 Seventh Avenue, New York 19, N.Y.

FAMILY SERVICE ASSOCIATION OF AMERICA, 215 Fourth Avenue, New York 17, N.Y.

NATIONAL CATHOLIC WELFARE CONFERENCE, DEPARTMENT OF SOCIAL ACTION, 1312 Massachusetts Avenue, N.W., Washington 5, D.C.

NATIONAL CONFERENCE OF JEWISH COMMUNAL SERVICE, 150 East 35th Street, New York 16, N.Y.

NATIONAL COUNCIL OF CATHOLIC CHARITIES, 1346 Connecticut Avenue, N.W., Washington 5, D.C.

NATIONAL COUNCIL OF THE CHURCHES OF CHRIST IN THE UNITED STATES OF AMERICA, DEPARTMENT OF SOCIAL WELFARE, 297 Fourth Avenue, New York 10, N.Y.

NATIONAL COUNCIL ON FAMILY RELATIONS, 1219 University Avenue S.E., Minneapolis 14, Minnesota

Social Welfare Departments of various Church Headquarters (address may be sought from local clergyman)

HOBBIES AND RECREATION

AMERICAN FEDERATION OF ARTS, 1083 Fifth Avenue, New York 28, N.Y., offers traveling exhibits, illustrated lectures, and an information service to promote interest in art.

AMERICAN NATURE ASSOCIATION, 1214 Sixteenth Street, N.W., Washington 6, D.C., offers illustrated lectures and audio-visual aids to encourage interest in the out-of-doors and use of National Parks.

AMERICAN YOUTH HOSTELS, 14 West Eighth Street, New York 11, N.Y., has information on hosteling the world over, arranges tours.

COOPERATIVE RECREATION SERVICE, P.O. Box 333, Delaware, Ohio, provides educational assistance in, and manufactures nonprofit equipment for, games, folk dancing, and other recreational activities.

NATIONAL FEDERATION OF MUSIC CLUBS, 445 West 23rd Street, New York 11, N.Y., has organized clubs in all states, Canada, and Mexico that offer financial assistance to music students and help young artists establish careers.

NATIONAL RECREATION ASSOCIATION, 8 West Eighth Street, New York 11, N.Y., offers extensive literature dealing with all types of recreation, has a leadership training program.

HOME MANAGEMENT

NATIONAL SAFETY COUNCIL, 425 No. Michigan Avenue, Chicago 11, Illinois, provides comprehensive literature on safety in the home, including baby sitter safety.

UNITED STATES DEPARTMENT OF AGRICULTURE, BUREAU OF HUMAN NUTRITION AND HOME ECONOMICS, Washington 25, D.C., offers evaluations of foods, textiles and clothing, housing and household equipment, and pamphlets containing advice on family economics.

HEALTH

Local and State Boards of Health can provide information about obtaining local health services. Helpful Federal agencies are the CHILDREN'S BUREAU and the PUBLIC HEALTH BUREAU OF THE UNITED STATES, DEPARTMENT OF HEALTH, EDUCATION AND WELFARE, Washington 25, D.C. The following organizations provide help in connection with specific diseases and handicaps.

AMERICAN ASSOCIATION ON MENTAL DEFICIENCY, P.O. Box 96, Cambridge, Ohio

AMERICAN CANCER SOCIETY, 521 West 57th Street, New York 19, N.Y.

AMERICAN DENTAL ASSOCIATION, 222 East Superior Street, Chicago 11, Illinois

AMERICAN DIABETES ASSOCIATION, 1 East 45th Street, New York 17, N.Y.

AMERICAN FOUNDATION FOR THE BLIND, 15 West 16th Street, New York 11, N.Y.

AMERICAN HEARING SOCIETY, 919 Eighteenth Street, N.W., Washington 6, D.C.

AMERICAN HEART ASSOCIATION, 44 East 23rd Street, New York 10, N.Y.

AMERICAN NATIONAL RED CROSS, 17th and D Streets, N.W., Washington 6, D.C.

AMERICAN PUBLIC HEALTH ASSOCIATION, 1790 Broadway, New York 19, N.Y.

AMERICAN SOCIAL HYGIENE ASSOCIATION, 1790 Broadway, New York 19, N.Y. (emphasis on sex education, control of venereal diseases)

JOHN TRACY CLINIC, 806 West Adams Boulevard, Los Angeles 7, California, offers correspondence courses for deaf children's parents.

LEAGUE FOR EMOTIONALLY DISTURBED CHILDREN, 10 West 65th Street, New York 23, N.Y.

MATERNITY CENTER ASSOCIATION, 48 East 92nd Street, New York 28, N.Y.

MUSCULAR DYSTROPHY ASSOCIATIONS OF AMERICA, 1790 Broadway, New York 19, N.Y.

NATIONAL ASSOCIATION FOR MENTAL HEALTH, 10 Columbus Circle, New York 19, N.Y.

NATIONAL ASSOCIATION FOR THE PREVENTION OF BLINDNESS, 1790 Broadway, New York 19, N.Y.

NATIONAL ASSOCIATION FOR RETARDED CHILDREN, 99 University Place, New York, N.Y.

NATIONAL EPILEPSY LEAGUE, 130 North Wells Street, Chicago 6, Illinois

NATIONAL FOUNDATION FOR INFANTILE PARALYSIS, 301 East 42nd Street, New York 17, N.Y.

NATIONAL HEALTH COUNCIL, 1790 Broadway, New York 19, N.Y.

NATIONAL MULTIPLE SCLEROSIS SOCIETY, 270 Park Avenue, New York 17, N.Y.

NATIONAL SOCIETY FOR CRIPPLED CHILDREN AND ADULTS, 2023 West Ogden Avenue, Chicago 12, Illinois

NATIONAL TUBERCULOSIS ASSOCIATION, 1790 Broadway, New York 19, N.Y.

UNITED CEREBRAL PALSY, 369 Lexington Avenue, New York 17, N.Y.

VOLTA SPEECH ASSOCIATION FOR THE DEAF, 1537–35th Street, N.W., Washington 7, D.C.

WAYNE STATE UNIVERSITY SPEECH AND HEARING CLINIC, 656 W. Warren St., Detroit 2, Michigan

EDUCATION

AMERICAN CAMPING ASSOCIATION, Bradford Woods, Martinsville, Indiana, encourages educational, recreational, character-developing camping, provides information on reputable camps.

AMERICAN COUNCIL ON EDUCATION, 1785 Massachusetts Avenue, N.W., Washington 6, D.C., is a coordination center in American education.

AMERICAN EDUCATION FELLOWSHIP, 105 Gregory Hall, University of Illinois, Urbana, Illinois, helps local chapters with community planning and action for better education.

ASSOCIATION FOR CHILDHOOD EDUCATION INTERNATIONAL, 1200 Fifteenth Street, N.W., Washington 5, D.C., offers excellent pamphlets on educational needs to parents and teachers.

EDUCATION POLICIES COMMISSION OF THE NATIONAL EDUCATION ASSOCIATION, 1201 Sixteenth Street, N.W., Washington 6, D.C., provides publications on experimentation and change in school programs.

NATIONAL ASSOCIATION FOR NURSERY EDUCATION, University of Rhode Island, Kingston, Rhode Island, is an organization of administrators.

NATIONAL CITIZENS COMMISSION FOR THE PUBLIC SCHOOLS, 9 East 40th Street, New York 16, N.Y., supplies guidance to groups working for school improvement on a local basis.

NATIONAL CONGRESS OF PARENTS AND TEACHERS, 700 North Rush Street, Chicago, Illinois, provides various P.T.A. publications.

NATIONAL KINDERGARTEN ASSOCIATION, 8 West 40th Street, New York 18, N.Y., guides the establishment of kindergartens in communities and schools.

RELIGIOUS EDUCATION ASSOCIATION, 545 West 111th Street, New York 25, N.Y., is an interfaith agency that suggests aids for religious education.

UNITED STATES DEPARTMENT OF HEALTH, EDUCATION AND WELFARE, OFFICE OF EDUCATION, Washington 25, D.C., offers information on all phases of education.

UNITED STATES DEPARTMENT OF LABOR, Washington 25, D.C., offers vocational guidance.

COMMUNITY LIVING

BOYS' CLUBS OF AMERICA, 381 Fourth Avenue, New York 16, N.Y.

BOY SCOUTS OF AMERICA, 2 Park Avenue, New York 16, N.Y.

CAMPFIRE GIRLS, 16 East 48th Street, New York 17, N.Y.

4-H CLUBS, EXTENSION SERVICE, U. S. DEPARTMENT OF AGRICULTURE, Washington 25, D.C.

GIRL SCOUTS OF THE UNITED STATES OF AMERICA, 830 Third Avenue, New York 22, N.Y.

NATIONAL ASSOCIATION FOR THE ADVANCEMENT OF COLORED PEOPLE, 20 West 40th Street, New York 18, N.Y.

NATIONAL CONFERENCE OF CHRISTIANS AND JEWS, 43 West 57th Street, New York 19, N.Y., promotes intergroup relations through mass media, through community organizations and in schools.

NATIONAL JEWISH WELFARE BOARD, 145 East 32nd Street, New York 16, N.Y., has information on Jewish Community Centers and Young Men's and Young Women's Hebrew Associations.

PLAY SCHOOLS ASSOCIATION, 41 West 57th Street, New York, N.Y., offers information on community sponsored after-school and summertime recreation programs.

RURAL YOUTH OF THE UNITED STATES OF AMERICA, 210 Fifth Street, Marietta, Ohio

YOUNG MEN'S CHRISTIAN ASSOCIATION, NATIONAL COUNCIL, 291 Broadway, New York 7, N.Y.

YOUNG WOMEN'S CHRISTIAN ASSOCIATION, NATIONAL BOARD, 600 Lexington Avenue, New York 22, N.Y.

INDEX

INDEX

D

I

J

N

O

W

Y